TAKEOVERS, RESTRUCTURING, AND CORPORATE GOVERNANCE

PRENTICE HALL FINANCE SERIES

Adelman/Marks, *Entrepreneurial Finance*

Aggarwal, *Capital Budgeting Under Uncertainty*

Alexander/Sharpe/Bailey, *Fundamentals of Investments*, Third Edition

Arshadi/Karels, *Modern Financial Intermediaries and Markets*

Baker, *International Finance: Management, Markets, and Institutions*

Bierman/Smidt, *The Capital Budgeting Decision*, Eighth Edition

Black/Skipper, *Life and Health Insurance*, Thirteenth Edition

Bodie/Merton, *Finance*

Click/Coval, *The Theory and Practice of International Financial Management*

Cornwall/Zang/Hartman, *Entrepreneurial Financial Management: An Applied Approach*

Danthine/Donaldson, *Intermediate Financial Theory*

Dietrich, *Financial Services and Financial Institutions*

Dorfman, *Introduction to Risk Management and Insurance*, Sixth Edition

Emery/Finnerty/Stowe, *Corporate Financial Management*, Second Edition

Emery/Finnerty/Stowe, *Principles of Financial Management*

Fabozzi, *Bond Markets, Analysis and Strategies*, Fourth Edition

Fabozzi, *Investment Management*, Second Edition

Fabozzi/Modigliani, *Capital Markets: Institutions and Instruments*, Third Edition

Fabozzi/Modigliani/Ferri/Jones, *Foundations of Financial Markets and Institutions*, Third Edition

Fischer/Jordan, *Security Analysis and Portfolio Management*, Sixth Edition

Francis/Ibbotson, *Investments: A Global Perspective*

Fraser/Ormiston, *Understanding Financial Statements*, Sixth Edition

Gallagher/Andrew, *Financial Management: Principles and Practices*, Third Edition

Grabbe, *International Financial Markets*, Third Edition

Handa, *FinCoach: Fixed Income* (software)

Handa, *FinCoach 2.0*

Haugen, *Modern Investment Theory*, Fifth Edition

Haugen, *The New Finance*, Second Edition

Haugen, *The Beast on Wall Street*

Haugen, *The Inefficient Stock Market*, Second Edition

Holden, *Spreadsheet Modeling: A Book and CD-ROM Series* (Available in graduate and undergraduate versions)

Hull, *Fundamentals of Futures and Options Markets*, Fourth Edition

Hull, *Options, Futures, and Other Derivatives*, Fifth Edition

Kaufman, *The U.S. Financial Systems*, Sixth Edition

Keown, *Personal Finance: Turning Money into Wealth*, Third Edition

Keown/Martin/Petty/Scott, *Financial Management*, Ninth Edition

Keown/Martin/Petty/Scott, *ActiveBook, Financial Management*, Ninth Edition

Keown/Martin/Petty/Scott, *Foundations of Finance: The Logic and Practice of Financial Management*, Fourth Edition

Keown/Martin/Petty/Scott, *ActiveBook, Foundations of Finance*, Third Edition

Mason/Merton/Perold/Tufano, *Cases in Financial Engineering*

Mastering Finance CD-ROM

Mathis, *Corporate Finance Live: A Web-based Math Tutorial*

For more information on Finance titles from Prentice Hall, visit us at www.prenhall.com/finance.

FOURTH EDITION

TAKEOVERS, RESTRUCTURING, AND CORPORATE GOVERNANCE

J. Fred Weston

The Anderson School
University of California, Los Angeles

Mark L. Mitchell

Harvard Business School and CNH Partners

J. Harold Mulherin

Claremont McKenna College

Assisted by

Juan A. Siu and **Brian A. Johnson**

PEARSON

Prentice
Hall

Upper Saddle River, New Jersey 07458

Library of Congress Cataloging-in-Publication Data

Weston, J. Fred (John Fred) [date]

 Takeovers, restructuring, and corporate governanance/J. Fred Weston,
 Mark Mitchell, J. Harold Mulherin; assisted by Juan A. Siu, Brian A. Johnson. —
 4th ed.
  p. cm.
 Includes bibliographical references and index.
 ISBN 0-13-140737-6
  1. Consolidation and merger of corporations—United States—Finance.
  2. Consolidation and merger of corporations—United States—Management.
  3. Corporate governance—United States. I. Mitchell, Mark, [date]— II. Mulherin,
 John Harold, [date]– III. Title.
 HG4028.M4W47   2003
 338.8′3′0973—dc21

                                                                    2003042988

Executive Editor: Mickey Cox
Editor-in-Chief: P. J. Boardman
Managing Editor (Editorial): Gladys Soto
Project Manager: Erika Rusnak
Media Project Manager: Victoria Anderson
Editorial Assistant: Francesca Calogero
Executive Marketing Manager: Debbie Clare
Marketing Assistant: Amanda Fisher
Managing Editor (Production): John Roberts
Production Editor: Kelly Warsak
Production Assistant: Joe DeProspero
Permissions Supervisor: Suzanne Grappi
Manufacturing Buyer: Michelle Klein
Cover Design: Kiwi Design
Cover Illustration: Albright-Knox Art Gallery/Corbis
Composition/Full-Service Project Management: BookMasters, Inc./Jennifer Welsch
Printer/Binder: Phoenix Color Corp.
Cover Printer: Phoenix Color Corp.

Credits and acknowledgments borrowed from other sources and reproduced, with permission, in this textbook appear on appropriate page within text.

Pearson Education LTD.
Pearson Education Singapore, Pte. Ltd
Pearson Education, Canada, Ltd
Pearson Education–Japan

Pearson Education Australia PTY, Limited
Pearson Education North Asia Ltd
Pearson Educatión de Mexico, S.A. de C.V.
Pearson Education Malaysia, Pte. Ltd

10 9 8 7 6 5 4 3 2 1
0-13-140737-6

To my wife Bernadine, with love,
Fred

To my wife Janet, with love,
Mark

To my parents,
Harold

BRIEF CONTENTS

CONTENTS

SHORT CASES AND COMPANY
EXAMPLES IN TEXT

In addition to end-of-chapter questions, 136 cases and company examples have been added for analysis. The case studies seek to provide further experience with spreadsheet analysis, valuation, and strategic considerations. The text itself is enriched by brief summaries of cases throughout the chapters. The book concludes with guidelines for the role of mergers and acquisitions in the strategic planning processes of firms. The following is a list of cases and company examples that you will see in the text:

Chapter	Topic	Case or Company Example	Page
1	The Takeover Process	Hewlett Packard/Compaq	10
		Sabre Corporation/Travelocity.com	12
		Sears Roebuck & Co/Land's End Inc.	13
		WorldCom/MCI	17
		AOL/Time Warner	20
2	The Legal and	PepsiCo/Quaker Oats	24
	Regulatory Framework	WorldCom/Sprint	39
		Staples/Office Depot	40
		Microsoft Antitrust Case	41
		CSX & Norfolk Southern/Conrail	45
		Boeing/McDonnell Douglas	48
		General Electric/Honeywell	48
		First Executive Corporation	49
		Pacific Lumber Company	50
		First Capital Life	50
		Broader Board Responsibilities	53
		Van Gorkom	54
		Revlon/Pantry Pride	55
		Maxwell/Macmillan	55
		Paramount/Time	56
		Paramount/QVC	56
		Sandoz/Gerber	57
		United Airlines/US Airways	57
3	Accounting for M&As	AT&T/NCR	79
		Wells Fargo/First Interstate	85
		Time Warner/Turner Broadcasting System	86
		AOL/Time Warner	87
		Pfizer/Pharmacia	89
4	Deal Structuring	Chevron/Texaco	92
		Univision/Hispanic Broadcasting Corporation	96
		Northrop Grumman/TRW	98

PREFACE

For individual firms, the economic role of mergers and acquisitions (M&As) is to assist in achieving or maintaining their competitive advantage by anticipating and adjusting to change. M&As include mergers, acquisitions, divestitures, alliances, joint ventures, restructuring, minority investments, licensing, and franchising, as well as international activities. For economies, M&As help move resources from lower-value uses to higher-value uses. Yet a high number of M&A investments fail to earn their cost of capital. The materials in this book seek to improve the success rate of M&A activities.

Powerful, long-term change forces have been driving M&A activity in recent decades. Foremost is technological change, impacting every industry. Changes in transportation and communications produced the internationalization of markets. The globalization of competition and its increased intensity produced deregulation in airlines, financial services, telecommunications, and even the traditional electrical and other public utilities industries. But the massive change forces also have impacted the pharmaceutical, chemical, auto, tire, and petroleum industries. Ways of doing business will continue to change. The forms of competition will continue to multiply, and the intensity of competition will continue to increase. Relations with suppliers, workers, consumers, and other stakeholders will continue to evolve. These forces are not likely to diminish in the years ahead.

Other developments have become superimposed on the longer-term trends. An economic downturn began in early 2000. Chain reactions set in. Slowing economies always impact the durable goods industries the most adversely. Strong new growth sectors were severely stunted. The promising Internet industries came to a virtual standstill. The world telecommunications industry was battered by overinvestment and overcapacity, resulting in a collapse of profit margins. Stock market values were shattered. Large stock price declines took place in industry leaders such as Intel, Cisco, Oracle, Sun Microsystems, IBM, and even Microsoft. These problems were aggravated by geopolitical developments. International terrorism was signaled by the September 11, 2001, tragedy. Political tensions in the Middle East, India–Pakistan, Russia–Chechnya, and so on continued.

Another adverse development was the collapse of several individual companies. Some were accompanied by disclosures of fraud. Among these were Enron, WorldCom, Tyco, and ImClone. *Fortune* in its September 2, 2002, issue calculated that executives at 25 companies whose stock price declined 75% from their peak in the period January 1999 through May 2002 sold out before the bad news and "walked away" with $66 billion. These developments shattered confidence in the integrity of the financial markets. As a consequence, the Sarbanes-Oxley Act was signed into law on July 30, 2002. By requiring that senior corporate officials be more responsible for the preparation of their companies' financial reports, it was hoped that investors' confidence would be restored.

The dollar value of mergers in 2001, adjusted for price level changes, was down 48% from 2000. For 2002, the dollar volume again declined about 50% from the previous year. The outlook for 2003 appears to be about the same level as for 2002. The slow rate of economic recovery has impacted all forms of investment activity negatively, including M&As. However, the role of M&As is to assist firms and economies in adjusting to opportunities and change. It follows, therefore, that M&A activity has a bigger job to do because of the new and stronger shocks that have occurred. Cash purchases of divisions of distressed companies are underway. An example is the purchase of Houghton-Mifflin from Vivendi Universal by Thomas Lee Partners and Bain Capital underway in November 2002. Deal activity in October 2002 was active and rising in the computer software, supply and services, brokerage, medical supplies, broadcasting, and retail industries. Industry consolidations to reduce excess capacity are occurring. In general, with the strong new shocks, many adjustments will be required. Hence, increased M&A activities are likely as economies and financial markets recover.

CHANGES IN THE FOURTH EDITION

With two new coauthors, we have revised every chapter of the book. We have tried to cover all of the major articles and books published since the last edition. We have added a new chapter on merger arbitrage and have updated all the empirical materials.

The accounting changes that have become effective since the prior edition have been included in Chapter 3. Chapter 4 has been retitled Deal Structuring and includes method of payment, taxes, collars, and contingent payments. A strong conceptual framework is further developed in Chapter 6. The empirical materials on merger performance are reworked completely in Chapter 8. Appendix A to Chapter 8 analyzes a recent M&A sample to illustrate and explain modern techniques of performance measurements. The valuation discussions in Chapters 9 and 10 are rewritten for clarification with new applications provided. Chapters 11, 12, and 13 on restructuring are rewritten with a strong conceptual framework. Appendix A to Chapter 11 presents a case study of restructuring in the natural gas industry. Appendix A to Chapter 12 analyzes a sample of divestitures. Chapter 14 on alliances and joint ventures is broadened and includes new applications. For Chapter 16 on leveraged buyouts, we have added the capital cash flow valuation model and illustrated its use. In Chapter 18 on share repurchases, a new conceptual framework is applied in the discussion of a substantial new volume of literature. Chapter 20 on corporate governance covers new developments in corporate behavior, fraud, and ethical responsibilities. Chapter 21 on merger arbitrage reflects some *Journal of Finance* articles by coauthor Mark Mitchell in addition to his experience as a partner in a merger arbitrage firm. Chapter 22 includes tables summarizing alternative strategies for growth and value enhancements, as well as a new section on value-based management.

SUPPLEMENTARY MATERIALS

On a Companion Web site to this text (*www.prenhall.com/weston*), we offer an ancillary package containing the following resources. For students, Excel computer models—formulated key analytical models contained in our book—enable the user to study a wide range of alternative concepts, assumptions, or company characteristics. Outlines of our PowerPoint presentation are also available to the student.

For the instructor, our resource manual includes a syllabus, Thoughts for Teaching an M&A Course, solutions to all end-of-chapter questions, problems, and cases, and a test bank containing true/false questions. Illustrative Examinations, and the complete PowerPoint Presentation Graphics are available. Instructors should contact their Prentice Hall sales representative for their password.

A related book of cases has been published under the title *Cases in Dynamic Finance: Mergers and Restructuring,* by J. Fred Weston. This casebook focuses on the adjustment processes of firms in increasingly dynamic environments. The cases in this compilation include firms that have succeeded and those that have floundered in the new environment. The content of the cases overlaps the traditional areas of microeconomics, business finance, mergers and takeovers, restructuring, and corporate governance. The title, *Dynamic Finance,* seeks to encompass multiple areas. A convergence of disciplines is emerging. We plan to continue to update cases and to add new cases as more companies adjust to the changing environment. They will be available in the Pearson Business Resource Case Series and periodically in compilations. (Please view information on this program at www.pearsoncustom.com). The availability of individual cases will enable users to select different compilations.

APPRECIATION

The theoretical framework of the book draws heavily on the work of Ronald Coase, Eugene Fama, Michael Jensen, Armen Alchian, Harold Demsetz, and Benjamin Klein. We are indebted to the many scholars whose writings have enriched the literature on M&As and corporate control. Those with the largest number of citations in the Author Index deserve our special gratitude. They include Tom Copeland, Harry and Linda DeAngelo, Eugene Fama, Kenneth French, David Ikenberry, Steven Kaplan, Kenneth Lehn, John McConnell, Chris Muscarella, Annette Poulsen, Richard Ruback, Michael Ryngaert, Bill Schwert, Andrei Shleifer, Clifford Smith, Robert Vishny, Jerold Warner, Michael Weisbach, Karen Wruck, and others from whom we have learned.

We also were helped by other scholars whose writings and discussions have stimulated our thinking: Edward Altman, Antonio Bernardo, Michael Brennan, Bhagwan Chowdhry, Bradford Cornell, Jack Farrell, Julian Franks, Gerald Garvey, David Hirshleifer, Patricia Hughes, John Matsusaka, Jim Miles, Jeff Pontiff, Todd Pulvino, Richard Roll, Eduardo Schwartz, James Seward, Erik Stafford, Laura Starks, Walt Torous, and Ivo Welch. Particular thanks to Matthias Kahl for his corrections and many penetrating comments.

We are grateful to the following people for their helpful comments on the first edition: Nickolaos Travlos, Boston College; Michael J. Sullivan, Florida State University; Kenneth W. Wiles, University of Texas at Austin; George J. Papaioannou, Hofstra University; Douglas V. Austin, University of Toledo; Maclyn L. Clouse, University of Denver; Matthew Spiegel and Michael Salinger, Columbia University; Nikhil P. Varaiya, Southern Methodist University; Robert F. Brunner, University of Virginia; and Ralph A. Walkling, the Ohio State University.

For help on the second edition, we thank Michael F. Toyne, LaSalle University; Kent Hickman, Gonzaga University; and Yun W. Park, Saint Mary's University.

For contributions to the third edition, we thank Mark Mitchell, Harvard University; J. Harold Mulherin, Penn State University; Ted Azami, Cal State at Long Beach; Theodore Peridis, York University; Mark Shrader, Gonzaga University; David Ikenberry, Rice University; and R. M. Karanjia, University of Notre Dame.

For this fourth edition, we benefited from the reviews by Ted Azarmi, California State University at Long Beach; David Ikenberry, Rice University; R.M. Karanjia, University of Notre Dame; Theodore Peridis, York University; and Mark Shrader, Gonzaga University.

We also offer our special appreciation to Juan A. Siu and Brian A. Johnson, whose contributions would have justified their designation as coauthors. We also received assistance from other associates in the M&A Research Program at The Anderson School at UCLA. They include Brigitta Schumacher-Bradley, Alex Duffy, Scott Morrow, Nam H. Le, Jamie Oh, and Kelley Coleman. We also appreciate the help from Lynda Pires, intern at CNH Partners.

We appreciate the cooperation of the people at Prentice Hall, particularly Gladys Soto, Managing Editor Business Publishing. We also value our association with Karen Houston, who handles the distribution of our merger cases at Pearson Custom Publishing.

This subject is so dynamic and the flow of articles and other materials is so voluminous that there will be need for future updating. We invite reactions, comments, and suggestions from our readers.

J. Fred Weston
Mark L. Mitchell
J. Harold Mulherin

J. Fred Weston
The Anderson School at UCLA
258 Tavistock Ave.
Los Angeles, CA 90049-3229
Tel. (310)472-5110
Fax. (310) 472-9471
E-mail: jweston@anderson.ucla.edu
Web site: www.anderson.ucla.edu/faculty/john.weston

CHAPTER 1
THE TAKEOVER PROCESS

After reaching a record $2.3 trillion in 1999, world merger and acquisition (M&A) activity increased by another 50% to $3.6 trillion in 2000, as shown in Table 1.1. As of 2000, merger activity had grown for nine straight years. That growth dramatically reversed in 2001, with merger activity plummeting to $2.0 trillion. The reversal was especially striking for non-U.S. M&A activity, which had been growing at a considerably faster rate during the prior few years.

A historical perspective of M&A activity in the United States is presented in Table 1.2. The data in Table 1.2 are from *Mergerstat*, which compiles announcement data. In contrast, Table 1.1 is from Securities Data Corporation (SDC) as reported in the *Mergers & Acquisitions* magazine, which compiles M&A completions and uses different selection criteria. For individual years, the numbers are sometimes higher for one source, but lower in other years. The trend patterns over time for the two sources convey the same economic implications.

During the 1980s, merger activity was considered to be at an all-time high. The peak year during the 1980s was 1988, when merger activity (in 1996 dollars) was $308 billion. This period has been studied extensively and is viewed as one of the greatest merger booms ever. Yet, the late 1990s broke numerous records with respect to M&A activity. For example, the 1999 level (in constant dollars) was more than four times that of the peak year of the 1980s. Even in 2001, when merger activity dropped considerably, the constant dollar amount was more than twice as high as that in 1988.

Large firms continue to be susceptible to takeover. Table 1.3 displays the 10 largest mergers, based on purchase price of the target equity, completed during 2000–2001. At the top of the list is the $115 billion acquisition of Warner-Lambert by Pfizer. All of these deals exceeded $25 billion in target value as of the close of the merger. The industries represented in descending order are telecommunications (four), drugs (two), oil (two), entertainment (one), and financial services (one). Table 1.3 also illustrates the internationalization of merger activity. BP PLC,

TABLE 1.1 Worldwide M&A Activity, 1998-2001 ($ billion)				
	1998	*1999*	*2000*	*2001*
World	$2,092	$2,373	$3,565	$2,063
United States	$1,343	$1,395	$1,786	$1,143
Rest of World[a]	$ 749	$ 979	$1,779	$ 920

[a]Non-U.S. targets and acquirers

Source: Mergers & Acquisitions Magazine, various issues.

TABLE 1.2 Merger Announcements: The Mergerstat Series

Years	Total Dollar Value Paid ($ billion)	Number Total	Number of Transactions Valued At		GDP Deflator (1996=100)	1996 Constant Dollar Consideration	Percent Change
			$100 Million or More	$1 Billion or More			
1975	11.8	2297	14	0	40	29.5	
1976	20	2276	39	0	42.3	47.3	60
1977	21.9	2224	41	1	45	48.7	3
1978	34.2	2106	80	0	48.2	70.9	46
1979	43.5	2128	83	3	52.2	83.3	17
1980	44.3	1889	94	4	57	77.7	-7
1981	82.6	2395	113	12	62.4	132.4	71
1982	53.8	2346	116	6	66.3	81.2	-39
1983	73.1	2533	138	11	68.9	106.2	31
1984	122.2	2543	200	18	71.4	171.1	61
1985	179.8	3011	270	36	73.7	244	43
1986	173.1	3336	346	27	75.3	229.8	-6
1987	163.7	2032	301	36	77.6	211	-8
1988	246.9	2258	369	45	80.2	307.8	46
1989	221.1	2366	328	35	83.3	265.5	-14
1990	108.2	2074	181	21	86.5	125.1	-53
1991	71.2	1877	150	13	89.7	79.4	-36
1992	96.7	2574	200	18	91.8	105.3	33
1993	176.4	2663	242	27	94	187.6	78
1994	226.7	2997	383	51	96	236.1	26
1995	356	3510	462	74	98.1	362.9	54
1996	495	5848	640	94	100	495	36
1997	657.1	7800	873	120	101.9	644.6	30
1998	1191.9	7809	906	158	103.2	1154.9	79
1999	1425.9	9278	1097	195	104.6	1362.6	18
2000	1325.7	9566	1150	206	107	1238.6	-9
2001	699.4	8290	703	121	109.4	639.5	-48

Source: Mergerstat Review, various issues.

TABLE 1.3 Top 10 Mergers Completed During 2000-2001

Rank	Target	Acquirer	Amount ($ billions)	Industry
1	Warner-Lambert	Pfizer	114.9	drugs
2	Time Warner	America Online	86.4	entertainment
3	GTE	Bell Atlantic	59.9	telecommunications
4	US West	Qwest Communications	43.5	telecommunications
5	MediaOne	AT&T	42.7	telecommunications
6	Texaco	Chevron	38.4	oil
7	Pharmacia & Upjohn	Monsanto	31.0	drugs
8	Atlantic Richfield	BP PLC	27.5	oil
9	Voicestream Wireless	Deutsche Telekom AG	26.7	telecommunications
10	JP Morgan	Chase Manhattan	26.6	financial services

Source: Mergerstat Review, various issues.

a U.K. oil company, acquired Atlantic Richfield, an American company, illustrating a cross-border transaction. In addition, VoiceStream Wireless, an American company, was acquired by Deutsche Telecom AG, a German firm.

Although merger activity during 2001 and 2002 dropped considerably from that of the late 1990s, the daily newspapers and wire services continue to be filled with case studies of mergers and acquisitions (M&As), tender offers (friendly and hostile), spin-offs, equity carve-outs and divestitures, corporate recapitalizations and restructurings, changes in ownership structures, and struggles for corporate control (see glossary for definitions). Although the traditional subject matter of M&As has been expanded to include these other types of activities, for brevity we refer to these and related activities as M&As. Investors, especially large institutional investors, are continually increasing their role in monitoring management with respect to merger plans. Even small retail investors, who have been empowered via a wealth of information from the Internet, are starting to scrutinize mergers rather than simply going along with management on every deal. The Securities and Exchange Commission (SEC) continues to actively pursue insider trading cases associated with mergers, as well as pursuing cases of financial fraud associated with merging parties.

CHANGE FORCES

Merger activities throughout history have been related to the economic and cultural characteristics of their time and place. The increasing pace of merger activity during the past two decades is related to the powerful change forces listed in Figure 1.1.

Overriding all other forces are technological changes, which include computers, computer services, software, servers, and the many advances in information systems, including the Internet. Improvements in communications and transportation have created a global economy. Nations have adopted international agreements such as the General Agreement on Tariffs and Trade (GATT) that have resulted in freer trade. The euro was launched in 1999 and became the sole currency for the 12 participating member states in 2002, continuing to result in an opening of boundaries and restrictions throughout Europe. The growing forces of competition have produced deregulation in major industries such as financial services, airlines, broadcasting, and medical services.

FIGURE 1.1 The 10 Change Forces

1. Technological change
2. Economies of scale, economies of scope, complementarity, and the need to catch up technologically
3. Globalization and freer trade
4. Changes in industrial organization
5. New industries
6. Deregulation and regulation
7. Favorable economic and financial conditions for much of the past two decades
8. Negative trends in certain individual economies and industries
9. Widening inequalities in income and wealth
10. Relatively high valuations for equities during the 1990s

Another set of change factors relates to efficiency of operations. Economies of scale spread the large fixed cost of investing in machinery or computer systems over a larger number of units. Economies of scope refer to cost reductions from operations in related activities. In the information industry, these would represent economies of activities in personal computer (PC) hardware, PC software, server hardware, server software, the Internet, and other related activities. Another efficiency gain is achieved by combining complementary activities—for example, combining a company that is strong in research with one that is strong in marketing. Mergers to catch up technologically are illustrated by the series of acquisitions AT&T made during the 1990s, many of which AT&T has been attempting to divest or spin off in the early 2000s.

A third group of change forces stimulating M&A and restructuring activities comprises changes in industry organization. An example is the shift in the computer industry from vertically integrated firms to a horizontal chain of independent activities. As industries continue to undergo rapid change, often leading to merger, it is important to note that the change does not end with the merger. It is difficult to combine organizations when industries undergo rapid change, and multiple adjustment processes typically are required.

A fourth group of change forces is the result of the favorable economic and financial conditions during the past two decades. Consequently, prior to the recent decline in equity values, stock valuations have been high relative to historical relationships. When corporate managers were optimistic about the future, they made large-scale investments, often via M&As. As the economy began to struggle in 2001 and the stock market dropped as well, corporate investment, at the internal and external levels, via M&A, also began a substantial pullback.

ISSUES RAISED BY M&A ACTIVITY

Mergers and industrial restructuring activities have raised important issues for business decisions and for public policy for formulation. No firm is considered safe from the possibility of takeover. Mergers and acquisitions can be critical to the healthy expansion of business firms as they evolve through successive stages of growth and development. Internal and external growth may be complementary in the long-range evolution of firms. Successful entry into new product markets and into new geographic markets may require M&As at some stage in the firm's development. Successful competition in international markets may depend on capabilities obtained in a timely and efficient fashion through M&As.

Some have argued that mergers increase value and efficiency and move resources to their optimal uses, thereby increasing shareholder value. Others are skeptical. They argue that acquired companies are already efficient and that their subsequent performance after acquisition is not improved. Yet others aver that the gains to shareholders merely represent a redistribution away from labor and other stakeholders. Another view is that the M&A activity represents the machinations of speculators who reflect the frenzy of a "casino society." This speculative activity is said to increase debt unduly and to erode equity, resulting in an economy highly vulnerable to economic instability.

Even individual businesspeople have expressed skepticism about the power of mergers.

Many managements apparently were overexposed in impressionable childhood years to the story in which the imprisoned handsome prince is released from a toad's body by a kiss from a beautiful princess. Consequently, they are certain their managerial kiss will do wonders for the profitability of Company T[arget]. . . . Investors can always buy toads at the going price for toads. If investors instead bankroll princesses who wish to pay double for the right to kiss the toad, those kisses had better pack some real dynamite. We've observed many kisses but very few miracles. Nevertheless, many managerial princesses remain serenely confident about the future potency or their kisses—even after their corporate backyards are knee-deep in unresponsive toads . . .

We have tried occasionally to buy toads at bargain prices with results that have been chronicled in past reports. Clearly our kisses fell flat. We have done well with a couple of princes—but they were princes when purchased. At least our kisses didn't turn them into toads. And, finally, we have occasionally been quite successful in purchasing fractional interests in easily identifiable princes at toadlike prices.

Warren Buffet made these remarks in his 1992 letter to the shareholders of Berkshire Hathaway. Despite Buffet's stated skepticism of the power of mergers, Berkshire under his leadership has engaged in numerous successful acquisitions over the past few decades, and recently completed acquisitions of large firms such as Fruit of the Loom, Johns Manville, Shaw Industries, and XTRA Corporation in 2001 and 2002.

In this volume, we seek to sort out these opposing views. We offer guidelines for such practical matters as M&A planning by firms and the valuation of combining firms. Further, the theory and empirical evidence have implications for social and economic policies toward mergers. Thus, this work provides a framework for the evaluation of alternative business and social policies involving M&As.

In this chapter, we provide a framework for understanding the many aspects of mergers and takeovers. We cover the topics of merger and tender offer terminology, types of mergers from an economic standpoint, mergers in a legal framework, and the nature or tender offers.

MERGER AND TENDER OFFER TERMINOLOGY

The words *merger* and *tender offer* are used frequently, but the distinctions are not precise. In general, *mergers* refers to negotiated deals that meet certain technical and legal requirements. *Tender offer* usually means that one firm or person is making an offer directly to the shareholders to sell (tender) their shares at specified prices. In one sense, the word *merger* refers to negotiations between friendly parties who arrive at a mutually agreeable decision to combine their companies. However, in practice, one firm in a merger might be stronger and might dominate the transaction. Similarly, tender offers can be friendly or hostile. In either mergers or tender offers, the negotiations may start out friendly and become hostile. Conversely, negotiations may start out hostile and become friendly. In addition, there may be wide variations in attitudes in either direction as negotiations proceed. However, mergers are mostly friendly. Some tender offers are hostile in the sense that an offer is made to the shareholders without the approval of the board of directors.

As a practical matter, it is useful to have some language to describe the M&A activities. Definitions are arbitrary but useful. In general, mergers reflect various forms of combining companies through some mutuality of negotiations. In tender offers, the bidder contacts share-holders directly, inviting them to sell (tender) their shares at an offer price. The directors of the company may or may not have endorsed the tender offer proposal. These distinctions are reflected in a practical way in business practice. That segment of investment banking firms engaged in providing advice an these activities usually is referred to as the Mergers and Acquisitions (M&A) Group. In this sense, mergers and tender offers are two forms of takeovers. It is appropriate, therefore, to refer to these activities interchangeably as takeovers or M&As or M&A activity.

With the foregoing as background, we describe some characteristics of mergers and then follow with a section in which some technical aspects of tender offers are discussed. Then we discuss the concept of restructuring, which involves changes in organizations or policies to alter the firm's approach to achieving its long-term objectives. Describing the activities related to the words and concepts conveys a practical understanding of their meaning. With experience, a judgmental feel for or understanding of how these terms are used is developed. They provide some useful handles for organizing data and studying important phenomena. However, the terms should be used thoughtfully and not in a mechanical way.

TYPES OF MERGERS FROM AN ECONOMIC STANDPOINT

Economists have grouped mergers based on whether they take place at the same level of economic activity—exploration, production or manufacturing, wholesale distribution, or retail distribution to the ultimate consumer. The element of relatedness is also important in defining economic categories of mergers.

HORIZONTAL MERGERS

A horizontal merger involves two firms that operate and compete in the same kind of business activity. Thus, the acquisition in 1999 of Mobil by Exxon represented a horizontal combination or merger. Forming a larger firm may have the benefit of economies of scale. The argument, that horizontal mergers occur to realize economies of scale is, however, not sufficient to be a theory of horizontal mergers. Although these mergers generally would benefit from large-scale operation, not all small firms merge horizontally to achieve economies of scale. Further, why do firms decide to merge at a particular time? Why do they choose a merger rather than internal growth? Because a merger theory should have implications with respect to these aspects, it must be more than a theory of large firm size or a theory of horizontally integrated operations.

Horizontal mergers are regulated by the government for possible negative effects on competition. They decrease the number of firms in an industry, possibly making it easier for the industry members to collude for monopoly profits. Some believe that horizontal mergers potentially create monopoly power on the part of the combined firm, enabling it to engage in anticompetitive practices. It remains an empirical question whether horizontal mergers take place to increase the market power of the combined firm or to augment the firm's capabilities to become a more effective competitor.

Industry roll ups are a special type of horizontal merger. In a roll up, a consolidator acquires a large number of small companies with similar operations. Roll ups generally occur in fragmented industries with small, yet mature firms. In most cases, the industry does not have a dominant leader, thereby allowing for the entry of the consolidator to merge several small firms together. The goal of the roll up is to achieve economies of scale in purchasing, marketing, information systems, distribution, and senior management.

The consolidator must have a strong management team in order for the roll up to succeed. The management team must exhibit strong industry experience and have a good background in merger execution strategies. The consolidator will either provide its own equity financing to start the venture or will obtain such financing from an equity financing. To implement the roll up strategy, the consolidator will often use debt to finance the purchase of the small companies in the fragmented industry. In recent years, a popular roll up technique has been to use an initial public offering (IPO) to provide the financing of the small companies. The IPO provides the consolidator with cash and liquid shares by which to carry out the strategy. Many consolidators that have taken the IPO route have since filed for bankruptcy, and thus it is not obvious as to the best way to achieve economies of scale.

VERTICAL MERGERS

Vertical mergers occur between firms in different stages of production operation. In the oil industry, for example, distinctions are made between exploration and production, refining, and marketing to the ultimate consumer. In the pharmaceutical industry, one could distinguish between research and the development of new drugs, the production of drugs, and the marketing of drug products through retail drugstores.

Firms might want to be vertically integrated for many reasons. There are technological economies such as the avoidance of reheating and transportation costs in the case of an integrated iron and steel producer. Transactions within a firm may eliminate the costs of searching for prices, contracting, payment collecting, and advertising and also might reduce the costs of communicating and coordinating production. Planning for inventory and production may be improved due to more efficient information flow within a single firm. When assets of a firm are specialized to another firm, the latter may act opportunistically. Expropriation can be accomplished by demanding the supply of a good or service produced from the specialized assets at a price below its average cost. To avoid the costs of haggling that arise from expropriation attempts, the assets are owned by a single, vertically integrated firm. Divergent interests of parties to a transaction can be reconciled by common ownership.

The efficiency and affirmative rationale of vertical integration rests primarily on the costliness of market exchange and contracting. The argument, for instance, that uncertainty over input supply is avoided by backward integration reduces to the fact that long-term contracts are difficult to write, execute, and police.

CONGLOMERATE MERGERS

Conglomerate mergers involve firms engaged in unrelated types of business activity. Thus, the merger between Mobil Oil and Montgomery Ward was generally regarded as a conglomerate merger. Among conglomerate mergers, three types have been distinguished. Product extension mergers broaden the product lines of firms. These are mergers between firms in related business activities they also can be called concentric mergers. A geographic market extension merger involves two firms whose operations have been conducted in nonoverlapping geographic areas. Finally, the other conglomerate mergers that are often referred to as pure conglomerate mergers involve unrelated business activities. These would not qualify as product extension or market extension mergers.

Investment Companies

By contrasting four categories of companies, the economic functions of conglomerate mergers may be illuminated. The four categories are: (1) investment companies such as mutual funds; (2) financial conglomerates that operate as internal capital markets; (3) managerial conglomerates in which staff groups in general management functions such as research, legal, and human resources provide services to diversified segments of operations; and (4) concentric companies in which diversified activities are related to core activities. A fundamental economic function of investment companies is to reduce risk by diversification. Combination of securities whose returns are not perfectly correlated reduce portfolio variance for a target rate of return. Because investment companies combine resources from many sources, their power to achieve a reduction in variance through portfolio effects is greater than that of individual investors. In addition, the managements of investment companies provide professional selection from among investment alternatives.

Conglomerate firms differ fundamentally from investment companies in that they control the entities to which they make major financial commitments. Two important characteristics define a conglomerate firm. First, a conglomerate firm controls a range of activities in various industries that require different skills in the specific managerial functions of research, applied engineering, production, marketing, and so on. Second, the diversification is achieved mainly by external acquisitions and mergers, not by internal development.

Within this broader category, two types of conglomerate firms can be distinguished. Financial conglomerates provide a flow of funds to each segment of their operations, exercise control, and are the ultimate financial risk takers. In theory, financial conglomerates undertake strategic planning but do not participate in operating decisions. Managerial conglomerates not only assume financial responsibility and control but also play a role in operating decisions and provide staff expertise and staff services to the operating entities.

Financial Conglomerates

The characteristics of financial conglomerates may be further clarified by comparisons with investment companies. The financial conglomerate serves at least five distinct economic functions. First, like investment companies, it improves risk/return ratios through diversification. Second, it avoids "gambler's ruin" (an adverse run of losses that might cause bankruptcy). If the losses can be covered by avoiding gambler's ruin, the financial conglomerate maintains the viability of an economic activity with long-run value. Without this form of risk reduction or bankruptcy avoidance, the assets of the operating entity might be shifted to less productive uses because of a run of losses at some point in its development.

Third, a potential contribution by financial conglomerates derives from their establishing programs of financial planning and control. Often, these systems improve the quality of general and functional managerial performance, thereby resulting in more efficient operations and better resource allocation for the economy.

Fourth, if management does not perform effectively but the productivity of assets in the market is favorable, then the management is changed. This reflects an effective competitive process because assets are placed under more efficient management to ensure more effective use of resources. This contributes to improved resource allocation.

Fifth, in the financial planning and control process, a distinction is made between performance based on underlying potentials in the product market area and results related to managerial performance. Thus, adverse performance does not necessarily indicate inadequate management performance. If management is competent but product market potentials are inadequate, executives of the financial conglomerate will seek to shift resources by diverting internal cash flows from the unfavorable areas to areas more attractive from a growth and profitability standpoint. From the standpoint of the economy as a whole, resource allocation is improved.

Managerial Conglomerates

Managerial conglomerates carry the attributes of financial conglomerates still further. By providing managerial counsel and interactions on decisions, managerial conglomerates increase the potential for improving performance. One school of management theory holds that the generic management functions of planning, organizing, directing, and controlling are readily transferable to all types of business firms. Those managers who have the experience and capability to perform general management functions can perform them in any environment.

This theory argues for management transferability across a wide variety of industries and types of organizations, including government, nonprofit institutions, and military and religious organizations. To the extent that this proposition is valid, it provides a basis for the most general theory of mergers. When any two firms of unequal management competence are combined, the performance of the combined firm will benefit from the impact of the superior management firm, and the total performance of the combined firm will be greater than the sum of the individual parts. This interaction defines synergy in its most general form. In the managerial conglomerate, these economic benefits are achieved through corporate headquarters that provide the individual operating entities with expertise and counsel on the generic management functions.

Concentric Companies

The difference between the managerial conglomerate and the concentric company is based on the distinction between the general and specific management functions. If the activities of the segments brought together are so related that there is carryover of specific management functions (manufacturing, finance, marketing, personnel, and so on) or complementarity in relative strengths among these specific management functions, the merger should be termed concentric rather than conglomerate. This transferability of specific management functions across individual segments has long been exemplified by the operations of large, multiproduct, multiplant firms in the American economy. The characteristic organizational structure of these firms has included senior vice presidents who perform as staff specialists to corresponding functional executives in operating departments.

Definitions are inherently arbitrary. Is there any reason to distinguish between managerial conglomerates and concentric companies? The two types have in common a basic economic characteristic. Each transfers general management functions over a variety of activities, using the principle of spreading a fixed factor over a larger number of activities to achieve economies of scale and to lower the cost function for the output range. Concentric companies achieve these economic gains in specific management functions as well as in general management functions. A priori, the potential economies for the concentric companies might be expected to be larger. However, the magnitude of economies gained in general rather than specific management functions may vary by industry and by industry mix. Further, in the multiproduct multiplant firms that have achieved economies of carryover of specific and general management functions, the interactions may be so great that it is impossible to differentiate between the two.

Similarly, a managerial conglomerate that originally provided expertise on general management functions may increasingly act on specific management functions as its executives become more familiar with the operations of the individual entities. Financial conglomerates also may increasingly provide staff service for general and specific management functions.

Additional illustrations will clarify these concepts and their economic implications. If one company has competence in research, manufacturing, or marketing that can be applied to the product problems of another company that lacks that particular competence, a merger will provide the opportunity to lower cost functions. For example, firms seeking to diversify from advanced technology industries may be strong on research but weaker on production and marketing capabilities than firms in industries with less advanced technology.

To this point, we have described the different kinds of mergers and explained some of the reasons why they appear to take place. In the following section, we look at mergers within a legal framework.

MERGERS IN A LEGAL FRAMEWORK

From a legal standpoint, the statutory merger is the basic form of transaction. The transaction is governed by the statutory provisions of the state or states in which the parties to the merger are chartered. The main elements of a statutory merger are the percentage vote required for approval of the transaction, who is entitled to vote, how the votes are counted, and the rights of the voters who object to the transaction or its terms.

The Delaware statute is typical of the merger provisions found in most states. After the boards of directors have approved the transaction, it is submitted for ratification to the shareholders of the respective corporations. Prior to the 1960s, most states required approval by two thirds of the shareholders who possessed the right to vote. In 1962, the model Business Corporation Act provided for a majority vote. In 1967, the state of Delaware adopted the majority vote provision. Other states that provide for a majority vote include California, Michigan, and New Jersey. The state of New York, in contrast, still requires a two-thirds majority for approval of a takeover proposal. In a merger, the traditional legal doctrine was that the minority must agree to the terms approved by the majority. The minority still has the right to sue on a number of issues such as the fairness of the pricing of ownership interests.

In most cases, shareholders of the respective corporations approve the merger by a wide margin. However, notable exceptions occur, most recently the merger of Hewlett-Packard and Compaq that was announced in September 2001. In that merger, much opposition was vocalized on the acquirer side from Walter Hewlett, board member of Hewlett-Packard and son of a cofounder, other family members and trusts associated with the cofounders, employees of Hewlett-Packard, and numerous financial institutions. Eventually, Hewlett-Packard management prevailed by a narrow margin, receiving roughly 51% of the vote, allowing the merger to close in May 2002.

After approval by the majority of those with voting rights, the act of "merger" takes place upon the filing of appropriate documents with the states in which the participant companies are chartered. One corporation survives, the others go out of existence. The surviving company assumes the assets and liabilities of the merging firms. When the Nabisco Corporation merged with Standard Brands, Standard Brands was dissolved and Nabisco survived. Nabisco itself was subsequently acquired by the RJ Reynolds tobacco company to form RJR Nabisco in 1986; split into two companies again in 1999. In some combinations, a new entity is created. For example, Citigroup was formed in 1998 as a result of the merger of Citicorp and Travelers Group. Each share in Citicorp received 2.5 Citigroup shares, and each share in Travelers Group received 1 share in Citigroup.

The law also makes provision for a short-form merger. The legal procedures are streamlined, and shareholder approval is not required. In such a transaction, the ownership of the corporation is concentrated in the hands of a small group, usually referred to as insiders. The threshold ownership requirement is usually 90%.

Sometimes the identity of one of the companies in the merger transaction is preserved. For example, when General Motors bought Electronic Data Systems (EDS) from Ross Perot, EDS became a subsidiary of General Motors. In 1996, General Motors spun off its EDS subsidiary.

Furthermore, when one firm controls a number of other firms held in the form of subsidiaries, the parent firm is referred to as a holding company. Each of the subsidiaries remains a separate legal entity. In a holding company system, the parent has a controlling interest in each of the subsidiaries.

The percentage of ownership required for a controlling interest varies. If a target has widely dispersed ownership, holdings of 25% to 50% probably give the parent effective control. Ownership of more than 50% conveys certain control. If a parent owns 80% or more of the shares of its subsidiary, the financial results of the subsidiary can be consolidated for income tax purposes.

The preceding discussion conveys much of the terminology of the legal rules governing merger transactions. Many of the same principles apply to tender offers.

THE NATURE OF TENDER OFFERS

In a tender offer, the bidder, which typically seeks the approval of the company management and board of directors of the target company, makes an offer directly to shareholders of the target firm. The bidder's obtaining 50% or more of the shares of the target firm is equivalent to having received shareholder approval. In this case, the shareholders have voted with their pocketbooks.

In a merger, the traditional legal doctrine held that the minority must agree to the terms negotiated. In a tender offer, the offer is extended to the individual shareholders so that management and the board of directors can be bypassed. The law is still not clear on whether merger doctrine applies. In some cases, after the bidder has obtained control, the terms may be "crammed down" on the minority. Sometimes the acquirer may decide not to complete the buyout. In this case, there is a "freeze-in" problem in that the minority is subject to the decision of the majority holders. The minority always has the right to bring legal action if it feels that it has been treated inequitably.

During 2001 and 2002, numerous minority squeeze outs occurred. For the most part, these cases arose when a parent corporation had previously issued shares of a subsidiary in an equity carve out, typically retaining majority ownership. Many of these carve outs occurred during the mid to late 1990s during a rising stock market. With the substantial market decline during 2000 and 2001, many of the parents chose to buy back the minority stakes at prices considerably below those paid when they were issued to the public via the carve out. Court decisions by the Delaware Chancery Court in 2001 have eased the standards by which majority holders can buy out the minority interest. In essence, the court decisions hold that the majority holder can make the takeover bid without demonstrating that it is offering a fair price. In addition, the subsidiary company can remain neutral on the buyout decision. Despite the apparent advantage given to the parent corporation, shareholders of subsidiaries have not been bought out at low premiums. A typical example is the 2002 case of Sabre Corporation offering a $23 cash tender to the shareholders of Travelocity.com, its 70%-owned subsidiary. The $23 offer represented a 19.8% premium to the stock price on the close of trading the day prior to the announced bid. Rather than immediately accepting the bid, Travelocity.com appointed a special committee of outside directors, who recommended that shareholders reject the bid. Sabre responded by increasing the bid to $28, thereby paying a premium of 45.8%. Most of the other minority squeeze outs in recent times have had a similar outcome. One explanation for the positive outcomes is that the parent corporations seek to avoid costly litigation instituted by target shareholders.

Different kinds of tender offers have different kinds of provisions. The financial press from time to time reports detailed tender offers, summarizing the provisions of the documents sent directly to shareholders. These, in effect, are public notices of the proposals mailed to the shareholders. The tender offer may be conditional or unconditional. For example, the offer may be contingent on obtaining 50% of the shares of the target. The tender offer may be restricted or unrestricted. A restricted tender offer prespecifies the number or percentage of shares the bidder will take. An "any-or-all" tender offer is unconditional and unrestricted.

If the tender offer is restricted, oversubscription may result in prorating by the bidder. For example, assume that the bidder tenders for 60% of a target company's 1,000 shares of stock and that 80% of the total shares are offered. The bidder may decide to accept all 800 or to accept only 600 shares, which is 75% of the amount tendered by the shareholders. Then, for example, if shareholder A offered 100 shares, the bidder would buy only 75.

The law requires a 20-day waiting period during which the target company shareholders may make their decision to offer their shares for sale. The bidder would then have to wait until after the 20-day waiting period to calculate the proration percentage. If the bidder decides to extend the offer, the proration period also is extended automatically.

Another complication arises when other bidders compete with the first bidder—a contested offer. The law requires that when a new tender offer is made, the stockholders of the target company must have 10 business days to consider that new offer. The effect is to extend the initial offer period. For example, suppose 18 days have elapsed since the first offer. If a second bid is made, the shareholders have an additional 10 days, which is equivalent to 28 days on the first bid and 10 days on the second bid. If the second bid occurred 5 days after the first bid was made, the original 20-day waiting period is not extended because 5 + 10 is less than the original 20-day waiting period.

Another variation is the use of a two-tier tender offer. The first tier, typically for cash, is to obtain 50% or more of the target's stock to obtain control. In the second tier, a smaller value may be offered because control already has been established. The second tier is often paid in securities such as debt rather than cash or equity of the bidder.

A variation of the two-tier offer is the "three-piece suitor." The three steps are (1) an initial toehold; (2) a tender offer to obtain control; and (3) after control and a majority of shareholders have tendered, a freeze-out purchase of the minority shareholders. As discussed earlier, the threat of litigation by target shareholders can often mitigate these freeze-out purchases.

The preceding by no means describes all of the different types of tender offers or merger patterns, nor does it cover the multitude of legal issues that can result. We simply convey the general patterns. The details would require legal and accounting expertise of a high order.

RISK ARBITRAGE IN M&A ACTIVITY

Arbitrage is defined as purchasing in one market for immediate sale in another at a higher price. Thus, arbitrageurs take advantage of temporary price discrepancies between markets. By their actions, the differences are eliminated, driving prices up by their purchases in one market and driving prices down by their sales in the other. Arbitrageurs may take offsetting positions in one security in two markets or in equivalent securities in one or two markets to make profits without assuming any risk under the theory of pure arbitrage.

In the area of mergers and acquisitions, risk arbitrage is the practice of buying the stock of takeover targets after a merger is publicly announced and holding the stock until the deal is officially consummated. The risk arbitrageur purchases the stock at a discount to its eventual value at the close of the merger. By taking a position in the stock of target firms, risk arbitrageurs are, in effect, betting that the merger will be successful. Thus, the term *risk arbitrage* is used differently from the true or original concept of arbitrage.

ILLUSTRATIVE EXAMPLE

An example will illustrate the arbitrage operation. In May 2002, Sears Roebuck & Company announced a definitive agreement to acquire Lands' End Incorporated in a cash tender offer for $62 for a total purchase price of $1.9 billion. On May 13, the day of the announcement, the stock of Lands' End rose to $61.72 from, $51.02 at the close on the prior trading day, yielding a return of 21% to the target shareholders. Existing shareholders faced the following choice—hold the stock until merger consummation and receive the cash tender price of $62 or sell the stock to a merger arbitrageur. Management of the merging parties forecasted that the merger would close in 45 days. Thus, the shareholder would expect to earn a return of 0.45%, yielding an annualized return of 3.7%. These returns assume that the deal will succeed with 100% probability. If the deal happens to fail, and deals fail for a wide variety of reasons, the stock price would likely drop considerably. In fact, the stock price will often fall below the price that it traded at before the deal was announced. Thus, the investor—faced with the possibility, albeit low, of a large loss in the case of deal failure—will often choose to sell soon after the announcement rather than holding the stock in order to capture the 0.45% return. To facilitate the investors' demand for liquidity, a risk arbitrageur steps in and purchases the shares at a discount to the promised cash tender price. In a stock merger, the risk arbitrageur does not simply buy the target stock and hold it until merger consummation. Rather, because arbitrageurs are betting on the deal going through, they will short the acquirer stock in order to hedge out market risk. For every target share purchased, the arbitrage will short a number of shares equal to the exchange ratio provided in the merger. For example, if the merger agreement calls for an exchange of two acquirer shares for each target share, the risk arbitrageur will short two acquirer shares for each target share long.

THE NATURE OF THE ARBITRAGE BUSINESS

Traditionally, arbitrageurs have responded to announced takeover bids. They evaluate the offer and assess its probability of success relative to the value of the target. They must consider the likelihood and consequences of a bidding war between alternative potential acquirers, various takeover defenses, a white knight, and so on.

Information is the principal raw material in the arbitrage business. The vast majority of this information comes from careful analysis of publicly available documents, such as financial statements and filings with the SEC and/or regulatory agencies. Arbitrageurs buy expert advice from lawyers and industry specialists. They may hire investment bankers to assist in their assessment of the offer. In some cases, the investment bankers involved in the transaction may double-check their own assessment of valuation against that of the arbitrageurs. They attempt to get all available information from the investment bankers representing the target and bidding firms and from the participants themselves. This phase of information gathering may cross over the boundary into the gray area of insider trading if the pursuit is too vigorous.

With the increased pace in the late 1990s, arbitrageurs have in some cases attempted to anticipate takeover bids to establish their stock position in advance of any public announcement, thus increasing their potential return. To do so, they try to identify undervalued firms that would make attractive targets and to track down rumors of impending bids; they may monitor price increases that might signal someone is accumulating stock in a particular company to ferret out potential bidders before the 5% disclosure trigger at which the purchaser has to announce his or her intentions. The risk of taking a position based upon this type of activity is clearly greater. Also, if one firm in an industry is acquired, other firms in the industry may be expected to become targets. Famed investor Mario Gabelli in early 2001 started a fund, Enterprise Mergers and Acquisition Fund, that specifically identifies companies that the fund manager believes will be acquired in the subsequent 12 to 18 months.

ARBITRAGE FUNDS

The basic philosophy of a merger arbitrage fund is to eliminate market risk by taking an arbitrage position in connection with multiple merger and takeover transactions. The fund engages in intensive research in order to mitigate deal risk and does not invest in rumors. The fund generally takes a position only after a public announcement has been made that two firms are likely to sign a definitive agreement. In most cases, the price of the target stock trades at a discount to the stated offer, whether it be in cash, stock, or a combination of cash and stock. The fund buys the target stock, and in the case of stock deals, the fund also shorts the stock of the acquirer in order to hedge against market risk. As a result of hedging out market risk, the main risk is deal risk, namely whether or not the deal is completed. To mitigate deal risk, most funds hold a sizable number of deals, generally at least 20 or so. During times when deal flow is especially high, a merger arbitrage fund might hold as many as 60 deals. The fund also will mitigate deal failure risk by holding high-quality deals, namely deals in which definitive agreements are made by two financially stable firms. The goal of these merger arbitrage funds is to provide annual returns of 10% or greater, and to provide returns that are relatively uncorrelated with the overall stock market, therefore adding diversification to the investor's portfolio.

Although the performance of these funds has often been high, turbulent periods have occurred as well. During the stock market crash of October 1987, the risk arbitrage firms and the arbitrage departments of most investment banks suffered huge losses. As a result of the crash, many deals were repriced or canceled outright. An arbitrageur betting on the outcome of the merger going through and expecting to receive a small return for this bet was suddenly faced with extraordinary losses. In addition, many of the arbitrage firms employed leverage in their merger arbitrage portfolios, thereby exacerbating the losses. Consequently, many of the arbitrage shops failed immediately and went out of business. Arbitrage funds also suffered large losses in August 1998 at the time of the well-known collapse of Long Term Capital Management, a hedge fund that bet heavily on merger arbitrage among its several trading strategies. After 1998, merger arbitrage funds have chosen to be more diversified across deals and to use less financial leverage in order to minimize the likelihood of fund failure.

Summary

This chapter has summarized some basic terminology and concepts, providing a foundation for developing further knowledge and understanding of M&As. Merger activity is driven by economic and cultural trends. Recent change forces driving mergers include globalization, technology, deregulation, favorable economic and financial conditions, and changes in industry organization. In tender offers, the bidder contacts shareholders directly, inviting them to sell (tender) their shares at an offer price. Mergers usually involve some mutuality of negotiations. In practice, the acquiring company may make a successful tender offer for the target followed by a formal merger of the two companies.

From an economic standpoint, different types of mergers or tender offers are grouped on the basis of the stage of economic activity and the degree of relatedness of the firms. Horizontal mergers involve firms operating in the same kind of business activity. Vertical mergers take place between firms in different stages of production operations. Pure conglomerate mergers involve firms engaged in unrelated types of business activity. Financial conglomerates develop financial planning and control systems for groups of segments that may be otherwise unrelated from a business standpoint. Financial conglomerates operate as an internal capital market in assigning funds to segments; future allocations of funds will depend on the performance of the segments. Managerial conglomerates provide managerial counsel and interactions with their segments. Concentric companies carry the idea further in having staff expertise in specific managerial functions such as production, marketing, and finance.

Statutory mergers meet the formal legal requirements of the state or states in which the parties to the merger are chartered. After the approval of the tender offer, followed by a merger agreement or the approval of a merger directly, the act of merger takes place upon the filing of appropriate documents with the state or states. Tender offers can have various types of conditions or restrictions.

Risk arbitrage in connection with M&As is the practice of making short-term gains from the relationship among the takeover bid price and the relative prices of the bidder's and target's stock. The announcement of a merger or tender offer causes the stock price of the target to rise because the bidder pays a premium. Arbitrageurs generally will take a long position in the target stock, and a short position in the bidder stock in the case of stock mergers. For example, if the bidder offers to trade 1.5 shares for 1 share of the target and, net of commissions, the bidder stock sells for $10 and the target stock sells for $14.25, the arbitrageur can lock in a

$0.75 gain by shorting 1.5 shares of the bidder and going long on 1 share of the target stock. If anything, the spread is likely to move in favor of the arbitrageur. The big risk is that the deal might not be completed. Some arbitrageurs also attempt to establish their stock position before the run-up of the target's stock price by trying to anticipate takeover announcements through careful research.

Questions

1.1 What is the difference between a merger and a tender offer?

1.2 What are some of the potential synergy advantages of horizontal mergers?

1.3 How do the economic advantages of vertical mergers differ from those of horizontal mergers?

1.4 Are there valid distinctions among pure conglomerates, managerial conglomerates, and a concentric company? If so, what are they?

1.5 An arbitrage firm (A) notes that a bidder (B) whose stock is selling at $30 makes an offer for a target (T) selling at $40 to exchange 1.5 shares of B for 1 share of T. Shares to T rise to $44; B stays at $30. A sells 1.5 B short for $45 and goes long on T at $44. One month later the deal is completed with B at $30 and T at $45. What is A's dollar and percentage annualized gain, assuming a required 50% margin and 8% cost of funds on both transactions?

APPENDIX A

MERGER PROCESS INFORMATION IN PROXY STATEMENTS

A rich source of information about the merger process is contained in the proxy statements to shareholders issued in connection with reviews by the U.S. Securities and Exchange Commission (SEC). These proxy statements include the designation of a future shareholders' meeting at which approval of the transaction is solicited. Also, the statements give the details of the merger agreement, company backgrounds, reasons for the merger, and opinions of legal and financial advisers. These proxy statements are available in hard copy from the companies involved. They also are available on the Internet at the SEC Web page (www.sec.gov) within the EDGAR database.

To illustrate the vast amount of information available in the proxy statements to mergers, we examine the proxy for WorldCom's acquisition of MCI. Many proxy statements begin with a list of questions and answers addressing potential concerns of investors. This provides a quick reference that avoids some of the "legalese" of the rest of the document. In the WorldCom/MCI proxy, the questions addressed concerns including the benefits of the merger, the other bids for MCI by British Telecommunications (BT) and GTE, how to vote on the merger, the terms of the deal, the tax consequences, dividends, regulatory approval, and other topics. These questions filled about the first 3 pages of the WorldCom proxy statement (out of 135 pages before appendices).

Following the investors' questions section is generally a summary of the topics covered in the rest of the material. In the case of the WorldCom Proxy statement, the summary provides a 10-page overview of the following 120 pages. It gives descriptions of the businesses, information about the shareholders' meetings, terms of the deal, and most of the other topics covered in the comprehensive proxy statement.

The proxy statement is very detailed. A proxy statement probably will address more issues and concerns than any individual investor will have. This is necessary to attempt to prevent liability if the firms are sued for not disclosing some piece of information. The WorldCom/MCI proxy contains a description of the risks associated with the transaction. It cautions investors about the risks concerning "forward-looking statements." It also lists 13 risk factors particular to the merger. These include uncertainties in integrating the acquired companies and achieving cost savings, risks associated with regulation and obtaining government approvals of the merger, dilution of voting interest for WorldCom shareholders, risks of international business, and so on.

Most merger proxy statements give a detailed outline of the merger agreement. MCI agreed to accept $51 in WorldCom stock. However, the firms included a table detailing how that consideration would increase if the value of WorldCom stock exceeded a certain point, or fall if the stock dropped below a designated value. As long as WorldCom remained within a window between $29 and $41, MCI would receive $51 of WorldCom stock.

The "Background of the Merger" section is an account of the negotiations between the two merging firms. In the case of WorldCom/MCI, this section begins as far back as 1994, when BT took a 20% stake in MCI. It details the merger agreement between BT and MCI (announced August 21, 1997), and the subsequent announcements of the WorldCom (October 1, 1997) and GTE (October 15, 1997) offers. The background includes details about board meetings and decisions, and meetings between the senior management of the merging firms. WorldCom had extensive negotiations with MCI as well as with BT to arrive at a deal to buy BT's shares of MCI.

The "Reasons for the Merger" section details management's views of the gains created by the merger. This section often includes estimates of synergies and a description of the overall strategic motivations for the merger. WorldCom and MCI looked to combine two leaders in long-distance telecommunication, as well as to capitalize on the booming Internet industry. The combined company would provide extensive telecommunications services. Synergies were projected to be $2.5 billion in 1999 and $5.6 billion in 2002.

The "Opinion of Financial Adviser" sections give insight into some of the findings of the investment banks involved in the deal. Salomon Smith Barney, WorldCom's adviser, used analyses including historical stock price performance, historical exchange ratio analysis, synergy analysis, and business division analysis. MCI used at least two advisers, Lazard Freres and Lehman Brothers, who did similar analyses of the deal.

Merger proxy statements also address the issues of taxability and accounting treatment. The tax sections usually tries to cover any possible scenario that would require payment of taxes. Accounting treatment details the effects of purchase or pooling on the resulting financial statements of the combined firm. The WorldCom/MCI deal was nontaxable to most shareholders. It was accounted for under the purchase method of accounting.

The accounting method will be reflected in the "Pro Forma Financial Information" section, which attempts to capture what the financials or the future combined firm will look like. However, as the WorldCom/MCI proxy states, the financials "are presented for comparative purpose only and are not intended to be indicative of actual results . . . nor do they purport to indicate results which may be attained in the future."

The foregoing is only a small portion of the information contained within a merger proxy statement. To illustrate, a partial list of the Table of Contents from the WorldCom/MCI proxy gives an indication of how much information is readily available.

MCI WorldCom Proxy Table of Contents

QUESTIONS

One of the valuable benefits of going through a proxy statement is that it gives you a good feel and understanding of the takeover process. With that objective in mind, the following questions required selection of one of the large mergers from 2001. Go to the EDGAR database on the SEC Web page (www.sec.gov) and look for "S-4" or "DEF14A" forms dated a few months after the merger announcement date for the company you select.

Choose one of the mergers from the table.

Approximate Announcement Date	Buyer	Seller
9/4/01	Hewlett-Packard	Compaq
11/18/01	Phillips Petroleum	Conoco
6/25/01	Washington Mutual	Dime Bancorp
6/18/01	Land O'Lakes	Purina Mills
7/31/01	Berkshire Hathaway	XTRA

A1.1 Was the merger taxable or nontaxable?

A1.2 What was the method of payment (stock, cash, debt)?

A1.3 Describe the major products of each company. Classify the transaction as related (10), unrelated (1), or somewhere in between (with a number). Give reasons.

A1.4 The Federal Trade Commission classifies mergers and tender offers as horizontal, vertical, or conglomerate. Explain what each of these terms means, and classify this one.

A1.5 Summarize the reasons given for the transaction. If an estimate of synergies is provided, summarize the dollar amounts with the specific sources of savings.

A1.6 What does the proxy say about what happens if the merger agreement is terminated?

A1.7 What does the proxy say about the rights of dissenting shareholders?

A1.8 What does the proxy say about the exercise of executive stock options as a result of the merger?

A1.9 Summarize the methods of valuation employed by the financial adviser to each of the companies. If comparable companies or transactions are cited, list them and explain the ratios used. Describe and explain the discounted cash flow (DCF) method or methods used by the financial advisers as the basis for the fairness opinion.

APPENDIX B

THE AOL AND TIME WARNER MERGER

This appendix provides a summary of the America Online (AOL) merger with Time Warner (TWX) as a symbol of important new directions in M&A activities. The AOL-TWX combination is an illustration of the broader industry implications of combining "new economy" companies with "old economy" companies. Many regard the merger as a precursor to more pervasive impacts of the Internet companies on more traditional industries.

A merger between AOL and Time Warner was announced on January 10, 2000. A new company named AOL Timer Warner Incorporated was the planned outcome of the merger. AOL shareholders would receive 1 new share for each AOL share, and TWX shareholders would receive 1.5 new shares for each TWX share.

The merger captured the imagination of the public. AOL agreed to pay stock worth about $165 billion for Time Warner, a 70% premium. At the announcement, it was estimated that the market value of the combined companies would be $350 billion. As important as the large value of the deal was the combination of "new economy" and "old economy" companies. AOL's stock price had boomed in the 1990s as a hot Internet stock. Investors saw its potential for significant future earnings growth based on its implementation of technology. Meanwhile, Time Warner was a leader of old-line media, owning publishing, television, cable, movie, and other entertainment properties. Although AOL only brought 18% of the revenues and 30% of the operating cash flows to the table, AOL shareholders would own 55% of the combined firm.

New technologies were crucial in transforming the industries of AOL and Time Warner. The Internet industry underwent rapid transformation in the 1990s. In the early part of the decade, it was seen as a kind of virtual library. The Internet would be the means to exchange tremendous amounts of academic information easily. The introduction of Netscape Navigator In 1994 made the Internet more accessible to the masses. During the late 1990s, e-commerce became a central function of the Internet, with shopping online becoming "the next big thing." Many analysts believe the AOL Time Warner merger is the sign that multimedia entertainment will be the next major step for the Internet and a precursor to combining more old and new economy industries.

For all the promise of the Internet as a source of multimedia entertainment many challenges have to be overcome. Although some believe that Internet sources eventually will replace print media, many find it cumbersome to read from a computer screen for long periods of time. Television on demand (where consumers pay to watch programming of their own choosing) has long been a dream for media companies, but so far it never has been implemented effectively. The movie and music industries have experienced challenges from the Internet in the form of piracy. In particular, some consumers are finding it easier to download their favorite songs from the Internet than to purchase CDs. However, virtually all these multimedia activities are eased by faster Internet connections, sparking the conversion to broadband.

The reasons for the AOL Time Warner merger reflect the challenges that both companies face in the changing business environment. AOL was a content distributor. As an Internet service provider (ISP), monthly fees are the source of 70% of its revenues. AOL faces competition from Microsoft and from free and low-cost Internet access providers. In order to continue its profit growth, AOL could no longer rely on subscription revenue. Instead, AOL had to pursue increased advertising and e-commerce. It needed unique content and services to distinguish itself from its competitors.

Furthermore, AOL was constricted in a world shifting toward high-speed Internet connections. AOL currently relies on dialup modems using regular telephone lines. The speed restrictions are a bottleneck for multimedia content delivery. Because AOL doesn't own any high-speed lines, it would have been forced to hash out deals with companies that do (e.g., AT&T). Once it became clear the broadband cable Internet access could become the future of the ISP industry, AOL became the most vocal supporter of government intervention to force cable firms to open their cables to outside ISPs. This would allow firms like AOL to offer its services to the cable customers of other firms without having to own the "pipes" that carry the information to the home. Uncertainty concerning the future of open access was a motivation for AOL to acquire its own cable system.

TWX was a content producer and a broadband content distributor. Its revenues were growing at 10% to 15% per year. Any opportunity for higher growth would require developing a successful Internet business. So far, it had no clear Internet strategy and had been frustrated by its inability to exploit its cable and media assets more effectively in the Internet. Its interactive TV, Full Service Network, failed. Its Pathfinder Web site was a fiasco. Its broadband distribution business over cable lines through its partial ownership of the Internet provider Road Runner had not grown as rapidly as was hoped. Thus, the merger answered AOL's concerns about how it would implement its broadband strategy without owning content or having access to high-speed lines. It allows TWX to leverage its entertainment assets more effectively online with the benefit of AOL Internet resources and expertise.

The merger will link AOL's broad customer relationships to TWX's content and service distribution. The premier Internet distribution company in the world will be paired with the leading owner of copyrights in the world. AOL brings its worldwide Internet services, AOL and CompuServe, with a combined 22.2 million subscribers base or 54% of the total ISP business; also portal sites such as Netscape Netcenter and AOL.com; Web browsers like Netscape Navigator and Communicator; and several leading Internet brands such as ICQ and A.I.M. instant messaging. Digital City, AOL MovieFone, and MapQuest.com.

TWX brings the second-largest U.S. cable television system with 13 million subscribers in Time Warner Cable and 350,000 subscribers in its partially owned broadband Internet provider, Road Runner; print media businesses that include Time Incorporated with 33 magazines such as *Entertainment Weekly, Fortune, Life, People, Sports Illustrated,* and *Time,* with an estimated 120 to 130 million readers and a 21% share of the 1998 consumer magazine advertising dollars; the eighth-largest book publishing business, which includes Book-of-the-Month Club, Time Life, Little Brown, and Warner Books; television broadcasting with 10 cable channels including CNN with a global reach of more than 1 billion, HBO with 30 million subscribers, TNT and TBS with 75 million homes, and the WB Network; movie and television production such as Warner Bros. and New Line Cinema with 8% of the domestic film market; and music with Warner Music Group, which accounted for 16% of all records sold. The new company embraces nearly all types of media including cable, magazine, movies, music, and online, offering new opportunities for cross promotion and expanded e-commerce.

It was estimated that the combination would save $1.0 billion in 2001. Potential cost savings would arise from administrative savings and from substantially lower advertising and promotion costs. The new management team states that layoffs are unlikely and the intention is to expand the company. In the future, broadband strategies could represent substantial savings; for example, it could dramatically cut manu-facturing and shipping costs associated with audio and video delivery.

Perhaps due to skepticism about the estimates of synergies or the overall strategic vision of the merger, the market had a negative initial reaction to the announcement of the merger. Although TWX stock took off, due to the large premium, AOL stock suf-fered, as illustrated by Figure B1.1. On February 19, 2000, AOL stock reached its low point of 54 and began to recover. By late March, AOL was trading at more than 80% of its pre-merger levels. Some people attributed the loss of value to the fact that investors did not yet "get" the merger. In some mergers, the complexity of the deal makes it hard to immediately recognize future revenue sources, cost savings, and other synergies that may arise. The AOL Time Warner deal was further complicated by the fact that AOL was covered by Internet financial analysts, and Time Warner was covered by media financial analysts. No analysts were fully conversant with both businesses.

This provides a summary of the economic and business aspects of the transaction. Strong views have been expressed on other issues. One concern is media independence. Another is editorial integrity. These issues were raised directly by Jim Lehrer in his January 12, 2000, interview with Steve Case, head of AOL, and Gerald Levin, head of TWX. Levin assured Jim Lehrer that Henry Luce had left a legacy that Time was to be operated not only in the interest of shareholders, but also in the interest of the public. Case emphasized that AOL would support the public service objective. He argued that individual segments of the combined firm in the future would be even more independent of other segments to demonstrate their integrity.

Some critics fear that a small number of firms increasingly control viewer choices. Others argue the opposite. In earlier decades, viewers were limited to the offerings of four major networks; today every viewer has a multiplicity of choices. At least dozens of choices are possible through cable television, although the majority of cable channels are owned by the few large media firms that control the networks. Thus, critics argue that although the number of choices has increased, fewer viewpoints are repre-sented in deciding what those choices will be. The AOL Time Warner merger is an indicator that the Internet may fall under the same media influences that control television and other media outlets. Indeed, the merger gave rise to speculation about other firms that could follow the same "new" and "old" media combination strategy. Prominently men-tioned were Yahoo! and Disney as potential partners.

The convergence between TV, the PC, and the Internet will continue to evolve. No one knows for sure what the nature of the ultimate development will be. Many firms and interest groups will shape the future of the media industry. Other media firms are going to have to decide if they will follow Time Warner and seek a strong Internet partner, or if they will con-tinue independently. Cable providers like AT&T and the new AOL Time Warner will have to resolve the debate with Internet service providers to determine who will bring broadband Internet access into peo-ple's homes. Entertainment firms will have to coordi-nate with technology firms if they are to achieve inter-active television. Such dynamic interactions will be shaped by mergers, joint ventures, strategic alliances, and other forms of interfirm relationships. For updates see Chapter 3.

QUESTIONS

B1.1 Are major problems likely when combining different cultures in this combination of "bricks and clicks"?

B1.2 Discuss the issue of the integration of diverse compensation structures between Time Warner and AOL.

B1.3 Has the merger yielded the synergies fore-casted for 2001 and 2002?

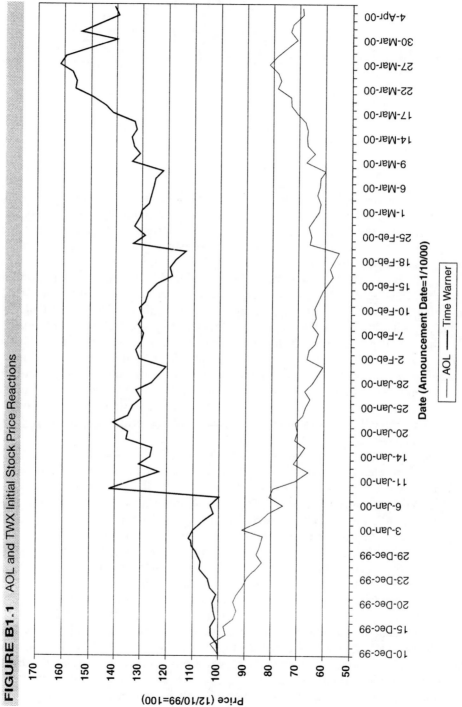

FIGURE B1.1 AOL and TWX Initial Stock Price Reactions

CHAPTER 2
THE LEGAL AND
REGULATORY FRAMEWORK

This chapter discusses the laws and rules or regulations promulgated to cover securities trading and takeover activity. We discuss securities trading generally as well as takeover activity, the central focus of this book, because the two are so interlinked that they cannot be separated. Indeed, the laws that were enacted to regulate takeover activity were made a part of the original securities acts enacted in the early 1930s. We also examine the leading cases related to the laws we cover, because they give more explicit content to the nature of the law and its intent.

As a preview, we briefly describe Securities and Exchange Commission (SEC) filings by the merging parties in a recent major merger. On December 4, 2000, PepsiCo, Incorporated, and Quaker Oats Company announced an agreement for PepsiCo to acquire Quaker Oats in a merger whereby PepsiCo would exchange 2.3 shares of its stock for each share of Quaker, up to a maximum value of $105 for each share of Quaker. The resulting firm would have a market capitalization in excess of $80 billion, making it one of the world's five-largest consumer products companies. The merger was completed successfully 8 months later on August 3, 2001. During the course of the merger transaction, the merging parties filed numerous documents with the SEC. Table 2.1 shows a time line and summary description of these SEC filings. Next, we describe the various filings associated with the merger.

On the day of the merger announcement, PepsiCo filed an 8-K with the SEC. The 8-K contained the press release that PepsiCo used to publicly disseminate its plan to acquire Quaker Oats. Form 8-K is a "current report" form required under the 1934 Securities Act to report the occurrence of any material event that would be of importance to investors. On the same day, Quaker Oats filed a Form 425 with the SEC, which provided a fact sheet regarding the merger, management's commentary about the merger, and anticipated questions with follow-up answers regarding the merger. Form 425 is required in the filing of various communications in connection with mergers. One day later, PepsiCo filed a 425, providing a transcript of the conference call that it held with analysts and investors on the prior day. That same day, Quaker filed an 8-K announcing the termination of an earlier merger agreement that it had with the Coca-Cola Company. Two days later, Quaker Oats filed another 8-K, containing the full copy of the merger agreement with PepsiCo. The merger agreement contains all the terms and stipulations of the planned merger. In accordance with the 1933 Securities Act, PepsiCo filed Form S-4 on January 9, 2001. Form S-4 is used in the registration of securities associated with mergers and was required in this particular case because PepsiCo was acquiring Quaker with stock. Note that 2 months later, on March 13, 2001, PepsiCo filed an amendment to the original S-4. On March 21, 2001, Quaker Oats filed a Form 14A, the definitive merger proxy statement that is required under the 1934 Securities Act. This form is intended to provide the shareholders with

TABLE 2.1 SEC Filings for the PepsiCo and Quaker Oats Merger

Firm	Form	Filing Date	# of Pages	Description
PepsiCo	8-K	12-4-2000	4	Merger announcement press release
Quaker Oats	425	12-4-2000	12	Merger fact sheet; questions and answers about merger; management discussion of merger
PepsiCo	425	12-5-2000	62	Transcript of conference call discussing merger with analysts and investors
Quaker Oats	8-K	12-5-2000	2	Termination announcement of Quaker Oats merger with Coca-Cola
Quaker Oats	8-K	12-7-2000	128	Merger agreement
Quaker Oats	425	12-8-2000	8	Quaker Oats employee information regarding merger
PepsiCo	S-4	01-9-2001	384	Joint proxy statement/prospectus
Quaker Oats	425	02-8-2001	3	Announcement that Federal Trade Commission (FTC) requires additional information regarding merger
PepsiCo	S-4A	03-13-2001	432	Amendment to registration statement
Quaker Oats	425	03-16-2001	4	Quaker Oats update of merger to employees
Quaker Oats	DEF 14A	03-21-2001	366	Merger proxy statement
Quaker Oats	8-K	03-27-2001	2	Notification of European Union approval
PepsiCo	425	04-17-2001	4	Merger information update to PepsiCo employees
PepsiCo	425	05-03-2001	4	Announcement that PepsiCo shareholders approved merger
Quaker Oats	8-K	07-03-2001	3	Announcement that Quaker is extending date for PepsiCo to divest assets
Quaker Oats	8-K	08-02-2001	2	Announcement of FTC clearance
Quaker Oats	15-12B	08-03-2001	2	Notification of securities registration completion

Compilation from Edgar Online.

all the necessary information in order for them to vote on the upcoming merger. Along the way, both firms continued to file Forms 8-K and 425, updating shareholders of important events that might materially impact the merger plans. Finally, on August 3, 2001, just one day after receiving FTC clearance to proceed with the merger, Quaker Oats filed Form 15-12B under the 1934 Securities Act. Form 15-12B is a notice as to the termination of registration of securities and to the suspension of the filing of periodic reports. These filings were all largely required by the Securities Act of 1933 and the Securities Exchange Act of 1934, two important securities laws implemented in the aftermath of the stock market crash of 1929.

THE MAIN SECURITIES LAWS

Because wide price fluctuations are likely to be associated with merger and acquisition activity, public policy has been concerned that investors be treated fairly. Legislation and regulations have sought to carry over to the takeover activity of recent decades the philosophy of the securities acts of the 1930s. The aim is prompt and full disclosure of relevant information in the effort to achieve a fair "playing field" for all participants. Some of the earlier legislation remains fully applicable, but it has been augmented with changes in statutes and regulations.

Because the takeover laws are so closely interlinked with securities laws generally, we begin with a summary of the major securities laws. This provides a framework to which we can relate the laws, rules, and regulations governing takeover activity.

FEDERAL SECURITIES LAWS

The federal securities laws consist mainly of eight statutes:

> Securities Act of 1933 (SA)
> Securities Exchange Act of 1934 (SEA)
> Public Utility Holding Company Act of 1935 (PUHCA)
> Trust Indenture Act of 1939 (TIA)
> Investment Company Act of 1940 (ICA)
> Investment Advisers Act of 1940 (IAA)
> Securities Investor Protection Act of 1970 (SIPA)
> Sarbanes-Oxley Act of 2002 (SOA)

We first summarize what each of the laws covers to provide an overview of the pattern of legislation. We then develop some of the more important provisions in greater detail. The early major acts were enacted beginning in 1933. There is a reason for the timing. The stock market crash of 1929 was followed by continued depressed markets for several years. Because so many investors lost money, both houses of Congress conducted lengthy hearings to find the causes and the culprits. The hearings were marked by sensationalism and wide publicity. The securities acts of 1933 and 1934 were the direct outgrowth of the congressional hearings.

The Securities Act of 1933 regulates the sale of securities to the public. It provides for the registration of public offerings of securities to establish a record of representations. All participants involved in preparing the registration statements are subject to legal liability for any misstatement of facts or omissions of vital information.

The Securities Exchange Act of 1934 established the Securities and Exchange Commission (SEC) to administer the securities laws and to regulate practices in the purchase and sale of securities.

The purpose of the Public Utility Holding Company Act of 1935 was to correct abuses in the financing and operation of electric and gas public utility holding company systems and to bring about simplification of the corporate structures and physical integration of the operating properties. The SEC's responsibilities under the act of 1935 were substantially completed by the 1950s.

The Trust Indenture Act of 1939 applies to public issues of debt securities with a value of $5 million or more. Debt issues represent a form of promissory note associated with a long document setting out the terms of a complex contract and referred to as the indenture. The 1939 act sets forth the responsibilities of the indenture trustee (often a commercial bank) and specifies requirements to be included in the indenture (bond contract) for the protection of the bond purchasers. In September 1987, the SEC recommended to Congress a number of amendments to establish new conflict-of-interest standards for indenture trustees and to recognize new developments in financing techniques.

The Investment Company Act of 1940 regulates publicly owned companies engaged in the business of investing and trading in securities. Investment companies are subject to rules formulated and enforced by the SEC. The act of 1940 was amended in 1970 to place additional controls on management compensation and sales charges.

The Investment Advisers Act of 1940, as amended in 1960, provides for registration and regulation of investment advisers, as the name suggests.

The Securities Investor Protection Act of 1970 established the Securities Investor Protection Corporation, (SIPCO). This corporation is empowered to supervise the liquidation of bankrupt securities firms and to arrange for payments to their customers.

The Securities Act Amendments of 1975 were passed after 4 years of research and investigation into the changing nature of securities markets. The study recommended the abolition of fixed minimum brokerage commissions. It called for increased automation of trading by utilizing data processing technology to link markets. The SEC was mandated to work with the securities industry to develop an effective national market system to achieve the goal of nationwide competition in securities trading with centralized reporting of price quotations and transactions. It proposed a central order routing system to find the best available price.

In 1978, the SEC began to streamline the securities registration process. Large, well-known corporations were permitted to abbreviate registration statements and to disclose information by reference to other documents that already had been made public. Before these changes, the registration process often required at least several weeks. After the 1978 changes, a registration statement could be approved in as little as 2 days.

In March 1982, Rule 415 provided for shelf registration. Large corporations can register the full amount of debt or equity they plan to sell over a 2-year period. After the initial registration has been completed, the firm can sell up to the specified amount of debt or equity without further delay. The firm can choose the time when the funds are needed or when market conditions appear favorable. Shelf registration has been actively used in the sale of bonds, with as much as 60% of debt sales utilizing shelf registration. Less than 10% of the total issuance of equities have employed shelf registration.

In 1995, the Private Securities Litigation Reform Act (PSLRA) was enacted by Congress. This law placed restrictions on the filing of securities fraud class action suits. It sought to discourage the filing of frivolous claims. In late 1998, the Securities Litigation Uniform Standards Act (SLUSA) was signed into law. It had been found that some class action plaintiffs had been circumventing the PSLRA by filing suits in state courts. SLUSA establishes a uniform national standard to be applied to securities class actions and makes clear that such suits will be the exclusive jurisdiction of the federal courts. SLUSA forces all class action plaintiffs alleging securities fraud to provide greater detail on the basis for their claims. It enables defendant companies to delay the expenses of discovery of evidence until the complaint has withstood a motion to dismiss. The 1998 act seeks to protect companies against unfounded securities fraud class actions. This reduces the pressure on defendant companies to enter into a settlement to avoid the litigation expenses that otherwise would be incurred.

In the wake of the recent allegations of fraud, insider trading, and questionable accounting practices by large companies such as Adelphia, Enron, Global Crossing, ImClone, Qwest, and

Tyco, President Bush signed into law on July 31, 2002, the Sarbanes-Oxley Act of 2002. The Sarbanes-Oxley Act is expected to have a huge impact on corporate governance, financial disclosures, auditing standards, analyst reports, insider trading, and so forth. Observers view the Act as the most comprehensive reform of securities laws since the 1933 and 1934 Acts. The Act contains eleven titles:

    I. Public Accounting Oversight Board
    II. Auditor Independence
    III. Corporate Responsibility
    IV. Enhanced Financial Disclosures
    V. Analyst Conflicts of Interest
    VI. Commission Resources and Authority
    VII. Studies and Reports
    VIII. Corporate and Criminal Fraud Accountability
    IX. White Collar Crime Penalty Enhancements
    X. Corporate Tax Returns
    XI. Corporate Fraud Accountability

Below is a brief summary of some of the Titles. Title I establishes a five member Public Company Accounting Oversight Board to oversee audits, establish standards, and monitor registered public accounting firms. Title II requires auditor independence by prohibiting auditors from performing certain non-audit services contemporaneous with an audit, requires auditor rotation, and requires that auditors report detailed material to the audit committee. Title III strengthens corporate responsibility by requiring each member of the audit committee to be an independent member of the board, requires the CEO and CFO to certify financial reports, requires the CEO and CFO to forfeit bonus and compensation if an accounting restatement is due to non-compliance of the firm, and requires that attorneys appearing before the SEC to report violations of securities by a firm or its management. Title IV provides for greater financial disclosures such as requiring financial reports to reflect all material adjustments and off-balance sheet items, prohibits loans to executives, requires insiders to disclose insider transactions within 2 business days of the transaction, and requires that at least one member of the audit committee be a financial expert. Title V attempts to separate analyst conflicts of interest by restricting the ability of investment bankers to pre-approve research reports, restricts employers from firing analysts for having written negative reports, and requires analysts to disclose any potential conflicts such as having owned stock in the company covered. Titles VIII, IX, and XI provide stringent penalties for corporate and financial fraud and other white-collar crimes by corporations and management.

The Sarbanes-Oxley Act went through Congress at a rapid pace without any opposition in the Senate and minimal opposition in the House of Representatives. Subsequent to President Bush's signing of the Act into law on July 31, 2002, the SEC and the stock exchanges have been proposing and implementing rules in accordance with the Act. Some of the provisions were effective immediately, whereas in other cases, the SEC has 180 and 270 days, in some instances longer, to implement the rules. There is no question that the Act will have an enormous impact on corporate governance. However, since the timing is so recent, it remains to be seen as to the effectiveness of the Act in curtailing corporate and financial fraud and providing greater financial disclosure to investors, while at the same time not impeding corporations from maximizing profits on behalf of shareholders.

THE OPERATION OF THE SECURITIES ACTS

The Securities Act of 1933 has primary responsibility for recording information. Section 5 prevents the public offering and sale of securities without a registration statement. Section 8 provides for registration and permits the statement to automatically become effective 20 days after it is filed with the SEC. However, the SEC has the power to request more information or to issue a stop order, which delays the operation of the 20-day waiting period. It was with accordance to the Securities Act of 1933 that PepsiCo on January 9, 2001, filed Form S-4 to register the new shares to be issued in the merger with Quaker Oats.

It is the Securities Exchange Act of 1934 (SEA) that provides the basis for the amendments that were applicable to takeover activities. Section 12(j) empowers the SEC to revoke or suspend the registration of a security if the issuer has violated-any provisions of the 1934 act. The SEC imposes periodic disclosure requirements under Section 13. The basic reports are (1) Form 10-K, the annual report; (2) Form 10-Q, the quarterly report; and (3) Form 8-K, the current report for any month in which specified events occur. As displayed in Table 2.1, Quaker Oats filed five 8-Ks and PepsiCo filed one 8-K associated with their planned merger.

Section 14 governs proxy solicitation. Prior to every meeting of its security holders, they must be furnished with a proxy statement containing specified information. The SEC provides procedural requirements for proxy contests. Under SEA Rule 14a-8, any security holder may require management to include a proposal for action in the proxy statement. If management opposes the proposal, it must include in the proxy material a statement by the security holder not more than 200 words in length in support of the proposal. It was with respect to Section 14 that Quaker Oats filed DEF-14A, the merger proxy statement for its upcoming acquisition by PepsiCo.

TENDER OFFER REGULATION—THE WILLIAMS ACT

Prior to the late 1960s, most intercorporate combinations were represented by mergers. This typically involved friendly negotiations by two or more firms. When they mutually agreed, a combination of some form might occur. During the conglomerate merger movement of the 1960s, corporate takeovers began to occur. Some were friendly and not much different from mergers. Others were hostile and shook up the business community.

In October 1965, Senator Harrison Williams introduced legislation seeking to protect the target companies. These initial efforts failed, but his second effort, initiated in 1967, succeeded. The Williams Act, in the form of various amendments to the Securities Exchange Act of 1934, became law on July 29, 1968. Its stated purpose was to protect target shareholders from swift and secret takeovers in three ways: (1) by generating more information during the takeover process that target shareholders and management could use to evaluate outstanding offers; (2) by requiring a minimum period during which a tender offer must be held open, thus delaying the execution of the tender offer; and (3) by explicitly authorizing targets to sue bidding firms.

SECTION 13

Section 13(d) of the Williams Act of 1968 required that any person who had acquired 10% or more of the stock of a public corporation must file a Schedule 13D with the SEC within 10 days of crossing the 10% threshold. The act was amended in 1970 to increase the SEC powers and to reduce the trigger point for the reporting obligation under Section 13(d) from 10% to 5%. Basically, Section 13(d) provides management and the shareholders with an early notification system.

The filing requirement does not apply to those persons who purchased less than 2% of the stock within the previous 12 months. Due to this exemption, a substantial amount of stock can be accumulated over several years without having to file Schedule 13D. Institutional investors (registered brokers and dealers, banks, insurance companies, and so forth) can choose to file Schedule 13G instead of Schedule 13D if the equity securities were acquired in the ordinary course of business. Schedule 13G is an abbreviated version of Schedule 13D.

The insider trading scandals of the late 1980s produced calls for a reduction below 5% and a shortening of the 10-day minimum period for filing. However, shortening the period would not stop the practice of "parking" violations that was uncovered in the Boesky investigation. Under parking arrangements, traders attempt to hide the extent of their ownership to avoid the 5% disclosure trigger by "parking" purchased securities with an accomplice broker until a later date. A related practice is to purchase options on the stock of the target; this is equivalent to ownership because the options can be exercised whenever the holder wishes to take actual ownership.

SECTION 14

Section 13(d) and 13(g) of the Williams Act apply to any large stock acquisitions, whether public or private (an offering to less than 25 people). Section 14(d) applies only to public tender offers but applies whether the acquisition is small or large, so its coverage is broader. The 5% trigger rule also applies under Section 14(d). Thus, any group making solicitations or recommendations to a target group of shareholders that would result in owning more than 5% of a class of securities registered under Section 12 of the Securities Act must first file a Schedule 14D with the SEC. An acquiring firm must disclose in a Tender Offer Statement (Schedule 14D-1) its intentions and business plans for the target as well as any relationships or agreements between the two firms. The schedule must be filed with the SEC "as soon as practicable on the date of the commencement of the tender offer"; copies must be hand delivered to the target firm and to any competitive bidders; and the relevant stock exchanges (or the National Association of Securities Dealers, NASD, for over-the-counter stocks) must be notified by telephone (followed by a mailing of the schedule).

Note, however, that the language of Section 14(d) refers to *any* group making recommendations to target shareholders. This includes target management, which is prohibited from advising target shareholders as to how to respond to a tender offer until it too has filed with the SEC. Until target management has filed a Schedule 14D-9, a Tender Offer Solicitation/Recommendation Statement, they may only advise shareholders to defer tendering their shares while management considers the offer. Companies that consider themselves vulnerable often take the precaution of preparing a fill-in-the-blanks schedule left with an agent in Washington to be filed immediately in the event of a takeover attempt, allowing target management to respond swiftly in making public recommendations to shareholders. Thus, Section 14(d) (1) provides the early notification system and information that will help target shareholders determine whether or not to tender their shares. SEA Sections 14 (d) (4)–(7) regulate the terms of a tender offer, including the length of time the offer must be left open (20 trading days), the right of shareholders to withdraw shares that they may have tendered previously, the manner in which tendered shares must be purchased in oversubscribed offers, and the effect of the bidder changing the terms of the offer. The delay period also gives shareholders time to evaluate the offer, but, more importantly, it enables management to seek competing bids.

Also, SEA Section 14(e) prohibits misrepresentation; nondisclosure; or any fraudulent, deceptive or manipulative acts or practices in connection with a tender offer.

INSIDER TRADING OVERVIEW

The SEC has three broad categories under which insider trading, fraud, or illegal profits can be attacked. Rule 10b-5 is a general prohibition against fraud or deceit in security transactions. Rule 14e-3 prohibits trading in nonpublic information in connection with tender offers. The Insider Trading Sanctions Act of 1984 applies to insider trading more generally. It states that those who trade on information not available to the general public can be made to give back their illegal profits and pay a penalty of three times as much as their illegal activities produced. To date, the term *insider trading* has not been clearly delineated by the SEC. The ambiguity of the three sources of power that may be used by the SEC in the regulation of insider trading gives the SEC considerable discretion in its choice of practices and cases to prosecute. Also, the SEC is empowered to offer bounties to informants whose information leads to the recovery of illegal gains and payment of a civil penalty.

It should be noted also that the traditional regulation of insider trading was provided for under SEA Sections 16(a) and 16(b). Section 16(a) applies to officers, directors, and any persons who own 10% or more of any class of securities of a company. Section 16(a) provides that these corporate insiders must report to the SEC all transactions involving their purchase or sale of the corporation's stock on a monthly basis. Section 16(a) is based on the premise that a corporate insider has an unfair advantage by virtue of his or her knowledge of information that is generated within the corporation. This information is available on a privileged basis because the insider is an officer, a director, or a major security holder who is presumed to have privileged communications with top officers in the company. Section 16(b) provides that the corporation or any of its security holders may bring suit against the offending corporate insider to return the profits to the corporation because of insider trading completed within a 6-month period.

The Sarbanes-Oxley Act of 2002 amended Section 16(a) of the 1934 Act by requiring that insiders disclose any changes in ownership within 2 business days of the transaction, sharply decreasing the time between the insider transaction and disclosure. In addition, the Act requires that changes in ownership be filed electronically, rather than on paper as was done prior, and that the SEC post the filing on the Internet within 1 business day after the filing is made.

THE RACKETEER INFLUENCED AND CORRUPT ORGANIZATIONS ACT OF 1970 (RICO)

The Racketeer Influenced and Corrupt Organizations Act of 1970 (RICO) was originally aimed at unions. It provides for triple damages, as do the antitrust laws. It also has been applied to securities trading in famous cases such as the legal action against Michael Milken. Its requirements are simple: (1) conspiracy and (2) repeated transactions. If more than one person in involved, it is a conspiracy. If, in addition, repeated acts occur, the two requirements for the applicability of RICO have been met. Its provisions are truly draconian.

The act is now aimed at companies that engage in acts that defraud consumers, investors, or public bodies such as cities or states and authorizes triple damages for winning plaintiffs.

TABLE 2.2   Summary of Securities Laws and Regulations

Rule 10b-5:	Prohibits fraud, misstatements, or omission of material facts in connection with the purchase or sale of any security.
Section 13(d):	Provides early warning to target firms of acquisitions of their stock by potential acquirers: 5% threshold, 10-day filing period. Applies to all large stock acquisitions.
Section 14(d) (1):	Requirements of Section 13(d) extended to all public tender offers. Provides for full disclosure to SEC by any group making recommendations to target shareholders.
Section 14(d) (4)–(7):	Regulates terms of tender offers: length of time offer must be held open (20 days), right of shareholders to withdraw tendered shares, and so on.
Section 14(e):	Prohibits fraud and misrepresentation in context of tender offers. Rule 14e-3 prohibits trading on nonpublic information in tender offers.
Section 16(a):	Provides for reporting by corporate insiders on their transactions in their corporations' stocks.
Section 16(b):	Allows the corporation or its security holders to sue for return of profits on transactions by corporate insiders completed within a 6-month period.
Insider Trading Sanctions Act of 1984:	Provides for triple damages in insider trading cases.
Racketeer Influenced and Corrupt Organizations Act of 1970 (RICO):	Provides for seizure of assets upon accusation and triple damages upon conviction for companies that defraud consumers, investors, and so on.

Furthermore, in a criminal suit brought by any representative of the Department of Justice, RICO permits the court to order that all of the assets of the accused be seized while the case is still being tried. This gives the prosecutor tremendous power. From a practical standpoint, it means that a mere accusation brought under RICO can bring the business of any accused to a halt. If its assets are seized, particularly if it is engaged in securities transactions, it no longer has the means of conducting business. Hence, whether the accused is guilty or not, the pressure to settle is tremendous, because the alternative is to have its business disrupted. Even if after months and months of trial the accused is found innocent, it is small solace, because the disruption may well have resulted in irreparable damage to its business.

We have thus brought together in one place the whole array of laws, rules, and regulations that apply to securities trading including the takeover process. For convenience of reference, we summarize them briefly in Table 2.2.

COURT CASES AND SEC RULES

To this point we have described the main statutory provisions that specify the various elements of fraud and insider trading in connection with trading in securities and takeover activities. The full meaning of these statutes is brought out by the subsequent court interpretations and SEC rules implementing the powers granted the SEC by the various statutes.

LIABILITY UNDER RULE 10B-5 OF THE 1934 ACT

As we have indicated, Rule 10b-5, issued by the Securities and Exchange Commission under the powers granted to it by the 1934 act, is a broad, powerful, and general securities antifraud provision. In general, for Rule 10b-5 to apply, a security must be involved. Technical issues have arisen regarding what constitutes a security. If securities are involved, all transactions are covered, whether on one of the securities exchanges or over the counter. A number of elements for a cause of action have been set forth in connection with Rule 10b-5, as follows.

1. There must be fraud, misrepresentation, a material omission, or deception in connection with the purchase or sale of securities.
2. The misrepresentation or omission must be of a fact as opposed to an opinion. However, inaccurate predictions of earnings may be held to be misrepresentations, and failure to disclose prospective developments may be challenged.
3. The misrepresentation or omission must be material to an investor's decision in the sense that there was a substantial likelihood that reasonable investors would consider the fact of significance in their decision.
4. There must be a showing that the plaintiff believed the misrepresentation and relied upon it and that it was a substantial factor in the decision to enter the transaction.
5. The plaintiff must be an actual purchaser or an actual seller to have standing.
6. Defendant's deception or fraud must have a sufficiently close nexus to the transaction so that a court could find that the defendant's fraud was "in connection with" the purchase or sale by plaintiff.
7. Plaintiff must prove that the defendant had scienter. *Scienter* literally means "knowingly or willfully." It means that the defendants had a degree of knowledge that makes the individual legally responsible for the consequences of their act and that they had an actual intent to deceive or defraud. Negligence is not sufficient.

These elements represent requirements for a successful suit under Rule 10b-5. Some of the elements were developed in a series of court decisions. The main thrust of Rule 10b-5 concerns fraud or deceit. The Supreme Court set forth the scienter requirement in two cases: *Ernst and Ernst v. Hochfelder*, 425 US 185 (1976); and *Aaron v. SEC*, 446 US 680 (1980).

In addition to its use in fraud or deceit cases, a number of interesting cases have brought out the meaning and applicability of Rule 10b-5 in connection with insider trading. For the present, we refer to insider trading merely as purchases or sales by persons who have access to information that is not available to those with whom they deal or to traders generally. However, many court decisions address what constitutes insider trading and a continual stream of proposals in Congress attempt to clarify the meaning of the term.

An early case was *Cady, Roberts & Company*, 40 SEC 907 (1961). In this case, a partner in a brokerage firm received a message from a director of the Curtiss-Wright Corporation that the board of directors had voted to cut the dividend. The broker immediately placed orders to sell the Curtiss-Wright stock for some of his customers. The sales were made before news of the dividend cut was generally disseminated. The broker who made the transactions was held to have violated Rule 10b-5.

The Texas Gulf Sulphur Corporation case of 1965 was classic [*SEC v. Texas Gulf Sulphur Company*, 401 F.2d 833 (2d. Cir. 1968)]. A vast mineral deposit consisting of millions of tons of copper, zinc, and silver was discovered in November 1963. However, far from publicizing the discovery, the company took great pains to conceal it for more than 5 months, to the extent of issuing a false press release in April 1964 labeling proliferating rumors as "unreliable . . . premature and possibly misleading." Meanwhile, certain directors, officers, and employees of Texas Gulf Sulphur who knew of the find bought up quantities of the firm's stock (and options on many more shares) before any public announcement. The false press release was followed only 4 days later by another that finally revealed publicly the extent of the find. In the company's defense, it was alleged that secrecy was necessary to keep down the price of neighboring tracts of land that they had to acquire in order to fully exploit the discovery. However, the SEC brought and won a civil suit based on Rule 10b-5.

The next case is *Investors Management Company*, 44 SEC 633 (1971). An aircraft manufacturer disclosed to a broker-dealer, acting as the lead underwriter for a proposed debenture issue, that its earnings for the current year would be much lower than it had previously publicly announced. This information was conveyed to the members of the sales department of the broker-dealer and passed on in turn to major institutional clients. The institutions sold large amounts of the stock before the earnings revisions were made public. Again, the SEC won the suit.

In the next two cases we cover, the SEC lost. The first case involved one of the leading investment banking corporations, Morgan Stanley. The Kennecott Copper Corporation was analyzing whether or not to buy Olinkraft, a paper manufacturer. Morgan Stanley began negotiations with Olinkraft on behalf of Kennecott. Later Kennecott decided it did not wish to purchase Olinkraft. The knowledge that Morgan Stanley had gained in its negotiations led it to believe that one of its other clients, Johns-Manville, would find Olinkraft attractive. In anticipation of this possibility, Morgan Stanley bought large amounts of the common stock of Olinkraft. When Johns-Manville subsequently made a bid for Olinkraft, Morgan Stanley realized large profits. A suit was brought against Morgan Stanley. However, the court held that Morgan Stanley had not engaged in any improper behavior under Rule 10b-5.

In the next case, Raymond Dirks was a New York investment analyst who was informed by a former officer of Equity Funding of America that the company had been fraudulently overstating its income and net assets by large amounts. Dirks conducted his own investigation, which corroborated the information he had received. He told the SEC and a reporter at the *Wall Street Journal* to follow up on the situation and advised his clients to sell their Equity Funding shares. The SEC brought an action against Dirks on the grounds that if tippees have material information knowingly obtained from a corporate insider, they must either disclose it or refrain from trading. However, the U.S. Supreme Court found that Dirks had not engaged in improper behavior [*Dirks v. SEC*, 463 US 646 (1983)]. In Texas Gulf Sulphur, the law made it clear that trading by insiders in shares of their own company using insider knowledge is definitely illegal. However, the court held that it was not illegal for Raymond Dirks to cause trades to be made on the basis of what he learned about Equity Funding because the officer who conveyed the information was not breaching any duty and Dirks did not pay for the information.

Therefore, the first principle is that it is illegal for insiders to trade on the basis of inside information. A second principle that has developed is that it is illegal for an outsider to trade on the basis of information that has been "misappropriated." The misappropriation doctrine began to develop in the famous Chiarella case [*United States v. Chiarella* 445 US 222 (1980)]. *United States v. Chiarella* was a criminal case. Vincent Chiarella was the "markup man" in the New York composing room of Pandick Press, one of the leading U.S. financial printing firms. In working on documents, he observed five announcements of corporate takeover bids in which the targets' identities had presumably been concealed by blank spaces and false names. However, Chiarella made some judgments about the names of the targets, bought their stock, and realized some profits. Chiarella was sued under Rule 10b-5 on the theory that, like the officers and directors of Texas Gulf Sulphur, he had defrauded the uninformed shareholders whose stock he had bought. Chiarella was convicted in the lower courts, and his case was appealed to the Supreme Court. In arguing its case before the Supreme Court, the government sought to strengthen its case. It argued that even if Chiarella did not defraud the persons with whom he traded, he had defrauded his employer, Pandick Press, and its clients, the acquiring firms in the documents he had read. He had misappropriated information that had belonged to Pandick Press and its clients. As a result, he had caused the price of the targets' stock to rise, thereby injuring his employer's clients and his employer's reputation for reliability. The Supreme Court expressed sympathy with the misappropriation theory but reversed Chiarella's conviction because the theory had not been used in the lower court.

However, in the next case that arose, the SEC used its misappropriation theory from the beginning and won in a criminal case. A stockbroker named Newman was informed by friends at Morgan Stanley and Kuhn Loeb about prospective acquisitions. He bought the targets' shares and split the profits with his friends who had supplied the information. He was convicted under the misappropriation theory on grounds that he had defrauded the investment banking houses by injuring their reputation as safe repositories of confidential information from their clients. He had also defrauded their clients, because the stock purchases based on confidential information had pushed up the prices of the targets.

The misappropriation theory also won in a case similar to Chiarella. Materia was a proofreader at the Bowne Printing firm. Materia figured out the identity of four takeover targets and invested in them. This time the SEC applied the misappropriation theory from the start and won [*SEC v. Materia*, 745 F.2d. 197 (2d. Cir. 1984)].

The SEC also employed the misappropriation theory in its criminal cast against a *Wall Street Journal* reporter, R. Foster Winans, the author of the newspaper's influential "Heard on the Street" column. Along with friends, Winans traded on the basis of what they knew would appear in the paper the following day. Although his conviction was upheld by the Supreme Court, the 4–4 vote could not be mistaken for a resounding affirmation of the misappropriation doctrine, and some suspect that without the mail and wire fraud involved in the Winans case, the outcome might have been different. Rulings in later cases strengthened the misappropriation doctrine.

OTHER DISCLOSURE REQUIREMENTS

Regulations and legislation have been applied to all phases of trading activity generally. We next describe some additional aspects of disclosure including interpretation and implementation of the regulations.

DISCLOSURE REQUIREMENTS OF STOCK EXCHANGES

In addition to the disclosure and notification requirements of federal and state securities regulation, the various national and regional stock exchanges have their own internal disclosure requirements for listed companies. In general, these amount to notifying the exchanges promptly (that is, by telephone) of any material developments that may significantly affect the trading volume and/or price of the listed firm's stock.

The exchanges are naturally reluctant to halt trading in a stock, particularly because institutional investors may continue to trade in the "third market" during a halt. However, it sometimes does so to allow the public time to digest important information that would otherwise result in an order imbalance. A listed company also may request a trading halt. Target companies have sometimes requested halts as a defensive strategy to buy time to find another bidder (a white knight) or to force the initial bid higher. As a result, the New York Stock Exchange (NYSE) has implemented a policy to limit the length of such voluntary halts. Once a halt is requested, a company has 30 minutes to disclose its news, after which the exchange, not the company, decides when to reopen trading.

DISCLOSURE OF MERGER TALKS

On April 4, 1988, the Supreme Court ruled by a 6–0 vote (three justices not participating) that investors may claim damages from a company that falsely denied it was involved in negotiations that resulted in a subsequent merger. Such denials would represent misleading information about a pending merger, which would provide investors who sold stock during the period with a basis for winning damages from the company officers.

The case involved the acquisition by Combustion Engineering of Basic Incorporated. Executives of Combustion Engineering began talks with Basic officers in 1976. The talks continued through 1977 and into early 1978, when Basic stock was selling for less than $20 per share. The stock began to rise in price, and in response to rumors of a merger, Basic issued three public statements denying that its officers knew of any reason for the rise in the price of its stock. It issued a denial as late as November 6, 1978.

On December 19, 1978, Basic's board voted to approve the sale of the company to Combustion at $46 per share. Some shareholders filed suit against Basic's board, claiming that they were misled into selling their stock at the low, premerger price. A district court judge in Cleveland rejected their suit, but a federal appeals court reinstated the suit in 1986 on grounds that the statements made were significant and misleading. The Supreme Court returned the case to the district court judge for trial. The Supreme Court decision written by Justice Blackmun stated that federal securities laws require that investors be informed about "material developments." What is "material" depends on the facts of the case, but corporate boards may not deny merger talks that reach the point of board resolutions, instructions to investment bankers, and actual negotiations between principals (Savage, 1988).

In a footnote, Justice Blackmun appeared to suggest that refusing to comment might shield a board. Apparently, silence is not misleading under Rule 10b-5 of the Securities Exchange Act. This has been interpreted as saying that either the board must put a sufficiently tight lid on any information about mergers that no rumors get started or, if leaks occur, the board must issue accurate statements of information. The decision appeared to be consistent with the spirit of federal laws and regulations governing securities transactions. Mergers simply represent an area of particular importance because of the large price fluctuations frequently associated with such activity.

REGULATION OF TAKEOVER ACTIVITY BY THE STATES

Before the Williams Act of 1968, virtually no state regulation of takeover activity existed. Even by 1974, only seven states had enacted statutes in this area. This is surprising became states are the primary regulators of corporate activity. The chartering of corporations takes place in individual states. State law has defined a corporation as a legal person subject to state laws. Corporate charters obtained from states define the powers of the firm and the rights and obligations of its shareholder, boards of directors, and managers. However, states are not permitted to pass laws that impose restrictions on interstate commerce or that conflict with federal laws that regulating interstate commerce.

Early state laws regulating hostile takeovers were declared illegal by the courts. For example, in 1982 the U.S. Supreme Court declared illegal an antitakeover law passed by the state of Illinois. The courts held that the Illinois law favored management over the interests of shareholders and bidders. The Illinois law also was found to impose impediments on interstate commerce and was therefore unconstitutional.

DEVELOPMENTS DURING THE 1980s

To the surprise of most observers, the Supreme Court in April 1987 upheld the Indiana Act. The Indiana Act provides that when an acquiring entity or bidder obtains shares that would cause its voting power to reach specified threshold levels, the bidder does not automatically obtain the voting rights associated with those shares. The transfer of voting rights must receive the approval of a majority of shareholders, not including the shares held by the bidder or insider directors and officers of the target company. A bidder can request a special shareholders meeting that must be held within 50 days of the request, with the expenses of the meeting to be borne by the bidder.

Critics of the Indiana Act regard it as a delaying tactic that enables the target to delay the process by at least 50 days. The special requirements in connection with voting make the outcome of the tender offer much more uncertain. The Indiana Act was tested in a case brought by Dynamics Corporation of America, which is chartered in Connecticut. It announced a tender offer to increase its holdings of CTS Corporation (incorporated in Indiana) from 9.6% to 27.5%. CTS invoked the Indiana Act. Dynamics would not be able to vote either the additional shares or the initial 9.6%. Dynamics filed suit, arguing that the Indiana Act was preempted by the Williams Act and violated the interstate commerce clause. Dynamics won in the U.S. district court and in the appeals court, but the decision was reversed in the U.S. Supreme Court.

Other states passed acts more moderate than the Indiana Act. The New York-New Jersey pattern provides for 5-year moratorium preventing hostile bidders from doing a second-step transaction, such as merging a newly acquired company with another (Veasey, 1988).

A Delaware law was enacted in early 1988. It followed the New York–New Jersey model. The Delaware moratorium on second-step transactions is for only 3 years, and it does not apply if the hostile bidder obtains the approval of the board of the target company and a two-thirds vote of the other stockholders for the transaction to proceed. The board of a Delaware corporation also may vote to "opt out" of the statute within 90 days of its effective date (Veasey, 1988).

The Delaware statute was regarded as having great significance because more than half of the Fortune 500 companies are incorporated in Delaware. Also, Delaware's statutes and regulations of corporations are widely regarded as a national model. However, in this instance it is argued that Delaware acted because the Delaware state legislators "apparently feared an exodus of companies in search of protection elsewhere" (Bandow, 1988, p. 2). Subsequent to the Delaware statutes, there has been little development of state antitakeover laws.

ISSUES WITH REGARD TO STATE TAKEOVER LAWS

One reason put forth for state takeover laws is that they permit shareholders a more considered response to two-tier and partial tender offers. The other argument is that the Williams Act provides that tender offers remain open for only 20 days. It is argued that a longer time period may be needed when the target is large to permit other bidders to develop information to decide whether or not to compete for the target.

However, in practice it has been found that 70% of the tender offers during the years 1981 to 1984 were for all outstanding shares. The other 30% of the offers were split between two-tier and partial offers. The proportion of two-tier offers declined over the period of the study (Office of the Chief Economist, SEC April 1985). Today, virtually all tender offers are for all outstanding shares.

Furthermore, many companies have adopted fair price amendments that require the bidder to pay a fair price for all shares acquired. Under the laws of Delaware, Massachusetts, and certain other states, dissenting shareholders may request court appraisal of the value of their shares. To do so, however, they must file a written demand for appraisal before the shareholders meeting to vote on the merger. Tendering shareholders must not vote for the merger if they wish to preserve the right to an appraisal.

Critics also point out that state antitakeover laws have hurt shareholders. Studies by the Office of the Chief Economist of the SEC found that when New Jersey placed restrictions on takeovers in 1986, the prices for 87 affected companies fell by 11.5% (Bandow, 1988). Similarly, an SEC study found that stock prices for 74 companies chartered in Ohio declined an average of 3.2%, a $1.5 billion loss, after that state passed restrictive legislation. Another study estimated that the New York antitakeover rules reduced equity values by 1%, costing shareholders $1.2 billion (Bandow, 1988).

For these reasons, critics argue that the state laws protect parochial state interests rather than shareholders. They argues that the states act to protect employment and increase control over companies in local areas. Furthermore, they argue that state laws are not needed. If more shareholder protection were needed, it could be accomplished by simply amending the Williams Act by extending the waiting period from 20 to 30 days, for example. It is argued further that securities transactions clearly represent interstate commerce. Thus, it is difficult to argue that the state laws are not unconstitutional. By limiting securities transactions, they impede interstate commerce.

The goal is to achieve a balance. Certainly it is desirable to protect the interests of shareholders. However, it must be recognized that two-tier offers and partial offers are used to prevent free riding. In the absence of two-tier pricing and post-takeover dilution, shareholders know that their shares will not decline in value if the takeover succeeds. Therefore, individual small shareholders will wait until after the takeover in hopes that the changes made by the acquirer will increase the value of the stock. Most individual shareholders might behave this way. Then this "free rider" behavior will prevent takeovers from being accomplished.

Similarly, if states make takeovers more difficult, the advantage is that time can be extended so that competing bids may be made. The data show that competing bids lead to higher prices for target shareholders. On the other hand, if the impediments to takeover are increased too greatly, bidders will be discouraged from even making the effort. In this case, target shareholders will lose all benefits. The argument then concludes that state takeover laws are unnecessary. Applicable federal laws should seek to strike a balance between protecting shareholders and stimulating reasonable competing bidding activity, but not to the point where all bidding activity is discouraged.

It also has been argued that federal laws should prevent "abusive takeovers" where "speculative financing" may be involved. But the critical concepts are ambiguous. What is regarded as abusive or speculative varies with the viewpoints of different decision makers. There may, however, be legitimate concerns that rising debt ratios, whether or not associated with takeovers or restructuring, may amplify financial problems when a future economic downturn takes place.

ANTITRUST POLICIES

When firms announce plans to merge, a great outcry often arises from consumer groups, suppliers, and other stakeholders that the merger will lead to less competition. Consequently, the U.S. government scrutinizes every merger in which the transaction value exceeds $50 million. In most cases, antitrust policy is handled by the Department of Justice (DOJ) and the Federal Trade Commission (FTC). Although the DOJ and the FTC have overlapping jurisdictions regarding antitrust policy, they generally coordinate the merger cases and decide which agency should handle each deal. In early 2002, they released plans to overhaul the merger review process whereby the DOJ would be responsible for mergers in certain industries, such as media and entertainment, and the FTC would be responsible for other industries, such as health care and auto manufacturing. The plan would eliminate duplicative efforts and eliminate potential conflict over which group is responsible for handling a specific merger. However, in May 2002, the DOJ and the FTC dropped their proposal due to threats from Senator Ernest Hollings (democrat, South Carolina) that he would cut the budgets of the respective agencies if they moved forward with the plan. Senator Hollings's objection was based on the argument that the Justice Department under President Bush would be less likely to challenge certain mergers, especially mergers in the media industry.

The DOJ challenged 48 transactions in 2000, which it believed to lessen competition were the merger to go forward. In 21 of the mergers, the DOJ filed a complaint in the U.S. District Court to stop the merger. Subsequent to the filing of the complaint, 18 were settled by consent decree, two were dropped, and one went to litigation with the DOJ winning the case. In the other 27 challenges, the DOJ did not formally sue to block the merger, but rather notified the merging parties that it would file suit unless the parties did not either drop the plans to merge or restructure the merger such as to avoid any competitive problems. In response, the merging parties restructured the merger plans in 16 of the cases and dropped the merger in the other 11 cases.

A high-profile merger that DOJ blocked in 2000 was the proposed acquisition of Sprint Corporation by WorldCom, Incorporated. The DOJ alleged that this merger would greatly reduce competition in telecommunications and would result in higher prices for millions of consumers and businesses. As two of the three largest telecommunications firms in the United

States along with AT&T, the DOJ felt that the surviving entity would be able to exhibit monopoly power in markets such as residential long-distance services, Internet services, international long-distance services, private-line services, data network services, and custom network services. In response to the suit by the DOJ, WorldCom and Sprint in July 2000 dropped their plans to merge.

In 2000, the FTC challenged 32 merger transactions. These challenges led to 18 consent orders, nine terminated transactions, and five preliminary injunction proceedings. Two of these challenges were with respect to two huge mergers in the petroleum industry. The first was that of BP Amoco and Atlantic Richfield. The FTC held that the merger would reduce competition in the exploration and production of Alaskan crude oil and in the market for pipeline and storage facilities in Oklahoma, thereby raising prices for crude oil used to produce gasoline and other petroleum products. The merging parties and the FTC agreed to end the lawsuit by negotiating a consent decree whereby BP Amoco, the acquirer, would divest all of Atlantic Richfield's assets relating to Alaskan oil production. The second large petroleum merger that the FTC challenged was the Exxon and Mobil merger. Here, the FTC argued that the merger would lessen competition in numerous markets throughout the United States in products such as gasoline, jet fuel, diesel fuel, paraffinic lubricant base oil, and so forth. Exxon and Mobil settled the suit with the FTC by agreeing to sell nearly 2,500 Exxon and Mobil gas stations, the largest retail divestiture in the history of the FTC.

The above examples suggest that in considering possible merger transactions, antitrust considerations are an important part of the planning process. Also, note that although these examples involve large mergers, the DOJ and the FTC have successfully challenged relatively small mergers, as well. For these reasons, we review the relevant antitrust statutes and the policies promulgated by the DOJ and the FTC.

THE BASIC ANTITRUST STATUTES

The two basic antitrust laws are the Sherman Act of 1890 and the Clayton Act of 1914.

SHERMAN ACT OF 1890

This law was passed in response to the heightened merger activity around the turn of the century. It contains two sections. Section 1 prohibits mergers that would tend to create a monopoly or undue market control. This was the basis on which the FTC stopped the merger between Staples and Office Depot in 1997. This merger would have combined two of the top three office supply superstore chains in the United States. These two chains competed in numerous metropolitan areas and in some cases were the only two superstore competitors. The key issue in the case was defining the relevant product market. The FTC held that the relevant market for office supplies was "office supply superstores." Because only one other major superstore existed, namely Office Max, this definition eliminated any potential competition that could arise from nonsuperstores, Internet, fax, mail order, warehouse clubs, and so forth. As evidence, the FTC used internal documents obtained from the merging parties, which suggested that raising prices was easier in the markets with only two superstores as opposed to three. Section 2 is directed against firms that already had become dominant in their markets in the view of the government. This was the basis for actions against IBM and AT&T in the 1950s. Both firms were required to sign consent decrees in 1956 restricting AT&T from specified markets and requiring that IBM sell as well as lease computer equipment. Under Section 2, IBM and AT&T were sued again in the 1970s. The suit against IBM, which had gone on for 10 years, was dropped in 1983. The suit against AT&T resulted in divestiture of the operating companies, effective in 1984.

A recent landmark Section 2 case is *United States v. Microsoft*. The Microsoft case dates back to 1990 when the FTC opened an antitrust investigation to see whether Microsoft's pricing policies illegally thwarted competition and whether Microsoft had written its operating system source code to hinder competing applications. Throughout the 1990s, Microsoft was continually involved in litigation with the FTC, the DOJ, and various state governments regarding the antitrust allegations. At one juncture in 2000, a federal court issued a judgment requiring Microsoft to split the company into an operating systems business and an applications business. This judgment eventually was reversed on appeal, and in late 2001 Microsoft reached a settlement with the U.S. government. Under the consent decree, Microsoft agreed to restrictions on how it develops and licenses software, works with independent software providers, and communicates about its software with competitors and partners. Microsoft had not cleared all suits from some individual states as of March 4, 2003. Possible action by the EU has also been rumored.

CLAYTON ACT OF 1914

The Clayton Act created the Federal Trade Commission for the purpose of regulating the behavior of business firms. Among its sections, two are of particular interest. Section 5 gives the FTC power to prevent firms from engaging in harmful business practices. Section 7 involves mergers. As enacted in 1914, Section 7 made it illegal for a company to acquire the stock of another company if competition could be adversely affected. Companies made asset acquisitions to avoid the prohibition against acquiring stock. The 1950 amendment gave the FTC the power to block asset purchases as well as stock purchases. The amendment also added an incipiency doctrine. The FTC can block mergers if it perceives a tendency toward increased concentration—meaning the share of industry sales of the largest firms appears to be increasing.

HART-SCOTT-RODINO ACT OF 1976

The Hart-Scott-Rodino Act of 1976 (HSR) consists of three major parts. Its objective was to strengthen the powers of the DOJ and the FTC by requiring approval before a merger could take place. Before HSR, antitrust actions usually were taken after completion of a transaction. By the time a court decision was made, the merged firms had been operating for several years, so it was difficult to "unscramble the omelet."

Under Title I, the DOJ has the power to issue civil investigative demands in an antitrust investigation. The idea, here is that if the DOJ suspects a firm of antitrust violations. it can require firms to provide internal records that can be searched for evidence. We have seen cases in which firms were required to provide literally boxcar loads of internal files for review by the DOJ under Title I.

Title II is a premerger notification provision. If the acquiring firm has sales or assets of $100 million or more and the target firm has sales or assets of 15 million or more, or vice versa, information must be submitted for review. Before the takeover can be completed, a 30-day waiting period for mergers (15 days for tender offers) is required to enable the agencies to render an opinion on legality. Either agency may request a 20-day extension of the waiting period for mergers or a 10-day extension for tender offers.

Title III is the Parens Patriae Act—each state is the parent or protector of consumers and competitors. It expands the powers of state attorneys general to initiate triple-damage suits on behalf of persons (in their states) injured by violations of the antitrust laws. The state itself does not need to be injured by the violation. This gives the individual states the incentive to increase the budgets of their state attorneys general. A successful suit with triple damages can augment the revenues of the states. In the Microsoft case, the attorneys general of 22 states joined in the suit filed by the DOJ.

The prenotification required by Title II is an important part of the merger process. For example, in 2000, out of 9,566 merger announcements, filings were required for 4,926 transactions. This implies that 51% of total transactions involved targets with total assets in excess of $15 million; the other 49% were relatively small deals. About 71% of the filings were reviewed and permitted to proceed before the end of the statutory 30-day waiting period. About 16% (809) of the transactions were assigned to either the DOJ or the FTC for further substantive review. Of the 809, the DOJ or the FTC issued "second requests" for 98 of the submissions. A second request is traumatic for applicants because onerous investigations may result. Furthermore, of the 80 second-request cases in 1998, 54 resulted in formal actions taken against the merger and 26 in abandonments.

The legal literature and our own experience suggest actions by the parties to a merger that may improve the odds of approval by the review authorities. Companies should follow a proactive strategy during the 30-day review period. The HSR process should be viewed as an educational endeavor to provide the necessary information to the government staff attorneys. The staff attorneys should be contacted with an offer to provide additional information voluntarily. A briefing package should fully develop the business reasons for the merger. Under the guidance of attorneys, high-level business executives should be made available for informal presentations or staff interviews.

In response to a second request, the companies should start with a rolling production of material. Two copies of the organization charts for both companies should be provided, with the second copy annotated with names of core groups of employees identified as sources of information. Relevant documents identified in discussions with staff should be offered promptly.

The overriding approach should be for the lawyers and executives to convey a factual, logical story, emphasizing the industry dynamics that make the transaction imperative for the preservation of the client as a viable entity for providing high-quality products to its customers at fair prices. The presentation should demonstrate how the industry dynamics require the transaction to enable the firm to fulfill its responsibilities to consumers, employees, the communities in which it has its plants and offices, and its owners and creditors.

THE ANTITRUST GUIDELINES

In the merger guidelines of 1982, and successively in 1987, 1992, and 1996, the spirit of the regulatory authorities was altered. In the merger guidelines of 1968, concentration tests were applied somewhat mechanically. With the recognition of the internationalization of competition and other economic realities, the courts and the antitrust agencies began to be less rigid in their approach to antitrust. In addition to the concentration measures, the economics of the industry were taken into account. For example, in its July 8, 1995, issue, the *Economist* had a lead article entitled, "How Dangerous Is Microsoft?" (pp. 13–14). In an article on antitrust in the same issue, the *Economist* commented that Microsoft held 80% of its market but advised that the trustbusters should analyze the economics of the industry.

The guidelines sought to assure business firms that the older antitrust rules that emphasize various measures of concentration would be replaced by consideration of the realities of the marketplace. Nevertheless, the guidelines start with measures of concentration. For many years, the antitrust authorities, following the academic literature, looked at the share of sales or value added by the top four firms. If this share exceeded 20% (in some cases even lower), it might trigger an antitrust investigation.

Beginning in the 1982 guidelines, the quantitative test shifted to the Herfindahl-Hirschman Index (HHI), which is a concentration measure based on the market shares of all firms in the industry. It is simply the sum of the squares of market shares of each firm in the industry. For example, if there were 10 firms in the industry and each held a 10% market share, the HHI would be 1,000. If one firm held a 90% market share and the nine others held a 1% market share, the HHI would be 8,109 ($90^2 + 9 \times 1$). Notice how having a dominant firm greatly increases the HHI. The HHI is applied as indicated by Table 2.3.

A merger in an industry with a resulting HHI of less than 1,000 is unlikely to be investigated or challenged by the antitrust authorities. An HHI between 1,000 and 1,800 represents moderate concentration. Investigation and challenge depend on the amount by which the HHI increased over its premerger level. An increase of 100 or more may invite an investigation. An industry with a postmerger HHI higher than 1,800 is considered a concentrated market. Even a moderate increase over the premerger HHI is likely to result in an investigation by the antitrust authorities.

But, beginning in 1982, the guidelines already had recognized the role of market characteristics. Particularly important is the ability of existing and potential competitors to expand the supply of a product if one firm tries to restrict output. On the demand side, it is recognized that close substitutes usually can be found for any product, so a high market share of the sales of one product does not give the ability to elevate price. Quality differences, the introduction of new products, and technological change result in product proliferation and close substitutes. The result is usually fluctuating market shares. For these reasons, concentration measures alone are not a reliable guide to measure the competitiveness of an industry.

OTHER MARKET CHARACTERISTICS

Most important is whether entry is easy or difficult. If output can be increased by expansion of noncooperating firms already in the market or if new firms can construct new facilities or convert existing ones, an effort by some firms to increase price would not be profitable. The expansion of supply would drive prices down. Conditions of entry or other supply expansion potentials determine whether firms can collude successfully regardless of market structure numbers.

TABLE 2.3 Critical Concentration Levels

Postmerger HHI	Antitrust Challenge to a Merger?
Less than 1,000	No challenge—industry is unconcentrated.
Between 1,000 and 1,800	If HHI increased by 100, investigate.
More than 1,800	If HHI increased by 50, challenge.

Next considered is the ease and profitability of collusion, because it is less likely that firms will attempt to coordinate price increases if collusion is difficult or impossible. Here the factors to consider are product differences (heterogeneity), frequent quality changes, frequent new products, technological changes, contracts that involve complicated terms in addition to price, cost differences among suppliers, and so on. Also, the DOJ challenges are more likely when firms in an industry have colluded in the past or use practices such as exchanging price or output information.

NONHORIZONTAL MERGERS

The guidelines also include consideration of nonhorizontal mergers. Nonhorizontal mergers include vertical and conglomerate mergers. The guidelines express the view that although nonhorizontal mergers are less likely than horizontal mergers to create competitive problems, "they are not invariably innocuous." The principal theories under which nonhorizontal mergers are likely to be challenged are then set forth. Concern is expressed over the elimination of potential entrants by nonhorizontal mergers. The degree of concern is greatly influenced by whether conditions of entry generally are easy or difficult. If entry is easy, effects on potential entrants are likely to be small. If entry is difficult, the merger will be examined more closely.

The guidelines set forth three circumstances under which vertical mergers may facilitate collusion and therefore be objectionable: (1) If upstream firms obtain a high level of vertical integration into an associated retail market, this may facilitate collusion in the upstream market by monitoring retail prices. (2) The elimination by vertical merger of a disruptive buyer in a downstream market may facilitate collusion in the upstream market. (3) Nonhorizontal mergers by monopoly public utilities may be used to evade rate regulation.

PRIVATE ANTITRUST SUITS

The attitudes of business competitors have always had a strong influence on antitrust policy. Writers have pointed out that even when government was responsible for most antitrust actions, the investigations usually followed complaints that were lodged by competitors against the behavior of other firms that were making life difficult for them in the marketplace (Ellert, 1975, 1976).

It also is argued that the private lawsuit has always been a temptation to lawyers. The cost of litigation is so high that the threat of a private lawsuit can sometimes be used as blackmail to pressure the prospective defendant to make a cash settlement (Grundman, 1987). Some basic statistics on private antitrust cases were developed under the auspices of the Georgetown Law School (Pitofsky, 1987; White, 1988). Most private antitrust cases are Sherman Act cases in which plaintiffs challenge cartel behavior. The average private, triple-damage case takes about 1.5 years to complete compared with 9 months for the average civil case, including relatively minor court cases. The median award in private antitrust cases is $154,000, about the same as the median award in civil litigation.

STATE ANTITRUST ACTIVITY

Another development said to be stimulated by the changed policies of the federal antitrust agencies has been an increase in state activity. The arguments here also are complex and require careful analysis. In the first place, the increased power of the states was granted in the Hart-Scott-Rodino (HSR) Act of 1976 described earlier in this chapter. This was 4 years before antitrust policies by the federal agencies began to change in 1980. In addition, the federal government gave $10 million to the states to increase their antitrust enforcement efforts under HSR. The Department of Justice reported that during the grant period, the number of state actions increased from 206 in 1977 to more than 400 in 1979 (Ewing, 1987). Again, all of this increase in activity was before the change in policies by the federal antitrust agencies after 1980.

The activity of the states has been increasing. The state attorneys general have formed the National Association of Attorneys General (NAAG), which has published merger and vertical restraint guidelines. In addition, it is developing a legislative program to change by statute the content of the federal antitrust laws.

Although the state attorneys general have been cooperating, it is potentially chaotic to have 50 different antitrust laws to which business operations may be subject. Cooperation between the state attorneys general may mitigate this problem, but some risk remains. Whenever jobs are threatened in any locality either by the functioning of active free markets or by merger activity, a risk exists, that parochial views will prevail over what is best for the national economy (Ewing, 1987).

REGULATORY BODIES

Several industries in the United States remain subject to regulation. Generally, regulated industries are still subject to antitrust review, requiring cooperation between the regulatory bodies involved. Our summary coverage will be limited to railroads, commercial banking, and telecommunications.

RAILROADS

The Interstate Commerce Commission (ICC) established in 1887, had long regulated the railroad industry. Under the ICC Termination Act of 1995, it was replaced by the Surface Transportation Board (STB). The STB has final authority on antitrust matters but must file notices with the Justice Department, which may file objections at STB hearings. Among the tests the STB is required to consider are (1) the effect on adequacy of transportation, (2) the effect on competition among rail carriers, and (3) the interests of rail carrier employees affected by the proposed transaction.

The Department of Justice strongly opposed the Union Pacific–Southern Pacific merger, but, after gaining the approval of the STB, the deal was completed in 1996. In October 1996, CSX offered $92.50 in cash for 40% of Conrail and stock for the remaining 60%. The Norfolk Southern Railroad shortly made an all-cash offer of $100 per share. A bidding war ensued, coupled with legal skirmishes. The STB urged the participants to negotiate an agreement in which two balanced east-west lines would be created. In the resulting compromise, CSX acquired what was the old New York Central Railroad, and Norfolk Southern acquired the old Pennsylvania Railroad system. The two examples demonstrate the strong role of the STB.

COMMERCIAL BANKS

Banking is another industry subject to regulation. The Board of Governors of the Federal Reserve System (FED) has broad powers over economic matters as well as antitrust. With regard to bank mergers, three agencies may be involved. The Comptroller of the Currency has jurisdiction when national banks are involved. The FED makes decisions for state banks that are members of the Federal Reserve System. The Federal Deposit Insurance Corporation (FDIC) reviews mergers for state-chartered banks that are not members of the FED but are insured by the FDIC. In conducting its reviews, each agency takes into account a review provided by the Department of Justice.

Bank mergers have long been subject to Section 7 of the Clayton Act of 1914. Modifications were enacted by the Bank Merger Act of 1966. Past bank mergers were legalized. Any merger approved by one of the three regulatory agencies had to be challenged within 30 days by the Attorney General. The Act of 1966 provided that anticompetitive effects could be outweighed by a finding that the transaction served the "convenience and needs" of the community to be served. The convenience and needs defense is not applicable to the acquisition by banks of nonbanking businesses. The review by one of the three agencies substitutes for filing under Hart-Scott-Rodino of 1976.

TELECOMMUNICATIONS

The Federal Communications Commission (FCC) has primary responsibility for the radio and television industries. Mergers in these areas are subject to approval by the FCC, which defers to the Department of Justice and the FTC on antitrust aspects. The Federal Communications Act of 1996 provided for partial deregulation of the telephone and related industries, with rather complicated provisions affecting the role of the former operating companies of the Bell System with their relatively strong monopoly positions in their regional markets.

INTERNATIONAL ANTITRUST

Most of the developed countries of the world have some form of merger control. Cross-border transactions will be subject to the multiple jurisdictions of the home countries of bidders and targets. At the end of February 2000, the International Competition Policy Advisory Committee released its 2-year study. It recommended that the more than 80 nations conducting antitrust enforcement make more explicit what their antitrust policies are. They proposed faster approval of transactions that do not present obvious problems. They recommended that the U.S. "second-request" process, in which the U.S. antitrust agencies ask for more information about a merger, should be streamlined. The report noted that about half of the mergers reviewed by the U.S. Federal Trade Commission or Justice Department have an international component.

Although variations in statutes and administrative bodies and procedures are observed, a central theme is market share percentages. The advisory committee report recommended that the merger-size threshold be raised to reduce the number of reviews. It also recommended that more definite time lines for the review process be established. However, antitrust authorities may even take action when a purely foreign transaction is perceived to have an impact in domestic markets.

CANADA

The Competition Act of 1976, amended in 1991 and 2002, is a federal statute that governs all aspects of Canadian competition. Unlike the United States, where merging parties deal with separate agencies such as the SEC and the FTC, the Competition Bureau provides one-stop shopping for the review and control of all mergers. Waiting periods for merger approval range from 2 weeks for the straightforward cases to 6 weeks for more complicated cases and up to 5 months for complex cases. Mergers generally will not be challenged on the basis of concerns relating to the exercise of market power where the post-merger market share of the merged entity would be less than 35%.

UNITED KINGDOM

The Monopolies and Mergers Act of 1965 created the Monopolies and Mergers Commission (MMC) (Gray and McDermott, 1989). A new era in merger control was established by the Fair Trading Act of 1973 in the United Kingdom (UK). The act created an Office of Fair Trading (OFT) headed by a director general (DG). The DG of the OFT is required to review all mergers in which the combined firm would have a 25% market share or where the assets of the target exceed 30 million British pounds. After review by the OFT, its DG advises the secretary of state for trade and industry whether a referral should be made to the MMC. The secretary of state has discretion whether or not to make the referral. If a referral is made to the MMC, the current bid lapses but may be renewed if the MMC approves. The MMC review may take as long as 6 months. Its report is made to the OFT and the secretary of state. If the MMC recommends approval, the secretary of state cannot override. However, if the MMC recommends prohibition, the secretary of state is not required to accept its findings, but such instances are rare. As a practical matter, a referral to the MMC, which lapses the current bid and involves a long time lag, is likely to kill the transaction. In 1999 its name was changed to the Competition Commission.

JAPAN

Immediately after the conclusion of World War II, the United States attempted to reduce the role of Japanese business groups (keiretsu). Also, a proposed merger requires a filing with a Japanese FTC. The government has 30 days to review the antitrust implications and can extend the review period another 60 days. However, in a stock-for-stock transaction, approval by the government is not required. The reasoning is that advanced review is not needed in a stock transaction, which is more easily reversed. The government can, however, still make an antitrust challenge within 90 days after the transaction.

As in the United States, the review focuses on market share. A combined market share below 25% is not likely to be challenged. A market share above the critical level is likely to be reviewed. The government is probably more flexible in reaching a compromise with the merging companies than are the U.S. antitrust agencies.

EUROPE

The European Union (EU) Merger Regulation grants the European Commission (EC) exclusive authority to review the antitrust implications of transactions that affect the economy of the European Community. Transactions have a community impact if total sales of the combined firm are greater than $4.5 billion annually and the EU sales of each party are greater than $250 million. However, if two thirds of the revenues of each firm are achieved in a single EU country, the EC will defer to that country's antitrust authorities.

Premerger notification is required. The minister of competition of the EU requires a 3-week waiting period but can extend it. The commission is required to decide upon further investigation within the waiting period and must render an approval decision within 5 months. The critical issue is whether the combination will create or strengthen a dominant position.

A dramatic example of the international reach of the EU competition policy is provided by the Boeing–McDonnell Douglas merger, announced in December 1996. U.S. defense procurement outlays between 1988 and 1996 had declined by more than 50%. A series of consolidating mergers had taken place among U.S. defense contractors. The EU competition commissioner was concerned that Boeing's position in the commercial aviation market would be further strengthened. However, the main concern was Boeing's aggressive program of signing exclusive purchase contracts with major U.S. airlines that would have made it more difficult for Airbus to increase its share of the U.S. commercial aviation market. On May 21, 1997, the EU issued its objections, requiring concessions to avoid its stopping the transaction. The EU had the authority to impose substantial fines, including the seizure of Boeing planes in Europe. Boeing made the requisite concessions to obtain approval from the EU competition commissioner. This case illustrates the potentially far reach of international antitrust to a merger between two U.S. firms.

Another example of the international reach of the EU involves the General Electric and Honeywell merger announced in October 2000. When this deal was announced, analysts believed that the DOJ and the FTC would likely issue an HSR second request due to potential concerns about segment concentration and pricing power, especially in the aircraft engine segment. The view held at the time would be that perhaps some divestitures would be required, but the merger would be permitted to go through. A second request was issued, but the DOJ formally approved the merger in May 2001, with some minimal conditions such as requiring General Electric to divest a military helicopter engine unit and let a new company service some of Honeywell's small commercial jet engines.

Whereas analysts and the merging parties had expected some resistance from the DOJ and the FTC, they exhibited little concern regarding the EU. After all, the EU had never blocked a U.S.-based merger that had received the prior approval of the DOJ or the FTC. Indeed, Jack Welch, chairman and CEO of General Electric, believed that the deal would easily obtain EU approval. General Electric waited until early February 2001 before formally filing for EU approval. They delayed the EU filing until well after the United States in order to learn something from the U.S. experience so as to make any necessary adjustments to the EU filing. Even though they filed relatively late, representatives of the merging parties had spent considerable time in Brussels engaged in discussions with the EU staff in preparation for the filing. The goal was to get it right the first time and obtain approval without any waiting period. However, in March of 2001, the EU announced a formal second-stage review, which is similar to the HSR second review. The second-stage review can last up to 4 months. The primary issue was with General Electric's aircraft-engines business. The EU was concerned that with the addition of Honeywell, General Electric would be able to bundle various product packages, and thus have the ability to hurt its competitors and to increase its price to consumers. As a result of this possibility, Rolls Royce and Airbus Industries, two European aircraft-engine manufacturers, lobbied heavily to prevent the merger. General Electric continued to remain optimistic that the merger would go through. In late May, Jack Welch indicated that he did not foresee major hurdles to completing the deal. Nonetheless, in early July, the EU formally voted against the merger as it believed the merger would create dominant positions in several areas including the markets for avionics and jet engines.

The EU decisions with respect to the General Electric and Honeywell merger resulted in great criticism from numerous groups in the United States, including analysts on Wall Street, politicians in Washington, D.C., and business leaders throughout the country. The perception was that the EU's dominance test as applied in the Honeywell merger would result in too many rejections of mergers. Moreover, many hold the view that the dominance test tends to benefit competitors, and in the case of the General Electric and Honeywell merger, tends to benefit Rolls Royce and Airbus Industries. The EU has rejected this notion, indicating that if a merger results in cheaper or better services to the customer base, then it would consider allowing a merger even if it meant a reduction in competition. In the case of General Electric and Honeywell, the EU did not foresee any obvious benefits to the customer. It is our view that in most cases, regulators in the United States and in Europe tend to agree on basic principles of antitrust enforcement, but the occasional substantive divergence of opinion does occur.

REGULATION BY PUBLICITY

Three in-depth studies [DeAngelo, DeAngelo, and Gilson (DDG), 1994, 1996; DeAngelo and DeAngelo (DD), 1998] document some propositions developed by Michael Jensen on the politics of finance (Jensen, 1979, 1991, 1993).

SEIZURE OF THE FIRST EXECUTIVE CORPORATION AND FIRST CAPITAL LIFE

In their 1994 study, DDG described the experience of the First Executive Corporation (FE) and its main subsidiary, the Executive Life Insurance Company (ELIC). In 1974, Fred Carr took over as chief executive officer of FE. Under his direction, ELIC's total assets grew from 355th in rank to 15th in 1988. Measured by insurance in force, FE grew from $700 million in 1974 to $60 billion in 1989.

This spectacular growth came from two major sources. One was innovative products such as single-premium deferred annuities. Another important innovation was interest-sensitive whole life products that put competitive pressure on traditional insurers locked into long-term and low-risk assets with low returns. On the management side, FE and ELIC followed some innovative cost reduction methods. The other major competitive advantage developed was to invest in higher-yielding junk bonds, which grew to 65% of the assets of ELIC. Until January 1990, ELIC enjoyed a AAA rating from Standard & Poor's with comparable ratings from Moody's and A. M. Best.

Carr was a tough competitor. His letters to stockholders criticized his competitors for their stodginess and refusal to mark assets to market values. The aggressive behavior by Carr was especially inflammatory because it was accompanied by a substantial increase in market share.

In 1989, when Milken and the Drexel Company became the target of regulatory and legal actions, the junk bond market in its entirety was unfavorably impacted. In 1989, the congressional enactment of the Financial Institutions Reform Recovery and Enforcement Act (FIRREA) essentially forced the savings and loans (S&Ls) to dispose of their junk bonds and caused the junk bond market to collapse. Although Carr had been calling for "mark-to-market" accounting in his letters to shareholders for many years, the timing of the enactment of the legislation made what otherwise might have been a minor adjustment a major collapse.

ELICs competitors publicized these adverse developments and encouraged the policyholders of FE and ELIC to cash in their policies, resulting in the equivalent of a bank run. The financial press ran numerous feature articles dramatizing the difficulties of FE. This adverse publicity gave John Garamendi, the insurance commissioner of California, a basis for placing ELIC in conservatorship on April 11, 1991. This seizure caused further policy surrender requests. Ultimately, in March 1992, California regulators sold $6.13 billions (par value) of ELIC's junk bonds for $3.25 billions; this was at least $2 billion below their then-current value.

Ironically, the more traditional insurers experienced declines in their real estate portfolios that were 2.5 times the decline in junk bonds. Furthermore, although junk bonds, real estate, and mortgages bottomed out toward the end of 1990, the value of junk bonds increased in value by almost 60% by July 1992, but real estate and mortgages had recovered by less than 20%. Without regulatory intervention, FE and ELIC would have been fully solvent within a year and a half after the junk bond market bottomed out. Insurance companies and S&Ls with heavy investments in real estate and mortgages experienced continued difficulties.

The story of First Capital Life is similar (DDG, 1996). The seizure of First Capital Life and its parent First Capital Holdings was related to the investment of 40% of its portfolio in junk bonds. DDG state that their evidence suggests that regulatory seizure reflected the targeting of insurers that had invested in junk bonds. However, these companies did not experience differentially poorer financial positions compared with other insurers.

THE HOSTILE TAKEOVER OF THE PACIFIC LUMBER COMPANY

In 1986, the Pacific Lumber Company (PL), the largest private owner of old redwood trees, was acquired in a leveraged hostile takeover by the MAXXAM Group headed by Charles Hurwitz, regarded as a corporate raider. The event resulted in a dramatic barrage of negative media coverage, linking junk bonds and takeover greed to the destruction of the redwoods.

In their careful analysis of the facts, DD (1998) reach a more balanced conclusion. They point out that basic timber economics explains the behavior of MAXXAM and the predecessor owners of PL. Timber economics predict that old growth forests will be harvested first because they will yield virtually no further growth in harvestable timber volume. Timber economic principles predict that under any private ownership, old growth forests will be harvested, a process that had been taking place for at least 100 years before the 1986 takeover of PL. Their study presents evidence that shows that 91% of PL's old growth redwoods had already been logged by the time of the takeover and that the old and new managements had similar timetables for the remaining acreage. Junk bonds and takeovers would have little effect on these timetables. DD outline the correct policies for saving the redwoods. One is to raise funds to purchase the old growth acreage for public holding. The other is to raise funds to purchase previously logged land to grow new redwood forests. These eminently sensible prescriptions were lost in the hysteria over the change of ownership of the Pacific Lumber Company.

REGULATION BY THE POLITICS OF FINANCE

The clinical studies of ELIC, First Capital Life, and PL illustrate how the use of junk bonds resulted in regulation by the politics of finance. The ultimate explanation for the bad reputation of junk bonds is that potentially they could finance the takeover of any firm that was not performing up to its potential. Thus, junk bonds became a vigilant monitoring instrument to pressure managements to achieve a high level of efficiency in the companies under their stewardship. The junk bond takeover threat was unsettling to the managers of the leading companies in the United States. Widespread animosity toward the use of junk bonds developed. Junk bonds filled an important financing gap for new and risky growth companies. Their use in takeovers led to value enhancement for shareholders. However, these three studies illustrate how junk bond use became a lightning rod for widespread hysteria, animosity, and pressures on government regulators to limit and penalize their use.

Summary

Regulation of securities trading is closely related to regulation of merger and acquisition activity, because takeovers are carried out by means of the securities markets. Special characteristics of securities that make them vulnerable to being used fraudulently mandate regulation to increase public confidence in securities markets. The earliest securities legislation in the 1930s grew out of the collapse of confidence following the stock market crash of 1929. The Securities Act of 1933 called for registration of public offerings of securities. The Securities Exchange Act of 1934 established the Securities and Exchange Commission to regulate securities market practices; it also specified disclosure requirements for public companies (Section 13) and set out the procedural requirements for proxy contests. A number of other securities laws in the late 1930s and 1940s applied to public utilities, bond indenture trustees, and investment companies. In response to recent allegations of corporate and financial fraud by large corporations, the Sarbanes-Oxley Act of 2002 extended the earlier securities acts by substantially strengthening corporate governance, disclosure, audit, and analyst standards.

The Securities Act of 1933 and the Securities Exchange Act of 1934 provided the framework for subsequent regulation. Most of the more recent legislation has been in the form of amendments to these two acts. The Williams Act of 1968 amended the 1934 act to regulate tender offers. Two main requirements were a filing with the SEC upon obtaining 5% ownership and a 20-day waiting period after making a tender offer. The disclosure requirements aim to give the target shareholders information that will enable them to receive more of the gains associated with the rise in the share price of the takeover target. The 20-day waiting period gives the target more time to evaluate the offer, tailor a defense, or seek multiple bids. Empirical studies on the impact of tender offer regulation on shareholder returns almost universally document significantly higher returns for target shareholders and lower (or negative) returns for bidder shareholders. To the extent that successful tender offers continue to take place, the legislation has achieved its goal of benefiting target shareholders. The risk, however, is that reductions in the returns to bidding firms reduce their incentives to engage in the kind of information-producing activities that lead to beneficial takeovers; thus, the lot of target shareholders in those tender offers that *might* have taken place is not improved.

Historically, insider trading has little to do with M&A activity; it refers to the trading in their own companies' stock by corporate officers, directors, and other insiders. It is largely controlled by Section 16 of the Securities Exchange Act, which requires insiders to report such transactions to the SEC on a regular basis. However, the volatility of stock price changes in connection with M&As creates opportunities for gains by individuals who may not fit the traditional definition of insiders. Rule 10b-5 is a general prohibition of fraud and deceit in the purchase or sale of securities. Rule 14e-3 applies to insider trading, particularly in connection with tender offers. The Insider Trading Sanctions Act of 1984 provides for triple damage penalties in insider trading cases, as does the Racketeer Influenced and Corrupt Organizations Act of 1970

(RICO), which also allows immediate seizure of assets and which is invoked in some of the more notorious cases of insider trading. The SEC rules are somewhat ambiguous, but it is illegal to trade on inside information, whether obtained as a result of one's fiduciary relationship to a firm or through misappropriation.

In addition to federal regulation of M&A activity, a number of states have enacted legislation to protect corporations headquartered within their boundaries. States are the primary regulators of corporate activities. However, there are problems in state regulation of takeovers. Securities markets represent interstate commerce, and state regulations that interfere with interstate commerce are, by definition, unconstitutional. Others argue that state regulations are not necessary, that federal regulations and corporate antitakeover amendments provide sufficient protection. Evidence even exists that shows that shareholders are damaged by restrictive state legislation that limits takeovers.

Antitrust policies in the United States continue to be suspicious of large firms and merger activity. Yet the increasing dynamism of the economy has intensified the forces of market competition. Some fundamental economic factors have changed.

1. International competition has clearly increased, and many of our important industries are now international in scope. Concentration ratios must take into account international markets and will be much lower than when measured on the assumption of purely domestic markets.
2. The pace of technological change has increased, and the pace of industrial change has increased substantially. This requires more frequent adjustments by business firms, including many aspects of restructuring that include acquisitions and divestitures.
3. Deregulation in a number of major industries requires industrial realignment and readjustments. These require greater flexibility in government policy.
4. New institutions, particularly among financial intermediaries, represent new mechanisms for facilitating the restructuring processes that are likely to continue.

Many see merger activity as a natural expression of strong change forces. Mergers during the 1980s and 1990s were associated with extraordinary growth in employment and in gross domestic product. Through mergers and restructuring, firms all over the world have become more efficient. In light of the increased dynamism of their environments and the greater intensity of competitive forces, firms should not be restricted by antitrust policies from making required adjustments to economic turbulence. (See publications by Weston, 1953, 1973, 1978, 1980a, 1980b, 1982.)

Questions

2.1 For a merger that has been completed recently, examine the various filings on Edgar Online. What are the similarities and differences among these filings and the filings discussed for the PepsiCo and Quaker Oats merger?
2.2 What is the rationale for tender offer regulation?
2.3 Discuss the pros and cons of trading halts as a measure to deal with significant information about a listed firm.
2.4 Discuss the pros and cons of *state* regulation of mergers and tender offers.
2.5 List and briefly explain the product characteristics and management decision variables that make collusion within an industry more difficult.

2.6 What other factors are considered along with the Herfindahl-Hirschman Index in the government's decision to initiate an antitrust case?

2.7 In light of the increasing globalization of companies, evaluate the feasibility of a world antitrust agency.

Case 2.1 BROADER BOARD RESPONSIBILITIES

An area of great practical importance to directors involved in the sale of their company is the obligation to prove that they received the best possible price for their shareholders. One reason this problem arises is that a target may receive an attractive proposal from a bidder. The board of the target and some of its key shareholders may believe the offer is an attractive one. To prove to other shareholders that the offer is the best that could be achieved, the board of the target might test the market (shop around) for other possible bidders. Alternatively, they might hire an investment banker or some other financial intermediary to test the market or even to conduct an auction.

One risk is that if the market feels that the target is being shopped, it may suspect some weakness and potential problems at the target. If no other offers are forthcoming or if other offers come in at much lower prices, the first bidder might lower its offer because its position has been clearly strengthened. Another possibility is that the initial bidder may drop out as soon as the target checks other alternatives rather than continue to incur the additional expenses required to investigate and evaluate the deal with the target.

The basic problem is that if bidding is costly, then the decision of the potential bidder to make an investigation is influenced by the probability that the investigated investments will be profitable. There are advantages to the target to encourage bids by reducing the investment risk of potential acquirers. Four types of techniques have been used to provide this kind of encouragement (Gilson and Black, 1995, pp. 1020–1023). One is a *no-shop* agreement by the target. This prohibits the target from seeking other bids or providing nonpublic information to third parties. A related agreement commits the target management to use its best efforts to secure shareholder approval of the offer by the bidder. These protections to the acquirer are subject to a **fiduciary out** when the target receives a legal opinion that the fiduciary duty of the target board requires it to consider competitive bids.

Another protection is the payment of a **breakup or termination fee** to the initial bidder. For example, the termination fee Paramount Communications agreed to pay to Viacom, the favored acquirer, was $100 million. The termination fee reflects investigation expenses and the executive time involved in formulating an offer, as well as opportunity costs of alternative investment options not pursued.

Another protection to a bidder is a *stock lockup* such as an option to buy the target's stock at the first bidder's initial offer when a rival bidder wins. This technique was used in the bidding contest between U.S. Steel (later USX) and Mobil Oil for the acquisition of Marathon Oil. In this case, Mobil has made an initial hostile bid. Marathon granted USX the right to purchase 10 million newly issued Marathon shares for $90 per share, which was the competing offer by USX. If Mobil or some other firm ultimately acquired Marathon for $95 per share, for example, the gain to USX would have been $5 times 10 millions shares, or $50 million.

Still another method of encouraging the initial bidder is to grant a *crown jewels lockup*. USX also was granted an option to purchase for $2.8 billion Marathon's 48% interest in the oil and mineral rights to the Yates Field in western Texas, one of the richest domestic oil wells ever discovered.

QUESTION

C2.1.1 What are the four techniques used to encourage bidders?

═══════ ·/·/·/· ═══════

Case 2.2   VAN GORKOM

The creation of techniques to favor an early bidder plus the economic environment of competitive bids raise practical and legal issues. How does the board of directors of the target demonstrate that it obtained the best price? A series of court cases illustrates the nature of the issues involved. The lead case in this area is *Smith v. Van Gorkom*, 488 A.2d 858 (Del. 1985). The plaintiff Smith represented a class action brought by the shareholders of the Trans Union Corporation (Trans Union). Van Gorkom had been an officer of Trans Union for 24 years during most of which he was either chief executive officer (CEO) or chairman of the board. Trans Union was a diversified company, but most of its profits came from its railcar leasing business. The company had difficulty generating sufficient taxable income to offset increasingly large investment tax credits (ITCs). Beginning in the late 1960s, Trans Union followed a program of acquiring many companies to increase available taxable income. A 1980 report considered still further alternatives to deal with the ITC problem. Van Gorkom was approaching 65 years of age and mandatory retirement.

One of the alternatives was a leveraged buyout. The chief financial officer (CFO) of Trans Union ran some numbers at $50 a share and $60 a share to check whether the prospective cash flows could service the debt in a leveraged buyout (LBO). The numbers indicated that $50 would be easy but that $60 would be difficult. Van Gorkom took a midway $55 price and met with Jay Pritzker, a well-known takeover investor and social acquaintance. Van Gorkom explained to Pritzker that the $55 share price represented a substantial premium and would still enable the buyer to pay off most of the loan in the first 5 years. Van Gorkom stated that to be sure the $55 was the best price obtainable. Trans Union should be free to accept any better offer. Pritzker stated that his organization would serve as a "stalking horse" for an "auction contest" only if Trans Union would permit Pritzker to buy 1.75 million shares at (the current) market price, which Pritzker could then sell to any higher bidder. After many discussions and negotiations, Salomon

Brothers over a 3-month period ending January 21, 1981, tried to elicit other bids. GE Credit was interested but was unwilling to make an offer unless Trans Union first rescinded its merger agreement with Pritzker. Kohlberg Kravis Roberts (KKR) also made an offer but withdrew it.

Ultimately, the Pritzker offer was submitted to the vote of shareholders. Of the outstanding shares, 69.6% voted in favor of the merger; 7.55% voted against; 22.85% were not voted. The class action suit was then brought. The defendants argued that the $55 represented a 60% premium and established the most reliable evidence possible, a marketplace test that the price was more than fair. Nevertheless, the court concluded that the directors of Trans Union had breached their fiduciary duty to their stockholders on two counts: (1) their failure to inform themselves of all information relevant to the decision to recommend the Pritzker merger, and (2) their failure to disclose all material information that a reasonable stockholder would consider important in evaluating the Pritzker offer. Interestingly enough, the court's measure of damages was the amount by which the fair value of the transaction exceeded $55 per share, and the case was ultimately settled for about $23.5 million.

Within a few months after the Trans Union decision, the Delaware legislature amended the Delaware general corporate law to provide directors with more protection in connection with a transaction such as the Trans Union. The new law made three points: (1) Once it was recognized that a company was "in play," meaning it was going to be sold, the directors had the responsibility to get the best price for shareholders. (2) The directors should be equally fair to all bidders. (3) The decision should not be tainted by the self-interest of management or directors.

It was in the same year, 1985, that the Delaware Supreme Court was confronted with the issues of *Unocal v. Mesa.* In the Unocal case, the directors paid a large special dividend to all shareholders except Mesa. The court distinguished Unocal as a case in which the directors were seeking to preserve the company. To do this, the court held that the directors had the right to take defensive actions in the face of a hostile takeover attempt. In particular, the court held that Mesa had made a two-tier offer with a second-tier price less than the first tier, so it was coercive. ▨

QUESTION

C2.2.1 On what basis did the courts conclude that the directors of Trans Union had breached their fiduciary duty to their stockholders?

Case 2.3 REVLON INC. V. PANTRY PRIDE

The defendant in the Revlon case, 506 A.2d 173 (Del. 1986), was technically MacAndrews & Forbes Holdings, which was the controlling stockholder of Pantry Pride. Ronald O. Perelman, chairman and CEO of Pantry Pride, met with the head of Revlon in June 1985 to suggest a friendly acquisition of Revlon. Perelman indicated that Pantry Pride (PP) would offer $45 per share. Revlon's investment banker (in August 1985) advised that $45 was too low and that Perelman would use junk bond financing followed by a bust-up of Revlon, which would bring as much as $70 a share. As defensive actions, Revlon was advised to repurchase at least one sixth of its shares and to adopt a poison pill.

In October, Revlon received a proposal from Forstmann Little and the investment group Adler & Shaykin. The directors agreed to an LBO plan. Each shareholder would receive $56 cash per share, and management would receive a substantial stock position in the new company by the exercise of their Revlon golden parachutes. Some initial bids and counterbids by Pantry Pride and Forstmann Little took place. At this point, the court observed that the duty of the board had changed from the preservation of Revlon as a corporate entity to getting the best price for the shareholders. This made the case different from Unocal. The Revlon board had granted Forstmann Little (1) a lockup option to purchase certain Revlon assets, (2) a no-shop provision to deal exclusively with Forstmann, and (3) a termination fee of $25 million. The Delaware Supreme Court concluded that it agreed with the Court of Chancery that the Revlon defensive measures were inconsistent with the directors' duties to shareholders. ▨

QUESTION

C2.3.1 What was the reasoning of the court in *Revlon Inc. v. Pantry Pride*?

Case 2.4 MAXWELL COMMUNICATIONS V. MACMILLAN

Macmillan was a large publishing company. In May 1987, Robert Maxwell had made a hostile bid for another publishing company, Harcourt Brace Jovanovich, Incorporated, which was defeated by a leveraged recap. Fearing that Maxwell would make a hostile bid, the management of Macmillan decided to restructure the company in order to increase its share of stock ownership to block a Maxwell takeover.

On October 21, 1987, the Bass Group of Texas announced that it had acquired 7.5% of Macmillan's stock. At a special board meeting, management painted an uncomplimentary picture of the Bass Group. Offers and counteroffers took place. On July 20, 1988, Maxwell intervened in the Bass-Macmillan bidding contest with an all-cash offer of $80 per share. Macmillan did not respond but instead started negotiations for Kohlberg Kravis Roberts (KKR) to do an LBO of Macmillan. In the subsequent offers and counteroffers, Macmillan gave preferential treatment to KKR in a number of ways. KKR asked for a "no-shop rule" and a lockup option to purchase eight Macmillan subsidiaries for $950 million. Maxwell countered by stating that he would always top whatever bid was made by KKR. Maxwell sued, requesting an injunction against the lockup option. A lower court denied the injunction.

The Supreme Court of Delaware concluded that the Macmillan board had not been neutral. To conduct a fair auction to get the best price for shareholders, fairness to all bidders must be achieved. The higher court reversed the lower court's decision, thus allowing Maxwell's motion for a preliminary injunction. This blocked the sale of the eight Macmillan subsidiaries to KKR. Maxwell succeeded in acquiring Macmillan in 1988 for $2,335 million.

QUESTION

C2.4.1 What was the reasoning in the Macmillan decision?

Case 2.5   PARAMOUNT V. TIME

In *Paramount Communications, Incorporated, v. Time, Incorporated*, Fed.Sec.L. Rep. (CCH) 94.514 (Del.Ch. 1989) and 571 A.2d 1140 (Del, 1990), the Revlon and Macmillan case issues were visited again. The Supreme Court of Delaware reached a different decision. The court held that Time did not expressly resolve to sell the company. The exchange of stock between Time and Warner did not contemplate a change in corporate control. Although the Paramount offer had a higher dollar value, the Time board argued

that it was following a program of long-term share value maximization for its shareholders. The court therefore upheld the right of the Time board to not accept the Paramount offer.

QUESTION

C2.5.1 On what basis did the court uphold the right of Time's board of directors not to accept the Paramount offer?

Case 2.6   PARAMOUNT V. QVC NETWORK

This case is cited as 637 A.2d 34 (Del. 1993). Paramount had a strategic vision in trying to acquire Time. It would have given Paramount entry into the cable television industry. Failing to acquire Time, Paramount negotiated an acquisition of Viacom. The form of the transaction sought to avoid any implication of a change in control of Paramount. Paramount tried to avoid the Revlon trigger and sought to take advantage of that avoidance by providing Viacom with important lockups. Viacom was controlled by Summer Redstone, who essentially owned about 90%

of the company. Viacom's equity coinvestors in the Paramount-Viacom transaction included NYNEX and Blockbuster Entertainment Corporation.

After some preliminary negotiations, on September 12, 1993, the Paramount board approved a merger agreement. It was understood that Martin Davis, the head of Paramount, would be the CEO of the combined company and Redstone would be its controlling stockholder. The merger agreement included a no-shop provision, and it provided a termination fee to Viacom of $100 million. It granted Viacom an option to purchase about 20% of Paramount's outstanding common stock at $69.14 per share if any of the triggering event related to the termination fee occurred.

Despite the attempts to discourage a competing bid, Barry Diller, the chairman and CEO of QVC Network, along with several equity coinvestors including Bell South and Comcast, proposed a merger paying $30 in cash and about 0.9 share of QVC common to total $80 per share. This started counterbids by Viacom and further bids by QVC. In their final offers, the Paramount management disparaged some aspects of the QVC bid but failed to mention that it was $1 billion higher than the best Viacom offer. The Supreme Court of Delaware held that the directors of Paramount had breached their fiduciary duty in not getting the best possible price. Rather than seizing opportunities to get the highest price, the Paramount directors walled themselves off from material information and refused to negotiate with QVC or to seek other alternatives. The bidding war continued, but ultimately Viacom became the successful buyer of Paramount.

QUESTION

C2.6.1 What was the reasoning of the court in the *Paramount v. QVC* decision? How did that affect Viacom?

Case 2.7   SANDOZ-GERBER

We have seen legal subtleties weave their way through a number of major merger transactions. The decisions of the court seem inconsistent to some. To others, each of the court decisions had a valid factual basis for distinguishing between distinct and different circumstances. To wrap up this story, when Gerber Products was acquired by Sandoz, a major Swiss drug firm, in May 1994, there were no stock option lockups (Steinmetz, 1994). It was generally recognized that the Paramount decision had an impact. It was pointed out that the purchase of Syntex by Roche Holdings for $5.4 billion had no option agreements whatsoever. In the Sandoz-Gerber deal, there was a $70 million breakup fee. Takeover lawyers have commented that as long as the compensation of stock options and breakup fees was less than 2.5% of the deal's value, the courts probably would not find preferential treatment. The $70 million Sandoz breakup fee represented 1.9% of the $3.7 billion deal value.

QUESTION

C2.7.1 How did the previous court decision affect the size of the breakup fee in the acquisition of Gerber Products by Sandoz?

Case 2.8   UNITED AIRLINES AND US AIRWAYS

On July 27, 2001, the U.S. Department of Justice blocked the merger of United Airlines and US Airways. According to Attorney General John Ashcroft, "if this acquisition were allowed to proceed, millions of customers . . . would have little choice but to pay higher fares and accept lower-quality air service." Legislators on Capitol Hill applauded the decision of the DOJ to block the merger. The view was that competition along the East Coast would be greatly reduced because United Airlines and US

Airways are the only two airlines in many markets offering connecting services between cities up and down the coast. When the merger was announced in May 2000, the stock price of US Airways increased from $26.31 to $49.00, nearly doubling in price. The bid by United Airlines was for $60 in cash. As investors expected the deal to take a considerably long time to complete, and because there was a good chance that the deal might be rejected by the regulations, the stock price of US Airways traded at a fairly large spread relative to the agreed-upon price. When the DOJ blocked the merger, the stock price of US Airways immediately dropped into the teens, and in August 2002, the company filed for federal bankruptcy protection. Interestingly, before the year 2002 had ended, United Airlines had also filed for federal bankruptcy protection. As of early 2003, the survivability of both firms is questionable.▩

QUESTIONS

C2.8.1 The DOJ's blocking of the merger rested on the case that it would greatly reduce competition along the East Coast because the merging parties were often the only two major airlines in some markets. Should potential competition, for example, arising from Southwest Airlines, a mover into the East Coast market, factor into the DOJ's decision?

C2.8.2 US Airways is a failing firm and has a substantial probability of bankruptcy. Should the antitrust authorities consider a "failing firm" defense from the merging parties? That is, should mergers be allowed to occur if otherwise the target firm faces bankruptcy?

References

Bandow, D., "Curbing Raiders Is Bad for Business," *New York Times*, February 7, 1988, p. 2.

DeAngelo, Harry, and Linda DeAngelo, "Ancient Redwoods and the Politics of Finance: The Hostile Takeover of the Pacific Lumber Company," *Journal of Financial Economics* 47, 1998, pp. 3–53.

———, and Stuart C. Gilson, "The Collapse of First Executive Corporation Junk Bonds, Adverse Publicity, and the 'Run on the Bank' Phenomenon," *Journal of Financial Economics* 36, 1994, pp. 287–336.

———, "Perceptions and the Politics of Finance: Junk Bonds and the Regulatory Seizure of First Capital Life," *Journal of Financial Economics* 41, 1996, pp. 475–511.

Economist, "How Dangerous Is Microsoft?" 8 July 1995, pp. 13–14.

———, "Thoroughly Modern Monopoly," 8 July 1995, p. 76.

Ellert, J. C., "Antitrust Enforcement and the Behavior of Stock Prices," Ph.D. dissertation, Graduate School of Business. University of Chicago, June 1975, pp. 66–67.

———, "Mergers, Antitrust Law Enforcement and Stockholder Returns," *Journal of Finance* 31, 1976, pp. 715–732.

Ewing, Ky P., Jr., "Current Trends in State Antitrust Enforcement: Overview of State Antitrust Law" *Antitrust Law Journal* 56, April 1987, pp. 103–110.

Gilson, Ronald J., and Bernard S. Black, *The Law and Finance of Corporate Acquisitions*, 2d ed., Westbury, NY: The Foundation Press, Inc., 1995.

Grass, A., "Insider Trading Report Addresses Reform of Section 16," *Business Lawyer Update*, July/August 1987, p. 3.

Gray, S. J., and M. C. McDermott, *Mega-Merger Mayhem*, London: Paul Chapman Publishing Ltd., 1989.

Grundman, V. Rock, Jr., "Antitrust: Public vs. Private Law," *Restructuring and Antitrust*, The Conference Board Research Bulletin No. 212, 1987, pp. 5–13.

Jensen, Michael C., "Corporate Control and the Politics of Finance," *Journal of Applied Corporate Finance* 4, 1991, pp. 13–33.

———, "The Modern Industrial Revolution, Exit, and the Failure of Internal Control Systems," *Journal of Finance* 48, 1993, pp. 831–880.

——, "Toward a Theory of the Press," in Karl Brunner, ed., *Economics and Social Institutions*, Boston, MA: Martinus Nijhoff Publishing, 1979, pp. 267–287.

Office of the Chief Economist, Securities and Exchange Commission, "The Economics of Any-or-All, Partial, and Two-Tier Tender Offers," April 1985.

Pitofsky, Robert, "Antitrust: Public vs. Private Law," *Restructuring and Antitrust*, The Conference Board Research Bulletin No. 212, 1987, pp. 5–13.

Savage, D. G., "Justices Say Firm Can't Lie About Merger Talks," *Los Angeles Times*, March 8, 1988, pp. 1, 17.

Steinmetz, Greg, "Stock-Option Lockups Are Absent from Takeover Deals," *Wall Street Journal*, May 24, 1994, pp. C1, C21.

U.S. Department of Justice, "1968 Department of Justice Merger Guidelines," May 30, 1968 p. 12.

——, "1977 Antitrust Guide for International Operations," *The Journal of Reprints for Antitrust Law and Economics* 16, 1986, pp. 307–375.

——, "1977 Guidelines for Sentencing Recommendations in Felony Cases Under the Sherman Act," *The Journal of Reprints for Antitrust Law and Economics* 16, 1986, pp. 379–397.

——, "1980 Antitrust Guide Concerning Research Joint Ventures." *The Journal of Reprints for Antitrust Law and Economics* 16, 1986, pp. 189–303.

——, "1982 Department of Justice Merger Guidelines," *The Journal of Reprints for Antitrust Law and Economics* 16, 1986, pp. 119–165.

——, "1982 Federal Trade Commission Horizontal Merger Guidelines," *The Journal of Reprints for Antitrust Law and Economics* 16, 1986, pp. 169–185.

——, "1984 Department of Justice Merger Guidelines," *The Journal of Reprints for Antitrust Law and Economics* 16, 1986, pp. 61–115.

——, "1985 Vertical Restraints Guidelines," *The Journal of Reprints for Antitrust Law and Economics* 16, 1986, pp. 3–57.

Veasey, N., "A Statute Was Needed to Stop Abuses," *New York Times*, February 7, 1988, p. 2.

Weston J. Fred. *Concentration and Efficiency: The Other Side of the Monopoly Issue*, Special Issues in the Public Interest No.4, New York: Hudson Institute, 1978.

——, "International Competition, Industrial Structure and Economic Policy," Chapter 10 in I. Leveson and J. W. Wheeler, eds., *Western Economies in Transition*, Hudson Institute, Boulder, CO: Westview Press, 1980a.

——, *The Role of Mergers in the Growth of Large Firms*, Berkeley: University of California Press, 1953.

——, "Section 7 Enforcement: Implementation of Outmoded Theories," *Antitrust Law Journal* 49, August 1980b, pp. 1411–1450.

——, "Trends in Anti-Trust Policy," *Chase Financial Quarterly* 1, Spring 1982, pp. 66–87.

——, and Stanley I. Ornstein. *The Impact of the Large Firm on the U.S. Economy*, Lexington, MA: Heath Lexington Books, January 1973.

White, Lawrence J., ed., *Private Antitrust Litigation*, in Richard Schmaler, ed., *Regulation of Economics Series*, Cambridge, MA: MIT Press, 1988.

LEGAL DUE DILIGENCE PRELIMINARY INFORMATION REQUEST

GENERAL OBSERVATIONS

The checklist that follows is a relatively extensive and generic due diligence information request form. It is probably longer than most and longer than generally necessary (except for larger transactions involving a target company that owns real estate and may be involved in an environmentally sensitive business). A form such as this is almost certain to intimidate the typical target company. The acquiring company's management and counsel must thoughtfully customize any due diligence information request form, taking into account such factors as what is truly material to the buyer as well as the target company's level of tolerance.

It should be emphasized further that despite its considerable length and the wide range of subjects covered, this due diligence outline is limited to legal aspects. Many types of business activities and operations are inextricably tied to the legal issues treated. In addition, the wide range of topics treated in the other chapters of this volume need to be evaluated in the merger planning and implementation analysis. Mr. Weiner has emphasized in his lectures to the Merger Week programs at the Anderson School, UCLA: "The goal is to achieve the greatest increase in value from the merger transaction while minimizing all types of risks."

TABLE OF CONTENTS

LEGAL DUE DILIGENCE PRELIMINARY INFORMATION REQUEST LIST

1. Corporate and Organizational

1.1 Certified copy of articles/certificate of incorporation of [company name] (the "Company"), as currently in effect.

1.2 Certified copy of bylaws of the Company, as currently in effect.

1.3 Copy of minute books of the Company.

1.4 Copy of stock books and stock transfer ledgers of the Company.

1.5 List of states and foreign countries in which the Company is qualified to do business, including names and addresses of registered agents and list of states and foreign countries in which the trade names of the Company are registered.

1.6 Long-form good standing certificate, including payment of taxes for state of incorporation and every state and foreign country in which the Company is qualified to do business.

1.7 List of states and foreign countries in which tax returns are filed because of the ownership of property or conduct of business by the Company.

1.8 List of states and foreign countries, if any, in which the Company is not qualified to do business and does not file tax returns but in which it maintains an office, any inventory or equipment, employees, or an agent who is a resident of any state in which he or she solicits orders.

1.9 Current organizational chart for the Company and subsidiaries, operating divisions, and hierarchy of officers.

1.10 All names under which the Company or any predecessor has done business in the past 5 years.

2. Subsidiaries

2.1 List of Subsidiaries of the Company.

2.2 Certified copies of articles/certificates of incorporation and bylaws of each subsidiary, and access to minute books and stock transfer ledgers of each subsidiary.

2.3 Information requested in item 1, shown separately for each subsidiary.

3. Securities

3.1 Statement of outstanding and treasury shares of common stock, preferred stock (including a complete description of the rights attaching to preferred shares), and any other securities of the Company and each subsidiary.

3.2 Stockholders list, giving name and address of each stockholder of the Company and its subsidiaries and of any voting trustees, his or her affiliation with the Company, the type of security held, the date of issue by the Company, the consideration received by the Company, and the number of shares of such security owned by each such stockholder or trust.

3.3 List of holders of any options or rights to purchase any securities of the Company (including warrants), giving name, number of options held, option prices, date(s) of grant expiration dates, position in the Company or subsidiary, and number of shares owned (excluding those subject to option).

3.4 Copies of all stock option agreements, stock option plans, and warrants.

3.5 Copies of all stockholder agreements and all other agreements with respect to securities of the Company or its subsidiaries.

3.6 All reports to stockholders of the Company prepared within the past 5 years.

3.7 Indication of whether there are any stockholders or stock certificates whose whereabouts are unknown, or any stockholders from whom it will be difficult to obtain approval of the transaction or stock certificates, as appropriate.

3.8 Description of all contractual restrictions on transfer of the Company's capital stock or assets.

3.9 Copies of registration rights or preemptive rights agreements.

4. Business Descriptions

4.1 All market studies, feasibility studies, analyses, and similar reports concerning the Company prepared within the past 5 years.

4.2 All marketing and other descriptive brochures regarding the Company prepared within the past 5 years.

4.3 All press releases issued by the Company during the past 5 years, and any press clippings that refer to the Company, if available.

4.4 Recent analyses of the Company or its industries prepared by investment bankers, engineers, management consultants, accountants, or others, including marketing studies, credit reports, and other types of reports, financial or otherwise.

5. Financing Documents

5.1 List and brief description of all long-term and short-term debt and other financial obligations (including capitalized leases, guarantees, indemnity undertakings, and other contingent obligations) to which the Company and each subsidiary is a party, and copies of all related material documentation.

5.2 List of all mortgages, liens, pledges, security interests, or other encumbrances to which any property (real or personal) of the Company and each subsidiary is subject, and copies of all related material documentation.

5.3 All correspondence with lenders and other debt security holders for the past 5 years (including all consents, notices, or waivers of default from lenders with respect to borrowings by the Company).

5.4 Any presentations given to creditors in connection with obtaining credit or prepared for potential lenders in connection with any proposed financings.

6. Financial Statements

6.1 Audited financial statements, both consolidated and consolidating, for the Company and its subsidiaries for the past 5 fiscal years.

6.2 All unaudited interim financial statements of the Company prepared since the date of the most recent audited financial statements.

6.3 Separate consolidating statement for significant subsidiaries or divisions.

6.4 Brief description of contingent liabilities involving the Company.

6.5 Name of accountants and length of relationship with accountants; indicate whether the accountants own any interest in or hold any position with the Company or its subsidiaries.

6.6 Management financial reports to the directors, or any board committee, of the Company prepared during the past 5 years.

6.7 Correspondence with the Company's accountants prepared or received during the past five years, including all management letters from accountants.

6.8 Brief description of depreciation policy.

6.9 Brief description of nature of prepaid or deferred income or expenses.

6.10 Copy of any sales projections and estimates, and copy of current budget and any budget projections, including a discussion of any assumptions used.

6.11 Brief description of any change in accounting policies or procedures during the past 5 years.

6.12 Brief description of outstanding commitments for capital expenditures in excess of $____.

6.13 Any documents relating to material write-downs or write-offs of notes, accounts receivable, or other assets other than in the ordinary course of business.

7. Tax Matters

7.1 Copies of all federal, state, local, and foreign income and franchise tax returns filed by the Company and its subsidiaries for the past 5 years concerning the business, assets, or income of the Company.

7.2 All correspondence with the Internal Revenue Service or state or local tax authorities concerning adjustments or questioning compliance.

7.3 List of returns and the years thereof that have been audited by federal, state, or local tax authorities, and copies of related determination letters.

7.4 List of state and local taxes to which the Company or any subsidiary is subject with respect to the business, assets, or income of the Company, showing assessment date, date return is to be filed, and date tax is due.

7.5 Description and copies of all agreements, consents, elections, and waivers filed or made with the IRS or other taxing authorities.

7.6 List and description of all pending or threatened disputes with regard to tax matters involving the Company or any of its subsidiaries.

7.7 Copies of S corporation elections, IRS notices of acceptance, and any other information pertinent to the Company's S corporation status, where applicable.

7.8 Copies of any tax indemnification, tax sharing, or tax allocation agreements involving the Company and other members of an affiliate group, including any joint venture agreements that have the effect of tax allocation agreements, and a statement setting forth how such agreements were carried out for the past 5 fiscal years.

7.9 Copies of all legal or accounting tax opinions received by the Company during the past 5 fiscal years relating to the Company's tax reporting.

8. Officers and Directors, Employees, Benefit Plans, and Labor Disputes

8.1 Name, address, and telephone numbers (home and business) of each director and officer of the Company and each subsidiary (and, if applicable, principal occupation), and aggregate compensation at present and for the previous fiscal year.

8.2 Copies of all liability insurance policies for directors and officers of the Company and each subsidiary.

8.3 Number of persons employed by the Company and by each subsidiary in terms of function (executive, sales, clerical, research, labor, or other appropriate classification).

8.4 Name and address of each person who has a power of attorney to act on behalf of the Company or any subsidiary. Furnish copies.

8.5 List of all labor union contracts and collective bargaining arrangements to which the Company or any subsidiary is a party, the number of employees covered by each agreement, and the anticipated expiration dates. Furnish copies.

8.6 Brief description of "labor unrest" situations, all pending or threatened labor strikes, or other trouble experienced by the Company and its subsidiaries during the past 5 fiscal years.

8.7 List and brief description of the current status of all unfair labor practices complaints lodged during the past 3 fiscal years against the Company and its subsidiaries.

8.8 Brief description of any pending or threatened request for arbitration, grievance proceedings, labor disputes, strikes, or disturbances affecting the Company or any subsidiary, and history of recent union negotiations.

8.9 All performance bonus plans adopted by the board of directors of the Company during the past 5 years.

8.10 a. Brief description and copies of all employee benefit plans, group life insurance plans, major medical plans, medical reimbursement plans, supplemental unemployment benefit plans or welfare plans (for hourly employees) or salary continuation plans, or other perquisites, and a brief description of policy regarding bonuses, salary review, severance pay, moving expenses, tuition reimbursement, loans, advances, vacations, holiday, sick leaves, and other benefits.

b. For each pension or profit-sharing plan, including multiemployer plans, if any, furnish copies of plan documents, including amendments (and a description of any changes in these plans proposed, agreed upon, or under consideration); actuarial reports, if applicable; trust instruments and trust balance sheets, if any, summary plan descriptions; the latest application for determination to the IRS; any IRS determination letter; and the latest Annual Report on Form 5500, 5500-C, or 5500-K. For each pension plan that is a "multiemployer plan," furnish a statement of the employer's "withdrawal liability" under ERISA §4211.

8.11 Details on any terminated pension plans and unfounded pension liabilities.

8.12 a. List of all employees of the Company who received compensation exceeding $50,000 in the last fiscal year, giving name, date of birth, date hired, position, and compensation for the last fiscal year, and, to the extent available, similar information for all other employees and for retired employees who are receiving or will be entitled to receive any payment not described previously in item 8.9.

b. Description of all written or oral employment or consulting agreements (other than union contracts) to which the Company or any subsidiary is a party or bound, and copies of any written agreements (except for employment contracts that can be terminated at will by the

Company or a subsidiary without cost or liability).

c. Brief description of all confidentiality, noncompetition, or similar agreements between the Company or any subsidiary and any of their present or former officers, employees, directors, consultants, or agents. If any are in writing, furnish copies.

d. Brief description of all consulting and management agreements, arrangements, or understandings to which the Company or any subsidiary is a party. If any are in writing, furnish copies.

e. Description of all deferred compensation programs affecting officers, directors, or employees of the Company. State the amount accrued and/or paid during the most recent fiscal year under such programs and amounts of accruals thereunder through a recent date.

8.13 A description of the manner in which the Company fulfills its workers compensation and unemployment compensation insurance obligations in each state (i.e., insured or self-insured, etc.).

8.14 Documents representing or relating to workers' compensation or disability policies, and any material claims with respect thereto.

8.15 Copy of employee handbook or any similar document.

9. Properties, Leases, and Insurance

9.1 a. List of real estate owned, leased, or used by the Company, stating whether owned or leased (whether as lessor or lessee), and brief description of property, structures, zoning, estoppel letters, reversions or remainders, lease provisions (including assignment and renewal), use, and location. Furnish copies of mortgages, deeds, surveys, maps, rights of way, easements, leases, and other contracts.

b. Copies of title insurance policies or lawyers' abstract reports covering real estate.

c. Copies of zoning variances and local permits.

9.2 a. List of fixed assets, machinery, and equipment (whether owned, leased, or used by the Company), giving for each material asset or group of assets cost, depreciation reserve, method of depreciation, insured value, estimated remaining useful life, condition suitability for use, and (if available) appraised value.

b. List of automobiles, trucks, and other registered equipment owned, leased, or used by the Company, giving a brief description of equipment and lease provisions (if any), year made, state of registration, registration number, cost, estimated remaining useful life, and insured value.

c. List of premises at which any assets of the Company are currently located or located from time to time, including (without limitation) terminals, plants, storage facilities, sales offices, and warehouses, and any related written agreements.

d. Brief description of portfolio investments of the Company (except in subsidiaries), including cost basis and current value.

e. All currently effective purchase contracts, leases, or other arrangements concerning material items of equipment used by the Company.

f. All appraisals of any material property of the Company.

9.3 Copies of all material leases of or security agreements for personal property of the Company, including conditional sales contracts, equipment leases, financing agreements, and factoring agreements.

9.4 List of all insurance policies relating to the business assets or properties of the Company (including directors' and officers' liability insurance), giving insurance company, policy number, term of coverage, property or risk covered, appraised value of covered property (where appropriate), extent of coverage, annual premium, and amount of premiums that are prepaid or are unpaid from prior years. Furnish copies of all policies.

9.5 A description of all insurance claims over $____ in amount currently pending.

9.6 Schedule of Company's loss experience per insurance year.

10. Intellectual Property (Patents, Trademarks, Copyrights, Trade Secrets)

10.1 Schedule of patent registrations and applications, identifying each patent by title, registration (application) number, date of registration (application), and country.

10.2 Schedule of trademark and service mark registrations and applications, identifying each mark, including date of registration (application), registration (application) number, status, and country or state where registered. Where registration has not been sought, identify the mark and its date of first use anywhere in the United States.

10.3 Schedule of copyright registrations and applications, identifying each copyright by title, registration number, and date of registration.

10.4 Manual or other written document detailing the procedures for maintaining the secrecy of trade secrets.

10.5 Licensing agreements, merchandising agreements (naming Company as licensee or licensor), or assignments relating to patents, technology, trade secrets, trademarks (service marks), and copyrights.

10.6 Communications to or from third parties relating to the validity or infringement of any of Company's intellectual property.

10.7 Studies or reports relating to the validity or value of Company's intellectual property and the licensing or merchandising thereof.

10.8 Agreements pursuant to which any intellectual property has been sold or transferred by or to the Company and evidence of recording thereof.

11. Contracts and Arrangements

11.1 All standard sales and purchase orders and other forms of agreements used by the Company.

11.2 All warranty agreements, including all forms of product warranties, of the Company currently in force for completed and executory material contracts.

11.3 List and description of all significant oral contracts and commitments.

11.4 All currently effective guarantees given by the Company concerning the payment or performance of obligations of third parties.

11.5 All sales agency and distribution agreements.

11.6 A list of all contracts and commitments under which a default has occurred or is claimed to have occurred, setting forth the following:
a. Nature of default
b. Name of party in default
c. Monetary amount claimed
d. Current status of contract or claim

11.7 A list of all contracts subject to renegotiation (indicating those contracts currently being renegotiated).

11.8 All agreements to which the Company or any subsidiary is (or was within the past 5 years) a party and in which any officer, director, employee, or shareholder of any such companies has (or had) an interest (whether directly or indirectly).

11.9 Copies of all agreements not to be performed within 3 months or involving over $—whether or not entered into in the ordinary course of business, except (a) agreements for the sale of merchandise or standard sales order forms entered into in the ordinary course of business and (b) agreements referred to elsewhere herein.

11.10 Copies of all contracts with advertising or public relations agencies.

11.11 A list of all significant suppliers (representing in excess of 5% of annual purchases) of the Company, with an indication of the amount paid to each such supplier during the Company's most recent fiscal year and the estimated number of alternative suppliers.

11.12 All executory contracts, as amended to date, with each of the above referenced suppliers, and all related purchase orders.

11.13 Brief description of contractual or customary credit terms available from suppliers and manufacturers, and copies of all agreements with suppliers and manufacturers.

11.14 List and brief description of all agreements and arrangements with distributors, dealers, sales agents, or representatives. Furnish copies of all such written agreements.

11.15 List and brief description of all agreements and arrangements whereby the Company or any subsidiary acts as a distributor. Furnish copies of all such written agreements.

11.16 List and brief description of all agreements relating to the supply of [principal raw material] and other raw materials and supplies. Furnish copies of all such written agreements.

11.17 Copies of all forms of product warranties or guarantees, if any, given by the Company or any of its subsidiaries.

11.18 Copies of all agreements and other documentation relating to the acquisition of any business constituting a part of the Company, or sale or proposed sale of any business owned by it in the past 5 years.

11.19 Copies of joint venture or partnership agreements to which the Company or any subsidiary is a party.

11.20 Copies of all franchise or distribution agreements between the Company or any of its subsidiaries and any third party concerning the manufacture, sale, or distribution of the Company's or its subsidiaries' products or services. If any such agreements are oral, summarize the terms thereof.

11.21 Copies of all agreements, not previously listed, with suppliers, independent agents, salespersons, or others involving the payment of commissions or other consideration or discounts with respect to the manufacture, sale, or distribution of the Company's or its subsidiaries products or services. If any such agreements are oral, summarize the terms.

11.22 Brief description of any contracts restricting the ability of the Company or any subsidiary to complete in any line of business with any person or entity, or committing the Company or any subsidiary to continue in any line of business.

11.23 Advise if there are any facts or circumstances that may give rise to the cancelation or termination of, or claim for damages or loss under, any of the agreements, arrangements, or understandings referred to herein.

11.24 List and description of all leases, licenses, and other agreements involving the payment of more than $____ in the aggregate, currently in the process of negotiation.

11.25 Copies of agreements granting to the Company any right of first refusal to acquire any business or assets or pursuant to which the Company has granted any such rights.

11.26 List of material terms of all contracts and arrangements for (a) trucking and other delivery and (b) warehouse space.

11.27 Copies of all material research and development agreements.

11.28 All technology license agreements to which the Company is a party as licensor or licensee:

11.29 Documents relating to the Company's internal determinations as to whether it can, or should, fulfill a particular contract.

12. Litigation

12.1 List and brief description of each threatened or pending claim, lawsuit, arbitration, or investigation involving a claim for belief of $_____ or more against the Company, any subsidiary, or any of their respective officers or directors.

12.2 List and brief description of any pending or threatened (a) claim or litigation involving alleged violations of laws or regulations for the health or safety of employees or others, (b) governmental or administrative proceeding, (c) equal employment opportunity claim or litigation, (d) antitrust claim or litigation, (e) claim or litigation seeking injunctive relief, or (f) other material claim or litigation to which, in either case, the Company or any subsidiary is a party.

12.3 A copy of all complaints, answers, and other material pleadings concerning any litigation not fully covered by insurance.

12.4 All letters from counsel to the Company to accountants relating to litigation or contingent liabilities involving the Company.

12.5 All correspondence relating to actual or alleged infringement by the Company of intellectual property rights of other.

12.6 List and brief description of all outstanding judgments, decrees, or orders to which the Company or any subsidiary is subject.

12.7 Copy of most recent response to auditors' request for information about litigation and/or contingent liabilities of the Company.

12.8 All material governmental permits, licenses, etc., of the Company.

12.9 Documents pertaining to any litigation involving an officer or director of the Company concerning bankruptcy, crimes, securities law, or business practice (past five years).

12.10 Description of any investigations of the Company, pending or threatened, by any federal, state, local, or foreign authorities.

12.11 All correspondence with, reports of or to, fillings with, or other material information about any other regulatory bodies that regulate a material portion of the Company's business.

13. Environmental and Related Matters

13.1 All internal Company reports concerning environmental matters relating to current or former Company properties.

13.2 Copies of any applications, statements, or reports filed or given by the Company or any of its subsidiaries with or to the Federal Environmental Protection Agency, any state department of environmental regulations, or any similar state or local regulatory body, authority, or agency.

13.3 All notices, complaints, suits, or similar documents sent to, received by, or served upon the Company or any of its subsidiaries by the Federal Environmental Protection Agency, any state department of environmental regulation, or any similar state or local regulatory body, authority, or agency.

13.4 All Company or outside reports concerning compliance with waste disposal regulations (hazardous or otherwise).

13.5 Copies of all permits, shipping authorizations, manifests, and waste stream authorizations.

13.6 Description of any processes of facilities currently or previously operated by the Company or any subsidiary (or by others on property currently owned by the Company or any subsidiary) that generate or are suspected of generating any hazardous material.

13.7 All pollution control capital expenditure reports (including budget requests) for the past 5 years.

13.8 All annual reports, manifests, or other documents relating to hazardous waste or pesticide management over the past 5 years.

13.9 All documents relating to equipment using PCBs, spills of PCBs, or worker exposure to PCBs, and all documents relating to the existence or removal of asbestos.

13.10 Any public records reflecting existing or recent environmental problems.

14. Receivables

14.1 Brief description of customary sales credit terms.

14.2 Brief description of aging of accounts receivable, giving collections since aging date and brief statement of reasons for receivables in excess of $____ past due.

14.3 Names of customers owing in excess of $____.

14.4 Description of basis for establishing bad debt reserve.

15. Inventories

15.1 List of products and services currently sold by the Company and its subsidiaries, together with applicable prices and discounts.

15.2 Brief description of inventory pricing procedure.

15.3   List of major sources of supply for material, dollar purchases from each in the last fiscal year, and brief description of available alternative supply sources for material items.

16. Acquisition Documents and Sales of Securities

16.1   All other agreements pursuant to which the Company has acquired securities or has issued (or may be obligated to issue) securities.

16.2   All private placement memoranda, prospectuses, or other documentation relating to the offering or acquisition of securities by the Company.

16.3   All reports to, documents filed with, and correspondence with the Securities and Exchange Commission for the past five years.

16.4   All reports to, documents filed with, and correspondence with any state securities commission.

16.5   All agreements and other documentation concerning any sale of material assets (including any agreements in principle) to which the Company is a party.

16.6   Copies of all agreements and plans entered into by the Company or any of its subsidiaries relating to the acquisition of, or merger with, a business or an interest in any business, whether by acquisition of shares, acquisition of assets, or otherwise.

17. Transactions with Officers, etc.

17.1   List and statement of amounts and other essential terms of any indebtedness or other obligations of or to the Company or its subsidiaries to or from any officer, director, stockholder, or employee.

17.2   List and description of assets or properties used by the Company in which any officer, director, stockholder, or employee has any interest.

17.3   List of all material transactions between the Company and its officers, directors stockholders, or employees not disclosed under items 17.1 or 17.2.

18. Customers

List of major customers, showing percentage of sales to each customer accounting for more than 5% of sales for any product line or service within the past fiscal year.

19. Filings and Reports

To the extent not covered elsewhere, copies of all filings and reports in the last 3 years made with or submitted to any governmental agencies.

20. Licenses

20.1   List of all federal, state, local, and foreign governmental permits, licenses, and approvals (excluding those listed elsewhere herein) either held or required to be held by the Company or its subsidiaries for the conduct of their businesses.

20.2   All correspondence, reports, and notices relating to laws and regulations administered by any federal, state, local, or foreign governmental agency for the past 5 years.

21. Consents

21.1   List and brief description of any of the Company contracts, leases, security agreements, licenses, authorizations, etc., that may require the consent of any third party (including any governmental agency or instrumentality) to the proposed transactions.

21.2   Indicate any other notification required to be given to or consents required from any third party (including any governmental agency or instrumentality) in connection with the proposed transactions.

22. Miscellaneous

22.1   List of all bank accounts and safe deposit boxes, naming authorized signatories.

22.2   List of memberships in trade associations.

22.3   List of all requirements and obligations imposed on the Company by the proposed or effective rules and regulations of any governmental agency.

Source: This legal due diligence checklist was provided by Jeffrey M. Weiner, a partner in the Los Angeles office of Piper Rodnick LLP, a national law firm. They have kindly granted permission to use their copyrighted material (and in turn acknowledge their debt to lawyers who have preceded them in due diligence checklist drafting, particularly a committee of the American Bar Association's Business Law Section).

QUESTIONS

A2.1 Is due diligence restricted to legal matters?

A2.2 What is the fundamental nature of legal due diligence?

A2.3 What are important procedural aspects of due diligence?

A2.4 What are three legal documents that are critical in the due diligence process?

A2.5 What are the issues involved in formulating a letter of intent?

A2.6 Is the scope of due diligence limited to information provided by the parties to the transaction?

CHAPTER 3
ACCOUNTING FOR M&As

The analysis of M&As and restructuring must begin with the accounting numbers. This is a necessary first step if only to get behind the numbers to see the validity and value of any investment plans. The rules follow the recommendations of professional accounting organizations. Securities and Exchange Commission (SEC) approval is required in connection with financial statements issued to investors.

The Financial Accounting Standards Board (FASB) of the Financial Accounting Foundation is a cooperative private research organization financed by individuals and corporations. FASB issues statements on accounting policy that have become recognized as accounting standards. They are policies that the SEC usually adopts.

In January 2001, FASB voted unanimously to eliminate formally the pooling-of-interests method of accounting for mergers and acquisitions, thereby mandating the purchase method of accounting for all mergers and acquisitions. At that time, FASB set a deadline of late June 2001 after which all mergers must use the purchase method. Two years prior, FASB already had voted to eliminate the pooling of interests as a method of accounting for business combinations. This vote caused substantial controversy as discussed subsequently in this chapter.

HISTORICAL BACKGROUND

On August 2, 1970, the 18-member Accounting Principles Board (APB) of the American Institute of Certified Public Accountants issued Opinion 16, which deals with guidelines for corporate mergers, and Opinion 17, which deals with goodwill arising from mergers. The recommendations, which became effective on October 31, 1970, modify and elaborate on previous pronouncements on the pooling of interests and purchase methods of accounting for business combinations. These 1970 rules prevailed for the rest of the twentieth century, although discussion memoranda and related statements were issued periodically.

In a business combination, one company usually will be the acquiring firm, with the other firm described as the acquired or target firm. Although a business combination can be structured in many ways, one board of directors and one CEO usually end up with control over the combined operations. When the operations of two companies are placed under common control through any form of business combination, financial reporting rules require that financial statements (at the date of combining) present numbers from the combining of the two accounting systems.

Accounting Principles Board Opinion 16, "Accounting for Business Combinations," prescribed two accounting methods for recording the acquisition of a target company by an acquiring company:

1. The pooling-of-interests method of accounting, which requires that the original "historical cost" basis of the assets and liabilities of the target company be carried forward.
2. The purchase method of accounting, which requires that a new "historical cost" basis be established for the assets and liabilities of the target company.

A second major difference between the two methods pertains to the reporting of earnings:

1. In the pooling-of-interests method of accounting, earnings of the combined entities are combined for any reporting periods. If in a subsequent financial report, data for a prior year are included, they would reflect the accounting for a pooling-of-interests combination.
2. In the purchase method of accounting, earnings of the acquired company are reported by the acquirer only from the date of acquisition forward.

In April 1997, FASB described a project to reconsider the 1970 APB Opinions 16 and 17. FASB stated that more than 50 issues related to business combinations and tangible assets had been considered by its Emerging Issues Task Force. A *Wall Street Journal* article at about the same time commented that business firms wanted to have the rules changed to make it easier to use pooling accounting but that FASB was considering proposals to restrict more narrowly the use of pooling. Investment bankers and corporate chieftains lobbied hard to derail any plans to narrow the use of pooling. A representative argument was made by Merrill Lynch in the June 1999 report entitled *Valuing the New Economy: How New Accounting Standards Will Inhibit Economically Sound Mergers and Hinder the Efficiency and Innovation of U.S. Business*. In the report, Merrill Lynch states:

> The (purchase) accounting method itself would prove an obstacle to a merger that both parties are eager to consummate. As a result, the wave of consolidations that has enhanced productivity, encouraged innovation, and stimulated dynamism in the U.S. economy may notably decline.

Another representative argument was provided by Dennis Powell, vice president and corporate controller of Cisco Systems. According to Mr. Powell:

> The use of pooling accounting has contributed significantly to technology development and job creation in this country and has resulted in the strongest capital markets in the world. Elimination of pooling as proposed by the Financial Accounting Standards Board could stifle technology development and erode the competitive advantage the U.S. currently enjoys.

According to Robert Willens, a Lehman Brothers managing director who specializes in accounting and tax issues:

> I must spend 50% of my time fielding questions from clients who wish to avoid goodwill and who want to know how to qualify for pooling treatment. Managements care about this issue intensely. They'll try to avoid goodwill at all cost.

In light of the major controversy surrounding the rule changes, this chapter provides background for evaluating the pooling versus purchase methods of merger accounting and provides insight regarding the impact of the rule changes on future mergers.

POOLING OF INTERESTS

Twelve criteria were prescribed to determine whether the conditions for the pooling-of-interest treatment are satisfied. If all of them are met, the combination is, in theory, a merger between companies of comparable size, and the pooling-of-interests method must be employed. In practice, comparable size was not a compelling requirement. Accounting practice with SEC approval permitted some flexibility. The tests are as follows.

1. None of the combining companies has been a subsidiary or division of another corporation within 2 years.
2. The combining companies have no significant equity investments (greater than 10%) in one another.
3. The combination is effected in a single transaction or is completed in accordance with a specific plan within 1 year after the plan is initiated.
4. Payment is effected by one corporation offering and issuing only common stock in exchange for substantially all (meaning 90% or more) of the voting common stock interest of another company.
5. None of the combining companies changes the equity interest of its voting common stock for 2 years before the plan to combine is initiated or between the dates the combination is initiated and consummated.
6. None of the combining companies reacquires shares of its voting stock except for purposes other than business combinations.
7. The ratio of the interest of an individual common stockholder to those of other common stockholders in the combination is unchanged before and after the combination.
8. Voting rights in the combined company are exercisable by the stockholders.
9. The combined corporation does not agree to issue additional shares of stock or other consideration on any contingency at a later date to former stockholders of the combining companies.
10. The combined corporation does not agree to retire or reacquire any of the common stock issued to effect the combination.
11. The combined corporation does not enter into other financial arrangements—such as a guaranty of loans secured by stock issued in the combination, which in effect negates the exchange of equity securities—for the benefit of former stockholders of a combining company.
12. The combined corporation does not intend to dispose of a significant part of the assets of the combining companies—other than disposals in the normal course of business or to eliminate duplicate facilities or excess capacity—within 2 years after the combination.

DEFECTS IN POOLING

Previous to the issuance of APB Opinion 16, a commonly cited stimulus to pooling was the opportunity to dispose of assets acquired at depreciated book values, selling them at their current values and recording subsequent profits on sales of assets. Opinion 16 dealt with this practice with the requirement that sales of major portions of assets not be contemplated for at least 2 years after the merger has taken place. For example, suppose firm A buys firm T, exchanging stock worth $1 billion for assets worth $1 billion but carried at $250 million. After the merger, A could, before the change in rules, sell the acquired assets and report the difference between book value and the purchase price, or $750 million, as earned income. Thus, pooling could arguably be used to manipulate accounting measures of net income.

Two of these rules relate directly to stock repurchases and were the subject of considerable discussion during the 1990s. One of the rules is a limitation on the amount of stock a company can repurchase during the 2 years prior to a pooling merger. Generally, shares that are not expected to be issued under executive compensation programs or stock mergers are considered "tainted" shares. At most, 10% of the shares to be issued in the pooling merger can be tainted. The second rule is that the firm after merger cannot retire any of the stock issued in the pooling merger until 3 months after the completion of the merger.

Under these rules, if a company begins to repurchase its shares, one can view the repurchase as an indirect purchase transaction, which could then be subject to taxes and goodwill creation. In a widely publicized case, the SEC in 1995 ruled that First Bank System Incorporated would have to suspend its share repurchase program for 2 years subsequent to the acquisition of First Interstate Bancorp. This decision led to First Bank dropping the plans for merger (see Case 3.1 at the end of the chapter). In 1996, the SEC issued a staff bulletin advising companies to wait 6 months after the close of a pooling merger before repurchasing shares, as opposed to the commonly recognized 3-month window. This ruling caused some firms to halt their share repurchase programs temporarily. In 1998, the SEC took action against two firms, U.S. Office Products and Corporate Express, both of which had announced large stock buybacks within 6 months of closing pooling mergers. For example, the SEC forced U.S. Office Products to change the accounting for 22 all-stock deals from pooling to purchase. In two 1998 high-profile mergers, those of Chrysler–Daimler Benz and Waste Management–USA Waste, Chrysler and Waste Management had to reissue 28 million and 20 million shares, respectively, in order to offset prior stock repurchases in order to qualify for pooling accounting.

FASB ELIMINATION OF POOLING

FASB created a task force in February 1997 that consisted of individuals from various constituencies. The task force began by reviewing the academic literature on pooling versus purchase. The task force then wrote various reports that it circulated to constituents for comments. The task force also made field trips to numerous companies. After substantial internal and external debate, FASB formally decided in January 2001 to move solely to the purchase method of accounting for merger. In the end, FASB decided that the pooling method (1) provides investors with less relevant information, (2) ignores values exchanged in a business combination, and (3) yields artificial accounting differences rather than real economic differences from the purchase method. FASB essentially is arguing that because the future cash flows are the same whether the pooling or the purchase method is used, it makes sense to use the method that best captures the economic cost of the transaction.

In June 2001, FASB released its Statement of Financial Accounting Standards No. 141, "Business Combinations." This statement indicated that based on a unanimous vote by the directors of FASB, all business combinations announced beginning July 1, 2001, are to be accounted for using one method—the purchase method. In summary, FASB stated that:

> Virtually all business combinations are acquisitions, and thus all business combinations should be accounted for in the same way that other asset acquisitions are accounted for—based on the values exchanged.

In Statement No. 141, FASB provided the background for arriving at its conclusion. The process began in August 1996 when FASB added the project on accounting for business combinations to its agenda. The purpose was to reconsider prior rules, specifically the requirements of APB Opinion 16, "Business Combinations," and APB Opinion 17, "Intangible Assets." FASB offered several reasons for taking on the project. A primary reason was the increase in merger activity, which brought considerable attention to the fact that two economically similar transactions could be accounted for by two different accounting methods that generate substantially different accounting financial statement results. A second reason was that many companies believed that if they could not qualify for pooling, they were at a disadvantage when competing with acquirers who did qualify for pooling. The final consideration was the issue of recent globalization and the increased need for comparable financial reporting across countries. For example, most other countries do not allow pooling-of-interest mergers.

PURCHASE ACCOUNTING

In purchase accounting, one company is identified as the buyer and records the company being acquired at the price it actually paid. All identifiable assets acquired and liabilities assumed in a business combination should be assigned a portion of the cost of the acquired company, normally equal to their fair market values at the date of acquisition. In taxable transactions, the new, stepped-up basis is depreciable for tax accounting purposes. The excess of the cost of the acquired company over the sum of the accounts assigned to identifiable assets acquired less liabilities assumed should be recorded as goodwill. This goodwill account was required under the old rules to be written off, for financial reporting, over some reasonable period but not longer than 40 years.

PURCHASE ACCOUNTING ADJUSTMENT ENTRIES

We illustrate the purchase method by use of the pro forma accounting statements contained in the proxy to shareholders in connection with the AOL–Time Warner (TWX) transaction. The merger was announced on January 10, 2000. The main purchase accounting adjustment entries were:

Debit (in billions)	
TWX shareholders' book equity	$ 10.0
Other miscellaneous adjustments, net	(30.9)
Goodwill and other intangibles	174.0
Total pro forma debit adjustments	$153.1

Credit (in billions)	
AOL common stock at par issued to pay for TWX	$ 0.1
Addition to AOL paid-in capital	153.0
Total pro forma credit adjustments	$153.1

Before the merger announcement, AOL had 2.6 billion shares outstanding trading at $72.88 per share. TWX had 1.4 billion shares outstanding trading at $64.75. AOL exchanged 1.5 of its shares for each TWX share, paying a total of 2.1 billion shares. Multiplying this amount times the AOL share price of $72.88 gives a market value paid of $153.1 billion, which needs to be allocated.

TABLE 3.1 Asset Structure Changes in AOL and TWX (in $ millions)

| | PREMERGER | | | | PRO FORMA POSTMERGER | |
| | AOL | | TWX | | Combined | |
	Amount	%	Amount	%	Amount	%
Total assets	$10,789	100.0	$50,213	100.0	$235,388	100.0
Less: Goodwill + other intangibles	432	4.0	24,507	48.8	199,325	84.7
Tangible assets	$10,357	96.0	$25,706	51.2	$36,063	15.3

The basic entries for purchase accounting were as follows. Eliminate TWX book equity by a debit of $10 billion. Next, miscellaneous adjustments of a negative debit of $30.9 billion were made. The total increase in goodwill was $174 billion. Therefore, the sum of the pro forma debit adjustments equaled the market value of AOL stock ($153.1 billion) paid for TWX. We next consider the credits. The AOL common stock at par issued to pay for the purchase of TWX was a credit of $0.1 billion (rounded). This was deducted from the amount paid for TWX to obtain $153.0 billion, which became the addition to AOL paid-in capital.

The effects on the asset structures of AOL and TWX are shown in Table 3.1. Only 4% of AOL's assets were goodwill. For TWX, the ratio of tangible assets to intangibles was slightly more than 1. AOL paid $153.1 billion for the Time Warner book equity of $10.3 billion, so the goodwill account of the combined firm was greatly increased. As a consequence, the ratio of tangible assets to total assets in the combined company dropped to about 15%.

The effects on leverage are summarized in Table 3.2. Before the transaction, AOL had only about $68 in liabilities for every $100 of shareholders' equity. For TWX, liabilities were $389 to $100. With the huge increase in the equity of the combined firm as a consequence of the $109.32 per share ($72.88 × 1.5) paid for TWX in relation to the penny-per-share par value of the AOL shares used in payment, the paid-in capital account of the combined company increased by a huge amount.

On January 30, 2003, AOL Time Warner announced its financial results for its fiscal year ended December 31, 2002. From the financial statements, we are able to extend the results in Tables 3.1 and 3.2. Table 3.3a. and Table 3.3b show that the total assets declined from $235 billion to $209 billion by December 31, 2001. By December 31, 2002, one year later, total assets had further declined to $115 billion. Tangible assets remained virtually the same. However, goodwill and other intangibles had declined by $91.2 billion, recognizing their impairment as

TABLE 3.2 Leverage Changes in the AOL and TWX Merger (in $ millions)

| | PREMERGER | | | | PRO FORMA POSTMERGER | |
| | AOL | | TWX | | Combined | |
	Amount	%	Amount	%	Amount	%
Total liabilities	$ 4,370	40.5	$39,949	79.6	$ 79,095	33.6
Shareholders' equity	6,419	59.5	10,264	20.4	156,293	66.4
Total claims	$10,789	100.0	$50,213	100.0	$235,388	100.0
Liabilities/equity		68.1		389.2		50.6

TABLE 3.3a Asset Structure Changes in AOL and TWX (in $ millions)

| | PREMERGER | | | | POSTMERGER | | | | | |
| | AOL | | TWX | | Pro Forma (6/23/00) | | Actual (12/31/01) | | (12/31/02) | |
	Amount	%	Amount	%	Amount	%	Amount	%	Amount	%
Total assets	$10,789	100.0	$50,213	100.0	$235,388	100.0	$208,504	100.0	$115,450	100.0
Goodwill + other Intangibles	432	4.0	24,507	48.8	199,325	84.7	172,417	82.7	81,192	70.3
Tangible assets	$10,357	96.0	$25,706	51.2	$ 36,063	15.3	$ 36,087	17.3	$ 34,258	29.7

TABLE 3.3b Leverage Changes in the AOL and TWX Merger (in $ millions)

| | PREMERGER | | | | POSTMERGER | | | | | |
| | AOL | | TWX | | Pro Forma (6/23/00) | | Actual (12/31/01) | | (12/31/02) | |
	Amount	%	Amount	%	Amount	%	Amount	%	Amount	%
Total liabilities	$ 4,370	40.5	$39,949	79.6	$ 79,095	33.6	$ 56,477	27.1	$ 62,633	54.3
Shareholders' equity	6,419	59.5	10,264	20.4	156,293	66.4	152,027	72.9	52,817	45.7
Total claims	$10,789	100.0	$50,213	100.0	$235,388	100.0	$208,504	100.0	$115,450	100.0
Liabilities/equity	68.1		389.2		50.6		37.1		118.6	

required by FASB Statement No. 142. AOL Time Warner adopted FASB Statement No. 142 effective January 1, 2002. AOL Time Warner announced accounting changes including goodwill impairment of $54.2 billion during the first quarter of fiscal 2002 in addition to the fourth-quarter impairment of $44.7 billion, a total for the year of $98.9 billion. Other adjustments of a positive $7.7 billion reconciled to the $91.2 billion net change. These accounting entries are explained in the following section.

AMORTIZATION AND IMPAIRMENT RULES

Contemporaneous with the elimination of pooling, FASB also eliminated goodwill amortization in purchase mergers in Statement of Financial Accounting Standards No. 142, "Goodwill and Other Intangible Assets," as part of the same comprehensive project of accounting for mergers. Since 1970, purchase acquirers have followed the guidelines of Opinion 17 of the Accounting Principles Board, which required goodwill amortization. Under Opinion 17, the presumption was that goodwill and other intangible assets were depreciating assets with finite lives, and thus should be amortized over their expected useful life in computing net income. The ceiling set for such amortization was 40 years.

In contrast to Opinion 17, Statement No. 142 explicitly recognized that goodwill and some intangible assets might have indefinite lives and do not require amortization. Statement No. 142 notes that the useful life of an asset is the period of time for which that asset is expected to contribute cash flows to the reporting firm. For example, if a firm acquires a consumer trademark that is expected to contribute to future cash flows over the indefinite future, that trademark should not be amortized, notwithstanding that it might indeed have a remaining legal life of only 10 years. This logic is consistent with the switch from the pooling to purchase method of accounting, as the latter explicitly recognizes the value of the purchased assets.

In addition to recognizing the potentially infinite life of some intangible assets and of goodwill, a second major change set by Statement No. 142 is the use of impairment tests. Because certain assets and goodwill no longer will be amortized, the method of adjusting the book value of such assets is to conduct impairment tests based on the market values of these assets annually.

We distinguish between the types of amortization to clarify the impairment rules. Intangible assets can be separated from goodwill (1) if they arise from contractual or other legal rights; or (2) if they can be separated from the acquired entity and sold, transferred, licensed, rented, or exchanged. Some intangible assets are subject to amortization; others are not. Intangible assets not subject to amortization are those for which a definite or measurable life cannot be assigned, such as registered trademarks. They are subject to impairment write-offs. Intangible assets subject to amortization are those to which a useful life can be assigned, such as computer software or patents.

An example based on the types of amortization is described in Appendix C of FASB Statement No. 141. Alpha acquired Beta on June 30, 20XX. The purchase price was $9.4 billion. Tangible assets acquired net of debt were $2.3 billion. The $7.1 billion was allocated as follows: to goodwill, $2.2 billion; to intangible assets not subject to amortization, $1.4 billion (registered trademarks); to research and development in process, $1.0 billion. The remaining $2.5 billion of acquired intangible assets were to be amortized (patents and computer software) over their weighted average useful life. The R&D in process can be written of immediately by including it in general and administrative expenses.

In the AOL Time Warner balance sheets (Table 3.4), the three remaining categories are shown. Between December 31, 2001, and December 31, 2002, intangible assets subject to amortization

TABLE 3.4 AOL Time Warner Incorporated Consolidated Balance Sheet (unaudited)

	December 31, 2002	December 31, 2001
	(in millions, except per-share amounts)	
ASSETS		
Current assets		
Cash and equivalents	$ 1,730	$ 719
Receivables, less allowances of $2.379 and $1.889 billion	5,667	6,054
Inventories	1,896	1,791
Prepaid expenses and other current assets	1,862	1,687
Total current assets	11,155	10,251
Noncurrent inventories and film costs	3,351	3,490
Investments, including available-for-sale securities	5,138	6,886
Property, plant, and equipment	12,150	12,669
Intangible assets subject to amortization	7,061	7,289
Intangible assets not subject to amortization	37,145	37,708
Goodwill	36,986	127,420
Other assets	2,464	2,791
Total assets	$115,450	$208,504
LIABILITIES AND SHAREHOLDERS' EQUITY		
Current liabilities		
Accounts payable	$ 2,459	$ 2,266
Participations payable	1,689	1,253
Royalties and programming costs payable	1,495	1,515
Deferred revenue	1,209	1,451
Debt due within 1 year	155	48
Other current liabilities	6,388	6,443
Total current liabilities	13,395	12,976
Long-term debt	27,354	22,792
Deferred income taxes	10,823	11,231
Deferred revenue	990	1,048
Other liabilities	5,023	4,839
Minority interests	5,048	3,591
Shareholders' equity		
Series LMCN-V common stock, $0.01 par value, 171.2 million shares outstanding in each period	2	2
AOL Time Warner common stock, $0.01 par value, 4.305 and 4.258 billion shares outstanding	43	42
Paid-in capital	155,134	155,172
Accumulated other comprehensive income (loss), net	(428)	49
Retained earnings	(101,934)	(3,238)
Total shareholders' equity	52,817	152,027
Total liabilities and shareholders' equity	$115,450	$208,504

Source: AOL Time Warner 4Q 2002 Financial Tables.

decreased from $7.3 to $7.1 billion. Intangible assets not subject to amortization decreased from $37.7 billion to $37.1 billion. Goodwill decreased from $127.4 billion to $37.0 billion—a substantial impairment.

In the income statement (Table 3.5), the amortization of goodwill and other intangible assets is shown as a deduction before operating income. The impairment of goodwill and other intangibles is also a deduction before operating income. The reported net income before income taxes, discontinued operations, and accounting changes was –$44.5 billion. Adding the cumulative effect of the accounting changes, the reported net income of AOL Time Warner was a $98.7 billion loss for 2002.

In the statement of cash flows (Table 3.6), the accounting changes plus impairment charges of $99.7 billion are added back to net income; the other items representing depreciation and amortization plus changes in operating assets and liabilities result in reported cash provided by operations of $7.0 billion.

This examination of AOL Time Warner illustrates the application of the new accounting rules set forth in FASB Statement Nos. 141 and 142. It also illustrates the relationships among income statements, balance sheets, and cash flow statements. The AOL-TWX example also demonstrates that the use of purchase accounting has some strange results. The higher the ratio is of the price paid to the book equity acquired, the greater the degree is to which a high book-leverage company will become a lower book-leverage company.

The rules for measuring impairment set forth in FASB Statement No. 142 are equivalent to standard valuation methods. The emphasis is on comparable transactions and applications of discounted cash flow methodologies.

EMPIRICAL STUDIES OF POOLING VERSUS PURCHASE

Despite the evidence of a preference by many CEOs for the use of the pooling method (see considerable evidence of this preference provided by Walter [1999]), empirical research has established that the stock prices of acquiring firms are not penalized when the purchase method of accounting is used. In fact, most previous studies, including our own, found that stock price reactions to the use of purchase accounting are more positive than for pooling accounting. However, generally, the reaction in favor of purchase accounting is not statistically significant. An exception is recent work by Andrade (2001), who found that the stock price reaction is slightly more positive for pooling mergers than for purchase mergers.

Many commentators have suggested that corporate managers are willing to purchase the pooling method, namely by paying relative higher acquisition premiums to target shareholders in order to do so. In support of this argument, Lys and Vincent (1995) provided a comprehensive clinical study of AT&T's $7.5 billion acquisition of NCR in 1991, concluding that AT&T paid as much $500 million in order to satisfy pooling accounting requirements. The merger did not start off on friendly terms as NCR rejected AT&T's initial offer of $85 per share, a bid that offered an 80% premium to NCR's stock price.

As indicated earlier, one of the 12 pooling requirements is that neither merging party can change the equity interests of the voting common stock within 2 years of a pooling merger. Because AT&T had publicly indicated its plan to undertake a pooling merger, NCR employed this pooling requirement as an antitakeover mechanism by setting up a qualified ESOP with 8% control of NCR's voting stock and contemporaneously paid a $1 special dividend. Both

TABLE 3.5 AOL Time Warner Incorporated Consolidated Statement of Operations (unaudited)

	2002 Historical	2001 Pro Forma	2001 Historical
	YEAR ENDED DECEMBER 31,		
	(in millions, except per-share amounts)		
Revenues:			
Subscriptions	$18,959	$16,809	$15,657
Advertising and commerce	7,680	8,461	8,260
Content and other	14,426	13,232	13,307
Total revenues	41,065	38,502	37,224
Costs of revenues	(24,419)	(21,918)	(20,591)
Selling, general and administrative	(9,916)	(9,808)	(9,079)
Amortization of goodwill and other intangible assets	(732)	(705)	(7,186)
Impairment of goodwill and other intangible assets	(45,538)	—	—
Merger and restructuring costs	(335)	(250)	(250)
Operating income (loss)	(39,875)	5,821	118
Interest expense, net	(1,783)	(1,784)	(1,353)
Other expense, net	(2,498)	(2,955)	(3,567)
Minority interest income (expense)	(278)	(159)	46
Income (loss) before income taxes, discontinued operations and cumulative effect of accounting change	(44,434)	923	(4,756)
Income tax benefit (provision)	(140)	(455)	(139)
Income (loss) before discontinued operations and cumulative effect of accounting change	(44,574)	468	(4,895)
Discontinued operations, net of tax	113	4	(39)
Income (loss) before cumulative effect of accounting change	(44,461)	472	(4,934)
Cumulative effect of accounting change	(54,235)	—	—
Net income (loss)	$(98,696)	$ 472	$(4,934)
Basic income (loss) per common share before discontinued operations and cumulative effect of accounting change	$ (10.01)	$ 0.11	$ (1.11)
Discontinued operations	0.03	—	—
Cumulative effect of accounting change	(12.17)	—	—
Basic net income (loss) per common share	$ (22.15)	$ 0.11	$ (1.11)
Diluted income (loss) per common share before discontinued operations and cumulative effect of accounting change	$(10.01)	$0.10	$ (1.11)
Discontinued operations	0.03	—	—
Cumulative effect of accounting change	(12.17)	—	—
Diluted net income (loss) per common share	$ (22.15)	$ 0.10	$ (1.11)
Diluted cash earnings (loss) per common share before discontinued operations and cumulative effect of accounting change	$ 0.35	$ 0.29	$ 0.56
Average basic common shares	4,454.9	4,429.1	4,429.1
Average diluted common shares	4,521.8	4,584.4	4,584.4

Source: AOL Time Warner 4Q 2002 Financial Tables.

TABLE 3.6 AOL Time Warner Incorporated Consolidated Statement of Cash Flows Year Ended December 31, (unaudited)

	2002 Historical	2001 Pro Forma	2001 Historical
		(in millions)	
OPERATIONS			
Net income (loss)	$(98,696)	$ 472	$(4,934)
Adjustments for noncash and nonoperating items:			
Cumulative effect of accounting change	54,235	—	—
Impairment of goodwill and intangible assets	45,538	—	—
Depreciation and amortization	3,069	2,523	8,936
Amortization of film costs	2,536	2,380	2,380
Loss on write-down of investments	2,227	2,537	2,537
Gain on sale of investments	(136)	(34)	(34)
Equity in losses of investee companies after distributions	399	305	975
Changes in operating assets and liabilities, net of acquisitions:			
Receivables	200	(489)	(469)
Inventories	(2,489)	(2,801)	(2,801)
Accounts payable and other liabilities	70	(1,968)	(1,973)
Other balance sheet changes	(176)	604	68
Adjustments relating to discontinued operations	265	553	596
Cash provided by operations	7,032	4,082	5,281
INVESTING ACTIVITIES			
Acquisition of Time Warner Inc. cash and equivalents	—	690	690
Investments in available-for-sale securities	—	(527)	(527)
Other investments and acquisitions, net of cash acquired	(7,779)	(3,040)	(3,650)
Capital expenditures and product development costs from continuing operations	(3,023)	(3,299)	(3,213)
Capital expenditures from discontinued operations	(206)	(408)	(408)
Investment proceeds from available-for-sale securities	134	30	30
Other investment proceeds	414	1,890	1,821
Cash used by investing activities	(10,460)	(4,664)	(5,257)
FINANCING ACTIVITIES			
Borrowings	23,535	11,148	10,692
Debt repayments	(18,984)	(10,101)	(9,900)
Redemption of redeemable preferred securities of subsidiaries	(255)	(963)	(575)
Proceeds from exercise of stock option and dividend reimbursement plans	297	926	926
Current period repurchases of common stock	(102)	(3,031)	(3,031)
Dividends paid and partnership distributions from discontinued operations, net	(11)	(59)	(59)
Dividends paid from continuing operations	—	(4)	(4)
Principal payments on capital leases	(61)	—	—
Other	20	24	36
Cash provided (used) by financing activities	4,439	(2,060)	(1,915)
INCREASE (DECREASE) IN CASH AND EQUIVALENTS	1,011	(2,642)	(1,891)
CASH AND EQUIVALENTS AT BEGINNING OF PERIOD	719	2,833	2,610
CASH AND EQUIVALENTS AT END OF PERIOD	$ 1,730	$191	$719
FREE CASH FLOW FROM CONTINUING OPERATIONS	$ 3,570	$222	$ 1,507

Source: AOL Time Warner 4Q 2002 Financial Tables.

events violated the change in equity restriction, thereby eliminating the possibility for pooling in the merger. Other barriers to pooling existed, including NCR's stock buybacks during the prior 2 years. Per discussions with the SEC, AT&T would be able to offset these various barriers; however, doing so would require cooperation on the part of NCR, which would be unlikely given NCR's rejection of the merger offer. In order to convince NCR to cooperate, AT&T raised the price of the offer to $110, a premium in excess of 230% of NCR's price preceding AT&T's initial offer for NCR.

Lys and Vincent calculated the costs of pooling. In order to offset the taint associated with the prior NCR stock repurchases, it was necessary for AT&T to have NCR reissue 6.3 million shares prior to the merger completion. AT&T accomplished this by arranging the sale of the 6.3 million shares to a large money manager at a 5% discount—a discount that amounted to roughly $50 million. Lys and Vincent pointed out that the indirect costs of obtaining pooling were even higher. For example, according to the *Wall Street Journal*, AT&T was prepared to pay an additional $7 per share in order to treat the merger as a pooling of interests. With 65 million NCR shares outstanding, this was roughly $450 million in total. In conversations that Lys and Vincent had with an AT&T representative, the willingness to pay the higher premium in order to obtain pooling was confirmed. AT&T's stated motivation for paying to obtain pooling was due to the notion that the stock market mechanically values companies based on reported earnings per share (EPS). To the extent that EPS under pooling would be $2.42 versus $1.97 for an all-stock purchase merger, AT&T management believed that using the purchase method of merger accounting would have a large detrimental impact on the value of AT&T stock. In effect, AT&T management believed that investors value companies based on accounting-based EPS rather than on cash flows.

Large sample studies by Aboody, Kasznik, and Williams (2000) and Ayers, Lefanowicz, and Robinson (2002) also provide evidence that managers appear to pay up in order to obtain pooling of interest, especially when there would be a large negative impact on EPS if the purchase method of accounting for merger were chosen.

Summary

Historically, there were two methods of accounting for mergers: the pooling of interests and the purchase method. Whereas the pooling of interests simply carried the historical cost basis of the target assets and liabilities forward, the purchase method set a new cost basis that was consistent with the purchase price. Many corporate executives preferred the pooling-of-interests method due to the lower drag on earnings per share, despite the lack of cash flow implications. In 2001, over strong objections, FASB eliminated the pooling method, requiring the purchase method for all transactions. In addition, FASB eliminated the amortization of goodwill and certain intangibles, instead requiring that these assets undergo periodic appraisal tests to determine if their values should be written down. FASB has taken the approach that merger accounting and subsequent asset values should be consistent with market valuations. These new regulations are consistent with the view that the most important consideration should be whether a merger makes sense from an economic standpoint and creates value.

FASB has taken the approach that when mergers occur, the acquiring firm should account for the merger in the same way it would when making any other asset purchases, that is, based on the market value of the assets purchased; hence, the demise of the pooling-of-interests method of merger accounting. Second, when long-lived assets such as intangibles and goodwill become impaired, the book values of those assets should reflect such impairments based on market tests, namely how much those assets would be worth in the marketplace.

Although the FASB regulations were met with considerable opposition from some investment bankers and corporate executives, these regulations received support from numerous constituents, including investment bankers and corporate executives. The new FASB regulations are consistent with the view that the most important consideration should be whether a proposed merger makes sense from an economic standpoint and creates value. The purpose of combining companies is to achieve improvements that the individual companies could not have achieved independently. If the merger was soundly conceived and effectively implemented, then the combined cash flows should be greater than the simple sum of the cash flows of the constituent firms had the merger not occurred. In this longer-term perspective, even if an acquisition results in initial dilution in earnings per share for the stockholders, the merger still might make business and economic sense. The initial dilution can be regarded as an investment that will have a payoff in future years in the form of magnified cash flows for the combined company. Thus, the elimination of pooling is not likely to have a significantly negative impact on mergers that are soundly conceived and implemented effectively.

Questions

3.1 Why is reported net income lower under purchase accounting than under pooling-of-interests accounting?

3.2 Are actual cash flows different in financial accounting for pooling versus purchase if the 40-year write-off period for non-tax-deductible amortization of goodwill is used?

3.3 Why are cash flows higher under purchase accounting when the amortization of goodwill is deductible for tax purposes under the conditions of the 1993 law changes?

3.4 Summarize the studies on the effects of pooling versus purchase on stock prices.

3.5 Rework Table 3.3 when the terms of the merger are 0.9 share of the acquirer (A) for one share of the target (T).

3.6 Why did FASB eliminate pooling of interests as a method of accounting for mergers?

Case 3.1   WELLS FARGO ACQUISITION OF FIRST INTERSTATE BANCORPORATION

On October 17, 1995, Wells Fargo Bank (WF) made an unsolicited bid for the First Interstate Bancorporation (FIB), both operating mainly in California. First Interstate Bancorporation rejected the bid as inadequate. It solicited a second bidder (white knight), the First Bank System (FBS) of Minneapolis, Minnesota, with branches in that area. The wealth effects of the WF initial bid are shown in Part A.

Part A. Walls Fargo Initial Bid	WF	FIB	FBS
1. October 3, 1995—Preannouncement (1) prices	$207	$105	$51
2. Number of shares (millions)	47	76	127
3. Total market value (billions) (1 × 2)	$9.7	$8.0	$6.5
4a. October 17, 1995—Initial WF offer	0.625 FIB		
4b. Dollar value to FIB (1 × 4a)		$129.375/sh	
5. Postannouncement price	$229	$140	
5a. Price change per share (5 – 1)	$22	$35	
5b. Shareholder wealth effect (billions) (2 × 5a)	$1.03	$2.66	
5c. New total market value (billions) (2 × 5)	$10.76	$10.64	

The results of the white knight bid by FBS on November 6, 1995, are shown in Part B.

Part B. FBS Bid	WF	FIB	FBS
6. November 6, 1995—FBS merger agreement			2.6/FIB
6a. Postannouncement (2) price	$211	$127	$51
6b. Implied dollar value of FIB		FBS offer: 2.6($51) = $132.60/sh	
6c. WF counteroffer		WF offer: 0.625($211) = $131.88/sh	

Further bids by WF are shown in Part C.

Part C. WF Further Bids	WF	FIB	FBS
7a. November 6, 1995—WF raises offer to 0.65		0.65($211) = $137.15/sh	
7b. November 13, 1995—WF raises offer to 0.667		0.667($211) = $140.74/sh	

On January 19, 1996, the SEC ruled that FBS could not use pooling accounting because its share repurchase program violated one of the conditions for the use of pooling. The price effects are shown in Part D.

Part D. SEC Rules That FBS Cannot Use Pooling	WF	FIB	FBS
8. January 19, 1996—SEC ruling			
9. From January 17, 1996, to January 23, 1996— Stock price movements	$215 to $229	$136.75 to $149.25	$48.25 to $50.50

The wealth effects of WF's winning bid on January 24, 1996, are shown in Part E.

Part E. WF Winning Bid		WF	FIB	FBS
10.	January 24, 1996—WF and FIB agree to merge			$51.75
10a.	Value of FIB		0.667($229) = $152.74/sh	
11.	January 24, 1996—Prices less initial prices	$229 − $207 = $22/sh	$149.25 − $105 = $44.25/sh	$51.75 − $51 = $0.75/sh
12.	Deflate by 6% rise in NASDAQ Bank stock index (October 3, 1995, to January 24, 1996)	$229/1.06 = $216/sh	$149.25/1.06 = $140.80/sh	$51.75/1.06 = $48.82/sh
12a.	Price change based on deflated prices	$216 − $207 = $9/sh	$140.80 − $105 = $35.80/sh	$48.82 − $51 = −2.18/sh
13a.	Wealth effect, nominal (millions)	47($22) = $1,034	76($44.25) = $3,363	127($0.75) = $95.25
13b.	Wealth effect, deflated (millions)	47($9) = $423	76($35.80) = $2,720.8	127(−$2.18) = −$276.86

Wells Fargo estimated that they could save at least $1 billion dollars a year by combining overlapping offices. This was not possible for FBS, because it was located in a different geographic area. One attraction of FIB was that its average interest cost on deposits in the first half of 1995 was 2.49% annualized, the lowest of 42 big regional banks. Wells Fargo's cost of funds was 3.14%, and that of FBS, 3.71%. For FBS, the inexpensive deposits of FIB were especially attractive because FBS was "an aggressive lender hungry for funds" (Petruno, 1995).

The offers by WF and FBS were exchanges of stock. In the attempt to make its stock exchange offer more attractive, FBS had embarked on an open market share repurchase program of 73 million shares. However, FBS was planning to treat the acquisition as a pooling-of-interests transaction for financial accounting purposes. It was announced on January 20, 1996, that the SEC ruled that to qualify for pooling accounting, FBS could not buy back its own stock for 2 years (Hansell, 1996).

On January 25, 1996, it was announced that WF and FIB had agreed to merge under the terms described in the chronology. Wells Fargo planned to use purchase accounting that involved a write-off of goodwill, reducing reported net income by $400 million per year. First Interstate Bancorporation had contracted to pay FBS a $200 million fee if their agreement was not consummated. In the early stages of counterbidding, WF sued to have this agreement declared illegal. After its merger agreement with FIB, WF paid the $200 million to FBS in two installments.

For additional background, see the *Wall Street Journal*, the *New York Times*, and the *Los Angeles Times* from October 3, 1995, to March 5, 1996, and the following journal articles: Davis, Michael L, "The Purchase vs. Pooling Controversy: How the Stock Market Responds to Goodwill," *Journal of Applied Corporate Finance* 9, Spring 1996, pp. 50–59; and Houston, Joel F., and Michael D. Ryngaert, "The Value Added by Bank Acquisitions: Lessons from Wells Fargo's Acquisition of First Interstate," *Journal of Applied Corporate Finance* 9, 1996, pp. 74–82.

QUESTIONS

C3.1.1 Why were greater savings available to WF than to FBS?

C3.1.2 Compare the two methods of accounting that FBS and WF planned to use.

C3.1.3 What were the wealth effects of the transaction, and what are their implications?

REFERENCES

Hansell, Saul, "S.E.C. Deals a Blow to First Bank's Bid for First Interstate," *New York Times*, 20 January 1996, pp. 17, 31.

Petruno, Tom, "Suitors Covet First Interstate's Low-Cost Deposits," *Los Angeles Times*, 10 November 1995, pp. D1, D12.

‌

Case 3.2 TIME WARNER (TWX) PURCHASE OF THE TURNER BROADCASTING SYSTEM (TBS) IN 1996

The major entries for purchase accounting were:

Debit ($ billion)	
TBS shareholders' equity	$0.5
Identifiable intangible assets	0.7
Goodwill	6.4
Total	$7.6

Credit ($ billion)	
TWX common stock at par issued to pay for TBS	$1.2
Addition to Time Warner Paid-in Capital	6.4
Total	$7.6

Turner had book equity of about $0.5 billion with liabilities of $4 billion. Time Warner paid $7.6 billion for Turner. The basic entries for purchase accounting were:

- Eliminate TBS book equity by a debit.
- The difference between book equity acquired and purchase price is first assigned to tangible assets and the rest to intangibles and goodwill. In the debits shown in the entries above, goodwill was $6.4 billion.

- On the credit side, first is the $1.2 billion par value of TWX common stock issued to pay for TBS.
- The difference between the $7.6 billion purchase price and $1.2 billion is added to TWX paid-in capital (a part of shareholders' book equity).

The effects on book leverage of the Time Warner purchase of Turner Broadcasting were:

	Time Warner Historical		New Time Warner Pro Forma	
	Amount	Percent	Amount	Percent
Long-term debt	$ 9,928	72.1	$12,690	56.3
Shareholders' equity	3,843	27.9	9,867	43.7
Total	$13,771	100.0	$22,557	100.0
Debt-to-equity relation		258.3		128.6

QUESTIONS

C3.2.1 Why did the new Time Warner partial pro forma balance sheet show such a large increase in shareholders' equity?

C3.2.2 Comment on the change in the ratio of long-term debt to equity for the new Time Warner partial balance sheet.

Case 3.3 THE AOL ACQUISITION OF TIME WARNER (TWX)

QUESTIONS

C3.3.1 Merger announcement date: January 7, 2000

Stand-Alone Firms				
	Share Price		*Number of Shares (in billions)*	*Market Cap Premerger (in billions)*
AOL	72.88	×	2.6	= $189.5
TWX	64.75	×	1.4	= 90.7
Total				$280.2

Combined AOL-TWX

New AOL shares for TWX stockholders = Exchange Ratio × TWX shares
$$= 1.5 \times 1.4 \text{ billion}$$
$$= 2.1 \text{ billion}$$

	Share Price		*Number of Shares (in billions)*	*Market Cap Postmerger (in billions)*
"TWX"	$72.88	×	2.1	= $153.1
AOL	$72.88	×	2.6	= 189.5
Total			4.7	$342.6

What was the premium paid by AOL for TWX?

C3.3.2 The value of AOL on September 10, 2002, was $13.36, and the number of shares outstanding was 4.45 billion. What was the decline in value of AOL from its immediate postmerger market capitalization?

C3.3.3 Explain the pro forma accounting adjustments (except for the miscellaneous items) as an example of purchase accounting.

Debit (in billions)	
TWX shareholders' book equity	$ 10.0
Other miscellaneous adjustments, net	(30.9)
Goodwill and other intangibles	174.0
Total pro forma debit adjustments	$153.1

Credit (in billions)	
AOL common stock at par issued to pay for TWX	$ 0.1
Addition to AOL paid-in capital	153.0
Total pro forma credit adjustments	$153.1

C3.3.4 Calculate the percent of goodwill and other intangibles to total assets for AOL and for TWX premerger and for the pro forma combined company postmerger. Discuss.

Asset Structure Changes in AOL and TWX (in millions)

	PREMERGER				PRO FORMA POSTMERGER	
	AOL		*TWX*		*Combined*	
	Amount	*Percent*	*Amount*	*Percent*	*Amount*	*Percent*
Total assets	$10,789	100.0	$50,213	100.0	$235,388	100.0
Goodwill + other intangibles	432	____	24,507	____	199,325	____
Tangible assets						

C3.3.5 Calculate the percent of total liabilities and of shareholders' equity to total assets for AOL and for TWX premerger and for the pro forma combined company postmerger. Discuss.

Leverage Changes in the AOL and TWX Merger

	PREMERGER				PRO FORMA POSTMERGER	
	AOL		*TWX*		*Combined*	
	Amount	*Percent*	*Amount*	*Percent*	*Amount*	*Percent*
Total liabilities	$ 4,370		$39,949		$ 79,095	
Shareholders' equity	6,419	____	10,264	____	156,293	____
Total claims	$10,789	100.0	$50,213	100.0	$235,388	100.0
Liabilities/equity						

Case 3.4   THE PFIZER ACQUISITION OF PHARMACIA

This case is based on the joint proxy statement/ prospectus sent to shareholders of the two companies shortly after its issue date of October 21, 2002. The merger was approved by shareholders of both companies in early December of 2002. Based on the exchange ratio, the price paid by Pfizer for Pharmacia was calculated in the prospectus to be $55.4 billion. The purpose of this exercise is to illustrate that the purchase accounting procedures following the elimination of pooling accounting by FASB in June 2001 are unchanged. The accounting entry adjustments pro forma are given in the table.

Accounting Entry Adjustments Pro Forma

Debit (in billions)	
Pharmacia shareholders' book equity	$12.2
Property, plant, and equipment	0.2
Identifiable intangible assets	27.0
Goodwill	18.5
Other miscellaneous adjustments, net	(18.7)
Total pro forma debit adjustments	$39.2

Credit (in billions)	
Pfizer common stock at par issued to pay for Pharmacia	$ 0.4
Addition to Pfizer paid-in capital	55.0
Other adjustments	(16.2)
Total pro forma credit adjustments	$39.2

QUESTION

C3.4.1   Explain the procedures illustrated by the accounting entries shown.

References

Aboody, David, Ron Kasznik, and Michael Williams, "Purchase versus Pooling in Stock-for-Stock Acqusitions: Why Do Firms Care?" *Journal of Accounting and Economics* 29, June 2000.

Andrade, Gregor. "Do Appearances Matter? The Impact of EPS Accretion and Dilution on Stock Prices," Harvard Business School working paper, 2001.

Ayers, Benjamin, Craig Lefanowicz, and John Robinson, "Do Firms Purchase the Pooling Method?" *Review of Accounting Studies* 7, March 2002, pp. 5–32.

Financial Accounting Standards Board, Financial Accounting Series, No. 141, "Business Combinations," June 2001.

Financial Accounting Standards Board, Financial Accounting Series, No. 142, "Goodwill and Other Intangible Assets," June 2001.

Financial Accounting Standards Board, Financial Accounting Series, No. 172-A, April 22, 1997, Status Report No. 287, p. 3.

Financial Accounting Standards Board, Financial Accounting Series, No. 200-B, August 1999.

Lys, Thomas, and Linda Vincent, "An Analysis of Value Destruction in AT&T's Acquisition of NCR," *Journal of Financial Economics* 39, 1995, pp. 353–378.

Merrill Lynch, "Valuing the New Economy: How New Accounting Standards Will Inhibit Economically Sound Mergers and Hinder the Efficiency and Innovation of U.S. Business," June 1999.

Walter, John R., "Pooling or Purchase: A Merger Mystery," Federal Reserve Bank of Richmond *Economic Quarterly* 85/1, 1999, pp. 27–46.

CHAPTER 4
DEAL STRUCTURING

The structuring of M&As often raises complex financing and tax issues in addition to the accounting issues discussed in Chapter 3. The issues are not only complex, but the regulations and rules can change dramatically, sometimes without much advance notice. Understanding these rules and regulations, and how to structure transactions within these rules in order to maximize the value of the deal, often requires the outside assistance of accounting, financial, and legal advisers.

TAXATION AND ACQUISITIONS

A considerable amount of literature has been produced on the relation between taxes and takeovers. This section provides a synthesis and assesses the results of the studies to date. The following topics are covered: taxable versus nontaxable or tax-deferred acquisitions; the Tax Reform Act of 1986; and the question of whether tax gains cause acquisitions, which include considerations of early empirical tax effects, later empirical studies of tax effects, and taxes and leveraged buyouts (LBOs).

TAXABLE VERSUS NONTAXABLE ACQUISITIONS

The basic tax rule with respect to acquisitions is simple. If the merger or tender offer involves exchanging the stock of one company for the stock of the other, it is a nontaxable transaction. If cash or debt is used, it is a taxable transaction. In practice, however, many complications exist.

The Internal Revenue Code makes a technical distinction among three types of "acquisitive tax-free reorganizations," which are defined in Section 368 of the code. They are referred to as type A, B, and C reorganizations. Type A reorganizations are statutory mergers or consolidations. In a merger, target firm stockholders exchange their target stock for shares in the acquiring firm; in a consolidation, the target and the acquiring firm shareholders turn in their shares and receive stock in the newly created company.

Type B reorganizations are similarly stock-for-stock exchanges. Following a type B reorganization, the target can be liquidated into the acquiring firm or maintained as an independent operating entity.

Type C reorganizations are stock-for-asset transactions with the requirement that at least 80% of the fair market value of the target's property be acquired. Typically, the target firm "sells" its assets to the acquiring firm in exchange for voting stock in the acquiring firm; the target then dissolves, distributing the acquiring firm's stock to its shareholders in return for its own (now-canceled) stock.

In practice, a three-party acquisition technique is employed. The parent creates a shell subsidiary. The shell issues stock, all of which is bought by the parent with cash or its own stock. The target as the third party is bought with the cash or stock of the parent held by the subsidiary. The advantage of creating the subsidiary as an intermediary is that the parent acquires control of the target without incurring responsibilities for the known and possibly unknown liabilities of the target. The transaction still qualifies as a type A reorganization. The target firm might remain in existence if the stock of the parent is used as the method of payment by the shell subsidiary. Because the parent-acquirer shareholders are not directly involved, they are denied voting and appraisal rights in the transaction. In a reverse three-party merger, the subsidiary is merged into the target. The parent stock held by the subsidiary is distributed to the target's shareholders in exchange for their target stock. This is equivalent to a type B reorganization.

The "tax-free" reorganization represents only tax deferral for the target firm shareholders. If the target shareholder subsequently sells the acquiring firm's stock received in the transaction, a capital gains tax becomes payable. The basis for the capital gains tax is the original basis of the target stock held by the target shareholder. Consider, for example, an individual who purchased 1,000 shares of Texaco in July 2000 at $53 per share. A few months later, in October 2000, Texaco agreed to be acquired by Chevron in a stock exchange merger of 0.77 Chevron shares for each Texaco share. When the merger closed in October 2001, the 1,000 Texaco shares held by the shareholder were converted into 770 Chevron Texaco shares. Assume that the shareholder sold the Chevron Texaco shares at a price of $88 in July 2002. The shareholder would realize a capital gain of $14.76 per each of the original 1,000 Texaco shares purchased. Or the shareholder realizes a capital gain of $19.17 ($88-$53/.77) per each of the 770 Chevron Texaco shares. In either case, the total capital gain is $14,760. Note, however, that if the shareholder dies without selling the shares in Chevron Texaco, the estate tax laws establish the tax basis at the time of death. That is, if the shareholder dies in 2040 and Chevron Texaco stock is trading at $800, then $800 would be the new basis with respect to taxes.

Table 4.1 summarizes the main implications of nontaxable versus taxable acquisitions. In a nontaxable (tax-deferred) reorganization, the acquiring firm generally can use the net operating loss (NOL) carryover and unused tax credits of the acquired firm. However, even though the value of the shares paid may be greater than the net book values of the assets acquired, no write-up or step-up of the depreciable values of the assets acquired can be made. For the shareholders of the target firm, taxes are deferred until the common shares received in the transaction are sold. Thus, the shareholders can defer the taxes.

TABLE 4.1 Nontaxable vs. Taxable M&As

	Acquiring Firm	*Target Firm*
A. Nontaxable reorganizations	NOL carryover Tax-credit carryover Carryover asset basis	Deferred gains for shareholders
B. Taxable acquisitions	Stepped-up asset basis Loss of NOLs and tax credits	Immediate gain recognition by target shareholders Depreciation recapture of income

In taxable acquisitions, the acquiring firm can assign the excess of purchase price over the book value of equity acquired to depreciable assets, as described under purchase accounting. The acquiring firm, however, is unable to carry over the NOLs and tax credits. The shareholders of the target firm in a taxable transaction must recognize the gain over their tax basis in the shares. In addition, if the target firm has used accelerated depreciation, a portion of any gain that is attributable to excess depreciation deductions will be recaptured to be taxed as ordinary income rather than capital gains, the amount of recapture depending on the nature of the property involved.

THE TAX REFORM ACT OF 1986

The Tax Reform Act of 1986 (TRA 1986) made many fundamental amendments to the prevailing 1954 code. Corporate income tax rates have been modified only slightly since TRA 1986. In 1993, the Omnibus Budget Reconciliation Act of 1993 increased the federal corporate income tax rate from 34% to 35%. TRA 1986 also had a number of impacts on merger and acquisition transactions: (1) It severely restricted the use of net operating loss carryovers; (2) the General Utilities doctrine was repealed; and (3) greenmail payments could not be deducted.

The Tax Reform Act of 1986 provides that if a greater than 50% ownership change occurs in a loss corporation within a 3-year period, an annual limit on the use of NOLs will be imposed. The amount of a NOL that may be used to offset earnings is limited to the value of the loss corporation at the date of ownership change multiplied by the long-term, tax-exempt bond. For example, assume that a loss corporation is worth $100 million immediately before an ownership change, the tax-exempt bond rate is 4%, and the corporation has a $70 million loss carryforward. Then $4 million ($100 million × 4%) of the NOL can be used annually to offset the acquiring firm's taxable income.

In addition, a loss corporation may not utilize NOL carryovers unless it substantially continues the same business for 2 years after the change in ownership. If this requirement is not met, all of the losses generally are disallowed (Curtis, 1987).

Under the General Utilities case decided in the 1930s and incorporated in later code sections, corporations did not recognize gains when they sold assets in connection with a "complete liquidation" in the sense of legal technicalities. This required adoption of a plan of liquidation and sale with distribution of assets within a 12-month period. Distribution of assets in kind in liquidation also was not subject to tax. The provisions were repealed by TRA 1986. Most of the exemptions from the new rules are for relatively small and closely held corporations or provide for limited transitional periods (Wood, 1987).

TRA 1986 also limited the extent to which amounts paid as greenmail to corporate raiders could be deducted for tax purposes. This change and others move in the direction of being less favorable to merger and acquisition activity.

STOCK VERSUS ASSET PURCHASES

Tax considerations are part of the general topic, structuring the deal. One issue is the effects on buyers and sellers of a stock versus asset purchase in a taxable transaction. We use a specific example to illustrate the factors involved.[1] The selling company in this example is a regular

---

[1]This presentation is based on the booklet "Tax Considerations—Mergers & Acquisitions," by Deloitte & Touche LLP, March 24, 1999.

C corporation (public or private), not a limited liability corporation (LLC) or S corporation. The other data assumed are as follows:

Purchase price, stock	$100
Purchase price, assets	$100
Liabilities of seller	$ 25
Basis in assets (seller)	$ 60
Basis in shares (of seller)	$ 50
Corporate tax rate (federal and state)	40%
Individual tax rate (federal and state)	25%
Applicable discount factor	10%

Based on these data, the net proceeds to the shareholders of the selling firm are compared in Table 4.2.

The explanation for the acquisition of stock alternative is straightforward. The assumed purchase price is $100. The tax basis for the shareholders of the seller is $50. Their capital gain is $50. With an assumed federal plus state capital gains tax of 25%, the tax to the shareholders would be $12.50. The net proceeds to the seller shareholders would be $87.50.

If the transaction is an acquisition of assets, the seller corporation must be included in the analysis. If the buyer pays $100 for the assets, its assumption of the liabilities of the corporation is added to the purchase price. We postulate that the seller corporation has a tax basis of $60 in the assets sold. Therefore, its gain is $65. With a combined state and federal corporate income tax rate of 40%, the tax on the sale of the assets would be $26. The amount available to the target shareholders would be $74. Their tax basis was postulated to be $50, so the capital gain would be $24. With the same individual tax rate of 25% (as previously named), the net proceeds to the seller shareholders would be $68.

The buyer might prefer the acquisition of assets to avoid unknown liabilities of the seller for which the buyer would otherwise be liable. In this asset acquisition with purchase account-

TABLE 4.2 Comparison of Net Proceeds

	(1) *Acquisition of Stock*	*(2)* *Acquisition of Assets*
Assumed purchase price	$ 100	$100
Assumed liabilities	—	25
Total purchase price	$ 100	$125
Basis in assets		(60)
Gain		65
Corporate tax rate		40%
Tax on sale of assets		26
Net to shareholders (SH)	$ 100	74
Basis in shares	(50)	(50)
Capital gain	50	24
Tax rate on individual	25%	25%
Tax on individual on sale	12.50	6
Net proceeds to seller SH	**$87.50**	**$ 68**

ing, the buyer is able to step up the tax basis of the assets acquired. The excess of the purchase price of $125 over the seller's original basis in assets can be allocated to tangible assets, intangible assets, and goodwill. The purchaser will have a step-up for book and tax purposes. In the present example, it is assumed that all of the differential is assigned to tangible assets, depreciable for tax purposes over 15 years.

The tax benefits of the step-up may influence the purchase price in a competitive corporate control market. The present value of the tax benefit can be added to the purchase price. The calculation of the present value of the tax benefit is as follows.

Purchase price	$ 100
Assumed liabilities	25
Total purchase price	$ 125
Basis in assets	(60)
Step-up of tangible asset	65
Life of tax benefit	15
Annual tax benefit	4.333
Expected future tax rate	40%
Actual cash savings	1.733
Discount rate	10%
PV of tax benefit	**$13.18**

The step-up of tangible assets of $65 is spread over 15 years, resulting in an annual tax benefit of $4.333. Using an expected future tax rate of 40%, the annual tax benefits would be $1.733. With a 10% discount factor, the present value of an annuity of $1 for 15 years would be 7.6061 to be multiplied times $1.733. The result is a present value of tax benefits of $13.18. If competition forces the buyer to pay this additional amount, the purchase price of the assets becomes $113. The total purchase price becomes $138. The net proceeds to the selling shareholders would rise from $68 to $74.

Even if the tax benefits to the buyer of the asset step-up in the purchase of assets are passed on to the selling shareholders, they still receive less than they would have from the sale of stock. For relatively small firms, the major shareholders are likely to be the founding executives. Tax and legal advisers usually counsel the closely held small corporations to be formed as LLCs or S corporations. For LLCs and S corporations, income from the entity flows directly to the shareholders. This avoids the double taxation that otherwise occurs when the business is sold as an asset acquisition.

EMPIRICAL STUDIES OF TAXES AND MERGERS

Several research papers have examined the influence of tax factors on takeover activity. A comprehensive discussion is provided by Gilson, Scholes, and Wolfson (1988). They focused on three main types of tax gains from acquisitions under the pre-1986 tax code when tax-related mergers were more likely to occur because TRA 1986 eliminated most of the tax advantages for mergers. The three types of tax gains include: increased leverage, NOL carryforwards, and the basis increase on acquired assets. Gilson, Scholes, and Wolfson argued that in efficient markets with low transaction costs, a merger is not required to achieve these types of tax gains, because a firm can realize them through other asset and financial restructuring measures. For example, there is no clear reason why a firm cannot leverage itself without an acquisition by issuing debt and repurchasing stock.

Empirical studies of tax effects confirm the prediction of the Gilson, Scholes, and Wolfson analysis. Tax factors are of significant magnitude in less than 10% of merger transactions. Individual case studies yield similar results. Leverage generally does increase following mergers. Although NOLs were present in some mergers, they are material in only a small percentage of mergers. Finally, although the increase in the basis of assets has the effect of increasing depreciation charges, and hence cash flows, this also seems to have a minimal impact on merger activity. Moreover, even when tax effects are significant, they are not the main motivation for merger transactions (Hayn, 1989).

A possible qualification of the role of taxes is in *going-private* transactions, such as leveraged buyouts (LBOs) and management buyouts (MBOs). See research by Kaplan (1989) on the influence of tax factors on MBOs. Kaplan found that the tax benefits of an MBO can explain a substantial part of the premium paid to the target shareholders. The initial financial structures of LBOs and MBOs can be as high as 90% debt. Although the tax savings from such high debt ratios can be substantial due to interest expense deductibility, subsequent studies show that the debt is paid down rapidly. In some cases, the firm continues to remain private and the debt is paid down out of retained earnings. In other cases, the firm is often taken public again within 3 to 5 years (Muscarella and Vetsuypens, 1990). The proceeds from such public offerings usually are used to pay down debt even further. All of this is evidence that tax savings from high leverage is not the dominant influence. Again, as noted, similar tax savings can be accomplished in a financial recapitalization without the firm going private due to interest expense deductibility. A more detailed discussion will follow in Chapter 16, Going Private and Leveraged Buyouts.

FORM OF PAYMENT

The method of payment in a merger or acquisition is generally cash, stock, debt, or some combination of the three. Table 4.3 displays the form of payment for mergers and acquisitions in which the form of payment was indicated. Cash accounts for 41%, stock accounts for 32%, and cash/stock combinations account for 27% of transactions. The cash/stock combination includes mergers in which target shareholders receive cash and stock in the merger or have a choice of receiving either cash or stock. The higher percentage of cash transactions is predominant throughout the past 20 years. Note, however, though not shown in Table 4.3, stock accounts for the form of payment in 44% of large transactions (greater than $1 billion in value) during 1997–2001 versus 37% for cash.

Cash as the form of payment occurs in cash tender offers and cash mergers. At the expiration of the tender offer or at the closing of the merger, the stockholders in the target firm receive cash in substitution for their shares, after which time the shares carry no value. In a stock merger, the merging parties negotiate a fixed number of acquirer shares that will be exchanged for each target share. The fixed-exchange ratio will be made available in the press release announcing the merger per the following press release of June 12, 2002.

Univision Communications Incorporated (NYSE: UVN) and Hispanic Broadcasting Corporation (NYSE: HSP) announced they have entered into a definitive merger agreement under which Univision will acquire Hispanic Broadcasting in an all-stock

TABLE 4.3 Method of Payment (1982–2001)

Year	Number of Acquirers Disclosing Payment	Cash	Percent	Stock	Percent	Combo	Percent	Other[a]	Percent
1982	1,083	405	37	317	29	338	31	23	2
1983	1,108	350	32	387	35	362	33	9	1
1984	1,079	465	43	281	26	320	30	13	1
1985	1,468	742	51	344	23	377	26	5	0
1986	1,303	545	42	411	32	345	26	2	0
1987	724	298	41	248	34	176	24	2	0
1988	777	437	56	166	21	170	22	4	1
1989	664	307	46	199	30	153	23	5	1
1990	657	260	40	207	32	186	28	4	1
1991	645	221	34	221	34	197	31	6	1
1992	818	178	22	328	40	303	37	9	1
1993	929	236	25	369	40	321	35	3	0
1994	1,202	317	26	466	39	412	34	7	1
1995	1,540	413	27	566	37	557	36	4	0
1996	2,433	830	34	900	37	687	28	16	1
1997	3,153	1,271	40	1,021	32	854	27	7	0
1998	3,440	1,509	44	1,014	29	905	26	12	0
1999	4,048	1,844	46	1,226	30	963	24	15	0
2000	3,602	1,766	49	1,150	32	666	18	20	1
2001	3,080	1,395	45	835	27	813	26	37	1
1982–2001	33,753	13,789	41	10,656	32	9,105	27	203	1

[a]Includes debt, warrants, etc.

Source: Mergerstat Review, 2002.

transaction currently valued at approximately $3.5 billion. Under the agreement, each share of Hispanic Broadcasting common stock will be exchanged for a fixed 0.85 shares of Univision Class A common stock, representing a premium of approximately 26% to Hispanic Broadcasting's 30-day average share price.

Once the merger is completed, each share of Hispanic is converted to 0.85 shares of Univision. To the extent that Univision's stock price drops between the merger announcement and merger completion dates, the share price of Hispanic will decline accordingly. The reverse is true if the share price of Univision increases during the merger period. Thus, stock as a form of payment has considerable market risk, unlike cash payment mergers that specify a dollar amount.

STOCK MERGERS WITH COLLARS

As in the Univision Communications and Hispanic Broadcasting merger described earlier, most stock mergers have a fixed-exchange ratio set as of the merger announcement date. However, in some stock mergers—roughly 25% during the past decade—the exchange ratio is not known as of the merger announcement date, but is instead dependent on the acquirer's stock price near the close of the merger. Various versions of this type of stock merger occur, commonly referred to as collar transactions (see Fuller, 2002; Officer, 2002). We will discuss a few examples in the following text.

The most widely used collar consists of a variable exchange ratio between a maximum and a minimum. An example is the recent acquisition of TRW, Incorporated by Northrop Grumman. This merger, announced in July 2002 and completed in December 2002, called for TRW shareholders to receive $60 in Northrop stock so long as the share price of Northrop traded within a range of $112 to $138 during a 5-day period just prior to the merger close. In the event that Northrop stock traded below $112 just before the merger closed, the exchange ratio would be fixed at 0.5357. If Northrop stock traded higher than $138 just before the merger closed, the exchange ratio would be fixed at 0.4348. Note that at the price of $112 for Northrop, the value to the TRW stock is $60 ($112 × 0.5357), and at the price of $138, the value to TRW stock is also $60 ($138 × 0.4348). At Northrop prices of less than $112 (greater than $138), TRW shares would receive less (more) than $60 in Northrop stock. Thus, the payoff structure is similar to a cash deal assuming Northrop stock is trading between $112 and $138 at the merger close, and a stock deal otherwise.

An alternative collar structure would be to specify a fixed exchange ratio within a certain range, with alterations to the exchange ratio outside the range. For example, an acquirer could specify that the target would receive $20 in acquirer stock if the acquirer's stock price is $30 or less when the merger closes, $24 in acquirer stock if the acquirer's stock price is $36 or greater, and a fixed-exchange ratio of 0.667 if the acquirer's stock price is between $30 and $36 near the close of the merger. This structure is like a cash deal outside the $30 and $36 acquirer range, and a fixed-exchange ratio merger within the range.

Finally, a third type of collar would be unrestrictive. It would provide that regardless of the market price of the acquirer, the exchange ratio would be adjusted so that the target would receive a fixed dollar amount in shares. For example, the merger agreement could specify that the target would receive $25 in acquirer stock, based on the acquirer's stock price near the close of the merger, irrespective of where the acquirer stock was trading.

In subsequent chapters, we will devote considerable attention to the form of payment in mergers, and especially to the distinction between cash and stock.

EARNOUTS IN MERGERS

In a merger or acquisition, the target firm generally will have more information about its value than will the acquiring firm. Thus, the acquirer often will seek to protect itself against future negative shocks at its new subsidiary. In addition, concern arises regarding how target managers will behave subsequent to the acquisitions. That is, will their incentives remain the same as before? One potential way for the acquirer to protect itself with respect to future negative shocks at its target subsidiary is to set earnouts or contingent payouts that provide for additional payments based on future performance.

Contingent payout transactions accounted for roughly 2.5% of total deals. Most acquired companies in such transactions are small, privately held firms (Datar, Frankel, and Wolfson, 2001; Kohers and Ang, 2000). They are often in high-technology and service-oriented establishments. In addition, the acquirers and targets are mostly from different industries with little integration between acquirer and target after the merger. Valuations of small, privately held firms are difficult because the future role of the owner-manager is uncertain. Contingent payouts might be employed to provide incentives for the owner-manager to continue with the firm, and empirical evidence suggests that earnouts do succeed in helping firms retain managers beyond the earnout period.

Despite the benefits of earnouts, they are not widely used financing mechanisms for mergers, as evidenced by the fact that they occur in only 2.5% of total deals. A problem with earnouts is the difficulty in measuring the postmerger performance of the target firm. Conflicts abound in this performance measurement as the acquirer (target) attempts to allocate smaller (larger) revenues and larger (smaller) costs to the target over the measurement period. Indeed, lawsuits occur frequently with respect to performance measurement subsequent to these transactions.

Summary

Deal structuring raises complex accounting, tax, and form-of-payment issues. Aside from whether or not the merger will increase value at the operational level, corporate managers also attempt to increase the value of the transaction by structuring it so as to minimize taxes, obtain the least expensive form of financing, and so forth.

Tax considerations affect the planning and structuring of corporate combinations. Even in mergers undertaken for other motives, transactions are structured to maximize tax benefits while complying with internal revenue code regulations. In some individual instances, the tax benefits might have been substantial and might have had a major impact. Unfavorable tax rulings by the IRS also have led to the abandonment of some proposed M&As. However, tax effects are not the dominant influence in merger and acquisition decisions.

In LBOs, taxes can have a significant influence because of the higher leverage employed. However, such leverage increases also can be accomplished without LBOs. Furthermore, LBOs reduce leverage from subsequent cash flows and public offerings of equity. As will be shown in later chapters, leverage is used as a device to increase the ownership position and to motivate key managers.

Form of payment is generally a choice between cash, stock, or a combination of cash and stock. Cash is the predominant form of payment, except in large mergers in which stock accounts for the highest percentage of financing. Most stock transactions specify a fixed exchange ratio of acquirer shares for each target share. However, roughly 25% of the time, a collar stock transaction is used, whereby the exchange ratio is no longer fixed but instead is a function of the acquirer's stock price during a period immediately around the close of the merger.

In some acquisitions, the acquirer conditions the form of payment on the postmerger operating performance of the target. These earnouts account for a small proportion of mergers and generally occur with small targets. In most cases, the objective is to align incentives properly and to retain key target management.

Questions

4.1 How can personal taxation affect mergers?

4.2 Discuss the advantages and disadvantages of stock-for-stock versus cash-for-stock transactions from the viewpoint of acquired and acquiring firm shareholders.

4.3 How do a firm's growth prospects affect its potential for being involved in a tax-motivated merger?

4.4 A selling company is a regular C corporation. Given the following data, calculate the net proceeds to the shareholders of the selling firm if the buyer makes a stock acquisition versus an acquisition of assets.

Purchase price, stock	$250
Purchase price, assets	250
Liabilities of seller	100
Basis in assets (seller)	150
Basis in shares (shareholders of seller)	125
Marginal corporate tax rate (federal and state)	35%
Individual capital gains tax rate (federal and state)	24%

4.5 Why are stock mergers the preferred form of payment for large mergers with greater than $1 billion in transaction value?

Case 4.1 FORM OF PAYMENT IN THE FIRST UNION AND THE MONEY STORE MERGER

On March 4, 1998, First Union Corporation announced the signing of a definitive merger agreement with The Money Store, Incorporated to create the largest coast-to-coast provider of home equity loans in the United States. For acquisitive-minded First Union, a leading financial services firm based in Charlotte, North Carolina, this acquisition would give the company access to low-and moderate-income borrowers. First Union would retain the brand name of The Money Store, as well as its management team. For Money Store, the buyout would allow cross-selling opportunities, for example, the ability to offer a credit card to its customers. In addition, the merger offers protection to Money Store against the recent shake-out in the subprime lending industry caused by loan losses and intense competition. Because the two firms have virtually no overlap, no layoffs or disruptions would result. Postmerger, Money Store would be managed as an autonomous unit of First Union.

First Union planned to account for the merger as a purchase transaction and would pay for Money Store with its stock. According to the press release announcing the merger on March 4, 1998, First Union would purchase Money Store for $34 per share in First Union stock.[2] The number of shares that ultimately would be exchanged would be determined by

dividing $34 by the average closing price of First Union stock over the trading days prior to the merger closing. When the merger closed on June 30, 1998, First Union set the exchange ratio at 0.585, equal to $34 divided by $58.11, where the latter is the average closing price of First Union stock during June 23–29. Mergers of this sort are known as floating-ratio stock mergers because they specify the value per share rather than the number of shares to be exchanged. In contrast, the commonly used fixed exchange ratio merger, as in the Hispanic Broadcasting example discussed in the text, specifies the exchange ratio at the time of the merger announcement. By fixing the value per share rather than the exchange ratio, the merging parties lock in the transaction value rather than have it vary with the price of the acquirer stock during the merger period.

QUESTIONS

C4.1.1 Why did First Union acquire The Money Store?

C4.1.2 On the day before the March 4, 1998, merger announcement, First Union stock closed at $52.75. Had First Union set an exchange ratio based on this predeal announcement stock price, what would it have been? What is the effect of the difference in this exchange ratio and the actual exchange ratio on the wealth of The Money Store shareholders?

---

[2]PR Newswire, "First Union and The Money Store Sign Merger Agreement," March 4, 1998.

References

Curtis, M. R., "Tempered Benefits on NOLs and Capital Gains," *Mergers & Acquisitions* 21, January/February 1987, pp. 48–49.

Datar, Srikant, Richard Frankel, and Mark Wolfson, "Earnouts: The Effects of Adverse Selection and Agency Costs on Acquisition Techniques," *Journal of Law, Economics, and Organization*, 17, April 2001, pp. 201–238.

Fuller, Kathleen, "Why Some Firms Use Collar Offers in Mergers," *Financial Review*, 38, February 2003, pp. 127–150.

Gilson, R. J., M. S. Scholes, and M. A. Wolfson, "Taxation and the Dynamics of Corporate Control: The Uncertain Case for Tax-Motivated Acquisitions," Chapter 18 in J. C. Coffee, Jr., L. Lowenstein, and S. Rose-Ackerman, eds., *Knights, Raiders, and Targets*, New York: Oxford University Press, 1988, pp. 271–299.

Ginsburg, M. D., "Taxing Corporate Acquisitions," *Tax Law Review* 38, 1983, pp. 177–319.

Hayn, C., "Tax Attributes as Determinants of Shareholder Gains in Corporate Acquisitions," *Journal of Financial Economics* 23, 1989, pp. 121–153.

Jensen, M., S. Kaplan, and L. Stiglin, "The Effects of LBO's on Tax Revenues," *Tax Notes*, 6 February 1989, pp. 727–733.

Kaplan, S., "Management Buyouts: Evidence on Taxes as a Source of Value," *Journal of Finance* 44, July 1989, pp. 611–632.

Kohers, Ninon, and James Ang, "Earnouts in Mergers: Agreeing to Disagree and Agreeing to Stay," *Journal of Business*, 73, July 2000, pp. 445–476.

Muscarella, C. J., and M. R. Vestuypens, "Efficiency and Organizational Structure: A Study of Reverse LBOs," *Journal of Finance* 45, December 1990, pp. 1389–1413.

Newport, J. P., Jr., "Why the IRS Might Love Those LBOs." *Fortune*, 5 December 1988, pp. 145–152.

Officer, Micah, "Collars and Renegotiations in Mergers and Acquisitions," University of Southern California working paper, 2002.

Wood, R. W., "General Utilities Repeal: Injecting New Levies Into M&A," *Mergers & Acquisitions* 21, January/February 1987, pp. 44–47.

CHAPTER 5
STRATEGIC PROCESSES

In Chapter 1, we described the change forces that have impacted the operations of business organizations, causing a wide range of acquisitions, restructuring, and other M&A activities. Strategies seek to provide a framework for continuity and adjustments in evolving environments and competitive conditions. The goal of strategy is to guide a firm to acquire capabilities and other resources to achieve a sustainable, competitive advantage. Competitive advantage means that a firm is able to achieve value growth above the average for the economy and its product-market areas. A central theme of this book is that M&A activities must be formulated within the framework of a company's overall strategic plans and processes. In this chapter, we discuss strategic planning processes and their implications for M&A activities.

THE NATURE OF STRATEGY

Strategies define the visions, plans, policies, and cultures of an organization over a long time period. Strategic decisions involve the future of the firm. Although the horizon is the long view, strategy also takes into account shorter-term decisions and actions. Strategies cannot be static but rather must be reassessed and reformulated continuously.

Strategy is formulated in different ways. Strategic planning processes can utilize formal procedures or develop through informal communications throughout the organization. Specific strategies, plans, policies, and procedures are developed, but they are not the whole story. Strategic planning is a behavior and a way of thinking that requires diverse inputs from all segments of the organization. Everyone must be involved in the strategic planning processes.

Because strategic planning is concerned with the future of the organization, it follows that ultimate responsibility resides in the top executive (or executive group). Although many others perform important roles and have responsibilities for strategic planning processes, the chief executive (or group) must take ultimate responsibility for its success or failure. The top manager of a division must be responsible for strategic planning for that division and for conformance to the strategic plan for the organization as a whole.

SUCCESSFUL STRATEGIES

The power of the formulation of a compelling vision and its effective implementation can be summarized for some illustrative companies. Southwest Airlines began with the recognition of the need for low-cost airline travel among key cities within the state of Texas: Houston, Dallas, and San Antonio. Low fares and peak versus off-peak pricing policies were developed. Food was limited to nuts, but warm, friendly treatment of customers was emphasized. The achievement of a 10-minute turnaround at airports reduced operating expenses by 25%. The airline fleet could be used 11.5 hours per day compared with an average of 8.6 for the other airline carriers. In recent years, Southwest Airlines has been the only consistently profitable airline in the United States.

Michael Dell started a made-to-order computer business selling directly to customers. From this basic concept, the vision developed to a broad supplier system to maximize choice and quality and minimize inventory and warehouses costs. Dell has become the world's leading computer systems company. It designs, builds, and customizes products and services to satisfy a range of customer information-technology needs.

Amazon recognized the potential and convenience of purchasing books through the Internet. Its business model reduced warehousing and other inventory costs and avoided investments in retail facilities and receivables. From books, Amazon has expanded into a wide range of products such as music CDs, electronics, online auctions, movies, toys and games, kitchenware, computers, and tools and hardware.

Starbucks started in a niche market selling high-quality coffee in an attractive setting. Mergers facilitated its expansion nationally and internationally. Starbucks has extended its product offerings to include coffee drinks, premium ice creams, and premium teas.

Borders provided a super bookstore in which to shop for books, music, and films in a comfortable environment. Its strategic vision had to be adjusted to meet the competition of the online bookstores. It teamed up in a partnership with Amazon.

McDonald's aimed to become the best low-priced, quick-service restaurant. It formulated its operations to sell hamburgers and other food items prepared with a consistent quality throughout its numerous franchise operations. McDonald's basic strategy was to open new restaurants domestically and internationally. In 1995, it added 1,130 outlets. By April 2002, it had reached 30,000 restaurants all over the world serving 46 million customers per day. Its presence worldwide stimulated *The Economist* to use the geographic patterns of the national prices of the Big Mac to calculate measures of purchasing price parity.

However, McDonald's became so big that it was difficult to find places for additional high rates of growth. Even worse, in 1996 McDonald's experienced four consecutive quarters of declining same-outlet sales, losing market share to Wendy's and Burger King. A new program, "Made for You," was launched in March 1998. Precooking was replaced by custom preparation of sandwiches on order. However, this resulted in complaints about waiting time, particularly when groups arrived at lunchtime. Adjusted for splits, McDonald's stock price had reached a high of almost $50 per share; it hit a low of $12.38 during the first quarter of 2003. McDonald's was seeking to achieve savings of $100 million per year by restructuring activities.

Wal-Mart began with the concept that establishing department stores in the less-populated areas made it possible to service a broader geographic area and achieve economies of inventory control, warehousing, and logistic support. Greater variety at lower prices could be achieved. Sam Walton implemented his Three Basic Beliefs—"respect for the individual, service to our customers, and strive for excellence"—to achieve the lowest prices and the highest customer satisfaction. From regional beginnings, Wal-Mart has moved worldwide, expanding into a broader range of products to offer one-stop shopping including full-line grocery departments and warehouse clubs.

Despite its spectacular achievements, the stock price of Wal-Mart peaked at $70 in 1999, reaching a low of $41.50 in late 2001, and recovering to almost $60 by April 2002. A price war with Kmart in 2001 caused Wal-Mart to cut its average markup. However, the bankruptcy filing of Kmart resulted in a rebound of Wal-Mart's gross margin in February 2002. The compound annual return to shareholders during the 10-year period ending February 28, 2002, was 17.2%, but Value Line's index of retail store returns to shareholders over the same period was 22.52%.

Memory chips were key to Intel's early strategy. Intel developed and refined new technologies for memory production. However, by 1984, Japanese companies were producing higher-quality memory chips at lower costs and selling them at lower prices. Intel decided to shift its strategy from memory to microprocessors. It continues to innovate its manufacturing processes and research and development programs to create new microchips with a wide range of applications in products such as personal computers, servers, automation instruments, and network and communications devices.

These examples illustrate how effective strategies can be formulated and launched. However, even the best-formulated strategies can encounter serious challenges. It is difficult to maintain an uninterrupted competitive advantage over long periods of time.

THE IMPORTANCE OF THE ECONOMIC ENVIRONMENT

The business cycle is not dead. The "New Economy" did not eliminate economic downturns or volatile stock prices. A business recession officially started in early 2001. It was aggravated by the events of September 11, 2001. Stock prices and merger activity overshoot on the upside and the downside. In addition, two other economic forces must be taken into account in strategic planning.

THE INVESTMENT ACCELERATOR PRINCIPLE

Textbooks on macroeconomics illustrate the accelerator principle using numerical examples. We shall provide an intuitive explanation. Firms that buy equipment to produce products they sell need to add to capacity as their sales increase. If their sales level off, their purchases of equipment will drop. Hence, the sales decline of the equipment maker will be magnified. The experience of Cisco Systems represents a clear example.

Cisco was one of the success stories in the exploding high-technology area of the New Economy. One dollar invested in Cisco in February 1990 would have grown in value 9 years later, in March of 1999, to $384.77, a compound annual rate of increase of 93.75%—almost a doubling in stock value every year! Cisco began by selling basic Internet routers to corporate customers. A router is a specialized computer that regulates traffic on the Internet and picks the most efficient route for each packet. When information is sent through the Internet, it is broken into smaller pieces called packets. Each packet travels independently through an Internet path; when packets arrive at their destination, they are reassembled. Cisco evolved from a single-product company in routers to become a complete data networking solutions provider.

What is most relevant for our subject is that between September 21, 1993, and October 26, 1999, Cisco engaged in more than 50 acquisitions. Most of the acquisitions were of relatively small size, ranging from $40 million to $400 million. Cisco's underlying strategy was to acquire the technology and people to enable it to perform an increasing role in the data networking industry. Cisco does not become attached to only one type of technology. Cisco concentrates on meeting customer needs, with an emphasis on customer service. Its acquisition strategy is defined by four main criteria: shared vision, beating competitors to the market, innovation, and chemistry.

Chemistry or culture, as explained by Michael Volpi, Cisco's vice president of business development, is of key importance. He points out that technology in their industry lasts only 18 months, so continued innovation is a necessity. Judgments are required, so debate and disagreements occur on the road to reaching decisions. The personalities involved have to be able to achieve bonding in the crucible of aggressive policy formulation. Cisco usually finances its acquisitions with its stock, and executives must be with the company for 4 years before they can exercise their options. Voluntary attrition at Cisco, including personnel from acquired companies, had been less than 5%.

As the economy expanded in the late 1990s, Cisco invested for continuation of growth. When the economy began to level off in the year 2000, Cisco's sales collapsed. This pattern was characteristic of all durable goods manufacturers, but especially the high-technology areas, which had become accustomed to high rates of growth. Cisco's revenues for 2002 had been projected by Value Line to be at about the same level as experienced in the year 2000, with a decline in its operating margin from 30% in 2000 to 24% in 2002. The impact of leveling sales and declining margins caused Cisco's stock price to decline from $82 in early 2000 to a low of $11 during 2001. Indeed, the accelerator principle had a severe impact on the manufacturers of durable goods. New orders for durable goods, measured by averages of monthly totals, declined from a peak of $209 billion to a low of $178 billion for January 2002—a decline of almost 15%. Over the same period, manufacturing and trade sales declined by 3% (Council of Economic Advisors, 2002, pp. 20–21). Thus, the moderate decline in sales caused a drop in orders for durable goods by a factor of almost five.

SALES-TO-CAPACITY RELATIONSHIPS

Favorable prospects in an industry can lead to overly optimistic expansion programs and too many competitors. The outlook might appear favorable for each individual competitor, but total investment might be excessive in relation to aggregate sales. The telecom industry illustrates the overinvestment problem. AT&T had a system of hardwired long-distance communications, which was its main business after its forced divestiture from the local operating telephone companies in 1984. MCI was able to underprice AT&T on high-density lines with microwave systems, starting the service between Chicago and St. Louis. Fiber-optic systems rapidly expanded the capacity for long-distance communications, both voice and data.

The Telecommunications Act of 1996 facilitated new entries of many forms. Capacity expanded and competitors multiplied, especially during the exuberant economic conditions of the late 1990s. The new technologies reduced costs of installation and service, and competition drove down prices. An article in *Barron's* discussed the dismal outlook for the telecom sector. It stated, "There is huge overcapacity in the system and no one can afford to take on more debt in order to cull the overcapacity" (February 25, 2002, p. 27). Mergers to eliminate overcapacity would have required more debt and substantial business risk, which even the relatively stronger firms were unwilling to attempt. The outlook was for continued price reductions with continued overcapacity.

A similar situation was described in *The Economist* in an article titled "Semiconductor Manufacturers—The Great Chip Glut." Often with government help, microchip capacity expansion developed sequentially in Japan, South Korea, Taiwan, Singapore, and Malaysia. The article noted that "The results could be chronic global overcapacity for this basic high-tech commodity" (August 11, 2001, p. 49). More generally, a *Business Week* article observed that overcapacity was causing the prices of metal-cutting machine tools, electric transformers, printing equipment, civilian aircraft, truck trailers, and computers to decline. The article noted that with weak pricing conditions for the goods and services produced by nonfarm businesses, "even cheap investment goods may be too expensive" (April 15, 2002, p. 76).

The experience of the telecoms, chip makers, and durable goods producers generally demonstrates that even a mild downturn in the general economy can produce a major decline through the accelerator principle. A favorable outlook for individual industries can lead to an investment trap. An expanding industry might stimulate overcapacity financed by debt. The combination of the accelerator principle and excess capacity causes downward price pressures, declining profits, and inability to service the debt.

When formulating a firm's strategy for the future, the economic forces described must be considered. In making investment decisions, individual firms must take into account worldwide investment activity and future sales-to-capacity relationships. The investment accelerator principle will severely aggravate overcapacity conditions in durable goods industries.

BASIC STEPS IN STRATEGIC PLANNING

Although different approaches to strategic planning can be found, they all include the steps set forth in Table 5.1, which lists the critical activities involved in strategic planning processes. These procedures are described at length in the vast literature on strategy. Whether these represent formal or informal procedures, they are elements to be covered in strategic planning. In each of these activities, staff and line personnel have important responsibilities in the strategic decision-making processes.

Some general elements required for any strategic planning activity have been identified. In other aspects of strategic planning, wide diversity is encountered. A number of different activities and aspects are involved in strategic planning.

TABLE 5.1 Essential Elements in Strategic Planning Processes

1. Assessment of changes in the organizational environment.
2. Evaluation of company capabilities and limitations.
3. Assessment of expectations of stakeholders.
4. Analysis of company, competitors, industry, domestic economy, and international economies.
5. Formulation of the missions, goals, and policies for the master strategy.
6. Development of sensitivity to critical external environmental changes.
7. Formulation of internal organizational performance measurements.
8. Formulation of long-range strategy programs.
9. Formulation of mid-range programs and short-run plans.
10. Organization, funding, and other methods to implement all of the preceding elements.
11. Information flow and feedback system for continued repetition of all essential elements and for adjustments and changes at each stage.
12. Review and evaluation of all processes.

MONITORING THE ORGANIZATIONAL ENVIRONMENT

As emphasized in the previous section, a key to all approaches to strategic planning is continuous monitoring of the external environment. The environmental monitoring should encompass domestic and international dimensions and include analysis of economic, technological, political, social, and legal factors. Different organizations give different emphasis and weight to each of the categories.

STAKEHOLDERS

Strategic planning processes must take into account the diverse stakeholders of the organization. These are the individuals and groups that have an interest in the organization and its actions. They include customers, stockholders, creditors, employees, governments, communities, media, political groups, educational institutions, the financial community, and international entities.

Writers disagree on the appropriate stake of each of the groups listed. One view is that the firm need only maximize profit or shareholder stock values to maximize the long-run interests of every group. Another is that by properly balancing the interests of major stakeholders, the long-range interests of all will be maximized.

ORGANIZATIONAL CULTURES

How the organization carries out the strategic thinking and planning processes also varies with its culture. Illustrative organizational cultures include:

1. Strong top leadership versus team approach.
2. Management by formal paperwork versus management by wandering around.
3. Individual decisions versus group consensus decisions.
4. Rapid evaluation based on performance versus long-term relationship based on loyalty.
5. Rapid feedback for change versus formal bureaucratic rules and procedures.
6. Narrow career paths versus movement through many areas.
7. Risk taking encouraged versus "one mistake and you're out."
8. Big-stakes (bet-your-company) decisions versus low-risk activities.
9. Narrow responsibility assignments versus "everyone in this company is a salesperson (or cost controller, or product quality improver, and so on)."
10. Learn from the customer versus "we know what is best for the customer."

This list conveys the wide differences in corporate cultures and how the strategic thinking and planning processes might be affected. Failure to mesh divergent cultures can be a major obstacle to the full realization of the potentials of a merger (*Economist*, 1997).

ALTERNATIVE STRATEGY METHODOLOGIES

We draw a distinction between different strategy methodologies and different analytical frameworks employed in developing strategy. First, some alternative approaches to methodologies used in strategy formulation are considered in Table 5.2.

The first 12 in the list are described somewhat more fully in the following pages. The remainder are well known or self-explanatory and do not require elaboration.

TABLE 5.2 Alternative Strategy Methodologies

1. SWOT or WOTS UP: Inventory and analysis of organizational strengths, weaknesses, environmental opportunities, and threats.
2. Gap analysis: Assessment of goals versus forecasts or projections.
3. Top-down and/or bottom-up: Company forecasts versus aggregation of segments.
4. Computer models: Opportunity for detail and complexity.
5. Competitive analysis: Assess customers, suppliers, new entrants, products, and product substitutability.
6. Synergy: Look for complementarities.
7. Logical incrementalism: Well-supported moves from current bases.
8. Muddling through: Incremental changes selected from a small number of policy alternatives.
9. Comparative histories: Learn from the experiences of others.
10. Delphi technique: Iterated opinion reactions.
11. Discussion group technique: Stimulating ideas by unstructured discussions aimed at consensus decisions.
12. Adaptive processes: Periodic reassessment of environmental opportunities and organizational capability adjustments required.
13. Environmental scanning: Continuous analysis of all relevant environments.
14. Intuition: Insights of brilliant managers.
15. Entrepreneurship: Creative leadership.
16. Discontinuities: Crafting strategy from recognition of trend shifts.
17. Brainstorming: Free-form repeated exchange of ideas.
18. Game theory: Logical assessments of competitor actions and reactions.
19. Game playing: Assign roles and simulate alternative scenarios.

WOTS UP Analysis

Identifying strengths and weaknesses and opportunities and threats would appear to be easily accomplished. However, much subjectivity is involved. Different managers might have different judgments. Even though opportunities might exist, the differences in cost might require a careful balancing of considerations. On balance, this approach may provide a useful starting point for developing a strategic planning process and for stimulating strategic thinking in an organization.

Gap Analysis

In the assessment of goals versus forecasts or projections, goals may be formulated first. These can be expressed in quantitative terms, such as sales of $2 billion by 20XX or net income of $100 million by 20XX or a return on shareholder equity of 15%. However, a reasonable assessment of the future based on the firm's existing capabilities may indicate that these goals cannot be achieved by the target dates. The divergence may stimulate an assessment of whether the goals should be revised or how the organization could augment its capabilities in order to close the gap between goals and projections.

Top-Down Versus Bottom-Up Forecasts

In the history of strategic planning, a variety of approaches can be observed. In some companies, overall projections are made with requirements assigned to individual segments so that the overall company results can be achieved. At the other extreme, the projections of individual segments could be added up, with the result representing the outlook for the company as a whole. Good practice avoids both extremes.

Evidence shows that successful companies begin with planning premises formulated at the overall corporate level. These planning premises begin with the outlook for the economy and the industry, translated into what appears plausible for the particular firm. The planning premises are supplied to the individual segments, which use them as a basis for their own individual forecasts. The individual segment forecasts are aggregated to provide an outlook for the company as a whole. Meetings and discussions between the corporate level and the individual segments take place. A communication process is developed, and iterations of meetings continue until a consensus is reached. The desired goal is a company plan that is understood and reasonable from the standpoint of the various segments and results in an overall company outlook that is satisfactory from the standpoint of top management.

Computer Models
Computer models provide the opportunity for considerable detail and complexity. However, the models must reflect a theory or logic to guide their content. Otherwise, risk is great that the methodology will be overwhelmed by the resulting complexity.

Competitive Analysis
A number of approaches to competitive analysis may be found (see, for example, Porter, 1979). Our approach is conveyed by Figure 5.1. A firm's competitive position is determined by 11 important factors involved in demand and supply conditions. On the demand side, what is critical is the degree of feasible product substitutability. On the supply side, the nature and structure of costs are critical. Of particular importance is the ability to switch among suppliers of inputs. This may be critically affected by switching costs—the costs involved in shifting from one

FIGURE 5.1 Competitive Analysis

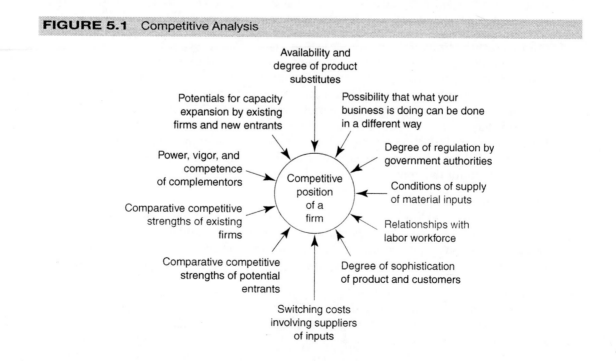

supplier to another. Supply competition from existing firms, including their potentials for capacity expansion, is also a major influence on the competitive position of the firm. Complementary firms are important. Is there a threat that your business could be carried out in another way?

Synergy

Synergy represents the $2 + 2 = 5$ effect. The concept of synergy was highly regarded at an earlier period but then subsequently came into disrepute. What is critical is how the extra gains are to be achieved. One example of synergy is found in the history of the pharmaceutical industry; after World War II, the major firms shifted from producing bulk chemicals for others to process to an emphasis on basic research and packaging products that were ready for final sale. They also needed a sales organization. After a number of years, synergistic mergers took place between companies strong in research or marketing and companies that had complementary strengths and weaknesses. Synergy can be a valid concept if it has a basis in reality.

Logical Incrementalism

After extensive field interviews, Quinn (1977, 1980) concluded that major changes in strategy are carried out most effectively when they can be broken down into numerous small changes, made on an incremental basis. In addition, he emphasized that a number of steps are required to involve the organization as broadly as possible. The process he emphasized also called for the exercise of effective leadership qualities.

Muddling Through

Another form of the incremental approach is one Lindblom (1959, 1965) called "muddling through." He also used the term *disjointed incrementalism* to describe the process. The basic idea is that instead of attempting to evaluate a wide range of alternatives, decision makers should focus on those policy alternatives that differ incrementally from existing policies. An iterative process is then employed to formulate and implement decisions.

Comparative Histories

The methodology of comparative histories is widely used by many firms in monitoring the behavior of their rivals. It was used in a fundamental research mode by Chandler (1962) in an analysis of the interrelationships among the economic environments of firms, their strategies, and their organizational structures. Chandler compared the histories of organizational changes among 50 large companies during a century beginning with the period after the Civil War in the United States. From his studies, he developed theories about the relationship between a firm's strategy and its organizational structure at various stages of development. Individual firms continuously monitor the policies, actions, and reactions of rivals.

Delphi Technique

A questionnaire developed to obtain information on problems or issues is distributed by mail to informed individuals. The responses are summarized into a feedback report, which is returned to the same people with a second questionnaire designed to probe more deeply into the ideas generated by the first questionnaire. Several iterations can be performed.

Discussion Group Technique

The group leader begins with a statement of the problem. An unstructured group discussion ensues for the purpose of generating ideas. Information and judgments are generated. The goal is to reach a consensus decision or to make a decision based on a majority voting procedure.

Adaptive Processes

In some sense, all approaches to strategy employ adaptive processes. The approach was first formalized by Ansoff (1965). The nature of the problem is structured on a tentative basis. Analysis is facilitated by a series of checklists or the analysis of matrix relationships. Successive iterations take place until a basis for formulating policies and reaching decisions is achieved. The method emphasizes developing a strong information feedback system to achieve flexibility in the organization's capability to adjust to its environmental changes. This approach is especially important in merger analysis.

The remainder of the approaches in Table 5.2 do not require further elaboration. The list conveys the profusion of methodologies encountered in strategic planning. The particular approaches to strategy adopted by individual firms and consultants involves selection from alternative strategy methodologies as listed in Table 5.2 combined with different groups of alternative analytical frameworks of the kind discussed next.

ALTERNATIVE ANALYTICAL FRAMEWORKS

Many different alternative analytical frameworks are employed in the formulation of strategy. Their nature is indicated by the list in Table 5.3.

Most of the items in Table 5.3 are self-explanatory. We will describe the many applications of matrix patterns of strengths and weaknesses or alternative approaches to markets.

A simple approach is the product-market matrix shown in Figure 5.2. It is based on the relatedness concept that is widely used in formulating strategy. The thrust of Figure 5.2 is that in developing new product markets, the lowest risk is to stay "close to home." The highest risk is to

---

TABLE 5.3   Alternative Analytical Frameworks

1. Product life cycles: Introduction, growth, maturity, decline stages with changing opportunities and threats.
2. Learning curve: Costs decline with cumulative volume experience resulting in competitive advantages for the firm that moves most quickly.
3. Competitive analysis: Industry structure, rivals' reactions, supplier-customer relations, product positioning.
4. Cost leadership: Low-cost advantages.
5. Product differentiation: Develop product configurations that achieve customer preference.
6. Value chain analysis: Control cost outlays to add product characteristics valued by customers.
7. Niche opportunities: Specialize to needs or interests of customer groups.
8. Product breadth: Carryover of organizational capabilities.
9. Correlations with profitability: Statistical studies of factors associated with high profitability measures.
10. Market share: High market share associated with competitive superiority.
11. Product quality: Customer allegiance and price differentials for higher quality.
12. Technological leadership: Keep at frontiers of knowledge.
13. Relatedness matrix: Unfamiliar markets and products involve greatest risk.
14. Focus matrix: Narrow versus broad product families.
15. Growth-share matrix: Aim for high market share in high-growth markets.
16. Attractiveness matrix: Aim to be strong in attractive industries.
17. Global matrix: Aim for competitive strength in attractive countries.
18. Resource-based view (RBV): Capabilities are inimitable.

Market \ Product	Present	Related	Unrelated
Present	Low risk		High risk
Related			
Unrelated	High risk		Highest risk

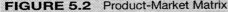

FIGURE 5.2 Product-Market Matrix

venture forth into unrelated products and unrelated markets. This analysis clearly depends on how risk is defined. It might be risky to stay where you are, if, for example, the prospects for growth of existing products and markets are unfavorable and the industry has excess capacity. This represents a strong motive for mergers to gain entry to markets with more favorable growth opportunities.

Figure 5.3 portrays one formulation of a competitive position matrix. It suggests a choice of emphasis between product differentiation and cost leadership. In addition, the focus may be on a narrow market segment or niche or product representation to provide presence in a broad range of markets.

The matrix shown in Figure 5.4, the growth-share matrix, has been associated particularly with the Boston Consulting Group. Products for which the firm has a high market share in an industry with favorable growth rates are potential "stars" with high profitability. As an industry matures, its growth slows, so that if a firm continues to have high market share, the attractive profits are available for investment in markets with more favorable growth rates, and the products become "cash cows." Products and markets with low growth where the firm has a small market share are "dogs," and the firm should discontinue such products, according to the simple product portfolio approach.

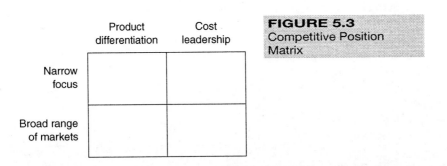

FIGURE 5.3
Competitive Position Matrix

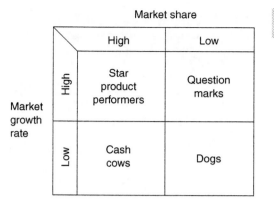

FIGURE 5.4 Growth-Share Matrix

A variant of the growth-share matrix is the strength-market attractiveness matrix shown in Figure 5.5. The greatest opportunities for investment and growth are where the outlook for an industry is attractive and the firm is highly capable of performing in that industry. In markets where the industry outlook is unfavorable and the firm has weakness, the firm should divest or close down such businesses.

Figure 5.6 moves the analysis to an international basis. In the international setting, the most attractive countries in terms of growth or political stability in which the firm has competitive strengths offer the most favorable growth opportunities. The opposite occurs in countries of low attractiveness and where the firm's competitive strengths are low.

In our view, the preceding examples of the matrix approach to strategy represent in spirit the checklist approach to formulating alternatives. They are useful devices for suggesting factors to take into account in formulating strategies.

The different analytical frameworks set forth in Table 5.3 are not mutually exclusive. In strategic planning, a wide range of analytical approaches may be employed. Their use is

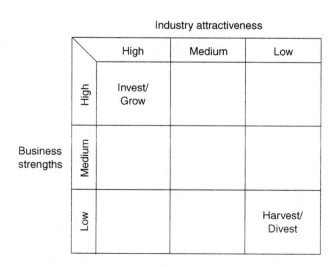

FIGURE 5.5 Strength-Market Attractiveness Matrix

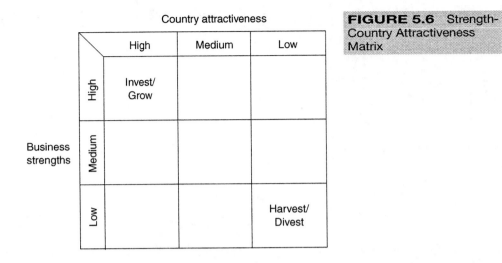

Country attractiveness

	High	Medium	Low
High	Invest/ Grow		
Medium			
Low			Harvest/ Divest

Business strengths

FIGURE 5.6 Strength-Country Attractiveness Matrix

facilitated by a checklist and an adaptive approach to strategic planning. Practicing consultants as well as individual firms have employed a combination of methodologies and analytical approaches with considerable success.

APPROACHES TO FORMULATING STRATEGY

Many different schools of thought in the strategy field can be observed. Each represents some combination of the methodologies and analytical frameworks from the preceding lists. Three approaches are discussed more fully to illustrate how alternative methodologies and analytical frameworks are used in practice. They are (1) the Boston Consulting Group approach, (2) the Porter approach, and (3) adaptive processes.

THE BOSTON CONSULTING GROUP

The Boston Consulting Group (BCG) historically emphasized three concepts; the experience curve, the product life cycle, and portfolio balance (Boston Consulting Group, 1985; Henderson, 1984; Thomas, 1986).

The experience curve represents a volume-cost relationship. It is argued that as the cumulative historical volume of output increases, unit costs will fall at a geometric rate. This results from specialization, standardization, learning, and scale effects. The firm with the largest cumulative output will have lower costs, suggesting a strategy of early entry and price policies to develop volume.

The product life cycle concept holds that every product or line of business proceeds through four phases: development, growth, maturity, and decline. During the first two stages, sales growth is rapid and entry is easy. As individual firms gain experience and as growth slows in the last two stages, entry becomes difficult because of the cost advantages of incumbents. In the decline phase of the product line (as other product substitutes emerge), sales and prices decline; firms that have not achieved a favorable position on the experience curve become unprofitable and either merge or exit from the industry.

Related to the product life cycle is the concept of portfolio balance. In the early stages of the product life cycle, rapid growth may require substantial investments. Such business segments are likely to require more investment funds than are generated by current profitability levels. As the requirements for growth diminish, profits might generate more funds than are necessary for current investment requirements. Portfolio balance seeks to combine attractive investment segments (stars) with cash-generating segments (cash cows), eliminating segments with unattractive prospects (dogs). Overall, total corporate cash inflows will roughly balance total corporate investments.

In recent years, the Boston Consulting Group has distinguished itself with newer approaches to strategy. Its executives have published innovative materials on the impact of the Internet and other technological innovations on the economics of information, "blowing apart the foundations of traditional business strategy" (Evans and Wurster, 1997, 2000). Implications for reconstructing value chain analysis are also developed. Other BCG publications have emphasized performance measurement by the use of "cash flow return on investment" (CFROI) and its implications for valuation.

THE PORTER APPROACH

Over the years, Michael Porter developed concepts that have become standard in strategy analysis. Michael Porter's (1980, 1985, 1987) approach has three parts: (1) Select an attractive industry, (2) develop a competitive advantage through cost leadership and product differentiation, and (3) develop attractive value chains.

First, Porter (1987, p. 46) defines an attractive industry or strategic group as one in which:

> entry barriers are high, suppliers and buyers have only modest bargaining power, substitute products or services are few, and the rivalry among competitors is stable. An unattractive industry like steel will have structural flaws, including a plethora of substitute materials, powerful and price-sensitive buyers, and excessive rivalry caused by high fixed costs and a large group of competitors, many of whom are state supported.

The difficulty of generalizing about industries is demonstrated by Porter's example. During the 1970s and 1980s, minimills flourished, and by 1988 some major steel firms had returned to profitability. In addition, there appears to be an inconsistency in that high fixed costs are considered to be an entry barrier in Porter's theory (Weston, 1978, 1982).

Second, Porter formulates a matrix for developing generic strategies. Competitive advantage can be based on cost leadership or on product differentiation. Cost advantage is achieved by consideration of a wide range of checklist factors including BCG's learning curve theory. The focus of cost advantage or of product differentiation can be on narrow market segments, or niches (for autos, the luxury car market—Cadillac, Continental, BMW, Mercedes, and so on), or on broader market groups (compact and standard cars), or across the board (GM).

Porter's third key concept is "the value chain." A matrix relates the support activities of infrastructure, human resource management, technology development, and procurement to the primary activities of inbound logistics, operations, out-bound logistics, marketing, sales, and service. The aim is to minimize outlays in adding characteristics valued by customers.

ADAPTIVE PROCESSES

Other writers have been more eclectic than the preceding two approaches. These writers view strategy more as an adaptive process or way of thinking (see, for example, Ansoff, 1965; Bogue and Buffa, 1986; Quinn, Mintzberg, and James, 1988; Steiner, 1979; Steiner, Miner, and Gray, 1986). Some writers also emphasize the uniqueness of each firm.

> In essence, the concept is that a firm's competitive position is defined by a bundle of unique resources and relationships and that the task of general management is to adjust and renew these resources and relationships as time, competition, and change erode their value (Rumelt, 1984, p. 557).

Mergers perform a role in these renewal efforts.

More generally the adaptive processes orientation involves matching resources to investment opportunities under environmental uncertainty compounded with uncertain competitors' actions and reactions. The methodology for dealing with these kinds of "ill-structured problems" requires an iterative solution process. Most managers in an organization have responsibilities for the inputs and studies required for the repeated "going around the loop" in the strategic planning processes outlined in Table 5.1.

In performing the iterated checklist procedures, difficult questions are encountered. For example, is the firm maximizing its potential in relation to its feasible environment? Does a gap exist between the firm's goals and prospects based on its present capabilities? Should the firm attempt to alter its environment, its capabilities, or both? Should the firm change its missions? What will be cost of each alternative? What are the risks and unknowns? What are the rewards for success and the penalties for failure?

The methodology involves not closed-form mathematical solutions but *iterative processes*. It involves ways of thinking that assess competitors' actions and reactions in relation to the changing environments. The process approach is especially applicable to merger analysis because it is difficult to find out all that is needed when combining with another entity.

EVALUATION OF THE ALTERNATIVE APPROACHES

Although some approaches emphasize generalizations, all make heavy use of checklists that have evolved into expert systems. Writers who have emphasized strategy implementation have shifted recently from a list of precepts to an emphasis on flexibility.

CHECKLISTS AND ITERATIONS

The adaptive processes methodologies emphasize the use of checklists to stimulate insights, and the BCG and Porter approaches to strategy formulation also rely heavily on similar techniques. For example, in his book *Competitive Strategy* (1980), Michael Porter utilized 134 checklists and checklist-like diagrams—one about every three pages. In his later *Competitive Advantage* (Porter, 1985), the number had expanded to 187 checklists and checklist-like diagrams—about one every 2.5 pages. Stryker (1986) (adaptive approach) had 174 checklists in 269 pages—one checklist per 1.5 pages. Thus, the process of strategic planning includes the art of making checklists, going around the loop iteratively, with the expectation that the thinking stimulated will lead to useful insights and sound strategies, policies, and decisions.

The BCG and Porter approaches emphasize prescriptions. However, in their actual implementation, they employ checklists not limited to the generalizations each emphasizes. In practice, all approaches to strategy become relatively eclectic.

With the greater use of computers in strategic planning, the different approaches appear to have more and more elements in common. Expert systems and other decision support systems have been developed. These represent a disciplined approach to strategic planning in which rules are used to guide implementation of the iterated checklist approach, making use of ideas from a wide range of philosophical perspectives (Chung and Davidson, 1987).

FLEXIBILITY AND RAPID ADJUSTMENTS

Publications by writers on strategy implementation present a different emphasis. In *In Search of Excellence*, Peters and Waterman (1982) asserted that the precepts for success could be reduced to a short checklist: (1) bias for action; (2) close to the customer; (3) autonomy and entrepreneurship; (4) productivity improvement; (5) hands-on, value-driven; (6) stick to core businesses; (7) simple form, lean staff; and (8) loose-tight properties.

Peters and Waterman (1982) admonished their readers to learn how the best-run American companies use eight basic principles to stay "on top of the heap!" Although *In Search of Excellence* was a commercial success, it also received criticisms (Carroll, 1983; Johnson, Natarajan, and Rappaport, 1985; Ramanujam and Venkatraman, 1988). Of particular interest to business economists was the analysis in the cover story of the November 5, 1984, issue of *Business Week* entitled, "Who's Excellent Now? Some of the Best-Seller's Picks Haven't Been Doing So Well Lately." *Business Week* studied the 43 "excellent" companies and concluded that many had encountered difficulties. The article observed:

> Of the 14 excellent companies that had stumbled, 12 were inept in adapting to a fundamental change in their markets. Their experiences show that strict adherence to the eight commandments—which do not emphasize reacting to broad economic and business trends—may actually hurt a company (p. 74).

Peters and Waterman appear to acknowledge the deficiencies in their earlier prescriptive approach by shifting their emphasis in later publications. In *The Renewal Factor*, Waterman (1987) emphasizes flexibility; he quotes with approval the executive who stated that he wanted his managers to be "Fred Astaires—intellectually quick, nimble, and ready to act" (p. 6). Similarly, Peters, Waterman's coauthor of *In Search of Excellence*, in his 1987 publication, begins, "There are no excellent companies. The old saw 'If it ain't broke, don't fix it' needs revision. I propose: 'If it ain't broke, you just haven't looked hard enough.' Fix it anyway" (Peters, 1987, p. 1). Similarly, two executives associated with the Boston Consulting Group proposed that to manage for increased competitiveness, companies need to "make decisions like a fighter pilot" (Hout and Blaxill, 1987, p. 3).

However, flexibility and rapid adjustments are more the stuff of tactics, not strategy. We believe that these developments in the literature on implementing strategy continue to suffer from the criticism conveyed by the *Business Week* article previously quoted. They make inadequate use of perspectives offered by economic analysis. Economics is forward looking, projecting market and supply conditions and patterns. Economic analysis can help identify prospective changes in such areas as demand, product differentiation, market growth segments, and behavior of rivals. Analysis of supply conditions can help identify areas of potential cost changes and thus targets for cost control. Economic analysis can delineate critical monitoring variables to indicate when changes in economic directions are likely to occur. Given this information, trade-off analysis (the bread and butter of economic marginal analysis) can identify and analyze alternative paths of action and their consequences. In short, economics aids in dealing with uncertainty and in anticipating change rather than reacting to events after they have occurred.

Economics seeks an understanding of environmental developments to identify the trends and discontinuities important to strategy formulation and implementation, as well as providing a framework within which flexibility and adjustments can be achieved efficiently. From the preceding analysis of alternative approaches to strategy, we can now develop guidelines for formulating a merger strategy.

FORMULATING A MERGER STRATEGY

The literature on long-range strategic planning indicates that one of the most important elements in planning is continual reassessment of the firm's environment. To determine what is happening in the environment, the firm should analyze its industry, competitors, and social and political factors.

Industry analysis allows the firm to recognize the key factors required for competitive success in the industry and the opportunities and threats present in the industry. From competitor analysis, the firm determines the capabilities and limitations of existing and potential competitors and their probable future moves. Through these analyses and with additional consideration of societal factors, the firm's strengths and weaknesses relative to present and future competitors can be ascertained.

The purpose of the environmental reassessment is to provide the firm with a choice among strategic alternatives. For this choice, the firm then considers whether its current goals and policies are appropriate to exploit industry opportunities and to deal with industry threats. At the same time, it is necessary for the firm to examine whether the goals and policies match the managerial, technological, and financial resources available to the firm, and whether the timing of the goals and policies appropriately reflects the ability of the organization to change.

The firm then works out feasible strategic alternatives given the results of the analyses. The current strategy (represented by its goals and policies) might or might not be included in the set of feasible alternatives. A strategic choice is made from this set such that the chosen strategy best relates the firm's situation to external opportunities and threats. Mergers represent one set of alternatives.

A brilliant exposition of how a company must be alert to important changes is set forth by Andrew S. Grove, president and CEO of Intel Corporation. Grove (1996) describes how a firm must adjust to six forces: existing competitors, potential competitors, complementors, customers, suppliers, and industry transformations. He presents illuminating case studies of the approach to strategy that we have called eclectic adaptive processes.

BUSINESS GOALS

General goals may be formulated with respect to size, growth, stability, flexibility, and technological breadth. Size objectives are established in order to use effectively the fixed factors the firm owns or buys. Size objectives also have been expressed in terms of critical mass. Critical mass refers to the size a firm must achieve to attain cost levels that enable it to operate profitably at market prices.

Growth objectives can be expressed in terms of sales, total assets, earnings per share, or the market price of the firm's stock. These are related to two valuation objectives. One is to attain a favorable price/earnings multiple for the firm's shares. A second is to increase the ratio of the market value of a firm's common stock to its book value.

Two major forms of instability can be distinguished. The first is exemplified by the defense market, which is subject to large, erratic fluctuations in its total size and abrupt shifts in individual programs. Another form of instability is the cyclical instability that characterizes producers of industrial and consumer durable goods.

The goal of flexibility refers to the firm's ability to operate in a wide variety of product markets. Such flexibility requires a breadth of research, manufacturing, or marketing capabilities. Of increased interest in recent years is technological breadth. With the increased pace of technological change in the U.S. economy, a firm may consider it important to possess capabilities in the rapidly advancing technologies.

Goals can be stated in general or specific terms, but both are subject to quantification. For example, growth objectives can be expressed in relationship to the growth of the economy or the firm's industry. Specific objectives can be expressed in terms of percentage of sales in specified types of markets. The quantification of goals facilitates comparisons of goals with the potential for achieving them.

Efforts to achieve multiple goals suggest a broader range of variables in the decision processes of the firm. Decisions require judgments of the nature of future environments; the policies of other firms with respect to the dimensions described; and new needs of customers, technologies, and capabilities. In short, to the requirements of operating efficiency and optimal output adjustments has been added the increased importance of the planning processes.

ALIGNING THE FIRM TO ITS CHANGING ENVIRONMENT

When it is necessary to take action to close a prospective gap between the firm's objectives and its potential based on its present capabilities, difficult choices must be made. For example, should the firm attempt to change its environment or capabilities? What would be the costs of such changes? What are the risks and unknowns? What are the rewards of success? What are the penalties of failure? Because the stakes are large, an iterative process is employed. A tentative decision is made. The process is repeated, perhaps from a different management function orientation, and the total-enterprise point of view is brought to bear on the problem. At some point, decisions are made that must involve entrepreneurial judgments. Mergers can help or hurt.

The emphasis is on the effective alignment of the firm with its environments and constituencies. Different approaches may be emphasized. One approach seeks to choose products related to the needs or wants of the customer that will provide large markets. A second approach focuses on technological bottlenecks or barriers, the solution of which might create new markets. A third strategy chooses to be at the frontiers of technological capabilities on the theory that some attractive product fall-out will result from such competence. A fourth approach emphasizes economic criteria including attractive growth prospects and appropriate stability.

If it is necessary for the firm to alter its product-market mix or range of capabilities to reduce or close the strategic gap, a diversification strategy may be formulated. Thus, the key connection between planning and diversification or mergers lies in the evaluation of current managerial and technological capabilities relative to capabilities required to reach objectives.

Thus far in the chapter, we have focused on strategy as the vision that guides the firm. We also reviewed alternative philosophies of strategy. We next turn to the relationships between strategy and structure and their implications for merger decisions.

STRATEGY AND STRUCTURE

A substantial body of literature discusses the relationship between strategy and structure. Some authors hold that structure determines strategy—the firm can access only those strategies that it is organized to undertake. Our view is that a feedback relationship exists between structure and strategy. The focus of our analysis here is on organizational architecture. We describe alternative organizational structures with emphasis on their implications for acquisition strategies. First, we describe the advantages and disadvantages of different types of organizational structures.

The unitary form, or U-form (Figure 5.7), is highly centralized under the president. It is broken into functional departments, and no department can stand alone. The president must stay close to the departments to know what needs to be improved, because it is not easy to measure each as a profit center. A long-term vision often is left solely to the president. Although this form allows rapid decision making, it is usually only successful in small organizations. It is difficult for the U-form to handle multiple products. Acquired firms have to fit into the limited span of control of the top executive group. Acquisitions are likely to be horizontal or closely related activities. The new units probably will be consolidated fully into the unitary organization.

The holding company, or H-form, is arranged, as shown in Figure 5.8, around various unrelated operating businesses. The leadership of the firm is able to evaluate each unit individually and can allocate resources according to projected returns. The firm has superior knowledge of the situation of each unit, allowing it to act as an "inside investor."

The holding company arrangement makes it possible for firms to acquire relatively unrelated activities. Each of the dissimilar operations is permitted to function almost as an independent company. The risk is that the H-form may be less than fully effective because of the requirement to guide activities that are widely diverse.

The multidivisional organization, or M-form, lies between the centralization of the U-form and the decentralization of the H-form. Each division is autonomous enough to be judged as a profit center, but all divisions share some endowments such as production or marketing. Hewlett-Packard, before it restructured in 1999, was arranged along product lines such as computers and measurement products. Although these divisions were largely separate, they shared

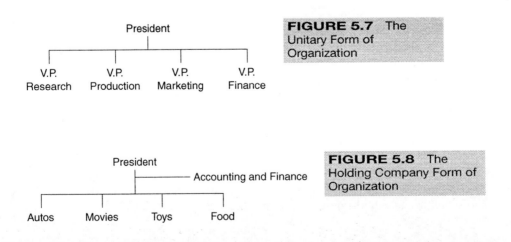

FIGURE 5.7 The Unitary Form of Organization

FIGURE 5.8 The Holding Company Form of Organization

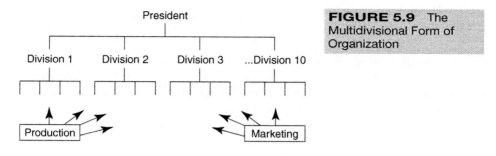

FIGURE 5.9 The Multidivisional Form of Organization

electrical engineering technology, as well as some facets of production (see Ouchi, 1984, for insights and extensions).

The multidivisional firm can handle related product and geographic market extensions. Its structure is represented in Figure 5.9. The acquisition of a firm with a related product line might result in designating it as a separate division. Because the products are related, the same functional staff groups might be able to serve the new division effectively. At some point, groups of divisions may have elements in common and require their own thrust with support staff groups having the required specialized knowledge. This appeared to be what developed at Hewlett-Packard when it restructured in 1999, separating the computer-related activities from the non-computer-related products. The latter group of activities was placed in a new company called Agilent. The new company had its own stock, a portion of which was sold to the public and was well received.

The matrix form of organization, as shown in Figure 5.10, consists of functional departments such as finance, manufacturing, and development. The employees of these functional departments are assigned to subunits that are organized around products, geography, or some other criterion. In such an organization, employees report to a functional manager as well as a product manager. The matrix form is most effective in firms characterized by many new products or projects. Intel, as of 1992, was structured around five major product groups.

The matrix form represents another way to handle the acquisition of related products or to engage in geographic market expansion. However, as new product groups are added, a heavier burden is placed on the communication system. The possibility of disputes and conflicts arising from multiple lines of authority is likely to be increased.

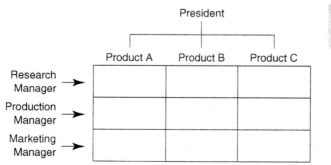

FIGURE 5.10 The Matrix Form of Organization

VIRTUAL INTEGRATION

A new method of organization has been developed by firms such as Dell, which are pursuing "virtual integration." Under such a system, the links of the value chain are brought together by an informal arrangement among suppliers and customers. Dell establishes close ties with suppliers, enabling many of the benefits of vertical integration. Shipments of the components that Dell needs can be arranged easily through the Internet or a networked computer system. This same type of arrangement allows Dell to fully serve customers in ordering, services, or any other areas of need. From the initial concept of selling computers by telephone or over the Internet, Dell has evolved into a sophisticated business organization. By recruiting top executives with strong track records in high-level positions in other successful companies, Dell has developed a strong management team. In addition, the emphasis on cost controls and high quality from suppliers has strengthened Dell's product reputation.

In this book, we emphasize that firms can follow many alternative paths to growth and value creation. In addition to mergers and acquisitions, other relationships include joint ventures, alliances, minority investments, licensing agreements, franchising, reorganizations, spinoffs, and divestitures. Peter Drucker (2001) observed that these developments transform corporations into confederations. He used General Motors (GM) as an example. GM has controlling investments in Fiat (Italy) and Saab (Sweden), as well as Suzuki and Isuzu (Japan). GM fully owns foreign subsidiaries such as Opel (Germany). In 1999, GM did an equity carveout and spin-off of a substantial portion of its parts and accessories manufacturing activities into Delphi, representing about 65% of its costs of production. Drucker stated that GM has joined with Ford and DaimlerChrysler to form a purchasing cooperative for buying parts and accessories using auctions and the Internet.

A qualification to such an arrangement being considered a "form of organization" is that it involves multiple firms, which likely have a variety of organizational forms. However, it is important to realize that virtual integration represents a blurring of company boundaries. As communication strengthens the ties among different firms in a value chain, it is easier to envision grouping them as an organization. Indeed, a firm's networks help create "inimitable" value in the resource-based view of the firm (Gulati, Nohria, and Zaheer, 2000; Lippman and Rumelt, 1982).

STRATEGY AND M&A DECISIONS

Mergers and acquisitions require changes in the organization structure of a firm. In major horizontal mergers such as Exxon-Mobil, the acquired firm is integrated into the structure of the acquiring firm. Usually one of the goals is to achieve savings by eliminating redundant facilities, officers, and employees. Sound business principles prescribe that the best facilities and the most highly qualified personnel be retained regardless of the previous company affiliation. Mergers of equals are said to protect the interests of the acquired firm. If efficiency principles are followed, no distinction should exist among mergers of equals and other kinds of mergers.

In acquisitions of more specialized firms, the entity might simply be added to the existing organization structure. The M-form of organization facilitates placing the new segment within an existing group of related firms. Systematic evidence on the principles of integration actually followed is fragmentary.

We have emphasized that M&As include alliances, joint ventures, investments, franchising, licensing, divestitures, spin-offs, split-ups, and many other forms of reorganization. The wide range of adjustment processes that we refer to as M&As must be consistent with the firm's overall strategy and organization structure.

Summary

In the process approach to strategy, each firm has a set of capabilities and opportunities. The firm must exploit these effectively in relation to its changing environments. It must recognize that the dynamics of competition and economic change will require continuous reassessment of its position and realignment to its new challenges and opportunities. In this view, the firm is required to make strategic decisions in the face of much uncertainty and considerable risk, especially with respect to mergers.

In this process view of strategy, divestitures represent a form of strategic adjustment process. Numerous case studies demonstrate that many divestitures were planned in advance in order to retain the desired parts of an acquisition. Or divestitures can represent a method of making acquisitions and paying them off in part or sometimes entirely by the segments sold off. At a minimum, this may help make the diversification effort a low-cost one. Hence, it is erroneous to conclude that divestitures represent management mistakes.

Internal and external investment programs can be successful or unsuccessful. Firms might try either or both approaches in their efforts to increase shareholder value. The generalization of writers on strategic planning contain valuable insights for helping firms carry out strategies with a higher degree of efficiency than they otherwise would have been able to attain. The critical need is a rapid information feedback system in the firm to improve its ability to adapt to change, correct errors, and seize new opportunities. It is in this framework that merger and takeover decisions are made.

A substantial body of literature develops the relationship between strategy and the structure of firms. Organizational form can be critical to implementing strategy. Our view is that a feedback relationship exists between strategy and structure. The unitary form is highly centralized under the president. The holding company form is decentralized and usually includes unrelated businesses. The multidivisional form has different units that share some common functions. The matrix form is organized around various products or projects. Virtual integration is a developing method of blurring the lines among organizations.

Questions

5.1   What is strategy?

5.2   What is an attractive industry according to Porter?

5.3   What does Porter mean by "competitive advantage" through cost leadership? Through product differentiation?

5.4   What are entry barriers, and what is their significance?

5.5   What is the adaptive approach to strategy? (Include a discussion of the role of checklists and iterative processes.)

5.6   Discuss different types of business goals.

5.7   What is meant by aligning a firm to its environment(s)?

5.8   Why does a firm seek to continue to exist after its main products are either obsolete or out of favor for health or other reasons?

5.9   What factors resulted in the conglomerate merger movement of the 1960s?

5.10 Explain the following forms of organization: unitary form (U-form), the holding company form (H-form), and the multidivisional form (M-form). Describe the strengths and limitations of each.

5.11 Explain what is meant by virtual integration taking place among firms resulting from modern communications systems such as the Internet.

Case 5.1   MERCK ACQUISITION OF MEDCO

On July 28, 1993, Merck & Company, then the world's largest drug manufacturer, announced that it planned to acquire, for $6.6 billion, Medco Containment Services Incorporated, the largest prescription benefits management company (PBM) and marketer of mail-order medicines in the United States. This merger reflected fundamental changes taking place in the pharmaceutical industry.

GROWTH IN MANAGED CARE

Perhaps the most significant change involves the growth of managed care in the health care industry. Managed care plans typically provide members with medical insurance and basic health care services, using volume and long-term contracts to negotiate discounts from health care providers. In addition, managed care programs provide full coverage for prescription drugs more frequently than do traditional medical insurance plans. Industry experts estimate that by the turn of the century, 90% of Americans will have drug costs included in some kind of managed health care plan, and 60% of all outpatient pharmaceuticals will be purchased by managed care programs.

The responsibility for managing the provision of prescription drugs is often contracted out by the managed care organizations to PBMs. The activities of PBMs typically include managing insurance claims, negotiating volume discounts with drug manufacturers, and encouraging the use of less expensive generic substitutes. The management of prescription benefits is enhanced through the use of formularies and drug utilization reviews. Formularies are lists of drugs compiled by committees of pharmacists and physicians on behalf of a managed care organization. Member physicians of the managed care organization are then strongly encouraged to prescribe from this list whenever possible. Drug utilization reviews consist of analyzing physician prescribing patterns and patient usage. They can identify when a patient may be getting the wrong amount or kind of medicine and when a member physician is not prescribing from a formulary. Essentially, this amounts to an additional opportunity for managed care or PBM administrators to monitor costs and consolidate decision-making authority.

The key aspect of the shift to managed care is that the responsibility for payment is linked more tightly to decision making about the provision of health care services than it is in traditional indemnity insurance plans. The implications for drug manufacturers are far reaching. With prescription decision-making authority shifting away from doctors to managed care and PBM administrators, drug manufacturers' marketing strategies similarly will shift their focus from several hundred thousand doctors to a few thousand formulary and plan managers. This, in turn, will result in a dramatic reduction in the sales forces of pharmaceutical manufacturers.

Several other significant changes in industry structure are expected to occur. Many industry experts predict that managed care providers will rely on a single drug company to deliver all of its pharmaceutical products and services rather than negotiating with several drug companies. This will favor those firms with manufacturing, distribution, and prescription management capabilities. In addition, many experts believe that only a handful of pharmaceutical companies will exist on the international scene in a few years. They point to intense competition, lower profits, and a decrease in the number of new drugs in the "research pipeline" as contributing factors.

BENEFITS OF THE ACQUISITION

Merck & Company and Medco Containment Services Incorporated believe that a merger between the two firms will create a competitive advantage that will allow for their survival. Merck executives identify Medco's extensive database as the key factor motivating the merger. Medco maintains a computer profile of each of its 33 million customers, amounting to 26% of all people covered by a pharmaceutical benefit plan. Medco clients include 100 Fortune 500 companies, federal and state benefit plans, and 58 Blue Cross/Blue Shield groups and insurance companies.

Numerous opportunities exist for Merck to utilize the information contained in Medco's database. First, the database will allow Merck to identify prescriptions that could be switched from a competitor's drug to a Merck drug. Merck pharmacists will then suggest the switch to a patient's doctor. This prospect of increasing sales is enormous. Second, the database will allow Merck to identify patients who fail to refill prescriptions. The failure to refill needed prescriptions amounts to hundreds of millions of dollars in lost sales each year. Finally, Merck will be able to use Medco's computerized patient record system as a real-life laboratory with the goal of proving that some Merck drugs are worth the premium price charged. This will take place by identifying who takes what pill and combining that information with the patient's medical records. This might allow Merck to establish the supremacy of its products.

Additional benefits of the merger include $1 billion annual savings in redundant marketing operations and a reduction in Merck's sales force as a result of more precise marketing strategies brought about by Medco's database and the industry emphasis on marketing to plan managers instead of doctors. Merck & Company's acquisition of Medco Containment Services Incorporated is essentially an attempt to increase market share in an industry with decreasing prices by capitalizing on the most valuable asset in the pharmaceutical industry—information. It also is intended to increase its competitive position in the growing managed care arena by aligning itself with a PBM.

Merck & Company's strategy was quickly emulated when British drug maker SmithKline Beecham announced plans to acquire Diversified Pharmaceutical Services Incorporated, one of the four largest drug wholesalers in the United States, from United Healthcare for $2.3 billion, and Roche Holdings Limited reported that it planned to acquire Syntex Corporation. Also, in the summer of 1994, Eli Lilly and Company announced its intention to acquire PCS Health Systems from McKesson Corporation for $4 billion. These mergers were not only a reaction to the changing industry structure but caused the change to accelerate. ▨

QUESTIONS

C5.1.1 What was the major force driving this acquisition?

C5.1.2 What is the role of prescription benefits management (PBM) companies?

C5.1.3 What role was envisaged for the use of Medco's database?

C5.1.4 What competitive reactions took place in response to Merck's acquisition of Medco?

Case 5.2 ACQUISITION OF LOTUS DEVELOPMENT CORPORATION BY IBM

Lotus Development Corporation, the second-largest PC software firm, was taken over via a hostile bid by IBM Corporation in 1995 for $3.52 billion.

THE TAKEOVER PROCESS

Previous Relations Between IBM and Lotus

According to executives familiar with the situation, Jim Manzi, the CEO of Lotus Development Corporation, offered to sell the company's desktop software applications to IBM but did not want to sell the entire company. In August 1994, Manzi suggested to James Cannavino, IBM's top strategist at the time, a joint venture in desktop applications or the sale of that part to IBM. IBM declined the offer. In January 1995, Manzi repeated the offer to the new IBM senior vice president in charge of the software group, John M. Thompson. Thompson offered to acquire the entire company, to which Manzi responded that Lotus was not for sale. Manzi ruled out anything but a minority stake for IBM of Lotus's communications business. The two met for the last time in March, when Manzi again objected to the acquisition.

Announcement of the Bid

On June 5, 1995, IBM announced its first-ever hostile bid in the form of a $60-cash-per-share tender offer. That day, Lotus's stock price soared $29 from $32.375, closing at $61.375 on the NASDAQ (a 90% premium), and IBM stock dropped $2.625 from $93.875, closing at $91.25 on the New York Stock Exchange (NYSE) (a 2.8% decline).

The bid was the culmination of months of strategy. In April 1995, IBM analyzed the fit of Lotus products with IBM software and decided to pursue Lotus. IBM realized that Lotus Development Corporation wanted to remain independent if they were to be acquired. With this in mind, Louis V. Gerstner, Jr., the chairman of IBM, approved the hostile deal on

May 12. On May 22, IBM incorporated White Acquisition Corporation, a subsidiary specifically created to execute the acquisition of Lotus. On June 5, 1995, IBM sent a message promising Lotus employees that they would not be assimilated into IBM after the merger. IBM agreed to this stipulation because they did not want to lose key Lotus employees such as the software developer of Lotus Notes, Raymond Ozzie.

Shortly after 8 A.M. on the morning of the bid, IBM's Delaware law firm filed a lawsuit challenging Lotus's poison pill. The activated Lotus pill with a trigger set at 15% would have increased dramatically the number of Lotus shares and the cost of the acquisition to a potential acquirer. At 8:25 A.M., Gerstner informed Manzi of the bid. Manzi agreed to consider the offer, knowing that he was not promised a position should Lotus be acquired. At 8:30 A.M., IBM informed the exchanges on which IBM and Lotus traded, the NYSE and NASDAQ, respectively. Gerstner also called the CEO of Hewlett-Packard and chairman of AT&T, two partners of Lotus who were also potential white knights, to inform them of IBM's intent.

At a 1:30 P.M. press conference, Gerstner spoke of the three different ages of computing. The first age of computing, the mainframe, was dominated by IBM, whereas the second age of personal computers remained competitive. The race is currently on for dominance of the third age, networked computing. Networked computing allows users of different software and hardware platforms to work together in a collaborative manner. A network offers the user friendliness and the applications of a desktop along with the security, dependability, and capacity of a large-scale system. IBM's acquisition of Lotus is an attempt to gain a significant share of the networked computing market.

In addition to the press conference on June 5, IBM took the first steps toward consent solicitation to put pressure on the Lotus board. Lotus bylaws permitted shareholders to vote at any time on whether to retain the board. With the threat of being ousted, the Lotus board would be forced to pay careful attention to the wishes of the shareholders. Shareholders were likely to want the premium, given the recent poor performance of the company stock. Institutions held the bulk of Lotus's stock. Directors and officers held only 3.3% of Lotus's stock, but 2.54% of that number, or 1.2 million shares, was held by Manzi, the largest individual holder of Lotus stock.

The announcement of the bid appeared to be anticipated given the 11% rise in the Lotus stock price on Friday, June 2, which triggered an SEC insider trader investigation. Rumors that IBM might acquire Lotus had existed for several months prior to the bid.

Acceptance of the Offer

On Sunday, June 11, Lotus accepted a sweetened $64 a share, or $3.52 billion, offer from IBM. The final price represented four times Lotus's 1994 revenues. IBM anticipated writing off approximately $1.8 billion in goodwill after a one-time charge. Also under the terms of the deal, Manzi would remain the CEO of Lotus and become a senior vice president of IBM. He would be allowed to run Lotus with a high degree of independence in addition to receiving a $78 million windfall from his Lotus stock.

In Manzi's own words, he was staying on, not in a "transitional role," but rather to help make Lotus Notes the industry standard for network software, to protect Lotus employees, and to protect the Lotus organization (Rifkin, 1995). Though analysts were surprised that Manzi would remain in charge of Lotus, they predicted that he would not stay with the company for long. Analysts spoke of the clash of egos they felt would occur between Gerstner and Manzi.

Manzi said that the previously announced restructuring of Lotus into four business units still would take place in spite of the merger. Some Lotus employees might have favored the merger because of the stability involved in joining IBM's team, the capital IBM could invest in the company, and the soaring value of their Lotus stock options. Prior to the merger, Lotus's future looked grim. Lotus was vulnerable due to its recent poor performance, lack of a white knight, and corporate bylaws that allowed a direct appeal to Lotus shareholders. Lotus shares traded at 66% below their 1994 high, and efforts to find a white knight might have been impeded by the fact that Lotus was a competitor of the powerful Microsoft, with which few companies were able or willing to compete.

On July 5, 1995, the acquisition was finally completed.

STRATEGIC ANALYSIS OF THE ACQUISITION

Previous History of Lotus

Lotus was founded by a college dropout named Mitch Kapor in 1982. Eight months later, the company successfully introduced Lotus 1-2-3, the first spreadsheet program to translate numbers into graphics. In 1983, a McKinsey and Company consultant by the name of Jim Manzi was assigned to help manage Lotus's rapid growth. Later that year, Manzi joined the Lotus board as vice president of marketing and sales. In 1986, Kapor left the firm and made Manzi his successor.

In the early 1980s, the Lotus 1-2-3 spreadsheet package was the most popular PC business application. But because Lotus was slow to develop a version of 1-2-3 for Windows, many users switched to Microsoft Excel or Borland's Quattro Pro for Windows.

The growing popularity of Windows created other problems for Lotus, as well. Late in developing software suites, the company tried to rectify this through acquisitions. In 1990, Lotus acquired Samna Corporation and its Ami Pro word processing line for $65 million, and in March 1991, Lotus purchased cc:Mail. Also, in June 1994, Lotus acquired SoftSwitch Incorporated for $70 million in stock, or 1.3 million shares. Unfortunately, these acquisitions did little to help improve Lotus's weakened state.

The reduction in its desktop applications and continued reputation for being weak on marketing and updating programs contributed to Lotus's subsequent decline. Lotus's desktop software accounted for two thirds of its revenues, so it was particularly troublesome when in 1994, these revenues declined 20% to $620 million. In the first quarter of 1995, Lotus lost another $17.5 million due in part to a 50% price cut on Notes announced in January 1995. The price cut was intended to increase the market share of Notes before the release of MS Exchange.

The company's troubles prompted Manzi to announce a restructuring on April 19, 1995. Cost cuts and reorganization meant layoffs and low employee morale. In 2 weeks, Lotus eliminated 32 high-level positions, with lower-level layoffs expected in the near future. This restructuring was directed by Richard S. Braddock, a powerful outside director and former president of Citicorp.

Motivations Behind the Merger

The main motivation behind the acquisition was IBM's desire to own Lotus's network software program called Notes. Released in December 1989, Notes had propelled Lotus to a 65% market share in groupware, a market that was anticipated to grow from $500 million to $5 billion by the end of the decade. In 1994, sales of Notes nearly doubled to $350 million, with the majority coming from existing customers. By January 1995, one million people used Notes in 4,500 companies, and third-party companies had created more than 700 commercial applications that work with Notes. Moreover, the Notes customer base had increased because although it was originally available only on OS/2 servers, it could now run on Windows NT and other operating systems.

Primarily used by large corporations and large networks, groupware enables groups of workers to communicate with one another and to share or have access to the same data. It often is used as the central framework for managing entire corporate systems and can be customized for use as a platform on which to build additional applications.

QUESTIONS

C5.2.1 What were IBM's strategic strengths and weaknesses in the computer industry?

C5.2.2 What role was the acquisition of Lotus expected to perform?

C5.2.3 What has been IBM's performance since this acquisition?

References

Ansoff, H. Igor, *Corporate Strategy*, New York: McGraw-Hill, 1965.

Bogue, Marcus C., III, and Elwood S. Buffa, *Corporate Strategic Analysis*, New York: The Free Press, 1986.

Boston Consulting Group, *The Strategy Development Process*, Boston: The Boston Consulting Group, 1985.

BusinessWeek, "Who's Excellent Now? Some of the Best-Seller's Pick Haven't Been Doing So Well Lately," 5 November 1984, p. 76.

Carroll, D. T., "A Disappointing Search for Excellence," *Harvard Business Review* 61, November-December 1983, pp. 78–88.

Chandler, Alfred D., Jr., *Strategy and Structure: Chapters in the History of the American Industrial Enterprise*, Cambridge, MA: The M.I.T. Press, 1962.

Chung, Mary, and Alistair Davidson, "Business Experts," *PCAI* 1, Summer 1987, pp. 16–21.

Council of Economic Advisors, *Economic Indicators*, February 2002, pp. 20–21.

Drucker, Peter, "The Next Society: A Survey of the Near Future," *The Economist*, 15 September 2001, pp. 1–30.

Economist, "Why Too Many Mergers Miss the Mark," 4 January 1997, pp. 57–58.

Economist, "Semiconductor Manufacturers—The Great Chip Glut," 11 August 2001, pp. 49–50.

Evans, Philip, and Thomas Wurster, *Blown to Bits*, Boston: Harvard Business School Press, 2000.

——, "Strategy and the New Economics of Information," *Harvard Business Review*, September-October 1997.

Grove, Andrew S., *Only the Paranoid Survive: How to Exploit the Crisis Points That Challenge Every Company and Career*, New York: Currency Doubleday, 1996.

Gulati, R., N. Nohria, and A. Zaheer, "Strategic Networks," *Strategic Management Journal*, March 2000, pp. 203–215.

Henderson, Bruce D., *The Logic of Business Strategy*, Cambridge, MA: Ballinger, 1984.

Hout, Thomas M., and Mark F. Blaxill, "Make Decisions Like a Fighter Pilot," *New York Times*, 15 November 1987, Sec. 3, p. 3.

Johnson, W. Bruce, Ashok Natarajan, and Alfred Rappaport, "Shareholder Returns and Corporate Excellence," *Journal of Business Strategy* 6, Fall 1985, pp. 52–62.

Lindblom, Charles E., *The Intelligence of Democracy: Decision Making Through Mutual Adjustment*, New York: The Free Press, 1965.

——, "The Science of 'Muddling Through'," *Public Administration Review* 19, Spring 1959, pp. 79–88.

Lippman, S., and R. Rumelt, "Uncertain Imitability: An Analysis of Interfirm Differences in Efficiency Under Competition," *The Bell Journal of Economics* 13, 1982, pp. 418–438.

Mandel, Michael, J., ed., "Equipment Is Going Cheap," *BusinessWeek*, 15 April 2002, p. 30.

Ouchi, William. *The M-Form Society: How American Teamwork Can Recapture the Competitive Edge*, Reading, MA: Addison-Wesley, 1984.

Peters, Thomas J., *Thriving on Chaos*, New York: Alfred A. Knopf, Publishers, 1987.

——, and Robert H. Waterman, Jr., *In Search of Excellence*, New York: Harper & Row, 1982.

Porter, Michael E., *Competitive Advantage*, New York: The Free Press, 1985.

——, *Competitive Strategy*, New York: The Free Press, 1980.

——, "From Competitive Advantage to Corporate Strategy," *Harvard Business Review*, May-June 1987, pp. 43–59.

——, "How Competitive Forces Shape Strategy," *Harvard Business Review* 57, March-April 1979, pp. 137–145.

Quinn, James Brian, *Strategies for Change: Logical Incrementalism*, Homewood, IL: Irwin, 1980.

——, "Strategic Goals: Process and Politics," *Sloan Management Review*, Fall 1977, pp. 21–37.

——, Henry Mintzberg, and Robert M. James, *The Strategy Process*, Upper Saddle River, NJ: Prentice Hall, 1988.

Ramanujam, Vasudevan, and N. Venkatraman, "Excellence, Planning, and Performance," *Interfaces* 18, May-June 1988, pp. 23–31.

Rifkin, Glenn, "How Shock Turned to Deal for Lotus Chief," *New York Times* 13 June 1995, p. 6.

Rumelt, Richard P., "Towards a Strategic Theory of the Firm," Chapter 26 in R. B. Lamb, ed., *Competitive Strategic Management*, Upper Saddle River, NJ: Prentice Hall, 1984.

Steiner, George A., *Strategic Planning*, New York: The Free Press, 1979.

——, John B. Miner, and Edmund R. Gray, *Management Policy and Strategy*, 3rd ed., New York: Macmillan, 1986.

Stryker, Steven C., *Plan to Succeed: A Guide to Strategic Planning*, Princeton, NJ: Petrocelli Books, 1986.

Thomas, Lacy Glenn, III, ed., *The Economics of Strategic Planning*, Lexington, MA: Lexington Books, 1986.

Ward, Sandra, "Stunted Growth," *Barron's*, 25 February 2002, pp. 27–30.

Waterman, Robert H., Jr., *The Renewal Factor*, New York: Bantam Books, 1987.

Weston, J. Fred, *Concentration and Efficiency: The Other Side of the Monopoly Issue*, Special Issues in the Public Interest No. 4, New York: Hudson Institute, 1978.

——, "Section 7 Enforcement: Implementation of Outmoded Theories," *Antitrust Law Journal* 49, 1982, pp. 1411–1450.

CHAPTER 6
THEORIES OF MERGERS
AND TENDER OFFERS

———≈/≈/≈———

This chapter presents the theories and concepts related to the causes and effects of mergers. The discussion is intended to apply to mergers, broadly defined, and includes tender offers and other forms of takeover activity. The analysis addresses the following three related queries:

1. Why do mergers occur?
2. What are the possible effects of merger activity on firm value?
3. How does the merger process unfold?

In addressing these important questions, we review a number of competing theories and also consider the relevance of the theory to several recent merger examples. The theoretical and conceptual material in this chapter provides the foundations for analysis in subsequent chapters. In particular, Chapter 7 presents the historical and industry evidence on the sources of merger activity. Chapter 8 reports the extensive empirical evidence on the wealth effects of mergers and acquisitions.

SOME INITIAL EXAMPLES OF THE MERGER PROCESS

To set the stage for the discussion of mergers and acquisitions, we review two major mergers: the merger of Hewlett-Packard and Compaq, and the acquisition of TRW by Northrop Grumman. We discuss the reasons given for the mergers, the market reaction to the announcements of the deals, and the details of the merger process in both cases. The two mergers are outlined in Table 6.1. The information used to construct the table was taken from the SEC EDGAR filings and from the financial media.

HEWLETT-PACKARD AND COMPAQ

The Hewlett-Packard (HP)–Compaq deal was made public on September 3, 2001, when the two companies jointly announced their prospective union. The primary reason offered for the merger was economies of scale. The companies projected cost synergies reaching $2.5 billion. The merger was offered as a strategic response to changing conditions in the computer and information technology sector.

The stock market was not as upbeat about the merger as the two companies were. On the first trading day following the announcement, Hewlett-Packard's stock price declined by 19%. The price of the target firm, Compaq, also fell by 10%.

TABLE 6.1 The Hewlett-Packard/Compaq and Northrop Grumman/TRW Mergers

	HP/Compaq	Northrop Grumman/TRW
Reasons for the Merger	Economies of scale in PCs	Economies of scale
	$2.5 billion in cost synergies	Complementary product mix
Price Reaction at Announcement	HP price declines 19%	Northrop Grumman declines 6.7%
	Compaq declines 10%	TRW increases 26.4%
Merger Process		
Private Activity	CEOs have initial discussion (6/2001)	Northrop Grumman makes $47 offer in letter (2/21/2002)
	Extensive business due diligence (6/2001)	Offer 2 days after TRW CEO takes job at Honeywell
	Retain financial advisers (7/2001)	Letter says offer responsive to nonpublic information
	Boards approve merger (9/3/2001)	Letter says Northrop Grumman plans to divest automotive
Public Activity	Joint press release (9/3/2001)	Northrop Grumman press release of offer (2/22/2002)
	Walter Hewlett opposes (11/5/2001)	TRW rejects offer as inadequate (3/3/2002)
	Packard foundation opposes (12/8/2001)	Northrop Grumman commences exchange offer (3/4/2002)
	Approval from FTC (3/7/2002)	TRW rejects upped bid of $53 in stock (4/18/2002)
	Compaq holders approve (3/21/2002)	TRW, Northrop Grumman confidentiality pact (5/7/2002)
	HP holders formally approve (5/1/2002)	Merger agreement for $60 in stock (7/2/2002)

Source: SEC EDGAR filings and financial media.

Although the merger was made public on September 3, 2001, the deal had been initiated privately several months before. As described in Table 6.1, the CEOs of the two firms had initial discussions of a possible alliance in June 2001. As noted in the merger documents filed with the SEC, this initial discussion was followed by extensive business due diligence whereby HP and Compaq worked, respectively, with the consulting firms McKinsey and Accenture to flesh out the strategic, operational, and other aspects of the possible merger. In July 2001, Goldman Sachs and Salomon Smith Barney were engaged, respectively, by HP and Compaq to provide financial advice on the merger. Hence, a great deal of analysis and negotiation occurred prior to the initial announcement of the deal.

As it turned out, the analysis and negotiation lasted well after the deal's initial announcement. Several members of the founding families of Hewlett-Packard came out against the merger. Walter Hewlett, a board member of HP, was especially vocal in his opposition to the deal. The Packard Foundation also elected to vote against the merger. In a close vote, however, the merger was formally approved by HP shareholders in May 2002.

NORTHROP GRUMMAN AND TRW

Another major merger occurring in 2002 was between the defense firms Northrop Grumman and TRW. As sketched in Table 6.1, the evolution of this deal differed in many respects from the HP-Compaq transaction. In this case, the deal was first made public on February 22, 2002, when the bidder, Northrop Grumman, publicly released the letter sent to TRW proposing the merger.

The letter was sent only 2 days after TRW's CEO resigned to take the helm at Honeywell. In the letter, Northrop Grumman indicated that it intended to immediately divest TRW's automotive business and that the remaining assets of TRW were complementary. Northrop Grumman also suggested that its offer of $47 in stock was responsive to nonpublic information.

The stock market reacted noticeably to the press release by Northrop Grumman. The price of the target firm, TRW, increased 26.4% from $39.80 to $50.30. By contrast, the price of Northrop Grumman fell by 6.7%.

TRW publicly rejected the $47 stock offer as inadequate on March 3, 2002. In spite of the opposition by the target, Northrop Grumman commenced its formal merger offer. Over the next several months, the two parties jockeyed and negotiated. For example, Northrop Grumman upped its offer, and TRW sought other bidders and also considered splitting up its automotive, aeronautic, and defense businesses.

After several months, the two companies came to terms. In May 2002, the companies signed a confidentiality pact to share nonpublic information. On July 2, 2002, they announced a merger agreement whereby Northrop Grumman would acquire TRW for $60 in stock.

MERGER OCCURRENCE: ECONOMIES OF SCALE AND TRANSACTION COSTS

In this section, we consider the fundamental question: Why do mergers occur? This analysis lays the groundwork for the competing theories regarding the wealth effects of merger announcements.

SIZE AND RETURNS TO SCALE

A common feature of all mergers is an increase in firm size. Consequently, a standard reason offered for a merger is that the union of the two firms will create economies of scale or synergies. The proponents of the HP-Compaq and Northrop Grumman–TRW mergers described in Table 6.1 motivated the deals with economies-of-scale arguments.

The concepts of "economies of scale" and "synergies" have several dimensions that are worth clarifying. One aspect of scale economies comes from technical and engineering relations such as those between volume and surface area. In pipeline transportation, for example, scale economies are created because volume increases disproportionately to surface area.

Another natural economy of scale occurs in holding inventories when demand is subject to random influences. The statistical law of large numbers maintains that the larger the scale of operations is, the lower the required investment in inventories is in relation to the average quantity sold. Such improvements in inventory management often are facilitated by technological change and have been associated with mergers in grocery stores and other retail sectors.

Another important source of returns to scale is specialization. This was observed by Adam Smith in his famous example of producing pins. Firms of larger size might be able to organize production into specialist groups that emphasize a single task. Such gains suggest one reason why growing industries often experience mergers.

Returns to scale can be distinguished from improved capacity utilization that spreads fixed costs over a larger number of units. In industries such as steel and autos, consolidating mergers have taken place to reduce industry capacity. Technological change is often a factor, as in the case of the tire industry following the development of radial tires, which last longer than their predecessors.

Another distinction is between economies of scale and economies of scope. Economies of scope enable a firm to produce related additional products at a lower cost because of experience with existing products. One example is the pharmaceutical industry, where adding new drugs to a particular therapeutic class such as antibiotics provides benefits because of production experience and marketing utilization.

TRANSACTION COSTS AND MERGERS

Concepts such as economies of scale, synergies, and economies of scope suggest reasons why a merger *might* be an efficient decision. However, the technological factors do not guarantee that a merger will enhance profits. Indeed, technological factors such as gains from specialization often suggest reasons why a merger should not occur. If a supplier can produce an input more cheaply or a buyer can distribute a product less expensively, then it will not profit a firm to merge.

A cogent framework for merger decisions is provided in the analysis of Ronald Coase. In his 1937 research, Coase asked the fundamental question What determines the size of a firm? Within his analysis, Coase also inquired why and when firms would engage in horizontal combination or in vertical integration.

Coase's central insight was that a firm faces a variety of costs whether it makes something internally or instead relies on an outside supplier or distributor. He argued that decisions about firm size and mergers should be determined by the relative transactions costs within and outside the firm. Coase's model provides an important guide for managers considering a merger decision. Rather than assume that bigger is always better, Coase guides the manager to weigh transactions costs of separate versus merged entities before proceeding with a merger transaction.

In summary, this section has discussed some of the possible gains from a merger including the cost savings from economies of scale and better capacity utilization. This section also cautions that specialization is sometimes better achieved by avoiding the urge to merge. A succinct guide is provided by the insight of Ronald Coase, who isolates the merger decision into determining the comparative costs of operating together versus apart.

THEORIES OF THE VALUATION EFFECTS OF MERGERS AND ACQUISITIONS

In this section, we discuss the different theories about the predicted effects of mergers on firm value. The different theories are presented in Table 6.2. The theories range from those predicting that mergers increase firm value to those arguing that mergers reduce firm value. In some respects, the theories vary according to whether the managers making the decision to merge follow the Coasian transaction cost framework.

MERGERS AS VALUE-INCREASING DECISIONS

The theory by Coase (1937) that already has been discussed argued that mergers increase value. Cross-sectionally, Coase argued that the organization of a given firm responds to the appropriate balance between the costs of using the market and the costs of operating internally. Dynamically, Coase (1937) argued that firms will respond to forces such as technological change that alter the balance between the transaction costs of markets and internal production. A specific application of the Coasian theory of moving equilibrium is provided by Mitchell and Mulherin (1996) and is discussed in detail in Chapter 7.

Work by Bradley, Desai, and Kim (1983, 1988) is among the research that argues that mergers create synergies. They include in their definition of *synergies* economies of scale, more effective management, improved production techniques, and the combination of complementary resources. Bradley, Desai, and Kim (1983, p. 184) emphasized that the valuation increase predicted by the synergy theory requires an actual merger, as distinguished from an information theory that merely relies on the revaluation of assets that are the object of a takeover attempt.

TABLE 6.2 Theories of the Value Effects of Mergers and Acquisitions

Theoretical Principle	*Research Paper*
Value Increasing	
Transaction Cost Efficiency	Coase (1937)
Synergy	Bradley, Desai, and Kim (1983, 1988)
Disciplinary	Manne (1965)
	Alchian and Demsetz (1972)
Value Reducing	
Agency Costs of Free Cash Flow	Jensen (1986)
Management Entrenchment	Shleifer and Vishny (1989)
Value Neutral	
Hubris	Roll (1986)

An alternative theory regarding why a takeover transaction creates value is based on disciplinary motives. Manne (1965) and Alchian and Demsetz (1972) posed corporate takeovers as an integral component of the market for corporate control. The takeover market facilitates competition among different management teams. If the executives at a given firm are viewed as responsible for poor performance, another firm or management team can use an acquisition to remove the existing officers and thereby improve the performance of the acquired firm's assets.

MERGERS AS VALUE-REDUCING DECISIONS

In contrast to the theories based on transaction cost efficiency and synergy, a number of theories argue that mergers are a source of value reduction. To some extent, these theories are related to the disciplinary motive for a takeover. Indeed, in some models, disciplinary takeovers are a possible response to a value-reducing merger.

Jensen (1986) argued that free cash flow is a source of value-reducing mergers. A firm with high free cash flow is one where internal funds are in excess of the investments required to fund positive net present value (NPV) projects. As an example of his theory, Jensen (1986) cited the oil industry in the 1970s and concluded that substantial free cash flow in the industry subsequently led to value-reducing diversification decisions.

Another value-reducing theory of mergers is the Shleifer-Vishny (1989) model of managerial entrenchment. In the model, managers make investments that increase the managers' value to shareholders. Such management-specific investments do not enhance value to the shareholders themselves. Consistent with the model of Jensen (1986), managers in the entrenchment model are hesitant to pay out cash to shareholders. Investments made by the managers can be in the form of acquisitions in which the managers overpay but lower the likelihood that they will be replaced.

MANAGERIAL HUBRIS AND MERGERS

In an intriguing article, Richard Roll (1986) suggested a novel theory of merger bidding based on managerial hubris. In his model, markets are strong-form efficient (private information does not produce above normal returns) but individual managers are prone to excessive self-confidence. In such a model, the manager who has the most optimistic forecast of another firm's value falls prey to the winner's curse in a bidding competition.

The concept of the winner's curse has a long history in auction models. The setting for such models is one where a number of competing bidders vie for an asset or a firm. In such bidding, a distribution of value estimates arises naturally, possibly centered on the actual value of the asset or firm. The winner in such a setting is the bidder who has the highest estimate in the distribution. This winner, however, is cursed by the fact that having the highest bid in the distribution implies that the bid was, in all likelihood, higher than the asset or firm's actual value.

As applied to mergers, the hubris theory suggests that mergers can occur even if they have no effects on value. In cases where a merger bid is less than the target firm's value, the target does not sell. In cases where the bid exceeds the target's value, the target sells and what is gained by the target shareholders is a wealth transfer from the bidding firm's owners.

When written, the hubris theory was by no means in the mainstream of merger analysis. However, the article, among other things, directed researchers to consider the combined valuation effects of a merger, rather than simply examining the gains to the target firms. Roll (1986, p. 212) stated that "the hubris hypothesis can serve as the null hypothesis of corporate takeovers."

THEORETICAL PREDICTIONS OF THE PATTERNS OF GAINS IN TAKEOVERS

A useful way to summarize the different theories of mergers is to distinguish the empirical predictions of the different merger theories regarding the effect of mergers on target, bidder, and combined value. Such a framework is provided in Table 6.3.

The value-increasing theories of mergers based on efficiency and synergy predict that the combined value of the two merging firms will increase and, therefore, the merger will have a positive effect on firm value. If the gain in value to the target is not positive, the target shareholders will not sell. The gains to the bidding firm should be non-negative. If the gains are negative, then the bidding firm will not complete the deal.

The value-decreasing theories make alternative predictions. The agency cost and entrenchment models predict that a merger will have a negative effect on combined firm value. This is because any positive return to target shareholders is more than offset by the negative effect on the value of the bidding firm.

The hubris theory of takeovers suggests that the gain to the combined firm in a merger is zero. Any positive gain borne by the target shareholders is merely an offset from the overbidding by the buyer.

The framework presented in Table 6.3 is a straightforward manner in which to empirically distinguish the content of the different merger theories. Berkovitch and Narayanan (1993) noted, however, that any or all of the three main merger motives can be present in the sample in a particular empirical study. These authors suggest some refined tests to better distinguish the merger theories. Chapter 8 discusses such refinements in the analysis of the empirical research on the valuation effects of mergers.

THE MERGER PROCESS

Thus far, we have analyzed why mergers occur and their possible effects on firm value. We next turn to the related question of how the merger process unfolds.

The cases illustrated previously in Table 6.1 provide two examples of the merger process. Both cases indicate that mergers involve private and public preparation and negotiation. In the HP-Compaq transaction, much of the negotiation between the firms and their advisers took place in private and occurred before the initial public announcement of the deal. By contrast, much of the merger analysis and negotiation between Northrop Grumman and TRW took place in the public arena. In some respects, Northrop Grumman's strategy was consistent with Schwert's (2000) observation that takeovers viewed as hostile use publicity as part of the bar-

TABLE 6.3 Theoretical Predictions of the Patterns of Gains in Takeovers

Theory	Combined Gains	Gains to Target	Gains to Bidder
Efficiency/Synergy	positive	positive	nonnegative
Agency Costs/Entrenchment	negative	positive	more negative
Hubris	zero	positive	negative

gaining process. In the Northrop Grumman case, a seemingly important aspect of the "publicity" used with TRW was an increase in the bid price from $47 to $60.

This section delves further into the merger bidding process. The analysis complements the prior analysis in that the various bidding models make assumptions about the reason mergers occur, as well as the anticipated valuation effects.

AN EXAMPLE OF THE BIDDING PROCESS: THE ACQUISITION OF SAVANNAH FOODS

To begin a detailed analysis of the takeover bidding process, we consider the acquisition of Savannah Foods & Industries in 1997. Savannah Foods was a leading sugar refiner but was by no means the size of HP-Compaq or Northrop Grumman–TRW. Yet this case was somewhat more distinct than the other deals in that the process was initiated by the ultimate target firm and entailed multiple bidders, the payment of termination fees, and a number of other bidding complexities. This case sets the stage for a review of the important aspects of takeover bidding models. The information presented in the case was taken from the SEC EDGAR filings and from the financial media.

The details of the Savannah Foods acquisition are outlined in Table 6.4. The merger process began in March 1996 when the board of directors of the company requested that management develop a plan to improve stockholder value. The plan that arose included maximizing the value of the core sugar business while at the same time considering acquisitions in related areas. The first stage of discussions in May and July of 1996 with possible acquisitions candidates and merger partners, however, produced no formal actions.

In mid to late 1996, Savannah Foods had sequential discussions with two possible merger partners. One company, Flo-Sun, Incorporated, was a privately held sugarcane grower that was interested in a vertical merger with Savannah Foods. The other company was in the food industry and was interested in a diversification move into sugar. In April and May of 1997, both of the potential bidders made merger proposals. After consideration, the board of Savannah Foods elected to terminate discussions with the diversification candidate and to enter serious discussions with Flo-Sun.

The negotiations with Flo-Sun led to a merger agreement that was announced on July 15, 1997. Under the terms of the agreement, the companies would merge and the shareholders of Savannah Foods would own 41.5% of the new entity. The stock market did not view the terms of this deal as favorable to holders of Savannah Foods. The price of the company fell 15.7%, from $18.6875 to $15.75, on the day the agreement was announced. Ten days later, a flurry of shareholder lawsuits arose over the terms of the merger.

Soon after the announcement of the deal between Savannah Foods and Flo-Sun, another sugar-refining company, Imperial Holly, contacted the investment banking firm Lehman Brothers. Imperial Holly asked Lehman Brothers to develop some possible acquisition strategies related to Savannah Foods. Following these efforts, Imperial Holly made a competing offer for Savannah Foods for $18.75 per share, with 70% to be paid in cash and 30% to be paid in stock. Flo-Sun was formally notified of this offer and on September 4, 1997, upped its bid by changing the ownership in its proposed merger so that Savannah Foods would own 45% of the new firm and the shareholders of Savannah Foods also would receive $4 in cash.

On September 8, 1997, Savannah Foods asked both bidders to submit their best and final offers. Imperial Holly responded by upping its bid to $20.25 per share. Flo-Sun stood by its most recent offer. On September 12, 1997, Savannah Foods ended the agreement previously made with Flo-Sun by paying a $5 million termination fee. Savannah Foods executed a merger agreement with Imperial Holly.

TABLE 6.4 Example of the Bidding Process: Acquisition of Savannah Food & Industries in 1997

Date	Event
March 1996	Meeting of the board of directors of Savannah Foods Board asks management for plan to improve stockholder value Management aims to maximize value of existing sugar business Also to consider diversifying, food-related acquisitions
May 1996	Investment banks present acquisition candidates; no action
July 1996	Discussions with firms in beet sugar industry; no action
August 1996	Preliminary discussions with Flo-Sun, Inc., sugarcane grower
February 1997	Confidentiality agreement with Flo-Sun, Inc.
May 12, 1997	Flo-Sun, Inc. privately proposes a business combination
November 1996	Firm outside sugar industry expresses interest in a combination
December 1996	Board of directors rejects proposed combination
April 1997	Same diversification candidate renews proposal
May 25, 1997	Discussions with diversification candidate terminated
July 15, 1997	Savannah Foods and Flo-Sun, Inc. announce a merger agreement Shareholders of Savannah Foods to own 41.5% of new company Price of Savannah Foods falls 15.7% (from $18.6875 to $15.75)
July 25, 1997	Savannah Foods sued by shareholders over proposed acquisition
July 16, 1997	Imperial Holly Corp., a sugar refiner, contacts Lehman Brothers
July 25, 1997	Lehman presents alternatives on an offer for Savannah Foods
August 25, 1997	Imperial offers $18.75 for Savannah Foods (70% cash; 30% stock)
September 4, 1997	Flo-Sun, Inc. revises offer Savannah Foods to own 45% of new company plus $4 in cash
September 8, 1997	Imperial and Flo-Sun both asked to submit best and final proposals
September 10, 1997	Imperial ups offer to $20.25 per share (70% cash; 30% stock) Flo-Sun stands by its offer of September 4
September 12, 1997	Savannah Foods pays Flo-Sun a $5 million termination fee; executes merger with Imperial Holly

Source: SEC EDGAR filings and the financial media.

MODELS OF THE TAKEOVER BIDDING PROCESS

The Savannah Foods case as well as the HP-Compaq and Northrop Grumman–TRW deals raise a number of questions related to the takeover bidding process. From the perspective of the bidding firm, these questions include whether to pay in cash or in stock, whether to negotiate directly with management or instead make an offer to shareholders, and whether to buy an initial stake in the target firm. From the perspective of the selling firm, or target, the questions include how to react to an initial bid, whether it makes sense to prescribe a termination fee for an initial bidder contractually, and whether to actively seek competing bids.

A number of models have been developed that address many of these questions. Assuming an efficiency motivation, the underlying issue considered in most of the models is simple: Both the buyer and the seller in a transaction want to make money. The models can quickly become complex, however, because of the many strategic interactions among the actual and potential players in a merger.

In this section, we touch upon some of the important aspects of the takeover bidding process. As shown in Table 6.5, we deal with issues faced by the bidder including responding to the winner's curse, whether to make a preemptive bid, and whether to obtain a toehold. From the seller's perspective, we address how exactly to sell the firm and whether to limit the number of bidders.

THE WINNER'S CURSE

As discussed in the context of Roll's (1986) hubris hypothesis of mergers, the bidders in a takeover attempt face a potential winner's curse. One response to the winner's curse would be to systematically shade any bid generated by the particular bidder's valuation models. Shading the bid too low, however, would lessen the likelihood of ever completing a wealth-enhancing merger.

As noted at the top of Table 6.5, Hansen (1987) suggested an alternative response to the winner's curse. At the root of the winner's curse problem is the lack of full knowledge about the target's value—knowledge that is presumably held by the target firm itself. In Hansen's (1987) model, a bidder that is concerned about the value of the target can offer stock rather than cash. With such an offer, the owners of the combined firm, both bidder and target shareholders, bear any costs of overbidding for the target at the time of the merger. In effect, the offer of stock is a contingent payment that internalizes the asymmetric information of the target firm.

BIDDER COSTS

In addition to the winner's curse, another important factor treated by the takeover bidding literature is the cost of making the acquisition that is borne by the bidder. For firms such as Northrop Grumman that initiate a takeover bid, significant legwork is required by the firm itself and its advisers to support the decision of what price to pay. Even in cases like that of Savannah Foods, where the ultimate target initiated the merger process, firms such as Flo-Sun or Imperial Holly incur expenses in developing their bids.

As modeled by Hirshleifer and Png (1989), the presence of bidding costs raises issues of especially interesting strategic interplay between the target firm and potential bidders. In their model, an initial bidder decides whether to make a preemptive bid that precludes other un-informed, potential bidders from making a competing offer. In this setting, the target firm can often receive a higher price if a single preemptive bid is made. In other words, because of the cost of bidding, it doesn't always pay the target to try to stimulate competing bids. The result that unencumbered bidding is not always beneficial to the target firm indicates the inherent complexity of the takeover process.

Another aspect of takeover bidding that is related to bidder costs is the termination fee. In many mergers, a bidder who makes a formal offer often requires a termination fee as part of

TABLE 6.5   Some Conceptual Issues in Takeover Bidding

Concept	Decision Variable	Research Paper
Winner's Curse	Cash versus Stock	Hansen (1987)
Bidder Costs	Preemptive Bid	Hirshleifer and Png (1989)
	Termination Fee	Officer (2003)
	Toehold	Chowdry and Jegadeesh (1994)
Seller Decisions	Auction Design	Bulow, Huang, and Klemperer (1999)
	Number of Bidders	French and McCormick (1984)

the merger agreement. For example, Flo-Sun was paid $5 million when its deal with Savannah Foods was terminated. One reason given for such fees is that in a world of costly bidding, the use of a termination fee is more likely to induce an initial offer. Officer (2003) offered analysis and empirical evidence on the use of termination fees in a sample of mergers.

A further choice variable faced by a potential bidder in a takeover is whether to obtain an initial stake, or toehold, prior to actively seeking control of the target firm. Chowdry and Jegadeesh (1994) modeled the decision of whether to obtain a toehold and how big the toehold should be. As in many models, the use of a toehold helps recoup bidding costs. The size of the toehold is shown to be a function of the expected synergies from the merger.

SELLER DECISIONS

Much of the auction literature focuses on the decisions from a bidder's perspective. However, any factor that affects bidders can have indirect and direct effects on sellers, meaning the target firms in takeovers.

Bulow, Huang, and Klemperer (1999) modeled the interactive effects of a bidder's toehold on the price received by the target firm. In cases where the competing bids come from financial bidders and an assumption of a common-values auction applies, an initial toehold by one bidder might deter active competition from other bidders and thereby lessen the gains to the selling firm. Bulow, Huang, and Klemperer (1999) suggested that a target firm can counteract this effect by the shaping of auction design.

French and McCormick (1984) more explicitly modeled the strategy of the selling firm in the face of costly bidding and an endogenous number of bidders. A central insight from their model is that in equilibrium, the selling firm bears the costs borne by the bidders in an auction. An implication of the model is that selling firms might want to limit the number of bidders making detailed evaluations of the value of the seller.

In summary, the real world of takeover bidding and the conceptual models of the process are complex. The information costs of valuing the target and determining the strategic fit of potential merger partners make the decision of the buyer and seller in a takeover bid important, yet difficult to specify.

Some of the results of the bidding models seem counterintuitive. For example, from different angles, Hirshleifer and Png (1989) and French and McCormick (1984) suggested that a seller might want to limit the competitiveness of the selling process. The logic behind such a result is that the number of bidders in an auction can indirectly affect the aggressiveness of any one bidder and also affects the combined net gains from the transaction.

To conclude the discussion of the takeover bidding process, we consider a final example that fits the auction setting of many of the formal models and that also has a sequential reduction of the number of bidders in the course of the auction.

AN EXAMPLE OF A TAKEOVER AUCTION

We conclude with the acquisition of Outlet Communications that occurred in 1995. The auction process that comprised the acquisition is outlined in Table 6.6. The example is taken from research on the restructuring process by Boone and Mulherin (2002).

Outlet Communications was an owner and operator of television stations. In late 1994, the firm's board of directors authorized management to explore various strategic alternatives to

TABLE 6.6 An Example of a Takeover Auction: Outlet Communications (1995)

Date	Event
Dec. 16, 1994	Board of Outlet Communications, an owner and operator of television stations, authorizes exploration of strategic alternatives
Feb. 7, 1995	Engages Goldman Sachs as financial adviser
March 21, 1995	Issues press release announcing retention of Goldman Sachs
March 1995	Board determines that offers be solicited via an auction process
March-May, 1995	Goldman Sachs contacts/is contacted by 80 interested parties
April-May 1995	Confidentiality agreements with 45 parties
May 17, 1995	Preliminary proposals from 12 parties; range of $32 to $38 8 preliminary bidders invited to further due diligence
June 28, 1995	Five bidders submit definitive proposals; range of $36.25 to $42.25 NBC's bid was $38 per share in GE common stock Bid from Renaissance Communications was $42.25 in cash
June 30, 1995	Board approves Renaissance merger agreement
July 28, 1995	Board receives written offer from NBC of $47.25 per share in cash
August 2, 1995	Terminates Renaissance agreement; approves NBC agreement

maximize shareholder value. In February 1995, the firm engaged Goldman Sachs to aid in the evaluation process.

In conjunction with publicly announcing the retention of Goldman Sachs, the board of directors determined that the firm be sold via an auction. In the initial stage of the auction, Goldman Sachs contacted or was contacted by 80 interested parties. Of these, 45 parties signed confidentiality agreements and received nonpublic information about the selling firm. By the middle of May 1995, preliminary bids were received from 12 parties with a price range from $32 to $38.

From the 12 preliminary bidders, 8 firms were invited to more extensive due diligence sessions. By June 28, 1995, 5 of these 8 firms submitted definitive proposals. The highest bid was $42.25 in cash by Renaissance Communications. Outlet Communications and Renaissance signed a merger agreement on June 30, 1995.

Before the deal between Renaissance and Outlet Communications was completed, NBC submitted a competing bid of $47.25 in cash. Note that NBC had participated in the previous round of bidding but offered only $38 in the stock of its parent firm, General Electric. After internal discussions and further interaction with Renaissance, the board of Outlet approved the merger with NBC.

This case of Outlet Communications conveys the complexity of the takeover bidding process. Moreover, the setting in the example is consistent with the structure of many of the formal models of takeover bidding that treat a takeover as a competitive auction.

An especially notable aspect of the Outlet Communications case is the sequential reduction of the number of potential bidders as the auction proceeds. For example, from the 12 firms that submitted preliminary bids, only 8 were invited to further due diligence. One possible reason that a selling firm would reduce the number of bidders at this stage would be to induce informative bids in the preliminary round. The complexities of the bidding process and the important decisions such as the number of firms invited to submit bids provide a ripe area for future theoretical and empirical research.

Summary

This chapter has reviewed theories and concepts on mergers and acquisitions. The questions that have been addressed include the underlying motivation for mergers, the possible effects of mergers on firm value, and the manner in which the merger process can unfold.

Economies of scale is a general term that often is used to motivate a merger. This concept can apply to technical relations between volume and surface area and also can stem from inventory management and the law of large numbers. A related reason for a merger is better capacity utilization that can lower a merged firm's average fixed costs.

The technological possibilities of economies of scale suggest why mergers *might* occur. However, bigger is not always better. Indeed, gains from specialization often suggest that firms should remain separate and weigh against having a merger.

The transaction cost framework of Ronald Coase provides a succinct standard for which managers can consider the desirability of a merger. The important question is whether it is cheaper to produce or distribute an item internally or instead to obtain the item from another firm.

A number of theories make predictions regarding the effects of a merger on firm value. Value-increasing theories based on efficiency and synergy predict that the combined value of the bidder and target firm will increase at the announcement of a merger. By contrast, theories based on agency costs and management entrenchment predict that the combined value of the merging firms will decline. Roll's hubris hypothesis predicts that mergers have no effect on combined value, because any gain to the target firm is merely a wealth transfer from the bidder.

The merger bidding process is often complex. The bidding firm faces decisions including how much to pay, whether to pay in cash or stock, and whether to obtain a stake in the target, or toehold, prior to actively pursuing the merger. The selling firm faces decisions such as whether to offer a termination fee in case the merger is canceled, whether to negotiate exclusively with a single bidder or instead conduct an auction, and whether to limit the number of bidding firms.

Questions

6.1 Compare and contrast economies of scale, specialization, and economies of scope.

6.2 Do the technological capabilities suggested by economies of scale and specialization always indicate that a merger should occur?

6.3 What is Ronald Coase's main insight on the size of a firm? How does Coase's theory relate to the decision of whether or not to merge?

6.4 What are some reasons why a merger can increase value?

6.5 What are some reasons why a merger can decrease value?

6.6 What is the underlying setting for Roll's hubris theory of takeovers? What is the prediction of this theory for the effect of a merger on firm value?

6.7 What is the winner's curse? How can a bidding firm avoid this problem?

6.8 Why might a bidder obtain a toehold?

6.9 Consider the two mergers discussed in Table 6.1. Why do you think Hewlett-Packard and Compaq negotiated the merger privately but the negotiation in the Northrop Grumman and TRW deal occurred in the public arena?

6.10 Review the facts in the merger discussed in Table 6.4. Why do you think Savannah Foods was willing to pay Flo-Sun a fee when their agreement was terminated?

6.11 Consider the merger discussed in Table 6.6. Note that on May 17, 1995, Outlet Communications invited 8 preliminary bidders to further due diligence and information sharing. Why didn't Outlet Communications invite all 12 preliminary bidders to the next round of bidding?

References

Alchian, Armen A., and Harold Demsetz, "Production, Information Costs, and Economic Organization," *American Economic Review* 62, December 1972, pp. 777–795.

Berkovitch, Elazar, and M. P. Narayanan, "Motives for Takeovers: An Empirical Investigation," *Journal of Financial and Quantitative Analysis* 28, September 1993, pp. 347–362.

Boone, Audra L., and J. Harold Mulherin, "Corporate Restructuring and Corporate Auctions," working paper, College of William and Mary and Claremont McKenna College, 2002.

Bradley, Michael, Anand Desai, and E. Han Kim, "The Rationale Behind Interfirm Tender Offers: Information or Synergy?" *Journal of Financial Economics* 11, 1983, pp. 183–206.

Bradley, Michael, Anand Desai, and E. Han Kim, "Synergistic Gains from Corporate Acquisitions and Their Division Between the Stockholders of Target and Acquiring Firms," *Journal of Financial Economics* 21, 1988, pp. 3–40.

Bulow, Jeremy, Ming Huang, and Paul Klemperer, "Toeholds and Takeovers," *Journal of Political Economy* 107, June 1999, pp. 427–454.

Chowdry, Bhagwan, and Narasimhan Jegadeesh, "Pre-Tender Offer Share Acquisition Strategy in Takeovers," *Journal of Financial and Quantitative Analysis* 29, March 1994, pp. 117–129.

Coase, R. H., "The Nature of the Firm," *Economica* 4, November 1937, pp. 386–405.

French, Kenneth R., and Robert E. McCormick, "Sealed Bids, Sunk Costs, and the Process of Competition," *Journal of Business* 57, 1984, pp. 417–441.

Hansen, Robert G., "A Theory for the Choice of Exchange Medium in Mergers and Acquisitions," *Journal of Business* 60, January 1987, pp. 75–95.

Hirshleifer, David, and I.P.L. Png, "Facilitation of Competing Bids and the Price of a Takeover Target," *Review of Financial Studies* 2, 1989, pp. 587–606.

Jensen, Michael C., "Agency Costs of Free Cash Flow, Corporate Finance, and Takeovers," *American Economic Review* 76, May 1986, pp. 323–329.

Manne, Henry G., "Mergers and the Market for Corporate Control," *Journal of Political Economy* 73, April 1965, pp. 110–120.

Mitchell, Mark L., and J. Harold Mulherin, "The Impact of Industry Shocks on Takeover and Restructuring Activity," *Journal of Financial Economics* 41, 1996, pp. 193–229.

Officer, Micah S., "Termination Fees in Mergers and Acquisitions," *Journal of Financial Economics*, forthcoming 2003.

Roll, Richard, "The Hubris Hypothesis of Corporate Takeovers," *Journal of Business* 59, April 1986, pp. 197–216.

Schwert, G. William, "Hostility in Takeovers: In the Eyes of the Beholder?" *Journal of Finance* 55, December 2000, pp. 2599–2640.

Shleifer, Andrei, and Robert M. Vishny, "Management Entrenchment: The Case of Manager-Specific Investments," *Journal of Financial Economics* 25, 1989, pp. 123–139.

APPENDIX A

A CHEMICAL INDUSTRY CASE STUDY

The chemical industry provides an excellent case study illustrating the concepts of Chapter 5 on strategy and Chapter 6 on theories of M&As. This appendix illustrates how patterns of restructuring and M&As have evolved in the chemical industry.

CHANGE FORCES

The major change forces that have propelled the increased pace of economic adjustment processes are technological change, the globalization of markets, and favorable financial and economic environments. The new technologies include advances in computers and related products that have transformed industrial processes, product proliferation, and new ways of doing business, illustrated by the Internet and "the Wal-Mart way." Improvements and cost reductions in communication and transportation have created a global economy. Industry boundaries have become blurred, with new competitive impacts coming from diverse and changing sources. These growing forces of competition have been reflected in deregulation in major industries such as financial services, medical services, and airlines and other forms of transportation. Strong economic growth, relatively favorable interest rate and financing environments, and rising equity and asset prices have facilitated the adjustment processes described.

CHARACTERISTICS OF THE CHEMICAL INDUSTRIES

Although the adjustment processes have followed the same general patterns exhibited by other segments of the economy, distinctive characteristics have influenced how the change forces have operated in the chemical industry. A rich body of literature is available on the characteristics of the chemical industries (see References to this appendix).

Mergers and acquisitions as a shorthand for adjustment and adaptive processes in firms are related to the economic characteristics of their industries. The U.S. chemical industry produces almost 2% of U.S. gross domestic product (GDP) making it the largest contributor to GDP among U.S. manufacturing industries (Arora, Landau, and Rosenberg, 1998, p. 6). The chemical industry is a high-tech, research-and-development–oriented industry that receives about 12% of patents granted annually. It produces more than 70,000 different products. Few industries exhibit the diversity and complexity of the chemical industry.

Certain characteristics are significant for an understanding of M&A processes within the chemical industry: The industry has many distinctive segments, a number of which overlap with the oil and other energy industries, as well as with pharmaceuticals and life sciences products. Two major types of firms have been identified. *All-around* companies operate in many areas. *Focused* firms operate in downstream specialized segments.

Research and development (R&D) performs a key role in the long-term viability of chemical firms. Because new R&D discoveries often do not fit into the firm's core businesses, the organization might require time to adjust effectively to the new products and might delay achieving significant economies of scope. A series of R&D efforts that result in "dry holes" will have a negative impact on sales and profitability, making the firm vulnerable to takeover.

In the chemical industry, innovations are imitated relatively rapidly by large competitors. The commoditization of products can occur relatively soon after innovations. This results in the familiar economic pattern of cobweb responses. Favorable profit margins induce large additions to capacity in existing and new entry firms, resulting in downward pressures on prices and returns. This problem has been aggravated in those segments of the chemical industry in which the process development of new products is performed by specialized engineering firms (SEFs) capable of installing turnkey chemical production plants. This speeds the diffusion of process information, making it more difficult for innovators to long sustain a competitive advantage. These market processes take place in a global setting and can affect even niche segments of the industry.

Chemical companies interact with other industries. As petrochemicals became a high percentage of chemical company production, oil refining and the chemical industries converged. Large oil companies were able to expand into the chemical industry more easily than the chemical companies could expand into oil refining. (Siu and Weston, 1996). The switch from coal to oil allowed the development of many organic chemicals, which revolutionized the industry with new products. In recent years, some firms shifted from oil to life sciences products. Synergies between the chemical business and life sciences activities have not been well established.

Chemicals is a keystone industry. Many products are related to chemicals. As an R&D–intensive industry, the chemical industry has been a source of new technologies that have diffused over many other industries. Chemicals are building blocks at every level of production in major economic segments of agriculture, construction, manufacturing, and the service industries (Arora, Landau, and Rosenberg, 1998). Chemical industry technological innovations have been important in individual industries, specifically textiles, petroleum refining, agriculture, rubber, automobiles, metals, health services, and construction.

The international competitiveness of other U.S. industries depends upon a strong U.S. chemical industry that can supply critical products of high quality and at competitive prices. For a number of chemical products, competition in foreign markets requires operations in foreign countries. Acquisitions are often a least-cost method of establishing operations abroad or a method of acquiring new capabilities and new product lines.

One of the adverse economic trends affecting the chemical industry stems from the changing structure of the economy. The increase in the service industries relative to manufacturing, construction, basic industries, and other major users of chemicals has caused a decline in the growth of chemical shipments in response to changes in GDP growth (U.S. Department of Commerce/ITC, 1999). In the 1960s, a 1% change in GDP growth was associated with a 2.9% change in growth of chemical shipments. By 1998, the 2.9% ratio had declined to 0.9%. Chemical shipments are not keeping up with the growth in the economy. Thus, secular trends represent a retardation factor for chemical industry growth. This is a massive influence that is difficult to overcome. This negative secular influence is aggravated further by the relative rapidity of commoditization of new products.

Entry into the chemical industries has been relatively easy. As noted, oil and gas companies have made substantial expansion into important segments of the chemical industry. The boundaries between pharmaceutical and chemical firms are blurred. Many important pharmaceutical firms started life as chemical companies. Important entrants into individual segments of the chemical industry have been established chemical, oil, and pharmaceutical firms. Thus, although some individual chemical firms may have a large market share in individual product segments of the chemical industry, their price and production policies are severely constrained by active and potential entrants. An important economic implication is that the relevant market for measuring the economic position of individual companies is the global chemical industry, not individual product segments in individual national markets. Especially important are foreign firms, many of which can make rapid entry by acquiring domestic firms whose capabilities provide an immediate market position with the potential for powerful expansion by combining strengths.

In many cases, new entrants into a segment have purchased activities divested by an established chemical firm. This is an empirical pattern for which the explanations are complex. Differences in bundles of capabilities and environments cause some activities to shrivel and fade in one firm and yet expand and thrive in another. Thus, substantial evidence supports the conclusion that entry into chemical industries is relatively easy, and movement between segments is taking place continuously.

M&AS IN THE CHEMICAL INDUSTRY

Mergers and acquisitions historically have performed a significant role in the evolution of the chemical industry. In Germany in 1926, the largest producers of organic chemicals consolidated into IG Farben. Apparently, this was the response of large dye makers to increasing competition from American companies (Da Rin, 1998). After World War II, the Allied powers restructured German industry. IG Farben was broken into its major constituent firms: Bayer, BASF, and Hoechst.

Also in 1926, the British government induced a merger to form Imperial Chemical Industries (ICI). Brunner, Mond was combined with another strong firm, Nobel, and joined with much weaker firms, United Alkali and the British Dye Corporation. This powerful aggregation had immediate access to the public equity markets. However, ICI suffered declines in market share over the years. A possible explanation is underperforming management with a lack of effective corporate governance due to its widely diffused ownership (Da Rin, 1998). In 1993, ICI spun off Zeneca, its pharmaceutical division. In May 1997, ICI bought four companies whose sales were 20% of ICI but whose operating profits were 68% of ICI. The four companies were National Starch, Quest, Unichema, and Crosfields. ICI's planned sale of $1 billion of chemical assets to DuPont and NL Industries in early 1999 was blocked by the U.S. Federal Trade Commission.

At the end of World War I, DuPont had substantial liquid assets from the wartime profits of its explosives division. This strong financial position and effective management led to innovation and diversification. This history is set forth in a detailed study covering the history of DuPont from 1902 to 1980 (Hounshell and Smith, 1988).

During the 1980s, DuPont was involved in more than 50 acquisitions and joint ventures, investing more than $10 billion. A major part of this investment was the purchase of Conoco and Consolidation Coal. In 1998, DuPont began spinning off Conoco. In 1999, it spent $7.7 billion to buy the 80% of Pioneer Hi-bred International it did not already own. *Fortune* magazine (April 26, 1999, p. 154) called this "trading oil for corn," saying that DuPont "hopes to use the corn grown with Pioneer seeds as the feedstocks for its bio-engineered chemicals." A DuPont release of July 7, 1999, announced plans to consolidate its coatings manufacturing facilities and to reorganize "other business activities" over a period of 9 months following the $1.8 billion acquisition of Herberts, a European coatings supplier.

These brief capsule histories of three major firms in the chemical industry illustrate the full panoply of acquisitions, alliances, restructuring, divestitures, and spin-offs. In the *Fortune* list of the global 500 (August 3, 1998), DuPont was ranked number 1 in chemicals, with sales of $41.3 billion. The offspring of IG Farben were ranked in the next three positions, each of which had sales of about $32 billion. Dow was fifth, with sales of $20 billion. ICI held the sixth position, with sales of $18 billion. It is interesting to note that ranks 7 through 12 were each from different countries, with sales of $15.4 billion for Rhone-Poulenc (France), $14.1 billion for Mitsubishi Chemical (Japan), $13.9 for Montedison (Italy), $13.6 for Norsk Hydro (Norway), $12.3 billion for Akzo

Nobel (Netherlands), and $11.6 billion for Henkel (Germany).

The size, complexity, dynamism, and turbulence of the chemical industry would be expected to produce a high level of merger activity. Our studies demonstrate that in any given year in the United States, five industries account for about 50% or more of total M&A activity by dollar value (*Mergerstat*, annual volumes). Yet, between 1981 and 1998, the category chemical, paints, and coatings was in the top five in only one year, placing number 5 in 1986. Over the total period 1981 to 1998, chemicals, paints, and coatings ranked 17th, accounting for some $83 billion of M&A activity in relation to a U.S. total for the 18 years of $4.7 trillion. The top three industries were banking and finance with $641 billion, communications with $385 billion, and oil and gas with $345 billion.

A partial resolution of the paradox between the size and complexity of the chemical industry and its relatively low ranking in M&A activity is provided by classification ambiguities. For example, a Chemical Manufacturer's Association listing of 31 mergers and acquisitions of more than $500 million in 1998 includes pharmaceutical and other life sciences firms, as well as oil and gas industry combinations. The two major producers of M&A statistical compilations, Mergerstat and the Securities Data Corporation, have separate categories for the latter two groups. Using the broader definition of chemical and related industries as a category establishes this area as one of the top ranking ones in M&A activity. Change forces have impacted industries generally but have had greater effect in industries such as chemicals that are characterized by a high rate of innovations in processes and products, as well as relatively easy entry conditions.

A number of important roles have been played by M&As in the chemical industry. They have been (1) to strengthen an existing product line by adding capabilities or extending geographic markets, (2) to add new product lines, (3) to make foreign acquisitions to obtain new capabilities or a needed presence in local markets, (4) to obtain key scientists for the development of particular R&D programs, (5) to reduce costs by eliminating duplicate activities and shrinking capacity to improve sales-to-capacity relationships, (6) to divest activities that were not performing well, (7) to harvest successful operations in advance of competitor programs to expand capacity and output, (8) to round out product lines, (9) to strengthen distribution systems, (10) to move the firm into new growth areas, (11) to expand to the critical mass required for effective utilization of large investment outlays, (12) to create broader technology platforms, and (13) to achieve vertical integration.

In summary, M&As can enable firms to revisit and refresh their strategic visions. M&As also may reduce the time required to catch up to other firms that have developed new technologies, new processes, and new products. M&As enable a firm to make changes more rapidly. The cost of new projects is known at the time of purchase. By obtaining an existing organization, the delays in the learning process are reduced or avoided.

However, M&As and internal new product programs are not mutually exclusive. One can reinforce the other. A disadvantage of internal programs is that the firm might lack the requisite experience, it might not have an effective operating organization in place, and the time required for achieving a profitable market position is uncertain.

Acquisitions have different kinds of disadvantages. Despite due diligence, it is impossible for the buyer to know as much about what is being acquired as the seller. Implementing two organizations is not easy. Considerable executive talent and time commitments are required. Implementation problems are magnified if the organizational cultures are different. This is often a serious challenge in cross-border transactions.

Joint ventures have been used widely in the chemical industries. Because the areas of expertise are so diverse, it is difficult for a firm to embrace all of them. Often the size of the investment and the risks involved can be reduced by combining the different areas of expertise and capabilities of different companies. Joint ventures, strategic alliances, and the joint use of facilities can minimize investment outlays and magnify capabilities. For every merger, many more joint venture types of activities exist. By forming alliances and joint ventures, outlays and risks are reduced, learning can be achieved, and returns can be attractive.

We emphasize that M&As represent a shorthand for a wide range of adjustments and adaptations to changing technologies, changing markets, and changing competitive thrusts. The many forms of restructuring include spin-offs and split-ups to realign organization systems. The goal, is to group activities so that the benefits of relatedness, focus, and the development of distinctive and superior expertise in each area

of activity can be achieved. Organization restructuring also is used to group related activities and to better measure their performance. Compensation systems can thereby be related to performance more effectively.

Restructuring and M&As include changes in financial policies and effectiveness. One aspect is to review cost structures to improve the utilization of investments in receivables, inventories, and plant and equipment. The other side of this coin is effective utilization of financing sources. Dow Chemical is legendary for its innovative use of dividend policy, equity financing, and aggressive debt leverage to facilitate its growth.

The chemical industry also has made considerable use of highly leveraged restructuring such as leveraged buyouts (LBOs) and management buyouts (MBOs) (Lane, 1993). The key logic of LBOs (covered in Chapter 16) can be summarized. A company is identified that has stable earnings or earnings growth potential from an improvement in strategy, operations, or management (a turnaround potential). High leverage is initially employed to finance investment requirements needed for the turnaround and to buy out previous owners. Management is given an opportunity to buy equity shares representing a significant fraction of the shrunken ownership base. The stable or augmented future cash flows are used to pay down debt and to increase the portion of cash flows available to equity holders. The aim is to increase equity prices so that within at least 3 years, the company could be taken public again, realizing large gains to the organizers of the buyout and management.

The early 1980s offered opportunities to buy segments or companies at low price-to-cash flow multiples, with opportunities to improve efficiency and financial performance. Early successes led to the expansion of large buyout funds, which in turn led to competition for the dwindling opportunities and payment of higher price-to-cash flow multiples. LBO activity revived in the 1990s with greater sophistication and more direct participation by financial investors. Cain Chemical and Vista Chemical were financial groups that were active in the chemical industry.

A scaled-down version of LBOs has been the use of share repurchases. The most prevalent form is open market repurchases of a firm's own shares. The announcement of share repurchases is taken as a signal of future improvements in cash flows. Such announcements on average have stimulated significant immediate share price increases, as well as superior market performance in the ensuing 3 years. The subsequent improvement in cash flows makes share repurchase announcements credible signals on average.

However, some manipulative financial engineering also can be involved. The reduction in the number of shares outstanding will increase reported earnings per share even if total net income does not increase. For given net income levels, the ratio of net income to shareholders' equity is artificially increased when the market-to-book ratio exceeds 1, because the reduction of book equity is magnified. For example, if book equity is $10 per share and the market price is $30 per share, the reduction in shareholders' equity from a share repurchase will be $30 per share, according to usual accounting practice, shrinking book equity per share by a factor of 3. For the share repurchase practice to remain a credible signal of improved future cash flows, this mechanical aspect must be supported by substance—superior operating performance and good cash flows. One positive aspect is that returning funds to shareholders can create confidence that management is responsibly giving shareholders the opportunity to invest the funds in alternatives that may provide higher returns. Another positive impact is that share repurchases might be regarded as a signal of broader management efforts to improve the efficiency and profitability of the firm.

We find evidence that M&As and restructuring in their broadest meaning have been important in the chemical industries. In one study, we analyzed the chemical companies followed by Value Line in three groups: basic chemicals, diversified chemicals, and specialty chemicals. We found that every firm in their listings had engaged in one or more of the forms of restructuring—M&As in the broad sense described above. The results are summarized in Table A6.1.

It is clear that each of these firms from this Value Line sample has engaged in some form of acquisition, divestiture, joint venture, share repurchase, and so on. These many forms of M&As and restructuring in the chemical industry parallel similar activities in other industries. The nature of the adjustment processes can be made more specific. Table A6.2 briefly describes the reasons for the M&A activities listed in Table A6.1, augmented by a Chemical Manufacturers Association (CMA) list of 31 M&A deals of more than $500 million that took place in 1998.

The diverse reasons for the merger activities described in Table A6.2 are summarized in Table A6.3. They reflect general change forces, as well as the particular characteristics of the chemical industry. The central influences are improving technology, broadening capabilities, adjusting to industry structure change, and responding to the pressures of commoditization of products.

These examples illustrate the multiple roles that M&As have performed in the adjustment processes in the chemical industry (Filipello, 1999).

EFFECTS ON CONCENTRATION

Concern has been expressed that the rising tide of M&A activity might have undesirable impacts on industry structures. Specifically, the issue has been raised of whether increases in industry concentration will have adverse effects on competition. Considerable evidence has demonstrated that the degree of concentration does not predict the nature or intensity of competition in an industry (see Weston, 1978). Nevertheless, some still believe in this numbers game, so it will be addressed.

In our description of the nature of the chemical industry, it was established that the relevant market for analysis would be the world industry. We begin with the U.S. market because of the availability of reliable data. We then make estimates for the world market.

Concentration will be measured by the Herfindahl-Hirschman Index (HHI), an index named after the economists who developed it, Herfindahl and Hirschman. This is the measure adopted in the antitrust guidelines first issued by the Federal Trade Commission and Department of Justice in 1982 and retained in subsequent modifications. The HHI is measured by the sum of the squares of the market shares of all firms in an industry. For example, if an industry has 20 firms, each with a market share of 5%, the HHI would be 20×25, or 500. If the industry included only 10 firms, each with a market share of 10%, the HHI would be 10×100, which equals 1,000. With 50 firms with a market share of 2% each, the HHI would be 50×4, which equals 200. This illustrates that more concentration results in a higher index, and less concentration results in a lower index. Assigning equal market shares is artificial, but it simplifies the arithmetic.

The guidelines have specified critical levels for the HHI. Below 1,000, concentration is considered sufficiently low that no further investigation is required to determine the possible effects of a merger

TABLE A6.1   M&A Adjustments in the Value Line Chemical Industries

Company	*Restructuring Activity*
Basic Chemical Companies	
Dow Chemical	Acquired Mycogen
DuPont	Divestiture of Conoco
Union Carbide	Repurchased shares
Diversified Companies	
Air Products	Repurchased shares
Eastman Chemical	Made deal to acquire Lawter International
W. R. Grace	Purchased Sealed Air
Imperial Chemical (ICI)	Sold commodity chemical divisions
Minnesota Mining and Manufacturing	Repurchased shares
Norsk Hydro	Made tender offer for Saga Petroleum
Novo-Nordisk	Various joint ventures
PPG Industries	Made or announced 15 acquisitions since 1997
Pall Corp.	Repurchased shares
Rhone-Poulenc	Planned merger with Hoechst
Specialty Companies	
Airgas	Acquired Oxygen Sales & Service
Crompton & Knowles	Agreed to merger with Witco Corp.
Engelhard	Repurchased shares
Great Lakes Chemical	Purchased NSC Technologies
Hercules	Purchased BetzDearborn
International Flavors and Fragrance	Divested aroma chemicals
Morton International	Purchased by Rohm & Haas
Nalco Chemical	Purchased by Suez Lyonnaise
Praxair	Acquired division of GP Industries
RPM	Repurchased shares
Rohm & Haas	Purchased Morton International
Sherwin-Williams	Purchased Marson Chilena
Sigma-Aldrich	Purchased Genosys
Valspar	Acquired Dexter

or joint venture on competition. If a premerger HHI was between 1,000 and 1,800 and the index has been increased by 100 or more, the merger will be investigated. If the industry HHI was more than 1,800 and has been increased by at least 50, the merger will be challenged. Thus, if the industry consisted of one firm with 40% and six firms each with 10% of industry revenues and one of the six was acquired by the largest firm, the new HHI would be 50 squared plus 500, resulting in an industry measure of 3,000. It would clearly violate the antitrust guidelines, because

the HHI exceeded 1,800 to begin with and was increased by 800 points.

Using data of annual chemical sales in the United States by firm presented in *Chemical & Engineering News (C&EN)*, we calculated HHIs for the U.S. chemical industry. The HHI in 1980 was 178, declining to 148 in 1990 and to 102 in 1998. Therefore, the HHI for the U.S. chemical industry is far below the critical 1,000 specified in the guidelines. Furthermore, the trend has been strongly downward. How can the HHI decline when M&A activity is

TABLE A6.2 Chemical Industry—Reasons for Merging or Divesting

Companies	Reasons	Type[a]
Dow Chemical/Mycogen	Leverage Mycogen's biotech capabilities throughout Dow and merge agricultural and medicine operations.	A, C, F, H
DuPont/Conoco (spin-off)	To avoid the volatility of the oil and gas industry.	F, I
Eastman/Lawter	To pursue growth opportunities in specialty chemicals, which are characterized by higher earnings and lower cyclicality.	A, C, F, I
W. R. Grace/Sealed Air	Combines specialty chemical business for synergies, expanded global reach, and ability to compete in changing marketplace.	F, I
Imperial Chemical (divestitures)	Strategic shift toward speciality products and paints.	B, I
Norsk Hydro/Saga Petroleum	Greater activity, lower cost, and increased expertise in the oil and gas industry.	F
PPG Industries (15 acquisitions)	To sustain growth with profitable acquisitions in higher-margin businesses.	A, B, C, I
Rhone-Poulenc/Hoechst	Focus on life sciences and divest all remaining chemical businesses.	A, B, I, J
Airgas/Oxygen Sales and Service	Invest in core distribution segment.	D, F
Crompton & Knowles/Witco	Consolidated industry size increases strategic options and lowers cost of capital.	C, F
Hercules/Betz Dearborn	Combined company will be able to meet paper manufacturers' growing demand for integrated services.	K
Rohm & Haas/Morton	Expanded product lines, greater technical depth, and broader geographic reach.	C, K
Suez Lyonnaise/Nalco	Will be better able to provide customers with range of services they desire; will take advantage of cross-selling opportunities.	F, K
Praxair/GP Industries	Strategic acquisition that is part of company focus on health care as a key growth area.	B, C, I
Sherwin-Williams/Marson Chilena	Acquisition is part of the companies' continued interest in Chile and South America.	D
Sigma-Aldrich/Genosys	Acquisition is part of Sigma's strategy to move into the molecular biology field.	A, B, I
Lyondell/Arco Chemical	Gains preeminent global market position in propylene oxide. Goal is to reduce cyclicality of earnings by broadening the product mix. Provides a platform for future domestic and international growth.	D, F
Equistar II (combination)	Diversify product line, improve distribution network	F, K

[a]See Table A6.3.

increasing? The answer lies in the intensity of competition. Manifestations include divestitures, spin-offs, carve-outs, and downsizing, among others. Also, in the chemical industry, many new firms have come into being as a result of divestitures.

We attempted to estimate the HHI for the world chemical industry. Compilations of chemical industry firms in the *Fortune* global list and other sources do not break out chemical sales as C&EN does for chemical sales in the United States. *Fortune* and other compilers overstate chemical sales, as the total company sales include products other than chemicals. These compilations also might not include in their chemical industry groupings petroleum and pharma-

TABLE A6.3   Reasons for Mergers

A. Technologically dynamic industries to seize opportunities in industries with developing technologies
B. To develop a new strategic vision
C. To apply a broad range of capabilities and managerial skills in new areas
D. International competition—to establish presence in foreign markets and strengthen position in domestic market
E. Deregulation—relaxation of government barriers
F. Industry excess capacity and need to cut costs
G. Industry roll ups—consolidation of fragmented industries
H. Change in strategic scientific segment of the industry
I. Shift from overcapacity area to area with more favorable sale-to-capacity ratios
J. Exit a product area that has become commoditized to area of specialty
K. Combined company can better meet customers' demands for a wide range of services; strengthens distribution systems.

ceutical companies with substantial sales in chemicals. Our best judgment of the HHI for the world chemical market is that it is significantly below the critical 1,000 level and that it is probably declining for the same reasons that the HHI for the U.S. market has been declining over time—new entries and competitive forces that have reduced firm size inequalities.

We conclude that concentration in the chemical industries has been relatively low and decreasing over time. Mergers and acquisitions and related activities in chemicals reflect the forces of change and the dynamics of competitive actions and reactions. The pace of new product introductions has increased. Product life cycles have been shortened. The numbers of competitors have increased. Competitors from one industry segment are invading other industry segments. Industry boundaries continue to blur. Concentration has declined, and competition has intensified in the evolution of the chemical industries.

SUMMARY

The high rate of M&A activity is being propelled by powerful change forces supported by favorable economic and financing environments. Rapid advances in technologies have led to the globalization of markets and increased intensity of competition. These forces have been magnified in the chemical industry, the most R&D–intensive in the economy.

The innovation activities in the chemical industry are reflected in its high ranking in the annual number of patents granted. Research and development efforts represent activities of high risk that should be associated with high returns—a basic principle of financial economics. However, the achievement of such results has faced formidable challenges in the chemical industry. A secular problem has been that structural changes in the economy have produced relatively higher growth in the service industries (where chemicals are less important) than in the other major users of chemicals. This problem is compounded by the rapidity with which innovations by one chemical firm are diffused to competitors. Innovative products become commodities in relatively short periods of time. Thus, the impacts of the major change forces are even stronger in the chemical industry.

As a consequence, the chemical industry throughout its long history has been characterized by adjustments and restructuring. The many forms of restructuring—mergers, joint ventures, cross-border transactions, divestitures, spin-offs, share repurchase programs—are actively employed by chemical companies. They represent competitive responses to turbulent environments and vigorous competitive moves and countermoves.

QUESTIONS

A6.1 Explain why the chemical industry's share of gross domestic product has been declining.

A6.2 What has been the impact of the specialized engineering firms (SEFs) in the industry?

REFERENCES

Arora, Ashish, Ralph Landau, and Nathan Rosenberg, eds., *Chemicals and Long-Term Economic Growth*, New York: John Wiley & Sons, 1998.

Chemical and Engineering News publications.

Chemical Manufacturers Association publications.

Da Rin, Marco in Arora, Ashish, R. Landau, and N. Rosenberg, eds., *Chemicals and Long-Term Economic Growth*, New York: John Wiley & Sons, 1998, p. 320.

Donaldson, Lufkin, and Jenrette, *Specialty Chemicals*, 21 June 1999.

Filipello, A. Nicholas, "The Evolution of Restructuring: Seizing Change to Create Value," *Business Economics*, January 1999, pp. 25–28.

"The *Fortune* Global 500," *Fortune*, 3 August 1998, p. F-17.

Houlihan Lokey Howard and Zukin, *Mergerstat Review*, annual volumes.

Hounshell, D. A., and J. K. Smith, *Science and Strategy: DuPont R&D 1902–1980*, Cambridge, U.K.: Cambridge University Press, 1988.

Lane, Sarah J., "Corporate Restructuring in the Chemicals Industry," in Margaret M. Blair, ed., *The Deal Decade*, Washington, DC: The Brookings Institution, 1993, pp. 239–287.

Siu, Juan A., and J. Fred Weston, "Restructuring in the U.S. Oil Industry," *Journal of Energy Finance & Development* 1, No. 2, 1996, pp. 113–131.

Standard & Poor's, *Industry Surveys*.

Taylor, Alex, III, "Why DuPont Is Trading Oil for Corn," *Fortune*, 26 April 1999, pp. 154–160.

U.S. Department of Commerce/International Trade Administration, *U.S. Industry & Trade Outlook 99*, Chapter 11, New York: McGraw-Hill, 1999.

Value Line Investment Survey, *Ratings & Reports*, April through July 1999.

Weston, J. Fred, *Concentration and Efficiency: The Other Side of the Monopoly Issue*, Special Issues in the Public Interest No. 4, New York: Hudson Institute, 1978.

APPENDIX B

MEASUREMENT OF ABNORMAL RETURNS

STEPS IN CALCULATION OF RESIDUALS

The first step in measuring the effect of an "event" (announcement of a tender offer, share repurchase, and so on) on stock value is to define an event period. Usually, this is centered on the announcement date, which is designated day 0 in event time. The purpose of the event period is to capture all the effects on stock price of the event. Longer periods will ensure that all the effects are captured, but the estimate is subject to more noise in the data. Many studies choose a period like days –40 to +40, that is, from 40 days before the announcement to 40 days after the announcement. Note, day 0 is the date the announcement is made for a particular firm and will denote different calendar dates for different firms.

The next step is to calculate a predicted (or normal) return, $\hat{R}_{jt}$, for each day t in the event period for each firm j. The predicted return represents the return that would be expected if no event took place. Three basic methods can be used to calculate this predicted return. These are the mean adjusted return method, the market model method, and the market adjusted return method. For most cases, the three methods yield similar results. Next the residual, r_{jt}, is calculated for each day for each firm. The residual is the actual return for that day for the firm minus the predicted return, $r_{jt} = R_{jt} - \hat{R}_{jt}$. The residual represents the abnormal return, that is, the part of the return that is not predicted and is, therefore, an estimate of the change in firm value on that day, which is caused by the event. For each day in event time, the residuals are averaged across firms to produce the average residual for that day, AR_t, where

$$AR_t = \frac{\sum_j r_{jt}}{N}$$

and N is the number of firms in the sample. The reason for averaging across firms is that stock returns are "noisy," but the noise tends to cancel out when averaged across a large number of firms. Therefore, the more firms that are included in the sample, the better the ability is to distinguish the effect of an event. The final step is to cumulate the average residual for each day over the entire event period to produce the cumulative average residual or return, CAR, where

$$CAR = \sum_{t=-40}^{40} AR_t$$

The cumulative average residual represents the average total effect of the event across all firms over a specified time interval.

The Mean Adjusted Return Method

In the mean adjusted return method, a "clean" period is chosen, and the average daily return for the firm is estimated for this period. The clean period can be before the event period, after the event period, or both, but it never includes the event period. The clean period includes days on which no information related to the event is released, for example days −240 to −41. The predicted return for a firm for each day in the event period, using the mean adjusted return method, is just the mean daily return for the clean period for the firm. That is:

$$\hat{R}_{jt} = \overline{R}_j = \frac{\sum_{t=-240}^{-41} R_{jt}}{200}$$

This predicted return is then used to calculate the residuals, average residuals, and cumulative average residual as explained above.

The Market Model Method

To use the market model, a clean period is chosen, and the market model is estimated by running a regression for the days in this period. The market model is:

$$R_{jt} = \alpha_j + \beta_j R_{mt} + \varepsilon_{jt}$$

where R_{mt} is the return on a market index (for example, the S&P 500) for day t, β_j measures the sensitivity of firm j to the market—this is a measure of risk, α_j measures the mean return over the period not explained by the market, and ε_{jt} is a statistical error term $\Sigma \varepsilon_{jt} = 0$. The regression produces estimates of α_j and β_j; call these $\hat{\alpha}_j$ and $\hat{\beta}_j$. The predicted return for a firm for a day in the event period is the return given by the market model on that day using these estimates. That is:

$$\hat{R}_{jt} = \hat{\alpha}_j + \hat{\beta}_j R_{mt}$$

where now R_{mt} is the return on the market index for the actual day in the event period. Because the market model takes explicit account of the risk associated with the market and mean returns, it is the most widely used method.

The Market Adjusted Return Method

The market adjusted return method is the simplest of the methods. The predicted return for a firm for a day in the event period is just the return on the market index for that day. That is:

$$\hat{R}_{jt} = R_{mt}$$

The market adjusted return method can be thought of as an approximation to the market model where $\hat{\alpha}_j = 0$ and $\hat{\beta}_j = 1$ for all firms. Because $\hat{\alpha}_j$ is usually small and the average $\hat{\beta}_j$ over all firms is 1, this approximation usually produces acceptable results.

Illustrations

The first step for any event study is to determine the date of the announcement. The actual date of the first release of the information to the public is not easily obtainable. The best one can do is to check a source such as the *Wall Street Journal Index (WSJI)* for the earliest date and use an event window sufficient to cover the period. In our example, the events of interest are three major mergers in the oil industry: Chevron–Gulf (March 5, 1984), Mobil–Superior Oil (March 9, 1984), and Imperial Oil–Texaco Canada (January 19, 1989). We chose 40 days prior and 40 days after the earliest announcement date found in the *WSJI*. We refer to [−40, 40] as our event window.

To quantify the effects of the event on the stock returns, we need to calculate the residuals during the event window interval. The residuals are the difference between the actual stock return and a benchmark of what would have been the expected return if the event had not happened. Three methods are used to calculate the expected return. One is the **mean adjusted return method**. We use the mean return of the stock in a clean period prior to the event window as the expected return. In our example, we took 200 trading days prior to our event window to calculate a mean expected return for each firm. For illustration, let us consider the case of Chevron. The mean return from date −240 to −41 was found to be 0.00037 (see Table B6.1). Chevron's return on date −40 was 0.0036. Then $R1$, the mean adjusted residual on date −40 will be Chevron's return on date −40 minus the estimated mean return, or $0.0036 − 0.00037 = 0.00323 \approx 0.003$ (see first row $R1$ under Chevron columns in Table B6.2).

Two is the **market model method**. We use an expected return that takes into account the riskiness of the firm with respect to the market. The procedure involves a regression of the firm return series against a market index. The calculations must involve a period not included in the event window. We again used the 200 trading days returns prior to the event window and regressed them against a market index represented by the value-weighted CRSP index, which represents an aggregate of stocks including dividends traded in the major exchanges such as NYSE and AMEX. The regression of Chevron's returns against the returns of the CRSP index for the period −240 to −41 yielded an intercept, $\hat{\alpha}$, of −0.0005 and a slope, $\hat{\beta}$, of 1.2096 (see Table B6.1). On date −40, Chevron's return was 0.0036, and the CRSP market index return was 0.00431. $R2$, the market model adjusted residual, for date −40 will be $0.0036 − (−0.0005) − 1.2096 (0.00431) = −0.0011 \approx −0.001$ (see first row $R2$ under Chevron column in Table B6.2).

Three is the **market-adjusted return method**. The expected return for any stock is postulated to be just the market return for that particular day. Going back to our Chevron example, $R3$, the market adjusted residual, for date −40 will be $0.0036 − 0.00431 = −0.00071 \approx −0.001$ (see first row $R3$ under Chevron column in Table B6.2).

Table B6.2 shows the residuals for the three acquiring firms in our sample using the above three methods. Table B6.3 is a similar table corresponding to the target companies. The residuals are averaged across firms to obtain an average residual (AR) for each day in the event period. Three average residuals are presented corresponding to each of the above three methods. For example, $AR1$ for the acquiring companies is the average of the mean adjusted residu-

als: $R1$ Chevron, $R1$ Mobil, and $R1$ Imperial Oil. For date −40, $AR1 = 1/3[0.003 + (−0.014) + 0.031] = 0.007$ (see first row $AR1$ under Average Residuals columns in Table B6.2). $AR2$ is for the market model. $AR3$ represents the average residuals using the market adjusted method.

Finally, the average residuals are cumulated over the entire event period to obtain the cumulative average residual (CAR). For the acquiring firms in Table B6.2, the cumulative average residual based on the mean adjusted residual is defined as $CAR1$. On day −40, $CAR1$ is equal to 0.007, the $AR1$ on day −40. On day −39, $CAR1$ is equal to the sum of the $AR1$ values on days −40 and −39, or $0.007 + 0.007 = 0.014$. On day −38, the corresponding $CAR1$ would be $0.007 + 0.007 + 0.003 = 0.017$, and so on (see the $CAR1$ columns in Table B6.2). $CAR2$ and $CAR3$ are calculated in the same way.

The residuals, average residuals, and CARs for the target companies shown in Table B6.3 are calculated by following the same procedures. The CARs in Table B6.2 for the acquiring firms are graphed in Figure B6.1. We see a picture of a sharp rise in the CAR values from −40 to −5. A small decline is followed by a strong recovery. For this illustrative sample of three firms, the three methods give somewhat different results, but the patterns are parallel. Figure B6.2 graphs the data from Table B6.3 for target firms. The patterns are again similar, but the CAR values are much larger for the target companies.

Absolute Gains and Losses

Residual returns are also known as *abnormal returns* because they represent the return that was unexpected or different from the return that would have been expected if the event had not occurred. The absolute dollar gain or loss at time $t(\Delta W_t)$ due to the abnormal return during the event period is defined by

$$\Delta W_t = CAR_t \times MKTVAL_0$$

where $MKTVAL_0$ is the market value of the firm at a date previous to the event window interval, and CAR_t is the cumulative residuals to date t for the firm. The percent return times the market value of the firm is the total dollar gain or loss.

Table B6.4 presents the market-adjusted residual returns ($R3$) that were previously displayed in Tables B6.2 and B6.3. In Table B6.4, the $CAR3$ values are the cumulative abnormal returns obtained by cumulating the daily abnormal returns $R3$ for each individual firm.

TABLE B6.1 Parameters for Measuring Abnormal Returns

		Targets			Acquirers	
		Gulf Corp.	Superior Oil	Texaco Canada	Chevron	Mobil	Imperial Oil
M1: Mean adjusted return model	$\overline{R}_j$	0.0022	0.0012	0.0015	0.0004	0.0010	−0.0007
$R1 = r_{jt}$ $= R_{jt} - \overline{R}_j$							
M2: Market model method	$\hat{\alpha}_j$	0.0015	0.0005	0.0012	−0.0005	0.0001	−0.0010
$R2 = r_{jt}$ $= R_{jt} - \hat{\alpha}_j - \hat{\beta}_j R_{mt}$	$\hat{\beta}_j$	0.9702	1.0807	0.6233	1.2096	1.3665	0.5136
M3: Market adjusted return method $R3 = r_{jt}$ $= R_{jt} - R_{mt}$							

TABLE B6.2 Event Study for Acquiring Companies

Event Date	Chevron Corp.			Mobil Corp.			Imperial Oil Ltd.			AR1	AR2	AR3	CAR1	CAR2	CAR3
	R1	R2	R3	R1	R2	R3	R1	R2	R3						
										AVERAGE RESIDUALS			*CAR*		
−40	0.003	−0.001	−0.001	−0.014	0.013	−0.013	0.031	0.032	0.032	0.007	0.006	0.006	0.007	0.006	0.006
−39	0.000	0.003	0.002	−0.005	0.000	−0.001	0.027	0.026	0.023	0.007	0.010	0.008	0.014	0.016	0.014
−38	0.007	0.012	0.011	−0.005	−0.004	−0.004	0.007	0.004	0.000	0.003	0.004	0.002	0.017	0.020	0.017
−37	0.000	0.001	0.001	0.008	0.004	0.006	0.032	0.035	0.036	0.013	0.014	0.014	0.030	0.033	0.031
−36	0.007	0.008	0.007	0.003	0.006	0.006	0.004	0.002	−0.001	0.005	0.005	0.004	0.035	0.039	0.035
−35	0.007	0.012	0.010	0.025	0.029	0.028	−0.005	−0.009	−0.014	0.009	0.011	0.008	0.043	0.049	0.043
−34	−0.011	−0.010	−0.011	0.003	0.012	0.010	−0.005	−0.010	−0.015	−0.004	−0.003	−0.005	0.039	0.046	0.038
−33	−0.007	−0.010	−0.010	−0.013	0.000	−0.004	0.001	0.002	0.001	−0.007	−0.003	−0.004	0.032	0.043	0.034
−32	−0.018	−0.016	−0.016	0.024	0.020	0.022	0.001	0.002	0.002	0.002	0.002	0.002	0.034	0.046	0.036
−31	0.025	0.029	0.028	−0.005	0.004	0.002	0.001	−0.003	−0.009	0.007	0.010	0.007	0.041	0.055	0.043
−30	0.017	0.025	0.023	−0.001	0.006	0.004	0.007	0.003	−0.002	0.008	0.011	0.009	0.049	0.067	0.052
−29	0.000	0.011	0.009	−0.001	0.003	0.002	0.001	0.000	−0.001	0.000	0.005	0.003	0.049	0.071	0.055
−28	−0.014	−0.018	−0.017	0.011	0.024	0.021	0.001	0.003	0.004	−0.001	0.003	0.003	0.048	0.074	0.057
−27	0.010	0.018	0.016	0.009	0.008	0.008	−0.005	−0.006	−0.008	0.004	0.007	0.006	0.053	0.081	0.063
−26	−0.004	0.002	0.001	−0.013	−0.007	−0.008	−0.006	−0.004	−0.005	−0.008	−0.003	−0.004	0.045	0.078	0.059
−25	−0.004	0.000	−0.001	0.007	0.004	0.005	−0.009	−0.008	−0.008	−0.002	−0.001	−0.001	0.043	0.077	0.057
−24	0.017	0.028	0.026	−0.005	0.014	0.009	−0.002	−0.001	0.000	0.003	0.014	0.012	0.046	0.090	0.069
−23	0.013	0.013	0.012	−0.022	0.001	−0.004	−0.002	−0.001	0.000	−0.004	0.004	0.003	0.043	0.095	0.072
−22	−0.007	−0.001	−0.003	−0.005	−0.007	−0.006	0.010	0.007	0.003	−0.001	0.000	−0.002	0.042	0.095	0.070
−21	0.020	0.017	0.018	−0.018	0.005	0.000	0.017	0.013	0.009	0.006	0.012	0.009	0.049	0.107	0.078
−20	−0.017	−0.001	−0.004	−0.005	0.002	0.000	0.016	0.018	0.018	0.002	0.006	0.005	0.046	0.113	0.083
−19	−0.025	−0.005	−0.008	−0.001	−0.007	−0.005	0.004	0.004	0.003	−0.007	−0.003	−0.003	0.039	0.110	0.080
−18	−0.008	−0.009	−0.009	0.003	0.017	0.014	0.001	0.001	0.001	−0.001	0.003	0.002	0.038	0.114	0.082
−17	−0.022	−0.001	−0.005	0.003	−0.009	−0.005	0.010	0.008	0.005	−0.003	−0.001	−0.002	0.035	0.113	0.080
−16	−0.008	−0.001	−0.003	−0.005	−0.003	−0.003	0.007	0.008	0.009	−0.002	0.001	0.001	0.033	0.114	0.081
−15	0.003	−0.002	−0.002	−0.001	0.002	0.001	0.004	0.003	0.002	0.002	0.001	0.001	0.035	0.115	0.082
−14	0.003	0.016	0.013	0.029	0.033	0.032	0.007	0.004	−0.001	0.013	0.017	0.015	0.048	0.133	0.096
−13	0.007	−0.004	−0.002	−0.022	−0.012	−0.014	0.001	0.002	0.002	−0.005	−0.004	−0.005	0.043	0.128	0.092
−12	0.003	0.005	0.005	0.012	0.016	0.015	0.004	0.008	0.011	0.006	0.010	0.010	0.049	0.138	0.102
−11	0.011	0.013	0.012	0.007	0.011	0.010	0.010	0.003	−0.004	0.009	0.009	0.006	0.059	0.147	0.108

-10	0.122	0.160	0.079	0.014	0.013	0.020	0.027	0.029	0.030	-0.020	-0.027	-0.001	0.035	0.036	0.032
-9	0.142	0.179	0.101	0.020	0.020	0.022	0.020	0.022	0.024	0.025	0.021	0.036	0.014	0.016	0.007
-8	0.158	0.198	0.113	0.017	0.019	0.012	0.026	0.028	0.029	0.021	0.026	0.007	0.002	0.003	0.000
-7	0.157	0.198	0.112	-0.001	-0.001	-0.001	-0.012	-0.012	-0.013	-0.003	-0.004	-0.001	0.012	0.013	0.010
-6	0.151	0.190	0.116	-0.006	-0.007	0.004	-0.007	-0.004	-0.002	0.005	0.003	0.011	-0.016	-0.020	0.003
-5	0.158	0.196	0.130	0.006	0.006	0.014	0.004	0.007	0.009	-0.011	-0.014	-0.005	0.026	0.024	0.037
-4	0.152	0.193	0.117	-0.006	-0.003	-0.013	-0.002	0.000	0.001	-0.016	-0.014	-0.025	0.000	0.003	-0.014
-3	0.142	0.185	0.106	0.009	0.008	-0.011	0.002	0.000	0.001	0.011	0.007	-0.021	0.016	-0.016	-0.014
-2	0.133	0.177	0.094	-0.009	-0.008	-0.012	-0.001	-0.001	-0.002	0.007	0.010	-0.005	-0.034	-0.035	-0.027
-1	0.127	0.172	0.094	-0.006	-0.005	0.000	-0.009	-0.004	0.001	0.005	0.004	0.007	-0.014	-0.015	-0.007
0	0.128	0.175	0.092	0.001	0.006	-0.003	-0.005	-0.003	-0.002	0.000	0.002	-0.005	0.007	0.009	0.000
1	0.100	0.146	0.064	-0.028	-0.028	-0.028	-0.022	-0.021	-0.021	-0.027	-0.031	-0.018	-0.036	-0.033	-0.046
2	0.090	0.137	0.050	-0.009	-0.009	-0.013	-0.023	-0.024	-0.028	-0.008	-0.010	-0.005	0.003	0.006	-0.008
3	0.081	0.130	0.045	-0.009	-0.007	-0.005	-0.030	-0.025	-0.020	-0.004	-0.004	-0.005	0.008	0.008	0.011
4	0.087	0.136	0.051	0.005	0.006	0.006	0.000	0.003	0.004	0.004	0.002	0.007	0.012	0.013	0.007
5	0.083	0.132	0.057	-0.003	-0.004	0.006	-0.002	0.003	0.007	0.002	-0.002	0.012	-0.010	-0.012	0.000
6	0.077	0.128	0.052	-0.006	-0.004	-0.006	-0.006	-0.002	0.001	-0.004	-0.001	-0.013	-0.008	-0.008	-0.004
7	0.074	0.125	0.051	-0.004	-0.003	-0.001	-0.003	-0.001	0.001	0.003	0.001	0.007	-0.011	-0.010	-0.011
8	0.083	0.135	0.063	0.009	0.010	0.012	-0.013	-0.009	-0.005	0.030	0.030	0.028	0.010	0.010	0.014
9	0.077	0.130	0.057	-0.006	-0.005	-0.006	0.003	0.004	0.004	-0.010	-0.007	-0.021	-0.011	-0.012	0.000
10	0.073	0.128	0.051	-0.003	-0.002	-0.007	0.003	0.004	0.004	-0.004	-0.004	-0.005	-0.009	-0.007	-0.018
11	0.074	0.130	0.054	0.001	0.002	0.003	-0.001	0.000	0.001	-0.004	-0.004	-0.005	0.009	0.009	0.014
12	0.077	0.132	0.057	0.003	0.003	0.003	0.001	0.002	0.001	0.005	0.004	0.007	0.001	0.002	0.000
13	0.065	0.121	0.049	-0.012	-0.011	-0.008	-0.010	-0.004	-0.002	-0.018	-0.023	-0.005	-0.008	-0.006	-0.019
14	0.068	0.124	0.050	0.003	0.003	0.001	-0.001	-0.001	-0.008	0.005	0.005	0.003	0.004	0.005	0.003
15	0.076	0.132	0.056	0.009	0.008	0.006	-0.002	-0.004	-0.002	0.009	0.010	0.007	0.019	0.019	0.018
16	0.081	0.136	0.056	0.005	0.004	0.000	0.009	0.004	0.001	-0.006	-0.004	-0.013	0.012	0.011	0.014
17	0.086	0.141	0.064	0.005	0.005	0.008	-0.001	0.001	0.001	0.003	0.004	-0.001	0.011	0.009	0.025
18	0.094	0.150	0.071	0.009	0.009	0.008	0.007	0.007	0.007	0.005	0.005	0.003	0.015	0.015	0.014
19	0.110	0.170	0.084	0.016	0.019	0.013	0.005	0.009	0.013	0.015	0.020	-0.001	0.029	0.029	0.027

(continued)

TABLE B6.2 (cont.)

Event Date	Chevron Corp.			Mobil Corp.			Imperial Oil Ltd.			Average Residuals			CAR		
	R1	R2	R3	R1	R2	R3	R1	R2	R3	AR1	AR2	AR3	CAR1	CAR2	CAR3
20	0.000	0.008	0.006	-0.009	-0.009	-0.009	-0.005	-0.006	-0.008	-0.005	-0.002	-0.003	0.079	0.167	0.107
21	0.003	0.007	0.006	-0.001	0.000	0.000	-0.002	-0.005	-0.008	0.000	0.001	-0.001	0.079	0.168	0.106
22	-0.014	-0.012	-0.013	-0.001	-0.003	-0.002	-0.011	-0.010	-0.010	-0.009	-0.008	-0.008	0.071	0.160	0.098
23	-0.014	0.005	0.001	0.003	0.011	0.010	-0.011	-0.004	0.002	-0.007	0.004	0.004	0.063	0.164	0.102
24	0.003	0.004	0.003	0.024	0.006	0.011	0.001	-0.001	-0.003	0.009	0.003	0.004	0.073	0.167	0.106
25	0.010	0.011	0.011	0.011	0.013	0.013	-0.002	0.005	0.010	0.006	0.009	0.011	0.079	0.177	0.117
26	0.010	0.008	0.008	0.007	0.001	0.003	0.010	0.010	0.008	0.009	0.006	0.006	0.088	0.183	0.124
27	0.000	0.007	0.005	-0.005	-0.011	-0.009	-0.002	-0.004	-0.006	-0.003	-0.002	-0.003	0.085	0.180	0.120
28	0.036	0.020	0.023	-0.013	-0.005	-0.007	-0.005	-0.003	-0.003	0.006	0.004	0.004	0.091	0.184	0.125
29	0.006	0.007	0.007	0.015	0.016	0.016	0.025	0.021	0.016	0.015	0.015	0.013	0.107	0.199	0.138
30	0.016	0.011	0.011	-0.001	0.009	0.006	0.013	0.011	0.008	0.009	0.010	0.009	0.116	0.209	0.146
31	0.009	0.004	0.005	0.003	-0.004	-0.002	0.004	-0.001	-0.007	0.005	0.000	-0.001	0.121	0.209	0.145
32	-0.016	-0.009	-0.010	0.003	-0.001	0.001	0.004	0.005	0.004	-0.003	-0.002	-0.002	0.118	0.207	0.143
33	-0.013	-0.013	-0.013	-0.005	-0.018	-0.014	0.013	0.012	0.011	-0.002	-0.006	-0.005	0.116	0.201	0.138
34	-0.023	-0.014	-0.016	-0.001	0.001	0.001	0.015	0.016	0.015	-0.003	0.001	0.000	0.113	0.202	0.138
35	0.019	0.013	0.014	-0.009	-0.009	-0.009	0.001	0.002	0.002	0.004	0.002	0.003	0.117	0.204	0.140
36	0.000	-0.004	-0.003	0.001	-0.012	-0.008	0.024	0.021	0.017	0.008	0.002	0.002	0.125	0.206	0.142
37	0.013	0.001	0.003	-0.005	-0.010	-0.008	0.012	0.012	0.012	0.006	0.001	0.002	0.131	0.207	0.144
38	0.000	0.001	0.001	-0.013	-0.009	-0.010	0.017	0.016	0.013	0.001	0.003	0.001	0.133	0.210	0.145
39	0.009	0.009	0.009	-0.009	0.005	0.002	0.006	0.002	-0.002	0.002	0.006	0.003	0.135	0.215	0.148
40	-0.010	-0.021	-0.019	-0.001	-0.002	-0.002	-0.007	0.003	0.012	-0.006	-0.007	-0.003	0.129	0.209	0.144

Source: University of Chicago Center for Research on Security Prices (CRSP) tapes.

TABLE B6.3 Event Study for Target Companies

| | RESIDUALS | | | | | | | | | AVERAGE RESIDUALS | | | CAR | | |
| | Gulf Corp. | | | Superior Oil Corp. | | | Texaco Canada Ltd. | | | | | | | | |
Event Date	R1	R2	R3	R1	R2	R3	R1	R2	R3	AR1	AR2	AR3	CAR1	CAR2	CAR3
−40	0.054	0.051	0.052	−0.008	−0.007	−0.006	0.019	0.020	0.022	0.022	0.021	0.022	0.022	0.021	0.022
−39	0.006	0.009	0.010	0.015	0.020	0.020	0.022	0.021	0.021	0.014	0.016	0.017	0.036	0.038	0.039
−38	0.035	0.039	0.041	0.002	0.003	0.003	0.010	0.006	0.005	0.016	0.016	0.017	0.052	0.054	0.056
−37	−0.025	−0.024	−0.022	0.012	0.009	0.010	0.006	0.009	0.012	−0.002	−0.002	0.000	0.049	0.052	0.056
−36	0.019	0.020	0.021	−0.014	−0.012	−0.011	−0.009	−0.011	−0.011	−0.001	−0.001	0.000	0.048	0.051	0.055
−35	0.011	0.015	0.016	0.044	0.048	0.048	0.018	0.013	0.011	0.024	0.025	0.025	0.072	0.076	0.081
−34	−0.012	−0.012	−0.010	−0.004	0.002	0.002	0.017	0.012	0.010	0.000	0.001	0.001	0.072	0.077	0.081
−33	−0.007	−0.010	−0.008	−0.017	−0.006	−0.007	0.002	0.003	0.005	−0.007	−0.004	−0.003	0.065	0.073	0.078
−32	−0.007	−0.005	−0.004	−0.001	−0.004	−0.004	−0.013	−0.011	−0.009	−0.007	−0.007	−0.006	0.058	0.066	0.072
−31	−0.028	−0.025	−0.023	0.024	0.031	0.031	0.006	0.001	−0.001	0.001	0.002	0.002	0.059	0.068	0.075
−30	−0.002	0.004	0.006	−0.035	−0.030	−0.030	−0.002	−0.006	−0.008	−0.013	−0.011	−0.011	0.046	0.057	0.064
−29	0.011	0.020	0.022	0.046	0.049	0.050	0.032	0.031	0.032	0.030	0.034	0.035	0.075	0.091	0.099
−28	0.053	0.050	0.052	−0.025	−0.016	−0.016	−0.002	0.001	0.004	0.009	0.012	0.013	0.084	0.103	0.112
−27	0.010	0.016	0.018	0.039	0.038	0.039	−0.002	−0.002	−0.001	0.016	0.018	0.019	0.100	0.120	0.130
−26	−0.010	−0.005	−0.003	−0.016	−0.011	−0.011	−0.002	0.000	0.002	−0.009	−0.005	−0.004	0.091	0.115	0.126
−25	0.050	0.053	0.054	−0.004	−0.007	−0.006	−0.005	−0.004	−0.002	0.013	0.014	0.015	0.104	0.129	0.142
−24	0.007	0.016	0.018	−0.010	0.004	0.004	−0.009	−0.007	−0.004	−0.004	0.005	0.006	0.100	0.134	0.147
−23	−0.009	−0.010	−0.008	−0.020	−0.001	−0.002	−0.002	0.001	0.003	−0.010	−0.004	−0.003	0.090	0.130	0.145
−22	0.036	0.041	0.042	0.011	0.010	0.011	0.006	0.002	0.001	0.018	0.018	0.018	0.108	0.148	0.163
−21	0.048	0.046	0.047	−0.023	−0.004	−0.005	0.016	0.012	0.011	0.014	0.018	0.018	0.122	0.166	0.180
−20	−0.033	−0.020	−0.018	−0.011	−0.005	−0.005	−0.002	0.001	0.003	−0.015	−0.008	−0.007	0.107	0.158	0.174
−19	0.007	0.023	0.025	0.005	0.000	0.001	−0.002	−0.001	0.000	0.003	0.007	0.009	0.110	0.165	0.183
−18	−0.020	−0.021	−0.020	−0.014	−0.003	−0.003	0.006	0.006	0.008	−0.009	−0.006	−0.005	0.101	0.159	0.178
−17	−0.009	0.008	0.010	−0.001	−0.011	−0.010	0.005	0.003	0.003	−0.002	0.000	0.001	0.099	0.159	0.179
−16	0.037	0.042	0.044	0.040	0.042	0.043	0.005	0.007	0.010	0.028	0.031	0.032	0.127	0.190	0.211
−15	0.002	−0.002	−0.001	−0.007	−0.005	−0.005	0.012	0.012	0.012	0.002	0.001	0.002	0.129	0.191	0.213
−14	−0.057	−0.047	−0.045	0.005	0.008	0.009	0.016	0.012	0.010	−0.012	−0.009	−0.009	0.117	0.182	0.204
−13	0.065	0.057	0.058	−0.023	−0.015	−0.015	−0.008	−0.007	−0.005	0.011	0.012	0.013	0.128	0.194	0.217
−12	−0.035	−0.033	−0.031	−0.004	−0.001	−0.001	−0.002	0.004	0.008	−0.014	−0.010	−0.008	0.115	0.183	0.209
−11	−0.031	−0.029	−0.028	−0.026	−0.024	−0.023	−0.002	−0.009	−0.013	−0.020	−0.021	−0.021	0.095	0.163	0.187

(continued)

159

Event Date	Gulf Corp. R1	R2	R3	Superior Oil Corp. R1	R2	R3	Texaco Canada Ltd. R1	R2	R3	AVERAGE RESIDUALS AR1	AR2	AR3	CAR CAR1	CAR2	CAR3
−10	−0.002	0.001	0.002	0.018	−0.003	0.000	0.022	0.021	0.021	0.013	0.006	0.008	0.108	0.169	0.195
−9	−0.028	−0.020	−0.019	0.024	0.012	0.013	−0.002	−0.003	−0.003	−0.002	−0.004	−0.003	0.106	0.165	0.192
−8	0.107	0.110	0.111	−0.009	0.006	0.005	0.005	0.004	0.005	0.034	0.040	0.041	0.140	0.205	0.233
−7	0.094	0.097	0.098	0.008	0.006	0.007	−0.008	−0.007	−0.005	0.031	0.032	0.033	0.172	0.237	0.266
−6	−0.024	−0.042	−0.041	0.030	0.023	0.024	−0.002	−0.004	−0.005	0.002	−0.008	−0.007	0.173	0.229	0.259
−5	0.092	0.081	0.082	−0.019	−0.026	−0.025	−0.011	−0.014	−0.014	0.020	0.014	0.014	0.193	0.243	0.273
−4	0.007	0.021	0.022	0.002	0.010	0.010	0.039	0.038	0.039	0.016	0.023	0.024	0.209	0.266	0.297
−3	−0.004	−0.006	−0.004	−0.016	−0.005	−0.006	−0.009	−0.010	−0.009	−0.010	−0.007	−0.006	0.199	0.259	0.291
−2	0.005	−0.001	0.000	−0.035	−0.023	−0.023	0.006	0.008	0.009	−0.008	−0.005	−0.005	0.191	0.254	0.286
−1	−0.002	−0.008	−0.007	−0.043	−0.046	−0.045	0.002	−0.003	−0.005	−0.014	−0.019	−0.019	0.177	0.235	0.267
0	0.016	0.024	0.025	0.049	0.054	0.055	0.002	0.001	0.002	0.022	0.026	0.027	0.199	0.261	0.294
1	−0.023	−0.013	−0.012	0.008	−0.002	−0.001	0.029	0.029	0.030	0.005	0.005	0.006	0.204	0.265	0.300
2	−0.067	−0.056	−0.054	−0.042	−0.046	−0.045	0.002	0.006	0.009	−0.036	−0.032	−0.030	0.168	0.233	0.270
3	0.033	0.030	0.031	−0.001	0.000	0.000	0.002	−0.004	−0.006	0.011	0.009	0.008	0.179	0.242	0.279
4	−0.030	−0.025	−0.024	−0.011	−0.015	−0.014	−0.002	−0.003	−0.003	−0.014	−0.015	−0.014	0.165	0.227	0.265
5	0.015	0.006	0.007	0.049	0.038	0.039	0.002	−0.003	−0.004	0.022	0.014	0.014	0.187	0.241	0.279
6	−0.034	−0.038	−0.036	0.011	0.022	0.021	0.000	−0.003	−0.004	−0.008	−0.006	−0.006	0.179	0.235	0.272
7	0.019	0.020	0.022	0.018	0.012	0.013	0.000	−0.002	−0.002	0.012	0.010	0.011	0.192	0.245	0.284
8	0.011	0.007	0.009	0.017	0.019	0.019	−0.002	−0.006	−0.008	0.009	0.007	0.007	0.201	0.252	0.290
9	0.083	0.073	0.074	−0.013	−0.002	−0.002	−0.009	−0.009	−0.007	0.020	0.021	0.022	0.221	0.273	0.312
10	0.006	0.016	0.017	−0.004	−0.003	−0.003	−0.002	−0.001	0.000	0.000	0.004	0.005	0.221	0.276	0.317
11	0.010	0.005	0.007	0.002	0.003	0.004	−0.002	−0.002	−0.001	0.003	0.002	0.003	0.224	0.278	0.320
12	0.028	0.030	0.032	−0.010	−0.013	−0.012	0.002	0.003	0.005	0.007	0.007	0.008	0.231	0.285	0.328
13	−0.002	0.008	0.010	0.008	−0.006	−0.004	−0.002	−0.008	−0.010	0.001	−0.002	−0.002	0.233	0.283	0.326
14	−0.002	−0.001	0.001	0.008	0.010	0.010	−0.002	0.000	0.002	0.001	0.003	0.004	0.234	0.286	0.330
15	0.001	0.002	0.004	0.011	0.013	0.013	0.006	0.010	0.014	0.006	0.008	0.010	0.240	0.295	0.341
16	0.001	−0.001	0.000	−0.001	0.006	0.006	−0.005	0.003	0.009	−0.002	0.003	0.005	0.238	0.297	0.346
17	0.011	−0.002	−0.001	−0.007	−0.003	−0.003	−0.002	−0.002	−0.001	0.001	−0.002	−0.001	0.239	0.295	0.344
18	0.001	0.003	0.004	−0.001	0.000	0.001	−0.002	−0.001	0.001	−0.001	0.001	0.002	0.238	0.296	0.346
19	−0.007	−0.005	−0.004	−0.001	0.016	0.015	0.004	0.000	−0.001	−0.001	0.003	0.003	0.237	0.299	0.349

20	0.004	0.011	0.013	-0.001	-0.001	0.000	-0.003	-0.004	-0.004	0.000	0.002	0.003	0.237	0.301	0.352
21	0.001	0.005	0.006	0.005	0.006	0.006	0.000	-0.003	-0.004	0.002	0.003	0.003	0.239	0.304	0.355
22	-0.001	0.001	0.002	-0.001	-0.003	-0.002	-0.005	-0.004	-0.002	-0.002	-0.002	-0.001	0.237	0.302	0.355
23	-0.005	0.010	0.012	-0.001	0.005	0.005	0.002	0.011	0.018	-0.001	0.009	0.012	0.235	0.310	0.366
24	-0.002	-0.002	0.000	-0.001	-0.016	-0.014	-0.002	-0.003	-0.003	-0.002	-0.007	-0.006	0.233	0.304	0.360
25	-0.002	-0.001	0.000	-0.004	-0.003	-0.003	0.005	0.014	0.020	0.000	0.003	0.006	0.233	0.307	0.366
26	0.003	0.001	0.002	-0.001	-0.006	-0.005	0.002	0.002	0.003	0.001	-0.001	0.000	0.234	0.306	0.366
27	-0.004	0.002	0.004	-0.004	0.009	-0.008	-0.016	-0.018	-0.018	-0.008	-0.008	-0.007	0.226	0.298	0.359
28	0.003	-0.010	-0.009	-0.004	0.002	0.002	-0.002	0.001	0.003	-0.001	-0.002	-0.001	0.255	0.295	0.358
29	0.003	0.004	0.005	-0.001	-0.001	0.000	-0.002	-0.007	-0.009	0.000	-0.001	-0.001	0.225	0.294	0.357
30	-0.001	-0.005	-0.003	-0.001	0.006	0.006	0.002	0.000	0.000	0.000	0.001	0.001	0.225	0.295	0.358
31	0.001	-0.003	-0.002	-0.001	-0.007	-0.006	0.024	0.018	0.016	0.008	0.003	0.003	0.233	0.297	0.361
32	-0.010	-0.004	-0.003	0.008	0.005	0.006	-0.034	-0.033	-0.031	-0.012	-0.011	-0.009	0.221	0.287	0.351
33	0.001	0.001	0.003	0.002	-0.008	-0.007	-0.005	-0.006	-0.005	-0.001	-0.004	-0.003	0.220	0.283	0.348
34	0.004	0.011	0.013	-0.001	0.000	0.001	-0.005	-0.005	-0.003	-0.001	0.002	0.003	0.220	0.285	0.352
35	0.003	-0.002	-0.001	-0.004	-0.004	-0.004	0.004	0.006	0.008	0.001	0.000	0.001	0.220	0.285	0.353
36	-0.001	-0.003	-0.002	0.002	-0.008	-0.007	-0.007	-0.011	-0.012	-0.002	-0.007	-0.007	0.218	0.277	0.346
37	0.002	-0.006	-0.005	0.002	-0.002	-0.001	0.000	0.001	0.002	0.002	-0.002	-0.001	0.220	0.275	0.345
38	-0.005	-0.004	-0.003	0.002	0.005	0.005	-0.003	-0.006	-0.006	-0.002	-0.002	-0.001	0.218	0.273	0.344
39	0.002	0.002	0.004	-0.004	0.007	0.007	0.002	-0.002	-0.004	0.000	0.002	0.002	0.218	0.276	0.346
40	-0.005	-0.014	-0.013	-0.004	-0.005	-0.005	-0.016	-0.004	0.005	-0.009	-0.008	-0.004	0.209	0.268	0.342

Source: University of Chicago Center for Research on Security Prices (CRSP) tapes.

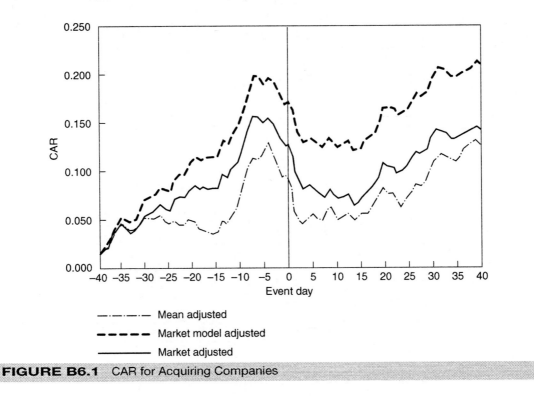

FIGURE B6.1 CAR for Acquiring Companies

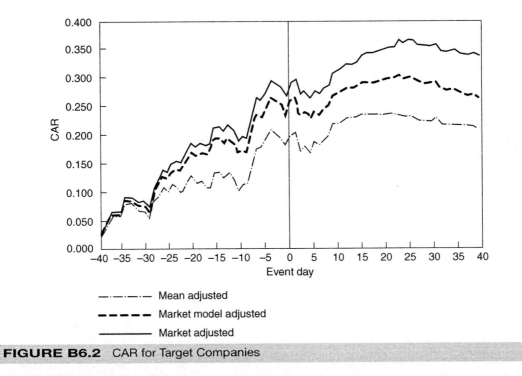

FIGURE B6.2 CAR for Target Companies

TABLE B6.4 Market-Adjusted CAR for Individual Companies

| Event Date | TARGETS | | | | | | ACQUIRERS | | | | | |
| | Gulf Corp. | | Superior Oil | | Texaco Canada | | Chevron | | Mobil | | Imperial Oil | |
	R3	CAR3	R3	CAR3	R3	CAR3	R3	CAR3	R3	CAR3	R3	CAR3
−40	0.052	0.052	−0.006	−0.006	0.022	0.022	−0.001	−0.001	−0.013	−0.013	0.032	0.032
−39	0.010	0.063	0.020	0.013	0.021	0.043	0.002	0.001	−0.001	−0.013	0.023	0.055
−38	0.041	0.104	0.003	0.017	0.005	0.048	0.011	0.012	−0.004	−0.018	0.000	0.055
−37	−0.022	0.081	0.010	0.026	0.012	0.060	0.001	0.013	0.006	−0.012	0.036	0.091
−36	0.021	0.102	−0.011	0.015	−0.011	0.049	0.007	0.020	0.006	−0.007	−0.001	0.091
−35	0.016	0.119	0.048	0.063	0.011	0.060	0.010	0.031	0.028	0.022	−0.014	0.077
−34	−0.010	0.108	0.002	0.066	0.010	0.070	−0.011	0.020	0.010	0.032	−0.015	0.061
−33	−0.008	0.100	−0.007	0.059	0.005	0.075	−0.010	0.010	−0.004	0.028	0.001	0.063
−32	−0.004	0.096	−0.004	0.055	−0.009	0.066	−0.016	−0.006	0.022	0.050	0.002	0.064
−31	−0.023	0.073	0.031	0.086	−0.001	0.064	0.028	0.022	0.002	0.051	−0.009	0.056
−30	0.006	0.079	−0.030	0.057	−0.008	0.056	0.023	0.045	0.004	0.055	−0.002	0.054
−29	0.022	0.101	0.050	0.106	0.032	0.088	0.009	0.054	0.002	0.057	−0.001	0.053
−28	0.052	0.153	−0.016	0.091	0.004	0.092	−0.017	0.037	0.021	0.078	0.004	0.057
−27	0.018	0.171	0.039	0.130	−0.001	0.091	0.016	0.053	0.008	0.087	−0.008	0.049
−26	−0.003	0.168	−0.011	0.119	0.002	0.092	0.001	0.054	−0.008	0.078	−0.005	0.045
−25	0.054	0.222	−0.006	0.113	−0.002	0.090	−0.001	0.052	0.005	0.084	−0.008	0.037
−24	0.018	0.240	0.004	0.117	−0.004	0.086	0.026	0.078	0.009	0.093	0.000	0.036
−23	−0.008	0.231	−0.002	0.114	0.003	0.089	0.012	0.091	−0.004	0.088	0.000	0.036
−22	0.042	0.273	0.011	0.125	0.001	0.090	−0.003	0.088	−0.006	0.082	0.003	0.039
−21	0.047	0.321	−0.005	0.120	0.011	0.101	0.018	0.106	0.000	0.082	0.009	0.048
−20	−0.018	0.303	−0.005	0.115	0.003	0.103	−0.004	0.102	0.000	0.082	0.018	0.066
−19	0.025	0.328	0.001	0.116	0.000	0.104	−0.008	0.093	−0.005	0.077	0.003	0.070
−18	−0.020	0.309	−0.003	0.113	0.008	0.111	−0.009	0.085	0.014	0.091	0.001	0.070
−17	0.010	0.319	−0.010	0.104	0.003	0.114	−0.005	0.079	−0.005	0.085	0.005	0.075
−16	0.044	0.362	0.043	0.146	0.010	0.124	−0.003	0.077	−0.003	0.082	0.009	0.084
−15	−0.001	0.361	−0.005	0.142	0.012	0.136	−0.002	0.075	0.001	0.084	0.002	0.086
−14	−0.045	0.316	0.009	0.150	0.010	0.147	0.013	0.088	0.032	0.116	−0.001	0.085
−13	0.058	0.374	−0.015	0.136	−0.005	0.142	−0.002	0.086	−0.014	0.102	0.002	0.087
−12	−0.031	0.342	−0.001	0.135	0.008	0.149	0.005	0.091	0.015	0.117	0.011	0.097
−11	−0.028	0.314	−0.023	0.111	−0.013	0.136	0.012	0.103	0.010	0.127	−0.004	0.093

(continued)

TABLE B6.4 (cont.)

| | TARGETS | | | | | | ACQUIRERS | | | | | |
| | Gulf Corp. | | Superior Oil | | Texaco Canada | | Chevron | | Mobil | | Imperial Oil | |
Event Date	R3	CAR3	R3	CAR3	R3	CAR3	R3	CAR3	R3	CAR3	R3	CAR3
−10	0.002	0.317	0.000	0.111	0.021	0.157	0.035	0.138	−0.020	0.108	0.027	0.120
−9	−0.019	0.298	0.013	0.124	−0.003	0.154	0.014	0.152	0.025	0.133	0.020	0.140
−8	0.111	0.410	0.005	0.129	0.005	0.159	0.002	0.154	0.021	0.154	0.026	0.166
−7	0.098	0.508	0.007	0.136	−0.005	0.154	0.012	0.166	−0.003	0.152	−0.012	0.155
−6	−0.041	0.466	0.024	0.160	−0.005	0.150	−0.016	0.150	0.005	0.157	−0.007	0.147
−5	0.082	0.548	−0.025	0.135	−0.014	0.136	0.026	0.175	−0.011	0.146	0.004	0.151
−4	0.022	0.571	0.010	0.146	0.039	0.174	0.000	0.175	−0.016	0.130	−0.002	0.150
−3	−0.004	0.566	−0.006	0.140	−0.009	0.165	−0.016	0.159	−0.011	0.119	−0.002	0.148
−2	0.000	0.567	−0.023	0.117	0.009	0.175	−0.034	0.126	0.007	0.125	−0.001	0.147
−1	−0.007	0.560	−0.045	0.072	−0.005	0.170	−0.014	0.112	0.005	0.131	−0.009	0.138
0	0.025	0.585	0.055	0.126	0.002	0.171	0.007	0.119	0.000	0.131	−0.005	0.134
1	−0.012	0.573	−0.001	0.126	0.030	0.202	−0.036	0.083	−0.027	0.104	−0.022	0.112
2	−0.054	0.519	−0.045	0.080	0.009	0.211	0.003	0.087	−0.008	0.096	−0.023	0.089
3	0.031	0.551	0.000	0.081	−0.006	0.205	0.008	0.094	−0.004	0.091	−0.030	0.058
4	−0.024	0.527	−0.014	0.066	−0.003	0.202	0.012	0.106	0.004	0.095	0.000	0.059
5	0.007	0.534	0.039	0.105	−0.004	0.197	−0.010	0.096	0.002	0.097	−0.002	0.057
6	−0.036	0.498	0.021	0.127	−0.004	0.193	−0.008	0.088	−0.004	0.094	−0.006	0.050
7	0.022	0.519	0.013	0.140	−0.002	0.191	−0.011	0.077	0.003	0.097	−0.003	0.047
8	0.009	0.528	0.019	0.159	−0.008	0.184	0.010	0.087	0.030	0.127	−0.013	0.033
9	0.074	0.602	−0.002	0.157	−0.007	0.176	−0.011	0.077	−0.010	0.117	0.003	0.036
10	0.017	0.620	−0.003	0.155	0.000	0.176	−0.009	0.067	−0.004	0.113	0.003	0.039
11	0.007	0.626	0.004	0.158	−0.001	0.175	0.009	0.077	−0.004	0.109	−0.001	0.037
12	0.032	0.658	−0.012	0.146	0.005	0.179	0.001	0.078	0.005	0.115	0.001	0.039
13	0.010	0.668	−0.004	0.142	−0.010	0.169	−0.008	0.070	−0.018	0.097	−0.010	0.028
14	0.001	0.668	0.010	0.152	0.002	0.171	0.004	0.074	0.005	0.102	−0.001	0.027
15	0.004	0.672	0.013	0.165	0.014	0.185	0.019	0.093	0.009	0.111	−0.002	0.025
16	0.000	0.673	0.006	0.171	0.009	0.193	0.012	0.104	−0.006	0.105	0.009	0.034
17	−0.001	0.672	−0.003	0.168	−0.001	0.193	0.011	0.116	0.003	0.108	−0.001	0.033
18	0.004	0.676	0.001	0.169	0.001	0.193	0.015	0.130	0.005	0.113	0.007	0.040
19	−0.004	0.672	0.015	0.184	−0.001	0.192	0.029	0.159	0.015	0.128	0.005	0.044

20	0.013	0.685	0.000	0.184	-0.004	0.188	0.006	0.165	-0.009	0.119	-0.008	0.036
21	0.006	0.691	0.006	0.190	-0.004	0.184	0.006	0.171	0.000	0.120	-0.008	0.028
22	0.002	0.693	-0.002	0.188	-0.002	0.183	-0.013	0.159	-0.002	0.117	-0.010	0.018
23	0.012	0.705	0.005	0.193	0.018	0.200	0.001	0.160	0.010	0.127	0.002	0.020
24	0.000	0.705	-0.014	0.179	-0.003	0.197	0.003	0.163	0.011	0.138	-0.003	0.017
25	0.000	0.705	-0.003	0.176	0.020	0.217	0.011	0.174	0.013	0.150	0.010	0.027
26	0.002	0.708	-0.005	0.172	0.003	0.220	0.008	0.182	0.003	0.154	0.008	0.035
27	0.004	0.711	-0.008	0.164	-0.018	0.202	0.005	0.187	-0.009	0.145	-0.006	0.029
28	-0.009	0.702	0.002	0.166	0.003	0.203	0.023	0.210	-0.007	0.138	-0.003	0.026
29	0.005	0.708	0.000	0.166	-0.009	0.197	0.007	0.217	0.016	0.154	0.016	0.042
30	-0.003	0.704	0.006	0.172	0.000	0.197	0.011	0.228	0.006	0.160	0.008	0.050
31	-0.002	0.703	-0.006	0.167	0.016	0.212	0.005	0.233	-0.002	0.159	-0.007	0.043
32	-0.003	0.700	0.006	0.172	-0.031	0.181	-0.010	0.222	0.001	0.159	0.004	0.047
33	0.003	0.730	-0.007	0.165	-0.005	0.177	-0.003	0.209	-0.014	0.145	0.011	0.058
34	0.013	0.716	0.001	0.166	-0.003	0.174	-0.016	0.193	0.001	0.146	0.015	0.073
35	-0.001	0.715	-0.004	0.162	0.008	-0.181	0.014	0.207	-0.009	0.137	0.002	0.076
36	-0.002	0.713	-0.007	0.155	-0.012	0.170	-0.003	0.204	-0.008	0.129	0.017	0.092
37	-0.005	0.708	-0.001	0.154	0.002	0.172	0.003	0.207	-0.008	0.121	0.012	0.104
38	-0.003	0.705	0.005	0.160	-0.006	0.166	0.001	0.207	-0.010	0.111	0.013	0.116
39	0.004	0.709	0.007	0.167	-0.004	0.162	0.009	0.216	0.002	0.113	-0.002	0.114
40	-0.013	0.696	-0.005	0.162	0.005	0.167	-0.019	0.197	-0.002	0.111	0.012	0.125

Source: Data from CRSP 1995 tape.

Table B6.5 illustrates the absolute dollar gain or loss at days +1 and +40 for the six firms of interest. The reference $MKTVAL_0$ is obtained one day prior to the event window interval or at day −41. Thus, the absolute gain for Chevron on day +1 was $11,888 million times the CAR from days −40 to +1 of 0.083, or a gain of $987 million.

Interpretation of Measurements

Residual analysis basically tests whether the return to the common stock of individual firms or groups of firms is greater or less than that predicted by general market relationships between return and risk. Most merger studies in recent years have made use of residual analysis. These studies have sought to test whether merger events provide positive or negative abnormal returns to the participants. The studies of abnormal returns provide a basis for examining the issue of whether or not value is enhanced by mergers.

The studies cover different time periods and different sample sizes. The studies are sometimes limited to conglomerate mergers. Other studies include horizontal and vertical mergers, as well. Many studies deal with tender offers only. Some studies use monthly data, some use daily data, and some focus on individual mergers. At least one study analyzes firms engaged in programs of merger and tender offer activity over a period of years (Schipper and Thompson, 1983).

On average, the event studies predict the longer-term performance of merging companies. Healy, Palepu, and Ruback (1992) find a strong positive relationship between the abnormal stock returns related to the announcement of mergers and the subsequent postmerger changes in operating cash flows. Their findings support the view that the event returns, on average, represent accurate predictions of the subsequent performance of merging companies.

STATISTICAL SIGNIFICANCE OF EVENT RETURNS

One Day, One Firm

Once the measures of abnormal returns have been estimated, we must interpret these results. Can we infer with a certain level of confidence that the residuals are significantly different from zero? If we assume that the returns for each firm are independently and identically normally distributed, then

$$\frac{r_{jt}}{\hat{S}(r_j)}$$

has a t-distribution. [r_{jt} is the residual for firm j on day t; $\hat{S}(r_{jt})$ is the estimated standard deviation of the residuals for firm j using data from the estimation period,

$$\left[\frac{1}{199} \sum_{t=-240}^{-41} (r_{jt} - \bar{r}_j)^2 \right]^{1/2}$$

TABLE B6.5 Absolute Event Gains (Losses) (in millions)

	Targets			Acquirers		
	Gulf Corp.	Superior Oil	Texaco Canada	Chevron	Mobil	Imperial Oil
Market value at −41[a]	$7,296	$4,867	$3,729	$11,888	$12,052	$6,034
On day +1						
CAR (market adjusted)[b]	0.573	0.126	0.202	0.083	0.140	0.112
Dollar gain (loss)	$4,183	$612	$752	$989	$1,254	$673
On day +40						
CAR (market adjusted)[b]	0.696	0.162	0.167	0.197	0.111	0.125
Dollar gain (loss)	$5,078	$789	$621	$2,339	$1,341	$757

[a]Data from CRSP 1995 tape.
[b]Here the CARs represent the cumulative abnormal returns obtained by cumulating the daily abnormal returns in each of the individual company R3 columns in Tables B6.2 and B6.3, which are repeated as the first of the two columns under each company name in Table B6.4.

and the degrees of freedom are 199.] For more than 30 degrees of freedom, the t-statistic has, approximately, a standard normal distribution. This statistic tests the null hypothesis that the 1-day residual for a single firm is equal to zero. Intuitively, we are comparing the value of the residual to its estimated sample standard deviation. Only if this ratio is greater than a specified critical value can we reject the null hypothesis with some degree of confidence. For instance, if this ratio is greater than 1.96, we can say that the 1-day residual is significantly different from zero at the 5% level. If the ratio is greater than 2.58, we can reject the null hypothesis at a confidence level of 1%. Table B6.6 presents the statistical significance (the t-stat) of the individual firm's residual on the announcement day (r_{j0}). The positive abnormal returns for Superior Oil are the only ones significant at the 1% level. For the other firms, we cannot reject the null hypothesis of a zero residual.

One Day, Average Over Firms

The corresponding test statistic for the hypothesis that the 1-day residual, averaged over three firms,

$$AR_t = \frac{1}{3} \sum_{j=1}^{3} r_{jt}$$

is zero is as follows:

$$\frac{AR_t}{\hat{S}(AR)} = \frac{AR_t}{\left[\frac{1}{199} \sum_{t=-240}^{-41} (AR_t - \overline{AR})^2 \right]^{1/2}}$$

where the sample standard deviation is

$$\hat{S}(AR) = \left[\frac{1}{199} \sum_{t=-240}^{-41} (AR_t - \overline{AR})^2 \right]^{1/2}$$

and

$$\overline{AR} = \frac{1}{200} \sum_{t=-240}^{-41} AR_t$$

In Table B6.6, the positive average residuals for the target companies are statistically significant. For the acquirers, the small average residuals are not distinguishable from zero.

Over 81 Days, Average Over Firms

The corresponding statistic for the cumulative average residual (CAR) for the three firms and cumulating over 81 days [−40, +40], is

$$\frac{CAR}{\hat{S}(CAR)} = \frac{\sum_{t=-40}^{+40} AR_t}{\sum_{t=-40}^{+40} \hat{S}(AR)} = \frac{\sum_{t=-40}^{+40} AR_t}{\sqrt{81}\hat{S}(AR)}$$

Note that the estimated standard deviation for each day in the event interval is the same because we are using the same estimation period for a sample drawn from independent and identically distributed excess returns. Table B6.7 presents the CAR for each individual firm and the average CAR for target and acquiring firms. Gulf Corporation is the only company that presents a significant abnormal return during the event interval. Both target and acquiring firms' average CARs are significant, except for the acquirers' average CAR using the mean adjusted return method.

The procedure we used to estimate the test statistics is the simplest to illustrate the calculations of statistical significance. Several adjustment factors must be recognized. For the mean adjusted return model and the market model, the estimation of $\hat{S}$ should be adjusted because the residuals involve prediction errors.

These errors derive from the estimation of the mean return of the mean adjusted model and from the estimation of the regression coefficients for the market model. In addition, we did not take into account the possible changes in the variance outside the estimation period, nor did we consider time dependence or non-normality in the returns. Finally, there is the possibility of cross-correlation in abnormal returns resulting, for example, from a government regulation that simultaneously impacts a number of different securities. For a more complete exposition of the issues involved in event studies, see Brown and Warner (1980, 1985) and Boehmer, Musumeci, and Poulsen (1991).

TABLE B6.6 One-Day Residuals (Announcement Day) Statistical Significance

		Targets				Acquirers			
		Gulf Corp.	Superior Oil	Texaco Canada	Average	Chevron	Mobil	Imperial Oil	Average
M1: Mean adjusted Return model	$R1 = r_{jt}$ $= R_{jt} - \bar{R}_j$								
	r_{j0}	0.0158	0.0489	0.0023	0.0223	-0.0004	-0.0051	-0.0020	-0.0025
	s_j	0.0160	0.0236	0.0160	0.0104	0.0172	0.0171	0.0103	0.0083
	t-stat	0.9890	2.0764	0.1430	2.1496	-0.0215	-0.2998	-0.1947	-0.3021
M2: Market model method	$R2 = r_{jt}$ $= R_{jt} - \hat{\alpha}_j - \hat{\beta}_j R_{mt}$								
	r_{j0}	0.0236	0.0544	0.0014	0.0265	0.0094	0.0018	-0.0028	0.0028
	s_j	0.0144	0.0223	0.0152	0.0103	0.0150	0.0142	0.0094	0.0074
	t-stat	1.6385	2.4381	0.0906	2.5615	0.6264	0.1248	-0.2911	0.3805
M3: Market adjusted return method	$R3 = r_{jt}$ $= R_{jt} - R_{mt}$								
	r_{j0}	0.0253	0.0546	0.0019	0.0273	0.0074	0.0003	-0.0047	0.0010
	s_j	0.0144	0.0223	0.0155	0.0104	0.0151	0.0145	0.0102	0.0074
	t-stat	1.7589	2.4450	0.1209	2.6126	0.4883	0.0194	-0.4577	0.1326

TABLE B6.7 Cumulative Average Residuals [−40, +40] Statistical Significance

		Targets				Acquirers			
		Gulf Corp.	Superior Oil	Texaco Canada	Average	Chevron	Mobil	Imperial Oil	Average
M1: Mean adjusted return model	$R1 = r_{ji}$ $= R_{ji} - \overline{R}_j$								
	CAR	0.4677	0.0079	0.1518	0.2091	0.1176	−0.0249	0.2932	0.1287
	s_j	0.1436	0.2121	0.1436	0.0935	0.1552	0.1543	0.0926	0.0746
	t-stat	3.2579	0.0370	1.0568	2.2371	0.7579	−0.1613	3.1673	1.7241
M2: Market model method	$R2 = r_{ji}$ $= R_{ji} - \hat{\alpha}_j - \hat{\beta}_j R_{mt}$								
	CAR	0.5715	0.1235	0.1084	0.2678	0.2470	0.1214	0.2575	0.2086
	s_j	0.1296	0.2008	0.1366	0.0930	0.1348	0.1280	0.0850	0.0663
	t-stat	4.4081	0.6151	0.7934	2.8807	1.8319	0.9481	3.0277	3.1465
M3: Market–adjusted return method	$R3 = r_{ji}$ $= R_{ji} - R_{mt}$								
	CAR	0.6960	0.1620	0.1667	0.3416	0.1967	0.1113	0.1254	0.1445
	s_j	0.1297	0.2009	0.1392	0.0939	0.1355	0.1301	0.0918	0.0670
	t-stat	5.3678	0.8066	1.1972	3.6372	1.4523	0.8555	1.3660	2.1575

169

REFERENCES

Boehmer, E., J. Musumeci, and A. Poulsen, "Event-Study Methodology Under Conditions of Event-Induced Variance," *Journal of Financial Economics* 30, 1991, pp. 253–272.

Brown, S., and J. Warner, "Measuring Security Price Performance," *Journal of Financial Economics* 8, 1980, pp. 205–258.

——, "Using Daily Stock Returns: The Case of Event Studies." *Journal of Financial Economics* 14, 1985, pp. 3–31.

Healy, Paul M., Krishna G. Palepu, and Richard S. Ruback, "Does Corporate Performance Improve After Mergers?" *Journal of Financial Economics* 31, 1992, pp. 135–175.

Schipper, K., and R. Thompson, "Evidence on the Capitalized Value of Merger Activity for Acquiring Firms," *Journal of Financial Economics* 11, 1983, pp. 85–119.

CHAPTER 7
THE TIMING OF
MERGER ACTIVITY

Possibly the most important question raised by the concepts presented in Chapter 6 is: Why do mergers occur? The present chapter addresses this query by reviewing the major merger movements that have taken place in the United States since the 1890s. The empirical evidence focuses on aggregate merger waves and industry patterns in merger activity. As we shall see, the historical evidence provides fascinating and useful insights for ongoing merger activity in the United States and abroad. The evidence confirms the importance of the change forces initially discussed in Chapter 1.

CONCEPTUAL FRAMEWORK

A useful framework with which to consider the timing of merger activity is provided by Professor Ronald Coase in his 1937 paper on the Nature of the Firm. In his research, Coase addressed the factors that influence the choice between production within a firm and exchange across markets. He isolated transaction costs as a central choice variable.

In analysis rather pertinent to merger activity, Coase (1937) identified technological change as a major determinant of firm size. Coase predicted, "Changes like the telephone and the telegraph which tend to reduce the cost of organizing spatially will tend to increase the size of the firm" (p. 397). An implication of this analysis is that merger activity will be related to technological change. As Professor Hal Varian noted in an article in the *New York Times*, the insights of Coase can be applied not only to the historical creation of the corporation but also are relevant to changing corporate organization that currently is being induced by innovations such as the Internet (Varian, p. C2).

Research by Professor Michael Jensen (1993) expanded on the economic forces that are associated with merger activity. Like Coase, Jensen associated merger activity with technological change. Indeed, Jensen drew parallels between the industrial revolution of the nineteenth century and the technological change in recent decades.

Jensen also pointed to several related factors that influence merger activity. One is input prices; Jensen tied the merger activity in the 1980s to energy price volatility that began with OPEC in 1973. Another important factor discussed by Jensen is the legal/political/regulatory system. Factors such as deregulation, privatization, and free trade ratification are important change forces. Finally, Jensen noted the importance of capital markets for merger activity and pointed out that innovations in financing can be tied to organizational change. With this framework as a guide, we now turn to the evidence on the timing of merger activity.

EARLY MERGER MOVEMENTS

Several major merger movements have occurred in the United States (Golbe and White, 1988), and each was more or less dominated by a particular type of merger. All of the merger movements occurred when the economy experienced sustained high rates of growth and coincided with particular developments in business environments. Mergers represent resource allocation and reallocation processes in the economy, with firms responding to new investment and profit opportunities arising out of changes in economic conditions and technological innovations impacting industries. Mergers rather than internal growth sometimes can expedite the adjustment process and in some cases can be more efficient in terms of resource utilization.

THE 1895 TO 1904 HORIZONTAL MERGERS

The combination movement at the turn of the century consisted mainly of horizontal mergers, which resulted in high concentration in many industries, including heavy manufacturing industries. The period was one of rapid economic expansion. The 1904 decision of the Supreme Court in the Northern Securities case [193 U.S. 197 (March 1904)] might have contributed to ending this merger wave. In the decision, the court established that mergers could be attacked successfully by Section I of the Sherman Act, which prohibited "every combination in the form of trust or otherwise" in restraint of trade. It should be noted, however, that the merger activity began its downturn in 1901, as some combinations failed to realize their expectations, and declined further by 1903, when the economy went into recession.

This merger movement at the turn of the century accompanied major changes in economic infrastructure and production technologies (Markham, 1955, p. 156; Salter and Weinhold, 1980, p. 7). It followed the completion of the transcontinental railroad system, the advent of electricity, and a major increase in the use of coal. The completed rail system resulted in the development of a national economic market, and thus the merger activity represented to a certain extent the transformation of regional firms into national firms.

In addition to the goal of achieving economies of scale, two other motivational factors have been ascribed to this first major merger movement. Stigler (1950) characterized the merger movement as "merging for monopoly." Of 92 large mergers studied by Moody (1904), 78 controlled 50% or more of the market. However, in reviewing the early literature on mergers, Markham (1955) concluded that "out of every five mergers ostensibly monopolistic in character only one resulted in considerable monopoly control" (pp. 161–162) and that "it is certain that many mergers formed during the early merger movement did not have monopoly power as their principal objective and, accordingly, must be explained on other grounds" (p. 162). In reviewing the early literature, authors such as Markham (1955) and Salter and Weinhold (1979) concluded that professional promoters and underwriters or "producers" of mergers added to the magnitude of the merger wave.

Several studies attempted to measure the success of the early mergers in terms of profitability and to determine the reasons for their success or failure. Livermore (1935) attributed success to "astute business leadership" and, in particular, to rapid technological and managerial improvement, development of new products or entry into a new subdivision of the industry, promotion of quality brand names, and commercial exploitation of research. The causes for failure as given by Dewing (1953) included lack of efforts to realize economies of scale by modernizing inherited plants and equipment, increase in overhead costs and lack of flexibility due to large size, and inadequate supply of talent to manage a large group of plants.

THE 1922 TO 1929 VERTICAL MERGERS

As in the first merger movement, the second wave of mergers also began with an upturn in business activity in 1922. It ended with the onset of a severe economic slowdown in 1929. Many combinations in this period occurred outside the previously consolidated heavy manufacturing industries. The public utilities and banking industries were among the most active. About 60% of the mergers occurred in the still-fragmented food processing, chemicals, and mining sectors (Salter and Weinhold, 1980, p. 4). Accordingly, the question of monopoly was not applicable in most cases, and the transformation of a near monopoly to an oligopoly by "merging for oligopoly" was more frequent (Stigler, 1950). Oligopoly provided a motive for many mergers, but it was limited to no more than a small fraction of the mergers (Markham, 1955, p. 169). A large portion of mergers in the 1920s represented product extension mergers, as in the cases of IBM, General Foods, and Allied Chemical; market extension mergers in food retailing, department stores, and motion picture theaters; and vertical mergers in the mining and metals industries.

As for the motivational factors of these mergers, Markham (1955) and Stocking (1955) emphasized major development in transportation, communication, and merchandising. A new transportation system utilizing motor vehicles broke down small local markets by enabling sellers to extend their sales areas and by making consumers more mobile. Mergers in such industries as food processing and chemicals accompanied the rise of automobile transportation just as mergers in heavy industries in the previous merger movement accompanied the rise of railroad transportation. The development of home radios facilitated product differentiation through national-brand advertising. By the 1920s, mass distribution with low profit margins became a new method of merchandising. Both of these developments caused an increase in the scale of operations and hence encouraged mergers. On the increase in vertical integration, Stocking noted that by the 1920s, business had come to appreciate the advantages of integration. The advantages were related to technological economies such as the shortening of processes or elimination of waste motions in a mechanical sense, or the reliability of input supply.

THE CONGLOMERATE MERGERS OF THE 1960s

The Celler-Kefauver Act of 1950 amended Section 7 of the Clayton Act of 1914 to close the "asset-purchase" loophole and granted the federal government additional power to declare illegal those mergers that tended to increase concentration. (The Clayton Act had prohibited a corporation from acquiring the stock of another corporation if competition were to be substantially lessened. The act had referred only to acquisition of stock, not that of assets.) Thereafter, the relative importance of horizontal and vertical mergers declined in relation to conglomerate mergers. By 1967 to 1968 when the merger activity peaked, horizontal and vertical mergers declined to 17% of the total number of mergers. Among the conglomerate type of mergers, product extension mergers increased to 60%, and market extension mergers became negligible in number. "Other" or pure conglomerates increased steadily to about 23% of all mergers (or 35% in terms of assets acquired). Merger activity reached its then historically highest level during the 3-year period of 1967 through 1969. The period was also one of a booming economy. The number of mergers declined sharply as general economic activity slowed after 1969.

Most acquirers in the period that have subsequently been known as conglomerates were small or medium-sized firms that adopted a diversification strategy into business activities outside their traditional areas of interest. The acquired firms were also small or medium-sized and "operating in either fragmented industries or on the periphery of major industrial sectors" (Salter and Weinhold, 1980, p. 6). Based on an analysis of backgrounds and acquisition histories of the acquiring firms, Weston and Mansinghka (1971) suggested that the conglomerates were

> diversifying defensively to avoid (1) sales and profit instability, (2) adverse growth developments, (3) adverse competitive shifts, (4) technological obsolescence, and (5) increased uncertainties associated with their industries (Weston and Mansinghka, 1971, p. 928).

The largest single category of firms was the aerospace industry. This industry was subject to wide fluctuations in total market demand as well as abrupt and major shifts in its product mix. The Department of Defense (DOD) emphasized high-technology weapons from 1945 through 1950. During the Korean War in the early 1950s, DOD procurement shifted to ammunition and ordinance. When Dwight Eisenhower became president in 1953, he quickly ended the Korean War, cut DOD spending substantially, and shifted to high-tech weapons. These shifts created substantial demand uncertainty for defense firms. Reduced DOD spending caused excess capacity, aggravated by partial entry of firms from other industries.

The industrial machinery and auto parts companies also were subject to considerable instability in sales. Low-growth prospects were associated with a major long-term decline in some markets. This was characteristic of the railway equipment industry, textiles, movie distribution (at an earlier period), and the tobacco industry.

Sometimes the conglomerate represented the personality of the chief executive, for example, Harold Geneen at ITT and Charles Bludhorn at Gulf & Western. Their successors sold off everything but a relatively focused core of activities. Some conglomerates were formed to imitate earlier conglomerates that appeared to have achieved high growth and high valuations. Many of the later conglomerates had no sound conceptual basis and were a substantial source of sell-offs in later years. Indeed, many writers view the merger activity of the 1980s as a correction to the unwise diversification of the 1960s (Shleifer and Vishny, 1990).

The rise of management theory that had begun in the 1950s led to the increased professionalization of business operations. The early success of the General Electric Company and Litton Industries in moving top executives from highly divergent types of business operations led some to generalize that "good managers can manage anything." This provided some intellectual underpinning for combining the unrelated activities in conglomerate firms.

Another influence was playing the differential price/earnings (P/E) game. When an acquiring firm with a high P/E ratio combines with a firm with a lower P/E ratio, the earnings per share (EPS) of the buyer will rise. Table 7.1 illustrates this generalization. The first three rows present assumed data for a buyer in column 1 and a seller in column 2 on P/E ratios, net income, and shares outstanding. Row 4 is calculated as net income divided by shares outstanding to obtain EPS. The final row is the indicated market value per share obtained by multiplying the P/E times EPS.

The results in column 3 for the combined firms are summarized briefly in column 4. The P/E ratio of the buyer is assumed to continue for the combined firm. The net income of $200 million is a simple addition. We postulate that the buyer pays a 20% premium for the seller, or $60 per share. Hence, the buyer pays the seller 0.6 of its $100 stock, so the buyer issues 12 million shares to replace the 20 million of the seller. The total shares in the combined column

TABLE 7.1 Playing the Relative P/E Game

	(1) *Buyer*	*(2)* *Seller*	*(3)* *Combined*	*(4)* *Explanation for Column 3*
Price Earnings Ratio (P/E)	20	10	20	Assumed
Net Income	$100 million	$100 million	$200 million	(1) + (2)
Shares Outstanding	20 million	20 million	32 million	(1) + 0.6(20 million)
Earnings per Share (EPS)	$5	$5	$6.25	$200 / 32
Market Value per Share	$100	$50	$125	20 × $6.25

are 32 million. Dividing this number into the combined net income of $200 million gives $6.25 as the new EPS. Applying the P/E of 20 gives a market price per share of $125.

In Table 7.2, the effects on buyers and sellers are summarized. The postmerger EPS for the buyer increases by $1.25, or 25%. Its market price per share also increases by 25% to $125. The EPS of the seller is 0.6 of the postmerger price of $6.25, which is $3.75. It suffers dilution in EPS. But the seller now owns 0.6 share of stock worth $125. So postmerger, for each share the seller owned premerger, the seller holds a value of $75. This represents an increase in market value of 50%. This is the nature of P/E magic.

The key assumption in this scenario is that the P/E ratio of the buyer will carry over to the combined firm. Because the buyer could announce that its earnings per share had increased by 25%, its actual postmerger P/E ratio was likely to increase even further. Although P/E magic works in the short run, in the longer run it is likely to come apart. The lower P/E ratio of the seller company must reflect either lower growth or higher risk. In the longer term, the lower growth of the seller will depress the earnings growth of the buyer. The higher risk implies the occurrence of unfavorable events, also depressing earnings. So P/E magic works only if the new acquisitions are sufficient to offset the depressing influences of the older acquisitions.

In 1968, Congress began to move against conglomerate firms in the antitrust and tax arenas. The Department of Justice (DOJ) began to file suits against conglomerate firms. Congressional hearings were held on the frightening increase in size and power of the big conglomerate firms. These actions adversely affected conglomerate prices. The Tax Reform Act of 1969 limited the use of convertible debt to finance acquisitions. The use of convertible debt had magnified P/E magic. The prospect of large future capital gains made it possible to sell convertible debt with low coupons, so the conglomerate firms obtained cash inflows from the sale of debt at low after-tax cost, which contributed to their growth in EPS and market prices. The act also provided that EPS would have to be calculated on a fully diluted basis, as if the debt had been converted into common stock.

TABLE 7.2 Effects on Buyers and Sellers

	Buyer		*Seller*	
	Premerger	*Postmerger*	*Premerger*	*Postmerger*
Earnings per Share	$5	$6.25	$5	$3.75
Market Price per Share	$100	$125	$50	$75
Total Market Value	$2 billion	$2.5 billion	$1 billion	$1.5 billion

The hostile public policy environment depressed the stock prices of conglomerate firms. In addition, the general stock market declined. The Dow Jones Industrial Average peaked in 1967 at slightly over 1,000, then declined to 631 by mid-1971. Thus, hostile antitrust policies, punitive tax laws, and declining stock prices brought the conglomerate merger movement to an end.

THE DEAL DECADE, 1981 TO 1989

The fourth merger movement during 1981 to 1989 excited the interest of the general public. The pace of activity exceeded even the conglomerate activity of the 1960s. There was a confluence of forces. The economy and the stock market began to surge upward in mid-1982. International competition was increasing, impacting mature industries such as steel and autos. As noted, the conglomerates became more streamlined. New technologies and managerial innovations brought new industries into existence and affected the old. Computers and microwave communication systems impacted the communication and entertainment industries.

This was the decade of big deals, as illustrated by Table 7.3. All of the 10 largest transactions of the 1980s exceeded $6 billion each. Five of the 10 involved oil companies, reflecting the increased price instability resulting from OPEC actions. The two drug mergers reflected the increased pressure to reduce drug prices because of the high proportion of spending by the rising proportion of the population represented by older people. Two of the remaining three reflected efforts by tobacco companies to diversify into the food industry.

The ability to undertake transactions was facilitated by the financial innovations of the 1980s. Michael Milken, through the Drexel Burnham investment banking firm, was able to underwrite the sale of large volumes of below-investment-grade (high-yield junk bonds) debt securities. The concept was that yields on portfolios of junk bonds net of defaults would provide a differential over less-risky portfolios commensurate with the risk differentials. The creation of a broad market for risky debt provided financing for aggressive acquirers, who came to be known as raiders. Holderness and Sheehan (1985) studied the activities of six "controversial

TABLE 7.3   Largest Transactions Announced in the 1980s

Buyer	Seller	Industry	Deal Value (in billions)	Year Announced
Kohlberg Kravis Roberts	RJR Nabisco	Food, tobacco	$ 27.5	1988
Beecham Group PLC	SmithKline Beecham	Drugs	16.1	1989
Chevron Corp.	Gulf Corp.	Oil	13.2	1984
Philip Morris	Kraft Inc.	Food, tobacco	13.1	1988
Bristol-Myers	Squibb	Drugs	12.0	1989
Time Inc.	Warner Communications	Media	11.7	1989
Texaco Inc.	Getty Oil	Oil	10.1	1984
DuPont Co.	Conoco	Oil	8.0	1981
British Petroleum	Standard Oil (Ohio)	Oil	7.8	1987
U.S. Steel	Marathon Oil	Oil	6.6	1981
			Total $126.1	

Source: Mergerstat Review, 1981–1989.

investors." They found that their stock purchases resulted in positive event returns, as well as positive returns to shareholders net of benchmarks for the subsequent 2 years. This evidence appeared consistent with two hypotheses: (1) The six investors were able to identify under-priced stocks, and (2) they influenced the improvement in the management of the target firms.

The 1980s also witnessed the rise of financial buyers such as Kohlberg Kravis Roberts (KKR) (Table 7.3). The financial buyers arranged going-private transactions, referred to as *leveraged buyouts* (LBOs). The LBO concept was to purchase a public company with substantial use of debt, provide managers with large equity interest for strong incentives, improve operations, reduce debt from operating cash flows, and harvest the investment by taking the firm public again within a 3- to 5-year holding period. (LBOs are discussed in greater detail in Chapter 16.)

Often the financial buyers bought segments of diversified firms. Thus, almost half of the annual acquisitions during the 1980s represented divestitures of selling firms. This was part of the process of unwinding the conglomerates, as firms sought to focus on their core capabilities.

Another process by which diversification was unwound was by the use of "bustup acquisitions." Corporate buyers and others would seek firms whose parts as separate entities were worth more than the whole. After the acquisition, segments would be divested. Proceeds of such sales often were used to reduce the debt incurred to finance the transaction.

The combined impact of raiders, financial buyers, and bustup merger activity was to put pressure on business firms, large or small, to defend against takeovers. Sophisticated acquisition activities began to be matched by the rise of a wide range of defensive measures (discussed in Chapter 19). So the increased use of hostile takeovers financed by debt gave rise to the increased use of defensive measures.

With growing reports of insider trading during the 1980s and concern about the general impact of mergers on the economy, government actions became restrictive. A number of well-publicized insider trading cases cast doubt on the integrity and soundness of merger activity. The 1980s began to be referred to as the decade of greed. In a highly publicized case, Dennis Levine, who had joined Drexel in 1984 after experience with other investment banking firms, pleaded guilty in mid-1986 to charges of insider trading. He also implicated Ivan Boesky, a prominent arbitrageur on mergers. In a deal with prosecutor Rudolph Giuliani to lighten his sentence, Boesky implicated Michael Milken, who was indicted in 1989. Giuliani invoked the use of the Racqueteer Influenced and Corrupt Organizations Act (RICO), which would have enabled him to seize the assets of the defendant to pressure Milken. Milken argued his innocence and did not implicate others. Ultimately, Milken pleaded guilty to 6 of the 98 charges. He was originally sentenced to 10 years in prison, but in 1992 the sentence was reduced to 24 months. Milken also was required to pay $1 billion to settle various other charges.

With the indictment of Michael Milken and the subsequent bankruptcy of Drexel on February 13, 1990, the junk bond market was severely wounded. Some major LBO deals could not be financed. The weakness in the junk bond market was exacerbated by the passage in 1989 of the Financial Institutions Reform, Recovery, and Enforcement Act (FIRREA). This law essentially required financial institutions to mark their junk bond holdings down to market. The effect was to force massive sales of junk bonds by financial institutions, which further devastated the junk bond market.

The economic recession associated with the war against Iraq also put a damper on M&A activity. The development of powerful takeover defenses, state antitakeover laws, the weakness in the junk bond market, and the economic downturn all combined to bring the deal decade to an end. Some predicted that these forces would reduce future merger activity, as well.

STRATEGIC MERGERS, 1992–2000

By 1992, another merger movement commenced. The Gulf War was over and economic recovery was strong. The stock market resumed its upward course. Other investment banking firms moved into the junk bond market, which recovered to levels above its peak in 1988. The period of strategic mergers was underway to bring levels of activity higher than ever before experienced. The major forces were (1) technology, (2) globalization, (3) deregulation, (4) the economic environment, (5) the method of payment, (6) share repurchases, and (7) stock options.

Technological change occurred at an explosive pace. Computer and software applications impacted all aspects of business. Microwave systems and fiber optics transformed the telecommunications industry. The Internet explosion created new industries and firms, changing the forms and nature of competitive relationships. Acquisitions by firms in all segments of the Internet economy were used to augment critical capabilities and to gain economies of scale and scope.

The globalization of markets matured in the 1990s. Competition came from distant places. Europe and other regions continued to move toward common markets. Just as the transcontinental railroads made the United States a common market at the end of the 1800s, technological developments in transportation and communications helped make the world a common market at the beginning of the new millennium.

The intensification of competition brought on by technological change and globalization led to deregulation in major industries. These include financial services, telecommunications, energy in all of its forms, airlines, and trucking. Increased competition forced deregulation, which in turn caused further massive reorganization of industries. M&As played a major role in the readjustment processes necessitated by deregulation.

M&A activities of all forms that resulted from the preceding three forces were facilitated by a favorable economic environment. Stock prices were rising. P/E ratios were moving upward. Interest rate levels were relatively low, and financing was available.

Many megamergers were made possible by stock-for-stock transactions. Deals of more than $500 million were predominantly stock for stock. Compared with the high-debt transactions of the 1980s, this placed less time pressure for achieving improvements in cash flows, permitting longer-term strategies to be executed.

Successful firms with superior revenue growth and favorable cost structures used programs of share repurchases to signal their favorable future prospects. The combination of strong performance and credible signals of future success produced impressive returns to shareholders.

Rising stock prices made the use of stock options a powerful tool for competing in the managerial labor market. High-tech firms added stock options as an important component of compensation to attract innovative, experienced executives. Some firms extended the use of stock options as a form of compensation widely throughout the organization. Stock options increase the number of shares outstanding; share repurchases provide a counterbalance. Both were widely used by firms in the "New Economy" sectors.

One measure of the impact of the 1990s is the size of M&As in relation to the level of economic activity as measured by gross domestic product (GDP). This is shown in Table 7.4. We have calculated annual averages for four time segments. During the deal decade of the 1980s, M&As represented less than 4% of GDP. For the period 1993 through 2000, M&As grew to about 9% of GDP. In 1999, the number was 15%. For perspective, the largest previous merger movement was at the beginning of the 1900s, when M&A activity was about 10% of the size of the economy.

TABLE 7.4 M&As in Relation to the Size of the Economy

Year	(1) Dollar Amount of M&As (in billions)	(2) GDP in Current Dollars (in billions)	(3) M&As as a Percent of GDP
1970	$ 16.4	$ 1,015.5	1.6%
1971	12.6	1,102.7	1.1
1972	16.7	1,212.8	1.4
1973	16.7	1,359.3	1.2
1974	12.4	1,472.8	0.8
1975	11.8	1,598.4	0.7
1976	20.0	1,782.8	1.1
1977	21.9	1,990.5	1.1
1978	34.2	2,249.7	1.5
1979	43.5	2,508.2	1.7
1980	44.3	2,732.0	1.6
1981	82.6	3,052.6	2.7
1982	53.8	3,166.0	1.7
1983	73.1	3,405.7	2.1
1984	122.2	3,772.2	3.2
1985	179.6	4,014.9	4.5
1986	173.1	4,240.3	4.1
1987	163.7	4,526.7	3.6
1988	246.9	4,880.6	5.1
1989	221.1	5,200.8	4.3
1990	108.2	5,463.6	2.0
1991	71.2	5,632.5	1.3
1992	96.7	6,318.9	1.5
1993	176.4	6,642.3	2.7
1994	226.7	7,054.3	3.2
1995	356.0	7,400.5	4.8
1996	494.9	7,813.2	6.3
1997	657.1	8,318.4	7.9
1998	1,191.9	8,781.5	13.6
1999	1,425.9	9,274.3	15.4
2000	1,325.7	9,824.6	13.5
2001	699.4	10,082.2	6.9
Annual Average:			
1970–1980	$ 22.8	$ 1,729.5	1.3
1981–1989	146.2	4,028.9	3.6
1990–1992	92.0	5,805.0	1.6
1993–2000	731.8	8,138.6	9.0
2001	699.4	10,082.2	6.9

Sources: Column 1: *Mergerstat Review, 2002*; Column 2: *Economic Report of the President*, various issues; *Economic Indicators.*

MERGER ACTIVITY AFTER THE BUBBLE

As shown in Chapter 1, the dollar value of mergers in 2001, adjusted for price level changes, was down 48% from 2000. For 2002, the dollar volume was estimated to be down about 40% from the previous year. The outlook for 2003 was estimated to be at about the same level as in 2002. The negative influences are a continuation of the factors causing the reduced level of activity in 2001 and 2002. The economic outlook for 2003 appears to be a continuation of the weak recovery of 2002. The level of M&As reflects the same influences as plant and equipment expenditures, which had not shown a recovery by early 2003. Corporate fraud and the dismal record of active acquirers such as Tyco and WorldCom also dampened the M&A market. The M&A activities in the media, telecom, and dot-com areas did not solve the overcapacity problem aggravated by the economic downturn that began in early 2000.

Yet our central theme is that M&As represent adjustments by industries and firms to change forces and economic turbulence, which have continued. In individual sectors, major mergers such as Northrop Grumman–TRW and Pfizer–Pharmacia have taken place. Financial buyers such as Bain Capital in October/November 2002 announced four transactions totaling $3.1 billion. Bain stated that since the middle of 2002, they had found opportunities to utilize the firm's strategy of turning around depressed situations. However, a full recovery of M&A activity, as in the past, requires a growing economy and a rising stock market.

TIMING OF MERGER ACTIVITY

The foregoing summary of the major merger movements in U.S. history suggests that somewhat different forces were operating in different historical economic and financial environments. The data show merger waves in the sense that in some groups of years, merger activity increases sharply. However, the evidence does not support merger waves in the sense of regular patterns of periodic rises and declines of merger activity.

Two broad generalizations can be made. One is that each of the major merger movements reflected some underlying economic or technological factors. The early twentieth century movement was triggered by the completion of the transnational railroads, which made the United States the first large common market. This was the major force behind the horizontal mergers that consolidated regional firms into national firms. The automobile and radio had an impact on distribution systems, stimulating the vertical mergers of the 1920s. (Some articles have disputed whether vertical mergers were predominant—our judgment of the evidence is that they were.) The conglomerate mergers of the 1960s reflected the view that good managers could manage unrelated activities. The use of differential P/E ratios to augment earnings growth in the near term produced spectacular stock price movements for major conglomerates such as ITT and Litton Industries. The deal decade of the 1980s was fueled by unwinding diversification and innovations in financing. The strategic mergers of the 1990s were produced by the combination of seven factors described earlier. In some respects, therefore, each major merger movement was associated with strong economic and technological factors. But the strength and nature of these factors were different for each of the five major merger movements.

A second generalization also can be made. Some common economic factors are associated with different levels of merger activity. Rising stock prices, low interest rates, favorable term structures of interest rates in the form of low short rates in relation to long rates, and narrow risk premiums in the form of small differentials between treasury bonds and medium- to low-rated corporate bonds are all favorable to higher levels of merger activity (Weston, 1953; Nelson, 1959; Melicher, Ledolter, and D'Antonio, 1983; Shughart and Tollison, 1984).

INDUSTRY CLUSTERING IN MERGER ACTIVITY

The evidence presented in this chapter, spanning well over 100 years, indicates that mergers cluster in time. Another important facet that we develop in this section is that merger activity in a given time interval tends to cluster in specific industries. Eis (1969) reported evidence of the industry clustering of merger activity during the 1919 to 1930 time period. Eis noted (p. 273) that although merger activity was widespread, "it was not equally important in every industry." Of the 25 industries studied, Eis (pp. 273–274) found that five industries represented more than two thirds of merger value. Gort (1969) found similar industry patterns in the 1950s. Gort (1969, p. 625) found that "the distribution both of acquisitions and of acquiring firms is highly concentrated in certain types of industries."

In this section, we review in detail several studies that document significant industry clustering in recent decades. The studies on industry clustering are summarized in Table 7.5. This analysis provides important insights about the question of why mergers occur.

INDUSTRY CLUSTERING IN THE 1980s

In an in-depth analysis of industry effects, Mitchell and Mulherin (1996) studied takeover and restructuring activity during the period 1982 to 1989. They began with 1,064 firms representing 51 industries and tracked which of the firms were the object of takeover or restructuring activity. Confirming the breadth of restructuring activity during the 1980s, Mitchell and

TABLE 7.5 Summary of Research on Industry Clustering in Merger Activity

Research Paper	Time Period	Number of Industries	Number of Mergers	Central Finding(s)
Eis (1969)	1919–1930	25	3,009	Five industries account for 67.5% of merger activity
Gort (1969)	1951–1959	101	5,534	Acquisitions concentrated in certain industries
Mitchell and Mulherin (1996)	1982–1989	51	440	Mergers cluster by industry and in time Change forces include deregulation and oil shocks
Mulherin and Boone (2000)	1990–1999	59	381	Mergers and divestitures cluster by industry Change forces include deregulation
Andrade and Stafford (2003)	1970–1994	55	1,536	Merger activity clusters through time by industry Mergers contractionary in 1970s, 1980s; expansionary in 1990s
Andrade, Mitchell, and Stafford (2001)	1973–1998	varied	4,300	Industry clustering varies across merger booms Deregulation an important force, especially in 1990s

Mulherin (1996) found that 57% of the sample firms were the object of a takeover attempt or experienced a major restructuring.

Confirming the importance of industry effects, Mitchell and Mulherin (1996) found significant differences in the rate and timing of merger activity across industries. For example, more than two thirds of the firms in industries such as broadcasting, petroleum producing, and air transport were acquired during the 1980s, but fewer than one third of the firms were acquired in the electronics, specialty chemicals, and metal-fabricating industries.

Moreover, takeover and restructuring activity was concentrated in time. Mitchell and Mulherin (1996) found that 50% of the mergers in a given industry clustered within an adjacent 2-year period; in other words, half of the takeovers in an industry occurred within one fourth of the time period studied.

Mitchell and Mulherin (1996) related the industry clustering during the 1980s to industry shocks, defined as economic factors that alter industry structure. One major force was federal deregulation, which led to above-average takeover and restructuring activity in industries such as air transport, broadcasting, entertainment, natural gas, and trucking.

Consistent with the model of Jensen (1993), a second major change force was the oil price shocks of 1973 and 1979. This factor affected not only firms in the oil industry, but also industries in which energy was a significant fraction of input costs. The industries most directly affected included integrated petroleum, natural gas, air transport, coal, and trucking.

Mitchell and Mulherin (1996) also found an above-average rate of takeover and restructuring activity in low-tech industries having small levels of R&D to sales. This finding is consistent with Jensen's (1993) observation that the ability to use public markets for leveraged financing increased the rate of takeover activity and the size of takeover targets.

Mitchell and Mulherin (1996) concluded that the interindustry patterns in takeovers and restructuring reflect the relative economic shocks to industries. Their results support the view that a major influence on the takeover activity of the 1980s was a combination of broad underlying economic, political, and financial forces.

INDUSTRY CLUSTERING IN THE 1990s

Mulherin and Boone (2000) performed related research on industry clustering in takeover and restructuring activity during the time period 1990 to 1999. They analyzed the restructuring activity for 1,305 firms from 59 industries. Comparable to evidence from the 1980s, Mulherin and Boone (2000) found that half of the sample firms were acquired or engaged in a major divestiture during the 1990s.

Also similar to the 1980's evidence, Mulherin and Boone (2000) found that merger activity tended to cluster by industry. However, the industries with an above-average incidence of activity in the 1990s were not identical to those of the 1980s. Some industries, such as broadcasting and petroleum producing, had high merger activity in both decades. However, heavy merger activity was a novel occurrence in the 1990s for industries such as banking and telecommunications.

In addition to studying merger activity, Mulherin and Boone (2000) examined industry patterns in divestiture activity during the 1990s. They found that divestitures tended to cluster within particular industries. For example, roughly half of the firms in the chemical, petroleum, and telecommunications industries engaged in a major divestiture during the 1990s. By contrast, few or no firms in the toiletries and cosmetics, securities brokerage, and grocery store industries conducted a major divestiture. These results suggest that economic change is an important factor affecting the corporate divestiture decision. Indeed, the change forces faced by firms can induce a variety of restructuring actions.

Comparable to the 1980s, Mulherin and Boone (2000) found that deregulation was an important force in inducing merger activity during the 1990s. However, many of the industries affected by deregulation differed between the two decades. Deregulation in the 1980s affected industries such as air transport, natural gas, and trucking; deregulation in the 1990s affected sectors such as banking, electric utilities, and telecommunications.

As a notable distinction from the 1980s, Mulherin and Boone (2000) found that mergers in the 1990s were not isolated to low-tech industries. Hence, mergers can be a response to industry growth as well as decline.

EXTENDED ANALYSIS OF INDUSTRY CLUSTERING

In comprehensive research, Andrade and Stafford (2003) studied industry patterns in merger activity during the period 1970 to 1994. They developed a sample of 1,536 mergers from 55 industries. Similar to prior research, Andrade and Stafford (2003) found that mergers tend to cluster by industry and over time. For example, the average industry in their sample experienced roughly 50% of its merger activity within a 5-year subperiod within the 25-year sample. In other words, half of the merger activity for a given industry occurred during one fifth of the sample period.

Andrade and Stafford (2003) also compared the value of industry merger activity with non-merger forms of investment such as capital expenditures and R&D and to capacity utilization. From this analysis, they concluded that mergers played a contractionary role in the 1970s and 1980s but played an expansionary role in the 1990s. These results resemble a juxtaposition of the findings from Mitchell and Mulherin (1996) and Mulherin and Boone (2000).

MERGERS AND DEREGULATION

An important finding in the analysis of industry patterns in merger activity is that deregulation is an important change force. In this section, we build on the evidence of the relation between deregulation and merger activity, and also consider the performance effects that this activity has on the deregulated industries.

INDUSTRY CLUSTERING AND DEREGULATION

A detailed analysis of deregulation and merger activity is included in the comprehensive evidence in Andrade, Mitchell, and Stafford (2001). Their main sample entailed 4,300 completed mergers during the time period 1973 to 1998. Consistent with previous work, they found that mergers tended to cluster in time. For the 1970s, Andrade, Mitchell, and Stafford found that the top five industries based on annual merger activity were metal mining, real estate, oil and gas, apparel, and machinery. During the 1980s, the top five industries in their sample were oil and gas, textile, miscellaneous manufacturing, nondepository credit, and food. In the 1990s, the top five industries were metal mining, media and telecommunications, banking, real estate, and hotels.

To study the importance of deregulation, Andrade, Mitchell, and Stafford (2001) classified the following industries as having substantial deregulation: airlines (1978), broadcasting (1984 and 1996), entertainment (1984), natural gas (1978), trucking (1980), banks and thrifts (1994), utilities (1992), and telecommunications (1996). The years listed in parentheses are the dates of major federal deregulation affecting the industries. Andrade, Mitchell, and Stafford (2001) defined a deregulation window as the 10-year period (3 years before through 6 years after) around each of the event years.

Using this classification scheme, Andrade, Mitchell, and Stafford (2001) measured the fraction of merger activity represented by industries in the deregulation window. They found that during most of the 1980s, the deregulated industries accounted for 10% to 15% of merger activity. After 1988, however, the deregulated industries made up roughly half of the merger volume. Indeed, Andrade, Mitchell, and Stafford (2001) concluded that the 1990s can be viewed as the "decade of deregulation."

DEREGULATION, MERGERS, AND PERFORMANCE

Related to the evidence linking mergers and deregulation is also a body of research that studies the effect of deregulation on industry performance. Winston (1998) surveyed the evidence on changes in industry efficiency and consumer welfare following deregulation. For sectors ranging from transport (airlines, trucking, and railroads) to natural gas to banking, the evidence generally indicated that deregulation has led to greater capacity utilization, lower firm costs, and reduced consumer prices.

Winston (1998, pp. 94–95) noted that deregulation generally is followed by merger activity. He suggested several reasons why mergers are related to the improved corporate performance and consumer welfare. For example, mergers have allowed firms to enter new markets, while at the same time providing consumers with expanded choices. Indeed, in many deregulated industries as diverse as natural gas and banking, mergers have enabled firms to form nationwide networks.

Significant internal corporate reorganization has occurred in many deregulated industries to match the external industry restructuring. Kole and Lehn (1999) provided a detailed analysis of the effect of deregulation on corporate governance in the airline industry. Zingales (1998) studied the interactions of deregulation and capital structure in the trucking industry.

A notable study of the joint effect of deregulation and mergers on corporate performance is contained in Becher's (2000) analysis of the banking industry. Becher (2000) studied 558 commercial bank mergers during the period 1980 to 1997. Because a large majority of the mergers in the sample occurred in the deregulated environment of the 1990s, the analysis provides a direct test of the effect of mergers and deregulation on corporate value. Using event study techniques, Becher (2000) found that bank mergers in the 1990s improved shareholder wealth. The combined return to target and bidder shareholders averaged 3.53%. These results indicate that mergers are not only a response to change forces, but that this response enhances wealth.

Weston 2001 provided a general review of the interrelations between change forces and merger activity. The appendix to this chapter studies the telecommunications industry as a means of illustrating the relation among mergers and change forces such as technology and deregulation.

INTERNATIONAL PERSPECTIVES

The data on M&A activities in other countries are not as complete as those for the United States. However, the evidence is clear that the increased M&A and restructuring activity is not unique to the United States. In all of the developed countries of the world, M&A activity in recent decades has paralleled the patterns in the United States. The underlying major force has been the internationalization of markets and the globalization of competition.

An interesting historical study on international merger activity is provided by McGowan (1971). He compared merger activity in four countries (United States, United Kingdom, Australia, and France) across 20 industries during the period 1950 to 1964. In results remarkably similar to recent studies from the United States, McGowan (1971, pp. 238–240) found that merger activity clustered significantly in particular industries during the sample period. Moreover, he reported (p. 240) "strong intercountry similarities in the industries" with above-average merger activity. McGowan (1971) interpreted the results to reflect the view that mergers are an adaptive response to changes in technology and market conditions.

Industries and firms in countries throughout the world have experienced the pressures of the increased intensity of competitive forces. Some have argued that relaxed government policies in the early 1980s stimulated an M&A wave in the United States. However, antimerger laws and regulations clearly were increased in the United Kingdom in the 1980s. Also, the policies of the European Economic Community have tightened antimerger regulations since the 1980s. Nevertheless, M&A activity increased in the United Kingdom and in all of Europe in the face of tighter legal restraints. This again suggests that M&A activity is determined primarily by underlying economic and financial forces.

Analysis by Mulherin, Netter, and Stegemoller (2002) found direct evidence of the effects of change forces on international mergers. They studied a set of non-U.S. firms that were first privatized and then became targets during the period 1990 to 1999. Of the 39 sample firms spanning 21 industries, 22 firms (57%) came from only 2 industries: banking and utilities. These results indicate that non-U.S. mergers cluster in time by industry and that the mergers respond to economic and political change forces. Indeed, privatization is the non-U.S equivalent of deregulation.

Summary

To place merger activity in perspective, we have traced the major merger movements since the turn of the twentieth century. All of the merger movements coincided with sustained growth of the economy and with significant changes in business environments. The horizontal merger movement in the 1890s was associated with the completion of national transportation systems and made the United States the first broad common market. Mergers in the 1920s were represented by forward and backward vertical integration. They appeared to represent responses to radio, which made national advertising feasible, and to the automobile, which facilitated national distribution systems. The conglomerate merger movement of the 1960s appeared to reflect the philosophy of management technology that had developed in the 1950s. The mergers of the 1980s were associated with innovations in financing and the reversal of the diversification of the 1960s. The strategic mergers of the 1990s were propelled by favorable economic environments and by new forces of technology, globalization, and deregulation.

Fluctuations in merger activity over the years stimulated a number of attempts to explain the determinants of merger timing. These studies have demonstrated an association among merger activity and various macroeconomic variables. The main macroeconomic forces are rising stock prices, low interest rates, and favorable conditions of financing availability.

Recent evidence indicates that mergers cluster not only in time but also in specific industries. Important industry forces related to merger activity include input costs such as energy prices and financing vehicles such as debt markets. Deregulation is a growing source of merger activity in the United States, and similar effects can be expected from the privatization movement in non-U.S. markets.

Questions

7.1 Describe each of the major merger movements that have occurred in the United States, indicating the major forces involved.

7.2 What percentage of gross domestic product is represented by M&A activity?

7.3 Discuss the effect of the following variables on merger activity:
   a. The growth rate of GDP.
   b. Interest rate levels.
   c. Interest rate risk premiums.
   d. Monetary stringency.

7.4 What are some reasons why merger activity clusters by industry?

7.5 What are some reasons why deregulation is associated with heightened merger activity?

References

Andrade, Gregor, and Erik Stafford, "Investigating the Economic Role of Mergers," *Journal of Corporate Finance*, forthcoming, 2003.

Andrade, Gregor, Mark Mitchell, and Erik Stafford, "New Evidence and Perspectives on Mergers," *Journal of Economic Perspectives* 15, Spring 2001, pp. 103–120.

Becher, David A., "The Valuation Effects of Bank Mergers," *Journal of Corporate Finance* 6, July 2000, pp. 189–214.

Coase, R. H., "The Nature of the Firm," *Economica* 4, November 1937, pp. 386–405.

Dewing, Arthur Stone, *The Financial Policy of Corporations*, Vol. 2, New York: The Ronald Press Company, 1953.

Eis, Carl, "The 1919–1930 Merger Movement in American Industry," *Journal of Law and Economics* 12, October 1969, pp. 267–296.

Golbe, Devra L., and Lawrence J. White, "A Time-Series Analysis of Mergers and Acquisitions in the U.S. Economy," chapter 9 in Alan J. Auerbach, ed., *Corporate Takeover: Causes and Consequences*, Chicago: The University of Chicago Press, 1988, pp. 265–309.

Gort, Michael, "An Economic Disturbance Theory of Mergers," *Quarterly Journal of Economics* 83, November 1969, pp. 624–642.

Holderness, Clifford G., and Dennis P. Sheehan, "Raiders or Saviors?: The Evidence on Six Controversial Investors," *Journal of Financial Economics* 14, 1985, pp. 555–579.

Jensen, Michael C., "The Modern Industrial Revolution, Exit, and the Failure of Internal Control Systems," *Journal of Finance*, July 1993, pp. 831–880.

Kole, Stacey R., and Kenneth M. Lehn, "Deregulation and the Adaptation of Governance Structure: The Case of the U.S. Airline Industry," *Journal of Financial Economics* 52, April 1999, pp. 79–117.

Livermore, Shaw, "The Success of Industrial Mergers," *Quarterly Journal of Economics* 50, November 1935, pp. 68–96.

Markham, Jesse W., "Survey of Evidence and Findings on Mergers," *Business Concentration and Price Policy*, National Bureau of Economic Research, Princeton, NJ: Princeton University Press, 1955.

McGowan, John J., "International Comparisons of Merger Activity," *Journal of Law and Economics* 14, April 1971, pp. 233–250.

Melicher, R. W., J. Ledolter, and L. D'Antonio, "A Time Series Analysis of Aggregate Merger Activity," *The Review of Economics and Statistics* 65, August 1983, pp. 423–430.

Mitchell, Mark L., and J. Harold Mulherin, "The Impact of Industry Shocks on Takeover and Restructuring Activity," *Journal of Financial Economics* 41, June 1996, pp. 193–229.

Moody, John, *The Truth About the Trusts*, New York: Moody Publishing Company, 1904.

Mulherin, J. Harold, and Audra L. Boone, "Comparing Acquisitions and Divestitures," *Journal of Corporate Finance* 6, July 2000, pp. 117–139.

Mulherin, J. Harold, Jeffry M. Netter, and Michael Stegemoller, "Privatization and the Market for Corporate Control," working paper, Claremont McKenna College and University of Georgia, 2002.

Nelson, R. L., *Merger Movements in American Industry, 1895–1956*, Princeton, NJ: Princeton University Press, 1959.

Salter, Malcolm S., and Wolf A. Weinhold, *Diversification Through Acquisition*, New York: The Free Press, 1979.

———, "Merger Trends and Prospects for the 1980s," U.S. Department of Commerce, Harvard University, December 1980.

Shleifer, Andrei, and Robert W. Vishny, "The Takeover Wave of the 1980s," *Science* 249, August 1990, pp. 745–749.

Shughart, W. F., II, and R. O. Tollison, "The Random Character of Merger Activity," *Rand Journal of Economics* 15, Winter 1984, pp. 500–509.

Stigler, George J., "Monopoly and Oligopoly by Merger," *American Economic Review* 40, May 1950, pp. 23–34.

Stocking, G. W., "Commentary on Markham, 'Survey of Evidence and Findings on Mergers,'" in *Business Concentration and Price Policy*, Princeton, NJ: Princeton University Press, 1955, pp. 191–212.

Varian, Hal, "If There Was a New Economy, Why Wasn't There a New Economics?" *New York Times*, 17 January 2002, p. C2.

Weston, J. F., *The Role of Mergers in the Growth of Large Firms*, Berkeley and Los Angeles: University of California Press, 1953, chapter 5.

Weston, J. Fred, "M&As as Adjustment Processes," *Journal of Industry, Competition, and Trade* 1, December 2001, pp. 395–410.

———, and Surenda K. Mansinghka, "Tests of the Efficiency Performance of Conglomerate Firms," *Journal of Finance* 26, September 1971, pp. 919–936.

Winston, Clifford, "U.S. Industry Adjustment to Economic Deregulation," *Journal of Economic Perspectives* 12, Summer 1998, pp. 89–110.

Zingales, Luigi, "Survival of the Fittest or the Fattest? Exit and Financing in the Trucking Industry," *Journal of Finance* 53, June 1998, pp. 905–938.

APPENDIX A

─────⋘∘⧸∘⧸∘⋙─────

TELECOMMUNICATIONS INDUSTRY CASE STUDY

The telecommunications sector provides a cogent illustration of the effects that change forces such as technology and deregulation have on corporate strategy and corporate restructuring activity. In this case, we first present the causes and effects of the major regulatory changes impacting the industry including the Bell breakup in 1984 and the Telecommunications Act of 1996. We discuss how deregulation and technology jointly alter the risks faced by the industry and, consequently, affect the strategic process of the telecommunications incumbents and potential entrants. We then study the merger activity during the 1990s, as well as since the year 2000. The specific mergers show the interacting effects of deregulation and technology on restructuring activity.

BACKGROUND ON TELECOMMUNICATIONS DEREGULATION

The telecommunications industry dates to the nineteenth century and Alexander Graham Bell. An important modern date is 1984, when AT&T was broken up. Under arrangements with the federal government, the new AT&T would provide long-distance phone service and would compete with firms such as MCI and Sprint. This settlement was the outcome of a long debate that began in the 1970s with a federal antitrust suit against AT&T.

In the 1984 breakup, local phone service was divided among seven regional operating companies, which were referred to as the Baby Bells: Ameritech, Bell Atlantic, BellSouth, Nynex, Pacific Telesis, Southwest Bell, and US West. These firms were granted monopolies in local phone service in their areas of the country. However, under the conditions of the breakup agreement, the regional operating companies were not to provide long-distance phone service.

Twelve years later, further significant regulatory change occurred in the industry. The Telecommunications Act of 1996 altered the terms of the Bell breakup. The regional operating companies were allowed to provide long-distance service, on the condition that their local market was deemed competitive. The 1996 act also removed restrictions on the combination of phone and cable service.

CAUSES AND EFFECTS OF TELECOMMUNICATIONS DEREGULATION

Deregulation and Technology

An important phenomenon illustrated by the telecommunications industry is that deregulation often occurs in the midst of substantial technological change. A case in point is the 1984 removal of the regulated monopoly status of long-distance phone service in the United States. As we noted in Chapter 5, this deregulation evolved contemporaneously with the development of microwave and fiber-optic technology by firms such as MCI and Sprint, which made these firms viable competitors against AT&T's wireline network. Indeed, the interaction of technology and deregulation was not isolated to the United States. The initial privatization of British Telecom, for example, occurred at the same time as the Bell breakup.

Further technological developments interacted with the causes and effects of the Telecommunications Act of 1996. Cellular technology greatly improved between 1984 and 1996. The wireless phone was invented by Bell Labs in 1947. However, commercial viability was noticeably enhanced in the 1990s when McCaw Cellular produced innovations that facilitated nationwide roaming networks. Such innovations enabled direct competition with local phone service.

Technological change has, more generally, blurred distinctions across sectors. Innovations related to satellite use of the electromagnetic spectrum have spurred more competition within media transmission as a whole, engaging companies that previously specialized in either phones or cable. As a whole, much of the deregulation in 1996 was spurred by technology and its effect on the competitive features of local phone service and cable transmission of media.

Deregulation and Industry Risk

The interaction of technological change and deregulation can be expected to alter the risk faced by the telecommunications industry. One source of changing risk stems from the buffering effect modeled by Sam Peltzman (1976). The regulatory buffering model predicts that a firm subject to governmental rate regulation will face an altered, less risky profit stream relative to a nonregulated firm. The intuition provided by Peltzman (1976) is that regulators will not permit the firm to gouge customers, but at the same time will always allow the regulated firm to cover costs and not let the firm go bankrupt. Support for Peltzman's (1976) model has been provided by Norton (1985) for electric utilities, and by Fraser and Kannan (1990) for a variety of industries including financial services and transportation.

Chen and Merville (1986) studied deregulation in the telecommunications industry to provide a novel test of the buffering hypothesis. They relied on the natural experiment of the 1984 Bell breakup to examine the effects of deregulation on risk within an industry. Consistent with Peltzman's (1976) model, Chen and Merville (1986) found that AT&T's risk increased after 1984.

Another reason that deregulation can be expected to be followed by an increase in industry risk stems from the fact that deregulation usually is associated with new entry. For example, the Telecommunications Act of 1996 was associated with a significant increase in the entry of competitive local exchange carriers, known in industry jargon as CLECs. These new entrants were generally smaller, younger firms that were seeking the opportunities provided by the removal of the monopoly control of the regional Bell companies (Gilpin, 2002, p. 8).

A case in point is Allegiance Telecom, a company that went public in 1998. In the firm's initial public offering (IPO) prospectus filed with the U.S. Securities and Exchange Commission, it is stated, "The Company believes that the Telecommunications Act of 1996, by opening the local exchange market to competition, has created an attractive opportunity for new facilities-based CLECs like the Company" (p. 3). Allegiance Telecom also alerted investors regarding the risks inherent in the new company's operations, stating in the prospectus:

> There can be no assurance that it will be able to achieve any of these objectives, generate sufficient revenues to make principal and interest

payments on its indebtedness or compete successfully in the telecommunications industry. (p. 9).

This entry of new, riskier firms such as Allegiance Telecom after the passage of the Telecommunications Act of 1996 would be expected to measurably increase industry risk. As a simple test of the effects of entry, we estimated the stock market beta of the Dow Jones Telecom Index, using the S&P 500 as a proxy for the market index. We indeed found that risk in the telecommunications industry increased subsequent to the 1996 act. The beta for the DJ Telecom Index was noticeably below 1 during the period 1991 to 1995. The beta increased to more than 1.5 during the period 1996 to 2000. This increase in industry risk is an important effect of deregulation and corresponding technological change.

Deregulation, Technology, and Corporate Strategy

The interacting forces of technology and deregulation directly affect the strategic process at the firms in the telecommunications industry. The obvious example is AT&T, a company that has tried to re-invent itself several times since the 1984 breakup. Most of AT&T's strategic initiatives attempt to incorporate new technologies or react to the new business opportunities provided by deregulation. AT&T dabbled in computers by acquiring NCR in 1991, cellular by acquiring McCaw in 1993, and broadband by acquiring TCI in 1999. As summarized in many media articles, the results of these efforts have been mixed at best.

The effect of deregulation and technology on corporate strategy is not isolated to AT&T. All of the firms in the industry must continually consider avenues for expansion, as well as areas that should be retrenched.

An interesting case on the strategic process in the telecommunications industry is provided in Hertzel, Smith, and Smith (2001). They studied the causes and effects of the different strategies in the cable and phone industries. They focused on the period surrounding the proposed merger of Bell Atlantic and TCI in 1993. Confirming the importance of strategy in an ever-changing business environment, Hertzel, Smith, and Smith (2001) concluded that strategic decisions of particular firms in the cable and phone industries have spillover effects on the valuation of other industry competitors. See also Maloney and McCormick (1995) and Green and Lehn (1995).

DEREGULATION, TECHNOLOGY, AND CORPORATE RESTRUCTURING

Deregulation and technological change jointly create new business opportunities for incumbent firms in an industry, as well as for potential entrants. One way to take advantage of such opportunities is through in-house production. An alternative is to enter a new opportunity by acquiring another firm. Such a choice will arguably be based on the transaction cost considerations modeled by Coase (1937). We maintain that the acquisition route is often the least-cost response to deregulation and technological change. In this section, we study many of the important mergers in the telecommunications industry during the decade of the 1990s, as well as since the year 2000.

Telecommunications Mergers in the 1990s

During the 1990s, the telecommunications industry experienced heavy merger activity. Indeed, in a number of research papers, the telecommunications sector was ranked as one of the top industries for mergers during the 1990s. See, for example, Mitchell and Mulherin (1996, Table 1); Mulherin and Boone (2000, Table 3); and Andrade, Mitchell, and Stafford (2001, Table 2).

Table A7.1 provides details of some of the major mergers in the telecommunications industry during the 1990s. The full table lists the 23 firms that comprised the Telecommunications Services Industry in the *Value Line Investment Survey* on January 19, 1990. This set of firms was part of the broader sample used by Mulherin and Boone (2000) in their study of merger activity during the 1990s.

The firms in Table A7.1 were the major telecom players as of 1990. The sample includes AT&T and the seven Baby Bells: Ameritech, Bell Atlantic, BellSouth, NYNEX, Pacific Telesis, Southwestern Bell, and US West. Also included are long-distance stalwarts MCI and Sprint as well as GTE, the operator of a major non-Bell communications system.

Table A7.1 reports the extent of merger activity within the telecommunications industry during the 1990s. The table reports the firms that were acquired, the announcement and completion dates of the merger, and the bidding firm in the acquisition. As shown, 10 of the 23 firms were the targets in a merger, an acquisition rate of 43%.

An important aspect of the telecommunications mergers in the 1990s was the remerger of many of the Baby Bells. SBC Communications (formerly Southwestern Bell) acquired Ameritech (in 1999) and Pacific Telesis (in 1997), and Bell Atlantic acquired NYNEX (in 1997). Notably, these mergers occurred in the midst of the passage of the Telecommunications Act of 1996, attesting to the association between deregulation and merger activity. Among other things, these mergers were a prelude for the entry of the former Baby Bells into long-distance service.

Several other mergers in Table A7.1 occurred following the Telecommunications Act of 1996. WorldCom acquired MCI in 1998 in a merger that *BusinessWeek* said could change the face of communications by combining local, long-distance, and Internet service (Elstrom, 1997, pp. 26–34). Global Crossing acquired Rochester Telephone (whose name had changed to Frontier Corporation) in 1999 as a means of linking its international fiber-optics network with the networks in the United States.

Several generalizations can be garnered from the merger data in Table A7.1. First, merger activity was broad in the telecommunications industry during the 1990s; 43% of the major firms were acquired. Second, a better part of the merger activity was related to deregulation; 7 of the 10 mergers listed in Table A7.1 were completed after the passage of the Telecommunications Act of 1996. Finally, the mergers responded to the opportunities presented by ongoing changes in technology such as the growth of the Internet and fiber optics.

The Telecommunications Industry in 2000

The telecommunications industry of today continues to be shaped by ongoing changes in technology and regulation, and by related organizational changes brought about by corporate restructuring. Some insights into this ongoing change can be gleaned by considering the list of telecommunications firms in Table A7.2

One thing to note is the difference in composition of the telecommunications industry in the year 2000 (Table A7.2) compared to the 1990s (Table A7.1). Relatively fewer of the firms are mainstream companies from the Bell family. This reflects, in part, the remerger of many of the Baby Bells reported in Table A7.1

Another reason for the changing composition of the industry is the entry of new firms following the Telecommunications Act of 1996. Ten of the 35 firms

TABLE A7.1   The Telecommunications Services Industry in the 1990s

Firm	Acquired?	Announce Date	Complete Date	Bidder
ALLTEL Corp.				
Ameritech	Yes	5/11/98	8/8/99	SBC Comm.
AT&T				
Bell Atlantic				
BellSouth Corp.				
C-TEC Corp.				
Centel Corp.	Yes	5/27/92	3/10/93	Sprint
Century Telephone				
Cincinnati Bell				
Citizens Utilities				
COMSAT Corp.	Yes	9/3/98	9/20/99	Lockheed Martin
Contel Corp.	Yes	7/13/90	3/15/91	GTE Corp.
GTE Corp.				
LIN Broadcasting	Yes	6/7/89	3/6/90	McCaw Cellular
MCI	Yes	11/2/96	9/15/98	WorldCom
NYNEX Corp.	Yes	12/18/95	8/15/97	Bell Atlantic
Pacific Telesis	Yes	4/1/96	4/2/97	SBC Comm.
Rochester Tel.	Yes	3/18/99	9/28/99	Global Crossing
Southern N.E. Tel.	Yes	1/5/98	10/26/98	SBC Comm.
Southwestern Bell				
Sprint				
Telephone & Data				
US West				

Number of firms acquired: 10
Number of firms in industry: 23
Rate of acquisition: 43%

(29%) in Table A7.2 went public in 1996 or later. These new entrants included several competitive local exchange carriers such as Allegiance Telecommunications, Level 3 Communications, RCN Corporation, and Teligent, which sought to utilize the opportunities created by the changing regulation of local phone service.

As reported in Table A7.2, merger activity in the telecommunications industry continued into the year 2000. Six of the 35 firms were acquired in 2000, a rate of 17%. These mergers included the large deal between Bell Atlantic and GTE Corp. that created Verizon and the acquisition of US West, another former Baby Bell, by Qwest. Another notable merger that was completed in 2000 was AT&T's acquisition of the broadband company MediaOne Group. Such mergers continue the trend from the 1990s that followed the Telecommunications Act of 1996.

SUMMARY

The telecommunications industry has witnessed significant restructuring since the Bell breakup of 1984. This restructuring activity has heightened following the passage of the Telecommunications Act of 1996.

This restructuring activity highlights the interacting effects of change forces such as technology and deregulation. Technological changes such as advancements in the use of microwave transmission and fiber optics altered the competitive structure of the telecommunications industry in the period leading up to the 1984 Bell breakup. More recent developments

TABLE A7.2 The Telecommunications Services Industry in 2000

Firm	Acquired?	Announce Date	Complete Date	Bidder
Adtran Inc.				
Allegiance Telecom				
ALLTEL Corp.				
AT&T				
Bell Atlantic				
BellSouth Corp.				
Billing Concepts				
Broadcom Corp.				
Broadwing Inc.				
CenturyTel Inc.				
Citizens Utilities				
Dycom Industries				
GTE Corp.	Yes	6/28/98	6/30/2000	Bell Atlantic (Verizon)
Global Crossing				
Level 3 Comm.				
MCI Worldcom				
MediaOne Group	Yes	3/22/99	6/16/2000	AT&T
Metromedia Fiber				
NTL Inc.				
Nextel Comm.				
Nextlink Comm.				
Omnipoint Corp.	Yes	6/23/99	2/28/2000	Voicestream Wireless
Paging Network	Yes	11/8/99	11/10/2000	Arch Comm.
PanAmSat Corp.				
RCN Corp.				
SBC Comm.				
Sprint Corp.				
Sprint PCS Group				
TV Guide	Yes	10/4/99	7/13/2000	Gemstar
Telephone & Data				
Teligent Inc.				
U.S. Cellular				
US West	Yes	5/17/99	7/3/2000	Qwest
Western Wireless				
WinStar Comm.				

Number of firms acquired: 6
Number of firms in industry: 35
Rate of acquisition: 17%

Source: Value Line Investment Survey, January 7, 2000.

in cellular, digital, satellite, and broadband technology played a part in the forces inducing the further regulatory changes in 1996. Indeed, the Telecommunications Act of 1996 reflected the growing evolution of substitute and lower-cost modes of media transmission and communication.

The specific examples of restructuring activity discussed in this appendix demonstrate how strategic merger decisions are predictable reactions to an ongoing, altered business environment. The remerger of many Baby Bells, the union of MCI and WorldCom, and the joining of AT&T with MediaOne Group were responses to the evolving, competitive conditions brought about by deregulation and technological change.

An important aspect of deregulation is that it adds to industry risk. The model of Peltzman (1976) poses regulation as a mechanism that prevents price gouging but at the same time does not allow regulated firms to go bankrupt. General evidence on industry betas indicates that risk increased in the telecommunications industry following deregulation in 1996. The serious difficulties of major industry entrants such as WorldCom and Global Crossing attest to the riskiness of a deregulated environment.

QUESTIONS

A7.1 What were the primary features of the Telecommunications Act of 1996? Why would this act be associated with subsequent merger activity?

A7.2 What are some reasons why industry risk increases after deregulation?

A7.3 Choose a merger listed in Table A7.1 or Table A7.2. Using financial media such as LexisNexis or merger documents from the SEC's EDGAR filings, summarize the reasons given for the transaction and the synergies expected. To what extent is the merger related to regulatory and technological change?

A7.4 Choose a merger listed in Table A7.1 or Table A7.2. Using the announcement date listed in the table, conduct an event study of the merger. What was the stock market reaction to the proposal of the merger for (1) the target and (2) the bidder?

REFERENCES

Andrade, Gregor, Mark Mitchell, and Erik Stafford, "New Evidence and Perspectives on Mergers," *Journal of Economic Perspectives* 15, Spring 2001, pp. 103–120.

Beker, Victor A., "Preparing Competition for the 21st Century: The U.S. Telecommunications Act of 1996," *International Journal of Development Planning Literature* 16, April-June 2001, pp. 7–29.

Chen, Andrew H., and Larry J. Merville, "An Analysis of Divestiture Effects Resulting from Deregulation," *Journal of Finance* 41, December 1986, pp. 997–1010.

Chen, Jim, "The Magnificent Seven: American Telephony's Deregulatory Shootout," *Hastings Law Journal* 50, August 1999, pp. 1503–1584.

Coase, R. H., "The Nature of the Firm," *Economica* 4, November 1937, pp. 386–405.

Elstrom, Peter, "The New World Order," *BusinessWeek*, 13 October 1997, pp. 26–34.

Frank, Robert, and Deborah Solomon, "Cable Industry Mergers? Let's Count the Ways," *Wall Street Journal*, January 22, 2002, p. C1.

Fraser, Donald R., and Srinivasan Kannan, "Deregulation Risk: Evidence from Earnings Forecasts and Stock Prices," *Financial Management* 19, Winter 1990, pp. 68–76.

Gilpin, Kenneth N., "The Strong Will Survive the Fallout in Telecom," *New York Times*, February 3, 2002, p. 8.

Green, Kevin C., and Kenneth M. Lehn, "The Effect of Enhanced Competition on the Equity Values of the Regional Bell Operating Companies," *Managerial and Decision Economics* 16, July-August 1995, pp. 469–477.

Hazlett, Thomas W., "Economic and Political Consequences of the 1996 Telecommunications Act," *Hastings Law Journal* 50, August 1999, pp. 1359–1394.

Hertzel, Michael, Janet Kiholm Smith, and Richard L. Smith, "Competitive Impact of Strategic Restructuring: Evidence from the Telecommunications Industry," *Industrial and Corporate Change* 10, 2001, pp. 207–246.

Maloney, Michael T., and Robert E. McCormick, "Realignment in Telecommunications," *Managerial and Decision Economics* 16, July-August 1995, pp. 401–425.

Mitchell, Mark L., and J. Harold Mulherin, "The Impact of Industry Shocks on Takeover and Restructuring Activity," *Journal of Financial Economics* 41, June 1996, pp. 193–229.

Mulherin, J. Harold, and Audra L. Boone, "Comparing Acquisitions and Divestitures," *Journal of Corporate Finance* 6, July 2000, pp. 117–139.

Norton, Seth W., "Regulation and Systematic Risk: The Case of Electric Utilities," *Journal of Law and Economics* 28, October 1985, pp. 671–686.

O'Donaghue, Jane, and David Caouette, "AT&T Wireless Is Separate," *Business Wire*, July 9, 2001.

Peltzman, Sam, "Toward a More General Theory of Regulation," *Journal of Law and Economics* 19, August 1976, pp. 211–241.

Weston, J. Fred, *Cases in Dynamic Finance: Mergers and Restructuring,* Upper Saddle River, New Jersey: Prentice Hall, 2002.

White, James A., Monica Longley, and Tim Carrington, "Bell's Legacy: AT&T Gives Details on How It Will Divide Its $152 Billion Assets," *Wall Street Journal*, November 17, 1983, p. 1.

Young, Shawn, Yochi J. Dreazen, and Rebecca Blumenstein, "How Efforts to Open Local Phone Markets Helped the Baby Bells," *Wall Street Journal*, February 11, 2002, p. A1.

Young, Shawn, "AT&T's Long, Troubled Trip Back to Its Past," *Wall Street Journal*, December 21, 2001, p. B4.

CHAPTER 8
EMPIRICAL TESTS OF M&A PERFORMANCE

This chapter reviews the large body of empirical research on mergers and acquisitions. The evidence provides direct tests of the theories discussed in Chapter 6. In relation to Chapter 7, which focused on the *causes* of merger activity, much of the evidence in this chapter reports analysis of the *effects* of mergers and acquisitions.

The chapter begins with the evidence on the combined return to target and bidder shareholders in M&A transactions. The chapter then reviews the factors found to affect the magnitude of target and bidder returns. The chapter also considers the measurement of postmerger performance, as well as antitrust issues related to mergers, efficiency, and market power.

THE COMBINED RETURNS IN MERGERS AND ACQUISITIONS

One of the most important empirical questions in merger research is whether the combined return to bidders and targets is positive or negative. In other words, are mergers positive net present value investments?

Merger theories based on synergy and efficiency predict that the combined return in a merger is positive. By contrast, theories based on the agency costs of free cash flow and managerial entrenchment argue that mergers destroy wealth and predict that the combined returns in a merger are negative. Roll's (1986) hubris hypothesis suggested that any wealth gain to target firms merely represents redistribution from bidders and predicts that the net merger gains are zero.

COMBINED RETURNS: EVENT STUDY EVIDENCE

Much of the empirical analysis of the combined returns in mergers has employed event study methods. The early evidence reviewed by Jensen and Ruback (1983) found that mergers created wealth for target shareholders and were roughly a break-even endeavor for bidders. This evidence was generally taken to indicate that mergers created wealth. Roll (1986) observed, however, that caution must be taken in interpreting merger gains. Among other things, bidders are often much larger than targets, implying that the proper consideration of merger gains must carefully match each target and bidder firm and estimate a combined return that weights the size of the two merger parties.

Subsequent analysis has reported evidence on the combined returns to target and bidder firms in mergers and acquisitions. A selection of this research is reported in Table 8.1. The evidence finds that, on average, the combined return to mergers and acquisitions is positive.

Bradley, Desai, and Kim (1988) studied a sample of 236 tender offers that occurred in the period 1963 to 1984. Using an event window from 5 days before the announcement of the first bid through 5 days after the announcement of the ultimately successful bid, they found that target shareholders gain 31.77% and bidder shareholders gain 0.97% at the announcement of the tender offer. The value-weighted portfolio of matched targets and bidders gains 7.43%. Bradley, Desai, and Kim concluded that, "Successful tender offers generate synergistic gains and lead to a more efficient allocation of corporate resources" (1988, p. 13).

Subsequent empirical research has resulted in similar conclusions. Kaplan and Weisbach (1992) and Servaes (1991) studied several hundred mergers and acquisitions that occurred in the 1970s and 1980s and estimated combined returns of roughly 4%. Mulherin and Boone (2000) analyzed a sample of 281 takeovers from the 1990s and found positive combined returns. Mulherin and Boone also found that the magnitude of the combined return is related directly to the relative size of the takeover event and conclude that their results "are consistent with the synergistic theory of the firm . . . and are inconsistent with nonsynergistic models based on management entrenchment, empire building and managerial hubris" (2000, p. 135).

Andrade, Mitchell, and Stafford (2001) performed a comprehensive analysis of the combined returns in a sample of 3,688 mergers from the period 1973 to 1998. They found that the combined return to targets and bidders is roughly 2%. They concluded that, "mergers create value on behalf of the shareholders of combined firms" (p. 112).

COMBINED RETURNS: EXTENDED ANALYSIS

Berkovitch and Narayanan (1993) proposed further tests to distinguish between the synergy, hubris, and agency theories of mergers and acquisitions. As an extension to the analysis of the *average* gains in mergers, the tests considered the *correlation* between target gains and total gains and between target gains and bidder gains. Berkovitch and Narayanan (1993) argued that if synergy is the driving force, these correlations will be positive. By contrast, if hubris is at play, the correlation between the target gain and total gain will be zero. If agency is the primary factor, this correlation will be negative.

In their sample of 330 tender offers from the period 1963 to 1988, Berkovitch and Narayanan (1993) found that 250, or 76%, achieved positive total gains. Moreover, the correlation between target and bidder returns is positive and significant. Berkovitch and Narayanan (1993) concluded that synergy is the dominant force in mergers and takeovers. However, they noted that agency and hubris also are at play in some takeovers.

COMBINED MERGER RETURNS: ANALYSIS OF THE BANKING INDUSTRY

We review recent analysis from the banking industry to provide further evidence regarding the effects of mergers on the combined returns to target and bidder shareholders. The focus on a particular industry also sheds light on the sources of the wealth gains in M&A transactions.

Becher (2000) studied the shareholder wealth effects of 558 bank mergers from the period 1980 to 1997. His research was motivated by the significant increase in bank merger activity that accompanied the deregulation of the industry in the 1990s. He used event study analysis to test whether the heightened merger activity that was spurred by deregulation led to synergistic combinations of banks or instead allowed empire building by entrenched bank executives.

TABLE 8.1 Research on the Combined Returns in Mergers and Acquisitions

Research Paper	Time Period	No. of Targets	No. of Bidders	Event Window	Target Return (%)	Bidder Return (%)	Combined Return (%)
Bradley et al. (1988)	1963–1984	236	236	(−5, +5 last bid)	31.77	0.97	7.43
Kaplan and Weisbach (1992)	1971–1982	209	271	(−5, +5 last bid)	26.90	−1.49	3.74
Servaes (1991)	1972–1987	704	384	(−1, resolve)	23.64	−1.07	3.66
Mulherin and Boone (2000)	1990–1999	281	281	(−1, +1)	20.2	−0.37	3.56
Andrade, Mitchell, and Stafford (2001)	1973–1998	3,688	3,688	(−1, +1)	16.0	−0.7	1.8
				(−20, close)	23.80	−3.8	1.9

Using an event window from 30 days prior to announcement through 5 days after, Becher (2000) found that bank mergers create wealth. For the full 1980 to 1997 time period, the average combined return to target and bidder shareholders was 3.03%. The combined return was slightly larger, 3.53%, for the deregulation period of the 1990s. From this evidence, Becher (2000) inferred support for the synergistic theory of mergers and concluded that bank deregulation has improved efficiency in the industry.

Related evidence on the effect of takeover deregulation in banking is provided by Brook, Hendershott, and Lee (1998). They studied the wealth changes of banks in the period around the passage of the Interstate Banking and Branching Efficiency Act of 1994, which effectively removed the barriers to takeovers in the U.S. banking industry. They found that the passage of the act had a positive stock price effect on a portfolio of 290 publicly traded banks and concluded that the takeover deregulation created value. Brook, Hendershott, and Lee (1998) conjectured that these gains stem from a better utilization of scale and scope economies.

To investigate the sources of gains in bank mergers, Houston, James, and Ryngaert (2001) used novel data on the projected estimates of cost savings and revenue enhancement made by management in 41 bank mergers during the period 1985 to 1996. They found that costs savings, rather than revenue enhancement, was the driving force behind bank mergers and that these cost savings were strongly related to the wealth improvements shown in the combined target and bidder stock returns.

In summary, the empirical research in financial economics generally shows that mergers and acquisitions, on average, create wealth for the combined target and bidder shareholders. This evidence supports the synergy and efficiency theory of mergers. We next consider the factors shown to affect the cross-sectional patterns in target and bidder returns.

FACTORS RELATED TO TARGET RETURNS

A consensus result in M&A research is that the announcement of corporate takeovers is associated with a large increase in the wealth of target shareholders. See, for example, the surveys by Jensen and Ruback (1983) and Jarrell, Brickley, and Netter (1988), as well as the more recent research summarized in Table 8.1. Moreover, the shareholder wealth effects appear to stem from actual merger effects rather than mere revaluation of target firms. Bradley, Desai, and Kim (1983) reported that the positive announcement returns revert to zero for targets in unsuccessful takeovers.

To better understand the effects of mergers and acquisitions, researchers have measured how factors such as the method of payment and the number of bidder firms affect the wealth gains borne by target shareholders. Related analysis has focused on the run-up in stock returns prior to an actual takeover announcement. This section reviews this research.

TARGET RETURNS: TYPE OF MERGER AND METHOD OF PAYMENT

In Table 1 of their survey of takeover research through 1983, Jensen and Ruback (1983) reported that target returns in tender offers were 30%, and target returns in mergers were 20%. Subsequent analysis by Huang and Walkling (1987) found that when method of payment and degree of resistance were taken into account, abnormal returns were no higher in tender offers than in mergers.

Huang and Walkling (1987) studied 169 transactions from the period 1977 to 1982. They analyzed a narrow $(-1, 0)$ window around the initial takeover announcement. They found that the most powerful influence on target returns was method of payment. As reported in Panel A of Table 8.2, they found that the average CAR for cash offers was 29.3%, compared with 14.4% for stock offers. For acquisitions where the payment was a combination of cash and stock, the average abnormal return was 23.3%, which fell between the values reported for cash and stock offers. Research by Asquith, Bruner, and Mullins (1990), also summarized in Table 8.2, reported similar findings. Both sets of authors suggested taxes as one plausible explanation for the higher return for cash offers.

In their comprehensive study of 3,688 M&A transactions from the period 1973 to 1998, Andrade, Mitchell, and Stafford (2001) also found that cash deals create more wealth for target shareholders than do stock deals. For the narrow (–1, +1) window, cash deals are associated with a 20.1% target return, and stock deals are associated with a 13% return. For the longer window, from 20 days pre-announcement through the close of the transaction, cash is associated with a 27.8% target return, and stock is associated with a 20.8% target return. Servaes (1991) reported similar results using a window from day-1 through deal resolution.

TARGET RETURNS: SINGLE VERSUS MULTIPLE BIDDERS

Another factor related to the magnitude of target returns is the number of bidders in the transaction. Relevant research is summarized in Panel B of Table 8.2. On average, target returns are larger when more than one firm publicly bids for the target. Servaes (1991), for example, found that in the window from day-1 through resolution, acquisitions with a single bidder have an average target return of 20.8%, compared with an average target return of 30.5% for multiple-bidder contests.

Consistent with a semistrong efficient market, the higher returns in multiple-bidder contests accrue in the period after the announcement of the initial bid. As noted in Panel B of Table 8.2, Bradley, Desai, and Kim (1988) found that returns in the (–20, +1) period around the initial announcement are similar in magnitude for single- and multiple-bidder contests. However, for a wider window that stretches through 40 days after announcement, and thereby often captures competing bids, the return to single-bidder contests is 26.65%, compared with 46.12% in multiple-bidder contests. These results resemble the authors' earlier study—Bradley, Desai, and Kim (1983)—which found that target announcement effects are only fleeting in takeovers that do not come to fruition.

Similar results can be found in Schwert's (1996) research on run-up and markup. As summarized in Panel B of Table 8.2, Schwert (1996) found that the target run-up in the (–42, –1) period is similar for single- and multiple-bidder contests. However, the mark-up in the period (0, +126) is noticeably larger for the multiple-bidder contests. This evidence is consistent with Schwert's statement that "the type of competition feared by the bidder is the best systematic explanation for variation in takeover premiums, and whether this type of competition will occur is not generally known before the first bid occurs" (1996, p. 187).

TARGET RUN-UP

A number of papers have noted that takeover targets experience a positive stock return run-up prior to acquisition announcements. Table 8.3 summarizes some of this research. Although the 10 papers in the table use slightly different measures of the run-up window, the basic results are similar. Taking a simple average across studies, the increase of target returns in the period prior to an actual takeover is 11.8%, which is comparable in magnitude to the target return surrounding public announcement.

TABLE 8.2 Research on Factors Affecting Target Returns

Panel A. Method of Payment

Research Paper	Time Period	No. of Observations	Event Window	Cash (%)	Mixed (%)	Stock (%)
Huang and Walkling (1987)	1977–1982	169	(−1, 0)	29.3	23.3	14.4
Asquith et al. (1990)	1973–1983	80	(−1, 0)	27.5	32.2	13.9
Servaes (1991)	1972–1987	688	(−1, resolve)	26.7	21.1	20.5
Andrade, Mitchell, and Stafford (2001)	1973–1988	3,688	(−1, +1) (−20, close)	20.1 27.8	NA NA	13.0 20.8

Panel B. Single Versus Multiple Bidders

Research Paper	Time Period	No. of Observations	Event Window	Single (%)	Multiple (%)
Bradley et al. (1988)	1963–1984	236	(−20, +1) (−20, +40)	23.95 26.65	25.98 46.12
Servaes (1991)	1972–1987	704	(−1, resolve)	20.8	30.5
Schwert (1996)	1975–1991	1,523	(−42, −1) (0, +126)	13.4 8.5	12.7 18.2

TABLE 8.3 Research on Target Stock Return Run-Up

Research Paper	Time Period	No. of Observations	Run-Up Window	Run-Up (%)	Annou. Return (%)
Dodd (1980)	1971–1977	151	(−40,−2)	11.2	13.0
Keown and Pinkerton (1981)	1975–1978	194	(−25,−1)	13.3	12.0
Dennis and McConnell (1986)	1962–1980	76	(−19,−2)	8.11	8.84
Huang and Walkling (1987)	1977–1982	204	(−50,−2)	9.1	23.4
Bradley et al. (1988)	1963–1984	236	(−20,−1)	10.07	14.5
Jarrell and Poulsen (1989a)	1981–1985	172	(−20,−1)	11.0	13.9
Meulbroek (1992)	1974–1988	145	(−20,−1)	13.0	17.6
Barclay and Warner (1993)	1981–1984	108	(−30,−2)	16.3	15.0
Schwert (1996)	1975–1991	1,523	(−42,−1)	13.3	10.1
Schwert (2000)	1975–1996	2,296	(−63,−1)	12.4	9.6
			Simple average	11.8	13.8

Several possible explanations exist for the positive target run-up. Keown and Pinkerton suggested that the run-up represents illegal insider trading, concluding that, "impending public merger announcements are poorly held secrets, and trading on this nonpublic information abounds" (1981, p. 866). Jarrell and Poulsen (1989a) countered that much of the run-up is related to media rumors and prebid share acquisition by eventual bidders.

More detailed analysis further addresses the source of run-up. Sanders and Zdanowicz (1992) used information from the Background section of 14D filings to determine when each of a sample of 30 tender offers was initiated. They found that the run-up does not begin until the date that the bidder or target initiates the transaction, a date that usually is known privately until the public announcement. These results indicate that the run-up is not simply due to idle speculation but is tied to the likelihood of an actual deal.

Meulbroek (1992) employed a proprietary database of illegal insider trades during the period 1980 to 1989. With these data, she was able to identify specific days on which illegal insiders trade prior to a takeover announcement. She found that the abnormal return on an insider trading day averages 3%, which represents roughly half of the run-up in her sample.

Schwert (1996) considered the relation between the run-up in the (−42, −1) period preceding a takeover and the markup that occurs in the (0, +126) period at and following a formal acquisition announcement. He found no correlation between the run-up and the markup and concluded that the run-up is an added cost to the bidder. Using more direct evidence, Meulbroek and Hart (1997) concluded that illegal insider trading increases takeover premiums.

Overall, the results clearly indicate a positive run-up in target returns prior to a takeover announcement. However, research conclusions differ regarding the source of the run-up and the complementary policy implications. As noted by Meulbroek and Hart, an attempt to tighten the reins on trading prior to takeovers might have "a chilling effect on the flow of non-insider information among market participants" (1997, p. 76).

TABLE 8.4 Takeover Premiums for Targets

Research Paper	Time Period	No. of Observations	Base Price Date	Premium (%)
Bradley (1980)	1962–1977	161	41 days before offer	49
Jarrell, Brickley, and Netter (1988)	1981–1984	225	1 month before offer	53
Jennings and Mazzeo (1993)	1979–1987	647	10 days before offer	23
Cotter and Zenner (1994)	1988–1991	141, initial	30 days before rumor	47
		141, final	30 days before rumor	60
Betton and Eckbo (2000)	1971–1990	697, initial, single bid	60 days before offer	51
		194, initial, multiple bids	60 days before offer	45

TAKEOVER BIDDING AND TAKEOVER PREMIUMS

As a final measure of the effects of corporate takeovers on the value of target firms, we report evidence on the premium offered in takeover deals. The premium is defined as the percentage difference between the price offered in a merger and a price based on a date prior to the merger offer. Empirical research of takeover premiums usually focuses on cash tender offers.

A selection of the research reporting takeover premiums is presented in Table 8.4. Bradley (1980) studied the premium in 161 successful tender offers from the time period 1962 to 1977. He used a base date of 41 days prior to the offer. He found an average premium of 49%.

Subsequent analysis, also reported in Table 8.4, confirms the substantial premiums received by target firms in tender offers. The research also reports evidence pertinent to the models of the bidding process that were discussed in Chapter 6. Cotter and Zenner (1994), for example, reported the straightforward result that the final premium in a takeover bid exceeds the premium initially offered by the first bidder.

Betton and Eckbo (2000) provided an in-depth treatment of the bidding process in their study of 2,335 takeover bids in 1,353 tender offer contests in the period 1971 to 1990. Table 8.4 provides only one example of the many results in their comprehensive analysis. They found that the initial premium in a tender offer with a single bidder is 51%, which exceeds the initial premium of 45% in a tender offer that ends up with multiple bidders. This result suggests that a bidder sometimes opts to make a preemptive bid to deter competition. Betton and Eckbo (2000) reported a variety of other results on bidding decisions such as toeholds and price revisions.

FACTORS RELATED TO BIDDER RETURNS

A parallel body of literature exists on the cross-sectional determinants of bidder returns. Similar to analysis of targets, the research on bidder returns includes analysis of the effects of the method of payment and the number of bidders.

BIDDER RETURNS AND METHOD OF PAYMENT

Panel A of Table 8.5 summarizes research on the effect of method of payment on bidder returns. The research finds that bidders have more negative returns in stock transactions compared with cash deals. Travlos (1987) studied 167 M&A transactions from the period 1972 to

TABLE 8.5 Research on Factors Affecting Bidder Returns

Panel A. Method of Payment

Research Paper	Time Period	No. of Observations	Event Window	Cash (%)	Mixed (%)	Stock (%)
Travlos (1987)	1972–1981	167	(−10,+10)	−0.13	NA	−1.60
Asquith et al. (1990)	1973–1983	186	(−1,0)	0.20	−1.47	−2.40
Servaes (1991)	1972–1987	380	(−1, resolve)	3.44	−3.74	−5.86
Andrade, Mitchell, and Stafford (2001)	1973–1998	3,688	(−1,+1)	0.4	NA	−1.5
			(−20, close)	−0.2	NA	−6.3

Panel B. Single Versus Multiple Bidders

Research Paper	Time Period	No. of Observations	Event Window	Single (%)	Multiple (%)	First Bid Acquirer (%)	Late Bid Acquirer (%)
Bradley et al. (1988)	1963–1984	236	(−20,+1)	2.75	−0.41	2.0	−2.5
			(−20,+40)	2.97	−0.21		
Servaes (1991)	1972–1987	384	(−1, resolve)	−0.35	−2.97		
Schwert (1996)	1975–1991	1,523	(−42,+1)	1.9	0.2		
			(0,+126)	−0.4	−3.5		

1981. He found that the average bidder return in stock transactions was –1.6%, and the bidder return in cash deals was –0.13%. Asquith, Bruner, and Mullins (1990) and Servaes (1991) also reported that bidder returns are lower, and indeed negative, in stock mergers as compared with cash mergers.

Andrade, Mitchell, and Stafford (2001) also studied the effects of method of payment on the returns to bidder firms. They bifurcated their sample based on whether any stock was used to finance the transaction. Similar to prior research, they found that 100% cash deals are associated with better bidder returns than transactions with stock. They noted that a stock transaction has aspects of both a merger and an equity offering and suggested that the results are tied to asymmetric information between bidder managers and investors along the lines of models such as Myers and Majluf (1984).

BIDDER RETURNS: SINGLE VERSUS MULTIPLE BIDDERS

Another important variable affecting bidder returns is the number of bidders publicly competing for the target. Research on this variable is summarized in Panel B of Table 8.5. The research indicates that bidder returns are lower when there are multiple bidders.

Bradley, Desai, and Kim (1988) compared the returns in 236 tender offers: 163 were single-bidder contests, and 73 were multiple-bidder contests. For the single-bidder contests, the bidder return was nearly 3% for both the (–20, +1) and (–20, +40) windows. For the multiple-bidder contests, the successful bidder experienced a negative announcement return, on average.

Bradley, Desai, and Kim (1988, p. 25) reported that the negative return in multiple-bidder contests stems from the fact that their sample contains only the successful bidder, who might or might not be the initial bidder in the contest. Of the 73 acquirers in the multiple-bidder sample, 24 were first-bidder acquirers and 49 were late-bidder acquirers. Bradley, Desai, and Kim (1988) found that the announcement return to the first-bidder acquirers was 2.0%, roughly the same as the return when there is only a single bidder. By contrast, for successful acquirers who were not the first bidder, the announcement return was –2.5%. Hence, even in multiple-bidder contests, the market reaction to the initial bid was positive but, as Bradley, Desai and Kim noted, "when competing bids are actually made . . . there is . . . a dissipation of the initial gains to the stockholders of bidding firms" (1988, p. 25). Indeed, Servaes (1991) found that bidder returns in the period from day –1 to resolution are more negative when the contest entails multiple bidders.

Schwert (1996) provided evidence consistent with a differential effect of single versus multiple bids on bidder returns. He found that the return in the (–42, –1) run-up period was positive for both contests with only a single bidder and contests that end up with multiple bidders. However, in the subsequent (0, + 126) period, bidder returns deteriorated more noticeably in the multiple-bidder contests.

The data on bidder returns in multiple-bid contests raise the question as to whether it is better to win or lose a publicly contested takeover. In analysis of multiple-bid contests during the period 1963 to 1980, Bradley, Desai, and Kim (1983) found that unsuccessful bidders lost value and successful bidders broke even, leading the authors to conclude that it was better to win than lose a bidding contest. However, in the later time period of 1981 to 1984, Bradley, Desai, and Kim (1988) found that successful bidders lost wealth during a multiple-bid takeover.

As a whole, the research summarized in Table 8.5 suggests a more mixed take on bidder returns compared with the same evidence on target firms. To better understand the wealth effects for bidders, we next review a study that uses novel means to distinguish between bidder ability in subsets of corporate takeovers.

DO BAD BIDDERS BECOME GOOD TARGETS?

A paper by Mitchell and Lehn (1990) asked the provocative question: Do bad bidders become good targets? This research was motivated by theoretical work such as that of Manne (1965) and Alchian and Demsetz (1972), which portrayed the corporate takeover market as a Darwinian world. In this world, managerial mistakes can occur, but not without sanction. From this theory, Mitchell and Lehn (1990) predicted that firms that make poor acquisition decisions are more likely to become targets themselves.

To conduct their analysis, Mitchell and Lehn (1990) started with a sample of 1,158 corporations listed on the Value Line Investment Survey in 1981. Each firm was then classified according to whether it was a takeover target in the period 1980 to 1988. The acquisition performance of the targets and nontargets was then compared using event study techniques.

Consistent with prior research, Mitchell and Lehn (1990) found that the acquisition performance of the sample firms was a roughly break-even endeavor: The announcement returns to all bidders averaged 0.14%. However, an analysis of the target and nontarget subsamples revealed the existence of good bids and bad bids. For firms that remain nontargets, the average bidder return was positive and statistically significant. By contrast, for firms that subsequently became targets themselves, the average bidder return was negative and significant. Logit regression analysis confirms that the more negative the market response is to a firm's acquisitions, the greater the likelihood is that the firm will become a takeover target.

The results indicate that bad bidders do indeed become targets. Mitchell and Lehn concluded that, "takeovers can be both a problem and a solution" (1990, p. 396). Their results are consistent with a corporate control world where the threat of takeover improves the performance of actual and potential target firms.

TAKEOVER REGULATION AND TAKEOVER HOSTILITY

A relevant feature in the market for corporate control is regulation. The Williams Act of 1968 imposed federal constraints on the tender offer process by forcing greater disclosure by bidders and setting a minimum bidding period. In the 1980s, state laws and firm-sponsored poison pills imposed further impediments on the takeover process. In this section, we study the effects of such regulation on target and bidder shareholders.

MEASURING THE EFFECT OF THE WILLIAMS ACT

Takeover research has addressed ways in which the Williams Act has affected the distribution of gains in corporate takeovers. Bradley, Desai, and Kim (1988), for example, compared the returns to targets, bidders, and combined firms in the period before and after 1968. They reported that following the act, the combined returns to takeovers did not change but that the distribution between targets and bidders was shifted. After the act, target premiums increased and bidder returns fell. Jarrell and Bradley (1980) and Jarrell and Poulsen (1989b) offered similar evidence.

Nathan and O'Keefe (1989) used a time series of takeovers from the period 1963 to 1985 to further study the effect of regulation on target premiums. Although they found an increase in target premiums over time, they did not attribute the change to the Williams Act. They attributed the changing premiums to an unspecified economic event that was not unique to the takeover market. More recent, refined analysis by Malatesta and Thompson (1993), however, concluded that the changes in the takeover market subsequent to the Williams Act were not coincidental.

TAKEOVER IMPEDIMENTS IN THE 1980s

Comment and Schwert (1995) studied the effect of 1980s impediments such as state anti-takeover laws and poison pills on the market for corporate control. When they initiated their analysis, a policy concern was whether these impediments had wrecked the takeover market permanently. Comment and Schwert's (1995) research suggested that the decline in the takeover market in the late 1980s was due to general economic conditions rather than factors such as state laws or poison pills. They concluded that, "Antitakeover measures increase the bargaining position of target firms, but they do not prevent many transactions" (p. 3).

IS HOSTILITY IN THE EYES OF THE BEHOLDER?

Although not unanimous, the research on takeover regulation suggests that the rules underlying the market for corporate control affect the distribution of gains between targets and bidders but do not necessarily affect the rate of takeover activity. Similar inferences suggest that the regulation might affect the form (hostile versus friendly) but not the substance of mergers and acquisitions.

G. William Schwert (2000) addressed these issues by asking whether the hostility in takeovers is in the eyes of the beholder? Schwert (2000) employed tests to determine whether the concept of a "hostile takeover" is best viewed as a reaction to entrenched, inefficient target managers or instead should be considered a choice variable in a bidder's bargaining arsenal. One result is that "the phrase 'hostile takeover' means different things to different people" (p. 2638). Schwert (2000) found that although the various classifications of hostility by the *Wall Street Journal*, Securities Data Corporation, and other sources are positively correlated, the correlation is not high.

Schwert (2000) also investigated the variation in the rate of hostile takeovers in a long-time series over the period 1975 to 1996. He found that proxies for poor target management performance contribute little explanatory power. Variables that Schwert (2000) interpreted as proxies for the bargaining power of the target firm, such as firm size and secular dummy variables, contributed the most explanatory power. Schwert concluded that, "most of the characteristics of takeover offers that are related to hostility seem to reflect strategic choices made by the bidder or target firm to maximize their respective gains from a potential transaction" (2000, p. 2639).

POSTMERGER OPERATING PERFORMANCE

In addition to studying stock returns in the period around merger announcements, researchers have measured the effects of mergers on subsequent performance. This is a difficult issue, as analysis in Chapter 7 has shown that mergers often follow industry shocks. Hence, mergers are often the message bearers of such fundamental changes facing an industry. Those studying merger performance must be careful in prescribing the benchmarks with which to compare the combined firms in their empirical samples.

Healy, Palepu, and Ruback (1992) studied the post-acquisition operating performance of the 50 largest U.S. mergers in the period 1979 to 1984. The sample included cases in which the two merging firms were classified as having high (LTV Group-General Steel), medium (Pan Am Corporation-National Airlines) and low (U.S. Steel-Marathon Oil) overlap. Their sample also included a large number of oil firms that conducted mergers within (e.g., Diamond Shamrock-Natomas Company and Occidental Petroleum-Cities Service) and outside (e.g., Exxon Corporation-Reliance Electric and Sohio-Kennecott Corporation) the energy sector.

In the main part of their analysis, Healy, Palepu, and Ruback (1992) determined the effect of the mergers on accounting variables. They garnered the accounting data from annual reports, merger prospectuses, proxy statements, and analyst reports. They compared pro-forma performance of the two combining firms in the 5 years prior to the merger with the actual performance of the merged entity in the 5 years after the merger. As a control for economic changes, they benchmarked the results to overall changes at the industry level.

Healy, Palepu, and Ruback (1992) reported that operating cash flows for the merged firms increased relative to industry benchmarks. They also decomposed into cash-flow margin on sales and asset turnover. Their analysis concluded that the increase in cash flows was driven by an improvement in asset turnover for the merged firms.

Healy, Palepu, and Ruback (1992) also related the operating improvements and the abnormal stock returns at the announcement of the mergers. Similar to other research, they found that the combined stock returns at the merger announcement were positive for their sample. Moreover, in regression analysis, they found that the cash-flow improvements following the merger were positively and significantly related to the announcement stock returns. These important results indicated that, consistent with efficient markets theory, the announcement returns accurately forecast postmerger performance.

Andrade, Mitchell, and Stafford (2001) used their comprehensive database of mergers during the period 1973 to 1998 to analyze further the effect of mergers on operating performance. In their analysis, they included roughly 2,000 mergers for which accounting data were available on Compustat. They found an improvement in operating performance by the merging firms relative to industry peers. They noted that the improvement in postmerger cash-flow performance is consistent with the evidence of positive combined stock returns at merger announcement.

LONG-TERM STOCK PRICE PERFORMANCE FOLLOWING MERGERS

GENERAL ISSUES

The event study evidence on mergers that has been reviewed in this chapter has pinpointed analysis on relatively narrow windows around merger announcement dates. This is by design. The efficient markets hypothesis maintains that any new information tied to an event such as a merger announcement will be incorporated into market prices quickly and accurately. Because of the emphasis on narrow windows of time, event studies are not sensitive to the manner in which abnormal returns are estimated. Hence, event studies avoid the joint-hypothesis problem of many tests of market efficiency (Fama, 1991).

A burgeoning body of empirical research has applied event study techniques over much longer periods of time. As summarized in Table 1 of Fama (1998), these studies deal with multi-year stock return performance around events such as equity offerings, proxy contests, and stock splits. Many of the studies report anomalous performance. For example, firms making equity offerings are reported to underperform the market, and firms conducting stock splits appear to outperform the market.

Fama (1998) provided a detailed critique of such analysis. A major problem is the lack of theory. Without an underlying theory, the finding of positive (or negative) abnormal returns in the years after an event is possibly due to random chance. A related concern is the lack of a robust asset pricing model. Even elegant models such as the Capital Asset Pricing Model (CAPM) do not capture all of the variation in a specific sample. A third concern is the sensitivity of results to measurement issues, such as the assumptions of normality and independence, the use of buy-and-hold returns versus calendar-time portfolios, and the choice of equal versus value weighting.

The assumption of the cross-sectional independence of events is an especially important matter for restructuring events. For a sample from the 1980s, Mitchell and Mulherin (1996) found evidence of industry clustering in corporate restructuring. Mulherin and Boone (2000) found that mergers and divestitures in the 1990s are industry specific and that the industries differ from the high-restructuring sectors in the 1980s. A failure to account for the nonindependence of corporate events driven by factors such as industry clustering can severely bias the studies of long-term stock returns.

LONG-TERM MERGER PERFORMANCE

One segment of the long-term performance research has studied mergers. Much of the work was purely data driven. Agrawal, Jaffe, and Mandelker (1992) reported a 5-year, postmerger abnormal return of –10%. Franks, Harris, and Titman (1991) argued that much of the observed evidence of poor performance following mergers was due to benchmark errors rather than mispricing.

The results in some of the empirical studies have motivated the creation of theoretical models. Shleifer and Vishny (2003) have developed a model of stock market–driven acquisitions. In their model, managers are rational and calculating and take advantage of misperceptions by investors. A key aspect of the theory is the bidder's choice of cash versus stock. Cash is used when the target is undervalued, and stock is used when the bidder is overvalued. An implication of the theory is that the long-term stock price performance following a cash-financed acquisition will be positive, and the long-term price performance following a stock acquisition will be negative.

The development of models such as that of Shleifer and Vishny (2003) indicates why careful study of postmerger performance is important. To assess the predictions of their model, we review the extant evidence on the long-term price performance following mergers. A summary of some of the recent papers is provided in Table 8.6.

The three papers covered in Table 8.6 are by Loughran and Vijh (1997), Rau and Vermalen (1998), and Mitchell and Stafford (2000). All three papers study a large sample of mergers over a long period of time. One difference among the papers is the method of estimating abnormal returns. Loughran and Vijh (1997) used equally weighted buy-and-hold returns. Rau and Vermaelen used cumulative abnormal returns. Mitchell and Stafford (2000) used a variety of methods and also used equal and value weighting.

For their full samples, reported in Panel A of Table 8.6, the estimates of long-term price performance are relatively small in magnitude and usually are not statistically significant. For example, the average 5-year return of –6.5% in Loughran and Vijh (1997) has a t-statistic of –0.96. In Mitchell and Stafford (2000), statistical significance is often sensitive to whether the abnormal returns are equally weighted or value weighted.

TABLE 8.6 Research on Long Term Stock Price Performance

Research Paper	Time Period	No. of Observations	Method	Stock Return (%)
Panel A. Overall Results				
Loughran and Vijh (1997)	1970–1989	947	5-year EW BHAR	–6.5
Rau and Vermaelen (1998)	1980–1991	2,823	3-year CAR	–4.04
Mitchell and Stafford (2000)	1961–1993	2,068	3-year EW BHAR	–1
			3-year VW BHAR	–3.8
			3-year EW Calendar	–5.0
			3-year VW Calendar	–1.4
Panel B. Results Based on Form of Payment				
Loughran and Vijh (1997)	1970–1989	314 Cash	5-year EW BHAR	18.5
		405 Stock	5-year EW BHAR	–24.2
Mitchell and Stafford (2000)	1961–1993	1,039 Cash	3-year VW Calendar	3.6
		1,029 Stock	3-year VW Calendar	–4.3
Panel C. Results Based on Book-to-Market Ratio				
Rau and Vermaelen (1998)	1980–1991	931 Value	3-year CAR	7.64
		932 Growth	3-year CAR	–17.3
Mitchell and Stafford (2000)	1961–1993	257 Value	3-year VW Calendar	1.1
		526 Growth	3-year VW Calendar	–7.2

Note: EW = equally weighted
VW = value weighted
BHAR = buy and hold abnormal return
CAR = cumulative abnormal return

Analysis of the effects of the method of payment are reported in Panel B of Table 8.6. A comparison of the findings of Loughran and Vijh (1997) and Mitchell and Stafford (2000) illustrates the sensitivity of the results to estimation methods. Loughran and Vijh (1997) employed 5-year buy-and-hold abnormal returns and found large differences between cash and stock mergers. By contrast, Mitchell and Stafford (2000) included analysis of calendar-time portfolios that account for the nonindependence of merger activity. The estimates in Mitchell and Stafford (2000) are much lower in magnitude.

Similar contrasts hold for the partitions based on book-to-market ratios reported in Panel C of Table 8.6. Rau and Vermalean (1998) reported that value firms with high book-to-market ratios have positive performance following mergers. On the other hand, they found that growth or glamour firms with low book-to-market ratios significantly underperform following mergers. Mitchell and Stafford (2000) conducted a similar bifurcation based on book-to-market ratios and found abnormal returns that are much smaller in magnitude and that are statistically insignificant.

SUMMARY COMMENTS ON LONG-TERM PRICE PERFORMANCE

One conclusion taken from the results summarized in Table 8.6 is that the average long-term price performance *following* a merger is insignificantly different from zero. This is completely consistent with an efficient market. Together with the event study evidence presented earlier in this chapter, such findings indicate that mergers create wealth.

A second conclusion taken from the evidence summarized in Table 8.6 is that the results based on partitioned samples such as method of payment and book-to-market ratio are sensitive to estimation method. This echoes Fama's (1998) general observation on the long-term performance literature. Moreover, the lack of any consistent, significant differences between the long-run performance of cash versus stock mergers fails to support the predictions of Shleifer and Vishny (2003).

EFFICIENCY VERSUS MARKET POWER

The general findings in this chapter are that mergers are associated with an increase in value. Based on the tests of the theories from Chapter 6, the interpretation of these results is that mergers enable firms to reap efficiencies and attain synergies.

An alternative explanation of the empirical results is that mergers facilitate collusion. In particular, especially in the case of horizontal mergers, the positive combined returns in the empirical studies may reflect the market's anticipation that the merging firms will have greater market power and be able to charge higher product prices. In this section, we review the research that has contrasted the efficiency explanation for merger gains with an explanation based on market power.

WHICH FIRMS ARE SUBJECT TO ANTITRUST ENFORCEMENT?

Ellert (1976) provided analysis on mergers and market power by studying 205 firms that were defendants in antitrust complaints in the period 1950 to 1972. His main interest was whether the sample firms had any evidence of abnormal, monopoly-driven stock returns prior to the antitrust enforcement and whether this enforcement reversed such gains from market power.

Ellert (1976) found that the equity performance of the firms in his sample was significantly positive in the period prior to the antitrust enforcement actions. However, the positive performance occurred before the mergers that led to the enforcement by the government. The initiation of the government actions had only a small, negative effect on the firm's equity value. Ellert (1976) concluded that his results were inconsistent with a market power explanation for merger gains and instead interpreted the results to indicate that mergers facilitated the efficient reallocation of resources across firms.

THE EFFECT OF MERGERS ON RIVAL FIRMS

As another test of the efficiency and market power explanations for merger gains, Stillman (1983) and Eckbo (1983) studied the effect of a merger on the stock price of rivals in the merging firms' industry. The underlying premise of these studies was that if a merger is collusive in nature, then industry rivals also will gain and should experience a positive stock return at merger announcement. By contrast, if the merger enables the combining firm to compete more effectively, this should have a negative effect on the stock price of rivals. Such predictions are less clear cut if a given merger in an industry reflects an underlying industry shock. As Stillman noted, "a merger announcement may signal the existence of hitherto unappreciated economies of scale that can be realized by rivals as well as by the merging firms" (1983, p. 228). To control for such efficiency spillovers to rivals, the empirical analysis also contrasts the overall effect on rivals with the effect in mergers contested by antitrust enforcers, and looks at stock price movements of rivals at the time of an antitrust complaint, as well.

Stillman (1983) studied the effect of 11 contested mergers in the time period 1964 to 1972. His sample firms represent a variety of industries including oil refining, drugs, and roofing materials. He found that the merger announcements had no discernible effect on the industry rivals. He concluded that the sample mergers had no anticompetitive effect.

Eckbo (1983) performed related tests of the efficiency and market power explanations for merger gains. His sample included 159 horizontal mergers from the period 1963 to 1978, of which 57 were challenged by federal antitrust authorities. Eckbo (1983) found that rivals experience a positive and significant stock return around the time of the merger announcement. Moreover, he found that the returns for rivals in challenged mergers, 2.45% in the (−20, +10) window, were greater than for unchallenged mergers, 1.10%. However, Eckbo (1983) also found that the announcement of an antitrust complaint had no effect on industry rivals, a result he interpreted as inconsistent with the market power explanation.

FURTHER ANALYSIS OF INDUSTRY SPILLOVERS

More recent analysis has addressed the effect of takeovers on industry rivals. Slovin, Sushka, and Bendeck (1991) measured the stock price effects on horizontal industry rivals of the announcement of 128 going-private transactions from the period 1980 to 1988. In a going-private transaction, the control of a firm is acquired by management or a financial investor. Because a going-private transaction does not affect the number of firms in an industry, any stock price effect on rivals must reflect some sort of efficiencies rather than collusion. Slovin, Sushka, and Bendeck (1991) found that the average return to industry rivals in the (−1, 0) announcement window is 1.32%. They interpreted the returns to represent positive intra-industry information.

As one implication of their analysis of industry shocks, Mitchell and Mulherin (1996) measured the spillover effects of the 607 takeover and restructurings in their sample. They found that the average abnormal return for other firms in an industry in the month of an announcement is 0.5%. They interpreted the positive return to other industry members as reflecting future restructuring in the given industry.

Song and Walkling (2000) more explicitly related the industry spillover effects of acquisition announcements to subsequent takeover activity. They studied a sample of 141 acquisitions and 2,459 rival firms in the period 1982 to 1991. Consistent with prior research, they found that other industry members experienced a positive return at the time of a merger announcement in the industry. They further found that the magnitude of this return is related to the probability that a given industry member will become a takeover target itself.

VERTICAL AND HORIZONTAL MERGERS

To wrap up the section on efficiency versus market power, and to summarize much of the analysis of the gains from mergers, we discuss a recent paper by Fan and Goyal (2002). These authors studied 2,162 completed mergers in the period 1962 to 1996. For their full sample, they found that mergers create wealth. The announcement return is 1.9% for the (−1, +1) window and 2.4% for the (−10, +10) window.

Fan and Goyal (2002) also studied the wealth effects based on whether the merger is vertical, horizontal, or diversifying. An important innovation in their study is that they carefully defined vertical relatedness based on input-output tables rather than relying on imprecise designations such as SIC codes. For the (−1, +1) window, they found that the wealth creation in vertical mergers is 2.5% and is statistically indistinguishable from that in horizontal mergers. These results have relevance for antitrust policy. Presumably, any gains due to market power would be restricted to horizontal mergers. The fact that vertical mergers result in valuation increases comparable to those in horizontal mergers adds to the other evidence in this section that supports the efficiency explanation for merger gains over the explanation based on market power.

EFFECTS OF CONCENTRATION

Another aspect of merger performance is the impact of mergers on concentration in the economy. Two dimensions of concentration have been analyzed. Macroconcentration measures the shares of the largest firms in the economy; microconcentration measures the shares of the largest firms in individual industries.

IMPACT ON MACROCONCENTRATION

Macroconcentration is important because if a small number of large firms dominate the economy, economic power potentially could spill over to political and social power. In addition, smaller enterprises have long been recognized as sources of new ideas, innovation, new products, and increased employment. Therefore, changes in macroconcentration are potentially important to the political, social, and economic vitality of a nation.

White (2002) has summarized trends in macroconcentration by a number of measures. Value added in manufacturing represents the increase in the value of shipments over the cost of input materials, a widely used measure of processing activities by firms. The share of the largest 200 companies declined from 44% in 1976 to 40% in 1997. Aggregate concentration also has been measured by the share of total assets of the largest 200 companies in the nonfinancial private sector. This measure declined from 44% in 1958, to 38.3% in 1977, to 32.2% in 1988.

To update the data, the Bureau of the Census performed special tabulations reported by White (2002). Aggregate concentration in the entire private sector measured by employment in the largest 1,000 companies was 27.1% in 1988, 26.1% in 1993, and 27.4% in 1999. The share of the largest 1,000 companies of total private sector payroll was 32.4% in 1988, 29.8% in 1995, and 31.1% in 1999. The patterns for both measures declined during the first half of the 1990s, returning to earlier levels by 1999. In addition, the Bureau of the Census provided data on the distribution of employment and payroll percentages by employment size for the period 1988 to 1999. The employment and payroll shares of the smallest-sized groups declined slightly, the shares of larger firms increased slightly, and aggregate concentration generally decreased slightly. The data give an upward bias in estimates of aggregate concentration, as significant ongoing change occurs in the 200 largest firms in the economy, attesting to the vigor of the competitive forces at work.

The data demonstrate that aggregate concentration has been virtually unchanged or lower during the last two decades despite increased merger activity. Possible explanations include the following. About one third of merger transactions represent divestitures in which the buyer becomes larger and the seller smaller. If the size distribution of merger activity were concentrated among small- and medium-sized firms, moderately large firms would grow relative to the largest. Entrepreneurs are motivated to establish firms in order to achieve capital gains by being acquired by larger firms; this could stimulate the creation of new firms over time. Innovation, technological change, and the creation of new industries could strengthen the creation and growth of new firms. Another possibility is that the growth of joint ventures and alliances reduces the need to conduct some activities inside the firm.

U.S. company purchases of non-U.S. firms during the period 1991 to 2000 averaged about 15% of total U.S. mergers and acquisitions; the reverse averaged about 10%. However, these are numbers of transactions not values. Potentially, cross-border transactions could reduce concentration in the United States. But even more importantly all of these measures of aggregate concentration are for the United States. With the increasing internationalization of markets, macroconcentration should be measured over the sum of global economies, as well as for individual national markets. Also, the import of goods and services in the United States increasingly exceeds exports by a substantial margin. This trend could reduce the relative role of the largest U.S. firms nationally and internationally.

IMPACT ON MICROCONCENTRATION

Concentration measures also are available for individual industries. Historically, such measures estimate the largest four firms' share of industry sales, assets, employment, or value added in manufacturing. The degree of concentration varies widely across industries. Figures by Scherer (1980) indicate that the weighted average level of concentration stayed relatively constant at about 40% over the decades of the 1960s and 1970s.

However, the published microconcentration measures are based on U.S. domestic data and do not account for international competition. A later study by Weston (1982) found that the domestic share of the four largest U.S. firms in steel production was 52%, and the share of the same four firms in world production was 14%. More generally, an analysis of 75 manufacturing industries found that the average four-firm concentration ratio fell from 50% when the base was U.S. production to 25% when world output was accounted for.

Summary

Empirical analysis of the value effects of mergers is guided by three distinct theories based on efficiency and synergy, agency costs of free cash flow and management entrenchment, and managerial hubris. The bulk of the evidence indicates that the combined returns at merger announcement are positive. These results support the efficiency/synergy explanation for mergers.

Target firm announcement returns are large and significantly positive. Target announcement returns are larger when a takeover bid is in cash vis-à-vis stock. Targets also gain when there are multiple bidders, with the added gains appreciating after the initial announcement. Targets also experience a positive run-up prior to a formal takeover announcement. Some of this run-up may be related to insider trading, but at least some of the run-up is related to the market reaction to rumors and to the research of analysts.

Bidder firm announcement returns equal roughly zero on average. This is consistent with expectations in a competitive takeover market. Bidder returns appear to be lower when stock is the method of payment vis-à-vis cash. Bidder returns are lower in multiple-bidder contests, with the deterioration appearing after the appearance of the competing bidder. Bidding firms that experience a negative return at merger announcement are themselves likely to become targets in a later acquisition.

Merger regulation such as the Williams Act has been associated with a lengthening of the merger process. Research suggests that this affects the distribution of the merger gains between targets and bidders. More recent firm-specific and state-induced antitakeover measures also appear to affect the bargaining power of target firms.

Recent research measures the long-term stock price performance following mergers. Such analysis is much more sensitive to estimation methods than event studies of announcement returns. The evidence suggests no reliable average abnormal stock price performance following mergers, which is what is expected in an efficient market.

A possible explanation for the positive combined returns at the announcement of a merger is an increase in market power. However, evidence suggests that any gains to rivals at merger announcement are a reaction to underlying change in the industry and to the anticipation of additional future restructuring activity.

Questions

8.1 What are the theoretical predictions on combined merger returns for the (1) efficiency and (2) entrenchment theories? Which theory is supported by the empirical evidence on combined returns?

8.2 What does the evidence of merger returns around banking deregulation say about the source of gains from takeover activity?

8.3 How are target stock returns affected by the use of (1) cash or (2) stock as the method of payment?

8.4 How does the presence of single versus multiple bidders affect the returns to the target (1) on the announcement date versus (2) subsequent to the announcement date?

8.5 Define target run-up. What are some possible reasons for run-up?

8.6 How might the premiums paid for target firms be expected to vary with single versus multiple bidders?

8.7 How do bidder returns vary with (1) the mode of payment and (2) the presence of single versus multiple bidders?

8.8 This question is related to AT&T's venture into cable. On Wednesday June 24, 1998, AT&T announced its intent to acquire TCI. The assets obtained in the acquisition helped create AT&T Broadband. Three years later, on Monday July 9, 2001, Comcast announced its intent to purchase the Broadband assets from AT&T.

A. Given the following data, what was AT&T's abnormal return at the announcement of the TCI acquisition?

Date	AT&T Stock Price	S&P 500 Index
June 23, 1998	$32.2566	1119.49
June 24, 1998	$29.6045	1132.88

B. Given the following data, what was AT&T's abnormal return at the announcement of the Comcast bid?

Date	AT&T Stock Price	S&P 500 Index
July 6, 2001	$16.6846	1190.59
July 9, 2001	$18.6604	1198.78

C. Do you think the results in Parts A and B are related?

8.9 How has the Williams Act affected the returns to target and bidder firms?

8.10 What are some possible reasons for the decline in takeover activity at the end of the 1980s and beginning of the 1990s?

8.11 What is the evidence on postmerger operating performance? How does this evidence relate to the event study results for combined returns at merger announcement?

8.12 How do the estimation issues differ between event studies of merger announcements and the analysis of the long-term performance following mergers?

8.13 What is the evidence on the market power explanation for merger announcement gains?

References

Agrawal, Anup, Jeffrey F. Jaffe, and Gershon N. Mandelker, "The Post-Merger Performance of Acquiring Firms: A Re-Examination of an Anomaly," *Journal of Finance* 47, September 1992, pp. 1605–1621.

Alchian, Armen A., and Harold Demsetz, "Production, Information Costs, and Economic Organization," *American Economic Review* 62, December 1972, pp. 777–795.

Andrade, Gregor, Mark Mitchell, and Erik Stafford, "New Evidence and Perspectives on Mergers," *Journal of Economic Perspectives* 15, Spring 2001, pp. 103–120.

Asquith, Paul, Robert F. Bruner, and David W. Mullins, Jr., "Merger Returns and the Form of Financing," August 1990, working paper, Massachusetts Institute of Technology, University of Virginia, and Board of Governors, Federal Reserve System.

Barclay, Michael J., and Jerold B. Warner, "Stealth Trading and Volatility: Which Trades Move Prices?" *Journal of Financial Economics* 34, 1993, pp. 281–305.

Becher, David A., "The Valuation Effects of Bank Mergers," *Journal of Corporate Finance* 6, 2000, pp. 189–214.

Berkovitch, Elazar, and M. P. Narayanan, "Motives for Takeovers: An Empirical Investigation," *Journal of Financial and Quantitative Analysis* 28, September 1993, pp. 347–362.

Betton, Sandra, and B. Espen Eckbo, "Toeholds, Bid Jumps, and Expected Payoffs in Takeovers," *Review of Financial Studies* 13, Winter 2000, pp. 841–882.

Bradley, Michael, "Interfirm Tender Offers and the Market for Corporate Control," *Journal of Business* 53, 1980, pp. 345–376.

Bradley, Michael, Anand Desai, and E. Han Kim, "The Rationale Behind Interfirm Tender Offers: Information or Synergy?" *Journal of Financial Economics* 11, 1983, pp. 183–206.

——, "Synergistic Gains from Corporate Acquisitions and Their Division Between the Stockholders of Target and Acquiring Firms," *Journal of Financial Economics* 21, 1988, pp. 3–40.

Brook, Yaron, Robert Hendershott, and Darrell Lee, "The Gains from Takeover Deregulation: Evidence from the End of Interstate Banking Restrictions," *Journal of Finance* 53, December 1998, pp. 2185–2204.

Comment, Robert, and G. William Schwert, "Poison or Placebo? Evidence on the Deterrence and Wealth Effects of Modern Antitakeover Measures," *Journal of Financial Economics* 39, 1995, pp. 3–43.

Cotter, James F., and Marc Zenner, "How Managerial Wealth Affects the Tender Offer Process," *Journal of Financial Economics* 35, 1994, pp. 63–97.

Dennis, Debra K., and John J. McConnell, "Corporate Mergers and Security Returns," *Journal of Financial Economics* 16, 1986, pp. 143–187.

Dodd, Peter, "Merger Proposals, Management Discretion, and Stockholder Wealth," *Journal of Financial Economics* 8, 1980, pp. 105–137.

Eckbo, B. Espen, "Horizontal Mergers, Collusion, and Stockholder Wealth," *Journal of Financial Economics* 11, 1983, pp. 241–273.

Ellert, James C., "Mergers, Antitrust Law Enforcement and Stockholder Returns," *Journal of Finance* 31, May 1976, pp. 715–732.

Fama, Eugene F., "Efficient Capital Markets: II," *Journal of Finance* 46, December 1991, pp. 1575–1617.

Fama, Eugene F., "Market Efficiency, Long-Term Returns, and Behavioral Finance," *Journal of Financial Economics* 49, 1998, pp. 283–306.

Fan, Joseph P. H., and Vidhan Goyal, "On the Patterns and Wealth Effects of Vertical Mergers," working paper, Hong Kong University of Science and Technology, January 2002.

Franks, Julian, Robert Harris, and Sheridan Titman, "The Postmerger Share-Price Performance of Acquiring Firms," *Journal of Financial Economics* 29, 1991, pp. 81–96.

Healy, Paul M., Krishna G. Palepu, and Richard S. Ruback, "Does Corporate Performance Improve After Mergers?" *Journal of Financial Economics* 31, 1992, pp. 135–175.

Houston, Joel F., Christopher M. James, and Michael D. Ryngaert, "Where Do Merger Gains Come From? Bank Mergers from the Perspective of Insiders and Outsiders," *Journal of Financial Economics* 60, 2001, pp. 285–331.

Huang, Yen-Sheng, and Ralph A. Walkling, "Target Abnormal Returns Associated with Acquisition Announcements," *Journal of Financial Economics* 19, 1987, pp. 329–349.

Jarrell, Gregg A., and Annette B. Poulsen, "The Returns to Acquiring Firms in Tender Offers: Evidence from Three Decades," *Financial Management* 18, 1989b, pp. 12–19.

Jarrell, Gregg A., and Annette B. Poulsen, "Stock Trading Before the Announcement of Tender Offers: Insider Trading or Market Anticipation?" *Journal of Law, Economics, and Organization* 5, Fall 1989a, pp. 225–248.

Jarrell, Gregg A., and Michael Bradley, "The Economic Effects of Federal and State Regulations of Cash Tender Offers," *Journal of Law and Economics* 23, 1980, pp. 371–407.

Jarrell, Gregg A., James A. Brickley, and Jeffry M. Netter, "The Market for Corporate Control: The Empirical Evidence Since 1980," *Journal of Economic Perspectives* 2, Winter 1988, pp. 49–68.

Jennings, Robert H., and Michael A. Mazzeo, "Competing Bids, Target Management Resistance, and the Structure of Takeover Bids," *Review of Financial Studies* 6, Winter 1993, pp. 883–909.

Jensen, Michael C., and Richard S. Ruback, "The Market for Corporate Control: The Scientific Evidence," *Journal of Financial Economics* 11, 1983, pp. 5–50.

Kaplan, Steven N., and Michael S. Weisbach, "The Success from Acquisitions: Evidence from Divestitures," *Journal of Finance* 47, March 1992, pp. 107–138.

Keown, Arthur J., and John M. Pinkerton, "Merger Announcements and Insider Trading Activity: An Empirical Investigation," *Journal of Finance* 36, September 1981, pp. 855–869.

Loughran, Tim, and Anand M. Vijh, "Do Long-Term Shareholders Benefit from Corporate Acquisitions?" *Journal of Finance* 52, December 1997, pp. 1765–1790.

Malatesta, Paul H., and Rex Thompson, "Government Regulation and Structural Change in the Corporate Acquisitions Market," *Journal of Financial and Quantitative Analysis* 28, September 1993, pp. 363–379.

Manne, Henry G., "Mergers and the Market for Corporate Control," *Journal of Political Economy* 73, April 1965, pp. 110–120.

Meulbroek, Lisa K., "An Empirical Analysis of Illegal Insider Trading," *Journal of Finance* 47, December 1992, pp. 1661–1699.

Meulbroek, Lisa K., and Carolyn Hart, "The Effect of Illegal Insider Trading on Takeover Premia," *European Finance Review* 1, 1997, pp. 51–80.

Mitchell, Mark L., and Erik Stafford, "Managerial Decisions and Long-Term Stock Price Performance," *Journal of Business* 73, July 2000, pp. 287–329.

Mitchell, Mark L., and J. Harold Mulherin, "The Impact of Industry Shocks on Takeover and Restructuring Activity," *Journal of Financial Economics* 41, 1996, pp. 193–229.

Mitchell, Mark L., and Kenneth Lehn, "Do Bad Bidders Become Good Targets?" *Journal of Political Economy* 98, 1990, pp. 372–398.

Mulherin, J. Harold, and Audra L. Boone, "Comparing Acquisitions and Divestitures," *Journal of Corporate Finance* 6, 2000, pp. 117–139.

Myers, Stewart C., and Nicholas S. Majluf, "Corporate Financing and Investment Decisions When Firms Have Information That Investors Do Not Have," *Journal of Financial Economics* 13, 1984, pp. 187–221.

Nathan, Kevin S., and Terrence B. O'Keefe, "The Rise in Takeover Premiums: An Exploratory Study," *Journal of Financial Economics* 23, 1989, pp. 101–119.

Rau, Raghavendra, and Theo Vermaelen, "Glamour, Value, and the Post-Acquisition Performance of Acquiring Firms," *Journal of Financial Economics* 49, 1998, pp. 223–253.

Roll, Richard, "The Hubris Hypothesis of Corporate Takeovers," *Journal of Business* 59, April 1986, pp. 197–216.

Sanders, Ralph W., and John S. Zdanowicz, "Target Firm Abnormal Returns and Trading Volume Around the Initiation of Change in Control Transactions," *Journal of Financial and Quantitative Analysis* 27, March 1992, pp. 109–129.

Scherer, F. M., *Industrial Market Structure and Economic Performance*, Chicago: Rand McNally College Publishing Company, 1980.

Schwert, G. William, "Hostility in Takeovers: In the Eyes of the Beholder?" *Journal of Finance* 55, December 2000, pp. 2599–2640.

Schwert, G. William, "Markup Pricing in Mergers and Acquisitions," *Journal of Financial Economics* 41, 1996, pp. 153–192.

Servaes, Henri, "Tobin's Q and the Gains from Takeovers," *Journal of Finance* 47, March 1991, pp. 409–419.

Shleifer, Andrei, and Robert W. Vishny, "Stock Market Driven Acquisitions," *Journal of Financial Economics*, forthcoming, 2003.

Slovin, Myron B., Marie E. Sushka, and Yvette M. Bendeck, "The Intra-Industry Effects of Going-Private Transactions," *Journal of Finance* 46, September 1991, pp. 1537–1550.

Song, Moon H., and Ralph A. Walkling, "Abnormal Returns to Rivals of Acquisition Targets: A Test of the 'Acquisition Probability Hypothesis,'" *Journal of Financial Economics* 55, 2000, pp. 143–171.

Stillman, Robert, "Examining Antitrust Policy Towards Horizontal Mergers," *Journal of Financial Economics* 11, 1983, pp. 225–240.

Travlos, Nickolas G., "Corporate Takeover Bids, Methods of Payment, and Bidding Firms' Stock Returns," *Journal of Finance* 42, September 1987, pp. 943–963.

Weston, J. Fred, "Domestic Concentration and International Markets," Chapter 7 in J. Fred Weston and Michael E. Granfield, eds., *Corporate Enterprise in a New Environment*, New York: KCG Productions, Inc., 1982, pp. 173–188.

White, Laurence J., "Trends in Aggregate Concentration in the United States," *Journal of Economic Perspectives*, 16, Fall 2002, pp. 137–160.

APPENDIX A

—————◆/◆/◆—————

ANALYSIS OF A RECENT M&A SAMPLE

This appendix reviews in detail a recent sample of mergers and acquisitions. The material provides a specific application of the financial economic research on corporate control transactions. The analysis first considers the acquisition type and payment method of recent mergers, and then presents event study evidence on target, bidder, and combined returns. The appendix also describes the use of negotiation and auctions in the merger process, discusses the role of investment banks, and sketches some of the valuation techniques employed during the sale of major corporations.

The transactions studied in the appendix are taken from research by Mulherin and Boone (2000). The sample comprises 16 deals announced in 1999 for which stock price data were available for the target and bidder firms. The information and data used in the appendix were obtained from LexisNexis, the *Wall Street Journal,* the SEC EDGAR filings, and the Standard & Poor's Daily Stock Price Record.

THE SAMPLE OF TARGETS AND BIDDERS

Table A8.1 describes the sample of targets and bidders. The announcement date in the table represents the first public statement of the transaction in the financial media. Usually this is the date on which a formal agreement is jointly announced by the target and the bidder, although the announcement date sometimes reflects a rumor or an unsolicited offer by the bidder or a third party. For example, Meulbroek and Hart (1997) found that between 25% to 30% of the mergers in their sample have a public announcement that the target is in play on a date that precedes the formal merger announcement.

The industry classification reported in Table A8.1 is based on the depiction of the target firm by the Value Line Investment Survey. Generally speaking, the target firms in the sample were acquired by bidder firms from the same industry. The sectors represented in the table include the environmental industry, which Mulherin and Boone (2000) reported had the highest rate of acquisition activity during the 1990s, as well as

the banking and thrift industries, which experienced deregulation in the 1990s. The chemical industry also is well represented in the sample.

Table A8.2 describes some of the characteristics of the transactions in 1999. Classifying by type, 12 of the transactions (75%) were by merger, and the remaining 4 transactions (25%) were by tender offer. The payment method was roughly equally distributed: 5 transactions employed cash, 6 employed stock, and 5 used a combination of cash and stock. In all 16 transactions, the acquiring firm was the only publicly announced bidder.

EVENT STUDY EVIDENCE

To estimate the wealth effects of the M&A transactions, we use event study analysis. We first compute the raw stock return of the target and bidder firms for the 3-day window around the announcement of the takeover: This is depicted as the return over the $(-1, +1)$ period, where day 0 is the announcement date. The 3-day window is employed because even when the news wires announcing a takeover can be pinpointed, there is still slight imprecision in discerning exactly when the takeover news first publicly reaches the stock market. The price formula for the 3-day return is $(P_{+1} - P_{-2})/P_{-2}$.

As a simple method of controlling for factors other than the announcement under study, we also estimate the movement in the stock market over the same 3-day window. As a proxy for the market, we employ the S&P 500. We then subtract the market return from the return of the particular target or bidder firm to estimate the net-of-market abnormal return related to a given transaction.

Estimating Target Returns

Table A8.3 reports the estimation of the returns to the targets in the sample. As an example, Armco Incorporated's stock return for the 3 days surrounding the announcement date is equal to $(6.44 - 5.63)/5.63 = 14.44\%$. The S&P 500 fell by 2.80% over the same window. Hence, the net-of-market return for Armco Incorporated is 17.24%.

TABLE A8.1 Sample of Targets and Bidders from 1999

Announcement Date	Target Firm	Shares Outstanding	Industry	Bidder Firm	Shares Outstanding
May 21	Armco Inc.	108,692,000	Steel	AK Steel	59,408,000
March 1	Aydin Corp.	5,220,000	Electronics	L-3 Communications	30,902,000
March 15	BankBoston	296,482,000	Banking	Fleet Financial Group	569,040,000
March 31	Blount Intl.	27,434,000	Building Materials	Lehman Brothers	119,411,000
March 8	Browning Ferris	158,136,00	Environmental	Allied Waste Ind.	182,737,000
April 23	Chock Full o' Nuts	11,084,000	Food Processing	Sara Lee	903,480,000
March 17	Daniel Ind.	17,515,000	Oilfield Services	Emerson Electric	437,380,000
April 28	Lawter Intl.	33,068,000	Chemical	Eastman Chemical	78,176,000
February 1	Morton Intl.	120,759,000	Chemical	Rohm & Haas	167,643,000
March 12	Pioneer Hi Bred Intl.	190,117,000	Food Processing	DuPont	1,126,944,000
May 19	Raychem Corp.	77,285,000	Chemical	Tyco Intl.	820,649,000
May 7	Shelby Williams	8,761,000	Furniture	Falcon Products	8,634,000
March 13	Sonat Inc.	110,039,000	Natural Gas	El Paso Energy Co.	120,989,000
May 17	St. Paul Bancorp.	39,926,000	Thrift	Charter One Financial	166,366,000
February 21	Sundstrand Corp.	54,748,000	Aerospace/Defense	United Technologies	225,140,000
June 1	Witco Corp.	57,644,000	Chemical	Crompton & Knowles	65,449,000
	Average shares	82,306,875		Average shares	317,646,750

TABLE A8.2 Merger Characteristics

Announcement Date	Target Firm	Bidder Firm	Type	Payment	Number of Public Bidders
May 21	Armco Inc.	AK Steel	Merger	Stock	1
March 1	Aydin Corp.	L-3 Communications	Tender Offer	Cash	1
March 15	BankBoston	Fleet Financial Group	Merger	Stock	1
March 31	Blount Intl.	Lehman Brothers	Merger	Combination	1
March 8	Browning Ferris	Allied Waste Ind.	Merger	Cash	1
April 23	Chock Full o' Nuts	Sara Lee	Merger	Stock	1
March 17	Daniel Ind.	Emerson Electric	Tender Offer	Cash	1
April 28	Lawter Intl.	Eastman Chemical	Tender Offer	Cash	1
February 1	Morton Intl.	Rohm & Haas	Merger	Combination	1
March 12	Pioneer Hi Bred Intl.	DuPont	Merger	Combination	1
May 19	Raychem Corp.	Tyco Intl.	Merger	Combination	1
May 7	Shelby Williams	Falcon Products	Tender Offer	Cash	1
March 13	Sonat Inc.	El Paso Energy Co.	Merger	Stock	1
May 17	St. Paul Bancorp.	Charter One Financial	Merger	Stock	1
February 21	Sundstrand Corp.	United Technologies	Merger	Combination	1
June 1	Witco Corp.	Crompton & Knowles	Merger	Stock	1

TABLE A8.3 Estimating Target Returns

Announcement Date	Target Firm	Estimating Target Return			Estimating Market Return (S&P 500)			Net of Market Return (%)
		P_{-2}	P_{+1}	Return (%)	P_{-2}	P_{+1}	Return (%)	
May 21	Armco Inc.	5.63	6.44	14.44	1344.23	1306.65	-2.80	17.24
March 1	Aydin Corp.	9.31	12.94	38.93	1245.02	1225.50	-1.57	40.49
March 15	BankBoston	45.88	46.38	1.09	1297.68	1306.38	0.67	0.42
March 31	Blount Intl.	27.31	27.94	2.29	1310.17	1293.72	-1.26	3.54
March 8	Browning Ferris	33.75	39.00	15.56	1246.64	1279.84	2.66	12.89
April 23	Chock Full o' Nuts	6.00	9.81	63.54	1336.12	1360.04	1.79	61.75
March 17	Daniel Ind.	11.50	14.81	28.80	1307.26	1316.55	0.71	28.09
April 28	Lawter Intl.	8.88	12.00	35.21	1360.04	1342.83	-1.27	36.48
February 1	Morton Intl.	25.88	35.69	37.92	1265.37	1261.99	-0.27	38.19
March 12	Pioneer Hi Bred Intl.	22.06	38.38	73.94	1286.84	1307.26	1.59	72.35
May 19	Raychem Corp.	29.38	35.00	19.15	1339.49	1338.83	-0.05	19.20
May 7	Shelby Williams	13.75	16.25	18.18	1347.31	1340.30	-0.52	18.70
March 13	Sonat Inc.	27.13	29.00	6.91	1297.68	1306.38	0.67	6.24
May 17	St. Paul Bancorp.	25.00	26.38	5.50	1367.56	1333.32	-2.50	8.00
February 21	Sundstrand Corp.	51.63	67.94	31.60	1237.28	1271.18	2.74	28.86
June 1	Witco Corp.	15.13	19.50	28.93	1281.41	1294.81	1.05	27.88
	Average			26.37			0.10	26.27

For the entire sample of 16 target firms, the net-of-market abnormal return averages 26.27%. All of the target returns are positive. Hence, the acquisitions in this sample create wealth for target shareholders. These results are in line with the body of M&A research done in financial economics.

As a methodological point, note that the average of the raw stock returns for the target firms in Table A8.3 is equal to 26.37%, which is virtually identical to the value of the net-of-market return. This similarity in magnitude stems from the fact that the average estimate of the 3-day return of the S&P 500, the proxy for the market, is a small value, 0.10%. The small average market movement reflects the small expected market return over a randomly selected, short time interval. This illustrates an important point emphasized by Fama (1991, 1998): Event-study analysis over a narrow window is scientifically clean because of the robustness to the control methods employed and the lack of sensitivity to a particular asset-pricing model.

Estimating Bidder Returns
Table 8A.4 reports the estimates of the returns to the 16 bidder firms in the sample. The estimation follows the same procedure as done for the targets: First estimate the 3-day return for the bidder, then subtract the market return over the same window to provide the net-of-market return.

As reported, the net-of-market return to the bidder firms averages –0.47%. Roughly half (44%) of the bidder returns were positive. Consistent with prior research, the announcement of an acquisition is roughly a break-even endeavor for bidders.

Estimating Combined Returns
The most important query concerning the wealth effects of mergers and acquisitions is whether the transactions create wealth. In other words, are mergers positive net present value (NPV) projects? This query is addressed by estimating the combined return to targets and bidders. The combined return is the weighted average of the returns of the two parties in the merger, where the weights are the equity value of the particular target and bidder. The formula is:

$$(\text{target value} \times \text{target return} + \text{bidder value} \times \text{bidder return})/(\text{target value} + \text{bidder value})$$

An example can be taken from Table A8.5. Consider the acquisition of Sundstrand Corporation by United Technologies. The equity value of the two firms is obtained by using the shares outstanding data

in Table A8.1 and the share price data 2 days prior to the announcement, as reported in Table A8.3 and Table A8.4. The return to Sundstrand is 28.86%, and the return to United Technologies is –1.11%. This implies a wealth gain of roughly $800 million for Sundstrand and a wealth loss of roughly $300 million for United Technologies. The combined wealth creation is roughly $500 million, which equates to a 1.66% return on the combined firm value of $30 billion.

The average combined return reported in Table A8.5 is 3.59%. Ten of the 16 transactions (62.5%) have a positive combined return. Consistent with overall research in financial economics, the sample mergers, on average, are positive NPV projects.

DETAILS ON THE MERGER PROCESS

The event study analysis provides succinct evidence on the wealth effects of the M&A transactions from 1999. However, the focus on the announcement date abstracts away from the lengthy procedure that occurs prior to the public revelation of the merger agreement. In this section, we address how the sample transactions are initiated and the nature of the process involved in the complex and often lengthy period in which the merger evolves. We also report that the sales process of the target firms is often much more competitive than suggested by the presence of only a single public bidder. This analysis complements the theory and cases on the bidding process that were discussed in Chapter 6.

How Is the Merger Initiated?
Table A8.6 provides some details on the initiation and evolution of the mergers that precede the public announcement of the sample transactions. The information to construct the table was garnered by employing documents filed in the EDGAR system of the U.S. Securities Commission. For the 16 transactions in the sample, we reviewed the merger background reported in 14A, 14D, S-4, and related filings.

As reported in the column labeled "Initiation Event," the transaction often was initiated by the target board or by a mutual meeting of the senior executives of the target and bidder: Six cases (38%) were initiated by the target board and seven cases (44%) were classified as a CEO meeting. In only three cases was the merger initiated via an unsolicited offer by the bidder or a third party. As a comparison, Sanders and Zdanowicz (1992) used similar SEC merger documents to study the initiation of 30 transactions from

TABLE A8.4 Estimating Bidder Returns

Announcement Date	Bidder Firm	Estimating Bidder Return			Estimating Market Return (S&P 500)			Net of Market Return (%)
		P_{-2}	P_{+1}	Return (%)	P_{-2}	P_{+1}	Return (%)	
May 21	AK Steel	24.00	24.44	1.82	1344.23	1306.65	-2.80	4.62
March 1	L-3 Communications	43.00	43.88	2.03	1245.02	1225.50	-1.57	3.60
March 15	Fleet Financial Group	44.63	41.06	-7.98	1297.68	1306.38	0.67	-8.65
March 31	Lehman Brothers	60.44	60.44	0.00	1310.17	1293.72	-1.26	1.26
March 8	Allied Waste Ind.	20.00	16.25	-18.75	1246.64	1279.84	2.66	-21.41
April 23	Sara Lee	25.88	23.88	-7.73	1336.12	1360.04	1.79	-9.52
March 17	Emerson Electric	58.50	56.88	-2.78	1307.26	1316.55	0.71	-3.49
April 28	Eastman Chemical	49.75	54.06	8.67	1360.04	1342.83	-1.27	9.93
February 1	Rohm & Haas	30.94	30.06	-2.83	1265.37	1261.99	-0.27	-2.56
March 12	DuPont	57.38	56.25	-1.96	1286.84	1307.26	1.59	-3.55
May 19	Tyco Intl.	88.25	91.38	3.54	1339.49	1338.83	-0.05	3.59
May 7	Falcon Products	8.00	10.56	32.03	1347.31	1340.30	-0.52	32.55
March 13	El Paso Energy Co.	38.69	31.56	-18.42	1297.68	1306.38	0.67	-19.09
May 17	Charter One Financial	31.06	29.13	-6.24	1367.56	1333.32	-2.50	-3.73
February 21	United Technologies	123.06	125.06	1.63	1237.28	1271.18	2.74	-1.11
June 1	Crompton & Knowles	17.94	19.94	11.15	1281.41	1294.81	1.05	10.10
	Average			-0.36			0.10	-0.47

TABLE A8.5 Estimating Combined Returns

Announcement Date	Target Firm	Equity Value	Net of Market (%)	Bidder Firm	Equity Value	Net of Market (%)	Combined Return (%)
May 21	Armco Inc.	$611.4 million	17.24	AK Steel	$ 1.4 billion	4.62	8.41
March 1	Aydin Corp.	48.6 million	40.49	L-3 Communications	1.3 billion	3.60	4.90
March 15	BankBoston	13.6 billion	0.42	Fleet Financial Group	25.4 billion	−8.65	−5.49
March 31	Blount Intl.	749.3 million	3.54	Lehman Brothers	7.2 billion	1.26	1.47
March 8	Browning Ferris	5.3 billion	12.89	Allied Waste Ind.	3.7 billion	−21.41	−1.05
April 23	Chock Full o' Nuts	66.5 million	61.75	Sara Lee	23.3 billion	−9.52	−9.32
March 17	Daniel Ind.	201.4 million	28.09	Emerson Electric	25.6 billion	−3.49	−3.24
April 28	Lawter Intl.	293.5 million	36.48	Eastman Chemical	3.9 billion	9.93	11.80
February 1	Morton Intl.	3.1 billion	38.19	Rohm & Haas	5.2 billion	−2.56	12.76
March 12	Pioneer Hi Bred Intl.	4.2 billion	72.35	DuPont	64.7 billion	−3.55	1.08
May 19	Raychem Corp.	2.3 billion	19.20	Tyco Intl.	72.4 billion	3.59	4.06
May 7	Shelby Williams	120.5 million	18.70	Falcon Products	69.1 million	32.55	23.75
March 13	Sonat Inc.	2.98 billion	6.24	El Paso Energy Co.	4.7 billion	−19.09	−9.22
May 17	St. Paul Bancorp.	998.2 million	8.00	Charter One Financial	5.2 billion	−3.73	−1.83
February 21	Sundstrand Corp.	2.8 billion	28.86	United Technologies	27.7 billion	−1.11	1.66
June 1	Witco Corp.	871.9 million	27.88	Crompton & Knowles	1.2 billion	10.10	17.68
	Average	2.4 billion			17.1 billion		3.59

TABLE A8.6 Details on the Merger Process

Target Firm	Private Initiation Date	Initiation Event	Merger Evolution	Public Announce Date	Length of Merger Process (in Months)
Armco Inc.	Feb. 1998	CEOs meet	mutual negotiation	May 1999	15
Aydin Corp.	August 1998	target board considers alternatives	controlled sale	March 1999	7
BankBoston	April 1998	CEOs meet	mutual negotiation	March 1999	11
Blount Intl.	August 1998	target board considers alternatives	private auction	March 1999	7
Browning Ferris	Feb. 1998	CEOs meet	mutual negotiation	March 1999	13
Chock Full o' Nuts	August 1997	bidder's unsolicited offer	cash tender; then merger	April 1999	20
Daniel Ind.	March 1999	third-party's unsolicited offer	private auction	March 1999	1
Lawter Intl.	July 1998	target board considers alternatives	controlled sale	April 1999	9
Morton Intl.	July 1998	target board considers alternatives	mutual negotiation	Feb. 1999	7
Pioneer Hi Bred Intl.	Jan. 1999	CEOs meet	mutual negotiation	March 1999	2
Raychem Corp.	March 1999	CEOs meet	mutual negotiation	May 1999	2
Shelby Williams	Nov. 1998	target investment bank contacts third party	controlled sale	May 1999	6
Sonat Inc.	Dec. 1998	target board considers alternatives	controlled sale	March 1999	3
St. Paul Bancorp.	July 1998	third-party initial inquiry	controlled sale	May 1999	10
Sundstrand Corp.	Sept. 1998	CEOs meet	mutual negotiation	Feb. 1999	5
Witco Corp.	Feb. 1999	CEOs meet	mutual negotiation	June 1999	4

Average time 7.6 months

the time period 1978 to 1986. They found that 15 of the transactions (50%) were initiated by the bidder, 10 (33%) were initiated by the target, and the remainder were initiated by other means.

The data in Table A8.6 indicate that the merger was often initiated well before the public announcement date. In these cases, the private initiation date reported in the SEC documents occurred between 1 month and 20 months prior to the public announcement of the transaction. The average time between private initiation and public announcement was 7.6 months.

How Does the Merger Evolve?

As described in the column entitled "Merger Evolution," the process of the merger can follow several possible paths between the private initiation and public announcement dates. In half of the cases (8 of 16), the merger agreement resulted from a direct, mutual negotiation between the bidder and the target. Most of these cases followed an initial meeting between the senior executives of the two firms. This mutual negotiation contrasts with only a single case, Chock Full o' Nuts, where the bidder, Sara Lee, engaged in an unsolicited tender offer before eventually completing a mutually agreed-upon merger.

In 7 of the 16 cases (44%), the sales process that led to the merger was implemented and administered by the target firm. In 5 cases, the target engaged in a controlled sale with a limited set of potential bidders. In 2 cases, the target sold itself via a full-scale, privately conducted auction.

Table A8.7 sketches the dimensions of the sales process for these seven target firms. As reported in Panel A, in the five cases labeled "controlled sales," the target firm and its investment bank contacted three to five possible bidders. Either all or a subset of these possible bidders signed confidentiality agreements whereby the target firm agreed to share nonpublic information and the bidding firm often agreed to a standstill restricting unsolicited takeover actions. The confidential information sharing was followed by preliminary indications of interest or an initial bid. The next round of the sales process entailed more detailed due diligence and information sharing.

The controlled sales process described in Panel A of Table A8.7 culminated in formal written bids. As reported, one to five firms submitted a bid for the target, with the number of bids averaging two. Hence, even though each of the five targets had only one public bidder, the actual sales process entailed multiple bidders.

The two firms reported in Panel B of Table A8.7 had an even more extensive private auction. In these two cases, the investment banks for the targets initially contacted 65 and 28 possible bidders. Confidentiality agreements were signed by 28 and 19 firms. Actual interest was indicated by 7 and 9 firms. Detailed due diligence was conducted by 6 and 8 firms. The auctions concluded with formal written bids by 2 firms in one case and a single firm in the other case. Similar to the controlled sales, the existence of only a single public bidder understates the competitiveness of the sales process conducted by the target firm and its investment bank.

INVESTMENT BANKS

Table A8.8 reports the investment banks for the targets and bidders in the sample. Most of the investment banks in the table are the major players in the profession. Moreover, a number of the listed banks, such as Goldman Sachs, Merrill Lynch, and Salomon Smith Barney, serve as financial advisers for both target firms and bidder firms.

The investment banks play an important role in the merger process. For bidders and targets that engage in mutual negotiation, the investment banks often provide advice during the negotiation process. In cases where the target conducts a controlled sale or private auction, the investment bank for the target usually is a prime player in the sales process.

Investment Banks and Merger Valuation

Another important function of investment banks in the merger process relates to valuation. As discussed by DeAngelo (1990), the fairness opinion produced by an investment bank provides shareholders with a benchmark with which to gauge the price in an M&A transaction. As noted by DeAngelo (1990), the valuation methods used by investment banks include (1) the comparable companies approach, (2) the comparable transactions approach, and (3) discounted cash flow analysis.

Table A8.9 sketches some of the valuation techniques employed by investment banks for the M&A transactions studied in this appendix. Due to limited data, the table considers only 11 of the 16 transactions. For any particular transaction, a variety of valuation methods can be employed. Table A8.9

TABLE A8.7 The Dimensions of Controlled Sales and Private Auctions

Panel A. Controlled Sales

Target Firm	Contact	Confidentiality Agreement	Preliminary Interest or Bid	Invited to Detailed Due Diligence	Formal Written Bid
Aydin Corp.	4	4	1	1	1
Lawter Intl.	3	2	2	2	2
Shelby Williams	5	3	3	3	1
Sonat Inc.	5	5	5	5	5
St. Paul Bancorp.	4	2	2	1	1
Average	4.2	3.2	2.6	2.4	2

Panel B. Private Auctions

Target Firm	Contact	Confidentiality Agreement	Preliminary Interest or Bid	Invited to Detailed Due Diligence	Formal Written Bid
Blount Intl.	65	28	7	6	2
Daniel Ind.	28	19	9	8	1
Average	46.5	23.5	8	7	1.5

TABLE A8.8 Target and Bidder Investment Banks

Announcement Date	Target Firm	Target Investment Bank	Bidder Firm	Bidder Investment Bank
May 21	Armco Inc.	Salomon Smith Barney	AK Steel	CS First Boston
March 1	Aydin Corp.	Pricewaterhouse Coopers	L-3 Communications	Lehman Brothers
March 15	BankBoston	Merrill Lynch	Fleet Financial Group	Goldman Sachs
March 31	Blount Intl.	Beacon Group	Lehman Brothers	Lehman Brothers
March 8	Browning Ferris	Goldman Sachs	Allied Waste Ind.	Donaldson Lufkin Jenrette
April 23	Chock Full o' Nuts	CS First Boston	Sara Lee	Goldman Sachs
March 17	Daniel Ind.	Simmons & Co.	Emerson Electric	Morgan Stanley
April 28	Lawter Intl.	ABN Amro	Eastman Chemical	Merrill Lynch
February 1	Morton Int	Goldman Sachs	Rohm & Haas	Wasserstein Perella
March 12	Pioneer Hi Bred Intl.	Lazard Freres	DuPont	Salomon Smith Barney
May 19	Raychem Corp.	Morgan Stanley	Tyco Int.	NA
May 7	Shelby Williams	Lazard Freres	Falcon products	Donaldson Lufkin Jenrette
March 13	Sonat Inc.	Merrill Lynch	El Paso Energy Co.	Donaldson Lufkin Jenrette
May 17	St. Paul Bancorp.	Merrill Lynch	Charter One Financial	Salomon Smith Barney
February 21	Sundstrand Corp.	Merrill Lynch	United Technologies	NA
June 1	Witco Corp.	Goldman Sachs	Crompton & Knowles	Salomon Smith Barney

TABLE A8.9 Techniques Used in Merger Valuation

Target	Comparable Companies			Comparable Transactions			Discounted Cash Flow Analysis			Target's Merger Price
	No. of Firms	Average or Range of P/E Multiples	Implied Prices or Target's Multiple	No. of Mergers	Average or Range of EBITDA Multiples	Implied Prices or Target's Multiple	Terminal Multiple	Discount Rate (%)	Estimated Price Range	
Armco Inc.	5	13.8x–16.3x	7.8x	10	5.8x–15.3x	$7–$10	6.5x–8.5x	10–12	$ 6.05–$8.01	$7.50
BankBoston	13	16.81x	14.81x	3	11.6x–24.9x	18.5x	12x–14x	13–15	39.94–48.88	53
Blount Intl.	26	12.5x–18.7x	$20.60–$30.82	19	13.3x–19.4x	$21.92–$31.97	6x–8x	11.5–15.5	28.43–41.79	30
Browning Ferris	6	12.0x–19.4x	13.4x	10	5.5x–13.4x	6.8x	6x–8x	9–11	37.27–55.08	45
Chock Full o' Nuts	15	not reported	$7–$9.25	22	not reported	$10–$11.75	5x–7x	9–10	10.75–13	11
Morton Intl.	10	9.2x–17.1x	14.5x	7	11.4x	10.2x	DCF analysis not reported			37.125
Pioneer Hi Bred Intl.	6	28.8x	$30–$40	8	17.5x–52.9x	$30–$50	10x–14x	10–12	34.69–50.70	40
Raychem Corp.	9	14.8x	13.4x	18	11.4x	11.4x	5.5x–7.5x	11.5	24–31	37
St. Paul Bancorp.	7	12.67x	$19.38	NA	21.7x	$28.43	11x–13x	12–14	18.78–22.33	28.62
Sundstrand Corp.	10	10x–13x	$45.30–$58.89	20	8.5x–10.5x	$62.78–$78.92	7x–9x	10–11	61.13–77.82	70
Witco Corp.	10	10.5x–19.6x	19.4x	Comparable transactions analysis not reported			6x–8x	9–11	18.75–30.02	18.14

Source: SEC EDGAR filings.

focuses on comparable companies, comparable transactions, and discounted cash flow.

For each of the target firms listed in Table A8.9, the firm's investment bank compared the price paid in the merger, listed at the far right of the table, against a range of prices implied by the different valuation techniques. For some methods in some transactions, the investment bank simply compared the target firm's pricing multiple against the multiple for the comparable companies or transactions.

An example illustrates the valuation approach. In the acquisition of Sundstrand by United Technologies, Merrill Lynch was the target firm's financial adviser. The payment method in the merger was a combination of cash and stock that had an implied price of $70 per share.

For the comparable companies approach, Merrill Lynch selected 10 publicly traded firms with operations similar to Sundstrand. The investment bank then estimated a variety of financial ratios of the comparable companies including the P/E ratio, which ranged from 10 to 13. Applying this range to earnings data from Sundstrand produced price estimates that ranged from $45.30 to $58.89.

For the comparable transactions analysis, Merrill Lynch selected 20 recent acquisition—9 from aerospace and 11 from the industrial sector. The investment bank then estimated the multiple of the transaction value to Earnings Before Interest, Taxes, Depreciation and Amortization (EBITDA) of the acquired businesses. This produced multiples ranging from 8.5 to 10.5. Applying these multiples to Sundstrand EBITDA data generated a price range of $62.78 to $78.92.

Merrill Lynch also performed a discounted cash flow analysis of the projected after-tax unlevered cash flows of Sundstrand. The analysis relied on projections of cash flow between 1999 and 2003 and assumed discount rates ranging from 10% to 11%. For the years after 2003, the analysis assumed terminal multiples of 2003 EBITDA ranging from 7 to 9. Using these data and these assumptions, the base case estimates of share price ranged from $61.13 to $77.82.

In the Sundstrand example, as in most of the cases reported in Table A8.9, the range of estimates generated by the valuation analysis usually spans the target's actual merger price. The fact that the valuation techniques and the actual merger price concur does not necessarily mean that the valuation techniques are completely accurate. Kaplan and Ruback (1995) provided an assessment of the various methods of valuation for a sample of transactions from 1983 to 1989 and concluded that the techniques, including discounted cash flow analysis, provide reliable estimates of value.

SUMMARY

This appendix has examined 16 M&A transactions from 1999. Using event study methods to determine the wealth effects of the transactions, the analysis finds results similar to prior research in financial economics: Target shareholders gain, bidder shareholders break even, and the average combined return in the transactions is positive. The analysis also notes the complexity of the merger process and notes some of the valuation techniques employed by investment banks in M&A transactions.

QUESTIONS

A8.1   Using information in Table A8.2 on merger characteristics and Table A8.3 on target returns, compare the average returns where cash is a means of payment versus where stock is the means of payment. How does this evidence from 1999 compare with prior empirical research?

A8.2   Repeat question 1 for (1) bidder returns and (2) combined returns.

REFERENCES

DeAngelo, Linda Elizabeth, "Equity Valuation and Corporate Control," *Accounting Review* 65, January 1990, pp. 93–112.

Fama, Eugene F., "Efficient Capital Markets: II," *Journal of Finance* 46, December 1991, pp. 1575–1617.

Fama, Eugene F., "Market Efficiency, Long-Term Returns, and Behavioral Finance," *Journal of Financial Economics* 49, 1998, 283–306.

Kaplan, Steven N., and Richard S. Ruback, "The Valuation of Cash Flow Forecasts: An Empirical

Analysis," *Journal of Finance* 50, September 1995, pp. 1059–1093.

Meulbroek, Lisa K., and Carolyn Hart, "The Effect of Illegal Insider Trading on Takeover Premia," *European Finance Review* 1, 1997, pp. 51–80.

Mulherin, J. Harold, and Audra L. Boone, "Comparing Acquisitions and Divestitures,"

Journal of Corporate Finance, July 2000, pp. 117–139.

Sanders, Ralph W., and John S. Zdanowicz, "Target Firm Abnormal Returns and Trading Volume Around the Initiation of Change in Control Transactions," *Journal of Financial and Quantitative Analysis* 27, March 1992, 109–129.

CHAPTER 9
ALTERNATIVE APPROACHES TO VALUATION

This chapter discusses valuation in relation to merger and acquisition activity. This subject is critical for the study of M&As because a major cause of acquisition failures is that the bidder pays too much. Sometimes a bidder makes a tender offer, which might stimulate competing bidders. The securities laws provide for a 20-day waiting period to give shareholders the opportunity to evaluate the proposal. This also gives other potential bidders time to evaluate the situation to determine whether a competitive bid will be made. In a bidding contest, the winner is the firm with the highest estimates of the target's value. A framework is essential to discipline valuation estimates.

The leading methods used in the valuation of a firm for merger analysis are the comparable companies or comparable transactions approach, the spreadsheet approach, and the formula approach. In this chapter, we explain and illustrate the logic or theory behind each of these three approaches. In Chapter 10, we develop further the implementation of the leading valuation methods.

COMPARABLES APPROACHES

In the comparable companies or comparable transactions approach, key relationships are calculated for a group of similar companies or similar transactions as a basis for the valuation of companies involved in a merger or takeover. This approach is widely used, especially by investment bankers and in legal cases. The theory is not complicated. Marketplace transactions are used. It is a commonsense approach that says that similar companies should sell for similar prices. This straightforward approach appeals to businesspersons, to their financial advisers, and to the judges in courts of law called upon to give decisions on the relative values of companies in litigation. For a full elaboration of this approach, emanating from considerable application in court cases, see Cornell (1993).

COMPARABLE COMPANIES ANALYSIS

First, a basic idea is illustrated in a simple setting, followed by applications to actual companies in an M&A setting. Table 9.1a illustrates the comparable companies approach. We are seeking to place a value on company W. We find three companies that are comparable. To test for comparability, we consider size, similarity of products, age of company, and recent trends, among other variables.

TABLE 9.1a Comparable Companies Ratios (Company W Is Compared with Companies A, B, and C)

Ratio	Company A	Company B	Company C	Average
Market/sales[a]	1.2	1.0	0.8	1.0
Market/book	1.3	1.2	2.0	1.5
Market/net income = price/earnings ratio	20	15	25	20

[a]"Market" refers to the market value of equity.

Assume that companies A, B, and C meet most of our comparability requirements. We then calculate the ratio of the market value of shareholders' equity to sales, the ratio of the market value of equity to the book value of equity, and the price/earnings ratio for the individual companies. The resulting ratios are given in Table 9.1a. These ratios are then averaged, and the average ratios are applied to the absolute data for company W. For the averages to be meaningful, it is important that the ratios we calculate for each company be relatively close in value. If they are greatly different, which implies that the dispersion around the average is substantial, the average (a measure of central tendency) is not meaningful. In the example given, the ratios for the three comparable companies do not vary widely. Hence, it makes some sense to apply the averages.

We postulate that for a relevant recent time period, company W had sales of $100 million, a book value of $60 million, and a net income of $5 million as shown in Table 9.1b. We next apply the average market ratios from Table 9.1a to obtain the indicated value of equity for company W. We have three estimates of the indicated equity value of W based on the ratio of market value to sales, to book, and to net income. The results are close enough to be meaningful. When we average them, we obtain $97 million for the indicated market value of equity for company W.

One of the advantages of the comparable companies approach is that it can be used to establish valuation relationships for a company that is not publicly traded. This is a method of predicting what its publicly traded price is likely to be. The methodology is applicable in testing for the soundness of valuations in mergers also. The buyer and the seller in a merger seek confirmation that the price is fair in relation to the values placed on other companies. For public companies, the courts will require such a demonstration if a suit is filed by an aggrieved shareholder.

COMPARABLE TRANSACTIONS ANALYSIS

The data in Table 9.1a can be reinterpreted to illustrate the comparable transactions approach. The data would then represent companies involved in the same kind of merger transactions as company W. In connection with merger transactions, a clarification should be made. When the

TABLE 9.1b Application of Valuation Ratios to Company W

Actual Recent Data for Company W		Average Market Ratio	Indicated Value of Equity (in millions)
Sales	= $100	1.0	$100
Book value of equity =	60	1.5	90
Net Income =	5	20	100
			Average = $ 97

TABLE 9.2a Comparable Transaction Ratios (Company W Is Compared with Companies TA, TB, and TC)

Ratio	Company TA	Company TB	Company TC	Average
Market/sales[a]	1.4	1.2	1.0	1.2
Market/book	1.5	1.4	2.2	1.7
Market/net income = price/earnings ratio	25	20	27	24

[a]"Market" refers to the transaction price of the deal.

term *market* is used, it does not refer to the prevailing market price of the companies' common stock before the merger announcement. In this context, "market" refers to the transaction price in a deal recently completed. Typically, merger transactions involve a premium as high as 30% to 40% over the prevailing market price (before news of the merger transaction has leaked out). The relevant valuation for a subsequent merger transaction would be the transaction prices for comparable deals.

Now let us reinterpret Table 9.1b as shown in Table 9.2a which covers comparable transactions. We postulate that the premiums over market that were paid caused the multiples (ratios) to be increased. We now view the companies as targets in acquisitions. The market values are now interpreted as the transaction market prices that were paid when these companies were acquired. Before a merger transaction, the prevailing market prices of companies include some probability that they will be acquired. But when they are acquired, the transaction price reflects the actual takeover event. Because takeover bids typically involve a premium over prevailing market prices, we accordingly illustrate this in the multiples reflected in Table 9.2b. We now observe that the average transaction ratios for the comparable transactions have moved up. The indicated market value of company W is now $114, compared with $97, reflecting a premium of 17.5% over general market valuation relationships.

The practical implication of this is that if company W here going to be purchased and no comparable transactions had taken place, we would take the comparable companies approach as illustrated in Tables 9.1a and 9.1b. However, this would be only a starting point. Some merger negotiations would follow and probably some premium would be paid over prevailing market prices for the comparable companies.

Tables 9.1a through 9.2b illustrate the comparable companies and comparable transactions approaches using the ratios of market value of equity to book value, market value to sales, and market value to net income of the company. In some situations, other ratios might be employed in the comparable companies or comparable transactions approach. Additional ratios could include sales or revenue per employee, net income per employee, or assets needed to produce

TABLE 9.2b Application of Valuation Ratios to Company W

Actual Recent Data for Company W		Average Transaction Multiple	Indicated Value of Equity
Sales	= $100	1.2×	$120
Book value of equity =	60	1.7×	102
Net Income	= 5	24×	120
			Average = $114

TABLE 9.3a	Data for Comparable Transactions (dollar amounts in billions)		
	BP Amoco	*Chevron Texaco*	*Phillips Conoco*
Total paid	$47.1	$35.8	$15.2
Market value target	$39.1	$30.4	$15.2
Market value combined	$113.3	$85.4	$34.9
Book value target	$15.7	$12.8	$6.6
LTM net income target	$2.1	$2.3	$2.0
LTM sales target	$34.2	$46.4	$40.6
Premium paid, % target	22.3%	17.7%	0.0%
Premium paid, % combined	7.7%	6.3%	0.0%

$1 of sales or revenue. Note that market values are not included in the ratios just listed. The additional ratios provide information on supplementary aspects of performance of the companies. This additional information could be used for interpreting or adjusting the average multiples obtained by using the comparable companies or comparable transactions approaches. Our experience has been that in actual merger or takeover transactions, investment bankers employ the comparable companies approach and the comparable transactions approach and develop additional comparative performance measures, as well.

APPLICATION OF COMPARABLE TRANSACTIONS ANALYSIS

The comparable transactions analysis is illustrated for the Exxon-Mobil merger. Table 9.3a uses three major oil mergers in the late 1990s as comparable transactions. The basic data for the target and combined companies are shown. The comparable transactions ratios are calculated in Table 9.3b. The average ratios calculated have considerable dispersion. In Table 9.3c, the ratios are applied to Mobil data. The resulting average indicated price that Exxon should have paid for Mobil is $56.8 billion. This is substantially below the $74.2 billion paid by Exxon. The values produced by the five tests range widely between $43.8 billion and $69.6 billion. In Table 9.4 we use the transaction multiples in the BP-Amoco transaction. The average indicated price for Mobil is $71.4 billion, which is closer to the $74.2 billion Exxon paid. The dispersion is again substantial. Among the important considerations the comparable transactions method does not take into account is the estimated synergies (cost and revenues improvements) that can vary between different transactions.

TABLE 9.3b	Comparable Transaction Ratios			
	Amoco	*Texaco*	*Conoco*	*Average*
Total paid/sales	1.38	0.77	0.37	0.84
Total paid/book	3.00	2.79	2.29	2.69
Total paid/net income	22.46	15.46	7.60	15.18
Premium paid, % target	22.3%	17.7%	0.0%	13.3%
Premium paid, % combined	7.7%	6.3%	0.0%	4.7%

TABLE 9.3c Application of Valuation Ratios to Mobil (dollar amounts in billions)

	Mobil	Average Transaction Multiple	Value of Equity
LTM sales	$ 63.0	0.84	$53.0
Book value	19.0	2.69	51.2
LTM net income	2.9	15.18	43.8
Market value target[a]	58.7	13.3%	66.5
Market value combined[b]	233.7	4.7%	69.6
			Average = 56.8

[a]Value of equity = market value target × (1 + average premium paid, % target)
[b]Value of equity = market value combined × (1 + average premium paid, % combined) – market value buyer

The advisory opinions of the investment bankers in the Exxon-Mobil merger obtained similar results. In the Exxon-Mobil merger, J. P. Morgan, financial adviser to Exxon, reviewed 38 large capitalization stock-for-stock transactions. Their data indicated that a premium of 15% to 25% for Mobil "matched market precedent" (Joint Proxy to Shareholders, April 5, 1999). Goldman Sachs for Mobil used six large oil companies judged to be similar to Mobil. The two ratios used were price/earnings (P/E) and price/cash flows. For 1999, the estimated P/E ratio range was 19.3 to 23.8 times. The estimated price/cash flows ratios were 8.5 to 12.5. The premium analysis by J. P. Morgan and the ratio ranges of Goldman Sachs result in a relatively wide spread of values.

The comparables method in practice fails to arrive at definitive values. This result occurs for important conceptual reasons. The companies used in the comparisons are likely to have different track records and opportunities even though they are in similar businesses and comparable in size. For example, they are likely to differ in their prospective: (1) growth rates in revenues, (2) growth rates in cash flows, (3) riskiness (beta) of companies, (4) stages in the life cycles of industry and company, (5) competitive pressures, or (6) opportunities for moving into new expansion areas.

Because of the limitations of the comparable approaches, we next describe the discounted cash flow (DCF) methodologies.

TABLE 9.4 Application of Valuation Ratios to Mobil (dollar amounts in billions)

	Mobil	Amoco Transaction Multiple	Value of Equity
LTM sales	$ 63.0	1.38	$86.7
Book value	19.0	3.00	57.0
LTM net income	2.9	22.46	64.9
Market value target[a]	58.7	22.3%	71.8
Market value combined[b]	233.7	7.7%	76.7
			Average = $71.4

[a]Value of equity = market value target × (1 + average premium paid, % target)
[b]Value of equity = market value combined × (1 + average premium paid, % combined) – market value buyer

THE DCF SPREADSHEET METHODOLOGY

The spreadsheet approach makes projections of the relevant cash flows. It begins with presentations of historical data for each element of the balance sheet, the income statement, and the cash flow statement. This provides the basis for a detailed financial ratio analysis to discover the financial patterns of the company. The detailed financial analysis covers data for the previous 5 to 10 years. For detailed and comprehensive illustrations of this approach, see Copeland, Koller, and Murrin (2000); see also Chapter 17 in Weston and Copeland (1992). In addition to a review of the historical financial data on a company involved in a merger or takeover, the analysts compile considerable material on the business economics of the industry in which the company operates; the company's competitive position historically and prospectively into the future and an assessment of financial patterns, strategies, and actions of its competitors—comparable companies.

Whereas in practice the spreadsheet approach involves many items of the balance sheets, income statements, and cash flow statements, the basic underlying logic builds on a basic capital budgeting analysis.

CAPITAL BUDGETING DECISIONS

Capital budgeting represents the process of planning expenditures that have returns that extend over a period of time. Examples of capital outlays for tangible or physical items are expenditures for land, building, and equipment. Outlays for research and development, advertising, or promotional efforts also may be regarded as investment outlays when their benefits extend over a period of years. Whereas capital budgeting criteria generally are discussed in relation to investment in fixed assets, the concepts are equally applicable to investments in cash, receivables, or inventory as well as to M&As and other restructuring activities.

Several methods for evaluating projects have been developed. The net present value methodology has been widely used for evaluation and ranking of investment proposals. The net present value (NPV) is the present value of all future cash flows discounted at the cost of capital, minus the cost of the investments made over time compounded at the opportunity cost of funds.

All of the formal valuation models widely used in practice reflect the basic capital budgeting NPV analysis. We begin by illustrating the idea of the spreadsheet approach by relating it to a basic capital budgeting NPV approach. An acquiring firm (A) has the opportunity to buy a target company (T). The target company can be purchased for $180 million. The relevant net cash flows that will be received from the investment in the target company will be $40 million for the next 10 years, after which no cash flows will be forthcoming. The relevant cost of capital for analyzing the purchase of the target is 14%. Does this acquisition represent a positive NPV project? The applicable formula for calculating the NPV is

$$NPV = \sum_{t=1}^{n} \frac{CF_t}{(1+k)^t} - I_0$$

$$NPV = \sum_{t=1}^{10} \frac{\$40}{(1.14)^t} - \$180$$

where

NPV = net present value
$PVIFA$ = present value interest factor for an annuity
CF_t = net cash flows in year t (after taxes) = \$40 million
k = marginal cost of capital = 14%
n = number of years, investment horizon = 10
I_0 = investment outlay in year zero = \$180

We can now calculate the NPV of the acquisition.

$$NPV = \$40\,[PVIFA\,(14\%, 10\text{ yr})] - \$180$$
$$= \$40\,(5.2161 - \$180)$$
$$= \$208.644 - \$180$$
$$NPV = GPV - I_0$$
$$= \$28.644 \text{ million}$$

The present value of the cash inflows is the gross present value of the acquisition (GPV). From the GPV, the present value of the investment outlays (I_0) is deducted to obtain the NPV of the acquisition.

With this simple illustration of the analysis of an acquisition in the framework of capital budgeting principles, we can illustrate a significant principle. Even acquisitions that achieve synergies will be unsound if the buyer (bidder, acquirer) pays too much. For example, if the bidder paid \$250 million for the target company, the NPV of the acquisition would then become a negative \$41.4 million.

$$NPV = \$208,644 - \$250,000$$
$$= -\$41.356 \text{ million}$$

The underlying concept that an acquisition is fundamentally a capital budgeting problem should be kept in mind even when the transactions involve great complications. Some mergers among firms have been called "marriages made in heaven." They make considerable sense from the business standpoint. The two companies blend beautifully. However, if the acquirer (A) pays too much, it is a negative NPV investment and the value of the bidder will decline. The market recognizes this, and the event return for A will be negative. The financial press will report, "A acquired T and as a consequence the market value of A fell by \$4 billion. A paid too much."

A REAL OPTIONS ANALYSIS

The NPV approach has been criticized for not recognizing the flexibility of postponing, abandoning, or otherwise modifying the investment project. In Chapter 1, we placed the M&A decision alternatives in a real options framework. We embrace and endorse the use of a real options analysis. The NPV approach can lead to similar results by doing a sensitivity (flexibility) analysis as we demonstrate later in this chapter. However, we also emphasize that the valuation process is most fundamentally guided by an analysis of the underlying business economic factors affecting the industries in which a merger, divestiture, or alliance is taking place.

We present a compact comparison between the NPV and real options approach. Company R needs to expand its distribution system. It seeks to analyze the returns if it postpones the investment until year 2. The NPV analysis would proceed as follows:

Investment in year 2 = $50 million
Present value of incremental cash flows = $40 million
Cost of capital = 10%

$$NPV = \$40 - \frac{\$50}{(1.10)^2} = \$40 - \frac{\$50}{1.21}$$
$$= \$40 - \$50(0.8264)$$
$$= 40 - \$41.322$$
$$NPV = -\$1.322 \text{ million}$$

In the NPV analysis, this investment appears to have a negative NPV. However, in a real options framework, the valuation might be positive. Alternative frameworks for performing a real options analysis are available. One useful technique is to view the real option as a call option in the Black-Scholes (1973) option pricing model:

$$C = S\,N(d_1) - Xe^{-r_F T} N(d_2),$$

where

$$d_1 = \frac{\ln(S/X) + r_F T}{\sigma\sqrt{T}} + \frac{1}{2}\sigma\sqrt{T}$$
$$d_2 = d_1 - \sigma\sqrt{T}$$

Five key variables in this model are shown in the following table:

Real Option	Variable	Call Option
Present value of incremental cash flows	S	Current stock price
Investment to create the option	X	Exercise price
Volatility of cash inflows	σ	Stock-price volatility
Life of option	T	Life of option
Risk-free rate of return	r_F	Risk-free rate of return

The present value of incremental cash flows corresponds to the current stock price (S), which is the $40 million from the previous NPV analysis. Similarly, the investment to create the option is equivalent to the price of $50 million at which the option can be exercised (X). It is recognized that the cash flows are subject to uncertainty, which is measured by the volatility of the cash flows (σ) calculated to be 20% in this example. The time (T) is 2 years. In the derivation of the Black-Scholes formula, the risk-free rate of interest is used in contrast to the applicable risk-adjusted cost of capital, which was 10% in the NPV example. The risk-free rate measured by the 2-year Treasury note rate is 3.7%.

We have defined all the terms in the formula except two probability expressions. $N(d_1)$ represents a probability term measuring the change in C in response to a change in S. $N(d_2)$ is the probability that the option will be exercised. A model for calculating the value of the call option, which determines whether the investment has a positive value, is provided in the Web site related to this book. The output of this model follows.

Inputs:

Risk-free rate = R_F = 3.70%
Time to maturity (years) = 2.00000
Strike price = X = $50.00
Standard deviation = σ = 0.15

Stock Price (S)	d_1	d_2	$N(d_1)$	$N(d_2)$	Call Price (C)
$ 3.00	−12.80764	−13.01977	0.00000	0.00000	$0.00
10.00	−7.13206	−7.34419	0.00000	0.00000	0.00
15.00	−5.22068	−5.43281	0.00000	0.00000	0.00
20.00	−3.86453	−4.07666	0.00006	0.00002	0.00
25.00	−2.81262	−3.02475	0.00246	0.00124	0.00
30.00	−1.95315	−2.16528	0.02540	0.01518	0.06
35.00	−1.22648	−1.43861	0.11001	0.07513	0.36
40.00	−0.59700	−0.80914	0.27525	0.20922	1.30
45.00	−0.04177	−0.25390	0.48334	0.39979	3.19
46.75	0.13808	−0.07405	0.55491	0.47048	4.10
50.00	0.45491	0.24277	0.67541	0.59591	6.10

At the present value of the incremental cash flows (S) of $40 million as given in the problem inputs, the investment outcome (C) now has a positive value of $1.3 million. Note the critical role of the volatility variable. If the volatility variable were reduced to 0.04, the value of the investment (C) would not become positive unless S were higher. If the volatility variable were 0.20, the investment value would rise to $2.3 million.

Because the growing body of real options literature is a separate subject, we shall not attempt more detailed coverage of it. We follow the more widely used DCF valuation methodology. We emphasize that the economics of the industry involved represents the most critical part of valuation analysis. The sensitivity analysis we employ can be used to reflect alternative economic scenarios and alternative management strategies in the spirit of a real options orientation.

SPREADSHEET PROJECTIONS

The basic idea of the spreadsheet approach can be conveyed in a somewhat more detailed capital budgeting analysis. Company A is considering the purchase of a target company T. A detailed spreadsheet analysis of the financial statements of the target has been made. On the basis of that analysis and of all aspects of the business economics of the target's industry, the acquiring firm has made the spreadsheet projections exhibited in Table 9.5.

The first row of Table 9.5 is projected revenues. They start at $1,000 and are expected to grow at a 20% rate. Row 2 is total costs related to the sales levels shown in row 1. From the historical patterns and the economic outlook, the investment bankers make the spreadsheet projections that net operating income will be 20% of sales. The net operating income is projected in row 3. Corporate taxes of 40% are postulated and shown in row 4. Deducting taxes paid, we

TABLE 9.5   Spreadsheet Projections of Company T

				Year		
	Percent of Revenue	*0*	*1*	*2*	*3*	*4 to* ∞
1. Revenues (R_t)	100	$1,000	$1,200	$1,440	$1,728	$1,728
2. Costs	80		960	1152	1382	1382
3. Net operating income (X_t)	20		240	288	346	346
4. Taxes (T)	40		96	115	138	138
5. Net operating income after taxes [$X_t(1-T)$]	12		144	173	207	207
Investment Requirements						
6. Net working capital (I_{wt})	4		$ 48	$ 68	$ 69	$ 0
7. Net property, plant, and equipment (I_{ft})	6		72	86	104	0
8. Total (I_t)	10		120	144	173	0
9. Free cash flows [$X_t(1-T)-I_t$]			$24	$29	$35	$207

obtain net operating income after taxes, shown in line 5. Total capital requirements consist of net working capital plus net property, plant, and equipment. Net working capital is 4% of revenues, and net property, plant, and equipment are 6% of revenues. So for the target company, a total capital investment of 10 cents is required for each dollar of revenues. This represents a capital turnover of 10, so row 8 is 10% of the figures in row 1. Company T represents an investment opportunity in which revenues will grow at 20% for 3 years, after which they will level off at $1,728 as shown in the right-hand columns. In rows 6 to 8, the annual investment requirements are shown. *Investment* is defined as "the addition to total capital made in a given year to have the total capital required to support sales in that year."

The column values for each row in Table 9.5 grow at a 20% per annum rate through year 3. These assumptions were made for the convenience of simplicity. One of the advantages of the spreadsheet approach is that the growth rates for the items listed in the rows could be different from one another and from year to year. The spreadsheet approach provides great flexibility in making the projections. However, it is equally important to recognize that when one is presented with a set of projections, as in the spreadsheet approach, it is useful to raise the question: What underlying growth patterns are illustrated by these projections? Further questions should be pursued including, but not limited to, the following. Are the growth rates in the projections consistent with the forecasts for the economy? For the industry? For market share in relation to competitors? Although the numbers shown in Table 9.5 are simplified, the basic principles that are illustrated are equally valid no matter how complicated the numbers turn out to be in real-life applications of the spreadsheet methodology.

Given the projections in the spreadsheets reflected in Table 9.5, we can illustrate the calculation of a value for the target that is the maximum the acquiring firm can pay if it is to earn its 10% cost of capital. Alternatively, we could say that if an acquirer pays more for the target than the value we calculate in Table 9.6, it will be making a negative net present value investment.

Table 9.6 is a worksheet to explain how free cash flows are measured. Each row is expressed in symbols that will be used throughout the book. Row 1 is before-tax cash flows

TABLE 9.6 Valuation of the Target

			YEAR	
			3	
	1	*2*	*Beginning*	*End*
1. Before-tax cash flow (X_t)	240	288	346	346
2. Taxes at 40% (T)	96	115	138	138
3. After-tax cash flow [$X_t(1 - T)$]	144	173	207	207
4. Investment (I_t)	120	144	173	0
5. Free cash flow [$X_t(1 - T) - I_t$]	24	29	35	207.4
6. Discount factor	$(1 + k)$	$(1 + k)^2$	$(1 + k)^3$	$k(1 + k)^3$
a. Discount factor	1/1.10	1/1.21	1/1.331	10/1.331
7. Present value	$21.82	$23.97	$26.30	$1,558.23

(X_t) taken from row 3 of Table 9.5. In row 2, the 40% tax rate (T) is applied. Row 3 is after-tax cash flows [$X_t(1 - T)$]. Annual investment outlays (I_t) are shown in row 4. Row 5 represents the free cash flows. When we discount the free cash flows at the applicable cost of capital (k), we obtain the NPV of the acquisition because the investment outlays have been deducted year by year.

We can now develop a spreadsheet valuation of the target company by discounting the free cash flows in Table 9.6 at the applicable cost of capital of 10%. The discount factor is $(1 + k)$ to the first power for the cash flow in year 1, to the second power for the cash flow in year 2, and to the third power in the cash flow in year 3.

At the beginning of the fourth year, the after-tax (free) cash flow is $207.4, which remains constant to infinity. Because no further growth occurs the net new investment required to support growth is also zero. Therefore, the after-tax cash flows from the end of year 3 (the beginning of year 4) are the free cash flows to be discounted back to the beginning of year 4. The value of these constant cash flows is obtained by dividing by the discount factor of 10%. This gives us the so-called exit value of the target firm as of the end of the third year. This value of $2,074 is discounted back for 3 years under the general principle that we begin discounting with next year's cash flow. This timing of the discounting of the constant cash flows to infinity is followed in the widely used formulas employed by investment bankers and consulting firms in actual applications.

The $2,074 is discounted back to the present by dividing by $(1 + k)^3$ or $(1.10)^3$ in our example. This gives a present value of the exit value of $1,558.23. The value of the firm V_0 is

Present value of the discounted cash flow in year 1	$ 21.82
Present value of the discounted cash flow in year 2	23.97
Present value of the discounted cash flow in year 3	26.30
Present value of the discounted terminal value or exit value	1,558.23
Total value of the target	$1,630.32

Thus, the value of the target firm that would enable the acquiring firm to earn its cost of capital would be $1,630.32. If the acquiring firm is able to obtain the target for something less than $1,630.32, and if the projections are fulfilled, this would be a positive net present value investment. If the acquiring firm pays more than $1,630.32, it will be making a negative net present value investment, and its own market value will decline.

BRIEF EVALUATION OF THE SPREADSHEET APPROACH

An advantage of the spreadsheet approach is that it is expressed in financial statements familiar to businesspersons. A second major advantage is that the data are year by year with any desired detail of individual balance sheet or income statement accounts. Judgment and flexibility can be reflected in formulating the projections.

The spreadsheet approach also has some pitfalls. The specific numbers used in the projections might create the illusion that they are the actual or correct numbers. This is misleading. Projections are subject to error. Sometimes the bases for the projections might be obscured. A clear link is not always established between the projected numbers and the economic or business logic by which they were determined. Another limitation is that the spreadsheet can become highly complex. The advantage of including many details is also subject to the risk that the detail obscures the forces that are important in making the projections. This is why in our initial explanation of the spreadsheet approach, we employed a simple numerical example. More complex applications are made to actual companies in the following sections.

COST OF CAPITAL

To this point in the valuation discussions, we have taken the cost of capital as given. We now describe the procedures for calculating it. To calculate the cost of capital of a firm, first calculate the costs of its major individual components of financing: equity, debt, and preferred stocks. Our discussion begins with calculating the cost of equity.

COST OF EQUITY

Capital Asset Pricing Model

The most widely employed method used in calculating the cost of equity is the capital asset pricing model (CAPM). In CAPM, the required return on equity is a risk-free return plus a risk component. For the economy as a whole, the risk-free rate would be related to the returns on U.S. government bonds. Because the discount factor used in valuation involves relatively long periods, the rates on relatively long-term bonds would be employed. We use the promised yield on 10-year Treasuries. Theory and practice generally begin with interest rate levels in the current economic environment because the long-term future is difficult to forecast. We use 5.6% as the estimate for the risk-free rate.

In the CAPM, the risk adjustment begins with the market-determined differential between equity yields and government bonds. The widely used historical data developed by Ibbotson Associates for the period January 1, 1926, to December 31, 2000, shows a geometric mean of 11% for large company stocks and 5.3% for long-term government bonds. This gives a spread of 5.7% as the market-determined differential, also called the market price of risk. Using the arithmetic mean, the spread is 13.0% −5.7%, which gives a 7.3% difference. The argument for the use of the geometric mean is that returns from investments should use compounded interest rates. The argument for the use of the arithmetic mean is that we are calculating an expected return that is calculated by some weighted arithmetic average of future returns. This view argues that when using historical data as a guide, the arithmetic means should be used. Each view has some logic behind it.

For many years, based on patterns of the long-term relationships among returns on long- and short-term government bonds, on long- and short-term corporate bonds, and on equity groups such as large caps, small caps, high techs, and so on, the market equity premium appeared to be in the range of 6.5% to 7.5%. However, by the mid-1990s, a paradigm for a new economy began to emerge. Analysts moved toward using 4% to 5% as the market price of risk. With the decline in stock prices from their peak levels in March 2000 and forecasts of a recession in the U.S. economy beginning to be reflected in declining revenue and profit reports during the first quarter of 2001, the arguments for lowering the expected market price of risk become weakened.

To illustrate the CAPM, we use 7% for the market price of risk. The 7% is multiplied by the firm's beta to obtain an estimate of the risk adjustment for an individual firm. The beta of a firm is a measure of how the return on its common stock varies with returns on the market as a whole. Returns on the market as a whole have been conveniently measured by use of the S&P 500, all stocks on the New York Stock Exchange, or other broad groupings. Thus, if the return on the market increased by 10%, a firm with a beta of 1.2 would experience a rise in its returns of 12% (conversely, if the market fell by 10%). Thus, high-beta stocks exhibit higher volatility than low-beta stocks in response to changes in market returns.

The beta for the market as a whole must necessarily be 1, by definition. With a risk-free rate of 5.6% and a market price of risk of 7%, we can write an equation for the expected return on the market:

$$\text{Expected return on the market} = 5.6\% + 7\% \ (1) = 12.6\%$$

From this relationship, we can generalize to individual firms.

$$\text{Required return on equity of a firm} = 5.6\% + 7\% \ (\text{beta})$$

If the beta of the firm were 1.2, its required return would be 14%. If the beta of the firm were 0.8, its required return would be 11.2%, according to CAPM. In our example, we will use a 1.2-beta-level firm. Thus, the cost of equity for a firm with a beta of 1.2 would be 14% compared with required return of 11.2% for a 0.8-beta firm. Betas have been calculated for individual firms by most of the brokerage houses and data sources such as Value Line.

We have illustrated how to calculate the cost of equity using the CAPM. To make comparisons with alternative calculations of the cost of equity, we call our firm the Smith Company, assign it a beta of 1.2, and use 14% as its CAPM measure of the cost of equity.

Bond Yield Plus Equity Risk Adjustment

A second approach provides a check. The yield on a firm's equity should be greater than the yield on its bonds, because equity claims are junior to the claims of creditors. Here, the firm's equity risk adjustment is in relation to the yield on its bonds. Smith Company's long-term bonds are rated Baa with a yield of 8.0%. Historical data on the equity returns to Smith Company shareholders suggest a spread over its bond yields of about 5%. We add 5% to the 8% bond yield to obtain 13%.

We have two estimates of the cost of equity capital. They average about 13.5%. This is the figure we shall employ as our component cost of equity. We next consider the cost of other methods of financing.

COST OF DEBT

The cost of debt should be on an after-tax basis because interest payments are tax deductible. Therefore, the cost of debt capital is calculated as follows:

$$k_b(1 - T) = \text{after-tax cost of debt}$$

Here, T is the corporate tax rate used previously. Thus, if the before-tax cost of debt were 8% and the firm's effective corporate tax rate were 35%, the after-tax cost of debt would be 5.2%.

We start with the firm's before-tax cost of debt and multiply it by the $(1-T)$ factor to obtain the relevant after-tax cost. How do we obtain the before-tax cost of debt in practice for an actual firm? Two main procedures can be used: (1) We can look in any investment manual to determine the rating of the firm's outstanding publicly held bonds. Various government agencies and investment banking firms periodically publish promised yields to maturity of debt issues by rating categories. (2) We can take a weighted average of the yield to maturity for all of the firm's publicly traded bonds.

Preferred stock is a third source of financing. Most preferred stocks have no maturity and pay a fixed dividend. Therefore, the cost of preferred stock is the promised dividend divided by its current market price. Preferred stocks have somewhat greater risk than debt because of their junior position. This makes for a higher required yield. However, preferred stock dividends received by another corporation are not fully subject to the corporate tax. This makes for a lower required yield. The two influences tend to balance out such that the yield on preferred stock is the same as the yields on long-term debt. Therefore, we would expect the Smith Company's yield on preferred stock to be about 8%. Most companies have little or no preferred stock shown in their balance sheet, so we will not use preferred stock in our example.

WEIGHTED AVERAGE COST OF CAPITAL

To calculate the marginal weighted cost of capital, we first calculate financing proportions at book values and at market values for the Smith Company.

Financial Proportions at Book Value (in millions)		
Interest-bearing debt	$ 4,000	40%
Shareholders' equity	6,000	60%
Total	$10,000	

Financial Proportions at Market Value (in millions)		
Interest-bearing debt^a	$ 4,000	14.3%
Shareholders' equity^a ($40 × 600)	24,000	85.7%
Total	$28,000	

^{a}The market value of shareholders' equity is calculated as the number of shares outstanding times the market price of the common stock. The market value of debt is assumed to be the same as its book value.

Taking these financial proportions as a guide, we use a target financial structure consisting of 35% debt and 65% equity to calculate the weighted average cost of capital for Smith Company as:

$$0.135(0.65) + 0.052(0.35) = 0.08775 + 0.0182 = 0.10595$$

CAPITAL STRUCTURE AND THE COST OF CAPITAL

A decision with respect to capital structure was required to obtain the proportions of debt and equity used in calculating the weighted average cost of capital (WACC or k). The following materials provide a basis for making such a decision.

A strong inducement to sell debt is that the interest on debt is deductible as an expense for tax purposes. Even without the tax consideration, a firm might seek to use debt, which carries a fixed interest payment, to magnify the gains on equity. This is called trading on the equity. We have seen many examples of this during the boom environment of the 1990s. A case in point is the telecommunications equipment industry. The great prospects for the use of fiber optics led to heavy investments in companies to produce fiber optics and in telecom companies, which use them in their operations. Existing as well as new companies made heavy use of debt, seeking high returns and high stock values. However, because the use of debt results in high debt-to-equity ratios, at some point the risk of financial distress affects the cost of debt and the required return on equity.

One consequence of rising debt ratios is a deterioration in bond ratings and an increase in the cost of debt. This is illustrated in Table 9.7. We continue to use 5% as the promised yield on 10-year Treasuries. AAA corporate bonds are shown to yield 7.2%, representing a differential of 160 basis points. Leverage ratios measured by debt-to-equity for top-grade corporates would be 25% or less. The associated EBIT-to-fixed charges ratio would be 7 times or better.

Table 9.7 shows that as the leverage ratios increase, associated with lower fixed charge coverage ratios, bond ratings decline and debt costs increase. BBB bonds carry leverage ratios in the 67% to 90% range and require yields about 80 basis points higher than AAAs.

Table 9.7 shows a required yield on junk bonds of 640 basis points above the AAAs, and 800 basis points higher than 10-year U.S. Treasuries. The market for junk bonds is subject to extreme fluctuations in market attitudes. In periods of optimism, the spread in relation to Treasuries can drop as low as 300 basis points.

TABLE 9.7 Leverage, Ratings, and Debt Costs

B/S	EBIT/Fixed Charges	Bond Rating	Debt Costs
25% or less	>7x	AAA	7.2%
25% to 43%	4x to 8x	AA	7.3%
43% to 67%	3x to 5x	A	7.6%
67% to 90%	1.75x to 2.5x	BBB	8.0%
90% to 233%	1x to 2x	BB	13.6%
233% and above	0.75x to 1.25x	B	16.0%

Bond ratings are related to leverage ratios and pre-tax fixed charge coverage.
Other factors include: firm size, prospective growth rates in sales and profitability, industry, and competitive factors.

The message of Table 9.7 is that high debt ratios associated with low fixed-charges coverage ratios can lead to high debt costs and higher cost of capital to business firms. Another method of measuring the risk of high leverage ratios is the impact on a firm's beta. The relationship between a levered equity beta and an unlevered beta is shown by the following equation:

$$\beta_e = \beta_u \left[1 + \frac{B(1-T)}{S} \right]$$

where:

β_e = levered equity beta
β_u = unlevered equity beta
B = market value of debt
S = market value of equity
T = tax rate

To see how this equation works, suppose a firm's unlevered beta is 0.8. Assume a tax rate of 40% and a leverage ratio (B/S) of 2/3. The levered equity beta is 0.8[1 + 2/3(0.6)] or 1.12. If the leverage ratio were 0.5, the levered beta would be 1.04.

The unlevered equity beta reflects the business risk of the firm. The difference between the levered beta and the unlevered beta reflects the financial risk resulting from the use of leverage. Therefore, the equation can be used to calculate a target leverage ratio based on the firm's target equity beta. Suppose the firm had a target equity beta of 1.12. From our previous analysis, we can use the equation to solve for the target B/S, which would be 2/3.

We can generalize this information by using Figure 9.1, which shows the relationship among leverage measured by B/S and the costs of debt, equity, and the resulting WACC or k. With no debt, the unlevered firm's cost of equity and WACC would be k_u. As shown in Table 9.7, for a

FIGURE 9.1   Effects of Bankruptcy Costs and Taxes on the Cost of Capital

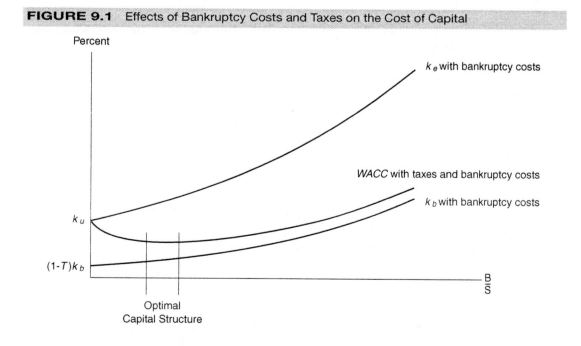

debt ratio of up to 25% equity, the debt rating remains at AAA. As the leverage ratio begins to rise beyond that point, its cost increases moderately until it reaches below-investment-grade status, when it rises sharply. The cost-of-equity curve is similar. However, equity is junior to debt, so as the cost of debt rises, the cost of equity rises even faster. The level of the WACC curve first falls because the proportion of lower-cost debt increases. At some point, the WACC curve rises because the increased costs of debt and equity offset the higher debt proportion. Because the WACC curve falls and then rises, it must have some low point. This optimum capital structure range is shown in Figure 9.1. The range is more like a flat saucer than a steep cup.

The aim of this section has been to provide a general framework for making cost-of-capital estimates required in valuation studies for analyzing M&As.

FORMULA APPROACH

In this section, we focus on the formula approach to valuation. No real distinction is evident between the spreadsheet approach and the formula approach. Both use a discounted cash flow (DCF) analysis. The spreadsheet approach is expressed in the form of financial statements over a period of years. The formula approach summarizes the same data in more compact expressions. Both give the same numerical results, as we shall illustrate.

Valuation formulas appear in many different shapes, sizes, and expressions. The four basic formulas are shown in Table 9.8 (derivations in Appendix A). The concepts follow from basic finance materials. They will be illustrated in the case examples we subsequently present on valuations in acquisitions. The leading practitioners in valuation employ these basic expressions in various forms.

THE BASIC FORMULA

To start, we set forth the formula for valuing free cash flows growing at a supernormal rate for a period of years followed by no growth. We use the data from Table 9.6, which illustrated the spreadsheet approach. We evaluate the same data using the equation (9.3) formula to demonstrate that we obtain exactly the same numerical result. The widely used equation (9.3) for free cash flows has a period of supernormal growth followed by no growth as shown in Table 9.8.

$$V_0 = R_0[m(1-T) - I] \sum_{t=1}^{n} \frac{(1+g)^t}{(1+k)^t} + \frac{R_0(1+g)^n[m(1-T)]}{k(1+k)^n} \qquad (9.3)$$

Using $1 + h = (1+g)/(1+k)$, equation (9.3) becomes

$$V_0 = R_0[m(1-T) - I](1+h)\left[\frac{(1+h)^n - 1}{h}\right] + \frac{R_0 m(1-T)}{k}(1+h)^n \qquad (9.3a)$$

We use the numbers from Table 9.6 to obtain equation (9.3b):

R_0 = initial revenues = \$1,000
m = net operating income margin = 20%
T = tax rate = 40%
I = investment as a percentage of revenues = 10%

TABLE 9.8 Formulas for Valuation of a Firm/Discounted Cash Flow

No growth:

$$V_0 = \frac{R_0[m(1-T)]}{k} \text{ for } k > 0 \qquad (9.1)$$

Constant growth:

$$V_0 = \frac{R_0(1+g)[m(1-T)-I]}{k-g} \text{ for } k > g \qquad (9.2)$$

Temporary supernormal growth, then no growth:

$$V_0 = R_0[m(1-T)-I]\sum_{t=1}^{n}\frac{(1+g)^t}{(1+k)^t} + \frac{R_0(1+g)^n[m(1-T)]}{k(1+k)^n} \qquad (9.3)$$

Temporary supernormal growth, then constant growth:

$$V_0 = R_0[m(1-T)-I_s]\sum_{t=1}^{n}\frac{(1+g_s)^t}{(1+k)^t} + \frac{R_0(1+g_s)^n[m(1-T)-I_c]}{(1+k)^n} \times \left(\frac{1+g_c}{k-g_c}\right) \qquad (9.4)^a$$

where

R_0 = initial revenues
m = net operating income margin
T = tax rate
I = investment as a percentage of revenues
g = growth rate of revenues
k = cost of capital
n = number of years of supernormal growth

[a]In equation (9.4), the subscript s indicates that I or g is for the supernormal growth period; the subscript c indicates that I or g is for the period of constant growth.

g = growth rate of revenues = 20%
k = cost of capital = 10%
n = number of years of supernormal growth = 3
$1 + h$ = calculation relationship $(1 + g)/(1 + k) = 1.09091$

$$V_0 = \$1,000[0.2(0.6) - 0.1](1.09091)\left[\frac{(1.09091)^3 - 1}{0.0909}\right] + \frac{1,000(0.2)(0.6)}{0.1}(1.09091)^3 \qquad (9.3\text{b})$$

$$= (20)(1.09091)(3.28) + \left(\frac{120}{0.1}\right)(1.09091)^3$$

$$= 72 + 1558$$

$$= \$1,630$$

The final result approximates the period-by-period calculations in Table 9.6. This demonstrates that the DCF spreadsheet method and the DCF formula method are conceptually the same and give the same numerical result. The two approaches are complementary. The spreadsheet approach allows flexibility in making projections on a year-by-year basis. The formula approach helps us focus on the underlying elements or drivers that determine value.

SENSITIVITY ANALYSIS

With the use of equation (9.3) we are able to do a sensitivity analysis of the impact of the size of the value drivers on the valuation. The results are shown in Table 9.9. In our initial case shown in line 1, the valuation was $1,630. In line 2, we reduce the growth rate in revenues. Predictably, the valuation declines. In line 3, we go back to the initial case but increase the investment requirement percentage to 15%. Again, valuation declines because free cash flows are reduced by the higher investment requirements.

In line 4, we return to the initial case but now lower the operating profit margin. Clearly, valuation would decline sharply, indicating that the profitability rate is a powerful value driver. In line 5, we return to the initial case but reduce the cost of capital. Valuation increases substantially, showing that the cost of capital is another powerful influence. Line 6 indicates that an increased cost of capital has a strong negative influence on valuation. The impact of the number of periods of supernormal growth or period of comparative advantage or variations in the tax rate operate in predictable directions, as shown in lines 7 through 10.

In Table 9.9, the second term (the present value of the terminal value) in the valuation model represents the higher proportion of the valuation. This is true in many practical cases. This should alert those who are performing the valuation to be careful regarding the assumptions made about the factors that affect so-called exit or terminal values.

Our experience has been that executives knowledgeable in the industry and firm for which the analysis is being made are likely to be interested in having a sensitivity analysis. They are aware of the many influences that could alter the size of the value drivers, so they are interested in checking the impact of a range of alternative possibilities.

The sensitivity analysis performs another valuable function. It provides a framework for planning and control. By improving performance on one or more of the value drivers, the valu-

TABLE 9.9 Sensitivity Analysis of Varying the Value Drivers[a]

	k	g	I	m	n	T	Valuation	2nd Term As Percent of Total
Initial case								
1.	10%	20%	10%	20%	3	40%	$1,630	96
Change g, I, and m:								
2.	10	15	10	20	3	40	1,437	95
3.	10	20	15	20	3	40	1,451	107
4.	10	20	10	15	3	40	1,133	103
Back to initial case, but vary k:								
5.	9	20	10	20	3	40	1,852	96
6.	11	20	10	20	3	40	1,449	95
Back to initial case, but vary n:								
7.	10	20	10	20	2	40	1,474	97
8.	10	20	10	20	5	40	1,985	93
Back to initial case, but vary T:								
9.	10	20	10	20	3	35	1,795	94
10.	10	20	10	20	3	45	1,464	98

[a]For meaning of column heads, see text.

ation of the firm can be increased. Tangible incentives are thereby created to stimulate improvements, particularly in areas where managers have responsibility.

Summary

Valuation uses historical data as a starting point to establish first approximation patterns. Valuations depend on forecasts. The reliability of the forecasts depends heavily on a thorough analysis of the industry, on how it is impacted by evolving changes in the economies of the world, and by competitive strategies and tactics. Valuation requires a thorough understanding of the business economics and financial characteristics of the industry.

Precision is not possible, nor is it required. Recognizing that forecasts are subject to revision has positive aspects as well as challenges. It can be a valuable planning framework for guiding the firm to sound strategies and improved efficiencies. Valuation depends on identifying the critical factors that influence the levels of the value drivers. The DCF valuation approach provides a valuable framework to help identify what is important to the future value of the firm.

Sensitivity analysis helps identify the most critical factors for the future. Such an analysis helps develop a business model for the firm with expectations of continuous reviews based on an effective information feedback system in the firm. It supports a flexible, long-range planning process as a basis for short-term and medium-term budgets. It requires in-depth understanding of the industry, its environment, and its competitors to guide strategies, policies, and decisions.

Questions

9.1   How are mergers and acquisitions related to capital budgeting?

9.2   List four methods of valuation, and briefly set forth the advantages and limitations of each.

9.3   What is the difference between gross basis and net basis cash flows?

9.4   The basic DCF sales growth model can be expressed in spreadsheets or in a formula, illustrated by equation (9.3) in Table 9.8 as follows:

$$V_0 = R_0[m(1 - T) - I]\sum_{t=1}^{n} \frac{(1 + g)^t}{(1 + k)^t} + \frac{R_0(1 + g)^n[m(1 - T)]}{k(1 + k)^n}$$

We will use the same symbols, definitions, and data inputs given in association with equation (9.3a) in the text except that we will change the number of years of supernormal growth (competitive advantage) to 10. Using a hand calculator, calculate the value beyond which you could not pay a target company with the characteristics illustrated, if you, as the buyer firm, are to earn the applicable cost of capital for the acquisition.

9.5   Some practitioners use an incremental profit rate instead of an average profit rate and normalize investment by dividing it by after-tax net operating income, defined as $X_t(1-T)$. This expression, $I_t/X_t(1-T)$, where I_t is in dollars, is defined as b. The new formula is shown here:

$$V_0 = X_0(1 - T)(1 - b)\sum_{t=1}^{n} \frac{(1 + g)^t}{(1 + k)^t} + \frac{X_0(1 - T)(1 + g)^n}{k(1 + k)^n}$$

Use this new expression to repeat the calculation in Question 9.4. How does your answer compare to your answer in Question 9.4?

9.6   In Rappaport (1998), our equation (9.3) is modified slightly. Investment is expressed as a ratio of the change in sales. Therefore, the first part of the first term in equation (9.3) will read:

$$R_0[m(1-T) - g\text{ "I"}]$$

If "I" is 50%, how does the new value compare with what you obtained in the previous two questions?

9.7   How are the following valuation parameters related to each other? How do they affect the general free cash flow valuation model?

Revenues

Investment

Net operating income

Profitability rate

Growth rate

9.8   The Alcindor Company is similar to and is in the same industry as the Walton Company. Both Alcindor Company and Walton Company have a cost of equity of 12%, cost of debt of 8%, and 30% debt. If Walton has revenues (R) of $1,000, operating margin (m) of 15%, a tax rate (T) of 40%, investment rate (I) of 8%, growth rate (g) of 18%, and 5 years of supernormal growth (n) and zero growth thereafter, what value should Alcindor Company be willing to pay for Walton Company?

9.9   Suppose Alcindor Company is instead interested in the Elway Company, a firm in a completely unrelated (and riskier) industry. Elway Company has the same parameters as Walton Company (Question 9.8), except Elway has a cost of equity of 15%, a cost of debt of 10%, and 20% debt. What value should Alcindor Company be willing to pay for Elway Company?

9.10 Kubrick Company decides to buy Hitchcock Company. Both firms have the same characteristics as Walton Company (Question 9.8), except Kubrick Company has a beta of 1.2, and Hitchcock Co. has a beta of 1.4. Both firms have 30% debt and a cost of debt of 8%. Because of the nature of the synergies anticipated in the acquisition, the combined firm is expected to have a beta of 1.1.

a. If the risk-free rate is 6% and the equity risk premium is 5%, calculate the cost of capital for the two firms and the combined firm.

b. Assuming the value drivers remain constant (and revenues are simply combined), what would be the value of the combined company?

9.11 Vonnegut Company and Heller Company are two identical firms that agree to merge. Both have revenues (R_0) of $1,500, operating margin (m) of 15%, a tax rate (T) of 40%, investment rate (I) of 10%, growth rate (g) of 11%, 5 years of supernormal growth (n) followed by zero growth thereafter, and a 9% cost of capital (k).

a. What are the values of the firms as stand-alone companies?

b. If the combined firm increases its operating margin by 2%, revenues are combined, and the other value drivers remain unchanged, what is the value of the combined firm?

References

Black, Fischer, and Myron Scholes, "The Pricing of Options and Corporate Liabilities," *Journal of Political Economy* 81, No. 3, May-June 1973, pp. 637–654.

Copeland, Tom, Tim Koller, and Jack Murrin, *Valuation: Measuring and Managing the Value of Companies*, 3rd ed., New York: John Wiley & Sons, 2000.

Cornell, Bradford, *Corporate Valuation*, Homewood, IL: Business One Irwin, 1993.

Rappaport, Alfred, *Creating Shareholder Value*, New York: The Free Press, 1998.

Weston, J. Fred, and Thomas E. Copeland, *Managerial Finance*, 9th ed., Fort Worth, TX: The Dryden Press, 1992.

APPENDIX A

DERIVATION OF REVENUE GROWTH VALUATION FORMULAS

We present a derivation of the free cash flow basis for valuation. It has its roots in a generalization of the basic capital budgeting equation. We develop four basic models, but we easily could derive many other variants reflecting any range of assumptions postulated for analysis. The four basic models are:

1. No growth
2. Constant growth
3. Supernormal growth followed by no growth
4. Supernormal growth followed by constant growth

We start with equation (A9.1):

$$V_0 = \frac{R_1[m(1-T)-I_1]}{(1+k)} + \frac{R_2[m(1-T)-I_2]}{(1+k)^2} + \dots$$
$$+ \frac{R_n[m(1-T)-I_n]}{(1+k)^n}$$

(A9.1)

Equation (A9.1) is a general capital budgeting expression. The symbols have all been defined in the main text of this chapter. The initial revenue, R_0, grows at some rate g, which can be positive, negative, or zero. We can replace R_t values in (A9.1) by $R_0 (1+g)^t$. We also assume that investment remains at a constant percentage of revenues, so I_t becomes I. We can rewrite equation (A9.1) as:

$$V_0 = \frac{R_0(1+g)[m(1-T)-I]}{(1+k)}$$

$$+ \frac{R_0(1+g)^2[m(1-T)-I]}{(1+k)^2} + \dots$$

$$+ \frac{R_0(1+g)^n[m(1-T)-I]}{(1+k)^n}$$

(A9.2)

We factor from each term in equation (A9.2) a common expression:

$$\frac{R_0(1+g)[m(1-T)-I]}{1+k}$$

This gives the equation:

$$V_0 = \frac{R_0(1+g)[m(1-T)-I]}{1+k} \times$$

$$\left[1 + \frac{1+g}{1+k} + \frac{(1+g)^2}{(1+k)^2} + \dots + \frac{(1+g)^{n-1}}{(1+k)^{n-1}}\right]$$

(A9.3)

The series inside the large brackets can be written as a summation expression, giving:

$$V_0 = \frac{R_0(1+g)[m(1-T)-I]}{1+k} \sum_{t=1}^{n} \frac{(1+g)^{t-1}}{(1+k)^{t-1}}$$

(A9.3a)

We can move the first $(1+g)/(1+k)$ term into the summation expression to obtain the equation:

$$V_0 = R_0[m(1-T)-I] \sum_{t=1}^{n} \frac{(1+g)^t}{(1+k)^t}$$

(A9.3b)

From the valuation equation (A9.3), (A9.3a), or (A9.3b), we can obtain all the valuation expressions by specifying how g, the growth rate, behaves.

THE NO-GROWTH CASE

First assume that $g = 0$. If $g = 0$, then the firm requires no investment, so $I_t = I = 0$ as well. Equation (A9.3) becomes:

$$V_0 = \frac{R_0[m(1-T)]}{1+k}$$

$$\times \left[1 + \frac{1}{1+k} + \left(\frac{1}{1+k}\right)^2 + \dots + \left(\frac{1}{1+k}\right)^{n-1}\right]$$

(A9.4)

The term in front of the large brackets has parameters that are all constants. The terms inside the large brackets form a geometric progression that starts with the constant term 1 and increases by the ratio $1/(1 + k)$. A geometric progression can be written as follows:

$$a + ar + ar^2 + ar^3 + \ldots + ar^{n-1} =$$
$$a[1 + r + r^2 + r^3 + \ldots + r^{n-1}]$$

Note that the constant term, a, can be factored out, and the form of the standard geometric progression is exactly as in equation (A9.4). When there is a finite number of terms, n, the sum of these terms is:

$$S^n = \frac{a(r^n - 1)}{r - 1}$$

When n goes to infinity, the sum of this geometric progression is equal to $S^\infty = a/(1-r)$ when $r<1$.

We can write equation (A9.4) (when $k > 0, r < 1$, and n goes to infinity) as

$$V_0 = \frac{R_0[m(1-T)]}{1+k}\left[\frac{1}{1 - 1/(1+k)}\right]$$
$$= \frac{R_0[m(1-T)]}{1+k}\left[\frac{1}{(1+k-1)/(1+k)}\right]$$
$$= \frac{R_0[m(1-T)]}{1+k}\left(\frac{1+k}{k}\right)$$

Cancel the $1 + k$ in the numerator and denominator to obtain equation (9.1) of Table 9.8:

$$V_0 = \frac{R_0[m(1-T)]}{k} \text{ for } k > 0 \tag{9.1}$$

The result in equation (9.1) (see Table 9.8) is the familiar formula for the valuation of a stream of receipts or cash flows that continues at a constant level to infinity. This is the standard valuation expression for a perpetuity or bond that has no maturity, often called a consol.

CONSTANT GROWTH

For the second basic case, assume that g is not zero but a constant. We return to equation (A9.3). The constant ratio is equal to $(1 + g)/(1 + k)$. We again use the expression for the summation of a geometric progression that continues to infinity, which is $a/(1 - r)$, where $r = (1 + g)/(1 + k)<1$. Equation (9.3) can be written as:

$$V_0 = \frac{R_0(1+g)[m(1-T)-I]}{(1+k)}\left[\frac{1}{1 - (1+g)/(1+k)}\right]$$
$$V_0 = \frac{R_0(1+g)[m(1-T)-I]}{1+k}\left(\frac{1+k}{k-g}\right)$$

Simplifying, we obtain equation (9.2) of Table 9.8:

$$V_0 = \frac{R_0(1+g)[m(1-T)-I]}{k-g} \text{ for } k > g \tag{9.2}$$

Equation (9.2) is the valuation expression (when k is larger than g) for cash flows that grow at a constant rate, g, to perpetuity.

SUPERNORMAL GROWTH FOLLOWED BY NO GROWTH

The third basic case is temporary supernormal growth followed by no growth. The valuation formula consists of two terms:

$$V_0 = V_1 + V_2 \tag{A9.5}$$

In the first term, the V_1 component of total value, V_0, the firm experiences temporary supernormal growth for n periods. The V_2 component of value shown for the second term has no further growth in revenues from $n + 1$ to infinity.

Equation (A9.3b) becomes the first term in equation (A9.5), which gives us:

$$V_1 = R_0[m(1-T)-I]\sum_{t=1}^{n}\frac{(1+g)^t}{(1+k)^t} \tag{A9.6}$$

At the end of the first term, the revenues are R_0 $(1 + g)^n$. Because no further growth occurs the same level of revenues is expected forever with no additional investment requirements. The free cash flows will remain constant at:

$$FCF = R_0(1+g)^n[m(1-T)]$$

The present value of the cash streams in the second term is:

$$V_2 = \frac{FCF}{(1+k)^{n+1}} + \frac{FCF}{(1+k)^{n+2}}$$
$$+ \frac{FCF}{(1+k)^{n+3}} + \ldots + \frac{FCF}{(1+k)^\infty}$$
$$= \frac{FCF}{(1+k)^n}\left(\frac{1}{1+k}\right)$$
$$\times \left[1 + \frac{1}{(1+k)} + \frac{1}{(1+k)^2} + \ldots + \frac{1}{(1+k)^\infty}\right]$$

Using the property of the sum of a geometric progression:

$$V_2 = \frac{FCF}{(1+k)^n}\left(\frac{1}{1+k}\right)\left(\frac{1+k}{k}\right) = \frac{R_0(1+g)^n[m(1-T)]}{k(1+k)^n}$$

the formula for our third case of temporary supernormal growth followed by zero growth reduces to equation (9.3) in Table 9.8 in Chapter 9:

$$V_0 = R_0[m(1-T) - I]\sum_{t=1}^{n}\frac{(1+g)^t}{(1+k)^t}$$

$$+ \frac{R_0(1+g)^n[m(1-T)]}{k(1+k)^n} \tag{9.3}$$

SUPERNORMAL GROWTH FOLLOWED BY CONSTANT GROWTH

By the same logic, we can develop the expression for the fourth case. The first term on the right in equation (A9.5) is given by equation (A9.6). Revenues grow at a supernormal rate, g_s with an investment requirement, I_s for the first n periods, so:

$$V_1 = R_0[m(1-T) - I_s]\sum_{t=1}^{n}\frac{(1+g_s)^t}{(1+k)^t} \tag{A9.7}$$

At the end of the first term, the revenues are $R_0(1+g_s)^n$, and they will increase from then on at a constant rate, g_c, to perpetuity. If the investment requirement during the second term is I_c, we can think of a level of free cash flow:

$$FCF = R_0(1+g_s)^n[m(1-T) - I_c]$$

growing at a rate g_c to perpetuity. The present value of the cash streams is:

$$V_2 = \frac{FCF(1+g_c)}{(1+k)^{n+1}} + \frac{FCF(1+g_c)^2}{(1+k)^{(n+2)}}$$

$$+ \frac{FCF(1+g_c)^3}{(1+k)^{n+3}} + \ldots + \frac{FCF(1+g_c)^\infty}{(1+k)^\infty}$$

$$= \frac{FCF}{(1+k)^n}\left(\frac{1+g_c}{1+k}\right)$$

$$\times \left[1 + \frac{(1+g_c)}{(1+k)} + \frac{(1+g_c)^2}{(1+k)^2} + \ldots + \frac{(1+g_c)^\infty}{(1+k)^\infty}\right]$$

which reduces to:

$$V_2 = \frac{FCF}{(1+k)^n}\left(\frac{1+g_c}{1+k}\right)\left(\frac{1+k}{k-g_c}\right)$$

$$= \frac{R_0(1+g_s)^n[m(1-T) - I_c]}{(1+k)^n}\left(\frac{1+g_c}{k-g_c}\right)$$

The formula for our fourth case of temporary supernormal growth followed by constant growth becomes equation (9.4) of Table 9.8.

$$V_0 = R_0[m(1-T) - I_s]\sum_{t=1}^{n}\frac{(1+g_s)^t}{(1+k)^t}$$

$$+ \frac{R_0(1+g_s)^n[m(1-T) - I_c]}{(1+k)^n}\left(\frac{1+g_c}{k-g_c}\right) \tag{9.4}$$

Thus, from a general capital budgeting equation, valuation expressions for four patterns of growth have been derived. The formulas for the four free cash flow patterns are summarized in Table 9.8 of Chapter 9.

CHAPTER 10
INCREASING THE VALUE
OF THE ORGANIZATION

In Chapter 9, we described and illustrated three approaches to valuation that would be useful in merger analysis: comparable companies or comparable transactions, the spreadsheet approach, and the formula approach. We discussed their strengths and weaknesses, and we concluded that each approach has something to offer. We recommended that in an acquisition analysis, all three be used for guidance they could provide. In addition, two other tests should be employed to judge the valuations in M&A transactions. Test four is whether the transaction makes business sense. Test five is whether the premium paid is justified by a realistic assessment of potential synergies.

In this chapter, we demonstrate how multiple approaches can be used in actual practice. Valuation must be related to the economic and strategic factors affecting business firms. To facilitate consideration of these broader influences that are involved in making valuations, it is necessary to focus on the industry in which the acquisition transaction takes place. We chose the oil industry because it is one of the three largest in the U.S. economy and has much economic as well as political and military importance.

THE EXXON-MOBIL MERGER

The oil industry illustrates an area of high M&A activity occurring in response to the general change forces discussed in earlier chapters. The early 1980s was a period of active merger activity. The Organization of Petroleum Exporting Countries (OPEC) sharply reduced supply, creating the oil price shocks of 1973 and 1979. Real oil prices increased fivefold over their 1972 level of $10.66 per barrel to almost $51 by 1981. Conservation by oil users and cheating by members of OPEC caused oil prices to drop to $10 per barrel by early 1986. The costs of finding and lifting oil by U.S. producers were substantially higher. Depressed oil prices caused the market prices of U.S. producers to decline so that it was cheaper to add oil reserves by buying other companies than by exploration activities. In the early 1980s, the major companies acquired included Gulf, Conoco, Marathon, Cities Service, and seven others for a total of more than $61 billion.

Similarly, in the late 1990s, depressed oil prices caused nine major mergers in efforts to reduce costs. The combined premerger market capitalization of the acquired firms was more than $218 billion. We analyzed the Exxon-Mobil transaction completed on November 30, 1999, as illustrative of major merger activity. Although our emphasis was on valuation, the analysis must be viewed relative to the broader factors related to the business economic characteristics of the industry. The topics we cover are industry characteristics, merger motivations, deal terms and event returns, valuation analysis, sensitivity analysis, and tests of merger performance.

INDUSTRY CHARACTERISTICS

The oil industry, like other industries, has been forced to adjust to the massive change forces of technology, globalization, industry transformations, and entrepreneurial innovations. The oil industry has some special characteristics, as well. Oil is a global market with 53% of volume traded internationally. It accounts for about 10% of world trade, more than any other commodity. Although the oil market is world in scope, oil varies in quality, and the requirements for pipelines and other specialized distribution and marketing facilities cause geographic market segmentation.

Because of low production costs, OPEC has a substantial influence on oil prices. However, the pricing power of OPEC is constrained. In the early 1970s, OPEC's share of the world market was about 55%. In response to OPEC price increases, factories altered production processes away from the use of oil. Consumers increased insulation in their homes, bought smaller cars, and practiced other energy-conservation measures.

At higher prices, exploration for oil was stimulated. Wells that had previously been shut down again became profitable, resulting in increased non-OPEC production. By 1985, the market share of OPEC had dropped to less than 30%. This experience demonstrated that the pricing power of OPEC is limited.

The M&A activity of the oil industry can be viewed as a response to price instability. Oil firms sought to invest in new technologies to reduce costs. Previous restructuring efforts and improvements in technologies had lowered costs to $16 to $18 per barrel. Oil prices declined to $9 per barrel in late 1998. Thus, the overriding objective for the mergers beginning in 1998 was to further increase efficiencies to lower break-even levels toward the $11 to $12 per-barrel range.

MERGER MOTIVATIONS

The motivations for the Exxon-Mobil merger, completed on November 30, 1999, reflect the industry forces described. By combining complementary assets, Exxon-Mobil would have a stronger presence in the regions of the world with the highest potential for future oil and gas discoveries. The combined company also would be in a stronger position to invest in programs involving large outlays with high prospective risks and returns.

Exxon's experience in deepwater exploration in West Africa would combine with Mobil's production and exploration acreage in Nigeria and Equatorial Guinea. In the Caspian region, Exxon's strong presence in Azerbaijan would combine with Mobil's similar position in Kazakhstan, including its significant interest in the Tengiz field, and its presence in Turkmenistan. Complementary exploration and production operations also existed in South America, Russia, and eastern Canada.

Near-term operating synergies of $2.8 billion were predicted. Two thirds of the benefits would come from eliminating duplicate facilities and excess capacity. It was expected that the combined general and administrative costs also would be reduced. Additional synergy benefits would come from applying each company's best business practices across their worldwide operations. In a news release on March 4, 2003, ExxonMobil reported that synergies had reached $4.0 billion. Analyst reports projected synergies could reach $8 billion by 2002 (Deutsche Bank, 2001).

TABLE 10.1 Exxon-Mobil Financial Relations

	Exxon		Mobil
Market value (in billions)[a]	$ 175.0		$ 58.7
Book value (in billions)[b]	$ 43.7		$ 19.0
Market value/Book value	4.0		3.1
LTM net income (in millions)[c]	$7,410		$3,272
P/E Ratio	23.6		17.9
Total paid (in billions)		$74.2	
Premium over market of Mobil			
Amount (in billions)		$15.5	
Percent		26.4%	
Premium over market, combined percent		6.6%	

[a]Market Value as of November 20, 1998.
[b]Book Value as of September 30, 1998; Source: 1998 3Q 10Q.
[c]LTM Net Income is through September 30, 1998; LTM is Last 12 Months.

DEAL TERMS AND EVENT RETURNS

The basic characteristics of the deal are set forth in Table 10.1. Exxon had a market value, premerger, of $175 billion, compared with $58.7 billion for Mobil. Exxon had a P/E ratio of about 23.6 versus 17.9 for Mobil. Exxon paid 1.32 shares for each share of Mobil. Because Mobil had 780 million shares outstanding, Exxon paid 1,030 million shares times the $72 share price of Exxon for a total of $74.2 billion. This was a 26.4% premium over the $58.7 billion Mobil market cap.

Table 10.2 shows that premerger, the equity value of Exxon shares represented 75% of the combined market value. The premium paid to Mobil caused the postmerger proportion of ownership to drop to about 70% for Exxon and rise to 30% for Mobil. This demonstrates the fallacy of the concept that in a stock-for-stock transaction, the terms of the deal don't matter because paper is only being exchanged. The terms of the deal determine the respective ownership shares in the combined company.

An event analysis of the announcement of the Exxon-Mobil combination is shown in Table 10.3. Adjusted by the Dow Jones Major World Oil Companies Index (DJWDOIL), the

TABLE 10.2 Exxon-Mobil Deal Terms

PREMERGER

	Dollar Amounts			Percentage	
	Exxon	Mobil	Total	Exxon	Mobil
Share price[a]	$72.00	$75.25			
Shares outstanding (in millions)[b]	2,431	780			
Total market value (in billions)	$175.0	$58.7	$233.7	74.9%	25.1%
Exchange Terms	1.32 for	1			
POSTMERGER					
Number of shares (in millions)	2,431	1,030	3,461	70.2%	29.8%

[a]Share prices as of November 20, 1998, a few days before runup in stock prices; announced December 1, 1998.
[b]Shares outstanding are as of 1998 3Q 10Qs.

TABLE 10.3 Exxon (XON) and Mobil (MOB) Initial Market Responses

Date	Dow Jones DJWDOIL Index	Returns on DJWDOIL Index (%)	Cumulative Actual Returns (%)	MOB	MOB Returns (%)	Cumulative Actual Returns (%)	Cumulative Adjusted Returns (%)	XON	XON Returns (%)	Cumulative Actual Returns (%)	Cumulative Adjusted Returns (%)
11/13/1998	216.62			73.44				72.88			
11/16/1998	215.41	-0.558	-0.558	72.63	-1.107	-1.107	-0.549	71.44	-1.972	-1.972	-1.414
11/17/1988	213.39	-0.938	-1.496	71.94	-0.946	-2.053	-0.557	70.56	-1.225	-3.197	-1.701
11/18/1998	213.86	0.219	-1.277	73.63	2.345	0.292	1.569	70.69	0.177	-3.020	-1.743
11/19/1988	212.18	-0.787	-2.064	73.50	-0.170	0.122	2.186	69.88	-1.150	-4.170	-2.106
11/20/1988	215.82	1.717	-0.347	75.25	2.381	2.503	2.850	72.00	3.041	-1.129	-0.782
11/23/1998	216.45	0.291	-0.056	76.19	1.247	3.750	3.805	72.06	0.086	-1.042	-0.987
11/24/1998	215.29	-0.535	-0.590	74.94	-1.641	2.109	2.699	72.69	0.869	-0.174	0.416
11/25/1998	215.13	-0.076	-0.666	78.38	4.586	6.696	7.361	72.69	0.000	-0.174	0.492
11/27/1998	223.59	3.935	3.270	86.00	9.729	16.424	13.155	74.38	2.321	2.147	-1.122
11/30/1998	220.66	-1.313	1.956	86.00	0.000	16.424	14.468	75.00	0.840	2.987	1.031
12/1/1998	214.08	-2.980	-1.023	83.75	-2.616	13.808	14.831	71.63	-4.500	-1.513	-0.489
12/2/1998	210.29	-1.772	-2.796	84.19	0.523	14.331	17.127	71.25	-0.524	-2.036	0.759
12/3/1998	208.45	-0.873	-3.669	84.50	0.371	14.702	18.370	70.56	-0.966	-3.002	0.667
12/4/1998	209.71	0.602	-3.067	86.00	1.775	16.477	19.543	71.50	1.329	-1.672	1.394
12/7/1998	211.28	0.749	-2.318	87.38	1.599	18.076	20.394	73.00	2.098	0.426	2.743
12/8/1998	213.80	1.195	-1.123	87.94	0.644	18.720	19.843	73.19	0.258	0.683	1.806
12/9/1998	216.66	1.338	0.215	88.25	0.355	19.075	18.860	73.94	1.025	1.708	1.493
12/10/1998	216.13	-0.245	-0.030	88.25	0.000	19.075	19.105	73.75	-0.254	1.454	1.484
12/11/1998	215.18	-0.441	-0.471	88.88	0.708	19.783	20.254	74.63	1.186	2.640	3.111
12/14/1988	214.87	-0.413	-0.614	89.38	0.563	20.346	20.960	74.44	-0.251	2.389	3.004
12/15/1988	213.36	-0.705	-1.319	88.44	-1.048	19.297	20.617	74.00	-0.588	1.801	3.120

cumulative return for the 11 trading days prior and through the announcement date of December 1, 1998, was 14.8% for Mobil (MOB) and 0.5% for Exxon (XON). By the tenth trading day after the merger announcement, the cumulative adjusted returns for Mobil were 20.6% and for Exxon, 3.1%. These event returns reflected the market view that the merger made economic sense.

COST OF CAPITAL CALCULATIONS

To obtain the discount factors needed for the DCF valuations, estimates of the cost of equity, of debt, and their weighted costs are needed. The Capital Asset Pricing Model (CAPM) is used most widely to calculate the cost of equity. As a check, the cost of equity should be higher than the before-tax cost of debt by 3 to 5 percentage points. The equation for the CAPM is:

$$k_e = r_f + ERP(\text{beta})$$

where:

k_e = firm's cost of equity
r_f = risk-free rate—measured by the expected yields on 10-year Treasury bonds
ERP = equity risk premium—measured by the expected market return less the risk-free rate
beta = the firm's systematic risk—the covariance of the firm's returns with the market returns divided by the market variance

The betas are discussed first. Published sources such as Value Line estimated a beta of 0.85 for Exxon and 0.75 for Mobil. Beta estimates are subject to estimation error. However, there is logic for beta levels below 1 for oil companies. The covariances of oil company stock returns with market returns are reduced by the oil industry's special economic characteristics.

We used a 5.6% yield on 10-year Treasuries as an estimate of the risk-free rate. We next considered the market equity risk premium (ERP). For many years, based on patterns of the long-term relationships between stock and bond returns, the market equity premium appeared to be in the range of 6.5% to 7.5%. By the mid-1990s, a new paradigm for a new economy began to emerge. Academics and practitioners had moved toward using 4% to 5% as the market price of risk (Welch, 2000). However, with the stock market adjustments beginning in 2000, the historical range of 6.5% to 7.5% is again reflected in market valuations.

Using CAPM, with a risk-free rate of 5.6% and a market equity risk premium of 7%, Exxon with a beta of 0.85 would have an estimated cost-of-equity capital of 11.55%. Mobil with a beta of 0.75 would have a cost-of-equity capital of 10.85%.

Cost of equity: $k_e = r_f + ERP(\text{beta})$
Exxon: $k_e = 5.6\% + 7\%(0.85) = 11.55\%$
Mobil: $k_e = 5.6\% + 7\%(0.75) = 10.85\%$

For the before-tax cost of debt (k_b), we followed the methodology used in the Paramount case by Kaplan (1995) and in Stewart (1991). Bond ratings and yield data have the virtue of being market based. Exxon had a AAA bond rating, with yields to maturity at about 160 basis points above Treasuries, for an expected before-tax cost of debt for Exxon of about 7.2%. Mobil had a AA bond rating, requiring an additional 30 basis points over the Exxon debt cost, for an expected before-tax cost of debt for Mobil of 7.5%. These pretax cost-of-debt estimates indicated a risk differential of about 3 to 4 percentage points between equity and debt costs, providing further support for our cost of equity estimates.

Theory calls for using market values in assigning weights to the cost of equity and the cost of debt to obtain a firm's weighted cost of capital. We have studied the leverage policies of the oil companies since 1980. Exxon has had debt–to–total capital (debt plus book equity) ratios as high as 30% to 40%, moving toward 20% in recent years. However, during major acquisitions or other major investment programs, these debt-to-capital ratios have been at the higher 40% level. At market values, these ratios would be lower. A similar analysis would apply for Mobil. Plausible target proportions are B/V_L equals 30% and S/V_L equals 70%, where B and S are the market values of debt and equity, respectively, and V_L equals the market value of the firm $(B + S)$. We followed the literature and general practice in using target debt-equity proportions for decisions at the margin (Kaplan, 1995; Stewart, 1991; Copeland, Koller, and Murrin, 2000). This also had the advantage of solving the circularity problem of obtaining leveraged firm valuations (Copeland, Koller, and Murrin, 2000, p. 204), which depend on the tax benefit of debt.

The prospective cash tax rates (T) were 35% for Exxon and 40% for Mobil. Accordingly, the weighted average cost of capital (WACC) for the two companies was:

$$WACC = (S/V_L)k_e + (B/V_L)\,k_b\,(1 - T)$$
$$Exxon = 0.7\,(0.1155) + (0.3)(0.072)(0.65) = 9.49\%$$
$$Mobil = 0.7(0.1085) + (0.3)(0.075)(0.60) = 8.95\%$$

The mix of upstream and downstream activities of the two companies, and the combination of different geographic areas of operations, increased the stability of the combined cash flows. The larger size of the combined companies enabled them to take on larger and riskier investment programs than either could do independently. The critical mass size requirements for research-and-development efforts in all segments of the oil industry have been increasing, so the combination would be risk reducing in that dimension as well. Value Line and other sources estimated a beta of 0.80 for the combined firm. Using a risk-free rate of 5.6% and an equity risk premium of 7% gives a cost of equity for ExxonMobil of 11.2%. The combined company had a strengthened AAA rating, so Exxon's 7.2% debt cost continues to be applicable. With a projected 38% tax rate and a capital structure with 70% equity, the base case WACC is 9.18% for ExxonMobil:

$$Combined\ WACC = 0.70(0.112) + 0.30(0.072)(0.62) = 9.18\%$$

APPLICATION OF THE DCF PERCENTAGE-OF-SALES METHOD TO EXXONMOBIL

Projections were developed for the combined company for the years 2001 and beyond, as shown in Table 10.4. The historical patterns provided a foundation for the projections. However, these were modified by a business-economic analysis of the future prospects for the oil industry. We studied contemporaneous analyst reports as well as materials from the Energy Information Administration of the U.S. Department of Energy, the *Oil & Gas Journal,* and consulting firms such as the *Energy Economic Newsletter* of the WTRG Economics. In Panel A of Table 10.4, the cash flow inputs are developed. We started with 1999 as the base net revenues of ExxonMobil and used the actual data for 2000. We then projected growth rate percentages for net revenues for the years 2001 through 2010 and for the terminal period from 2011 forward.

TABLE 10.4 DCF Spreadsheet Valuation of ExxonMobil (dollar amounts in millions except per share)

	2000	2001E	2002E	2003E	2004E	2005E	2006E	2007E	2008E	2009E	2010E	2011E On
					Panel A. Inputs for Present Value Calculations							
1. Net revenues[a]	$206,083	$185,475	$191,039	$198,680	$208,615	$224,261	$238,838	$253,168	$265,826	$276,459	$284,753	$293,296
2. Revenue growth rate	28.1%	−10.0%	3.0%	4.0%	5.0%	7.5%	6.5%	6.0%	5.0%	4.0%	3.0%	3.0%
3. NOI	$25,179	$22,257	$28,656	$31,789	$34,421	$40,367	$40,602	$43,039	$45,190	$45,616	$46,984	$45,461
4. Cash tax rate	39.9%	38.0%	38.0%	38.0%	38.0%	38.0%	38.0%	38.0%	38.0%	38.0%	38.0%	38.0%
5. Income taxes	10,056	8,458	10,889	12,080	13,080	15,339	15,429	16,355	17,172	17,334	17,854	17,275
6. NOPAT	$15,123	$13,799	$17,767	$19,709	$21,341	$25,027	$25,173	$26,684	$28,018	$28,282	$29,130	$28,186
7. + Depreciation	8,130	7,419	7,642	7,947	8,345	8,970	9,554	10,127	10,633	11,058	11,390	11,732
8. − Change in working capital	5,463	2,782	2,866	2,980	3,129	3,364	3,583	3,798	3,987	4,147	4,271	4,399
9. − Capital expenditures	8,446	8,346	7,642	7,947	8,345	10,092	10,748	11,393	11,962	12,441	12,814	7,332
10. − Change in other assets net	583	(2,318)	(2,388)	(2,484)	(2,608)	(2,803)	(2,985)	(3,165)	(3,323)	(3,456)	(3,559)	293
11. Free cash flows	$8,761	$12,408	$17,289	$19,212	$20,820	$23,346	$23,382	$24,785	$26,024	$26,208	$26,995	$27,892
12. WACC	9.18%	9.18%	9.18%	9.18%	9.18%	9.18%	9.18%	9.18%	9.18%	9.18%	9.18%	9.18%
13. Discount factor	0.91592	0.83891	0.76837	0.70376	0.64459	0.59039	0.54075	0.49529	0.45364	0.41550	0.38056	
14. Present values	$8,025	$10,409	$13,284	$13,521	$13,420	$13,783	$12,644	$12,276	$11,806	$10,890	$10,273	
					Panel B. Operating Relationships (as a % of revenues)							
NOI	12.2	12.0	15.0	16.0	16.5	18.0	17.0	17.0	17.0	16.5	16.5	15.5
NOPAT	7.3	7.4	9.3	9.9	10.2	11.2	10.5	10.5	10.5	10.2	10.2	9.6
Depreciation	3.9	4.0	4.0	4.0	4.0	4.0	4.0	4.0	4.0	4.0	4.0	4.0
Change in working capital	2.7	1.5	1.5	1.5	1.5	1.5	1.5	1.5	1.5	1.5	1.5	1.5
Capital expenditures	4.1	4.5	4.0	4.0	4.0	4.5	4.5	4.5	4.5	4.5	4.5	2.5
Change in other assets net	0.3	−1.25	−1.25	−1.25	−1.25	−1.25	−1.25	−1.25	−1.25	−1.25	−1.25	0.1
Free cash flow	4.3	6.7	9.1	9.7	10.0	10.4	9.8	9.8	9.8	9.5	9.5	9.5

[a]Net revenues exclude excise taxes and earnings from equity interests. End-of-year revenues for 1999 were $160,883 million.

The percentage relationships to revenues are developed in Panel B of Table 10.4. The product of revenues times the net operating margin gives net operating income (NOI). The NOI margin for the combined company increases as synergies are realized; however, this ratio is also dependent on the price of oil. Oil prices fluctuating around $20 per barrel (real) would balance OPEC production targets and noncompliance by some producers, with the objective of OPEC to maintain a 40% world market share of oil and oil-equivalent revenues. Projections of revenue growth reflect the economics of the industry. However, oil price volatility makes revenue and operating income estimates in individual years provisional.

Continuing in Panel A, the cash tax rates are applied to the NOI to calculate cash income taxes paid, which are deducted to obtain net operating profit after taxes (NOPAT). Depreciation is added back because it is a noncash expense. Capital expenditures and changes in working capital are deducted. The disposal of duplicate facilities represents negative outlays shown in "change in other assets net," Line 10 in Panel A. The result is the projected "free cash flows" for ExxonMobil shown in Table 10.4, Panel A, Line 11.

The patterns of free cash flows projected in Table 10.4 reflect the economic environment of the oil industry, as well as the integration of the two companies. The discount factors calculated in the previous section are applied to the free cash flows in Table 10.4 to obtain the present values of the free cash flows for the period 2000 to 2001, shown in Line 14 of Panel A. These items sum to a total present value of $130,331 million.

The exit value, or terminal value, is calculated next. The formula for calculating terminal value with constant growth is the free cash flow in the $(n + 1)$ period discounted at the difference between the terminal period WACC and the growth estimate for the terminal period. (In the special case where the terminal period growth is zero, the numerator becomes the $n + 1$ period NOPAT, and the denominator becomes the terminal period WACC.) The projected continuing growth rate of the free cash flows of 2011 and beyond for ExxonMobil is 3% per year. The estimated terminal value in 2010 is:

$$\text{Terminal Value}_n = \frac{FCF_{n+1}}{WACC - g} = \frac{\$27,892}{0.0918 - 0.03} = \$451,327 \text{ million}$$

The present value of the terminal value is obtained by discounting the terminal value back to the present using WACC.

$$\frac{\$451,327}{(1.0918)^{11}} = \$451,327 \times 0.38056 = \$171,757 \text{ million}$$

The sum of (1) the discounted cash flows of the high-growth period, plus (2) the discounted cash flows of the terminal period, plus (3) the initial marketable securities balance, gives (4) the total value of the firm of $302,161 million.

PV of cash flows, 2000–2010	$130,331
PV of terminal value	$171,757
Marketable securities	73
Total value of the firm	$302,161

From total firm value, we deducted total interest-bearing debt ($18,972 million) to obtain the indicated market value of equity of $283,189 million. We divided by the total number of shares outstanding to obtain the intrinsic value per share of $81.45, or $40.725 after the two-for-one split of July 19, 2001. The resulting indicated share price reflects the projections of the key value drivers. Such provisional results are used in a continuing process of reassessing economic and competitive impacts related to the firm's operating performance and adjustments.

Table 10.5 summarizes all the steps in the valuation procedures, obtaining the same result of $81.45 as developed in the text discussion. A general expression for the valuation procedure is set forth in Table 10.6. (This is Model 10-03B in our models compilation available on our Web site www.anderson.ucla.edu/faculty/john.weston). We express the years as 0 to 10; 0 is the base year for which the valuation is made. Growth takes place during years 1 to 10. The n + 1 year is the 11th year. At the end of the chapter in Problem 10.1, we use the general valuation model set forth in Table 10.6 (Model 10-03B) in our analysis of Intel.

The results reflect the value driver estimates that determine the firm's projected intrinsic value. The intrinsic value projections are planning benchmarks to be monitored by the firm. They can provide the basis for setting performance targets and performance-based compensation systems. Sensitivity analysis establishes that small changes in these value drivers can have a substantial impact on estimates of firm values.

DCF FORMULA VALUATION

The formula approach to DCF valuation summarizes the value driver inputs in a compact framework that relates the input variable to broader economic forces. For example, suppose we have a forecast of the growth of the U.S. economy of 5.0% for the next 10 years, with 2.5% real and 2.5% inflation. In this overall economic environment, we postulate that revenues in the oil industry will grow at 3% per year. We project ExxonMobil to grow at a somewhat higher rate per year for the next 10 years. This implies some growth in the firm's market share. Some increased competitive pressures will develop. This might influence not only ExxonMobil's revenue growth rates, but the magnitudes of other value drivers, as well. Individual value drivers might need to be adjusted upward or downward. This establishes the planning relationships among value drivers, performance results, and the resulting projected intrinsic value levels of the firm. This is at the heart of value-based management.

We can build on the spreadsheet approach to make estimates of the patterns of the value drivers for the initial growth period and for the terminal period in a systematic way. This is illustrated in Panel A of Table 10.7. Using ExxonMobil for illustration, we present projections of nine value drivers for the growth period and eight value drivers for the terminal period (the number of years is not applicable). The formula projections represent trend patterns for the up-and-down movements that might occur for individual years in the spreadsheet projections.

Panel B presents the formulas that are a mathematical summary of the steps in the spreadsheet procedure. The resulting firm values are shown in Panel C. The estimate of intrinsic value per share is about the same as in the spreadsheet calculation. We attach no significance to their equality. The exercise simply illustrates that the spreadsheet valuations and the formula valuations produce similar results.

SENSITIVITY ANALYSIS

Much analysis and many judgments are required in estimating the future behavior of the value drivers. To assess the impact of possible changes in the future behavior of the key value drivers, it is useful to perform sensitivity studies. These can be helpful in management planning and control systems and in other forms of enterprise resource planning. The sensitivity analysis can

TABLE 10.5 DCF Spreadsheet Valuation of ExxonMobil (dollar amounts in millions except per share)

	2000	2001E	2002E	2003E	2004E	2005E	2006E	2007E	2008E	2009E	2010E	2011E On
Panel A. Inputs for Present Value Calculations												
1. Net revenues[a]	$206,083	$185,475	$191,039	$198,680	$208,615	$224,261	$238,838	$253,168	$265,826	$276,459	$284,753	$293,296
2. Revenue growth rate	28.1%	−10.0%	3.0%	4.0%	5.0%	7.5%	6.5%	6.0%	5.0%	4.0%	3.0%	3.0%
3. NOI	$ 25,179	$ 22,257	$ 28,656	$ 31,789	$ 34,421	$ 40,367	$ 40,602	$ 43,039	$ 45,190	$ 45,616	$ 46,984	$ 45,461
4. Cash tax rate	39.9%	38.0%	38.0%	38.0%	38.0%	38.0%	38.0%	38.0%	38.0%	38.0%	38.0%	38.0%
5. Income taxes	10,056	8,458	10,889	12,080	13,080	15,339	15,429	16,355	17,172	17,334	17,854	17,275
6. NOPAT	$ 15,123	$ 13,799	$ 17,767	$ 19,709	$ 21,341	$ 25,027	$ 25,173	$ 26,684	$ 28,018	$ 28,282	$ 29,130	$ 28,186
7. +Depreciation	8,130	7,419	7,642	7,947	8,345	8,970	9,554	10,127	10,633	11,058	11,390	11,732
8. −Change in working capital	5,463	2,782	2,866	2,980	3,129	3,364	3,583	3,798	3,987	4,147	4,271	4,399
9. −Capital expenditures	8,446	8,346	7,642	7,947	8,345	10,092	10,748	11,393	11,962	12,441	12,814	7,332
10. −Change in other assets net	583	(2,318)	(2,388)	(2,484)	(2,608)	(2,803)	(2,985)	(3,165)	(3,323)	(3,456)	(3,559)	293
11. Free cash flows	$ 8,761	$ 12,408	$ 17,289	$ 19,212	$ 20,820	$ 20,820	$ 23,382	$ 24,785	$ 26,024	$ 26,208	$ 26,995	$ 27,892
12. WACC	9.18%	9.18%	9.18%	9.18%	9.18%	9.18%	9.18%	9.18%	9.18%	9.18%	9.18%	9.18%
13. Discount factor	0.91592	0.83891	0.76837	0.70376	0.64459	0.59039	0.54075	0.49529	0.45364	0.41550	0.38056	
14. Present values	$ 8,025	$ 10,409	$ 13,284	$ 13,521	$ 13,420	$ 13,783	$ 12,644	$ 12,276	$ 11,806	$ 10,890	$ 10,273	
Panel B. Operating Relationships (as a % of revenues)												
NOI	12.2	12.0	15.0	16.0	16.5	18.0	17.0	17.0	17.0	16.5	16.5	15.5
NOPAT	7.3	7.4	9.3	9.9	10.2	11.2	10.5	10.5	10.5	10.2	10.2	9.6
Depreciation	3.9	4.0	4.0	4.0	4.0	4.0	4.0	4.0	4.0	4.0	4.0	4.0
Change in working capital	2.7	1.5	1.5	1.5	1.5	1.5	1.5	1.5	1.5	1.5	1.5	1.5
Capital expenditures	4.1	4.5	4.0	4.0	4.0	4.5	4.5	4.5	4.5	4.5	4.5	2.5
Change in other assets net	0.3	−1.25	−1.25	−1.25	−1.25	−1.25	−1.25	−1.25	−1.25	−1.25	−1.25	0.1
Free cash flow	4.3	6.7	9.1	9.7	10.0	10.4	9.8	9.8	9.8	9.5	9.5	9.5

Panel C. Valuation Calculations

Part I—Cost of Capital Inputs

(a) Risk-free rate	5.60%
(b) Beta	0.80
(c) Equity risk premium	7.00%
(d) Tax rate	38.0%
(e) Cost of equity	11.20%
(f) Cost of debt (before tax)	7.20%
(g) Cost of debt (after tax)	4.46%
(h) Capital structure, % equity	70.00%
(i) Base WACC	9.18%

Part II – Terminal Value (TV)

$$TV = \text{Free Cash Flows}_{n+1}/(WACC - g)$$
$$= 27892/(0.0918 - 0.030)$$
$$= \$451,327$$

Part III – Valuation Calculation

(1) PV of cash flows, 2000–2010	$130,331
(2) PV of terminal value	$171,757
(3) Marketable securities	73
(4) Total value of the firm	$302,161
(5) Value of debt	18,972
(6) Value of equity	$283,189
(7) Shares outstanding	3,477
(8) Intrinsic share price	$ 81.45

[a]Net revenues exclude excise taxes and earnings from equity interests. End-of-year revenues for 1999 were $160,883 million.

TABLE 10.6 General DCF Spreadsheet Valuation Model (Model 10-03B) (dollar amounts in millions except per share)

	Year 0	Year 1	Year 2	Year 3	Year 4	Year 5	Year 6	Year 7	Year 8	Year 9	Year 10	Year n+1
						Panel A. Inputs for Present Value Calculations						
1. Net revenues	$100,000	$104,000	$108,160	$112,486	$116,986	$121,665	$126,532	$131,593	$136,857	$142,331	$148,024	$152,465
2. Revenue growth rate		4.0%	4.0%	4.0%	4.0%	4.0%	4.0%	4.0%	4.0%	4.0%	4.0%	3.0%
3. NOI		$ 12,480	$ 16,224	$ 17,998	$ 19,303	$ 21,900	$ 21,510	$ 22,371	$ 23,266	$ 23,485	$ 24,424	$ 23,632
4. Cash tax rate		38.0%	38.0%	38.0%	38.0%	38.0%	38.0%	38.0%	38.0%	38.0%	38.0%	38.0%
5. Income taxes		4,742	6,165	6,839	7,335	8,322	8,174	8,501	8,841	8,924	9,281	8,980
6. NOPAT		$ 7,738	$ 10,059	$ 11,159	$ 11,968	$ 13,578	$ 13,336	$ 13,870	$ 14,425	$ 14,560	$ 15,143	$ 14,652
7. + Depreciation		4,160	4,326	4,499	4,679	4,867	5,061	5,264	5,474	5,693	5,921	6,099
8. – Change in working capital		1,560	1,622	1,687	1,755	1,825	1,898	1,974	2,053	2,135	2,220	2,287
9. – Capital expenditures		4,680	4,326	4,499	4,679	5,475	5,694	5,922	6,159	6,405	6,661	3,812
10. – Change in other assets net		1,300	1,352	1,406	1,462	1,521	1,582	1,645	1,711	1,779	1,850	152
11. Free cash flows		$ 4,358	$ 7,084	$ 8,065	$ 8,751	$ 9,624	$ 9,224	$ 9,593	$ 9,977	$ 9,935	$ 10,332	$ 14,499
12. WACC		9.18%	9.18%	9.18%	9.18%	9.18%	9.18%	9.18%	9.18%	9.18%	9.18%	9.18%
13. Discount factor		0.91592	0.83891	0.76837	0.70376	0.64459	0.59039	0.54075	0.49529	0.45364	0.41550	
14. Present values		$ 3,991	$ 5,943	$ 6,197	$ 6,158	$ 6,203	$ 5,446	$ 5,188	$ 4,941	$ 4,507	$ 4,293	
					Panel B. Operating Relationships (as a % of revenues)							
NOI		12.0	15.0	16.0	16.5	18.0	17.0	17.0	17.0	16.5	16.5	15.5
NOPAT		7.4	9.3	9.9	10.2	11.2	10.5	10.5	10.5	10.2	10.2	9.6
Depreciation		4.0	4.0	4.0	4.0	4.0	4.0	4.0	4.0	4.0	4.0	4.0
Change in working capital		1.5	1.5	1.5	1.5	1.5	1.5	1.5	1.5	1.5	1.5	1.5
Capital expenditures		4.5	4.0	4.0	4.0	4.5	4.5	4.5	4.5	4.5	4.5	2.5
Change in other assets net		1.25	1.25	1.25	1.25	1.25	1.25	1.25	1.25	1.25	1.25	0.1
Free cash flow		4.2	6.6	7.2	7.5	7.9	7.3	7.3	7.3	7.0	7.0	9.5

Panel C. Valuation Calculations

Part I – Cost of Capital Inputs

(a) Risk-free rate	5.60%
(b) Beta	0.80
(c) Equity risk premium	7.00%
(d) Tax rate	38.0%
(e) Cost of equity	11.20%
(f) Cost of debt (before tax)	7.20
(g) Cost of debt (after tax)	4.46%
(h) Capital structure, % equity	70.00%
(i) Base WACC	9.18%

Part II – Terminal Value (TV)

$$TV = \text{Free Cash Flow}_{n+1}/(WACC - g)$$
$$= 14499/(0.0918 - 0.030)$$
$$= \$234,619$$

Part III – Valuation Calculation

(1) PV of cash flows, Years 1–10	$ 52,868
(2) PV of terminal value	$ 97,484
(3) Marketable securities	10,000
(4) Total value of the firm	$160,351
(5) Value of debt	20,000
(6) Value of equity	$140,351
(7) Shares outstanding	3,500
(8) Intrinsic share price	$ 40.10

TABLE 10.7   DCF Formula Valuation of ExxonMobil (Model 09-02)
                (dollar amounts in millions except per share)

Panel A. Value Drivers

R_0 = Base year revenues (EOY 1999)[a]	$160,883

Initial growth period

m_s = Net operating income margin	16.5%
T_s = Tax rate	38.0%
g_s = Growth rate	5.1%
d_s = Depreciation	4.0%
I_{ws} = Working capital requirements	1.5%
I_{fs} = Capital expenditures	4.5%
I_{os} = Change in other assets net	−1.25%
k_s = Cost of capital	9.18%
n = Number of growth years	11

Terminal period

m_c = Net operating income margin	15.5%
T_c = Tax rate	38.0%
g_c = Growth rate	3.0%
d_c = Depreciation	4.0%
I_{wc} = Working capital requirements	1.5%
I_{fc} = Capital expenditures	2.5%
I_{oc} = Change in other assets net	0.1%
k_c = Cost of capital	9.18%
$1 + h$ = calculation relationship = $(1+g_s)/(1+k_s)$	0.9626

Panel B. Formula

$$V_0 = R_0\Big[m_s\big(1-T_s\big)+d_s-I_{ws}-I_{fs}-I_{os}\Big]\sum_{t=1}^{n}\frac{\big(1+g_s\big)^t}{\big(1+k_s\big)^t}+\frac{R_0\big(1+g_s\big)^n\big(1+g_c\big)\Big[m_c\big(1-T_c\big)+d_c-I_{wc}-I_{fc}-I_{oc}\Big]}{\big(k_c-g_c\big)\big(1+k_s\big)^n}$$

$$V_0 = \frac{R_1\Big[m_s\big(1-T_s\big)+d_s-I_{ws}-I_{fs}-I_{os}\Big]}{1+k_s}\left(\frac{\big(1+h\big)^n-1}{h}\right)+\frac{R_0\big(1+g_s\big)^n\big(1+g_c\big)\Big[m_c\big(1-T_c\big)+d_c-I_{wc}-I_{fc}-I_{oc}\Big]}{\big(k_c-g_c\big)\big(1+k_s\big)^n}$$

Panel C. Calculating Firm Value

Present value of initial growth period cash flows	$134,466
Present value of terminal value	167,724
Enterprise operating value	$302,191
Add: Marketable securities	73
Total value of the firm	$302,264
Less: Total interest-bearing debt	18,972
Equity value	$283,292
Number of shares	3,477
Value per share	$ 81.48

[a]Revenues exclude excise taxes and earnings from equity interests.

be performed with either the spreadsheet or formula approaches. The formula method is used for simplicity of exposition.

In Table 10.8, we calculated the elasticities of the responses in the ExxonMobil intrinsic value levels to upward and downward changes in each of the value drivers. The analysis changes one value driver, holding constant the levels of the others. The elasticities calculated and shown in the bottom of Table 10.8 are based on the maximum percent changes calculated. The elasticities are positive for the growth rate in revenues, the net operating income margin, and the duration of the period of competitive advantage. The elasticities are negative for tax rates, cost of capital, and total investment requirements.

The negative elasticity for investment requirements results from the construction of the sales growth DCF spreadsheet model. In this model, when the investment requirements ratios change, the growth rate remains unchanged, so the profitability ratio changes in the opposite direction. In other models, such as in the Miller and Modigliani (1961) dividend paper, *growth* was defined as "the product of profitability and investment requirements," so investment can have a positive elasticity.

Another dimension of sensitivity is shown in Table 10.9, in which paired value drivers are analyzed. The top part of the table reflects the critical relationship between the operating margin and the cost of capital. When the spread between the operating margin and the discount rage widens, the impact on valuation is magnified (and conversely). In the lower part of Table 10.9, the relationship between the growth rates in revenues and in the net operating margin is shown. In some business circumstances, a trade-off between revenue growth and operating margin might be encountered. Hence, it can be useful to analyze various combinations of revenue growth operating margins.

The sensitivity analyses shown in Tables 10.8 and 10.9 enable the decision maker to identify the relative strength of the value drivers on the valuation of the enterprise. Valuations reflect changes in the economy and competitive developments. Valuation estimates are useful because they sensitize decision makers to how the economic and competitive changes affect critical value drivers. In the strategic planning processes of firms, valuations perform an important role in a firm's information-feedback system. Through the process of identifying the impact of value drivers on valuation changes, sensitivity analysis is used in planning processes for improving the performance of the firm and in making valuation estimates by outside analysts.

TEST OF MERGER PERFORMANCE

Table 10.10 illustrates how to test for increases in shareholder value by analysis of the combined operations. Table 10.10 begins with the respective premerger values, totaling $233.7 billion. The base equity valuation of the combined companies from Table 10.7 is $283.3 billion. Deduct the $74.2 billion paid to Mobil. This leaves $209.1 billion. The premerger value of Exxon was $175 billion. Hence, the gain from the merger was $34.1 billion. The Mobil $10.2 billion share of the estimated value increase, combined with the $15.5 billion premium, represents a total gain of $25.7 billion to its shareholders. The gain of $23.9 billion to the original Exxon shareholders represents approximately the same as total gains to Mobil shareholders.

More generally, Healy, Palepu, and Ruback (1992) find that event returns are statistically significant predictors of subsequent market value changes, as well as accounting performance measures. For the nine major oil industry mergers during the period 1998 to 2001, Table 10.11 summarizes value changes (industry adjusted) over a window from 10 days before the

TABLE 10.8 ExxonMobil
Sensitivity of Equity Values ($ billions) to the Value Drivers

% Change	g_s (%)	V_0	m_s (%)	V_0	T (%)	V_0	k (%)	V_0	I_s (%)	V_0	n	V_0
-20	4.08	$259.1	13.20	$254.3	30.40	$301.1	7.34	$331.3	3.80	$296.8	8.80	$275.4
-14	4.39	$266.2	14.19	$263.0	32.68	$295.7	7.89	$316.0	4.09	$292.7	9.46	$277.8
-10	4.59	$270.9	14.85	$268.8	34.20	$292.2	8.26	$306.2	4.28	$290.0	9.90	$279.4
-6	4.79	$275.8	15.51	$274.6	35.72	$288.6	8.63	$296.8	4.47	$287.3	10.34	$281.0
-4	4.90	$278.3	15.84	$277.5	36.48	$286.8	8.81	$292.2	4.56	$286.0	10.56	$281.8
-2	5.00	$280.8	16.17	$280.4	37.24	$285.1	9.00	$287.7	4.66	$284.6	10.78	$282.5
0	5.10	$283.3	16.50	$283.3	38.00	$283.3	9.18	$283.3	4.75	$283.3	11.00	$283.3
2	5.20	$285.8	16.83	$286.2	38.76	$281.5	9.36	$279.0	4.85	$281.9	11.22	$284.0
4	5.30	$288.4	17.16	$289.1	39.52	$279.7	9.55	$274.7	4.94	$280.6	11.44	$284.8
6	5.41	$291.0	17.49	$292.0	40.28	$278.0	9.73	$270.5	5.04	$279.2	11.66	$285.5
10	5.61	$296.2	18.15	$297.8	41.80	$274.4	10.10	$262.4	5.23	$276.6	12.10	$287.0
14	5.81	$301.5	18.81	$303.6	43.32	$270.8	10.47	$254.6	5.42	$273.9	12.54	$288.5
20	6.12	$309.7	19.80	$312.3	45.60	$265.5	11.02	$243.3	5.70	$269.8	13.20	$290.6

Elasticities

	g_s (%)		m_s (%)		T (%)		k (%)		I_s (%)		n	
+20%	0.466		0.512		-0.314		-0.704		-0.238		0.129	
-20%	0.427		0.512		-0.314		-0.847		-0.238		0.139	

Notes: Illustration of calculation of elasticity for n and V:

Elasticity of V wrt $n = (\Delta V/V)/(\Delta n/n) = [(290.6 - 283.3)/283.3]/[(13.2-11.0)/11.0] = (7.3/283.3)/(2.2/11.0) = 0.02577/0.20 = 0.129$

The table shows that for the value drivers with positive elasticities, the cost of capital (k) has the greatest influence. The cost of capital (k) has the greatest negative relationship with value. These numerical relationships are specific to the magnitudes of the value drivers in Table 10.7, Panel A. The signs of the relationship will always hold. More general expression for the elasticities can be obtained by taking the derivative of value with respect to (wrt) each of the value drivers in the formula shown in Table 10.7, Panel B.

TABLE 10.9 DCF Sensitivity Matrix ExxonMobil Corporation

		EQUITY VALUE (IN $ BILLIONS)				
		Net Operating Income Margin, m_s				
		10.5%	*12.5%*	*16.5%*	*18.5%*	*20.5%*
	7.50%	$269.3	$288.5	$326.9	$346.1	$365.3
	8.00%	$257.0	$275.7	$313.1	$331.8	$350.6
	8.50%	$245.4	$263.6	$300.1	$318.3	$336.5
	9.00%	$234.4	$252.1	$287.6	$305.4	$323.1
Discount Rate, k_s	9.18%	$230.5	$248.1	$283.3	$300.9	$318.5
	9.50%	$223.9	$241.2	$275.8	$293.1	$310.4
	10.00%	$213.9	$230.8	$264.5	$281.4	$298.3
	10.50%	$204.5	$220.9	$253.8	$270.3	$286.7
	11.00%	$195.5	$211.5	$243.6	$259.7	$275.7

		EQUITY VALUE (IN $ BILLIONS)				
		Revenues Growth Rate, g_s				
		3.00%	*4.00%*	*5.10%*	*6.00%*	*7.00%*
	13.0%	$208.2	$228.3	$252.5	$274.1	$300.2
	14.0%	$216.1	$236.6	$261.3	$283.4	$310.0
	15.0%	$223.9	$244.9	$270.1	$292.6	$319.7
	16.0%	$231.8	$253.2	$278.9	$301.8	$329.4
Net Operating Margin, m_s	16.5%	$235.7	$257.3	$283.3	$306.4	$334.3
	17.0%	$239.7	$261.5	$287.7	$311.1	$339.2
	18.0%	$247.5	$269.8	$296.5	$320.3	$348.9
	19.0%	$255.4	$278.0	$305.3	$329.5	$358.7
	20.0%	$263.3	$286.3	$314.1	$338.7	$368.4

TABLE 10.10 Tests of Merger Performance Exxon-Mobil Example (Model 10-02) (in $ billions)

Premerger

	Market Caps	Ownership Proportions (%)
Exxon	$175.0	74.9
Mobil	58.7	25.1
Total	$233.7	100.0

Postmerger

Combined value	$283.3	
Paid to Mobil	74.2	
Remainder	209.1	
Exxon premerger	175.0	
Gain from merger		$ 34.1
Portion to Exxon 70%		23.9
Portion to Mobil 30%		10.2
Plus premium to Mobil		15.5
Mobil total gain		$ 25.7

TABLE 10.11 Value Changes in 9 Major Oil Industry Mergers, 1998–2001 (in $ billions)

| Target | Acquirer | Announcement Date | Market Cap, –10 days | | | Value Changes (–10, +10) | | |
			Target	Acquirer	Combined	Target	Acquirer	Combined
Amoco	BP	8/11/1998	$38.7	$79.7	$118.4	$10.6	$1.9	$12.5
PetroFina	Total	12/1/1998	8.1	29.6	37.7	2.5	(4.7)	(2.2)
Mobil	Exxon	12/1/1998	56.7	173.7	230.3	11.7	5.4	17.1
Arco	BP	4/1/1999	20.8	161.5	182.3	4.7	7.9	12.6
Elf Acquitaine	TotalFina	7/5/1999	41.6	46.2	87.8	5.9	(3.2)	2.7
Texaco	Chevron	10/16/2000	29.4	56.6	86.0	3.8	(1.1)	2.7
Tosco	Phillips	2/4/2001	5.0	14.0	19.1	1.2	(0.2)	1.0
Gulf Canada	Conoco	5/29/2001	3.0	19.2	22.2	1.1	(0.3)	0.7
Conoco	Phillips	11/18/2001	15.5	20.6	36.1	2.3	2.1	4.5
Totals			$218.8	$601.1	$819.9	$43.8	$7.8	$51.6

Note: Market capitalizations are calculated 10 days before the merger announcement date. The value changes are calculated from 10 days before the announcement date to 10 days after. The measurement of the value changes adjust for market changes using the Dow Jones Major World Oil Companies Index (DJWDOIL).

announcement date to 10 days after the announcement date. Targets increased in value by $43.8 billion. Acquirers increased in value by $7.8 billion. The combined value increase was $51.6 billion. The acquisition by Total (French) of PetroFina (Belgian) was the sole transaction for which the value change was negative. Analysts were critical of the 54.8% premium offered by Total, because it was exposing itself to the substantial cyclical risks of the petrochemical industry and to PetroFina's low margins on its retail operations. This example also illustrates how the event returns reflect the market's evaluation of the underlying economics of the deal. Table 10.11 demonstrates that the nine major oil merger deals during the period 1998 to 2001 overall were value increasing for both targets and acquirers.

TESTS OF MERGER THEORY

Three major types of merger motivations were identified by Berkovitch and Narayanan (1993): synergy, hubris, and agency problems. In the Exxon-Mobil merger, synergy and efficiency objectives were promised and achieved. The initial synergies were estimated at $2.8 billion. As a result of rapid and effective integration of the two companies, Chairman Lee Raymond announced within 7 months of the completion of the merger that synergies of $4.6 billion had been achieved. Analysts' reports were projecting a further increase in synergies to the $7 billion level.

Synergies can result from cost reductions or revenue increases. ExxonMobil benefited from sales of duplicate facilities and employment reductions. Costs were reduced by adoptions of best practices from both companies, particularly in combining advanced technologies. Revenue increases can come from strengthening the market positions of each. In addition, joint ventures with major oil-producing countries such as Saudi Arabia were facilitated by strengthening Exxon's position as one of the three largest international oil companies.

Hubris can be reflected in overpaying for the target. Exxon paid a premium of $15.5 billion. The equity market cap of the combined firm increased from $234 billion to actual values of $280 billion by the end of 1999 and to $301 billion by the end of 2000. Thus, the capitalized value of the synergies was $46 billion to $67 billion. In his news release of August 1, 2000, Raymond stated that an improvement of at least 3 points above the historic Exxon level of return on capital employed (ROCE) was being achieved. These results are inconsistent with agency problems.

Other motives for mergers discussed in the literature include tax savings, monopoly, and redistribution. Tax aspects were not a major factor. Regulatory agencies found no antitrust problems in the upstream activities (exploration and development). However, divestitures were required in downstream activities (distribution and marketing). Redistribution from bondholders did not occur. Redistribution from labor took place in the sense that employment reshuffling occurred and reductions were made.

In their review of merger activity, Holmstrom and Kaplan (2001) described the positive influence of a number of developments in the 1990s. These included an increase in equity-based compensation, an increased emphasis on shareholder value, a rise in shareholder activism, improved and more active boards of directors, increased CEO turnover, and an increase in the role of capital markets. The goal of improving through the Exxon-Mobil merger reflected these general developments.

In their companion review, Andrade, Mitchell, and Stafford (2001) further developed the earlier Mitchell and Mulherin (1996) emphasis on the role of shocks in causing mergers. Their analysis is applicable to the oil industry mergers. However, the pressures have been more than periodic shocks. Price instability has been a continuing problem for oil firms. Large price changes in downward as well as upward directions have been destabilizing. Price drops reduce profit margins and investment returns. Price rises increase margins and returns, but stimulate production expansion and new entrants. Hence, price uncertainty created strong continuing pressures for improved efficiency to reduce oil finding and production costs.

Another oil industry characteristic is high sensitivity to changes in overall economic activity. The East Asian financial problems in 1997 and 1998 led to reduced demand, resulting in a decline in world oil prices to less than $10 per barrel in late 1998. The decline in growth in the U.S. economy beginning in 2000 contributed to the drop in oil prices from $37 to less than $20 per barrel during 2001. By February 2003 the threat of war with Iraq moved oil prices to over $38 per barrel.

The rise of 15 government-connected national oil companies created increased competitive pressures. The increased application of technological advances in exploration, production, refining methods, and transportation logistics created new competitive opportunities and threats. Price instabilities (like persistent overcapacity in the steel, auto, and chemical industries) caused continuing pressures for M&A activities to reduce costs and increase revenues. In addition, the $2 billion synergy in the BP acquisition of Amoco stimulated competitive responses resulting in other mergers, alliances, and joint ventures. The oil industry M&A activities during the period 1998 to 2001 are consistent with the industry shocks theory, an industry structural problems theory, and a theory of competitive responses.

REVIEW

The Exxon-Mobil combination is an archetype of a successful merger. Fundamentally, the reasons, structures, and implementation of the transaction reflected the characteristics of the oil and gas industry. The industry increasingly utilizes advanced technology in exploration, production, and refining, and in the logistics of its operations. It is international in scope. World demand is sensitive to economic conditions. The weakness in the Asian economies pushed prices below $10 per barrel at the end of 1998. The U.S. recession, which began in March 2001, helped push oil prices from $32 per barrel down to $17 per barrel by November 2001. During the Middle East crisis in April 2002, oil prices had moved up to the $37-per-barrel level.

Critics of merger activities have argued that the likelihood of successful mergers is small. In addition, they argue that purchase prices include substantial premiums requiring increases in values of acquired firms that are not likely to be achieved. The Exxon-Mobil combination provides counterevidence. Synergies include improvements in the performance of all the parties in the transaction. Premiums usually are expressed as a percentage of the premerger market cap of the target. These percentages can run high; however, more relevant is the amount of the premium in relation to the size of the combined firm. The $15.5 billion premium to Mobil was 26.4% of its market cap but represented only 6.6% of the combined premerger market cap. The $2.8 billion premerger synergy estimate ($7 billion postmerger) required only a modest valuation multiple to recover the $15.5 billion premium. More generally, Table 10.11 demonstrates that in total, the nine major oil transactions were value increasing for acquirers as well as targets.

This chapter develops a framework for an analysis of how M&As can perform a positive role in aiding firms as they adjust to changing environments. We emphasize a multiple approach. Critical factors are the economics of the industry, the business logic of the combination within the framework of the industry and the economy, the behavior of the value drivers in the financial analysis of the merger, regulatory factors, and competitive interactions.

MULTIPLE-STAGE VALUATION

Thus far in the analysis, we have followed the general practice of using two-stage DCF spreadsheet and formula valuation models. In the first stage, the firm is postulated to have a competitive advantage in which growth and profitability rates are high relative to long-run average patterns. The second stage or terminal period runs to infinity so growth can be no larger than the economy as a whole. In a mature industry, real growth could be zero or negative. However, even with zero growth, nominal growth (growth in current dollars) will reflect general price level movements as they impact individual economic segments.

A more general valuation approach could use multiple stages related to the growth and decline of industries and firms. Table 10.12 illustrates a DCF spreadsheet valuation model using four stages. Stage 1 is the introduction stage in which free cash flows may be negative. Stage 2 is a period of strong competitive advantage and high growth. During Stage 3, as the industry reaches maturity, revenue growth decays until it reaches a constant growth level, which continues throughout Stage 4, the terminal period. We hold the cost of capital constant throughout the periods, but the model permits the use of a cost of capital that varies for each stage. Revenues in period 0 are $1,000, so our model can be readily generalized to actual companies whose revenues will be some multiple of this initial value.

The spreadsheet shows details for revenues and costs elements. In Line 11, NOPAT is defined as the sum of net income plus the interest tax shield. However, as in our previous spreadsheet, NOPAT also is equal to NOI (assumed equal to EBIT) times $(1 - T)$. For example, for period 1, the pretax operating income (NOI) in Line 5 is $60. Multiplying $60 by 0.85 gives $51, the NOPAT listed in Line 11.

The remainder of the spreadsheet follows the formats employed previously in the chapter. The calculations also proceed as before. We summarized all forms of investments including capital expenditures and working capital investments into one rate, giving the same results as would have been obtained by listing them separately and then adding. The total present value of free cash flows for the first three stages covering years 1 to 20 is $3,225. To this we added the present value of the stage 4 terminal period calculated in Table 10.13. In Table 10.13, we began with the calculation of the free cash flows for year 21, the n + 1 year. This is discounted at the cost of capital minus the growth rate to obtain the terminal value of $29,355. Its discounted value uses the present value factor at the cost of capital of 15% for year 20, which, is 0.061, to obtain $1,794. This amount added to the total present value of the free cash flows of the first three stages gives a total operating value of $5,019. In Table 10.13, the present value of the free cash flows for each of the individual stages is shown to obtain the same result.

In the lower-left corner of Table 10.12, we also calculated multiples of operating value in the base year to revenues, NOI, EBITDA, and net income in years 1 and 6. The multiples are not meaningful for a newly borne firm. However, based on the values achieved at the end of stage 1, the multiples begin to be useful in a comparables analysis.

We also present a general four-stage model in Table 10.14. By using a formula approach with investment requirements net of depreciation and other cash inflows, our results can be presented compactly. The valuation is expressed as the base period total present value. This

TABLE 10.12 Four-Stage Spreadsheet DCF Valuation, Value Driver Method

Input Relations

Revenue year 0: $1,000

	Stage 1	Stage 2	Stage 3	Stage 4
	1-5	6-15	16-20	21-∞
Revenues growth rate (g)	20.0%	33.0%	⇒ 3.0%	3.0%
Operating margin (% Rev.)	5.0	20.0	15.0	10.0
Interest expense (% Rev.)	2	2	2	2
Depreciation (% Rev.)	5	5	5	4
Investment rate (% Rev.)	15	15	8	6
Tax rate (% EBT)	15	20	40	40
Cost of capital (k) or (WACC)	15	15	15	15

($ in millions)

	1	2	3	4	5	6	7	8	9	10	11	12	13	14	15	16	17	18	19	20 or n
Incremental Free Cash Flow:																				
1. Revenues growth rate	20.0%	20.0%	20.0%	20.0%	20.0%	33.0%	33.0%	33.0%	33.0%	33.0%	33.0%	33.0%	33.0%	33.0%	33.0%	27.0%	21.0%	15.0%	9.0%	3.0%
2. Revenues	$1,200	$1,440	$1,728	$2,074	$2,488	$3,309	$4,402	$5,854	$7,786	$10,355	$13,773	$18,318	$24,362	$32,402	$43,095	$54,730	$66,223	$76,157	$83,011	$85,501
3. −Cost of goods sold, SG&A	1,080	1,296	1,555	1,866	2,238	2,482	3,301	4,391	5,839	7,767	10,329	13,738	18,272	24,301	32,321	43,784	52,979	60,926	66,409	68,401
4. −Depreciation	60	72	86	104	124	165	220	293	389	518	689	916	1,218	1,620	2,155	2,737	3,311	3,808	4,151	4,275
5. Pretax operating Income (NOI = EBIT)	60	72	86	104	124	662	880	1,171	1,557	2,071	2,755	3,684	4,872	6,480	8,619	8,210	9,934	11,424	12,452	12,825
6. −Interest expense	24	29	35	41	50	66	88	117	156	207	275	366	487	648	862	1,095	1,324	1,523	1,660	1,710
7. Income before taxes (EBT)	36	43	52	62	75	596	792	1,054	1,401	1,886	2,479	3,297	4,385	5,832	7,757	7,115	8,609	9,900	10,791	11,115
8. −Income Taxes	5	6	8	9	11	119	158	211	280	373	496	659	877	1,166	1,551	2,846	3,444	3,960	4,317	4,446
9. Net Income (NI)	31	37	44	53	63	477	634	843	1,121	1,491	1,983	2,638	3,508	4,666	6,206	4,269	5,165	5,940	6,475	6,669
10. +Tax shield: (1 − T) × (6)	20	24	29	35	42	53	70	94	125	166	220	293	390	518	690	657	795	914	996	1,026
11. NOPAT (9+10)	51	61	73	88	106	530	704	937	1,246	1,657	2,204	2,931	3,898	5,184	6,895	4,926	5,960	6,854	7,471	7,695
12. +Depreciation	60	72	86	104	124	165	220	293	389	518	689	916	1,218	1,620	2,155	2,737	3,311	3,808	4,151	4,275
13. −Investment	180	216	259	311	373	496	660	878	1,168	1,553	2,066	2,748	3,654	4,860	6,464	4,378	5,298	6,093	6,641	6,840
14. Free cash flow (FCF)	$(69)	$(83)	$(99)	$(119)	$(143)	$199	$264	$351	$467	$621	$826	$1,099	$1,462	$1,944	$2,586	$3,284	$3,973	$4,589	$4,981	$5,130
15. Discount factor (DF)[a]	0.870	0.756	0.658	0.572	0.497	0.432	0.376	0.327	0.284	0.247	0.215	0.187	0.163	0.141	0.123	0.107	0.093	0.081	0.070	0.061
16. Discounted FCF	$(60)	$(63)	$(65)	$(68)	$(71)	$86	$99	$115	$133	$154	$178	$205	$238	$275	$318	$351	$369	$369	$350	$313
17. Total present value of FCF:	$3,225																			

Ratios

	t = Year 1	t = Year 6
18. Operating value_t/revenue_t	4.18	1.52
19. Operating value_t/NOI_t	83.64	7.58
20. Operating value_t/EBITDA_t	41.82	6.07
21. Operating value_t/NI_t	164.01	10.53

[a] Discount factor = $DF_t = 1/(1+k_1) \times 1/(1+k_2) \times 1/(1+k_3) \times \ldots \times 1/(1+k_t)$ and k_t = cost of capital for year t.

TABLE 10.13 Four-Stage Spreadsheet DCF Valuation, Value Driver Method

	Year 21 or $n+1$
1. Revenues growth rate	3.0%
2. Revenues	$88,066
3. −Cost of goods sold, SG&A	75,737
4. −Depreciation	3,523
5. Pretax operating income (NOI = EBIT)	8,807
6. −Interest expense	1,761
7. Income before taxes (EBT)	7,045
8. −Income taxes	2,818
9. Net income (NI)	4,227
10. + Tax shield: $(1 - T) \times (6)$	1,057
11. NOPAT $(9 + 10)$	5,284
12. + Depreciation	3,523
13. −Investment	5,284
14. Free cash flow (FCF)	$ 3,523

Terminal Value (TV) = $FCF_{n+1}/(k_{stage4} - g_{stage4}) = 3523/(0.15 - 0.03) = $29,355$

PV of FCF stage 1	$ (327)
PV of FCF stage 2	1,799
PV of FCF stage 3	1,753
Present value of TV (PVTV) = $TV \times DF_n = 29355 \times 0.061 =$	1,794
Operating value$_0$	$5,019
Plus: Marketable securities	—
Less: Total interest bearing debt	—
Equity value	$5,019
Number of shares	1,000
Price per share	5.02

TABLE 10.14 General Four-Stage Model (Model 10-05A) (revenue growth model)

Revenue period 0 (R_0) $1,000

	Stage 1	Stage 2	Stage 3	Stage 4
Number of periods (n)	5	10	5	∞
Growth rate of revenues (g)	55.6%	33.0%	5.0%	3.0%
Operating margin (m)	−5.0%	30.0%	15.0%	10.0%
Tax rate (T)	0.0%	20.0%	40.0%	40.0%
Cost of capital (k)	15.0%	15.0%	15.0%	15.0%
Investment requirements rate (I)	6.0%	6.0%	6.0%	2.0%
h = (1 + g)/(1 + k)	1.353	1.157	0.913	0.896

Stage 1: Period 1–5
$$V_0^1 = R_0 \cdot \left[m_1(1 - T_1) - I_1 \right] \cdot \sum_{t=1}^{n_1} h_1^t \qquad = (1,490)$$

Stage 2: Period 6–15
$$V_0^2 = R_0 \cdot h_1^{n_1} \cdot \left[m_2(1 - T_2) - I_2 \right] \cdot \sum_{t=1}^{n_2} h_2^t \qquad = 19,788$$

Stage 3: Period 16–20
$$V_0^3 = R_0 \cdot h_1^{n_1} \cdot h_2^{n_2} \cdot \left[m_3(1 - T_3) - I_3 \right] \cdot \sum_{t=1}^{n_3} h_3^t \qquad = 2,235$$

Stage 4: Period 21 → Inf
$$V_0^4 = R_0 \cdot h_1^{n_1} \cdot h_2^{n_2} \cdot h_3^{n_3} \cdot \left[m_4(1 - T_4) - I_4 \right] \cdot \frac{(1 + g_4)}{(k_4 - g_4)} \qquad = 4,229$$

Total PV = $24,762

Notes:
V_0^i = PV of stage i free cash flows at time 0. For example, V_0^1 = PV of stage 1 free cash flows at time 0.
Terminal value = V_n^4 = (NOI$_{N+1}$(1 − T_4) − $R_{N+1}I_4$)/(k_4 − g_4).
NOI$_{N+1}$ = NOI for period 1 in stage 4.

result can be used to calculate the ratio of market values to period 1 revenues as was done often in the valuation of Internet firms that had not reached profitability. This ratio is almost 16 times initial revenues, but if calculated for later years, it is more likely to be closer to two to five times the amount usually observed for companies in stages 2 or 3.

We also calculate the ratio of value of NOI at the beginning of stage 2, obtaining 6.8 times. This result can be used in comparables analysis with other companies in similar circumstances. The multiplier used in stage 4 can be obtained by taking the reciprocal of the cost of capital less the growth rate. The cost of capital in period 4 of 0.15 less the projected constant growth rate of 0.03 for stage 4 is 0.12. The reciprocal of 0.12 is 8.33. The software for these multiple-stage models is available on Web sites for this text.

Summary

The goal of valuation analysis is to provide a disciplined approach to analyzing acquisition premiums and their recovery. This chapter illustrates alternative approaches to achieving this basic objective. The Exxon-Mobil merger analysis presented illustrates a general framework for analyzing mergers.

First, the underlying economics of the industry must be understood. This provides the basis for the second step, which is to understand the potential benefits and synergies from the merger. Third is the application of the DCF valuation procedures, which quantifies potential synergies and permits a comparison of whether the value increases will recover the premiums paid by the acquiring firm. This analysis is based on financial projections of the value drivers. Fourth, all aspects of potential regulatory factors need to be taken into account. Fifth, the competitive reactions of rival firms and the changes in industry dynamics need to be taken into account. These five major financial factors must be related to the challenges of combining two organizations' cultures and achieving effective implementation of the merger plans.

We place the analysis in a dynamic framework by analyzing how the key value drivers behave for firms at different stages of their life cycles. The key value drivers identified were: the growth rate in revenues, the net operating income-to-revenue margin, working capital requirements in relation to revenue growth, plant and equipment expenditures in relation to revenue growth, applicable tax rates, applicable cost of capital, and the years of competitive advantage producing above-average growth and profitability.

We used this dynamic framework in assessing valuation patterns in Internet companies. We presented a four-stage DCF valuation model to show the relationship between the value drivers and the resulting revenue valuation relationships.

Key valuation relationships are used in some industries. For example, cable companies were bought at $5,000 to $8,000 per subscriber (or "pop"). In the high-tech area, the price paid for a company could be $2 million to $4 million per engineer, depending upon the nature of their capabilities in relation to the acquiring firm's needs.

Problems

10.1 **Intel (INTC)** In his article on the valuation of Intel, Cornell(2001) discussed the market reaction to a press release issued by Intel late on September 21, 2000. Intel stated that it expected revenue growth for the third quarter over the second quarter to be 3% to 5%. This was a downward revision from the company's previous forecast of 7% to 9% and of the analysts' consensus projection of 8% to 12%. By September 26, 2000, Intel had declined from $61.48 on the press release date to $43.31.

Intel reached a high of $75.80 in mid 2000 and experienced a low of $18.96 during the market weakness following the terrorist attacks of September 11, 2001. By May 13, 2002, Intel had recovered to $28.52. Intel closed on July 29, 2002, at $18.89. The critical factors influencing Intel valuation were its revenue growth, gross margin percentage, and operating income percentage margin. Data on these variables are presented for the seven years 1995 to 2001 in Table P10.1.1

The net revenue annual growth rate fluctuated from 29% in 1996, down to 5% in 1998, recovering to 15% by 2000, and falling to –21% in 2001. The gross margin fluctuated from a high of more than 60% in 1997 and 2000 to a low of 49.2% in 2001. The operating income margin declined from a high of 39.4% in 1997 to a low of 8.5% in 2001.

QUESTIONS

Use the format of Table P10.1.2, based on Table 10.7 in the text (Model 09-02), to answer the questions.

10.1.1 Fill in your judgment of the blank items in Table P10.1.2 using the software from our Web site for Model 09-02. What is the resulting indicated intrinsic value per share of Intel?

10.1.2 Verify your result using the format of Table 10.6 in the text (based on Model 10-03B) using the software from our Web site.

	1995	1996	1997	1998	1999	2000	2001
Net revenue (in millions)	16,202	20,847	25,070	26,273	29,389	33,726	26,539
Net revenue growth rate		29%	20%	5%	12%	15%	−21%
Gross margin (in millions)	8,393	11,237	15,117	14,187	17,553	21,076	13,052
Gross margin as a percent of revenues	51.8%	53.9%	60.3%	54.0%	59.7%	62.5%	49.2%
Operating income (in millions)	5,252	7,103	9,887	8,600	9,767	10,395	2,256
Operating income as a percent of revenues	32.4%	34.1%	39.4%	32.7%	33.2%	30.8%	8.5%

Source: Intel Annual Reports.

Value Drivers

R_0 = Base year revenues	$33,726

Initial growth period

m_s = Net operating income margin	
T_s = Tax rate	33.00%
g_s = Growth rate	
d_s = Depreciation	9.00%
I_{ws} = Working capital requirements	1.00%
I_{fs} = Capital expenditures	12.25%
I_{os} = Change in other assets net	0.00%
k_s = Cost of capital	10.00%
n = Number of growth years	10

Terminal period

m_c = Net operating income margin	20.00%
T_c = Tax rate	33.00%
g_c = Growth rate	6.00%
d_c = Depreciation	9.00%
I_{wc} = Working capital requirements	1.00%
I_{fc} = Capital expenditures	12.00%
I_{oc} = Change in other assets net	0.00%
k_c = Cost of capital	10.00%
$1 + h$ = calculation relationship = $(1 + g_s)/(1 + k_s)$	

Calculating Firm Value

Present value of initial growth period cash flows	
Present value of terminal value	
Enterprise operating value	
Add: Marketable securities	3,600
Entity value	
Less: Total interest-bearing debt	1,000
Equity value	
Number of shares	6,710
Value per share	

10.1.3 Discuss some alternative scenarios for the future of Intel, and do a sensitivity analysis of its valuation with respect to its alternative projections of the growth rate in revenues and the net operating income margin.

10.2 **Dow-Union Carbide** The chemical industry has a long history of M&A activity. In the 1920s, Imperial Chemical was formed in England, and Germany's largest chemical firms combined to form IG Farben. Following World War II, IG Farben was broken up into Bayer, BASF, and Hoechst. These and other large firms, such as Dow and DuPont, have long dominated the chemical industry. New developments in the chemical industry and the changing nature of the economy have contributed to the resurgence of M&A activity within the industry. This problem studies Dow Chemical Company's merger with Union Carbide announced on August 4, 1999.

THE CHARACTERISTICS OF THE CHEMICAL INDUSTRY

Sound analysis of any merger transaction requires knowledge of the economic characteristics of the industry(ies) of the companies involved. The nature of the industry is key to explaining the economic and business logic of the transaction.

The chemicals industry requires that firms be high tech and R&D oriented in order to maintain relatively high margins of profitability. Even innovative firms are threatened by the relative ease with which new technology diffuses through the industry. This has led to a distinction between specialty and commodity chemicals. Commodity chemicals have been established for a period of time, and many firms compete to distribute high volumes. The margins on such chemicals are low. Specialty chemicals result from firm innovation and provide firms with high margins during a period of competitive advantage. However, as more firms enter the market segment, the margins will be reduced by the increasing industry capacity. Specialized engineering firms have aided the rapid dispersal of technology. These firms install turnkey chemical production plants, making it difficult for firms to maintain a competitive advantage based on production procedures.

One factor that has a negative effect on the chemical industry is the changing nature of the economy. Although the chemical industry represents 2% of U.S. GDP, this figure has been greatly reduced in the last 30 years. As the growth in the service sector of the economy outpaces the growth in the production sector (which is a major consumer of chemicals), chemicals are growing at a slower rate than the economy as a whole. Because this dynamic is most pronounced in the United States, it is increasingly important for chemical firms to have a global scope of operation and sales.

THE COMPANIES

Dow Chemical Company

Dow manufactures and sell chemicals, plastics materials, and agricultural and other specialized products and services. Dow is a global science and technology-based company that develops and manufactures a portfolio of chemicals, plastics, and agricultural products and service for customers in 168 countries around the world. Dow conducts its operations through subsidiaries and 14 global businesses, including 121 manufacturing sites in 32 countries; it supplies more than 3,500 products through the efforts of its 39,000 employees.

Union Carbide Corporation

Union Carbide operates in two business segments of the chemicals and plastics industry. The specialties and intermediates segment converts basic and intermediate chemicals into a diverse portfolio of chemical and polymers serving industrial customers in many markets. This segment also provides technology services, including licensing, to the oil and gas and petrochemicals industries. The basic chemicals and polymers segment converts hydrocarbon feedstocks, principally liquefied petroleum gas and naphtha, into ethylene or propylene used to manufacture polyethylene, polypropylene, ethylene oxide, and ethylene glycol for sale to third parties, as well as for consumption by Union Carbide's specialties and intermediates segment. Union Carbide, with nearly 12,000 employees worldwide, operates 32 principal manufacturing facilities in 13 countries to provide products to customers in more than 100 countries. In addition to these operations, Union Carbide participates in the global market through 10 principal corporate joint ventures and partnerships.

DEAL TERMS

The deal was announced on August 4, 1999. Dow, which closed at $ 124.68 on August 3, offered 0.537 shares of its stock for each share of Union Carbide stock. This represented a premium of 37% for Union Carbide shareholders; Union Carbide had been trading at $48.81. Union Carbide's market capitalization had been $6.5 billion, but under the terms of the deal, Dow paid $8.9 billion. Following the merger, Dow held 75% of the shares, and Union Carbide held 25%.

PREMERGER

	Dollar Amounts			*Percentage*	
	Dow	*U. Carbide*	*Total*	*Dow*	*U. Carbide*
Share price	$124.68	$ 48.81			
Share outstanding (in millions)	217	133			
Total market value (in billions)	$ 27.1	$ 6.5	$ 33.5	80.6%	19.4%
Exchange Terms	0.537 for	1			

POSTMERGER

Number of shares (million)	217.0	71.4	288.4	75.2%	24.8%

PREMIUM ANALYSIS

Paid to target (in billions) = Bidder Share Price × Exchange Terms × Target Shares
$$= \$124.68 \times 0.537 \times 0.133$$
$$= \$8.9$$

Premium (in billions) $= \$8.9 - \$6.5$
$$= \$2.4$$

Premium over target value $= \$2.4/\$6.5$
$$= 37.2\%$$

Premium over combined premerger value $= \$2.4/\$33.5$
$$= 7.2\%$$

The Federal Trade Commission (FTC) delayed approval of the merger. The FTC agreed to the merger only on the condition that Union Carbide first divest some promising products that has strong market positions that would have been strengthened further by synergies with Dow's product lines.

QUESTIONS

10.2.1 Table P10.2.1 uses Model 10-04 (from our Web sites) to calculate the premerger stand-alone values of Dow and Union Carbide. Dow had a higher net operating margin and a higher growth rate. Because of its higher credit rating it had a somewhat lower cost of capital. Analysts'

TABLE P10.2.1   (Model 10-04) Dow-Union Carbide

	Dow	Union Carbide	Combined (Dow)
Panel A — Value Drivers			
R_0 = Base-year revenues	$18,500	$6,000	$24,500
Super growth period			
m_s = Net operating income margin	10.0%	8.0%	
T_s = Tax rate	35.0%	30.0%	32.0%
g_s = Growth rate	8.6%	6.0%	
d_s = Depreciation	5.5%	5.5%	5.5%
I_{ws} = Working capital requirements	1.0%	1.0%	2.0%
I_{fs} = Capital expenditures	4.0%	5.0%	5.0%
I_{os} = Change in other assets net	0.0%	0.0%	0.0%
k_s = Cost of capital	9.0%	9.4%	9.6%
n = Number of super growth years	10	10	10
Terminal period			
m_c = Net operating income margin	7.1%	7.0%	
T_c = Tax rate	35.0%	30.0%	32.0%
g_c = Growth rate	4.0%	4.0%	
d_c = Depreciation	4.0%	4.0%	4.0%
I_{wc} = Working capital requirements	1.0%	1.0%	1.0%
I_{fc} = Capital expenditures	2.0%	3.0%	2.0%
I_{oc} = Change in other assets net	0.0%	0.0%	0.0%
k_c = Cost of capital	9.0%	9.4%	9.6%
$1 + h$ = calculation relationship = $(1 + g_s)/(1 + k_s)$	0.9963	0.9689	
Panel B—Calculating Values			
Present value of super growth cash flows	$12,691	$2,583	
Present value of terminal value	20,923	4,129	
Enterprise operating value	$33,615	$6,712	
Add: Marketable securities	267	–	267
Entity value	$33,882	$6,712	
Less: Total interest-bearing debt	5,900	2,200	8,100
Equity value	$27,982	$4,512	
Number of shares	660	133	660
Value per share	$ 42.40	$33.93	

reports predicted that the combined operating margin would reflect the benefits of synergies in the total amount of $2 billion. They also predicted that the combined growth rate would raise Union Carbide's growth rate toward the higher of Dow. In the combined column (Dow, the surviving company), of Table P10.2.1, are blanks for the operating income margins and growth rates for the initial period and the terminal period. Make your best estimate to fill in the blanks to calculate the values for the third column of the table.

10.2.2 Use Model 10-02 to test the performance of the Dow–Union Carbide merger based on your results from question 10.2.1.

References

Andrade, Gregor, Mark Mitchell, and Erik Stafford, "New Evidence and Perspectives on Mergers," *Journal of Economic Perspectives* 15, Spring 2001, pp. 130–120.

Berkovitch, Elazar, and M. P. Narayanan, "Motives for Takeovers: An Empirical Investigation," *Journal of Financial & Quantitative Analysis* 8, 2 September 1993, pp. 347–362.

Copeland, Tom, Tim Koller, and Jack Murrin, *Valuation: Measuring and Managing the Values of Companies,* 3rd ed., New York: John Wiley & Sons, 2000.

Cornell, Bradford, "Is the Response of Analysts to Information Consistent with Fundamental Valuation? The Case of Intel," *Financial Management,* 30, Spring 2001, pp. 113–136.

Deutsche Bank, "ExxonMobil: The Emperor's New Groove," September 2001.

ExxonMobil, *Joint Proxy to Shareholders,* April 5, 1999.

Healy, Paul M., Krishna G. Palepu, and Richard S. Ruback, "Does Corporate Performance Improve After Mergers?" *Journal of Financial Economics,* 31, April 1992, pp. 135–175.

Holmstrom, Bengt, and Steven N. Kaplan, "Corporate Governance and Merger Activity in the United States: Making Sense of the 1980s and 1990s," *Journal of Economic Perspectives* 15, Spring 2001, pp. 121–144.

Kaplan, Steven N., "Case Teaching Package for: Paramount–1993," Boston, MA: CaseNet, South Western College Publishing, 1995.

Miller, Merton H., and Franco Modigliani, "Dividend Policy, Growth, and the Valuation of Shares," *Journal of Business* 34, October 1961, pp. 411–433.

Mitchell, Mark L., and J. Harold Mulherin, "The Impact of Industry Shocks on Takeover and Restructuring Activity," *Journal of Financial Economics* 41, June 1996, pp. 193–229.

Stewart, G. Bennett, III, *The Quest for Value,* New York: HarperBusiness, 1991.

U.S. Department of Commerce, *1992 Census of Manufacturers: Concentration Ratios in Manufacturing, Report MC92-S-2,* Washington, DC: Government Printing Office 1996.

U.S. Energy Information Administration, *Performance Profiles of Major Energy Producers,* Washington, DC: Government Printing Office, January 1999, January 2000, January 2001.

Welch, Ivo, "Views of Financial Economists on the Equity Premium and on Professional Controversies," *Journal of Business* 73, October 2000, pp. 501–537.

APPENDIX A

CALCULATING GROWTH RATES

Growth rates play a crucial role in many areas of financial analysis. This appendix describes three ways to calculate the growth rate of a particular variable, such as net operating income (NOI) or stock price, over a series of time. The data in Table A10.1 represent net operating income (NOI) for a company that has grown at a steady annual rate of 20%.

The first method calculates a discrete compound annual growth rate, d, as discussed in the text. It is a geometric average based on the end points of the time series, and is found by dividing the final year by the initial year, then taking, for this example, the tenth root. This is done as follows.

$$(61.9/10.0)^{(1/10)} = 1.20 = 1 + d$$

Thus, the discrete growth rate is 20%. Note that these data plot as a curved line (concave from above) on arithmetic graph paper and as a straight line on semilog paper (Figures A10.1 and A10.2).

The second method calculates a continuously compounded growth rate, c, as shown in Table A10.2. It is found as the slope of the regression line where the natural logarithm of NOI (in this case) is the dependent variable, and the year (designated as 1, 2, 3, . . . rather than as the actual year number such as

TABLE A10.1	Data to Illustrate Growth at 20%
Time Period	*NOI*
1	$10.0
2	12.0
3	14.4
4	17.3
5	20.7
6	24.9
7	29.9
8	35.8
9	43.0
10	51.6
11	61.9

1996) is the independent variable. This is easily accomplished on a personal computer using Excel or other software packages, and even on some handheld calculators. For our data, the slope of the regression equation tells us that the continuously compounded growth rate is 18.23%.

Because of the nature of the data, the only difference in the growth rates is caused by the compounding assumption in each case. The regression method results in a continuously compounded growth rate, the end-points method implicitly assumes annual compounding. This is illustrated using the standard formula relating discrete and compound growth rate: $d = e^c - 1$. We first solve the equation for d, the discrete rate, using the continuously compounded growth rate we obtained in the regression.

$$d = e^{0.182302} - 1 = 1.20 - 1 = 20\%$$

Alternatively, we can solve for c, using the d we obtained in the end-point method:

$$0.20 = e^c - 1$$
$$1.20 = e^c$$

Taking the natural logarithm of both sides of the equation we have:

$$\ln(1.20) = \ln(e^x)$$

Because the natural logarithm of (e^x) is simply x, we have:

$$\ln(1.20) = c = 0.1823$$

These results obtain only for the special case we have illustrated in which the discrete growth rate has no fluctuations. Now consider a case where the NOI does fluctuate, while still exhibiting overall growth, as depicted in Table A10.3.

Figure A10.3 portrays the greater variability. The discrete growth rate, d, using end points, is calculated as:

$$(3,700/1,000)^{(1/10)} = 1.1397 = 1 + d$$

Thus, $d = 14\%$.

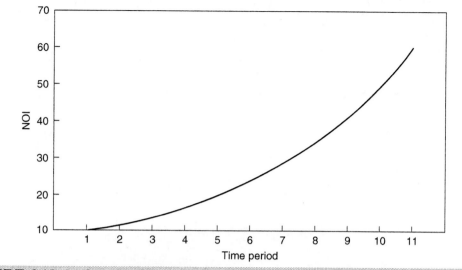

FIGURE A10.1 Constant Growth Rate, 20%

FIGURE A10.2 Constant Growth Rate (20%) Graphed on Semilog Paper

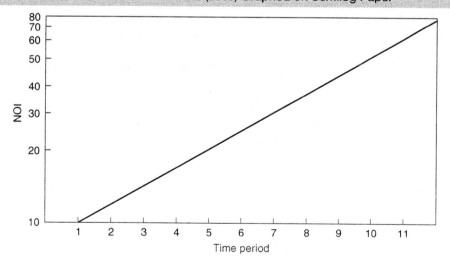

TABLE A10.2 Regression Method of Calculating Growth Rate—Constant Growth

Time Period	NOI	ln (NOI)	Regression Output	
1	10.0	2.302585	Constant	2.120411
2	12.0	2.484906	Std. err. of Y est.	0.000909
3	14.4	2.667228	R squared	0.999997
4	17.3	2.850706	No. of observations	11
5	20.7	3.030133	Degrees of freedom	9
6	24.9	3.214867		
7	29.9	3.397858	X coefficient(s)	0.182302
8	35.8	3.577947	Std. err. of coef.	0.000086
9	43.0	3.761200		
10	51.6	3.943521		
11	61.9	4.125520		

TABLE A10.3 Data to Illustrate Fluctuating Growth Rates

Time Period	NOI($)
1	1,000
2	1,400
3	1,250
4	1,600
5	1,250
6	2,000
7	3,300
8	2,800
9	2,600
10	3,000
11	3,700

FIGURE A10.3 Fluctuating Growth Rates

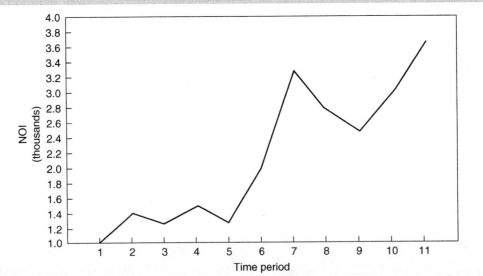

TABLE A10.4 Regression Method of Calculating Growth Rate—Fluctuating Growth

Time Period	NOI	ln (NOI)	Regression Output	
1	1000	6.907755	Constant	6.835528
2	1400	7.244227	Std. err. of Y est.	0.189571
3	1250	7.130898	R squared	0.844064
4	1600	7.377758	No. of observations	11
5	1250	7.130898	Degrees of freedom	9
6	2000	7.600902		
7	3300	8.101677	X coefficient(s)	0.126157
8	2800	7.937374	Std. err. of coef.	0.018074
9	2600	7.863266		
10	3000	8.006367		
11	3700	8.216088		

Using the regression method, the continuously compounded growth rate, c, is 12.6% as shown in Table A10.4. As before, the continuously compounded growth rate is lower than the discrete rate. In this example, the difference is not due solely to the compounding method, but also because the regression method considers the fluctuations. If we again use the standard relationship between d and c, we obtain the discrete rate. Solving for d, using c, we have:

$$d = e^{0.126157} - 1 = 1.13446 - 1 = 13.45\%$$

which is below the end-point result of $d = 14\%$.

Alternatively, the annual compounding 14% result found by the end-points method can be converted into a continuously compounding rate:

$$0.14 = e^c - 1$$
$$1.14 = e^c$$
$$\ln(1.14) = c = .1310 = 13.1\%$$

This is above the 12.6% continuously compounded rate found using the regression method. The end-points method is a useful, rough method of calculating growth rates. However, the end-points method may be seriously flawed if the end values are not representative. The regression method takes into account all data points.

CHAPTER 11
CORPORATE RESTRUCTURING AND DIVESTITURES

⸻ ❧❧❧ ⸻

This chapter and the next discuss the theory and evidence on corporate restructuring and divestitures. We will examine the causes and effects of a firm's decision to dispose of some assets. This chapter emphasizes concepts, theories, and examples of corporate restructuring. Chapter 12 highlights the empirical research on divestitures, as well as related analysis on corporate focus and diversification. The analysis of restructuring and divestitures is an integral complement to the prior chapters on mergers and acquisitions. Indeed, the conceptual and empirical interfaces between M&As and divestitures represent dynamic interactions.

CORPORATE RESTRUCTURING STRATEGIES

An important point to stress when discussing corporate restructuring is that corporate managers face an ever-changing environment. Symmetrically, managers have a variety of strategic options when evaluating the choices to be made in responding to such change. The various forms of corporate restructuring to be discussed in the following chapters illustrate the many possible organizational and financial options available to a corporate manager. The extended discussion of the many available organizational strategies indicates not only the array of options but also the lack of a one-size-fits-all approach to corporate decision making.

To place the subject matter in perspective and to provide a road map for the coming analysis, Table 11.1 sketches a general framework for corporate restructuring and reorganization. As noted in the table, this chapter and the next will address issues tied to asset and ownership structure. Chapter 13 deals with financial restructuring issues such as recapitalization, bankruptcy, and liquidation. Subsequent chapters take up other strategies in the corporate arsenal ranging from joint ventures to share repurchase programs.

DEFINITIONS OF CORPORATE RESTRUCTURING

We begin the discussion of corporate restructuring with some definitions and examples of different types of divestitures. As outlined in Table 11.2, we consider the three main forms of restructuring and divestitures: asset sales, equity carve-outs, and spin-offs. We also describe three restructuring variations: split-ups, tracking stock, and exchange offers.

TABLE 11.1	General Framework for Corporate Restructuring and Reorganization

1. Reorganization of assets and ownership (Chapters 11 and 12)
   a. Asset sales
   b. Equity carve-outs
   c. Spin-offs
2. Reorganizing financial claims (Chapter 13)
   a. Debt-equity exchange offers
   b. Dual-class recapitalizations
   c. Leveraged recapitalizations
   d. Financial reorganization (bankruptcy)
   e. Liquidation
3. Other strategies
   a. Alliances and joint ventures (Chapter 14)
   b. ESOPs and MLPs (Chapter 15)
   c. Going-private and leveraged buyouts (Chapter 16)
   d. Using international markets (Chapter 17)
   e. Share repurchase programs (Chapter 18)

ASSET SALES, EQUITY CARVE-OUTS, AND SPIN-OFFS

An **asset sale** is defined as the sale of a division, subsidiary, product line, or other assets directly to another firm. In an asset sale, the transferred subsidiary or division is absorbed within the organizational structure of the buying firm. The payment in this form of divestiture is usually in cash, although the payment in some asset sales is in the stock of the buying firm. An example of an asset sale in the 1990s was the sale of Snapple by Quaker Oats in May 1997. The buyer was Triarc Companies.

An **equity carve-out** is defined as the offering of a full or partial interest in a subsidiary to the investment public. In effect, an equity carve-out is an IPO of a corporate subsidiary, or a split-off IPO. This mode of restructuring creates a new, publicly traded company with partial or

TABLE 11.2	Types and Definitions of Restructuring and Divestiture Methods

Type of Divestiture	Definition
A. Primary Methods of Divestiture	
Asset sale	Sale of a division, subsidiary, product line, or other assets to another firm, usually for cash.
Equity carve-out	Offering of a full or partial interest in a subsidiary to the investment public; creates a separate, publicly traded company
Spin-off	Pro rata distribution of the shares in a subsidiary to existing shareholders of the parent; creates a separate, publicly traded company
B. Variations of Divestiture Methods	
Split-up	Separation of the company into two or more parts, often via spin-off
Tracking stock	Creation of a separate class of stock with value based on the cash flows of a specific division; sometimes part of a public offering
Exchange offer	Distribution giving shareholders a choice to retain parent or exchange for shares in new subsidiary; creates a separate, publicly traded company

complete autonomy from the parent firm. An example is Pharmacia's carve-out of a 14% stake in Monsanto in October 2000.

A **spin-off** is defined as a pro rata distribution of shares in a subsidiary to the existing shareholders of the parent. In other words, a spin-off is a stock dividend in a subsidiary. No cash is generated by the parent in this form of divestiture, although the debt allocation between the parent and the subsidiary has capital structure implications. This form of restructuring creates a new, publicly traded company that is completely separate from the former parent firm. An example is the spin-off by Sears of its Dean Witter Discover operation in 1993.

These three main forms of corporate restructuring have similarities and differences. All three partially or fully remove assets from the control of the former parent firm. Equity carve-outs and spin-offs create new corporate entities, but asset sales merely transfer assets to another entity.

The different forms of restructuring sometimes are used in tandem or employed sequentially. For example, an equity carve-out can be the first stage of a broader divestiture strategy. Indeed, equity carve-outs often are followed by either a sale of the remaining interest of the subsidiary to another firm or the spin-off of the remaining ownership to shareholders. For example, Ford Motor Company carved out a fraction of its interest in Associates First Capital in May 1996 and later spun off the remaining portion to shareholders in April 1998.

SPLIT-UPS, TRACKING STOCK, AND EXCHANGE OFFERS

In addition to the three main forms of restructuring just presented, there are variations on the main theme. These variations usually are interrelated with the main restructuring methods.

A **split-up** is defined as the separation of a company into two or more parts. This term is applied to a restructuring where the firm is not merely divesting a piece of the firm but is instead strategically breaking up the entire corporate body. This break-up strategy usually is accomplished with one or more equity carve-outs or spin-offs. For example, as the first stage in a split-up in November 1999, Hewlett-Packard offered 15% of Agilent in an equity carve-out. The split-up was completed in June 2000, when Hewlett-Packard spun off the remaining 85% as a stock dividend.

Tracking stock is a separate class of common stock of a parent corporation. The value of this stock is based on the cash flows of a specific division. Tracking stock was first issued in 1984 as part of the acquisition of EDS by General Motors. More recently, the issuance of tracking stock has been employed as part of the public offering of a corporate subsidiary, such as the case of AT&T Wireless described in the following section.

An **exchange offer** is defined as a distribution of the ownership of a subsidiary in which shareholders have a choice to retain the parent shares or exchange their existing shares for the new shares in the subsidiary. An exchange offer resembles a spin-off in that shares are issued in a separate, publicly traded company. The difference is that the shares in the new firm are received only by those holders who opt to trade in the shares in the parent. An example is the Limited's divestiture of Abercrombie and Fitch in 1998.

EXAMPLES OF CORPORATE RESTRUCTURING: AT&T CORPORATION

To more fully describe the different forms of corporate restructuring, we consider various restructuring choices by AT&T Corporation. As outlined in Table 11.3, since 1984, AT&T has employed virtually every possible form of restructuring in the book. A review of AT&T also

TABLE 11.3 Examples of Restructuring and Divestitures: AT&T Corporation

Subsidiary	Date	Divestiture Type	Implementation
Baby Bells	Feb. 1984	Spin-off	AT&T holders get 1 share of each Baby Bell for every 10 shares of AT&T
AT&T Capital	July 1993	Equity carve-out	Raised $107.5 million in a public offering of 14% of the subsidiary
	Oct. 1996	Asset sale	Sold the subsidiary to an investor group for $2.2 billion
Lucent	April 1996	Equity carve-out	Raised $3 billion in a public offering of 18% of the subsidiary
	Sept. 1996	Spin-off	AT&T holders get 0.324 shares of Lucent for each share of AT&T
NCR	Dec. 1996	Spin-off	AT&T holders get 0.0625 shares of NCR for each share of AT&T
Universal Card	April 1998	Asset sale	Sold the credit card subsidiary to Citicorp for $3.5 billion
AT&T Wireless	April 2000	Tracking stock	Raised $10.6 billion in a public offering of 15.6% of the subsidiary
	June 2001	Exchange offer	372 million shares of AT&T exchanged for 438 million shares of AT&T Wireless
	July 2001	Spin-off	AT&T holders get 0.32 shares of AT&T Wireless for each share of AT&T
Liberty Media	August 2001	Spin-off	Holder of 1 tracking share gets 1 share of separate Liberty Media
AT&T Broadband	July 2002	Asset Sale	Shareholders approve sale to Comcast

illustrates how the different restructuring methods interact with corporate strategy and often are used in tandem or employed sequentially.

THE BABY BELL BREAKUP IN 1984

The first major restructuring action by AT&T reported in Table 11.3 is known as the Baby Bell breakup. As discussed in Chapter 7, Appendix A, this breakup was mandated by the federal government as part of telecommunications deregulation in the United States. In the breakup, the parent company, AT&T, maintained its long-distance operations. Local phone service was divided among seven regional operating companies, referred to as the Baby Bells: Ameritech, Bell Atlantic, BellSouth, Nynex, Pacific Telesis, Southwest Bell, and US West.

To implement the organizational breakup, AT&T spun off ownership interests in the seven Baby Bells in February 1984. The share ratio was 1 to 10. As described in Table 11.3, each holder of AT&T got 1 share of each Baby Bell for every 10 shares of AT&T that the shareholder held. For example, someone owning 1,000 shares in AT&T prior to the spin-off would own 1,000 shares in the new AT&T and 100 shares in each of the seven Baby Bells.

RESTRUCTURING IN THE 1990s

During the 1990s, AT&T undertook several restructuring steps as it altered its corporate strategy. These decisions also are outlined in Table 11.3.

In July 1993, AT&T carved out a portion of its interest in AT&T Capital. This raised $107.5 million for the parent and also created a separate, publicly traded firm. Consistent with the tenure of many equity carve-outs, AT&T Capital was later fully severed from the parent firm when an investor group paid $2.2 billion for the entire interest in the subsidiary.

In the mid-1990s, AT&T undertook a substantial split-up. Reversing an ill-fated venture to combine computers with its other operations, the company sequentially broke itself into three publicly traded, global companies. This restructuring was announced by AT&T Chairman Robert E. Allen on September 20, 1995, and implemented the following year.

One part of the split-up was the creation of Lucent Technologies. This company produced telecommunications equipment and also included Bell Labs. The divestiture of Lucent was accomplished in two steps. In April 1996, 18% of the subsidiary was sold to investors in a public offering that raised $3 billion. The remaining ownership in Lucent was spun off to AT&T shareholders in September of the same year. In the spin-off, AT&T holders received 0.324 shares of Lucent for every share held in AT&T.

Another major piece of the AT&T split-up occurred in December 1996, when NCR was fully spun off to shareholders. In the spin-off, AT&T holders received 0.0625 shares of NCR for each share they held in AT&T. NCR had been obtained by AT&T in 1991 as part of the firm's strategy at the time to enter the computer business. The spin-off in 1996 represented a recognition that the strategy had not worked.

To complete its restructuring in the 1990s, AT&T divested Universal Card, its credit card subsidiary, in April 1998. The divestiture was implemented via an asset sale in which Citicorp paid $3.5 billion for the subsidiary.

In addition to implementing the split-up of the company, AT&T underwent a change in top management. Robert Allen was replaced as chairman and CEO by Michael Armstrong. (See "How AT&T Directors Decided It Was Time for Change at the Top," *Wall Street Journal,* October 20, 1997, p. A1.) As the new strategic leader for the company, Mr. Armstrong moved AT&T into the cable industry, which led to subsequent restructuring at the beginning of the following decade.

RESTRUCTURING SINCE 2000

Entering the new millennium, AT&T had interests in three main areas: traditional wireline long-distance phone service, wireless phone, and cable (often referred to as broadband). As a further refinement of its strategy, AT&T sequentially split up these three interests.

AT&T split off its wireless business in multiple steps. In April 2000, a tracking stock in AT&T Wireless was offered to the public. The offering of a 15.6% interest in the subsidiary raised $10.6 billion. As the next step in the complete severance of the subsidiary, AT&T conducted an exchange offer in which shareholders in the parent firm could choose whether to retain AT&T shares or swap their current holdings for shares in AT&T Wireless. Through this offer, 372 million shares of AT&T were exchanged for 438 million shares of AT&T Wireless, a 1 for 1.176 ratio. To complete the divestiture, a spin-off was implemented in July 2001 in which AT&T holders received 0.32 shares in AT&T Wireless for each share held in AT&T.

As another part of its restructuring, AT&T spun off the tracking stock of Liberty Media in August 2001. AT&T had obtained the interest in Liberty in 1999 when it acquired TCI.

The final step in AT&T's latest restructuring involved AT&T Broadband. This portion of the company was obtained when AT&T ventured into cable by acquiring TCI and Media One. As early as October 2000, AT&T had announced its intention of divesting the broadband assets. In July 2001, Comcast made an unsolicited bid for AT&T Broadband. This was followed by an auction where, in addition to Comcast, bidders included AOL and Cox. In December 2001, Comcast was declared the winner of the auction, and in July 2002 shareholders of AT&T and Comcast approved the transaction. A December 21, 2001, story in the *New York Times* details the evolution of the AT&T-Comcast transaction ("AT&T's Cable Deal," p. C1).

OTHER EXAMPLES OF RESTRUCTURING AND DIVESTITURES

To extend the discussion of restructuring, we next cover several other recent examples. In addition to describing the various methods of divestitures, the examples also indicate the choices entailed in the divestiture decision and suggest some of the change forces at play in the restructuring process.

THE AUTO PARTS INDUSTRY: GM-DELPHI AND FORD-VISTEON

In the auto industry, the two major players in the United States, Ford and General Motors, have recently divested their auto parts subsidiaries. We compare the methods by which these divestitures were implemented.

General Motors divested its auto parts subsidiary, Delphi Automotive Systems, in 1999. The divestiture proceeded in two stages. In February, GM offered 17.3% of the subsidiary to the public in an equity carve-out. The separation was completed in May when the remaining 82.7% of Delphi was spun off. GM shareholders received 0.7 shares of Delphi for every share owned in the parent.

Ford Motor Company also spun off its parts-making unit in 2000. The new company was called Visteon. The divestiture was accomplished via a stock dividend in which holders of Ford common stock received one Visteon share for every 7.63 shares they held.

These two divestitures in the auto industry indicate that corporate restructuring can alter long-standing business relations. As noted in a May 25, 1999, article in the *New York Times* ("GM Is Set to Spin Off Parts Division," p. C2), "the spin-off ends a 90-year tradition of vertical integration" at General Motors. The two examples also show that similar restructuring decisions can be accomplished by different means. GM opted for a two-stage divestiture process that employed an equity carve-out and a spin-off, and Ford accomplished its restructuring in one fell swoop with a spin-off.

RESTRUCTURING AT PHILIP MORRIS

Philip Morris recently used a series of acquisitions and divestitures to restructure its operations and implement a changing business strategy. Historically, the company's core business has been tobacco. It has been in the beer business since its purchase of Miller Brewing in 1969. It also has major interests in the food industry stemming from its acquisition of General Foods in 1985 and Kraft Foods in 1988. In December 2000, Philip Morris increased its presence in the food sector by acquiring Nabisco.

As part of its restructuring in 2001, Philip Morris divested a portion of its interest in Kraft Foods. In an equity curve-out in May 2001, Philip Morris offered 16% of Kraft to the public. The offering raised $8.7 billion. According to the prospectus for the offering filed with the SEC, these proceeds were used to pay down some of the debt amassed in the acquisition of Nabisco the previous year.

In a further restructuring move in 2002, Philip Morris sold its Miller Brewing subsidiary. The buyer was South African Breweries, and the asset sale was valued at $5.6 billion. In a somewhat complex transaction reflecting tax matters, the payment to Philip Morris was in the form of stock and the assumption of debt by the buyer. Media coverage considered the transaction a win-win deal in that Philip Morris could implement its new strategic direction, and South African Breweries could increase its scale in order to compete better in a consolidating global brewing industry.(See "Philip Morris Drops Beer to Concentrate Elsewhere: Focus on Food, Tobacco and Expansion," and "Deal for Miller Brewing May Be First in a Series," *New York Times,* May 31, 2002, p. C2.)

The recent divestitures by Philip Morris further illustrate the interaction of strategy and restructuring. The two examples of Kraft and Miller also confirm that the same company often employs different methods of divesting assets.

RESTRUCTURING AT PETE'S BREWING

Pete's Brewing Company is another beer manufacturer that recently has undergone restructuring. The company's restructuring process is described in SEC EDGAR filing DEFM14A, June 24, 1998.

In the early and mid-1990s, the company's Wicked Ale was successful in the craft beer segment of the industry. However, by 1997, sales trends ebbed and the company's management and board began to explore strategic alternatives. The officers and directors believed that greater scale and lower costs were required to remain competitive. Among the options considered were increased scale through (1) acquisition of other craft beer companies, (2) joint ventures, or (3) strategic distribution alliances. The company also considered methods to alter overhead structure or to downsize.

The board and management considered the option of selling the company to a buyer that could facilitate an increase in scale. As part of the exploration of this option, the company engaged Morgan Stanley as an adviser in November 1997. During the next several months, Morgan Stanley contacted 28 potential strategic and financial buyers. From this process, the high bidder was the Gambrinus Company, a privately held beer importer. Gambrinus completed the acquisition of Pete's Brewing in July 1998.

SOME DISCUSSION OF RESTRUCTURING MOTIVES

The various methods of divestitures provided by the examples in this chapter indicate that a firm can restructure in many ways. The variety of divestiture methods also suggest that many motives can exist for corporate restructuring. The many phases of restructuring at AT&T illustrate the direct relation between corporate strategy and corporate restructuring. At the same time, the ongoing restructuring at AT&T indicates the evolving change brought about by forces such as deregulation and technological change.

Corporate focus often is cited as a prime reason for corporate restructuring. The recent sale of the brewery operations at Philip Morris appears consistent with a more focused strategy. However, the example of restructuring as Pete's Brewing Company indicates that even a focused company periodically will review strategic alternatives in response to changing conditions in product markets.

These recent examples relate to research on divestitures by Weston (1989) of earlier time periods. He found that the reasons for divestitures included changing strategies, reversing mistakes, and learning. Weston (1989, p.76) concluded that the rates of acquisitions and divestitures in the U. S. economy reflected "a healthy and dynamic interplay between the strategic planning of U. S. companies and continually shifting market forces."

In general, firms restructure to remain competitive and to respond to the change forces in the economy. To further analyze the causes and effects of corporate restructuring, we next address some theoretical issues related to corporate divestitures. The following two related questions will be addressed: (1) Why might divestitures create wealth? (2) Why do divestitures occur?

WHY MIGHT DIVESTITURES CREATE WEALTH?

In this section, we synthesize the many possible sources of wealth gains from corporate divestitures by borrowing from the primary theories in corporate finance. We start with the concepts developed by Modigliani and Miller (1958, 1961) that frame research in the area. We build on this foundation by considering the information effects and incentive changes related to corporate restructuring.

MODIGLIANI, MILLER, AND IRRELEVANCE

Franco Modigliani and Merton Miller developed the foundations of modern corporate finance theory in their research papers on capital structure and dividends that were published in 1958 and 1961. The heart of their analysis argued that in a world of zero transaction or information costs, the value of a firm is independent of its choice of debt or equity or its dividend policy. In other words, the products, services, and ideas offered by a firm, rather than financial doctoring, determine value. In concurrent but independent work, Ronald Coase (1960) offered a similar theory of legal liability and ownership, and William Vickrey (1961) applied a related framework to auction design.

The theory of Modigliani and Miller (1958, 1961), Coase (1960), and Vickrey (1961) can be applied to corporate restructuring and divestitures. Their concepts suggest that in a world of zero information and transaction costs, corporate organization is irrelevant. In other words, whether a firm is comprised of two divisions, or the two divisions are instead separate firms, the combined value will be the same.

The lessons from the theoretical research for corporate restructuring are twofold. First, a corporate manager cannot improve firm value by arbitrarily chopping a company into pieces. Second, the theory guides analysis of restructuring toward factors such as information and transaction costs as possible sources of wealth creation. We next consider the role of incentives and information costs in corporate restructuring.

CORPORATE RESTRUCTURING, INCENTIVES, AND EFFICIENCY

Table 11.4 outlines several theories that are relevant to the study of corporate restructuring. One body of research addresses the importance of the incentive structure and the monitoring costs in an efficiently operating corporation. Alchian and Demsetz (1972) suggested that the essence of a firm is team production where the joint production of the firm's assets exceeds the

TABLE 11.4 Theories of Corporate Restructuring

Theory	Research Paper	Concepts Pertinent to Corporate Restructuring
Incentives/ Monitoring Costs	Alchian and Demsetz (1972) Jensen and Meckling (1976)	Corporate governance geared toward monitoring performance; restructuring can enhance monitoring
Information/ Signaling	Myers and Majluf (1984) Nanda (1991)	Corporate managers possess information not known to the market; restructuring can signal information
Transaction Costs	Coase (1937) Williamson (1975) Klein, Crawford, and Alchian (1978)	Choice between firm and market a function of transaction costs; restructuring responds to changes in transaction costs

feasible output of the assets in separate uses. In such a setting, the monitoring of inputs is important and is performed by the residual claimants of the firm—the shareholders. An important monitoring function is assessing the performance of the firm's management.

Jensen and Meckling (1976) offered a similar model of the firm that incorporates the interaction among managers, stockholders, and bondholders. In their model, the optimal scale of the firm is determined by the monitoring and bonding costs of writing contracts among these interacting parties.

The concepts presented in work such as Alchian and Demsetz (1972) and Jensen and Meckling (1976) suggest one reason why corporate divestitures might create wealth. If the divestitures improve managerial incentives or better enable shareholders to monitor managerial performance, then the separation of a corporation into different pieces can improve the efficiency of operations and thereby increase the combined value of the assets.

CORPORATE RESTRUCTURING AND INFORMATION

Another body of research considers the importance of information in corporate valuation. Myers and Majluf (1984) pointed out that in the modern corporation, managers often know more about a firm's investment opportunities than outside investors do. In this setting of asymmetric information, management actions regarding financing or restructuring can convey information about firm value to investors.

Nanda (1991) extended the model of Myers and Majluf (1984) to a particular form of restructuring, an equity carve-out. Nanda (1991) noted that equity carve-outs have two aspects. Carve-outs create a new public entity but also raise money for the parent. Nanda (1991) suggested that carve-outs also convey the further piece of information that the parent firm has chosen not to raise money by issuing its own shares. Nanda (1991) predicted that the announcement of an equity carve-out would convey positive information to the market about the parent firm's value.

To summarize this section, we have considered the important question regarding why corporate restructuring and divestitures might create wealth. The irrelevance propositions of Modigliani and Miller (1958, 1961) alert the corporate manager that random changes in corporate organizational structure cannot be expected to be wealth enhancing. Subsequent conceptual analysis suggested that incentive changes or information revelation are two plausible sources of wealth creation from corporate restructuring. We present the empirical evidence on restructuring and wealth creation in Chapter 12.

WHY DO DIVESTITURES OCCUR?

In addition to addressing why restructuring has wealth implications, related theoretical research provides a framework to assess why restructuring takes place at all. The beginnings of such analysis are usually traced to Coase's (1937) work on the nature of the firm. Coase (1937) modeled the choice to contract within a firm or across a market as a function of transaction costs. An implication of his model is that restructuring will occur when change forces such as technology alter the relative costs of using the market vis-à-vis operating within a firm.

Subsequent analyses by Williamson (1975) and Klein, Crawford, and Alchian (1978) proposed that an important factor in the choice between market transactions and firms is the presence of specialized assets. An example of a specialized asset is an oil pipeline in a remote location. When deciding whether to build the pipeline, the owners would consider their expected risks and rewards from the investment. However, once the pipeline is laid in the ground, much of the investment is a sunk cost. In effect, incentives change once specialized assets are in place.

According to Williamson (1975) and Klein, Crawford, and Alchian (1978), such specialized assets are subject to contracting problems. For example, a customer of the pipeline such as an oil refinery might threaten to renege on a written agreement once the pipeline investment was sunk. Given that the enforcement of contracts is costly, an alternative is for the pipeline and the refinery to integrate vertically. Williamson (1975) and Klein, Crawford, and Alchian (1978) predicted that the more specialized the assets are, the more likely it is that vertical integration will occur.

We next review two industry studies to extend the analysis of corporate restructuring, transaction costs, and change forces. We first study evidence from the petrochemical industry and then review research on the natural gas industry.

CORPORATE RESTRUCTURING AND TRANSACTION COSTS: THE PETROCHEMICAL INDUSTRY

This section reviews research by Fan (1996, 2000) on organizational restructuring in the petrochemical industry. Fan considered the effect of transaction costs and uncertainty on the extent of vertical integration between petrochemical firms and their energy feedstock during the 1960s, 1970s, 1980s, and 1990s.

The petrochemical industry can be described by a vertical chain that begins with energy inputs, traces through primary petrochemicals, and includes intermediate products. For example, natural gas can be used to extract methane for fuel but also is used to develop petrochemicals such as methanol and ethylene. Ultimate products include ammonia, plastics, and polyester.

Fan (1996) reported significant changes over time in the extent of vertical integration between petrochemical firms and energy inputs. Prior to the OPEC oil embargo that occurred in 1973, Fan (1996, Figure 1, p.10) found that only 13% of the petrochemical firms in his sample owned oil and gas assets. Following the oil embargo, this fraction increased to more than 50%. However, by 1992, the fraction of petrochemical firms with integration into oil and gas had reverted back to 26%.

Fan (2000) argued that the changing extent of vertical integration reflected the uncertainty in input prices brought about by the oil embargo. Such uncertainty and actual energy price volatility made contracts more difficult to write and to enforce. Such transaction cost factors shifted the least-cost method of transacting away from market contracts and toward internal firm arrangements. These results from the petrochemical industry also support Jensen's (1993) argument that much of the restructuring in the 1980s can be traced back to OPEC.

These findings indicate that transaction costs are an important determinant of corporate restructuring. The heightened input volatility following OPEC and the subsequent reduction in the level and volatility of energy prices in more recent years have affected the decision whether to integrate vertically. By implication, such change forces have affected the decisions to merge or divest.

Restructuring decisions at DuPont provide a specific example of the patterns in the level of integration between the energy and chemical sectors. In 1981, DuPont, a major chemical company, acquired Conoco, an energy producer. The acquisition price was $ 7.54 billion, which Ruback (1982) noted was the largest acquisition in U.S. history at the time.

Consistent with the trends noted by Fan (1996, 2000), DuPont subsequently divested its interest in Conoco. In October 1998, DuPont offered 30% of Conoco in an equity carve-out. The remaining 70% was divested in an exchange offer in August 1999.

More recently, Conoco agreed to merge with Philips Petroleum. The merger occurred in the midst of significant consolidation in the energy industries with deals including BP and Amoco in 1998, Exxon and Mobil in 1999, Total Fina and Elf Aquitaine in 2000, and Chevron and Texaco in 2001. The Conoco and Philips agreement was announced on November 19, 2001, and the shareholders of both companies approved the transaction in March 2002. In addition to illustrating an example of transaction cost theory, the evolving ownership of Conoco suggests that change forces inducing divestitures in one industry also can affect mergers in related sectors.

CORPORATE RESTRUCTURING AND CHANGE FORCES: THE NATURAL GAS INDUSTRY

Similar to petrochemicals, the natural gas industry can be described by a series of vertical steps beginning with production in the field; followed by transmission through pipelines; and continuing to distribution to end users such as power plants, factories, and residential users. In the past 100 years, the organizational arrangements in the natural gas industry have varied significantly.

Mulherin (1986) noted that at the beginning of the twentieth century, most of the natural gas production in the United States was in the Appalachian area near the consumers in the Midwest and Northeast. In the 1920s, however, major gas finds occurred in the Southwest. To transmit the gas to the major population centers, several new, large pipelines were constructed. Consistent with transaction cost theory such as that of Klein, Crawford, and Alchian (1978), these new pipelines were owned by production and distribution companies such as Columbia Gas and Electric, Cities Service Company, and Standard Oil Company of New Jersey.

As described by Mulherin (1986), however, federal regulation in the 1930s induced restructuring in the natural gas industry. In 1935, the Public Utility Holding Company Act led to divestitures in the industry. This piece of legislation empowered the Securities and Exchange Commission to vertically dissolve the holding companies in the natural gas and electric utility industries. Of the four major holding companies in the natural gas industry at the time, only

Columbia Gas and Electric was allowed to continue as a holding company. However, even Columbia was required to divest a major transmission entity, the Panhandle Eastern Pipeline Company.

A related piece of federal legislation was the Natural Gas Act of 1938. This legislation gave the Federal Power Commission the authority to establish the rates charged by interstate natural gas pipelines. To implement this authority, the Federal Power Commission imposed original cost rate regulation. This created a strong disincentive for interstate pipelines to produce their own gas. Any in-house production would enter the rate base at the original cost, and any gas purchased from an unaffiliated producer would be put in the rate calculation at the actual price paid. Subsequent to this legislation, a sustained decline occurred in vertical integration between natural gas production and transmission.

To summarize the historical discussion, the natural gas industry in the United States illustrates the effect of change forces on corporate restructuring. Energy discoveries in the 1920s, combined with technological changes, led to vertical integration in the industry from production, through transmission, to distribution. However, federal regulation in the 1930s induced a reversal of the vertical integration and induced a trend of divestitures.

This discussion of the natural gas industry is more than a mere historical exercise of transaction cost economics. The natural gas industry of today is experiencing a further set of changes in federal regulation. As discussed in the Appendix to this chapter, these ongoing regulatory changes are having noticeable effects on the structure of the natural gas industry that have direct parallels to the previous century. The changing regulatory environment has induced mergers and divestitures in natural gas and related industries.

Summary

Corporate restructuring can take many forms. The three primary methods of divesting assets are asset sales, equity carve-outs, and spin-offs. Variations on these main themes include split-ups, tracking stock, and exchange offers. Corporations such as AT&T often employ several of these restructuring methods in tandem or sequentially.

Conceptually, corporate finance theory warns managers from arbitrarily attempting to improve firm value by breaking a firm into pieces. Theory suggests that corporate restructuring and divestitures can create value by improving incentives and thereby altering corporate efficiency. Divestiture decisions also can reveal information to outside investors.

An important query is why restructuring occurs. Such a query shows the interaction between decisions to merge and decisions to divest. Ultimately, the question reduces to the expected effects on the costs of operating within a firm vis-à-vis across markets.

Questions

11.1 What are the three primary forms of corporate restructuring and divestitures?

11.2 What are the three variations on the methods of corporate restructuring and divestitures? How do these variations interact with the primary divestiture methods?

11.3 Using AT&T Corporation, provide an example of each restructuring method and describe how each method is implemented.

11.4 What are two theoretical reasons why divestitures might create wealth?

11.5 Why might energy price volatility be associated with corporate restructuring?

11.6 How can changes in regulation affect the rate of restructuring activity?

References

Alchian, Armen A., and Harold Demsetz, "Production, Information Costs, and Economic Organization," *American Economic Review* 62, December 1972, pp. 777–795.

Coase, R. H., "The Nature of the Firm," *Economica* 4, November 1937, pp. 386–405.

Coase, R. H., "The Problem of Social Cost," *Journal of Law and Economics* 3, October 1960, pp. 1–44.

Fan, Po-Hung Joseph, "Essays on Vertical Integration and Corporate Governance," Ph.D. Dissertation, University of Pittsburgh, 1996.

Fan, Po-Hung Joseph, "Price Uncertainly and Vertical Integration: Examination of Petrochemical Firms," *Journal of Corporate Finance* 6, 2000, pp. 345–376.

Jensen, Michael C., "The Modern Industrial Revolution, Exit, and the Failure of Internal Control Systems," *Journal of Finance* 48, 1993, pp. 831–880.

Jensen, Michael C., and William H. Meckling, "Theory of the Firm: Managerial Behavior, Agency Costs, and Ownership Structure," *Journal of Financial Economics* 3, 1976, pp. 305–360.

Klein, Benjamin, Robert G. Crawford, and Armen A. Alchian, "Vertical Integration, Appropriable Rents, and the Competitive Contracting Process," *Journal of Law and Economics* 21, October 1978, pp. 297–326.

Modigliani, Franco, and Merton H. Miller, "The Cost of Capital, Corporation Finance, and the Theory of Investment," *American Economic Review* 48, June 1958, pp. 261–297.

Modigliani, Franco, and Merton H. Miller, "Dividend Policy, Growth, and the Valuation of Shares," *Journal of Business* 34, October 1961, pp. 411–433.

Mulherin, J. Harold, "Specialized Assets, Governmental Regulation, and Organizational Structure in the Natural Gas Industry," *Journal of Institutional and Theoretical Economics* 142, 1986, pp. 528–541.

Myers, Stewart C., and Nicholas S. Majluf, "Corporate Financing and Investment Decisions When Firms Have Information That Investors Do Not Have," *Journal of Financial Economics*, 13, 1984, pp. 187–221.

Nanda, Vikram, "On the Good News in Equity Carve-Outs," *Journal of Finance* 46, December 1991, pp. 1717–1737.

Ruback, Richard S., "The Conoco Takeover and Stockholder Returns," *Sloan Management Review* 23, Winter 1982, pp. 13–33.

Vickrey, William, "Counterspeculation, Auctions, and Competitive Sealed Tenders," *Journal of Finance* 16, March 1961, pp. 8–37.

Weston, J. Fred, "Divestitures: Mistakes or Learning," *Journal of Applied Corporate Finance* 2, 1989, pp. 68–76.

Williamson, Oliver E., *Markets and Hierarchies*, New York: Free Press: 1975.

RESTRUCTURING IN THE DIVERSIFIED NATURAL GAS INDUSTRY IN THE 1990s

This appendix studies the restructuring in the diversified natural gas industry during the 1990s It provides examples of the various forms of divestitures discussed in Chapter 11 and notes the interrelation between divestitures and other forms of corporate reorganization such as mergers and acquisitions. The appendix also considers the major change forces at play in the natural gas industry during the 1990s and the effects of such forces on the strategies of the firms in the industry.

The sample of firms studied in this appendix comes from the broader analysis of 59 industries by Mulherin and Boone (2000). The sample begins with the firms in the diversified natural gas industry of the Value Line Investment Survey as of the first quarter of 1990. The restructuring activities of those firms during the 1990s were determined by searching LexisNexis, the *Wall Street Journal*, and other financial media. Further detail was obtained from the SEC EDGAR fillings. The analysis reported in the appendix extends the original work by Mulherin and Boone (2000) by considering restructuring events through the year 2000.

THE DIVERSIFIED NATURAL GAS INDUSTRY

The Value Line Investment Survey defines the diversified natural gas industry as "firms with at least two major business segments within the overall natural gas sector that spans from the wellhead in the field to end users such as residences, factories, and power generators." These segments include (1) local distribution, (2) pipeline transmission, (3) gathering and processing, and (4) exploration and production.

The 22 firms that comprised the diversified natural gas industry in 1990 are listed in Table A11.1. A large number of the firms were involved in both pipeline transmission and petroleum exploration and production. Many also were engaged in local gas distribution. Several firms had other energy business interests ranging from coal, to oil field services, to liquid fuels. Some firms had more distinct segments, such as Eastern Enterprise's barge fleet; Tenneco's automotive parts, farm equipment, and shipbuilding; and Williams Companies' fiber-optics system.

INDUSTRY AND REGULATORY BACKGROUND

In 1999, the Value Line Investment Survey described the diversified natural gas industry by the phrase, "It's a MADD World" (p. 43). This world was one where mergers, acquisitions, dispositions, and divestitures (MADD) had been and were expected to continue to be a feature of the industry.

To understand the ongoing restructuring in the diversified natural gas industry, a sketch of the regulatory changes in the 1990s faced by natural gas and related energy sectors is useful. For a detailed treatment, see Joskow (2000, 2001). For an extended discussion of the Public Utility Holding Company Act, see U.S. SEC (1995). For the analysis of the effects of changes in natural gas regulation, see Hollas(1999) and Leitzinger and Collette (2002). For analysis of electric utility deregulation, see Leggio and Lien (2000) and Besanko, D'Souza, and Thiagarajan (2001).

Regulation of the natural gas industry and related sectors such as electric utilities is conducted at the state and the federal level. Federal regulation affecting these sectors is administered by the Federal Energy Regulatory Commission (FERC) and other agencies such as the SEC, which is responsible for the Public Utility Holding Company Act (PUHCA). Several changes in regulation and in the approach of the regulators impacted the diversified natural gas industry in the 1990s.

A major piece of federal regulation in the 1990s was the Energy Policy Act of 1992. As noted by Joskow (2000, p. 23), this act removed many of PUHCA's barriers to ownership in electric power and also expanded FERC's authority in mandating the provision of energy transmission service.

TABLE A11.1 The Diversified Natural Gas Industry in 1990

Firm	Business Areas
Arkla Inc.	Natural gas pipeline; petroleum exploration and production
Burlington Resources	Natural gas pipeline; petroleum exploration and production
Coastal Corp.	Natural gas pipeline; petroleum exploration and production; oil refining
Columbia Gas	Local distribution; natural gas pipeline; petroleum production
Consolidated Natural Gas	Natural gas pipeline; petroleum exploration and production; utility subsidiaries
Eastern Enterprises	Natural gas distribution; coal; barge fleet
Enron Corp.	Natural gas pipeline; petroleum exploration and production; liquid fuels; cogeneration
ENSERCH Corp.	Local distribution; natural gas pipeline; petroleum production
Equitable Resources	Local distribution; natural gas pipeline; petroleum production
Hadson Corp.	Petroleum production; natural gas marketing; power generation
KN Energy	Local distribution; natural gas pipeline; natural gas storage
Mitchell Energy	Natural gas pipeline; petroleum exploration
National Fuel Gas	Local distribution; natural gas pipeline; petroleum exploration and production
ONEOK Inc.	Local distribution; natural gas pipeline; petroleum exploration and production
Panhandle Eastern	Natural gas pipeline; liquid natural gas
Seagull Energy	Natural gas pipeline; gathering and marketing; petroleum exploration and production
Sonat Inc.	Natural gas pipeline; offshore drilling; oil field services
Southwestern Energy	Local distribution; natural gas pipeline; petroleum exploration and production
Tenneco Inc.	Natural gas pipeline; construction and farm equipment; shipbuilding; automotive parts
Transco Energy	Natural gas pipeline; petroleum exploration and production; coal
Valero Energy	Natural gas pipeline; petroleum refinery
Williams Cos.	Natural gas and oil pipelines; fiber-optics telecommunications system

FERC Order 636 in 1992 implemented the open transmission policy and the unbundling of energy production, transmission, and distribution. A story in the *New York Times* ("Arkla Selling Unit to Seagull Energy," p. 5) described the change brought about by unbundling.

Under the current system, pipeline companies can charge users a fee that reflects the cost of natural gas and services like transportation and storage, whether or not customers use the services. Under the rules approved in April and effective next winter, the companies must separate the cost of their sales and transportation services so customers can be charged only for the services they use. (November 18, 1992, p. 5)

FERC Orders 888 and 889 further opened energy transmission to third parties in 1996.

Contemporaneous with these regulatory changes, the various federal agencies began to take a more lenient approach toward mergers in the natural gas and electric utility sectors. Joskow (2000, p. 59) noted that FERC began to focus on competition, rather than structural or technical standards, in its review of proposed mergers. The SEC adopted a similar, broader framework toward the implications of PUHCA for gas and electric mergers (U.S. SEC, 1995). But also see, "Court Rules SEC Exceed Authority with AEP Merger," *Wall Street Journal*, January 21, 2002, p. A8.

These changes in the United States and similar changes brought about by privatization in Europe have been followed by significant restructuring activity in the natural gas and electric utility sectors. See, for example, a January 23, 1996, *Financial Times* article ("Market Deregulation Is Reshaping Power Industry," July 23, 1996, p. 22). The following sections describe the divestiture and merger activity in the diversified natural gas industry in the 1990s.

RESTRUCTURING ACTIVITY IN THE 1990s: DIVESTITURES AND MERGERS

This section reports the restructuring activity for the 22 firms in the diversified natural gas industry during the 1990s. We first consider spin-offs and equity carve-outs and then discuss asset sales. Together, the analysis indicates that 10 of the 22 firms (45%) engaged in major asset divestitures during the 1990s. We then conclude this section with analysis of the mergers and acquisitions in the industry over the same time period.

Spin-Offs and Equity Carve-Outs

Table A11.2 reports the spin-offs and equity carve-outs for the sample firms in the 1990s. Six of the firms undertook equity carve-outs, where the parent firm sold an interest in a subsidiary to the investing public. Most of the carve-outs entailed energy assets. However, Tenneco used a series of equity carve-outs to sequentially divest its entire interest in J.I. Case, its farm equipment subsidiary.

The divestiture of El Paso Natural Gas by Burlington Resources also evolved sequentially. The parent announced the divestiture in 1991. In March 1992, 15% of El Paso was carved out to investors. The remaining 85% was spun off to the shareholders of Burlington Resources in July 1992. El Paso undertook a number of acquisitions subsequent to becoming a separate, publicly traded corporation.

The other spin-off in Table A11.2 was related to the acquisition of ENSERCH Corporation by Texas Utilities. In the merger negotiations between the target and the bidder, the management of Texas Utilities indicated that it was not interested in acquiring the exploration assets of ENSERCH. (See TUC Holding Co., SEC EDGAR Form 424B3, September 27, 1996, p. 32.) Hence, Enserch Exploration was spun off on the same day that the merger closed.

Asset Sales

Table A11.3 reports the major asset sales by the sample firms during the 1990s. The table reports the parent and the subsidiary in the divestiture, as well as the buyer and the buyer's industry. The sales generally

represent a transfer of energy assets in one segment of the industry to a buyer in that same segment. Examples include SONAT's sale of oil field services, Tenneco's sale of energy, and Williams Companies' sale of coal.

The divestiture by Valero Energy also transferred assets within the energy sector. In a somewhat complex transaction described in a February 1, 1997, story in the *New York Times* ("PG&E to Buy Valero Energy, a Marketer of Natural Gas," p. 33), Valero merged its natural gas pipeline with PG&E Corporation. At the same time, Valero spun off its refinery operations as an independent, publicly traded company that maintained the Valero name. This transaction was one of the many cases of an electric utility entering into the natural gas sector in the second half of the 1990s. We discuss several other cases in the following section on mergers.

Mergers and Acquisitions

The substantial rate of divestiture activity in the diversified natural gas industry during the 1990s was matched by the rate of mergers during the same period. As reported in Table A11.4, 11 of the 22 sample firms (50%) were involved in a major merger or acquisition between 1995 and 2000.

Note that some of the sample firms changed their names prior to or in conjunction with the merger activity. Two of the acquired firms had changed their names prior to merging: Arkla had become Noram Energy, and Panhandle Eastern had become Panergy. Two other firms adopted the name of their merger partner: KN Energy took the name Kinder Morgan, and Seagull Energy took the name Ocean Energy.

The buyers in the acquisitions were of two types. Six of the acquiring firms were from the electric utility sector. The other five mergers were between firms in the natural gas sector. As noted in an SEC filing related to the ENSERCH–Texas Utilities deal, the mergers reflected "trends toward consolidation in the electric utility industry, vertical integration in the natural gas industry, and potential for consolidation and integration of the natural gas and electric utility industries." (See TUC Holding Co. SEC EDGAR Form S-4, September 20, 1996, p. 29.)

DEREGULATION AND RESTRUCTURING

The significant amount of restructuring in the diversified natural gas industry illustrates the effect of change forces on the rate of restructuring activity.

TABLE A11.2 Spin-Offs and Carve-Outs in the Diversified Natural Gas Industry During the 1990s

Firm	Spin-Off or Carve-Out?	Announce Date	Completion Date	Divestiture Type	Subsidiary/Division
Arkla Inc.					
Burlington Resources	Yes	Sep. 23, 1991	July 1, 1992	Carve-out/spin-off	El Paso Natural Gas
Coastal Corp.					
Columbia Gas					
Consolidated Natural Gas					
Eastern Enterprises					
Enron Corp.	Yes	June 1, 1992	July 30, 1992	Equity carve-out	Enron Liquids Pipeline
ENSERCH Corp.	Yes	Apr. 15, 1996	Aug. 5, 1997	Spin-off	Enserch Exploration
Equitable Resources					
Hadson Corp.	Yes	Jan. 4, 1990	Jan. 31, 1990	Equity carve-out	Hadson Energy Resources
KN Energy					
Mitchell Energy					
National Fuel Gas					
ONEOK Inc.					
Panhandle Eastern					
Seagull Energy					
Sonat Inc.	Yes	Apr. 13, 1993	May 28, 1993	Equity carve-out	Sonat Offshore Drilling
Southwestern Energy					
Tenneco Inc.	Yes	Apr. 25, 1994	Mar. 9, 1996	Equity carve-out	J.I. Case farm equipment
Transco Energy					
Valero Energy					
Williams Cos.	Yes	Oct. 23, 1992	Jan. 13 1993	Equity carve-out	Coal Seam Gas Royalty Trust

TABLE A11.3 Asset Sales in the Diversified Natural Gas Industry During the 1990s

Firm	Subsidiary	Announce Date	Completion Date	Buyer	Buyer Industry
Arkla Inc.	Arkla Exploration	Nov. 11, 1992	Dec. 31, 1992	Seagull Energy	Natural gas
Burlington Resources					
Coastal Corp.					
Columbia Gas					
Consolidated Natural Gas					
Eastern Enterprises					
Enron Corp.					
ENSERCH Corp.					
Equitable Resources					
Hadson Corp.					
KN Energy					
Mitchell Energy					
National Fuel Gas					
ONEOK Inc.					
Panhandle Eastern					
Seagull Energy	ENSTAR gas pipeline	July 15, 1999	Nov. 2, 1999	Semco Energy	Gas distribution
Sonat Inc.	Telco Oilfield Svcs.	Jan. 6, 1992	Apr. 23, 1992	Baker Hughes	Oilfield services
Southwestern Energy					
Tenneco Inc.	Tenneco Energy	Mar. 21, 1996	Dec. 12, 1996	El Paso Energy	Natural gas
Transco Energy					
Valero Energy	Natural gas pipeline	Nov. 22, 1996	June 20, 1997	PG&E	Electric and gas utility
Williams Cos.	Transco Coal	May 16, 1995	May 31, 1995	James River Coal	Coal

TABLE A11.4 Mergers & Acquisitions in the Diversified Natural Gas Industry During the 1990s

Firm	Event	Announce Date	Completion Date	Buyer/ Merger Partner	Buyer Industry
Arkla Inc. (Noram Energy)	Acquired	Aug. 12, 1996	Aug. 6, 1997	Houston Industries	Electric utility
Burlington Resources					
Coastal Corp.					
Columbia Gas	Acquired	June 7, 1999	Nov. 1, 2000	NiSource	Electric utility
Consolidated Natural Gas	Acquired	Feb. 22, 1999	Jan. 28, 2000	Dominion Resources	Electric utility
Eastern Enterprises	Acquired	Nov. 5, 1999	Nov. 8, 2000	KeySpan Corp.	Gas distribution
Enron Corp.					
ENSERCH Corp.	Acquired	Apr. 15, 1996	Aug. 5, 1997	Texas Utilities	Electric utility
Equitable Resources					
Hadson Corp.	Acquired	Feb. 10, 1995	May 15, 1995	LG&E Energy	Electric utility
KN Energy	Merger	Feb. 22, 1999	Oct. 7, 1999	Kinder Morgan	Natural gas
Mitchell Energy					
National Fuel Gas					
ONEOK Inc.					
Panhandle Eastern (Panergy)	Acquired	Nov. 25, 1996	June 18, 1997	Duke Power	Electric utility
Seagull Energy	Merger	Nov. 26, 1998	Mar. 30, 1999	Ocean Energy	Natural gas
Sonat Inc.	Acquired	Mar. 13, 1999	Oct. 25, 1999	El Paso Energy	Natural gas
Southwestern Energy					
Tenneco Inc.					
Transco Energy	Acquired	Dec. 12, 1994	May 1, 1995	Williams Cos.	Natural gas
Valero Energy					
Williams Cos.					

In particular, deregulation was an important impetus for the changing structure of the industry during the 1990s.

Restructuring as a Response to Deregulation

A number of the companies in the industry cited specific regulatory changes as the reasons for restructuring. One change was the movement from cost-based pricing to unbundled services in natural gas transmission induced by rulings such as FERC Order 636. For example, commenting on Arkla's 1992 sale of its exploration assets in a *New York Times* story, a company spokesperson stated that FERC Order 636 "would change the competitive rules of the natural gas exploration business and that the company would now focus on its pipelines network" (November 18, 1992, p. 5). Similar factors were cited by Noram Energy (the successor to Arkla) as being part of the underlying strategy behind its merger with Houston Industries in 1997. (See Houston Industries, SEC EDGAR Form S-4, September 4, 1996, p. 30.)

Both Panergy (the target) and Duke Power (the bidder) cited deregulation as the motivating force behind their combination of an electric utility and a natural gas company in 1997. In a filing related to the merger, Panergy gave reasons for the merger from the perspective of a natural gas company:

> The natural gas and electric industries have been undergoing a fundamental transformation toward increased competition over the past several years, initiated, in the case of the natural gas industry, as a result of the issuance by FERC in 1991 of Order 636, which further deregulated the natural gas business and created a more competitive environment in the natural gas industry. (See Duke Power, SEC EDGAR Form S-4, March 13, 1997, p. 34.)

On page 32 of the same filing, Duke motivated the merger from the perspective of an electric utility:

> The electric utility industry has been undergoing dramatic structural change for several years. This rapid evolution has been marked by the Energy Policy Act of 1992 and the issuance of FERC in 1996 of Orders 888 and 889, which further opened the transmission systems of electric utilities to use by third parties.

According to the comments in the filing, Duke aims to use the merger, "to better compete in this changing and more competitive environment."

The financial press also cites the competition induced by deregulation as the underlying motivation for much of the restructuring in the natural gas and electric utility sectors. As a precursor to its merger with KeySpan, an August 17, 1999, story in the *New York Times* ("Eastern Gas Utility May Offer Itself for Sale," p. C4) noted that Eastern Enterprises might "put itself up for sale to stay competitive in the region's deregulating energy markets" (August 17, 1999, p. C4). Commenting on the bid by Dominion Resources for Consolidated Natural Gas, a February 23, 1998, story in the *Times-Picayune* ("Virginia Company Will Purchase CNG; No Cuts Planned in New Orleans," p. C1) stated, "The strategy is to prepare for deregulation, when many customers are expected to be up for grabs"(February 23, 1999, p. c1). Discussing the Columbia Energy–NiSource union, a February 29, 2000, story in the *Washington Post* ("Columbia Energy Agrees to Takeover," p. E1) reported that the merger reflects:

> electric power and natural gas companies struggling to come up with the right combination of strengths to survive a major shakeout in an industry that is shifting from a system of regional monopolies to nationwide competition. (February 29, 2000, p. E1)

In addition to the view that deregulation mandated new strategies, commentators also observed that the uncertainty associated with deregulation precluded obvious, uni-dimensional strategic choices. As described in a December 10, 1996, article in the *New York Times*, ("A New Breed of Power Broker," p. D1) a utility consultant observed, "Nobody has a crystal ball that shows the winning strategy, so people will be trying different kinds of combinations" (December 10, 1996, p. D1). This view is echoed in another article in the *New York Times* ("Acquirers Take on Greater Risks to Become More Competitive in a New-Era Utilities Business," p. C9):

> Utilities are changing rapidly. Some are selling their power plants and shrinking to become mainly transmission companies; others are buying and building power plants to become major sellers of electricity and natural gas; some are seeking mergers to become bigger so as to compete more effectively. (November 3, 1998, p. C9)

One clear example of this adaptive approach toward strategy is Duke Power. In 1998, Duke sold CMS Energy two pipeline companies: the Panhandle Eastern Pipeline Company and the Trunkline Gas Company, assets that Duke had obtained in 1997 as part of its acquisition of Panergy. According to a statement of Duke's chairman and CEO on the PR Newswire ("Duke Energy Sells Panhandle Eastern and Trunkline Pipelines to CMS Energy," November 2, 1998), "This is a great example of how being true to your strategy can yield new opportunities to create or extract value" (November 2, 1998).

The Many Dimensions of Strategy: Hadson Corporation

Hadson Corporation provides an interesting example of the variety of strategic choices and combinations faced by firms in the diversified natural gas industry during the 1990s. As noted in Table A11.1, the company began the 1990s with interests in petroleum production, natural gas marketing, and power generation. As reported in Table A11.2, the company carved out a portion of its petroleum production interests in 1990.

As described in an SEC EDGAR filing, in 1994 Hadson's board of directors began to assess its competitive position in the natural gas industry. (See Hadson Corporation, Form PREM14C, March 8, 1995.) In August 1994, the board formally considered whether to remain as an independent company or instead seek strategic alternatives such as the sale of the company. In September 1994, the company engaged S.G. Warburg as a financial adviser to consider transactions including (1) a gas supply transaction in exchange for equity of the company; (2) a purchase or sale of assets; (3) a purchase, sale, or merger of all of the company's assets; or (4) a restructuring of the company's equity or debt.

As part of this strategic process, Hadson's management and its financial adviser contacted approximately 30 companies between March 1994 and October 1994. Seven of these companies entered into confidentiality agreements to facilitate more detailed discussions. Five of these companies made preliminary proposals to purchase Hadson. On December 6, 1994, El Paso Natural Gas Company made a formal proposal to acquire Hadson that was publicly announced on December 15, 1994.

In response to the proposal from El Paso Natural Gas, a special committee of Hadson's board requested Dillon Read to make further inquiries of possible bidders for Hadson. Through this process, LG&E Energy, an electric utility, became involved in the bidding. As shown in Table A11-4, LG&E signed a definitive merger agreement with Hadson on February 10, 1995, and the merger was completed on May 15, 1995.

As a whole, Hadson faced a series of choices including what to do and who to do it with. The firm considered possibilities including recapitalization, asset sales, and an outright takeover. After putting themselves in play, they considered offers from natural gas companies and electric utilities. The ultimate acquisition by an electric utility was one of the first of the many such gas-electric mergers in the 1990s.

THE DIVERSIFIED NATURAL GAS INDUSTRY IN 2000

The status of the 22 sample firms in circa 2000 is reported in Table A11.5. To some extent, the table answers the query, Where are they now? Nine of the firms were acquired and are now divisions of other firms, either in natural gas or in the electric utility sector. The remaining firms are somewhat more streamlined than their 1990 versions. These surviving firms have tended to divest assets that were not in the natural gas area, and many have expanded through the acquisition of other natural gas companies.

One company that clearly streamlined in the 1990s was Tenneco. As noted in a December 8, 1996, story in the *Houston Chronicle* ("As Tenneco Fades Away," p. 1), the company first was named Tennessee Gas and Transmission Company, and its primary asset was a pipeline between the Gulf of Mexico and West Virginia. The company entered the 1990s as a broad-based conglomerate with interests not only in natural gas but also construction and farm equipment, shipbuilding, and automotive parts. Today, the Tenneco name is attached only to Tenneco Automotive. In some sense, the original assets of the company returned to their roots when purchased by El Paso Natural Gas Company in 1996.

Another member of the diversified natural gas industry also might ultimately return to its roots along a rockier path. Enron Corporation began the decade of the 1990s as a natural gas pipeline with interests in exploration and production, liquid fuels, and cogeneration. By contrast, the Value Line Investment Survey dated December 24, 1999, indicated that the majority of Enron's profits had moved to its Wholesale Energy Operations and Services Group. Consistent with the rewards and risks of a deregulated environment, Enron's business strategy concluded with bankruptcy. The company is sequentially auctioning assets, and as noted in a January 15, 2002, story in the *Los Angeles Times* ("Enron could End Up where It Started"), the surviving company could be a natural gas pipeline.

TABLE A11.5 The Diversified Natural Gas Industry in 2000

Firm	Business Emphasis
Arkla Inc.	Division of an electric utility
Burlington Resources	Petroleum production
Coastal Corp.	Natural gas transmission
Columbia Gas	Division of an electric utility
Consolidated Natural Gas	Division of an electric utility
Eastern Enterprises	Division of a natural gas distribution company
Enron Corp.	Natural gas (delisted in 2002)
ENSERCH Corp.	Division of an electric utility
Equitable Resources	Natural gas distribution
Hadson Corp.	Division of an electric utility
KN Energy	Natural gas transmission (name change to Kinder Morgan)
Mitchell Energy	Natural gas production and transmission
National Fuel Gas	Natural gas production and transmission
ONEOK Inc.	Natural gas distribution
Panhandle Eastern	Sold to CMS Energy (electric utility)
Seagull Energy	Petroleum exploration and production (name change to Ocean Energy)
Sonat Inc.	Division of a natural gas company
Southwestern Energy	Natural gas production and transmission
Tenneco Inc.	Automotive parts
Transco Energy	Division of a natural gas company
Valero Energy	Petroleum refinery
Williams Cos.	Natural gas transmission

SUMMARY

The analysis in the appendix indicates that the 22 firms in the diversified natural gas industry as of the first quarter of 1990 underwent substantial change during the subsequent decade. Factors emanating from deregulation were associated with a variety of restructurings including equity carve-outs, spin-offs, assets sales, and outright acquisitions.

An important point illustrated by the industry analysis is that change forces such as deregulation add uncertainty to corporate strategy. In such an altered environment, there is often no single best decision. Indeed, some firms in the industry chose to emphasize natural gas, some divested natural gas assets and sought growth in other segments of the energy industry, and still other firms joined with electric utilities.

QUESTIONS

A11.1 What are some of the segments in the natural gas industry? What are some of the potential efficiencies to be gained via vertical integration among some of these segments?

A11.2 What are some of the efficiencies to be gained by the linkage of the assets of natural gas companies such as pipelines and electric utilities?

A11.3 How might changes in regulation alter the efficiencies discussed in the first two questions?

A11.4 How might restructuring allow firms to respond to the alteration in efficiencies brought about by deregulation?

REFERENCES

Besanko, David, Julia D'Souza, and S. Ramu Thiagarajan, "The Effect of Wholesale Market Deregulation on Shareholder Wealth in the Electric Power Industry," *Journal of Law and Economics* 45, April 2001, pp. 65–88.

Hollas, Daniel R., "Gas Utility Prices in a Restructured Industry," *Journal of Regulatory Economics* 16, 1999, pp. 167–185.

Joskow, Paul L., "Deregulation and Regulatory Reform in the U.S. Electric Power Sector," working paper, MIT, February 17, 2000.

Joskow, Paul L., "U.S. Energy Policy During the 1990s," working paper, MIT, July 11, 2001.

Leggio, Karyl B., and Donald Lien, "Mergers in the Electric Utility Industry in a Deregulatory Environment," *Journal of Regulatory Economics* 17, 2000, pp. 69–85.

Leitzinger, Jeffrey, and Martin Collette, "A Retrospective Look at Wholesale Gas: Industry Restructuring," *Journal of Regulatory Economics* 21, 2002, pp. 79–101.

Mulherin, J. Harold, and Audra L. Boone, "Comparing Acquisitions and Divestitures," *Journal of Corporate Finance* 6, July 2000, pp. 117–139.

U.S. Securities and Exchange Commission, Division of Investment Management, "The Regulation of Public Utility Holding Companies," June 1995.

CHAPTER 12
EMPIRICAL TESTS OF CORPORATE RESTRUCTURING AND DIVESTITURES

This chapter considers the evidence on the effects of corporate restructuring and divestitures on firm value. The research provides tests of the theories presented in Chapter 11. This material is especially important for managers facing decisions to grow or decisions to downsize.

The chapter first asks whether restructuring and divestitures create wealth for corporate shareholders and considers some of the sources of wealth changes. The chapter then addresses the role of corporate focus in restructuring and divestiture decisions. This is followed by a broader discussion of corporate focus that includes analysis as to whether or not firms face a diversification discount. The chapter concludes by addressing some of the factors that might influence the particular form of restructuring that a firm chooses to undertake.

THE WEALTH EFFECTS OF RESTRUCTURING AND DIVESTITURES

ARE DIVESTITURES A POSITIVE NPV PROJECT?

A central question to consider in the study of corporate restructuring is whether divestitures create wealth. In other words, is the decision to engage in a spin-off, equity carve-out, or asset sale a positive NPV project?

Research presented in Table 12.1 provides evidence related to these queries. The findings come from event studies at the time of the announcement of the particular types of divestitures. In all of the listed research papers, corporate divestitures, on average, create wealth for parent shareholders. The results collectively span a time period from 1962 through 1999. The results indicate that corporate divestitures are positive NPV projects.

The magnitude of the wealth creation reported in Table 12.1 ranges from 1.12% to 4.51%. One reason for this variation is that the relative size of the divestitures varies to some extent across samples and across types of divestitures. In results not provided in the table, several of the studies (e.g., Miles and Rosenfeld, 1983; Mulherin and Boone, 2000) also reported that the greater the relative size is of the divestiture, the greater the announcement return is to the parent firm.

In their study of spin-offs, Copeland, Lemgruber, and Mayers (1987) extended the basic event study procedure. First, they employed a sample that includes unsuccessful divestitures.

TABLE 12.1 Event Study Analysis of Corporate Restructuring and Divestitures

Research Paper	Divestiture Type	Time Period	Number of Observations	Event Window	Parent Return (%)
Miles and Rosenfeld (1983)	Spin off	1963–1980	55	(0, +1)	3.34
Hite and Owers (1983)	Spin-off	1963–1981	123	(−1, 0)	3.30
Schipper and Smith (1983)	Spin-off	1963–1981	93	(−1, 0)	2.84
Copeland et al. (1987)	Spin-off	1962–1981	73	(0, +1)	2.49
Mulherin and Boone (2000)	Spin-off	1990–1999	106	(−1, +1)	4.51
Schipper and Smith (1986)	Carve-out	1965–1983	76	(−4, 0)	1.83
Mulherin and Boone (2000)	Carve-out	1990–1999	125	(−1, +1)	2.27
Klein (1986)	Asset sale	1970–1979	202	(−2, 0)	1.12
Lang, Poulsen, and Stulz (1995)	Asset sale	1984–1989	93	(−1, 0)	1.41

Second, they accounted for the fact that many firms make a series of announcements about the proposed divestiture. By cumulating the returns for the series of announcement dates, they estimated that the full return to the parent firm is 5.02%, which is twice as large as their estimate for the initial announcement date.

SOURCES OF WEALTH GAINS: EVIDENCE FROM ASSET SALES

Given that divestitures have been found to create wealth, the next question is: What is the source of the wealth gain? Asset sales provide one piece of evidence on this query, as one can study the parent that sells the assets as well the firm that purchases the assets. This analysis results in the determination as to whether the restructuring gains are particular to the divesting firm or instead reflect shared efficiencies between the buyer and the seller.

Table 12.2 reports event study evidence on the gains to sellers and buyers in asset sale transactions. Across all five of the research papers, the evidence indicates that on average, asset sales create wealth for the seller and the buyer. These results support the view that asset sales represent an efficient transfer of resources between corporations.

The results on seller and buyer returns share similarities and differences from the research on corporate mergers that was presented in Chapter 8. Similar to the merger research, the combined return in asset sales is positive. These results are reported in two of the papers reported in Table 12.2. Hanson and Song (2000) and Mulherin and Boone (2000) estimated a positive combined return in asset sales, where the combined return is the weighted average of the seller and buyer returns, and the weights are the equity values of the seller and the buyer.

One notable difference in the asset sale studies from much of the merger research is in the distribution of gains between the seller and buyer. In the research in Table 12.2, the seller and buyer consistently have positive returns. As noted by Rosenfeld, "Unlike the merger studies, this result demonstrates that the transaction's synergistic effects are not restricted to the selling firm" (1984, p. 1447).

As a complement to the event study evidence, Maksimovic and Phillips (2001) used plant level data for manufacturing firms to analyze the productivity effects of asset transfers between corporations. They found an increase in productivity following asset transfers. From their results, Maksimovic and Phillips concluded "The market for corporate assets facilitates the redeployment of assets from firms with a lower ability to exploit them to firms with higher ability," (2001, p. 2021). The results are consistent with a neoclassical model of profit maximization.

TABLE 12.2 Seller and Buyer Returns in Corporate Asset Sales

Research Paper	Time Period	Number of Sellers	Number of Buyers	Event Window	Seller Return (%)	Buyer Return (%)	Combined Return
Rosenfeld (1984)	1969–1981	30	30	(−1, +1)	2.76	2.10	Not reported
Jain (1985)	1976–1978	1,062	304	day −1	0.44	0.34	Not reported
Hite, Owers, and Rogers (1987)	1963–1981	55	51	(−1, 0)	1.66	0.83	Not reported
Hanson and Song (2000)	1981–1995	326	326	(−1, +1)	0.602	0.477	0.269%
Mulherin and Boone (2000)	1990–1999	83	83	(−1, +1)	1.75	1.34	1.18%

SOURCES OF WEALTH GAINS: INFORMATION VERSUS EFFICIENCY

An important question raised by the theories in Chapter 11 is whether the wealth effects of corporate restructuring reflect information signals or instead reflect efficiencies in operations. Hite, Owers, and Rogers (1987) provided one test that distinguishes between the information and efficiency theories by analyzing unsuccessful asset sales. They found that although the announcement effect of such sales is positive, the initial gains are given up when the sales are terminated. They interpreted this result to indicate that actual asset transfers are required to create wealth, which is consistent with an efficiency explanation.

Vijh (2002) used equity carve-outs to provide additional tests of theories based on information and efficiency. As a test of Nanda's (1991) asymmetric information model, Vijh (2002) analyzed the relation between the wealth effects in a carve-out and the ratio of subsidiary to nonsubsidiary assets. Vijh (2002) found that the wealth effects are positively related to the ratio of subsidiary to nonsubsidiary assets, a result he interpreted to be inconsistent with the asymmetric information model. From a series of related tests, Vijh (2002) concluded that the wealth effects of equity carve-outs emanate from improved corporate efficiency.

Hulburt, Miles, and Woolridge (2002) performed tests that directly discriminate between the information and efficiency theories. They examined the stock returns of *rival* firms at the time a parent firm announces an equity carve-out. If the carve-out conveys information that the parent firm is undervalued, then the announcement should have a positive effect on rival firms. By contrast, if the carve-out will enable the parent to operate more efficiently, and thereby be more competitive, then the announcement should have a negative effect on the rival firms. The results indicated a negative effect on the rival firms, which Hulburt, Miles, and Woolridge (2002) interpreted to be in support of the efficiency theory of divestitures.

CORPORATE FOCUS

FOCUS AND THE WEALTH EFFECTS OF CORPORATE DIVESTITURES

One possible source of the efficiency gains in corporate divestitures is an improvement in corporate focus. Presumably, if the business of a firm is more narrowly positioned, the executives will be easier to monitor and will make better decisions.

In the divestiture and restructuring literature, the effect of corporate focus has been studied by comparing the effects of divestitures in related industries with those in unrelated industries. The definition of *related* usually is based on SIC codes. For example, if a parent and a subsidiary share the same two-digit SIC code, they are classified as related. If not, they are classified as unrelated. The prediction of the focus explanation of corporate restructuring is that the wealth gains will be found in the divestiture of unrelated subsidiaries.

One paper on divestitures and corporate focus is by John and Ofek (1995). They studied 258 asset sales during the period 1986 to 1988. In an event study of the (−2, 0) window, they found that on average, the divesting firms experienced a 1.5 increase in wealth. In regression analysis, they found that the wealth effects are greater when the subsidiary's assets are from a different four-digit SIC code than the parent's.

Several event studies on spin-offs also examined the effects of corporate focus. As reported in the top three rows of Table 12.3, Krishnaswami and Subramaniam (1999); Daley, Mehrotra, and Sivakumar (1997); and Desai and Jain (1999) all found that spin-offs of unrelated assets have larger announcement returns than spin-offs of related assets. The authors interpret the

TABLE 12.3 Related Versus Unrelated Divestitures

Research Paper	Divestiture Type	Time Period	Related Definition	Number Related	Number Unrelated	Event Window	Related Return (%)	Unrelated Return (%)
Krishnaswami and Subramaniam (1999)	Spin-off	1979–1993	2-digit SIC	30	88	(-1, 0)	1.86	3.59
Daley, Mehrotra, and Sivakumar (1997)	Spin-off	1975–1991	2-digit SIC	25	60	(-1, 0)	1.6	4.5
Desai and Jain (1999)	Spin-off	1975–1991	2-digit SIC	41	103	(-1, +1)	2.71	4.45
Boone (2000)	Spin-off	1985–1990	2-digit SIC	15	43	(-1, +1)	0.85	4.07
	Spin-off	1991–1996	2-digit SIC	30	60	(-1, +1)	3.29	4.82
Allen and McConnell (1998)	Carve-out	1978-1993						
		Payout	2-digit SIC	16	56	(-1, +1)	6.56	5.83
		Retain	2-digit SIC	28	67	(-1, +1)	-0.11	-0.16
Boone (2000)	Carve-out	1985–1996	2-digit SIC	79	145	(-1, +1)	2.91	2.76
Vijh (2002)	Carve-out	1980–1997	2-digit SIC	100	221	(-1, +1)	0.80	2.34
Hulburt, Miles, and Woolridge (2002)	Carve-out	1981–1994	4-digit SIC	30	153	(-1, +1)	0.98	2.10

results to indicate that the improvement in focus and the reduction in information asymmetry are the sources of wealth gains in corporate spin-offs.

Several pieces of evidence, however, suggest that improved focus is not the only source of wealth gains from corporate spin-offs. For one, the returns in the divestitures of related assets are positive in all three studies. More importantly, more recent research by Boone (2000) indicated that the results for related and unrelated divestitures are not robust over time.

As reported in the fourth row of Table 12.3, Boone (2000) studied the effect of related and unrelated spin-offs in the period 1985 to 1996. In the first half of her sample during the period 1985 to 1990, which spans the period of earlier work, Boone (2000) found that the wealth creation of corporate spin-offs emanates from the divestiture of unrelated assets. In the more recent time period, 1991 to 1996, however, the wealth effects of the spin-off of related and unrelated assets are both positive and are comparable in magnitude. These latter results indicate that although an improvement in focus can create wealth, the source of wealth gains in corporate spin-offs stems from a broader set of efficiency factors.

Analysis of equity carve-outs provides further evidence on the effect of related and unrelated divestitures. The bottom rows of Table 12.3 report four event studies of equity carve-outs that bifurcate the announcement returns based on whether the parent and subsidiary have related or unrelated assets. In two of the studies—Allen and McConnell (1998) and Boone (2000)—the returns in the related sample are slightly higher. In the two other studies—Vijh (2002) and Hulburt, Miles, and Woolridge (2002)—the returns to the related sample are slightly lower. These results confirm that focus is not the only source of wealth gains from corporate divestitures.

Boone (2000) further cautioned against the naïve use of SIC codes or industry segments as a measure of corporate focus and related assets. She noted that theories in transaction cost economics point to vertical integration as an important choice variable in the theory of the firm. The use of SIC codes and industry segments obfuscates such important corporate interrelations. Boone (2000) offered the carve-out of El Paso Natural Gas (SIC code = 4922) by Burlington Resources (SIC codes = 1311, 1321) as an example of a vertically related transaction that would be naïvely classified as unrelated based solely on SIC codes. Such misclassification can cloud the understanding of the causes and effects of corporate divestitures. Similar measurement issues are discussed next in the broader analysis of corporate focus, diversification, and firm value.

FOCUS, DIVERSIFICATION, AND FIRM VALUE

The literature on focus and divestitures is one aspect of a broader treatment of the relation among corporate focus, diversification, and firm value. The central question is whether a strategy toward greater focus can improve firm value. Alternatively, the issue is whether diversification is an aid or instead a hindrance to firm performance.

Comment and Jarrell (1995) provided an interesting analysis of trends in corporate focus during the 1980s. They found that focus increased during this time period in that the fraction of firms reporting multiple business segments declined between 1979 and 1988. They also reported that the improvement in focus corresponds to an improvement in corporate value, although the authors express several reservations about their results.

Related analysis of corporate focus, diversification, and firm value is provided by Lang and Stulz (1994). As a normalized proxy for value, they used Tobin's q, defined as the market value of the firm divided by the replacement value of the firm's assets. They found that multiple-segment firms have lower values of q than single-segment firms (i.e., diversification appears to impinge on firm value). Lang and Stulz (1994) tempered the implications of their results by noting that the diversified firms in their sample had lower performance even before opting to diversify.

Berger and Ofek (1995) also estimated the valuation effects of corporate diversification. They employed the Compustat Industry Segment tapes during the period 1986 to 1991 to impute values of multiple-segment firms relative to single-segment firms. In their technique, the median ratios of total capital to assets, sales, and earning for single-segment firms are computed for a given industry. For multiple-segment firms, these ratios are multiplied by the firm's values in each segment and then summed to create an imputed value. The ratio of the firm's actual value to its imputed value provides a measure of excess value. Using this methodology, Berger and Ofek (1995) inferred a 13% to 15% average loss from diversification.

IS THERE REALLY A DIVERSIFICATION DISCOUNT?

The analysis by Comment and Jarrell (1995), Lang and Stulz (1994), and Berger and Ofek (1995) suggested that diversification reduces value. One immediate query is Why do firms diversify? In the extreme, why don't all firms focus on a single segment?

Recent research examines more closely the estimates of the effect of diversification on value and raises several concerns about the prior work. Many of these concerns emphasize measurement issues. Whited (2001) detailed the significant measurement error in estimates of q. Villalonga (2003) and Schoar (2002) presented evidence on the noisiness of segment data. Chevalier (2000) and Villalonga (2000) both noted the importance of accounting for the non-randomness of diversification.

In a detailed study, Graham, Lemmon, and Wolf (2002) asked the question, "Does corporate diversification destroy value?" They studied a sample of 356 acquisitions during the period 1980 to 1995. Using a (−1, +1) event window, they found that the acquisitions created wealth: The combined return was 3.4%. In spite of this wealth creation, Graham, Lemmon, and Wolf (2002) found that the merged entities experienced a reduction in excess value when they applied the technique of Berger and Ofek (1995). Graham, Lemmon, and Wolf (2002) concluded that acquisitions, on average, are wealth enhancing, and that the prior measures of conglomerate discounts should be reconsidered carefully.

CORPORATE CHOICE: HOW TO DIVEST?

A specific critique of the diversification discount literature is the apparent assumption that two-digit SIC codes provide the model to which corporate managers should aspire. Boone (2000) and Chevalier (2000), in particular, pointed out that many related factors of production span the dimensions set by SIC codes.

A more general critique is that the diversification discount literature fails to appreciate the important dynamics faced by corporate managers. As first laid out by Coase:

> Business men will be constantly experimenting, controlling more or less, and in this way, equilibrium will be maintained. This gives the position for static analysis. But it is

clear that dynamic factors are also of considerable importance, and an investigation of the effect changes have on the cost of organizing within the firm and on marketing costs generally will enable one to explain why firms get larger and smaller. We thus have a theory of moving equilibrium. (1937, pp. 404–405)

In this section, we discuss some research that, in the spirit of Coase (1937), addressed why firms choose a certain form of divestiture. The evidence indicates that the particular form of divestiture is not chosen at random. Instead, restructuring decisions respond to factors such as the changing transactions costs faced by corporate managers.

The early event study analysis on corporate divestitures outlined various differences in the forms of divestiture. Rosenfeld (1984), for example, noted that spin-offs and asset sales had potential differences in tax implications. Jain (1985) noted differences between the predivestiture performance of parents that elect to spin-off or engage in an asset sale and conjectured that the divestiture decision was affected by financial planning. Recent research by Maydew, Schipper, and Vincent (1999) indeed found that taxes and financial constraints affect the choice between a spin-off and an asset sale.

Jongbloed (1992) studied factors affecting the choice between spin-offs and equity carve-outs. Using data from the period 1980 to 1988, he found that a carve-out is more likely to be chosen when the subsidiary has more growth options. In a study of spin-offs, carve-outs, and asset sales from the period 1981 to 1998, Powers (2001) also found that the choice of a carve-out is related to growth opportunities. In related analysis, Lehn, Netter, and Poulsen (1990) found that growth opportunities are an important determinant in the choice between dual-class recapitalizations, where a firm maintains access to capital markets, and leveraged buyouts, where a firm is taken private.

Boone (2001) employed a sample of 220 equity carve-outs from the period 1985 to 1996 to study the variation in organization form that follows a partial divestiture. Unlike research of an earlier time period by Klein, Rosenfeld, and Beranek (1991), Boone (2001) found that in more recent equity carve-outs, the parent firms often maintain a long-term ownership stake in the subsidiaries. She found that the retained ownership interest by the parent is higher when the parent and subsidiary share a product market relationship. Consistent with Coase (1937), Boone (2001) interpreted the results to indicate that the organizational choice of a firm balances the cost of market transactions with the costs of operating in a hierarchical structure.

Summary

This chapter has reviewed evidence on the effects of corporate divestitures. Consistent with theory, event study evidence indicates that divestitures create wealth. Whether an asset sale, equity carve-out, or spin-off, the decision by a parent firm to divest is a positive NPV project. The source of the wealth gains in divestitures appears to arise from a more efficient use of assets.

Corporate focus often is cited as a motivation for restructuring and divestitures. The empirical evidence indicates that focus is a driver of divestiture gains. Yet focus is not the sole source of efficiency improvements. Moreover, recent research suggests care in naïvely defining focus by the dissimilarity of SIC codes.

Broader research on corporate focus has suggested that a diversification discount occurs. Ongoing studies, however, suggest caution in the use of single-segment firms to value conglomerates and in stringently basing levels of diversification on SIC codes.

Studies of the choice of divestiture mode indicate that factors such as transaction costs influence the decisions of management in implementing restructuring.

Questions

12.1 How are event studies used to determine the wealth effects of restructuring and corporate divestitures? Are asset sales, equity carve-outs, and spin-offs positive NPV projects?

12.2 What are the wealth gains to (1) sellers and (2) buyers in asset sales? How do these results compare to those for targets and bidders in mergers?

12.3 What are the wealth effects to parent firms in *unsuccessful* asset sales? What do these results say about the efficiency of *completed* asset sales?

12.4 What does the empirical evidence say about (1) information and (2) efficiency as a source of wealth gains in equity carve-outs?

12.5 How are related and unrelated assets usually defined?

12.6 How is diversification measured? What is meant by a diversification discount?

12.7 How can event study methods be used to test for a diversification discount?

12.8 What are some factors that might determine whether a firm engages in (1) an asset sale, (2) an equity carve-out, or (3) a spin-off?

References

Allen, Jeffrey W., and John J. McConnell, "Equity Carve-Outs and Managerial Discretion," *Journal of Finance* 53, February 1998, pp. 163–186.

Berger, Phillip G., and Eli Ofek, "Diversification's Effect on Firm Value," *Journal of Financial Economics* 37, 1995, pp. 39–65.

Boone, Audra L., "Can Focus Explain Carve-Out Gains?" paper presented at the meeting of the Western Finance Association, Sun Valley Idaho, June 2000.

Boone, Audra L., "The Interaction of Ownership, Governance, and Product Markets: Evidence from Equity Carve-Outs," paper presented at the meeting of the Western Finance Association, Tucson, Arizona, June 2001.

Chevalier, Judith A., "What Do We Know About Cross-Subsidization? Evidence from the Investment Policies of Merging Firms," working paper, University of Chicago and NBER, March 2000.

Coase, R. H., "The Nature of the Firm," *Economica* 4, November 1937, pp. 386–405.

Comment, Robert, and Gregg A. Jarrell, "Corporate Focus and Stock Returns," *Journal of Financial Economics* 37, 1995, pp. 67–87.

Copeland, Thomas E., Eduardo Lemgruber, and David Mayers, "Corporate Spinoffs: Multiple Announcements and Ex-date Abnormal Performance," Chapter 7 in *Modern Finance and Industrial Economics*, T.E. Copeland (ed.), New York: Basil Blackwell, 1987.

Daley, Lane, Vikas Mehrotra, and Ranjini Sivakumar, "Corporate Focus and Value Creation: Evidence from Spinoffs," *Journal of Financial Economics* 45, 1997, pp. 257–281.

Desai, Hemang, and Prem C. Jain, "Firm Performance and Focus: Long-Run Stock Market Performance Following Spinoffs," *Journal of Financial Economics* 54, October 1999, pp. 75–101.

Graham, John R., Michael L. Lemmon, and Jack G. Wolf, "Does Corporate Diversification Destroy Wealth?" *Journal of Finance* 57, April 2002, pp. 695–720.

Hanson, Robert C., and Moon H. Song, "Managerial Ownership, Board Structure, and the Division of Gains in Divestitures," *Journal of Corporate Finance* 6, 2000, pp. 55–70.

Hite, Gailen L., and James E. Owers, "Security Price Reactions Around Corporate Spin-Off Announcements," *Journal of Financial Economics* 12, 1983, pp. 409–436.

Hite, Gailen L., James E. Owers, and Ronald C. Rogers, "The Market for Interfirm Asset Sales: Partial Sell-Offs and Total Liquidations," *Journal of Financial Economics* 18, 1987, pp. 229–252.

Hulburt, Heather M., James A. Miles, and J. Randall Woolridge, "Value Creation from Equity Carve-Outs," *Financial Management* 31, Spring 2002, pp. 83–100.

Jain, Prem C., "The Effect of Voluntary Sell-Off Announcements on Shareholder Wealth," *Journal of Finance* 40, March 1985, pp. 209–224.

John, Kose, and Eli Ofek, "Asset Sales and Increase in Focus," *Journal of Financial Economics* 37, 1995, pp. 105–126.

Jongbloed, Auke, "A Comparison of Spin-Offs and Equity Carve-Outs," working paper, University of Rochester, December 1992.

Klein, April "The Timing and Substance of Divestiture Announcements: Individual, Simultaneous, and Cumulative Effects," *Journal of Finance* 41, July 1986, pp. 685–696.

Klein, April, James Rosenfeld, and William Beranek, "The Two Stages of an Equity Carve-Out and the Price Response of Parent and Subsidiary Stock," *Managerial and Decision Economics* 12, 1991, pp. 449–460.

Krishnaswami, Sudha, and Venkat Subramaniam, "Information Asymmetry, Valuation, and the Corporate Spin-Off Decision," *Journal of Financial Economics* 53, 1999, pp. 73–122.

Lang, Larry, Annette Poulsen, and Rene Stulz, "Asset Sales, Firm Performance, and the Agency Costs of Managerial Discretion," *Journal of Financial Economics* 37, 1995, pp. 3–37.

Lang, Larry, and Rene Stulz, "Tobin's q, Corporate Diversification, and Firm Performance," *Journal of Political Economy* 102, 1994, pp. 1248–1280.

Lehn, Kenneth, Jeffry Netter, and Annette Poulsen, "Consolidating Corporate Control: Dual-Class Recapitalizations versus Leveraged Buyouts," *Journal of Financial Economics*: 27, 1990, pp. 557–580.

Makismovic, Vojislav, and Gordon Phillips, "The Market for Corporate Assets: Who Engages in Mergers and Asset Sales and Are There Efficiency Gains?" *Journal of Finance* 56, December 2001, pp. 2019–2065.

Maydew, Edward L., Katherine Schipper, and Linda Vincent, "The Impact of Taxes on the Choice of Divestiture Method," *Journal of Accounting and Economics* 28, 1999, pp. 117–150.

Miles, James, A., and James D. Rosenfeld, "The Effect of Voluntary Spin-Off Announcements on Shareholder Wealth," *Journal of Finance* 38, December 1983, pp. 1597–1606.

Mulherin, J. Harold, and Audra L. Boone, "Comparing Acquisitions and Divestitures," *Journal of Corporate Finance* 6, 2000, pp. 117–139.

Nanda, Vikram, "On the Good News in Equity Carve-Outs," *Journal of Finance* 46, December 1991, pp. 1717–1737.

Powers, Eric A., "Spinoffs, Selloffs and Equity Carve-outs: An Analysis of Divestiture Method Choice," working paper, University of South Carolina, September 2001.

Rosenfeld James D., "Additional Evidence on the Relation Between Divestiture Announcements and Shareholder Wealth," *Journal of Finance* 39, December 1984, pp. 1437–1448.

Schipper, Katherine, and Abbie Smith, "A Comparison of Equity Carve-Outs and Seasoned Equity Offerings: Share Price Effects and Corporate Restructuring," *Journal of Financial Economics* 15, 1986, pp. 153–186.

Schipper, Katherine, and Abbie Smith, "Effects of Recontracting on Shareholder Wealth: The Case of Voluntary Spin-Offs," *Journal of Financial Economics* 12, 1983, pp. 437–467.

Schoar, Antoinette, "Effects of Corporate Diversification on Productivity," *Journal of Finance*, 57, December 2002, pp. 2379–2403.

Vijh, Anand M., "The Positive Announcement-Period Returns of Equity Carve-Outs Asymmetric Information or Divestiture Gains?" *Journal of Business* 75, 2002, pp. 153–190.

Villalonga, Belen, "Diversification Discount or Premium? New Evidence from BITS Establishment-Level Data," *Journal of Finance*, forthcoming, 2003.

Villalonga, Belen, "Does Diversification Cause the 'Diversification Discount'?" working paper, UCLA, July 2000.

Whited, Toni M., "Is It Inefficient Investment That Causes the Diversification Discount?" *Journal of Finance* 56, October 2001, pp. 1667–1691.

APPENDIX A

ANALYSIS OF A SAMPLE
OF RECENT DIVESTITURES

This appendix studies a sample of recent corporate divestures. The analysis first reports the reasons given by the firms for the divestitures and also considers some of the broader change forces at play. For the subsample of asset sales, the motivation of the buying firm also is discussed. The value and implementation of the specific divestitures are then presented. The appendix concludes with an event study analysis of the wealth effects of the transactions on the divesting firms.

The divestitures studied in the appendix are taken from research by Mulherin and Boone (2000). The sample comprises 19 divestitures that were announced in 1998. The transactions were completed in either 1998 or 1999. The information and data used in the appendix were obtained from LexisNexis, the *Wall Street Journal*, the Value Line Investment Survey, the SEC EDGAR filings, and the Standard & Poor's Daily Stock Price Record.

THE SAMPLE OF DIVESTITURES

Table A12.1 describes the sample of divestitures. The sample comprises 19 transactions that were announced in 1998. The announcement date represents the first public statement by the parent firm that the subsidiary or division would be sold. Media stories on this date often identify the form of the divestiture and, in the case of asset sales, the firm buying the divested assets. However, on some of the announcement dates, the initial story merely reported that the subsidiary would be divested and later stories developed the details on the restructuring.

Within the full sample of 19 divestitures, 11 took the form of asset sales, whereby the parent firm sold the subsidiary to another corporation. An example is Cincinnati Milacron's sale of its machine tool operations. Four of the transactions were equity carve-outs, whereby the parent sold shares in the subsidiary in a public offering. An example is Du Pont's carve-out of Conoco. The four other transactions were spin-offs, whereby the parent created separate stock in the subsidiary and issued the shares to existing shareholders. An example is Olin Corporation's spin-off of its Arch Chemicals subsidiary.

MOTIVATION FOR THE DIVESTITURES

The far right column in Table A12.1 reports statements made in the media by the parent firms regarding why the divestiture was undertaken. A general reason given for the sample restructurings was to sharpen focus in order to improve performance.

Related information on the motivation of the divestitures is provided in Table A12.2, which compares the industry of the parent firm with the industry of the divested subsidiary. Several of the divestitures represented cases in which the business of the subsidiary was somewhat removed from that of the parent. The divestiture by Xerox of its insurance unit, Crum & Forster, is a prime example. In this case, the divestiture was part of major restructuring whereby Xerox fully exited the financial services sector.

In other cases, the divestiture of the subsidiary was intended to enable more clear-cut valuation. The equity carve-out of Time Warner Telecom is one example. The spin-offs by Rockwell and Varian Associates of their semiconductor divisions are other such cases. Indeed, Varian split itself into three separate companies—medical systems, instruments, and semiconductors—to remove a perceived conglomerate discount.

In some cases, however, the restructuring represented a change in strategy rather than an obvious inefficiency in organization. Bausch & Lomb, for example, chose to sell its prestigious sunglass business and emphasize eye-related health care. Similarly, CIGNA Corporation chose to divest one arm of its insurance business, property/casualty, in order to concentrate on the health care sector.

Further information on the motivation of the sample divestitures can be garnered from Table A12.3, which reports the identity of the buyer in the 11 transactions in the sample that were asset sales. In several cases, the buyer in the asset sale was able to use the transaction to expand market share and thereby lower costs. The acquisition of Bausch & Lomb's sunglass business by Luxottica Group and of CIGNA Corporation's property/casualty business by Ace Limited serve as examples. The acquisition of C.R. Bard's coronary catheter lab business by Arterial

321

TABLE A12.1 Sample of Divestitures from 1998

Announce Date	Divestiture Type	Parent	Subsidiary/Division	Divesting Firm's Motivation
Nov. 18	Asset sale	Bausch & Lomb	Sunglass business	Strategic focus on eye-related health care
Dec. 22	Asset sale	CIGNA Corp.	Property/casualty business	Focus on health care and employee benefits
Aug. 21	Asset sale	Cincinnati Milacron	Machine tool operations	Focus on high-margin businesses
July 9	Asset sale	C.R. Bard	Coronary catheter lab business	Focus and efficiency
Nov. 2	Asset sale	Duke Energy	Midwest gas pipelines	Regional focus
Nov. 17	Asset sale	Eli Lilly	PCS Health Systems	Concentrate on core drug business
Aug. 3	Asset sale	Entergy Corp.	Australia and UK power business	Sharpened growth and back to basics
Sept. 1	Asset sale	IBM	Global Network operations	Focus on main business
May 18	Asset sale	PG&E Corp.	Power-generation plants	Strategy to focus on electricity sales
Mar. 11	Asset sale	Xerox Corp.	Crum & Forster	Exit from financial services
June 1	Asset sale	Yellow Corp.	Preston Trucking	Lack of synergy
Apr. 27	Equity carve-out	Cincinnati Bell	Convergys Corp.	Focus for growth
May 11	Equity carve-out	DuPont	Conoco	Enhance value and growth
Feb. 2	Equity carve-out	Thermo Instr. Sys.	ONIX Systems	Repay indebtedness
Apr. 6	Equity carve-out	Time Warner	Time Warner Telecom	Facilitate valuation
June 30	Spin-off	Hilton Hotels	Park Place Entertainment	Separate valuation of hotel and gaming
July 30	Spin-off	Olin Corp.	Arch Chemicals	Sharpen management focus
June 29	Spin-off	Rockwell Intl.	Conexant Systems	Focus to unlock value
Aug. 21	Spin-off	Varian Associates	Instruments and Semiconductor	Eliminate conglomerate discount

TABLE A12.2 Industry of Parent and Subsidiary

Parent	Parent Industry	Subsidiary/Division	Subsidiary Industry
Bausch & Lomb	Eye-related health care	Sunglass business	Sunglasses
CIGNA Corp.	Insurance	Property/casualty business	Property/casualty insurance
Cincinnati Milacron	Industrial products	Machine tool operations	Machine tool
C.R. Bard	Medical supplies	Coronary catheter lab business	Coronary devices
Duke Energy	Electric utility east	Midwest gas pipelines	Natural gas transmission
Eli Lilly	Drug	PCS Health Systems	Pharmacy benefits
Entergy Corp.	Electric utility	Australia and UK power business	Non-U.S. power
IBM	Computer	Global Network operations	Information services
PG&E Corp.	Electric utility	Power-generation plants	Electric utility
Xerox Corp.	Office equipment	Crum & Forster	Insurance
Yellow Corp.	Long-haul trucking	Preston Trucking	Regional trucking
Cincinnati Bell	Telecom services	Convergys Corp.	Customer billing services
DuPont	Basic chemical	Conoco	Petroleum
Thermo Instr. Sys.	Precision instruments	ONIX Systems	Precision instruments
Time Warner	Publishing	Time Warner Telecom	Business telecom
Hilton Hotels	Hotel	Park Place Entertainment	Gaming
Olin Corp.	Basic chemical	Arch Chemicals	Specialty chemicals
Rockwell Intl.	Aerospace/defense	Conexant Systems	Semiconductors
Varian Associates	Medical systems	Varian and Varian Semiconductor	Instruments and semiconductor

TABLE A12.3 The Buyer in Asset Sales

Parent (Seller)	Buyer in the Asset Sale	Buyer Industry	Buying Firm's Motivation
Bausch & Lomb	Luxottica Group	Eyeglasses	Broadened global presence
CIGNA Corp.	Ace Ltd.	Specialty insurance	Cost savings and geographic expansion
Cincinnati Milacron	UNOVA Inc.	Machine tool	Economies of scale
C.R.Bard	Arterial Vascular Engineering	Angioplasty systems	Complementary products
Duke Energy	CMS Energy	Electric utility midwest	Regional vertical integration
Eli Lilly	Rite Aid Corp.	Drugstores	Growing strategy in health care services
Entergy Corp.	American Electric Power	Electric utility	Strategy of global portfolio of energy assets
IBM	AT&T	Telecom services	Complement to strategy in business networks
PG&E Corp.	Southern Co.	Electric utility	Develop energy supply business
Xerox Corp.	Fairfax Financial Holdings	Insurance	Complementary assets
Yellow Corp.	Management group	Regional trucking	Specialization

Vascular Engineering and of Xerox's Crum & Forster unit by Fairfax Financial Holdings are other cases in which the buying firm obtained complementary assets.

BROADER CHANGE FORCES

In addition to the firm-specific motivation for the divestitures, much of the restructuring in the sample of divestitures resulted from broad, underlying change forces. Several of the divestitures in the 1998 sample occurred in the electric utility industry, which has been undergoing deregulation. In commenting on the ongoing restructuring represented by the acquisition by CMS Energy of the gas pipelines of Duke Energy, a *Financial Times* article dated November 3, 1998, stated, "The deals are part of efforts to take up and strengthen strategic regional positions as deregulation of the power industry spreads across the country" ("Restructuring Continues in the U.S. Energy Industry," p. 30). Similar points are made in the *New York Times* regarding the sale by PG&E of its power-generation plants ("Pacific Gas to Receive $1.01 Billion for Power Plants," p. C4).

The divestiture of Conoco by DuPont also reflected changing conditions in the energy industry. As noted in a May 12, 1998, article in the *New York Times:*

> DuPont bought the oil company in 1981 as insurance against the pricing and supply tactics of the Organization of Petroleum Exporting Countries. But oil prices have been far less volatile than it feared, and DuPont continues to de-emphasize the petrochemical side of its business, so having Conoco as a captive source of raw material is of less strategic importance. ("DuPont to Spin Off 20% of Conoco, the Rest to be Sold Later," p. D4.)

THE COMPLETION AND VALUE OF THE DIVESTITURES

As reported in Table A12.4, each of the divestitures was completed in 1998 or 1999. The far-right column in the table reports the value of each transaction and the manner in which the transaction value was estimated.

The 11 asset sales represented cash payments from the buyer to the selling parent firm. Several of these sales, such as Eli Lilly's sale of PCS Health Systems to Rite Aid, had values in the billions of dollars. The values of the equity carve-outs were computed by multiplying the number of shares offered times the offer price. The $4.4 billion Conoco deal stands out. The values of the spin-offs were computed by multiplying the number of shares received by stockholders times the closing price on the first day of trading. For example, Hilton Hotels distributed 260.8 million shares in its casino gaming division, Park Place Entertainment. The newly public subsidiary had a closing price of $7.50 on the first day of trading, implying an equity value of $1.96 billion.

For some of the equity carve-outs in the sample, the initial divestiture was only the first step in a full severance from the parent firm. For example, the carve-out of Convergys by Cincinnati Bell represented only about 10% of the subsidiary's shares. The remaining stock in the subsidiary was divested by the parent via a spin-off in January 1999.

The divestiture of Conoco by DuPont also entailed a two-stage transaction. The equity carve-out in October 1998 represented 30% of Conoco's shares. The remaining 70% was subsequently divested in August 1999. The divestiture was accomplished via a variant of a spin-off called an exchange offer whereby DuPont shareholders had the choice of either maintaining their DuPont shares or exchanging their stock in the parent for shares in the subsidiary.

In contrast to the above examples, the post-carve-out life of ONIX Systems followed a different path. Its parent, Thermo Instrument Systems, reacquired the subsidiary in April 2000. This "spin-in" is one of the many interesting financial transactions by subsidiaries of Thermo Electron Corporation. (See Allen, 1998, for a detailed analysis of Thermo Electron.)

EVENT STUDY ANALYSIS OF THE DIVESTITURE SAMPLE

As a means of measuring the wealth effects of the sample divestitures, this section reports event study analysis of the stock returns to the parent firms around the announcement date of the transactions. The data used to conduct the analysis were taken from the Standard & Poor's Daily Stock Price Record. The estimates employ a $(-1,+1)$ window, where day 0 is the initial announcement date of the divestiture in the financial media.

The event study results are reported in Table A12.5. The raw returns of each parent firm as well as the proxy for the market, the S&P 500, are reported. The difference between the firm's return and the market proxy equals the net-of-market return.

The results of the event study analysis indicate that the sample divestitures created wealth for the parent firms. The average net-of-market announcement

TABLE A12.4 Completion and Value of the Divestiture

Completion Date	Divestiture Type	Parent	Subsidiary/Division	Value
June 29, 1999	Asset sale	Bausch & Lomb	Sunglass business	$640 million (in cash)
July 2, 1999	Asset sale	CIGNA Corp.	Property/casualty business	$3.45 billion (in cash)
Oct. 5, 1998	Asset sale	Cincinnati Milacron	Machine tool operations	$180 million (in cash)
Oct. 1, 1998	Asset sale	C.R. Bard	Coronary catheter lab business	$550 million (in cash)
Mar. 29, 1999	Asset sale	Duke Energy	Midwest gas pipelines	$2.2 billion ($1.9 bil cash; $300 mil debt)
Jan. 22, 1999	Asset sale	Eli Lilly	PCS Health Systems	$1.6 billion (in cash)
Dec. 30, 1998	Asset sale	Entergy Corp.	Australia and UK power business	$4.28 billion (in cash)
May 3, 1999	Asset sale	IBM	Global Network operations	$5 billion (in cash)
Apr. 16, 1999	Asset sale	PG&E Corp.	Power-generation plants	$1.01 billion (in cash)
Aug. 13, 1998	Asset sale	Xerox Corp.	Crum & Forster	$680 million (in cash)
July 15, 1998	Asset sale	Yellow Corp.	Preston Trucking	$20 million (in cash)
Aug. 13, 1998	Equity carve-out	Cincinnati Bell	Convergys Corp.	$195 million (13 million shrs @ $15)
Oct. 22, 1998	Equity carve-out	DuPont	Conoco	$4.4 billion (191.5 million shrs @ $23)
Mar. 25, 1998	Equity carve-out	Thermo Instr. Sys.	ONIX Systems	$47.85 million (3.3 million shrs @ $14.50)
May 11, 1999	Equity carve-out	Time Warner	Time Warner Telecom	$252 million (18 million shrs @ $14)
Jan. 4, 1999	Spin-off	Hilton Hotels	Park Place Entertainment	$1.96 billion (260.8 million shrs @ $7.50)
Feb. 9, 1999	Spin-off	Olin Corp.	Arch Chemicals	$432 million (22.962 mil shrs @ $18.8125)
Jan. 4, 1999	Spin-off	Rockwell Intl.	Conexant Systems	$1.78 billion (94.9 million shrs @ $18.81)
Apr. 5, 1999	Spin-off	Varian Associates	Instruments and semiconductor	$620 million (shares in 2 new entities)

TABLE A12.5 Event Study Analysis for Divestiture Sample from 1998

Announce Date	Divestiture Type	Parent	Firm Return (−1, +1)%	Market (−1, +1)%	Net of Market (−1, +1)%
Nov. 18	Asset sale	Bausch & Lomb	7.27	1.47	5.79
Dec. 22	Asset sale	CIGNA Corp.	4.77	3.41	1.36
Aug. 21	Asset sale	Cincinnati Milacron	4.21	−0.90	5.12
July 9	Asset sale	C.R. Bard	0.94	0.84	0.11
Nov. 2	Asset sale	Duke Energy	0.89	2.29	−1.40
Nov. 17	Asset sale	Eli Lilly	1.49	1.67	0.17
Aug. 3	Asset sale	Entergy Corp.	0.00	−6.20	6.20
Sep. 1	Asset sale	IBM	−1.68	−3.57	1.89
May 18	Asset sale	PG&E Corp.	0.83	−0.70	1.53
Mar. 11	Asset sale	Xerox Corp.	2.63	1.67	0.96
June 1	Asset sale	Yellow Corp.	3.55	−0.40	3.95
Apr. 27	Equity carve-out	Cincinnati Bell	3.07	−3.08	6.15
May 11	Equity carve-out	DuPont	8.39	1.89	6.50
Feb. 2	Equity carve-out	Thermo Instr. Sys.	6.40	2.08	4.32
Apr. 6	Equity carve-out	Time Warner	2.01	−0.93	2.94
June 30	Spin-off	Hilton Hotels	−6.52	1.36	−7.87
July 30	Spin-off	Olin Corp.	8.51	−0.85	9.35
June 29	Spin-off	Rockwell Intl.	−1.92	0.40	−2.32
Aug. 21	Spin-off	Varian Associates	11.51	−0.90	12.42
		Average	2.97	−0.02	2.99

return for the divestiture sample is 2.99%. Sixteen of the 19 net-of-market estimates (84%) are positive. These results are in tune with the general research on the wealth effects of corporate divestitures.

SUMMARY

This appendix examines a sample of 19 divestitures announced in 1998. The firm-specific motivation of the divesting parents generally aimed at a new focus either as a means to improve performance or to reflect a changing emphasis in corporate strategy. A number of the divestitures also were tied to broader economic change forces such as deregulation and energy markets. Similar to general research on corporate restructuring, the divestitures in the sample created wealth for the shareholders of the parent corporations.

QUESTIONS

A12.1 Pick an asset sale reported in Table A12.3. What were the advantages of the sale of the assets for the divesting parent? What were the advantages to the buying firm?

A12.2 Several of the sample divestitures were conducted by firms in the deregulated electric utility industry. Why might deregulation be associated with divestitures?

REFERENCES

Allen, Jeffrey, W., "Capital Markets and Corporate Structure: The Equity Carve-Outs of Thermo Electron," *Journal of Financial Economics* 48, 1998, pp. 99–124.

Mulherin, J. Harold, and Audra L. Boone, "Comparing Acquisitions and Divestitures," *Journal of Corporate Finance* 6, July 2000, pp. 117–139.

CHAPTER 13
FINANCIAL RESTRUCTURING

W e emphasize throughout this book that M&A policies should take place within the framework of the strategic planning processes of the firm. Equally important, M&A decisions are not separate compartments. It is impossible to separate internal programs for growth and the use of external M&A markets. Financial and M&A decisions also interact. In this chapter, we illustrate the implementation of these generalizations, particularly in some of the areas of traditional financial management. We include the following topics: leverage and leveraged recapitalizations, dual-class stock recapitalizations, exchange offers, reorganization processes, financial engineering, and liquidations and takeover bust-ups.

UNLOCKING THE VALUE IN THE FIRM

As an overview, we utilize the relationships depicted in Figure 13.1, which presents some major factors affecting the value of the firm. First is the value of a firm when it is all equity financed. To this can be added the present value of tax shields. A third source of value growth is the present value of other benefits of leverage such as pressures for efficiency to meet debt obligations (Jensen, 1986; Wruck, 1990, pp. 430–433).

A fourth group of benefits involves top management changes and changing roles of other control groups such as banks, insurance companies, and pension funds. Fifth, M&As can perform a constructive role in augmenting the capabilities and product-market spans of firms.

FIGURE 13.1 Sources of Value Increases

$$
\begin{array}{l}
\text{Value of the firm} = \begin{bmatrix} \text{Value} \\ \text{all equity} \\ \text{financed} \end{bmatrix} + \begin{bmatrix} \text{PV of} \\ \text{tax} \\ \text{shields} \end{bmatrix} + \begin{bmatrix} \text{PV of other} \\ \text{benefits of} \\ \text{leverage} \end{bmatrix} + \begin{bmatrix} \text{PV of benefits} \\ \text{of control} \\ \text{change} \end{bmatrix} \\[4em]
+ \begin{bmatrix} \text{PV of} \\ \text{benefits} \\ \text{from M\&As} \end{bmatrix} + \begin{bmatrix} \text{PV of benefits} \\ \text{of changes in} \\ \text{strategies, policies,} \\ \text{operations,} \\ \text{organization} \\ \text{structure} \end{bmatrix} - \begin{bmatrix} \text{PV of} \\ \text{costs of} \\ \text{financial} \\ \text{distress} \end{bmatrix}
\end{array}
$$

Sixth, in taking positive actions for growth and improvement, such as expansion, M&As, leverage changes, and dealing with financial distress, performance improvement is essential. The present value of benefits of changes in strategies, policies, and operations, as well as organizational structure and processes, can be substantial (Wruck, 1990, pp. 434–435). A demonstration of a leveraged recap plus efficiency improvements can be found in a case study of the Sealed Air Corporation developed by Wruck (1994). Finally, the present value of the costs of financial distress would reduce the value of the firm. Figure 13.1, therefore, summarizes major factors that influence the success of the individual restructuring efforts we now describe.

LEVERAGE AND LEVERAGED RECAPITALIZATIONS

Capital structure and leverage decisions often are involved in mergers and takeovers. A firm with zero leverage might be vulnerable to takeover by a firm seeking to capture the tax benefits of debt. Capital structure and leverage decisions represent potentials for value enhancement, for acquiring other firms, or for defending against acquisition by others. We start with a simple example that provides a foundation for more complex financial recapitalizations.

Table 13.1 presents the initial input values for the analysis. Table 13.2 presents a series of balance sheets to illustrate the effects of increasing leverage. Before the financial recapitalization, the firm has no debt. The next two columns illustrate taking on debt equal to 20% or 40% of the market value of the firm before adding leverage. Table 13.2 depicts $600 of debt or $1,200 of debt. Table 13.3 presents the effects of tax shields on share prices. The present value of tax shields is calculated by multiplying the amount of debt by the tax rate of the firm, which was given in Table 13.1 as 40%. This is a simplified version of the tax effects, but the qualifications would not change the central principles, we are illustrating (DeAngelo and DeAngelo, 1998, Mitchell and Mitchell, 1996). Line 4 of Table 13.3 shows that the market value of the firm has been increased by the present value of the tax shields.

Table 13.4 illustrates other effects of increasing leverage. We start with the total market value of the firm from Table 13.3. In Line 2, the amount of debt is deducted to obtain the market value of equity. The values shown in Lines 3 to 5 are calculated simultaneously because the shares repurchased and the share price must be determined simultaneously. For example, with 20% debt, we would have the following expression for the new share price, P.

$$P = \frac{2.640}{100 - 600 / P}$$

$$(13.1)$$

TABLE 13.1 Initial Input Values

1. Operating income (millions)	$300
2. Shares outstanding (millions)	100
3. Management ownership	20%
4. Market value per share	$30
5. Market value of the firm (millions)	$3,000
6. Tax rate	40%

TABLE 13.2 Balance Sheets with Increasing Leverage

	Before Recap	*20% Debt*	*40% Debt*
1. Cash	$ 10	$ 10	$ 10
2. Other current assets	100	100	100
3. Long-term assets, net	90	90	90
4. Total assets	$200	$200	$ 200
5. Debt	$ 0	$600	$1,200
6. Equity at book	200	–400	–1,000
7. Total claims	$200	$200	$ 200

In words, the expression says

$$\text{New Share Price} = \frac{\text{Market Value of Equity}}{\text{Previous Shares Outstanding} - \text{Shares Purchased}}$$

Solving equation (13.1), we obtain $32.40 for the share price. The second term in the denominator of (13.1) represents shares repurchased with the debt proceeds and equals 18.52. When this number is subtracted from the previous shares outstanding of 100, we obtain the new shares outstanding with 20% debt of 81.48. The amount for Lines 3 to 5 with 40% debt are calculated in the same way.

In the remainder of Table 13.4, we calculate some ratios and coverages. Line 6 is developed by using the data in Table 13.2 on the balance sheets. For example, in Table 13.2 the total assets remain the same after $600 of debt is incurred. This is because the proceeds of debt were used to retire equity shares outstanding. Because total assets and total claims remain at $200, equity at book, which had been $200, must be a negative $400 for total claims to continue to equal assets of $200. Book equity becomes negative. This is what is observed in actual cases of leveraged recapitalizations. Whereas book equity becomes negative, the debt-to-market equity ratio is positive because market equity is positive.

In Lines 8 through 11, we calculate the interest coverage. Some plausible levels of the pretax cost of debt are shown in Line 8. When these percentages are multiplied by the level of debt outstanding, we obtain the amount of interest expense. Operating income was given in Table 13.1 at $300. The ratio of operating income to interest expense gives the interest coverage shown in Line 11.

In this base case example of increasing leverage, we can draw a number of generalizations. Using the original Modigliani–Miller measure of the tax shield benefits of debt, we have demonstrated that management has increased the value of the firm by adding leverage where

TABLE 13.3 Effect of Tax Shields on Share Prices

	Before Recap	*20% Debt*	*40% Debt*
1. Debt as percent of original firm value	0%	20%	40%
2. Amount of debt	$0	$600	$1,200
3. Present value of tax shields	$0	$240	$480
4. Market value of the firm	$3,000	$3,240	$3,480

TABLE 13.4 Leverage Ratios and Interest Coverage

	Before Recap	*20% Debt*	*40% Debt*
1. Market value of the firm	$3,000	$3,240	$3,480
2. Market equity	$3,000	$2,640	$2,280
3. Shares repurchased with debt proceeds	0.00	18.52	34.48
4. Shares outstanding	100.00	81.48	65.52
5. Share price	$30.00	$32.40	$34.80
6. Book equity	$200	–$400	–$1,000
7. Debt-to-market equity ratio	0.00	0.23	0.53
8. Pretax cost of debt	8.0%	9.5%	11.5%
9. Interest expense	$0.0	$57.0	$138.0
10. Operating income	$300	$300	$300
11. Interest coverage	—	5.3	2.2

there was none before. Other measures of tax benefits might produce different levels of value increases for the firm. However, adding leverage where there had been none before is likely to move the firm away from a suboptimal (zero) level of debt.

Table 13.5 illustrates the impact of a leveraged recapitalization on the percentage of control by the management of the firm. In the previous examples, the funds were used to repurchase shares. Table 13.5 illustrates the effects of using the funds from selling debt to pay a cash dividend to nonmanagement shareholders, who are assumed to hold 80% of the outstanding shares. The funds raised from selling debt are divided by 80 to obtain dividends of $7.50 per share when the funds raised by debt are $600 and $15 per share for the $1,200 level of debt, as shown in Line 3. Recall that before debt was sold, the value per share of stock was $30. Therefore, for management to receive the equivalent in shares of stock, they would receive 0.25 share of stock of each share held. When the dividend per share is $15, the share fraction due

TABLE 13.5 Leveraged Recapitalization: Alternative I

	20% Debt	*40% Debt*
1. Amount of debt	$600	$1,200
2. Shares held by nonmanagement shareholders	80	80
3. Dividend per share	$7.50	$15.0
4. Fraction of shares received by management	0.25	0.50
5. Original number of management shares in total	20	20
6. Additional number of management shares	5	10
7. New total number of management shares	25	30

	Before Recap		*After Recap*		
			Ownership %		
Shareholders	80.0%	80	76.2%	80	72.7%
Managers	20.0%	25	23.8%	30	27.3%
		105		110	

management is 0.50. Taking into account the original number of management shares, as shown in Line 5, the new total number of management shares would be 25 and 30, as shown in Line 7.

As shown in Table 13.5, it is straightforward to see that the share of ownership by management would rise as high as 27.3% when the amount of debt sold is $1,200. If higher levels of debt were incurred and paid out as a dividend, the patterns in Table 13.5 would become even more pronounced.

Table 13.6 goes through an analysis in which the interest-bearing debt becomes 77.5% of the pre-recap market value of equity. In this example, each shareholder receives all the funds raised not only by selling new debt (add $176 new debt to $10 old debt; multiplying $24 market value per share times 10 equals 240; then 186 divided by 240 equals 77.5), but also by drawing down $40 of available cash, a total of $216. The accounting entry is to credit cash $216 and debit "equity" $216. So equity after recap becomes a negative $16. The example illustrates the case where the shareholders receive in cash the full pre-recap market value of the equity. In addition, it is assumed that the market value per share of stock falls to $4 and that the nonmanagement shareholders receive in exchange for their old shares one share of the new equity stub. The common equity is referred to as a *stub* when a financial recap results in the decline of its market value to 25% or less of its previous market value. Management receives no cash but instead receives seven equity stubs for each equity share to obtain the same value received by each nonmanagement share. As a result, as shown in section D of Table 13.6, the ownership proportion held by managers rises from 10% to 44%. Thus, the higher the percentage is of original equity raised in debt form and distributed to nonmanagement, the larger the increase is in management's share of ownership.

THE EFFECTS OF THE USE OF LEVERAGED RECAPS

In the preceding section, we presented models of leveraged recaps (LRs). In this section, we discuss the rationale for their use. From the preceding examples, we see that a leveraged recap involves (1) a relatively large issue of debt, (2) the payment of a relatively large cash dividend to nonmanagement shareholders, and (3) as an alternative to the cash dividend or combined with it, a repurchase of common shares.

A number of empirical studies show that book leverage measured by total debt to total capitalization increases from about 20% to about 70% (Gupta and Rosenthal, 1991; Handa and Radhakrishnan, 1991; Kleiman, 1988). The ownership share of management increases from 9% to 24% on average.

The market response to announcements of leveraged recaps depends on whether the action was defensive or proactive. In defensive LRs, the actions are taken in response to actual takeovers or indications of a likely takeover bid. Proactive LRs are part of a longer-term program of improving the performance of the firm. Event returns in a proactive LR experience a cumulative abnormal return of about 30%, similar to the level in tender offers (Gupta and Rosenthal, 1991; Handa and Radhakrishnan, 1991; Kleiman, 1988). Surprisingly, in such LRs the event returns to bond shareholders have been a positive 5% even though leverage has been increased substantially.

For defensive LRs, the abnormal returns include negative as well as positive values. The range is so wide that making a generalization is difficult (Kleiman, 1988). Gupta and Rosenthal (1991), however, show cumulative abnormal returns of 48% over a window beginning 30 days before the start of the takeover and ending 150 days after the completion of the leveraged recapitalization and a positive 5% to bondholders.

TABLE 13.6   Recap to Increase Management Control

A. Basic Data Inputs

Market value of equity per share		$24
Net operating income (NOI), millions		$30
Shares outstanding, millions		10
Shares owned by management, millions		1
Each shareholder share (SH) receives		
Cash		$24.00
Stub	1 @ $4	$ 4.00
		$28.00
Each management share receives		
Stub	7 @ $4	$28.00

B. Sources and Uses of Cash

Sources of cash		Uses of cash	
Cash on books	$ 40	Cash offer per SH	$24.00
Short-term interest-bearing debt	0	Number of stubs for SH	× 9
Senior long-term debt	100		$ 216
Subordinated debt	76		
	$216		

C. Balance Sheets

	Before Recap	After Recap
Cash	$ 50	$ 10
Other current assets	100	100
Long-term assets, net	120	120
Total assets	$270	$230
Non-interest-bearing ST debt	$ 60	$ 60
Short-term interest-bearing debt @ 10%	10	10
Senior long-term debt @ 12%	0	100
Subordinated debt @ 15%	0	76
Equity	200	−16
Total liabilities and shareholders' equity (SHE)	$270	$230
Difference	0	0

D. Ownership Proportions

	Before Recap	After Recap
Total number of shares (millions)		
Owned by shareholders	9 (90%)	9 (56%)
Owned by managers	1 (10%)	7 (44%)
	10	16

E. Interest Coverage

Net operating income (NOI)	$30	$30
Interest expense		
Short-term interest-bearing debt (STIBD)	$ 1.0	$ 1.0
Senior long-term debt	0.0	12.0
Subordinated debt	0.0	11.4
	$ 1.0	$24.4
NOI/Interest expense ratio	30.0	1.2

SUBSEQUENT PERFORMANCE

A defensive LR might succeed by returning cash to shareholders that is close to or more than the takeover offer. In addition, share owners continue to hold the equity stubs received. The substantial increases in leverage also might discourage outside bidders. The high leverage ratios may represent a form of scorched earth policy. Prospective bidders might be reluctant to face the task of returning the firm to leverage ratios closer to historical industry patterns. Although LRs are used as a takeover defense, a high percentage of firms that adopt them are subsequently acquired.

One study (Denis and Denis, 1995) found that 31% of their 29-firm sample completing LRs between 1985 and 1988 encountered financial distress. The high rate of financial distress, however, resulted mainly from unexpected and adverse macroeconomic and regulatory developments. The main factors influencing subsequent performance appear to have been (1) industry conditions, (2) whether the LRs were defensive or proactive, and (3) whether operating improvements were achieved.

Critical to the performance of the firm following an LR (proactive or defensive) is whether other operating improvements are made. This has been demonstrated in a number of case studies (Healy and Palepu, 1995; Mitchell and Mitchell, 1996; Stewart, 1991; Wruck 1994). The evidence is also consistent with a positive disciplinary role of debt (Dann, 1993; Gupta and Rosenthal, 1991). The large overhang of debt stimulates management to improve operations to generate sufficient cash flows to pay down the debt.

A leveraged recapitalization is likely to achieve the best results if it is part of a strategic plan to improve the performance of a firm in relation to its changing environments. In addition to the financial restructuring, the success of an LR depends heavily on programs to improve operating performance.

We now present a series of examples to illustrate the proposition that organizational restructuring can produce more basic improvements than financial engineering.

The Sealed Air Corporation illustrates the policy changes required as a result of moving from a position of competitive advantage from strong patent positions in the early 1960s to increased competition by the late 1980s after the expiration of its major patents (Wruck, 1994). During the period of patent protection, its profit margins were high and its cash flows were high, with little pressure to control costs. With the expiration of its patents, new firms entered its product line. Price pressures developed, which put Sealed Air at a competitive disadvantage because of its inefficient operations and high costs. In response, the management of Sealed Air initiated major policy changes. It increased financial incentives to focus on efficiency and cash flow. It developed capital budgeting procedures to improve investment decisions. It substantially increased leverage, which created pressures to develop cash flows to service the debt. However, the increased leverage without the other policy changes to increase efficiency would have resulted in bankruptcy. The policy changes were successful in improving earnings performance and Sealed Air's stock price.

After years of dominating the copier market, Xerox Corporation faced competition from an increasing number of competitors who produced cheaper and better copiers in the early 1980s. Xerox responded by focusing on improving the reliability of its products. It redefined its strategy in a 1990 initiative called "Xerox 2000" from a maker of machines to a manager of documents. Its organizational restructuring involved moving from a classic functional form to an M-form of organization (recall our discussion of organization and strategy in Chapter 5), providing increased decentralized decision making in nine strategic business units, each focusing on a distinct type of customer. Xerox also introduced a contingent executive compensation system. Bonuses and long-term incentives were determined by a combination of individual achievement, business unit success, and overall company performance. The increased efficiency resulted in a 10% cut in its workforce in October 1993; note that this downsizing was the result of major policy changes. The Xerox example illustrates that successful restructuring requires improvements in strategy and organizational structure, as well as new incentive compensation programs to motivate better performance. Downsizing alone is an indication of weakness.

In summary, the Sealed Air and Xerox examples illustrate that increased efficiency is critical in strategic programs to improve a firm's performance. If such a program is successful, a firm's vulnerability to a takeover offer will be reduced. On the positive side, restructuring can help the firm enhance long-run benefits for its stakeholders.

DUAL-CLASS STOCK RECAPITALIZATIONS

In dual-class recapitalizations (DCRs), firms have created a second class of common stock that has limited voting rights and usually a preferential claim to the firm's cash flows. Most firms create the new class by distributing limited voting shares pro rata to current shareholders. A typical DCR creates a class A type of shares with one vote per share but with a higher dividend rate than the other class. The class B shares can cast multiple votes such as 3, 5, or 10 per share; their dividend rate is lower than for the class A shares. As a result of a DCR, officers and directors as a group will usually have 55% to 65% of common stock voting rights (DeAngelo and DeAngelo, 1985; Partch, 1987). However, the officers and directors have a claim on about 25% of the total cash flows from common stock. In a substantial proportion of companies with dual classes of common stock, the control group represents founding families or their descendants (DeAngelo and DeAngelo, 1985). In one third of a sample of firms, two or more of the top executives were related by either blood or marriage.

REASONS FOR DUAL-CLASS RECAPITALIZATIONS

A positive reason for DCRs is to enable top management to solidify its control so that long-term programs can be carried out. This avoids the pressure to show good results every quarter. The motive is particularly applicable if the operations of the firm are relatively complex so that it is difficult for acquirers to evaluate managerial performance.

A related rationale is that managers may develop firm-specific abilities that are fully compensated when long-range plans come to fruition. Before the longer-term results are in, these managers would suffer the risk that their prospective rewards would be appropriated when outside shareholders responded favorably to an acquisition offer. Alternatively, it is also possible that managers who are not performing well might be motivated to entrench their positions against a takeover so that they will not be replaced.

MARKET RESPONSE TO DUAL-CLASS RECAPS

One way to test the alternative motives for DCRs is to measure the market response. In such studies, the 90-day period preceding the announcement of a DCR represents a period of positive abnormal returns of more than 6% (Lease, McConnell, and Mikkelson, 1984; Partch, 1987). When the event return is measured over a narrow window of 2 or 3 days including the day of announcement of plans to create limited voting common stock, the market response is about a

1% significantly positive gain. When the average stock price reaction is cumulated over the time period from the announcement of the plan to the shareholder meeting at which it is approved, the response is negative but not significantly different from zero. The conclusion is that shareholder wealth is not adversely affected by the adoption of a DCR.

However, it was found that when a firm was taken over, the holders of superior voting right shares received a differentially higher payment than the holders of inferior voting shares (DeAngelo and DeAngelo, 1985). Other studies found that few firms with dual-class stock have experienced takeover bids. A virtual laboratory test of this issue was provided when the Ontario Securities Commission, on March 2, 1984, adopted a policy that it would not approve a prospectus offering inferior voting shares unless they were given coattails that would permit them to participate equally in any takeover bid for the superior shares. After some experience, the commission reversed this policy on October 12, 1984. The premium to superior shares was then increased again (Maynes, 1996). The consensus view appears to be that superior shares sell at a premium and mainly because they receive more in a takeover (Lease, McConnell, and Mikkelson, 1983).

PARADOX OF THE ENTRENCHMENT

Shareholder approval is required for the adoption of a DCR. Why do DCRs continue to be approved if their purpose is management entrenchment? In some cases, the voting power of insiders will be sufficient to achieve shareholder approval, but this cannot explain all approvals. Ruback (1988) developed a model that explains shareholders' behavior in exchange offers in which shareholders are given the opportunity to exchange common stock for shares with limited voting rights but higher dividends. These offers induce shareholders to exchange their shares for limited-voting-rights shares carrying higher dividends, even though such shareholders are harmed by the exchange as a result of the decline in the share price. In these offers, the wealth of shareholders who retain the superior-vote shares is transferred to shareholders who elect the inferior-vote shares with higher dividends. Thus, all outside shareholders rationally choose the higher dividend. This leads to the approval of the exchange plan and in turn to the decline in their wealth. If collective action were possible, outside shareholders would collude to defeat the exchange offer in order to avoid the reduced probability of receiving a takeover bid caused by the recapitalization.

Lehn, Netter, and Poulsen (LNP) (1990) found DCRs to be comparable with leveraged buyouts, reasoning that both are forms of increasing ownership by management. However, they also found that DCRs experienced significantly higher growth rates in sales and number of employees than LBO firms. This is predictable, because during the period of their study, 1977 through 1987, LBOs were mainly in relatively mature industries with stable cash flows. The ratios of research and development expenditures to sales and of advertising expenditures to sales were higher for the DCR firms. The recap firm also had lower pretransaction tax liabilities.

With respect to performance after the transaction, LNP found that the dual-class firms use a higher percentage of their cash flows for capital expenditures than the LBO firms. A large proportion of the dual-class firms issue equity following the recapitalization. For the period studied, the LBOs were in more mature industries, whereas the dual-class firms were in industries with higher growth prospects. Significant increases in industry-adjusted operating income to sales ratios are achieved by dual-class firms. The LBO firms outperform dual-class firms in terms of size of improvement and performance, reflecting the turnarounds associated with managers with substantially increased equity stakes in LBOs. Insiders of dual-class firms already held 43.1% of the common equity before the transaction. In contrast to LBOs, which often were used as antitakeover transactions, takeover rumors or bids preceded recaps in only 3 of the 97 firms. Dual-class firms have relatively lower leverage policies and do not alter them as a consequence of the transaction.

All of the preceding findings on DCRs are consistent with the other studies. Insiders in DCR firms seek to consolidate their control in order to carry through their long-range plans. They are willing to sacrifice some current dividend income for the prospect of larger, long-term capital gains.

Moyer, Rao, and Sisneros (MRS) (1992) examined the hypothesis that DCRs are accompanied by ways to decrease managerial control of the corporation—specifically by increasing leverage, dividends, and monitoring by security analysts and institutional investors. Their sample consisted of 114 firms that announced in the *Wall Street Journal* or in some SEC document (on a date that could be identified) DCRs during the period 1979 to 1987. The average asset size per firm was $517.1 million. MRS show that the mean proportion of outside directors on the board changed from 53.7% to 59.1% over the two years preceding the announcement. Only the changes in debt ratio and the mean number of analysts following the firm showed significant change. Changes in dividend payout and changes in the number of institutions holding the stock after the recapitalization were statistically insignificant. For prior ownership levels of up to 7.5%, the change in debt ratio was significantly greater in the low-prior-ownership groups than in the high-prior-ownership groups. The mean number of analysts following the sample firms was 5.72 prior to announcement and 7.47 after the announcement. Thus, a moderate increase in external control took place.

EXCHANGE OFFERS

An exchange offer provides one or more classes of securities the right or option to exchange part or all of their holdings for a different class of securities of the firm. Like a tender offer repurchase, an exchange offer is usually open for about 1 month. However, the offer frequently is extended. To induce the securities holders to make the exchange, the terms of exchange offered necessarily involve new securities that are of greater market value than the market value prior to the exchange offer. Exchange offers usually specify the maximum number of securities that can be exchanged. Also, many exchange offers are contingent upon acceptance by holders of a minimum number of the securities to be exchanged. Masulis (1980) reports that initial announcement dates precede the beginning of the exchange offer by, on average, 9 weeks. He states that the average life of the offer is about 7 weeks.

TAX ASPECTS OF EXCHANGE OFFERS

When a company sells bonds at a discount, this generally implies that the coupon interest rate is below the market rate of interest. If the amount of the discount is material, the discount for tax purposes must be amortized over the life of the debt instrument. The amount of the amortized discount is treated as an additional interest payment to make up for the low coupon. It is, therefore, a tax expense to the corporation. When a corporation sells a bond at a premium, this means that the coupon payment is higher than the market rate. The amortization of the premium is a reduction in the interest tax expense to the corporation.

TABLE 13.7 Exchange Offers with Positive Returns

P1. Debt for common stock (Masulis, 1983)	+14.0%
P2. Preferred for common stock (Masulis, 1983; Pinegar and Lease, 1986)	+ 8.2%
P3. Debt for preferred stock (Masulis, 1983)	+ 2.2%
P4. Income bonds for preferred stock (McConnell and Schlarbaum, 1981)	+ 2.2%

When a firm redeems debt at a price below the issue price, the difference is treated as ordinary income. If debt is redeemed at a price above the issue price, the difference is treated as an ordinary loss to the corporation and a gain to the seller of debt (Masulis, 1980). When stock is tendered for debt, stockholders incur a capital gains tax liability just as if they had sold their stock for cash. Masulis (1980) therefore observes that an exchange of debt for common stock is likely to occur when stocks are selling at relatively low prices and most shareholders would incur little or no capital gains liability as a consequence.

EMPIRICAL EVIDENCE ON EXCHANGE OFFERS

With some of the characteristics of exchange offers as a background, we next turn to the empirical data. Table 13.7 shows that an exchange of debt for common stock involves the largest positive returns to shareholders. It is 14%, about the order of magnitude of wealth effects observed in stock repurchase tender offers. The exchange of preferred stock for common also carries a large gain of more than 8%. The exchange of debt or the exchange of income bonds for preferred stock carries small but significant positive returns.

Table 13.8 summarizes the results of exchange offers with negative returns. Why do some types of exchange offers result in negative returns and others achieve positive returns? A number of theories or explanations are possible. The effects appear to depend on whether the exchanges have one or more of the following consequences:

1. Leverage increasing or decreasing.
2. Implied increases or decreases in future cash flows.
3. Implied undervaluation or overvaluation of common stock.
4. Increases or decreases in management share ownership.
5. Increases of decreases in control of management use of cash.
6. Positive or negative signaling effects.

The exchange offers in Table 13.7 have positive returns. They appear to have in common a number of characteristics: They increase leverage, they imply an increase in future cash flows, and they imply undervaluation of common stock. In two of the four cases, management share ownership is increased; in three of the four cases, the control over management's use of cash is

TABLE 13.8 Exchange Offers with Negative Returns

N1. Common stock for debt (Masulis, 1983)	−9.9%
N2. Private swaps of common for debt (Finnerty, 1985: Peavy and Scott, 1985)	−0.9%
N3. Preferred stock for debt (Masulis, 1983)	−7.7%
N4. Common for preferred stock (Mauslis, 1983: Pinegar and Lease, 1986)	−2.6%
N5. Calls forcing debt conversion (Mikkelson, 1981)	−2.1%

decreased. It is difficult to judge whether the leverage effect is also a signaling effect or whether it is purely a tax effect. It could be argued that the exchange of preferred for common stock does not carry tax implications for the corporation. On the other hand, because 80% of the dividends (85% before 1986) on preferred stock (for the period of these studies) could be excluded as income for a corporate investor, the incidence of this tax advantage accrued at least partially to the issuing corporation. Copeland and Lee (1991) judged the signaling effects to be most consistent with theory and empirical evidence.

Another curiosity in connection with the leverage-increasing exchange offers is noted by Vermaelen (1981). He pointed out that 30.1% of the leverage-increasing exchange offers in the sample developed by Masulis were announced during the period of dividend controls, roughly from mid-1971 through mid-1974. This suggests that they were by relatively smaller firms that were seeking to avoid the requirement that dividend increases could be no more than 4% per year. Another strong external effect came about on the swaps that were stimulated by a tax law change in 1984 documented by Finnerty (1985). Because multiple explanations could account for the positive returns shown by Table 13.7, it is difficult to assign weights to each explanation.

Similarly, in Table 13.8, for exchange offers causing negative returns, it appears that the five explanations will run in the opposite direction. Swaps of common stock or preferred stock for debt carry about the same relatively large negative returns. However, private swaps of common stock for debt carry a small but significant return. Much more detailed studies would be required to attempt to assess the relative weight of each of the potential explanations for the pattern of abnormal returns observed.

One study introduces the q-ratio as an additional variable (Born and McWilliams, 1993). In a study of 127 equity-for-debt exchange offers, firms with q-ratios less than 1 experienced significantly negative abnormal returns on announcement. This confirms the studies reported previously. However, firms with q-ratios greater than 1 did not experience a significant event response. These findings suggest that the equity-for-debt exchanges with low q values may be used to rescue the firm from pressures resulting from the inability to service debt obligations.

Distressed exchanges have been widely used by firms that issued high-yield junk bonds and tried to work out what they felt was a short-term problem caused by overleveraging a basically sound operating company. Exchanges usually involve either a total exchange of preferred or common equity for the old debt or a combination of some equity and some new, but extended, debt for the old debt.

The classic distressed exchange involves a firm whose operating and financial condition has deteriorated due to chronic and cyclical problems. It attempts to restructure its assets and its liabilities. For example, International Harvester Corporation—a large farm equipment, truck, and bus manufacturer—was on the verge of total collapse in 1980 to 1982. The firm first exchanged preferred stock for its interest payment obligations to banks and extended its interest payments to creditors and payables to suppliers. Next, it converted its short-term bank debt (1 to 3 years) to longer-term junk bonds (10 to 12 years). Finally, it exchanged common equity in its newly named entry, Navistar International, for the "old" junk bonds. These distressed restructuring strategies helped the firm improve its operations; it eventually paid its short- and long-term creditors in full (Chen, Weston, and Altman, 1995).

Lie, Lie, and McConnell (2001) provided a comprehensive study of exchange offers by distressed firms. Their sample comprised 126 firms that announced debt-reducing exchange offers during the time period 1980 to 1994. As provided in the appendix to their paper, the sample includes International Harvester and other well-known firms such as BF Goodrich, Lockheed, and LTV.

Lie, Lie, and McConnell (2001) addressed two queries. They asked why firms perform debt-reducing exchange offers and also inquired about the information provided by the offers. They found that the answers to these two questions are related. Firms perform debt-reducing exchange offers to stave off further financial distress. The bad news, however, is that the announcement of the debt-reducing offer conveys financial weakness to the market. Lie, Lie, and McConnell (2001) concluded that debt-reducing exchange offers represent actions by management to avoid Chapter 11 filings and thereby preserve value for stockholders.

REORGANIZATION PROCESSES

Several forms of financial restructuring can take place when a firm experiences financial distress. Financial distress is defined here as the condition in which the liquidation value of the firm's assets is less than the total face value of creditor claims.

OUT-OF-COURT PROCEDURES

Figure 13.2 provides an overview of alternative adjustments that a firm might make to relieve financial distress. The three main alternatives are informal procedures, merger, and legal proceedings. In out-of-court procedures, the firm can either continue or be liquidated. If the firm continues, (1) a residual or equity claim can be substituted for a debt priority claim, or (2) the

FIGURE 13.2   Alternative Adjustments to Financial Distress

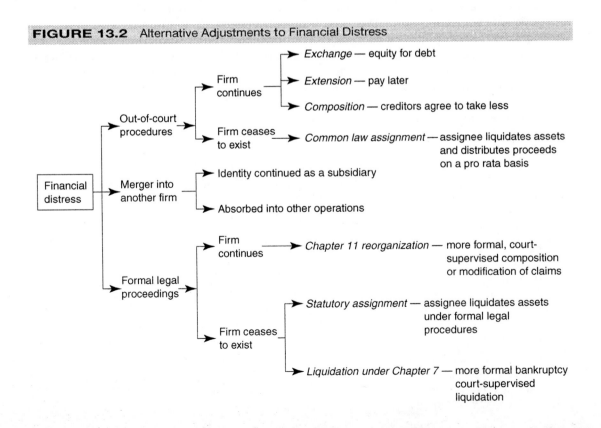

maturity of the debt can be postponed. A third alternative is to scale down the obligation. All three procedures are based on the idea that if the distressed firm is given some breathing room to improve operations, the creditors ultimately will receive more than they would otherwise.

MERGER INTO ANOTHER FIRM

Mergers also can be used to rescue a floundering or failing firm. A study of 38 takeovers of distressed firms between 1981 and 1988 (Clark and Ofek, 1994) revealed that such combinations were more likely to involve firms in the same industry and less likely to be hostile takeovers than general patterns. In the sample of 38 restructuring efforts that used mergers, Clark and Ofek classified 20 as failures, 9 as marginally successful, and 9 as clearly successful. These evaluations were based on the use of 5 different measures to evaluate the postmerger performance of the combined and target firms: (1) ratio of earnings before interest, taxes, and depreciation (EBITD) to sales; (2) return to the bidder on its investment in the target; (3) beta excess return during the 2 years after completion of the merger; (4) the bidder's excess equity return over its industry 3-digit SIC code median during the 2 years after merger completion; and (5) a qualitative variable that equals +1 if it was successful, 0 if marginal, and –1 if a failure.

Clark and Ofek also studied the relationship between the announcement period cumulative abnormal return (CAR) and each of their five performance variables. The bidder CAR was positively related to each of the five performance measures. This is another study that demonstrates the ability of market event returns to forecast postmerger results.

They found also that bidders overpay for the distressed targets. Postmerger performance results appear to be dominated largely by industry factors. Takeovers of target firms that are financially distressed are more likely to be successfully restructured than takeovers of target firms whose operating performance is poor. Distressed targets that are small compared to the bidder yield positive returns to the bidder. Clark and Ofek concluded that in the majority of cases, takeovers do not successfully restructure a distressed target. They observe, however, that the effort to do so might appear to be the best alternative available at the time.

FORMAL LEGAL PROCEEDINGS

When an informal extension or scaling down of the obligations as well as the merger alternative do not appear to solve the problems of a distressed firm, more formal legal proceedings are required. The formal court proceedings follow the bankruptcy law adopted in 1978. Its five major provisions are (1) an automatic stay, (2) debtor in possession (DIP), (3) increased power of managers in the recontracting process, (4) new voting rules for creditors, and (5) some flexibility in applying absolute priority rules.

An automatic stay permits the firm to stop all payments of principal and interest, preventing secured creditors from taking possession of their collateral. This makes it easier for the firm to obtain additional financing. Debtor-in-possession financing makes it possible to issue new debt claims with priority over existing debt.

Managers retain considerable power after a firm has filed for bankruptcy. Managers are able to continue to make operating decisions, and, for 120 days after the Chapter 11 filing, managers have the exclusive right to propose a reorganization plan. The court often grants one or more extensions of this deadline. Management has 180 days from the filing date to obtain creditor and shareholder approval. If management fails to propose a plan or its plan is rejected, creditors can propose their own plan. To do so, they must provide proof of values for claims to be issued and assets to be retained or sold. This requires costly appraisals and hearings compared with a management plan that requires the bankruptcy judge to evaluate it as "fair and reasonable."

The 1978 Bankruptcy Code introduced new voting rules for approval by creditors of a reorganization plan. It specifies majority (in number) requirements for approval of the plan and provides that dissenters must accept the terms approved by the majority.[1] In this sense, each class of creditors behaves as one part in which minority creditors cannot hold out. The new voting rules facilitate renegotiation of the debt, so the potential for investment efficiency is improved by reducing bargaining costs.

The code also provides for absolute priority rules in establishing the order of claims under reorganization. Frequent but small (2.3% to 7.6%) deviations from absolute priority occur. Here are two possible explanations: (1) One or more classes of claimants may provide new or future financing as a basis for improving their position over what it would have been under absolute priority; (2) estimated market values are used as a basis for establishing priority positions. However, market values depend on the success of the restructuring and the future performance of the firm. The value estimates are subject to negotiation among the claimants. Thus, deviations from absolute priority might facilitate approval of a plan earlier than would otherwise be possible.

The basic goal for the legal bankruptcy-restructuring process is to preserve organization value. The aim of recontracting with claimants is to restore the firm to operating and financial health. Thus, there is a positive side to the procedures for restructuring financially distressed firms.

BANKRUPTCY

In this section, we look further into the reorganization process related to bankruptcy. We first consider evidence on major examples of bankruptcies. Then we discuss some of the theory and evidence on the incentive effects of bankruptcy on corporate managers. We also review the applicability of the tools of financial valuation for firms facing the bankruptcy process.

RECENT DATA ON BANKRUPTCY

Table 13.9 provides data on the 20 largest corporate bankruptcies in the United States since 1980. The firms are presented in the order of the dollar value of pre-bankruptcy assets.

The data in the table allow some generalizations on the incidence of bankruptcy. In some instances, bankruptcy emanates from firm-specific sources. For example, Texaco filed for bankruptcy in 1987 due to the loss of a multibillion dollar lawsuit with Pennzoil related to the 1984

---

[1]If the reorganization is proposed in an out-of-court distressed restructuring (i.e., not under Chapter 11), then a virtually unanimous acceptance by those creditors who are impaired must be received. This explains the relatively recent phenomenon known as a "prepackaged Chapter 11," whereby the required (but not necessarily unanimous) proportion of accepting creditor votes is assembled for a plan *prior to* the filling of the petition for relief (which initiates the bankruptcy process). In most cases, the formal Chapter 11 reorganization that follows the prepack agreement is a relatively simple procedure. The actual time spent in the bankruptcy process has been as little as one month, and it generally averages only a few months. The money spent in a prepackaged bankruptcy is also typically less. See Altman (1993), Betker (1995), McConnell and Servaes (1991), and Salerno and Hansen (1991) for discussions of prepackaged plans and their recent experience. Berker analyzed 49 cases and concluded that although direct costs of prepacks are comparable to those of traditional Chapter 11, gains come from the binding of holdouts and from favorable tax treatment on tax loss carryforwards.

TABLE 13.9   The 20 Largest U.S. Bankruptcies Since 1980

Firm	Industry	Filing Date	Pre-Bankruptcy Total Assets (in $ billion)
WorldCom, Inc.	Telecom	July 21, 2002	103.9
Enron Corp.	Energy	Dec. 2, 2001	63.4
Conseco, Inc.	Insurance	Dec. 18, 2002	61.4
Texaco, Inc.	Petroleum	Apr. 12, 1987	35.9
Financial Corp. of America	Savings and loan	Sept. 9, 1988	33.9
Global Crossing Ltd.	Telecom	Jan. 28, 2002	30.2
UAL Corp.	Airline	Dec. 9, 2002	25.2
Adelphia Communications	Cable	June 25, 2002	21.5
Pacific Gas and Electric Co.	Electric utility	Apr. 6, 2001	21.5
MCorp	Banking	Mar. 31, 1989	20.2
First Executive Corp.	Insurance	May 13, 1991	15.2
Gibratar Financial Corp.	Savings and loan	Feb. 8, 1990	15.0
Kmart Corp.	Retail	Jan. 22, 2002	14.6
FINOVA Group, Inc. (The)	Financial services	Mar. 7, 2001	14.1
HomeFed Corp.	Savings and loan	Oct. 22, 1992	13.9
Southeast Banking Corporation	Banking	Sept. 20, 1991	13.4
NTL, Inc.	Cable	May 8, 2002	13.0
Reliance Group Holdings, Inc.	Insurance	June 12, 2001	12.6
Imperial Corp. of America	Savings and loan	Feb. 28, 1990	12.3
Federal-Mogul Corp.	Auto parts	Oct. 1, 2001	10.2

Source: BankruptcyData.Com.

takeover of Getty Oil. In another case, the bankruptcy of Kmart can be attributed to a specific source: competition from Wal-Mart.

Many of the bankruptcies, however, appear to reflect industry conditions. For example, two of the large bankruptcies at the end of the 1980s, Financial Corporation of America and Mcorp, occurred in the financial services industry. Two of the more recent cases, Enron Corporation and Pacific Gas and Electric Company, are firms in energy-related sectors.

Several of the recent large bankruptcies—WorldCom, Global Crossing, Adelphia Communications and NTL Incorporated—have occurred in the telecom and cable sectors. Such industries have been faced with increasing risk due to deregulation and technological change. Cases such as WorldCom and Global Crossing have brought forth media stories of fraud. It is important to note, however, that leading telecom firms throughout the world, such as British Telecom, Deutsche Telekom, and France Telecom, also experienced financial problems at the same time as the failures of the U.S. firms. See, for example, a July 26, 2002, article in the *New York Times* ("Telecom Giants Retrench in Europe," p. W1).

BANKRUPTCY PROCEDURES

In the United States, bankruptcy procedures for corporations are governed by the Bankruptcy Reform Act of 1978 (with minor modifications through 2003). We illustrate the procedures using a composite example reflecting actual companies in recent years. The Newton Company had expanded rapidly, both internationally and through acquisitions. It began suffering losses and filed for bankruptcy with the following balance sheet.

Newton Company Balance Sheet

Assets		Liabilities	
Current assets	$2,000,000	Accounts payable	$ 950,000
Fixed assets	2,250,000	Note payable (bank), 8%	220,000
		Accrued wages	90,000
		Taxes payable	230,000
		Current liabilities	$1,490,000
		Mortgage, 6%	315,000
		Subordinated debentures[a],12%	300,000
		Long-term debt	$ 615,000
		Preferred stock	250,000
		Common stock	1,500,000
		Retained earnings	395,000
		Net worth	$2,145,000
Total Assets	$4,250,000	Total claims	$4,250,000

[a]Subordinated to $220,000 notes payable to bank.

The outlook for Newton was so unfavorable that liquidation was unavoidable. The total legal fees and administrative expenses of the bankruptcy proceedings were $350,000. Upon liquidation of the firm's assets, only $1,500,000 was realized, as shown:

Current assets	$1,200,000
Net property	300,000
	$1,500,000

The proceeds were distributed as follows:

Cash received from sale of current assets		$1,200,000
Less priority claims:		
1. Fees and expenses of bankruptcy proceedings	$350,000	
2. Wages due workers	90,000	
3. Taxes due	230,000	670,000
Available for general claims		$ 530,000
Cash received from sale of property	$300,000	
Mortgage claims	315,000	
Unsatisfied portion of mortgage claims	$ 15,000	

The preceding illustrates the priority of claims. First is the legal fees and expenses of the bankruptcy proceedings (the lawyers wrote the laws, so they come first). Second are wages due workers (this makes sense because their income has been interrupted). Third are taxes due. The difference between the cash received and the amount of the priority claims, $530,000 is available for general claims. As shown, to the extent that mortgage claims are not covered by the proceeds from the sale of real property, they become a general claim. We next illustrate the allocation to general creditors as follows.

(1)	(2)	(3)	(4)	(5)
Claims of General Creditors	Amount	Application of 35.7%[a]	After Subordination	% of Original Claim Received
Unsatisfied portion of mortgage	$15,000	$5,355	$5,355	96.90[c]
Bank notes payable	220,000	78,540	185,640	84.40
Accounts payable	950,000	339,150	339,150	35.70
Subordinated debentures	300,000	107,100	0	0
	$1,485,000	$530,000[b]	$530,000[b]	46.50[d]

[a]$530,000/$1,485,000 = 35.7%
[b]Does not add to total because of rounding.
[c]($5,355 + $300,000)/$315,000 = 96.9%
[d]($530,000 + $300,000)/($1,485,000 + $300,000) = 46.5%

The claims of general creditors listed in column 2 total $1,485,000. However, amount available for general claims is only $530,000. General claimants receive only 35.7% of their claims. However, the debentures were subordinated to the notes payable to the bank. So, in column 4, the $107,100 that the subordinated debentures would have received as a general creditor is added to the claim of the bank notes payable. Column 5 shows that the mortgage holders received almost all of their claims because they received the total amount of the proceeds of the sale of property. They have double protection. The banks do well because of the subordination. The trade creditors to whom the accounts payable are owed receive 35.7%. The holders of subordinated debentures, preferred stock, and common stock received nothing.

This is an example of a Chapter 11 bankruptcy liquidation. As an alternative, management might propose a reorganization plan in which the going concern value of the company is preserved so that creditors and owners can receive more. In this example, the common stockholders have a strong incentive to keep the firm in operation to preserve some equity value. Workers also have an incentive to accept some reduction in wages so that the firm can continue to operate and save their jobs.

Management proposes a reorganization plan calling for: (1) an exchange of the accounts payable creditors' existing claims for 20% of the equity in the reorganized firm, (2) the preferred stockholder invest an additional $200,000 for 10% of the equity, (3) the common stockholders invest an additional $800,000 for 60% of the equity, (4) in return for the wage concessions, the workers receive 10% of the equity. In the reorganization plan, management demonstrates that with the cash infusion of $1,000,000, the wage concessions, and the new business model, the firm would be able to earn $1.2 million per year after paying interest on the notes payable, the mortgage, and the subordinated debentures. The applicable (post reorganization) weighted-average cost of capital is estimated to be 12%. Using a simple, no-growth valuation model, the expected market value of equity would, therefore, be $10 million. If these expectations are realized, the creditors would hold equity with a value of $2 million, the preferred shareholders would hold $1 million of equity, the common stockholders would have equity with a value of $6 million, and the workers would hold equity with a value of $1 million.

These expectations might be optimistic. However, they illustrate that with a cash infusion to support a new business model and with lower operating costs and improved profitability, value might be preserved and even increased. In practice, many variations of this example can be observed. Considerable negotiations may be involved. The basic elements in the reorganization processes of companies like those listed in Table 13.9, which have entered into Chapter 11 bankruptcy proceedings, are illustrated by the preceding example. A better strategic plan, an improved business model, cash infusions, an exchange of debt claims or wage claims for equity, and improved operating efficiency can achieve the preservation and potential increase in economic value.

Bankruptcy and Incentives: Ex-Ante Effects

For all of the firms in Table 13.9, bankruptcy was not an expected outcome. Stockholders and bondholders invested in the firm with the common goal of reaping positive returns. The financial distress and bankruptcy of the firms, however, often puts stockholders and bondholders in conflict.

Daigle and Maloney (1994) offered a positive theory of bankruptcy that addresses responses to the stockholder-bondholder conflicts in bankruptcy. In their research, they provided a summary of bankruptcy law and the reorganization process. They focused on developing an explanation for the deviation of the absolute priority of debt over equity in the reorganization process.

Daigle and Maloney (1994) modeled the incentives of corporate managers in this process. They noted that if equity holders never receive any share of a post-reorganization firm, then corporate managers, acting in shareholders' interests, have an incentive to shift investments to high-risk projects if the firm experiences financial distress. Such a strategy of betting the ranch can possibly create large gains for shareholders. Because the firm is already in financial distress, any greater chance of default is effectively passed on to bondholders.

The stockholder-bondholder incentive conflict modeled by Daigle and Maloney (1994) is a classic agency cost issue. Jensen and Meckling (1976, Section 4.1) posed such incentive effects as one reason that outside corporate financing is not solely from debt. In the spirit of Jensen and Meckling (1976), firms can be expected to develop bonding and monitoring mechanisms to alleviate the wealth losses posed by the potential incentive problems. Extending this line of thought, Daigle and Maloney (1994) argued that one response to the stockholder-bondholder conflict is for stockholders to receive a piece of the post-bankruptcy firm. If stockholders receive a part of the reorganized firm, then corporate managers, acting in shareholders' interests, have less of an incentive to engage in high-risk projects prior to bankruptcy.

To test their model, Daigle and Maloney (1994) compared the attributes of bankrupt firms with the fraction of stock received by equity holders in the post bankruptcy reorganization. They argued that the more malleable the assets of the firms are and, therefore, the more potential risk shifting there is when in financial distress, the greater the potential stockholder-bondholder conflicts. To ameliorate such a conflict, Daigle and Maloney (1994) predicted that the greater the malleability of assets is, the greater will be the fraction of the reorganized firm received by equity holders. In an analysis of 56 firms from the period 1980 to 1986, they found support for their model.

Bankruptcy and Incentives: Ex-Post Outcomes

In addition to potential stockholder-bondholder conflicts, Jensen and Meckling (1976) also modeled the possible incentive discrepancies between managers and stockholders. One question that arises for firms that become financially distressed is whether corporate managers bear costs resembling those losses experienced by shareholders. Similarly, do the members of the board of directors, whose job it is to monitor managers, bear any costs if the firms for which they serve undergo financial distress?

Research by Gilson (1989, 1990) addressed the effect of bankruptcy and financial distress on management and board of director turnover. In his 1989 paper, Gilson studied the replacement of senior management (chairman, CEO, and president) at 381 financially distressed firms during the period 1979 to 1984. He found that in any given year, more than half of the distressed firms experienced a change in senior management. Gilson (1989) interpreted the evidence to indicate that corporate senior management experiences significant costs when their firms default.

Gilson (1990) performed related analysis of the boards of directors of financially distressed firms. He studied 111 firms that either filed Chapter 11 bankruptcy or privately restructured their debt in the period 1979 to 1985. He found that less than half of the directors of the distressed firms remained with their firms after reorganizing or restructuring. Moreover, the directors who resign from the boards of distressed firms are less likely to serve on the boards of other publicly traded firms in the future. These results suggest that board members are monitored for the performance of their firms.

Bankruptcy and Valuation

An important issue for a firm in financial distress or in formal bankruptcy is the value of the firm's assets. One question is whether the firm can cover debt obligations. A related issue is whether the firm should continue operations or instead liquidate. The answers to such questions are complicated by the costs of valuing the assets of distressed firms.

Gilson, Hotchkiss, and Ruback (2000) analyzed the valuation of firms undergoing bankruptcy. They studied 63 firms that reorganized under Chapter 11 during the period 1984 to 1993. They found that traditional financial techniques such as discounted cash flow analysis provide accurate estimates of value, on average. However, they found a relatively large dispersion in valuation forecasts of the bankrupt firms compared with nondistressed firms. They attributed the dispersion in the estimates for the distressed firms to the paucity of information on these firms compared with the representative publicly traded corporation.

The information costs associated with bankrupt firms suggest that the manner in which a distressed firm is reorganized or liquidated may affect the value received by claim holders. Stromberg (2000) investigated this issue by studying cash auction bankruptcy. He relied on a unique data set of 205 Swedish corporations that filed for bankruptcy between 1988 and 1991. He found that the sale back to incumbent management is a common auction outcome. This suggests that bankruptcy auctions have some resemblance to the reorganization process under Chapter 11 in the United States. Moreover, the auction outcome in the Swedish setting suggests that the costs associated with the reorganization and liquidation of distressed firms are driven primarily by the underlying source of the financial distress rather than by a particular set of legal rules in a given country.

FINANCIAL ENGINEERING

Financial engineering involves the use of calls, puts, swaps, and forward and futures contracts to influence the payoffs from taking on various types of financial exposure. These instruments have helped limit the financial exposures of business firms as well as other types of investors. A rich body of literature is available on this subject. We limit our discussion to one example, of how financial engineering can facilitate a merger transaction (Mason et al., 1995; Tufano, 1996).

In 1991 in its strategic planning processes, Amoco, a major oil company, made a decision to dispose of its marginal oil and gas properties. It created a new organization, MW Petroleum

Corporation, as an entity with interest in 9,500 wells in more than 300 producing fields. The Apache Corporation, a smaller independent oil and gas company, was interested in purchasing Amoco's unit. Apache's strategy was to acquire properties that others regarded as marginal and use its lower-cost operations to achieve higher returns. The negotiations were taking place during the spring of 1991, just after Iraq's invasion of Kuwait had pushed up oil prices. Future oil prices were highly uncertain. Financial engineering provided a solution.

Amoco was willing to write Apache a guarantee that if oil prices fell below a specified level during the first 2 years after the sale. Amoco would make compensating payments to Apache. Apache, in turn, agreed to pay Amoco if oil prices exceeded a specified level over a 5- to 8-year period. Thus, the commodity risk of the transaction was shared. In financial engineering terms, Amoco and Apache had created a "collar"—a combination of a call option and a put option. Option pricing theory can price a collar.

After the merger was completed, each company was approached with an offer to purchase its option position. Thus, the financial markets gave the companies the opportunity to monetize (sell) their options and thereby close their risk exposures if they so desired. The body of literature on financial engineering is rich with creative transactions. This example illustrates their implications for facilitating M&As.

LIQUIDATIONS AND TAKEOVER BUST-UPS

Corporate liquidations can be involuntary or voluntary. Corporate liquidations associated with bankruptcy proceedings are usually involuntary. Creditors force a firm to liquidate if it is worth more "dead" than "alive." In other words, attempting to operate an unsuccessful firm can cause values to deteriorate even further. But voluntary liquidations have a more positive orientation. When a firm can be sold in parts or as a whole for an amount that exceeds the market value of the firm's securities, liquidation will realize more for the security holders. Managers may be encouraged to take such actions because of the threat that an acquirer will mount a proxy contest for control or launch a tender offer to buy the firm and then liquidate it. Even the threat of such "bust-up" takeovers may stimulate voluntary liquidations.

Voluntary liquidations partake of the characteristics of divestitures and spin-offs. Divestitures have the advantage of realizing gains by moving resources to other companies for whom the operations are worth more. In voluntary liquidations, the seller may have different types of activities for which larger gains could be achieved by selling to different types of buyers. This is superior to the alternative of a merger in which one buyer obtains three types of businesses and seeks to sell off the types that do not fit into its own operations. The original owner probably can obtain more because it can justify more fully the value of the business. Liquidations can substitute for a spin-off when the key managers might otherwise have left the company to start up a competing operation.

An important tax advantage of liquidations was removed by the Tax Reform Act of 1986. Under the General Utilities Doctrine, the corporate capital gains to the selling firm were not taxable if it adopted a plan of complete liquidation and all liquidating dividends were paid to shareholders within 12 months after the plan was adopted. One effect of the repeal of the General Utilities Doctrine by the 1986 act was to eliminate the tax incentive for firms to liquidate voluntarily after partial sell-offs. The 1986 act also eliminated the preferential personal capital gains tax rate, which makes the deferral of realization in nontaxable mergers more attractive. It appears that the Tax Reform Act of 1986 reduced the tax advantages of liquidations compared with nontaxable mergers.

EMPIRICAL STUDIES

Skantz and Marchesini (1987) studied a sample of 37 firms that announced liquidation between 1970 and 1982. They found that the announcement-month average excess return was +21.4%. Interestingly, they found that their sample firms were "not highly dissimilar to their industry members" (p. 71) in profitability prior to the liquidation decision.

Of the possible reasons for the positive abnormal return. Skantz and Marchesini found only one to be applicable. Although divestitures had been generally subject to capital gains taxes, voluntary liquidations could be structured to qualify for preferential tax treatment on a major portion of the gains. This does not explain the much higher positive gains to liquidations (21.4% for the announcement with a cumulative average excess return of 41.3%) than for spin-offs, which also are treated as tax-free exchanges. The reason might be that spin-offs average only 20% of the original parent; if the abnormal returns found by Copeland, Lemgruber, and Mayers (1987) of 5.02% are multiplied by 5 for comparable sizing of investment, the gains are similar.

Hite, Owers, and Rogers (1987) included an analysis of total liquidations in their study of the market for interfirm asset sales. They analyzed 49 voluntary liquidations during the period 1963 to 1983. The median market value of equity was $41 million. The median book value of total assets was about $72 million. Although mergers were eliminated, they found that 21 of the 49 firms had been targets in earlier merger, tender offer, or leveraged buyout bids in the 24 months preceding the liquidation proposal. An additional three firms had been involved in proxy solicitation control contests.

Hite, Owers, and Rogers observed a 2-day announcement period average abnormal return of 12.24% for total liquidations, and more than 80% of the sample observations were positive. They estimated that for the seven liquidating firms that had senior securities, an equally weighted portfolio yielded a 2-day holding period average return of 8.57%. Their analysis of the source of the positive returns to both the shareholders and senior claimants is that assets are being moved to higher-valued uses.

The study of voluntary liquidations by Kim and Schatzberg (1987, 1988) covered a sample of 73 liquidating firms over the period 1963 to 1981. They observed that their sample was composed of relatively small firms. The median market value of equity was $23 million. The median ratio of the market value of equity of the liquidating firm to the market value of equity of the acquiring firm was 0.28. Kim and Schatzberg found that the liquidation announcement was associated with an average 3-day market-adjusted return of 14% to the shareholders of liquidating firms. An additional 3% abnormal return took place at shareholder confirmation. Acquiring shareholders experienced a small positive return at a liquidation announcement and a small negative return at confirmation, but these returns were not statistically significant.

As in the Hite, Owers, and Rogers (1987) study, liquidation announcements often were associated with prior news related to mergers, tender offers, or partial sell-offs. At the time of the prior announcements, an abnormal return of 9% was realized. When Kim and Schatzberg took into consideration all public announcements, they obtained even higher returns. They measured the abnormal returns for shareholders from 2 days before the earliest announcement date until 2 days after the last announcement date, obtaining total gains of 30% for firms without prior announcements and 34% for firms with prior announcements. The average gain to the shareholders of acquiring firms was not statistically significant.

The Kim and Schatzberg (KS) (1987, 1988) papers confirmed the beneficial effect on senior claimants found by Hite, Owers, and Rogers (1987). The majority of the firms in the KS sample retired debt that had a market value less than the face value. Kim and Schatzberg also analyzed the question of why liquidations increase market values. They observed that one advantage of liquidations is that there may be several purchasers, whereas in a merger there is likely to be only one. This enables the selling firm to move its assets to the individual purchasers from whom the greatest value can be realized.

Kim and Schatzberg also compared the tax effects of liquidations with those of nontaxable mergers, and they discussed the impact of the Tax Reform Act of 1986. In general, a nontaxable merger had the advantage of deferring the recognition of a gain to the stockholders of the selling firm until a subsequent sale occurred of the securities involved. First, in a liquidation, the selling stockholders must recognize the gain immediately. Second, unused tax credits and losses belonging to either of the pre-merger firms are carried over in a nontaxable merger, but those of the selling firm are lost at liquidation. Third, a liquidation permits the acquiring firm to step up the tax basis of the assets acquired, but this cannot be done in a nontaxable merger.

Berger and Ofek (1996) found that between 1986 and 1991, the average diversified firm destroyed about 15% of the value its individual segments would have had if they had been operating as independent business units. For a sample of 100 large acquisitions, they found that half of the large diversified targets were broken up. The negative value of diversification that was recovered by the bust-up ranged from 21% to 37%. The large targets that were not broken up after they were taken over had a mean value effect of diversification of only 5%, implying that they were not broken up after the acquisition because not much could be gained by doing so. Berger and Ofek studied the buyers of the divested divisions in the bust-up group and found that 75% of the buyers were LBO associations (financial groups taking segments private in a leveraged buyout) or focused, related firms. This indicates that the bust-up was carried out to move the segments to firms with experience in related businesses.

A paper by Mehran, Nogler, and Schwartz (MNS) (1998) studied the influence of executive ownership and executive compensation incentives on voluntary liquidation decisions. They covered 30 firms for the period 1975 to 1986 related to a sample of control firms in the SIC 1000 to 3999 categories. They found that the probability of a voluntary liquidation increases as the percent ownership of the firm's shares by top executives increases. The greater the use of stock options and other executive compensation incentives is the higher the probability of voluntary liquidation is. The median total asset size of the liquidating firm sample was $46 million; the control sample had a median size of $44 million.

The abnormal event returns for their sample of voluntary liquidations over an 11-day window beginning 5 days before the announcement were 15.5%, significant at the 1% level. So voluntary liquidation decisions increase value for shareholders. MNS noted that their study generalized the earlier Dial and Murphy (1995) case study of General Dynamics's partial liquidation in which the executive compensation plans motivated them to shrink the firm's assets, sometimes eliminating their own jobs.

Six firms in their sample had received takeover bids. The average gain to the shareholders measured by the discounted value of payments in liquidation was 10.3% higher than the average of the takeover bids. They found that 70% of the CEOs in the liquidating firms did not find another CEO position for at least 3 years.

Summary

The firm's internal growth program is tied closely to the external market for corporate control. Capital structure and leverage decisions represent potentials for value enhancement, for acquiring other firms, or for defending against being acquired by others. These are illustrated in the financial restructuring transactions currently in use.

In leveraged recapitalizations, a relatively large issue of debt is used for the payment of a relatively large cash dividend to nonmanagement shareholders or for the repurchase of common shares, or a combination of the two. The end result is an increase in the ownership share of management. Leveraged recaps should be proactive as part of a long-run program to improve the performance of the firm rather than defensive in response to actual or possible takeovers.

In dual-class stock recapitalizations (DCRs), firms create a second class of common stock that has limited voting rights but usually has a preferential claim to the firm's cash flows. Top management may use DCRs as a way to solidify their control to pursue long-run improvement programs or, alternatively, to entrench their position against takeovers or against being replaced. As a result of a DCR, officers and directors will have, on average, from 55% to 65% of the common stock voting rights but a claim on only about 25% of the total cash flows.

An exchange offer provides the holders of one or more classes of securities the right or option to exchange part or all of their holdings for a different class of securities of the firm. Positive returns are associated with exchange offers that increase leverage, imply an increase in future cash flows, suggest undervaluation of common stock, increase management share ownership, or decrease management control over cash. These are illustrated by debt–for–common stock and preferred–for–common stock exchanges. In recent years, distressed exchanges have been used widely by firms in attempts to restructure assets and liabilities.

Financial distress becomes a driving force for financial restructuring. A distressed firm can make many alternative adjustments. Out-of-court procedures allow the firm's obligations to be restructured to give it some breathing room. Mergers can be used to rescue a floundering or failing firm. However, takeovers do not, in the majority of cases, successfully restructure a distressed target firm. Takeovers are more likely to be successful for financially distressed target firms than for target firms whose operating performance is poor. As a last resort, formal legal proceedings such as filing for a Chapter 11 reorganization or for bankruptcy may be employed.

Firms have used financial engineering to limit their financial exposure. Financial engineering also has been used to facilitate merger transactions. If the acquiring firm and the prospective target firm are able to share the risk exposures of their mutual transaction, then it is more likely that the deal will be completed.

If the firm is worth more "dead" than "alive," creditors will force the firm to liquidate. The firm can be sold in parts or as a whole for an amount that exceeds the preliquidation market values of its securities. Liquidation also can be voluntary when there is the threat of a "bust-up" takeover. Managers might prefer to liquidate if outsiders are likely to mount a proxy contest for control or launch a tender offer to buy the firm and conduct the liquidation themselves.

The examples in the chapter illustrate that the best forms of restructuring involve strategy, structure, efficient operations, and compensation systems that provide the correct incentives. Compensation systems that balance the performance of individuals, business units, and the corporation can help implement programs to reduce costs and improve quality. A solid foundation is thereby established for gaining the benefits of financial engineering.

Questions

13.1 What are the goals of a leveraged recapitalization?

13.2 What are the pros and cons of dual class recapitalizations?

13.3 What types of exchange offers have positive event returns, and what types have negative event returns?

13.4 Discuss the relationship among financial reorganizations of various types, including a Chapter 11 reorganization.

13.5 How can financial engineering be used to facilitate M&As?

13.6 How do bust-up takeovers and subsequent liquidation of the parts increase the total value realized over the market price of the firm prior to its sale by parts?

Case 13.1   MANAGEMENT ASSISTANCE, INCORPORATED

Liquidating for profit is discussed from the standpoint of case studies plus the analysis of what is going on. When a firm "liquidates," its economic resources have not necessarily been destroyed. Indeed, even though an individual firm might cease to exist, it typically sells some or most of its assets to other ongoing firms. In the hands of the buying companies, the assets can be put to a higher economic use than when they were held by the seller.

The case study of Management Assistance, Incorporated, (MAI) illustrates a number of the concepts involved in liquidating a company (Rosenberg, 1985). MAI had started as a company that leased punch card equipment. Then in the late 1950s, it became a computer-leasing company. It was somewhat unique as a leasing company in that it emphasized the need for strong marketing and customer engineering organizations. In particular, it emphasized customer engineering as a method of assuring customers that the products it leased would receive prompt and effective attention to maintain their serviceability.

In the 1970s, MAI was a leader in the development of personal computers with its Basic Four Information Systems. This enabled MAI to record a $19 million profit in 1979. With increased competition in personal computers, the company recorded a $17 million loss in fiscal 1984. The reported losses caused the price of its stock to decline substantially.

MAI caught the attention of Asher Adelman early in his career in corporate takeovers. "But where others saw only red ink, Adelman discerned hidden value" (Rosenberg, 1985, p. 9). The customer engineering and service activity of MAI had been placed in a corporate subsidiary named Sorbus Service. Adelman says that he judged that this activity alone would sell for more than two times the then-current market price of the common stock of MAI as a whole. The personal computer business of MAI had been placed in a corporate subsidiary with the name Basic Four Information Systems. The division was experiencing losses, but Adelman saw potential in the strong marketing organization as a distribution operation, selling not only the products of MAI but the products of other companies, as well. By January 1985, Adelman had won control of the board of directors and sold off Sorbus and Basic Four. In February 1985, MAI began to distribute liquidating dividends of about $26 per share to stockholders. It is said that Adelman made a profit of $11 million on his investment of $15 million, a gain of 73%.

QUESTIONS

C13.1.1 Were the main assets of MAI destroyed?

C13.1.2 What happened to Sorbus and Basic Four?

C13.1.3 Why didn't the previous control group at MAI liquidate MAI?

References

Altman, E. I., *Corporate Financial Distress and Bankruptcy,* 2d ed., New York: John Wiley & Sons, 1993.

Berger, Philip G., and Eli Ofek, "Bustup Takeovers of Value-Destroying Diversified Firms," *Journal of Finance* 51, September 1996, pp. 1175–1200.

Betker, B., "An Empirical Examination of Prepackaged Bankruptcy," *Financial Management,* Spring 1995, pp. 3–18.

Born, Jeffery A., and Victoria B. McWilliams, "Shareholder Responses to Equity-for-Debt Exchange Offers: A Free-Cash-Flow Interpretation," *Financial Management* 22, Winter 1993, pp. 19–20.

Chen, Yehning, J. Fred Weston, and Edward I. Altman, "Financial Distress and Restructuring Models," *Financial Management* 24, Summer 1995, pp. 57–75.

Clark, Kent, and Eli Ofek, "Mergers as a Means of Restructuring Distressed Firms: An Empirical Investigation," *Journal of Financial and Quantitative Analysis* 29, December 1994, pp. 541–565.

Copeland, Thomas E., E. F. Lemgruber, and D. Mayers, "Corporate Spinoffs: Multiple Announcement and Ex-Date Abnormal Performance," chapter 7 in *Modern Finance and Industrial Economics,* T. E. Copeland (ed.), New York: Basil Blackwell, 1987.

Copeland, Thomas E., and Won Heum Lee, "Exchange Offers and Stock Swaps—New Evidence," *Financial Management* 20, Autumn 1991, pp. 34–48.

Daigle, Katherine H., and Michael T. Maloney, "Residual Claims in Bankruptcy: An Agency Cost Explanation," *Journal of Law and Economics* 37, April 1994, pp. 157–192.

Dann, Larry Y., "Highly Leveraged Transactions and Managerial Discretion over Investment Policy: An Overview." *Journal of Accounting & Economics,* 16, January-April-July 1993, pp. 237–240.

DeAngelo, Harry, and Linda DeAngelo. "Ancient Redwoods and the Politics of Finance: The Hostile Takeover of the Pacific Lumber Company." *Journal of Financial Economics* 47, January 1998, pp. 3–53.

——, "Managerial Ownership of Voting Rights: A Study of Public Corporations with Dual Classes of Common Stock," *Journal of Financial Economics* 14, 1985, pp. 33–69.

Denis, David J., and Diane K. Denis, "Causes of Financial Distress Following Leveraged Recapitalization," *Journal of Financial Economics* 37, February 1995, pp. 129–157.

Dial, J., and K. Murphy, "Incentives, Downsizing, and Value Creation at General Dynamics," *Journal of Financial Economics* 37, 1995, pp. 261–314.

Finnerty, John D., "Stock-for-Debt Swaps and Shareholder Returns," *Financial Management* 14, Autumn 1985, pp. 5–17.

Gilson, Stuart C., "Bankruptcy, Boards, Banks, and Blockholders: Evidence on Changes in Corporate Ownership and Control When Firms Default," *Journal of Financial Economics* 27, 1990, pp. 355–387.

Gilson, Stuart C., "Management Turnover and Financial Distress," *Journal of Finacial Economics* 25, 1989, pp. 241–262.

Gilson, Stuart C., Edith S. Hotchkiss, and Richard S. Ruback, "Valuation of Bankrupt Firms," *Review of Financial Studies,* 13, Spring 2000, pp. 43–74.

Gupta, Atul, and Leonard Rosenthal, "Ownership Structure, Leverage, and Firm Value: The Case of Leveraged Recapitalizations," *Financial Management* 20, Autumn 1991, pp. 69–83.

Handa, Puneet, and A. R. Radhakrishnan, "An Empirical Investigation of Leveraged Recapitalizations with Cash Payout as Takeover Defense," *Financial Management* 20, Autumn 1991, pp. 38–68.

Healy, Paul M., and Krishna G. Palepu, "The Challenges of Investor Communication: The Case of CUC International, Inc." *Journal of Financial Economics* 38, 1995, pp. 111–140.

Hite, Gailen, James E. Owers, and R. C. Rogers, "The Market for Interfirm Asset Sales: Partial Sell-Offs and Total Liquidations," *Journal of Financial Economics* 18, 1987, pp. 229–252.

Jensen, Michael C., "Agency Costs of Free Cash Flow, Corporate Finance and Takeovers," *American Economic Review* 76, May 1986, pp. 323–329.

Jensen, Michael C., and William H. Meckling, "Theory of the Firm: Managerial Behavior, Agency

Costs, and Ownership Structure," *Journal of Financial Economics* 3, October 1976, pp. 305–360.

Kim, E. H., and J. D. Schatzberg, "Voluntary Corporate Liquidations," *Journal of Financial Economics* 19, 1987, pp. 311–328.

———, "Voluntary Liquidations: Causes and Consequences," *Midland Corporate Finance Journal* 5, Winter 1988, pp. 30–55.

Kleiman, R. T., "The Shareholder Gains from Leveraged Cashouts: Some Preliminary Evidence," *Journal of Applied Corporate Finance* 1, Spring 1988, pp. 46–53.

Lease, R., J. McConnell, and W. Mikkelson, "The Market Value of Control in Publicly Traded Corporations," *Journal of Financial Economics* 11, 1983, pp. 439–472.

———, "The Market Value of Differential Voting Rights in Closely Held Corporations," *Journal of Business* 75, 1984, pp. 443–467.

Lehn, Kenneth, Jeffry Netter, and Annette Poulsen, "Consolidating Corporate Control; Dual-Class Recapitalizations Versus Leveraged Buyouts," *Journal of Financial Economics* 27, October 1990, pp. 557–580.

Lie, Erik, Heidi J. Lie, and John J. McConnell, "Debt-Reducing Exchange Offers," *Journal of Corporate Finance* 7, 2001, pp. 179–207.

Mason, Scott P., Robert C. Merton, Andre F. Perold, and Peter Tufano, *Cases in Financial Engineering: Applied Studies of Financial Innovation,* Upper Saddle River, NJ: Prentice Hall, 1995.

Masulis, Ronald W., "The Impact of Capital Structure Change on Firm Value: Some Estimates," *Journal of Finance* 38, March 1983, pp. 107–126.

———, "Stock Repurchase by Tender Offer: An Analysis of the Causes of Common Stock Price Changes. "*Journal of Finance* 35, 1980, pp. 305–319.

Maynes, Elizabeth, "Takeover Rights and the Value of Restricted Shares," *The Journal of Financial Research* 19, Summer 1996, pp. 157–173.

McConnell, J., and H. Servaes "The Economics of Prepackaged Bankruptcy." *Journal of Applied Corporate Finance* 4, Summer 1991, pp. 93–97.

McConnell, John J., and Gary G. Schlarbaum, "Evidence on the Impact of Exchange Offers of

Security Prices: The Case of Income Bonds." *Journal of Business* 54, 1981, pp. 65–85.

Mehran, H., G. Nogler, and K. Schwartz, "CEO Incentive Plans and Corporate Liquidation Policy," *Journal of Financial Economics* 50, 1998, 319–349.

Mikkelson, W. H., "Convertible Security Calls and Security Returns," *Journal of Financial Economics* 9, 1981, pp. 237–264.

Mitchell, Mark, and Janet Mitchell, "UST, Inc.," CaseNet, Boston: South-Western College Publishing, 1996.

Moyer, R. C., Ramesh Rao, and P. M. Sisneros, "Substitutes for Voting Rights: Evidence from Dual Class Recapitalizations," *Financial Management* 21, Autumn 1992, pp. 35–47.

Partch, M. Megan, "The Creation of a Class of Limited Voting Common Stock and Shareholder Wealth," *Journal of Financial Economics* 18, 1987, pp. 313–339.

Peavy, J.W., and J. A. Scott, "A Closer Look at Stock-for-Debt Swaps," *Financial Analysis Journal,* May/June 1985, pp. 44–50.

Pinegar, J. Michael, and Ronald C. Lease, "The Impact of Preferred-for-Common Exchange Offers of Firm Value," *Journal of Finance* 41, September 1986, pp. 795–814.

Rosenberg, Hilary, "Newest Kid on the Takeover Block," *Barron's,* March 11, 1985, pp. 8–9, 11.

Ruback, R. S., "Coercive Dual-Class Exchange Offers," *Journal of Financial Economics* 20, January/March 1988, pp. 153–173.

Salerno, T., and C. Hansen, "A Prepackaged Bankruptcy Strategy," *Journal of Business Strategy* 12, January/February 1991, pp. 36–41.

Sikora, Martin, ed., *Capturing the Untapped Value in Your Company,* Philadelphia: MRL Publishing Company, 1990.

Skantz, Terrance R., and Roberto Marchesini, "The Effect of Voluntary Corporate Liquidation on Shareholder Wealth," *The Journal of Financial Research* 10, Spring 1987, pp. 65–75.

Stewart, G. Bennett, *The Quest for Value,* New York: HarperBusiness, 1991.

Stromberg, Per, "Conflicts of Interest and Market Illiquidity in Bankruptcy Auctions: Theory and Tests," *Journal of Finance* 55, December 2000, pp. 2641–2692.

Tufano, Peter, "How Financial Engineering Can Advance Corporate Strategy," *Harvard Business Review* 74, January/February 1996, pp. 136–146.

Vermaelen, Theo, "Common Stock Repurchases and Market Signaling: An Empirical Study," *Journal of Financial Economics* 9, 1981, pp. 139–183.

Wruck, Karen Hopper, "Financial Distress, Reorganization, and Organizational Efficiency," *Journal of Financial Economics* 27, October 1990, pp. 419–444.

——, "Financial Policy, Internal Control, and Performance: Sealed Air Corporation's Leveraged Special Dividend," *Journal of Financial Economics* 36, 1994, pp. 157–192.

CHAPTER 14
ALLIANCES AND JOINT VENTURES

Thomson Financial Securities Data (TFSD), a segment of International Thomson Organization, Limited, has a database on alliances and joint ventures starting in 1985. For the period 1988 to 1999, it lists 75,330 transactions. All types of alliances are covered including joint ventures, strategic alliances, licensing agreements, research and development agreements, manufacturing agreements, marketing agreements, and supply agreements. These categories represent agreements by two or more entities to combine resources to form a new business arrangement. The emphasis of this chapter will be on joint ventures, strategic alliances, and minority equity investments because they involve broader, interfirm relationships. We also will discuss licensing and related activities covered by more specific legal contracts.

We emphasize two aspects. (1) Alliances and joint ventures should be seen as examples of multiple paths to value enhancement along with internal growth, as well as mergers and acquisitions. (2) Although it is necessary to evaluate the merits of individual transactions, they also should be understood in a broader framework of strategic planning for the long term. Schipper and Thompson (1983) were the first to emphasize the evaluation of firms' merger programs over time rather than individual merger events. Geis and Geis (2001) use this extended time framework in analyzing alliances, minority equity investments, and licensing, as well as mergers and acquisitions.

Using the TFSD database, we compiled for an illustrative sample of 10 companies their merger and alliance transactions per year since 1985, as shown in Table 14.1. The cumulative M&A transactions of General Electric for the 17-year period exceeded 1,000 transactions. The cumulative alliance transactions for Microsoft for the 17-year period totaled 782. For the two technology firms, Intel and Microsoft, the alliances exceeded M&As.

In a broader sample, Robinson (2002) compiled 43,900 alliances involving U.S. firms or transactions covering activities in the United States for the period 1985 through 1999. He compared this with 59,759 merger transactions measured by Mergerstat data over the same time period. Merger rates averaged 2,599 compared to 726 per year for alliances from 1985 through 1989. Alliances increased to an average of 4,196 per year between 1990 and 1995, compared with an average of 2,616 mergers (Table 14.2). The surge in alliance activities reflected a change in antitrust legislation and policies of regulatory agencies. Initially, the aim was to encourage joint research and development activities, but later it extended to production activities. Pieces of legislation beginning in 1985 with subsequent amendments have been named the National Cooperative Research and Production Act (NCRPA). The business and economic benefits of alliances caused the activities to surge when antitrust policies were changed.

TABLE 14.1   Illustrative Merger and Alliance
Transactions, 1985 to June 15, 2002

	Transactions per Year	
	Alliances	*M&A*
Coca-Cola	5	14
Dow Chemical	7	16
Exxon/ExxonMobil	3	17
Ford	10	20
General Electric	11	67
General Motors	13	30
Intel	16	12
Merck	5	4
Microsoft	46	12
Procter & Gamble	5	12

Notes: Alliances include joint ventures and strategic alliances.
M&As include mergers, acquisitions, and repurchase agreements.
    Transactions done by firms' subsidiaries are not included in
the count.
    Transactions per year are calculated by dividing total transac-
tions during the period by the corresponding number of years for
the period. These are rounded to the nearest integer.
Source: Thomson Financial Securities Data.

TABLE 14.2   Alliances and Mergers, 1985–1999

	Number of Transactions, *Yearly Averages*	
	Alliances	*M&As*
1985–1989	726	2,599
1990–1995	4,196	2,616
1996–1999	3,773	7,768

Source: Robinson (2002), Table 1.

This chapter will cover: (1) joint ventures, (2) strategic alliances, (3) minority equity investments, (4) licensing and related agreements, and (5) franchising.

JOINT VENTURES

A joint venture represents a combination of subsets of assets contributed by two (or more)
business entities for a specific business purpose and a limited duration. Joint venture participants continue to exist as separate firms with a joint venture representing a newly created business enterprise. The joint venture can be organized as a partnership, a corporation, or any other
form of business organization the participating firms choose to select.

In contract law, joint ventures usually are described as having the following characteristics.

1. Contribution by partners of money, property, effort, knowledge, skill, or other asset to a common undertaking.
2. Joint property interest in the subject matter of the venture.
3. Right of mutual control or management of the enterprise.
4. Expectation of profit, or presence of "adventure."
5. Right to share in the profit.
6. Usual limitation of the objective to a single undertaking or ad hoc enterprise.

Thus, joint ventures are of limited scope and duration. Typically, they involve only a small fraction of each participant's total activities. Each partner must have something unique and important to offer the venture and simultaneously provide a source of gain to the other participants. However, the sharing of information or assets required to achieve the objective need not extend beyond the joint venture. Hence, the participants' competitive relationship need not be affected by the joint venture arrangement. Sometimes the joint arrangement is relatively informal, involving only an exchange of ideas and information while the participants work on similar challenges. The term *strategic alliances* has been used to describe relationships among companies that are something short of establishing a joint venture entity.

Joint ventures and mergers display similar timing characteristics. The correlation between completed mergers and joint venture start-ups is more than 0.95, highly significant from a statistical standpoint. Merger activity is also highly correlated with plant and equipment outlays. Joint ventures and mergers are likely to be stimulated by factors that affect total investment activity generally.

USES OF JOINT VENTURES

Joint ventures have been used for many years. In an early study, Bachman (1965) described the entry of oil and gas companies into the chemicals industry using joint ventures to a considerable degree. For the early 1960s, some illustrative joint ventures and the products they produced included the following:

Alamo Polymer (Phillips Petroleum and National Distillers)—polypropylene
American Chemical (Richfield Oil and Stauffer)—vinyl chloride, ethylene
Ancon Chemical (Continental Oil and Ansul)—methyl chloride
Avisun (Sun Oil and American Viscose)—polypropylene resins
Goodrich-Gulf (Gulf Oil and Goodrich Rubber)—S-type rubber
Hawkeye Chemical (Skelly Oil and Swift)—ammonia
Jefferson Chemical (Texas Company and American Cyanamid)—ethylene, propylene, and others
National Plastics Products (Enjay and J. P. Stevens)—polypropylene fiber
Sun Olin (Sun Oil and Olin)—urea, ethylene, and others
Witfield Chemical (Richfield Oil and Witco Chemical)—detergent alkylate

The value of combining different skills is demonstrated by the relationship between USX Corporation, a large integrated steel producer, and Nucor Corporation, the leading minimill steel producer. USX researchers developed a theory for a new process of making steel from iron carbide, eliminating blast furnaces and supporting coke batteries. If successful, the new process would cut steel production costs by as much as one fourth. In 1994 the two companies entered into an agreement to study the feasibility of the process. Nucor possessed considerable experience and expertise in constructing the types of plants that would be required. They would inter-

CHAPTER 14 ♦ Alliances and Joint Ventures **359**

act with the physicists at USX, who had formulated the new concepts. Additional examples of joint ventures are described in the following sections.

JOINT VENTURES AND BUSINESS STRATEGY

A succession of joint ventures can enable a firm to achieve market penetration into new areas over time. Geis and Geis (2001) described how Microsoft employed a series of joint ventures to enter and develop new product markets, expand into new geographic areas, and participate in new technology-driven value activities. The joint ventures were a part of the multiple paths to value growth including internal developments, mergers, minority investments, alliances, and contractual agreements.

Microsoft has aggressively sought to develop a strong position in online games. Microsoft purchased the Internet Gaming Zone from Electric Gravity in 1996. It made minority investments in game content developers (Digital Anvil and Gas Powered Games). In 1995, Microsoft formed a joint venture with DreamWorks SKG to establish DreamWorks Interactive. In February 2000, the joint venture was sold to Electronic Arts at a price that stamped the effort as a failure despite the hit status of games such as Lost World: Jurassic Park and Medal of Honor. Microsoft launched its Xbox game console in 2001.

In online gambling, NineMSN was established in 1997 as a 50–50 joint venture between Microsoft and ecorp. In 1995, Microsoft formed a joint venture with NBC-TV to establish MSNBC Cable. In 1999, Microsoft obtained a 2% interest in InsWeb Japan, a joint venture created in 1998 by Softbank and InsWeb. In 1999, Microsoft partnered with Ford Motor in an MSN CarPoint joint venture to sell autos via the Internet. Microsoft already had participated in a joint venture with Softbank and Yahoo! to develop an online car-buying service in Japan. In wireless communications, Microsoft formed a joint venture with Ericsson, the Swedish equipment manufacturer. Wireless Knowledge was formed as a 50–50 joint venture with Qualcomm to blend computer and wireless communication.

These are examples of the 782 joint ventures and alliances of Microsoft totaled in Table 14.1. The list is a small sample of the many activities described by Geis and Geis (2001) as a part of Microsoft's broader strategic objective to penetrate new attractive product markets and its geographic scope. Some of the efforts were less successful than others, but they all represented a part of a long-range program of learning and growth by expanding the capabilities of Microsoft.

Joint ventures also can be used by smaller firms protectively as an element of long-range strategic planning. The spider's web strategy is used to provide countervailing power among rivals in a product market and among rivals for a scarce resource. Thus, a small firm in a highly concentrated industry can negotiate joint ventures with several of the industry's dominant firms to form a self-protective network of counterbalancing forces. Indeed, it is reported that large companies such as General Electric are involved in more than 100 joint ventures and that IBM, GM, AT&T, and Xerox participate in more than a dozen joint ventures. Companies of the type listed have both financial resources and managerial and technical competence to bring to a joint venture (*BusinessWeek*, 1986). This strategy presupposes that the small firm has something unique to offer the industry leaders (Templin, November 1, 1995).

JOINT VENTURES AND RESTRUCTURING

Joint ventures perform a useful role in assisting companies in the process of restructuring. A number of case studies have been described (Nanda and Williamson, 1995). In the late 1980s, Philips, a large Dutch electronics company, decided to divest its appliances division, whose revenues had been running at $1.55 billion. The division had a history of poor performance because of a number of problems. It was trying to sell nine different brands and lacked coordination in marketing efforts. Production was spread across 10 plants in 5 countries, and large investments were needed for modernization. Nevertheless, the division had strong design and manufacturing skills.

Whirlpool was seeking to expand beyond its U.S. base and saw a potential for developing the appliance business of Philips into a global, coordinated production and sales activity. However, many uncertainties arose about the investment required, the future relationship with dealers, and the ability to turn around the operations. In 1989, Philips proposed a joint venture in which Whirlpool would own 53% of the appliance operation for $381 million and would have an option to buy the remaining 47% within 3 years. The joint venture enabled Whirlpool to gain knowledge about the appliance division before committing further funds. Whirlpool also benefited from Philips's continued participation in a number of ways. For a period of time, the products were double branded as Philips-Whirlpool appliances. The incentive for Philips to help was that it would receive more for the remaining 47%, which it sold to Whirlpool in 1991 for $610 million. It was estimated that by the use of the temporary joint venture, Philips received about $270 million more than if it had tried to complete the transaction before the start of the joint venture 2 years earlier.

This example illustrates how the buyer can use the joint venture experience to better determine the value of brands, distribution systems, and personnel. Through direct involvement with the business, the risk of making mistakes is reduced.

How costly mistakes can be made is illustrated by the method used by the Maytag Corporation when it sought to enter the European appliances market in 1989. It bought the Hoover appliances line from the Chicago Pacific Corporation. In seeking to penetrate the British market, the Hoover executives on behalf of Maytag sought to build on Hoover's historically strong relationships with small retailers in fragmented markets. However, in Britain, six major retailers accounted for most of the market. Because of the difficulties of penetrating this market, the Hoover executives mounted a special promotional campaign offering free airplane tickets with the purchase of a major appliance in Great Britain and Ireland. In the United States, discounted airline tickets are widely available, but in Europe airfares are regulated and higher. About 1 of every 300 people in Britain and Ireland bought an appliance to receive the free flights. The people who bought the appliances for the free tickets soon put the appliances into an active market in secondhand Hoover appliances. In honoring the commitments of its promotion, Hoover incurred a $50 million charge. Maytag became discouraged by this unfortunate experience and disposed of the European portion of the Hoover appliances line in June 1995, booking a $130 million loss.

Nanda and Williamson (1995) described how the Corning Company in 1985 used a joint venture to exit the U.S. medical diagnostics business. In that year, Ciba-Geigy was studying how to enter the U.S. pharmaceuticals market. The two companies formed a 50–50 joint venture called Ciba Corning with a payment of $75 million from Ciba-Geigy to Corning. The activity was operated as a joint venture until 1989. During the intervening years, Ciba-Geigy demonstrated its commitment to the new-product market area by making long-term investments. The business was integrated into the global operations of Ciba-Geigy. Customers, vendors, and employees remained loyal to the joint venture enterprise. Corning was able to demonstrate the value of the unit it was seeking to sell. In 1989, Ciba-Geigy purchased the remaining 50% portion of the joint venture at a price double the $75 million paid to establish Ciba Corning. This example illustrates the value of continuity, which retains the loyalty of stakeholders.

The time-phased aspect of the joint venture also is illustrated by the disposal of the Rolm Systems Division by IBM to Siemens of Germany. IBM had purchased Rolm with a view to exploiting some computer applications to PBX systems. These potentials were not realized, and IBM found it had no particular advantages in the thin-margin PBX market. Siemens was interested in broadening its position in the U.S. telecommunications market. The transaction illustrates the differences in treatment of tangible and intangible assets. The manufacturing activities of the Rolm business were sold outright in 1989 to Siemens, but a 50–50 joint venture was formed between IBM and Siemens to handle marketing distribution and service for the Rolm products. This provided continuity for customer relationships and gave Siemens a basis for judging the value of Rolm's brand franchise. After 3 years, the joint venture moved entirely to Siemens, which during the course of the joint venture had paid $1.1 billion. This was a good price from IBM's standpoint. For Siemens, it provided a controlled cost for wider penetration of the U.S. telecommunications market.

These examples from Nanda and Williamson (1995) illustrate how, in a broad restructuring process, joint ventures can be used as a transitional mechanism. Several advantages have been illustrated by the examples: (1) The customers are moved to the buyer over a period of time in which the seller and buyer continue to be involved. (2) The buyer builds experience with the new line of business. (3) The buyer receives managerial and technical advice and assistance from the seller during the transition period. (4) The experience and knowledge developed during the life of the joint venture enable the buyer to obtain a better understanding of the value of the acquisition. (5) Consequently, the seller is able to realize a larger value from the sale than it could have under an immediate, outright sale when the buyer must necessarily discount the purchase price because of lack of knowledge about the asset being purchased.

RATIONALE FOR JOINT VENTURES

The foregoing discussion provides a background for focusing on the potential benefits of the use of joint ventures.

Strategic Planning

The previous materials demonstrate that joint ventures are used in combination with internal developments, mergers, minority investments, and so on as a time-phased program in formulating and executing a firm's long-term strategy for value-increasing growth.

Knowledge Acquisition

The expressed purpose of 50% of all joint ventures is knowledge acquisition (Berg, Duncan, and Friedman, 1982). The complexity of the knowledge to be transferred is a key factor in determining the contractual relationship between the partners.

When the knowledge to be transferred is complex or embedded in a complicated set of technological and organizational circumstances, learning by doing and teaching by doing might be the most appropriate means of transfer. Successive adaptations to changing internal and environmental events might be necessary to achieve efficiency in the process being taught. It might be costly or even impossible to give training in complex production tasks in a classroom situation—the atmosphere (operations, machines, work group) can be essential. In addition, job incumbents, no matter how skilled, might be unable to describe job skills to trainees except in an operational context. The demands of the task sometimes make joint venture the most appropriate vehicle for the knowledge transfer.

Risk Reduction

Risk is reduced in a number of ways. Activities can be expanded with smaller investment outlays than if financed independently. This has been a strong motive for joint ventures beginning in biblical times. Later, exploration for gold, silver, copper, and petroleum resources involved some form of joint venture.

Tax Aspects

Tax advantages are a significant factor in many joint ventures. If a corporation contributes a patent or licensable technology to a joint venture, the tax consequences might be less than on royalties earned through a licensing arrangement. For example, one partner contributes the technology, and another contributes depreciable facilities. The depreciation offsets the revenues accruing to the technology, the joint venture may be taxed at a lower rate than any of its partners, and the partners pay a later capital gains tax on the returns realized by the joint venture if and when it is sold. If the joint venture is organized as a corporation, only its assets are at risk; the partners are liable only to the extent of their investment. This is particularly important in hazardous industries where the risk of worker, product, or environmental liability is high.

A number of other more technical tax advantages can tip the scale toward the use of joint ventures in many circumstances. These include the limitation on operating loss carryover, the partnership status of unincorporated commercial joint ventures, the use of the equity method of incorporating the joint venture into the partners' financial statements, and the benefits of multiple surtax exemptions.

International Aspects

Joint ventures can be used to reduce the risk of expanding into a foreign environment. In fact, some foreign countries legally require a local joint venturer. The contribution of the local partner is likely to be in the form of specialized knowledge about local conditions, which can be essential to the success of the venture. International joint ventures might enable a firm to take advantage of favorable tax treatment or political incentives.

FAILURE AND SUCCESS

Joint ventures are a form of long-term contract. Like all contracts, they are subject to difficulties. As circumstances change in the future, the contract might be too inflexible to permit the required adjustments to be made. In many joint ventures, the participants become enamored of the idea of the joint activity early on but do not spend sufficient time and effort to lay out a program for implementing the joint venture. *BusinessWeek* (1986) refers to independent studies by McKinsey & Company and Coopers & Lybrand that found that about 70% of joint ventures fell short of expectations or were disbanded. Other studies suggest that on average, joint ventures do not last as long as half the term of years stated in the joint venture agreement (Berg, Duncan, and Friedman, 1982). We conducted an independent survey that uncovered many examples of joint ventures that came apart before they started or early into the venture. Some of the reasons for the abortive lives of joint ventures are as follows.

1. The hoped-for technology never developed.
2. Preplanning for the joint venture was inadequate.
3. Agreements could not be reached on alternative approaches to solving the basic objectives of the joint venture.

4. Managers with expertise in one company refused to share knowledge with their counter-parts in the joint venture.

5. Management difficulties might be compounded because the parent companies are unable to share control or compromise on difficult issues.

The requirements for successful joint ventures include the following.

1. Each participant has something of value to bring to the activity.

2. Participants should engage in careful preplanning.

3. The resulting agreement or contract should provide for flexibility in the future as required.

4. The planning should include provisions for termination arrangements including provisions for a buyout by one of the participants.

5. Key executives must be assigned to implement the joint venture.

6. It is likely that a distinct unit in the organization structure needs to be created with authority for negotiating and making decisions.

EMPIRICAL TESTS

Berg, Duncan, and Friedman (1982) identified three primary incentives for joint venture participation: (1) risk avoidance, (2) knowledge acquisition, and (3) market power. To carry out a cross-firm and cross-industry analysis on a large sample of joint ventures from the period 1964 to 1973, they used multiple regression to evaluate the relationships among joint ventures and concentration, research and development (R&D), financial variables, and firm size.

They found that industry joint venture participation rose with average firm size, average capital expenditure, and average profitability. Technologically oriented joint venture participation also rose with average R&D intensity. Within each industry, Berg, Duncan, and Friedman attempted to distinguish the characteristics of those large firms that engaged in joint ventures from those that did not and found firm size to be the *only* pervasive influence across industries.

Cross-firm patterns indicated that joint ventures substitute for research and development in the chemical and engineering industries but not in resource-based industries, and Berg, Duncan, and Friedman found that the long-term R&D substitution effect was stronger than the short-term substitution effect. Joint ventures also were found to have a significant negative impact on large firms' rates of return in chemicals and engineering in the short run, although the long-run effect on rate of return was not significant.

At the industry level, technologically oriented and nonhorizontal joint ventures showed strong positive effects on R&D intensity, indicating that joint ventures and R&D are complements at the industry level. These same types of joint ventures also have a significant negative impact on industry average rates of return, consistent with the reduced risk or reduced time lag that may result from technological or commercial knowledge acquisition joint ventures. The result is also consistent with using joint ventures as a vehicle for new market entry.

McConnell and Nantell (1985) studied the performance of joint ventures using residual analysis. Their study covered a selection from all joint ventures reported in *Mergers and Acquisitions* for the period 1972 to 1979. Their sample consisted of 210 firms engaged in 136 joint ventures. The average size of the joint ventures was about $5 million. The 2-day announcement period abnormal return was 0.73%, which was significant at the 0.01 level. The cumulative average residual (abnormal return) over the 62-day period ending on the event day (announcement day) was 2.15%, significant at the 0.10 level. The cumulative average residual remained at 2.15% after 50 days subsequent to the joint venture announcement, indicating no further valuation effect following the initial announcement.

McConnell and Nantell compared the size of the abnormal return with the results for companies involved in mergers using a representative study of mergers by Asquith (1983). Asquith found excess returns for the 2 days ending in the announcement to be 6.5% for the target firm and 0.3% for the bidding firm. Because joint ventures do not identify the acquiring and acquired firm, their results should fall between the two, which they do. Asquith found that over a 60-day period prior to the merger announcement, the CAR increased by 11% for acquired firms and was unchanged for the acquiring companies. Again, the CAR for joint ventures lay between the CARs for the individual firms.

Because real estate and entertainment joint ventures constituted 23% of their sample, McConnell and Nantell also tested for overrepresentation by calculating results without this group. Their results were similar. They also eliminated firms for which other information was released near the joint venture announcement date. Again, the results were unchanged.

McConnell and Nantell also studied the relative size effect. They noted that in mergers, the dollar value of gains appeared to be evenly divided between the two companies. However, if the acquiring company is 20 times as large as the target that gains 10% in market value, the acquiring company will gain only 0.5% in stock value. Accordingly, the firms in their joint venture sample were divided into large and small groups based on the total market value of their common stock 61 trading days before the announcement of the joint venture. Information was available to do this for 65 joint ventures but not for 80 other companies that were placed into a third, "all other" category. The statistical tests were repeated for the three groups. The small firms gained 1.10%, the large firms gained 0.63%, and all others gained 0.57% — all of these statistically significant. The dollar gain to the small-firm sample was $4.538 million and to the large-firm sample $6.651 million. Thus, as in mergers, the dollar gain was about evenly divided, but the percentage gains were much higher for the smaller firms.

When the dollar gains are scaled by the amounts invested in the joint venture, the average premium is 23% (after removing one outlier). This result lies in the range of premiums observed in mergers and tender offers. McConnell and Nantell observed that the gains in mergers and tender offers could be from either synergy or the displacement of less-effective management. Because joint ventures do not change the managements of the parents, McConnell and Nantell (1985, p. 535) concluded that "we are inclined to interpret our results as supportive of the synergy hypothesis as the source of gains in other types of corporate combinations."

Event studies subsequent to the 1985 study by McConnell and Nantell supported their results. Woolridge and Snow (1990) studied stock market reactions to strategic investment decisions represented by joint ventures, R&D projects, capital expenditures, and product/market diversification. Treating joint ventures as one of a number of strategic investments is consistent with our analysis of the economic role of joint ventures. Their data covered a 15-year span for 767 investment announcements from 1972 to 1987. Their measurements covered a 2-day window of the announcement date and the day before (−1, 0). The 2-day abnormal returns were significant for all categories except expansion into new markets with old products, which already might have been anticipated by investors. For joint ventures, the returns for the day before the announcement were positive 2.45%, significant at the 1% level. The 2-day return was 2.17%, significant at the 5% level. Thus, extending the time period strengthened the results of the earlier study.

The Koh and Venkatraman (1991) study covered the period 1972 to 1986 for 239 firms in the information technology sector defined as electrical and electronic products, measuring instruments, communication, data processing, electronic imaging, and video products. The mean

2-day abnormal returns for joint ventures was 0.87%, and for technology exchanges it was 0.80%, both significant at the 1% level. Their further analysis showed that joint ventures have positive effects on the market value of the firms if they are in the existing market-product segment or place new products in existing markets. However, no significant increase in market value occurred in joint ventures that seek to develop new customers or enter new, unrelated product-market segments.

Crutchley, Guo, and Hansen (1991) studied 146 joint ventures between Japanese and U.S. companies for the period 1979 to 1987. Announcement week excess returns were positive and significant—1.05% for U.S. partners and 1.08% for Japanese partners. U.S. firms earned larger excess returns when they were smaller than their Japanese partner. Roughly half of the joint ventures do not realize significant abnormal returns, reflecting our earlier discussion of requirements for successful joint ventures.

Chen, Hu, and Shieh (1991) studied U.S. joint ventures in China. Since 1979, China has approved more than 21,000 foreign investment projects; 90% were joint ventures. The database consists of 517 joint ventures established between 1979 and 1990. The 2-day $(-1, 0)$ cumulative portfolio excess returns were a positive 0.71%, significant at the 1% level. The positive wealth gain is negatively related to the size of the foreign investment. They observed that a real options framework helps explain the results. Foreign firms face high risks in investments in China. Small investments increase the flexibility for further expansion under favorable conditions, limiting the risks to initial investments.

Johnson and Houston (2000) studied a sample of 191 joint ventures that were announced in the *Wall Street Journal* during the period 1991 to 1995. The authors found that the announcement of the joint ventures created wealth. The average announcement excess return for the $(-1, 0)$ window was 1.67%. In horizontal joint ventures, the wealth gains appeared to be shared between the two parties. In vertical joint ventures, the suppliers experienced the better portion of the wealth gains.

Johnson and Houston (2000) also studied a sample of 345 vertical contracts engaged in between publicly traded firms during the same time period. The announcement of these contracts also is associated with a positive return. In comparing the choice between joint ventures and simple contracts, Johnson and Houston (2000) concluded that firms elect joint ventures when the transaction costs of specific investments are high.

The results of the multiple-event studies of joint ventures are consistent with the nature of joint-venture investments. Joint ventures permit knowledge acquisition while limiting risks, but they must be well conceived and managed effectively.

STRATEGIC ALLIANCES

Strategic alliances are informal or formal decisions or agreements between two or more firms to cooperate in some form of relationship. Rapid advances in technology, the globalization of markets, and deregulation have created economic turbulence. These change forces have stimulated the reorganization of capabilities, resources, and product market activities of business firms. Methods by which firms have responded to the increased pace of change have included mergers or takeovers, joint ventures, and strategic alliances. Mergers and joint ventures have been methods by which firms have increased the intensity of competition. Value chains have been altered, and product life cycles have been shortened. Industry boundaries have become blurred, with firms eyeing a wide range of other products and markets as potential new growth opportunities. This ambiguity in the nature of industries and the scope of firms has given rise to a new form of relationship—the strategic alliance.

USES OF STRATEGIC ALLIANCES

At the beginning of the chapter, we noted that the TFSD database on alliances and joint ventures for the period 1988 to 1999 lists more than 75,000 transactions. Table 14.1 provides a sample of companies, indicating that most large companies are likely to have engaged in as many as 100 alliances (not including joint ventures) during the period 1985 to mid 2002. Illustrative examples of strategic alliances follow.

AT&T, Lucent, and Motorola entered into a joint cooperation on a software language that would allow users to access the Internet by voice. The companies wanted to establish a voice extensible markup language (VXML) as a standard for voice commands to the Internet (*Wall Street Journal*, March 2, 1999, p. 88).

An alliance between Xerox and Microsoft aimed at bridging the worlds of paper documents and computers was announced in May 1999. The new relationship included Xerox licensing a Web-surfing technology to Microsoft. Xerox would incorporate Microsoft's embedded NT operating system in a future generation of its high-end copying systems. Xerox stated that its relationship with Microsoft would have no impact on a similar arrangement Xerox had with Sun Microsystems (*New York Times*, May 19, 1999, p. C5).

The *New York Times*, in 1999, described an investment by AOL in Hughes Electronics "as part of a wide-alliance" providing online service to achieve high-speed Internet access using the Hughes satellite data delivery system (June 22, p. C6). This broadened a deal that had been announced by the companies a month earlier.

Also in 1999, the *Wall Street Journal* reported "multi-million-dollar collaboration agreements" between Glaxo Wellcome and SmithKline Beecham to extend the therapeutic qualities of existing drugs (July 28, p. B8). One objective was to develop a version of the antibiotic tetracycline that would be effective against drug-resistant bacteria. Other potential drug developments that could be furthered by the alliance were described. Apparently, this kind of collaboration laid the groundwork for the announcement on January 17, 2000, of an agreement on a merger that the two companies were unable to achieve a year earlier.

In March of 1999, an alliance was formed between Abbott Laboratories and Germany's Boehringer Ingelheim GmbH (*Wall Street Journal*, March 4, p. B2). Abbott acquired U.S. comarketing rights to Mobic, a pain medication aimed at arthritis. The article described how the competitive landscape for this therapeutic drug class would be altered by adding Abbott's powerful marketing force to the German company's efforts in the U.S. market. Monsanto and Pfizer were already comarketing the drug Celebrex for arthritis pain relief with great success.

The U.S. Postal Service (USPS) formed an alliance with DHL Worldwide Express to jointly offer a 2-day delivery service between 18 major U.S. cities and 18 foreign countries (*Wall Street Journal*, March 2, 1999, p. A4). Customers could track the shipments by telephone or at the United States Postal Service (USPS) Internet site. John F. Kelly, the head of packing services for USPS, stated that "a series of international alliances" would be used for further growth. The article also noted that spokespersons for FedEx and UPS stated that the alliance made it necessary for tighter controls on forays into private-sector competition by USPS, financed by its monopoly profits on first-class mail.

It was widely announced on February 3, 1999 (*Wall Street Journal*, p. A3), that Goodyear Tire & Rubber had formed a "broad alliance" with Sumitomo Rubber Industries. Some cross investments would be made, and the two companies would combine research and purchasing activities in six joint ventures. A number of duplicate efforts would be combined, saving a total of more than $300 million per year in combined costs.

As we emphasized in our discussion on mergers and joint ventures, strategic alliances are best understood in the framework of a program of planned transactions of multiple types over a period of years to achieve carefully formulated strategic plans. Geis and Geis's (2001) case study of AOL illustrates our framework. During the 1990s, AOL engaged in a series of transactions that included acquisitions, joint ventures, alliances, advertising-commerce deals, co-marketing partnerships, and minority equity investments. Geis and Geis (2001) formulated a five-part rationale for the AOL transactions: (1) expand its subscriber base, (2) use its subscriber base to augment its revenues, (3) expand its product lines, (4) augment its technology capabilities, and (5) expand internationally. Its agreement with Columbia House in 1999 was a 3-year alliance to cross sell products. AOL also sought to increase its subscriber base through brick-and-mortar partnerships with Wal-Mart, Barnes & Noble, Blockbuster Video, and United Artists movie houses. Similar deals were signed with AmericanGreetings.com, Travelocity, and Electronic Arts (EA). The details of the revenue-enhancing nature of the deal with EA, a leading game software developer, are summarized by Geis and Geis (2001) from EA's proxy statements. AOL sought to develop its technologies by investments in mobile Internet devices and interactive TV. In late 1999, AOL invested in Palm Computing. AOL acquired MapQuest in a $1.1 billion stock-for-stock transaction.

On January 10, 2000, AOL announced the acquisition of Time Warner (TWX) in which 1.5 shares of AOL were exchanged for 1 share of TWX. Premerger, the combined companies had a market value of $280 billion as shown in the table.

	Share Price (1/10/00)		Number of Shares		Market Cap Premerger
AOL	$72.88	×	2.6 billion	=	$189.5 billion
TWX	$64.75	×	1.4 billion	=	$ 90.7 billion
Total					$280.2 billion

The 1.4 billion TWX shares multiplied by 1.5 became 2.1 billion AOL shares, which when added to the 2.6 billion premerger AOL shares gives a total of 4.7 billion shares. At AOL's closing price of $12.45 on July 18, 2002 (a major reorganization was announced), this gives a total market value of approximately $59 billion. The difference of $221 billion represents a 79% decline from the premerger $280 billion combined market value. The $221 billion question is whether the value erosion between January 10, 2000, and July 18, 2002, reflected a flawed strategy or the severe deterioration of the macroeconomic and stock price environments. The more relevant observation for our analysis on alliances is that AOL's early strategy had created $189.5 billion of value between 1989 when America Online was launched and the merger announcement of January 10, 2000.

AOL's model of monetizing adcom partnerships was profitable in the 1990s. It is not clear what the relative roles of the following possibilities were in the subsequent failures. The general recession beginning in early 2000 caused a decline in advertising expenditures generally and adcom revenues particularly. In the altered market environment of the Internet, was it inherently more difficult to structure partnerships to support AOL service and revenues? Alternatively, did AOL fail to work at partnerships as vigorously or effectively? Did AOL fail to adjust its strategy and business model to its new market environment? Did an alternative strategy and business model exist that could have enabled AOL to do better? Or finally, in its changed business environment was AOL doomed to shrink—no change in strategy or model could have prevented its revenue declines?

According to an analyst report from Prudential Financial (on January 30, 2003), Yahoo's share of the combined online advertising revenues of AOL plus Yahoo increased from 18.9% in the 4th quarter 2001 to 34.6% in the 4th quarter of 2002. Yahoo has created novel sponsored search services for a wide range of businesses and has achieved effective new partnerships. Its stock price increased from $16.35 on December 31, 2002, to $24.76 on March 26, 2003—a gain of 51%. This compares with a price decline of 14% for AOL Time Warner during the same time period. It appears that AOL has not executed effectively relative to its competition.

OTHER ISSUES

Other aspects of strategic alliances have been developed in the literature. One issue is whether inter-firm alliances lead to mergers and acquisitions. This issue was addressed in an empirical study by Hagedorn and Sadowski (1999), who used two large data sets. A data set on more than 6,000 strategic technology alliances was related to information on 16,000 M&As of the same group of nearly 3,000 firms. Only 2.6% of the alliances led to an M&A between the same partners. These findings were inconsistent with the encroachment hypothesis that larger firms use their strategic technology alliances to take over their smaller partners. It appears that the strategic alliances represent a form of exploratory learning. In high-technology industries, where turbulence and change dominate, strategic alliances are used to scan market-entry possibilities, to monitor new technological developments, and to reduce the risks and costs of developing new products and processes. As industries mature, learning and flexibility become less important, so integration through M&As is more likely.

Another study predicted the success or failure of alliances depending on their characteristics (Bleeke and Ernst, 1995). Six types of alliances are discussed:

1. Collisions between competitors: The core businesses of two strong, direct competitors form an alliance. Because of competitive tensions, they are short lived and fail to achieve their strategic and financial goals.
2. Alliances of the weak: Two weak companies join forces in the hope that they will improve. However, the weak grow weaker, and the alliance fails.
3. Disguised sales: A weak company joins with a strong competitor. The alliance is short lived, and the weak is acquired by the strong.
4. Bootstrap alliances: By forming an alliance with a strong company, the weak company might be improved so that the partnership develops into an alliance of equals.
5. Evolution to a sale: Two strong and initially compatible partners initiate an alliance. These alliances might succeed in meeting the initial objectives and exceed the 7-year average life span for alliances. When competitive tensions develop, one partner ultimately sells out to the other.
6. Alliances of complementary equals: Complementarity and compatibility lead to mutually beneficial relationships likely to last longer than the 7-year average.

Robinson (2002) built on recent developments in the theory of internal capital markets. Programs with equal or higher average returns but larger variances might have their resource allocations reduced by headquarters. Because strategic alliances involve contractual relations with another entity, they provide a commitment to provide continuing support. Robinson considered a number of alternative explanations including a real options framework. His major emphasis was on risk considerations. He found that alliances are positively related to industry risk, industry growth, and with the number of acquisition targets in an industry. He also found support for the view that alliances cluster in R&D-intensive industries. He observed that alliances are more common than mergers when the parent firm is less risky and the alliance or target activity is more risky. Among multidivision firms, alliance activity tends to take place in the relatively more risky segments.

EVENT STUDIES

Chan, Kensinger, Keown, and Martin (1997) investigated the stock price response to the formation of 345 strategic alliances during the period 1983 to 1992. On the announcement date, they found positive abnormal returns of 0.64%, significant at the 0.01 level. The magnitude of these returns is similar to the magnitude of those for the announcement of joint ventures as reported by McConnell and Nantell (1985). No evidence was found to support the idea that the observed wealth effect is due to wealth transfer between the partners in the alliance. For a sub-sample of high-tech firms, the abnormal returns were a highly significant 1.12%, and low-tech firms had an insignificant 0.10% return.

Partitioning the sample by industry focus and presence of technological transfer reveals that horizontal alliances between firms in the same three-digit SIC class that involved the transfer or pooling of technology experienced the highest average abnormal return, 3.54%, significant at the 0.01 level. Nonhorizontal alliances whose main objective was to position or enter a new market encountered a significant 1.45% return. For the remaining cases, horizontal non-technical and nonhorizontal technical alliances, the returns were positive but not significant.

Finally, Chan et al. found no evidence that firms enter into strategic alliances because of deteriorating past performance. In fact, in their sample, firms that entered into strategic alliances exhibited better operating performance than their industry peers over a 5-year period around the formation of the alliance.

Das, Sen, and Sengupta (1998) studied 119 strategic alliances for the period 1987 to 1991. Technological alliances consisted of research and development, technology transfers/licensing, and manufacturing. Marketing alliances included distribution, marketing/promotion, and customer service. The event study methodology used nine different windows ranging from 7 days $(-3, +3)$ to 2 days $(-1, 0)$ or $(0, +1)$. Cumulative abnormal returns of slightly more than 1% were significant for all windows of technological alliances. Marketing alliances had insignificant negative returns. The researchers argued that the market perceives technological alliances as having greater positive impact on future income streams. In technological alliances, larger firms depend on their smaller partners for resources (technology). The stronger bargaining power of smaller partners is associated with significantly higher returns than those of the larger partners.

Another dimension of alliances is analyzed by Kale, Dyer, and Singh (2002). They studied 78 firms with 1,572 alliances during the period 1988 to 1997. Firms with greater alliance experience, which create a dedicated alliance function, achieved cumulated average returns (CARs) of 1.35% and a 63% success rate. Firms without an alliance function achieved CARs of only 0.18% and a 50% success rate. The critical dedicated alliance function has an executive group with its own resources aimed at coordinating all alliance-related activity within the firm. This group is likely to codify alliance-management knowledge by creating guidelines and manuals covering partner selection, alliance negotiation, alliance contracts, alliance termination, and so on. When a firm sets up an alliance group, it facilitates the development of alliance metrics to monitor alliance performance on an ongoing basis. Finally, Kale et al. found that the event study results are highly correlated to the long-term alliance benefits measured by managerial assessments or accounting data.

SUCCESSFUL STRATEGIC ALLIANCES

A considerable body of literature discusses the requirements for achieving the positive benefits of alliances observed in the empirical studies. Book-length treatments include Dyer (2000), BenDaniel and Rosenbloom (1998), Doz and Hamel (1998), Marks and Mirvis (1998), and Gomes-Casseres (1996). The major findings of this literature are summarized next.

The critical factors in forming and operating value-increasing strategic alliances stem from their fundamental characteristics, summarized in Table 14.3. Strategic alliances can range from informal communications to carefully formalized legal agreements. A simple illustration of a strategic alliance would be an understanding among automobile companies to share information on research and development activities, such as improved methods of smog control. Another example would be agreements between pharmaceutical companies to share research findings in gene mapping. These kinds of problems involve advanced technologies, as well as large continuing investments.

Key characteristics included in Table 14.3 are the pooling of resources and expertise in an evolving relationship, which requires change and adaptability over time. A firm can be a participant in multiple strategic alliances. A strategic alliance can involve multiple firms organized into some form of constellation.

TABLE 14.3 Characteristics of Strategic Alliances

1. The creation of a new entity is unnecessary.
2. A contract need not be specified.
3. The relative sizes of the firms can be highly unequal.
4. The alliance might involve relations with competitors and complementor firms.
5. Synergistic value is created from combining different resources.
6. Both companies might learn and internalize new knowledge and capabilities from the relationship.
7. The alliance can add more value to the partnering firms by creating an organizational mechanism that better aligns decision authority with decision knowledge.
8. The alliance can add value to the partnering firms through the organizational flexibility they provide.
9. Partner firms pool resources and expertise rather than transferring the specialized knowledge, so the partners will have a continuing need for each other.
10. The relationship is an evolving one.
11. Adaptability and change are required over time.
12. Deliberate efforts might be made to change the direction of at least one partner.
13. The alliance blurs corporate boundaries.
14. The alliance members can have multiple partners.
15. An alliance requires mutual trust.
16. The speed of change is increased.
17. Participating companies move to other alliances as attractive possibilities emerge.
18. An alliance can provide access to creative people who want to work with smaller firms, not giants. A strategic alliance with small firms enables the larger to attract and provide incentives to more creative people.

The requirements for successful strategic alliances flow from their basic characteristics. First, strategic alliances must have well-defined strategic themes. Without focus, strategic alliances can be wasteful. This is consistent with a theme we have emphasized: There are multiple paths to growth that are implemented over extended planning periods. Developing multiple-growth opportunities requires a strategic framework for guiding and coordinating activities. As emphasized in Chapter 5 on strategy, strategic frameworks evolve and develop over time as part of a learning process.

Second, it follows that organization relationships in a strategic alliance should facilitate communication to achieve shared control on the decision-making process. Third, strategic alliance activities should be viewed in the framework of real-options theory. In the face of complex decision making, small investments might be sufficient to gain information and experience. A portfolio of potential growth opportunities can be developed. Strategic alliances provide flexibility for choosing among alternative decision paths over time.

Fourth, to conduct strategic alliances, a high-level management group must occupy an important place in the firm's organizational structure. To initiate and manage interfirm relationships over time requires continuing communications and personal interactions to develop trust and effective working relationships.

Fifth, the tensions arising from relationships among competitors and potential competitors require dominating positive incentives. The gains to be shared by members of an alliance make it worthwhile to give up part of the values that are created.

Sixth, because a firm might be involved in different types of strategic alliances, different models for alliance governance must be employed. Again, interactions and communications are required to achieve evolving sets of rights and responsibilities.

Seventh, the alliance seeks to develop growth opportunities that will augment existing core capabilities. Hence, continuous integration is required between existing activities and the evolving redefinition of the firm's capabilities and resources.

The foregoing summarizes some key elements for successful collaborations. They will evolve over time. In their implementation, they require flexibility and adaptability. Central is the existence of the potential for value creation, which provides incentives for making ambiguous relationships succeed.

RELATIVE ROLES

The nature of strategic alliances can be further developed by comparing characteristics of acquisitions and joint ventures. These relationships are summarized in Table 14.4. They are not mutually exclusive paths to increasing value; they can be complementary and reinforcing. Acquisitions achieve significant augmentations of capabilities and resources in a short time period. The consequences are long lasting and might involve the commitment of substantial resources. Mergers involve the challenges of combining organizations and cultures.

Joint ventures can reduce the relative size of investments and limit risks. However, new organization entities and relationships are created. Mutual learning and new growth opportunities can be developed.

Strategic alliances broaden the range of potential market product opportunities. Evolving relationships are less formal and more ambiguous. Greater capabilities for developing governance relationships and effective communication are required.

TABLE 14.4 Acquisitions, Joint Ventures, and Strategic Alliances

Acquisition	*Joint Venture*	*Strategic Alliance*
Allows 100% control	Firms intersect over narrow, well-defined segments	Useful for creation of complex systems among multiple firms
No need for interfirm consensus	Exploits distinctive opportunities	Blurs corporate boundaries
Less flexible	Generally involves only two firms	Partner is usually larger than in joint venture (10/1 vs. 5/1)
Larger commitment of resources	Limits risk	Allows firms to focus on fewer core competencies
Greater risk	Enables joint production of single products	Difficult to measure contributions of participants and to measure or assign benefits
Often acquire more than is needed	Combines known resources	Difficult to anticipate consequences
May cause upheaval in corporate culture	Requires interaction of high-level management	Gives firms access to people who would not otherwise work directly for them
Requires combining and harmonizing information systems	Can be used to avoid risks in a merger transaction	Often small initial resource commitments
Requires combining different corporate cultures	Often crosses borders	Limited time duration
Requires rapid, effective integration	Tensions: Each firm seeks to learn as much as possible but not to convey too much	Must be managed actively by senior executives
Affords the most cost-cutting possibilities		Likely to evolve in directions not initially planned
Can have partial investments as an interim step		Requires adaptability to change and new knowledge for management over time
Can cross borders		Especially useful across borders
Can be used to try to correct previous errors in strategy selection		Substitute for government-prohibited, cross-border mergers

OTHER INTERFIRM RELATIONSHIPS

This section covers minority investments, licensing, and franchising. A comprehensive analytical framework for understanding these relationships is found in Brickley, Smith, and Zimmerman (2000).

MINORITY EQUITY INVESTMENTS

Successful, high-technology firms with substantial cash balances (measured by short-term liquid investments) such as Intel and Microsoft have been active in developing minority equity investment programs. Based on in-depth knowledge of related activities, minority equity investments in promising start-ups can yield high returns, especially in a period of rising stock prices.

Such investments also can yield substantial long-term benefits, regardless of general stock price movements. These investments can be a source of information on a wide range of promising growth opportunities. They also can serve as a method of learning more about industries and companies and can contribute to the development of significant information and new ideas. Through minority equity investments, an effective radar screen can be developed for new technologies and business strategies, and they can help in identifying promising new managerial talent. They also can represent a form of efficient research and development investments. In assisting in the development of firms whose inputs represent the investor's products (such as Intel's microprocessors), the market might be expanded. Other value chain linkages also can be achieved.

Recipient firms also can benefit in a number of ways. Their financing sources are expanded. Communication and advisory relationships can be mutually beneficial, and advice and other forms of R&D assistance might be received. A strong halo effect sometimes results from the visibility and endorsement implied by the relationship with a leading company.

Strategic alliances in the form of minority equity investments also have broader implications. From a strategy perspective, resources and capabilities can be mutually augmented. From the perspective of organizational architecture, the nature of the firm is modified. Thus, the boundaries of the firm and the structure of product market relationships can be modified in important ways over time.

TECHNOLOGICAL AND MARKETING AGREEMENTS

Our summary of studies of event returns included the paper by Das, Sen, and Sengupta (1998), which discussed forms of technological and marketing alliances. Sometimes the two may be related as in the agreement between Pfizer and Warner-Lambert. Warner-Lambert's R&D team successfully developed Lipitor, an important turbostatin. It entered into an agreement with Pfizer to comarket the product. This reflected the highly regarded marketing prowess of Pfizer. Unable to produce a statin on its own, the deal enabled Pfizer to shore up its strength in cardiovascular drugs (Dow Jones News Service, March 27, 1997).

Exclusive agreements represent special relationships among companies. In the previous example Warner-Lambert granted an exclusive arrangement for Pfizer to comarket. The example also illustrates the reasons for exclusive agreements. They enable firms to combine complementary strengths more quickly and at lower costs. Such agreements also may lead to other forms of interdependence between firms.

Licensing agreements are formal legal arrangements in which the licensee is permitted to use the knowledge or processes of the licensor for a fee. Licensing agreements represent a method of expanding a market for a firm's product advantages. An example is the global licensing between Abbott Laboratories and a biotechnology company, Antisoma PLC, based in the United Kingdom. The licensing agreement provided Abbott's funding to Antisoma in a program to develop and market Theragyn, a treatment for ovarian cancer (*Wall Street Journal*, November 1, 1999).

More generally, licensing agreements enable a firm to build market acceptance for a promising product more rapidly than otherwise might be possible. For the licensee, its marketing organization can augment returns by adding successful products. Additional knowledge about the nature of the product also can be obtained. The expanded market provides higher immediate returns for the licensor; however, over time, it might be creating a new competitor.

FRANCHISING

Franchising represents another method of expanding a firm's reach. Of McDonald's 28,000 restaurants worldwide, about 80% of the outlets are franchised. Franchise agreements are contracts between the franchisor (parent) and the franchisee that grant the rights to use the parent's name, brand, reputation, and business model at a specified location within a designated market area.

Mail Boxes Etc. (MBE) is a classic example of the use of franchising. Its first outlet was established in 1980. The founders wanted to expand but lacked financial resources to do so. It grew by franchising to 4,000 centers worldwide by 1999. The outlets originally provided services that included 24-hour mailbox access, packaging, stamp sales, and parcel shipping. Services expanded to include copying; printing; faxing; and selling money orders, office supplies, passport photos, and duplicate keys. Its subsequent history illustrates interactions between alliances and mergers. By 1986, MBE was able to go public with about 275 locations. In 1990, UPS invested in 15% of MBE stock. In 1997, MBE formed a joint venture with USA Technologies to comarket MBE Express. U.S. Office Products acquired MBE in 1997 for $267 million. In 1999, MBE formed an alliance with iShip.com, and on March 2, 2001, it was announced that MBE had been acquired by UPS in a cash transaction. The story of MBE illustrates the dynamics of multiple paths to growth.

The benefits provided by a franchisor include: (1) established brand name with wide consumer recognition; (2) training program; (3) preopening support, ongoing support, quarterly business evaluation program, and marketing support; (4) advantageous buying arrangements with vendors; and (5) national advertising campaigns.

The economic role of franchising is to minimize monitoring costs by having independent operators whose returns are tied to their own efforts and performance. The operations of outlets with independent owners can be compared to the performance of outlets owned by the franchisor. Franchising is used widely in fields such as motels and hotels, automobile dealerships, tax services, travel agents, pest-control services, and weight control. Ongoing monitoring is critical because the business activities are labor intensive, and expansion requires individual operations that are widely dispersed geographically.

The key decision area is the negotiation of the original investment required and the size of initial and ongoing franchising fees. A major risk to the franchisor is the failure of owner-operators to conform to the standards required to maintain brand name reputation. Conflicts can arise because the franchisees might prefer to use vendors different from the franchisor when their size and experience enable them to obtain better terms. Disagreements also can occur with respect to the size of areas that will be exclusive to individual franchisees.

Summary

Joint ventures are new enterprises owned by two or more participants. They typically are formed for special purposes for a limited duration. This brings the participants into what is essentially a medium- to long-term contract that is specific and flexible. It is a contract to work together for a specified period of time. Each participant expects to gain from the activity but also must make a contribution.

To some degree, the joint venture represents a relatively new thrust by each participant, so it is often called a strategic alliance. Probably the main motive for joint ventures is to share risks. This explains why joint ventures frequently are found in bidding on oil contracts and in drilling oil wells; in large real estate ventures; and in movies, plays, and television productions. The second-most-frequently cited aim in joint ventures is knowledge acquisition. One or more participants are seeking to learn more about a relatively new product market activity. This might concern all aspects of the activity or a limited segment such a R&D, production, marketing, or product servicing.

International joint ventures magnify the potential advantages and weaknesses of joint venture activity. The GM-Toyota joint venture in Case 14.1 illustrates the kind of potentials that can be achieved in a joint venture. GM hoped to gain new experience in the management techniques of the Japanese in building high-quality, low-cost compact and subcompact cars. Toyota was seeking to learn from the management traditions that had made GM the number-one auto producer in the world and in addition to learn how to operate an auto company in the environment of the United States, dealing with contractors, suppliers, and workers. It appears that differences in cultures and management styles have provided a valuable learning experience for both parties in this joint venture.

Other reasons for joint ventures are numerous. One frequently encountered is the small firm with a new product idea that involves high risk and requires relatively large amounts of investment capital. A larger firm might be able to carry the financial risk and be interested in becoming involved in a new business activity that promises growth and profitability. By investing in a large number of such ventures, the larger firm has limited risk in any one and the possibility of high financial payoffs. In addition, the larger firm might thereby gain experience in a new area of activity that may represent the opportunity for a major new business thrust in the future. Case studies illustrate how joint ventures can facilitate different types of restructuring activities for either or both participant firms in the joint venture.

Event studies of joint ventures are in agreement that the returns are positive and significant. These results reflect the functions and benefits of the joint ventures described.

Strategic alliances are commitments between two or more firms to cooperate in some form of relationship. They enable firms to manage risk, gain knowledge, increase expertise, and learn about new technologies. Strategic alliances are likely to evolve in directions not initially planned. An experienced, high-level management group must develop continuing relationships and communications with alliance partners. Adaptability to change is required. Event analyses of strategic alliances also have yielded positive returns. The establishment of an alliance function in the organizational structure of the firm has been shown to improve alliance performance.

Other forms of interfirm relationships include minority investments, licensing agreements, and franchising. Minority investments can provide information on new growth opportunities. They are a method for identifying promising new managerial talent and can represent a form of efficient R&D activity. They also can develop important value chain linkages. Recipient firms benefit from augmented financing, advisory relationships, R&D assistants, and the endorsement implied by the investors.

Licensing agreements enable the firm to build markets for new products more rapidly. For the licensee, the new products can add additional revenues and knowledge. Franchising is another method a firm can use to expand its markets. Franchising is found in labor-intensive business activities that are widely dispersed geographically. The franchisor sells its business model, reputation, and brand name. The franchisee provides labor management, as well as some financing.

Conceptually, joint ventures and the several forms of strategic alliances perform several functions. They can be understood in the framework of real options. Strategic options provide flexibility and sequential learning. Real options create value for projects of high risk in changing environments. Joint ventures and strategic alliances have the characteristics of real options. In addition, they expand the boundaries of firms and interfirm relationships.

The event studies of joint ventures and strategic alliances summarized in the present chapter consistently found positive returns to participating firms. In addition, the positive returns can be differentially higher when joint ventures and strategic alliances are managed well. Effective performance starts with an organizational structure that includes a high-level, experienced management group adequately supported to carry out a dedicated function over time. When the organization commitment is established, other requirements for success are more likely to follow. These include good planning in a sound strategic framework, effective integration in the evolving organizational relationships, and continuing adaptation and learning.

Questions

14.1 How do joint ventures differ from merger activity? In what ways are they similar?

14.2 What are the advantages and disadvantages of joint ventures?

14.3 How does the concept of complex learning relate to joint ventures?

14.4 What is the primary difference between a joint venture and a strategic alliance?

14.5 How can joint ventures be affected by public policy on antitrust?

14.6 How do joint venture returns compare with returns in mergers and tender offers?

14.7 What are the critical requirements for a successful strategic alliance?

14.8 What are the event returns for strategic alliances?

14.9 What are the advantages and disadvantages of minority equity investments from the standpoint of the investor and recipient?

14.10 What are benefits and disadvantages of licensing agreements?

14.11 What are the key characteristics of industries that employ franchising?

14.12 Compare the strategies of growth employed by McDonald's and Cisco Systems.

Case 14.1 GM-TOYOTA JOINT VENTURE

This case study brings together a number of the theoretical arguments and legal issues involved in connection with evaluating joint ventures. The GM-Toyota joint venture provided for production of a subcompact car in a GM plant in Fremont, California, that previously had been closed down. The plan was approved by a 3–2 majority of the Federal Trade Commission in December 1983. After approval by the FTC, Chrysler brought suit to stop the joint venture. After a series of legal skirmishes, Chrysler withdrew its suit. The following discussion is from an extended analysis of the joint venture (Weston, 1984).

The business reasons underlying the GM-Toyota joint venture are straightforward. GM hoped to obtain hands-on experience in the advanced management technology of building small cars and to add this experience to other efforts underway to become more cost efficient in producing a family of small cars.

For its part, Toyota aimed to test its production methods in a new setting with different labor and supplier relationships. Each firm was seeking to become more efficient to meet the tough competition in the automobile industry. Because the cars would be produced at an unused plant in Fremont, California, the new investment costs would be reduced. Hence, the risk/return prospects of the venture were better than those of alternative methods of achieving their objectives.

In contrast to earlier joint ventures that had been found illegal, this agreement expressed the intention of both parties to compete vigorously in all their markets for every product. This joint venture, as codified by the conditions of the FTC consent order, was quite circumscribed. It limited the annual volume of the one model the joint venture could produce for GM to 250,000. It limited the duration of the venture to a maximum of 12 years. It restricted the exchange of information between the parties. The order also required that records be kept of certain contacts between the parties and that both companies file annual compliance reports with the FTC.

The FTC majority weighed efficiency benefits against anticompetitive costs: "To the extent the Fremont venture can demonstrate successfully that the Japanese system can work in America, the Commission finds that this will lead to the development of a more efficient, more competitive U.S. auto-mobile industry." The FTC determined that the GM-Toyota joint venture would achieve an important management technology transfer to the United States; it reinforced GM's strong commitment to the small-car market and provided incentives for other U.S. firms to do likewise.

QUESTIONS

C14.1.1 What did GM hope to gain from the joint venture?

C14.1.2 What did Toyota seek to gain?

C14.1.3 In your judgment, was the joint venture pro-competitive or anticompetitive?

C14.1.4 Do you think that the Fremont joint venture influenced Toyota's subsequent decision to establish its own manufacturing operations in the United States while continuing the Fremont activity?

References

Asquith, Paul, "Merger Bids, Uncertainty, and Stockholder Returns," *Journal of Financial Economics* 11, 1983, pp. 51–83.

Bachman, Jules, "Joint Ventures in the Light of Recent Antitrust Developments," *Antitrust Bulletin* 10, 1965, pp. 7–23.

BenDaniel, David J., and Arthur H. Rosenbloom, eds., *International M&A, Joint Ventures, and Beyond: Doing the Deal*, New York: John Wiley & Sons, 1998.

Berg, Sanford V., Jerome Duncan, and Philip Friedman, *Joint Venture Strategies and Corporate Innovation*, Cambridge, MA: Oelgeschlager, Gunn, and Hain, 1982.

Bleeke, Joel, and David Ernst, "Is Your Strategic Alliance Really a Sale?" *Harvard Business Review* 73: 1, January–February, 1995, pp. 97–105.

Brickley, James A., Clifford W. Smith Jr., and Jerold L. Zimmerman, *Managerial Economics and Organizational Architecture*, 2nd ed. Boston: Irwin/McGraw-Hill, 2000.

BusinessWeek, "Corporate Odd Couples," July 21, 1986, pp. 100–105.

Chan, Su Han, John W. Kensinger, Arthur J. Keown, and John D. Martin, "Do Strategic Alliances Create Value?" *Journal of Financial Economics* 46: 2, November 1997, pp. 199–221.

Chen, Haiyang, Michael Y. Hu, and Joseph C. P. Shieh, "The Wealth Effect of International Joint Ventures: The Case of U.S. Investment in China," *Financial Management* 20: 4, Winter 1991, pp. 31–41.

Crutchley, Claire E., Enyang Guo, and Robert S. Hansen, "Stockholder Benefits from Japanese–U.S. Joint Ventures," *Financial Management* 20: 4, Winter 1991, pp. 22–30.

Das, Somnath, Pradyot K. Sen, and Sanjit Sengupta, "Impact of Strategic Alliances on Firm Valuation," *Academy of Management Journal* 41: 1, February 1998, 27–41.

Doz, Yves L., and Gary Hamel, *Alliance Advantage: The Art of Creating Value Through Partnering*, Boston: Harvard Business School Press, 1998.

Dyer, Jeffrey H., *Collaborative Advantage: Winning Through Extended Enterprise Supplier Networks*, New York: Oxford University Press, 2000.

Geis, George T., and George S. Geis, *Digital Deals: Strategies for Selecting and Structuring Partnerships*, New York: McGraw-Hill, 2001.

Gomes-Casseres, Ben, *The Alliance Revolution: The New Shapes of Business Rivalry*, Boston: Harvard University Press, 1996.

Hagedorn, John, and Bert Sadowski, "The Transition from Strategic Technology Alliances to Mergers and Acquisitions: An Exploratory Study," *Journal of Management Studies* 36, January 1999, pp. 87–107.

Johnson, Shane, and Mark B. Houston, "A Reexamination of the Motives and Gains in Joint Ventures," *Journal of Financial and Quantitative Analysis* 35: 1, March 2000, pp. 67–85.

Kale, Prashant, Jeffrey H. Dyer, and Harbir Singh, "Alliance Capability, Stock Market Response, and Long-Term Alliance Success: The Role of the Alliance Function," *Strategic Management Journal* 23: 8, August 2002, pp. 747–767.

Koh, Jeongsuk, and N. Venkatraman, "Joint Venture Formations and Stock Market Reactions: An Assessment in the Information Technology Sector," *The Academy of Management Journal* 34: 4, December 1991, pp. 869–892.

Marks, Mitchell Lee, and Philip H. Mirvis, *Joining Forces: Making One Plus One Equal Three in Mergers, Acquisitions, and Alliances*, San Francisco: Jossey-Bass Publishers, 1998.

McConnell, John J., and Timothy J. Nantell, "Corporate Combinations and Common Stock Returns: The Case of Joint Ventures," *Journal of Finance* 40, June 1985, pp. 519–536.

Nanda, Ashish, and Peter J. Williamson, "Use Joint Ventures to Ease the Pain of Restructuring," *Harvard Business Review* 73: 6, November–December 1995, pp. 119–128.

Robinson, David T., "Strategic Alliances and the Boundaries of the Firm," working paper, Columbia University, May 1, 2002.

Schipper, Katherine, and Rex Thompson, "Evidence on the Capitalized Value of Merger Activity for Acquiring Firms," *Journal of Financial Economics* 11: 1–4, April 1983, pp. 85–119.

Templin, Neal, "More and More Firms Enter Joint Ventures with Big Competitors," *Wall Street Journal*, November 1, 1995, pp. A1, A9.

Weston, J. Fred, "The GM–Toyota Vows: A Reply to the Critics," *Across the Board, The Conference Board Magazine* 21, March 1984, pp. 3–6.

Woolridge, J. Randall, and Charles C. Snow, "Stock Market Reaction to Strategic Investment Decisions," *Strategic Management Journal* 11: 5, June 1990, pp. 353–363.

CHAPTER 15
EMPLOYEE STOCK OWNERSHIP AND MLPs

The collapse of Enron, Global Crossing, and WorldCom caused widespread public outrage resulting in the passage of a Corporate Reform Law in late July 2002. Employees' savings in the corporate 401(k) plans were virtually wiped out. Job losses were coupled with investment losses. These events caused a fundamental reassessment of the role of employee stock ownership. Particularly, employee stock ownership plans (ESOPs) exempted from investment diversification requirements were under continued review in congress during the summer of 2002. ESOPs also have been involved in takeovers, takeover defense activities, and buyouts—central subjects of this book. This chapter is divided into two parts. The first part covers ESOPs. The second part deals with master limited partnerships (MLPs), which also have tax advantages and have been used in takeover and takeover defense activities. The discussion of ESOPs will cover (1) the nature and history of ESOPs, (2) ESOPs as pension plans, (3) the uses of ESOPs, (4) data on ESOP characteristics, (5) tax advantages, (6) performance of ESOPs, (7) economic issues, (8) ESOPs event returns, and (9) evaluation of ESOPs.

NATURE AND HISTORY OF ESOPs

To analyze the role that ESOPs perform, it is necessary to understand their fundamental nature as an employee benefit plan and their relationship to other employee benefit plans. The employee benefit plans involved are pension plans. A pension plan is established by an organization to provide for payments to plan participants after retirement. Such plans are subject to federal government regulation established by the Employee Retirement Income Security Act (ERISA) of 1974.

TYPES OF PENSION PLANS

ERISA divides employee pension plans into two major types: (1) defined benefit plans and (2) defined contribution plans. The defined benefit plans are what people usually have in mind when they think about a pension plan. It is the type used by most large corporations. According to a formula set in advance, these plans specify the amounts that participants will receive in retirement. A flat benefit formula is a fixed amount per year of service, such as $10 for each year of service. An employee with 30 years of service would receive a pension of $300 per month, subject to a maximum percentage (for example, 60%) of (average) final salary. Under a unit benefit formula, the participant receives a fixed percentage of earnings per year of service, such as 2% of the average of the last 5 years. An employee with 30 years of service would receive a monthly pension based on 60% of the average final salary. Plans must meet federal fiduciary standards to quality for favorable tax treatment. They are subject to minimum funding standards and are guaranteed by the Pension Benefit Guarantee Corporation (PBGC).

Defined contribution plans make no fixed commitment to a pension level. Only the contributions into the plan are specified, and participants receive over the period of their retirement what is in their accounts when they retire. Defined contribution plans can be of three kinds: stock bonus plans, profit-sharing plans, and money purchase plans. In a stock bonus plan, the firm contributes a specified number of shares of its common stock into the plan annually. The value of the contribution is based on the price of the stock at a recent date if it is traded; otherwise, an appraisal is required. The other two forms of defined contribution plans provide for the payment of cash into the plan. Contributions to qualified profit-sharing plans are related to profitability rates, so they can vary in dollar amounts from year to year. Defined contribution plans are required by law to make "prudent" investments. They are not subject to minimum funding standards and are not covered by the PBGC.

ESOPs are defined contribution employee benefit pension plans that invest at least 50% of their assets in the common shares of the sponsoring corporation. Under ERISA, ESOPs are stock bonus plans or combined stock bonus plans and money purchase plans designed to invest primarily in qualifying employer securities. The plans can receive stock or cash, the latter being used by the plan managers to buy stock. A stock bonus plan can determine each year the amount to invest. A money purchase plan has a specific contribution schedule, such as 4% of ESOP salaries per year. ESOPs also can provide for employee contributions.

Since 1977, Treasury Department regulations have permitted ESOP contributions to represent a portion of a profit-sharing plan. However, an ESOP is different from an employee stock purchase plan. Stock purchase plans are programs whereby a firm enables employees to buy company stock at a discount. The Internal Revenue Code specifies that all or most employees must participate and that the shares must be sold at 85% or more of the prevailing market price of the shares.

ESOPs also should be differentiated from executive incentive programs. The latter are provided mainly to top management and other key employees. These programs are part of executive compensation packages aimed to align the interests of managers with those of the stockholders. Although many forms can be used, the tax laws since 1981 govern two types of plans: incentive stock options (ISOs) and stock appreciation rights (SARs). The exercise price of ISOs must be equal to or greater than the stock price at the time of issue. The SARs can have an exercise price as low as 50% of the stock price. Both can have a maximum life of 10 years from the date of issue.

The nature of different incentive stock option programs is discussed more fully in Chapter 18, in which their relationships to stock repurchases are discussed.

TYPES OF ESOPs

In its reports on ESOPs, the U.S. General Accounting Office (GAO) (1986) identified four main kinds: leveraged, leveragable, nonleveraged, and tax credit. Leveraged ESOPs were recognized under ERISA in 1974. In a leveraged ESOP, the plan borrows funds to purchase securities of the employer firm. The employer firm makes contributions to the ESOP trust in an amount that meets the annual interest payments on the loan as well as repayments of the principal. It is well known that corporations can deduct interest as a tax expense but not principal.

However, contributions by the corporations to ESOPs to cover interest and principal (subject to some limitations) are fully deductible. Leveragable and nonleveraged ESOPs, also recognized under ERISA, are plans that have not used leveraging. In a leveragable ESOP, the plan is authorized but is not required to borrow funds. The plan documents for nonleveraged ESOPs do not provide for borrowing. Nonleveraged ESOPs are essentially stock bonus plans that are required to invest primarily in the securities of the employer firm.

The Tax Reduction Act of 1975 provided for tax credit ESOPs. In addition to the regular investment credit in existence at that time, an additional investment credit of 1% of a qualified investment in plant and equipment could be earned by a contribution of that amount to an ESOP. The plans were called Tax Reduction Act ESOPs or TRASOPs. An additional 0.5% credit was added in 1976 for companies that matched contributions of their employees of the same amount to the TRASOP. In 1983, the basis for the credit was changed from plant and equipment investments to 0.5% of covered payroll. These types of plans were called payroll-based ESOPs or PAYSOPs. TRASOPs and PAYSOPs have been called tax credit ESOPs. The other three types of ESOPs are referred to as ERISA-type ESOPs.

ESOPs AS PENSION PLANS

It is helpful in understanding how ESOPs are used to continue to view them in the setting of a form of employee benefits, particularly as a pension plan. The basic relationships involved in a pension plan are shown in Figure 15.1. An individual corporation is responsible for setting up the pension fund. It makes dollar contributions in the form of either a defined benefit plan or a defined contribution plan, as discussed earlier. The pension fund uses the dollar contributions to make investments in a wide range of securities, real estate, and so on. The implication of ERISA is that prudence generally requires diversification of the pension fund investments. The benefits of the pension fund accrue to and are finally paid to the pension beneficiaries, who are the employees of the company. It is presumed that, at least to some degree, wages are lower than they otherwise would be because of contributions by the company to the pension fund on behalf of its employees.

Contributions by a company to a qualified pension fund are tax-deductible expenses at the time of payment by the company. However, these dollar flows are not taxable to the recipient at the time the pension fund is set up. They are taxable to the recipient only when the benefits are received. Because the income of the employees would be expected to be lower after retirement, the employee has the benefit of a lower tax rate on the value of the contributions into the pension fund. In addition, the pension fund earns income that augments the amount of benefits

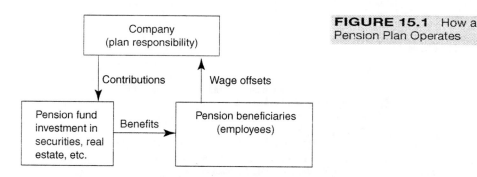

FIGURE 15.1 How a Pension Plan Operates

payable to the employees in the future. Both the original payments by the employer into the pension fund and earnings thereon receive the benefit of tax deferral until received by employees.

CONCEPT OF A LEVERAGED ESOP

In an ESOP, the logic of the arrangement is the same as in Figure 15.1. The pension fund would be called an ESOP fund or trust. In a basic ESOP, the contribution by the company could be either cash or securities of the sponsoring company as described earlier. Like ordinary pension funds, ESOPs also can provide for employee contributions. Unlike the general pension fund, which is expected to diversify its investments widely for financial prudence, an ESOP is set up to invest in the securities of the sponsoring company. In practice, ESOPs are likely to use leverage to increase the tax benefits to the sponsoring company. The nature of a leveraged ESOP is shown in Figure 15.2.

We now have an additional element in the arrangement. This is the financial institution, which is the source of the borrowing by the ESOP. As shown in Figure 15.2, the lender transfers cash to the ESOP trust in return for a written obligation. The sponsoring firm generally guarantees the loan. The ESOP trust (ESOT) purchases securities from the sponsoring firm. Because the sponsoring firm has a contingent liability, it does not transfer the stock to the name of the ESOP trust until payments are made that reduce the principal that the firm has guaranteed. As portions of the principal are repaid, the firm transfers stock to the name of the ESOP trust. The source of payment of interest and principal to the financial institution is the cash

FIGURE 15.2 Illustration of a Leveraged ESOP

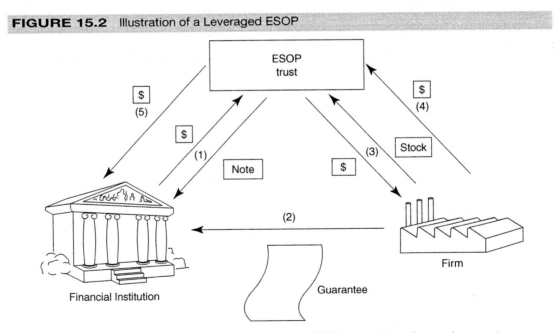

1. Financial institution lends cash to ESOP trust in return for promissory note.
2. Sponsoring firm guarantees note.
3. ESOP trust purchases stock from sponsoring firm.
4. Firm contributes cash to ESOP trust.
5. ESOP trust uses cash to make principal and interest payments on loan.

Source: United States General Accounting Office, *Employee Stock Ownership Plans: Benefits and Costs of ESOP Tax Incentives for Broadening Stock Ownership,* Washington, DC, December 1986, p. 49.

contributed to the ESOP trust by the company. The interest and principal amounts transferred by the company are deductible expenses for tax purposes.

USES OF ESOPs

An example with numbers can illustrate the nature of a leveraged ESOP. John Jones is the president and 100% owner of Ace Company. His entire estate is represented by the value of Ace. His children are grown and have no interest in running the business. His attorney has recommended the sale of Ace because Jones does not have other investments. In the case of his death, his estate would be unable to pay the required estate taxes and would be forced to sell the company under unfavorable conditions.

Jones has received an offer from Universal Company. It is to be a share-for-share stock exchange for each of the 300,000 Ace shares outstanding. Universal is trading at around $15 per share. Investment bankers have placed a value on Ace at around $20 per share. Because Jones is only 54 years old, he is reluctant to relinquish ownership and control of his company. Jones recognizes the need to increase his liquidity but does not want to sell the company at this time.

We can now illustrate how an ESOP could be helpful. An ESOP is established with all of the employees of Ace Company as beneficiaries. The ESOP borrows $2 million from a bank. These funds are used to purchase 100,000 shares of Ace Company stock from Jones. The loan from the bank to the ESOP is guaranteed by Ace Company and is secured by the 100,000 shares held in trust. Ace Company agrees to make ESOP contributions to cover interest and repayment of principal. These are tax-deductible expenses for Ace Company. Note that at this point, Jones has received $2 million in cash; presumably, he will place this in a diversified portfolio with a relatively high degree of liquidity and/or marketability. As long as these funds are invested in other U.S. corporations within 12 months, the proceeds are not taxable to Jones at this time, as will be explained.

As the ESOP repays the loan, the stock held in trust will be allocated to each individual employee's account. When the loan is completely paid off, the ESOP will have received and will own 100,000 shares of stock representing 33.3% of the outstanding stock of Ace Company. These relationships are illustrated in Figure 15.3.

COMPARISON WITH A MERGER

Another example will sharpen the advantages of the use of an ESOP compared with a merger. It is similar to the previous illustration, which was streamlined to bring out the essential nature of a leveraged ESOP. In the present example, more variables are considered in the analysis. Consider John Doe, the aging owner of 100% of the stock of Doeskin Textiles. Most of his personal wealth is tied to the firm's fortunes; he is thinking about retirement and worries about his relatively illiquid position, as well as about having all his eggs in one basket. In addition, declining health has caused him to consider the effect of substantial estate taxes, which might necessitate a hasty sale of the firm by his heirs in the event of his death. All these factors led him to consider seriously a recent overture from Polyestech Corporation to acquire Doeskin in a tax-free exchange of securities for $8 million. The offer is acceptable in terms of price, although Doe is somewhat concerned that the value received would deteriorate if Polyestech's stock price declined. Also, Polyestech has a rather unsavory reputation in terms of labor relations and social responsibility. Doeskin has been the mainstay of the Minnesota community where it is located, and Doe feels

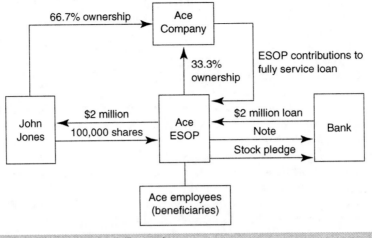

FIGURE 15.3 Leveraged ESOP Example

paternalistic toward his employees and managers. He is uneasy about turning over the firm to outsiders and would like to find another solution. ESOPs offer such a solution.

Suppose Doe would like to withdraw $2.5 million of Doeskin's $8 million value to invest in a diversified portfolio of publicly traded corporate securities to provide diversification and liquidity. He should take the following steps.

1. Doeskin should establish an ESOP.
2. The ESOP should borrow $2.5 million from a bank, insurance company, or other lender. Doeskin most likely would be required to guarantee the ESOP loan.
3. Doe should sell 31.25% of his stock to the ESOP for $2.5 million.

As long as Doe invests the $2.5 million in securities of other U.S. corporations within 12 months, he can defer any federal tax on the transaction. This tax-free rollover is allowable under the 1984 Deficit Reduction Act as long as the ESOP owns at least 30% of the firm's stock following the sale, and neither the owner nor his family participates in the ESOP once it is formed. (If Doe sells less than 30%, he will have to pay capital gains tax on the sale, but he will be able to participate in the ESOP, reducing over time the extent of his ownership dilution.) Doeskin would make tax-deductible contributions to the ESOP sufficient to repay the loan principal and to pay interest. As the loan was repaid, the Doeskin shares belonging to the ESOP would be allocated to Doeskin employees participating in the plan. Thus, the owner of a privately held firm can achieve tax-free liquidity without selling his firm to outsiders and can even maintain control, depending on his need for cash and thus the proportion of stock sold to the ESOP.

Among the advantages and disadvantages of the ESOP versus the Polyestech offer are the following.

ESOP

1. Employee loyalty increases as a result of stock ownership through an ESOP.
2. Liquidity and diversification increase for Doe.
3. Dilution of ownership is not critical here because Doe maintains control.
4. The tax-free rollover is only a tax deferral until the replacement securities are sold.

5. The ESOP establishes a market value for Doeskin stock that might help in estate valuation. This could be a positive or negative effect.
6. An ESOP provides a market for Doeskin shares if heirs must sell shares to pay estate taxes. This avoids a "fire sale," and furthermore, 50% of the proceeds from the sale of stock to an ESOP can be excluded from the estate's value.

SALE TO POLYESTECH

1. Liquidity is not improved until Polyestech shares are sold.
2. There is potential deterioration of the value received.
3. Doe completely loses control over the firm.
4. The tax advantage in tax-free exchange of securities is one of timing only. Tax must be paid when securities are sold to achieve liquidity.
5. There is no diversification effect, because all eggs would still be in one basket, albeit a different and perhaps more marketable basket.

ESOPs IN LIEU OF SUBSIDIARY DIVESTITURES

Large corporations often have subsidiaries or plants that they wish to divest for one reason or another. The usual alternatives are to sell the subsidiary to another corporation (although it might be difficult to find a buyer at an acceptable price) or to liquidate the subsidiary's assets, which is disruptive for the subsidiary's employees and often for others, as well. An ESOP can function well in this type of situation. The subsidiary's employees are likely to be willing purchasers (through an ESOP), because they have a great deal at stake and the alternatives are highly uncertain.

First, a shell corporation is established. The shell establishes an ESOP; the debt capacity of the shell and the ESOP (with the guarantees of the parent corporation) is used to arrange financing to purchase the subsidiary from the parent. The shell corporation (now no longer a shell) operates the former subsidiary, and the ESOP holds the stock. If successful, enough income will be generated to make the most of allowable tax-deductible contributions to the ESOP, which will enable it to service its debt. As the debt is reduced, the ESOP will allocate shares to the employees' accounts, and over time the former subsidiary will come to be owned by its employees.

This entire transaction is predicated on the subsidiary's viability as an independent entity and its ability to generate sufficient income to cover its financing. In many cases, the original motivation for divestiture is that the subsidiary is in a dying industry or requires extensive modernization of inefficient facilities. If so, selling the subsidiary to the employees benefits neither them nor the economy as a whole in the long run, even though short-term disruption might be kept to a minimum. In such cases, liquidation might be the preferred solution.

OTHER USES OF ESOPs

Employee stock ownership plans have been used in a wide variety of corporate restructuring activities (Bruner, 1988, U.S. General Accounting Office, 1986). Fifty-nine percent of leveraged ESOPs were vehicles used to buy private companies from their owners. This enabled the owners to make their gains tax free by investing the funds received into a portfolio of U.S. securities. ESOPs also have been used in buyouts of large private companies.

Thirty-seven percent of leveraged ESOPs were employed in divestitures. In a substantial ESOP transaction, the Hospital Corporation of America sold more than 100 of its 180 hospitals to Health Trust, a new corporation created and owned by an employee-leveraged ESOP.

Leveraged ESOPs also have been used as rescue operations. An ESOP was formed in 1983 to avoid the liquidation of Weirton Steel, which subsequently became a profitable company. ESOPs used in the attempt to prevent the failure of Rath Packing, McLean Trucking, and Hyatt Clark Industries were followed by subsequent bankruptcies.

A number of leveraged ESOPs were formed as a takeover defense to hostile tender offers. Early examples of ESOPs established as takeover defenses were those set up by Dan River in 1983, by Phillips Petroleum in 1985, and by Harcourt Brace Jovanovich in 1987.

Especially noteworthy was the use of an ESOP by Polaroid to defeat a takeover attempt in 1988 by Shamrock Holdings, the investment vehicle of Roy E. Disney. Shamrock Holdings had purchased a 6.9% stake in Polaroid with the expectation of making a tender offer for control. Polaroid created an ESOP that purchased 14% of its common stock. Polaroid was chartered in Delaware, which has an antitakeover statute that prevents a hostile acquirer from merging with the target for at least 3 years unless 85% of the target's voting shares are tendered. (This generally is referred to as the Delaware "freeze-out" law.) By creating its ESOP, Polaroid made it virtually impossible for Shamrock to obtain the necessary 85% in a tender offer. Shamrock fought this ESOP defense by Polaroid in the courts but ultimately lost. After Polaroid, ESOPs became a widely used antitakeover weapon.

The Tax Reform Act of 1986 also permits excess pension assets to be shifted tax free if they are placed into an ESOP. Ashland Oil reverted $200 million and Transco Energy Co. $120 million into new ESOPs.

Employee stock ownership plans represent one among a number of restructuring activities. They can be used as a substitute for or in connection with the purchase of private companies, divestiture activities, efforts to save failing companies, as a method of raising new capital, and as a takeover defense.

DATA ON ESOP CHARACTERISTICS

Table 15.1 presents an overview of some relevant statistics on ESOP characteristics. Recall that ESOPs are a type of defined contribution plan in which payments into pension plans are promised, in contrast to defined benefit plans in which payments to pension recipients are specified. Table 15.1 draws on testimony by Douglas Kruse (Rutgers) on February 13, 2002, to the Committee on Education and the Workforce, U.S. House of Representatives based on the Form 5500 Research File for fiscal year 1998 made available by the Pension and Welfare Benefits Administration. A total of almost 51,000 defined contribution plans were in place. The total 2,669 ESOP plans—both 401(k) and non-401(k) types—were 5.16% of the total number of plans and 24% of total plan assets. Table 15.1 does not detail 8,988 profit-sharing defined contribution plans, which are predominantly without employer stock, the focus of this analysis. Non-ESOP 401(k) plans with total plan assets of $472 billion have 28.1% invested in employer stock. Non-ESOP 401(k) plans without employer stock have total plan assets of $567 billion; this category represents 73% of the total number of plans and 34% of total plan assets.

In the compilations by Kruse, 666 of the ESOP plans were in publicly held firms representing 25% of the 2,669 total by number, but 84% of total ESOP plan assets of $402.3 billion. Thus, 75% of ESOP plans were in privately held firms, but they represented only 16% of total ESOP plan assets. We described earlier the advantage to the owner of a privately held firm to receive as high as 30% of the market value of the firm in tax-deferred, diversified investments by establishing an ESOP. This might provide a partial explanation of the predominance of ESOP plans

TABLE 15.1 Employer Stock Held in Pension Plans

	(1) Number of Plans	(2) Number of Participants (in millions)	(3) Employer Stock per Participant	(4) Total Employer Stock (in billions)	(5) Total Plan Assets (in billions)	(6) Employer Stock Percent
All Defined Contribution Plans[a]	50,764	50.9	$ 6,489	$331	$1,672	19.8
ESOP Non-401(k) Plans	2,056	3.2	16,933	54	70	77.1
ESOP 401(k) Plans	613	4.8	27,244	130	333	39.0
Non-ESOP 401(k) with Employer Stock	2,275	11.0	12,040	133	472	28.1
Non-ESOP 401(k) Without Employer Stock	36,832	23.5	0	0	567	0.0

[a]Includes 8,955 profit-sharing, defined contribution plans.

Source: Developed from Table 1 in Douglas Kruse, "Research Evidence on Prevalence and Effects of Employee Ownership," testimony before the Committee on Education and the Workforce, U.S. House of Representatives, February 13, 2002.

in privately held firms. However, the benefit of the tax deferral goes mostly to the owners, not the employees. Kruse's data show that the value of employer stock in non-401(k) ESOP plans was about $15,000 per participant in publicly held firms and about $20,000 in privately held firms. In ESOP 401(k) plans, the employer stock per participant in privately held companies is about $13,000, with $30,000 in publicly held firms. These numbers are all relatively modest in absolute amounts, raising questions about the motivation power of the ESOP plans. Furthermore, recall that the data are for 1998 and potentially subject to substantial erosion by the stock market declines during the period 2000 to 2002. In companies like Enron, WorldCom, and Global Crossing, employee stock ownership accounts were virtually wiped out. In addition, analytically it has been demonstrated that the certainty equivalent of investing $1 in a single stock over a 10-year period is only $0.36 (Brennan and Torous, 1999; Benartzi, 2001). These considerations suggest that ESOPs and 401(k) plans invested primarily in employer stock could potentially have strong negative consequences.

TAX ADVANTAGES

Scholes and Wolfson (1992) cautioned that many of the claimed tax advantages of ESOPs might be illusory. Expenses incurred by business firms to create pension benefits for their employees are generally tax deductible. The full deductibility of payments to an ESOP for the amortization debt is claimed to have tax advantages because principal is being repaid as well as interest. However, Scholes and Wolfson pointed out that viewing such payments as pension benefits demonstrates that providing pension benefits directly would yield substantially the same tax benefits.

The Scholes and Wolfson argument can be illustrated by an example. Suppose a firm spends $100,000 in year X to add to its pension fund for employees. The total $100,000 would be a tax-deductible expense for that year. Alternatively, assume that the firm had borrowed an amount in an earlier year to set up an ESOP and that the tax-deductible amount paid in year X to amortize the debt was $100,000. The amount of tax deduction for the firm with an ESOP is no different than if the same amount had been paid into its pension fund.

Other studies have discussed tax benefits that are associated with the use of ESOPs.

INTEREST EXCLUSION

Beatty (1995) described tax provisions that appear to apply exclusively to leveraged ESOPs, making their tax treatment different from that of other retirement plans. A bank, insurance company, or investment company could exclude from taxable income 50% of the interest income earned on loans to ESOPs that own more than 50% of the employer's equity. Although the 50% interest exclusion is accorded to the lender, competitive markets would result in lower interest rates on ESOP loans than on non-ESOP loans. As part of the Small Business Job Protection Act of 1996, this loan interest exclusion provision of the Internal Revenue Code was repealed (P.L. 104–188, Section 1602(a)).

DIVIDEND DEDUCTION

Another possible tax benefit is that the employer can deduct the dividends paid on ESOP shares if they are allocated to employee accounts or used to repay ESOP debt. These benefits were strengthened by the Economic Growth and Tax Relief Reconciliation Act of 2001.

When dividends are used to repay ESOP debt, the value of the ESOP shares declines by the amount of the dividend. However, the employer can deduct the entire market value of the shares at the time they are placed in the ESOP. Beatty (1995) presented an example. On May 9, 1988, the Berry Wright Corporation (BWC) loaned $24 million to its new ESOP, which purchased 1.525 million newly issued BWC common shares at $15.75 each. On the same day, a dividend of $8 per share was announced with a record date of May 31, 1988. The ESOP shares received $12.2 million of dividends that were then used to repay about one half of the ESOP loan. The BWC shares dropped by exactly $8 per share on the ex-dividend date. Because the ESOP was not able to keep the dividend, it bought shares worth $7.75. The ESOP contribution, therefore, was worth $11.8 million, representing the balance of the ESOP loan that was repaid during 1988 by BWC. The corporation was permitted to deduct $24 million but made only an $11.8 million contribution to the ESOP. Beatty observed that this example illustrates the Chaplinsky and Niehaus (1990, 1994) position that dividends used to repay ESOP debt provide a distinctive tax benefit.

DEFERMENT OF CAPITAL GAINS TAX

As noted earlier in the Ace Company and Doeskin Textiles cases, an owner of a closely held firm can defer capital gains taxes resulting from the sale of his or her firm by selling at least 30% of the outstanding shares to an ESOP.

TAX LOSS CARRYFORWARDS

The Tax Reform Act of 1986 placed a number of restrictions on the ability of a corporation to carry losses forward after a change in control unless an ESOP purchases at least 50% of the equity.

EXCESS PENSION ASSET REVERSIONS

Also in 1986, an excise tax was placed on reversions of excess assets from a defined benefit plan. However, if the excess pension assets are placed in an ESOP, the excise tax rate is lower.

CONCLUSIONS ON TAX BENEFITS

In the opposite direction, the method of allocating ESOP assets to the accounts of employees results in a smaller expected present value tax deduction for leveraged ESOPs than other retirement plans. Shares purchased by a leveraged ESOP are initially placed in a temporary company account. The shares are allocated to employees on a percentage basis related to the repayment of principal and interest in each year of the loan. Other retirement plans provide for immediate allocation of assets to the employees. The value of the ESOP tax deduction is based on the market value of the shares when they were placed in the ESOP, but the deduction cannot be taken until the debt is repaid and the assets are allocated some years in the future. The present value factor is applied to the future value of the shares but on the generally lower value at the time they are placed into the suspense account.

Beatty (1995, p. 229) estimated that for ESOPs established in 1987 and later, the average net tax benefit was 0.3% of equity value. The General Accounting Office (1986) estimated that for the period 1977 to 1983, the federal revenue losses from ESOPs were about $13 billion, an annual average of $1.9 billion. When an S corporation is owned by an ESOP, large tax benefits are possible (Mergers and Acquisitions, 2003).

THE PERFORMANCE OF ESOPs

Five dimensions of the performance of ESOPs have been studied: (1) corporate control or anti-takeover defense, (2) a method of financing, (3) comparison with profit sharing, (4) effects on productivity, and (5) economic consequences.

ESOPs AS A TAKEOVER DEFENSE

Many individual case studies document how ESOPs have been used as a takeover defense. Beatty (1995) documented this evidence systematically from her sample of 145 ESOP announcements. Seventy-five percent of the transactions occurred in 1987 or later when the interest exclusion for lenders and the dividend deduction used to repay ESOP debt became effective. This is consistent with her data for tax benefits discussed previously. She noted also that 57% of the transactions took place in 1988 and 1989 after the Polaroid decision and enactment of the related Delaware "freeze-out" law that increased the effectiveness of ESOPs as a takeover defense. This finding that more than half of a substantial sample of ESOPs was motivated to establish a takeover defense for existing managers raises questions about the benefits for employees.

Empirical studies generally find that when a firm is subject to a takeover attempt, the announcement of an ESOP has a negative effect on equity values (Beatty, 1995, and references cited therein). If the firm is not subject to a takeover attempt, the announcement of an ESOP is not associated with a change in equity values if the company was subject to the Delaware freeze-out law and the size of the ESOPs results in the establishment of an effective blocking percentage ownership.

ESOPs VERSUS ALTERNATIVE METHODS OF RAISING FUNDS

Bruner (1988) analyzed ESOPs as an alternative to other methods of raising funds. In one example, the outlays in a leveraged ESOP represented by interest expense and principal repayment represented a substitute for pension payments that otherwise would have been made. Another plausible assumption is that the interest rate charged by the lender will reflect all or some of the tax advantage that permits the financial institution to exclude from taxable income 50% of the income on loans to ESOPs. This would make the debt interest expense under a leveraged ESOP arrangement lower than under straight debt financing.

Another issue is control of the stock that is placed in the ESOP. Some people argue that management continues to control the ESOP, so the stock remains in friendly hands. On the other hand, the stock technically belongs to the individual employees, and with a strong union speaking on behalf of the employees there is always the risk that the employees or their union might vote the stock in a way that conflicts with the interests of management. The point was made in connection with Polaroid's establishment of an ESOP that the employees who wished to maintain the status quo and who did not want an outside firm to take over the company would be even more strongly opposed to the takeover than management. Typically, after a takeover, employment is reduced, and to protect their positions the employees are likely to be supporters of management when ESOPs are used as a takeover defense.

The view has been set forth that ESOP transactions represent economic dilution. Potentially, they transfer shareholders' wealth to employees (Bruner, 1988). As we observed at the beginning of this chapter, ESOPs represent a form of an employee pension program. If the

ESOP contribution is not offset by a reduction to some degree in other benefit plans or in the direct wages of workers, employees gain at the expense of shareholders. The argument also has been made that any borrowing by the ESOP uses some of the debt capacity of the firm (Bruner, 1988). It also could be argued that such borrowing substitutes for other forms of borrowing that the firm would otherwise use. To the extent that there is a valid belief that ESOP transactions represent economic dilution to the original shareholders, the price charged to the ESOP for the company stock transferred to it may be at a premium to compensate for economic dilution. The Department of Labor's reviews of such transactions may be a source of its disagreements about the fairness of the price charged by management to the ESOP.

The impact of moving equity shares into the ownership of the employees is apparently an important disadvantage of ESOPs despite their considerable tax advantage. Kaplan (1988, note 12) expressed this view in the following terms:

> The infrequent use of ESOP loans in the sample analyzed in this paper (5 of 76 companies) suggests that the non-tax costs of using an ESOP are high. One such cost is the large equity stake that eventually goes to all contributing employees and significantly reduces the equity stake that can be given to managers and the buyout promoter.

A potential advantage is that shares can be sold at higher prices over the years as the ESOP contributes to higher earnings through tax advantages and through the increased incentives and improved motivations of employees as a result of their stock ownership through the ESOP.

COMPARISON WITH PROFIT SHARING

A study by Mitchell (1995) compared profit sharing with ESOPs. He noted that deferred profit-sharing plans are found in about 16% of all medium-sized and large establishments compared with only 3% for ESOPs. So, despite the tax subsidies to ESOPs, their coverage of workers is relatively small. Mitchell stated that noninsured private pensions held $1.2 trillion in equity in 1991. Insured pensions account indirectly for additional equity holdings. Equity holdings by ESOPs for 1991 were estimated at only $47 billion. Thus, the worker coverage of ESOPs is relatively small compared with other pension plans in terms of its impact on helping workers achieve equity holdings.

Mitchell argued that profit sharing from an economic standpoint has advantages over ESOPs. Profit sharing introduces flexibility in worker compensation so it might improve the stability of employment, which is desirable because of the macroeconomic aspects of stabilizing the economy. ESOPs do not have the same macroeconomic benefits. An ESOP involves a form of bonus to employees in the form of equity shares in their own firm. An ESOP does not add to pay flexibility.

Mitchell considered the ability of the firm to deduct the repayment of interest and principal in payments to retire the debt of an ESOP as a tax subsidy. He reasoned that in publicly held companies, the principal repayment reflects the value of stock given to employees. If the valuation of the stock is accurate, the value of the stock represents a true cost to the employer and should be deductible just as wages are. However, owners of closely held companies have the incentive to overvalue the stock assigned to employees, which according to Mitchell would represent a form of tax evasion. Mitchell accordingly argued that if tax subsidies are to be employed, they should be made to profit-sharing schemes that have macroeconomic benefits.

EFFECTS ON COMPANY PRODUCTIVITY

Because one of the objectives expressed in the writings in support of the ESOP idea was to achieve "people's capitalism," it is of interest to consider the stock ownership and control of ESOPs. However, most studies indicate that ownership percentages have been relatively small—10% or less. Even when stock carries voting rights, the voting rights associated with the stock of ESOP accounts may be exercised by the plan trustees (usually the company management) without input by participants. This has given rise to the charge that ESOPs can be used by management to obtain tax benefits without sharing control with employees. This has been justified in the following terms:

> "Our programs are the antithesis of workplace democracy," says Joseph Schuchert, managing partner of Kelso & Co., the firm founded by Louis Kelso, which has installed about 800 ESOPs for companies since 1956 and has arranged 80 buy-outs with ESOP participation since 1970. "We've been criticized for not giving workers more participation, but we believe workers are natural shareholders, not natural managers." (Hiltzik, 1984, p. 2)

Interesting issues are raised in connection with the preceding quote. Apparently, the aim of ESOPs is to enable workers to participate in ownership for the purpose of augmenting their income from dividends and capital gains. However, ownership carries the ultimate control power in a corporation. If workers are not to participate in the decision-making process or to exercise ultimate control in their role as shareholders, some unresolved issues are posed.

With regard to productivity performance, the most exhaustive study was performed by the U.S. General Accounting Office (1987), which reviewed a number of prior studies on ESOPs and corporate performance. Few of these earlier studies found significant gains in either profitability or productivity. Only one of the studies reported a significant improvement in the growth rate of sales. No study reported a significant improvement in the growth rate of employment.

Later studies reported mixed evidence. For example, Park and Song (1995) found that, on average, firms sponsoring ESOPs experience a permanent improvement in performance. However, when they partition their sample between firms with large outside block holders (block firms) and firms without them (nonblock firms), important differences are observed. The improvement in performance is limited to block firms. Their regression analysis finds a negative relation between the fraction of ownership held by the ESOPs and changes in performance for nonblock firms. No systematic relationship is observed for block firms.

Conte, Blasi, Kruse, and Jampani (1996) found that the financial returns of public companies with ESOPs are significantly higher than those of comparable non-ESOP companies. Paradoxically, after companies adopt an ESOP, their financial returns decline, indicating a negative incentive effect. Conte et al. observed that these patterns are consistent with the proposition that most ESOPs in large, publicly traded companies are adopted as takeover defenses.

Most systematic studies of the effects of ESOPs in the United States have not documented performance improvements. Considerable anecdotal evidence can be found that suggests that ESOPs have had positive effects on individual companies. Some positive effects of an ESOP adopted in July 1994 by United Airlines have been reported (Bernstein, 1996). Following the 1994 ESOP, operating revenue per employee increased, the number of employee grievances fell, the market share of United inched up, and pretax operating margins reached about 7.5%. Between June 30, 1994, and March 5, 1996, the stock price of United Airlines increased by almost 150%, compared with an increase of only about 50% over the same period for four other major airlines. The establishment of the United ESOP was associated with concessions representing an average of 15% in pay cuts for 55% of the employees and reduced wage costs overall by 7% in 1995. Thus, the employees who accepted wage cuts became equity holders in the company. The effects on profitability and stock prices are similar to those experienced at TWA earlier when Carl Icahn obtained control. The positive results were only temporary, and 3 years later TWA faced severe financial problems again. TWA has gone through Chapter 11 bankruptcy twice. While in its second bankruptcy in 1995, employees agreed to forgo wage increases and to reduce their equity ownership share from 45% to 30%.

The use of an ESOP at United has not been an unqualified success (Chandler, 1996). Flight attendants were unwilling to participate because they felt that the pay cuts were too large. With regard to individual measures of performance, United still had problems. "UAL's ESOP: From Milestone to Millstone?" *BusinessWeek*, March 20, 2000. (On December 9, 2002, UAL announced bankruptcy.)

Weirton Steel Corporation was formed in 1984 when workers bought 100% of the company to avoid a shutdown. In the following decade, they had to accept successive wage and job reductions and sold 30% of their stock to pay for plant improvements and to reduce debt. In 1994, top management spent $550 million on plant modernization. To help finance this, the ESOP sold more stock, reducing its voting share to 49%.

One problem with ESOPs is that management generally has been unwilling to grant employees full shareholder rights when ESOPs are formed. Employees own an average of 13% of their companies at 562 public corporations, according to a *BusinessWeek* article citing Joseph R. Blasi of Rutgers University (Bernstein, 1996). Most of the 562 companies are unionized, and employees hold board seats in fewer than a dozen.

As discussed in the 1997 *Human Resource Management Handbook*, Kruse and Blasi reviewed 11 studies comparing the productivity of ESOP to non-ESOP firms. Only three studies found significant positive effects of ESOPs. However, referring to a study of signs and significant levels (Weitzman and Kruse, 1990), they concluded that the overall association between ESOPs and performance is positive.

Borstadt and Zwirlein (1995) partitioned their sample of 85 publicly traded firms by the reason for ESOP adoption. ESOPs put in place as a takeover defense have little effect on productivity or performance. They found some evidence that ESOPs established as an incremental employee benefit resulted in a productivity increase but not improved overall firm performance. ESOPs used to obtain wage concessions have no effect on company productivity or performance. After adjustments for industry data, no significant changes are observed in productivity or performance. They conjecture that in firms in which ESOP ownership is coupled with substantial employee participation in decision making, "benefits may be realized" (p. 12).

In his testimony on February 13, 2002, Kruse states that "productivity improves by an extra 4–5% on average in the year an ESOP is adopted, and the higher productivity level is maintained in subsequent years." His citation is to Logue and Yates (2001), which details the possibilities for productivity improvements. However, the only data on productivity in Logue and Yates are on page 208. This section presents a frequency distribution of survey responses on productivity in which only 10.1% of respondents reported a "strong positive impact"; the remaining 89.9% reported weak, negative, or no impact.

In contrast to the uneven experience with ESOPs in the United States, in a study of Japanese manufacturing companies for the period 1973 to 1988, Professors Derek C. Jones of Hamilton College and Takao Kato of Colgate University found positive results for ESOPs in

Japan. They found that since 1973, the portion of publicly traded Japanese firms that had ESOPs jumped from 61% to more than 90%. By 1989, the average holdings per employee had reached about $14,000. Jones and Kato also found that 3 to 4 years after setting up an ESOP, companies averaged a 4% to 5% increase in productivity. A 10% increase in employee bonuses relative to the bonuses of competitors resulted in a 1% increase in productivity in the next year (*BusinessWeek*, 1995, p. 24).

The mixed results for ESOPs suggest that the potential for performance improvements does exist. However, the performance results depend on how management uses the ESOPs.

ECONOMIC ISSUES

ESOPs have been analyzed from an economic standpoint as a bargaining game with asymmetrical information. Ben-Ner and Jun (1996) postulated that management has information about the firm's future cash flows superior to that of employees. They formulated a model in which employees attempt to overcome this informational handicap by making simultaneous offers on wages and a purchase price for the firm. Their model predicted that owners of relatively unprofitable firms will establish ESOPs in lieu of paying higher wages. Owners of more profitable firms will prefer to pay higher wages rather than dilute control by establishing an ESOP.

Of concern are the charges that ESOPs have been used by management not only as instruments for increasing their control, but also to conduct financial transactions in their own interests and to the detriment of the ESOPs and the workers they represent. Some of the court cases in which these issues were at least raised include the following. In Hall-Mark Electronics, employees owned one third of the company stock through their retirement plan. The issue in the court case is the allegation that three Hall-Mark executives arranged to have the ESOP sell its shares back to the company at $4 per share shortly before they participated in the sale of the company for $100 per share (Hiltzik, 1986, p. 1).

Another example is the Chicago Pneumatic Tool Company, which established an ESOP in 1985. The controlling trustee was the chief executive of the company. In March 1986, the company became the target of a hostile takeover. To defeat the bid, it is alleged that the chief executive transferred 1 million shares from the company's treasury to the ESOP under his own voting control. The U.S. Department of Labor (which has responsibility for implementing the provisions of ERISA and of employee pension plans generally) stated that the cost of the transaction to the ESOP was $32.4 million for the shares, which were trading at about 30% over their historical average because of takeover speculation (Hiltzik, 1986, pp. 1, 6).

In 1985, the Department of Labor blocked an ESOP-financed $500 million leveraged buyout of Scott & Fetzer, the publisher of *The World Book Encyclopedia*. The department objected to the arrangement, which provided that the Scott & Fetzer ESOP would invest $182 million in borrowed funds to receive 41% of the company in the leveraged buyout. A group consisting of Scott & Fetzer's top management plus Kelso & Company, were to invest $15 million, for which they would receive 29% of the company. The General Electric Credit Corporation, which financed the $182 million ESOP loan and provided other financing, would receive the remaining 30%. The Department of Labor alleged that the ESOP was putting up more than 92% of the equity investment for only 41% of the company. The rebuttal view was that the ESOP investment represented a purchase of shares at market value (or takeover value), not an initial equity contribution. Another issue raised by this case is whether it was appropriate for Kelso &

Company, a leading investment banking firm specializing in setting up ESOPs and formulating the terms of the deal, to have a substantial equity participation. There would appear to be the possibility of a conflict of interest.

The broader economic consequences of ESOPs also have been analyzed (Chen and Kensinger, 1988). If managements also control the ESOPs that are created, then employee influence on the company does not increase. Although employees might receive stock that can be sold, the additions to their wealth may be relatively small. The amounts received might be insufficient to provide motivation for increased efforts by workers or to achieve harmonious relations between workers and management. On the other hand, if workers did receive substantial increases in control over the company through ESOPs, other harmful results might follow. Workers might use their increased ownership powers to redistribute wealth away from the original shareholders and other shareholders in the firm.

ESOP EVENT RETURNS

The event return effects of establishing an ESOP depend on the circumstances. Chang (1990) calculated the 2-day abnormal portfolio returns for 165 announcements of employee stock ownership plans. The overall return was a positive 11.5%. However, the announcement produces small positive event returns if the ESOP is used as a leveraged buyout (LBO) or as a form of wage concession. However, if the ESOP is established as a defense against a takeover, the event returns will be negative. Managers of such firms, on average, hold smaller ownership interest in their firms than do managers of comparable firms.

Sellers, Hagan, and Siegel (1994) sharpened the analysis of event returns to ESOPs. They eliminated from the sample those ESOPs that provide tax incentives. A positive market 2-day return of 1.5% is consistent with other favorable effects of ESOPs, such as improvements in employee productivity. Similarly, Chang and Mayers (1992) found nontax influences on event returns from the establishment of ESOPs. The largest positive event returns were observed when officers and directors initially controlled between 10% and 20% of share ownership. The positive effects on shareholder wealth were smaller when the initial control was less than 10% or more than 20%. When officers and directors controlled 40% or more of total shares, a negative association was found between event returns and the fraction of shares added to the ESOP.

Event return studies of ESOPs have obtained different results reflecting the multiple motives for ESOPs. Anne Beatty published two empirical studies of ESOPs (1994, 1995). In the first study, she examined three motivations for leveraged ESOPs: (1) as a takeover defense, (2) as incentives to employees, and (3) for tax savings. Her empirical study suggested that companies that adopt ESOPs are likely to have adopted other types of takeover defenses, as well. However, companies that adopt ESOPs are likely to have characteristics consistent also with tax and incentive effects.

In her 1995 study, Beatty analyzed a sample of 122 ESOP transaction announcements during the period 1976 to 1989. She found an average 1% two-day cumulative positive return over the days −1 to 0. This increase in equity value primarily reflects tax effects. She also found some relationship between a positive share price reaction and the size of ESOP benefits, and found that equity values decline for firms that are subject to takeovers. The latter again supports the view that ESOPs are used as a takeover defense.

Event returns also were calculated in the Chaplinsky, Niehaus, and Van de Gucht (1998) study. Market-adjusted returns for the 3-day window covering the days before and after the announcement were 13.3% for ESOPs and 14.9% for management buyouts, with which their study made comparisons.

EVALUATION OF ESOPs

The role of ESOPs is illuminated further by a study of comparisons with management buyouts (MBOs). In Chapter 16, we explain that in MBOs, officers and directors, not workers, substantially increase their percentage ownership; in ESOPs, workers do not effectively increase their control rights. Chaplinsky, Niehaus, and Van de Gucht (1998) first made comparisons prior to the buyout transaction. The transaction size for ESOPs, measured by the median, was $209 million, compared with $172 million for MBOs. ESOP firms had poorer stock price performance. Leverage measured by the ratio of long-term debt to total capitalization (defined as long-term debt plus market value of equity) was significantly lower for ESOPs—12% versus 27%. ESOP firms were more likely to have experienced takeover threats. The ESOP firms had lower ratios of ownership by officers and directors.

Second, they analyzed the relationships after the transaction. Compensation to employees was reduced by 56% of the ESOPs but by only 2.6% of the MBOs. This suggests that ESOPs are used to reduce direct employment costs. The median postbuyout leverage rose for both ESOPs and MBOs. Including the effects of the reversion of excess pension fund assets, the median post-buyout leverage for ESOPs was about 80%, compared to about 75% for MBOs, which is statistically different. ESOP firms did not differ greatly from MBO firms with regard to post-buyout, industry-adjusted employment growth over a 3- to 5-year period. They found also that employees failed to obtain substantial control rights through the formation of ESOPs.

ESOPs are not panaceas for productivity improvement. Their effect on the performance of the firm depends heavily on how they are employed. Some of the notable examples of the use of ESOPs have occurred in industries such as steel and airlines. These are industries where changed economic circumstances forced employees to give up a portion of their wages for a partial equity position in the firm. Even in these circumstances, management continued to exercise major control over decision processes in the firm. Thus, even where ESOPs have been used in a major way, employees have not received full shareholder rights, and ownership incentives have been severely diminished. Many ESOPs were established as takeover defenses. However, the proliferation of a broad arsenal of other takeover defenses has reduced the role of ESOPs in this area.

Finally, the supposed tax advantages have sometimes been confused with the tax deductibility of employee benefits. A major tax advantage for closely held corporations is the tax shelter for the owners, but there are no clear effects on employee incentives. Arguments also have been made that the tax subsidies involved with ESOPs might have perversely negative effects. Similar positive effects also might be achieved through alternative compensation arrangements.

The evidence suggests that ESOPs established as takeover defenses or to enable owners of privately held firms to diversify their wealth positions on a tax-deferred basis while maintaining control of their companies are not likely to benefit employees or improve company productivity or performance. However, if owners truly seek to achieve increased employee participation in decision processes and convey a sense of identity with the firm to achieve performance improvements that will be shared, the results might be positive. However, ESOPs and 401(k) plans invested mainly in employer stocks can result in poorly diversified portfolios with potentially negative effects in declining markets.

MASTER LIMITED PARTNERSHIPS

The corporation has been the dominant form of business organization in the United States when measured by total assets. When measured by numbers, proprietorships and partnerships are the most numerous, applying mostly to relatively small businesses. A corporation has four major advantages in raising large sums of money.

1. It provides for limited liability of stockholders. Stockholders are not personally liable if the firm is unable to pay its debts.
2. The corporation has an unlimited life. Managers can come and go and owners can change, but this does not affect the continuity of the corporation.
3. The ownership shares carry the residual risk, but they are divided into many units. Hence, investors can limit their risk exposure in any one firm, and this facilitates diversification by investors across many firms.
4. The shares of common stock are bought and sold freely. This facilitates tradability and transferability of ownership interest in the firm.

THE NATURE OF MLPs

The master limited partnership (MLP) is a type of limited partnership whose shares are publicly traded. The limited partnership interests are divided into units that trade as shares of common stock. In addition to tradability, it has the advantages of limited liability for the limited partners. The tradability also provides for continuity of life. The MLP retains many of the advantages of a corporation, but it has an advantage over the corporation in that it eliminates the double taxation of corporate earnings. The MLP is not taxed as an entity; it is treated like any other partnership for which income is allocated pro rata to the partners. Unit holders reflect all income deductions and credits attributable to the partnership's operation in determining the unit holder's taxable income.

The Internal Revenue Service has focused on four characteristics in distinguishing between a corporation and a master limited partnership (MLP): unlimited life, limited liability, centralized management, and transferability. To avoid being taxed as a corporation, an MLP can have only two, and no more, of the four corporate characteristics, which are usually centralized management and transferability. Master limited partnerships typically specify a limited life of 100 years more or less. The general partner or manager of the partnership has unlimited liability even though the limited partners do not.

Probably in part because the general partner has unlimited liability, it also has virtually autocratic powers. Once a general partner and the formation of an MLP have been approved by the courts and have been reviewed at least by the Securities and Exchange Commission, it is difficult to change the general partner in the absence of readily provable fraud or the equivalent. The probability of success of an MLP is increased if it is structured to achieve an alignment of interests between the general partner and the public unit holders. One way to do this is by using management incentive fees such as providing the general partner with a sharing rule of 4% to 6% of the distributable cash flows from the MLP. Alignment of incentives also is achieved since the management of the general partnership owns a significant number of the limited partnership units.

THE BOSTON CELTICS EXAMPLE

The Boston Celtics example illustrates many aspects of MLPs, including important tax changes in 1987 and 1997. In October 1986, the Boston Celtics MLP was formed. A hoped-for offering price of $20 per unit had to be reduced to $18 for the public offering. For 1997, the 52-week range in price for the units was a high of 25 1/8 and a low of 20 1/8. Based on the average price and dividend payments of $2.50 during the previous 52 weeks, the units were yielding 11.05%.

The Revenue Act of 1987 provided that publicly traded limited partnerships (MLPs or PTPs) would become taxed as corporations for federal income tax purposes, except for partnerships involving oil and gas, timber, and real estate. However, other PTPs existing on December 17, 1987, would be grandfathered until their first taxable year beginning after December 31, 1997. In August 1997, congress passed the Taxpayer Relief Act of 1997, which permitted PTPs to elect, as an alternative to taxation as a corporation, to pay a federal tax at a rate of 3.5% of gross income from the active conduct of trades or businesses ("Toll Tax") in taxable years beginning after December 31, 1997. Accordingly, the Boston Celtics Limited Partnership (BCLP) would have become taxable as a corporation during its taxable year beginning July 1, 1998, if it remained a PTP unless it elected to pay the Toll Tax. As a result of the two major tax changes, the BCLP was reorganized on April 13, 1998. The reorganization created multiple corporations and limited partnerships with cross-ownership relationships, described in the 10K—Annual Report of the BCLP filed on September 17, 1999.

The BCLP's most significant operating asset was its indirect investment in Celtics Basketball, which owned the Boston Celtics. Reflecting the subsequent declining fortunes of the Celtics basketball operations, the quotation on the BCLP on April 19, 2000, was slightly under $10. In 2002, BCLP changed its name to Henley Limited Partnership when a local investment group, Boston Basketball Partners LLC (BBP), bought control of the team. BBP planned to buy all the publicly traded shares of Henley during the first quarter of 2003.

ADVANTAGES OF MLPs

A strong motivation for the formation of an MLP is the tax advantage. The MLP is taxed as a partnership and, therefore, avoids the double taxation to which corporate dividends are subject. The nature of the advantage to the use of an MLP is shown by Table 15.2. The marginal corporate rate of 40% is below the marginal personal rate of 45%. For company income of

TABLE 15.2 Tax Benefits of MLPs

	Corporation	*MLP*
Company income	$100	$100
Company tax (federal 35%, state 5%)	40	0
After-tax income	60	100
Retained income	0	0
Payout	60	100
Personal tax (federal plus state @ 45%)	27	45
Investor after-tax income	$ 33	$ 55

$100, the investor would receive $55 under the MLP, compared with $33 under the corporation. This is 67% more income.

INITIAL PRICING OF MLPs

Muscarella (1988) analyzed the price performance of MLP units. His sample consisted of all initial public offerings of MLP units from January 1983 to July 1987. He analyzed the price performance of the MLPs for the 20 days following the initial public offerings. He found no significant underpricing or overpricing for his total sample or any subsample except for a slight overpricing of oil and gas and hotel/motel limited partnerships. This contrasts with substantial underpricing of initial public offerings (IPOs) of corporate securities. Ritter (1984), for example, reported initial average returns of 26.5% for 1,028 IPOs from 1977 to 1982. Chalk and Peavy (1987) reported 22% initial returns for 649 firms from 1975 to 1982. Muscarella and Vetsuypens (1989) found an initial return of 7.61% for 1,184 firms for the period 1983 to June 1987. All of these studies indicated substantial underpricing. Theoretical models of IPO underpricing argue that the level of IPO underpricing is related to the degree of uncertainty about the market value of the common stock of the issuing firm. The study of initial price performance of MLP units implies much less uncertainty in the valuation of MLP units. Muscarella was unable to provide an explanation regarding why there should be relatively little uncertainty about the valuation of MLP units.

Moore, Christensen, and Roenfeldt (1989) found a 2-day return $(-1, 0)$ of 4.61% (significant) and some evidence of anticipation of the MLP announcement. The reasons they gave for the positive market reaction include (1) tax advantages, (2) reduced information asymmetry, (3) improved asset management, and (4) information signaling.

Summary

Employee stock ownership plans were designed ostensibly to promote employee stock ownership and to facilitate the raising of capital by employers. They have a number of shortcomings in the performance of both functions. Nevertheless, ESOPs can be valuable in a number of circumstances, particularly for privately held companies engaged in ownership transfer or for firms near the limit of their debt capacity.

The argument for employee stock ownership holds that employees who own stock in their employer are more productive, because as part owners they have a greater stake in the firm's profitability. However, ESOPs provide a good deal less than direct stock ownership. Participants typically do not receive any distribution of securities from the plan until they separate from service. Dividends and voting rights are passed through only with respect to shares actually allocated to participants' accounts. However, most participants are not allowed to sell even those shares that have been allocated to them and thus cannot achieve a level of diversification in their benefit plans. (ERISA excludes ESOPs from the requirement to diversify.) A 1987 report by the U.S. General Accounting Office (GAO) concluded that although ESOPs do broaden stock ownership within participating firms, given the limited number of ESOPs within the economy as a whole, the effect is modest overall. Perhaps more importantly it found little evidence of improved performance in terms of either profitability or productivity.

As a financing tool, ESOPs provide benefits midway between those of debt financing and equity financing. They can bring additional debt capacity to highly leveraged firms or provide a market for equity financing for closely held firms. They are useful devices for transferring ownership. The same 1987 GAO report indicated that the use of ESOPs in corporate finance had not lived up to its potential—most leveraged ESOP funds were being used to buy back stock from existing shareholders (for instance, retiring major shareholders) and not for capital expansion by the sponsoring firms. Thus, ESOP contributions to corporate finance had been limited.

The MLP is an organizational form that offers investors the structure and tax attributes of more traditional partnerships but differs in one key respect. MLPs offer investors liquidity via an organized secondary market for the trading of partnership interests.

Tax advantages were an important motivating factor in the early development of MLPs. However, some of these advantages have been eroded. The Tax Reform Act of 1986 (TRA 86) eliminated an important tax benefit of corporate–MLP conversions with its repeal of the General Utilities doctrine. Before TRA 86, in a liquidation MLP, the corporate sponsor would contribute assets to the MLP in exchange for units in a roll-out transaction. The units would then be distributed to the corporate sponsor's shareholders in a complete liquidation of the corporation. This transaction would be completely tax free. However, with the repeal of the General Utilities doctrine, this was no longer the case. The general rule had been that corporate gains from the sale of appreciated assets were taxed at the corporate level at the time of the sale and at the shareholder level when this income was distributed as dividends. Under the General Utilities doctrine, a significant portion of the assets involved in a corporate MLP conversion would escape corporate taxation at the time of conversion. However, TRA 86 eliminated this exception and taxed at the corporate level the entire difference between the adjusted basis of the assets and their fair market value. In addition, the shareholders at the time of conversion after TRA 86 continued to be taxed on the difference between their basis in the common stock and the market value of the MLP units at conversion.

The main tax advantages of MLPs were the result of the status of MLPs as nontaxable entities. All profits and losses of an MLP flow through to individual investors to be taxed at lower personal rates while avoiding the double taxation at the corporate and personal levels of corporate dividend distributions to shareholders. However, these tax advantages are highly sensitive to an MLP's need to retain earnings, because MLP earnings are taxable to investors whether or not they are distributed. Thus, the liquidity advantages of MLPs assume even greater importance. Siciliano (1987, p. 1) suggested that this aspect of MLPs had led to "a distinctly different investment and marketing thesis," appealing to investors to view MLP units as simply another component of their equity securities portfolio rather than "as a long-term method of sheltering income from taxes."

Questions

15.1 What are the advantages and limitations of ESOPs?

15.2 How successful have ESOPs been in achieving their goals of increasing employee stock ownership and facilitating capital raising by employers?

15.3 Explain the differences between leveraged and nonleveraged ESOPs. Compare the EPS and control dilution under equity financing versus financing through an ESOP.

15.4 Why are ESOPs particularly suited for service businesses and franchise operations?

15.5 How do MLPs differ from ordinary limited partnerships?

15.6 What are the advantages and limitations of MLPs?

15.7 How are MLPs similar to corporations? How do they differ?

15.8 What were the significant tax changes involving MLPs?

Case 15.1 PAN PETROLEUM MLP

Most of the literature on MLPs has emphasized tax aspects. This case study of the Pan Petroleum MLP, whose formation was reviewed by the courts on April 26, 1989, illustrates the underlying business and economic rationales, as well. The 1989 transaction involved a consolidation of a group of 45 oil and gas limited partnerships with Pan Petroleum MLP, a publicly traded master limited partnership. The consolidated partnership had approximately 4,300 limited partners. It was predicted that as a result of the consolidation, general and administrative expenses would be reduced by as much as $300,000 per year. These savings would result from several types of economies of scale resulting from the consolidation. The savings in general and administrative expenses became possible because of the need for only one set of financial records rather than 46, one annual appraisal of mineral properties, the maintenance of one legal entity, and one partnership tax return.

Many of the limited partners in the constituent partnerships consolidating with Pan Petroleum MLP were limited partners in more than one partnership. This made possible further cost savings with respect to record keeping and participant reporting. Many of the constituent partnerships owned interests in the same mineral properties. Duplicate accounting and record keeping could be eliminated as a result of the consolidation. The constituent partnerships participated mainly in wells drilled by two different major exploration companies. The consolidation provided Pan Petroleum MLP with a majority of the working interest in many of the properties. This enabled the MLP to conduct negotiations with the two large exploration companies on a more effective basis.

The basis for the consolidation appeared to be efficient and equitable. Engineering surveys established the proved reserves in developed producing properties, as well as nonproducing or undeveloped properties. From the estimates of proved reserves of oil and gas, the amounts of cash flows and their duration were projected. Similar projections were made for the nonproducing or undeveloped properties. The cash flows for this latter group were reduced by 30% as an uncertainty factor. The resulting cash flows for the developed producing properties and for the non-producing or undeveloped properties were discounted at a 10% rate over the expected future economic producing lives of each of the properties. The MLP into which the other constituent partnerships were consolidated had its future cash flows discounted into a value figure on the same basis. For each constituent limited partnership and the Pan Petroleum MLP, the value of other assets and liabilities also were taken into account to arrive at a total "formula value." These were summed to arrive at a total figure of approximately $23 million. Of this amount, something over $11 million represented the "formula value" of Pan Petroleum MLP, 49.2% of the total. Pan Petroleum MLP had 2,571,670 limited partnership units already outstanding. Using these as the reference factor, a total of 5,226,191 MLP units were issued, of which Pan Petroleum accounted for 49.21%. The other constituent partnerships received MLP units representing the same percentage of the total MLP units issued that their formula value represented in relation to the total formula value. Inherently, forecasts and projections were required, but the methodology appears to have represented a rational and equitable basis for making the apportionment of ownership and income rights.

Clearly one of the major advantages to the owners of the constituent limited partnerships is that they would now have ownership rights that could be freely traded, bought, and sold. A number of the constituent limited partnerships would have had to be liquidated and would have ceased to exist except for the consolidation with Pan Petroleum MLP. In addition, by exchanging their limited partnership units for units in the Pan Petroleum MLP, the limited partners now have pro rata ownership rights in an efficient business operation.▦

QUESTIONS

C15.1.1 What were the economics in grouping 45 oil and gas limited partnerships into one MLP?

C15.1.2 What were some advantages to the owners of the constituent limited partnerships of the formation of the MLP?

Case 15.2   UAL CORP

The UAL case involves bankruptcy (Chapter 13) and ESOPs (Chapter 15) due to sharp declines in revenues and net income (Figure C15.2.1). UAL formed an ESOP in 1994 in which employees agreed to pay cuts for ownership of 55% of the equity. Flight attendants did not participate in the plan. The labor contract with the 9,900 members of the Air Line Pilots Association (ALPA) expired on April 12, 2000, and it expired on July 12, 2000, with the 48,600 machinists. Tensions developed because both the pilots and machinists argued for restoration of the earlier pay concessions. In 1998, the International Association of Machinists (IAM) succeeded in organizing 20,000 nonunion United reservation and gate agents to form an IAM local. The rival Aircraft Mechanics Fraternal Association (AMFA) represented the skilled union mechanics, some of whom believed that the IAM was seeking to use the ESOP to raise wages of the unskilled employees. The pilots appeared to have the strongest bargaining position with management through their board representation. It was said that the wage levels of the UAL pilots were higher than the industry average and that the wage levels of the mechanics were lower than the industry average.

Despite these tensions, the performance of UAL measured by its net income and its operating margins held up well until weakness developed in 2000, as shown in Figure C15.2.1. The events of September 11, 2001, resulted in sharp declines in revenues and profitability. UAL needed a cash infusion and was seeking to obtain a federal loan guarantee. In late November 2002, UAL needed $5.2 billion in wage reductions over a 5.5-year period to obtain a $1.8 billion federal loan guarantee. However, the mechanics' unit of the machinists' union would not agree to the concessions requested. As a result, the government rejected the loan request on December 4, 2002.

The inability of UAL to reduce costs sufficiently resulted in a bankruptcy announcement on December 9, 2002. Four bank lenders agreed to provide UAL with $1.5 billion debtor-in-possession (DIP) financing conditional on UAL's meeting specified cash flow projections each month.

To meet the cash flow projections, UAL needed labor concessions of $2.4 billion per year over 5 years. The union resisted, so UAL requested the bankruptcy judge to grant the company the power to void its union contracts. UAL stated that it would withdraw this request if the unions agreed to pay cuts of $70 million per month through May 1, 2003, giving it time to develop longer-term plans. On December 27, 2002, the pilots, flight attendants, flight dispatchers, and meteorologists agreed to accept their respective shares of the short-term cuts. The machinists refused. UAL requested the bankruptcy court to order the cutbacks. On January 10, 2003, Judge Eugene R. Wedoff made a written ruling that the 35,000 workers represented by the IAM would have to accept the pay cuts of 14% through May 1, 2003. "Judge Orders Pay Cut for Machinists at United," (*New York Times*, January 11, 2003, p. C1). He stated that the reduction was necessary to keep crucial financing in place and to avoid "irreparable damage to the company."

QUESTIONS

C15.2.1 Did the ESOP at United promote a sense of worker democracy that gave the employees a sense of ownership of the company?

C15.2.2 What is the broader significance of Judge Wedoff's ruling?

C15.2.3 What were the objectives of the new business plan that the top management of UAL was seeking to develop by May 1, 2003?

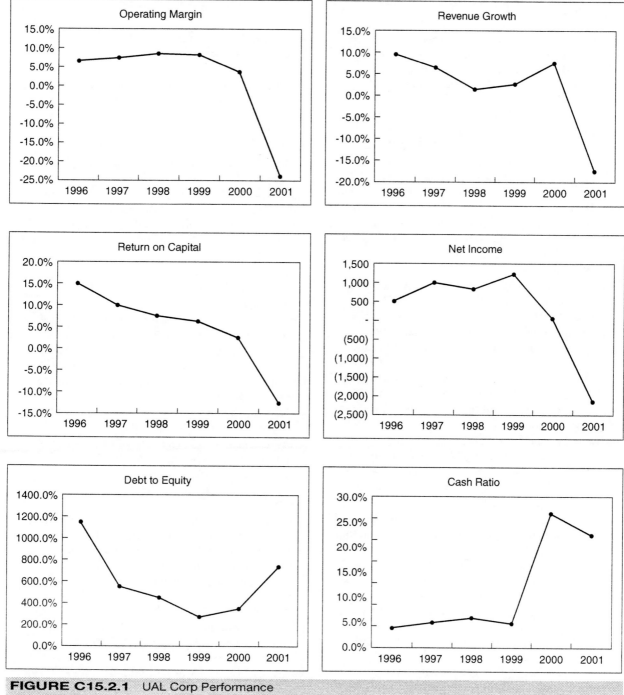

FIGURE C15.2.1 UAL Corp Performance

References

Beatty, Anne, "An Empirical Analysis of the Corporate Control, Tax and Incentive Motivations for Adopting Leveraged Employee Stock Ownership Plans," *Managerial and Decision Economics* 15, 1994, pp. 299–315.

———, "The Cash Flow and Informational Effects of Employee Stock Ownership Plans," *Journal of Financial Economics* 38, June 1995, pp. 211–240.

Ben-Ner, Avner, and Byoung Jun, "Employee Buyout in a Bargaining Game with Asymmetric Information," *American Economic Review* 86, June 1996, pp. 502–523.

Benartzi, Shlomo, "Excessive Extrapolation and the Allocation of 401(k) Accounts to Company Stock, *Journal of Finance* 56:5 October 2001, pp. 1747–1764.

Bernstein, Aaron, "Why ESOP Deals Have Slowed to a Crawl," *Business Week*, March 18, 1996, pp. 101–102.

Borstadt, Lisa F., and Thomas J. Zwirlein, "ESOPs in Publicly Held Companies: Evidence on Productivity and Firm Performance," *Journal of Financial and Strategic Decisions* 6:1, Spring 1995, pp. 1–13.

Brennan, Michael, and Walter N. Torous, "Individual Decision-Making and Investor Welfare," working paper, UCLA, 1999.

Bruner, Robert F., "Leveraged ESOPs and Corporate Restructuring," *Journal of Applied Corporate Finance* 1, Spring 1988, pp. 54–66.

BusinessWeek, "How Japan Perks Up Productivity," August 28, 1995, p. 24.

Chalk, A. J., and J. W. Peavy III, "Initial Public Offerings: Daily Returns, Offering Types, and the Price Effect," *Financial Analysts Journal* 43, September/October 1987, pp. 65–69.

Chandler, Susan, "United We Own," *BusinessWeek*, March 18, 1996, pp. 96–100.

Chang, Saeyoung, "Employee Stock Ownership Plans and Shareholder Wealth: An Empirical Investigation," *Financial Management* 19, Spring 1990, pp. 48–58.

———, and David Mayers, "Managerial Vote Ownership and Shareholder Wealth," *Journal of Financial Economics* 32, August 1992, pp. 103–131.

Chaplinsky, Susan, and Greg Niehaus, "The Role of ESOPs in Takeover Contests," *Journal of Finance* 49, September 1994, pp. 1451–1470.

———, "The Tax and Distributional Effects of Leveraged ESOPs," *Financial Management* 19:1, 1990, pp. 29–38.

Chaplinsky, Susan, Greg Niehaus, and Linda Van de Gucht, "Employee Buyouts: Causes, Structure, and Consequences," *Journal of Financial Economics* 48, 1998, pp. 283–332.

Chen, A. H., and J. W. Kensinger, "Beyond the Tax Effects of ESOP Financing," *Journal of Applied Corporate Finance* 1, Spring 1988, pp. 67–75.

Conte, Michael A., Joseph Blasi, Douglas Kruse, and Rama Jampani, "Financial Returns of Public ESOP Companies: Investor Effects vs. Manager Effects," *Financial Analysts Journal* 52, July/August 1996, pp. 51–61.

Hiltzik, Michael A., "Do ESOPs Aid Workers or Managers?" *Los Angeles Times*, May 25, 1986, Part IV, pp. 1, 6.

———, "ESOPs Now a Boon for Management," *Wall Street Journal*, December 30, 1984, pp. 1–2.

Kaplan, Steven, "A Summary of Sources of Value in Management Buyouts," Presentation at the Conference on Management Buyouts, Graduate School of Business Administration, New York University, Salomon Brothers Center for the Study of Financial Institutions, May 20, 1988.

Kruse, Douglas, "Research Evidence on Prevalence and Effects of Employee Ownership," testimony before the Committee on Education and the Workforce, U.S. House of Representatives February 13, 2002.

Kruse, Douglas L., and Joseph R. Blasi, "Employee Ownership, Employee Attitudes, and Firm Performance: A Review of the Evidence," in *The Human Resource Management Handbook, Part I*, David Lewin, Daniel J. B. Mitchell, and Mahmood A. Zaidi (eds), Greenwich, CT: JAI Press Inc., 1997, pp. 113–151.

Logue, John, and Jacquelyn Yates, *The Real World of Employee Ownership*, Ithaca, NY: Cornell University Press, 2001.

Mentz, J. Roger, Department of the Treasury, Statement on June 30, 1987 in *Master Limited Partnerships*, Hearings Before the Subcommittee on Select Revenue Measures of the Committee on Ways and Means, House of Representatives, 100th Congress, First Session, Serial 100–39.

Mergers & Acquisitions, "Illinois School Goes the ESOPs Route," February 2003, pp. 8–9.

Mitchell, Daniel J. B., "Profit Sharing and Employee Ownership: Policy Implications," *Contemporary Economic Policy* 13, April 1995, pp. 16–25.

Moore, W. T., D. G. Christensen, and R. L. Roenfeldt, "Equity Valuation Effects of Forming Master Limited Partnerships," *Journal of Financial Economics* 24, 1989, pp. 107–124.

Muscarella, C. J., "Price Performance of Initial Public Offerings of Master Limited Partnership Units," *The Financial Review* 23, November 1988, pp. 513–521.

Muscarella, Chris J., and Michael R. Vetsuypens, "The Underpricing of 'Second' Initial Public Offerings," *Journal of Financial Research* 12, Fall 1989, pp. 183–192.

Pan Petroleum MLP, Proposal, March 8, 1989.

Park, Sangsoo, and Moon H. Song, "Employee Stock Ownership Plans, Firm Performance, and Monitoring by Outside Blockholders," *Financial Management* 24, Winter 1995, pp. 52–65.

Ritter, J. R., "The 'Hot' Issue Market of 1980," *Journal of Business* 57, April 1984, pp. 215–240.

Scholes, Myron S., and Mark A. Wolfson, *Taxes and Business Strategy: A Planning Approach*, Upper Saddle River, NJ: Prentice Hall, 1992.

Schultz, Ellen, "All That Payout and Capital Gains Too," *Fortune* 118, October 10, 1988, p. 28.

Sellers, Keith F., Joseph M. Hagan, and Philip H. Siegel, "Employee Stock Ownership Plans and Shareholder Wealth: An Examination of the Market Perceptions of the Non-Tax Effects," *Journal of Applied Business Research* 10, Summer 1994, pp. 45–52.

Siciliano, John M., "Investment Banking Considerations," in Lionel M. Allan, *Master Limited Partnerships for Real Property Investments*, Berkeley, CA: California Continuing Education of the Bar, 1987, pp. 1–13.

U.S. General Accounting Office, *Employee Stock Ownership Plans: Benefits and Costs of ESOP Tax Incentives for Broadening Stock Ownership*, Washington, DC: December 1986.

——, *Employee Stock Ownership Plans: Little Evidence of Effects on Corporate Performance*, Washington, DC, October 1987.

Weitzman, M., and D. Kruse, "Profit Sharing and Productivity," in *Paying for Productivity: A Look at the Evidence*, Alan S. Blinder (ed), Washington, DC: Brookings Institution Press, 1990, pp. 95–140.

CHAPTER 16
GOING PRIVATE AND LEVERAGED BUYOUTS

*G*oing private refers to the transformation of a public corporation into a privately held firm. A leveraged buyout (LBO) is the purchase of a company by a small group of investors using a high percentage of debt financing. Whether performed by an outside financial group or mainly by the managers or executives of the company (management buyout, or MBO), an LBO results in a significant increase in the ownership of equity shares by the managers. A turnaround or improvement in performance usually is associated with the formation of an LBO.

A summary of the largest LBOs in 2001 illustrates the range of participants involved. *Mergers & Acquisitions* magazine lists the top 10 LBOs for 2001 (February 2002, p. 52). Berkshire Hathaway, in combination with the management of Shaw Industries Incorporated (carpeting), bought 87.5% of Shaw's equity for $2.1 billion. Forstmann Little did an LBO of Citadel Communication Corporation (radio stations) for $2 billion. First Reserve Corporation and Odyssey Investment Partners combined with management to buy the Dresser Equipment Group (energy-related equipment) for $1.6 billion. First Reserve is a private equity firm specializing in the energy industry. Odyssey is a private equity fund focused on management-backed, leveraged acquisitions. AEA Investors, DLJ Merchant Banking Partners, and DB Capital Partners joined to purchase the performance material division (textile coatings) from B.F. Goodrich Company for $1.4 billion. AEA Investors was founded in 1969 by the Rockefeller, Harriman, and Mellon families. DLJ Merchant Banking Partners is a segment of Donaldson, Lufkin, & Jenrette, Incorporated. This group also bought the stock and assumed the debt of IBP (part of Tyson Foods) for $3.8 billion with the aim to further develop its beef and pork business in late 2000. The third partner in the B.F. Goodrich deal was DB Capital Partners, the private equity arm of Deutsche Bank. Citigroup bought the remaining 63.6% of Delco Remy International (motor vehicle parts) for $0.7 billion. On July 26, 2002, Diageo PLC announced the sale of its Burger King fast-food chain for $2.26 billion to the Texas Pacific Group, Bain Capital, and Goldman Sachs. A close competitor in the bidding was Thomas H. Lee, a buyout firm (*New York Times*, July 26, 2002, p. C5).

This sample of transactions illustrates the relatively wide range of participants in the LBO market. They are generally referred to as financial buyers. Berkshire Hathaway and Citigroup are leading financial holding companies. Forstmann Little represents LBO companies such as KKR and Thomas Lee. Most of the other examples described are private equity or venture capital segments of commercial banks or investment banking firms. Many types of financial firms are involved through merchant banking or partnership groups.

An example will illustrate how a financial buyer operates. In March 1993, Hicks, Muse, Tate, and Furst purchased from DuPont for $370 million a small division that it named Berg Electronics Incorporated. Hicks Muse replaced top management and bought six more related companies for $135 million. Berg moved from the seventh-ranked electrical supplier in 1993 to number four by 1995, during which time earnings doubled to $113 million. In March 1996, Hicks Muse was able to make a public offering of Berg at $21 per share. By midyear, it traded at $25, compared to the original purchase price of $4.11 paid by Hicks Muse. Berg was acquired in 1998 for $35 per share.

THE CHARACTERISTICS OF LEVERAGED BUYOUTS

Leveraged buyout activity reached its peak during the years 1986 to 1989. The largest was RJR Nabisco (in 1988), with a purchase price of $24.6 billion. The next-largest LBOs were the Beatrice Companies (in 1985) at $5.4 billion, the Safeway Stores (in 1986) at $4.2 billion, and the Borg Warner Corporation (in 1987) at $3.8 billion. The total purchase price of the 20 largest LBOs formed between 1983 and 1995 was $76.5 billion (*Mergerstat Review*, 1996, p. 43).

Incumbent management is usually included in the buying group. Sometimes an entire company is acquired. Sometimes only a segment, a division, or a subsidiary of a public corporation is acquired from the parent company. These are usually of relatively smaller size, and key executives perform such an important role that these going-private transactions are called unit management buyouts (MBOs). Notable examples of unit management buyouts announced in 1995 include the Merck & Co., Inc. sale to a management group of its Medco Behavioral Care Corporation at a purchase price of $340 million. Another example is the sale by Torchmark Corporation of a unit involved in energy asset management (Torch Energy Advisors, Incorporated) for $115 million (*Mergerstat Review*, 1996, p. 34).

Especially when financial groups such as venture capital companies or other types of buyout specialists are involved, the LBO transaction is expected to be reversed with a public offering. The aim is to increase the profitability of the company taken private and thereby increase market value. The buyout firm seeks to harvest its gains within a 3- to 5-year period of time.

THE MAJOR STAGES OF LEVERAGED BUYOUTS

Leveraged buyout activity can be placed into three distinct time periods: the 1980s, the early 1990s, and post-1992. Leveraged buyouts did not begin with the 1980s; they actually have a long history. Before 1980, they often were referred to as bootstrap transactions characterized by highly leveraged deals. During the 1980s, the economic and financial environments that stimulated M&A activity were also fertile environments for LBOs.

Economic and legislative changes, as well as some unsound patterns in LBO transactions of the late 1980s, resulted in a correction period. From a peak of a total of $65.7 billion in LBO transactions in 1989, the volume declined to $7 billion in 1991. New developments in the nature of LBO transactions and market participants led to a revival in LBO transactions to a level of $62 billion in 1999.

The percentage relationships underscore the changing relative importance of LBOs, as shown in Table 16.1. For the years 1986 to 1989, LBOs accounted for more than one fifth of the total dollar value of completed mergers. From 1990 to 1992, LBOs dropped to 11.3% of the

TABLE 16.1	Value of LBO Transactions (in $billions)		
Year	Total Value Offered All M&A	Leveraged Buyouts	% of Total Mergers
1982	53.8	3.5	6.5
1983	73.1	4.5	6.2
1984	122.2	18.7	15.3
1985	179.8	19.7	11.0
1986	173.1	45.2	26.1
1987	163.7	36.2	22.1
1988	246.9	47.0	19.0
1989	221.1	65.7	29.7
1990	108.2	15.2	14.1
1991	71.2	7.0	9.8
1992	96.7	9.6	9.9
1993	176.4	11.0	6.2
1994	226.7	13.0	5.7
1995	356.0	20.0	5.6
1996	495.0	29.0	5.9
1997	657.1	28.7	4.4
1998	1,191.9	41.0	3.4
1999	1,425.9	62.0	4.3
2000	1,325.7	51.5	3.9
2001	699.4	18.6	2.7
Yearly Averages			
1982–1985	107.2	11.6	9.7
1986–1989	201.2	48.5	24.2
1990–1992	92.0	10.6	11.3
1993–1995	253.0	14.7	5.9
1996–2000	1,019.1	42.4	4.4
2001	699.4	18.6	2.7

Source: *Mergers & Acquisitions Almanac* issues, *Mergerstat Review* (2002).

total dollar value of merger activity. For the years 1996 to 2000, LBOs represented only 4.4% of total M&A activity.

The weakness in the economy during 2001 resulted in a decline in both M&A activity and LBO activity. LBOs continue to perform an important role in improving the utilization of corporate resources. The rising absolute dollar amounts of LBO activity are consistent with the material we present later in the chapter that describes the well-articulated business logic of the LBO transactions.

Table 16.2 sets forth the relative premiums paid during the four different time periods. For all acquisitions, the mean or median premium did not change greatly except in 2001. However, the mean and median premium were substantially lower for going-private transactions in all three periods. The decline in the premiums paid in going-private transactions was relatively

TABLE 16.2 Relative Premium Offered

| | All Acquisitions | | Going Private | |
Period	Mean Premium	Median Premium	Mean Premium	Median Premium
1986–1989	39.9%	30.2%	33.9%	26.5%
1990–1992	39.4	32.0	27.6	19.9
1993–2000	41.4	32.2	35.1	27.1
2001	57.2	40.5	67.6	52.2

Source: Mergerstat Review (2002).

sharp during 1990 to 1992, but for the period 1993 to 1998, the premiums paid in going-private transactions were slightly above the levels of the period 1986 to 1989. The premiums paid in acquisitions and going-private transactions during 2001 were surprisingly high. A possible explanation is that stock prices had declined so much during 2001 that prices paid represented some probability that the targets would return to higher values in the future.

In Table 16.3, it is clear that the mean and median price earnings ratios (P/Es) reflected in the purchase price of the going-private transactions established dropped sharply in the period 1990 to 1992 compared with 1986 to 1989. P/Es paid in the period 1986 to 1989 appeared to be higher for the going-private transactions than for the benchmark S&P 500 during the same time period. The P/Es in the going private transactions in 1990 to 1992, however, were much lower than in the benchmark S&P 500 for the period.

For the period 1993 to 2000, the P/E ratio of the S&P 500 had risen to 23.3. For going-private transactions, the mean P/E ratio also rose. However, the median going-private P/E ratio was only slightly higher than during the period 1986 to 1989. This indicates that a few high P/E ratio transactions during the time period 1993 to 2000 increased the arithmetic average. For the year 2001, the S&P 500 average P/E ratio increased sharply, because prices did not fall as much as earnings. The median P/E ratio in going-private transactions dropped to about the same level as in the recession period of 1990 to 1992.

It is clear from the foregoing data that distinct differences can be discerned in the LBOs of the three periods. Accordingly, we first describe the basic pattern of LBO and MBO activity during the 1980s. We next describe the factors that caused LBO activity to drop sharply in the early 1990s. The final section of the chapter describes the new developments associated with the revival of leveraged buyouts after 1992.

TABLE 16.3 Relative P/E Ratios

Period	S&P 500 Mean P/E	Going-Private Mean P/E	Going-Private Median P/E
1986–1989	15.3	20.5	17.8
1990–1992	19.3	14.6	12.3
1993–2000	23.3	22.7	17.8
2001	48.3	22.7	12.1

Source: Mergerstat Review (2002).

CHARACTERISTICS OF LBOs IN THE 1980s

In the traditional LBOs of the 1980s, debt financing typically represented more than 50% of the purchase price. Debt was secured by the assets of the acquired firm or based on the expected future cash flows. The cash flows typically were measured by earnings before depreciation and amortization, before interest and taxes (EBITDA, also called EBDIT). Debt was scheduled to be paid off either from the sale of assets or from future cash flows generated by operations. Following completion of the buyout, the acquired company became a privately held corporation. It was expected that the firm would go public again after a period of 3 to 5 years at a gain. Before developing in some detail the financial patterns in an illustrative LBO, we first discuss the general economic and financial factors that stimulated the LBOs in the 1980s.

GENERAL ECONOMIC AND FINANCIAL FACTORS

In substantial measure, the increase in the number and dollar volume of mergers and restructuring activities in the 1980s reflected underlying forces in the economic and financial environments. The same general forces that produced mergers and restructuring also appear to have stimulated increased use of leveraged buyouts and management buyouts. Indeed, sometimes an LBO or MBO is a defensive measure against an unwanted takeover. On the other hand, sometimes the announcement of a going private plan, an LBO, or an MBO will stimulate competing bids by outsiders. Thus, interactions occur between takeover activity and LBO activity. We briefly summarize here materials on the factors that stimulated M&A and LBO activity in the 1980s.

One fundamental influence was the period of sustained economic growth between 1982 and 1990. A new peak in all categories of M&A activity was reached in this period of sustained business expansion, as all previous major merger waves were also observed in periods of expansionary environments. Total M&A transactions, divestitures, and leveraged buyouts of public companies and divisions all followed similar patterns in the 1980s; total M&A transactions and divestitures peaked in 1986 in terms of the number of transactions, and leveraged buyouts peaked in 1988 (*Mergerstat Review*, 1996).

Another pervasive influence was (somewhat unanticipated) persistent inflation, which began to accelerate in the late 1960s and continued through 1982. The gross national product implicit price deflator during the period 1968 to 1982 increased by no less than 5%. Measured by the Consumer Price Index on all items, double-digit inflation or close to that level was experienced in 6 out of the 14 years. The persistence of a relatively high level of inflation had a number of consequences. One was to cause the q-ratio to decline sharply. The q-ratio is the ratio of the market value of a firm to the replacement cost of its assets. When this ratio is less than 1, it is cheaper to buy capacity in the financial markets than in the real asset markets. The q-ratio moved from a peak of 1.3 in 1965 to a low of 0.52 in 1981. It began to rise in 1982 with the rise in stock prices after mid-1982. When the q-ratio was as low as 0.52 in 1981, this meant that a firm could be purchased in the financial markets at almost half of what it would cost to replace the firm's assets in brick and mortar and inventories. This undoubtedly motivated some takeovers, although takeovers also can be stimulated by the value creation reflected in high q-ratios.

In addition, the persistent inflation provided opportunities to realize tax savings through recapitalization. Because coupon payments on existing debt were not adjusted for inflation, real debt obligations declined with rising price levels. Thus, the real levels of debt-to-equity ratios declined over the period of persistent but largely unanticipated inflation. Thus, opportunities existed for greater interest tax shields by releveraging business firms. On the other hand, increased free cash flows reflecting inflation and fixed interest payments (on old debt) might have allowed managers to increase self-aggrandizing but unprofitable expenditures, as suggested by Jensen (1986). For these reasons, firms that lagged in increasing leverage became inviting targets to outsiders who were ready, willing, and able to bring about the restructuring (Shleifer and Vishny, 1988). This, in turn, stimulated new forms of debt financing such as the use of high-yield bonds in the innovative financial markets. Developments in the financial markets were further stimulated by a succession of laws that deregulated financial institutions.

Other legislative factors also played a role. New tax laws stimulated restructuring and takeover activity. In particular, the Economic Recovery Tax Act (ERTA) enacted in 1981 permitted old assets to be stepped up on purchase. These newly established high values could then be depreciated on an accelerated basis. In the period of high inflation, the nominal value of corporate assets was increased above their historical cost, enabling a large step-up in basis. Depreciation recapture was relatively small. Also under the General Utilities doctrine, the sales of assets in the liquidation process (actual or under technical legal terms) were not subject to capital gains taxes at the corporate level. (The General Utilities doctrine was repealed in the 1986 tax reform.)

Another legislative change that encouraged MBOs involved employee stock ownership plans (ESOPs). Although these had been around for some years, the 1981 ERTA increased the ability of ESOPs to borrow from a bank to invest the funds in the firm's shares. The firm was able to treat as a deductible expense for tax purposes contributions to the ESOP sufficient to cover the interest and the principal payments on the loan. In addition, in 1984 a further tax law change permitted banks to deduct half of their interest income on loans to ESOPs. This enabled the banks to make loans to ESOPs on relatively more favorable terms. This loan interest exclusion provision was repealed in 1996.

A new antitrust climate began in 1980. New appointees to the Federal Trade Commission and to the Department of Justice made it clear through public speeches and agency actions that the stringent prohibitions against horizontal and vertical mergers would no longer be supported. Efficiency considerations and a "new economic realism" were substituted for the older structural view that held that the effects on competition could be judged by market concentration ratios. At least three competing explanations for the change in the antitrust regulatory environment have been proffered. First, the new administration had different political views. Second, the culmination of more than a decade of new empirical research from the academic community provided support for a dynamic competition view of the interactions among large firms. Third, most significant U.S. industries had become subject to intense competition from foreign firms. Thus, competitive pressures provided the stimulus for restructuring, and the recognition of these pressures was the basis for changed public opinion and regulatory policy toward mergers, takeovers, and restructuring.

It was these forces that increased merger activity and restructuring in a wide range of forms. LBOs and MBOs were part of this general pattern. Sometimes LBOs and MBOs were responses to the increased threat of takeover, and their announcements often stimulated rival offers by outsiders.

ILLUSTRATION OF AN LBO

A simplified example illustrates the nature of a leveraged buyout transaction during the 1980s. Wavell Corporation, a successful, publicly traded manufacturer of glassware, was purchased in the 1970s by Eastern Pacific (EP), a large conglomerate that during this period seemed bent on buying everything in sight. Eventually, however, Eastern Pacific began to focus its interests predominantly in the transportation, communications, and real estate industries. Wavell did not fit into the EP mold and languished for a number of years. In 1983, when a small group of disgruntled Wavell executives began to consider the possibility of a leveraged buyout, EP was more than willing to consider divestiture; Wavell's growth rates did not meet EP's objectives, and EP had never been comfortable with Wavell's product line. Although the glassware industry was not growing rapidly, Wavell's product enjoyed a steady demand. The company had stable production costs and good contribution margins, which consistently resulted in a strong, steady cash flow. The production equipment was old but in good condition, and its replacement cost far exceeded its book value. Up until the EP acquisition, Wavell had always been managed well, if conservatively, and had little debt.

Wavell's current sales were $7 million with EBIT of $650,000 and net income of $400,000. Negotiations between Wavell management and EP resulted in a purchase price of $2 million. Because of the high replacement cost of Wavell's assets, its strong cash flow, and its relatively unencumbered balance sheet, Wavell was able to take on a large amount of debt. Banks supplied $1.2 million of senior debt at an interest rate of 13%; this debt was secured by the finished goods inventory and by net property, plant, and equipment and was to be amortized over a 5-year period. An insurance company loan of $600,000 also was arranged in the form of subordinated debt, likewise to be amortized over a 5-year period. The insurance company also took an equity position worth $100,000; Wavell was expected to repurchase this equity interest after 5 years for an amount that would provide the insurance company with a 40% annual yield. Finally, the Wavell management team put up $100,000 as their own equity position.

The following calculations illustrate the cash flow patterns that might be expected following the LBO. First, amortization tables are provided for the bank and insurance company loans in Tables 16.4 and 16.5:

TABLE 16.4 Bank Loan Amortization Schedule[a]

Year	Interest	Principal	Balance
1	$156,000	$185,177	$1,014,823
2	131,927	209,250	805,573
3	104,724	236,453	569,120
4	73,986	267,191	301,929
5	39,248	301,929	—

[a]$1.2 million at 13%; annual payment = $341,177.

TABLE 16.5 Insurance Company Loan Amortization Schedule[a]

Year	Interest	Principal	Balance
1	$96,000	$ 87,245	$512,755
2	82,041	101,204	411,551
3	65,848	117,397	294,154
4	47,065	136,180	157,974
5	25,271	157,974	—

[a]$600,000 at 16%; annual payment = $183,245.

In Table 16.6, pro forma cash flow calculations are made on the basis of a number of conservative assumptions. First, no growth is assumed. The tax rate is assumed to be 40%. Depreciation is calculated on a straight-line basis over a period of 16.67 years (or 6%); accelerated depreciation would clearly enhance cash flows. Furthermore, it is unlikely that debt levels would decline to zero. As the original debt was repaid, it is likely that Wavell would take on additional debt, perhaps long-term debt, to augment the declining interest tax shelter.

If we now assume that Wavell is sold at the end of year 5 for book value (again a conservative assumption given the track record in the pro forma cash flows), we can calculate the annual compounded rate of return on equity as follows:

$$ROE = \left(\frac{1,656,734}{200,000} \right)^{1/5} - 1 = 53\% \text{ annual compounded rate of return}$$

Because Wavell is required to pay only 40% annually on the insurance company's equity interest, a payment of $537,824 would be sufficient to repurchase this equity. This would leave $1,118,910 for the management group, or an annual return of more than 62% on their investment.

ELEMENTS OF A TYPICAL LBO OPERATION

The preceding analysis was a simplified example of an LBO operation. If we abstract from this example and many more real-world LBOs, the following picture emerges. The first stage of the operation consists of raising the cash required for the buyout and devising a management incentive system. Typically, about 10% of the cash is put up by the investor group headed by the company's top managers or buyout specialists. This becomes the equity base of the new firm. Outside investors provide the remainder of the equity. The managers also receive stock price-based incentive compensation in the form of stock options or warrants. Thus, the equity share of management (not including directors) will grow to a higher percentage, possibly to more than 30%. Frequently, managers also are provided with incentive compensation plans based on measures such as increases in share price values.

TABLE 16.6 Pro Forma Cash Flows for Wavell Corporation

	Year 0	Year 1	Year 2	Year 3	Year 4	Year 5
EBIT	$ 650,000	$ 650,000	$ 650,000	$ 650,000	$ 650,000	$ 650,000
− Interest		252,000	213,968	170,572	121,051	64,519
EBT		398,000	436,032	479,428	528,949	585,481
− Taxes		159,200	174,413	191,771	211,580	234,192
NI		238,800	261,619	287,657	317,369	351,289
− Depreciation		120,000	120,000	120,000	120,000	120,000
CFBDR[a]		358,800	381,619	407,657	437,369	471,289
− Principal repaid		272,422	310,454	353,850	403,371	459,903
Cash flow cushion		86,378	71,165	53,807	33,998	11,386
Equity	200,000	438,800	700,419	988,076	1,305,445	1,656,734
Debt	1,800,000	1,527,578	1,217,124	863,274	459,903	—
Total assets	2,000,000	$1,966,378	$1,917,543	$1,851,350	$1,765,348	$1,656,734
% Debt	90%	78%	63%	47%	26%	0%

[a]CFBDR: Cash flow before debt repayment.

About 50% to 60% of the required cash is raised by borrowing against the company's assets in secured bank acquisition loans. The bank loan may be syndicated with several commercial banks. This portion of the debt also can be provided by an insurance company or limited partnership specializing in venture capital investments and leveraged buyouts. The rest of the cash is obtained by issuing senior and junior subordinated debt in a private placement (with pension funds, insurance companies, venture capital firms, and so on) or public offering as "high-yield" notes or bonds (that is, junk bonds). Subordinated debt often is referred to as "mezzanine money" and may carry payment-in-kind provisions. If adverse surprises result in the inability to meet interest obligations on portions of mezzanine financing, the debt holders receive more of the same paper in lieu of cash interest payments.

In the second stage of the operation, the organizing sponsor group buys all the outstanding shares of the company and takes it private (in the stock purchase format) or purchases all the assets of the company (in the asset purchase format). In the latter case, the buying group forms a new, privately held corporation. To reduce the debt by paying off part of the bank loan, the new owners sell off some parts of the acquired firm.

In the third stage, management strives to increase profits and cash flows by cutting operating costs and changing marketing strategies. It will consolidate or reorganize production facilities; improve inventory control and accounts receivables management; improve product quality, product mix, customer service, and pricing; trim employment; and try to extract better terms from suppliers. It might even lay off employees and cut spending on research and new plants and equipment as long as these are necessary to meet payment on the swollen debt. (However, in reviewing business plans, lenders would require that provisions for capital expenditures be adequate.)

In the fourth stage, the investor group might take the company public again if the "leaner and meaner" company emerges stronger and the goals of the group are achieved. This reverse LBO is effected through a public equity offering, referred to as a secondary initial public offering (SIPO). One purpose of this reconversion to public ownership is to create liquidity for existing stockholders. Aside from this, a study of 72 firms engaging in reverse LBOs over the period 1976 to 1987 reveals that 86% of the firms intended to use the SIPO proceeds to lower the company's leverage (Muscarella and Vetsuypens, 1990). Only 8 out of 72 firms raised the funds for capital expenditures. The reverse LBOs are undertaken mostly by ex post successful LBO companies, and indeed the equity participants at the time of the LBO realized a median return of 1,965.6% on their equity investment, or a median annualized rate of return of 268.4% by the time of the SIPO. (The median length of time between the LBO and the SIPO was 29 months.)

OTHER ASPECTS OF GOING-PRIVATE BUYOUTS IN THE 1980s

For LBOs of the 1980s, typical targets included manufacturing firms in basic, non-regulated industries with at least predictable or low financing (capital expenditure) requirements. Stability and predictability of earnings were essential in the face of substantial interest payments and loan amortization. The financing needs of very high-growth firms might put a strain on debt service capability. High-tech firms were considered less appropriate because they generally have a shorter history of demonstrated profitability, as well as greater business risk; they generally have fewer leveragable assets. Furthermore, they command high P/E multiples well above book value because of future growth opportunities.

These generalizations are supported by the empirical data developed by Lehn and Poulsen (1988), who studied a sample of 108 leveraged buyouts during the period 1980 to

1984. Almost half of the firms were in five industries: retailing, textiles, food processing, apparel, and bottled and canned soft drinks. Note that these are all consumer nondurable goods industries for which the income elasticity of demand would be relatively low. Hence, these industries would be least subject to fluctuations in sales as the level of gross national product fluctuated. Note also that all of these are mature industries with limited growth opportunities.

The success of an LBO in the 1980s was enhanced by a track record of capable management. The company should have a strong market position in its industry to enable it to withstand economic fluctuations and competitors' assaults. The balance sheet should be highly liquid; it should show a large, relatively unencumbered asset base for use as collateral, and in particular a high proportion of tangible assets whose fair market value exceeds net book value.

The transaction required sufficient leverage to maximize return on equity but not so much as to drain funds needed to sustain growth. Lenders were attracted by interest rates three to five percentage points above the prime rate and by the characteristics of the company and its collateral. Borrowing capacity was favorably affected by large amounts of cash or cash equivalents, and undervalued assets (hidden equity) whose market value exceeded depreciated book value. Lenders might also look to subsidiaries of the LBO candidate whose liquidation would not impact ongoing operations. In addition, lenders such as venture capital and insurance companies, which also take an equity interest in the LBO, look to the high rate of return they expect on their equity participation. Last, but by no means least, lenders must have confidence in the management group spearheading the LBO, whether incumbent or external. The managers involved typically have a proven record as highly capable executives. They are betting their reputations on the success of the venture and are highly motivated by the potential for large personal wealth gains that might not be achievable in larger public corporations.

Among the sources of MBO targets are divestitures of unwanted divisions by public companies, privately owned businesses whose current growth rate is insufficient to provide opportunities for capable management or to attract corporate acquirers, and public companies whose shares are selling at low earnings multiples representing a substantial discount from book value.

EMPIRICAL RESULTS OF GOING PRIVATE IN THE 1980s

The earliest comprehensive study of going-private transactions was by DeAngelo, DeAngelo, and Rice (1984). Their sample consisted of 72 firms that made 72 initial and 9 subsequent (revived) going-private proposals during the period 1973 to 1980. The median market value of total equity was about $6 million for the sample of 45 pure/going-private proposals (that is, without third-party equity participation in the private firm) and somewhat more than $15 million for 23 leveraged buyout proposals. Thus, the firms were relatively small. In addition, management held a relatively large ownership position. In 72 going-private proposals, management's mean preoffer ownership fraction was 45%, with a median measure of 51%. For the 23 LBOs with third-party participation, the mean and median were 32% and 33%, respectively.

DeAngelo, DeAngelo, and Rice found that the average change in stockholder wealth at announcement was a positive 22%, which was highly significant from a statistical standpoint. The cumulative increase in stockholder wealth over the 40 days including the announcement date was more than 30%. They note that public stockholder gains measured as the average premium above market (2 months before the proposal) were more than 56% in 57 sample proposals involving all payment in cash.

DeAngelo, DeAngelo, and Rice also tested for the effects of the announcement of a going-private withdrawal. Their sample was 18 firms for the period 1973 to 1980. The announcement effect was a negative change in stockholder wealth of almost 9%. However, because the cumulative prediction error for the 40 days up to the announcement date was almost 13%, the cumulative prediction error for the 40 days through the announcement date was +4%. During the subsequent 40 days, the cumulative prediction error rose to about 8%. They noted three potential explanations for the positive returns net of proposal and withdrawal announcement effects. First, an information effect causes a permanent upward revaluation of the firm's prospects. Second, a positive probability might remain that managers will revive the going-private proposal at a future date. Third, the positive return might reflect the possibility that another party will offer to acquire the firm.

The Lehn and Poulsen study (1989) covered 284 going-private transactions for the period 1980 to 1987. The mean equity value for the Lehn and Poulsen sample was $191 million. The size of going-private transactions increased significantly during the period covered. In a separate study, Lehn and Poulsen (1988) reported that the average pre-LBO debt-to-equity ratio for a sample of 58 firms was about 46%. For the post-LBO period, the average debt-to-equity ratio rose to more than 552%. Thus, substantial increases in leverage took place.

Lehn and Poulsen (1988) found that the average net-of-market stock price reaction to the announcement for 92 leveraged buyouts was slightly more than 20%, measured over a period of 20 days before the announcement to 20 days after the announcement. The result was highly significant from a statistical standpoint. The average value of the premium paid in the LBO offer compared to the market price of the firm's common stock 20 trading days prior to the announcement was 41%, calculated for the 72 leveraged buyouts in the sample that were all-cash offers. These results are somewhat lower than those found by DeAngelo, DeAngelo, and Rice. The Lehn and Poulsen sample represented larger firms for a later period. Also, the Lehn and Poulsen study covered LBOs during the period 1980 to 1984, when the takeover and restructuring market was much more active. In addition, they measured the premium from a reference point 20 days prior to the announcement, whereas DeAngelo, DeAngelo, and Rice measured the premium from a reference point 2 months before the announcement.

Another empirical study was performed by Lowenstein (1985). His sample was 28 management buyout proposals made from 1979 to 1984; each was worth at least $100 million to the shareholders at the winning bid price. The percentage of shares owned by management for the Lowenstein sample was much smaller than for the DeAngelo, DeAngelo, and Rice sample. It was only 3.8% when measured by the median and 6.5% when measured by the mean. In 15 new companies formed as the result of going-private, management shares increased to 10.4% measured by the median and to 24.3% measured by the mean.

Lowenstein also measured the premium of the winning bid over the market price 30 days before the first significant announcement. He found that on all bids, the premium was 58% measured by the median and 56% measured by the mean. However, when a greater number of bids was involved in the going-private transactions, the size of the premium also was higher. When three or more bids were received, the premium rose to 76% when measured by the median and 69% when measured by the mean. The premium of 11 successful third-party bids over the management bid was 8% (median) and 14% (mean). Lowenstein argued strongly for the creation of an auction that would ensure that multiple bids would be received. He acknowledged difficulties in implementing such a proposal. In addition, we would observe that the relatively small percentage increase in third-party bids over the management bids casts doubt on the need for such a proposal. Furthermore, the Lowenstein findings corroborate those of

DeAngelo, DeAngelo, and Rice in observing premiums for public stockholders of 50% or more over their market price 1 to 2 months before the announcement. This would appear to be a substantial reward to public shareholders. If they left nothing "on the table" for the entrepreneurs involved in the LBO activity, it would leave little incentive for the transactions to take place. The subsequent losses to the public shareholders would be much greater than the relatively small increase in the bid when third-party offers are involved. Besides, market competition ensures that if the entrepreneurs are taking too much, this will stimulate other nonmanagement outside offers. In any event, it is difficult to feel that a great injustice is done to the public shareholders or the subsequent minority shareholders, because they have received premiums exceeding 50%. Later studies also found large premiums and abnormal announcement returns to prebuyout shareholders (Kaplan, 1989a; Muscarella and Vetsuypens 1990; Travlos and Cornett, 1993).

For divisional management buyouts, Hite and Vetsuypens (1989) found small but statistically significant wealth gains to parent company shareholders. The mean abnormal return during the 2-day period surrounding the buyout announcement was 0.55% for their sample of 151 unit MBOs. Because the mean sale price of the divisions represented only 16.6% of the market value of equity of an average seller, the abnormal return would translate into 3.3% for a full LBO, which is much lower than the gains found for the previously discussed LBOs. Hite and Vetsuypens suggested that divisional buyouts reallocate ownership of corporate assets to higher-valued uses and that parent company shareholders share in the expected benefits of this change in ownership structure. For a sample of 45 divisional buyouts that subsequently went public (after an average period of 34 months), Muscarella and Vetsuypens (1990) reported a mean abnormal return of 1.98% to the seller in the two days (−1 and 0) around the announcement.

Harlow and Howe (1993) found that there was little insider trading before third-party LBOs. However, they found evidence that insider trading prior to management LBOs was associated with private managerial information, but the net buying by insiders resulted from decreased levels of insider sales of stock rather than from increased levels of purchases. In the MBO subsample, they found a positive correlation between the offer premium and the amount of abnormal net buying by insiders.

Most of the LBOs were highly leveraged transactions (HLTs). Andrade and Kaplan (1998) studied a sample of 136 HLTs completed between 1980 and 1989 that subsequently became distressed. As of December 1995, out of the 136 studied, 31 had defaulted, and an additional 8 attempted to restructure debt because of problems in meeting debt payments. Of these 39 financially distressed firms, data were available on 31. The median EBITDA-to-interest expense ratio pre-HLT was 7.95. Post-HLT, the median had dropped to 1.16, indicating that for more than half of the sample, the debt coverage was precarious.

All of the sample firms had positive operating margins in the distressed years, typically exceeding their industry median, so the firms were financially distressed but not economically distressed. Surprisingly, the sample firms experienced a small increase in value from pretransaction to distress resolution. The implication is that the HLTs overall earn significantly positive market-adjusted returns. Thus, for this HLT sample, despite financial distress, performance was positive.

Another study looked at 41 leveraged buyout firms that made 134 divestments in response to financial distress (Easterwood, 1998). Most of the LBOs were formed during the years 1984 to 1988. The common stock in the companies was privately owned. Bond returns for their publicly traded debt were used to measure the wealth effects of the divestment announcement. The divestments on average are not associated with significant wealth effects for the total sample of firms. Firms that suffered financial distress experienced significant negative abnormal returns associated with the divestments. Firms that were not distressed experienced positive bond returns when the asset sales were announced.

SOURCES OF GAINS

The empirical evidence is consistent among studies in finding that the premiums paid are 40% or more of the market price of the stock 1 to 2 months before the announcement of the buyout. The standard residual analysis shows that these gains are substantially sustained in stock price performance after the completion of the change in ownership control. What are the sources of these large gains? A number of explanations have been offered: (1) taxes, (2) management incentives, (3) wealth transfer effects, (4) asymmetrical information and underpricing, and (5) efficiency considerations. Each is considered in turn.

Tax Benefits

The tax benefits are clearly there. The question is whether they are the only factor, the major factor, or simply a facilitating factor added to more fundamental business and economic forces. It is difficult to quantify the degree. Some students of the subject ascribe a major role to taxes. Lowenstein (1985), for example, argued that most of the premium paid is financed from tax savings. He stated that the new company can expect to operate tax-free for as long as 5 to 6 years. An LBO often is sold after about this period of time when its debt-to-equity ratio has been pulled down from about 10 to 1 or under.

The sources of the tax gain are standard and have been detailed in previous pages. They include the following. The high leverage provides the benefits of interest savings. Asset step-ups can provide higher asset values for depreciation expenses. This tax advantage became much more difficult under the Tax Reform Act of 1986. The accelerated depreciation provisions of the 1981 ERTA had enhanced this benefit. Lowenstein (1985, p. 760) pointed out that the extent of write-up of assets depended in part on the ability to assign larger value to items for which there is little recapture (inventory, film libraries, mineral resources, or real estate) than to items for which recapture may be substantial (equipment).

Tax benefits were further augmented by the Tax Reform Act of 1984, which broadened the benefits of the use of ESOPs. The ESOP purchases the shares using borrowed funds. The borrowings are secured by the employer's schedule of contributions to the fund. The interest and principal on the ESOP are deductible, and the lender could exclude half of the interest income from taxable income. These are substantial benefits indeed. These changes increased the use of ESOPs in management buyouts, representing tangible evidence that this particular tax factor was of importance. However, Kaplan (1989a) suggested that ESOP loans are infrequently used due to nontax costs. One such cost pointed out by Kaplan is that all contributing employees share in the equity, which will not leave an adequate equity stake to the managers and the buyout promoter.

Kaplan (1989b) also provided empirical evidence on the potential value of tax benefits. Although it is not difficult to estimate current tax savings on new buyout debt, valuation of these savings flows is dependent on, among other factors, whether the debt is permanent and the appropriate marginal tax rate applied to the interest deduction. Further, there is the argument that the interest rate on corporate debt is higher to compensate for higher personal taxation on interest income than on equity income, and thus the use of debt to obtain tax savings might have no value. When Kaplan assumed a marginal tax rate of 46% and permanent new debt, interest deductions were worth a median 1.297 times the premium. A 30% tax rate and a maturity of 8 years for new debt implied a median value equal to 0.262 times the premium. In Kaplan's sample of 76 companies, 33 were known to have elected to step up the basis of their assets, and the median value was estimated at 0.304 times the premium.

These tax benefits appear large, but Kaplan argued that they are predictable and thus appropriable by the prebuyout shareholders. However, Kaplan found that only a portion of the tax benefits could be attributed to unused debt capacity or the inefficient use of tax benefits prior to buyout. This implies that a large portion of the tax benefits were the result of buyout and that the buyout structure might be necessary to realize those benefits. It turns out that the buyout companies eliminated their federal taxes in the first 2 years after the buyout.

In regression analyses, the excess return to prebuyout shareholders is significantly related to the potential tax benefits generated by the buyout, but the excess return to postbuyout shareholders is not. Kaplan interpreted this result as indicating that prebuyout shareholders capture most of the tax benefits. The premium paid to prebuyout shareholders also is found to be positively related to the pre-LBO tax liability-to-equity ratio by Lehn and Poulsen (1988). This is interpreted as evidence that tax benefits play a significant role in LBOs.

The preceding findings on strong tax benefits are at odds with the regression result of Travlos and Cornett (1993) that capital structure change–induced effects fail to explain the abnormal returns experienced at the announcement of buyouts. One reason for this result might be that the dependent and independent variables only partly capture the full effects that they are supposed to measure. Travlos and Cornett (1993) defended their results by stating that increased leverage serves no long-term purpose but rather "functions primarily as a part of the mechanism to take the company private." The temporary nature of at least some portion of the new debt was also shown by Muscarella and Vetsuypens (1990). Their sample of 72 reverse LBO firms had an average debt–to–total value ratio of more than 0.90 at the time of the LBO, and average debt–to–total asset ratios of 0.78 prior to the SIPO and 0.60 after the SIPO.

The preceding results indicate that tax factors can improve a deal but come into play only if some underlying positive business factors are also operating. This is where other factors come into consideration.

Management Incentives and Agency Cost Effects

It is argued that management's ownership stake is enhanced by the LBO or MBO so that their incentives are stronger for improved performance. Some profitable investment proposals call for disproportionate efforts on the part of managers, so they will be undertaken only if managers are given a correspondingly disproportionate share of the proposal's income (Easterbrook and Fischel, 1982). However, such managerial compensation contracts might be viewed as overly generous by outside shareholders. In this case, going-private buyouts facilitate compensation arrangements that induce managers to undertake those proposals (DeAngelo, DeAngelo, and Rice, 1984; Travlos and Cornett, 1993). This reasoning is similar to the argument that the threat of a hostile takeover decreases incentives for managers and employees to invest in firm-specific human capital (DeAngelo and DeAngelo, 1987, p. 107). Going-private buyouts can guarantee compensation for those investments.

When information on managerial performance is costly, incumbent management can be mistakenly replaced. Managers waste resources to defend their position to potential proxy contestants and to outside shareholders. They might undertake projects that are less profitable but have payoffs more easily observed by outsiders (DeAngelo and DeAngelo, 1987). Going private might eliminate these costs. In many buyouts, the promoters retain a large equity stake and serve on the board. Their equity stake and their desire to protect their reputation as efficient promoters give them the incentive to closely monitor postbuyout management. This will decrease the information asymmetry between the managers and shareholders. In this view, the concentrated ownership resulting from an LBO represents reunification of ownership and control, which must reduce agency costs.

Finally, free cash flows motivate managers to use them in self-aggrandizing expenditures rather than to pay them out as dividends. Increasing debt through leveraged buyouts commits the cash flows to debt payment, which is an effective substitute for dividend payment. Managers have less discretion over debt payments than over dividends. Thus, the increased debt reduces managerial discretion in the allocation of free cash flows; the agency costs of free cash flows will be decreased in LBOs (Jensen, 1986). If managers are risk averse, the increased debt also will put pressure on them and give them an incentive to improve the firm's performance to prevent bankruptcy (because bankruptcy will cause a decline in their compensation and the value of human capital). The LBO thus represents a debt-bonding activity; it bonds (precommits) managers to meet newly set targets.

These agency cost arguments contrast with the notion that the internal controls of the firm already align managers' interests to those of the stockholders. The internal controls are compensation arrangements and settling up, stock options, bonuses based on performance, and surveillance by the board of directors. If internal controls do not take hold sufficiently, the market for corporate control and the threat of takeovers will ensure that managers operate to their full potential. However, a study by Baker, Jensen, and Murphy (1988) found that actual executive compensation contracts are insufficient to provide optimal incentives for managers and that most CEOs hold trivial fractions of their firm's stock, although stock ownership generally swamps incentives generated by compensation. The median fractional ownership of CEOs in their sample of 73 large manufacturing firms was only 0.16%, and the average was 1.2%. The CEO salary plus bonus changes by only two cents for every $1,000 change in equity value. Baker, Jensen, and Murphy ascribed the low ratio between pay and performance to pressures from other stakeholders and the public, including the media.

Roden and Lewellen (1995) analyzed capital structures of LBOs to test traditional theories of capital structure. Their sample covered 107 LBOs formed during 1981 to 1990, accounting for about two thirds of the total dollar volume of LBO activity during that period. The postbuyout capital structure of their LBO sample resembled what they called "an inverted pyramid." At the top was senior secured debt financing by banks, representing just over 60% of total funds raised. The next layer was mezzanine financing, consisting of unsecured, subordinated, long-term debt securities (junk bonds), about 25%. Preferred stock was 4%, and common equity about 7%. These patterns were consistent with prior studies. Within these averages, cross-sectional variations were observed. Their econometric analysis suggested that the prospective cash flow profile of the firm greatly influenced the capital structure. They presented a balancing model of the capital structure decision process. Leverage-related benefits included the motivating and disciplining effects of debt on management and the tax shields provided by debt.

Empirical evidence consistent with the management incentive rationale is reported in other studies. First, ownership shares of management are increased substantially after MBOs. For a sample of 76 MBOs in 1980 to 1986, Kaplan (1989a) reported prebuyout and postbuyout equity ownership of management. The median prebuyout ownerships of the CEO, all managers, and all managers and directors were 1.4%, 5.88%, and 19.3%, respectively. (The corresponding mean values were 7.13%, 12.20%, and 22.89%.) The median postbuyout ownership fractions of the CEO and all managers were 6.40% and 22.63%, respectively. Thus, in terms of median values, management ownership increased by about three times the prebuyout levels. For a reverse LBO sample, Muscarella and Vetsuypens (1990) reported the before-SIPO (post-buyout) and after-SIPO management equity ownership fractions. The median before-SIPO fractions for the most highly paid officer, three most highly paid officers, and all officers and directors were 9.2%, 26.1%, and 61.6%, respectively. The management ownership remained high even after the firm went public through a SIPO. The median after-SIPO fractions were 6.5%, 18.8%, and 44.2%. Evidence on the concentration of ownership is provided by Smith (1990). The median post-MBO ownership share of all officers, outside directors, and other major holders was 95.26%. The corresponding pre-MBO ownership share was 75.45%.

The second set of evidence on management incentives was provided by Muscarella and Vetsuypens. They documented various management incentive plans in LBO firms. Almost all firms in their sample (69 out of 72) had implemented at least one type of incentive plan under private ownership, and about 75% of the sample firms had at least two separate incentive plans. Among the different types of incentive plans, stock option plans and stock appreciation rights were the most popular. The importance of incentive plans also was described in most anecdotes on individual LBOs. For example, see Anders (1988).

The third and most important item of evidence is the operating performance of LBO firms. However, it should be pointed out in advance that the following results on operating performance may be subject to a selection bias because the reverse LBO firms or firms with postbuyout data available might be only the more successful ones. Muscarella and Vetsuypens described the multiple restructuring activities under private ownership. Based on examination of the SIPO prospectuses of the firms that went public again after the LBO, they found that more than two thirds of all firms (54 out of 72) disclosed at least one restructuring activity undertaken since the LBO. Among the activities were asset redeployment (reorganization of production facilities, divestitures, and so on); initiation of cost reduction programs; changes in marketing strategies involving product mix, product quality, and pricing; and customer service. Judging from the tone of the offering prospectuses, the authors suggested that these activities "represent a significant departure from pre-LBO strategies which would not have been implemented by the predecessor company" (p. 1390). As a result of these restructuring activities, the firms under private ownership realized substantial improvements in operating performance. In 35 cases for which data were available, total sales increased by 9.4% in real terms for the median firm between the LBO and SIPO (a median period of 29 months), and gross profits and operating profits increased 27.0% and 45.4%, respectively.

Kaplan (1989a) also provided evidence of improved operating performance following an LBO. The level of operating income in LBO firms increased more than in other firms in the same industry during the first 2 years after the LBO, but sales growth rates were lower. The results on operating income and sales suggested that the operating margins of LBO firms would improve relative to their industries. Statistical tests by Kaplan confirmed this proposition. One potential source of operating improvement was found to be in the area of working capital management as the inventory-to-sales ratio declined in the postbuyout years.

Similar results were obtained by Smith (1990). She found that both the profit or before-tax operating margin and the ratio of sales to operating assets or employees increased significantly relative to other firms in the same industry. Improvement in working capital management was evidenced by a reduction in the inventory holding period and the receivables collection period. There was little evidence that cutbacks in research and development, advertising, and maintenance were responsible for the increase in operating cash flows. Although the ratio of capital expenditures to sales was reduced after the MBO, this should not affect the short-run operating gains. Smith also provided regression results that suggested a positive relationship between the change in operating returns and the changes in financial leverage and percentage stock holdings by officers, outside directors, and other major stockholders. These results were consistent with the debt bonding effect, managerial incentive effect, and the improved monitoring (concentrated ownership) effect. Smith conducted various empirical analyses to provide evidence that the improved post-MBO performance was not attributable to the sample selection procedures in her study. Overall, the results did not tend to indicate selection bias. Smith also considered whether favorable inside information on future cash flows explained the observed increase in operating returns associated with MBOs and provided indirect evidence that the improved performance did not reflect the realization of gains privately anticipated by the buyout group.

Travlos and Cornett (1993) found a statistically significant negative correlation between the abnormal return to prebuyout shareholders and the P/E ratio of the firm relative to its industry. They interpreted this result as being consistent with the joint hypothesis that the more severe the agency problems were of the going-private firms, the lower their P/E ratios were, and that the lower this ratio is the greater the room is for improvement and thus the greater the efficiency gains are to be obtained by taking the firm private. This interpretation might not be correct though, because a low P/E ratio might simply mean lower growth opportunities. The Jensen hypothesis predicted that the LBO firms were mature firms with limited growth opportunities.

The theory of agency costs involving free cash flow also has empirical support. Lehn and Poulsen (1989) posited that a direct relationship between measures of cash flows and premiums paid to prebuyout shareholders was consistent with Jensen's hypothesis. Their data for 149 LBOs in the period 1984 to 1987 showed highly significant direct relationships between the undistributed cash flow–to–equity value ratio and the premium paid even after controlling for the effects of tax savings (by using the tax-to-equity variable). The likelihood of going private also was related directly to the cash flow–to–equity value ratio in their data for LBOs and matched control firms. Further evidence that appeared consistent with the free cash flow argument of Jensen included the findings that most LBOs took place in mature industries and that the growth rates and capital expenditures of LBO firms (without controlling for divestitures after the buyout) were lower than those of their industry control sample in the pre- and post-buyout periods (Kaplan, 1989a; Lehn and Poulsen, 1989).

However, one potential difficulty of the free cash flow argument is that it does not directly predict the strengthened incentive compensation schemes after the buyout, which are evidenced in the study by Muscarella and Vetsuypens. They also found an elasticity of compensation (defined as salary plus bonus) to sales of 0.46 for the most highly paid officer in their sample, whereas Murphy (1985) reported that the typical elasticity appeared to be about 0.3. It might be that going private enabled the firm to institute more incentive compensation plans, which might not be possible for public firms due to the political process (Baker, Jensen, and Murphy, 1988). Holthausen and Larcker (1996) argued that the performance and equity ownership incentive have not been fully demonstrated.

Wealth Transfer Effects

Critics of leveraged buyouts argue that the payment of premiums in these transactions might represent wealth transfers to shareholders from other stakeholders including bondholders, preferred stockholders, employees, and the government. Increased efficiency cannot be inferred automatically from the rise in the equity value. Because debt is increased in LBOs, at least part of the increased value can be offset by a reduction in the value of the firm's outstanding bonds and preferred stock. Many bond covenants do protect existing bondholders in the event of changes of control, debt issues, and so forth, but some do not. The newly issued debt might not be subordinated to the outstanding bonds or they might have shorter duration than the outstanding bonds. Further, the "absolute priority rule" for a senior security might not be strictly adhered to in bankruptcy court decisions.

Empirical evidence on the change in the value of outstanding debt at the time of the LBO announcement is mixed. Although Lehn and Poulsen (1988) found no evidence that (nonconvertible) bondholders and preferred stockholders lose value, Travlos and Cornett reported statistically significant losses at the announcement of going-private proposals. However, the losses were small relative to the gains to the prebuyout shareholders, which implies that wealth transfer cannot be an economically significant factor in explaining the shareholder gain. Such anecdotes as the lawsuit filed against RJR Nabisco by large bondholders do suggest that bondholders can lose substantially in certain cases (Quigley, 1988, pp. 1,5). In the Nabisco case, it was charged that its $5 billion in highly rated bonds had lost nearly 20% ($1 billion) in market value since the announcement of a management-led buyout proposal involving new borrowing of $16 billion (Greenwald, 1988, p. 69).

Warga and Welch (1993) demonstrated that the source of bond price data greatly influences the empirical results. Previous studies used exchange-based data such as the Standard & Poor's Bond Guide data. Warga and Welch used trader-quoted data from a major investment bank. They gave an illustration of the role of the data source. In an earlier study, Asquith and Wizman (1990) found LBO risk-adjusted announcement bondholder returns of −3.2%. Warga and Welch found returns of about −7% in a set of overlapping bonds for which the Asquith and Wizman data show a −3.8% return. They noted that when they "either properly aggregate returns among correlated bonds or if we exclude RJR Nabisco," the S&P data source suggests no significant loss of bondholder wealth. When they used their trader-quoted data, however, they found a risk-adjusted bondholder loss of about 6%. However, these losses in the value of debt were only 7% of the size of shareholder gains. Their conclusion is that although bondholders do suffer negative returns, their losses account for only a small percentage of shareholder gains.

Wealth can also be transferred from current employees to the new investors in hostile takeovers (Shleifer and Summers, 1988). The hostile bidder can break implicit contracts between the firm and employees by reducing employment and lowering wages to expropriate quasi-rents accruing to their past firm-specific investments. Whether this argument can be extended to leveraged buyouts is an empirical question, although the supposed hostility against existing employees does not appear to be present in most LBOs. Management turnover in buyout firms is lower than in an average firm, although sometimes a new management team is brought in after the LBO (Muscarella and Vetsuypens, 1990). The number of employees grows more slowly in an LBO firm than in others in the same industry and sometimes even decreases, but this appears to be the result of postbuyout divestitures and more efficient use of labor (Kaplan, 1989a; Muscarella and Vetsuypens, 1990).

The argument also can be made that the tax benefits in an LBO constitute a subsidy from the public and cause a loss in tax revenues of the government (Lowenstein, 1985). Evidence exists that the premiums paid in LBOs are positively related to potential tax benefits at the corporate level. However, the net effect of an LBO on government tax revenues may be positive (Morrow, 1988). Shareholders pay ordinary income taxes on the capital gains realized on the sale of their stock in the LBO tender offer. These gains might be realized even without the LBO, but the shareholders could postpone the capital gains taxes to a later date or even eliminate them by bequeathing stocks in an estate. If the firm becomes stronger and goes public at a later date, which is suggested by the empirical evidence reviewed earlier, then the LBO investor group will pay capital gains taxes and the firm will pay more corporate taxes.

Asymmetrical Information and Underpricing

Large premiums paid by the buyout investors are also consistent with the argument that the managers or investors have more information on the value of the firm than the public shareholders. In this theory, a buyout proposal signals to the market that future operating income will be larger than previously expected or that the firm is less risky than perceived by the public.

A variant of this theory is that the investor group believes the new company is worth more than the purchase price, and thus the prebuyout shareholders are receiving less than adequately informed shareholders would receive. This theory amounts to the claim that the MBO proposal cannot reveal much of the information and establish a competitive price for the target firm (despite the fact that a special committee of the board of directors who do not participate in the new company has to approve the proposal).

Kaplan (1989a) provided evidence that runs counter to these arguments. He found that informed persons (managers and directors) often do not participate in the buyout even though these nonparticipants typically hold large equity stakes in the buyout firm (a median share of 10% compared with 4.67% held by the management participants). Also, as indicated earlier, Smith (1990) provided indirect evidence that asymmetrical information cannot explain the improved performance of bought-out firms. For instance, MBO proposals that fail due to board/stockholder rejection, withdrawal, or a higher outside bid are not followed by any increase in operating returns among the involved firms.

Efficiency Considerations

The other arguments are related to efficiency considerations. The decision process can be more efficient under private ownership. Major new programs do not have to be justified by detailed studies and reports to the board of directors. Action can be taken more speedily, and sometimes getting a new investment program underway early is critical for its success. In addition, a public firm must publish information that might disclose vital and competitively sensitive information to rival firms. These arguments are difficult to evaluate, and empirical evidence on these has yet to appear. Stockholders' servicing costs and other related expenses do not appear to be a major factor in going private (Travlos and Cornett, 1993).

EVIDENCE OF POSTBUYOUT EQUITY VALUE

We now turn to statistical evidence on how the investment in an LBO has fared and what has determined the rate of return. Muscarella and Vetsuypens (1990) first compared the total value of the firm at the time of the LBO (the purchase price paid plus the book value of debt assumed) to the value of the firm at the time of its SIPO (the book value of outstanding debt plus the market value of equity minus any proceeds from the SIPO used to retire existing debt). The median rate of change in firm value for the 41 companies that went public again was 89.0% for the entire period between an LBO and the subsequent SIPO. The mean rate was 169.7%. The median annualized rate of change was 36.6%.

The total shareholder wealth change was positively and statistically, significantly correlated with the fraction of shares owned by officers and directors. Thus, larger shareholder gains under private ownership are associated with greater managerial stock ownership. Also, the correlation between the size-adjusted measure of salary and shareholder wealth was positive and statistically significant. This finding is consistent with the notion that well-compensated managers work harder to increase shareholder wealth. However, the causality might be the reverse. The change in equity values also was associated with the improvements in accounting measures of performance. Thus, it is possible that the improved corporate performance led to both increased managerial compensation and higher equity value. Further, the improved corporate performance does not disprove that exploiting inside information alone can explain postbuyout shareholder gains.

Other interesting results were obtained by Kaplan (1991). He first noted that returns on *leveraged* equity in a period of rising stock prices should be large because interest payments are fixed. Thus, the interesting comparison should be between the total return to all capital (debt and equity) invested in the buyout and the return on a stock index such as the S&P 500. He found for his sample of 21 buyouts that the median excess return to postbuyout investors (both debt and equity) was 26.1% higher than the benchmark return on the S&P 500 (the length of time is not stated). He suggested that this excess return is close to the premium earned by prebuyout shareholders. This implies that the prebuyout shareholders share handsomely in the gains to the buyout. Because the 21 companies in the sample had publicly available valuation of their securities, the result might be subject to selection bias; that is, they might represent the more successful LBOs.

Finally, Kaplan's regression analysis shows that the excess return to postbuyout investors was significantly related to the change in operating income but not to the potential tax benefits. It is shown that the prebuyout shareholders capture most of the tax benefits that become publicly available information at the time of the LBO.

Degeorge and Zeckhauser (1993) analyzed a particular aspect of reverse LBO decisions. They found that on average, reverse LBOs experienced an industry-adjusted rise in operating performance of 6.90% during the year before an initial public offering (IPO). In the year following an IPO, these same firms saw an industry-adjusted decline in operating performance of 2.59%.

Degeorge and Zeckhauser attributed the rise and fall of operating performance to information asymmetries and pure selection. More specifically, if management, and not the market, knew the expected profitability of the company, management would use this asymmetry and take the firm public only during exceptional years. Managers also have an incentive to quietly improve current performance at the expense of future profitability. The complementary theory of pure selection relies on the behavior, or perceived behavior, of IPO purchasers. Degeorge and Zeckhauser hypothesized that purchasers look at the strength of current performance and future growth. Subsequently, only strong companies have the ability to go public and experience normal mean reversion following the IPO.

Trends in operating performance do not translate into market inefficiencies. The market apparently understands the manager's incentive for performance manipulation and pure selection. Stock returns do not penalize the company for expected poor performance following the reverse LBO. In fact, reverse LBOs tend to outperform their peer group, although not significantly.

Mian and Rosenfeld (MR) (1993) studied the long-run performance of reverse LBOs. They observed that their results were consistent with those of Muscarella and Vetsuypens (1990). They studied 85 firms that had reverse LBOs during the period 1983 to 1989. They measured stock price performance for a 3-year period beginning 1 day after the firm went public. They found evidence of significant positive cumulative abnormal returns. They observed that this performance differed from the performance of IPOs as reported by Ritter (1991).

MR found that about 39% of their sample firms were taken over within 3 years after going public. The CARs using their comparable firm index for the first 3 years were 4.65%, 21.96%, and 21.05%. Most of the takeovers took place during the second year when the CARs were the highest. Firms that were taken over outperformed comparable investments by more than 100%. For the sample of firms that were not taken over, the CAR was essentially zero. This suggests that the firms that were taken over had qualities that were attractive to the bidding firm. Mian and Rosenfeld also found that 79% of the acquired firms had gone private with an active investor. This suggests that the firm's interest in being taken over reflects the desire of the main investor to liquidate ownership.

Holthausen and Larcker (1996) also studied the financial performance of reversed leveraged buyouts. They analyzed a sample of 90 LBOs that returned to public ownership between 1983 and 1988. They related changes in accounting performance to incentive variables. The firms outperformed their industries for the 4 years following the reverse LBO, with some weak evidence of a decline in accounting performance over the period. The firms increased capital expenditure subsequent to the public offering; working capital levels also increased. The authors observed that firm performance decreased with declines in levels of equity ownership by management and other insiders. They found no evidence that performance after the IPO was related to changes in leverage. The fact that capital expenditures increased after the LBO was consistent with these firms being cash constrained while they were LBOs. This would suggest that the high leverage during an LBO constrained investments but that the reduced leverage after the IPO facilitated efficient investments.

Holthausen and Larcker also found that for the firms that were still public 3 years after the IPO, a median decline in ownership by management insiders was 15% and by nonmanagement insiders, 20%. They also found that board structure moves toward the standard patterns of non-LBO firms.

THE CORRECTION PERIOD 1991 TO 1992

We have seen from the previous materials on LBOs that the investors in the companies that were bought out received substantial premiums. The mean premiums were on the order of magnitude of 35%, similar to the premiums found in cash takeovers. The groups that formed the LBOs and MBOs, on average, made returns in excess of the S&P 500 over the holding period as private companies. Returns to shareholders in the LBOs that again went public (the SIPOs) outperformed comparable companies over a 4-year period following the reverse LBO. These performance results had at least two forms of selection bias. LBOs that were able to return to the public markets were the relatively more successful ones. In addition, most published empirical studies to date cover LBOs formed mostly during the early part of the 1980s. LBOs formed in the latter half of the 1980s did not perform as well (Kaplan and Stein, 1993).

Opler (1992) found that LBOs in 1985 to 1989 were associated with operating improvements comparable to those in earlier transactions. Kaplan and Stein (1993) found similar results for the later LBOs. However, despite improvements in operating performance, many of the later buyouts experienced financial distress. The defects in the later LBO deals were due to the relatively high prices paid and weakened financial structures for the LBOs formed. In addition, management, investment bankers, and other deal promoters were able to take more cash up front, which also weakened the structure and incentives in the later deals (Kaplan and Stein, 1993).

General economic principles and factors more specific to LBO activity explained the deterioration in the quality of LBOs in the second half of the 1980s. In an enterprise system, high-return segments of the economy attracted more financial resources. Investments flowed to areas of high prospective returns (Weston and Chen, 1994). This occurred with the LBOs. Many specialized LBO funds were formed. More banks and other financial intermediaries participated. The dollar volume of funds seeking to organize LBO deals began to exceed the number of good prospects available. The successful LBOs of the early 1980s were able to make purchases on favorable terms; purchase prices were as low as three to four times prospective cash flows (EBITDA). However, in the late 1980s, the quantity of funds exceeded the availability of good prospects. As a consequence, the price–to–expected cash flow multiples rose sharply. The difference between the winning price and the next-highest bid was often substantial. Winner's curse operated in the extreme.

Public high-yield debt substituted for private subordinated debt and "strip" financing in which subordinated debt holders also received equity stakes. This raised the cost of reorganizing companies that encountered financial difficulties.

Commercial banks took smaller positions. They sought to reduce their commitments and shorten maturities, and required an accelerated program for required principal repayments. As a consequence, the coverage of debt service declined. In some cases, coverage ratios were less than 1. Sometimes the first interest payment in the buyout could be achieved only if asset sales were accomplished and substantial cost reductions were achieved. Some deals utilized high-yield bonds with either zero coupons or interest payments consisting of more of the same securities, payment in kind (PIK). Cash requirements for debt service were postponed for several years after the formation of the LBO.

Consistent with the general economic principles about the flow of resources to high-return areas, the leveraged buyout market began making some "corrections." Allen (1996, p. 22) observed that movement toward lower transactions prices, larger equity commitments, lower debt ratios, and lower up-front fees were underway. Despite the corrections underway, the rules of the game and the general economic environment were altered. Legislative and regulatory rule changes interacting with the economic downturn devastated the LBO market. The main legislative change was the S&L legislation in 1989, the Financial Institutions Reform, Recovery and Enforcement Act (FIRREA). Its major effect was to push masses of high-yield debt from S&L portfolios onto the marketplace. The downward impact on the prices of high-yield debt was predictable. Bank regulators put pressures on banks to reduce their exposures in highly leveraged transactions (HLTs). The recession of 1990 and 1991 brought to an end the rising levels of economic activity that supported the revenue growth and profitability of individual companies. Leveraged buyout activity in 1991 dropped to $7.0 billion, 10.7% of the $65.7 billion in 1989.

THE ROLE OF JUNK BONDS

Junk bonds are high-yield bonds either rated below investment grade or unrated. Using Standard & Poor's ratings, junk bonds are defined at below BBB; using Moody's, the level is below Baa3. Allegations have been made that junk bonds have contributed to excessive takeover activity and LBOs and have resulted in unsound levels of business leverage.

High-yield bond have always existed. However prior to 1977, high-yield bonds were "fallen angels," bonds that initially had been rated investment grade but whose ratings had been subsequently lowered. The first issuer of bonds rated below investment grade from the start is said to have been Lehman Brothers in 1977. Drexel Burnham Lambert (Michael Milken) soon became the industry leader. Competition followed, but Drexel still had 45% of the market in 1986 and 43.2% of the market through mid-November 1987 (Frantz, 1987). However, as a result of its legal problems, Drexel's share of public underwritings of junk debt fell to only 16% in the first quarter of 1989 (Laing, 1989). Subsequently, Drexel declared bankruptcy and dropped from the market. By the early 1990s, the volume of high-yield bond financing had exceeded the peak levels of the 1980s. Other investment banks took over the market share previously held by Drexel.

Between 1970 and 1977, junk bonds represented on average about 3% to 4% of total public straight-debt bonds. By 1985, this share had risen to 14.4%. These are shares of the totals of public straight bonds outstanding. As a percentage of yearly flows of new public bond issues by U.S. corporations, the straight–junk bond shares had risen from 1.1% in 1977 to almost 20% by 1985. Clearly, junk bonds began to play a significant role.

The use of high-yield or junk bonds represented a financial innovation in making it possible for relatively high-risk firms to obtain financing from public sources. They also were used in takeovers. Acquiring firms could obtain debt financing to make cash tender offers for targets. This made even the largest firms subject to unwanted takeovers.

The default or mortality rate of corporate bonds has varied by rating (Altman and Arman, 2002). For the period 1971 to 2001, the cumulative 10-year mortality rates for bonds rated A or AA were slightly above 0.5%; for AAA bonds, the default rate was 0.03%. For below–investment grade bonds, the cumulative 10-year default rates were much higher. For BB, the rate was about 17% for B, 33%, and for CCC, 51%.

Weighted averaged recovery rates vary by debt seniority. For the period 1971 to 2001, the median average recovery rate for defaulted senior secured debt was 57.2%. The median recovery rate for subordinated debt was about 32%. For all seniorities, the median weighted average recovery rate was 40.5%, implying a loss of principal and 1-year interest of almost 60%. During the period 1978 to 2001, the promised yield on high-yield debt has averaged 12.87%; the promised yield on 10-year Treasury has averaged 8.0%. The average spread was, therefore, 4.87%. However, during the period the spread has varied from 10.5% in 1990 to as low as 2.81% in 1978; for 1999, the spread was 4.9%. It rose to 9.44% in 2000 and dropped back to 7.27% in 2001. Clearly the spread on promised yield reflects the market's attitude toward risk, which in turn reflects the economic outlook. The compound annual average realized spread between 1978 and 2001 was 1.88%; the arithmetic average was 1.86%. Thus, the differential return required for bearing the extra risk was less than 200 basis points (Altman and Arman, 2002).

A study by Glenn Yago (1991) covered all public firms issuing junk bonds during the period 1980 to 1986. About one fourth of the proceeds were used for acquisition financing, whereas about three fourths of the proceeds were used to finance internal corporate growth. Although high-yield bonds facilitated takeover activity, their significance was much broader. Junk bonds made financing available to high-risk growth firms and helped them realize their potentials. A high percentage of employment growth in the economy had been accounted for by the growth of firms using high-yield financing. These high-yield firms had higher-than-average rates of sales growth, capital expenditures, and productivity improvements.

High-yield financing was not the fundamental cause of the problems of the savings and loan (S&L) industry during the 1980s. Their basic problem was that the changing nature of financial markets removed the economic basis for the existence of the industry. By 1980, before the era of takeovers and high-yield financing had started, the S&L industry had a negative net worth on a market value basis of more than $100 billion. Ninety percent of the firms in the S&L industry were suffering losses in 1980 and 1981.

Investments in junk bonds in total represented 1% or less of their total assets. Some individual S&Ls had high ratios of junk bonds in their portfolios. Legislation enacted by congress in 1989 essentially required S&Ls to liquidate the high-yield bonds they currently held and prohibited them from further investing in high-yield bonds. This artificial interference with normal supply-and-demand conditions in the high-yield bond market caused temporary losses. However, by 1993, the junk bond market was achieving record-high returns for investors, and the size of the high-yield bond market reached new highs, suggesting a sound fundamental economic basis for this financial innovation.

Much has been written on the role of Michael Milken, with opposing views, reflected in two contrasting studies. The first was written by Ralph S. Saul (Saul, 1993), who served as a court-appointed member of the oversight committee to monitor the liquidation of Drexel; he later served as the chairman of its board in reorganization. From his close and long association in overseeing the liquidation of Drexel, Saul also reviewed closely the activities of Michael Milken. His detailed review of Milken and his activities can be summarized into three charges: that Milken engaged in (1) securities parking, (2) market stabilization, and (3) market monopolization.

Securities parking entails having an associate or cooperating firm or firms hold securities in their account names. Historically, this was a common practice used by investment banking firms to avoid technical violations of net equity or capital requirements in relation to assets held or obligations outstanding. The need to add to an investment banking firm's equity or net worth on a permanent basis was avoided by having other nominees hold temporary surges in asset holdings and related debt obligations incurred. However, parking became a more serious violation when the Williams acts, initially enacted in 1968 and subsequently amended, made it illegal to engage in parking to avoid triggering the Rule 13(d) requirement of filling a report with the SEC when 5% ownership of the equity securities of a firm had been reached. The main evidence of the charge against Milken for parking was from the testimony of Ivan Boesky.

Saul placed heaviest emphasis on the market stabilization activities of Milken. He stated that Milken was able to develop underwriting and investment participation by other institutions by guaranteeing them against losses on their high-yield bond investments during the time required for the markets to absorb them. In addition, Saul (1993, p. 44) stated that Milken did not make "public disclosure in high-yield bond offering documents of the hundreds of millions in equities or warrants that he took as underwriting compensation." Furthermore, Saul pointed out, "In the most egregious cases, he made side payoffs, awarding interests in his investment partnerships to portfolio managers in return for investing institutional funds in his issues" (p. 43). Saul further stated that "such reprehensible conduct" helped Milken achieve his third crime of becoming the dominant firm or monopolist of the high-yield bond market. He then described the advantages that Milken achieved as the innovator or first mover in developing the high-yield bond market.

Saul then posed the question, "Why—in the fiercely competitive world of Wall Street, where a new financial product rarely has an edge for more than a few years at most—was no competitor able to challenge Milken?" (p. 42). The answer Saul gave was in three parts. First, they did not have Milken's network to be "highly confident" that it could successfully "place" or sell a high-yield offering. "Second, and most important, no other firm on Wall Street was prepared to commit so much of its capital to inventory high-yield bonds in secondary market trading" (p. 42). Third, Milken over time developed close relationships with client issuers, institutional customers, and his employees.

A positive case for Milken was developed by Daniel Fischel (1995), who was a consultant on the Milken case and other lawsuits in the 1980s. Fischel also has served as an expert witness on behalf of several government agencies. Fischel addressed the question, "Was Milken guilty?" His summary view is as follows. "Milken was a tough and formidable competitor. . . . His success made him the envy of many. . . . After the most thorough investigation, the government came up with nothing" (p. 158).

Fischel described the action against Milken as a part of the hysteria against the "excesses of the 1980s" and the ability of the government to invoke the Racketeer Influenced and Corrupt Organizations Act (RICO), which would have enabled the government to seize all of Milken's assets at the start of a trial. At the time of his decision to avoid the application of RICO by his guilty plea, so many other defendants had lost their court cases that it appeared that Milken simply could not win. However, in 1991, the Second Circuit Court reversed numerous convictions that the U.S. attorney's office had previously achieved in the lower courts (Fischel 1995, p. 183). Fischel argued that these reversals supported his position that Milken was not, in fact, guilty of breaking any security law violations.

LBOs IN THE 1992 TO 2000 PERIOD

After 1992, the economy experienced sustained economic growth, stock prices reached new highs, the size of the total market for high-yield debt reached new highs, and the size of aggregate LBO transactions moved to $62.0 billion in 1999, almost 900% of the volume in 1991. This more favorable economic environment was a major factor in the resurgence of LBOs. In addition, the financial structure of the deals changed. Innovative approaches were developed by LBO sponsor companies, LBO sponsor specialists, investment banks, and commercial banks. Because of innovative approaches, LBOs were applied increasingly beyond mature, slow-growing industries to high-growth, technology-driven industries.

The changed financial structure of the transactions after 1992 are first described. The price-to-EBITDA ratios paid moved down toward 5 to 6 from the 7–8–10 multiples of the late 1980s. The percentage of equity in the initial capital structure moved up to 20% to 30% compared with equity ratios as low as 5% to 10% in the late 1980s. Interest coverage ratios moved up. The ratio of EBITDA to interest and other financial requirements moved to a standard of 2. This contrasts with the deals in the late 1980s when asset sales and immediate improvements in profitability margins were required to cover interest and other financial outlays in the first year of the LBO.

A major restructuring of the intermediaries also was taking place. Milken and Drexel were no longer present to dominate LBO activity as in the 1980s. However, the LBO resumed its growth through other investment banking houses, the larger commercial banks, the traditional LBO sponsors such as Kohlberg Kravis Roberts (KKR), and innovative approaches by investment banking–sponsoring firms. For example, Forstmann Little, and Company emphasized using its own funds and participation in management over a period of time (Antilla, 1992, 1993). A general partner of Forstmann Little stated in a *New York Times* interview of December 27, 1992, "We're looking more and more to finance our deals without any bank debt—substituting what was once bank debt with more of our own capital." This represents a strategy of substituting sponsor equity for bank debt. Sometimes deals are structured so that principal repayments are not required until 10 years after the deal. This reduces the pressure for immediate performance improvement or asset sales.

Clayton, Dubilier, and Rice Incorporated (CD&R) has emphasized a partnership structure with members who have considerable previous managerial experience. It structures the transaction, owns the majority of the equity, controls the company it acquires, and establishes management incentives by linking compensation to performance. Detailed examples of CD&R activities are provided in a *BusinessWeek* story of November 15, 1993, pp. 70, 74. CD&R has emphasized buying undermanaged segments of larger companies to achieve a turnaround. Financial buyers also might develop joint deals with corporate strategic buyers to purchase companies on a leveraged basis.

The financial press provides numerous examples of innovative approaches by LBO sponsors. The increased participation by commercial banks is described in detail in a comprehensive survey by Allen (1996). He described the increased use of syndication of HLT transactions to other banks and the development of a highly liquid secondary loan trading market. He emphasized a continued close, client-focused relationship by the commercial bank. This embraces not only LBO and M&A activity but the broad gamut of financial services the client company may require. He also described a range of capital structure strategies tailored to the characteristics of the transaction. Similar innovative approaches have been developed by investment banking firms and other financial intermediaries.

Financial buyers (LBO sponsors, investment banks, commercial banks) have faced increased competition from corporate buyers. All have adopted new strategies. One is the leveraged buildup. The leveraged buildup identifies a fragmented industry characterized by relatively small firms. Buyout firms based on partners with industry expertise purchase a firm as a platform for further leveraged acquisitions in the same industry (Allen, 1996, p. 27). They seek to build firms with strong management, developing revenue growth while reducing costs, with the objectives of improved margins, increased cash flow, and increased valuations.

VALUATION OF LBOs

The preceding section described the characteristics of going-private transactions and LBOs. It pointed out that initially debt can be as high as 90% of total assets. In the Wavell Company illustration, pro forma cash flows were presented in Table 16.6. In that example, the initial debt of $1.8 million was paid down to zero by the end of year 5. Empirical studies presented later in this chapter show that if the LBO were sold before the debt was paid down, a substantial portion of the proceeds would be used to pay down the debt. The central point of significance here is that the financial leverage ratios are changed over time. In Chapters 9 and 10, the discounted free cash flows (DCF) methodology used the weighted average cost of capital (WACC) as the discount factor. Ruback (2002) calls this the FCF method. With changing debt-to-equity ratios, the WACC would have to be recalculated at each time period to reflect the changing weights. Because this would be cumbersome, the capital cash flows (CCF) method is employed. In the CCF method, the interest tax shields are added to the other free cash flows and the sum is discounted at the expected asset return rate. Ruback (2002) demonstrated that the CCF method and the FCF method obtain the same results if the WACC is recalculated each year.

Table 16.7 illustrates the capital cash flows model. In Panel A, Lines 1 through 11 calculate the free cash flows following exactly the same format that we used in Chapters 9 and 10. Line 12 introduces the planned pattern of interest payments. They are estimated to decrease each year. The interest tax shield is the cash or actual tax rate given in Line 4 multiplied times the interest expense listed in Line 12. The capital cash flows shown in Line 14 add the interest tax shields to the free cash flows from Line 11.

TABLE 16.7 Capital Cash Flow Model (Model 16–03)

	Year 0	Year 1	Year 2	Year 3	Year 4	Year 5 = n	Year n + 1
Panel A. Inputs for Present Value Calculations							
1. Net revenues	$5,000	$5,400	$5,832	$6,299	$6,802	$7,347	$7,567
2. Revenue growth rate		8.0%	8.0%	8.0%	8.0%	8.0%	3.0%
3. NOI = EBIT	$ 500	$ 540	$ 583	$ 630	$ 680	$ 735	$ 605
4. Cash tax rate (T)	40.0%	40.0%	40.0%	40.0%	40.0%	40.0%	40.0%
5. Income taxes	200	216	233	252	272	294	242
6. NOPAT	$ 300	$ 324	$ 350	$ 378	$ 408	$ 441	$ 363
7. + Depreciation	250	270	292	315	340	367	265
8. – Change in working capital	50	54	58	63	68	73	38
9. – Capital expenditures	100	108	117	126	136	147	76
10. – Change in other assets net	50	54	58	63	68	73	76
11. Free cash flows	$ 350	$ 378	$ 408	$ 441	$ 476	$ 514	$ 439
12. Interest expense		$ 400	$ 380	$ 300	$ 200	$ 150	$ 100
13. Interest tax shield		$ 160	$ 152	$ 120	$ 80	$ 60	$ 40
14. Capital cash flow (CCF) (11 + 13)		$ 538	$ 560	$ 561	$ 556	$ 574	$ 479
15. Discount rate (k$_a$)		10.70%	10.70%	10.70%	10.70%	10.70%	10.70%
16. Discount factor		0.90334	0.81603	0.73715	0.66590	0.60154	
17. Present values		$ 486	$ 457	$ 413	$ 370	$ 345	
Panel B. Operating Relationships (as a % of revenues)							
NOI	10.0%	10.0%	10.0%	10.0%	10.0%	10.0%	8.0%
NOPAT	6.0	6.0	6.0	6.0	6.0	6.0	4.8
Depreciation	5.0	5.0	5.0	5.0	5.0	5.0	3.5
Change in working capital	1.0	1.0	1.0	1.0	1.0	1.0	0.5
Capital expenditures	2.0	2.0	2.0	2.0	2.0	2.0	1.0
Change in other assets net	1.0	1.0	1.0	1.0	1.0	1.0	1.0
Free cash flow	7.0	7.0	7.0	7.0	7.0	7.0	5.8

The discount factor employed in the CCF is the expected asset return, k$_a$. This discount factor is obtained by using a CAPM model, which requires estimates of the risk-free rate, a risk premium, and the asset beta of the firm (Ruback, 2002). For the estimates shown in Panel C, Part II, the expected asset return factor is 10.7%. The expected asset return is also a weighted average in which the before-tax cost of debt is employed. The derivation of this relationship is shown in Appendix A to Chapter 16. Using the data estimates in Part II of Table 16.7, we illustrate that the expected asset return using a weighted average is also 10.7%. In Appendix B to Chapter 16, we demonstrate that the adjusted present value model (APV) gives the same result as the CCF model if the before-tax cost of debt is used.

The valuation calculations shown in Table 16.7, Panel C, Parts III and IV proceed exactly as in Chapters 9 and 10. For this example, the operating value to initial revenue ratio is slightly higher than 1. The operating value to initial net operating income is 11.63. The operating value to initial EBITDA is 7.75. These ratios are widely used in making comparisons among firms.

TABLE 16.7   (cont.)

Panel C. Valuation Calculations

Part I—Expected Asset Return Inputs		Part III—Terminal Value (TV)	
(a) Risk-free rate (R_f)	6.00%	$TV = \text{Capital cash flows}_{n+1}/(k_a - g)$	
(b) Asset beta (β_a) = β_U	0.723	$= 479/(0.107 - 0.03) = 479/0.077 =$	$6,219
(c) Risk premium (RP)	6.50%		
(d) Tax rate (T)	40.00%	Part IV—Valuation Calculation	
(e) Cost of equity (k_c)	12.50%	(1) PV of cash flows	$2,072
(f) Before-tax cost of debt (k_b)	8.00%	(2) PV of terminal value	$3,741
(g) Target equity (S) to value (V)	60.0%	(3) Operating value (V)	$5,814
(h) Target debt (B) to value (V)	40.0%	(4) Add: Marketable securities	—
		(5) Total value	$5,814
Part II—Expected Asset Return Calculation		(6) Less: Initial book debt (D)	2,000
Using CAPM		(7) Value of equity	$3,814
$k_a = R_f + (RP)\beta_a = 6.0\% + 6.5\%\ (0.723) =$	10.70%	(8) Shares outstanding	100.0
		(9) Intrinsic share price	$38.14
Using weighted average			
$k_a = k_c(S/V) + k_b(B/V)$		Part V—Ratios	
$= 12.50\%(0.600) + 8.00\%(0.400) =$	10.70%	Operating Value/Revenues$_0$	1.16
		Operating Value/NOI$_0$	11.63
		Operating Value/EBITDA$_0$	7.75

Table 16.7 illustrates that ratios for comparable companies or transactions reflect a number of value drivers in a fundamental valuation analysis.

Table 16.7 provides a format for using the capital cash flow model when debt levels change year to year. It is generalized in Appendix A to Chapter 16 in a format labeled Model 16–03 for a 5-year period of growth and in Model 16–04 for a 10-year period of growth.

Summary

The 1980s were characterized by LBOs focused on mature industries with stable cash flows. High leverage was used to provide owners and LBO sponsors with a high percentage of the equity. The cash flows were used to pay off the debt. In the standard case, debt was 90%, and equity was 10% of total capital. When the debt was paid off, the equity holders became owners of 100% of the company. It could then be sold with strong management incentives. A turn-around could achieve substantial operating improvements. The value of the company when sold represented good returns to the equity holders.

In the late 1980s, buyers paid too much, and leverage was excessive for realistic future cash flows. The deals were unsound from a strategic and financial structure standpoint. In 1990 to 1991, the LBO market had almost dried up.

The LBO market revived in 1992. The volume of high-yield debt outstanding by 1995 was greater than it had ever been before. In addition, investments in the LBO market by sponsors' investment banks and commercial banks also increased. Innovative approaches augmented more traditional financial strategies. Financial structures have been related to the characteristics of the companies involved. Leveraged transactions have moved from mature industries to growth-oriented, technology-driven industries. There is often greater equity participation by financial buyers. In addition, financial buyers increasingly offer management expertise and close interaction with or control of operating management. In short, LBO activity appears to have moved to an age of renewal.

Questions

16.1 Discuss the typical types of financing involved in LBOs and MBOs.

16.2 What were the characteristics of industries and firms in which LBOs and MBOs took place in the 1980s?

16.3 What are the advantages and disadvantages of LBOs and MBOs?

16.4 What were the magnitudes of abnormal returns for LBOs and MBOs during the early 1980s?

16.5 What were the sources of these gains?

16.6 What were the reasons for the increase in LBO activity during the early 1980s?

16.7 Why were LBOs and MBOs able to use such high-leverage ratios compared with other forms of business organizations?

16.8 What were some of the unsound developments in the LBO market that began to take place in the late 1980s?

16.9 How were these developments corrected during the resurgence of the LBO market after 1992?

Problems

SOURCES OF VALUE IN LBOs

16.1 In the text, we use spreadsheets to convey how an LBO is set up and how cash flows can be used to pay down debt in a successful LBO. A firm with the characteristics of the usual LBO candidate in the early 1980s would have value drivers that could be improved by a turnaround. In Table P16.1.1, we present the relevant operating relationships and financial information for Coleman Textiles, which has not been managed well.

New England Partners, an investment group, made a leveraged buyout of Coleman Textiles. They replaced management with a new team with a track record of high-quality performance in the textile business. After a turnaround was accomplished by the new management group, the operating relationships and financial information were changed to the patterns shown in Table P16.1.2.

QUESTIONS

(Use the software provided by Model 16–03 (the same as Table 16.7) in the text available at our Web sites.)

16.1.1 Based on the patterns in Table P16.1.1, what is the indicated share price of Coleman Textiles?

16.1.2 Based on the new patterns in Table P16.1.2, calculate the new intrinsic share price of Coleman Textiles.

16.1.3 Comment on your results.

RJR NABISCO LBO

16.2 Many studies set forth materials on the 1988 RJR Nabisco LBO. Two examples are Allen Michel and Israel Shaked, "RJR Nabisco: A Case Study of a Complex Leveraged Buyout," *Financial Analysts*

TABLE P16.1.1 Operating Relationships and Financial Information—Coleman Textiles

Initial revenues (in millions)		$10,000	Marketable securities			$ 0
Expected asset return		11.00%	Initial book debt			$2,000
Tax rate		40.00%	Shares outstanding (in millions)			100

	Year 1	Year 2	Year 3	Year 4	Year 5	Year n + 1
Revenue growth rate	6.0%	6.0%	6.0%	6.0%	6.0%	3.0%
Interest expense (in millions)	$400	$380	$300	$200	$150	$100
(as a % of revenues)						
NOI	8.0%	8.0%	8.0%	8.0%	8.0%	6.0%
NOPAT	4.8	4.8	4.8	4.8	4.8	3.6
Depreciation	5.0	5.0	5.0	5.0	5.0	4.0
Change in working capital	2.0	2.0	2.0	2.0	2.0	3.0
Capital expenditures	4.0	4.0	4.0	4.0	4.0	2.5
Change in other assets net	1.0	1.0	1.0	1.0	1.0	1.0
Free cash flow	2.8	2.8	2.8	2.8	2.8	1.1

Journal, September–October 1991, pp. 15–27; and Richard S. Ruback, "RJR Nabisco," *Harvard Business School Case No. 9-289-056,* May 28, 1997. Both articles project the cash flows from 1989 through 1998. In competition with other bidders, KKR won with a bid of $109 per share.

QUESTIONS

16.2.1 Using the format of Model 16–04 and the inputs provided by Table P16.2.1, calculate the indicated value of RJR Nabisco.

16.2.1 In Table P16.2.2, the net operating income percentages are increased as shown. Calculate the new indicated value of RJR Nabisco.

TABLE P16.1.2 Operating Relationships and Financial Information—Coleman Textiles LBO

Initial revenues (in millions)		$10,000	Marketable securities			$ 0
Expected asset return		13.00%	Initial book debt			$4,000
Tax rate		40.00%	Shares outstanding (in millions)			100

	Year 1	Year 2	Year 3	Year 4	Year 5	Year n + 1
Revenue growth rate	8.0%	8.0%	8.0%	8.0%	8.0%	3.0%
Interest expense (in millions)	$800	$760	$600	$400	$300	$200
(as a % of revenues)						
NOI	12.0%	12.0%	12.0%	12.0%	12.0%	8.0%
NOPAT	7.2	7.2	7.2	7.2	7.2	4.8
Depreciation	5.0	5.0	5.0	5.0	5.0	3.5
Change in working capital	1.0	1.0	1.0	1.0	1.0	0.5
Capital expenditures	4.0	4.0	4.0	4.0	4.0	3.0
Change in other assets net	1.0	1.0	1.0	1.0	1.0	1.0
Free cash flow	6.2	6.2	6.2	6.2	6.2	3.8

TABLE P16.2.1 Operating Relationships and Financial Information—RJR Nabisco Projections

(in millions)

Initial revenues (1988)	$15,173	Risk-free rate (R_f) 8.0%
Marketable securities	0	Asset beta (β_a) = β_U 0.9
Initial book debt	$5,204	Risk premium (RP) 7.5%
Shares outstanding	229.0	Tax rate (T) 34.0%

	1989	*1990*	*1991*	*1992*	*1993*	*1994*	*1995*	*1996*	*1997*	*1998*	*Year n + 1*
Revenue growth rate	6.7%	6.7%	6.7%	6.6%	6.6%	6.5%	6.5%	6.0%	6.0%	6.0%	3.0%
Interest expense (in millions)	$2,754	$2,341	$1,997	$1,888	$1,321	$1,088	$806	$487	$21	$0	$590
Operating relationships (as a % of revenues)											
NOI	17.0%	17.0%	17.0%	17.0%	17.0%	17.0%	17.0%	17.0%	17.0%	17.0%	15.0%
NOPAT	11.2	11.2	11.2	11.2	11.2	11.2	11.2	11.2	11.2	11.2	9.9
Depreciation	7.0	6.0	6.0	5.5	5.5	5.5	5.0	5.0	4.0	3.0	2.0
Change in working capital	0.5	0.5	0.5	0.5	0.5	0.5	0.5	0.5	0.5	0.5	0.5
Capital expenditures	4.8	4.0	3.0	3.0	2.0	2.0	1.0	1.0	0.5	0.5	0.5
Change in other assets net	−21.6	−15.6	0.0	0.0	0.0	0.0	0.0	0.0	0.0	0.0	0.0
Free cash flow	34.5	28.3	13.7	13.2	14.2	14.2	14.7	14.7	14.2	13.2	10.9

TABLE P16.2.2 Operating Relationships and Financial Information—RJR Nabisco Projections

(in millions)

Initial revenues (1988)	$15,173	Risk-free rate (R_f)	8.0%
Marketable securities	0	Asset beta (β_a) = β_u	0.9
Initial book debt	$ 5,204	Risk premium (RP)	7.5%
Shares outstanding	229.0	Tax rate (T)	34.0%

	1989	1990	1991	1992	1993	1994	1995	1996	1997	1998	Year n + 1
Revenue growth rate	6.7%	6.7%	6.7%	6.6%	6.6%	6.5%	6.5%	6.0%	6.0%	6.0%	3.0%
Interest expense (in millions)	$2,754	$2,341	$1,997	$1,888	$1,321	$1,088	$806	$487	$21	$0	$590
Operating relationships (as a % of revenues)											
NOI	17.0%	18.0%	19.0%	20.0%	20.0%	20.0%	20.0%	20.0%	20.0%	20.0%	15.0%
NOPAT	11.2%	11.9%	12.5%	13.2%	13.2%	13.2%	13.2%	13.2%	13.2%	13.2%	9.9%
Depreciation	7.0%	6.0%	6.0%	5.5%	5.5%	5.5%	5.0%	5.0%	4.0%	3.0%	2.0%
Change in working capital	0.5%	0.5%	0.5%	0.5%	0.5%	0.5%	0.5%	0.5%	0.5%	0.5%	0.5%
Capital expenditures	4.8%	4.0%	3.0%	3.0%	2.0%	2.0%	1.0%	1.0%	0.5%	0.5%	0.5%
Change in other assets net	−21.6%	−15.6%	0.0%	0.0%	0.0%	0.0%	0.0%	0.0%	0.0%	0.0%	0.0%
Free cash flow	34.5%	29.0%	15.0%	15.2%	16.2%	16.2%	16.7%	16.7%	16.2%	15.2%	10.9%

16.2.3 In Table P16.2.2, consider the possibility that asset sales (change in other assets net) yield only $1 billion for each of the years 1989 and 1990. The applicable operating relationships for the change in other assets net in 1989 and 1990 as a percent of net revenues should be calculated in using Model 16–04.

References

Allen, Jay R., "LBOs—The Evolution of Financial Structures and Strategies," *Journal of Applied Corporate Finance* 8, Winter 1996, pp. 18–29.

Altman, Edward I., "Measuring Corporate Bond Mortality and Performance," *Journal of Finance* 44, September 1989, pp. 909–922.

Altman, Edward I., and Pablo Arman, "Defaults and Returns on High Yield Bonds: Analysis Through 2001," *Journal of Applied Finance* 12:1, Spring/Summer 2002, pp. 98–112.

Anders, George, "Leaner and Meaner: Leveraged Buy-Outs Make Some Companies Tougher Competitors," *Wall Street Journal*, September 15, 1988, pp. 1, 14.

Andrade, Gregor, and Steven N. Kaplan, "How Costly Is Financial (Not Economic) Distress? Evidence from Highly Leveraged Transactions That Became Distressed," *Journal of Finance* 53, October 1998, pp. 1443–1493.

Anslinger, Patricia L., and Thomas E. Copeland, "Growth Through Acquisitions: A Fresh Look," *Harvard Business Review* 74, January–February 1996, pp. 126–135.

Antilla, Susan, "A Different Face on the L.B.O. Front," *New York Times*, December 27, 1992, Section 3, p. 13.

———, "Forstmann Turns Toward the Future," *New York Times*, November 14, 1993, Section 3, p. 13.

Asquith, P., and T. A. Wizman, "Event Risk, Covenants, and Bondholder Returns in Leveraged Buyouts," *Journal of Financial Economics* 27, 1990, pp. 195–214.

Baker, G. P., M. C. Jensen, and K. J. Murphy, "Compensation and Incentives: Practice vs. Theory," *Journal of Finance* 43, 1988, pp. 593–616.

DeAngelo, Harry, and Linda DeAngelo, "Management Buyouts of Publicly Traded Corporations," Chapter 6 in *Modern Finance & Industrial Economics*, Thomas E. Copeland, (ed.), New York: Basil Blackwell Inc., 1987, pp. 92–113.

———, and Edward Rice, "Going Private: Minority Freezeouts and Stockholder Wealth," *Journal of Law and Economics* 27, October 1984, pp. 367–401.

Degeorge, Francois, and Richard Zeckhauser, "The Reverse LBO Decision and Firm Performance: Theory and Evidence," *Journal of Finance* 48, September 1993, pp. 1323–1348.

Easterbrook, F. H., and D. R. Fischel, "Corporate Control Transactions," *Yale Law Journal* 92, 1982, pp. 698–711.

Easterwood, John C., "Divestments and Financial Distress in Leveraged Buyouts," *Journal of Banking & Finance* 22, 1998, pp. 129–159.

Fischel, Daniel, *Payback*, New York: HarperCollins Publishers, 1995.

Frantz, Douglas, "Crash Hasn't Shaken Drexel's Faith in the Value of 'Junk Bonds,'" *Los Angeles Times*, November 19, 1987, Part IV, p. 1.

Greenwald, J., "Where's the Limit?" *Time*, December 5, 1988, pp. 66–70.

Harlow, W. V., and J. S. Howe, "Leverage Buyouts and Insider Nontrading," *Financial Management* 22, Spring 1993, pp. 109–118.

Hite, G. L., and M. R. Vetsuypens, "Management Buyouts of Divisions and Shareholder Wealth," *Journal of Finance* 44, 1989, pp. 953–970.

Holthausen, Robert W., and David F. Larcker, "The Financial Performance of Reverse Leveraged Buyouts," *Journal of Financial Economics* 42, 1996, pp. 293–332.

Jensen, M. C., "Agency Costs of Free Cash Flow, Corporate Finance, and Takeovers," AEA Papers and Proceedings, May 1986, pp. 323–329.

Kaplan, Steven, "The Effects of Management Buyouts on Operating Performance and Value," *Journal of Financial Economics* 24, 1989a, pp. 217–254.

———, "Management Buyouts: Evidence on Taxes as a Source of Value," *Journal of Finance* 44, July 1989b, pp. 611–632.

——, "The Staying Power of Leveraged Buyouts," *Journal of Financial Economics* 29, 1991, pp. 287–313.

——, and Jeremy C. Stein, "The Evolution of Buyout Pricing and Financial Structure (Or, What Went Wrong) in the 1980s," *Journal of Applied Corporate Finance* 6, 1993, pp. 72–88.

Laing, J. R., "Up and Down Wall Street," *Barron's*, April 10, 1989, pp. 1, 49–50.

Lehn, Ken, and Annette Poulsen, "Free Cash Flow and Stockholder Gains in Going Private Transactions." *Journal of Finance* 44, 1989, pp. 771–788.

——, "Leveraged Buyouts: Wealth Created or Wealth Redistributed?" Chapter 4 in *Public Policy Towards Corporate Takeovers*, M. Weidenbaum and K. Chilton (eds.), New Brunswick, NJ: Transaction Publishers, 1988.

Lowenstein, Louis, "Management Buyouts," *Columbia Law Review* 85, 1985, pp. 730–784.

Mian, Shehzad, and James Rosenfeld, "Takeover Activity and the Long-Run Performance of Reverse Leveraged Buyouts," *Financial Management* 22, Winter 1993, pp. 46–57.

Michel, Allen, and Israel Shaked, "RJR Nabisco: A Case Study of a Complex Leveraged Buyout," *Financial Analysis Journal*, September–October 1991, pp. 15–26

Morrow, D. J., "Why the IRS Might Love Those LBOs," *Fortune*, December 5, 1988, pp. 145–146.

Murphy, K. J., "Corporate Performance and Managerial Remuneration: An Empirical Analysis," *Journal of Accounting and Economics* 7, 1985, pp. 11–42.

Muscarella, C. J., and M. R. Vetsuypens, "Efficiency and Organizational Structure: A Study of Reverse LBOs," *Journal of Finance* 45, December 1990, pp. 1389–1413.

Opler, Tim, "Operating Performance in Leveraged Buyouts: Evidence from 1985–1989," *Financial Management* 21, Spring 1992, pp. 27–34.

Quigley, E. V., "Big Bondholders Launch Revolt Against Nabisco," *Los Angeles Times*, November 18, 1988, Part IV, pp. 1, 5.

Ritter, Jay R., "The Long-Run Performance of Initial Public Offerings," *Journal of Finance* 46, March 1991, pp. 3–27.

Roden, Dianne M., and Wilbur G. Lewellen, "Corporate Capital Structure Decisions: Evidence from Leveraged Buyouts," *Financial Management* 24, Summer 1995, pp. 76–87.

Ruback, Richard S., "Capital Cash Flows: A Simple Approach to Valuing Risky Cash Flows," *Financial Management* 31:2, Summer 2002, pp. 85–103.

Ruback, Richard S., "RJR Nabisco," *Harvard Business School Case No. 9-289-056*, May 28, 1997.

Saul, Ralph S., "DREXEL," *The Brookings Review* 11, Spring 1993, pp. 41–45.

Shleifer, A., and L. H. Summers, "Breach of Trust in Hostile Takeovers," Chapter 2 in *Corporate Takeovers: Causes and Consequences*, A. J. Auerbach (ed.) Chicago: University of Chicago Press, 1988, pp. 33–56.

Shleifer, A., and R. W. Vishny, "Management Buyouts as a Response to Market Pressure," Chapter 5 in *Mergers and Acquisitions*, A. J. Auerbach(ed), Chicago: University of Chicago Press, 1988.

Smith, Abbie, "Corporate Ownership Structure and Performance: The Case of Management Buyouts," *Journal of Financial Economics* 27, September 1990, pp. 143–164.

Travlos, N. G., and M. M. Cornett. "Going Private Buyouts and Determinants of Shareholders' Returns," *Journal of Accounting, Auditing and Finance* 8, 1993, pp. 1–25.

United States Government Printing Office, *Economic Report of the President*, Washington, DC, 1996.

Warga, Arthur, and Ivo Welch, "Bondholder Losses in Leveraged Buyouts," *Review of Financial Studies* 6, 1993, pp. 959–982.

Weston, J. Fred, and Yehning Chen, "A Tale of Two Eras," *Business Economics* 29, January 1994, pp. 27–33.

Yago, Glenn, *Junk Bonds: How High Yield Securities Restructured Corporate America*, New York: Oxford University Press, 1991.

RELATION BETWEEN WACC AND CCF MODELS

In an infinite horizon framework, the equivalence of the FCF and CCF models is shown.

Inputs and Definitions:

Cost of equity = $k_e = 15\%$
Cost of debt = $k_b = 10\%$
Cost of assets = k_a
WACC = weighted average cost of capital
FCF = Free Cash Flows = 1140
CCF = Capital Cash Flows
Tax = $T = 40\%$
V = Value of the firm = $B + S$
L = leverage ratio = $B/V = 40\%$
Amount of Debt = B
Amount of Equity = S

Valuation Formula:

$$V = \frac{FCF}{WACC} = \frac{FCF}{k_b(1-T)(B/V) + k_e(S/V)}$$

$$FCF = V\left[k_b(1-T)(B/V) + k_e(S/V)\right]$$

$$FCF = V\frac{\left[k_bB - k_bTB + k_eS\right]}{V}$$

$$FCF = V\left[\frac{k_bB + k_eS}{V}\right] - k_bTB$$

$$FCF = Vk_a - k_bTB$$

$$Vk_a = FCF + k_bTB$$

$$V = \frac{FCF + k_bTB}{k_a} = \frac{CCF}{k_a}$$

$$\therefore V = \frac{FCF}{WACC} = \frac{CCF}{k_a}$$

Note that $V = \dfrac{FCF + k_bTB}{k_a} = \dfrac{FCF}{k_a} + \dfrac{k_bTB}{k_a}$

$$= V_U + V_{TS} \text{ where:}$$

V_U = value of unlevered firm = FCF/k_a
V_{TS} = value of tax shield = k_bTB/k_a

Example:

$$WACC = k_b(1-T)(B/V) + k_e(S/V)$$
$$= 10\%(1-0.40)(0.40) + 15\%(0.60) = 11.4\%$$
$$V = FCF/WACC = 1140/0.114 = 10,000$$
$$k_a = k_b(B/V) + k_e(S/V) = 10\%(0.40)$$
$$+ 15\%(0.60) = 13\%$$
$$CCF = FCF + k_bTB = 1140 + 0.10(0.40)(4000) = 1300$$
$$V = CCF/k_a = 1300/0.13 = 10,000$$

The equivalence of the WACC and asset return model holds in an infinite horizon model because implicitly, the leverage ratio is held constant. However, the whole point of the capital cash flow model is to provide a methodology for handling changing leverage ratios. Therefore, in Table A16.1, we provide Model 16–03, which is a general format for using the capital cash flow model for a 5-year period of growth. In Table A16.2, Model 16–04 provides a format for a 10-year period of growth. The software for these two models enables users to insert the relevant numbers for their study. This software is found at our Web sites.

TABLE A16.1 Model 16–03: Capital Cash Flow Model

	Year 0	Year 1	Year 2	Year 3	Year 4	Year 5 = n	Year n + 1
Panel A. Inputs for Present Value Calculations							
1. Net revenues	$5,000	$5,400	$5,832	$6,299	$6,802	$7,347	$7,567
2.　Revenue growth rate		8.0%	8.0%	8.0%	8.0%	8.0%	3.0%
3. NOI = EBIT	$ 500	$ 540	$ 583	$ 630	$ 680	$ 735	$ 605
4.　Cash tax rate (T)	40.0%	40.0%	40.0%	40.0%	40.0%	40.0%	40.0%
5.　Income taxes	200	216	233	252	272	294	242
6. NOPAT	$ 300	$ 324	$ 350	$ 378	$ 408	$ 441	$ 363
7.　+ Depreciation	250	270	292	315	340	367	265
8.　− Change in working capital	50	54	58	63	68	73	38
9.　− Capital expenditures	100	108	117	126	136	147	76
10.　− Change in other assets net	50	54	58	63	68	73	76
11. Free cash flows	$ 350	$ 378	$ 408	$ 441	$ 476	$ 514	$ 439
12. Interest expense		$ 400	$ 380	$ 300	$ 200	$ 150	$ 100
13. Interest tax shield		$ 160	$ 152	$ 120	$ 80	$60	$40
14. Capital cash flow (CCF) (11 + 13)		$ 538	$ 560	$ 561	$ 556	$ 574	$ 479
15. Discount rate (k_a)		11.85%	11.85%	11.85%	11.85%	11.85%	11.85%
16. Discount factor		0.89405	0.79933	0.71465	0.63893	0.57124	
17. Present values		$ 481	$ 448	$ 401	$ 355	$ 328	
Panel B. Operating Relationships (as a % of revenues)							
NOI	10.0%	10.0%	10.0%	10.0%	10.0%	10.0%	8.0%
NOPAT	6.0	6.0	6.0	6.0	6.0	6.0	4.8
Depreciation	5.0	5.0	5.0	5.0	5.0	5.0	3.5
Change in working capital	1.0	1.0	1.0	1.0	1.0	1.0	0.5
Capital expenditures	2.0	2.0	2.0	2.0	2.0	2.0	1.0
Change in other assets net	1.0	1.0	1.0	1.0	1.0	1.0	1.0
Free cash flow	7.0	7.0	7.0	7.0	7.0	7.0	5.8

Panel C. Valuation Calculations

Part I — Expected Asset Return Inputs

(a) Risk-free rate (R_f)	6.00%
(b) Asset beta (β_a) = β_U	0.900
(c) Risk premium (RP)	6.50%
(d) Tax rate (T)	40.00%

Part II — Expected Asset Return Calculation

$k_a = R_f + (RP) \beta_a$

$= 6.0\% + 6.5\% \ (0.900) = $　　11.85%

Part III — Terminal Value (TV)

TV = Capital cash flows$_{n+1}$/(k_a − g)

$= 479/(0.1185 - 0.03) = 479/0.0885 = $　$5,411

PVTV = TV/$(1 + k_a)^n$

$= 5411 \times 0.57124 = $　$3,091

Part IV — Valuation Calculation

(1) PV of cash flows	$2,013
(2) PV of terminal value	$3,091
(3) Operating value (V)	$5,104
(4)　Add: Marketable securities	—
(5) Total value	$5,104
(6)　Less: Initial book debt (D)	2,000
(7) Value of equity	$3,104
(8) Shares outstanding	100.0
(9) Intrinsic share price	$31.04

Part V — Ratios

Operating Value/Revenues$_0$	1.02
Operating Value/NOI$_0$	10.21
Operating Value/EBITDA$_0$	6.81

TABLE A16.2 Model 16-04: LBO Valuation

	Year 0	Year 1	Year 2	Year 3	Year 4	Year 5	Year 6	Year 7	Year 8	Year 9	Year 10	Year n+1
Panel A. Inputs for Present Value Calculations												
1. Net revenues	$10,000	$10,670	$11,385	$12,148	$12,949	$13,804	$14,701	$15,657	$16,596	$17,592	$18,648	$19,207
2. Revenue growth rate		6.7%	6.7%	6.7%	6.6%	6.6%	6.5%	6.5%	6.0%	6.0%	6.0%	3.0%
3. NOI = EBIT		$ 1,814	$ 2,049	$ 2,308	$ 2,590	$ 2,761	$ 2,940	$ 3,131	$ 3,319	$ 3,518	$ 3,730	$ 2,881
4. Cash tax rate (T)		34.0%	34.0%	34.0%	34.0%	34.0%	34.0%	34.0%	34.0%	34.0%	34.0%	34.0%
5. Income taxes		617	697	785	881	939	1,000	1,065	1,129	1,196	1,268	980
6. NOPAT		$ 1,197	$ 1,353	$ 1,523	$ 1,709	$ 1,822	$ 1,941	$ 2,067	$ 2,191	$ 2,322	$ 2,461	$ 1,902
7. + Depreciation		747	683	729	712	759	809	783	830	704	559	384
8. – Change in working capital		53	57	61	65	69	74	78	83	88	93	96
9. – Capital expenditures		512	455	364	388	276	294	157	166	88	93	96
10. – Change in other assets net		(1,003)	(1,002)	–	–	–	–	–	–	–	–	–
11. Free cash flows		$ 2,382	$ 2,525	$ 1,827	$ 1,968	$ 2,236	$ 2,382	$ 2,615	$ 2,772	$ 2,850	$ 2,834	$ 2,094
12. Interest expense		$ 2,754	$ 2,341	$ 1,997	$ 1,888	$ 1,321	$ 1,088	$ 806	$ 487	$ 21	$ –	$ 590
13. Interest tax shield		$ 936	$ 796	$ 679	$ 642	$ 449	$ 370	$ 274	$ 166	$ 7	$ –	$ 201
14. Capital cash flow (CCF) (11+13)		$ 3,318	$ 3,321	$ 2,506	$ 2,610	$ 2,685	$ 2,752	$ 2,889	$ 2,937	$ 2,857	$ 2,834	$ 2,294
15. Discount rate (k_a)		14.70%	14.70%	14.70%	14.70%	14.70%	14.70%	14.70%	14.70%	14.70%	14.70%	14.70%
16. Discount factor		0.87184	0.76010	0.66269	0.57776	0.50371	0.43916	0.38287	0.33380	0.29102	0.25373	
17. Present values		$ 2,893	$ 2,524	$ 1,661	$ 1,508	$ 1,353	$ 1,208	$ 1,106	$ 980	$ 831	$ 719	
Panel B. Operating Relationships (as a % of revenues)												
NOI		17.0%	18.0%	19.0%	20.0%	20.0%	20.0%	20.0%	20.0%	20.0%	20.0%	15.0%
NOPAT		11.2%	11.9%	12.5%	13.2%	13.2%	13.2%	13.2%	13.2%	13.2%	13.2%	9.9%
Depreciation		7.0%	6.0%	6.0%	5.5%	5.5%	5.5%	5.0%	5.0%	4.0%	3.0%	2.0%
Change in working capital		0.5%	0.5%	0.5%	0.5%	0.5%	0.5%	0.5%	0.5%	0.5%	0.5%	0.5%
Capital expenditures		4.8%	4.0%	3.0%	3.0%	2.0%	2.0%	1.0%	1.0%	0.5%	0.5%	0.5%
Change in other assets net		–9.4%	–8.8%	0.0%	0.0%	0.0%	0.0%	0.0%	0.0%	0.0%	0.0%	0.0%
Free cash flow		22.3%	22.2%	15.0%	15.2%	16.2%	16.2%	16.7%	16.7%	16.2%	15.2%	10.9%

Panel C. Valuation Calculations

Part I – Expected Asset Return Inputs

(a) Risk-free rate (R_f)	9.00%
(b) Asset beta (β_a) = β_U	0.760
(c) Risk premium (RP)	7.50%
(d) Tax rate (T)	34.00%

Part II – Expected Asset Return Calculation

$k_a = R_f + (RP)\ \beta_a$ = 14.70%
= 9.0% + 7.5%(0.760) =

Part III – Terminal Value (TV)

TV = Capital cash flows$_{n+1}$/(k_a – g)
= 2294/(0.147 – 0.03) = 2294/0.117 = $19,608

PVTV = TV/$(1 + k_a)^n$
= 19608 × 0.25373 = $4,975

Part IV – Valuation Calculation

(1) PV of capital cash flows	$14,784
(2) PV of terminal value	$ 4,975
(3) Operating Value (V)	$19,759
(4) Add: Marketable securities	–
(5) Total value	$19,759
(6) Less: Initial book debt (D)	5,204
(7) Value of equity	$14,555
(8) Shares outstanding	229.0
(9) Intrinsic share price	$63.56

APPENDIX B

RELATION BETWEEN CCF AND APV MODELS

The APV is first illustrated in Table B16.1 with a tax shield discounted at k_b. The same free cash flows as in the CCF model are discounted at the cost of equity of an unlevered firm equal to the expected asset return rate. The interest payment pattern is assumed to be the same as in the CCF Model in Table 16.7. However, the interest tax shield is discounted at the before-tax cost of debt rather than at the expected

asset return rate in the CCF model. Applying a lower discount rate results in a higher valuation than in Table 16.7 using the CCF model. In Table B16.2, the interest tax shield is discounted at the cost of assets, because the interest tax shields are subject to the same uncertainties as cash flows from assets (Ruback, 2002). Now the results are equal to the capital cash flow methodology shown in Table 16.7 in the text.

REFERENCE

Ruback, Richard S., "Capital Cash Flows: A Simple Approach to Valuing Risky Cash Flows," *Financial Management* 31:2, Summer 2002, pp. 85–103.

TABLE B16.1 APV Method with Tax Shield Discounted at k_b

	Year 0	Year 1	Year 2	Year 3	Year 4	Year 5 = n	Year n + 1
Panel A. Inputs for Present Value Calculations							
1. Net revenues	$5,000	$5,400	$5,832	$6,299	$6,802	$7,347	$7,567
2. Revenue growth rate		8.0%	8.0%	8.0%	8.0%	8.0%	3.0%
3. NOI = EBIT	$ 500	$ 540	$ 583	$ 630	$ 680	$ 735	$ 605
4. Cash tax rate	40.0%	40.0%	40.0%	40.0%	40.0%	40.0%	40.0%
5. Income taxes	200	216	233	252	272	294	242
6. NOPAT	$ 300	$ 324	$ 350	$ 378	$ 408	$ 441	$ 363
7. + Depreciation	250	270	292	315	340	367	265
8. − Change in working capital	50	54	58	63	68	73	38
9. − Capital expenditures	100	108	117	126	136	147	76
10. − Change in other assets net	50	54	58	63	68	73	76
11. Free cash flows (FCF)	$ 350	$ 378	$ 408	$ 441	$ 476	$ 514	$ 439
12. Discount rate (k_a)		10.70%	10.70%	10.70%	10.70%	10.70%	10.70%
13. Discount factor		0.90334	0.81603	0.73715	0.66590	0.60154	
14. Present values of FCF		$ 341	$ 333	$ 325	$ 317	$ 309	
15. Interest expense		$ 400	$ 380	$ 300	$ 200	$ 150	$ 100
16. Interest tax shield (TS)		$ 160	$ 152	$ 120	$ 80	$ 60	$ 40
17. Discount rate (k_b)		8.00%	8.00%	8.00%	8.00%	8.00%	8.00%
18. Discount factor		0.92593	0.85734	0.79383	0.73503	0.68058	
19. Present value of tax shield		$ 148	$ 130	$ 95	$ 59	$ 41	

TABLE B16.1 (cont.)

Panel B. Operating Relationships (as a % of revenues)

NOI	10.0%	10.0%	10.0%	10.0%	10.0%	10.0%	8.0%
NOPAT	6.0	6.0	6.0	6.0	6.0	6.0	4.8
Depreciation	5.0	5.0	5.0	5.0	5.0	5.0	3.5
Change in working capital	1.0	1.0	1.0	1.0	1.0	1.0	0.5
Capital expenditures	2.0	2.0	2.0	2.0	2.0	2.0	1.0
Change in other assets net	1.0	1.0	1.0	1.0	1.0	1.0	1.0
Free cash flow	7.0	7.0	7.0	7.0	7.0	˜7.0	5.8

Panel C. Valuation Calculations

Inputs

(a) Risk-free rate (R_f)	6.00%
(b) Asset beta (β_a)	0.723
(c) Risk premium (RP)	6.50%
(d) Tax rate (T)	40.00%
(e) Before-tax cost of debt (k_b)	8.00%
(f) Target equity (S) to value (V)	60.0%
(g) Target debt (B) to value (V)	40.0%

Calculations

Cost of assets (k_a) = R_f + (RP) β_a
= 6.0% + 6.5% (0.723) =   10.70%

Terminal value free cash flows = $FCF_{n+1}/(k_a - g)$
= 439/(0.107 − 0.03) = 439/0.077 = $5,700

Terminal value interest tax shield = $TS_{n+1}/(k_b - g)$
= 40/(0.08 − 0.03) = 40/0.05 = $ 800

(1) PV of free cash flows	$1,626
(2) PV of interest tax shield	$ 473
(3) PV of terminal free cash flows	$3,429
(4) PV of terminal interest tax shield	$ 544
(5) Operating Value (V)	$6,073
(6) Add: Marketable securities	—
(7) Total value	$6,073
(8) Less: Book debt (D)	2,000
(9) Value of equity	$4,073
(10) Shares outstanding	100.0
(11) Intrinsic share price	$40.73

Ratios:

Operating Value/Revenues$_0$	1.21
Operating Value/NOI$_0$	12.15
Operating Value/EBITDA$_0$	8.10

TABLE B16.2 APV Method with Tax Shield Discounted at k_a

	Year 0	Year 1	Year 2	Year 3	Year 4	Year 5 = n	Year n + 1
Panel A. Inputs for Present Value Calculations							
1. Net revenues	$5,000	$5,400	$5,832	$6,299	$6,802	$7,347	$7,567
2. Revenue growth rate		8.0%	8.0%	8.0%	8.0%	8.0%	3.0%
3. NOI = EBIT	$ 500	$ 540	$ 583	$ 630	$ 680	$ 735	$ 605
4. Cash tax rate	40.0%	40.0%	40.0%	40.0%	40.0%	40.0%	40.0%
5. Income taxes	200	216	233	252	272	294	242
6. NOPAT	$ 300	$324	$ 350	$ 378	$ 408	$ 441	$ 363
7. + Depreciation	250	270	292	315	340	367	265
8. − Change in working capital	50	54	58	63	68	73	38
9. − Capital expenditures	100	108	117	126	136	147	76
10. − Change in other assets net	50	54	58	63	68	73	76
11. Free cash flows (FCF)	$ 350	$ 378	$ 408	$ 441	$ 476	$ 514	$ 439
12. Discount rate (k_a)		10.70%	10.70%	10.70%	10.70%	10.70%	10.70%
13. Discount factor		0.90334	0.81603	0.73715	0.66590	0.60154	
14. Present values of FCF		$ 341	$ 333	$ 325	$ 317	$ 309	
15. Interest expense		$ 400	$ 380	$ 300	$ 200	$ 150	$ 100
16. Interest tax shield (TS)		$ 160	$ 152	$ 120	$ 80	$ 60	$ 40
17. Discount rate (k_a)		10.70%	10.70%	10.70%	10.70%	10.70%	10.70%
18. Discount factor		0.90334	0.81603	0.73715	0.66590	0.60154	
19. Present value of tax shield		$ 145	$ 124	$ 88	$ 53	$ 36	
Panel B. Operating Relationships (as a % of revenues)							
NOI	10.0%	10.0%	10.0%	10.0%	10.0%	10.0%	8.0%
NOPAT	6.0	6.0	6.0	6.0	6.0	6.0	4.8
Depreciation	5.0	5.0	5.0	5.0	5.0	5.0	3.5
Change in working capital	1.0	1.0	1.0	1.0	1.0	1.0	0.5
Capital expenditures	2.0	2.0	2.0	2.0	2.0	2.0	1.0
Change in other assets net	1.0	1.0	1.0	1.0	1.0	1.0	1.0
Free cash flow	7.0	7.0	7.0	7.0	7.0	7.0	5.8

Panel C. Valuation Calculations

Inputs

(a) Risk-free rate (R_f)	6.00%
(b) Asset beta (β_a)	0.723
(c) Risk premium (RP)	6.50%
(d) Tax rate (T)	40.00%
(e) Before-tax cost of debt (k_b)	8.00%
(f) Target equity (S) to value (V)	60.0%
(g) Target debt (B) to value (V)	40.0%

Calculations

Cost of assets (k_a) = R_f + (RP) β_a
= 6.0% + 6.5% (0.723) =   10.70%

Terminal value free cash flows = $FCF_{n+1}/(k_a - g)$
= 439/(0.107 − 0.03) = 439/0.077 = $5,700

Terminal value interest tax shield = $TS_{n+1}/(k_a - g)$
= 40/(0.107 − 0.03) = 40/0.077 = $ 519

(1) PV of free cash flows	$1,626
(2) PV of interest tax shield	$ 446
(3) PV of terminal free cash flows	$3,429
(4) PV of terminal interest tax shield	$ 312
(5) Operating Value (V)	$5,814
(6) Add: Marketable securities	—
(7) Total value	$5,814
(8) Less: Book debt (D)	2,000
(9) Value of equity	$3,814
(10) Shares outstanding	100.0
(11) Intrinsic share price	$38.14

Ratios:

Operating Value/Revenues$_0$	1.16
Operating Value/NOI$_0$	11.63
Operating Value/EBITDA$_0$	7.75

CHAPTER 17
INTERNATIONAL TAKEOVERS
AND RESTRUCTURING

The annual reports of individual business firms make increasing reference to international markets as sources of future growth. The world has truly become a global marketplace. A significant proportion of total takeover activity has an international dimension. U.S. firms are buying foreign firms, foreign firms are buying U.S. entities, and U.S. and foreign firms are buying one another.

HISTORICAL PATTERNS

Table 17.1 displays data on trends in foreign versus U.S. merger activity during the period 1991 to 2001. M&A activity is grouped by the U.S. alone and by three categories of international deals. As displayed in Panel A, all measures of M&A activity show a large positive trend in activity through 2000, followed by a steep drop-off in 2001 due to the global recession and stock market plunge. With respect to relative activity, acquisitions by non-U.S. companies of U.S. companies range from 5% to 11% of total M&A activity. U.S. company acquisitions of non-U.S. companies are in the range of 4% to 7% of total world M&A activity. Deals not involving U.S. companies, including cross-border and within-border transactions, account for 37% to 57% of total world M&A activity. By dollar volume, total international deals account for 52% to 68% of total world activity. Measured by number of deals, the U.S.-alone category accounts for 22% to 39% of M&A activity, with international deals accounting for 61% to 78%.

The main reason for the large levels of foreign M&A activity can be summarized briefly. Europe continues to become a common market thus, it continues to experience the kind of M&A activity that took place in the United States when it first became a common market as a result of the completion of the transnational railroad systems in the late-1880s. In addition to that is globalization and the increased intensity of international competition, which has been impacting U.S. M&A activity, as well. The impact of rapid technological change and the consolidation of major industries represent additional forces for increased M&A activity throughout the world.

LARGE CROSS-BORDER TRANSACTIONS

To give real-life content to the broad statistical compilations of these tables, we present tables listing the 25 largest cross-border transactions in history, completed as of December 31, 2001, for four categories. Table 17.2 presents data for cross-border transactions in which U.S. firms

TABLE 17.1 Foreign vs. U.S. Merger Activity, 1991–2001

Panel A. Dollar Volume

| | UNITED STATES | | INTERNATIONAL DEALS | | | | | | | | | Total |
| | U.S. Alone | | U.S. by Non-U.S. | | Non-U.S. by U.S. | | Deals outside U.S. | | Total International | | | |
Year	$ in Billions	% of Total	$ in Billions	% of Total	$ in Billions	% of Total	$ in Billions	% of Total	$ in Billions	% of Total	$ in Billions
01	$ 846	41.0%	$ 189	9.2%	$ 108	5.2%	$ 920	44.6%	$1,217	59.0%	$2,063
00	1,308	36.7	337	9.5	141	4.0	1,779	49.9	2,257	63.3	3,565
99	998	42.0	247	10.4	150	6.3	979	41.3	1,376	58.0	2,373
98	1,005	48.1	221	10.6	117	5.6	749	35.8	1,086	51.9	2,092
97	626	46.5	86	6.4	85	6.3	550	40.8	721	53.5	1,348
96	516	48.1	70	6.5	61	5.7	426	39.7	557	51.9	1,072
95	285	41.1	54	7.8	47	6.7	308	44.3	409	58.9	694
94	205	44.8	46	10.1	24	5.1	183	40.0	253	55.2	458
93	131	40.9	22	6.8	19	5.9	149	46.4	189	59.1	320
92	95	32.3	15	5.2	15	5.2	168	57.3	199	67.7	294

Panel B. Number of Deals

| | UNITED STATES | | INTERNATIONAL DEALS | | | | | | | | | Total |
| | U.S. Alone | | U.S. by Non-U.S. | | Non-U.S. by U.S. | | Deals outside U.S. | | Total International | | | |
Year	No. of Deals	% of Total	No. of Deals	% of Total	No. of Deals	% of Total	No. of Deals	% of Total	No. of Deals	% of Total	No. in Billions
01	4,241	21.5%	889	4.5%	1,084	5.5%	13,478	68.4%	15,451	78.5%	19,692
00	6,243	32.3	1,306	6.8	1,634	8.5	10,151	52.5	13,091	67.7	19,334
99	6,209	32.5	1,034	5.4	1,452	7.6	10,413	54.5	12,899	67.5	19,108
98	7,584	39.1	922	4.7	1,586	8.2	9,329	48.0	11,837	60.9	19,421
97	6,030	36.8	777	4.7	1,336	8.2	8,227	50.3	10,340	63.2	16,370
96	5,453	37.0	652	4.4	1,127	7.6	7,517	51.0	9,296	63.0	14,749
95	4,465	33.5	597	4.5	994	7.4	7,291	54.6	8,882	66.5	13,347
94	3,748	33.8	476	4.3	765	6.9	6,104	55.0	7,345	66.2	11,093
93	3,096	33.1	385	4.1	636	6.8	5,250	56.0	6,271	66.9	9,367
92	2,807	29.6	394	4.1	552	5.8	5,744	60.5	6,690	70.4	9,497

Source: Mergers and Acquisitions Annual Almanac, issues 1993–2002.

TABLE 17.2 Major Cross-Border Transactions Involving U.S. Targets

	Date Announced	Date Effective	Target Name	Target Business Description	Acquirer Full Name	Acquirer Business Description	Acquirer Nation	Value of Transaction (in millions)
1	1/18/1999	6/30/1999	Air Touch Communications	Mobile telecommunications	Vodafone Group PLC	Mobile telecomm.	UK	$ 60,287
2	8/11/1998	12/31/1998	Amoco Corp.	Oil and gas company	British Petroleum Co. PLC	Integrated oil and gas company	UK	48,174
3	5/7/1998	11/12/1998	Chrysler Corp.	Mfr. automobiles and trucks	Daimler-Benz AG	Mfr. automobiles and trucks	GER	40,467
4	7/24/2000	5/31/2001	VoiceStream Wireless Corp.	Cellular communications services	Deutsche Telekom AG	Telecomm. services	GER	29,404
5	4/1/1999	4/18/2000	Atlantic Richfield Co.	Oil and gas exploration	BP Amoco PLC	Integrated oil and gas company	UK	27,223
6	5/2/2000	10/4/2000	Bestfoods	Food producer	Unilever PLC	Food producer	UK	25,065
7	7/12/2000	11/3/2000	PaineWebber Group Inc.	Investment bank	UBS AG	Bank: investment bank	SWI	16,542
8	12/7/1998	11/30/1999	PacifiCorp	Electric utility; telecom services	Scottish Power PLC	Electric utility	UK	12,600
9	12/6/1999	5/23/2000	Ernst & Young LLP-Consulting Business	Consulting services	Cap Gemini SA	Consulting services	FRA	11,774
10	8/30/2000	1/3/2001	AXA Financial Inc.	Life insurance company	AXA Group	Insurance company	FRA	11,189
11	2/18/1999	7/21/1999	TransAmerica Corp.	Insurance company	Aegon NV	Insurance company	NETH	10,814
12	12/14/2001	5/7/2001	USA Networks Inc-Entertainment Assets	TV stations	Vivendi Universal SA	Media, communications services	FRA	10,749
13	1/15/2001	12/12/2001	Ralston Purina Co.	Pet foods	Nestle SA	Chocolate and food producer	SWI	10,479
14	11/30/2000	1/22/2001	AT&T Wireless Group (partial interest)	Wireless voice, data services	NTT DoCoMo Inc.	Telecomm. services	JPN	9,805
15	6/18/1998	8/31/1998	Bay Networks	Mfr. date networking products	Nortel Networks Corp.	Mfr. telecomm. equipment	CAN	9,269
16	11/30/1998	6/4/1999	Bankers Trust New York Corp.	Banking	Deutsche Bank AG	Banking	GER	9,082
17	9/5/2000	1/31/2002	Niagara Mohawk Holdings Inc.	Electric and gas utility	National Grid Group PLC	Electric utility	UK	8,047
18	3/31/1989	7/26/1989	SmithKline Beckman Corp.	Mfr. pharmaceutical products	Beecham Group PLC	Mfr. pharmaceutical products	UK	7,922
19	3/26/1987	7/7/1987	Standard Oil Co. of Ohio	Oil and gas company	British Petroleum Co. PLC	Integrated oil and gas company	UK	7,858
20	3/8/1999	5/12/1999	RJ Reynolds International (RJR Nabisco)	Mfr. tobacco products	Japan Tobacco Inc.	Mfr. tobacco products	JPN	7,832
21	5/10/1999	12/31/1999	Republic New York Corp.	Banking	HSBC Holdings PLC	Banking	UK	7,703
22	7/20/2000	12/13/2000	Aetna Inc-Financial Services & Intl. Bus.	Financial services, insurance	ING Group NV	Insurance, brokerage services	NETH	7,632
23	9/24/1990	1/3/1991	MCA Inc.	Motion picture production	Matsushita Electric Industrial Co.	Mfr. home audio, video products	JPN	7,406
24	2/28/1995	7/18/1995	Marion Merrell Dow (Dow Chemical)	Mfr. pharmaceuticals	Hoechst AG	Mfr. chemicals and fibers	GER	7,265
25	7/28/2000	10/5/2000	Alteon Websystems Inc.	Internet solutions	Nortel Networks Corp.	Mfr. network solutions	CAN	7,057
							TOTAL =	$411,645

Source: Thomson Financial Services.

were acquired. Announcement and effective dates are given. The lag of effective dates behind announcement dates ranges mostly from 4 to 10 months. The table gives the target and buyer names plus a brief description of their business activities. All of these 25 transactions would be classified as horizontal mergers. The predominance of these mergers became effective after 1997; only four took place prior to 1998. The predominance of the large mergers during the recent time period is attributed to two factors: (1) the value of the transaction is based on nominal U.S. dollars, and thus the bull market of the 1980s and 1990s naturally results in larger transactions during the latter years, and (2) high levels of merger activity during the latter-1990s. Foreign acquirers of large U.S. companies were domiciled in 7 different nations, with 9 of the 25 mergers associated with U.K. acquirers.

In Table 17.3, we present a similar analysis of the largest 25 transactions in which U.S. firms acquired foreign firms. Almost all of these transactions are horizontal or consolidating mergers. Eleven different countries accounted for the U.S. acquisitions of foreign firms, with Canada and the U.K. accounting for the bulk of the acquisitions with 7 each. The total of the 25 largest cross-border acquisitions with U.S. acquirers is $151.5 billion, only 36.8% of the value of the transactions in Table 17.2 in which U.S. firms were targets. This statistic reflects the protection that foreign governments provide to target companies relative to the level of protection provided by the U.S. government to U.S. targets of foreign acquirers.

Table 17.4 lists the top 25 in history in which cross-border transactions took place without the involvement of U.S. firms. It can be readily seen that most of these transactions involve European firms. The U.K. led the way with 6 target companies and 7 acquirer companies represented, followed by Germany with 4 targets and 3 acquirers. France and Switzerland were active acquires with 5 and 4 acquisitions, respectively. Similar to the prior tables, these cross-border mergers are largely of the horizontal category.

Although the focus of this chapter is on cross-border transactions, Table 17.5 presents the 25 largest intranational mergers by foreign companies. Japan and the U.K. dominate the top 25 with 7 transactions each. Again, these mergers are largely of the horizontal type. Banking transactions account for roughly half of the 25 mergers.

The cross-border transactions listed in Tables 17.2 through 17.4 can be placed in industry groups, as shown in Table 17.6. We emphasize that the companies listed represent only the largest transactions in each category. For example, in Appendix A to Chapter 6 on the chemical industry we present a list of companies with reason for merging or divesting in Table A6.2. Similarly, we compiled an extended list of large M&As in the drug industry, as displayed in Table 17.7. The major reasons for the transactions listed in Table 17.7 were to combine complementary capabilities, to strengthen distribution networks, and to achieve the greater size required for the new approaches to R&D.

The industries represented in the combined company listing in Table 17.6 can be regrouped into eight categories. All have been greatly impacted by the broad forces of technological change and the globalization of markets. These, in turn, have produced deregulation, the blurring of industry boundaries, and unequal growth patterns among industries. These and other industries' specific influences have combined to produce some high-takeover industries. The industry characteristics related to M&A pressures can be summarized as follows.

1. **Telecommunications:** Technological change and deregulation in the United States and abroad (particularly Europe) have stimulated efforts to develop a global presence.
2. **Media** (movies, records, magazines, newspapers): Technological changes have impacted the relationship between the content and delivery segments. Potential overlap exists in

TABLE 17.3 Major Cross-Border Transactions Involving U.S. Acquirers

	Date Announced	Date Effective	Target Name	Target Business Description	Target Nation	Acquirer Full Name	Acquirer Business Description	Value of Transaction (in millions)
1	3/2/1998	8/19/1998	Energy Group PLC	Electric utility, coal mining	UK	Texas Utilities Co.	Electric and gas utility	$ 10,947
2	6/14/1999	8/20/1999	ASDA Group PLC	Op food; clothing superstores	UK	Wal-Mart Stores Inc.	Mass merchandising retail	10,805
3	8/21/1995	11/2/1995	Pharmacia AB	Mfr. pharmaceuticals	SWE	Upjohn Co.	Mfr. pharmaceutical products	6,989
4	1/28/1999	5/11/1999	Lucas Varity PLC	Provide engineering services	UK	TRW Inc.	Provides advanced tech products and services	6,827
5	1/26/1999	3/5/1999	Japan Leasing Corp.	Provide business credit services	JPN	General Electric Co.	Conglomerate	6,566
6	1/28/1999	3/31/1999	Volvo AB-Worldwide Psgr. Veh. Bus	Mfr. passenger vehicles	SWE	Ford Motor Co.	Mfr. autos, trucks, auto parts	6,450
7	5/22/1995	2/15/1996	CarnaudMetalbox SA	Mfr. metal cars	FRA	Crown Cork & Seal Co.	Mfr. cans, crowns	4,982
8	4/13/1987	9/1/1988	Dome Petroleum Ltd.	Oil and gas exploration production	CAN	Amoco Corp.	Oil and gas exploration, production	3,616
9	3/2/1998	4/30/1998	BTR PLC-Global Packaging & Materials	Mfr. packaging	AUS	Owens-Illinois	Mfr. glass, plastic containers	3,600
10	1/26/1998	3/3/1998	Noreen Energy Resources Ltd.	Oil and gas exploration production	CAN	Union Pacific Corp.	Oil and gas exploration, production	3,449
11	3/24/1999	6/1/1999	Bell Canada (BCE Inc.)	Telecomm. services	CAN	Ameritech Corp.	Telecomm. services	3,383
12	10/27/1997	1/20/1998	Tele Danmark A/S	Telecomm. services	DEN	Ameritech Corp.	Telecomm. services	3,160
13	10/16/1998	1/31/1999	Telus Corp.	Telecomm. equipment	CAN	Anglo-Canadian Telephone Co.	Telecomm. equipment	3,107
14	1/28/1999	6/30/1999	JDS Fitel Inc. (Furukawa Electric Co. Ltd.)	Fiberoptics components	JPN	Uniphase Corp.	Fiberoptics components	3,058
15	5/17/2001	8/6/2001	Grupo Financiero Banamex Accival SA	Bank	MEX	Citigroup Inc.	Insurance company	12,821
16	7/26/1999	5/30/2000	CWC ConsumerCo	Provide telecomm. services	UK	NTL Inc.	Provide communication services	11,004
17	4/11/2000	8/1/2000	Robert Fleming Holdings Ltd.	Merchant bank	UK	Chase Manhattan Corp.	Bank holding company	7,698
18	9/20/2001	3/14/2002	Westcoast Energy Inc.	Provider gas transmission services	CAN	Duke Energy Corp.	Electric utility	7,422
19	12/15/2000	3/2/2001	Knoll AG (BASF AG)	Mfr. pharmaceuticals	GER	Abbott Laboratories	Mfr. pharmaceuticals, med. equip.	6,900
20	5/29/2001	7/13/2001	Gulf Canada Resources Ltd.	Oil and gas exploration production	CAN	Conoco	Integrated oil company	6,300
21	2/12/2001	4/10/2001	Sema PLC	Computer consulting, software	UK	Schlumberger Ltd.	Energy services	5,300
22	11/19/1997	1/16/1998	Mercury Asset Management Group PLC	Investment management services	UK	Merrill Lynch & Co. Inc.	Financial services holding company	5,256
23	9/4/2001	11/8/2001	Anderson Exploration Ltd.	Oil and gas exploration production	CAN	Devon Energy Corp.	Oil and gas exploration, production	4,562
24	12/13/1999	3/28/2000	Cablecom Holding AG	Provider cable television services	SWI	NTL Inc.	Provider communication services	3,674
25	9/27/2000	12/12/2000	Pirelli SpA-Optical Compnts. and Devices	Mfr. optical components	ITA	Corning Inc.	Mfr. cable, fiber optic, glass	3,580
							TOTAL	$151,456

Source: Thomson Financial Services.

TABLE 17.4 Major International Cross-Border Transactions (non-U.S.)

	Date Announced	Date Effective	Target Name	Target Business Description	Target Nation	Acquirer Full Name	Acquirer Business Description	Acquirer Nation	Value of Transaction (in millions)
1	11/14/1999	6/19/2000	Mannesmann AG	Mobile telecomm.	GER	Vodafone Air Touch PLC	Mobile telecomm.	UK	$202,785
2	5/30/2000	8/22/2000	Orange PLC (Vodafone AirTouch PLC)	Mobile telecomm.	UK	France Telecom SA	Mobile telecomm.	FRA	45,967
3	6/20/2000	12/8/2000	Seagram Co. Ltd.	Mobile telecomm.	CAN	Vivendi SA	Water utility, electric utility	FRA	40,428
4	12/9/1998	4/19/1999	Astra AB	Mfr. pharmaceuticals	SWE	ZENECA Group PLC	Chemicals	UK	34,637
5	10/21/1999	1/12/2000	Orange PLC	Provide radiotelephone comm. services	UK	Mannesmann AG	Steel products	GER	32,595
6	5/17/1999	12/15/1999	Hoechst AG	Mfr. chemical and fibers	GER	Rhone-Poulenc SA	Mfr. chemicals and cosmetics	FRA	21,918
7	4/17/2000	10/16/2000	Allied Zurich PLC	Insurance company	UK	Zurich Allied AG	Insurance company and agency	SWI	19,399
8	10/13/1997	9/7/1998	BAT Industries PLC-Fin. Srvc. Ops.	Insurance agency, company	UK	Zurich Versicherungs GmbH	Insurance holding company	SWI	18,355
9	7/17/2000	12/29/2000	Airtel SA (increased stake)	Mobile telecomm.	SPA	Vodafone AirTouch PLC	Mobile telecomm.	UK	14,365
10	8/17/2001	2/16/2001	Viag Interkom GmbH & Co. (increased stake)	Mobile telecomm.	GER	British Telecommunication PLC	Mobile telecomm.	UK	13,813
11	7/28/1999	10/1/1999	One 2 One (Cable & Wireless, MediaOne Grp.)	Mobile telecomm.	UK	Deutsche Telecom AG	Mobile telecomm.	GER	13,629
12	4/29/1999	6/24/1999	YPF SA	Oil and gas exploration production	ARG	Repsol SA	Petroleum	SPA	13,152
13	12/1/1998	6/9/1999	Petrofina SA	Mfr. oil and petroleum	BEL	Total SA	Oil and gas exploration and production	FRA	12,769
14	3/19/2001	6/29/2001	Billiton PLC	Aluminum, zinc, nickel mining	UK	BHP Ltd.	Diversified mining company	AUS	11,511
15	4/1/2000	7/18/2000	Credit Commercial de France	Bank	FRA	HSBC Holdings PLC	Bank holding company	UK	11,100
16	2/15/2001	6/8/2001	De Beers Consolidated Mines Ltd.	Diamond mining	SAFR	DS Investments	Investment holding company	UK	11,078
17	5/21/1998	12/24/1998	Polygram NV (Philips Electronics)	Mfr. prerecorded records	NETH	Universal Studios Inc. (Seagram Co. Ltd.)	Motion pictures	CAN	10,236
18	1/13/2000	7/10/2000	Telecommunicacoes de Sao Paulo SA	Mobile telecomm.	BRA	Telefonica SA	Mobile telecomm.	SPA	10,213
19	5/26/1997	3/5/1998	Corange Ltd.	Mfr. pharmaceuticals	BER	Roche Holding AG	Mfr. pharmaceuticals	SWI	10,200
20	2/4/1999	6/27/1999	ABB AB	Mfr. electrical equipment	SWE	ABB AG	Mfr. electrolyzers, electrical equip.	SWI	9,812
21	12/10/1999	2/24/2000	E-Plus Mobilfunk GmbH (Vodafone AirTouch)	Mobile telecomm.	GER	BellSouth GmbH (KPN, BellSouth)	Mobile telecomm.	NETH	9,400
22	3/26/2001	9/17/2001	Cable & Wireless Optus Ltd. (Cable & Wireless)	Mobile telecomm.	AUS	Singapore Telecomm. Ltd.	Mobile telecomm.	SIN	8,481
23	2/2/1999	6/15/1999	Ing C Olivetti & Co. SpA-Telecom Interests	Mobile telecomm.	ITA	Mannesmann AG	Steel products	GER	8,404
24	8/19/1999	12/8/1999	Cies Reunies Electrobel et Tractionel	Electric and gas utility	BEL	Suez Lyonnaise des Eaux SA	Water utility	FRA	8,178
25	12/19/2000	12/21/2001	Seagram Co. – Alcohol & Spirit Division	Mfr. alcohol & spirits	CAN	Diageo PLC and Pernod Ricard SA	Investor group	UK	8,170
								TOTAL	$600,605

Source: Thomson Financial Services.

TABLE 17.5 Major Intranational Transactions (non-U.S.)

	Date Announced	Date Effective	Target Name	Target Nation	Target Business Description	Acquirer Full Name	Acquirer Business Description	Value of Transaction (in millions)
1	1/17/2000	12/27/2000	SmithKline Beecham PLC	UK	Mfr. pharmaceuticals	Glaxo Wellcome PLC	Mfr. pharmaceuticals	$ 75,961
2	7/5/1999	3/27/2000	Elf Aquitaine	FRA	Oil and gas exploration, production	Total Fina SA	Oil and gas exploration, production	50,070
3	10/13/1999	4/1/2001	Sakura Bank Ltd.	JPN	Bank	Sumitomo Bank Ltd.	Bank	45,494
4	8/20/1999	9/29/2000	Dai-Ichi Kangyo Bank Ltd.	JPN	Bank	Fuji Bank Ltd.	Commercial bank	40,097
5	11/29/1999	3/13/2000	National Westminster Bank PLC	UK	Bank holding company	Royal Bank of Scotland Group	Bank, bank holding company	38,525
6	2/29/2000	8/17/2000	Cable & Wireless HKT (Cable & Wireless)	HK	Provide telecomm. services	Pacific Century CyberWorks Ltd.	Internet service provider (ISP)	37,442
7	2/20/1999	5/21/1999	Telecom Italia SpA (stake)	ITA	Provide telecomm. services	Ing C Olivetti & Co. SpA	Provide telecomm. services, mfr. office equipment	34,758
8	3/27/1995	4/1/1996	Bank of Tokyo Ltd.	JPN	Bank	Mitsubishi Bank Ltd.	Bank	33,788
9	8/20/1999	9/29/2000	Industrial Bank of Japan Ltd. (IBJ)	JPN	Bank	Fuji Bank Ltd.	Commercial bank	30,760
10	3/7/1996	12/17/1996	Ciba-Geigy AG	SWI	Mfr. wholesale pharmaceutical products	Sandoz AG	Mfr. dyestuffs	30,090
11	8/28/1989	4/2/1990	Taiyo Kobe Bank Ltd.	JPN	Bank	Mitsui Bank Ltd.	Bank	23,017
12	12/8/1997	6/29/1998	Schweizerischer Bankverein	SWI	Bank; investment bank	Union Bank of Switzerland	Bank; investment bank	23,009
13	4/1/2001	7/20/2001	Dresdner Bank AG	GER	Bank	Allianz AG	Insurance company	19,656
14	3/16/2000	11/16/2000	Seat Pagine Gialle SPA	ITA	Publishing, Internet services	Telecom Italia SpA	Provide telecomm. sves.	18,206
15	5/12/1997	12/17/1997	Guinness PLC	UK	Produce beer; publish books	Grand Metropolitan PLC	Prod. milk, beer; own, op. pubs	15,968
16	8/30/1999	1/25/2000	Promodes	FRA	Own, operate grocery stores	Carrefour SA	Operate retail grocery stores	15,837
17	12/16/1999	10/1/2000	Kokusai Denshin Denwa Corp.	JPN	Provide telecomm. services	DDI Corp.	Provide telecomm. services	15,822
18	10/9/1995	12/28/1995	Lloyds Bank PLC	UK	Bank	TSB Group PLC	Bank	15,316
19	3/14/2000	4/1/2001	Tokai Bank Ltd.	JPN	Bank	Sanwa Bank Ltd.	Bank	14,984
20	5/4/2001	9/10/2001	Bank of Scotland PLC	UK	Bank	Halifax Group PLC	Provider financial sves.	14,904
21	1/20/1995	5/1/1995	Wellcome PLC	UK	Mfr. pharmaceuticals	Glaxo Holdings PLC	Mfr. pharmaceuticals	14,285
22	3/9/1999	8/6/1999	Paribas SA	FRA	Bank holding company	Banque Nationale de Paris	Bank	13,201
23	9/27/1999	6/16/2000	VIAG AG	GER	Electric utility; mfr. chemical	VEBA AG	Electric utility; holding company	13,153
24	1/19/1999	11/29/1999	Marconi Electronic Systems (General Electrical)	UK	Mfr. electronic equipment	British Aerospace PLC	Mfr. space vehicles, aircraft	12,863
25	5/31/1999	12/2/1999	Banca Commerciale Italiana SpA	ITA	Bank holding company	Banca Intesa SpA	Bank holding company	12,791
							TOTAL	$584,034

Source: Thomson Financial Services.

TABLE 17.6 Industrial Classification of Selected Cross-Border Mergers

Telecommunications
Vodafone-Mannesmann
Deutsche Telekom–VoiceStream Wireless
Vodafone–AirTouch Communications
Ameritech-TeleDanmark
Mannesmann-Olivetti (some units)
France Telecom–Orange
NTL–CWC Consumer

Media
Seagram-Polygram
Vivendi Universal–USA Networks (assets)
Matsushita Electric–MCA
Vivendi-Seagram

Financial
Aegon-TransAmerica
HSBC Holdings–Republic New York
Deutsche Bank–Bankers Trust
UBS-PaineWebber
GE Capital–Japan Leasing
Merrill Lynch–Mercury Asset Mgt.

Pharmaceuticals
Upjohn-Pharmacia
Abbott Labs–Knoll
Zeneca-Astra
Roche-Corange
Hoechst–Marion Merrell Dow
Beechman–Smithkline Beckman

Autos
Daimler Benz–Chrysler
Ford-Volvo (passenger vehicles)

Oil
BP Amoco–Atlantic Richfield
British Petroleum–Amoco
Total-Petrofina
Union Pacific–Norcen
Conoco–Gulf Canada

Packaging
Crown Cork–CarnaudMetalbox
Owens Illinois-BTR (assets)

Electric
National Grid–Niagara Mohawk
Scottish Power–PacifiCorp
Texas Utilities–Energy Group
Suez Lyonnaise–Tractebel

Food
Nestle–Ralston Purina
Unilever-Bestfoods
Diageo-Seagram (alcohol unit)

Retail
Wal-Mart–ASDA

Mining
BHP-Billion
DB Investments–De Beers

content of different media outlets. This is attractive and glamorous industry (attracted Japanese companies beginning in late-1980s)

3. Financial (investment banks, commercial banks, insurance companies): Globalization of industries and firms requires financial services firms to go global to serve their clients.

4. Chemicals and Pharmaceuticals: Both require extensive R&D but suffer rapid imitation. Chemicals become commodities. Pharmaceuticals enjoy a limited period of patent protection but are eroded by me-too drugs and generics. Changes in the technology of basic research and increased risks due to competitive pressures have created the stimulus for larger firms through M&As.

TABLE 17.7 Largest Recent Drug M&As

Target (country)	Acquirer (country)	Date Announced	Deal Value (in billions)
SmithKline Beecham (UK/U.S.)	Glaxo Wellcome (UK)	Jan. 17, 2000	$76
Warner-Lambert (U.S.)	Pfizer (U.S.)	Nov. 4, 1999	70
Astra (SWE)	Zeneca (UK)	Dec. 9, 1998	37
Ciba-Geigy (SWI)	Sandoz (SWI)	Mar. 7, 1996	30
Pharmacia & Upjohn (U.S.)	Monsanto (U.S.)	Dec. 20, 1999	23
Hoechst (GER)	Rhone-Poulenc (FRA)	Nov. 16, 1998	22
Wellcome (UK)	Glaxo (UK)	Jan. 20, 1995	14
Synthelabo (FRA)	Sanofi (FRA)	Dec. 2, 1998	11
Corange (GER)	Roche (SWI)	May 26, 1997	10
American Cyanamid (U.S.)	American Home (U.S.)	Aug. 2, 1994	10
Marion Merrell Dow (U.S.)	Hoechst (GER)	Feb. 28, 1995	7
Pharmacia (SWE)	Upjohn (U.S.)	Aug. 21, 1995	7
Knoll (GER)	Abbott Laboratories (U.S.)	Dec. 15, 2000	7

Source: Thomson Financial Services.

5. Autos, Oil and Gas, and Industrial Machinery: All face unique difficulties that give advantages to size, stimulating M&As to achieve critical mass. Autos face global excess capacity. Oil faces the uncertainty of price and supply instability due to actions of the OPEC cartel.
6. Utilities: Deregulation has created opportunities for economies from enlarging geographic areas. New kinds of competitive forces have created the need to broaden managerial capabilities.
7. Food, Retailing: Hampered by slow growth. Food consumption will grow only at the rate of population growth. Expanding internationally offers opportunities to grow in new markets.
8. Mining, Timber: Sources of supply are being exhausted. There are problems with matching raw material supplies with manufacturing capacity.

EXAMPLES OF CROSS-BORDER TRANSACTIONS

To convey further content and understanding of the forces operating in transnational M&As, we present summaries of some of the leading cross-border transactions organized by the three types covered in Tables 17.2, and 17.3, and 17.4.

DEUTSCHE TELEKOM AG–ONE2ONE
ANNOUNCED JULY 28, 1999; EFFECTIVE OCTOBER 1, 1999; $13.629 BILLION

Deutsche Telekom (DT) acquired One2One, Britain's smallest mobile telephone business, which was jointly owned by London-based Cable and Wireless and MediaOne Group. The deal allowed DT to shore up its presence in the changing European telecommunications arena as it sought to expand beyond the competitive German market into Britain and other high-growth regions.

The acquisition came after DT had suffered a serious blow to its international strategy when it failed to merge with Italian phone giant Telecom Italia SpA, a setback that also damaged its partnership with France Telecom S.A. DT was pressured to revise its strategy when France Telecom agreed to invest $5.5 billion in British cable operator NTL Inc. to gain a major foothold in the British telecommunications market.

DT and other telecom giants were attracted to the British market not only for the possibility of huge demands for their services but also for the prospects of technological innovation. Both Britain and Japan were in line to be among the first countries to offer the next generations of voice and data mobile phone services. These cutting-edge services would not be available for the next 3 or 4 years, but the British government planned to sell five licenses for such services by the end of 1999. By owning One2One, DT hoped to have an edge in acquiring one of those licenses.

FRANCE TELECOM SA–ORANGE PLC
ANNOUNCED MAY 30, 2000; EFFECTIVE AUGUST 22, 2000; $45.97 BILLION

When the German conglomerate Mannesmann purchased UK telecom Orange PLC in October of 1999 for a record $32.5 billion, it started a new wave of mergers and acquisitions in the European telecommunications market. Soon after the deal, UK telecom Vodafone made a play for Mannesmann in another record-breaking deal worth $203 billion. In order to appease European Union regulators who feared Vodaphone's oligopolistic dominace, Mannesmann was asked to divest itself of Orange. In addition, EU rules barred Vodafone from holding two UK mobile phone licenses at one time.

France Telecom faced difficulties when strong relations with former ally Deutsche Telekom dissolved and it lost bids for mobile licenses in Spain, in addition to its bid for control of German-owned E-Plus Mobilfunk. France Telecom's interest in Orange stemmed from Orange's extensive European network. At the same time, Vodafone needed to spin off Orange as a separate entity if it could not find a buyer quickly. The sale to France Telecom quickly provided Vodafone with the sorely needed cash for new mobile license purchases.

The deal launched France Telecom to a new level. By combining France Telecom and Orange's wireless operations, the new entity projected 30 million customers a year, second only to Vodafone in Europe. The transaction continued to give Vodafone a 9.9% indirect stake in France Telecom via Mannesmann in France, and the French company acquired 1.3% of Vodafone's shares in Mannesmann. The complex deal was sealed through a cash, share, and debt exchange. France Telecom paid Vodafone 55% of the acquisition price in cash ($20.7 billion) and the rest in France Telecom shares. France Telecom assumed $2.7 billion in debt and the $6.2 billion purchase of Orange's third-generation license in the UK. The transaction diluted the French government's 63% stake in its leading mobile carrier to 54%. By acquiring Orange, France Telecom finally gained footing in the British market and new wireless channels throughout the rest of the European Union.

DEUTSCHE BANK AG–BANKERS TRUST NEW YORK CORPORATION
ANNOUNCED NOVEMBER 30, 1998; EFFECTIVE JUNE 4, 1999; $9.082 BILLION

Deutsche Bank's (DB) dominant position in Germany had eroded from increasing competition and from the big American investment banks taking over the lucrative work advising large European companies. DB needed to expand its investment banking business, which was badly battered by its ill-considered acquisition of Morgan Grenfell, and it needed to compete in the United States, the world's largest capital market.

The acquisition of Bankers Trust (BT) secured a foothold in the United States. BT had a middle-rank investment banking firm, BT Alex Brown, with a strong reputation in underwriting young, high-tech companies. BT also had a sizable business issuing high-yield bonds.

The deal created the world's largest financial services company. The firm became a global leader in leveraged finance and one of the largest issuers of high-yield bonds. Its portfolio included one of the largest global custody and processing business as well as a huge asset-management operation.

The new company could reap the benefits of an expanding European market for new stocks and high-yield corporate bond issues for smaller companies, especially as the advent of a common currency was expected to boost European securities issuance and trading volume. High-yield bonds also were attracting new interest as more European companies underwent management buyouts.

UBS AG–PAINEWEBBER GROUP
ANNOUNCED JULY 12, 2000; EFFECTIVE NOVEMBER 3, 2000; $16.542 BILLION

After several years of tumultuous scandal, re-invention, and change, UBS AG, a Swiss global, integrated investment services firm and bank, set out to improve its image worldwide and establish itself as a serious European player in the U.S. market. UBS AG had been searching for the right acquisition to extend its global infrastructure into the United States and was strongly attracted to PaineWebber's substantial retail distribution platform. Through PaineWebber's platform, UBS was able to capitalize on synergies relating to the sales of fixed income and structured products and derivatives including the ability to provide investors with new access to IPOs and convertibles. The merger created a stronger equity presence for both companies.

The companies believed that synergies also could be realized by using the expanded retail base as an audience for its bond underwriting program. Like Morgan Stanley, UBS AG now has a good audience for its electronic bond offerings. PaineWebber brought 2.7 million new clients to UBS's customer franchise and approximately $490 billion in client assets. PaineWebber shareholders received $73.50 per share in cash or 0.4954 of UBS shares for every PaineWebber share. The merger helped boost product offerings, increase distribution, and increase assets under management.

With the purchase of PaineWebber, UBS also was able to improve its equity profile. PaineWebber provided UBS with an elite client base in the United States. and access to middle-American investors through PaineWebber's strong brand name recognition. With PaineWebber's strong Main Street presence, UBS could emulate the Merrill Lynch and Morgan Stanley Dean Witter models, which succeeded in becoming household names by launching major media campaigns directed at the average investor.

RHONE-POULENC SA–HOECHST AG
ANNOUNCED NOVEMBER 16, 1998; EFFECTIVE DECEMBER 15, 1999; $21.918 BILLION

The merger created Aventis SA, the world's largest life sciences company. It became the number 1 agrochemical company and one of the world's biggest pharmaceutical firms. By joining forces, the two companies could achieve the critical mass necessary to sustain an ambitious R&D program and the global marketing muscle to push new drugs. The projected annual cost savings of more than $1 billion would allow them to continue their profit growth until promising new drugs were in the pipeline. The size of the combined company could attract a U.S. partner on an equal footing if they decided to boost their presence in the American pharmaceuticals market.

Both companies were disposing of their industrial chemical operations in an attempt to narrow their strategic focus to life sciences. Hoechst planned to spin off its industrial chemical operation as a separate company named Celanese AG.

DAIMLER-BENZ–CHRYSLER
ANNOUNCED MAY 7, 1998; EFFECTIVE NOVEMBER 12, 1998; $40.467 BILLION

As the automobile industry entered a period of brutal competition, Daimler-Benz and Chrysler were trying to become a full-line global automobile company. The merger signified huge economies of scale in engineering and purchasing, broader complementary product lines, and a worldwide network of manufacturing and distribution.

They combined the famous Mercedes-Benz line of luxury sedans and limousines with Chrysler's mass-market cars and light trucks, including pickups, minivans, and sport utility vehicles. Daimler was known for its engineering and technical knowhow. Chrysler had design and production expertise. The combination gave Daimler a huge U.S. distribution network that the company had lacked. Chrysler obtained a much stronger base in Europe, where it had 1% of the Western European market compared to 12% each for GM and Ford. Substantial cost savings would come from combined purchasing operations, economies of scale in automobile components, and combined technical product developments.

FORD MOTOR COMPANY–VOLVO AB-WORLD WIDE PASSENGER VEHICLE BUSINESS
ANNOUNCED JANUARY 28, 1999: EFFECTIVE MARCH 31, 1999; $6.45 BILLION

The automotive industry was in a period of fierce consolidations and competition. Ford Motor Company was the world's most profitable car and truck manufacturer. It was the largest pickup-truck maker and the second-ranked producer of cars and trucks, behind General Motors. Brands under its control included Aston Martin, Ford, Jaguar, Lincoln, and Mercury. On the heels of the enormous Daimler-Benz–Chrysler merger, Ford looked to acquire a company that would help it intensify competition in the luxury market and shore up its market presence in Europe. In March of 1999, it completed a purchase of Volvo AB-World Wide Passenger Vehicle Business.

In this large, cross-border transaction, Ford expanded its economies of scale through its ability to use Ford parts in Volvos and expanded delivery of all brands through Ford's extensive distribution network. Ford acquired a distinctive brand in the medium-priced luxury category that appealed to a younger baby boomer and more affluent suburban audience. Traditionally, the Ford name had been synonymous with the middle-class American buyer. Even with the acquisition of Jaguar, Ford lacked a strong presence in the more moderate luxury arena. Volvo's reputation for quality, safety, and environmental responsibility were important to Ford's profile. Synergies also helped Volvo, the second-largest manufacturer of heavy-duty trucks. Ford's share in the European auto market moved from 10.2% to 11.9%, from sixth place to second, trailing only behind Volkswagen AG. The merger signaled a continued trend toward restructuring in the global auto sector and placed pressure on remaining European auto manufacturers to consolidate.

BRITISH PETROLEUM CORPORATION PLC–AMOCO CORPORATION. ANNOUNCED AUGUST 11, 1998; EFFECTIVE DECEMBER 31, 1998; $48.174 BILLION

The merger of BP and Amoco came at a time of low oil and chemical prices. Oil companies were struggling to boost their profits but were unable to increase production or find additional ways to cut costs. The merger added more oil reserves and assets from which to squeeze out costs.

BP got Amoco's large reserves of oil and gas, which would have taken BP an extraordinary amount of time and capital to accumulate. The two companies were complementary. Amoco had lots of gas, and BP had lots of oil. Amoco brought in its U.S. presence, and BP had extensive international assets. Amoco was the largest natural gas producer in North America and had a vast U.S. gasoline marketing network. BP had a huge worldwide exploration and production operation and a strong European retail network.

The two companies could do more together than they could as stand-alone firms and could do it more efficiently. There were plenty of possibilities for synergy: There would be cost reductions from the elimination of duplicate operations, BP could bring its expertise in deepwater exploration and production to Amoco's fields in the Gulf of Mexico, and BP could combine its cheaper finding cost with Amoco's lower development costs. The cost savings were projected to amount to $2 billion annually by the end of 2000.

The size of the new company made it comparable to Exxon and Royal Dutch. It could give BP even greater market clout, enabling it to finance more development, keep costs down, and help win more auctions of oil reserves.

TOTAL SA–PETROFINA SA
ANNOUNCED DECEMBER 1, 1998; EFFECTIVE JUNE 9, 1999; $12.77 BILLION

In a year marked by megamergers in the petroleum sector, the merger between Belgian oil group Petrofina SA and French oil group Total SA saw the creation of the fifth-biggest oil group in the world. Weak oil prices and industry consolidations put pressure on oil companies to seek mergers to capitalize on greater economies of scale. Total and its French rival Elf Aquitaine engaged in a bidding war over the Belgian concern. After several rounds of bidding. Total paid a premium price of $12.77 billion in a cash and 9-for-2 stock swap for Petrofina.

Petrofina, though midsize, was a strong presence in refining and marketing and continued to outperform companies in its peer group. In addition, it had strong links to the petrochemical industry. This was a solid complement to Total, a company with a concentration on oil, coal, and uranium reclamation and exploration.

The new entity, under the name Totalfina, sold off nonstrategic assets to finance its development program for exploration and production and was able to combine its refining capacity to 1.6 million barrels per day. It immediately realized cost savings by streamlining business ventures, office integration, tax benefit optimization, and improvement in financing charges linked through Total's superior, long-term debt rating.

The deal was almost derailed when the companies filed for EU regulatory approval. The companies withdrew notification when they suspected that the commission would launch a full investigation, potentially delaying or rejecting approval. By making modifications in the fuel-storage arena, Total negotiated approval with the commission, and the EU authorities approved the merger shortly before the deal closed.

UNION PACIFIC RESOURCES GROUP–NORCEN ENERGY RESOURCES LIMITED
ANNOUNCED JANUARY 26, 1998; EFFECTIVE MARCH 3, 1998; $3.449 BILLION

Canada's weak currency had made acquisition opportunities much more attractive. In addition to the lower acquisition prices, Canada's energy businesses received much of their revenues in U.S. dollars although their expenses were in Canadian dollars.

Union Pacific Resources, an independent oil and gas company, acquired the Canadian oil producer Norcen Energy. Union Pacific Resources was trying to diversify its reserve portfolio. After its failed attempt to acquire Pennzoil, the weakness of the Canadian dollar allowed it greater leverage in its bid for Norcen. The deal gave Union extensive oil and natural gas reserves in western Canada and the Gulf of Mexico, and exploration acreage in Venezuela and Guatemala. This represented a doubling of its reserves, access to international operations, and a lessening of investor fear that Union's aggressive drilling and production strategy would deplete the capital needed to replace reserves over the long run.

SCOTTISH POWER PLC–PACIFICORP
ANNOUNCED DECEMBER 7, 1998; EFFECTIVE NOVEMBER 30, 1999; $12.60 BILLION

The deal represented the first major foreign acquisition of a U.S. electric utility. It was driven by global liberalization of electricity markets. Scottish Power became one of the world's 10 largest electricity and utility companies. The company has been looking to acquire a U.S. utility for some time. Its officials believed that the United States was 4 to 5 years behind the United Kingdom in deregulating its power markets and that the U.S. industry was ripe for consolidation. Deregulation activity also was occurring in continental Europe, but Scottish Power believed the U.S. market offered better potential.

TEXAS UTILITIES CORPORATION–ENERGY GROUP PLC
ANNOUNCED MARCH 2, 1998; EFFECTIVE AUGUST 19, 1998; $10.947 BILLION

As the U.S. market continued to deregulate, U.S. electric utilities were trying to find new sources of revenues as they were forced to open their service area to competitors. U.S. electric utilities had been purchasing British utilities since the United Kingdom privatized the industry in 1990. They were looking for cash-rich utilities in a more relaxed regulatory environment with high growth prospects.

Texas Utilities decided to enter the UK market for the first time. The deal allowed it to become a major player in Britain, which opened its electricity market to full retail competition in late 1998. Texas Utilities was able to bid successfully over another American suitor, PacifiCorp. The acquisition doubled Texas Utilities's revenues and gave it the necessary marketing muscle to compete in Britain and possibly enter into other European markets.

NESTLE SA–RALSTON PURINA
ANNOUNCED JANUARY 15, 2001; EFFECTIVE DECEMBER 12, 2001; $10.479 BILLION

Swiss food giant Nestle's acquisition of Ralston Purina created the largest, publicly owned, pet-food producer. Already the world's largest human-food company, Nestle wanted to shore up its 12% share in the pet-food market by acquiring Ralston Purina, which had strong annual sales of $2.76 billion and 27% control of the pet-food market. The deal came during a flurry of food-industry consolidations, and signaled a commitment by the two companies to capitalize on growth trends in the dog- and cat-food industry. Analysts speculated that dog and cat food were the two highest-growth areas in the food industry, with overall sales increasing 5% in 2000 alone. The longer-term growth estimate was seen as a possible 6.5% annually, twice as fast as the projected growth figure for the human-food sector. Trends indicated that the pet-food industry, unlike the human-food sector, was generally impervious to market downfalls: Trends saw owners as resistant to shortchanging their pets even in tougher economic times. Nestle paid 36% over Ralston's final previous closing price in an all-cash $33.50-per-share deal, or $10.48 billion. The street believed that at 15 times earnings before interest, taxes, depreciation, and amortization (EBITDA), it was a fair price considering the potential synergies between the two companies. Ralston Purina had become more attractive when it spun off its Energizer division. The acquisition clearly signaled Nestle's targeted desire to accelerate dominance, growth, and performance in the pet-food market.

The deal resulted in combined yearly sales of $6.3 billion. By combining their market power, they wanted to present a full line of strong brands including Puppy Chow, Tender Vittles, Purina One, Friskies, and Alpo through which they could dominate supermarket shelf space and gain added influence with retailers while cutting expenses in distribution and product development.

WAL-MART STORES INCORPORATED–ASDA GROUP PLC
ANNOUNCED JUNE 14, 1999; EFFECTIVE AUGUST 20, 1999; $10.805 BILLION

Wal-Mart, the giant retailer, was trying to gain critical mass outside the United States. Wal-Mart had expanded to several countries but had not achieved a dominant position except in Mexico and Canada. The acquisition of the British supermarket chain ASDA Group gave it a strong presence in Europe and fulfilled its long-standing goal of doubling its international business. Wal-Mart achieved immediate economies of scale and got a chain of stores with a nearly identical operating strategy. The deal shifted European retailing to a more efficient, low-price, long-hours model that could allow Wal-Mart to dominate its competitors.

FORCES DRIVING CROSS-BORDER MERGERS

The data and examples just presented provide a basis for identifying the major forces driving cross-border mergers. Some of the forces are similar to those for purely domestic transactions, whereas others apply more strongly to international M&As. We first outline 10 major forces to serve as a road map for the discussion that follows.

1. Growth
2. Technology
3. Advantages in differentiated products
4. Roll ups
5. Consolidation
6. Government policy

7. Exchange rates
8. Political and economic stability
9. Following clients
10. Diversification

GROWTH

Growth is the most important motive for international mergers, and it is vital to the well-being of any firm. Mergers provide instant growth, and merging internationally adds a whole new dimension to this instant growth. The size of a market and the growth rates of markets are relevant for achieving growth objectives. The United States had long been highly regarded by foreign firms for exports, direct investment, and M&As because of its large and attractive markets. Firms in the United States have looked abroad to countries in relatively earlier stages of their life cycles, characterized by industries with rates of growth higher than in the United States. This has been especially true of U.S. food companies.

Leading firms in the domestic market might have lower costs because of economies of scale. Overseas expansion might enable medium-size firms to attain the size necessary to improve their ability to compete. Finally, even with the most efficient management and technology, the globalization of world markets requires a critical size level to even be able to carry out worldwide operations. Size enables firms to achieve the economies of scale necessary for effective global competition. Most of the firms listed in Table 17.6, whose characteristics were conveyed in our summary descriptions, were motivated by growth objectives in their international M&As.

TECHNOLOGY

Technological considerations impact international mergers in two ways: (1) a technologically superior firm may make acquisitions abroad to exploit its technological advantage, or (2) a technologically inferior firm may acquire a foreign target with superior technology to enhance its competitive position at home and abroad. It is generally accepted that for an investment project (in this case, the acquisition of a foreign firm) to be acceptable, the present value of benefits must exceed the present value of costs. If an asset (the target firm) is priced correctly, the present value of benefits should equal the present value of costs. For positive net present values to occur, an acquiring firm must be able to buy the target for less than the present value of its benefits (the target must be underpriced) or be able to increase the present value of future benefits. It is unlikely that target firms are systematically underpriced (even if they were, underpricing would be more difficult to detect in foreign firms in an unfamiliar market than in domestic firms). Hence, the acquiring firm must bring something to the target that will increase the present value of benefits, or the target firm must bring something to the acquirer that enables the combined benefits of the merged firm to be greater than the sum of what the individual firms could have achieved separately. It must exhibit synergy.

In domestic mergers, increased benefits often result when the superior management efficiency of the acquiring firm is applied to the target firm's assets. In international mergers, the acquiring firm might have an advantage in general management functions such as planning and control or research and development. However, capabilities in specific management functions such as marketing or labor relations, for example, tend to be environment specific and are not readily transferred to different surroundings. Such factors might help explain the predominance of the United Kingdom and Canada as international merger partners of the United States; that is, the common language and heritage and similar business practices minimize the drawbacks, making such skills more transferable. Likewise, note that none of the 25 large, non-U.S. cross-border transactions involved European firms merging with Asian firms.

Technological superiority, on the other hand, is a far more portable advantage and can be exploited more easily without a lot of cultural baggage. The acquirer might deliberately select a technologically inferior target that, because of this inferiority, is losing market share and thus market value. By injecting technology into the acquired firm, the acquirer can improve its competitive position and profitability at home and abroad. Most of the firms in our sample also were strongly motivated by technology considerations. Some sought to buy into foreign markets to exploit their technological knowledge advantage. The Wal-Mart–ASDA transaction is an example. By using its superior inventory technologies, Wal-Mart could achieve lower prices. This would be a basis for expansion into widening foreign markets.

A primary motive for cross-border transactions is to acquire new technologies. This was true of many of the chemical, pharmaceutical, oil, and auto mergers. Renault's investment in Nissan was motivated in part by the desire to learn some of Nissan's manufacturing techniques, as well as to establish a presence in Japan.

ADVANTAGES IN DIFFERENTIATED PRODUCTS

A strong correlation exists between multinationalization and product differentiation (Caves, 1982). This may indicate an application of the parent's (acquirer's) good reputation. A firm that has developed a reputation for superior products in the domestic market might find acceptance for the products in foreign markets, as well. In the 1920s, the early days of the U.S. automobile industry, cars were exported to Europe in large numbers. This was before the auto industry was developed in European countries. The advantage of the U.S. mass-production facilities and know-how made the American cars cheaper despite the high foreign tariffs and motivated foreign direct investments. The tables were then turned. First, Volkswagens came from Germany to the United States. Then cars from Japan became widely accepted in the United States. Later, manufacturing operations were established by foreign makers in the United States. In the other direction, Ford's acquisition of Jaguar brought modern assembly lines and other production systems to achieve improved design, quality, and costs to the Jaguar operations.

ROLL UPS

Roll ups to combine firms in fragmented industries have been taking place within the United States, as well as internationally. US Filter had achieved a roll up of water-improvement facilities in the United States. In early 1999 U.S. Filter was acquired by Vivendi, a French conglomerate. Similar motives appear to be at work in the energy industry, as exemplified by Scottish Power's acquisition of PacifiCorp. The acquisition by Texas Utilities of the UK Energy Group in 1998 reflected deregulation of energy markets, which created opportunities for energy industry roll ups abroad as well as in the United States.

CONSOLIDATION

The ultimate aim of consolidation M&As has been to reduce worldwide excess capacity. The Daimler-Chrysler merger is a prime example.

GOVERNMENT POLICY

Government policy, regulation, tariffs, and quotas can affect international mergers and acquisitions in a number of ways. Exports are particularly vulnerable to tariffs and quotas erected to protect domestic industries. Even the threat of such restrictions can encourage international mergers, especially when the market to be protected is large. Japan's huge export surplus, which led to voluntary export restrictions coupled with threats of more binding restrictions, was a major factor in increased direct investment by Japan in the United States.

Environmental and other governmental regulations (such as zoning, for example) can greatly increase the time and cost required to build facilities abroad for de novo entry. The added cost of compliance with regulation amplifies other effects that may be operating. Thus, the rationale for acquiring a company with existing facilities in place is reinforced by regulation.

The Deutsche Telekom acquisition of One2One is an example of the many influences of government policy. Deutsche Telekom had been a monopoly protected by the German government. German deregulation created competition from international and German firms. Similarly, Deutsche Telekom acquired One2One because of the possibility of purchasing a coveted mobile phone license from the British government. The influence of government policy also is reflected in the European Union's decision to open previously regulated industries, such as electric utilities, to competition.

EXCHANGE RATES

Foreign exchange rates affect international mergers in a number of ways. The relative strength or weakness of the domestic versus foreign currency can have an impact on the effective price paid for an acquisition, its financing, production costs of running the acquired firm, and the value of repatriated profits to the parent. Accounting conventions can give rise to currency translation profits and losses. Managing exchange rate risk is an additional cost of doing business for a multinational firm. The acquisitions by Union Pacific Resources and the CIT Group (both U.S. companies) of Canadian firms were facilitated by the decline in the value of the Canadian dollar in 1998 and 1999.

POLITICAL AND ECONOMIC STABILITY

The relative political and economic stability of the United States has been an important factor in attracting foreign buyers. Political and economic instability can increase greatly the risk of what is already a riskier situation than purely domestic investments or acquisitions. Acquiring firms must consider the frequency with which the government changes, how orderly the transfer of power is, and how much government policies differ from one administration to the next, including the degree of difference between the dominant political parties. They must assess the likelihood of government intervention on the upside and the downside (for example, subsidies, tax breaks, loan guarantees, and so forth, on the one hand, all the way to outright expropriation on the other hand).

Desirable economic factors include low, or at least predictable, inflation. Labor relations are another important consideration in economic stability. Western European labor unions appear to have a greater voice in the management of companies than do American unions.

The United States excels in virtually every measure of economic and political stability (except exchange rate uncertainty in early 2003). It is also a superior target because of the size and homogeneity of the market and the sophistication of the infrastructure. Transportation and communications networks in the United States are among the best in the world; the depth and breadth of U.S. financial markets are attractive; there is little risk of expropriation. Indeed, most states offer inducements to investment, and the labor force is relatively skilled and tractable. The high levels of foreign acquisitions described in Table 17.2 provide many examples.

FOLLOWING CLIENTS

The importance of long-term financial relationships is a major factor in international mergers in the financial services industry. If enough of a financial firm's clients move abroad, it makes economic sense for the firm to expand abroad, as well. Foreign firms abroad might want to remain loyal to their long-standing, home country banks. However, if a financial firm does not have offices available for servicing its clients, it runs the risk of losing business to more convenient, local financial firms.

For some time, foreign financial services firms operating in the United States had an advantage over U.S. firms, especially in interstate banking, in that they were allowed to have branches in more than one state (with restrictions), whereas this was denied to U.S. banks. Over the years, the playing field has become more equal. Because of their weak presence in the United States, especially in investment banking, Deutsche Bank acquired Bankers Trust and UBS acquired PaineWebber. Similarly, Ownes-Illinois's foreign acquisitions were made in part to support their major industrial customer as they expanded their businesses worldwide.

DIVERSIFICATION

International mergers can provide diversification geographically and by product line. To the extent that various economies are not perfectly correlated, merging internationally reduces the earnings risk inherent in being dependent on the health of a single domestic economy. Thus, international mergers can reduce systematic as well as nonsystematic risk. The cross-border oil mergers have provided geographic diversification, as well as opportunities for reducing excess capacity, increasing efficiency to reduce costs, and achieving the larger size required by global operations.

PREMIUMS PAID

Academic studies as well as the *Mergerstat* data show that foreign bidders pay higher premiums to acquire U.S. companies than the average of premiums paid in total acquisitions. In the Harris and Ravenscraft (1991) study of a sample of companies between 1970 and 1987, foreign bidders paid higher premiums by 10 percentage points. They found also that high foreign currency values led to increased premiums. Their data show that when foreign firms buy U.S. firms, they concentrate on research and development intensive industries. They found that the R&D intensity of foreign acquisitions is 50% higher than in purely domestic transactions. The Harris and Ravenscraft study found also that U.S. bidders earn only normal returns in both domestic and cross-border acquisitions. These results are consistent with other studies of bidder and target returns.

In Table 17.8, we pick up with 1987, the final year of the Harris and Ravenscraft study. A simple average of the percentages in Table 17.8 shows that the premiums in foreign acquisitions exceeded the average of all acquisitions by about four percentage points. One reason offered as an explanation is that foreign buyers offer higher premiums to preempt potential domestic bid-

TABLE 17.8 Mean Premium in Foreign vs. Total Announcements, 1987–2001

Year	Foreign Acquisitions	All Acquisitions
1987	39.4%	38.3%
1988	56.2	41.9
1989	38.9	41.0
1990	48.1	42.0
1991	39.8	35.1
1992	54.1	41.0
1993	41.8	38.7
1994	46.2	41.9
1995	41.9	44.7
1996	47.8	36.6
1997	33.0	35.7
1998	45.2	40.7
1999	43.2	43.3
2000	53.8	49.2
2001	60.0	57.2
1987–2001 average	46.0%	41.8%

Source: Mergerstat Review, 2002.

ders. Another possible reason is that U.S. targets have less knowledge of foreign buyers and need a higher premium to resolve some uncertainty. A third possible influence is that prospective future exchange rate movements give an edge to the U.S. dollar.

EVENT RETURNS

An early study (Doukas and Travlos, 1988) found that the announcement of international acquisitions was associated with positive abnormal returns for U.S. multinational enterprises that previously had not been operating in the target firm's country. When American firms expand internationally for the first time, the event returns are positive but not significant. When the American firm already has been operating in the target firm's home country, the event returns are negative but not significant. Shareholders of multinational enterprises gain the greatest benefits from foreign acquisitions when there is simultaneous diversification across industries and geographically.

Harris and Ravenscraft (1991) investigated shareholder returns for 1,273 U.S firms acquired during the period 1970 to 1987. They found that in 75% of cross-border transactions, the buyer and seller were not in related industries and that the takeovers were more frequent than domestic transactions in R&D-intensive industries. The percentage gain to the U.S. targets of foreign buyers was significantly higher than to the targets of U.S. buyers. The cross-border effects were positively related to the weakness of the U.S. dollar, indicating an important role for exchange movements in foreign direct investment.

A study of Japanese takeovers of U.S. firms (Kang, 1993) found that significant wealth gains are created for both Japanese bidders and U.S. targets. Returns to Japanese bidders and to a portfolio of Japanese bidders and U.S. targets increased with the leverage of the bidder, the bidder's ties to financial institutions, and the depreciation of the dollar in relation to the Japanese yen. A study that controlled for relative corporate wealth and levels of investment in different countries found no statistically significant relationship between exchange rate levels and foreign investment relative to domestic investment in the U.S. chemical and retail industries (Dewenter, 1995).

Eun, Kolodny, and Scheraga (1996) studied 225 foreign acquisitions of U.S. firms that occurred during the period 1979 to 1990. For an 11-day event window, (–5, +5), the CAR was 37.02% for the whole sample of U.S. targets, significant at the 1% level. Those acquired by firms from countries other than Japan were similar, with a CAR between 35% and 37% Cakici, Hessel, and Tandon (1996) examined the wealth gains for 195 foreign firms that acquired U.S. target firms during the period 1983 to 1992 compared to a sample of 112 U.S. acquisitions of foreign firms during the same period. The foreign acquiring firms experienced positive CARs of 0.63% for a 2-day period, (0, +1), and 1.96% over a (–10, +10) window, both significant at the 1% level. Meanwhile, the U.S. acquirers had negative CARs of –0.36% and –0.25%, respectively, neither being significant.

Doukas (1995) used a sample consisting of 234 U.S. bidding firms involved in 463 international acquisitions over the period 1975 to 1989 to study the relationship between bidders shareholders gains and their q-ratios. The sample was divided into value maximizers and overinvestors based on Tobin's q. The 2 day (–1, 0) CAR for firms with average q-ratios greater than 1 (value-maximizing firms) was 0.41%, significant at the 5% level. Bidders with average q-ratios less than 1 (overinvested firms) had a negative CAR of –0.18%, not significant. The difference was significant at the 1% level. The impact of exchange rates was consistent with Froot and Stein's (1991) hypothesis of a negative relationship between the dollar exchange rate and the level of foreign direct investment. The method of payment and industry relatedness did not appear to be significant.

Seth, Song, and Pettit (2000) studied a sample of 100 cross-border acquisitions of U.S. targets during 1981 to 1990. The average CAR of acquirers was 0.11% for an event window (–10, +10), not statistically significant. For targets, the average CAR was 38.3%, significant at the 1% level. Hudgins and Seifert (1996) looked at the announcement gains and losses for a sample of 88 American acquirers and 72 American targets involved in cross-border transactions of financial firms during 1968 to 1989. Announcement effects for U.S. financial firms acquiring foreign firms were not significant and were not statistically different from the effects experienced by U.S. financial firms acquiring domestic firms. Target shareholder of foreign bids gained significant positive returns of 9.2%.

Markides and Oyon (1998) used a sample of 236 acquisitions made by U.S. companies in the period 1975 to 1998. The total sample consisted of 189 U.S. acquisitions in Europe and 47 U.S. acquisitions in Canada. Using standard event-study. methodology, they found significant but small gains for the acquiring firms. For a 2-day event window (–1, 0) the acquirers' CAR for the whole sample was 0.38%, significant at the 5% level. However, the gains came from continental European acquisitions, a CAR of 0.47% significant at the 10% level. Canadian and British acquisitions created no significant value for the acquiring U.S firms. Wider event windows, (–5, +5) and (–10, +10), yielded positive nonsignificant CARs for all cases.

In one study, Eckbo and Thorburn (2000) examined 390 acquisitions of Canadian targets by U.S. acquirers over the period 1962 to 1983 and documented negative (–0.19 percent) and insignificant abnormal returns during the month of the merger announcement.

Finally, a paper by Moeller and Schlingemann (2002) used a large sample of 4,430 mergers between 1985 and 1995 to compare and contrast cross-border acquisitions from domestic acquisitions for U.S. acquirers. Moeller and Schlingemann found that U.S. acquirers realize significantly lower stock returns and operating performance for cross-border acquisitions than for domestic acquisitions.

Event studies involving U.S. buyers of foreign targets and foreign buyers of U.S. targets gave results similar to those of domestic transactions. Targets received large abnormal returns regardless of the direction of the transactions. Buyers similarly earned nonsignificant percentage returns regardless of whether they were U.S. firms of foreign firms engaged in cross-border acquisitions.

INTERNATIONAL JOINT VENTURES

International joint ventures magnify the potentials and the weaknesses of joint ventures. In general, joint ventures should involve complementary capabilities. The risks posed by different cultural systems among firms from different countries might increase the tensions normally found in joint ventures.

Despite the increased challenges of international joint ventures, the advantages of joint ventures can be expanded. Some of the particular benefits of international joint ventures may be noted (Zahra and Elhagrasey, 1994): (1) The joint venture might be the only feasible method for obtaining access to raw material. (2) Different historical backgrounds and different managerial and technological skill might be associated with firms in different countries. International joint ventures, therefore, may involve different capabilities and link together complementary skills. (3) Having local partners may reduce the risks involved in operating in a foreign country. (4) The joint ventures might be necessary to overcome trade barriers. In addition, some of the advantages of domestic joint ventures might be enhanced. These include the achievement of economies of scale in providing a basis for a faster rate of corporate growth.

Management style may be different for companies from different countries. However, it appears that over time there has been increasing convergence of western and Asian management styles(Swierczek and Hirsch, 1994). In the past, the basic values of western management emphasized the individual, legal rules, and confrontation. In contrast, the Asian approach emphasized the group, trust, and compromise. With regard to management style, the western approach was emphasized by rationally and structured relationships. The Asian approach involved relationships, consensus, flexibility, and adaptive behavior. Over time, however, a convergence of the different management styles has been taking place.

Because of the complexity of relationships of international joint ventures, some principles have been suggested for the management of successful collaborations (Shaughnessy, 1995). Because joint ventures are a temporary alliance for combining complementary capabilities, joint venture contracts should make it easy to terminate the relationship. The initial contract should take into account which firm will become the outright owner of the joint venture activity and formulate the terms under which one company can buy out the other. The control and ultimate decision makers should be specified in advance. The activities and information flows in the joint venture should be tied into normal communication structures.

Criteria for evaluation of performance should be part of the contractual relationship. Because of the inherent uncertainties of the future alternative outcomes, scenarios should be visualized as a basis for allocation of rewards and responsibilities under different types of outcomes. Finally, it is in the international area particularly that the knowledge acquisition potential of joint ventures can be substantial. However, contractual differences might also put these potentials at considerable risk of failure of realization.

A study of 88 international joint venture announcements found statistically significant positive portfolio excess returns (Chen, Hu, and Shieh, 1991) when U.S. firms invested relatively small amounts in joint ventures that gained significantly positive excess returns. When firms made relatively large investments in the joint ventures, the positive excess returns were no longer significant.

An in-depth,book-length study of joint ventures in the steel industry documents the diverse motives and effects (Mangum, Kim, and Tallman, 1996). These authors placed the steel industry in the setting of an industrial staircase that moves from the agrarian age to an industrial age and finally to the present information age. The steel industry is put in the setting of a basic intermediate product with a capital resource emphasis. Summary data are provided on the investments by 17 foreign steel-makers in U.S. joint ventures. The foreign partners are mainly from Japan. In-depth case studies of seven joint ventures in steel are presented. The initial motive was the availability of foreign capital for modernizing the U.S. steel industry. Another important objective was to transfer the superior process technologies of the Asian partners to American plants. Cross-cultural differences added to the tensions usually found in joint ventures. Nevertheless Mangum et al. judge the joint ventures to be generally successful. The only joint venture that experienced great difficulties was the combination between NKK of Japan and the National Steel Corporation of the United States. NKK was Japan's second-largest steel producer but accounted for only 15% of Japan's total output of finished steel, compared with 72% for number-one Nippon Steel. National Steel had been formed in 1929 and was number seven in the United States. In the fall of 1983, it reorganized itself as National Intergroup Incorporated (NII), announcing that it would withdraw from the steel business and diversify into pharmaceuticals, aluminum, financial services, and computer services. Early in 1984, NII sold its Weirton works to its employees under an ESOP. It offered the remainder of its steelmaking facilities to USX. However, the Department of Justice blocked the sale on antitrust grounds.

Among the alternatives, the joint venture with NKK seemed the least unpalatable. NKK considered itself to be a world leader in steel technology but was unable to exploit its capabilities fully because of domestic overcapacity and rising obstacles to international trade. The joint venture with NII was viewed as the first step in its broader globalization plans. Despite considerable progress, the economic downturn in the United States in 1989 and 1990 caused losses. National Steel made a public offering of common stock as a device for NII to sell its ownership to the public. NKK's ownership share moved from 50% to 75%. NII "bailed out" of the joint venture. NKK took over ownership in an effort to restore its profitability. Net income of $168.5 million was achieved in 1994. Mangum et al. concluded, that although the joint venture came asunder, National Steel survived under a new management team.

Desai, Foley, and Hines (2002) provided a comprehensive analysis of international joint ventures by U.S. firms that reveals a marked decline in activity during the period 1982 to 1997. In that prior surveys had documented a positive trend in international joint venture activity by U.S. firms, and insofar as continued increased globalization would seem to lead to greater international joint venture activity, the analysis by Desai, Foley, and Hines is at first counterintuitive. These authors provided empirical evidence that decreases in coordination costs, as proxied by ease of communication, reduced transportation costs, and integration of worldwide financial and commodity markets, have actually made it relatively easier for U.S. firms to own 100% or the majority of the foreign assets rather than to engage in joint ventures. They found that over the sample period, 1982 to 1997, minority-owned affiliates declined from 17.9% to 10.6%, whereas wholly owned affiliates increased from 72.3% to 80.4%.

COST OF CAPITAL IN FOREIGN ACQUISITIONS AND INVESTMENTS

The calculation of the appropriate cost of capital to apply to the free cash flows of a foreign entity requires the use of the principles of international finance. Two main sets of concepts are involved. First are the fundamental international parity or equilibrium relationships. Second are the issues of whether the global capital markets are integrated or segmented. The first provides some insights for understanding the relationship between the cost of domestic debt and the cost of debt in foreign countries. The capital market integration issues relate to measuring the cost of equity capital in different countries.

COST OF DEBT RELATIONSHIPS

International business transactions are conducted in many different currencies. However, a U.S. exporter selling to a foreigner generally expects to be paid in U.S. dollars. Conversely, foreign importers buying from an American exporter might prefer to pay in their own currency. The existence of the foreign exchange markets allows buyers and sellers to deal in the currencies of their preference. The foreign exchange markets consist of individual brokers, the large international banks, and other commercial banks that facilitate transactions on behalf of their customers. Payments can be made in one currency by an importer and received in another by the exporter.

Exchange rates can be expressed in U.S. dollars per foreign unit or in foreign currency (FC) units per U.S. dollar. An exchange rate of $0.50 to FC 1 shows the value of one foreign currency unit in terms of the dollar. We shall use E_0 to indicate the spot rate, E_f to indicate the forward rate at the present time, and E_1 to indicate the actual future spot rate corresponding to E_f. An exchange rate of FC 2 to $1 shows the value of the dollar in terms of the number foreign currency units it will purchase. We will use the symbol X with corresponding subscripts to refer to the exchange rate expressed as the number of foreign currency units per dollar. We follow these conventions in developing four fundamental equilibrium relationships of international finance.

The model of international parity relationships is based on the assumptions required for perfect markets: Financial markets are perfect; goods markets are perfect; the future is known with certainty; the markets are in equilibrium. We can then establish the following equilibrium relationships.

1. The interest rate parity theorem (IRPT)
2. The forward parity theorem (FPT)
3. The purchasing power parity theorem (PPPT)
4. The international Fisher relation (IFR)

The Interest Rate Parity Theorem (IRPT)

The interest rate parity theorem holds that the ratio of the forward and spot exchange rates will equal the ratio of foreign and domestic nominal interest rates. The formal statement of the IRPT may be expressed as follows:

$$\frac{X_f}{X_0} = \frac{1 + R_{f0}}{1 + R_{d0}} = \frac{E_0}{E_f}$$

Where:

X_f = current forward exchange rate expressed as FC units per \$1 = \$11.24
E_f = current forward exchange rate expressed as dollars per FC unit = \$0.089
X_0 = current spot exchange rate expressed as FC units per \$1 = \$10.31
E_0 = current spot exchange rate expressed as dollars per FC unit = \$0.097
R_{f0} = current foreign interest rate = ?
R_{d0} = current domestic interest rate = 0.05

We now illustrate a practical way of developing numerical examples. We begin by looking at the foreign exchange rates and current future prices in the *Financial Times*. Suppose we find that the spot price for the Mexican peso is \$0.097 in dollars, which is 10.31 pesos per dollar. The 1-year futures value of the peso is \$0.089; in pesos per dollar, this is 11.24. Therefore, it takes more pesos to buy a dollar in the futures market than in the spot market. We use a U.S. prime rate of 5% as an indication of the borrowing cost to a prime business customer in the United States. These are the values shown in the foregoing list explanation of symbols.

We now apply the interest rate parity theorem to obtain the current foreign interest rate.

$$11.24/10.31 = x/1.05$$

Solving for x, we obtain 1.144, or a Mexican interest rate to a prime borrower in Mexico of 14.4%. We next set forth the forward parity theorem.

The Forward Parity Theorem (FPT)

Under the perfect and efficient market assumptions postulated, spot futures or forward exchange rates should be unbiased predictors of future spot rates. Hence, X_f should equal X_1, or the future spot rate (X_1) should equal the current forward rate. In our numerical example, the future spot rate should be 11.24 pesos to the dollar. We can now make use of the purchasing power parity theorem.

The Purchasing Power Parity Theorem (PPPT)

The purchasing power parity theorem is an expression of the law of one price: In competitive markets, the exchange-adjusted prices of identical tradable goods and financial assets must be equal worldwide (taking into account information and transactions costs). PPPT deals with the rates at which domestic goods are exchanged for foreign goods. Thus, if X dollars will buy a bushel of wheat in the United States, the X dollars also should buy a bushel of wheat in Mexico. In formal terms, the PPPT can be stated as:

$$X_1/X_0 = T_f/T_d$$

Where:

T_f = 1 + foreign country inflation rate = ?
T_d = 1 + domestic inflation rate = 1.015

Using the data we have developed to this point, we have:

$$11.24/10.31 = x/1.015$$

We can now calculate Mexico's expected inflation rate based on the parity relationships by solving for the unknown in the foregoing equation, which is 10.6% per annum. We now can illustrate the international Fisher relation.

The International Fisher Relation (IFR)

The Fisher relation states that nominal interest rates reflect the anticipated rate of inflation. The Fisher relation can be stated in a number of forms. We shall use:

$$1 + R_n = (1 + r)(T)$$

Where:

$T = 1 + $ rate of inflation
$r = $ real rate of interest
$R_n = $ nominal rate of interest

For Mexico, we have $1.144 = (1 + r)(1.106)$, so $r = 0.034$; for the United States, we have $1.05 = (1 + r)(1.015)$, so again $r = 0.034$. The real rates are the same, but the nominal rates differ by the inflation factor.

We now can summarize what the four parity relationships tell us. Interest rate parity states that current interest rate relationships will be consistent with a country's ratio of forward exchange rates to current spot rates. The forward parity condition says that the current forward rate is a good predictor of the expected future spot rate. Purchasing power parity states that the ratios of inflation rates will be consistent with the ratio of the future spot rate to the current spot rate. Finally, the Fisher relationship states that if the other parity conditions hold, real rates of interest will be the same across countries and nominal interest rates will reflect different inflation rates.

Many real-world frictions can cause departures from parity conditions in the short run. However these are the relationships toward which international financial markets are always moving. Experience and empirical evidence teach us that these parity conditions provide a useful guide for business executives. For individual managers to believe that they can outguess the international financial markets, which reflect the judgments of many players, is hubris in the extreme. They put their companies at the peril of severe losses.

Standard textbooks in finance describe how the use of futures markets can be used to hedge foreign exchange risks. In addition, many strategies can be used in conjunction with the futures markets. These include borrowing in foreign markets for foreign projects, conducting manufacturing operations in multiple countries as a buffer for inflation and foreign exchange rate movements, and making sales in multiple countries to offset strong and weak currency buyers, among others. Details on such strategies are beyond the scope of this book. Our objective is to estimate the applicable cost of capital for foreign acquisitions or investments. Our discussion of the parity relationships provides a basis for understanding the applicable cost of capital for foreign acquisitions or investments.

COST OF EQUITY AND COST OF CAPITAL

We begin with the basic idea behind the capital asset pricing model (CAPM), which is widely used to calculate the cost of equity and the cost of capital. CAPM states that the cost of equity is the risk-free return plus a risk adjustment that is the product of the return on the market as a whole multiplied by the risk measure of the individual firm or project. How the market is defined depends on whether the global capital market is integrated or segmented. If integrated, investments are made globally and systematic risk is measured relative to a world market index. If capital markets are segmented, investments are predominantly made in a particular segment or country and systematic risk is measured relative to a domestic index. With the rise of large financial institutions investing worldwide and mutual funds that facilitate international or foreign investments, the world is moving toward a globally integrated capital market. We are not there yet because of the home-bias phenomenon: Investors place only a relatively small part of their funds abroad. For recent data, see Hulbert (2000). The reasons are not fully understood. One possibility is there may be extra costs of obtaining and digesting information. Another possibility is the greater uncertainty associated with placing investments under the jurisdiction of another country whose authorities might change the rules of the game. If capital markets are not fully integrated, there are gains from international diversification. A multinational corporation (MNC) would apply to a foreign investment a lower cost of capital than a local (foreign) company would (see Chan, Karolyi, and Stulz, 1992; Stulz 1995a, 1995b; Stulz and Wasserfallen, 1995; and Godfrey and Espinosa, 1996).

Let us continue with the Mexico example. A firm domiciled in Mexico will have a beta based on market returns for investments in Mexico. An MNC domiciled outside Mexico will have cost of equity capital related to its beta measured with respect to the markets in which it operates. A world market index might be a reasonable approximation, but measurement problems and availability would be formidable. The examples we used in Chapters 9 and 10 on valuation were firms like Exxon and Mobil, which participate in global oil markets. Their betas, calculated by Value Line and others, are based on the U.S. market, so the betas used for MNCs already reflect the benefits of their foreign activities. Because a part of their cash flow patterns reflects foreign market conditions, their total cash flow patterns in relation to the U.S. market are likely to have a smaller covariance or beta. Thus, the betas we used in Chapters 9 and 10 for the Exxon-Mobil example were lower than if the firms had only domestic U.S. operations. The cost of equity capital used for Exxon was 11.55%, and for Mobil it was 10.85%. These are relatively low costs expressed in U.S. dollars.

If we calculated the cost of equity for an investment in Mexico in nominal peso terms, it necessarily would reflect a risk differential above the cost of debt borrowing in Mexico. If the cost of debt borrowing in Mexico is about 14.4% based on our prior analysis, then the cost of equity is likely to be 4 to 7 percentage points higher. Assuming a leverage ratio of debt to equity at market of 40%, a cost of equity of 20%, and a tax rate of 40%, we can calculate the weighted costs as follows:

$$\text{WACC} = (0.144)(0.6)(0.4) + (0.20)(0.6) = 0.155$$

We could use this discount factor of 15.5% in calculating the present value of an investment in Mexico. The cash flows expressed in pesos discounted by the peso cost of capital would give us a present value expressed in pesos. This present value converted to dollars at the spot rate should give us the net present value of the investment in dollars.

Table 17.9 displays the calculation of the present value in pesos of an investment in Mexico. The project yields cash flows over a 5 year period, at the end of which it hopefully can be sold to a local buyer for 10,000 pesos. Line 1 of Table 17.9 represents the preliminary estimates of cash flows from the project expressed in pesos. In Line 2, we recognize that these projections are subject to error. We are particularly concerned that the foreign country might change the rules of the game. For example, political instability might bring a government with an anti-foreign business philosophy into power, discriminatory taxes might be imposed, restrictions on repatriation of funds might be enacted, or militant unions might raise wage costs, reducing net cash flows. We believe it is better to recognize these risk adjustments in the cash flows explicitly

TABLE 17.9 Calculation of Present Value in Pesos

	0	1	2	3	4	5	5
				Year			
1 Cash flow in pesos		1,000	1,100	1,200	1,400	1,600	10,000
2 Probability (risk) factors		0.9	0.9	0.8	0.8	0.6	0.5
3 Expected cash flows in pesos		900	990	960	1,120	960	5,000
4 Discount factor (pesos)		1.155	1.133	1.539	1.777	2.052	2.052
5 Discounted peso cash flows		779.46	742.56	623.62	630.11	467.75	2436.21
6 Present value (pesos)	5,679.71						

rather than fudge the discount factor. The discount factor should reflect systematic risk and not the idiosyncratic factors described.

Therefore, Line 3 of Table 17.9 represents the risk-adjusted expected peso cash flows. In Line 4, we apply the discount factor of 15.5%, which reflects the peso cost of capital for the project. Line 5 presents the discounted peso cash flows using the data in Lines 3 and 4. In Line 6, the present values from Line 5 are summed to obtain the total present value of the project of 5,679.7 pesos. The U.S. firm could incur investment outlays with a present value of up to 5,679.7 pesos to earn its cost of capital. We convert the present value of 5,679 in pesos to dollars at the spot rate of 10.31 to obtain a present value of $550.90.

We should get the same result by beginning with the cash flows in pesos, converting them to dollars over time, and discounting them by the WACC of the U.S. firm. In Table 17.10, we will illustrate this second method as well, using the same cash flows in pesos. Again, the project yields cash flows over a 5 year period, at the end of which it hopefully can be sold to a local buyer for 10,000 pesos.

Lines 1 through 3 in Table 17.10 are identical to Lines 1 through 3 in Table 17.9. Line 1 displays the cash flows without adjustments, Line 2 provides the adjustment factor, and Line 3 displays the risk-adjusted cash flows in pesos. Line 4 provides the expected future exchange

TABLE 17.10 Calculation of Present Value in Dollars

	0	1	2	3	4	5	5
				Year			
1 Cash flows in pesos		1,000	1,100	1,200	1,400	1,600	10,000
2 Probability (risk) factors		0.9	0.9	0.8	0.8	0.6	0.5
3 Expected cash flows in pesos		900	990	960	1,120	960	5,000
4 Exchange rate in year t		11.236	12.246	13.347	14.546	15.854	15.584
5 Expected dollar cash flows		80.10	80.84	71.93	77.00	60.55	315.38
6 Discount factor (dollars)		1.059	1.122	1.189	1.260	1.335	1.335
7 Discounted dollar cash flows		75.61	72.03	60.49	61.12	45.37	236.31
8 Present value in dollars	550.93						

rate by which to convert pesos to dollars. We start with the spot rate of 10.31 pesos per dollar. From interest rate parity, for each subsequent year we multiply the 10.31 times $(1.106/1.015)^t$, the relative inflation rates. For example, the forecasted exchange rate in year 5 is equal to 15.85. In Line 5, the exchange rates are applied to the expected peso cash flows of Line 3 to give us the expected cash flows expressed in dollars.

In Line 6, we apply a U.S. WACC of 5.9%. To obtain this dollar discount factor, we multiplied 1.155 (1 plus the discount rate in pesos) times the relative inflation rates (1.015/1.106). Line 7 presents the discounted cash flows in dollars using the data in Lines 5 and 6. In Line 8, the present values from Line 7 are summed to obtain the total present value of the project of $550.93. Note that is identical to the first method in which we computed the present value of the project in pesos and then converted to dollars at the current spot rate.

We have illustrated a systematic methodology for valuing foreign acquisitions or making direct investments. The numbers used in the example were simplified to facilitate the exposition. The underlying principles and concepts would be the same if we were using a complex, sophisticated computer program. The method is similar to the valuation of domestic investments. The complications are mainly foreign exchange risks and foreign country risks. The parity relationships provide useful guidelines for thinking about foreign exchange rates, relative inflation, and relative interest rates. In Table 17.10, we do not mean to imply that the risk factors applied in Line 2 are to be approached passively. A company can use a wide range of strategies to minimize the unfavorable possibilities. A sound project or the purchase of a foreign firm can contribute to increased employment, productivity, and output in the foreign county. The technological and management practices the parent brings to the subsidiary can make its continued participation indispensable. Also, the foreign operation can be so organized that it could not function without the unique parts provided by the parent. Another possibility is that the investment is part of an international agency program to develop the infrastructure of the host country. Arbitrary changes in the rules of the game could injure the reputation and reduce future international support of a self-serving government.

As we noted at the beginning of this chapter, the number and magnitude of cross-border mergers are growing faster than those of U.S. mergers. Cross-border mergers involve international factors that need to be taken into account. Our aim has been to improve decision making in the area of international transactions.

Summary

International mergers are subject to many of the same influences and motivations as domestic mergers. However, they also present unique threats and opportunities. The issue of mergers versus other means of achieving international business goals (such as import/export, licensing, joint ventures) builds on the fundamental issue in the theory of the firm: whether to transact across markets or to internalize transactions using managerial coordination within the firm.

When firms choose to merge internationally, it implies that they have concluded that this will result in lower costs or higher productivity than alternative contractual means of achieving international goals. In horizontal mergers, intangible assets play an important role in domestic and international combinations. The exploitation of an intangible asset such as knowledge may require merger because of the "public good" nature of the asset. Attempts to exploit intangibles short of merger require complex contracting, which is not only expensive but likely to be incomplete (especially when compounded by the problems of dealing with a foreign environment), possibly leading to dissipation of the owner's proprietary interest in the asset. Similarly, vertically integrated firms exist to internalize markets for intermediate products on the domestic and international levels.

Among the special factors impacting international mergers more than domestic mergers are tariff barriers and exchange rate relationships. Operating within a tariff barrier might be the only means of obtaining competitive access to a large market, for example, the European Common Market. Exchange rates are also an important influence. A strong dollar makes U.S. products more expensive abroad but reduces the cost of acquiring foreign firms. The reverse holds when the dollar is weak, encouraging U.S. exports and foreign acquisitions of U.S. companies, all other factors held constant.

Although the risks of operating in a foreign environment are greater, they can be reduced through careful planning or by an incremental approach to entering the foreign market. Furthermore, to the extent that the foreign economy is imperfectly correlated with the domestic economy, the systematic risk to the company as a whole may be reduced by international diversification.

The increasing globalization of competition in product markets is extending rapidly into internationalization of the takeover market. The best method by which to achieve a firm's expansion goals may no longer be the takeover of a domestic firm but of a foreign one. International M&A activity has grown substantially over the past 20 years, and it is likely to continue to increase into the future.

Questions

17.1 Why is M&A activity in Europe in recent years growing at a more rapid rate than in the United States?

17.2 Why is M&A activity increasing in Japan in recent years?

17.3 Why is M&A activity increasing in the People's Republic of China in recent years?

17.4 Why is M&A activity increasing in other Asian areas, such as Taiwan, Korea, and Malaysia?

17.5 Describe the two most important reasons behind each of the cross-border transactions discussed in the brief examples in the text?

17.6 What has been driving the big pharmaceutical mergers in recent years?

17.7 Are there any forces driving cross-border mergers that operate more strongly than the reasons for transactions that take place within a given country's border?

17.8 How would you explain why foreign bidders pay higher premiums for U.S. targets than U.S. domestic bidders pay for U.S. targets?.

17.9 Suppose you go to the Web page of the Central Bank of Mexico and find that the inflation rate in Mexico during the last 5 years has been 10% per annum. You check a number of other research sources and find that this inflation rate is expected to continue for the next 5 years?

   a. With a current spot rate of 10.0 Mexican pesos to the U.S. dollar and an expected inflation rate in the U.S. for the next 5 years of 2%, use PPPT to calculate the expected future spot rate in 1 year.

   b. The forward parity theorem holds so that the spot futures or forward exchange rate is equal to the expected future spot rate. Use IRPT to calculate the current interest rate in Mexico when the comparable U.S. interest rate is 5%.

Case 17.1 THE SAGA OF GERBER PRODUCTS

The case study of Gerber Products is a more detailed analysis of the role of international markets in the growth of food companies. For years, Gerber saw the necessity of expanding abroad. Somehow though, Gerber was unable to implement its goals of expanding internationally. The M&A market accomplished what Gerber was unable to do on its own.

GERBER REBUFFS ANDERSON CLAYTON

In 1977, Gerber Products was approached by Anderson Clayton Company. Anderson Clayton wanted to continue to expand its diversified operations, which already included processing soy beans, coffee, and a life insurance company. Anderson Clayton's overtures were rebuffed by Gerber Products. Nevertheless, Anderson Clayton made a tender offer for Gerber Products at $40 a share.

Gerber management mounted a strong defense. Gerber Products filed suit against Anderson Clayton in a federal court in Grand Rapids, Michigan, relatively near the Gerber headquarters in Fremont, Michigan. Gerber charged that the acquisition by Anderson Clayton would represent a serious antitrust conflict. It charged that potential competition between the companies in the future would be stifled by the merger. Gerber argued that Anderson Clayton could develop a baby products business in the future. Gerber also stated that it had been considering entrance into the salad oil market, in which Anderson Clayton already was doing business. Gerber's lawsuit also charged that in its tender offer, Anderson Clayton did not make adequate disclosure of $2.1 million in questionable payments it had made overseas. This charge obviously sought to embarrass Anderson Clayton by the adverse publicity that would be generated by raising this issue. In addition, Gerber complained that Anderson Clayton had not made adequate disclosure of its financing arrangements in its tender offer filing. Michigan's antitakeover law includes a requirement for a 60-day waiting period after a tender offer. Gerber Products used this time to seek out an acceptable white knight. Gerber began discussions with Unilever as a possible alternative purchaser. Anderson Clayton secured a financing agreement from several New York banks to establish compliance with this requirement under Michigan's antitakeover law.

At its July 1977 annual meeting, Gerber reported that second quarter earnings had dropped by one third. Anderson Clayton indicated that Gerber was deliberately understating its earnings and lowered its offer from $40 to $37.

In the meantime, the Michigan courts issued a series of rulings, all favorable to Gerber. A trial on the securities charges was scheduled for September 1977. After this trial, there would be another in which the antitrust charges would be litigated. Faced with uncertain and expensive litigation and the possibility that over the extended period of time, other bidders might force higher bids, Anderson Clayton withdrew its offer. In response to this announcement, the stock price of Gerber fell from $34.375 to $28.25.

GERBER'S STRATEGIC PROBLEMS

In the following years, Gerber sought to reduce its vulnerability to a takeover. Gerber attempted to diversity into other areas such as children's apparel, furniture, farming, day care centers, trucking, humidifiers, and life insurance. None of these appeared to have any real synergy with Gerber's baby food business.

Although Gerber held 70% of the U.S. baby food market, it was relatively weak abroad. Higher growth for Gerber would have meant increasing in sales in countries outside the United States, which annually account for 98% of births worldwide. Over the years, Gerber made some efforts to expand its overseas operations but hesitated to commit the funds that would have had a near-term negative impact on its profitability rates. Because it was an inexpensive way to go, Gerber often would license overseas manufactures to make and distribute its baby food. Licensing has at least two drawbacks. First, the fees that can be charged for licensing are relatively small. Second, the licensee develops the critical capability and can always play one product against another. Sometimes the licensing arrangements came to an end because the foreign manufacturer decided to shift to other products. As a consequence, increasingly Gerber was supplying Asia and the Middle East from its U.S. plants.

THE AUCTION OF GERBER

As a consequence of its weak performance abroad, Gerber's revenues stayed flat at about $1.2 billion from 1990 through 1994 (Gibson, 1994). Its net income for the years 1990 through 1994 averaged less than $100 million. Gerber had stock splits in 1982, 1984, 1989, and 1992. However, adjusted for all splits, the Gerber stock stayed relatively flat in the range of $30 per share. Gerber realized it needed to go abroad but was reluctant to commit the resources that would have a negative impact on earnings. In early 1994, Gerber requested Goldman Sachs to explore a possible friendly buyout that would help Gerber become stronger in the overseas markets. Essentially, an auction was conducted. The winner was Sandoz AG, a Swiss company that bid $53 a share on May 23, 1994. When takeover speculation started, the price of Gerber shares moved up by 33% between early February 1994 and the period just before the Sandoz offer. After the Sandoz offer, Gerber shares increased another $15.50 to $50.125. The $53 price was high because it represented 30 times current earnings, 20 times after-tax cash flow, and 3 times sales.

For Sandoz, the acquisition would expand its position in the food business and in nutritional product sales. Sandoz already had a strong position in food sales in Europe and Asia, but only 14% of its food sales came from North America.

It was pointed out that the Sandoz bid would not include any form of stock option lockup. This followed from the court decision in the QVC takeover of Paramount. Paramount had granted Viacom, its preferred buyer, the right to buy 24 million Paramount shares for $69.14. When Paramount went to $80 a share, the option was worth $500 million to Viacom. Nevertheless, the Sandoz agreement involved a breakup fee. In a breakup fee arrangement, the original bidder receives a fee if it does not succeed in the takeover. Gerber agreed to pay $70 million to Sandoz if the Sandoz bid did not succeed.

Some writers argued that differences in tax laws made the acquisition more attractive to Sandoz than to a U.S. buyer (Sloan, 1994). The tangible net worth of Gerber was about $300 million. For a U.S. buyer, the difference between the $3.7 billion paid and the $300 million tangible net worth of Gerber would have represented goodwill. A U.S. company would have had to charge its after-tax profits, $85 million per year for 40 years, which was 75% of the $114 million net income of Gerber in its 1994 fiscal year. Sandoz, on the other hand, could charge the goodwill against its own net worth without affecting annual earnings. It was stated that the $114 million net income would represent a 38% return on the $300 million tangible assets Sandoz would add to its balance sheet (Sloan, 1994). In addition, there was also a possibility of a tax write-off by Sandoz in connection with the goodwill purchase and write-off.

QUESTIONS

C17.1.1 Why was Gerber interested in expanding in international markets?

C17.1.2 Why was Gerber unable to succeed on its own in developing international markets?

C17.1.3 Why did Gerber reject the earlier efforts by Anderson Clayton to acquire it?

C17.1.4 Why did Gerber request its investment banker to find a buyer that could develop its potential in international markets?

C17.1.5 Why was Sandoz interested in Gerber?

———✦⌇✦⌇✦———

Case 17.2   CIBA-GEIGY MERGER WITH SANDOZ[1]

In Basel, Switzerland, on March 7, 1996, Ciba-Geigy and Sandoz issued a joint statement by the chairmen of both companies that they would merge into one company with the new name Novartis (Olmos, 1996). The company would focus on its core businesses, which are pharmaceuticals, agribusiness, and nutrition. Each company would divest its divisions that did not relate to the core life sciences focus of the new company, Novartis. This included Ciba's division of specialty chemicals (Tanouye, Lipin, and Moore, 1996).

Ciba was well known for its New Vues disposable contact lens, Habitrol nicotine patches, Ritalin for hyperactive children, Sunkist vitamins, Maalox, Zantac, and Efidac, an over-the-counter cold medicine. Sandoz was known for its nutrition division, which included Gerber baby foods, Ovaltine, and Wasa crispbreads.

The new name Novartis was partly due to the strategy that the merger was between two equals that wanted to become innovators for the next century (Guyon, 1996). The new name was developed by London's Siegal and Gale consultants, who were hired to create a powerful new marketing strategy for the company. The word derives from the Latin *novo*, which means "new," and *artis*, which means "skill." The new name had to be tested in 180 countries to make sure that it did not have any negative connotations.

Ciba-Geigy was the world's 9th-largest drugmaker, and Sandoz was the 14th. The merger created a new company that was to be the world's number-one supplier in agricultural chemicals, a world leader in biotechnology, and a large presence in the nutrition products field. The new firm would still have only 4.4% of the global market. The new company would have the third-largest pharmaceuticals revenue, with drug sales at $10.94 billion (1995 revenue).

On April 24, 1996, in Basel, Switzerland, the merger was put to a vote at the final Ciba annual general meeting. The meeting counted 6,896 people in attendance with 70% of share capital with voting privileges. The CEO of Ciba, Dr. Alex Krauer, told shareholders that the merger "will not only improve shareholder value, but also open a promising future for the majority of our employees." The merger was approved by 98.7% of the members present and 69.4% of the share capital. The Sandoz shareholders approved the merger on April 24, 1996. The next phase of merger approval involved regulatory agencies of the European Union and to a lesser extent those of the United States.

Shareholders of Ciba stock received 1.067 shares of Novartis, and shareholders of Sandoz stock received 1 share of Novartis for each share they currently held. Sandoz shareholders held 55% of the new company, whereas Ciba shareholders held 45% of Novartis.

The merger took many analysts by surprise, but most agreed that it was an excellent strategic move because it was a proactive reaction to the general consolidation of the industry. The bankers who negotiated the deal also were praised because it was structured as a share swap instead of an outright purchase. This caused the deal to be virtually taxfree, and there was also no write-down of "goodwill." Goodwill compensates for the difference between sale price and the book value of assets but can be a negative force because it reduces reported profits.

The news of the merger sent stock prices of the large pharmaceutical companies soaring. It also affected smaller companies that were seen as possible takeover targets for the large companies looking to compete with the new Novartis. Both companies were traded on the Swiss stock market, and reaction to the news was positive for both companies; Sandoz shares rose 20% and Ciba's 30%. This also can be attributed to the intended cut of 10% of the workforce of the newly created company. The new company was to have an estimated total market value of $60 billion.

---

[1]Written by Erica Clark and J. F. Weston.

STRATEGIC REASONS FOR THE CIBA-SANDOZ MERGER

The consolidation of these two large companies reflected a growing trend in the fiercely competitive pharmaceuticals industry (Kraul, 1996). This was partly attributable to the high cost of research and development that is specific to the industry. An estimated $80 billion in mergers have occurred since 1993 in the pharmaceutical industry. However, the top 20 companies still make up only 50% of total sales worldwide (*Economist*, 1994).

Both companies were facing the fundamental challenges that most drug companies are encountering in the current, highly competitive market. The challenge was to develop a continuing supply of significant new drugs. This constant push for innovation based on the research and development of new products causes the pharmaceutical business to be inherently risky, because research and development is extremely costly but does not guarantee a constant stream of new products. In addition, the creation of new products is heavily dependent on the approval of regulatory agencies such as the U.S. Food and Drug Administration (FDA). Of every 10 drugs that pass the initial investigation stage, only 1 ultimately will receive approval of the FDA. Of the few products that ultimately do gain regulatory approval, only a fraction generate sufficient sales to earn the cost of capital for a drug company, even a modest 10% to 12%.

Another major challenge facing these companies is that the pharmaceutical industry seems to produce important scientific breakthroughs in cycles. There are periods of great productivity and periods when the foundations for new research are in the development state. This causes incredible pressure on the pharmaceutical companies to produce, even when their research is in the slow development phase. This particular issue was of great concern to Ciba and Sandoz. The companies viewed the merger as a way to create a more powerful research arsenal, which would help them into the important new research frontiers of the new century, such as biotechnology. Sandoz had invested heavily in gene research, but newly developed products were still years away (Taber, 1996).

The highly aggressive nature of the current industry trend of merge or be an acquisition target caused Ciba and Sandoz to make a decisive move toward consolidation. The merger can be attributed to the rapid pace of other mergers that have taken place in the industry. Cost-containment efforts by governments and managed health care organizations have squeezed profits and forced industry restructuring. Through mergers, firms have sought to economize on research costs, combine product lines, and increase marketing effectiveness. The Glaxo-Wellcome merger in 1995 produced a company with almost $12 billion in 1995 pharmaceutical revenues, making it number one worldwide. Glaxo planned to reduce costs by closing plants and reducing employment by 7,500 out of a workforce of 62,000.

BACKGROUND ON COMPANIES

Ciba-Geigy and Sandoz share a long corporate relationship dating back to Basel in the 1850s. The Ciba company merged with the Geigy company in 1970. The Geigy company was founded in 1758 by Johann Geigy, who traded organic compounds such as spices and natural dyes. It had grown into a large company by the 1900s. Another Basel citizen started a synthetic dye trade around the turn of the century called Gesellschaft für Chemische industrie im Basle, which was later shortened to CIBA. Sandoz was founded in 1886 in Basel as Kern & Sandoz.

In the 1970s, Ciba-Geigy had several public setbacks, including the discovery of the way the company had tested the chemical Galecron. In 1976, they paid six Egyptian boys to stand in a field and have the chemical sprayed on them. The result was public outrage, and the company was forced to improve its tarnished image. Then in 1978, more than 1,000 deaths in Japan were linked to a Ciba-Geigy diarrhea medication.

In the 1980s, Ciba-Geigy decided to focus its operations on specialty chemicals and the health care products field. In 1988, Ciba sold its Ilford Group, a photographic products division, to International Paper. Subsequently, Ciba formed alliances with high-technology companies, including a joint venture with a Carlsbad, California, company, Isis Pharmaceuticals, and with Affymax of Palo Alto, California, to study computer-aided screening of its products.

Sandoz spent the post-World War II era concentrating on product development based on internal research and development. In the 1950s and 1960s, Sandoz expanded its production units across Europe and into Japan. In 1967, Sandoz acquired Dr. Wander A.G., which gave Sandoz a consumer products presence and strengthened its international holdings. In 1976, it continued to diversify its product scope by acquiring Northrup King & Corporation, one of the largest U.S. seed companies.

Crucial moves occurred in 1980 and 1981 with the acquisitions of a French dye company, SA Cardoner, a

U.S. seed company, McNair, and a U.S. pharmaceutical company, Ex-Lax. In the mid-1980s, Sandoz enjoyed strong cash flows and was able to continue to strengthen itself with new investments and acquisitions, including Sodyeco, a division of Martin Marietta, and Zoecon Corporation from Occidental Petroleum.

In 1989, Sandoz had to reorganize due to harsher worldwide trading conditions. In 1990, a new structure was formed in which Sandoz Limited, holds 100% of six operating companies: Sandoz Chemicals, Sandoz Pharma, Sandoz Agro, Sandoz Seeds, Sandoz Nutrition, and MBT Holdings.

QUESTIONS

C17.2.1   What were the individual strengths and weaknesses of Sandoz and Ciba-Geigy?

C17.2.2   How would the merger help each company?

C17.2.3   What was the expected future strategic focus of Novartis, and why?

Case 17.3   VODAFONE AIRTOUCH TAKEOVER OF MANNESMANN[2]

Due to increased liberalization and a relaxation in regulatory regimes in many countries, the late-1990s witnessed a merger mania in the telecommunications industry. Companies in this sector moved to reposition themselves for an increasingly competitive landscape and sought to redefine themselves through increased size and market diversity.

On November 13, 1999, the world's largest mobile phone group, Vodafone AirTouch, announced a takeover bid for the German engineering and telecommunications group, Mannesmann AG. The UK-based telecom, Vodafone, had approached Mannesmann with an uninvited offer that was rejected immediately by Mannesmann's executive board. Management and the supervisory board expressed that the offer was not only inadequate, but strategically unsound due to their different infrastructures and growth prospects. A week later, Vodafone presented an improved proposal, appealing directly to shareholders to exchange their shares in the ratio of 53.7 Vodafone AirTouch shares for 1 Mannesmann share. When Mannesmann's executive board continued to fight the merger attempt, the Vodafone offer became the world's largest hostile bid in history.

The timing of Vodafone's bid for Mannesmann was due to a confluence of events. In January of 1999, Vodafone acquired AirTouch in a $66 billion cash/stock deal, making it the largest telecommunica-tions company in the world. The acquisition made Vodafone and Mannesmann partners in multiple European wireless markets with ventures covering 95% of the European Union. Later, in October 1999, Mannesmann broke what had been seen by many analysts in the market as a gentleman's agreement by winning a $34.2 billion bid on Orange PLC, a competitor of Vodafone in the United Kingdom. The move was a surprise because Mannesmann, only a month before its bid on Orange, pulled out of a much smaller bid on UK telecom One2One bought by Deutsche Telekom AG for $13.4 billion. Mannesmann's purchase of Orange sent Vodafone into the number three position in Europe. By entering the competitive field in their own backyard, Vodafone believed that Mannesmann created an adversarial situation where joint ventures with Mannesmann would suffer because the companies would be competing directly in each others' markets. As a result, Vodafone began its bid to take over Mannesmann.

POLITICAL DEBATES SURROUNDING THE VODAFONE-MANNESMANN MERGER

No foreign group had ever succeeded in taking over a German company against the wishes of the target management. German corporate bylaws are written

---

[2]Written by Lynda Pires.

to discourage predatory behavior. After public announcement of Vodafone's takeover plans, the response by Germany's left was almost immediate. By the end of November, German workers' unions had organized against the hostile bid and implored shareholders to reject the bid. In an unexpected event, Mannesmann workers and management received the support of the American trade unions' AFL-CIO. As trade union criticism gained public momentum, German politicians entered the public debate over the future integrity of the German business model. At its peak, German Chancellor Gerard Schroeder accused the hostile bid of working to "destroy corporate cultures." ("Blair Counters Schroeder on Telecoms Takeover Bid," Reuters News, November 21, 1999). He stated that a deal of this nature would work against German traditions of worker participation in company management. The media focused on a public fear of new German involvement in a no-holds-barred form of "global business cannibalism" even though Mannesmann was already in a sense foreign owned with 60% of shares in the hands of non-Germans.

The German outcry provoked an equally fervent reply on the part of the British press and political establishment. British Prime Minister Tony Blair heartily supported the Vodafone takeover, rejecting Chancellor Schroeder's claim as "exaggerated", and not in line with the new European market mechanism. Several market-oriented members of the German Right mirrored this sentiment by lamenting that Germany would remain in a state of nationalistic stagnation if it continued its political ethos of consensus building and reluctance to change and engage in globalizing trends. The Vodafone-Mannesmann struggle appeared to underscore the tensions between the Anglo-Saxon model of unfettered capitalism and the Rhineland model of a social market economy ("We're Talking Telephone Numbers," *The Guardian*, November 23, 1999).

The size of the transaction also encouraged policy makers to draft new EU takeover provisions. The need for pan-EU takeover rules had been discussed for more than a decade, but the newly highlighted fear over collective market dominance and oligopolies moved legislation to the table.

In the midst of complex political developments, Mannesmann also made a sudden move to gain time in staving off the transaction by seeking a court injunction in London against Vodaphone advisor Goldman Sachs, citing "conflict of interest."

COMPLETION OF "FRIENDLY" TAKEOVER

On February 3, 2000, after 3 months of public opposition, Mannesmann reached an agreement with Vodafone whereby shareholders would receive a 49.5% share in Vodafone. This offer increased the initial 53.7 exchange ratio to 58.96 Vodafone shares for every 1 Mannesmann share. The $203 billion deal consolidated four of Europe's biggest mobile companies—Omnitel in Italy, SFR in France, Mannesmann in Germany, and Vodafone in the UK—making it the fourth-largest company in the world with market capitalization of $393 billion (£228 billion) and a customer base of 42 million.

Preliminary negotiations, which had been hostile, continued until it appeared that Mannesmann shareholders would be receptive to a direct tender offer. By accepting Vodafone's offer at the 11th hour, Mannesmann management could formally position the deal as a "friendly" merger, preventing an embarrassing hostile takeover and situating Vodafone AirTouch to gain regulatory approval in the EU and Germany with greater ease. Analysts feared that Mannesmann would move to involve the German government in efforts to squelch the deal, but in late-evening negotiations between Vodafone Chairman Chris Gent and Mannesmann Director Klaus Esser the decision was made to end the takeover on positive terms.

STRATEGIC REASONS FOR VODAFONE-MANNESMANN MERGER

The deal resulted in significant gains for both companies. Their combined global assets created a company positioned to build a pan-European wireless network with strategies for growth in Asian, Australian, and U.S. markets. In addition, during negotiations, Vodafone entered into an alliance with Vivendi, which hinged on a Vodafone acquisition of Mannesmann. When the Mannesmann deal was confirmed, Vodafone simultaneously entered into a deal with Vivendi to develop a joint, multi-access, wireless Internet network with the potential for a pan-European, fixed-line network that would combine Mannesman's and Vivendi's fixed assets. (CIO, Analysts Corner, "Mannesmann Finally Succumbs to Vodafone," Current Analysis, Inc., February 7, 2000, www2.cio.com/analyst/report233.html). This massive merger confirmed the European trend to move e-commerce to a "internet-via-the-mobile" plan.

The merger signaled an attempt by Vodafone to take an early lead in the wireless Internet market. The Vodafone-Mannesmann-Vivendi conglomerate was positioned to exert greater influence in procuring deals with suppliers and distributors. The merger not only represented the largest takeover in history, but also serves to illustrate the ongoing debate and tensions in increasingly globalized industrial and market organizations. ▨

QUESTIONS

C17.3.1 Why was Vodafone AirTouch interested in acquiring Mannesmann?

C17.3.2 Why did Mannesmann reject the initial bid?

C17.3.3 What caused Mannesmann to eventually accept the takeover offer by Vodafone?

References

Cakici, N., G. Hessel, and K. Tandon, "Foreign Acquisitions in the United States: Effect on Shareholder Wealth of Foreign Acquiring Firms," *Journal of Banking & Finance* 20, 1996, pp. 307–329.

Caves, Richard E., *Multinational Enterprise and Economic Analysis,* Cambridge, MA: Cambridge University Press, 1982.

Chan, K. C., G. A. Karolyi, and R. M. Stulz, "Global Financial Markets and the Risk Premium of U.S. Equity," *Journal of Financial Economics* 32, 1992, pp. 137–167.

Chen, Haiyang, Michael Y. Hu, and Joseph C. P. Shieh, "The Wealth Effect of International Joint Ventures: The Case of U.S. Investment in China," *Financial Management* 20, Winter 1991, pp. 31–41.

Desai, Mihir A., C. F. Foley, and J. R. Hines, "International Joint Ventures and the Boundaries of the Firm," Harvard Business School working paper, 2002.

Dewenter, Kathryn L. "Do Exchange Rate Changes Drive Foreign Direct Investment?" *Journal of Business* 68, July 1995, pp. 405–433.

Doukas, J., "Overinvesting, Tobin's q and Gains from Foreign Acquisitions," *Journal of Banking & Finance* 19, 1995, pp. 1285–1303.

Doukas, John, and Nickolaos G. Travlos, "The Effect of Corporate Multinationalism on Shareholders' Wealth: Evidence from International Acquisitions," *Journal of Finance* 43, December 1988, pp. 1161–1175.

The Economist, "Drug Mergers: Understanding the Pill Poppers," August 6, 1994, p. 53.

Eckbo, Espen, and K. S. Thorburn, "Gains to Bidder Firms Revisited: Domestic and Foreign Acquisitions in Canada," *Journal of Financial and Quantitative Analysis* 35:1, March 2000, pp. 1–25.

Eun, C. S., R. Kolodny, and C. Scheraga, "Cross-Border Acquisitions and Shareholder Wealth: Tests of the Synergy and Internationalization Hypotheses," *Journal of Banking & Finance* 20, 1996, pp. 1559–1582.

Froot, K., and J. Stein, "Exchange Rates and Foreign Direct Investment. An Imperfect Capital Markets Approach, *The Quarterly Journal of Economics* 106, 1991, pp. 1191–1217.

Gibson, Richard, "Gerber Missed the Boat in Quest to Go Global, So It Turned to Sandoz," *Wall Street Journal,* May 24, 1994, pp. A1, A4.

Godfrey, Stephen, and Ramon Espinosa, "A Practical Approach to Calculating Costs of Equity for Investments in Emerging Markets," *Journal of Applied Corporate Finance* 9, Fall 1996, pp. 80–89.

Guyon, Janet, "What Is Novartis?" *Wall Street Journal,* March 11, 1996, p. B1.

Harris, Robert S., and David Ravenscraft, "The Role of Acquisitions in Foreign Direct Investment: Evidence from the U.S. Stock Market," *Journal of Finance* 46, 1991, pp. 825–844.

Hudgins, S. C., and B. Seifert, "Stockholder Returns and International Acquisitions of Financial Firms: An Emphasis on Banking," *Journal of Financial Service Research* 10, 1996, pp. 163–180.

Hulbert, Mark, "A Plan to Overcome Investors' Home Bias," *New York Times,* January 23, 2000, Sec. 3, p. 9.

Kang, Jun-Koo, "The International Market for Corporate Control: Mergers and Acquisitions of U.S. Firms by Japanese Firms," *Journal of Financial Economics* 34, December 1993, pp. 345–371.

Kraul, Chris, "Pain-Relieving Compound: Ciba-Sandoz Plan Is Part of the Bigger Survival Picture," *Los Angeles Times*, March 8, 1996, p. D1.

Mangum, Garth L., Sae-Young Kim, and Stephen B. Tallman, *Transnational Marriages in the Steel Industry*, Westport, CT: Quorum Books, 1996.

Markides, C., and D. Oyon, "International Acquisitions: Do They Create Value for Shareholders?" *European Management Journal* 16, 1998, pp. 125–135.

Moeller, Sara B., and Frederik P. Schlingemann, "Are Cross-Border Acquisitions Different from Domestic Acquisitions? Evidence on Stock and Operating Performance for U.S. Acquirers," University of Pittsburgh working paper, 2002.

Olmos, David, "Two Swiss Drug Firms Agree to Merge in $27 Billion Deal," *Los Angeles Times*, March 8, 1996, p. A1.

Seth, A., K. P. Song, and R. Pettit, "Synergy, Managerialism or Hubris? An Empirical Examination of Motives for Foreign Acquisitions of U.S. Firms," *Journal of International Business Studies*, 2000.

Shaughnessy, Haydn, "International Joint Ventures: Managing Successful Collaborations," *Long Range Planning*, 28, June 1995, pp. 10–17.

Sloan, Allan, "As Swiss Sandoz Scoops Up the Gerber Baby, Blame U.S. Accounting Law," *Los Angeles Times*, June 5, 1994, p. D1.

Stulz, René M., "The Cost of Capital in Internationally Integrated Markets: The Case of Nestlé," *European Financial Management* 1, March 1995a, pp. 11–22.

——, "Globalization of Capital Markets and the Cost of Capital: The Case of Nestlé," *Journal of Applied Corporate Finance* 8, Fall 1995b, pp. 30–38.

——, and Walter Wasserfallen, "Foreign Equity Investment Restrictions, Capital Flight, and Shareholder Wealth Maximization: Theory and Evidence," *The Review of Financial Studies* 8, Winter 1995, pp. 1019–1057.

Swierczek, Frederic, and Georges Hirsch, "Joint Ventures in Asia and Multicultural Management," *European Management Journal* 12:2, June 1994, pp. 197–209.

Taber, George, "Remaking an Industry," *Time*, September 4, 1996.

Tanouye, Elise, Steve Lipin, and Stephen D. Moore, "In Big Drug Merger Sandoz and Ciba-Geigy Plan to Join Forces," *Wall Street Journal*, March 7, 1996, p. A1.

Zahra, Shaker, and Galal Elhagrasey, "Strategic Management of International Joint Ventures," *European Management Journal* 12:1, March 1994, pp. 83–93.

CHAPTER 18
SHARE REPURCHASES[1]

S hare repurchases are cash offers made by companies for outstanding shares of their own common stock. Share-repurchase activities began increasing in the early 1980s and began accelerating by the end of the 1990s. Multiple motivations for share-repurchase activities have been discussed in the finance literature. This chapter will cover the following topics: the growth of share-repurchase activity, major types of share repurchases, fixed-price tender offers, Dutch auctions, transferable put rights, event studies, a model of undervaluation, accounting treatment of share repurchases, empirical studies of share repurchases, the measurement of share-repurchase growth, related dividend studies, and the substitution issue.

GROWTH OF SHARE-REPURCHASE ACTIVITY

Share repurchases have increased in absolute terms and relative to the use of cash dividends in returning cash to shareholders. However, the magnitudes vary with data sources and method of measurement. SDC data are based primarily on announcements in company press releases and newswires. An alternative source is Compustat where an indirect measure can be calculated using changes in equity accounts. *Wall Street Journal* announcements also have been used. Data measurement procedures are subject to error. As an initial estimate, Table 18.1 uses mainly the SDC data on share-repurchase announcements. It shows that in the 1970s, share repurchases were a small percentage of cash dividend payouts. A large, upward shift took place in 1984. Between 1984 and 2001, cash dividends grew at a rate of 9.3% per year; gross share repurchases grew at a compound annual rate of 13.6% per year.

Compilations based on Compustat data show time patterns of the percent of gross stock repurchases to dividends, similar to the SDC data in Table 18.1 through 1996 when the ratio was 59% (Grullon and Michaely, 2002, Table 1). Thereafter, the Compustat percent of gross repurchases to dividends rose to 113% in 2000. For the S&P 500, share repurchases exceeded cash dividends beginning in 1997 (Liang and Sharpe, 1999). Despite alternative data sources and measurement methods, the empirical evidence establishes that gross share repurchases have grown at a higher rate than cash dividends since 1980. Especially between 1995 and 1998, gross share repurchases grew at a compound annual rate of more than 25%, compared with 11% for aggregate cash dividends. From 1998–2002 dividends grew at 6.6%; share repurchases declined at a –12.5% per annum rate, a significant drop.

---

[1]This chapter draws on a manuscript by J. F. Weston and J. A. Siu entitled "Changing Motives for Share Repurchases."

TABLE 18.1 Share Repurchases vs. Cash Dividends, 1972–2001

Year	Dividends (in billions)	Share Repurchases (in billions)	% Share Repurchase to Dividends
1972	$ 26.8	$ 1.5	5.6%
1973	29.9	3.1	10.4
1974	33.2	1.6	4.7
1975	33.0	0.8	2.6
1976	39.0	1.6	4.1
1977	44.8	3.6	8.1
1978	50.8	4.3	8.5
1979	57.5	5.4	9.5
1980	64.1	6.6	10.3
1981	73.8	6.3	8.5
1982	76.2	10.6	13.9
1983	83.6	9.2	11.0
1984	91.0	27.3	30.0
1985	97.7	20.3	20.8
1986	106.3	28.2	26.5
1987	112.2	55.0	49.0
1988	129.6	37.4	28.9
1989	155.0	63.7	41.1
1990	165.6	36.1	21.8
1991	178.4	20.4	11.4
1992	185.5	35.6	19.2
1993	203.1	38.3	18.9
1994	234.9	73.8	31.4
1995	254.2	99.5	39.1
1996	297.7	176.3	59.2
1997	335.2	181.8	54.2
1998	348.7	224.2	64.3
1999	328.4	154.1	46.9
2000	379.6	158.1	41.6
2001	409.6	156.1	38.1
2002	434.3	119.2	27.4
Growth Rates			
1984–2001	9.2%	13.2%	
1984–1998	9.9%	14.4%	
1995–1998	10.7%	24.7%	
1998–2002	6.6%	−12.5%	

Source: Economic Report of the President, 2003, Table B-90; Thomson Financial Securities Data; share-repurchase data for 1972–1983 are from Grullon and Michaely (2002).

Although gross share repurchases have grown faster than cash dividends, Table 18.2 shows that aggregate dividend payouts have increased. These findings are consistent with the Fama and French (2001) dividend paper; they also found an increase in aggregate dividend payouts. Table 18.2 shows that dividends plus gross repurchases related to after-tax profits rose from 55% in 1984 to more than 100% in 1998 and 2001.

The decline in the shares outstanding for individual companies shown in Table 18.3 is additional evidence of a high rate of repurchase activity. For example, between January 31, 1995, and

TABLE 18.2 Dividends Plus Share Repurchases to After-Tax Profits, 1972–2001 (in billions of dollars)

					As Percent of After-Tax Profits	
Year	After-Tax Profits	Dividends	Share Repurchases	Total	Dividends	Dividends + Repurchases
1972	$ 67.9	$ 26.8	$ 1.5	$ 28.3	39.5%	41.66%
1973	74.7	29.9	3.1	33.0	40.0	44.18
1974	62.7	33.2	1.6	34.8	53.0	55.46
1975	82.1	33.0	0.8	33.8	40.2	41.23
1976	96.4	39.0	1.6	40.6	40.5	42.11
1977	117.9	44.8	3.6	48.4	38.0	41.06
1978	133.7	50.8	4.3	55.1	38.0	41.22
1979	134.5	57.5	5.4	62.9	42.8	46.80
1980	113.7	64.1	6.6	70.7	56.4	62.18
1981	137.8	73.8	6.3	80.1	53.6	58.11
1982	138.2	76.2	10.6	86.8	55.1	62.78
1983	176.9	83.6	9.2	92.8	47.3	52.46
1984	215.7	91.0	27.3	118.3	42.2	54.84
1985	225.9	97.7	20.3	118.0	43.2	52.24
1986	194.2	106.3	28.2	134.5	54.7	69.26
1987	219.5	112.2	55.0	167.2	51.1	76.17
1988	267.9	129.6	37.4	167.0	48.4	62.34
1989	254.2	155.0	63.7	218.7	61.0	86.03
1990	268.0	165.6	36.1	201.7	61.8	75.26
1991	297.7	178.4	20.4	198.8	59.9	66.78
1992	309.9	185.5	35.6	221.1	59.9	71.35
1993	345.1	203.1	38.3	241.4	58.9	69.95
1994	386.5	234.9	73.8	308.7	60.8	79.87
1995	457.8	254.2	99.5	353.7	55.5	77.26
1996	530.4	297.7	176.3	474.0	56.1	89.37
1997	596.6	335.2	181.8	517.0	56.2	86.66
1998	538.6	348.7	224.2	572.9	64.7	106.37
1999	558.0	328.4	154.1	482.5	58.9	86.47
2000	528.7	376.1	152.6	528.7	71.1	100.0
2001	532.3	409.6	156.1	565.7	76.9	106.27
2002	574.1	434.3	119.2	553.5	75.6	96.41

Source: Economic Report of the President, 2003, Table B-90; Thomson Financial Securities Data; share-repurchase data for 1972–1983 are from Grullon and Michaely (2002).

TABLE 18.3 Dow Jones Industrial Companies with Share Reductions, 1994–2001

	Adj. Shares Outstanding (in millions)		
	12/31/1994	*12/31/2001*	*% Change*
American Express Co.	1,488	1,331	−10.5%
Caterpillar, Inc.	401	343	−14.3
Coca-Cola Co.	2,552	2,486	−2.6
E.I. DuPont de Nemours & Co.	1,362	1,002	−26.4
Eastman Kodak Co.	340	291	−14.4
General Electric Co.	10,236	9,926	−3.0
General Motors Corp.	754	559	−25.9
Hewlett-Packard Co.	2,039	1,939	−4.9
International Business Machines Corp.	2,351	1,723	−26.7
McDonald's Corp.	1,387	1,281	−7.7
Merck & Co., Inc.	2,496	2,273	−8.9
Minnesota Mining & Manufacturing Co.	420	391	−6.8
Philip Morris Cos.	2,559	2,153	−15.9
Procter & Gamble Co.	1,369	1,296	−5.3
United Technologies Corp.	493	472	−4.1
Wal-Mart Stores, Inc.	4,594	4,453	−3.1

Source: Compustat.

December 31, 2001, the adjusted number of shares outstanding of IBM declined from 2,351 million to 1,723 million, representing a reduction of 26.7%. Similarly, the number of Coca Cola shares outstanding declined from 3,258 million in 1982 to 2,486 million in 2001, a decrease of 23.7% over the period. The share reductions have been widespread. For the period from the end of 1994 to the end of 2001, 16 of the 30 Dow Jones Industrial companies reduced the number of shares of stock outstanding. For this period, 7 of the 16 reduced the number of shares outstanding by more than 10%. These large reductions in shares outstanding reflect the high rates of share-repurchase activity.

MAJOR TYPES OF SHARE REPURCHASE

We first briefly describe four major types of share repurchases. After this overview, we analyze in greater depth the nature and implications of each. The four major types are:

1. Fixed-price tender offers (FPTs)
2. Dutch auctions (DAs)
3. Transferable put rights (TPRs)
4. Open-market repurchases (OMRs)

FIXED-PRICE TENDER OFFERS (FPTs)

A firm offers to buy a specified fraction of shares within a given time period. The fixed tender price offered is usually higher than the prevailing market price of the stock at the time of the offer. Most fixed-price tender offers are at least fully subscribed. If the offer is oversubscribed—more shares are offered than are sought—the firm can buy the shares back on a pro rata basis.

Alternatively, the firm can elect to buy back all shares (more than the original target number or fraction) at the tender offer price. If the tender offer is undersubscribed, the firm can extend the offer, hoping to have more shares tendered over time, or the firm can cancel the offer if it includes a minimum acceptance clause, or the firm can simply buy back whatever number or percentage of shares were tendered. In a fixed-price tender offer, the firm usually pays any transfer taxes involved, and the shareholder pays no brokerage fees.

DUTCH AUCTIONS (DAs)

In a Dutch auction, the firm announces the number of shares it will buy in a specified time period and the price range in which shareholders may offer to tender. For example, the current price of the stock might be $14. The company might offer to buy 4 million shares at a price range of $15 to $19 per share. Typically, the price offers will be at intervals such as 10¢ or 25¢. At the offer price that results in 4 million shares being offered, all shares offered at or below that price will be purchased at that price. Thus, even though some shareholders might all have offered to sell at $16, if $17 is the price at which the 4 million shares are offered, they all will receive the $17 per share. Oversubscription is possible in a Dutch auction if the reservation prices of the shareholders are lower than the lower-range price terms. Oversubscription also can occur from the lumpiness of bidding schedules. For example, if at $16.70 fewer than 4 million shares were offered but at $16.80, shareholders offered 4.1 million shares, the company might accept only a fraction of shares (4.0/4.1) of the amount tendered by each shareholder, or it might take the full 4.1 million shares at the $16.80.

TRANSFERABLE PUT RIGHTS (TPRs)

A firm seeks to purchase 5% of its outstanding common shares. Each shareholder would receive one TPR for every 20 shares held. Thus, if a firm has 100 million shares outstanding and is seeking to repurchase 5 million shares or 5%, then 5 million TPRs will be issued, and for every 100 shares a shareholder will receive five TPRs. A secondary market develops in which TPRs are bought and sold. If the prevailing market price of the stock is $14 and the TPR gives the shareholder the right to put the stock to the company at $15.50, trading may take place in the TPRs. Shareholders who believe that the stock is worth less than $15.50 will be glad to have the opportunity to put the stock to the company at $15.50. These shareholders or other investors will be buyers of the TPRs. On the other hand, shareholders who believe that the stock is worth more than $15.50, for example $16 or even $18, will want to continue to hold their stock and sell their TPRs.

OPEN-MARKET REPURCHASES (OMRs)

A firm announces that it will repurchase some dollar amount (e.g., $500 million) of its common stock from time to time in the open market. This is the most frequent type of share repurchase, outnumbering the other three methods by a factor of 10 to 1. However, open-market repurchases generally involve a smaller percentage of total shares outstanding than the other methods. OMRs probably average about 5% of shares outstanding versus about 16% for fixed-price tender offers.

The foregoing provides an overview of each of the four major types of share repurchases. Each one will be examined at greater depth in an attempt to understand the theory and practical decision making involved in choosing the form and terms of a share repurchase. We start the analysis with the fixed-price tender offers because they represent a convenient vehicle for developing the basic logic of share repurchases. We defer the discussion on OMRs to the section on event studies because their characteristics are best explained in that context.

FIXED-PRICE TENDER OFFERS (FPTs)

In a cash tender offer, the company usually sets forth the number of shares it is offering to purchase and the price at which it will repurchase them, as well as the period of time during which the offer will be extended. The tender offer price is generally higher than the market price at the time of offer (by approximately 20% on average). The tender offer price is usually the net price received by the shareholders who tender their shares, because the tendering shareholders pay no brokerage fees and the company generally pays any transfer taxes that are levied.

The number of shares set forth in the tender offer typically represents the maximum number that the company seeks to repurchase. If the number of shares tendered exceeds this limit, the company can purchase all or a fraction of the shares tendered in excess of the amount initially set forth. The company also may reserve the right to extend the time period of the offer. If a company purchases less than all shares tendered, the purchases must be made on a pro rata basis from each of the tendering shareholders. The adoption of SEC Rule 13e-4 in September 1979 made mandatory the pro rata repurchase of shares when the number tendered exceeds the number the company purchases.

If fewer shares are tendered during the initial offer period than were targeted by management, the company may decide to extend the length of the offer period. If the offer period is lengthened, the company is likely to purchase all shares tendered before the first expiration date and then purchase shares offered during the extension period either pro rata or in the order in which the shares are offered.

BASIC STOCK REPURCHASE MODEL

To understand the implications of stock-repurchasing and exchange offers, let us first set out some of the quantitative relationships involved. As is customary, it is necessary to set forth the assumptions of the model employed. The literature on the subject suggests a number of basic conditions involved in the equilibrium pricing of securities (Vermaelen, 1981).

1. The market is efficient in that at any time, market prices reflect all publicly available information that influences the prices of securities.
2. This also implies that markets are informationally efficient, which specifies that information is costless and is received simultaneously by all individuals. In the economic literature, these conditions generally are referred to as the condition of pure competition.
3. Perfect competition exists in securities markets. This implies that individual investors are price takers and cannot influence the outcome of a stock-repurchase offer.
4. Investors seek to maximize the value of their wealth after taking into account taxes and transactions costs.
5. After the announcement date, investors have homogeneous expectations with respect to the change in value that will be caused by the share repurchase and with respect to the fraction of shares that will be purchased by the company.
6. Offers are maximum-limit offers. This means that if the offer is undersubscribed, the firm will buy all shares tendered. However if the offer is oversubscribed, the company will buy

all shares tendered or will allocate shares pro rata—the company buys back the same fraction of shares from every tendering shareholder.

7. The price changes analyzed in connection with share repurchase are after adjusting for marketwide price changes.

In the analysis that follows, we employ a number of symbols:

P_0 = preannouncement share price
P_T = tender price
P_E = postexpiration share price
N_0 = preannouncement number of shares outstanding
N_E = number of shares outstanding after repurchase
W = shareholder wealth effect caused by the share repurchase
F_p = fraction of shares repurchased = $(N_0 - N_E)/N_0$
$1 - F_P$ = fraction of untendered shares = N_E/N_0

The basic condition that must be met is set forth in the equation

$$P_E N_E = P_0 N_0 - P_T(N_0 - N_E) + W \qquad (18.1)$$

Equation (18.1) states that the value of the shares outstanding after expiration of the repurchase offer equals the value of the shares existing before the announcement of the repurchase offer less the value of the shares repurchased plus the change in shareholder wealth associated with the repurchase offer. The source of W, the shareholder wealth effect, will be analyzed subsequently. If we then divide equation (18.1) by N_0 and substitute for the definitions of fraction of shares repurchased and fraction of shares not repurchased, we obtain the equation

$$P_E(1 - F_p) = P_0 - P_T F_p + W/N_0 \qquad (18.2)$$

We next divide by P_0 and solve for the rate of increase in value or the rate of return created by the repurchase offer:

$$\frac{W}{N_0 P_0} = F_p\left(\frac{P_T - P_0}{P_0}\right) + (1 - F_p)\left(\frac{P_E - P_0}{P_0}\right) \qquad (18.3)$$

Equation (18.3) reveals the two components of rate of return associated with the repurchase offer. The first component is the rate of return received by the tendering shareholders weighted by the percentage of shares purchased. The second component is the rate of return received by nontendering shareholders weighted by the percentage of nontendered shares.

Dann (1981) found for his sample of FPT share repurchases totaling 143 observations over the period 1962 to 1976 that the fraction of shares repurchased averaged 20%. The shareholder wealth effect was 15%. The initial premium represented by the tender offer was 23%. From this information, using the equation (18.3) relation, we can solve for the relationship between the price premium (X) of the stock at expiration of the repurchase offer and the initial price, P_0:

$$15\% = (20\%)(23\%) + 80\% X \qquad (18.4)$$

The premium of the expiration price after the share repurchase is, therefore, 13% over the initial share price. Thus, as shown in equation (18.4a), of the 15% wealth effect associated with the share-repurchase offer, 4.6% goes to the tendering shareholders and 10.4% goes to the nontendering shareholders.

$$15\% = 0.2(23\%) + 0.8(13\%)$$
$$15\% = 4.6\% + 10.4\%$$ **(18.4a)**

The relationship is similar for the Vermaelen (1981) study, which covered 131 FPT share repurchases over the period 1962 to 1977. The initial average premium was the same, 23%, but the fraction repurchased averaged 15%. The wealth effect was 16%. The relationships are shown in equation (18.5).

$$16\% = 15\%(23\%) + 85\%X$$
$$0.16 = 0.0345 + 0.85X$$
$$X = 0.1476 = 14.76\%$$
$$16\% = 0.15(23\%) + 0.85(14.76\%)$$
$$= 3.45\% + 12.5\%$$ **(18.5)**

The indicated postexpiration price is 14.76% over the initial price. Thus, using Vermaelen's data, the 16% wealth effect is composed of 3.45% to the tendering shareholders and 12.55% to the nontendering shareholders. Other studies of FPT share repurchases for sample periods prior to 1980 found similar results; these include Bradley and Wakeman (1983), Brickley (1983), Masulis (1980), and Vermaelen (1984).

The study by Comment and Jarrell (1991) covered the period 1984 to 1989. The median premium paid was 16%, with about 14% of the shares purchased. The postexpiration premium indicated by the event returns for a three-day window was about 11% for fixed-price tender offers. The wealth effect would, therefore, be:

$$11.7\% = 0.14(16\%) + 0.86(11\%)$$

This equation treats the event returns as an approximation to the postexpiration percentage price increase over the price of the stock before the share-repurchase announcement. It appears that the premiums offered during later fixed-price tender offer programs declined. This was associated with a decline in the event returns and in the post-expiration percentage price gain.

The still later study by Lie and McConnell (1998) extended the Comment and Jarrell sample through December 1994. The event returns for a three-day window were 7.9% mean and 6.8% median. The fraction of shares purchased and the premium offered were not significantly different from those of the earlier study. This suggests that the market expectation of future cash flow improvements was not as strong for later periods.

RATIONALE FOR THE POSTEXPIRATION PRICE CHANGES

The earlier studies covering data prior to 1980 disagreed on the sources of the postexpiration stock price increases associated with share-repurchase programs. Masulis (1980) emphasized the benefits of increased leverage. Vermaelen argued that although the leverage hypothesis might play a role, it is not the predominant explanation for the observed abnormal returns following the share-repurchase offer. He argued that the more plausible explanation is the signaling or information effect. He reported that tender offers for share repurchase are associated with per-share earnings of tendering firms that subsequently are above what would have been predicted by a time series model using preannouncement data.

Nohel and Tarhan (1998) also added to the Comment and Jarrell sample, covering the period 1978 through 1991 with a sample of 290 companies. Building on prior work by Lang and Litzenberger (1989), Howe, He, and Kao (1992), and Perfect, Petersen, and Petersen (1995), they divided the sample into low q-ratio firms and high q-ratio firms. They also focused their measurements on event returns of share-repurchase firms in excess of a control group of non-share repurchase firms. They used monthly returns to compute event returns. They found that the share-repurchase firms, net of the control group, have significantly positive event returns. However, the improvement comes entirely from the low q firms.

Nohel and Tarhan tried to explain the reasons why the low q firms outperform the high q firms. They used five measures of operating performance and five measures of investment characteristics, similar to those employed in the study by Healy, Palepu, and Ruback (1992). They found that the low q firms have higher asset turnover ratios relative to control firms before and after the repurchase. The difference widens following the repurchase. The improvement in asset turnover is associated with asset sales by the low q firms. They observed that successful repurchasing firms dispose of poorly performing assets as part of a corporate-restructuring program. The foregoing studies agree that fixed-price tender offers up to 1990 result in postexpiration stock price increases on the order of magnitude of 8% to 10%. These conclusions are further reinforced by studies of Dutch auction repurchases, discussed next.

DUTCH AUCTION REPURCHASES

A fundamental difference between fixed-price tender offers and Dutch auction repurchases (DARs) is brought out by the description of the first firm to utilize the Dutch auction (Bagwell, 1992). In 1981, Todd Shipyards was planning a fixed-price tender offer at $28 for about 10% of its 5.5 million shares outstanding. Bear Stearns, the investment banker for Todd, suggested instead a Dutch auction repurchase at a range of prices not to exceed $28. The fee paid to Bear Stearns would be 30% of the savings if the clearing price was less than $28. Todd employed the Dutch auction. The clearing purchase price was $26.50.

This example illustrates one of the basic differences between the FPT and the DAR. In the FPT, the tender offer is made for one price. In the DAR, a range of prices is made available within which investors can choose a price at which their shares will be tendered. In the Bagwell (1992) study, data were obtained for 32 firms employing Dutch auctions between 1981 and 1988. These firms supplied schedules of the quantity of shares offered at each price within the specified range. Bagwell analyzed these data, setting the preannouncement price equal to $100, and expressed the price range as a percentage of the preannouncement price. She also calculated the percentage of total shares sought in the Dutch auction repurchase offer. Schedules were developed in which quantity is normalized to measure the cumulative percentage of outstanding shares tendered at or below each price within the price range. Bagwell presented supply curves for 17 firms that did not require confidentiality. We have directly contacted other firms conducting Dutch auctions to request supply schedules. These supply schedules are consistent with the data presented in Appendix II in the Bagwell study.

An important finding from the Dutch auction supply curves is evidence of shareholder heterogeneity (Bagwell, 1992). Consistently upward-sloping supply curves are obtained from shareholders tendering responses in the Dutch auctions. An upward-sloping supply or valuation schedule is illustrated by the following equation:

$$V(r) = 80 + 0.04r \qquad \textbf{(18.6)}$$

The meaning of equation (18.6) and the definition of the terms in it can be clarified with the help of Figure 18.1. The horizontal axis shows the number of shareholders (r), and each

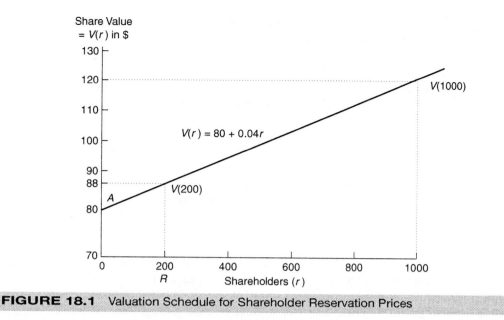

FIGURE 18.1   Valuation Schedule for Shareholder Reservation Prices

point up through 1,000 is for an individual shareholder holding one share of stock. The total number of shares outstanding (N) is also equal to 1,000. Each rth shareholder has a reservation price $V(r)$. The reservation price $V(r)$ is the price at which the rth shareholder would be willing to sell the share of stock held. $V(r)$ means that the reservation price (or value) depends on which rth shareholder we are talking about. For example, the 1st shareholder has a reservation price of $80 + $0.04 (1), or $80.04. The 100th shareholder has a reservation price of $80 + $0.04 (100) = $84 and so on. Equation (18.6) and its graph in Figure 18.1 show the relationship between the rth shareholder and his or her associated reservation price $V(r)$. The vertical axis in Figure 18.1 depicts these reservation prices, $V(r)$, for the r shareholders. The intercept term, $V(r) = 80$, represents the prevailing market price of the stock. Shareholders with reservation prices at or below the prevailing market price of $80 already would have sold their shares.

We show what happens when the firm seeks to repurchase 200 shares (R) representing 20% of the shares outstanding. It offers to repurchase the shares at a range of prices between $84 and $90. If the reservation prices of the shareholders are depicted by the illustrative equation, $V(r) = 80 + 0.04r$, we would have the following result. The price that would elicit 200 shares in the Dutch auction would be $88. We can check this using equation (18.6).

$$V(r) = \$80 + 0.04(200) = \$88 \qquad \textbf{(18.6a)}$$

The gain to the tendering shareholders can be measured by triangle A:

$$0.5(88 - 80)200 = \$800$$

Because the prevailing market price of the stock before the tender offer was $80, the 200 shares had a market value of $16,000. The gain of $800, therefore, represents 5% of the pre-tender market value of the 200 shares ($80 × 200 = $16,000).

Let us next consider the situation of the nontendering shareholders (this analysis is based on Gay et al., 1991). The nontendering shareholders now have a claim on the valuation curve less what was paid out to the tendering shareholders. The new upward-sloping supply curve for the nontendering shareholders is given for $V'(r)$ by the following equation:

$$V'(r) = (0.04r + 80)/0.8 - 88(200)/800 = 0.05r + 78 \qquad \text{(18.7)}$$

Thus, the new valuation schedule will have a lower implied intercept but a steeper slope.

The practical significance of the more steeply sloped valuation schedule is that the reservation prices of the remaining shareholders are higher than the reservation prices of the original valuation schedule. The role of share repurchase as a takeover defense is highlighted. The reservation price of the marginal shareholder after the share repurchase is something over $88 versus the original $80. In addition, the reservation price of the 1,000[th] shareholder is now $50 + $78 = $128. Therefore, to compete with the share-repurchase alternative, a bidder would have to pay a higher premium than would have been required under the original supply schedule. In a fixed-price tender offer, the tender offer price probably would have been in excess of $88 to obtain 20% of the shares. The premium paid in the Dutch auction share repurchase is somewhat lower (Kamma, et al., 1992).

Comment and Jarrell (1991) pushed the analysis still further. They investigated the influence of pro rata transactions and the role of the risk exposure of officers and directors. The logic of the necessity of prorationing is straightforward. If the reservation prices of the shareholders are so low that the tender offer stimulates a flood of tenders by shareholders, it is not likely that wealth effects will be high.

Comments and Jarrell (1991) also investigated the impact of whether officers and directors are exposed to a personal wealth loss if their signaling is not credible. Comment and Jarrell considered that officers and directors (OD) are at risk if two conditions hold. First, their collective proportionate ownership interest in their company's stock must increase as a result of the tender offer. Second, the premium in the tender offer is more than 2% above the market price of the stock four days before the offer is announced.

We summarize the empirical data for wealth effects that take into account the pro rata influence and the risk of officers and directors in Table 18.4. Average wealth effects in fixed-price tender offers are in the range of 12% to 13% as discussed previously. For Dutch auctions, the wealth effect is smaller, about 8%. This is plausible because the average premium paid in Dutch auctions is lower, as shareholder heterogeneity results in an upward-sloping supply schedule. If prorationing is involved, then shareholder reservation prices are low. Signaling of future value increases is less likely to be credible. With prorationing, the wealth effects are virtually zero for both fixed-price tender offers and for Dutch auctions. Where there is no prorationing, the reservation prices of shareholders are relatively high. They are more likely to view the premiums offered in the share repurchases as credible signals of future value increases. The wealth effects are relatively large.

Similarly, if officers and directors are at risk, the signaling will be credible and the wealth effects large. If officers and directors are not at risk, the wealth effects will be small or negligible.

TABLE 18.4 Wealth Effects

	Average	Pro Rata		OD at Risk	
		Yes	*No*	*Yes*	*No*
FPT	12–13%	0–5%	15%	16%	4%
DA	8%	0	8%	8%	0

After considering the kinds of evidence presented in Table 18.4 Comment and Jarrell (1991, pp. 1258–1259) concluded that Dutch auctions are favored by relatively large firms that are widely followed by security analysts and other informed investors. These are companies in which management owns a relatively low percentage of stock. Because their stock is widely followed and management stakes are relatively low, these firms are "ill-suited" to send strongly credible signals in premium repurchase offers. For such firms, Comment and Jarrell concluded that Dutch auctions are likely to be substitutes for open-market repurchases. They argued that the firms are not substituting Dutch auctions for fixed-price tender offers but rather would have switched to open-market programs.

A further comparison of fixed-price versus Dutch auctions is made by Lie and McConnell (1998). Their study covered 130 fixed-price and 102 Dutch auction self-tender offers between 1981 and 1994. Dutch auctions started in 1981 and accounted for fewer than 10 transactions per year through 1987. For the peak years 1988 and 1989, the number of Dutch auction share repurchases moved up to slightly more than 20 per year. In 1991, one fixed-price and two Dutch auctions occurred. In 1993, there were six Dutch auctions, and in 1994 only four. The dollar value of share repurchases grew 30% per year over the period of their study (1981 to 1994), so the sharp decline in the number of self-tenders in their sample after 1989 suggests that open-market share repurchases were substituting for fixed-price and Dutch auction repurchases. Most of the fixed-price transactions in their sample were pre-1990. Thus, their findings may in part reflect the economic characteristics of the 1980s. versus the 1990s.

Over a three-day window centered on the announcement date, the mean and median abnormal return for fixed-price tender offers were 7.9% and 6.8%. respectively, and for Dutch auctions they were 7.7% and 6.4%. Lie and McConnell noted that Comment and Jarrell recognized that the excess returns for fixed-price tenders were higher than for Dutch auction tenders only when offers with coincident confounding news were excluded. The mean and median abnormal returns become 10.2% and 8.6%, respectively, for fixed-price versus 7.6% and 6.2% for Dutch auctions. This difference is significant at the 5% level.

The emphasis of the Lie and McConnell study was on a comparison of earnings patterns and on a refinement of the estimate of expected earnings developed by Barber and Lyon (1996). The Barber and Lyon methodology proposed that when firms in a sample exhibit abnormal (earnings) performance, the benchmark should be firms with similarly abnormal performance. The logic is that performance might exhibit mean reversion, which means that over time firms with earnings higher than the mean will move down toward the mean, and conversely with firms with earnings below the mean. The deviation from the expected mean reversion is a measure of performance. Lie and McConnell found that their sample firms in both sets of tender offers exhibited superior performance during the year of the tender offer. They exhibited slower mean reversion in their operating performance than firms not undertaking tender offers. They observed that if there is an earnings signal in the two types of self-tenders under analysis, it is that these firms continued to exhibit superior performance longer than what otherwise would have been expected. They emphasized however, that no significant difference is evident in the performance (as measured) between the fixed-price versus Dutch auction samples.

TRANSFERABLE PUT RIGHTS (TPRs)

As summarized earlier, transferable put rights (TPRs) represent options granted to shareholders in proportion to the number of shares owned. In our previous example, we noted that if a company sought to repurchase 20% of its shares using TPRs, it would issue 20 TPRs for every

100 shares held by stockholders. If the put price represents a substantial premium over the prevailing market price, the TPRs will have value and trading in them will take place. Because all shares put to the firm are repurchased, the possibility of prorationing that occurs in a fixed-price tender offer is avoided. This point is illustrated by the first company to use TPRs, which was Millicom, a small cellular telephone and electronic paging company (Kale et al., 1989, p. 141). In April 1987, Millicom issued TPRs to its shareholders as a method of share repurchase. Millicom explained its choice of TPRs with reference to the prorationing problem. Under a fixed-price tender offer (FPT), because of the possibility of prorationing, shareholders cannot be sure what percentage of their tendered shares will be repurchased. Shareholders can avoid this risk by selling to arbitrageurs, who thereby achieve a strong bargaining position, particularly if a takeover or a control contest develops.

In their study, Kale et al., (1989) reported the announcement by Vista Chemical Company in May 1989 of a plan to repurchase one third of its 15 million shares outstanding at $70 share through the issuance of TPRs. They also described in some detail the use of TPRs by Gillette, the second company to initiate a share repurchase program with the use of TPRs. Gillette, the well-known maker of razor blades, pens, and other personal products, was subject to series of hostile takeover attempts for various reasons. In 1986, Revlon's Ronald O. Perelman made a series of takeover bids that were fought off by a targeted share repurchase (greenmail) plus a standstill agreement.

In February 1988, Coniston Partners announced that it owned 6.8% of Gillette stock and was seeking four seats on Gillette's board. Gillette accelerated its open-market share repurchase program. In the proxy fight for control, Gillette defeated Coniston by obtaining 52% of shareholder votes. Coniston filed a lawsuit claiming that Gillette had made false and misleading claims during the proxy contest. With the court contest under way, Gillette and Coniston reached a settlement, announced August 1, 1988, associated with the initiation of a stock repurchase through TPRs. Gillette, with 112 million shares outstanding, issued one put per seven shares, which would result in the repurchase of 16 million shares. Each TPR enabled the holder to sell back one share to the company at $45 (the prevailing market rate was about $39) by September 19, 1988. The TPRs were issued to shareholders of record as of August 12, 1988. Trading in the TPRs started on August 16, 1988, and took place through September 19, 1988. Over that period of time, the stock price of Gillette averaged about $35, with the TPR price fluctuating slightly above and below $10. Thus, one TPR plus one share of stock approximated the put price of $45. The average daily volume of trading during the period August 16 to September 19 was about 359,000 TPRs.

The logic of the TPR trading documented for Gillette can be conveyed by the numerical example we developed in connection with our discussion of Dutch auction repurchases (DARs). Recall that we postulated a reservation supply price schedule for shareholders:

$$V(r) = 80 + 0.04r \qquad \textbf{(18.6)}$$

In our example for the DAR, if a firm had announced that it would repurchase 20% of its 1,000 shares at a schedule of prices from $80 to $88, the market would have cleared at a price of $88. Using the Kale, Noe, and Gay notation of LR for a low-reservation price shareholder and HR for a high reservation price shareholder, we can see that the LR shareholders would have tendered and the HR shareholders would not have tendered. At the end of the DAR, the new marginal shareholder would have a reservation price of $88.

However, in practice the firm knows that the supply schedule is positively sloped but does not know the price and quantity that would just clear the market with neither prorationing nor an undersubscription to the tender offer. We can illustrate how the use of TPRs solves this problem. Assume that a firm facing the shareholder valuation schedule depicted by Figure 18.1 offered to buy 20% of its shareholders who would be interested in selling at $96. Based on the valuation schedule, the number of shares and shareholders who would be interested in selling at $96 would be determined by the following equations:

$$\$96 = \$80 + 0.04r$$

Solving for r, 400 shares would be offered, but only 200 TPRs were issued. Hence, trading in the TPRs would take place. Shareholders with a reservation price below $88 (the LRs) would place the greatest value on the TPRs and would end up buying TPRs from the shareholders with the higher reservation prices (the HRs). By the end of the trading period when the TPRs would be exercised, the LRs would own the 200 TPRs and the HRs would have been net sellers. Two hundred shares, along with the 200 TPRs, would be put to the company. The result would be that the TPR trading discovered the market clearing price for the 20% of the shares that the company is seeking to repurchase.

Another use of the TPRs is in consolidating the control position of a group. We can identify three types of shareholders: the control group, dissidents fighting for control, and others. Before the issuance of TPRs, the ownership position of each group is given in column 1 of Table 18.5. If one TPR is issued for each three shares held, and assuming that the number of shares is identical to the percentages indicated in column 1, 33.3 TPRs would be issued. Column 2 suggests that the control group would sell their TPRs but not their stock. Postulating that the put price represents a substantial premium over the prevailing market price of the stock, the dissidents would be happy to accept the substantial premium. The third group would use the 14 TPRs received plus the 11.3 TPRs purchased from the control group to sell 25.3 of their shares. Column 3 shows the number of shares each group owns after the TPRs plus stock are put to the company. The company now has only 66.7 shares outstanding. Column 4 expresses each group's ownership as a percent of the total number of shares outstanding. The control group has moved from 34% to 51%. The share of the dissidents is unchanged at 24%. The percentage ownership of the other shareholders has dropped from 42% to 25%.

From the illustrative examples, from the real-life cases, and from the theoretical framework, we can understand the advantages of the use of TPRs. The trading in TPRs results in the low-reservation-price shareholders putting their shares for repurchase. The remaining shareholders will be high-reservation-price shareholders. Thus, the TPRs are useful as a takeover defense. In addition, the TPRs may rearrange control positions, as well.

We conclude this section with a consideration of why the reservation price schedule is upward sloping. The empirical data presented by Bagwell (1992) is solid evidence of upward-sloping reservation price schedules. We have checked her findings by directly corresponding

TABLE 18.5 TPRs and Control

	(1) Before %	(2) Sell	(3) After	(4) After %
1. Control group	34	0.0	34.0	51
2. Dissidents	24	8.0	16.0	24
3. Others	42	25.3[a]	16.7	25
Total	100	33.3	66.7	100

[a]25.3 = 14.0 + 11.3.

with a sample of companies that have used Dutch auctions in recent years. Although we do not have permission to publish their data, we can confirm that they are consistent with the data published in Bagwell (1992). This leaves no question of the evidence of upward-sloping reservation price schedules. However, in our idealized example, we have used a slope that seems to be higher than that exhibited in the Bagwell data and in the data we developed. So one question is: How strong is the upward-sloping effect?

A second question is: Why does the upward-sloping schedule exist? Most authors refer to the possibility of a different tax basis for LRs and HRs. Beyond that, shareholder heterogeneity and differing expectations and valuations are possible explanations. This is an area that requires more investigation.

EVENT STUDIES

This section present a panoramic view of event studies and other evidence related to changing motives for share repurchase activities over time.

UNDERVALUATION IN THE 1970s

Earlier event studies were primarily of FPTs. The use of DAs did not begin until 1981. In recent years (1994 to 1999), OMRs represented 95% to 98% of repurchase activity (Grullon and Ikenberry, 2000). For that time period, FPT offers were generally 1% to 1.5%; DAs were about 2% to 3% of total repurchases. Our discussion of the event studies will seek to explain the changing relative importance of the types of repurchases used.

Table 18.6 presents an overview of representative event studies using data covering time periods beginning in 1962 and ending in 1997. The changing patterns of the results reported by the event studies reflect changes in the economic and financial environments. The studies present different patterns of pre-event data, near post-event data, or longer-term post-event performance.

Dann (1981) calculated for his sample of 143 FPTs during the period 1962 to 1976 a 17% cumulative abnormal return (CAR) for a 3-day window. The initial premium averaged 23% offered for an average 20% fraction of shares outstanding. At the expiration of the FPT, share prices on average were 13% (the shareholders' wealth effect) above their pre-announcement level. The results are similar to the Vermaelen (1981) study, which covered 131 FPTs over the period 1962 to 1977. The initial average premium was the same, 23%, but the fraction repurchased averaged 15%. The wealth effect was 16%.

The dominant explanation for the positive CARs for this period was undervaluation. The FPT announcements were signals of this undervaluation. Of this period, Warren Buffet was quoted as saying that in the mid-1970s, many stocks traded below their intrinsic values and "the wisdom of making these [share repurchases] was virtually screaming at managements" (McGough et al., 2000).

SHARE REPURCHASES AROUND THE OCTOBER 1987 STOCK MARKET DROP

Another pioneering study reported in Table 18.6 is the analysis of the share-repurchase activity associated with the stock market crash in October 1987 by Netter and Mitchell (1989). They analyzed OMRs for 337 NYSE/AMEX companies and 181 OTC companies. They observed significant, positive CARs over a 3-day window for both groups. The CARs for the near post-event period (+2, +40) were also significant, positive. They also observed that firms that announced repurchases had underperformed the market in the period immediately before the

TABLE 18.6 Representative Event Studies on Share-Repurchase Activities (CARs in percent)

Author	Period	Source	n	Type	Benchmark	Pre-Event Period	CAR	Event Announcement Period	CAR	Near Post-Event Period	CAR	LONGER TERM Period	All n	CAR	Value Stocks n	CAR
Dann (1981)	1962–1976	WSJ, IDD	143	FPT	portfolio mean			−1 to +1	17.01***	+3 to +20	2.86					
Netter and Mitchell (1989)	Oct. 1987	SEC	337	OMR NYSE/AMEX	CRSP EW			−1 to +1	2.71***	+2 to +40	3.45***					
	Oct. 1987	SEC	181	OMR OTC	CRSP EW			−1 to +1	5.46***	+2 to +40	10.57***					
Comment and Jarrell (1991)	1984–1989	DJNR	64	DA w/o CCN	CRSP EW			−1 to +1	7.90^{NA}							
	1984–1989	DJNR	68	FPT w/o CCN	CRSP EW			−1 to +1	11.00^{NA}							
	1984–1989	DJNR	84	DA, FPT ODR w/o CCN	CRSP EW			−1 to +1	11.70^{NA}							
	1984–1989	DJNR	48	DA, FPT not ODR w/o CCN	CRSP EW			−1 to +1	5.60^{NA}							
Bagwell (1992)	1981–1988	WSJ, BPI	31	DA	CRSP EW			−1 to 0	7.67***	−1 to EXP	6.728***					
Ikenberry, Lakonishok and Vermaelen (1995)	1980–1990	WSJ	1239	OMR	CRSP VW	−20 to −3	−3.07***	−2 to +2	3.54***	+3 to +10	0.21	4-yr BH	893	12.14***	169	45.29***
Grullon and Michaely (2002)	1980–1997	SDC, WSJ	3935	OMR	NA			−1 to +1	2.57***							
Kahle (2002)	1993–1996	SDC	712	OMR	NA	−43 to −4	−3.64^{NA}	−1 to +1	1.61^{NA}							

Notes:

Source: WSJ-*Wall Street Journal*, DJNR = Dow Jones News Retrieval, IDD-*Investment Dealer's Digest*, SEC = Division of Market Regulation of the SEC, SDC = Securities Date Corp., BPI = Business Periodicals Index

Type: DA = Dutch auction, FPT = fixed-price tender, OMR = open-market repurchase, ODR = officers & directors at risk, CCN = coincident confounding news

Benchmark: EW = equal weighted, VW = value weighted, NA = not available

Period: BH = Buy-and-Hold

Significance level *** 1%, ** 5%, * 10%, NA = not available

announcement. Their results were with the theory that the repurchases announced at the time of the October 19 stock market crash signaled undervalued stock prices.

Netter and Mitchell (1989) also presented evidence that for 530 publicly traded firms that announced stock repurchases, 347 insiders purchased stock and 33 insiders sold. For companies with no stock-repurchase announcements, 1,566 insiders purchased stock and 22 sold. The value of insider purchases relative to the value of all insider transactions was much higher in repurchase firms (86%) than in firms not announcing repurchases (56%). The purchases by officers and directors reflected their judgments that the stock price declines in October 1987 were only temporary. This contrasts with stock repurchases during the stock market declines beginning in 2000.

COMPARISONS BETWEEN FPTs, DAs, AND OMRs

Comment and Jarrell (1991) compared event returns among the three types of share-repurchase programs. FPTs have somewhat higher CARs than DAs for their total sample. For their sample without confounding events, FPT offers have substantially higher event returns, 11% versus 8%. The event returns to OMRs are much lower, 2.3%. Bagwell (1992) published an in-depth analysis of DAs. Her event return results were similar to those of Comment and Jarrell (1991) for DAs. The effects for prorationing were also similar.

LAGGED RESPONSES

Ikenberry et al. (1995) performed an in-depth analysis of OMRs for a sample of 1,239 for the period 1980 to 1990; the results are shown in Table 18.6. As in other studies, pre-event returns are negative. Event announcement returns for a 5-day window are 3.54%. A 4-year buy-and-hold portfolio of 893 OMRs has a 4-year return of 12.14%. For a portfolio of 169 value stocks, the 4-year return is 45.29%. Ikenberry et al. "hypothesize that the market treats repurchase announcement with skepticism, leading prices to adjust slowly over time." They also examined the potential influence of takeovers. They compared long-run performance overall with firms that survived for at least 4 years following the purchase announcement. For announcements between 1980 and 1988, the 3-year compounded abnormal performance is 13.0%; for survivors, it drops to 6.7%, still significant. For high book–to–market ratio firms, the 3-year abnormal performance drops from 39.7% to 31.6% for survivors. They infer that the takeovers that occurred in their original sample do not explain the abnormal returns of firms that repurchased shares.

Howe, Vogt, and He (2003) find higher initial and longer term returns for share repurchases when equity ownership of management is higher. The higher equity ownership increases the signaling credibility of the repurchase decision. Repurchases may be part of a longer term restructuring program whose soundness is also signaled by high equity ownership by management.

THE MITCHELL AND STAFFORD (2000) METHODOLOGY CRITIQUE

Persistent, long-term, abnormal returns following major corporate events are inconsistent with the efficient market hypothesis. Mitchell and Stafford (2000) found that with the proper statistical methodology, virtually no evidence of long-term, abnormal performance remains. They noted that the usual methodology in the literature calculates average multiyear buy-and-hold abnormal returns (BHAR), using a bootstrapping procedure to draw inferences. Mitchell and Stafford demonstrated that this methodology is biased because it assumed independence of multiyear abnormal returns. However share repurchases cluster by industry and take place in programs of successive announcements over a period of years. They recommended a methodology that accounts for the dependence of event-firm abnormal returns as illustrated by the calendar-time portfolio approach recommended by Fama (1998). After taking into account the positive cross correlations of event-firm abnormal returns, little evidence of long-term abnormal performance remains for major corporate events such as share repurchases.

EVENT RETURNS IN THE 1990s

Two subsequent studies of share repurchases focused on other issues (discussed in the next section) but also included materials on event returns.

Grullon and Michaely (2002) studied 3,935 OMR repurchases for the period 1980 to 1997 using SDC and *Wall Street Journal* sources. They found a positive CAR of 2.57% over a 3-day window, statistically significant at the 1% level. These results are much lower than the Ikenberry et al. results. The performance results in a post-event period are not studied.

Kahle (2002) analyzed 712 OMRs for the period 1993 to 1996 from the SDC M&A database. Similar to Ikenberry et al., she found a negative CAR of –3.64% for the pre-event period from –43 to –4 days. For a 3-day window around the share-repurchase announcement date, she found a mean CAR of 1.61% and a median of 1.30%. She pointed out that these CARs are much lower than in previous studies. She observed that the lower announcement returns are consistent with a reduced role for undervaluation and an increased role for reversing the dilution effects of the exercise of stock options.

THE IMPACT OF STOCK MARKET DECLINES

The stock market declines that began in 1999 accelerated in 2000, with subsequent fluctuations in a range below peak levels by year-end 2002. Nevertheless, some buybacks continued during this time interval. For example, Table 18.7 presents a sample of data on buybacks totaling $56.6 billion beginning in 1999. The closing prices on December 15, 2000, were $13 billion less than the share-repurchase prices paid. By October 9, 2002 the closing prices were $31 billion lower than the purchase prices. For some of the companies in the list, the downward pressure on stock prices reflected unfavorable industry developments that severely impacted individual companies, as well as movements in the general economy and financial markets. However such continuing large losses raise issues with respect to the rationales for these shares repurchases.

IMPLICATION OF GAINS AND LOSSES FROM SHARE REPURCHASES

The patch-quilt nature of the findings in Table 18.6 on event returns makes it difficult to formulate generalizations. Clearly, the findings of studies with data before 1980 based on FPTs were consistent with undervaluation as the main motive for the share buybacks. The Netter and Mitchell (1989) analysis of OMRs related to the October 1987 market crash demonstrated that companies correctly anticipated that the stock market declines were of relatively short duration. The 1987 stock market crash, in contrast to the market declines of 1999 to 2001, were not associated with a recession in the general economy (defining a recession as two successive quarters of declines in real gross domestic product).

Although contagion effects caused temporary declines in world stock markets in October 1987, Mitchell and Netter (1989) presented evidence that a tax bill containing antitakeover provisions caused the October 19, 1987, crash. A tax bill with antitakeover provisions was proposed by the U.S. House Ways and Means Committee on October 13, 1987, and approved by the committee on October 15. The antitakeover provisions would have limited the deductibility of interest on debt incurred to finance corporate takeovers, recapitalizations, and leveraged buyouts; it also would have imposed other restrictions on hostile takeovers. These provisions were associated with a greater

TABLE 18.7 Stock Repurchases in Down Markets (in millions of dollars except per share)

Company	Amount Spent on Buybacks	Time Period	Shares Sought	Average Price	Price Close 12/15/00	Paper Loss 12/15/00	Price Close 10/9/02	Paper Loss 10/9/02
1. AT&T	$ 3,940	Feb/Mar. 1999	69.8	$ 57.31	$ 21.000	($ 2,534)	$10.75	($ 3,250)
2. GM	2,600	1999	36.0	72.22	53.813	(663)	31.01	(1,484)
	310	1/1/00–9/30/00	5.0	62.00	53.813	(41)	31.01	(155)
3. Gillette	2,054	1999	46.7	42.53	33.813	(407)	30.06	(582)
	911	1/1/00–12/8/00	24.5	35.85	33.813	(50)	30.06	(142)
4. Hewlett-Packard	2,643	11/1/98–10/31/99	62.0	42.63	31.625	(682)	11.16	(1,951)
	5,570	11/1/99–10/31/00	97.0	57.44	31.625	(2,504)	11.16	(4,489)
5. IBM	7,280	1999	67.5	107.88	87.813	(1,355)	55.07	(3,565)
	5,279	1/1/00–9/30/00	45.8	115.31	87.813	(1,259)	55.07	(2,759)
6. Intel	4,600	1999	71.3	64.52	32.438	(2,287)	13.46	(3,641)
	3,000	1/1/00–9/30/00	50.7	59.17	32.438	(1,355)	13.46	(2,317)
7. McDonald's	933	1999	24.2	38.55	31.500	(171)	16.56	(532)
	1,700	1/1/00–9/30/00	48.0	35.42	31.500	(188)	16.56	(905)
8. Microsoft	4,852	7/1/99–12/31/99	54.7	88.70	49.188	(2,161)	43.99	(2,446)
	1,752	8/1/00–9/30/00	25.5	68.71	49.188	(498)	43.99	(630)
9. P&G	1,770	fiscal year 2000[a]	17.6	100.34	71.375	(510)	88.19	(214)
10. CIGNA	7,400	1997–2002	90.1	81.92	119.350	3,372	57.50	(2,200)
Total	$56,594					($13,293)		($31,262)

[a]Ended June 30.

Source: Based on McGough et al. (2000) and Norris (2002).

than 10% decline in the stock market from October 14 to 16, triggering the crash on October 19. The tax bill was subsequently enacted without most of the antitakeover provisions. Thus, the negative influences were temporary and the strong positive event returns associated with the share repurchases following the October 19 crash were motivated by judgments of undervaluation.

The Netter and Mitchell (1989) study also measured the behavior of executives and other insider investors. They found that insiders were heavy purchasers of their company equities during this period. Other empirical studies support these findings (Lee et al. 1992; D'Mello and Shroff, 2000). It is plausible that if management uses share repurchases to signal undervaluation, they also would increase their ownership in the company by additional stock purchases.

Similar issues are involved in reconciling the Comment and Jarrell (1991) findings with Ikenberry et al. (1995). The former found that in FPTs and DAs, event returns were substantially lower when officers and directors (ODs) were not at risk. OMRs do not provide information about whether ODs are at risk. Yet the OMRs in the Ikenberry et al. study yielded, very large abnormal returns at announcement and longer term.

We present a possible explanation for the large, abnormal returns from OMRs found in Ikenberry et al. and other studies of OMRs for data through the mid-1990s. A share repurchase by a firm is not an isolated event, but rather is part of a series of repeated actions. Table 18.8 shows that IBM authorized a series of share repurchases of $2.0 to $3.5 billion per year from the mid-1980s

TABLE 18.8 Authorized Repurchases by IBM

Date of Authorization[a]	Authorized Value (in millions)
2/24/1987	$ 574
10/27/1987	1,000
9/27/1988	2,000
10/18/1989	5,000
1/31/1995	2,500
7/25/1995	2,500
11/28/1995	2,500
4/30/1996	2,500
11/26/1996	3,500
4/29/1997	3,500
10/28/1997	3,500
4/28/1998	3,500
10/27/1998	3,500
4/27/1999	3,500
10/26/1999	3,500
4/25/2000	3,500
10/31/2000	3,500
4/24/2001	3,500
10/30/2001	3,500
4/30/2002	3,500
Total	$60,574

[a]Data before 1995 are incomplete.

Source: SDC Database on Share Repurchases.

TABLE 18.9   Frequency of Repurchase Announcements of Large Companies

	Number of Announcements[a]	Year Range	Frequency (Yrs/Announcement)
Abbott Laboratories	13	1982–2000	1.46
Alcoa, Inc.	9	1989–2001	1.44
Amgen, Inc.	8	1992–2002	1.38
Anheuser-Busch Cos., Inc	7	1984–2000	2.43
Baxter International, Inc.	9	1983–1999	1.89
Boeing Co.	5	1987–2000	2.80
ChevronTexaco Corp.	2	1989–1997	4.50
Cisco Systems, Inc.	3	1994–2001	2.67
Coca-Cola Co.	6	1984–1996	2.17
Colgate-Palmolive Co.	7	1985–1998	2.00
Dell Computer Corp.	6	1996–2002	1.17
Dow Chemical Co.	15	1983–1997	1.00
Eastman Kodak Co, Inc.	5	1984–1999	3.20
E.I. du Pont de Nemours and Co.	21	1984–2000	0.81
Eli Lilly & Co.	8	1984–2001	2.25
ExxonMobil Corp.	18	1984–2002	1.06
Ford Motor Co.	7	1984–2000	2.43
General Electric Co.	8	1984–1997	1.75
General Motors Corp.	15	1986–2000	1.00
Gillette Co.	6	1986–1997	2.00
IBM Corp.	16	1987–2002	1.00
Intel Corp.	6	1987–2001	2.50
Johnson & Johnson	6	1984–2002	3.17
Kimberly-Clark Corp.	9	1987–2000	1.56
McDonald's Corp.	6	1992–2001	1.67
Merck & Co, Inc.	13	1984–2002	1.46
Microsoft Corp.	4	1989–1996	2.00
Oracle Corp.	2	1997–1999	1.50
PepsiCo, Inc.	6	1985–2002	3.00
Pfizer, Inc.	8	1991–2002	1.50
Philip Morris Cos., Inc	8	1989–2001	1.63
Procter & Gamble Co.	5	1984–1996	2.60
Sun Microsystems, Inc.	7	1990–2001	1.71

[a]Includes major subsidiaries.

Source: SDC.

through 2002. More generally, Table 18.9 shows that for a sample of 33 large companies, share repurchases were authorized with high frequency. The number of announcements was as high as 21 for the period 1994 to 2002 for DuPont, a frequency of 1 every 10 months. The frequency for General Motors and IBM was 1 per year. Yet studies of OMRs treat their observations as independent, when actually they might represent related events in a program of repurchases followed over an extended time period.

A MODEL OF UNDERVALUATION

A formal model of the empirical findings of Ikenberry et al. (1995) is suggested by Rappaport (1998). If a company's shares are undervalued and if stock is repurchased near the undervalued price, the firm will earn a rate of return greater than its market-required cost of equity. The relationship can be expressed in a formula, where the symbols are defined as follows:

R = rate of return on share repurchase
k_s^* = market required cost of equity of the firm
V = intrinsic value of the firm
P = market price or market value of the firm

The initial relationship is shown by equation 18.8.

$$\text{Rate of return on share repurchase } = \frac{\text{Cost of equity}}{1 - \text{Percent undervaluation}} \qquad \textbf{(18.8)}$$

In symbols:

$$R = \frac{k_s^*}{1 - (V - P)/V} = \frac{k_s^*}{\left(V - V + P\right)/V} = \frac{k_s^*}{P/V}$$

In words:

$$R = \frac{\text{Cost of Equity}}{\text{Ratio of Actual Market to Intrinsic Value}}$$

For example, let k_s^*=10%, P=$20, and V=$30. Then:

$$R = \frac{10\%}{\$20\,/\,\$30} = 15\%$$

A share repurchase financed by foregoing value-creating investments is rational only if the investment would have yielded a rate of return less than the rate of return on a share repurchase, as calculated previously. A numerical example illustrates equation 18.8. The data inputs are shown in Table 18.10. An all-equity firm has an annual cash flow of $300, and a 10% cost of equity, and, therefore, has an initial intrinsic value of $3,000. With 100 shares outstanding, it has an intrinsic value per share of $30. The market price per share is $20. In an open market repurchase, assume it buys 20 shares at $20. This represents a market value discount of one-third, as shown in Line 6. Using equation 18.8, the rate of return on the share repurchase is 15%.

Table 18.11 provides numerical examples comparing returns from repurchases to returns from real investments. Case 1 represents the share-repurchase investment of $400 (Line 4) in which 20 shares are repurchased at their market value of $20. The new equity value is the original value of $3,000 less the $400 outlay. The new shareholder intrinsic value per share divides the $2,600 by 80, the new number of shares, to obtain $32.50 per share as shown in Line 12. The market value per share is one-third lower or $21.67, as shown in Line 15. This represents an increase in the initial market price per share of $20, or 8.33%. We next consider the Case 2

TABLE 18.10 Basic Relationships

1. Cash flow per year		$300
2. Cost of capital		10%
3. Intrinsic value before repurchase = (1)/(2)		$3,000
4. Number of shares		100
5. Intrinsic value per share = (3)/(4)		$30.00
6. Market value discount	33.3%	
7. Market price per share = (5) × (6)		$20.00
8. Rate of return on share repurchase = (2)/[(7)/(5)]	15.0%	
9. Share repurchase	$400	
10. Dollar gain on share repurchase = (8) × (9)		$60

alternative in which the $400 is invested in a project that returns 15% or $60. At the 10% cost of capital, the total intrinsic value is $3,600. We deduct the $400 investment to obtain a new equity value of $3,200, as shown in Line 5. Dividing by the original 100 shares, we obtain a new shareholder intrinsic value per share of $32. With the one-third market value discount, the new market value per share is $21.33, representing a 6.67% increase over the original market price per share of $20.

This analysis demonstrates that if the share repurchases can be made without paying a premium, the return on the share-repurchase investment is greater than 15%. Equation 1 makes an implicit assumption that the share repurchase requires a premium equal to the percent increase in market price that the 15% real investment achieved. These results are illustrated in Table 18.12. We go through the same analysis as we did for Table 18.11; however, the share,

TABLE 18.11 Investment vs. Repurchase (no premium)

		Case 1 Repurchase $400	Case 2 Invest $400
1. Cash flow		$300	$360
2. Cost of capital		10%	10%
3. Intrinsic value = (1)/(2)		$3,000	$3,600
4. Investment		$400	$400
5. New equity value = (3) − (4)		$2,600	$3,200
6. Initial number of shares		100	100
7. Share repurchase premium	0.00%		
8. Market price per share	$20.00		
9. Price per share under share repurchase = (8) × [1 + (7)]	$20.00		
10. Number of shares repurchased = (4)/(9)		20.00	0.00
11. New number of shares = (6) − (10)		80.00	100.00
12. New shareholder intrinsic value per share = (5)/(11)		$32.50	$32.00
13. Market value discount	33.3%		
14. New market value = (5) × [1 − (13)]		$1,733	$2,133
15. New market value per share = (14)/(11)		$21.67	$21.33
16. Percent increase in market price = [(15) − (8)]/(8)		8.33%	6.67%

TABLE 18.12 Investment vs. Repurchase (with premium)

		Case 1 Repurchase $400	Case 2 Invest $400
1. Cash flow		$300	$360
2. Cost of capital		$10%	$10%
3. Intrinsic value = (1)/(2)		$3,000	$3,600
4. Investment		$400	$400
5. New equity value = (3) – (4)		$2,600	$3,200
6. Initial number of shares		100	100
7. Share repurchase premium	6.67%		
8. Market price per share	$20.00		
9. Price per share under share repurchase = (8) × [1 + (7)]	$21.33		
10. Number of shares repurchased = (4) × (9)		18.75	0.00
11. New number of shares = (6) – (10)		81.25	100.00
12. New shareholder intrinsic value per share = (5)/(11)		$32.00	$32.00
13. Market value discount	33.3%		
14. New market value = (5)×[1 – (13)]		$1,733	$2,133
15. New market value per share = (14)/(11)		$21.33	$21.33
16. Percent increase in market price = [(15) – (8)]/(8)		6.67%	6.67%

repurchase premium is 6.67%, so only 18.75 shares are purchased instead of 20. Both the share repurchase price (Line 9) and the new market price per share after share repurchase (Line 15) rise to $21.33 in the example. Table 18.12 shows that the post-repurchase percent increase in market price is 6.67% (Line 16). This is now the same as the result obtained when a 15% return real investment is made. Thus, equation 18.8 requires modification. However, the critical issue is whether the market undervaluation is actually present. Some form of market inefficiency is required for undervaluation to persist (Isawaga, 2002).

In actual practice, the results from equation 18.8 may be modified further. OMRs can be increased somewhat by the use of puts. For example, a company with a stock selling at $40 sells one-year put warrants for 1 million shares at $3 per share, with an exercise price at $40. This $3 million income is net, because the tax code allows corporations to sell options on their stock free of taxes. The buyer of the warrants is likely to be a large financial concern, which will hedge the warrant by buying the company's shares in the open market. Using an options-based hedging model, they buy 400,000 shares to cover the 1 million warrants. If the stock price rises, the warrants are worthless, but the stock part of the hedge can be sold in the open market for profit. As the stock rises, the put owner can begin to sell shares because fewer shares are needed to hedge the position. If the stock falls below the exercise price, the financial concern can exercise the puts at $40 per share, regardless how low the price of the stock might fall. An example is Microsoft, which had sold 30 million to 40 million puts a year; none had been "put" back to the company through 1999. According to its 1998 Annual Report, Microsoft had 60 million puts outstanding on June 30, 1998. In its 10-K for its fiscal year ending June 30, 2002, Microsoft cash-flow statements show that sales of put warrants in 2000 were $472 million; repurchases in 2001 (a cash outflow) were $1.367 billion. Microsoft stated, "All outstanding put warrants were either retired or exercised during fiscal 2001."

Similarly, a Morgan Stanley Analyst Report of July 15, 2002, noted that Dell Computer in fiscal 1997, with sharply rising stock prices, began to buy call options financed by selling put options. The put options were not exercised because the Dell stock price was rising; the stock purchases could be accomplished at lower-than-market prices by exercising the calls. The put/call arrangement is estimated to have saved Dell $3.7 billion. However, as the price of the stock began to fall in 2000, the call options were out of the money, and the put options enabled the holders to sell shares back to the company at levels above market prices. The report estimated that Dell had an off balance sheet liability of $1 billion, expected to be retired by the end of fiscal 2003. Also, the report noted that Dell was cash-flow positive and had more than $8 billion in short-term and long-term investments at the end of the first quarter, fiscal 2003.

ACCOUNTING TREATMENT OF SHARE REPURCHASES

The accounting treatment of share repurchases is conveyed by the procedures in the Compustat compilations. Annual data item number 88 explains that the total dollar amount of treasury stock is expressed in units of millions of dollars and that the cost method or retirement method can be used. Generally Accepted Accounting Principles (GAAP) permits the charge (debit) to the shareholders' equity account to be at book or at cost—the amount paid for the repurchased stock (which will be related to its market price). Under the cost method, treasury stock is debited for the amount paid and is shown "on the Balance Sheet as a deduction to equity" (Compustat, chapter 5, Data Definitions, p. 274, April 2001). The second procedure states that "the retirement method records shares as if formally retired." The net balance sheet effect is the same in both methods: The book equity is debited by the purchase price (cost) of the share repurchased, and cash is credited (reduced) to reflect the outlay.

These procedures can be illustrated by a simplified accounting model of a stock buyback, shown in Table 18.13. Panel A of the table postulates a firm with a net income of $1,000 million, shares outstanding of 500 million, a P/E multiple of 20 times, and a buyback of 50 million shares. Panel B presents the balance sheet before and after the buyback. The results in panel C are calculated in panel D. Before the buyback, earnings are $2 per share. The market price per share, applying the P/E multiple, is $40. The book value per share is $6,000 million divided by 500 million shares, which is $12 per share. Market cap is $40 times the 500 million shares outstanding, which gives $20,000 million. The return on book equity is the $1,000 million divided by $6,000 million, which is 16.67%. The debt to equity ratio is $4,000 million debt less $2,000 million excess cash, equals $2,000 million divided by $6,000 million equals 33.33%.

We can now illustrate the accounting effects of the stock buyback. We postulate that in an open-market share-repurchase program, 50 million shares are bought at $40, for a total of $2,000 million. This is the debit to the book shareholders' equity, which is reduced to $4,000 million. The net income is postulated to be reduced by the 3% after-tax earnings on the $2,000 million excess cash used for the buyback, or $60. The resulting $940 million is divided by 450 million shares to give $2.09 as the new EPS after the buyback. If the P/E ratio of 20 continues to hold, the resulting market price per share rises to$41.80. Market cap declines to $18,810 million. The book shareholders' equity per share is the $4,000 million divided by the 450 million shares remaining, or $8.89. The return on book equity rises from 16.67% to 23.50%. The debt ratio rises to 100%. The return on shareholders' equity has risen by 41%. This is an impressive improvement. It occurs because the firm has a market-to-book ratio (M/B) of 3.3 times. Because the debit to the

TABLE 18.13 (Model 18–02A) Accounting for a Stock Buyback—P/E Ratio Unchanged

Panel A: Inputs

Excess cash	$2,000 million
Net income	$1,000 million
Earnings rate on excess cash	5%
Shares outstanding	500 million
P/E ratio	
Pre-buyback	20
Post-buyback	20
Tax rate	40%
Shares for buyback	50 million
Share price buyback	$40.00
Buyback	50 million shares @ $40 = $2,000 million

Panel B: Balance Sheets (in millions)

	Before Buyback		*After Buyback*	
Cash	$4,000		$2,000	
Other assets	6,000		6,000	
Total assets		$10,000		$ 8,000
Total debt		$ 4,000		$ 4,000
Book shareholders' equity		6,000		4,000
Total claims		$10,000		$ 8,000

Panel C: Financial Effects

Net income	$ 1,000	$ 940
EPS	$ 2.00	$ 2.09
P/E ratio	20	20
Market price per share	$ 40.00	$ 41.80
Book value per share	$ 12.00	$8.89
Market capitalization (in millions)	$20,000	$18,810
Return on book equity	16.67%	23.50%
Net debt-to-equity ratio	33.33%	100%

Panel D: Calculations After Buyback

Net income = Net income less after-tax 5% (1 − T) earnings on $2,000 excess cash
      = $1,000 − 60 = $940

EPS = Net income/New shares
    = $940/(500 − 50) = $940/450
    = $2.09

Market price per share = $2.09 × 20 = $41.80; 1.80/40.00 = 4.5% increase

Book value per share = $4,000/450 = $8.89

Market capitalization = $41.80 × 450 = $18,810

Return on book equity = $940/$4,000 = 23.50%

Net debt-to-equity ratio = $4,000/$4,000 = 100.00%

equity account is 3.3 times the book value of equity, the book value of equity is sharply decreased. The new net income has decreased by the loss of the after-tax earnings on the short-term investments (the excess cash), which is modest compared to the substantial decline in book equity.

EMPIRICAL STUDIES OF SHARE REPURCHASES IN THE 1990s

Econometric studies of share repurchases are consistent with the hypothesis that a major motive has been to offset the dilution effects of the exercise of stock options. The study by Bens et al. (2002) focused directly on the issue. They performed a statistical analysis comparing the antidilution motive versus plausible alternatives. They used hand-collected data on repurchases and employee stock option (ESO) activity for all employees of S&P 500 industrial firms from 1996 to 1999. As the dilutive effects of outstanding ESOs on reported (GAAP defined) earnings per share (EPS) rises, firms increase the amount of their stock repurchases. Furthermore, when the earnings growth targets of firms are threatened, they are more likely to increase share-repurchase activities. They also found that the incentives to repurchase in response to the potentially dilutive effects of ESOs are stronger for firms with high price-to-earnings (P/E) ratios. In their multiple-regression studies, they are able to control for other possible influences on repurchase decisions including the proceeds from the exercise of ESOs, deviations from target leverage, and firm characteristics—size, growth rates, book-to-market ratios, and levels of operating cash flows.

Fenn and Liang (2001) found similar results. They studied 1,108 firms for the period 1993 to 1997. They obtained data on dividends, repurchases, and firm characteristics from Compustat; data on managerial stock incentives were obtained from Execucomp. In addition to the positive relationship between ESOs and repurchases, they found that managerial share ownership furnishes incentives to increase payouts at firms where the most severe agency problems were associated with high free cash flows, limited investment opportunities, and low management stock ownership. Using a 3- to 5-year time horizon, they found dividends and repurchases increasing with free cash flows and decreasing with external financing costs. They found, as have other researchers, that firms distribute permanent cash-flow increases as cash dividends and use share repurchases for temporary cash-flow shocks. However, they found that a one-standard-deviation increase in their management stock option variable is related to a significant reduction of 38 basis points in dividend yields. They observed that although flexibility and undervaluation reasons for share repurchases had not changed during the accelerated use of share repurchases in the late 1990s, the use of ESOs had greatly increased. Hence, they concluded that the growth of ESOs has been significantly associated with the increased use of stock repurchases.

Kahle (2002) provided an in-depth analysis of the variables influencing repurchasing policies. Her sample for repurchases is based on the Securities Corporation's Mergers and Acquisitions database for the six-year period January 1, 1991, to December 31, 1996. Data on managerial options outstanding and exercisable are obtained from the Standard & Poor's Execucomp database. Compustat data are used for company characteristics. Annual reports were used to collect data on options exercised, total options outstanding, and total options exercisable held by all employees. The final sample analyzed 712 repurchase announcements.

She first compared the characteristics of dividend-increasing firms versus repurchase firms. The average dividend increase measured as a percent of the last previous dividend paid is 9.8%

and earns an abnormal return of 0.5% over the 3-day window (−1, +1). Repurchasing firms announce buybacks of an average of 6.4% of shares outstanding associated with an abnormal return of 1.6%, lower than the findings for earlier time periods.

Her regression analysis found that larger firms with higher ratios of free cash flows to assets are more likely to repurchase than to increase cash dividends. The coefficients on executive options as well as total options outstanding are positive and significant. Cash dividend payments would decrease the value of managerial options whether or not they are currently exercisable.

In open-market repurchases, firms may not follow through on the total amounts announced. Kahle next turned to an analysis of the determinants of the actual level of repurchases. She found that firms repurchase more shares as free cash flows increase, as firms are larger, have low growth opportunities (low market-to-book ratios), and are undervalued (larger post-announcement returns). Her data provide evidence that firms repurchase stocks in anticipation of future option exercises, which would cause earnings dilution. She noted also that firms concerned about dilution buy back shares as options move into the money when they are more likely to be exercised. This analysis further supports her findings of the role of total options exercisable in explaining share repurchases. Her finding that the announcement returns to repurchasing firms have declined over time is consistent with a decreasing influence of undervaluation and an increasing influence of the potential dilution effects of an increased number of employee stock options outstanding.

THE MEASUREMENT OF SHARE-REPURCHASE GROWTH

The measurement of share-repurchase growth is subject to disagreement. Stephens and Weisbach (1998) pointed out that open-market share repurchases can not be calculated at the announcement or directly measured after share repurchases begin to take place. They described four possible proxies: (1) firms' shares outstanding from CRSP, (2) firms' shares outstanding from Compustat, (3) the statement of cash flows or flow of funds statement from Compustat, and (4) changes of the dollar value of treasury stock reported by Compustat. The primary method they employed is the first. Because the primary interest of Stephens and Weisbach (1998) was the measurement of the percent of shares acquired after OMR announcements, they did not present a time series of share repurchases. They estimated that for their sample of 450 programs, 1981 to 1990, 74% to 82% of share announcement quantities take place within 3 years. They noted that the flexibility in OMRs is one of the reasons why they account for more than 95% of share-repurchase programs.

In the Grullon and Michaely (2002) study summarized previously, share repurchases use the Compustat measure of expenditures on the purchase of common and preferred stocks (adjusted to remove preferred stock). They stated that their evidence is consistent with the Fama and French (2001) findings of a lower propensity to pay dividends. However, they presented the view that firms have been substituting share repurchases for dividends. They stated that their results differ from those of Fama and French, who use a net measure of repurchase activities.

Whether the gross share-repurchase measure or the net measure should be used depends on the nature of the application. In studies of the influences on the growth of share repurchases by Kahle (2002), it was appropriate for her to use the gross measure to arrive at her finding that the number of exercisable options had the strongest explanatory power. In comparing share repurchases to cash dividends from firms to individuals, net distributions would be relevant. For example, if a firm sold equity whose proceeds were used in share repurchases, the distribution from firms to individuals would be offsetting. The option transaction is similar. At the time of option exercise, the firm is selling equity and raising cash. If the proceeds are used for share repurchases, no net cash payout by the firm is made. The firm's net cash balance remains the same, and the cash in the hand of investors is also unchanged.

If a firm makes an acquisition for cash, a net cash disbursement has occurred; the firm has less cash and investors have more. However, suppose the target prefers a non taxable event and the acquiring firm makes a share repurchase for cash, using the shares acquired in a stock-for-stock, non taxable transaction. From a funds-flow standpoint, the linked sequence of transactions for the acquiring firm represents an outflow of cash and no change in shares outstanding. However, although firms sometimes declare that the purpose of a buyback is to obtain shares to be used in acquisitions, that is not likely the real reason.

A more efficient procedure is for firms to have a cushion of authorized shares in excess of shares issued and outstanding. The authorized number of shares is just a number set forth in a company's articles of incorporation, as filed with the secretary of the state of incorporation, typically Delaware. The relatively minor expense relates to some state franchise taxes based on authorized capitalization. If a firm does not have an ample cushion of authorized shares in excess of shares outstanding, it might not have shares needed for acquisitions or the exercise of stock options, as well as for antitakeover defensive actions. The firm then would incur delays to authorize more shares by amending its corporate charter, which requires shareholders' approval. The benefits of having a substantial excess of authorized shares over outstanding shares are so great that it is predictable that most corporations would always have that cushion.

Empirical evidence is consistent with the proposition that firms have incentives to hold a cushion of authorized shares in excess of outstanding shares. Table 18.14 presents a tabulation of authorized shares versus outstanding shares for the Dow Jones 30 Industrial companies. The mean excess of shares authorized over shares outstanding is 162.2%. The median excess is 141.5%.

The empirical studies summarized found a strong association between share-repurchase activity and the use of stock options. The exercise of stock options was associated with share repurchases that offset the dilution effects of an increase in shares outstanding. These activities are consistent with the use of share repurchases on a net basis to measure total corporate payouts. This treatment is required for accurate flow-of-funds behavior for firms and the economy. Although measures of share repurchases on a net basis are not available, the gross measures as illustrated by our Table 18.2 data overstate net-share repurchases. A reduction by a 30% to 35% factor would bring the dividends plus repurchases percentages in the final column of Table 18.2 to more plausible levels.

RELATED DIVIDEND STUDIES

Fama and French (2001) reported that in 1973, 52.8% of publicly traded nonfinancial, non-utility firms paid dividends. This rose to 66.5% in 1978 and then declined to 20.8% in 1999. They attributed the decline in part to a shift of publicly traded firms toward characteristics of firms that have never paid dividends. The number of publicly traded firms grew from 3,638 in 1978 to 5,670 in 1997 then declined to 5,113 in 1999. The increase in the number of firms was associated with a shift to newer and smaller firms, which mostly have not paid dividends. These firms are characterized by higher rates of investment, higher R&D rates, and higher ratios of market

TABLE 18.14 Dow Jones 30 Industrial Companies, Shares Outstanding and Authorized (in millions as of 12/31/01)

	Shares Outstanding	*Shares Authorized*	*Authorized Less Outstanding*	*Excess over Outstanding*
ALCOA Inc.	848	1,800	952	112.4%
American Express Co.	1,331	3,600	2,269	170.5
AT&T Corp.	3,542	6,000	2,458	69.4
Boeing Co.	798	1,200	402	50.4
Caterpillar, Inc.	343	900	557	162.1
Citigroup, Inc.	5,149	15,000	9,851	191.3
Coca-Cola Co.	2,486	5,600	3,114	125.2
E.I. DuPont de Nemours & Co.	1,002	1,800	798	79.6
Eastman Kodak Co.	291	950	659	226.5
ExxonMobil Corp.	6,809	9,000	2,191	32.2
General Electric Co.	9,926	13,200	3,274	33.0
General Motors Corp.	559	2,000	1,441	257.8
Hewlett-Packard Co.	1,939	9,600	7,661	395.1
Home Depot, Inc.	2,346	10,000	7,654	326.3
Honeywell International, Inc.	815	2,000	1,185	145.4
Intel Corp.	6,690	10,000	3,310	49.5
International Business Machines Corp.	1,723	4,688	2,964	172.0
International Paper Co.	482	991	509	105.7
J.P. Morgan Chase & Co.	1,973	4,500	2,527	128.0
Johnson & Johnson	3,047	4,320	1,273	41.8
McDonald's Corp.	1,281	3,500	2,219	173.3
Merck & Co., Inc.	2,273	5,400	3,127	137.6
Microsoft Corp.	5,383	12,000	6,617	122.9
Minnesota Mining & Manufacturing Co.	391	1,000	609	155.6
Philip Morris Cos.	2,153	12,000	9,847	457.5
Procter & Gamble Co.	1,296	5,000	3,704	285.9
SBC Communications, Inc.	3,354	7,000	3,646	108.7
United Technologies Corp.	472	2,000	1,528	323.6
Wal-Mart Stores, Inc.	4,453	11,000	6,547	147.0
Walt Disney Co.	2,010	3,600	1,590	79.1
			Mean	162.2%
			Median	141.5%

Source: Compustat and Mergent FIS.

value of assets to their book value; their investments exceed pre-interest earnings. Their size is about one-tenth the size of payers. Fama and French stated that "the aggregate payout ratio for all firms masks the kind of widespread evidence of lower propensity to pay dividends, among individual firms of all types . . ." (p. 39). Fama and French also stated that the "Lower propensity to pay is quite general" (p. 40). Fama and French defined *propensity* as "the probability that a firm in a given category of firms will be a dividend payer."

In their paper on dividend concentration, DeAngelo et al. (2002) presented data (in their Appendix Table A1) on real dividends and real earnings in 1978 and 2000 for the 25 industrial firms that paid the largest dividends in 2000 when they accounted for 53.5% of the aggregate for all industrials. From their data, we calculated in Table 18.15 the percentage changes in the real dividend payouts between 1978 and 2000 for 23 firms with data for both years. Twelve firms reduced their payout ratios; 11 firms increased payouts. Therefore, the large firms that increased their dividend payouts are the engines behind the rise in aggregate payouts.

In Table 18.15, we also ranked the percentage change in payouts and ranked the compound annual growth rates in real earnings between 1978 and 2000. We calculated the Spearman's correlation coefficient between the ranked pairs. The resulting ρ of 0.53 for the 23 observations is significant at the 1% level. This finding that dividend payouts over time are related to underlying real earnings growth rates as one of the underlying causal variables is consistent with economic principles. We conclude that the dividend-paying group of firms increased their dividend payouts, and among the dividend payers, those with the highest rates of earnings improvements also had the highest rates of increase in their dividend payouts. Lower propensities, as defined by Fama and French, can, therefore, coexist with higher payouts for some dividend payers.

THE SUBSTITUTION ISSUE

The growth of share repurchases raises the issue of whether they have substituted for cash dividends. Aggregate dividends and the aggregate payout ratio have increased. Nevertheless, the probability that a firm in a given class of firms will be a dividend payer has decreased, as shown by the Fama and French data for 1978 to 1999. They stated: "The perceived benefits of dividends . . . have declined through time" (Fama and French, 2001, p. 5). Nondividend payers are mainly smaller firms with investment opportunities that use a high percentage of operating cash flows. The time span of the Fama and French data coincide with the period of strong growth in stock prices, as shown in Table 18.16. The capital gains element in shareholder returns offered much higher returns than dividends because price-earnings ratios also were rising. Increased use of stock options took place in growing firms with rising stock prices. As stock options were exercised, share repurchases were made. The growing firms that initiated share repurchases would not have paid dividends because this would have negative effects on the value of stock options.

It was the strong economy and rising stock prices that provided opportunities for the formation of new firms with high growth. The strong economy also made possible the growth in earnings in the larger, more mature firms. This enabled the traditional dividend-paying group to increase payouts from rising earnings. In this environment, the growth of dividends and share repurchases was produced by common factors: a strong economy associated with highly favorable financial performance associated with optimistic expectations of their continuation into the future. Dividends and share repurchases perform different functions in different segments of the economy.

TABLE 18.15 Real Dividend Payout in 1978 and in 2000 of the 25 Industrial Firms That Pay the Largest Dividends in 2000

	Real Dividend Payout			Real Earnings			Rank		Square Change in Rank
	1978	2000	Change in Payout	1978	2000	CAGR	Change in Payout	CAGR	
ExxonMobil	53.3%	38.3%	-15.0%	2,763	6,054	3.6%	19	14	25
General Electric	46.3	44.3	-2.0	1,230	4,822	6.4	14	10	16
Philip Morris	30.6	53.4	22.9	409	3,222	9.8	3	3	0
SBC	—	43.2	—	—	3,017	—	—	—	—
Merck	42.9	42.6	-0.3	308	2,583	10.1	12	2	100
Ford	26.2	50.6	24.3	1,589	2,048	1.2	2	16	196
Pfizer	39.8	69.1	29.3	206	1,408	9.1	1	6	25
AT&T	57.6	53.2	-4.4	5,273	1,768	-4.8	17	22	25
Bristol Myers Squibb	37.9	47.1	9.2	203	1,551	9.7	7	4	9
Johnson & Johnson	33.8	35.9	2.2	299	1,817	8.5	11	7	16
Chevron	39.3	32.6	-6.8	1,106	1,963	2.6	18	15	9
Coca-Cola	57.3	77.4	20.1	375	824	3.6	4	13	81
Procter & Gamble	43.6	47.4	3.9	512	1,341	4.5	10	12	4
DuPont	44.2	62.9	18.7	787	876	0.5	5	19	196
General Motors	48.8	29.1	-19.8	3,508	1,686	-3.3	20	21	1
American Home Products	59.5	-133.4	-192.9	348	-314	-10.0	23	23	0
Abbott Labs	31.5	42.3	10.7	149	1,055	9.3	6	5	1
Eli Lilly	41.9	37.9	-4.0	277	1,158	6.7	16	9	49
Texaco	63.7	38.5	-25.3	852	962	0.6	21	18	9
3M	41.6	49.5	7.9	563	703	1.0	8	17	81
IBM	56.7	11.2	-45.4	3,111	3,064	-0.1	22	20	4
Wal-Mart	9.1	16.0	6.9	22	2,111	23.1	9	1	64
Schering-Plough	33.5	33.2	-0.4	194	917	7.3	13	8	25
PepsiCo	38.9	36.6	-2.3	226	827	6.1	15	11	16
UPS	—	26.8	—	—	1,111	—	—	—	—
									Sum = 952

Note: Spearman's Rank Correlation (ρ) = 0.530.

Source: Based on DeAngelo et al. (2000) Appendix Table A1.

TABLE 18.16 Stock Price Movements 1959–2001

				% Change		
Year	S&P Composite	Dow Jones	Nasdaq	S&P Composite	Dow Jones	Nasdaq
1959	57.38	632.12	......	......	......	......
1960	55.85	618.04	......	−2.7	−2.2	......
1961	66.27	691.55	......	18.7	11.9	......
1962	62.38	639.76	......	−5.9	−7.5	......
1963	69.87	714.81	......	12.0	11.7	......
1964	81.37	834.05	......	16.5	16.7	......
1965	88.17	910.88	......	8.4	9.2	......
1966	85.26	873.60	......	−3.3	−4.1	......
1967	91.93	879.12	......	7.8	0.6	......
1968	98.70	906.00	......	7.4	3.1	......
1969	97.84	876.72	......	−0.9	−3.2	......
1970	83.22	753.19	......	−14.9	−14.1	......
1971	98.29	884.76	107.44	18.1	17.5	......
1972	109.20	950.71	128.52	11.1	7.5	19.6
1973	107.43	923.88	109.90	−1.6	−2.8	−14.5
1974	82.85	759.37	76.29	−22.9	−17.8	−30.6
1975	86.16	802.49	77.20	4.0	5.7	1.2
1976	102.01	974.92	89.90	18.4	21.5	16.5
1977	98.20	894.63	98.71	−3.7	−8.2	9.8
1978	96.02	820.23	117.53	−2.2	−8.3	19.1
1979	103.01	844.40	136.57	7.3	2.9	16.2
1980	118.78	891.41	168.61	15.3	5.6	23.5
1981	128.05	932.92	203.18	7.8	4.7	20.5
1982	119.71	884.36	188.97	−6.5	−5.2	−7.0
1983	160.41	1,190.34	285.43	34.0	34.6	51.0
1984	160.46	1,178.48	248.88	0.0	−1.0	−12.8
1985	186.84	1,328.23	290.19	16.4	12.7	16.6
1986	236.34	1,792.76	366.96	26.5	35.0	26.5
1987	286.83	2,275.99	402.57	21.4	27.0	9.7
1988	265.79	2,060.82	374.43	−7.3	−9.5	−7.0
1989	322.84	2,508.91	437.81	21.5	21.7	16.9
1990	334.59	2,678.94	409.17	3.6	6.8	−6.5
1991	376.18	2,929.33	491.69	12.4	9.3	20.2
1992	415.74	3,284.29	599.26	10.5	12.1	21.9
1993	451.41	3,522.06	715.16	8.6	7.2	19.3
1994	460.42	3,793.77	751.65	2.0	7.7	5.1
1995	541.72	4,493.76	925.19	17.7	18.5	23.1
1996	670.50	5,742.89	1,164.96	23.8	27.8	25.9
1997	873.43	7,441.15	1,469.49	30.3	29.6	26.1
1998	1,085.50	8,625.52	1,794.91	24.3	15.9	22.1
1999	1,327.33	10,464.88	2,728.15	22.3	21.3	52.0
2000	1,427.22	10,734.90	3,783.67	7.5	2.6	38.7
2001	1,194.18	10,189.13	2,035.00	−16.3	−5.1	−46.2

TABLE 18.16 (cont.)

| Year | CAGR (%) | | |
	S&P Composite	Dow Jones	Nasdaq
1959–1982	3.2	1.5	
1967–1982	1.8	0.0	
1971–1982	1.8	0.0	5.3
1982–2000	14.8	14.9	18.1
1982–1990	13.7	14.9	10.1
1990–1999	16.5	16.3	23.5
1994–1999	23.6	22.5	29.4

Source: Economic Report of the President, February 2002, Table B-95, averages of daily closing prices.

Summary

We have described four methods of share repurchase: (1) Fixed-price tender offers (FPTs), (2) Dutch auctions (DAs), (3) Transferable put rights (TPRs), and (4) Open-market repurchases (OMRs).

We have explained the mechanisms and logic behind each of the four types. Each has a different signaling effect and wealth effect. All result in significant positive abnormal returns to shareholders.

Multiple forces produce the growth in share repurchases, and their relative influences have changed over time. We present 12 factors that have caused share repurchases to grow in importance.

1.   Greater flexibility. Patterns of dividend behavior by individual firms and in the aggregate became established over time. The finance literature documents that corporate earnings rise with fluctuations, whereas dividends increase in a stair-step fashion and lag behind the growth in corporate cash flows. The market rewards a history of consistent increases in dividends. The market sharply punishes a company that announces a decline in dividends or failure to achieve historical patterns of annual percentage increases. With share repurchases, the expectation is that cash will be returned to shareholders when funds are available in excess of needs to finance sound investment programs. Share-repurchase programs thereby facilitate improved information exchange with shareholders. The data in Table 18.8 show that IBM, beginning on January 31, 1995 made four successive OMR authorizations of $2.5 billion; beginning on November 26, 1996, through April 30, 2002, a total of 12 successive authorizations of $3.5 billion were made. Just as special dividends began to be so regular that sophisticated institutional investors began to expect them as regular dividends (DeAngelo et al., 2000), share repurchases may lose their flexibility.

2.   Tax savings. Cash dividends to shareholders are subject to a maximum individual tax rate of 39.6%. The return of cash to shareholders in the form of share repurchases may qualify for the long-term capital gains rate of 20%. This represents a tax savings of potentially as much as 19.6 cents on each dollar received. The tax law of 2003 makes substantial changes.

3.   Timing of taxes. Shareholders can choose whether or not to participate in a stock-buyback program. They can defer their tax payments to make their own selection regarding when to sell.

4.   Change financial structure. The debt-to-equity ratio is one measure of the firm's financial structure. The standard procedure for measuring debt is to first deduct excess cash and

marketable securities holdings, so a share repurchase with excess cash not only reduces equity, but increases debt. Thus, the leverage ratio can be increased quickly. A similar result occurs if a firm sells additional debt in order to make share repurchases. If the firm has been operating with less than the optimal debt-leverage ratio, the share repurchase will move the firm toward that ratio. If so, it might lower the firm's cost of capital, with a resulting increase in share price and market value.

5.   Takeover defense. Share repurchases can be used as a takeover defense for two reasons. One, the share-repurchase plan might be viewed more favorably than the takeover. Two, when a firm tenders for a percentage of its shares, the shareholders who offer their shares for sale are those with the lowest reservation prices. Those who do not tender have the higher reservation prices. Hence, for a takeover bidder to succeed with the remaining higher-reservation-price shareholders, the premium offered will have to be higher. The required higher premium might deter some potential acquirers from making bids.

6.   Management incentives. Share repurchases increase the percentage ownership of the firm for the nonsellers. Because officers and directors might hold a significant percentage of ownership of the firm, their nonparticipation in share repurchases will increase their proportionate ownership by an even greater degree. If the percentages are substantial, the incentives of officers and directors to think like owners of the firm will be strengthened. Agency problems will be reduced.

7.   Management responsibility. When officers and directors return excess cash to shareholders through share-repurchase programs, they might be acting in the best interest of the shareholders (the owners). By not using the funds for unwise diversification or negative net-present-value investments in the firm's traditional lines of business activity, officers and directors increase the trust and confidence of the shareholders. This might have a positive influence on share prices.

8.   Undervaluation. Officers and directors usually do not tender or sell into share-repurchase programs because they might judge that the price of the stock is likely to increase in future years. Their nonparticipation might therefore, serve as a signal that the stock is undervalued. A special case of the undervaluation scenario is when a sharp decline in overall stock prices has taken place. When the stock market suffered a sharp decline in October 1987, many firms initiated substantial share-repurchase programs in the subsequent weeks. These share-repurchase programs represented a statement by their managements that the overall market decline did not justify the sharp drops in the share prices of their individual firms. We have demonstrated that when a firm's shares are undervalued, the returns from purchasing their own shares can be high. We presented examples where the returns from investing in undervalued shares are higher than some real investments.

9.   Signaling. Share repurchases can signal future improvements in cash flows. Dividends have even stronger signaling power because they are tied more closely to long-term cash-flow patterns.

10.   Accounting treatment. The basic accounting entry when shares are repurchased is to reduce (debit) shares outstanding and to reduce (credit) cash by the outlay required. Accounting principles permit the charge (debit) to the shareholders' equity account to be at cost or market. The common practice is for firms to charge the shareholders' equity account with the actual amount paid for the shares (at market). Because market is greater than book, book equity is reduced. The stock buyback, using Generally Accepted Accounting Principles (GAAP), would increase EPS, market price per share, and the return-on-book equity.

11. Restructuring. The financial literature also reports that share repurchases may be part of a more general restructuring program in which the firm is engaged (Nohel and Tarhan, 1998). If the firm has embarked on a general program to improve its efficiency and performance and a share-repurchase program is a part of that restructuring, the influence on share prices is likely to be positive. However the restructuring may be the stronger causal force.

12. Offset dilution from the exercise of stock options. Stock options are being used more frequently by firms in executive compensation programs and extended broadly to recruit or retain target employees. As stock options are exercised, the number of the firm's shares outstanding increases. Conceivably, this could create downward pressure on the firm's stock prices. Share repurchases can be used to offset this potential dilutive effect. The examples of IBM and Coca-Cola illustrate that share repurchases have been used to more than offset the effect of the exercise of stock options and may, therefore, have had an accretive effect on share prices.

The relative influences of the multiple forces behind the increase in share repurchases appear to have changed over time. The early literature on share repurchases (Dann, 1981; Vermaelen, 1981) developed models based on undervaluation. With the safe harbor policies of the SEC in 1983, supported by similar actions by the IRS, tax savings and tax flexibility motives became stronger. The increased threats of takeovers that emerged at about the same time increased the role of share repurchases as a takeover defense. The explosive growth in the use of share repurchases in the late 1990s was associated with the growth in the award of stock options and their exercise. Empirical associations were observed between the growth of stock options exercised or exercisable and share-repurchase activity.

Questions

18.1 What are four ways to carry out a share repurchase?

18.2 In a tender offer for share repurchase, how is the wealth increase distributed among tendering and non-tendering shareholders?

18.3 What theory most plausibly explains the positive shareholder wealth effect observed in share repurchases?

18.4 A company has 8 million shares outstanding. It offers to repurchase 2 million shares at $30 per share; the current market price of the stock is $25. Management controls 500,000 shares and does not participate in the repurchase. What is the signaling cost of the repurchase if the true value of the stock is $20? If the true value of the stock is $29?

18.5 What is the wealth effect of share repurchases when there is prorationing or not, and whether officers and directors (OD) are at risk or not?

18.6 Do open-market share repurchases meet the requirements of achieving credible signaling?

18.7 In an interview with Louis V. Gertsner, who had just retired as chairman of IBM, *Business Week* in its issue of December 9, 2002, raised questions about the use of financial engineering to increase the price of IBM stock. Particularly, they questioned him about IBM's use of $43 billion for share repurchases during his 9 years at the head of IBM. Mr. Gertsner responded that IBM had an unchanging plan for the use of its free cash flows after taxes. First, they made capital and working capital investments for future growth. Second, they funded research. Third, they increased employee compensation. Fourth, they paid down company debt. Fifth, what remained was returned to shareholders through share buybacks, not dividends, because of tax advantages to shareholders. "We always bought, right through thick and thin. If your were talking about financial engineering, then you would buy at certain times and not buy at other times." Comment on the share buyback policy at IBM.

18.8 The CEO and CFO of a successful company described the situation of their company. It had 80% of its market; a higher share would risk antitrust problems. Their capabilities were specialized to their industry, so they were reluctant to make unrelated acquisitions. They asked us if a share buyback could keep the price of their stock rising. How would you answer their question?

Case 18.1   FPL

A Harvard case published on March 15, 1995 (Esty and Schreiber) and an article published in spring 1996 (Soter, Brigham, and Evanson) highlight the flexibility aspect of share repurchase. The FPL group is a holding company whose principal operating subsidiary is Florida Power and Light Company (FPL), which serves most of the east coast and lower west coast of Florida, a population of about 6.5 million. Its energy mix consists of purchased power (17%), oil (31%), nuclear (26%), gas (20%), and coal (6%).

Deregulation had been increasing competition in the public utility industry since 1978. The Public Utilities Regulatory Policies Act (PURPA) in 1978 encouraged the creation of power plants using renewable or non-traditional fuels. If specified efficiency and size standards were met, PURPA required local utilities to buy all of their electrical output. In 1992, the National Energy Policy Act (NEPA) was enacted by congress. It required utilities to permit use of their transmission systems at the same level of quality and at fair cost. In early 1994, some states permitted retail wheeling, under which customers could buy power from utilities other than the local franchise supplier. The local utility would be required to permit competitors' use of its transmission and distribution network. Major utilities in states that proposed to phase in retail wheeling experienced substantial declines in market values. Electric utility companies faced increased competition.

Florida Power and Light embarked on a diversification program into life insurance, cable television, information services, and citrus production between 1985 and 1988. In 1989, the new president emphasized a return to the core utility business. An aggressive capital expenditure program was launched to meet projected demand increases. Quality and efficiency programs increased plant availability above industry averages and lowered operating expenses.

The improved outlook for growth and profitability caused FPL to reassess the relationship between its long-term business strategies and its financial strategies. Increased growth opportunities were associated with increased competitive risks. Increased financial flexibility was required. With increased business risk, financial leverage was reduced.

A major reassessment of dividend policy was also made. With prospects for increased investment requirements and possible acquisition opportunities, a lower dividend payout policy made sense. The traditional utility company policy of consistent annual dividend increases was breached. A share-repurchase program was announced. The initial stock price reaction to the dividend cut was negative. The share-repurchase program signaled a favorable outlook for FPL and conveyed assurances that management would return cash to shareholders (by share repurchases), if not required by its basic business strategy. In addition, a tax advantage resulted from the maximum personal rate on long-term capital gains at 28% versus a rate on dividend income as high as 39%.

The earnings of FPL continued to improve, and its share price increased sharply above previous high levels. The stock price range in 1994 was $27 to $37; for 1995, it was $34 to $46.50. This case illustrates a number of the elements of share-repurchase programs developed in the chapter. ▨

QUESTIONS

C18.1.1 What was the major force that stimulated the diversification program by FPL?

C18.1.2 How successful were the diversification efforts of FPL?

C18.1.3 What was the impact of increased competitive risks and increased growth and profitability opportunities on the financial policies of FPL?

C18.1.4 What caused FPL to reduce its dividend payout?

C18.1.5 What kinds of signals were conveyed by the announcement of a share-repurchase program?

Case 18.2 RETURNS FROM OPEN-MARKET REPURCHASE ANNOUNCEMENTS

The following table show event returns for two open-market share repurchases that occurred in early 2000. (These two cases were discussed in Justin Pettit, "Is a Share Buyback Right for Your Company?" *Harvard Business Review* 79: 4, April 2001, pp. 141–147.

Returns to Merck from Open-Market Repurchase Announcement

	Date	MRK Close	MRK Return (%)	S&P Close	S&P Return(%)	Abnormal Return (%)	CAR (%)
−10	2/7/00	72.92	0.25	1424.24	−0.01	0.26	0.26
−9	2/8/00	73.10	0.25	1441.72	1.23	−0.98	−0.72
−8	2/9/00	69.17	−5.39	1411.71	−2.08	−3.30	−4.02
−7	2/10/00	66.86	−3.33	1416.83	0.36	−3.69	−7.71
−6	2/11/00	63.23	−5.43	1387.12	−2.10	−3.34	−11.05
−5	2/14/00	64.02	1.25	1389.94	0.20	1.04	−10.01
−4	2/15/00	63.59	−0.66	1402.05	0.87	−1.53	−11.54
−3	2/16/00	63.47	−0.19	1387.67	−1.03	0.84	−10.71
−2	2/17/00	61.29	−3.44	1388.26	0.04	−3.48	−14.19
−1	2/18/00	60.08	−1.98	1346.09	−3.04	1.06	−13.12
0	2/22/00	63.47	5.65	1352.17	0.45	5.19	−7.93
1	2/23/00	61.17	−3.63	1360.69	0.63	−4.26	−12.19
2	2/24/00	60.08	−1.78	1353.43	−0.53	−1.25	−13.43
3	2/25/00	58.32	−2.92	1333.36	−1.48	−1.44	−14.88
4	2/28/00	59.66	2.28	1348.05	1.10	1.18	−13.69
5	2/29/00	59.66	0.00	1366.42	1.36	−1.36	−15.06
6	3/1/00	58.42	−2.08	1379.19	0.93	−3.01	−18.07
7	3/2/00	57.69	−1.25	1381.76	0.19	−1.44	−19.50
8	3/3/00	55.98	−2.95	1409.17	1.98	−4.94	−24.44
9	3/6/00	55.01	−1.74	1391.28	−1.27	−0.47	−24.91
10	3/7/00	52.52	−4.54	1355.62	−2.56	−1.97	−26.88

Returns to Payless ShoeSource from Open-Market Repurchase Announcement

	Date	PSS Close	PSS Return(%)	S&P Close	S&P Return(%)	Abnormal Return(%)	CAR(%)
−10	2/23/00	39.44	−3.37	1360.69	0.63	−4.00	−4.00
−9	2/24/00	39.38	−0.16	1353.43	−0.53	0.38	−3.62
−8	2/25/00	39.19	−0.48	1333.36	−1.48	1.01	−2.62
−7	2/28/00	39.38	0.48	1348.05	1.10	−0.62	−3.24
−6	2/29/00	39.50	0.32	1366.42	1.36	−1.05	−4.29
−5	3/1/00	40.69	3.01	1379.19	0.93	2.07	−2.21
−4	3/2/00	41.56	2.15	1381.76	0.19	1.96	−0.25
−3	3/3/00	43.06	3.61	1409.17	1.98	1.63	1.38
−2	3/6/00	42.81	−0.58	1391.28	−1.27	0.69	2.06
−1	3/7/00	41.75	−2.48	1355.62	−2.56	0.08	2.15
0	3/8/00	48.38	15.87	1366.70	0.82	15.05	17.20
1	3/9/00	48.25	−0.26	1401.69	2.56	−2.82	14.38
2	3/10/00	48.13	−0.26	1395.07	−0.47	0.21	14.59
3	3/13/00	47.91	−0.45	1383.62	−0.82	0.37	14.96
4	3/14/00	47.38	−1.11	1359.15	−1.77	0.66	15.62
5	3/15/00	47.75	0.79	1392.14	2.43	−1.64	13.98
6	3/16/00	48.56	1.70	1458.47	4.76	−3.06	10.92
7	3/17/00	48.63	0.13	1464.47	0.41	−0.28	10.64
8	3/20/00	49.00	0.77	1456.63	−0.54	1.31	11.94
9	3/21/00	49.06	0.13	1493.87	2.56	−2.43	9.51
10	3/22/00	48.94	−0.25	1500.64	0.45	−0.71	8.81

QUESTIONS

C18.2.1 What difference do you observe in the cumulative abnormal returns for the 21-day windows provided?

C18.2.2 Present some explanations for the differences in results.

References

Bagwell, Laurie Simon, "Dutch Auction, Repurchases: An Analysis of Shareholder Heterogeneity," *Journal of Finance* 47: March 1992, pp. 71–106.

Barber, B. M., and J. D. Lyon, "Detecting Abnormal Operating Performance: The Empirical Power and Specification of Test-Statistics," *Journal of Financial Economics* 41, 1996, pp. 359–399.

Bens, Daniel A., Venky Nagar, Douglas J. Skinner, and M. H. Franco Wong, "Employee Stock Options, EPS Dilution, and Stock Repurchases," working paper, University of Chicago, February 2002.

Bradley, Michael, and Lee M. Wakeman, "The Wealth Effects of Targeted Share Repurchases," *Journal of Financial Economics* 11, 1983, pp. 301–328.

Brickley, James, "Shareholder Wealth, Information Signalling, and the Specially Designed Dividend: An Empirical Study," *Journal of Financial Economics* 12, 1983, pp.103–114.

Comment, Robert, and Gregg A. Jarrell, "The Relative Signalling Power of Dutch-Auction and Fixed-Price Self-Tender Offers and Open-Market Share Repurchases," *Journal of Finance* 46: 4, September 1991, pp. 1243–1272.

Dann, Larry Y. "Common Stock Repurchases: An Analysis of Returns to Bondholders and Stockholders," *Journal of Financial Economics* 9, 1981, pp.113–138.

DeAngelo, Harry, Linda DeAngelo, and Douglas J. Skinner, "Are Dividends Disappearing? Dividend Concentration and the Consolidation of Earnings," working paper No. 02–9, University of Southern California—Marshall School of Business, September 2002.

DeAngelo, Harry, Linda DeAngelo, and Douglas J. Skinner, "Special Dividends and the Evolution of Dividend Signaling," *Journal of Financial Economics* 57: 3, September 2000, pp. 309–354.

D'Mello, Ranjan, and Pervin K. Shroff, "Equity Undervaluation and Decisions Related to Repurchase Tender Offers: An Empirical Investigation," *Journal of Finance* 55: 5, October 2000, pp. 2399–2424.

Esty, Benjamin C., and Craig F. Schreiber, "Dividend Policy at FPL Group, Inc.," HBS Case N9–295–059, March 15, 1995.

Fama, Eugene F., "Market Efficiency, Long-Term Returns, and Behavioral Finance," *Journal of Financial Economics* 49: 3, September 1998, pp. 283–306.

Fama, Eugene, and Kenneth R. French, "Disappearing Dividends: Changing Firm Characteristics or Lower Propensity to Pay," *Journal of Financial Economics*, 60: 1, April 2001, pp. 3–43.

Fenn, George W., and Nellie Liang, "Corporate Payout Policy and Managerial Stock Incentives," *Journal of Financial Economics* 60: 1, April 2001, pp. 45–72.

Gay, Gerald D., Jayant R. Kale, and Thomas H. Noe, "Share Repurchases Mechanisms: A Comparative Analysis of Efficacy, Shareholder Wealth, and Corporate Control Effects," *Financial Management* 20, Spring 1991, pp. 44–59.

Grullon, Gustavo, and David L. Ikenberry, "What Do We Know About Stock Repurchases?" *Journal of Applied Corporate Finance* 13: 1, Spring 2000, pp. 31–51.

——, and Roni Michaely, "Dividends, Share Repurchases, and the Substitution Hypothesis," *Journal of Finance* 4, August 2002, pp. 1649–1684.

Guay, Wayne, and Jarrad Harford, "The Cash-Flow Permanence and Information Content of Dividend Increases Versus Repurchases," *Journal of Financial Economics* 57: 3, September 2000, pp. 385–415.

Healy, P., K. Palepu, and R. Ruback, "Does Corporate Performance Improve After Mergers?" *Journal of Financial Economics* 19, 1992, pp. 135–175.

Howe, Keith M., Jia He, and G. Wenchi Kao, "One-Time Cash Flow Announcements and Free Cash-Flow Theory: Share Repurchases and Special Dividends," *Journal of Finance* 47, December 1992, pp. 1963–1975.

Howe, Keith M., Steve Vogt, and Jia He, "The Effect of Managerial Ownership on the Short- and Long-Run Response to Cash Distributions," *Financial Review* 38, May 2003, pp. 179–196.

Ikenberry, David, Josef Lakonishok, and Theo Vermaelen, "Market Underreaction to Open Market Share Repurchases," *Journal of Financial Economics* 39: 2–3, October-November 1995, pp. 181–208.

Isawaga, Nobuyuki, "Open-Market Repurchase Announcements and Stock Price Behavior in Inefficient Markets," *Financial Management* 31: 3, Autumn 2002, pp. 5–20.

Kahle, Kathleen M., "When a Buyback Isn't a Buyback: Open Market Repurchases and Employee Options," *Journal of Financial Economics* 63: 2, February 2002, pp. 235–261.

Kale, Jayant R., Thomas H. Noe, and Gerald D. Gay, "Share Repurchase Through Transferable Put Rights," *Journal of Financial Economics* 25, 1989, pp. 141–160.

Kamma, Screenivas, George Kanatas, and Steven Raymar, "Dutch Auction Versus Fixed-Price Self-Tender Offers for Common Stock," *Journal of Financial Intermediation* 2, 1992, pp. 277–307.

Lang, L., and R. Litzenberger, "Dividend Announcements: Cash Flow Signaling vs. Free Cash Flow Hypothesis," *Journal of Financial Economics* 24, 1989, pp. 181–191.

Lee, D. Scott, Wayne H. Mikkelson, and M. Megan Partch, "Managers' Trading Around Stock Repurchases," *Journal of Finance* 47: 5, December 1992, pp. 1947–1961.

Liang, J. Nellie, and Steven A. Sharpe, "Share Repurchases and Employee Stock Options and Their Implications for S&P 500 Share Retirements and Expected Returns," working paper, Federal Reserve Board—Division of Research and Statistics, November 1999.

Lie, Erik, and John J. McConnell, "Earnings Signals in Fixed-Price and Dutch Auction Self-Tender Offers," *Journal of Financial Economics* 49, 1998, pp. 161–186.

Masulis, Ronald W., "Stock Repurchase by Tender Offer: An Analysis of the Causes of Common Stock Price Changes," *Journal of Finance* 35, 1980, pp. 305–319.

McGough, Robert, Suzanne McGee, and Cassell Bryan-Low, "Heard on the Street: Poof! Buyback Binge Now Creates Big Hangover," *Wall Street Journal*, December 18, 2000, p. C1.

Mitchell, Mark L., and Erik Stafford, "Managerial Decisions and Long-Term Stock Price Performance," *Journal of Business* 73: 3, July 2000, pp. 287–329.

Mitchell, Mark L., and Jeffry M. Netter, "Triggering the 1987 Stock Market Crash: Antitakeover Provisions in the Proposed House Ways and Means Tax Bill?" *Journal of Financial Economics* 24: 1, September 1989, pp. 37–68.

Netter, Jeffry M., and Mark L. Mitchell, "Stock-Repurchase Announcements and Insider Transactions After the October 1987 Stock Market Crash," *Financial Management* 18: 3, Autumn 1989, pp. 84–96.

Nohel, Tom, and Vefa Tarhan, "Share Repurchases and Firm Performance: New Evidence on the Agency Costs of Free Cash Flow," *Journal of Financial Economics* 49: 2, August 1998, pp. 187–222.

Norris, Floyd, "Cigna's Buyback Plan Has Created a Cash Crunch," *New York Times,* October 29, 2002, p. C1.

Perfect, S., D. Petersen, and P. Petersen, "Self Tender Offers: The Effects of Free Cash Flow, Cash Flow Signaling, and the Measurement of Tobin's Q," *Journal of Banking and Finance* 19, 1995, pp. 1005–1023.

Rappaport, Alfred, *Creating Shareholder Value*, New York: The Free Press, 1998.

Soter, Dennis, Eugene Brigham, and Paul Evanson, "The Dividend Cut 'Heard Round the World': The Case of FPL," *Journal of Applied Corporate Finance* 9, Spring 1996, pp. 4–15.

Stephens, Clifford P., and Michael S. Weisbach, "Actual Share Reacquisitions in Open-Market Repurchase Programs," *Journal of Finance* 53: 1, February 1998, pp. 313–333.

Vermaelen, Theo, "Common Stock Repurchases and Market Signalling: An Empirical Study," *Journal of Financial Economics* 9, 1981, 138–183.

———, "Repurchase Tender Offers, Signalling and Managerial Incentives," *Journal of Financial and Quantitative Analysis* 19, 1984, pp. 163–181.

CHAPTER 19
TAKEOVER DEFENSES

Not all merger proposals are welcomed by the target. During the 1980s, arsenals of devices were developed to defend against unwelcome proposals. Examples of resistance to takeover offers abound. We present two illustrative cases. In August 1998, AMP received a cash bid from AlliedSignal. AMP was a leading producer of electronic connectors. AlliedSignal was regarded as an advanced-technology company with operations in diversified areas. AMP resisted and ultimately accepted a proposal by Tyco International, another diversified firm.

On November 14, 1999, Vodafone AirTouch (based in Britain) made an unsolicited bid to Mannesmann AG (based in Germany). Despite many defenses put up by Mannesmann, it finally agreed to the Vodafone offer on February 3, 2000.

Multiple issues are raised by the use of takeover defenses. One is whether the target is resisting mainly to get a better price. Recall the TRW case in Chapter 6. A second possibility is that management of the target judges that the company will perform better on its own. A third reason might be that management is seeking to entrench itself against loss of authority in the combined firm. So many issues are raised by the subject that we provide a road map in Table 19.1. We discuss each of the topics listed in the sections that follow.

STRATEGIC PERSPECTIVES

In Chapter 1, we described how strong change forces like advances in technology and globalization have redefined industries and increased the intensity of competition between firms. It is imperative that management and the board of a company, with the assistance of its legal advisers and its financial advisers, continuously reassess the competitive landscape. Management and the board must evaluate on a continuing basis how all the forms of M&A activities described in the previous chapter may impact the firm as threats and as opportunities. Wasserstein (1998) described how large public companies review takeover defense issues on a regular basis. He described the innovative contributions of Martin Lipton, the founder of Wachtell, Lipton, Rosen, and Katz, who developed the poison pill defense (Wasserstein, 1998, pp. 461–463).

Wide-ranging subjects are covered, including the following:

1. What are the main developments in the industry?
2. Are there opportunities for adding critical capabilities to participate in attractive growth areas?

TABLE 19.1   An Overview of Takeover Defenses

1. Strategic perspectives
2. Financial defensive measures
3. Corporate restructuring and reorganization
   a. Reorganization of assets
   b. Other strategies (leveraged recaps, LBOs, etc.)
4. Duty of directors
5. Greenmail
   a. Wealth effects of greenmail
   b. Antigreenmail developments
6. Methods of resistance
   a. Pac Man defense
   b. White knight
   c. White squire
7. Antitakeover amendments
   a. Supermajority amendments
   b. Fair-price amendments—to avoid two-tier offers
   c. Staggered or classified board of directors
   d. Dual class or create new classes of securities with magnified voting power
   e. Other antitakeover actions
   f. Antitakeover amendments and corporate policy
   g. Antitakeover amendments and shareholder returns
8. State laws
9. Poison pills—right to purchase securities at low prices
   a. Types of plans
   b. Dead-hand provisions
   c. Case studies
   d. Effects on shareholder returns
10. Shareholder activism
11. Poison puts—permit bondholders to put (sell) bonds to the issuer in the event of a takeover
12. Golden parachutes
    a. Rationale
    b. Silver and tin parachutes
    c. Returns to shareholders and golden parachutes

---

3. Are there opportunities for rolling up fragmented industries into stronger firms?
4. Is our firm likely to be rolled up?
5. Are sales-to-capacity relationships improving or deteriorating in our industry?
6. Will consolidating mergers to reduce capacity and cost impact our firm?
7. Is one of the top six to eight firms in our industry a likely target for takeover by a competitor whose capabilities would thereby be significantly enhanced?
8. Should our firm make preemptive moves?
9. How should our firm respond to a takeover bid?

In short, every firm needs to reevaluate its strategies on a continuing basis with particular reference to the possibilities of M&A activity that will impact it.

FINANCIAL DEFENSIVE MEASURES

It is often proposed that the best defense against a takeover is for the firm to be highly efficient, its sales growth favorable, and its profitability margins high. However, the firm could become a takeover target of another firm seeking to benefit from an association with such an efficient firm. In addition, if it has long-range investment plans with payoffs that are not reflected in its current stock price, the firm might be viewed as undervalued.

Other characteristics that make a firm vulnerable to a takeover include:

- A low stock price in relation to the replacement cost of assets or their potential earning power (a low q-ratio).
- A highly liquid balance sheet with large amounts of excess cash, a valuable securities portfolio, and significant unused debt capacity.
- Good cash flow relative to current stock prices; low P/EPS ratios.
- Subsidiaries or properties that could be sold off without significantly impairing cash flow.
- Relatively small stock holdings under the control of incumbent management.

A combination of these factors can simultaneously make a firm an attractive investment opportunity and facilitate its financing. The firm's assets act as collateral for an acquirer's borrowings, and the target's cash flows from operations and divestitures can be used to repay the loans.

A firm fitting the aforementioned description would do well to take at least some of the following steps. (1) Increase debt with borrowed funds used to repurchase equity, thus concentrating management's percentage holdings and using up debt capacity. (2) Increase dividends on remaining shares. (3) Structure loan covenants to force acceleration of repayment in the event of takeover. (4) Liquidate securities portfolios and draw down excess cash. (5) Invest continuing cash flows from operations in positive net-present-value projects or return it to shareholders. (6) Use some of the excess liquidity to acquire other firms. (7) Divest subsidiaries than can be eliminated without impairing cash flow, perhaps through spin-offs to avoid large sums of cash flowing in. (8) Analyze the profitability of all operations in depth to get at the true picture beneath such accounting devices as transfer pricing and overhead allocation, and divest low-profit operations. (9) Realize the true value of undervalued assets by selling them off or restructuring.

CORPORATE RESTRUCTURING AND REORGANIZATION

In academic journals and business magazines, the topics of corporate restructuring and reorganization to increase value have been kept separate from the topics of defensive corporate restructuring and reorganization. After reading both types of literature, the insight came to us that this is one subject, not two. We will review the topics of value-increasing activities and then show their application and extension in defensive programs. It is useful to recall the outline of Chapters 11 to 18 in Table 11.1. In the initial treatment of those chapters, the emphasis was on the development of value increasing strategies. Here we use the same framework to demonstrate how the entire panoply of activities can be employed as takeover defenses. We cover each of the four major topics in turn.

REORGANIZATION OF ASSETS

In the earlier discussion, assets were acquired to extend the firm's capabilities. However asset acquisitions also can be used to block takeovers. In 1984, Disney bought the Arvida real estate firm with equity to dilute the ownership position as a defense against Saul Steinberg and his

Reliance Group. Acquisitions also can be used to create antitrust problems for the bidder. The Marshall Field department store used this defense several times. For example, when Carter Hawley Hale (CHH) made a tender offer, Field's directors expanded into the Galleria in Houston and acquired five Liberty House stores in the Northwest. Because CHH was active in these areas, on February 22, 1978, it withdrew its tender offer, citing the impact of Field's expansion plan.

In Chapters 11 and 12, we described how sell-offs and divestitures can be used to move resources to their higher-valued uses, creating values for both the seller and buyer. To block a tender offer, however, a firm may dispose of those segments of its business in which the bidder is most interested. This is called "selling off the crown jewels."

In Chapter 13, we discussed reorganizing financial claims. By using exchange offers, a firm can either increase or decrease leverage. A debt-for-equity expansion can be used to increase leverage to levels that would be unacceptable to the bidder. Dual-class recapitalizations can be used to increase the voting powers of an insider group to levels that would enable it to block a tender offer. Leveraged recapitalizations can be used to unlock potential values for the company. However, a firm might also incur huge amounts of debt, using the proceeds to pay a large cash dividend and increase the ownership position of insiders. This tactic has been called a "scorched earth" policy. The crown jewel and scorched earth actions can be combined. The firm sells off attractive segments of the company and adds large amounts of debt, using the cash for a large dividend that might even exceed the tender offer price from the bidder.

OTHER STRATEGIES

In Chapter 14. we described how joint ventures can be used to extend the capabilities of the firm. Joint ventures also can be used to block a takeover. A close involvement with other firms could represent liaisons that the potential bidder might prefer to avoid.

In Chapter 15, we explain how ESOPs are often used to block takeovers, and we described the famous example of Polaroid and Shamrock Holdings. Chapter 16 discussed MBOs and LBOs, which are widely used as a defense against an outside tender offer. Sometimes the financing of the MBO or LBO comes from financial institutions. Sometimes the competitive bidder is an LBO specialist firm such as KKR. One of the incentives management might have for turning to the LBO specialist firm is that its stock ownership position might thereby be increased more than in the outside tender offer.

In Chapter 17, we discussed how international liaisons and other transactions can be used to defend against unwanted takeovers. A domestic bidder might not offer as great a potential for augmenting the firm's capabilities and growth as an international partner.

In Chapter 18, we discussed share-repurchase programs. One purpose of share-repurchase programs is to signal that the current price of the stock represents under-valuation. However, share-repurchase programs are widely used to defend against takeovers. They increase the ownership of insiders. With respect to outside shareholders, the low-reservation-price investors are bought out in a share-repurchase program. The tender offer price to succeed, therefore, is higher than it otherwise would be.

GREENMAIL

In one sense, greenmail says to the bidder, "Here is some money. Now go away." More formally, greenmail represents a targeted repurchase of a large block of stock from specified shareholders at a premium. The purpose of the premium buyback presumably is to end a hostile takeover threat by the large blockholder or greenmailer. The term ***greenmail*** connotes blackmail, and both payers and receivers of greenmail have received negative publicity. Proponents of antigreenmail charter amendments or legislation that would prohibit targeted repurchases argue that greenmailers cause damage to shareholders. In this view, the large block investors are corporate "raiders" who expropriate corporate assets to the detriment of other shareholders. Allegedly, raiding takes the form of the raiders using their corporate voting power to accord themselves excessive compensation and perquisites, receiving on their shares a substantial premium over the market price through greenmail or "looting" the corporate treasury in some unspecified manner (Holderness and Sheehan, 1985).

An alternative view is that the large block investors involved in greenmail help bring about management changes, either changes in corporate personnel or changes in corporate policy, or have superior skills at evaluating potential takeover targets (Holderness and Sheehan, 1985). In this view, proposals to prohibit targeted repurchases are antitakeover proposals in disguise (Jensen, 1988). Jensen (1988, p.41) argued that "management can easily prohibit greenmail without legislation; it need only announce a policy that prohibits the board or management from making such payments." He suggested that managers make greenmail payments to protect themselves from competition in the corporate control market.

Often, in connection with targeted repurchases, a standstill agreement is written. A standstill agreement is a voluntary contract in which the stockholder who is bought out agrees not to make further investments in the target company during a specified period of time (for example, 10 years). When a standstill agreement is made without a repurchase, the large blockholder simply agrees not to increase his or her ownership, which presumably would put him or her in an effective control position.

The St. Regis Paper Company provides an example of greenmail. When an investor group led by Sir James Goldsmith acquired an 8.6% stake in St. Regis and expressed interest in taking over the paper concern, the company agreed to repurchase the shares at a premium. Goldsmith's group acquired the shares for an average price of $35.50 per share, a total of $109 million. It sold its stake at $52 per share, netting a profit of $51 million. Shortly after the payoff in March 1984, St. Regis became the target of publisher Rupert Murdoch. St. Regis turned to Champion International and agreed to a $1.84 billion takeover. Murdoch tendered his 5.6% stake in St. Regis to the Champion offer for a profit.

WEALTH EFFECTS OF GREENMAIL

The announcement of a greenmail transaction by a company generally results in a negative abnormal return to shareholders of about 2% to 3%, which is statistically significant (Bradley and Wakeman, 1983; Dann and DeAngelo, 1983; Mikkelson and Ruback, 1991). However, further analysis is required. Consider a number of possibilities.

When the large blockholder starts buying the shares that provide him with a threatening position, the price of the company stock is likely to increase. Other empirical studies find that when these initial stock purchases are taken into account, positive abnormal returns are earned during the initial period when the foothold is being established and in the full "purchase-to-repurchase" period (Holderness and Sheehan, 1985; Klein and Rosenfield, 1988; Mikkelson and Ruback, 1985, 1991).

However, even at the announcement of a greenmail repurchase, a decline in stock prices generally does not occur unless the greenmail is associated with a standstill agreement or is preceded by a control contest (Mikkelson and Ruback, 1991). The standstill agreements may be viewed as reducing the probability of a subsequent takeover. Nevertheless, even with standstill agreements, about 40% of the firms experience a subsequent control change within 3 years of the greenmail.

We should not read the empirical results without thinking about some real-world possibilities, such as the hostile bid for Disney in 1984 by Saul Steinberg and his associates. Among other things, Disney paid Steinberg greenmail in the amount of about $50 million, but it was widely recognized that Disney needed some top management changes (Taylor, 1987). After fending off the Steinberg group, a new management team was brought in, headed by Michael D. Eisner. Taking into account stock splits, the Disney stock increased from about $6 in 1984 to $34 by 1989, representing a compound rate of increase in the common stock price for shareholders of 41.5%. From 1989 to 1996, Disney stock increased to $60 per share, representing a further compound annual rate of increase of 8.5%. The initial jump in stock prices reflected the ability of Disney directors to make the top management changes needed. The slower rate of growth in stock prices after 1989 might have contributed to the Disney acquisition of Cap Cities/ABC in August 1995.

The moral of this story is that the impact of greenmail can be different, depending on the circumstances. If it gives the directors time to work out a better solution, then the market reaction could be positive rather than negative.

ANTIGREENMAIL DEVELOPMENTS

The negative view of greenmail resulted in efforts to restrict its use. In 1986, congress included in the tax law changes a provision in Section 5881 of the Internal Revenue Code that imposes a 50% excise tax on the recipient of greenmail payments. In addition, antigreenmail charter amendments began to be enacted by companies.

Antigreenmail charter amendments prohibit or discourage the targeted repurchase by requiring management to obtain the approval of a majority or supermajority of nonparticipating shareholders prior to a repurchase. Proxy statements proposing antigreenmail amendments typically state that greenmailers pressure the company for a premium buyback with "threats of disruption" including proxy contests and tender offers, that greenmail is inherently unfair to the nonparticipating shareholders, and that the decision-making power for any targeted repurchases should be transferred properly to the hands of those most affected by the repurchase decision. According to Bhagat and Jefferis (1991), proxy statements proposing antigreenmail amendments frequently include one or more of (other) antitakeover amendment proposals. Among a sample of 52 NYSE-listed firms proposing antigreenmail amendments in the period 1984 to 1985, 40 firms also offered one or more antitakeover amendments in the proxy material. In 29 cases, shareholders had to approve or reject the antitakeover provisions and antigreenmail amendment jointly.

For a subsample in which the antigreenmail amendments are not associated with other antitakeover proposals, the antigreenmail amendment itself does not decrease shareholder wealth. Eckbo (1990) demonstrated the complexity of the effects of greenmail prohibitions. He found that the average market reaction to charter amendments prohibiting greenmail payments was weakly negative, indicating some value to retaining managerial flexibility. He found, however, that for a subsample of firms with an abnormal stock price run-up over the 3 months prior to the mailing of a proxy providing for greenmail prohibitions, the market reaction was strongly positive. This was particularly true if the prior run-up was associated with evidence or rumors of takeover activity. The logic here is that the prohibition against greenmail would remove a barrier to a takeover with positive gains to shareholders. It would follow that greenmail payments themselves would tend to decrease the firm's value. Eckbo suggested the possibility of alternative methods for remunerating takeover entrepreneurs.

METHODS OF RESISTANCE

Firms can employ several other types of strategies to resist a particular bidder. These include the Pac Man defense, the use of a white knight, and resorting to a white squire.

PAC MAN DEFENSE

Making a counterbid for the bidder is similar to the video game from which it gets its name. The Pac Man defense in essence involves the target counteroffering for the bidder. This severe defense is rarely used and in fact usually is designed not to be used. The defense is more likely to be effective if the target is much larger than the bidder, a phenomenon common in the 1980s. The risk of using the defense is that it implies that the target finds combining the two firms desirable but prefers control of the resulting entity. The user of the Pac Man essentially gives up using antitrust issues as a defense.

In most takeovers, target managements that resist maintain that the combination is undesirable. If the Pac Man defense is used, it is extremely costly and could have devastating financial effects for both firms involved. If both firms employ a large amount of debt to buy each other's stock, the resulting entity could be crippled by the combined debt load. Also, there is a risk that under state law, should both firms buy substantial stakes in each other, each would be ruled as subsidiaries of the other and be unable to vote its shares against the corporate parent. Curiously, the severity of the defense may lead the bidder to disbelieve that the target actually will employ the defense.

One famous example of the use of the Pac Man defense involves Bendix and Martin Marietta. On August 25, 1982, Bendix Corporation announced a previously rumored tender offer for Martin Marietta of $43 per share. The case is noteworthy because Martin Marietta became the first firm to remain independent by employing the Pac Man defense. Marietta, with the advice of its investment banker, announced a $75 per share countertender for half of Bendix, with a $55 back-end price.

Although Marietta announced its tender offer after Bendix and would be able to buy Bendix shares only after Bendix could purchase Marietta shares, it believed that it might be able to gain control first due to differences in state laws concerning the calling of a special meeting to approve a merger. United Technologies, a large defense contractor that was interested in the complementary fit of Bendix's automotive business and Bendix's consumer electronics business, later joined Marietta and agreed to tender for half of Bendix for $75 per share and a $50 back-end price.

Efforts to convince Bendix of the seriousness of the counterbid were not effective in getting Bendix to back down. On September 17, Bendix bought 70% of Marietta shares for $48 a share. On September 23, Marietta purchased 42.4% of Bendix shares, despite news that Allied Corporation and Bendix would merge. Allied, whose main businesses were oil and gas production and chemicals, had been searching for a profitable company to enable it to use its more than $100 million in U.S. federal income tax credits and to reduce its dependence on gas and oil profits.

After Marietta declined Allied's offer to buy both Bendix and Marietta, the two sides agreed to a stock swap at cost. Marietta reacquired some of its shares, but Allied retained possession of a 39% stake in Marietta. Allied signed a 10 year standstill agreement. Due to the purchase of Bendix stock, Marietta had a debt-to-equity ratio of 85%, and the new debt of $930 million raised total debt to $1.3 billion. To raise funds, it sold stock, businesses, plants, and other assets. The restructuring included the divestiture of its chemicals, cement, and aggregates businesses. In late 1983, Marietta bought back all its shares held by Allied for $345 million.

WHITE KNIGHT

The white knight defense involves choosing another company with which the target prefers to be combined. An alternative company might be preferred by the target because it sees greater compatibility, or the new bidder might promise not to break up the target or engage in massive employee dismissals.

Examples of the use of white knights abound. Frequently, T. Boone Pickens would make an offer for a company on behalf of his Mesa Petroleum. For example, in 1982, Mesa made a bid for the Cities Service Oil Company. Cities Service responded with a Pac Man defense. Then Cities Service invited Gulf Oil to make a bid. Gulf made a bid, but when the Federal Trade Commission raised antitrust objections, Gulf dropped out. Ultimately, Cities Service was purchased by Occidental Petroleum. In 1984, Mesa bid for Gulf Oil. Gulf responded by holding an auction. Chevron (then SOCAL) ultimately won the bidding contest.

WHITE SQUIRE

The white squire is a modified form of a white knight, the difference being that the white squire does not acquire control of the target. In a white squire transaction, the target sells a block of its stock to a third party it considers to be friendly. The white squire sometimes is required to vote its shares with target management. These transactions often are accompanied by a standstill agreement that limits the amount of additional target stock the white squire can purchase for a specified period of time and restricts the sale of its target stock, usually giving the right of first refusal to the target. In return, the white squire often receives a seat on the target board, generous dividends, and/or a discount on the target shares. Preferred stock enables the board to tailor the characteristics of that stock to fit the transaction and so usually is used in white squire transactions.

Here is a famous example of a white squire investment. Although Champion International did not face a direct takeover threat, the company became concerned about the possibility of an attempted takeover following the first hostile takeover bid in the paper industry, that of Georgia Pacific for Great Northern Nekoosa in 1989. Champion's management approached Warren Buffett about investing in the company. In December 1989, Buffett purchased $300 million of new Champion convertible preferred stock that carried a 9.25% annual dividend rate. This was about $6 million per year over the market rate of 7% for investment-grade, convertible preferred stock. Buffett held an 8% voting equity stake, one that he was allowed to raise to 18%.

ANTITAKEOVER AMENDMENTS

Other defense mechanisms are referred to as antitakeover amendments to a firm's corporate charter. These often are called "shark repellents." As with all charter amendments, antitakeover amendments must be voted on and approved by shareholders. Although 95% of antitakeover amendments proposed by management are ratified by shareholders, this might be because a planned amendment might not be introduced if management is unsure of its success (Brickley,

Lease, and Smith, 1988). Failure to pass might be taken as a vote of no confidence in incumbent management and may provide a platform for a proxy fight or takeover attempt where none had existed before. The evidence provided by Brickly, Lease, and Smith (1988) indicated that institutional shareholders such as banks and insurance companies were more likely to vote with management on antitakeover amendments than others such as mutual funds and college endowments. Note that the former institutions generally have ongoing business relationships with management and thus are more likely to be influenced by management. Brickley, Lease, and Smith also found that blockholders more actively participate in voting than nonblockholders and might oppose proposals that appear to harm shareholders. This result is consistent with Jarrell and Poulsen (1987), who found that those amendments having the most negative effect on stock price (amendments other than fair-price amendments) are adopted by firms with the lowest percentage of institutional holdings and the highest percentage of insider holdings. Jarrell and Poulsen suggested that these results helped explain how harmful amendments receive approval of shareholders. The evidence also suggested that blockholders do play a monitoring role. Institutional holders are sophisticated and well informed, so they vote in accordance with their economic interest more consistently than less well informed small investors.

Antitakeover amendments generally impose new conditions on the transfer of managerial control of the firm through a merger or tender offer or by replacement of the board of directors. There are four major types of antitakeover amendments: supermajority, fair-price, classified boards, and authorization of preferred stock.

SUPERMAJORITY AMENDMENTS

Supermajority amendments require shareholder approval by at least two-thirds vote and sometimes as much as 90% of the voting power of outstanding capital stock for all transactions involving change of control. In most existing cases, however, the supermajority provisions have a board-out clause that provides the board with the power to determine when and if the supermajority provisions will be in effect. Pure supermajority provisions would seriously limit management's flexibility in takeover negotiations.

FAIR-PRICE AMENDMENTS

Fair-price amendments are supermajority provisions with a board-out clause and an additional clause waiving the supermajority requirement if a fair price is paid for all purchased share. The fair price commonly is defined as the highest price paid by the bidder during a specified period and sometimes is required to exceed an amount determined relative to accounting earnings or book value of the target. Thus, fair-price amendments defend against two-tier tender offers that are not approved by the target's board. A uniform offer for all shares to be purchased in a tender offer and in a subsequent cleanup merger or tender offer will avoid the supermajority requirement. Because the two-tier tender offer is not essential in successful hostile takeovers, the fair-price amendment is the least restrictive in the class of supermajority amendments.

CLASSIFIED BOARDS

Another major type of antitakeover amendment provides for **staggered**, or **classified**, boards of directors to delay effective transfer of control in a takeover. Management's purported rationale in proposing a staggered board is to ensure continuity of policy and experience. For example, a nine-member board might be divided into three classes, with only three members standing for election to a 3-year term each year. Thus, a new majority shareholder would have to wait at least two annual meetings to gain control of the board of directors. Effectiveness of cumulative voting is reduced under the classified-board scheme because a greater shareholder vote is required to elect a single director. Variations on antitakeover amendments relating to the board of directors include provisions prohibiting the removal of directors except for cause and provisions fixing the number of directors allowed to prevent "packing" the board.

AUTHORIZATION OF PREFERRED STOCK

The board of directors is authorized to create a new class of securities with special voting rights. This security, typically preferred stock, may be issued to friendly parties in a control contest. Thus, this device is a defense against hostile takeover bids, although historically it was used to provide the board of directors with flexibility in financing under changing economic conditions. Creation of a poison pill security could be included in this category but generally is considered to be a different defensive device. (We examine the poison pill defense in the following section.)

OTHER ANTITAKEOVER ACTIONS

Other amendments that management may propose as a takeover defense include:

1. Abolition of cumulative voting where it is not required by state law.
2. Reincorporation in a state with more accommodating antitakeover laws.
3. Provisions with respect to the scheduling of shareholders' meetings and introduction of agenda items, including nomination of candidates to the board of directors.

Another refinement is the passage of lock-in amendments, making it difficult to void previously passed antitakeover amendments by requiring, for example, supermajority approval. Shareholders might propose antigreenmail amendments that restrict a company's freedom to buy back a raider's shares at a premium.

Iqbal et al. (1999) analyzed whether the termination of overfunded pension plans to deter takeover attempts was viewed negatively by shareholders. Termination could be viewed as a takeover defense because by liquidating the excess assets, the firm removes a significant source of cash flow to the bidder firm. The sample analyzed consisted of 123 firms with defined benefit pension plan terminations with excess asset reversions exceeding $1 million during the period May 1980 to October 1990. The event date was defined as the earlier of the *Wall Street Journal* announcement date or the filing date. No other financial news occurred around a 6-day window surrounding the event date. The sample was subdivided by managerial ownership level. Of the sample firms, 63 were classified as low ownership (5% or less direct insider ownership) and 60 were considered high ownership (higher than 5% ownership). The sample also was classified by whether they received a takeover bid in a period 2 years before through 2 years after the termination date. Twenty-eight firms were classified as takeover susceptible, whereas the remaining 95 firms were classified as nontakeover firms.

For the event window $(-1, 0)$, the full sample had CARs of 0.5% and 0.6% based on filing date and event date, respectively, both significant at the 10% level. The high ownership group exhibited a positive CAR of 1.0%, significant at the 10% level, consistent with the notion that terminations were favorable when managers had a high ownership interest in the firm. The CAR for the takeover-susceptible firms was a positive 1.6%, significant at the 5% level. One explanation given by Iqbal et al. was that shareholders viewed takeover attempts as a direct threat to their claim on the excess pension assets.

Additional analysis examined the effects of managerial ownership on the stock price reactions for the takeover-susceptible and nontakeover sample. For takeover-susceptible firms, high level of ownership had a highly significant CAR of 4.6%, significant at the 1% level. Low level of ownership did not show significant results. For the nontakeover sample, there was no significant reaction for either level of managerial ownership. Thus, stockholders favored terminations only when terminating firms faced takeover and managerial ownership was high in the firm.

Similarly, Boyle, Carter, and Stover (1998) studied autitakeover provisions adopted by mutual savings and loan associations converting to stock ownership (SLAs). For a sample of 51 SLAs receiving conversion approval during 1985 and 1986 (years of highest conversion activity), relatively low insider ownership after conversion was associated with strong antitakeover protection. Firms with relatively high resulting insider ownership adopted less "extraordinary" antitakeover protection; the strength of ownership position appeared to substitute for strong antitakeover provisions.

ANTITAKEOVER AMENDMENTS AND CORPORATE POLICY

The effects of antitakeover statutes on firm leverage were studied by Garvey and Hanka (1999), based on a sample of 1,203 firms and covering data for the period 1983 to 1993. This is a further test of the previous literature with models in which managers increased debt as a method of reducing the threat of hostile takeovers. By 1982, 37 states had first-generation antitakeover laws that in *Edgar v. MITE* were ruled to be preempted by the federal 1968 Williams Act. In 1987, the Supreme Court reversed in *Dynamics v. CTS*, ruling that state antitakeover laws are enforceable as long as they do not prevent compliance with the Williams Act. After this ruling, a majority of the states passed new antitakeover statutes between 1987 and 1990. Garvey and Hanka compared a sample of firms protected by the second generation of laws with a control sample of firms in states without such laws. Protected firms substantially reduced their debt ratios compared to the control group over a period of 4 years. The results are not influenced by variations in size, industry, or profitability. Garvey and Hanka found weak evidence that protected managers undertake fewer major restructuring programs. They also found that firms eventually covered by antitakeover legislation used greater leverage in the years preceding the adoption of the statutes. This is further evidence of the substitution between increased leverage and protection by the state antitakeover laws.

Johnson and Rao (1997) studied the impact of antitakeover amendments on the financial performance of the firm. Their study was based on the original sample of 649 firms that adopted antitakeover amendments between 1979 and 1985 used in the Jarrell and Poulsen (1987) study. The usable sample was reduced to 421 firms. The firms were classified by whether or not they adopted fair-price amendments. Of the total firms used, 311 firms were fair price and 110 were not.

The study compared financial attributes before and after the amendment adoption. Specifically, preantitakeover variables based on 3-year averages of financial attributes prior to the antitakeover amendment were compared to the postannouncement variables in each of the 5 years after the adoption. Four categories of financial performance were used in the analysis: income (ratio of operating and net income to total assets), expenses (ratio or operating and overhead expenses to sales), investment (ratio of R&D and capital expenditures to sales), and debt (ratio of debt to total assets). Raw and industry-adjusted data changes were analyzed.

For the overall sample, firms exhibited no significant differences from industry means except for a decline in net income but not in operating income, most likely due to an increase in leverage. For the non-fair-price subsample, there were no significant differences from the industry mean for any of the financial attributes. For the fair-price group, the results were similar to those of the full sample.

Meulbroek, Mitchell, Mulherin, Netter, and Poulsen (1990) more specifically analyzed the effect of antitakeover amendments, or shark repellents, on long-term managerial decision making. They examined whether shark repellents are associated with changes in research and development expenditures. The analysis used 203 firms from the Jarrell and Poulsen (1987) study that had available data. In contrast to models of managerial myopia, Meulbroek et al. (1990) found a reduction in R&D/sales following the implementation of antitakeover amendments.

ANTITAKEOVER AMENDMENTS AND SHAREHOLDER RETURNS

A substantial body of literature has studied the effects of antitakeover amendments on shareholder returns (Dodd and Leftwich, 1980; McWilliams, 1990; Pound, 1987; Romano, 1985, 1987, 1993; Ryngaert and Netter, 1988). The first edition of this book presented a review of the effects of several individual antitakeover measures in painstaking detail. Fortunately, a definitive, up-to-date analysis of the subject by Comment and Schwert (1995) enables us to compress our present discussion.

The literature predicts possible positive and negative effects of takeover amendments. Positive effects could result from the announcement of an antitakeover measure as a signal of the increased likelihood of a takeover with gains in value to shareholders of the order of magnitude of 30% to 50%. DeAngelo and Rice (1983) noted that shark repellents may have positive benefits in helping shareholders respond in unison (through management) to takeover bids. Negative effects of antitakeover amendments could result from discouraging or deterring takeovers because managers seek to prevent control changes. This is the management entrenchment hypothesis. Let us look at a review of the evidence.

Malekzadeh, McWilliams, and Sen (1998) analyzed the market reaction to antitakeover charter amendments, taking into account the governance and ownership structure of the firms. They used a sample of 213 firms that proposed antitakeover amendments during the period 1980 through 1987. Regressions showed significantly higher negative abnormal returns to firms where the CEO had a lower share ownership or to firms where the board had a lower share ownership. The relationship was more significantly negative when the CEO was also the board chair.

Loh and Rathinasamy (1997) studied the impact of the adoption of antitakeover devices on the announcement effect of voluntary spin-offs. The sample included in the study consisted of 268 U.S. firms that underwent voluntary sell-offs during the period 1981 to 1991. A firm was classified as a device firm if over a period of 6 months prior to the sell-off announcement, it announced the adoption of an antitakeover device; otherwise, it was classified as a non device firm. Of the total sample, 104 were classified as device firms. The top three antitakeover devices were poison pills (25 firms), leveraged recapitalizations (15 firms), and fair-price amendments (13 firms).

For the whole sample, the sell-off event generated a CAR of 4.18% from day –1 to day +1, significant at the 5% level. The subsample of device firms had an insignificant CAR of 0.65% for the same window. In contrast, the non device firms had a significant and positive corresponding CAR of 5.37%, significant at the 1% level. The market seemed to interpret the no-device sell-offs as a way for firms to reallocate assets to their higher-valued uses. On the other hand, the adoption of antitakeover devices seemed to indicate that the sell-off was part of a managerial entrenchment strategy.

The stock price reactions to antitakeover amendments were studied by McWilliams and Sen (1997) for a sample of 265 firms proposing antitakeover amendments from 1980 through 1990. They focused on board composition. The stock price reaction to antitakeover amendments was significantly lower when the board was dominated by inside and affiliated outside board members. The most negative reaction was when the CEO was also chair of the board and the inside and affiliated outside board members increased their ownership in the firm and their representation on the board.

Sundaramurthy, Mahoney, and Mahoney (1997) analyzed a sample of 261 firms that adopted 486 antitakeover provisions (supermajority, classified boards, fair-price, reduction in cumulative voting, antigreenmail, and poison pills) in the period 1984 to 1988. They found that the adoption of antitakeover provisions caused negative CARs, significant at the 1% level, for a range of event windows. The market reacted less negatively when the board of directors had a chairperson who was not the CEO. However, the market reacted more negatively to antitakeover provisions adopted by boards with higher proportions of outside members. The implications are that the use of outside directors does not ensure their independence. They might be chosen because they are aligned with top management.

The prior studies reviewed by Comment and Schwert (1995) showed a "typical decline" of less than 1% for most types of antitakeover measures and often under 0.5% (Jarrell and Poulsen, 1987; Karpoff and Malatesta, 1989; Malatesta and Walkling, 1988; Romano, 1993; Ryngaert, 1988). Two other studies found no statistically significant negative effects from the adoption of antitakeover charter amendments (DeAngelo and Rice, 1983; Linn and McConnell, 1983). Furthermore, a later study showed that corporate governance efforts through shareholder-initiated proposals to repeal antitakeover amendments had no statistically significant effects (Karpoff, Malatesta, and Walkling, 1996). The finding that the repeal of antitakeover amendments is a nonevent further buttresses the likelihood of little effect when they were announced in the first place.

Counterevidence is provided by Mahoney and Mahoney (1993). They found that although antitakeover amendments had no significant effects for the period 1974 to 1979, effects were significant for the period 1980 to 1988. However, they studied only classified board amendments and the supermajority provision. For 1980 to 1988, the effects of supermajority provisions were not statistically significant, but the effects of the adoption of a classified board of directors were. These results were the reverse of what logic would suggest. Supermajority provisions could be used to block takeovers by managers with some equity ownership. The effects of time-staggering fractions of director elections would be expected to be somewhat attenuated.

It is difficult to disentangle a number of influences. For example, if antitakeover amendments are adopted after a takeover is already underway, the purpose might be to help management obtain a better deal for the shareholders. The situation is similar if a takeover is rumored. Also, if one takeover has occurred in an industry, contagion effects might occur. When one takeover is completed, often the financial press observes that other takeovers in that industry are likely to occur. If the positive run-up in abnormal returns prior to the announcement of antitakeover amendments is considered, then a possible 1% decline in shareholder wealth should be netted against the prior positive returns. The 1% decline could be viewed as a reflection of the reduced probability of the takeover being completed. If 30% is taken as the average positive wealth effect of mergers and takeovers of all types, a wealth decline of 1% following the adoption of antitakeover amendments would mean a decrease of 3.3% (0.01/0.30) in the probability of the takeover. If the event effect is a −0.5%, the decline in the probability of the takeover would be 1.67%. We concur with the Comment and Schwert judgment that these relationships suggest that even small negative event returns from the announcement of antitakeover measures would have little power to deter takeovers.

TAKEOVER DEFENSES OF NEWLY PUBLIC FIRMS

A recent study by Field and Karpoff (2002) provided intriguing evidence on the role of anti-takeover devices in corporate strategy. They studied a sample of roughly 1,000 industrial firms that went public in the period 1988 to 1992. More than half of these firms had at least one takeover defense at the time of the IPO. These results indicate that corporate control issues are relevant even at the early stages of a corporation's public life.

STATE LAWS

We discussed the history of state antitakeover laws in the previous section. Here we look at decisions to opt out of the protection of state antitakeover laws. Janjigian and Trahan (1996) studied the factors that influenced firms to opt out of the Pennsylvania Senate Bill 1310 and the long-term performance of those firms after the bill announcement. The bill severely restricted hostile takeovers and was introduced on October 20, 1989. The sample analyzed was 39 firms incorporated in Pennsylvania. Of these, 21 firms opted out of at least one provision of the bill, and the remaining 18 did not opt out of any provision.

Using monthly returns, the mean CARs for the pre-event period defined as January 1988 to August 1989 were an insignificant 2.15% for the whole sample, a significant –12.79% (10% level) for firms opting out, and a significant 19.72% (10% level) for firms not opting out. The difference in the mean CARs for the two groups was significant at the 1% level. Six firms were targeted for takeover or rumored to be targets during this pre-event period. Excluding these firms resulted in mean CARs that were an insignificant –2.15% for the full sample of 33 firms, a significant –9.50% (10% level) for 20 firms that opted out, and an insignificant 9.15% for 13 firms that did not. The difference in the mean CARs for the two groups dropped to a 10% level of significance. Of the original 21 firms that opted out, 7 opted out of all provisions. The mean CAR for these 7 firms was –26.4%, significant at the 10% level. The mean CAR for firms that opted out of one or two provisions was an insignificant –4.26%.

Pre-event accounting performance in 1989 showed no significant difference between the firms that opted out and those that did not. However, the performance of both groups deteriorated substantially from 1989 to 1992. Nevertheless, firms that opted out had significantly better net profit margins, net return on assets, and operating return on assets in 1992 than firms that did not opt out.

Swartz (1996) examined a larger sample of 120 Pennsylvania firms. The event date was defined as April 27, 1990, the date of the passage of the Pennsylvania Antitakeover Law (Act 36 based on Senate Bill 1310). The mean CAR for the full sample for a 190-day (–130, +60) window was a negative 9.23%, significant at the 5% level. For a narrower window of 80 days, (+60, +20), the mean CAR was an insignificant –0.98%. Approximately 70% of the firms opted out of the legislation. The mean CAR was –5.24% from day –130 to day +60 for the firms that opted out and 0.70% from day –60 to day +20, neither one significant. The firms that did not opt out had a mean CAR of –23.35% for (–130, +60) and of –4.71% for (–60, +20) significant at the 1% and 5% level, respectively. The firms that opted out outperformed the firms that did not in both periods; from day –130 to day +60, the difference in the means was 18.11%, and from day –60 to day +30, the difference was 5.41%. Both differences were significant at the 5% level.

State laws appear to differ in provisions for facilitating takeover defenses. Heron and Lewellen (1998) studied 364 reincorporations during the period 1980 to 1992. Reincorporations made to establish stronger takeover defenses had significant negative returns. Reincorporations to limit director liability to attract better-qualified outside directors had significant positive returns. Heron and Lewellen also found that the firms giving limits on director liability as their prime motive did expand outside representation on their boards; firms citing other motives did not.

POISON PILLS

Poison pills represent the creation of securities carrying special rights exercisable by a triggering event. The triggering event could be the accumulation of a specified percentage of target shares (such as 20%) or the announcement of a tender offer. The special rights take many forms, but they all make it more costly to acquire control of the target firm. Poison pills can be adopted by the board of directors without shareholder approval. Although not required, directors often will submit poison pill adoptions to shareholders for ratification.

TYPES OF PLANS

Considerable jargon is involved. The basic distinction is between flip-over and flip-in plans. As an oversimplification, flip-over plans provide for a bargain purchase of the *bidder's* shares at some trigger point. The flip-in plans provide for a bargain purchase of the *target's* shares at some trigger point. Flip-in plans became more widely used after the weakness of the flip-over plans was demonstrated in the Crown Zellerbach case in 1984 to 1985. Crown Zellerbach was a paper and forest products company. Because its market price did not fully reflect the value of its forest lands, it was vulnerable to a takeover. Crown Zellerbach adopted a flip-over poison pill plan that enabled its shareholders to buy $200 worth of stock in the merged firm for $100. The pill was in the form of rights that would be triggered when either (1) an acquirer bought 20% of its stock or (2) a bidder made a tender offer for 30% of its stock. The rights or calls became exercisable when the bidder obtained 100% of the company stock.

Sir James Goldsmith (a famous raider) purchased just over 50% of Crown Zellerbach stock in order to achieve control. The rights were issued when Goldsmith's purchasing program brought his holdings to more than 20% of the stock. However the rights never became exercisable because he did not plan to complete the purchase of the company until after the flip-over rights had expired. Crown Zellerbach continued to resist but ultimately agreed to the takeover by Goldsmith.

The ownership flip-in provision allows the rights holder to purchase shares of the target at a discount if an acquirer exceeds a shareholding limit. The rights of the bidder who has triggered the pill become void. Some plans waive the flip-in provision if the acquisition is a cash tender offer for all outstanding shares (to defend against two-tier offers).

CASE STUDIES

The nature of ownership flip-in shareholder rights plans can be illustrated by a case study of the Bank of New York (BONY) pursuit of the Irving Bank Corporation (IB). On September 25, 1987, BONY launched an unsolicited cash bid of $80 per share for 47.4% of IB's shares. The remaining shares would receive 1.9 shares of BONY per IB share. On October 9, 1987, IB rejected the BONY offer as inadequate and adopted a flip-in poison pill. The poison pill rights to the IB shareholders when triggered would permit them to purchase $400 of IB stock for $200.

The IB shares held by BONY would be excluded from the rights distribution. The Bank of New York challenged the pill's legality. On October 4, 1988, the appellate division of the New York State Supreme Court upheld a lower court ruling. This ruling held that the flip-in provision violated New York law that shares of the same class should be treated equally. The court held that BONY should be allowed to buy shares at half price as well. On October 5, 1988, IB accepted BONY's offer. Irving Bank shareholders would receive $15 cash, 1.675 BONY shares, and a warrant to purchase BONY stock. The offer was valued at $77.15 per share. States subsequently modified their anti-takeover statutes to exclude the discriminatory effect of flip-in poison pills.

On May 17, 1985, the Delaware court upheld a discriminatory self-tender offer that was essentially a triggered back-end pill employed by UNOCAL against a bid by Mesa Petroleum. The court noted that Mesa had proposed a grossly inadequate coercive two-tier offer. The standard employed by the court was the "business judgment rule." The court stated that unless it could be shown that the directors' decisions were based primarily on perpetuating themselves in office or some other breach of judiciary duty, the court would not substitute its judgment for that of the board. The court's decision drew criticism, and in 1986 the Securities and Exchange Commission changed its rules to prevent discriminatory tender offers of the kind that UNOCAL had employed.

Later in the year, on November 19, 1985, the Delaware Supreme Court in *Moran v. Household International,* again upheld the adoption of the poison pill. It noted that any such defense by the directors must be justified on the basis of protection to the corporation and its stockholders. In 1986, the courts blocked a poison pill adopted by the CTS Corporation. The court held that the board had inadequately considered the bidders' offer and acted without adequate outside consultation. CTS formed a special committee of outside directors and solicited advice from investment bankers and legal counsel. It then adopted another poison pill that was upheld by the courts.

This brief review of court decisions demonstrates that the use of poison pills requires justification. Directors must establish that they were adopted not for their own entrenchment but in the best interests of the shareholders of the corporation. Thus, some ambiguity remains regarding whether the adoption of a poison pill will be effective and also whether it will be upheld by the courts.

DEAD-HAND PROVISIONS

A common feature of a poison pill is the board's ability to redeem it. This gives the board flexibility in negotiating with bidders. A hostile bidder can put considerable pressure on the board by making a premium cash bid that is conditional on the redemption of the pill. The board might find it difficult to refuse redemption. A dead-hand provision strengthens the board's position by granting the ability to redeem or amend the pill only by continuing directors—directors on the board prior to a bidder's takeover attempt. The dead-hand provision prevents a bidder from achieving control of the target's board, which then removes the pill.

In the 1988 *Bank of New York v. Irving Bank* case, a New York court invalidated a dead-hand pill. However other state courts have upheld the dead-hand provision. For example, in *Invacare v. Healthdyne Technologies,* a Georgia court in 1997 approved a dead-hand pill. A *Wall Street Journal* article (Plitch, 2000) quoted an estimate that of some 3,000 poison pills nationwide, 200 contained dead-hand features.

Some shareholder groups are critical of poison pills because they can be used to block a takeover carrying a substantial premium. Pension fund TIAA-CREF has described dead-hand poison pills as "a nefarious corporate-governance practice." TIAA-CREF sent letters and made phone calls to 35 companies with dead-hand pills, urging them to remove the dead-hand provisions from their pills. Many companies complied; the others are under continuing pressure to do so.

Sometimes stockholder pressure is sufficient to cause a company to eliminate the entire poison pill takeover defense plan. Such was the case with Phillip Morris (Hwang, 1995). In 1989, Philip Morris distributed rights to shareholders to buy additional Phillip Morris stock at reduced prices if a third party purchased 10% or more of the company's common stock. Pressure against the poison pill came from the Counsel for Institutional Investors, which represents more than 100 pension funds. Also, the International Brotherhood of Teamsters, whose pension funds held 3.38 million Phillip Morris shares, described the poison pill as "inappropriate, antiquated, and unnecessary." In removing the pill, the president of Phillip Morris stated that this was "a prudent course of action given the concern of some of our shareholders." Phillip Morris paid its shareholders 1 cent per share to redeem the poison pill rights, adding the penny to its quarterly dividends of 82.5 cents per share. The redemption cost totaled $8.5 million.

EFFECTS OF POISON PILLS ON SHAREHOLDER RETURNS

The early event studies of the wealth effect of poison pills found about a 2% negative impact (Malatesta and Walkling, 1988; Ryngaert, 1988). Comment and Schwert (1995) observed that these studies covered only the earlier one fourth of adopted pills. The Comment and Schwert paper updated the earlier studies by using the entire population of 1,577 poison pills adopted from 1983 through December 1991. They observed that the wealth effect of a poison pill adoption reflected a number of elements. The possibility that managers might wait to adopt pills until they know that an offer is likely to be made can cause the pill to be viewed as a signal that the probability of a takeover attempt has increased. This would cause the event return to be positive. Also, the poison pill might enable managers to obtain a better price in negotiations with bidders. This also would have a positive influence. However, if poison pills deterred takeovers, there would be a negative influence representing the expected present value of future takeover premium lost.

Datta and Iskandar-Datta (1996) examined the valuation effects of poison pill adoption announcements on bondholder and stockholder wealth. The sample analyzed contained 91 poison pill announcements between January 1985 and December 1989. Excess bond returns were calculated by matching the corporate bonds with treasury bonds according to maturity and coupon rate. The 2-day (0, +1) bond CAR was –0.67%, significant at the 1% level. In contrast, the (0, +1) stock CAR was an insignificant –0.25%. The stock excess returns were not sensitive to the time period. However, for firms that were the subject of takeover speculations in the year preceding the poison pill adoption, the 3-day period (–1, 0, +1) stock CAR was a significant –2.253%. The stock CAR for firms that were not targets was an insignificant 0.094%.

Additional long-run analyses were performed of changes in leverage and firm performance during 3 years centered around the poison pill announcement. The results indicated that the sample firms were not underleveraged compared to the industry median before the poison pill adoption. There was a significant increase in the median debt ratios during the year prior to the announcement, and the median debt ratio remained higher than the industry in the year following the poison pill adoption. Performance measures based on return on assets and profit margins revealed that the sample firms performed consistently worse than the industry during and around the year of the poison pill adoption.

Johnson and Meade (1996) examined the market reactions to the announcement of poison pills used as the first antitakeover measure compared with poison pills enacted after existing antitakeover amendments. Their sample consisted of 191 firms with poison pill announcements from November 1983 through December 1987. Of these 191 firms, 160 had adopted some prior form of antitakeover amendments. Thirty-one firms were implementing poison pills as their first antitakeover device.

Using a 2-day $(-1, 0)$ event window, the mean CAR for the full sample was 0.21%, not significant. For the subsample with no prior existing antitakeover amendments, the CAR was -0.94%, not significant. For the subsample with one or more preexisting antitakeover amendments, the CAR was 0.43%, not significant. The difference between the mean CARs of the two groups was significant at the 10% level.

The Comment and Schwert (1995) analysis considered several influences using the familiar cumulative abnormal return (CAR) measure and a regression analysis. One variable takes into account whether rumors of a bid or an actual takeover bid made it likely that a control premium was built into the issuer's stock price at the time of the announcement of a poison pill. The wealth effect was about -2%. Another variable accounts for whether merger and acquisition news was announced at the same time as the pill. This test found a positive wealth effect of about 3% to 4%. Dummy variables for the year of adoption distinguished the early pills from the later ones. In the year-by-year results for 1983 to 1991, only 1984 had a negative wealth effect of between 2.3% and 2.9%. For 1985 through 1991, the wealth effect usually was positive by about 1% or less, but it was significant only for the year 1988.

Comment and Schwert (1995) performed various sensitivity analyses, but the main thrusts of their findings remained unchanged. They observed that in some individual cases, potential takeovers were likely to have been deterred by poison pills. However, their systematic evidence indicates small deterrence effect. They observed that only the earliest pills (before 1985) were associated with large declines in shareholder wealth. Their new evidence indicated that takeover premiums were higher when target firms were protected by state antitakeover laws or by poison pills. Thus, the gains to targets were increased, raising the cost to bidders. This suggested some deterrence, but they also found that target shareholders gained even after taking into account deals that were not completed because of poison pills.

A major emphasis of the Comment and Schwert study was to evaluate whether the decline in the level of takeover activity that took place in 1991 and 1992 was primarily due to the effectiveness of antitakeover legislation and defensive measures by targets. Their empirical analysis led them to the conclusion that it was more general economic factors that caused the decline in takeover activity, not the widespread use of antitakeover measures adopted by governments and firms. Their conclusion is supported by the evidence we presented in Chapter 1 showing the return of significant merger activity in the 1990s. Thus, the carefully reasoned analysis of Comment and Schwert successfully predicted the resurgence in M&A activity as the economic environment changed after 1993.

SHAREHOLDER ACTIVISM

Shareholder resolutions to rescind poison pills were studied by Bizjak and Marquette (1998). They covered 190 shareholder-initiated proposals over the period 1987 to 1993. They started with a sample of firms that received shareholder proposals for poison pill rescissions. They made comparisons with a control sample of firms that had adopted poison pills but did not receive shareholder proposals to rescind them. Using a 3-day $(-1, +1)$ event window, they found a CAR for the proposals sample of -0.43% relative to a positive 1.35% for the matched sample.

The difference is statistically significant. They found that the average flip-in percentage for the rights plan was 14.20% for the proposal sample versus 17.87% for the matched sample. These relationships hold up for various forms of multivariate analysis.

Using different announcement dates and event return windows, they found a negative market reaction to the initial shareholder proposal but a positive market reaction to pill restructurings defined as rescissions or changes in the percentage trigger or similar characteristics. The positive management response to shareholder concerns yields positive information about management quality and indicates that shareholder proposals can influence managers' actions. The authors conclude that shareholders become active when they become concerned about managerial actions to create impediments to the market for corporate control. This activism can influence management to be responsive to shareholder recommendations.

POISON PUTS

Poison puts, or event risk covenants, give bondholders the right to put (sell) target bonds in the event of a change in control at an exercise price usually set at 100% to 101% of the bond's face amount. This poison put feature seeks to protect against risk of takeover-related deterioration of target bonds, at the same time placing a potentially large cash demand on the new owner, thus raising the cost of an acquisition. Merger and acquisition activity in general has had negative impacts on bondholder wealth. This was particularly true when leverage increases were substantial. As a consequence, poison put provisions began to be included in bond covenants beginning in 1986.

Cook and Easterwood (1994) analyzed the economic role of poison put bonds. They observed that poison puts could be included in corporate debt for three possible reasons. First, the entrenchment hypothesis was that the puts made firms less attractive as takeover targets. Second, the bondholder protection hypothesis was that the poison puts protect bondholders from wealth transfers associated with debt-financed takeovers and leveraged recapitalizations. If the poison puts had this purpose, their use would not reduce the probability of all takeovers, only those involving wealth transfers from bondholders to shareholders. If puts and related covenants did not increase the protection to existing debt, the bondholder protection hypothesis predicted no effect on the price of the firm's outstanding debt.

The impact on stock returns would be the net of two opposite influences. Takeovers motivated primarily by wealth transfers were deterred by puts which represented a negative influence on shareholder returns. Debt with event risk covenants could be issued at an interest cost lower than unprotected debt. If interest cost savings outweighed the forgone wealth transfers, there would be a positive stock price reaction to the sale of protected debt.

The bondholder protection hypothesis had been tested in two ways. One looked at the difference in yield spreads at the offering date for samples of protected and unprotected bonds. Two empirical studies suggested that the inclusion of event risk protection reduced the required yields on protected bonds by 25 to 50 basis points; a third study found no effect. A second type of test analyzed wealth transfers from bondholders in leveraged buyouts. One study (Marais, Schipper, and Smith, 1989) found no evidence of bondholder losses. Another, by Warga and Welch (1993), found small losses. Other studies showed that whether bondholders lose depends on the covenant protection. Protected bonds did not experience losses, but unprotected debt experienced significant losses. These findings were evidence that alternative contracting technologies could substitute for the use of poison puts.

TABLE 19.2 Effects of Poison Puts on Shareholder and Debt Holder Returns

	Managerial Entrenchment Hypothesis	*Bondholder Protection Hypothesis*	*Mutual Interest Hypothesis*
Effect on shareholder returns	–	0	–
Effect on outstanding debt	0	0	+

The third hypothesis was the mutual interest hypothesis. This postulated that both managers and bondholders sought to prevent hostile debt-financed takeovers. The managers sought to protect their control positions, and the bondholders sought to avoid losses from deterioration in credit ratings. Under this hypothesis, stock price reactions would be negative, whereas the effects on the price of existing debt would be positive. The wealth effects for debt and equity would be negatively correlated because more protective puts would make the price response more positive for existing debt and more negative for stock prices. These three alternatives are summarized in Table 19.2.

In their empirical analysis, Cook and Easterwood found that that the issuance of bonds with poison puts caused negative returns to shareholders and positive returns to outstanding bondholders. A control sample of straight bond issues without poison puts had no effect on stock prices. Note that the finding of no stock price effect of straight bond issues is different from the findings of earlier studies and could be related to the economic environment that prevailed in 1988 and 1989, the years covered by their sample. A cross-sectional regression for the put sample showed a strong negative relation between the returns for stocks and the returns for outstanding bonds. This relation was not found for the nonput sample. The study concluded that the empirical results were consistent with the mutual interest hypothesis, which holds that the use of poison put bonds protects managers from hostile takeovers and bondholders from event risk while lowering returns to shareholders.

GOLDEN PARACHUTES

Golden parachutes (GPs) are separation provisions of an employment contract that compensate managers for the loss of their jobs under a change-of-control clause. The provision usually calls for a lump-sum payment or payment over a specified period at full or partial rates of normal compensation. This type of severance contract was used increasingly even by the largest Fortune 500 firms as M&A activity intensified in the 1980s and these firms became susceptible to hostile takeover.

A brief case study will convey the role of golden parachutes. On May 23, 1983, Diamond Shamrock Corporation launched a hostile tender offer for Natomas Company. The offer at $23 per share, represented a 25% premium over-the closing price of Natomas on May 20, 1983. Natomas began arranging bank financing to defend itself. It also adopted golden parachutes that would give its top four executives a $10.2 million severance payment if they decided to quit within 6 months after the merger. These four top executives had received $1.3 million in compensation and benefits in 1982. Diamond Shamrock had been in the process of transforming itself from a chemical company into an energy company under W. H. Bricker, its chairman. It was seeking additional oil reserves to feed its refineries. The oil reserves of Natomas in the

Pacific Basin were especially attractive to Diamond. On May 29, 1983, a merger agreement was reached between Diamond and Natomas. The new terms were 1.05 shares of Diamond per share of Natomas. Diamond would retain the Natomas management, with Dorman Commons remaining as chairman of Natomas and becoming vice chairman of Diamond. Kenneth Reed would remain president of Natomas. The combination was completed in August 1983. In October 1983, Commons and Reed resigned, departing the company with the severance payments provided by the golden parachutes.

Extreme cases of golden parachutes created a stir among the public and were often viewed as "rewards for failure."[1] An example is the payment of $23.5 million to six officers of Beatrice Companies in connection with its leveraged buyout in 1985. One of the officers received a $2.7 million package even though he had been with the company for only 13 months. Another received a $7 million package after being recalled from retirement only 7 months before. Also in 1985, the chairman of Revlon received a $35 million package consisting of severance pay and stock options. Even in these extreme cases, the golden parachutes were small compared to the total acquisition prices of $6.2 billion in the Beatrice LBO and $1.74 billion in the Revlon acquisition. Indeed, the cost of golden parachutes is estimated to be less than 1% of the total cost of a takeover in most cases.[2] For this reason, golden parachutes are not considered to be an effective takeover defense.

Excessive use of golden parachutes appears to be infrequent, and tax law imposes specific limits. The Deficit Reduction Act of 1984 denies corporate tax deductions for parachute payments in excess of three times the base amount on a present value basis, where the base amount is the executive's average annual compensation over the 5 years prior to takeover. An executive has to pay an additional 20% income tax on "excess parachute payments." To be legally binding, the golden parachutes have to be entered into at least 1 year prior to the date of control change for the entire corporation or a significant portion of the corporation. In many employment contracts, the severance payment is triggered either when the manager is terminated by the acquiring firm or when the manager resigns voluntarily after a change of control. Coffee (1988, p. 131) reported several cases in which the court invalidated or granted preliminary injunctions against the exercise of golden parachutes, especially when the payment could be triggered at the recipient's own election.

RATIONALE

The use of golden parachutes has been defended by some (Coffee, 1988; Jensen, 1988; Knoeber, 1986). One argument is based on the concept of *implicit contracts* for managerial compensation. In general, managers' real contribution to the firm cannot be evaluated exactly in the current period but can be estimated better as time passes and more information becomes available on the firm's long-term profitability and value. In this situation, an optimal contract between managers and shareholders will include deferred compensation (Knoeber, 1986). Seniority-based compensation and internal promotion partly reflect this deferred compensation process. Because detailing all the future possibilities and contingent payments in a written contract is costly and likely futile, a long-term deferred contract will be largely implicit. Another argument presumes existence of firm-specific investments by managers. When the likelihood of an unexpected transfer of control and the loss of their job is high, managers will not be willing to

---

[1]See, for example, *New York Times*, "Golden Chutes Under Attack," November 4, 1985, p. D1.
[2]*Fortune*, "Those Executive Bailout Deals," December 13, 1982, p. 86.

invest in firm-specific skills and knowledge. A related argument is that the increased risk of losing one's job through a takeover might result in managers focusing unduly on the short term or even taking unduly high risks (Eisenberg, 1988).

Another rationale for golden parachutes is that they encourage managers to accept changes of control that would bring shareholder gains and thus reduce the conflict of interest between managers and shareholders and the transactions costs resulting from managerial resistance. Berkovitch and Khanna (1991) further analyzed the role of golden parachutes in takeover markets in which the bidder had a choice between a merger and a tender offer. In their model, a tender offer was more desirable for target shareholders as more information was released in tender offers, and this frequently led to an auction in which potential acquirers competed for the target. Excessive payment will tend to motivate managers to sell the firm at too low a gain. By tying the payment to synergy gains in the case of mergers, the firm can avoid the misuse of golden parachutes. Stock options that are exercisable in the event of a change of control are an appropriate solution, and in general increased stock ownership by management will tend to reduce the conflict of interest (Jensen, 1988).

SILVER AND TIN PARACHUTES

The terms *silver parachutes* and *tin parachutes* also have been employed. Silver parachutes provide less generous severance payments to executives. Tin parachutes extend relatively modest severance payments to a wider coverage of managers, including middle management, and in some cases cover all salaried employees. Tin parachutes were employed by General American Oil of Texas when it faced a takeover threat from T. Boone Pickens in 1982. It adopted tin parachutes that would give all employees at least 3 months' pay whether they were terminated or chose to leave after any adverse changes in their pay or duties. Workers would be entitled to at least 4 weeks' pay for each year of service.

There is disagreement on the number of employees to be covered. Focusing on the conflict-of-interest problem in control-related situations, Jensen (1988) argued that the contract should cover only those members of the top-level management team who would be involved in negotiating and implementing any transfer of control. On the other hand, Coffee (1988) emphasized the implicit contract for deferred payments and the incentive for managers to make investments in firm-specific human capital. This led Coffee to propose that the control-related severance contracts should be extended to members of middle management as well as top management.

GOLDEN PARACHUTES AND RETURNS TO SHAREHOLDERS

Mogavero and Toyne (1995) formulated three central hypotheses to be tested by the empirical evidence: (1) The **alignment hypothesis** is that prearranged severance agreements reduce conflict of interest between managers and shareholders. Golden parachutes will make executives more willing to support takeover offers beneficial to the firm's shareholders. (2) The **wealth transfer hypothesis** predicts that GPs reduce stock values by shifting gains from shareholders to managers. By increasing costs to bidders, GPs reduce the probability of takeover bids. By providing some insulation from the market for corporate control, GPs reduce the incentives for executives to manage firms efficiently. In addition, GPs also can indicate a level of influence over boards exercised by management that might increase the potential for other forms of executive benefit consumption. (3) Adoption of GPs may *signal* the likelihood of a future takeover, which would be associated with positive gains to shareholders. Alternatively, GPs might signal an increase in management influence over boards, which would have negative implications.

The empirical study by Lambert and Larcker (1985) covered the period 1975 to 1982. They found that the adoption of GPs resulted in abnormal positive returns to shareholders of about 3%. This finding was consistent with the alignment hypothesis, suggesting that the cost of reducing conflicts of interest between management and shareholders was low relative to potential gains from takeover premiums. Alternatively, the signaling hypothesis might be supported in that from 1975 to 1982, relatively few firms had adopted GPs, so that GPs could be interpreted as signals of a likely takeover bid. The study by Born, Trahan, and Faria (1993) looked at two samples. One sample for the period 1979 to 1989 contained firms that announced GPs while in the process of being acquired. Hence, there should be no takeover signal effect. If the alignment of interests hypothesis is accurate, the returns should be positive; if the wealth transfer hypothesis is accurate, the returns should be negative. However, no significant abnormal stock returns were found. The second sample from 1979 through 1984 contained firms not in the process of a takeover when the GPs were adopted. They found positive stock returns. The authors argued that the combined evidence is consistent with a takeover signaling hypothesis but not with an alignment hypothesis.

Hall and Anderson (1997) studied the impact of the adoption of golden parachute compensation plans on shareholder wealth. They used a sample of 52 firms that announced the adoption of golden parachutes between 1982 and 1990. The adoptions were for new contracts and not amendments to preexisting contracts. These firms did not experience preexisting takeover bids for the 3 years prior to the golden parachute adoption. The mean CAR for the whole event window (−20, +20) was a statistically insignificant −1.21%. The mean abnormal return on the announcement day was an insignificant 0.46%. CARs for other event windows were also not significant except for the window (−5, −2) which was −1.19%, significant at the 10% level. When three firms were excluded because of possible outliers, the event window (−5, 0) was a significant −1.29% at the 10% level.

The study by Mogavero and Toyne (1995) used a sample of 41 large firms with adoption dates from 1982 through 1990. For their full sample, the CAR was −0.5% but not statistically significant. They divided their sample into two subsamples. The first contained 18 observations from 1982 to 1985 for which the CAR was +2.3% but not statistically significant. The second subsample was of 23 observations and covered the years 1986 through 1990. Its CAR was −2.7% and statistically significant at the 1% level. This finding was consistent with the wealth transfer hypothesis. The authors noted that the stock returns associated with GPs changed from positive for the 1975 to 1982 period of the Lambert and Larcker study to negative for the 1986 to 1990 period of their own study. This change was associated with the initiation of legislative restraints on GPs that might have encouraged boards to adopt them to avoid further restrictions. Thus, shareholders in the later years may have perceived GP adoptions as unfavorable signals of management's ability to control directors in management's interest at the expense of shareholder interest.

Summary

Takeover defenses and antitakeover measures have become part of management's long-range strategic planning for the firm. One view justifies these actions on the basis of the desirability of creating an auction for the target, preventing coercive tender offers, and increasing management's ability to obtain better transaction terms in the bargaining process. Opposing views emphasize the increased cost of takeovers and the resulting inefficiency in the market for corporate control.

Just saying no to a takeover is not that simple. Target directors must present shareholders with a sound business reason to expect that the shareholders will gain more by not accepting the takeover offer. Even if the target company agrees to an acquisition, directors must demonstrate that the price is fair to shareholders and is the best offer that could be obtained.

A firm can be vulnerable to takeovers because of its financial characteristics. The firm's stock price might be low in relation to the replacement cost of assets or its potential earning power. It might possess a large amount of excess cash or unused debt capacity. Such characteristics make it an attractive investment opportunity and facilitate the financing of the takeover. The firm can take defensive adjustments to make itself less attractive. For example, it could sell assets, increase debt, and use its excess cash to increase cash dividends or share repurchases.

A target might counteroffer for the bidder in a Pac Man defense. This is a costly defense and is rarely used. Another defense strategy is for the target to seek a white knight as an appropriate company for the combination. Alternatively, in a white squire transaction, the target could sell a block of its stock to a third party it considers friendly.

Corporate restructuring and reorganizations that increase a firm's value are also extensions to a defensive program. Acquisitions of assets are used to extend a firm's capabilities, to block a takeover by diluting the ownership position of the pursuer, or to create antitrust issues. Sell-offs and divestitures move resources to their higher valued uses but also can involve selling off the "crown jewels." Spin-offs, split-ups, and equity carve-outs can be used to clarify organizational structures and to increase managerial incentives, motivations, and performance.

The target firm also can reorganize its financial claims to make itself less attractive. Exchange offers such as debt-for-equity offers can increase leverage to unattractive levels. Dual-class recapitalizations can increase the voting power of target insiders to levels that make tender offers less likely to succeed. "Scorched earth" tactics such as leveraged recapitalizations may incur a huge amount of debt and increase the ownership position of insiders. Joint ventures could represent liaisons that potential bidders might prefer to avoid. Employee stock ownership plans can prevent a successful tender offer by making it difficult to meet supermajority requirements. Management buyouts and LBOs are other leverage-increasing defenses favorable to the managers' stock ownership position. Share repurchase can be used to pay premium prices to shareholders to compete with takeover bids. Low-reservation-price shareholders will tender, leaving high-reservation-price shareholders who, with the increased ownership position of insiders, will require higher tender-offer prices.

In greenmail transactions, the target firm repurchases a large block of its shares at a premium price from large blockholders to end a hostile takeover threat. A standstill agreement might be included to prevent the greenmailer from making other takeover efforts for a specified period of time. The view that greenmail damages shareholders has prompted tax law penalties and antigreenmail charter amendments to discourage or prohibit its use. Antigreenmail amendments do not seem to decrease shareholder wealth but appear to remove a barrier to takeovers with positive gains to shareholders.

Antitakeover amendments or "shark repellents" impose new conditions on the transfer of managerial control. Supermajority amendments require shareholders' approval of takeover negotiations by a two-thirds vote or higher. Fair-price amendments hinder two-tier tenders by requiring the bidder to pay the "fair" price to all purchased shares. A staggered, or classified, board of directors can delay effective transfer of control. New securities with special voting rights may be issued to friendly parties in a takeover contest. Previously enacted antitakeover measures can be reinforced with lock-in amendments, making them difficult to void.

The empirical literature on antitakeover amendments is extensive but difficult to interpret because multiple influences are operating. In general, positive returns will result if the announcement of the antitakeover amendment is interpreted as a signal of an increased likelihood of a takeover or is associated with management's intention to obtain a better price in negotiations or a better solution. Negative effects could result if the amendment is interpreted as a management entrenchment tactic. Studies find small declines of about 1% but no statistical significance.

Poison pills are securities carrying special rights exercisable by a triggering event such as the announcement of a tender offer or a specified ownership position in the firm's stock. Poison pills make it more costly to acquire control of the firm and can be adopted without shareholders' approval. However, the adoption of poison pills requires justification that they are in the best interests of the shareholders if they are to be upheld by the courts. Studies by Comment and Schwert found small deterrence effects of poison pills. Takeover premiums are higher when target firms are protected by state antitakeover laws or by poison pills. Even the decline in the level of takeover activity in 1991 and 1992 is attributable to general economic factors and not to antitakeover measures.

Poison puts or event risk covenants give bondholders the right to sell target bonds in the event of takeover at a price set at the bond's face value or higher. This feature seeks to protect bondholders' wealth and at the same time place potentially large requirements on the new owner. The negative returns found by Cook and Easterwood are consistent with the mutual interest hypothesis in which bondholders and managers gain at the expense of shareholders.

Golden parachutes (GPs) are severance contracts that compensate managers for losing their jobs after a takeover. Extreme cases of golden parachutes have often been viewed as a reward for failure, but GPs are estimated to be less than 1% of the total cost of a takeover. For this reason, they are not considered to be a strong takeover defense. The rationale for their use is the reduction in the agency problem between managers and shareholders. This reduced conflict or alignment hypothesis is supported by the positive returns found by Lambert and Larcker. However, the golden parachute adoption also could be interpreted as a signal of future takeovers. The study by Mogavero and Toyne found negative returns for the period 1986 to 1990, indicating some influence over boards exercised by managements, increasing the potentials for wealth transfers from shareholders to managers.

Questions

19.1 What are three types of antitakeover amendments, and how do they work to defend a target from an unwelcome takeover?

19.2 What is the effect of the passage of antitakeover amendments on stock price?

19.3 What is the role of litigation against a bidder in takeover contests?

19.4 Under what circumstances are share repurchase and exchange offers useful as antitakeover measures?

19.5 How can legislation and regulation serve as merger defenses?

19.6 Explain the difference between flip-in and flip-over poison pills.

Case 19.1   CARTER HAWLEY HALE VERSUS MARSHALL FIELD & COMPANY

In 1977, the president of Marshall Field & Company died unexpectedly and was replaced by Angelo R. Arena, the former head of Carter Hawley Hale's (CHH) Neiman Marcus division. Carter Hawley Hale, which had long been interested in Field, then approached Marshall Field with the idea of a merger and continued to pursue the idea despite Field's lack of interest. On December 10, 1977, Philip Hawley, the CEO of CHH, gave Marshall Field an ultimatum: Either Field's directors would agree to merger negotiations by December 12 or he would make a public exchange proposal. Arena was unwilling to enter into negotiations, and Field directors rejected the $36 per share CHH offer, saying that the merger would not be in the best interests of Field stockholders, employees, and customers and that the price was inadequate. Field filed an antitrust suit.

Carter Hawley Hale was the nation's eighth-largest department store group, and Field was the largest of the department store independents. Carter Hawley Hale, which had grown through acquisitions, sought to expand further by taking over Field. Field owned valuable real estate, was established in the Chicago market, possessed large cash reserves, and had a conservative debt-to-equity ratio of 28% even with lease capitalization. Carter Hawley Hale had been looking to break into the Chicago market and believed it could bring operating improvements to Field. The takeover battle drew attention to CHH's highly leveraged position. Carter Hawley Hale had a debt-to-equity ratio of 42%, or 113% with lease capitalization, and was planning to finance the merger on the strength of Field's balance sheet.

Field previously had been targeted for takeover by Associated Dry Goods in 1969, Federated Department Stores in 1975, and Dayton-Hudson in 1976. In each battle, Field used the antitrust defense and/or made a major acquisition. Under the advice of lawyer Joseph Flom, Field believed expansion would help the firm remain independent. In 1976, CHH had sales of $1.4 billion compared with Field's sales of $610 million. At the time of the offer, Field shares,

which had a book value of $27, were trading at $23. In the prior 5 years, Field earnings per share had fallen by 20% as it struggled with declining profit margins and shrinking market share.

In early February 1978, CHH announced a tender offer of $42 in cash and CHH stock for each share of Field stock tendered. Field's board continued to oppose the merger and agreed to expand into the Galleria in Houston and to acquire five Liberty House stores in the Northwest. The two transactions would total $34 million. Carter Hawley Hale already had a store in the Galleria, Neiman Marcus. Field had considered acquiring the Liberty House stores in the context of another takeover battle, but at the time Field's vice president of corporate development judged the earnings potential to be minimal. It was rumored that CHH also had planned to expand to the Northwest. Field had the ambitious vision of becoming a national retailer. On February 22, CHH withdrew its proposed tender offer, citing doubts of the impact of Field's expansion plan. Through the expansion program, Field increased its debt, making it less attractive to CHH. Upon announcement of the withdrawal of CHH's offer, Field shares plummeted to $19.

Field's directors were sued by some of its shareholders for resisting the CHH offer regardless of shareholders' interests and breaching their fiduciary duty as directors. The court found that the plaintiffs failed to show that there was a breach of fiduciary duty, and the directors were protected by the business judgment rule.

Under Arena, the number of Field stores tripled and the firm took on $120 million in debt. Problems continued to plague Field, and by 1981 its share price had fallen to less than $20 per share. In February 1982, Field came under attack by Carl Icahn. Icahn continued to purchase Field stock despite lawsuits filed against him. Field turned to a white knight, Batus Incorporated, the American subsidiary of B.A.T. Industries of London. Batus owned the nation's third-largest tobacco company, as well as Gimbel's and

Saks Fifth Avenue. Other bidders included CHH and May Department Stores. Although Batus's initial offer was $25.50 per share, it eventually paid $30 per share for the front and back ends of the offer. Icahn walked away with a profit of $30 million.▨

QUESTIONS

C19.1.1 What defensive actions did Marshall Field take in response to Carter Hawley Hale's interest?

C19.1.2 Why did Carter Hawley Hale want to acquire Marshall Field?

C19.1.3 Over the years, which defense did Marshall Field employ several times?

C19.1.4 Which characteristics attracted Marshall Field's suitors to bid for the company?

C19.1.5 Who was Marshall Field's white knight?

≈≈≈≈

Case 19.2   MATTEL–HASBRO[3]

After some preliminary discussions on January 24, 1996, Mattel made an unsolicited proposal to buy the second-largest toy company, Hasbro Incorporated. Their proposal indicated a fundamental reorganization in the toy industry. The *Financial Times* (January 27, 1996) stated, "Barbie fluttered her eyelashes at GI Joe and all the hearts in Toy Town skipped a beat!" Mattel was strong in dolls with its market leaders Barbie and Ken and was developing joint products with Disney and others. Hasbro was strong in toys for boys such as GI Joe and Tonka trucks, as well as in board games. Hasbro's reaction was to cry, "Monopoly" (one of its board games). Both firms had gaps in creating electronic toys in which foreign competitors such as Nintendo and Sony were leaders.

The preannouncement price of Mattel was $32 per share and that of Hasbro was $30.625. The Mattel offer of 1.67 shares for 1 share of Hasbro placed a value of $53.44 per share on Hasbro, representing a premium of 74%. Because Hasbro objected immediately, the Hasbro price never went above $40. The price of Mattel moved up by about $1. With 225 million shares, the wealth of Mattel shareholders increased about $225 million. For Hasbro, with 97 million shares outstanding, shareholder wealth increased by almost $1 billion.

Negotiations continued, but Hasbro continued to raise antitrust objections. Finally, on February 3, 1996,

it was announced that Mattel would withdraw its offer for Hasbro. John Amerman, the Mattel chairman, stated that in a friendly deal the antitrust barriers could have been resolved in about 5 months (*Wall Street Journal*, February 8, 1996, p. B8).

However, with the obstacles thrown up by Hasbro, the legal complications would have continued for as long as 2 years. Mr. Amerman stated that at the end of 3 years, the earnings per share for Mattel would have been unchanged from current projections. He concluded by stating, "Why raise our risks?"

The Hasbro stock dropped back to $34.625. The Mattel stock stayed at about $33, about $1 above its prebid price. Mattel said that the costs related to the failed bid would lower their earnings per share for 1996 by about $0.01.▨

QUESTIONS

C19.2.1 What would have been the business advantages of the combination?

C19.2.2 Would the combination have created market power in the production and distribution of toys?

C19.2.3 From the standpoint of U.S. public policy, evaluate the desirability of the combination.

---

[3]This case was written by J. F. Weston, Aaron Cheatham, and Girish Kulai.

Case 19.3   HERSHEY FOODS SAGA[4]

The Hershey story is of interest because it demonstrates that public opinion can be effective in thwarting an acquisition. For background, we present a time line of Hershey beginning with the birth of its founder in 1857.

1857: Milton Hershey, of Pennsylvania Dutch, Mennonite origin, was born.

1872: Apprenticed at age 15 to a candy maker.

1887: Milton Hershey started the Lancaster Caramel Company at age 30.

1893: Milton Hershey saw a new chocolate-making machine at the World's Colombian Exposition in Chicago.

1898: Milton Hershey married Catherine Sweeney.

ORIGINS AND GROWTH OF THE CHOCOLATE MAKER

1900: Milton Hershey sold the caramel operations for $1 million to start a chocolate factory.

1905: Chocolate factory completed in Derry Church, Pennsylvania (renamed Hershey the next year).

1907: Hershey Chocolate Kisses were introduced.

(Hershey pioneered mass-production techniques for chocolates and developed much of the machinery for making and packaging its own products.)

1909: Saddened by the fact that he and his wife could not have children, Milton Hershey created the Deed of Trust establishing the Hershey Industrial School for orphan boys, which is now known as The Milton Hershey School.

1918: Milton Hershey gifted the Hershey Chocolate Company stock to the school.

1927: Hershey Chocolate Company went public, changing its name to Hershey Chocolate Corporation.

(Hershey did not advertise, believing that high quality was the best advertising.)

1945: Milton Hershey passed away at age 88.

DIVERSIFICATION PROGRAM

1963: Hershey Chocolate Corporation acquired H.B. Reese Candy Company, Incorporated, maker of the Reese's peanut butter cup. Reese was a former employee of Milton Hershey.

1966: Hershey entered the pasta business by purchasing San Giorgio Macaroni. Hershey also purchased Delmonico Foods, Incorporated.

1968: Hershey Chocolate Corporation changed its name to Hershey Foods Corporation to reflect its diversified businesses.

1969: Hershey acquired a 50% interest in National de Dulces, S.A. de C.V., a joint venture company in Mexico.

1970: Hershey Foods assumed U.S. distribution of KitKat through an agreement with Rowntree MacKintosh of Great Britain.

1970: Hershey lost market share to Mars due to a sluggish candy market and a diet conscious public. Began advertising.

1973: Hershey acquired the Cory Coffee Food Services business.

1977: Hershey Foods acquired Y&S Candies, Inc., the maker of Twizzlers, Nibs, and Bites.

1978: Hershey Foods acquired Procino-Rossi (P&R) Corporation's pasta business.

1979: Hershey purchased the Friendly Ice Cream chain (sold in 1988).

1979: Hershey Foods acquired Skinner Macaroni Company.

---

[4]This case was coauthored with S. C. Weaver, Lehigh University.

1984: Hershey bought the American Beauty Macaroni Company.

1985: Hershey divested the Cory Coffee Food Services business.

1985, 1986 Hershey purchased two small family restaurant chains, Marvin Franklin Enterprises, Incorporated and Idlenot Farm Shops, Incorporated, and converted them to Friendly Ice Cream units.

1986: Hershey Foods purchased the Dietrich Corporation, including the 5th Avenue bar and Luden's Throat Lozenges.

1988: Hershey purchased Cadbury Schweppes's U.S. candy business (Peter Paul, Cadbury, Caramello).

1988: Hershey sold the Friendly Ice Cream Corporation.

1990: Hershey formed a joint venture with Fujiya to distribute Hershey products in Japan.

1990: Hershey Foods purchased Ronzoni's pasta, cheese, and sauce operations, making Hershey the number one pasta company in the United States.

1991: Hershey acquired the remaining 50% interest in National de Dulces, S.A. de C.V.

1991: Hershey acquired assets of Dairyman, Incorporated.

1991, 1993: Hershey began its European thrust. Purchased Gubor, OZF Jamin, and Sperlari. In 1992, Hershey failed in acquiring Freia, a Norwegian company, for $1.2 billion. Kraft General Foods was the eventual purchaser of Freia.

1993: Hershey acquired Ideal Macaroni and Weiss Noodle companies.

1993: Hershey Trust sold $100 million of its stock to Hershey to diversify its holdings.

1994: Kenneth Wolfe was named chairman and CEO.

BACK TO THE CORE STRATEGY

1995: Acquired Henry Heide and boosted its presence in the nonchocolate candy market (Jujyfruits).

1995: Hershey Trust sold $500 million of its stock to Hershey to diversify its holdings.

1996: Acquired the North American operations of Leaf from Finnish candy maker Huhtamaki Oyj. Hershey entered into a trademark and license agreement to manufacture and distribute Huhtamaki's confectionery brands in North, Central, and South America.

1996: Hershey sold its European operation, to the Finnish candy maker Huhtamaki Oyj.

1997: Hershey Trust sold $500 million of its stock to Hershey to diversify its holdings.

1999: Hershey sold its pasta business (San Giorgio Macaroni) to New World Pasta, LLC, for $450 million and a 6% interest in that company.

1999: Hershey Trust sold $100 million of its stock to Hershey to diversify its holdings.

1999: Companywide computer system delayed orders during the critical Halloween season (Hershey lost more than $100 million in sales).

2000: Hershey bought Nabisco Holdings's breath freshener mints and gum business for about $135 million.

2001: Richard Lenny (Nabisco veteran) replaced Wolfe as CEO.

2001: Hershey established a manufacturing presence in South America by acquiring the chocolate and confectionary business of Brazilian company Visagis.

The Hershey story illustrates how many large corporations were developed from the entrepreneurship of a single individual. From 1905 to the early 1960s, Hershey remained a chocolate manufacturer. The chocolate products were produced in varied sizes and shapes. Hershey chocolate Kisses were developed in 1907 but continue to represent a strong concept. It was not until 1993 that the companion Hugs product was created. In 1963, the diversification program began with a different type of candy featuring the Reese's peanut butter cup. In 1966, Hershey launched a series of pasta purchases. It also bought and divested restaurants and ice-cream units and attempted international diversification in chocolate products. In the early 1990s, it was recognized that pasta was a low-margin business. As part of a refocusing of the company, the pasta business was sold. Hershey also sold its international operations. When Hershey started its refocusing in the early 1990s, its stock price was in the low $40s. After its reorganization in the late-1990 its stock price was in the low $60s.

Rumors began to circulate in 2001 that Hershey Trust would sell more of its stock. On November 31, 2001, its price per share closed at $65.46 with a market cap of $8.9 billion. At a meeting on December 1, 2001, with representatives from the Pennsylvania attorney general's office, a deputy attorney general, Mark Pacella, was reported to have urged the trustees to diversify their holdings and implied that they would be violating their fiduciary duty of missing potential large gains from the sale of the company. Later, Pacella said that diversification was discussed but that he never told them to sell the company. In May 2002, the trust board asked CEO Richard H. Lenny to solicit bids for Hershey. CEO Lenny protested and proposed that Hershey buy back the trust shares over time at a small premium. The trust directed that CEO Lenny and the Hershey board lead the sale process. On July 25, 2002, Robert C. Vowler, chief executive officer of the Milton Hershey School Trust, confirmed that the trust was exploring steps to divest its controlling interest in Hershey Foods. The indicated asking price was $11 billion ($80.53 per share).

On July 31, 2002, Nestle, Kraft Foods, Cadbury Schweppes, and Wrigley expressed an interest. August 27, 2002, Cadbury Schweppes told Hershey they would not submit an offer. Nestle and Kraft Foods were the two most interested remaining bidders. An auction was considered for the sale. Bids were due on September 14, 2002. A joint offer from Nestle and Cadbury Schweppes was submitted for $10.5 billion ($75 per share). CEO Lenny had developed an offer from the Wrigley company for $12.5 billion ($89 per share)—part cash, part stock. Objections to the sale were raised by the attorney general of the state of Pennsylvania, Mike Fisher, who was campaigning for governor as a Republican. The community of Hershey, Pennsylvania, was concerned that the sale of the company might result in movement of some or all operations out of the area.

Hershey and Wrigley began negotiating over the weekend beginning on September 14. Tuesday morning, September 17, they "had all but signed a deal" (*Wall Street Journal,* September 19, 2002, pp. B1, B5). Wrigley promised to uphold the company's commitment to the community. The Wrigley board was meeting to approve the purchase when it received a phone call from the trust saying the deal was off. "Mr. Wrigley was stunned. Mr. Lenny was livid. CEO Lenny believed that once he had developed a deal with a large premium as in the Wrigley offer, the sale would have been completed. On September 18, 2002, Hershey Trust called off the sale of Hershey Foods (10 of 17 trust members opposed the sale). The market capitalization was $8.9 billion ($65.00 per share) on September 18, 2002.

Comparative data for the three companies are presented in Table C19.3.1 and Table C19.3.2.

QUESTIONS

C19.3.1 Comment on Hershey's diversification program initiated in the 1960s.

C19.3.2 Evaluate the Hershey acquisition from the standpoint of Nestle.

C19.3.3 Evaluate the Hershey acquisition from the standpoint of Wrigley.

TABLE C19.3.1 Hershey vs. Wrigley and Nestle (amounts in millions)

	Hershey	Wrigley		Nestle S.A.[a]	
	2001	*2001*	*Relative to Hershey*	*2001*	*Relative to Hershey*
Revenue/Net Sales	$4,557	$2,430	53.3%	$50,144	1100.3%
Total Assets	3,247	1,766	54.4%	55,472	1708.2%
Book Value of Equity	1,147	1,276	111.2%	19,924	1736.7%
Market Value of Equity	9,183	11,576	126.1%	21,486	234.0%
NOI Margin	9.05%	21.11%	233.3%	10.88%	120.2%

[a]Nestle values converted from Swiss Francs to U.S. Dollars using 1.6891 Swiss Franc per U.S. Dollar.

Source: Annual Reports.

TABLE C19.3.2 Growth Rates 1996–2001 (6-year CAGR)

	Hershey	*Wrigley*	*Nestle S.A.*
Revenues	2.24%	4.78%	0.41%
NOI	−4.02%	5.84%	2.37%
Net Income	−4.51%	7.90%	6.24%
Total Assets	0.33%	6.16%	5.04%

Source: Annual Reports.

References

Bae, S. C., and D. P. Simet, "A Comparative Analysis of Leveraged Recapitalization Versus Leveraged Buyout as a Takeover Defense," *Review of Financial Economics* 7, 1998, pp. 157–172.

Bagli, Charles V., "A New Breed of Wolf at the Corporate Door: It's the Era of the Civilized Hostile Takeover," *New York Times*, March 19, 1997, pp. C1, C4.

Berkovitch, E., and N. Khanna, "A Theory of Acquisition Markets: Mergers Versus Tender Offers, and Golden Parachutes," *Review of Financial Studies* 4, 1991, pp. 149–174.

Bhagat, S., and R. Jefferis, "Voting Power in the Proxy Process: The Case of Antitakeover Charter Amendments," *Journal of Financial Economics* 30, 1991, pp. 193–225.

Bizjak, J. M., and C. J. Marquette, "Are Shareholder Proposals All Bark and No Bite? Evidence from Shareholder Resolutions to Rescind Poison Pills," *Journal of Financial and Quantitative Analysis* 33, 1998, pp. 499–521.

Born, Jeffery A., Emery A. Trahan, and Hugo J. Faria, "Golden Parachutes: Incentive Aligners, Management Entrenchers, or Takeover Bid Signals?," *Journal of Financial Research* 16, Winter 1993, pp. 299–308.

Boyle, G. W., R. B. Carter, and R. D. Stover, "Extra-ordinary Antitakeover Provisions and Insider Ownership Structure: The Case of Converting Savings and Loans," *Journal of Financial and Quantitative Analysis* 33, 1998, pp. 291–304.

Bradley, M., and L. Wakeman, "The Wealth Effects of Targeted Share Repurchases," *Journal of Financial Economics* 11, 1983, pp. 301–328.

Brickley, J. A., R. C. Lease, and C. W. Smith, Jr., "Ownership Structure and Voting on Antitakeover Amendments," *Journal of Financial Economics* 20, 1988, pp. 267–292.

Coffee, J. C., "Shareholders Versus Managers: The Strain in the Corporate Web," Chapter 6 in *Knights, Raiders, and Targets*, J. C. Coffee, L. Lowenstein, and S. Rose-Ackerman (eds.), New York: Oxford University Press, 1988, pp. 77–134.

Comment, Robert, and G. William Schwert, "Poison or Placebo? Evidence on the Deterrence and Wealth Effects of Modern Antitakeover Measures," *Journal of Financial Economics* 39, 1995, pp. 3–43.

Cook, Douglas O., and John C. Easterwood, "Poison Put Bonds: An Analysis of Their Economic Role," *Journal of Finance* 49, December 1994, pp. 1905–1920.

Dann, Larry Y., and Harry DeAngelo, "Standstill Agreements, Privately Negotiated Stock Repurchases, and the Market for Corporate Control," *Journal of Financial Economics* 11, 1983, pp. 275–300.

Datta, S., and M. Iskandar-Datta, "Takeover Defenses and Wealth Effects on Securityholders: The Case of Poison Pill Adoptions," *Journal of Banking & Finance* 20, 1996, pp. 1231–1250.

DeAngelo, Harry, and Edward M. Rice, "Antitakeover Charter Amendments and Stockholder Wealth," *Journal of Financial Economics* 11, April 1983, pp. 329–359.

Dodd, P. R., and J. B. Warner, "On Corporate Governance: A Study of Proxy Contests," *Journal of Financial Economics* 11, 1983, pp. 401–438.

Dodd, P. R., and R. Leftwich, "The Market for Corporate Control: 'Unhealthy Competition' Versus Federal Regulation," *Journal of Business* 53, 1980, pp. 259–283.

Eckbo, B. Espen, "Valuation Effects of Greenmail Prohibitions," *Journal of Financial and Quantitative Analysis* 25, December 1990, pp. 491–505.

Eisenberg, M. A., "Comment: Golden Parachutes and the Myth of the Web," Chapter 9 in *Knights, Raiders, and Targets,* J. C. Coffee, L. Lowenstein, and S. Rose-Ackerman (eds.), New York: Oxford University Press, 1988, pp. 155–158.

Field, Laura Casares, and Jonathan M. Karpoff, "Takeover Defenses of IPO Firms," *Journal of Finance* 57, October 2002, pp. 1857–1889.

Garvey, G. T., and G. Hanka, "Capital Structure and Corporate Control: The Effect of Antitakeover Statutes on Firm Leverage," *Journal of Finance* 54, 1999, pp. 519–546.

Hall, P. L., and D. C. Anderson, "The Effect of Golden Parachutes on Shareholder Wealth and Takeover Probabilities," *Journal of Business Finance and Accounting* 23, April 1997, pp. 445–463.

Heron, Randall A., and Wilbur G. Lewellen, "An Empirical Analysis of the Reincorporation Decision," *Journal of Financial and Quantitative Analysis* 33, 1998, pp. 549–568.

Holderness, C. G., and D. P. Sheehan, "Raiders or Saviors? The Evidence on Six Controversial Investors," *Journal of Financial Economics* 14, 1985, pp. 555–579.

Hwang, Suein L., "Philip Morris Throws Away Its Poison Pill," *Wall Street Journal,* March 2, 1995, B8.

Iqbal, Z., S. Shetty, J. Haley, and M. Jayakumar, "Takeovers, Managerial Ownership, and Pension Plan Termination," *American Business Review* 17, January 1999, pp. 1–6.

Janjigian, V., and E. A. Trahan, "An Analysis of the Decisions to Opt Out of Pennsylvania Senate Bill 1310," *Journal of Financial Research* 19, Spring 1996, pp. 1–19.

Jarrell, G. A., and A. Poulsen, "Shark Repellents and Stock Prices: The Effects of Antitakeover Amendments Since 1980," *Journal of Financial Economics* 19, 1987, pp. 127–168.

Jensen, Michael C., "Takeovers: Their Causes and Consequences," *Journal of Economic Perspectives* 2, Winter 1988, pp. 21–48.

Johnson, D. J., and N. L. Meade, "Shareholder Wealth Effects of Poison Pills in the Presence of Anti-Takeover Amendments," *Journal of Applied Business Research* 12, Fall 1996, pp. 10–19.

Johnson, M. S., and R. P. Rao, "The Impact of Antitakeover Amendments on Corporate Financial Performance," *Financial Review* 32, November 1997, pp. 659–690.

Karpoff, Jonathan M., and Paul H. Malatesta, "The Wealth Effects of Second Generation State Takeover Legislation," *Journal of Financial Economics* 25, 1989, pp. 291–322.

———, and Ralph A. Walking, "Corporate Governance and Shareholder Initiatives: Empirical Evidence," *Journal of Financial Economics* 42, 1996, pp. 365–395.

Klein, A., and J. Rosenfeld, "The Impact of Target Share Repurchases on the Wealth of Non-Participating Shareholders," *Journal of Financial Research* 11, Summer 1988, pp. 88–97.

Knoeber, C. R., "Golden Parachutes, Shark Repellents, and Hostile Tender Offers," *American Economic Review* 76, March 1986, pp. 155–167.

Lambert, R., and D. Larcker, "Golden Parachutes, Executive Decision Making, and Shareholder Wealth," *Journal of Accounting and Economics* 7, April 1985, pp. 179–204.

Linn, S. C., and J. J. McConnell, "An Empirical Investigation of the Impact of Antitakeover Amendments on Common Stock Prices," *Journal of Financial Economics* 11, April 1983, pp. 361–399.

Loh, C., and R. S. Rathinasamy, "The Impact of Antitakeover Devices on the Valuation Consequences of Voluntary Corporate Selloffs," *The Financial Review* 32, November 1997, pp. 691–708.

Mahoney, James M., and Joseph T. Mahoney, "An Empirical Investigation of the Effect of Corporate Charter Antitakeover Amendments on Stockholder Wealth," *Strategic Management Journal* 14, 1993, pp. 17–31.

Malatesta, Paul H., and Ralph A. Walkling, "Poison Pill Securities: Stockholder Wealth, Profitability, and Ownership Structure," *Journal of Financial Economics* 20, 1988, pp. 347–376.

Malekzadeh, A. R., V. B. McWilliams, and N. Sen, "Implications of CEO Structural and Ownership Powers, Board Ownership and Composition on the Market's Reaction to Antitakeover Charter

Amendments," *Journal of Applied Business Research* 14, Summer 1998, pp. 53–62.

Marais, L., K. Schipper, and A. Smith, "Wealth Effects of Going Private for Senior Securities," *Journal of Financial Economics* 23, 1989, pp. 151–191.

McWilliams, V. B. "Managerial Share Ownership and the Stock Price Effects of Antitakeover Amendment Proposals," *Journal of Finance* 45, 1990, pp. 1627–1640.

——, and N. Sen, "Board Monitoring and Anti-takeover Amendments," *Journal of Financial and Quantitative Analysis* 32, 1997, pp. 491–505.

Meulbroek, Lisa K., Mark L. Mitchell, J. Harold Mulherin, Jeffry M. Netter, and Annette B. Poulsen, "Shark Repellents and Managerial Myopia: An Empirical Test," *Journal of Political Economy* 98, October 1990, pp. 1108–1117.

Mikkelson, W. H., and R. S. Ruback, "An Empirical Analysis of the Interfirm Equity Investments Process," *Journal of Financial Economics* 14, 1985, pp. 523–553.

——, "Targeted Repurchases and Common Stock Returns," The *RAND Journal of Economics* 22, Winter 1991, pp. 544–561.

Mogavero, Damian J., and Michael F. Toyne, "The Impact of Golden Parachutes on Fortune 500 Stock Returns: A Reexamination of the Evidence," *Quarterly Journal of Business and Economics* 34, 1995, pp. 30–38.

Moran v. Household International, Inc., Del. Ch. 490A. 2d 1059 (1985).

Mulherin, J. H., and A. B. Poulsen, "Proxy Contests and Corporate Change: Implications for Shareholder Wealth," *Journal of Financial Economics* 47, 1998, pp. 279–313.

Plitch, Phyllis, "Pension Fund TIAA-CREF Targets 'Dead-Hand' Antitakeover Provisions," *Wall Street Journal*, January 31, 2000, p. B12.

Pound, J., "The Effects of Antitakeover Amendments on Takeover Activity: Some Direct Evidence," *Journal of Law and Economics* 30, October 1987, pp. 353–367.

Romano, Roberta, "Competition for Corporate Charters and the Lesson of Takeover Statutes," *Fordham Law Review* 61, 1993, pp. 843–864.

——, "Law as a Product: Some Pieces of the Incorporation Puzzle," *Journal of Law, Economics and Organization* 1, 1985, pp. 225–269.

——, "The Political Economy of Takeover Statutes," *Virginia Law Review* 73, 1987, pp. 111–199.

Ryngaert, Michael, "The Effect of Poison Pill Securities on Shareholder Wealth," *Journal of Financial Economics* 20, 1988, pp. 377–417.

——, and J. M. Netter, "Shareholder Wealth Effects of the Ohio Antitakeover Law," *Journal of Law, Economics and Organization* 4, Fall 1988, pp. 373–384.

Sundaramurthy, C., J. M. Mahoney, and J. T. Mahoney, "Board Structure, Antitakeover Provisions, and Stockholder Wealth," *Strategic Management Journal* 18, 1997, pp. 231–245.

Swartz, L. M., "The 1990 Pennsylvania Antitakeover Law: Should Firms Opt Out of Antitakeover Legislation?" *Journal of Accounting, Auditing and Finance* 11, Spring 1996, pp. 223–245.

Taylor, John, *Storming the Magic Kingdom,* New York: Ballantine Books, 1987.

Warga, A., and I. Welch, "Bondholder Losses in Leveraged Buyouts," *Review of Financial Studies* 6, 1993, pp. 959–982.

Wasserstein, Bruce, *Big Deal*, New York: Warner Books, 1998.

CHAPTER 20
CORPORATE GOVERNANCE AND PERFORMANCE

A s the stock market began to decline in early 2000, a number of companies collapsed. Most dramatic was the demise of Enron. Enron's stock price was still $90 per share in August 2000; on December 2, 2001, Enron entered into Chapter 11 bankruptcy. Problems were reported at WorldCom, Adelphia, Global Crossing, Tyco, and others. *Fortune* magazine in its September 2, 2002, issue published an article entitled, "You Bought. They Sold." They listed 26 companies whose stock prices declined 75% or more off their peak from January 1999 through May 2002, a period during which the top executives "walked away" with $66 billion.

GOVERNANCE FAILURE

The revelations gave rise to anguished complaints of corruption, fraud, and self-dealing at major corporations. Hubris (overweening pride) joined with avarice (consuming greed). The following summaries offer examples of corporate deception and fraud.

CORPORATE FRAUD

SUNBEAM—ALBERT J. DUNLAP (CHAINSAW AL)
- To inflate sales, the company arranged with major customers (Wal-Mart) to accept delivery of appliances in warehouses supplied by Sunbeam. These shipments were booked as sales. Dunlap argued to auditor Arthur Andersen that they were no different from sales that resulted in account receivables; in both cases, the company does not receive the cash in hand.
- Desperately sought to sell Sunbeam and when couldn't, made an acquisition, overpaid, but had the opportunity to take restructuring charges that would reduce costs in the future.

ENRON
- Entered into long-term contracts but booked sales in first year; arbitrarily underestimated costs, so showed large profits early.
- Partnerships—Special Purpose Entities (SPEs) controlled by Enron executives. Engaged in deals with Enron. Booked artificial profits for the SPEs and Enron. The partnership executives received large payments.

DYNEGY

- Engaged in cross selling with Enron and others at artificially high prices to book high profits for each.

WORLDCOM (WORLDCON PER BARRON'S)

- Treated operating expenses as capital expenditures.
- Made large loans to top executives.

ADELPHIA

- Signed contracts with imaginary customers, which are the basis for valuation of cable companies; inflated share prices.
- Top executives looted the company.

TYCO

- Manipulated the accounting, achieved high P/E ratios to put together a conglomerate that showed earnings accretion for each acquisition because of differentially higher P/E ratios.
- Made loans to top executives, then canceled them. Provided large cash bonuses plus extras to pay their taxes.

SOME OIL COMPANIES

- Lent executives money to buy subsidiaries at inflated prices. Reported profits on sale of segments (divestitures). Price of stock rose. Executives unloaded stock in the open market. As market recognized the reality, stock prices fell.

GLOBAL CROSSING (GLOBAL DOUBLE CROSSING PER BARRON'S)

- Illustrative of top executives selling out before the bad news.

INSIDER TRADING

- ImClone is illustrative. Stock peaked at $75. 45 on excitement about anticancer drug Erbitux. Top executives on December 26, 2001 (stock price was $63.62), learned that on December 28, 2001, it would not receive FDA approval. Before this became public knowledge, on December 27, 2001, they and friends sold stock (opened at $63, closed at $58). Later, the stock dropped to about $7. The SEC on June 12, 2002, filed charges against Samuel Waksal, CEO, who had resigned in late May and was succeeded by his brother, Harlan.

These nine examples of types of corporate fraud represent only a small sample of what occurs. A number of book-length treatments have become available. Howard Schilit published the first edition of his book entitled *Financial Shenanigans* in 1993. He established a Center for Financial Research and Analysis (CFRA) to detect early warning signs of operating problems or accounting "anomalies." In his 2002 edition, he listed 30 techniques of financial shenanigans or practices that intentionally distort a company's reported financial performance or condition. He presents examples of these practices for public companies. A similar book with many other examples was published by Mulford and Comiskey (2002).

The impact of earlier accusations of fraud was studied by Agrawal, Jaffe, and Karpoff (1999). They identified 103 firms accused of fraud from the Wall Street Journal Index from 1981 to 1992. They also developed 103 matched control firms with the same 2-digit Compustat primary

SIC code, with net sales closest to the fraud firm. The firms in the fraud sample have significantly more frauds than the control group in the 2 years before and the 2 years after the year of the fraud event keyed upon this study. The operating performance changes that occurred around the time of the fraud events were not statistically significant between the two groups.

With respect to managerial turnover, they found "no evidence that the revelation of fraud leads to a subsequent changing in leadership structure," as defined by the single top executive; the CEO and chairman are the same individual. However, turnover is also measured for persons holding the three top positions of chairman, CEO, and president. In year −1 relative to the keyed fraud, an average of 1.57 individuals held these top positions among the fraud firms (1.61 for the control firms) Higher turnover occurs for the fraud sample mainly in year +2 and +3, consistent with early studies that managerial turnover and takeovers lag poor firm performance. During the year of the keyed fraud and the 3 years following, the fraud firms reduced their board size slightly, decreasing the number of inside and outside directors; the control firms increased their outside board representation slightly but not significantly. These results are surprising because fraud surely would injure the reputation of the firm. However, the relatively modest impacts of fraud reported in this study might reflect the favorable economic and financial characteristics of the 1981 to 1992 period of the study.

REGULATORY RESPONSES

For the period 2000 to 2002, the fraud revelations were of such magnitude and inflicted such injury on investors that company reputations were irreparably destroyed. Stock price declines and the erosion of 401(k) values had widespread impacts. The fraud and self-dealing revelations resulted in investigations by congress, the SEC, and the State Attorney General in several jurisdictions, particularly New York. The Sarbanes-Oxley Act (SOA) was enacted into law on July 30, 2002.

In Chapter 2 we discussed the Sarbanes-Oxley Act as a part of the general legal and regulatory framework in which M&As take place. In the present chapter we emphasize its corporate governance implications. The summary of SOA which follows keys on the items with greatest impact on corporate governance issues.

1.   PCAOB: Title I provides for the establishment of the Public Company Accounting Oversight Board (PCAOB). The PCAOB is not an agency of the U.S. government. It is a private, nonprofit corporation subject to SEC regulation and oversight. The PCAOB is responsible for overseeing the auditing of public companies and for establishing standards for audit reports. Every auditing firm must be registered with the PCAOB. SOA adds greater responsibilities for company audit committees. Each company is required to report that its audit committee is comprised of at least one member who is a financial expert as defined by the SEC.

2.   Auditor Independence: Title 2 outlines the requirements for auditor independence. Audit firms are prohibited from providing nonaudit services such as consulting. Audit partner rotation is required every 5 years. Auditor reports should be made to audit committees rather than management. The auditing firm shall not have employed an accounting or financial officer of the audited company during the 1-year period preceding the initiation of an audit.

3.   Certification: The CEO and CFO must certify, as to each 10-K and 10-Q, that the report complies with SEC regulations and fairly presents the financial position of the company (Section 906). It is a crime punishable by up to $1 million and up to 10 years in prison to give

the certification knowing that it is false, and a crime punishable by up to $5 million and up to 20 years in prison to willingly give the certification knowing that it is false.

4. Disclosure: Each annual and quarterly report filed with the SEC is required to disclose all material off–balance sheet transactions. Pro forma financial statements should not be untrue or misleading. The filing deadline for the occurrence of a disclosable event is shortened to 2 days.

5. Insider Trading: Insider trading in their company's securities is considered a disclosable event to be reported on a Form 4 within 2 days. This supercedes the previous rule of the 10th day of the month following the transaction. Form 4 is to be filed electronically. During any blackout period imposed under a 401(k) or other profit-sharing or retirement plans, insiders are prohibited from trading any equity securities of the company.

6. Conflicts of Interest: Personal loans to officers and directors corporations are prohibited. To improve the objectivity of research and to provide investors with reliable information, new rules should be reasonably designed to address conflicts of interest that can arise when security analysts recommend equity securities.

7. Professional Responsibility: New SEC rules will establish minimum standards for professional conduct of attorneys who practice before the SEC. The rules will require that an attorney report evidence of securities law violations to the company's CEO or chief legal officer.

8. Studies and Reports: A wide range of GAO and commission studies shall be conducted.

9. Fraud Accountability: Destruction, alteration, or falsification of records in federal investigations and bankruptcy is criminal fraud. Debts are nondischargeable if incurred in violation of securities fraud laws. Protections for whistle-blowers are strengthened.

10. Penalties: All audit or work papers shall be maintained for 5 years. Violators shall be fined or imprisoned for up to 10 years. False certification or falsifying financial reports shall result in fines of up to $5 million and/or imprisonment of no more that 20 years. The statute of limitations for securities fraud is extended.

11. SEC Powers: Any person who has violated the antifraud provision of federal securities law may be prohibited by the SEC from serving as an officer or director. During investigations of possible violations of the federal securities laws, the SEC can petition a court to freeze extraordinary payments by the company.

On August 16, 2002, the New York Stock Exchange (NYSE) submitted revised listing requirements to the SEC for final approval. The NYSE new listing rules go beyond the auditor independence requirements of SOA. The company must have an ongoing independent audit committee with at least three directors. The committee must have a written charter covering the committee's activities. Detailed specifications of board independence are set forth. Within 2 years, the majority of the board of directors must be independent. Nonmanagement directors must meet periodically without management. Within 2 years, boards must have wholly independent compensation and nominating committees. Shareholders must vote on all stock option plans. Each listed company is required to adopt a set of governance guidelines. With regard to directors, the guidelines must cover their qualifications, responsibilities, compensation, and access to management. Each listed company must disclose a code of business conduct and ethics.

The NYSE new listing requirements also apply to all foreign companies with a stock market listing in the United States. They must create and maintain an audit committee that meets independence standards. Foreign firms must disclose in English any significant ways its corporate governance practices differ from those followed by domestic companies. The NYSE may continue to provide waivers to companies whose corporate governance practices comply with home company laws. However, foreign issuer filing with the SEC will be required to comply with SOA.

Implementation of the PCAOB got off to a shaky start. John Biggs of TIAA-CREF was proposed by SEC Chairman Harvey Pitt to head the new accounting oversight board. Under pressure, Pitt chose William Webster instead. Subsequently, it was found that Webster was the chairman of the audit committee of U.S. Technologies Incorporated, a company now considered insolvent and facing investors' lawsuits alleging fraud. The turmoil resulting from these appointment changes caused Pitt to resign on November 15, 2002. William Donaldson, a cofounder of the Donaldson, Lufkin & Jenrette investment banking firm and the chairman of the NYSE in the early 1990s, was appointed as a replacement for Pitt; William J. McDonough became chairman of PCAOB.

AN OVERVIEW OF CORPORATE GOVERNANCE

The subject matter is clearly important and exciting. It has many dimensions, so we begin with an overview to provide the big picture that will guide the organization of the chapter. Running a business requires funds. Once funds are supplied, what is to prevent the managers from taking advantage of all the other stakeholders? This is the problem of a separation of ownership and control; it also has been termed the agency problem or the relationship between the principal and agents. In theory, the shareholders elect a board of directors to represent their interests. However, the managers may subvert this process. If boards are ineffectual, can other mechanisms outside the firm help? Does the stock market serve as a regulator by penalizing poor performance with reduced security prices? Do proxy contests help? Or are M&As—the market for corporate control—the ultimate mechanism for the regulation of corporate governance? On the other hand, do completely different governance systems, such as banking control in Germany and Japan, work better? These are the issues covered in the following sections.

The materials that follow reflect our own conceptual framework plus a considerable body of empirical literature (see the valuable framework presented in the 168-page survey by Becht, Bolton, and Röell, 2002, and the March 2003 *Journal of Financial and Quantitative Analysis* special issue on international corporate governance, Malatesta and McConnell, eds.) The published research covers data sets mostly for the 1980s through the mid-1990s. This 15-year period was predominantly a time of a booming economy and rising stock prices. The studies, therefore, do not cover the downturn beginning in early 2000 and the spectacular revelations of corporate fraud and executive self-dealing. In the earlier periods, there was shareholder activism, especially in underperforming companies. Top executives were replaced and with the powerful tide of a strong economy, restructurings were successful and improvements were achieved.

However, the revelations beginning in 2000 resulted in the enactment of the Sarbanes-Oxley Act of July 30, 2002. This enactment of legislation was a warning sign that if business did not reform itself, the government would. One of the early responses was the adoption of the new corporate governance rules by the New York Stock Exchange during the following month. It is in this broader framework that the empirical studies reflected in the following analysis should be evaluated.

CORPORATE GOVERNANCE SYSTEMS IN THE UNITED STATES

In the United States, the system of corporate enterprise that developed was the limited liability public corporation, whose ownership in theory was widely dispersed among individual shareholders. After legislation in 1933, commercial banks were not permitted to make equity investments and insurance companies had long been circumscribed in the percentage of their funds they could invest in equities. In contrast, the system that grew up in Germany and Japan was characterized by large equity and loan investments by banks and insurance companies. In addition, substantial cross holding of ownership shares among corporations developed. We begin with an analysis of the U.S. model of corporate governance.

DIFFUSE STOCK OWNERSHIP

For many years, the dominant form of corporate ownership in the United States was diffuse limited liability ownership of the voting equity shares by a large number of individual investors. The growth of this form of ownership reflected some distinct advantages. Under limited liability, the investor could lose no more than was paid for the equity stock of the corporation. Relatively small investments could be made in a number of corporations, so the individual investor could achieve the benefits of diversification. Asset pricing models hold that diversification enables the investor to ignore the idiosyncratic risks of individual companies to earn the risk-free rate plus a market risk premium weighted by systematic risk, which implies that relatively little direct monitoring of the operations of individual business firms is required by investors.

In addition, the equity ownership shares of the corporation are readily bought and sold in active and relatively liquid markets. In the United States, by tradition and by legislation enacted in the 1930s, commercial banks and insurance companies are limited in their ability to hold large equity positions in individual corporations. Under this idealized scenario, issues of corporate governance and control are muted. However, over time, the effectiveness of this governance system has been questioned. The Gramm-Leach-Bliley Financial Modernization Act of 1999 relaxed the above restrictions. To understand the issues, we begin with a brief summary of the theory of the firm.

CONTRACTUAL THEORY OF THE FIRM

The contractual theory of the nature of the firm has become widely held (Alchian, 1982; Alchian and Woodward, 1988; Fama and Jensen, 1983a, 1983b). It views the firm as a network of contracts, actual and implicit, that specify the roles of the various participants or stakeholders (workers, managers, owners, lenders) and defines their rights, obligations, and payoffs under various conditions. The contractual nature of the firm implies multiple stakeholders. Their interests must be harmonized to achieve efficiency and value maximization. A basic issue is the role of market transactions (and their relative costs) versus organization processes as alternative modes of governance (Williamson, 1999).

Although contracts define the rights and responsibilities of each class of stakeholders in a firm, potential conflicts can occur. Contracts are unable to envisage the many changes in conditions that develop over the passage of time. Also, participants might have personal goals, as well.

Most participants contract for fixed payoffs. Workers receive wages. Creditors receive interest payments and are promised the repayment of principal at the maturity of debt contracts. The shareholders hold residual claims on cash flows. In recent years, wage earners have been paid in part in the common stock of the firm in ESOPs or in return for wage concessions. Warrants and convertibles add equity options to debt contracts.

In this framework, the literature has expressed concern about the separation of ownership and control (Berle and Means, 1932). In general, the operations of the firm are conducted and controlled by its managers without major stock ownership positions. In theory, the managers are agents of the owners, but in practice they may control the firm in their own interests. Thus, conflicts of interest arise between the owners and managers.

Jensen and Meckling (1976) developed a number of aspects of the divergence of interest between owners (the principal) and management (their agent). They described how the agency problem results whenever a manager owns less than the total common stock of the firm. This fractional ownership can lead managers to work less strenuously and to acquire more perquisites (luxurious offices, furniture, and rugs; company cars) than if they had to bear all of the costs.

To deal with agency problems, additional monitoring expenditures (agency costs) are required, Agency costs include (1) auditing systems to limit this kind of management behavior, (2) various kinds of bonding assurances by the managers that such abuses will not be practiced, and (3) change in organization systems to limit the ability of managers to engage in the undesirable practices.

DIVERGENT INTERESTS OF STAKEHOLDERS

Traditionally, corporate governance has focused on the problem of the separation of ownership by shareholders and control by management. However, increasingly we have come to recognize a broader framework. Firms must respond to the expectations of more categories of stakeholders. These include employees, consumers, large investors such as pension funds, government, and society as a whole. These diverse interests need to be harmonized. Firms must respond to the expectations of diverse stakeholders to achieve long-run value maximization (Cornell and Shapiro, 1987).

In recent years, externalities such as product safety, job safety, and environmental impacts have increased in importance. A business firm must be responsive to new and powerful constituencies for long-run viability. This point of view argues that business firms must recognize a wide range of stakeholders and external influences.

INTERNAL CONTROL MECHANISMS

We first consider the internal control mechanisms available to balance the interests of the multiple stakeholders. In theory, under widely dispersed ownership, shareholders elect the board of directors to represent their interests. This poses issues of how other stakeholders obtain representation of their views and interests. These problems have not been fully resolved. Increasingly, public expectations look to the board of directors to balance the interests of all stakeholders. Some criticize such a view as soft-headed, unrealistic "do-goodism." An alternative view is that if the needs and goals of the multiple stakeholders—shareholders, creditors, consumers, workers, government, the general public—are not addressed, the political-economic systems will not function effectively in the long run. These are matters of great importance with respect to which the board of directors has considerable responsibilities.

Campbell, Gillan, and Niden (1999) analyzed how shareholders used the proxy mechanism on issues concerning corporate governance and social policy in the 1997 proxy season. The shareholder proposal rule (Rule14a-8) allowed shareholders to include a proposal and a 500-word supporting statement in the company's proxy materials subject to certain constraints.

Campbell et al.'s sample consisted of 287 social policy proposals and 582 corporate governance proposals at 394 companies. The data source was the Investor Responsibility Center's compilation of shareholder proposals, the nature of which is described in the following paragraph.

Only 43.3% of all proposals were considered for vote. For the corporate governance proposals, 49.2% were voted on and 35.2% were either omitted or withdrawn. For social policy proposals, 31.4% were voted on and 61.6% were either omitted or withdrawn. For proposals that were submitted to a vote, corporate governance received a higher level of support, with a mean of 23.6% of the votes cast in favor, particularly those related to antitakeover measures, board pensions, and shareholders voting. Low support was associated with executive compensation, board stock ownership, and board tenure. Social policy issues received only weak support, with a mean of 6.6% of the votes cast in favor. Campbell et al. concluded that Rule 14a-8 remains an important avenue for shareholders seeking change in corporate behavior on issues of corporate governance and social policy.

ROLE OF THE BOARD OF DIRECTORS

Monitoring by boards of directors can, in theory, deal with at least some problems of corporate governance. The alternative view is that boards have been ineffective in recognizing the problems of the firm and standing up to top officers, especially when tough decisions are necessary to solve the problems (Jensen, 1986). External control devices such as hostile takeovers have multiplied because of the failure of the board, according to this view.

The work by Morck, Shleifer, and Vishny (1989) was motivated by these opposing views and provided evidence on when the board could deal effectively with the problems of the firm and when the external control market comes into play. It is the view of Morck, Shleifer, and Vishny that when the company underperforms its relatively healthy industry, it is easier for the board to evaluate top management. The board's task is much harder when the whole industry is suffering. When the industry is having problems, it is difficult to judge whether the management is making mistakes. The boards of directors of firms in problem industries might be reluctant to force the CEO to take the painful measures (for example, divest divisions, lay off workers, or cut wages) often required in slow-growth, mature, or declining industries. Under these circumstances, an external challenge (M&A) to shake up the management and the board might be necessary to enforce maximization of shareholder wealth.

COMPOSITION OF THE BOARD

It is widely believed that outside directors play a larger role in monitoring management than inside directors. Fama (1980), for instance, argues that the inclusion of outside directors as professional referees enhances the viability of the board in achieving low-cost internal transfer of control. This also lowers the probability of top management colluding and expropriating shareholders. Outside directors are usually respected leaders from the business and academic communities and have incentives to protect and develop their reputation as experts in decision control (Fama and Jensen, 1983a).

A study by Weisbach (1988) formally tested the hypothesis that inside and outside directors behave differently in monitoring top management and found that firms with outsider-dominated boards were significantly more likely than firms with insider-dominated boards to remove the chief executive officer (CEO). In Weisbach's study, firms were grouped according to the percentage of outsiders (directors who neither work for the corporation nor have extensive dealings with the company) on the board. In his samples of 367 New York Stock Exchange

(NYSE) firms, the proportion of outside directors on the board centered around 50%, with few firms in the tails of the distribution. In the study, outsider-dominated firms (128 firms) were those in which at least 60% of the board were outsiders. Insider-dominated firms (93 firms) had outsiders making up no more than 40% of the directors. Firms with between 41% and 59% outsiders were considered mixed (146 firms). For all the firms in the sample, 286 CEOs resigned in the period 1974 to 1983. In the actual analysis, CEO resignations for reasons that are clearly unrelated to performance were eliminated from the sample.

When stock returns are used as predictors of CEO removal, the results show a statistically significant inverse relation between a firm's market-adjusted share performance in a year and the likelihood of a subsequent change in its CEO. The responsiveness of the removal decision to stock performance is three times as large for the outsider-dominated boards as for the other board types. Resignations are not sensitive to returns from periods preceding the event by more than a year, which suggests that the board's decision to replace the CEO takes place relatively quickly following poor share return performance. Using accounting earnings changes (net of industry effects) as the performance measure gives similar results. Also, there is an indication that the board of directors looks at accounting numbers (earnings before interest and taxes) to evaluate a CEO's performance, possibly more than at stock returns.

Weisbach (1988) provided evidence that the larger the shareholdings are of the top two officers of the firm and the rest of the board, the smaller the number of outsiders on the board is. As expected, increased shareholdings of the CEO reduced the probability that he or she resigned. However, share ownership by noncontrolling directors (that is, directors excluding the top two officers) does not appear to have any explanatory power other than board composition. Thus, Weisbach suggested that the composition of the board rather than its equity ownership was what drove the level of monitoring. He also measured price responses to the announcement of CEO resignations. His results showed that the excess returns from a market model are significantly positive and thus imply that new information is revealed by these resignations.

Corporate governance reformers believe that outside directors are better monitors and, therefore, recommend that nominating committees should be composed of only independent outside directors. Outside directors are not officers of the firm and do not have a direct business relationship with the firm. It was GM's outside board members who played the pivotal role in ousting the chairman, Robert C. Stempel, in November 1992.

Using the *Wall Street Journal's* "Who's News" section, Rosenstein and Wyatt (1990) examined the impact of the announcement that a company is appointing an outside director. The cumulative average prediction error (CAPE) for the total sample was significantly positive, which provided support for the argument that the appointment of outside directors adds to shareholder wealth.

Borokhovich, Parrino, and Trapani (1996) discussed the role of outside directors and CEO selection. They found a positive monotonic relation between the proportion of outside directors and the likelihood that an outsider is appointed CEO. This relation holds after controlling for firm size, firm performance, CEO stock ownership, and regulatory effects. Evidence from the stock returns around the succession announcements suggests that the market views the appointment of an outsider to the CEO position more favorably than the appointment of an insider, especially when the incumbent CEO is forced to resign. A new CEO from outside the firm appears to be perceived as more likely to alter firm policies in a way that benefits shareholders. On average, a significant positive abnormal return is observed when a CEO is replaced by an outsider following either voluntary or forced turnover. In contrast, whereas inside appointments following voluntary successions are associated with small positive abnormal returns, large negative abnormal returns are observed when insiders replace fired CEOs.

COMPENSATION OF BOARD MEMBERS

Part of the solution might be a well-structured compensation system. Although director compensation is a relatively recent phenomenon, it goes hand in hand with the increased director responsibility. In the past, directors did little monitoring and their own performance was not evaluated. They received a token fee for their services. Board members today take a greater leadership role by overseeing the appointment and assessment of officers, helping implement strategy, representing shareholders, and seeing that the company fulfills its public responsibilities. Critics of the compensation as a motivating factor model point out that in some fields, particularly nonprofit, many directors volunteer their services without financial compensation.

If compensation is a significant motivating factor for directors, director stock ownership aligns director interests more closely with those of shareholders. Some companies have adopted stock ownership requirements for directors and/or pay part or all the directors' annual retainer in stock and stock options. Some finance their directors retirements with stock. Studies find that directories of top-performing companies hold more stock than do their counterparts at poor performers, suggesting a positive link between director stock ownership and company performance.

EVALUATING A BOARD OF DIRECTORS

BusinessWeek (Byrne, 1996) carried a cover story entitled "The Best & Worst Boards." Boards were rated by how close they came to meeting recommendations, which we summarize into nine items: (1) Evaluate CEO performance annually. (2) Link CEO pay to clear performance criteria. (3) Review and evaluate strategic and operating plants. (4) Require significant stock ownership and compensate directors in stock. (5) Consist of no more than three insiders. (6) Require election each year and mandatory retirement at 70. (7) Have key committees composed of outside directors. (8) Impose limits on number of boards and ban interlocking directorships. (9) Disqualify anyone receiving fees from the company.

The article listed the "best" and "worst" 25 companies based on the aforementioned criteria. Such listings throw the glare of publicity on the performance of boards of directors. The article also noted that some pension funds and mutual funds judge boards by the stock market performance of their companies. This is called a "blinkered view." It is argued that sound governance will improve the odds of good performance.

In its cover story of October 7, 2002, *BusinessWeek* (Louis Lavelle) covered the same subject with the subtitle, "How the Corporate Scandals Are Sparking a Revolution in Governance." The principles of good governance emphasize four areas: independence, stock ownership, director quality, and board activism. Independence was defined to mean that no more than two directors should be current or former company executives. None should do business for fees with the firm. Each director should have an equity stake of at least $150,000. The board should include at least one independent director with experience in the firm's core activities. Multiple directorships should be limited, and each director should participate in a minimum of 75% of meetings. To promote board activism, *BusinessWeek* recommends that boards should have regular meetings without management attendance. Audit committees should meet at least four times per year.

The story listed five companies in which improvements have been made. It listed nine companies whose boards were deficient on important criteria. It placed six companies in the Hall of Shame: Enron, Adelphia, Tyco, WorldCom, Global Crossing, and Metromedia Fiber Network. Other recommendations were made for further improvements including the following. More power should be given to shareholders to choose and replace directors. Firms should have two candidates for each seat. Results ought to be decided by a simple majority. Role call votes on important issues such as executive pay should be disclosed. Shareholder resolutions should require only a majority vote for passage. Shareholder rights and improved performance of the board of directors clearly remain unfinished business.

Published research also has evaluated board effectiveness. Millstein and MacAvoy (1998) developed two metrics for board independence and performance, using them to predict whether a company is adding wealth to its shareholders. The first metric for board performance is based on a survey by CalPERS of 300 large corporations in which they requested a response to a questionnaire on board procedures. The responses were graded by CalPERS with ranks from A+ to F based on criteria such as the nine aforementioned items. In addition, Millstein and MacAvoy assigned an associate to review the responses to the CalPERS questionnaire to develop a binary criterion of board independence. At least one of the following had to be present: a nonexecutive chairman of the board, meetings of outside directors without management present, or substantial adherence to recommended guidelines. These metrics were the independent variables in a regression on the company spread between ROIC (the return on invested capital) and WACC (the cost of capital), using data for 1991 to 1995. Calculations were made using the CalPERS grade of A+ to F and another using the binary measure of board independence. By either metric, the better the board rating was, the higher was the geometric mean of the 1991 to 1995 spread of ROIC over WACC. Their study demonstrated that the relationship between board procedures and performance can be quantified.

Similar results were found by Seward and Walsh (1996) in their study of 78 voluntary corporate spin-offs between 1972 and 1987. The new companies were typically headed by an inside CEO from the parent company. The CEO received a market-based performance-contingent compensation contract. The boards of directors in the new entities included a majority of outsiders. Incentive contracts for top managers were designed by a compensation committee composed of a majority of outside directors. Seward and Walsh concluded that the spin-off form of equity reorganizations has been associated with the implementation of efficient internal governance and control practices. As in earlier studies of spin-offs, the event returns were positive, with abnormal returns averaging 2.6%. However, their variables measuring the efficiency of the governance and control of the spin-offs did not explain the positive announcement returns.

OWNERSHIP CONCENTRATION

Equity ownership by managers must balance convergence or alignment of interests versus entrenchment considerations. When management share ownership increases, managers' interests are better aligned with shareholder interests, and thus deviation from value maximization will decline (convergence). However, managerial ownership and control of voting rights might give managers enough power to guarantee their employment with the firm and pursue self-interest at the expense of shareholder wealth (entrenchment).

OWNERSHIP AND PERFORMANCE

Stulz (1988) formulated a model in which at low levels of management ownership, increased equity holdings improve convergence of interests with shareholders, enhancing firm value. At higher levels of insider ownership, managerial entrenchment blocks takeovers or makes them more costly. This decreases the probability of a takeover, which is likely to decrease the value of the firm.

In Morck, Shleifer, and Vishny (1988), performance (measured by the q-ratio) was related to management or insider ownership percentages. As ownership concentration increased from

0 to 5%, performance improved. In the ownership range from more than 5% to 25%, performance deteriorated. As ownership concentration rose above 25%, performance improved, but slowly. A simple explanation of this pattern is that in the 0 to 5% range, the alignment-of-interest effect improved performance. In the more than 5% to 25% range, management entrenchment influence may have a dampening effect on performance. In the over 25% range, incremental entrenchment effects were attenuated. However, Morck et al. questioned this simple interpretation. In the 0 to 5% range, they observed that the direction of causality may be reversed. (See also Jensen and Warner, 1988.) High-performance firms were more likely to give managers stock bonuses or make it profitable for them to exercise their stock options, resulting in large ownership percentages for management. They also referred to the point made by Demsetz and Lehn (1985) that firms with high performance might have substantial intangible assets that require greater ownership concentration to induce proper management of these assets. Morck, Shleifer, and Vishny agreed that it appeared plausible that above the 25% ownership concentration additional entrenchment effects would be small.

McConnell and Servaes (1990) replicated the Morck et al. study, which used 1980 data, for the years 1976 and 1986. For 1976, McConnell and Servaes found that the relationship between concentration and performance, measured by the q-ratio, was relatively flat with a moderate convergence of interest effect up to 50%, after which the curve appears to flatten and then decline moderately. For their 1986 data, they found that the curve rose relatively sharply to 40%, after which it was relatively flat to 50%, followed by a sharp decline. McConnell and Servaes also tested for the influence of leverage, institutional ownership, R&D expenditures, and advertising expenditures, concluding that including these control variables did not change their initial findings.

Another follow-up study was made by Cho (1998). Cho, using 1991 data, was able to replicate the Morck et al. patterns using ordinary least squares (OLS) regression. He noted that the previous studies treat ownership structure as given by outside factors (exogenous). He tested for the hypothesis of Demsetz and Lehn (1985) that ownership structure is endogenous—reflecting decisions made by owners based on considerations such as choices between salaries and the receipt of stock options. When Cho estimated a simultaneous equation regression instead of OLS, he found that corporate value affects ownership structure, but not the reverse. This reverses the interpretation of the relationship between ownership structure and corporate value.

Bristow (1998) examined the issues using a new database of consistently derived insider holdings on 4,000 firms covering the years 1986 through 1995. He calculated the relationship between management ownership and performance for each of the 10 years. For some years, he obtained the Morck et al. results; for others, he obtained the McConnell and Servaes roof-shaped patterns, and for still other years, a bowl pattern (inverted roof). Bristow's findings suggest that other economic variables, such as the relative growth rates of industries, differences in demand-supply relationships among industries, the relative value change patterns among industries and firms within them, and stock price movements, may influence the ownership-performance relationship. Bristow's results also may reflect the econometric identification problems discussed by Cho. The true relationship may be that of the Demsetz-Lehn theory of no relationship between ownership and performance. Another possibility is suggested by the considerable literature concluding that corporate governance in the United States had suffered from widely diffused ownership. Holderness, Kroszner, and Sheehan (1999) found that the mean and median percentages of managerial equity ownership increased from 12.9% and 6.5%, respectively, in 1935 to 21.1% and 14.4% in 1995. This is roughly a doubling of managerial ownership, possibly implying a general improvement in corporate governance in the United States.

OTHER STUDIES OF OWNERSHIP EFFECTS

Holderness and Sheehan (1988) analyzed 114 listed firms with ownership concentration of more than 50% but less than 100%. Among the 114 firms, 27 became majority shareholder firms during the period 1978 to 1984, but only 13 ceased to be such firms during the same period. Thus, there was little net outflow from majority ownership. This result also is confirmed for a much larger base of publicly traded forms. It appears that majority ownership was surviving as a viable organizational form. In the sample, the majority shareholders were approximately equally divided between individuals and corporations. Firms with individual majority shareholders were typically smaller than, and firms with corporate majority shareholders slightly larger than, the typical NYSE or AMEX firms.

The average majority holding was 64% (median 60%) for all firms in the sample, which is substantially more than the minimum 50% that ensure voting control. This evidence appears inconsistent with the proposition that majority blocks are held to expropriate minority shareholders. Expropriation-oriented majority shareholders might want to hold above 66% because of supermajority voting provisions in the firm's bylaws or articles of incorporation. However, only 36% of the sample firms involved blocks above 66%, the typical supermajority requirement, and for these firms the authors found no cases in which the requirement was mentioned in proxy statements.

Holderness and Sheehan (1988) also analyzed stock price reaction to 31 announcements of majority block trades to study the effect on firm value of changing shareholders. On average, stock prices increased over the 2-day window of the day before announcement and the announcement day by an abnormal 7.3%, and over the 30-day period around the announcement by an abnormal 12.8%. The results also indicated that on average, firm value increases more when both the buyer and the seller are individuals rather than corporations. The abnormal return was higher for announcements that involved simultaneous tender offers to minority shareholders (10 out of 31 cases) than announcements with no such tender offers (21 cases). In most of the consummated cases, new directors and officers were appointed after the trades.

When majority shareholder firms were compared to firms with relatively diffuse stock ownership, Holderness and Sheehan (1988) found no statistical difference in investment expenditures, frequency of control changes, accounting rates of return, or Tobin's q. However, evidence indicated that *individual* majority shareholder firms underperformed their comparison firms in terms of q-ratios and accounting rates of return, whereas *corporate* majority shareholder firms did not (see also Barclay and Holderness, 1991.)

Slovin and Sushka (1993) analyzed the influence of ownership concentration of firm value by studying the effects of the deaths of inside blockholders. They found that the abnormal returns for the 2-day event interval from day-1 to the report of the executive's death were a positive 3.01%, statistically significant. They found also that ownership concentration fell and increased corporate control activity followed. A majority of the firms in which an inside blockholder died subsequently became the target of a takeover bid. Two thirds of the bids were friendly, and three fourths of them succeeded.

The preceding empirical studies yielded several implications. First, the positive stock price reactions were inconsistent with the proposition that the majority shareholders' primary objective was to expropriate or consume corporate wealth. If the expropriation hypotheses were valid, majority shareholders would not offer to buy out minority shareholders at substantial premiums. Yet such offers were made in one third of the majority-block trading announcements. Second, majority shareholders or their representatives did not merely monitor management teams but actively participated in management. That the majority shareholder played a central role in management was consistent with the management and board turnover following majority-block trading. Third, the apparent premise for the antagonism toward large block shareholders (reflected in state regulations limiting their voting rights, antitakeover laws, poison pill charter amendments, and other "shareholder rights" initiatives) was not consistent with the empirical evidence.

MANAGERIAL OWNERSHIP AND BOND RETURNS

The relationships between concentration of managerial ownership and bond returns were tested by Bagnani, Milonas, Saunders, and Travlos (1994). They employed the three-stage analysis of Morck, Shleifer, and Vishny (1988) discussed previously. Their empirical analysis found no relationship between bond returns and managerial ownership of 0 to 5%, a positive relationship between more than 5% to 25%, and a weak negative relationship for ownership above 25%.

Some reasons for these findings were suggested by Bagnani et al. The 5% to 25% range represented a concentration of stock ownership that resulted in increased incentives for managers to act in shareholders' interests, taking risks that were potentially harmful to bondholders. In this range, rational bondholders required higher returns on their bonds.

At ownership above 25%, managers became more risk averse. As their stake increased, their wealth was less diversified with firm-specific, nondiversifiable human capital and they had greater incentives to protect their private benefits and objectives. Thus, their interests were more aligned with those of bondholders, implying lower bond return premiums.

FINANCIAL POLICY AND OWNERSHIP CONCENTRATION

In share repurchases financed by debt, the amount of equity is reduced. Because the insider group does not tender its shares in the repurchase, its percentage of equity shares is increased. This may increase the convergence-of-interest effect. We have seen in Chapter 16 that LBOs and MBOs increase management ownership shares. Incentive effects of high management ownership percentages have played a positive role in LBOs and MBOs.

Safieddine and Titman (1999) studied a sample of 573 firms that successfully resisted takeover attempts during the period 1982 to 1991. Target stock prices declined an average of 5.14% around the date of the termination announcement. For 328 companies, data were available to calculate effects on leverage. In 207 firms, the median level of the total debt to total book value of assets increased from about 60% 1 year before the unsuccessful takeover attempt to 71.5% 1 year later. The increased leverage is one form of defensive strategy. Only 38% of the targets that increased their leverage ratio by more than the median during a 3-year window around the initial failed takeover attempt were taken over in the subsequent 5 years. For the target firms that increased their leverage ratios by less than the median, 57% were taken over during the 5-year period.

The higher leverage ratio increases are associated with corporate restructuring activity. The turnover of top management during the 3-year window was 30% for the group with low leverage increase and about 37% for the firms with higher leverage increases. In hostile takeover attempts, 44% of the top managers are replaced; in friendly takeover attempts, only 29% are replaced. In addition to management turnover, labor force reductions and asset sales to increase corporate focus take place. Operating performance improves. As a result, the long-run, post-termination performance of leverage-increased targets is superior to that of benchmark control groups. The returns realized by the shareholders of the targets with leverage increases grow by about 55% within 5 years or within a shorter time if the firm is delisted, possibly because of the takeover. This is approximately the same level of returns that would have been realized by accepting the takeover offer. Shareholders of targets with less than median leverage increases are worse off. The strong long-term abnormal stock price performance indicates that for the leverage-increasing firms, despite the initial drop at the termination announcement, the associated productivity improvements are consistent with target manager behavior aligned with the longer-run interests of their shareholders.

Other effects have been noted. The Amihud, Lev, and Travlos (1990) study measured whether the likelihood of an acquisition being financed by cash was an increasing function of the managerial ownership in the acquiring firm. Increasing debt also increases the probability of bankruptcy but it can be used to increase management's equity stake if the debt is used to retire equity held by the public. The Amihud et al. sample consisted of firms that appeared on the 1980 list of Fortune 500 companies and made cash acquisitions of more than $10 million of other firms during the period 1981 to 1983. The results showed that cash acquisitions are associated with significantly larger insider ownership levels than stock-financed acquisitions.

EXECUTIVE COMPENSATION

We have presented materials on the relationship between managerial concentration of ownership and the convergence of interests of managers with those of owners. Executive compensation plans also have been proposed to achieve alignment of interests.

One view is that the conflict of interest between owners and managers would be substantially reduced if executive compensation plans more tightly related pay to performance. The view is widely held that executive compensation is not closely linked to performance measured by changes in the value of the firm. Jensen and Murphy (1990) found that executive pay changes by only $3 for a $1,000 change in the wealth of a firm, an elasticity of 0.003, or 0.3%. This is argued to demonstrate that executive pay is not linked to performance. However, this relationship may be at least partially explained by the large value of the firm in relation to executive compensation.

For example, the Disney Company at the end of 1995 had 524 million shares outstanding. At a price of $60 per share, this represented $31.44 billion. If its top executive received compensation of $10 million, this was 0.0318% of total firm value.

In 1996 its president, Michael Eisner, realized $200 million mainly from the exercise of stock options. From a low of $7 in 1986, the price of Disney stock, adjusted for splits, increased to a high of $64.25 in 1995. Based on the 524 million shares outstanding at the end of 1995, this represented an increase in value to Disney shareholders of approximately $30 billion. Thus, Eisner's salary change in the one unusual year represented about $6.7 for each $1,000 change in the wealth of Disney shareholders, an elasticity of 0.0067 or 0.67%. The result was not greatly different from the Jensen and Murphy relationship. This example suggested that although the elasticity of executive pay in relation to changes in firm value was small, the impact on the wealth position of executives could be large.

A large impact on executive wealth position could have strong motivational influences. Haubrich (1994), using some reasonable parameter assumptions, derived the Jensen and Murphy results from some leading models of principal-agent theory. Haubrich's analysis led Shleifer and Vishny (1997) to observe that the Jensen and Murphy relationship would generate large swings in executive wealth and require considerable risk tolerance for executives.

Core, Holthausen, and Larcker (1999) examined the association between the firm's corporate governance structure and level of CEO compensation and the future performance of the firm. The sample consisted of 495 observations for 205 publicly traded U.S. firms over the period 1982 to 1984. The compensation data were collected by a major consulting firm using mail surveys.

The cross-sectional regression, controlling for the economic factors, showed that board of director characteristics and ownership structure were significantly related to the level of CEO compensation. With regard to board of director variables, CEO compensation was higher when the CEO was also the board chair, the board was larger, there was a greater percentage of outside directors appointed by the CEO, there were more outside directors considered "gray" (the director or his or her employer received payments from the company in excess of his board pay), and outside directors were older and served on more than three other boards. CEO compensation was lower the greater the percentage of inside directors that sat in the board. With respect to ownership variables, CEO compensation was lower when the CEO's ownership stake was higher and when the large blockholders were present (either non-CEO internal board members or external blockholders who owned at least 5% of the equity).

Core, Holthausen, and Larcker used a second set of regressions between the compensation predicted by the board and ownership variables and the subsequent operating and market performance of the firm. They found a significant negative relationship. This result suggested that the board and ownership variables were proxies for the effectiveness of the firm's governance structure in controlling agency problems and not for the determinants of the CEO's equilibrium wage. The board and ownership structures affected the extent to which CEOs obtained compensation in excess of the level implied by the economic determinants. Thus, firms with weaker governance structures had greater agency problems. CEOs of firms with greater agency problems were able to obtain higher compensation. Firms with greater agency problems did not perform as well.

Another criticism of past patterns in executive compensation was that bonuses and stock options had been based on accounting measures rather than on stock market–based performance measures. Rappaport (1986) provided some perspective on the choice of performance measure. He observed that early executive compensation performance plans *were* market based. However, during the 1970s, stock price movements were essentially flat. The average of daily closing prices for the Dow Jones Industrial Average was 911 for 1965 and was still only 884 for 1982. The broader S&P 500 Index also remained essentially flat over the same time period. As a consequence, performance measures for granting options shifted from market-based to accounting-based measures over this period (Rappaport, 1986, p. 177).

However, in recent years, performance is again moving to market-based measures. The data in Chapter 16 on leveraged buyouts demonstrate that in going-private transactions, top management increased its percentage ownership of equity shares in the company by substantial percentages. This was an important element in the strong motivational influences that led to the well-documented performance improvement in the LBOs during the first part of the 1980s.

Other proposals for improved pay versus performance policies have been made in recent years:

1. Limit the base salaries of top executives.
2. Base bonus and stock option plans on stock appreciation.
3. Stock appreciation benchmarks should consider
   a. close competitors.
   b. a wider peer group.
   c. broader stock market indexes such as the Dow or the S&P 500.

4. Base stock options on a premium of 10% to 20% over the current market and do not reprice them if the shares of the firm fall below the original exercise prices.
5. Institute company loan programs that enable top executives to buy substantial amounts of the firm's stock so that subsequent stock price fluctuations substantially impact the wealth position of the top executives.
6. Pay directors mainly in stock of the corporation with minimum specified holding periods to heighten their sensitivity to firm performance.

Executive pay is still an unsettled issue. A major criticism is that executives were not properly controlled in their virtually self-awards of stock options. Frequently expressed views can be summarized as "The imperial chief executive set his own compensation and was lavish in awarding himself stock options." An example of the widespread criticism was a *Wall Street Journal* article (June 4, 2001, pp. C1, C17) entitled "Options Overdose: Use of Stock Options Spins Out of Control; Now a Backlash Brews." The article refers to academic studies describing the disadvantages of the excessive grants of stock options. In a similar vein, Michael Jensen was quoted in *The Economist* of November 16, 2002 (p. 60):

> The way in which executive pay was typically tied to share performance through options meant that, in the bubble, the carrots became what he calls "managerial heroin," encouraging a focus on short-term highs with destructive long-term consequences.

The *Economist* goes on to argue that the incentive of managers became perverse in seeking to encourage even more overvaluation, leading to being "less than honest with shareholders." One proposed solution is customized stock options granted by effective boards, indexed properly and exercisable only after a long period of time.

It is now widely agreed that option grants should be expensed immediately, reducing reported earnings. Alternative methods of valuing option grants have been proposed. The theoretical solution is complicated by various restrictions on the conditions and times under which the options can be exercised. A flexible proposal has been made by Mark Rubinstein (*Economist*, November 9, 2002, p.102). Options initially would be expensed on the grant date using a properly modified Black-Scholes model. In subsequent public accounting reports, these estimates could be adjusted. If the option is exercised, the actual value could be determined, at which time the company would take an extraordinary gain or loss to match to amounts previously recorded.

OUTSIDE CONTROL MECHANISMS

To this point we have discussed internal control mechanisms for effective corporate governance. We have discussed the role of the board of directors, ownership concentration, and executive compensation. We now turn to outside control mechanisms, which include stock price performance, institutional investors, proxy contests, and takeovers.

STOCK PRICES AND TOP MANAGEMENT CHANGES

Warner, Watts, and Wruck (1988) investigated the relationship between a firm's stock price performance and subsequent changes in its top management including the CEO, president, and chairman of the board. They also provided new evidence on mechanisms for replacing inefficient managers and encouraging managers to maximize shareholder wealth. The data set used by Warner et al. included top management changes for 269 NYSE and AMEX firms in the period 1963 to 1978.

Consistent with studies of CEO changes (Coughlan and Schmidt, 1985; Weisbach, 1988), Warner et al. found that poor stock price performance was likely to result in an increased rate of management turnover. They also documented evidence of several internal control mechanisms such as monitoring by large blockholders, competition from other managers, and discipline by the board.

A number of earlier studies found significant positive price effects of changes in top management. Some found insignificant price reactions. In a later study, Denis and Denis (1995) also found insignificant announcement period abnormal returns for all management changes. However, forced resignations are associated with a positive 1.5% significant period abnormal return. Normal retirements have insignificant effects. Interestingly, for the preannouncement period of −251 to −2 days, the forced resignations were associated with a −24% CAR. Normal retirements were associated with a −4% CAR but not statistically significant.

Denis and Denis also found that forced top management changes were preceded by significantly large operating performance declines and followed by significant improvements. Forced management changes were associated with significant downsizing measured by declines in employment, capital expenditures, and total assets. Denis and Denis observed that improvements did not result from effective board monitoring. Only 13% of their large sample (853) were forced changes. More than two thirds of the forced resignations were associated with blockholder pressure, financial distress, shareholder lawsuits, and takeover attempts. They found that 56% of the firms with a forced top executive change became the target of some corporate control activity, generally in the form of a block investment or some form of takeover. They concluded that internal control mechanisms were inadequate to do the job alone and required the pressure of external corporate control markets.

The Shleifer and Vishny (1997) survey did not develop the potential role of the stock market and security price movements in disciplining managers in the United States. Security price movements provide a scorecard for measuring management performance. The evidence is clear that bad scores on the stock market increase managerial turnover. The potential of higher scores also might stimulate superior performance, bringing rewards to all of the stakeholders. The companies with performance like General Electric, Cisco Systems, and Intel do not raise issues of corporate governance.

INSTITUTIONAL INVESTORS

Public pension funds have the ability and size to become significant factors in corporate governance, yet only a small fraction have involved themselves in these issues. One of the more active pension funds is the California Public Employees' Retirement System (CalPERS), which invests $68 billion in pension funds for nearly 1 million public employees in California. In March 1992, CalPERS publicly announced the names of 12 companies with which it had failed to negotiate the adoption of corporate reforms. CalPERS accused these poorly performing companies of excessive executive pay or failing to maintain independent boards of directors.

In October 1993, the world's largest pension plan with $125 billion in assets, TIAA-CREF (formerly known as the Teachers Insurance and Annuity Association–College Retirement Equities Fund), announced a "corporate governance" policy. Although Chairman John Biggs said he was unwilling to sacrifice more than 0.1 percentage point in the annual return to fight for better corporate governance practices, TIAA encouraged companies to have independent, diverse boards with a majority of independent directors, and to have directors held more accountable to shareholders (Scism, 1994, p.C1).

Carleton, Nelson, and Weisbach (1998) found similar results for TIAA-CREF. They described the negotiation process between financial institutions and target firms on governance issues. TIAA-CREF contacted 45 firms during the period 1992 to 1996. All the firms agreed to institute confidential voting. Most of the firms contacted added women or minorities to the board. Most of the firms that were asked to limit the use of blank-check preferred stock as an antitakeover defense complied.

Wahal (1996) studied the activities of nine activist pension funds, from 1987 to 1993, with assets totaling $424 billion at the end of 1994. He noted that these funds averaged about 1% of the market value of equity of 146 targeted firms. In dollar terms, the ownership ranged from $8 million to $86 million. Inactive institutions as a group own approximately 51% ($3 billion) of the firms targeted by activist pension funds. The average inactive institution owns 0.3% ($14 million) of targeted firms. Takeover-related proxy proposals covered poison pills, greenmail, and antitakeover provisions. Governance-related targeting involved golden parachutes, board composition, and compensation. The activist proposals shifted from takeover-related proxy proposals in the late 1980s to governance-related proposals in the 1990s.

Wahal's results showed approximately a zero average abnormal return for shareholder proposals and small positive abnormal returns for attempts to influence target firms by using shareholder proposals (nonproxy targeting). However, no evidence of significant long-term improvement was found in either stock price movements or accounting measures of performance in the post-targeting period.

Strickland, Wiles, and Zenner (1996) studied the United Shareholders Association (USA) from 1986 to 1993. The USA was founded in August 1986 by T. Boone Pickens as a not-for-profit organization for shareholder rights. It was disbanded on October 25, 1993, by a vote of the USA board of directors. USA developed a Target 50 list of firms on the basis of poor financial performance, executive compensation plans not tied to firm performances, and policies that limited shareholder input on governance issues. If the targeted firms did not respond, the USA, through its 65,000 or so members, sought to sponsor proxy proposals to change the governance structure.

Strickland, Wiles, and Zenner recognized that proxy proposals do not bind the firm's board of directors. To judge whether USA was effective, Strickland et al. documented that USA successfully negotiated corporate governance changes covering 53 proposals before inclusion in proxy statements. At the announcement of such negotiated agreements, target firms' shareholders receive a 0.9% abnormal return, representing a wealth increase of $1.3 billion ($30 million per firm). The association was most effective when the target firm was a poor performer with high institutional ownership.

Gillan and Starks (2000) analyzed shareholder proposals related to corporate governance as reported by the *Investor Responsibility Response Center (IRRC) Corporate Governance Bulletin*. They developed a data set of 2,042 shareholder proposals made at 452 companies between 1987 and 1994. Pension fund investment groups and investor associations accounted for one third of the proposals; individual investors and religious organizations submitted the other two thirds. Three individuals (the Gilbert Brothers, Evelyn Davis, and the Rossi family group) accounted for 42% of the total proposals—more than the 33% by institutional investors and investment groups. These three individual activists were referred to by the press as "gadfly" investors. The issues on which proposals were submitted were mainly related to repealing antitakeover devices. Cumulative and confidential voting issues were the subject of almost as many proposals. Board of director independence and executive compensation were the subject of a high percentage of proposals. For the 8 years studied, the mean percentage of votes in favor of shareholder proposals was 23.0 (median 21.1). Proposals submitted by individuals obtained less support, associated with a small significant impact on stock prices. Proposals by institutions had greater support but negative nonsignificant abnormal returns. On some issues, voting support was as high as 35%, which gave the activists some leverage in discussions with corporate management. Overall, the influence of shareholder activism was modest. However, the period covered was mainly one of a strong economy and rising stock prices.

MULTIPLE CONTROL MECHANISMS

Most of the studies reviewed up to now considered the influence of individual control mechanisms. The study by Agrawal and Knoeber (1996) considered seven mechanisms: insider shareholdings, outside representation on the board, debt policy, activity in the corporate control market, institutional shareholdings, shareholdings of large blockholders, and the managerial labor market. Their sample comprised the 400 largest firms for which they could obtain the data required to measure the seven mechanisms Firm performance is measured by Tobin's q. Measuring the influence of each separately, the first four control mechanisms are statistically related to firm performance. Considering all of the mechanisms together but not within a simultaneous equation system, the influence of insider shareholdings drops out. Finally, when the interdependence among the mechanisms is accounted for in a simultaneous system estimation, only the negative effect on firm performance of outsiders on the board remains. Agrawal and Knoeber concluded that the control mechanisms are chosen optimally except for the use of outsiders on boards. Most other studies found a positive benefit from the use of outside directors.

PROXY CONTESTS

Proxy contests represent another corporate control mechanism. Proxy contests are attempts by dissident groups of shareholders to obtain board representation. Even though technically most contests are unsuccessful to the extent that the dissident group fails to win a majority on the board of directors, proxy contests can and do have significant effects on target firm shareholder wealth regardless of outcome. Some have argued that a better measure of success is whether the dissident group gains at least two members on the board of directors.

> We want one person to propose a motion and a second person to second it. Then discussion of the motion will be in the minutes of the board meeting. In this way, we can monitor the majority group and record our views on important policy issues.

This quote summarizes the view we have encountered in our experience with proxy contests.

A major change occurred in October 1992, when the SEC adopted proxy reform rules. Under the old rule, any shareholder who wanted to communicate with more than 10 other shareholders was required to submit the comments for SEC approval prior to circulation. The new rules ease requirements for communications among shareholders not seeking control of the company.

Studies of proxy contests explain the shareholder wealth effects that take place in terms of the disciplinary value of proxy contests in the managerial labor market, the relationship between proxy contests and other forms of takeover activity, and the value of the vote, which takes on greater importance during a proxy contests. The study of Pound (1988) empirically identified the sources of inefficiency of the present system of proxy contests.

WEALTH EFFECTS—EARLY STUDIES

Dodd and Warner (1983) examined 96 proxy contests for board seats on NYSE- or AMEX-listed firms over the period 1962 to 1978. They considered several hypotheses to explain why target shareholder returns were positive and significant on average (6.2% over the period from 39 days before the contest announcement through the contest outcome) in spite of the fact that dissidents won a majority on the board in only one fifth of the cases studied.

First, even minority board representation allows the dissident group to have a positive impact on corporate policy leading to a permanent share price revaluation.

In cases where no board seats change hands, the fact of the challenge itself might cause incumbent management to implement changes in policy that benefit shareholders (Bradley, Desai, and Kim, 1983; the "kick-in-the-pants" hypothesis). Scenarios that hypothesize stock price declines when proxy contests fail were not supported. These hypotheses emphasize the direct costs (in terms of corporate resources) of defending against the dissident group and ignore the possibilities for increased efficiency that might be exposed during the course of the contest. Abnormal returns at the contest outcome announcement were, in fact, negative for contests in which the dissidents failed to win any seats at all; however, the negative return was only −1.4%, not large enough to offset earlier gains and not significant.

The mechanics of waging a proxy contest almost guarantee that there will be leakage of information about dissident activity well before the proxy contest announcement in the *Wall Street Journal*. This is confirmed by significant abnormal returns of 11.9% over the period starting 60 days before the announcement through the announcement itself. The returns are not attributle to merger activity, because the results are similar whether the dissident group included another firm or not; the sample did not exhibit unexpectedly higher earnings in the preannouncement period. Thus, the positive returns seem attributable to the changes that may be stimulated by the proxy contest itself.

A later study by DeAngelo and DeAngelo (1989) of 60 proxy contests from 1978 to 1985 corroborated many of Dodd and Warner's (1983) results. They found significant positive abnormal returns of 6.02% from 40 days before the contest through the outcome announcement and significant returns of 18.76% in the 40 days preceding any public indication of dissident activity. As in the earlier study, the gains (particularly those in the precontest period) were not dependent on contest outcome. Like Dodd and Warner, they found negative returns at the contest outcome when the dissidents failed to win any seats on the board. These negative returns were larger than in the Dodd and Warner study: −5.45% over the 2-day outcome announcement period. However, most of these negative returns resulted from the means by which the dissidents were defeated. When the incumbents prevailed in a shareholder vote, the negative return was only −1.73% and not significant; when the dissidents were defeated by other means, the return was a −7.19% (significant). The other means included the expenditure of corporate assets to buy off the dissidents, a white knight acquisition of the target, or court approval of the validity of the incumbent's defense in the face of which the dissidents withdrew. This result appeared to imply than when the incumbent management was securely entrenched or the probability of future control contest was reduced, the value of a vote or the expected takeover premium capitalized in the share price declined.

As in the prior study, the dissidents were successful in only about one third of the proxy contests. However, DeAngelo and DeAngelo (1989) went on to examine events in the target firm for 3 years after the contest. It was found that by the end of 3 years, fewer than 20% of the target firms remained as independent, publicly held corporations under the same management as before the contest. For example, in 20 of the 39 firms in which dissidents failed to win a majority, there were 38 resignations of the CEO, president, or chairman of the board over the next 3 years. These resignations were clearly linked to the proxy contest either explicitly in the financial press or by the fact that the vacancy was filled by a member of the dissident group. The 60-firm sample included 15 cases where sale on liquidation of the firm in the 3-year period following the contest was linked directly to the dissident activity.

In fact, DeAngelo and DeAngelo (1989) concluded that most of the gains to proxy contest activity are closely related to merger and acquisitions activity. The initial gains in the precontest period (approximately 20%) are attributed to the increased likelihood that the firm eventually will be sold at a premium at some time following the proxy contest. To support this conclusion, they divided their sample into two groups: those that were eventually sold or liquidated and those that were not. For the "sold" subsample, abnormal returns over the full period of dissident activity were significant 15.16%; for the "unsold" group, the gain was a less significant 2.90%. The fact that the initial run-up was similar for the two groups simply indicates that the market revises its opinion of the likelihood of a sale as more information becomes available. To the extent that proxy contests are indeed linked to takeover activity, the goal seems to be to get some representation on the board to persuade the rest of the board to sell or liquidate.

Sridharan and Reinganum (1995) sought to explain why tender offers occur in some cases and proxy contests take place in others. Their sample was composed of 79 hostile tender offers and 38 proxy contests. A proxy fight is more likely to take place when target firm performance is relatively poor, measured by return on assets and stock market returns. Managerial inefficiency leads to a proxy contest; failure to pursue new and profitable investment opportunities leads to a tender offer.

When shareholdings of management are high, they are more likely to be able to block a tender offer so dissidents will engage in a proxy contest. Sridharan and Reinganum found that tender offer targets tend to be less leveraged than firms experiencing proxy fights. The reason they give is that the lower the leverage is, the greater is the supply of shares available for purchase in a tender offer.

WEALTH EFFECTS—LATER STUDIES

Borstadt and Zwirlein (1992) sampled 142 NYSE and AMEX firms that were involved in proxy contests waged between July 1, 1962, and January 31, 1986. The sample was further divided into full-control and partial-control subsamples. The dissident success rate was 42% for the full-control subsample and 60% for the partial-control subsample. The turnover rate of top management after the proxy contest was higher than average. On average, shareholders realized a positive abnormal return of 11.1% (significant) during the proxy contest period, defined as 60 days prior to the announcement of the contest through the contest resolution announcement.

Ikenberry and Lakonishok (1993) tested the hypothesis that the proxy contest, in challenging the management's slate for the board of directors, represents a referendum on management's ability to operate the firm and can act as a disciplinary mechanism. Their sample of 97 election contests during the period 1968 to 1987 came from the *Weekly Bulletin* for NYSE and AMEX firms. Firms not followed by Compustat or cases where there was an earlier election contest within the 60 months prior were eliminated. For the period from month –60 to month –5 relative to the announcement of the contest, the CAR of proxy contest targets was –34.4% (significant). Compared with growth in operating income before depreciation, contest targets underperformed control firms by 39.3% (significant) over the 5-year period prior to the announcement of election contests. Thus, proxy contests appear to be stimulated by poor performance.

When the incumbent board members retained all their seats, the CAR was not significantly different from zero for the 5-year period following the contest. In cases where dissidents gained at least one board seat, the CAR from month +3 to +24 was –32.4% (significant). The negative returns over the same time period were more severe in cases where the dissidents gained control of the board, –48%(significant). When dissidents gained control of the board, Ikenberry and Lakonishok speculated that the negative stock price behavior might be explained by either overoptimistic expectations of improved performance or the dissidents' discovery that the company faced more serious problems than anticipated.

The Ikenberry and Lakonishok findings of abnormal negative returns are different from those of the earlier studies, which found predominantly positive returns associated with proxy contests. Mulherin and Poulsen (1998) reexamined the shareholder wealth implications in proxy contests. They used a sample of 270 proxy contests for board seats during the period 1979 to 1994. For the event study analysis, day 0 was the date of the contest initiation and day R was the contest resolution data. The event windows analyzed were the initiation period (–20, +5) the post initiation period (+6, R), the full contest period (–20, R), and the post contest period of 1 year following the contest resolution. For the full sample using continuous compounding, the CAR in the initiation period was a significant 8.04%; in the post initiation period, it was an insignificant –2.82%; in the full contest period it was a significant 5.35%; in the postcontest period it was a borderline significant –3.43%. Using simple compounding, the results followed the same patterns except that the postcontest CAR was not significant.

The results contradicted the substantial decline in the postcontest period reported by Ikenberry and Lakonishok (1993). Further analysis showed that performance measurements were sensitive to the survivorship bias arising from minimum data requirements. Ikenberry and Lakonishok's requirement that a firm be listed on Compustat in the period around the contest led to a downward bias in estimated wealth changes. This occurred because the Compustat requirement excluded a sizeable number of firms that were acquired in the period surrounding the proxy contest.

The full sample results suggested that shareholders benefited from proxy contests during the full-contest period. Mulherin and Poulsen next looked for the sources of the value created. Subsamples were analyzed according to whether the firm was a takeover target, whether dissidents attained seats, and whether the senior officers of the target firm were replaced.

There were 116 proxy contests accompanied by a takeover bid. The acquisition attempts were successful in 63 of these cases. Both at the contest initiation and in the post-initiation period, the CARs were positive and significant, resulting in an abnormal return of 20.1% for the full-contest period. In the year following the resolution of the contest, the CAR was 12.4%, borderline significant, the CAR for the full contest period was a negative and not significant return of –4.88%, followed by a further significant decline of –23.7% in the year following the contest resolution.

For the 154 contests not accompanied by a takeover bid, the full-contest period had a positive and significant CAR of 3.27%. In the year following the contest, the CAR was effectively zero. The subsample of 154 contests not accompanied by takeover was further analyzed for possible interactions between whether dissidents attained seats and whether the senior officer was replaced within 3 years of the contest. Of the 85 contests in which dissidents won seats, management was replaced in 68 cases. The contests in which management were replaced experienced an increase in shareholder wealth, a significant 9.56% for the full-contest period but an insignificant 2.55% return in the postcontest period. The remaining 17 firms that retained the incumbent management suffered a significant decline, −13.8% in the full-contest period and −18.5% in the postcontest period. In both cases, the CAR during the initiation period was positive and significant. Investors anticipated that contests in which dissidents won would be followed by management changes. However, if the expectation was not fulfilled, investors revised the firm value downward.

In the 69 cases in which dissidents did not win seats, 25 firms replaced their senior management and experienced an average CAR increase of 5.07% in the full-contest period, not significant, and a significant positive 31.3% in the postcontest period. This postcontest wealth gain was significantly greater than the decline in wealth of −12.7% for the 44 firms that did not replace their senior management. These results demonstrated that management turnover should be an integral part of the interpretation of the changes in shareholders' wealth in the postcontest period. Ikenberry and Lakonishok reported a wealth decline whether dissidents attained seats or not, but they failed to observe that wealth changes following proxy contests were positive when there was management turnover.

THE M&A MARKET FOR CONTROL

In one sense, proxy contests, discussed in the preceding section, represent a form of external control if the dissidents are from outside the company, which is usually the case. The most widely recognized form of external pressure is the market for corporate control. Several empirical measures demonstrate the M&As do indeed impact business firms. One good metric is provided by Mitchell and Mulherin (1996). They analyzed the 1,064 firms listed in the *Value Line Investment Survey* at year-end 1981. By 1989, 57% of these firms either had been a takeover target or had engaged in substantial defensive asset restructuring. That more than half of the universe of firms with a relatively wide investment following were subjected to the pressures of the M&A market is a measure only of the direct impacts. Surely a high percentage of the remaining 43% had to be aware that poor performance would subject them to a possible takeover. Also, superior performance might enable such firms to augment their resources by taking over firms when performance could be improved.

Furthermore, the proprietary database of Robert Comment with information about all M&As for NYSE and AMEX listed target firms from 1975 to 1991 covered 1,814 companies, a substantial number (Schwert, 1996). The total number of M&A announcements tracked by the annual *Mergerstat Review* was 3,510 in 1995, jumping to 9,278 in 1999. Another metric is MBO activity, which represented 11.4% of the main sample of 1,523 firms in the Schwert study.

Thus, the M&A market is clearly a major source of external control mechanisms on business firms. However, the need to resort to the M&A market is an indication of at least some degree of failure in internal control mechanisms.

ALTERNATIVE GOVERNANCE SYSTEMS

A number of studies provide background for assessment of alternative governance systems (Kaplan, 1994; *The Economist,* 1994; Shleifer and Vishny, 1997; Franks and Mayer, 1998, 2001; Bruner, 1999). In the United States, managerial stock ownership has increased over time (Holderness, Kroszner, and Sheehan, 1999). Both large shareholders and small are protected by a well-developed system of laws, court decisions, and financial markets that facilitate efficient transactions in securities, protect minority rights, and enable shareholders to sue directors for violations of their fiduciary responsibilities. Companies are quickly penalized for poor performance and rewarded for excellence in stock market price changes. Although a vigilant stock market facilitates control, it also can have the disadvantage of causing managers to emphasize short-term results rather than longer-term strategies. The bankruptcy laws in the United States are highly protective of managers. After entering into bankruptcy, management (the debtor) remains in possession of the company (debtor in possession, or DIP). Provision is made for an automatic stay, which provides that no payment of interest or payment on principal need be made until the reorganization is complete. Interest continues to accrue only on fully secured debt. Financing after filing is facilitated, because it has priority status(DIP financing).

Shleifer and Vishny (1997) observed that in Germany, creditors have stronger rights than in the United States, but shareholder rights are weaker. Large shareholders, often the major banks, exercise control over the large firms as permanent investors. Shleifer and Vishny observed that small investors had virtually no participation in the stock market (p. 770).

Franks and Mayer (2001) provided a detailed analysis of ownership and control of German corporations. Germany has fewer than 800 quoted companies in contrast to about 3,000 in the United Kingdom. In Germany, 85% of the largest quoted companies have concentrated ownership; one shareholder (primarily families or other companies) owns more than 25% of the voting share. Company ownership often takes the form of pyramids of intercorporate holdings. When shareholdings are dispersed, bank influence and control is strong.

Franks and Mayer found virtually no market for corporate control in Germany as in the United States and the United Kingdom. They observed an active market in large ownership shares. In these block transactions, the premiums are much lower than those received by takeover targets in the United States and the United Kingdom. The sellers of large blocks of shares receive all of the gains with no benefits for minority holders. This is consistent with the Shleifer and Vishny findings of little participation by small investors in the German stock market. Franks and Mayer observed little relation between concentration of ownership and the effective discipline of the management of underperforming firms.

Japan is described as falling between the United States and Germany in the degree of protection to shareholders and regarding creditor rights. Shleifer and Vishny observed that the powerful banks and long-term shareholders in Japan are not as powerful as those in Germany. Anecdotal evidence questions this conclusion. Japanese companies financed in the United States during the earlier periods of time when Japan was supposed to have lower financing costs than in the rest of the world. The reasons given were that the Japanese firms were seeking to avoid the strong controls that came with financing from Japanese banks. In Japan, industrial firms own shares in one another, and groups of firms become tied together by cross share holdings (Kaplan, 1994). The Japanese governance system has facilitated participation in the stock market by small investors.

The three countries just described have in common a well-articulated set of rules of the game that provide effective legal protection for "at least some types of investors" (Shleifer and

Vishny, p. 770). Studies of Italy indicate that firms are predominantly family controlled, have difficulty raising outside funds, and finance their investment internally. Most bank financing is state bank financing of state-controlled firms.

Limited evidence suggests that most of the rest of the world is similar to Italy. At least in part this would reflect the absence of a system of laws, regulations, and courts to protect minority investors and creditors. The rules of the game are deficient. Large firms are mostly family controlled, rely on internal financing, or obtain help from government-controlled banks.

Clearly, the United States, Germany, and Japan benefit from having well-formulated rules of the game that are enforced by the courts and regulatory agencies. However, Germany and Japan differ in giving banks and financial groups a stronger role. In theory, the large ownership position of owners-lenders with business expertise and high financial stakes will lead to effective monitoring of business performance. In a survey of corporate governance, *The Economist* (January 29, 1994) presented material that raised doubts about the effectiveness of the German and Japanese corporate governance models. The articles cited studies that indicate that the banks have not monitored closely the firms to which they have provided equity and debt capital. These studies suggest that the banks became active only when their client firms experienced substantial difficulties.

The Economist also argued that German and Japanese governance appeared to be good only because the earlier economic environment was so favorable. With growing economies, favorable productivity improvements, high employment, and rising exports, stock prices were moving continuously upward. In favorable economies, commitments could be made to provide employees with lifetime employment. Cross holdings of common stocks led to an increase in trust among partners. The system works well if all parties have the same long-term interests and goals.

The Economist, in completing its survey of corporate governance, concluded that the increased activism of pension funds in the United States helped make that system work better. An active market for corporate control in the form of mergers and takeovers provide a marketplace test of performance. The strength of the American and British systems of shareholder control is that they are ultimately market based. In the long run, this is held to be superior to the direct supervision and judgments of the large banking corporation, which have their own governance problems. These conclusions of *The Economist* are weakened by the emergence of egregious examples of corporate misconduct resulting in the enactment of new legislation and the issuance of new listing stock exchange regulations.

Summary

Because a substantial body of literature is available on corporate governance, this summary provides a logical framework for the subject. Traditionally, corporate governance focused on conflicts of interest between managers and owners. It is increasingly recognized that conflicts of interest occur across a wide range of stakeholders: owners with a small number of shares, owners with large ownership positions, creditors, managers, employees, consumers, government, and society as a whole. Most of the literature discusses problems of the separation of ownership and control. Historically, in the United States, the main form of corporate ownership was small ownership stakes diffused among a large number of individual investors. The advantages were limited liability, broad diversification of investments, small monitoring requirements, and easy purchase or sale of ownership rights. But increasingly, several forms of agency problems became recognized. Managements may act in their own self-interest.

Compensation arrangements and competition among managers provide internal control mechanisms. In addition, poor stock price performance is likely to cause changes in management. In theory, the board of directors monitors management. In practice, boards tend to be dominated by management insiders. The use of outside directors provides for greater independence but does not solve the problem of effective monitoring of managers. The increased activism of large institutional holders of equity such as pension funds has demonstrated increased effectiveness in monitoring corporate managers and their performance.

Increased stock ownership by management has been proposed as a method of reducing conflicts of interest between owners and managers. Some studies suggest that performance improves with rising management ownership share in the 0 to 5% range, deteriorates in the 5% or 25% range, and improves above 25%. Large block purchases have had positive event returns. When the shareholdings of a group are large, monitoring is increased. In addition, large blockholders are more likely to monitor management.

The holding of voting stock that achieves control of the firm commands a price premium. Because control is valued by the capital markets, dual-class recapitalizations are employed by majority owners to further consolidate their control position. Larger managerial holdings can have incentive effects. The voting rights premium also may result from the possibility that in a takeover, superior voting rights will receive a higher price.

Proxy contests represent another method of improving managerial performance. In most studies, the initiation of proxy contests is associated with substantial positive event returns. The challenge of a proxy contest might be sufficient to cause incumbent management to improve policies. Minority board representation enables dissidents to have a continuing impact. A strong link has been found between proxy contests and subsequent takeover activity. The positive event returns associated with proxy contests reflect the increased likelihood of improved performance or the eventual sale of the firm at a premium. Mergers and acquisitions represent an important external control mechanism.

Executive compensation plans have been suggested as another mechanism for influencing managerial performances. The elasticity of management compensation in relation to changes in the value of the firm is apparently small. However, the elasticity of wealth changes of managers to changes in the value of the firm may be substantial. The increased ownership share of managers and LBOs in the early 1980s demonstrated strong motivational influences. Proposals have been made to improve the influence of executive pay on corporate performance. One is to base bonus, stock, and option plans on benchmarked stock price changes. The benchmarks can be based on the stock price performance of close competitors, wider peer groups, broader stock market indexes, or other criteria. Another proposal is to adopt policies that result in substantial stock holdings by executives so that they think more like owners. Also, the bonus and stock ownership arrangements with executives should cause their wealth positions to increase with good performance and to deteriorate with poor performance. These arrangements should be benchmarked appropriately and related to the long-range planning processes of the firm.

Finally, it has been proposed that the alternative governance systems of Germany and Japan provide a better model for improving corporate governance. In these alternative governance systems, commercial banks hold large ownership shares in industrial firms and are major lenders, as well. Also, groups of firms become tied together by cross shareholdings. However, some observers state that the alternative governance systems worked well when the general macroeconomic framework was favorable. With reduced economic growth, tensions and conflicts of interest also have arisen in the German and Japanese governance systems. Furthermore, even under favorable macroeconomic conditions, the system had strains. Monitoring by the large banking corporations with their own governance problems often was not effective.

The strength of the U.S. system of corporate governance was argued to be that it was ultimately market based. If so, market failure occurred. The corporate fraud and executive self-dealing caused such widespread complaints and pressures that new legislation and changes in NYSE listing requirements resulted. The Sarbanes-Oxley Act of 2002 covers 11 areas. It establishes the Public Company Accounting Oversight Board (PCAOB) and outlines new requirements for auditors' independence. It requires CEO and CFO certification of financial reports and prohibits pro forma financial statements that may be untrue or misleading. Off-balance sheet transactions must be disclosed. Insider trading must be reported within 2 days, and personal loans to officers and directors are prohibited. Standards for professional conduct of attorneys who practice before the SEC will be established. All auditor work papers shall be maintained for 5 years, and destruction of records is criminal fraud. Protections for whistle-blowers are strengthened. Falsification of financial reports shall result in fines up to $5 million and/or imprisonment up to 20 years. The statute of limitation for securities fraud is extended. This litany of prohibitions and penalties is a mirror of the wrongdoing by corporations and its officers. The failures of corporate governance in U.S. corporations have brought on a substantial increase in government intervention.

Cautionary admonitions also have been expressed. Nobel prize winner Gary S. Becker argued that the corporate scandals demonstrate the underlying strength of the U.S. economy. He expressed concern that overly aggressive implementation of the new legislation could weaken risk taking by CEOs and reduce innovation and efficiency. J. L. Jordan, the president of the Federal Reserve Bank of Cleveland, in its *Economic Commentary* of January 1, 2003, expressed similar concerns. He observed that sound principles of good corporate management are difficult to formulate. He also stated that government interference in markets is often wrong, retarding the natural processes of the marketplace. The operation of market forces improves a wide range of activities "from products and prices to accounting practices and corporate management practices." Corruption in a relatively small fraction of the some 16,300 publicly owned companies in the United States might result in overregulation, reducing the flexibility, productivity, and relative performance of the economy.

Questions

20.1 What was the role of enterprise governance in the history of the Russian economy?

20.2 What complaints have been made about corporate governance systems in the United States?

20.3 What are the effects of the size of the fraction of equity share ownership by top management on:
   a. q-ratio?
   b. Agency problems?
   c. Probability of a hostile bid?
   d. Level of premium required for a takeover bid to succeed?

20.4 List four of the *BusinessWeek* criteria for evaluating effective governance by boards of directors.

20.5 What were the findings by Millstein and MacAvoy?

20.6 Discuss the issue of the elasticity of executive pay in relation to changes in firm value versus the impact of incentive executive compensation on the wealth position of executives.

20.7 What is the potential role of the stock market and security price movements in corporate governance?

20.8 Evaluate the potential of activist pension funds for improving corporate governance.

20.9 What effect do proxy contests have on shareholder returns?

20.10 Compare the United States, Germany, and Japan with respect to protection of shareholder rights and creditor rights.

20.11 What criticisms have been made of corporate governance in Germany?

20.12 The *Economist* of November 16, 2002, quoted Michael Jensen as saying that the Sarbanes-Oxley Act increases government monitoring by putting new demands on corporate boards and on how contracts with managers are structured, increasing costs sharply. Other commentators have pointed out that despite reforms in new regulations, business executives still will find ways to deceive and defraud other stakeholders. Discuss these two views.

Case 20.1   CHRYSLER CORPORATION VERSUS TRACINDA CORPORATION—A STRUGGLE FOR CONTROL

The control struggle between Kirk Kerkorian and the Chrysler Corporation continued over the period from early April 1995 until early February 1996, when a compromise agreement was reached. The battles and skirmishes reflected a number of twists and turns in strategies that involved many episodes. The following is a time line of events:

4/11/95	Robert Eaton, chairman of Chrysler, received a phone call from Kirk Kerkorian saying that he and former Chrysler Chairman Lee Iacocca were planning a takeover bid of $55 per share, totaling $22.8 billion. The stock reaction was a 24% increase, closing at $48.75 on the announcement date, April 13, 1995. Kerkorian charged that Chrysler was too conservative in holding cash reserves of $7.5 billion.
4/24/95	Chrysler formally rejected the Kerkorian bid, saying it did not want to gamble with Chrysler's future.
5/31/95	Kerkorian withdrew his bid due to lack of financing but stated that he would continue his efforts to help Chrysler management improve the value of its common stock. Kerkorian hired the investment banking firm Wasserstein

Perella & Company to develop a full range of possible options.

6/26/95	Kerkorian announced his intention to buy 14 million Chrysler shares at $50 each to raise his stake to 13.6%.
7/1/95	Chrysler's board adopted golden parachutes for its 30 highest-ranking officers.
7/15/95	Chrysler moved to prevent Iacocca from exercising Chrysler stock options because he had violated the prohibition from taking actions "which adversely affect the Chrysler Corporation."
8/25/95	Kerkorian achieved his goal of increasing his ownership of Chrysler to 13.6%.
9/5/95	Kerkorian announced that he had hired Jerome York, the CFO of IBM and before that the treasurer of Chrysler, to be his main strategist.
9/7/95	Chrysler's board announced that it would double its share repurchase program to $2 billion.
9/10/95	York stated that Tracinda Corporation was considering a proxy fight. He criticized Chrysler's management for holding too much cash, stating that $4.5 billion would be an ample reserve rather

	than $7.5 billion. He also stated that $2.5 billion of Chrysler assets were "non-core."
9/20/95	Tracinda hired Ralph Whitworth, widely regarded as an expert on corporate governance and an influential shareholder activist.
10/1/95	Chrysler began a publicity campaign against York's criticisms and called attention to Chrysler's earnings and product successes.
10/25/95	York met with Chrysler's CFO and general counsel, requesting a seat on the board for himself and the addition of two independent members.
11/6/95	Iacocca filed a suit over his Chrysler stock options. Tracinda agreed to cover up to $2 million of his legal fees and make up the difference between $42 million and his award.
11/20/95	Tracinda announced that it would file preliminary proxy-soliciting materials with the SEC including a proposal to replace board member Joseph Antonini with Jerome York.
11/23/95	Antonini announced that he would resign from the Chrysler board.
12/7/95	Chrysler announced a 20% dividend increase, its fifth dividend increase in 2 years.
1/19/96	Chrysler announced strong fourth-quarter earnings.
2/7/96	Chrysler announced that it would recommend for membership on its board John R. Neff, a respected asset manager who retired in the previous year as manager of the $4.5 billion Windsor Fund.
2/8/96	The two sides agreed to a 5-year truce in the form of a 5-year standstill agreement. Kerkorian would reserve a board seat to be occupied by James Aljian, a Tracinda executive, in return for agreeing not to launch a proxy fight or to increase his shareholdings during the 5-year period. Within 30 days, Kerkorian also would terminate his arrangement with Wasserstein Perella, with Ralph Whitworth, and with D. F. King & Company, a proxy-soliciting firm. Chrysler would add another $1 billion to its share repurchase program and would continue its efforts to sell its nonautomotive units. Chrysler would increase the accountability of its board by switching from cash to stock compensation. In exchange for Iacocca's agreement to terminate his position as consultant to Tracinda and to refrain from publicly criticizing Chrysler for the 5-year period, Iacocca's stock option lawsuits would be settled; Chrysler would pay Iacocca $21 million, and Tracinda would contribute $32 million
5/17/96	Chrysler announced a dividend increase of 17% and a 2-for-1 stock split. The stock closed up $2.25 to $67.125, compared with its price in the low 40s in May 1995, about 1 year earlier.

QUESTION

C20.1.1 What are the lessons from the Kerkorian-Chrysler case?

Case 20.2   WORLDCOM

In early 2002, WorldCom joined the growing list of American companies that had committed accounting fraud. WorldCom's troubles were the end of a period that saw the company grow from a small Mississippi startup reselling long distance to one of the highfliers of the bull market of the 1990s, and ultimately becoming a symbol of corporate excesses. The headlines focused on securities fraud, but the WorldCom story is fundamentally the tale of a company operating in an industry that was experiencing overcapacity with demand lower than anticipated.

WorldCom originated in Mississippi as a small firm looking to resell long-distance telecom services. In 1983, with the breakup of AT&T set to be implemented in the near future, opportunities were emerging in the telecom market. Four investors, including Bernard Ebbers, decided to take advantage of this new market opportunity. In September 1983, they bought LDDS (Long Distance Discount Service). The company's first line of business was reselling AT&T long-distance services to small and mid-sized businesses. LDDS eventually became WorldCom and grew through acquisitions to become the second-largest telecom firm in the United States. The following time line chronicles some of the major events in the history of the company.

Year	Events
1985	Bernard Ebbers became president of LDDS.
1988–1992	LDDS's acquisition program expanded its scale and geographic coverage to the point that the firm became the fourth-largest telecom firm in the United States.
1993	In a $1.2 billion, three-way transaction, LDDS acquired Resurgens Communications and Metromedia Communications.
1994	LDDS acquired WilTel Network Service for $2.5 billion, gaining its large fiber-optic and wireless network.
1995	LDDS changed its name to WorldCom and entered the Fortune 500.
1996	WorldCom entered, the S&P 500 and acquired MFS Communications (local telephone and UUNET Internet services) for $12.4 billion.
1997	WorldCom outbid British Telecom and GTE to purchase MCI for $36 billion, becoming the second-largest U.S. telecom firm.
1999	WorldCom reached an agreement to purchase Sprint for $115 billion, a deal that gave the firm scale comparable to AT&T; the deal did not receive regulatory approval.

In early 2000, the stock market began to fall, and with it went WorldCom's stock price. The telecom industry as a whole was recognized for its overcapacity and failure to bring in returns on the massive capital investments of the 1990s. Long-distance prices continued to fall, and Internet bandwidth demand was lower than expected. As a result, WorldCom found itself forced to begin revising its earnings forecasts downward. However, the firm was unable to make even these lower numbers. To make its performance meet earnings forecasts, top executives began to shuffle accounting entries. At least $9 billion of expenses were booked improperly as capital expenditures. These dishonest maneuvers did not come to light until mid-2002.

In April 2002, Ebbers resigned from his CEO post under the pressure of the board of directors. His successor, John Sidgmore, launched an internal audit of WorldCom's books. In June 2002, WorldCom revealed that it had uncovered $3.8 billion of improper accounting. The revelation made the firm's high level of debt all the more critical and technically forced the company into default on some of its outstanding bonds. After unsuccessfully trying to negotiate a deal with lenders, WorldCom filed for bankruptcy in July 2002. Bankruptcy discussions were complicated by the discovery of further accounting irregularities. By the end of 2002, WorldCom had admitted that it misstated its financial position by at least $9 billion. In December 2002, Sidgmore was replaced by Michael Capellas, a former Compaq and HP executive. The new leader of WorldCom was left with the task of settling not only WorldCom's bankruptcy, but also ongoing negotiations with the SEC regarding the firm's accounting fraud.

WHY WORLDCOM FAILED

WorldCom has become symbolic of the rise and fall of the so-called New Economy. The firm was able to build itself from a small, failing long-distance reseller to a darling of Wall Street through a long series of acquisitions. However, due to managerial errors, industry overcapacity, and outright illegal actions, the company descended into Chapter 11 bankruptcy. Following are five major factors that contributed to WorldCom's spectacular downfall.

Adverse Industry Conditions

In the booming years of the 1990s, the rising use of the Internet led forecasts for required telecom capacity to become overly optimistic. Analysts and telecom executives anticipated that a massive growth in capacity would be necessary to serve the growing need for bandwidth. Although some growth was needed, the telecom system became overbuilt, far outpacing demand.

Compounding the unprofitability of WorldCom's Internet strategy was the faster-than-anticipated decline in long distance. Like AT&T, WorldCom did not anticipate how quickly revenues would fall. During 2001 and 2002, WorldCom began slashing some prices to business customers in half in the hopes of retaining them (also with the hope of dishonestly booking the deals twice, making them appear to be at the same price).

Poor Execution of Merger Integration

In retrospect, it is clear that postmerger integration by WorldCom was ineffective. It had a patchwork array of CLECs (competitive local exchange carriers), many in the same local markets with redundant services. Following the MCI acquisition, the difficulties within the firm were magnified. Many WorldCom executives were promoted to oversee former MCI properties, creating disillusion. A decision was made to shut down MCI's 3 national system maintenance centers and replace them with 12 more-cumbersome centers. Also, for years following the merger, the company was running at least 2 billing programs, making it difficult to track receivables. As a result, estimates are that by June 2000, collection of receivables had increased to 77 days from 63 days for collection in 1999.

Unscrupulous Accounting Practices

With pressure from Wall Street to make earnings numbers and show a profit to keep the stock price moving upward, WorldCom executives began to cook the books. The most blatant examples were revealed in 2002 when it came to light that the company had been booking regular expenses as capital expenditures. By December, it was evident that the firm had misstatements in excess of $9 billion. These misstatements likely accounted for most, if not all, of the company's profits from 1999 to 2002. They had the effect of keeping the stock price inflated, allowing the firm to first near a deal with Sprint and later appear to be meeting its forecasted earnings numbers.

Furthermore, the argument has been made that WorldCom pushed the limits of accounting for most of its mergers, perhaps also crossing the border of legality. With the benefit of hindsight, some analysts have characterized the firm as a house of cards created by playing games with merger accounting. Beginning with its acquisitions in the early 1990s, insiders have claimed that WorldCom would overstate its write-downs of assets relating to the merger. As a result, it was able to build in reserves to help it show future profits at the expense of the quarter following an acquisition. This characterization of WorldCom suggests that it needed to continue to make larger and larger acquisitions to camouflage the true health of the firm.

Relaxed Regulatory Environment

Making the WorldCom accounting deceptions easier was the relaxed regulatory environment that was exposed by the scandal. WorldCom's auditors never challenged the illegal accounting, which had dated back as far as 1999 (if not before). In addition, Wall Street analysts did not manage to detect any dishonesty among WorldCom management. The combination of the WorldCom and Enron collapses helped spur the U.S. congress to pass corporate reform laws as a future deterrent for such flagrant disregard for shareholders and securities law.

Poor Top Management

Ultimately, when so many problems emerge in a company, a large degree of blame must rest on top management. When WorldCom was the darling of Wall Street, Ebbers was embraced by the press as an outsider who had come in and taken the telecom world by storm. He was seen as a shrewd acquirer who had built an empire through acquisitions. Ebbers ultimately faced a decision of admitting he was complicit in WorldCom's accounting fraud, or admitting that he was a poor enough manager that he did not know it occurred. Under Ebbers, it is likely the upper management of WorldCom placed too much focus on making the next acquisition rather than on integrating what it had already acquired.

QUESTIONS

C20.2.1 What are the advantages and disadvantages of an aggressive merger policy like that at WorldCom?

C20.2.2 What motivations could explain the fraudulent account of WorldCom?

Case 20.3   AOL TIME WARNER

During the late 1990s, when the Internet firms were at their height, their market capitalization was such that it became feasible to acquire "brick and mortar" rivals. It was in this climate that AOL acquired Time Warner. AOL and other Internet service providers (ISPs) were believed to be a new channel for the delivery of entertainment content, which would be provided by Time Warner and other entertainment firms. Beginning in 2000, the stock prices of Internet firms were pummeled as hundreds of "dot-coms" went out of business. During this time period, AOL undertook many strategies to make the firm look more attractive, thereby allowing the merger to be executed. By 2002, some analysts were calling the AOL Time Warner merger a terrible mistake by Time Warner.

AOL

AOL built its large user base by attracting certain types of consumers. AOL's main target was the PC owner who had little knowledge of the Internet. AOL mailed millions of CDs with its easy to install and operate software. Unlike most other ISPs, AOL aimed to make the Internet simple and easy for its customers to access. AOL was more expensive than many of its dial-up ISP competitors, but it justified the price with its customer service, reliability (after some difficulties in the mid-1990s when the company allowed unlimited hourly access to users and overloaded its systems), and proprietary software like "chat rooms." By using the strategy of bringing in new users, AOL managed to build its user base to approximately 27 million users by mid-2002.

AOL also managed to use its captive users to make many lucrative deals with advertisers and retailers. No other ISP offered access to as many users as AOL. Because it was the largest ISP, AOL was able to negotiate favorable deals. For many dot-com companies, a deal with AOL gave fledgling companies instant credibility on the stock market. AOL capitalized and accepted large amounts of cash and/or stock from the firms.

However, by the time AOL announced its deal to acquire Time Warner, many analysts were pointing out the flaws of the AOL model. First, by building its base primarily of new Internet users, AOL's potential pool of new customers would decline as a higher percentage of the general population became connected to the Internet. The trend had been that AOL customers would leave as they became more Internet savvy. The second major flaw of the AOL model was its weakness in the broadband arena. By mid-2002, AOL had managed to capture fewer than 500,000 subscribers to its services through broadband connections.

TIME WARNER

Prior to its combinations with AOL, Time Warner was one of the largest firms in the entertainment industry. The firm had a large combination of holdings. Time, Incorporated was the flagship of the firm's large portfolio of publishing properties, which included approximately 25% of the advertising revenue among U.S. magazines. In addition, Time Warner's Warner Music Group was a leader in the music industry. Time Warner also was involved in cinema through its ownership of movie production companies. Time Warner's television holdings included the WB network and several cable channels, including HBO. However, some of these holdings were complicated by their partial ownership by Time Warner Entertainment (TWE), a complex entity that was partially owned by several cable companies. With such a large portfolio of entertainment properties, Time Warner was seen as a key controller of "content" in the industry.

THE MERGER

AOL and Time Warner announced their intention to merge on January 10, 2000. Many analysts were optimistic that the combination would prove to be an effective match between content, provided by Time Warner, and the new form of distribution represented by the Internet, provided by AOL. The basic financial relationships of the deal are summarized in Table C20.3.1. The merger terms specified that Time Warner shareholders would receive 1.5 AOL shares per Time Warner share. The market reacted negatively to the announcement. AOL stock declined

TABLE C20.3.1 AOL Time Warner Merger Terms

	AOL	TWX	Combined
Premerger			
Market price 1/7/00	$74	$65	
Number of shares (in billions)	2.460	1.287	
Market cap (in billions)	$182.0	$83.7	$265.7
Shares of market cap	68.5%	31.5%	100.0%
Postmerger			
Number of shares (in billions)	2.460	1.930	4.390
Percent ownership	56.0%	44.0%	100.0%
Total paid by AOL (in billions)		$142.8	
Premium paid		70.7%	

greatly following the announcement of the deal. The losses of the combined shareholders for the period of 20 days before and 30 days after the announcement were about $8 billion, with AOL shareholders' $38.7 billion of losses offset by Time Warner shareholders' $30.7 billion of gains.

AOL TIME WARNER'S DIFFICULTIES

By mid-2002, the combined AOL Time Warner had lost more than 80% of its value. AOL shares had been valued at more than $70 before the merger was announced, but by the summer of 2002, the price had fallen to approximately $10. Numerous factors were cited to explain this dramatic decline.

Economic/Advertising Recession

Beginning in 2000, the U.S. economy entered a downturn. The stock market began to fall significantly, drastically tightening the money that was available for Internet firms in the capital markets. Toward the end of the year, many of the dot-com firms were failing. These firms had spent heavily on advertising, particularly online. This downturn had serious effects for AOL's business model, which relied largely on advertising for profitability. In addition, the overall effectiveness of online advertising came into question. Advertisers became more discriminating and began to track carefully the number of sales that resulted from online advertising. The combined AOL Time Warner was officially formed in January 2001, and coincidentally, that was also the first year since the early 1990s that overall advertising revenues declined. As a result, the AOL Time Warner media juggernaut was suddenly operating in a poor advertising market.

The Overvaluation of AOL

Another possible explanation for the dramatic decline in value of AOL Time Warner is that AOL was overvalued by the market. This is supported by the dramatic decline in all of the Internet stocks. In January 2000, when the merger was announced, AOL was valued at $180 billion by the market. By the middle of 2002, most analysts were looking at AOL Time Warner with the caveat "even if the AOL division is valued at $0." With such a large change of value in 2 1/2 years, there seems to be credence for the argument that AOL was propelled by a "bubble," "irrational exuberance," or some other explanation for the market simply misvaluing a firm.

Differences in Corporate Culture

To make the complicated task of merging two different firms even more difficult, the management teams of the two firms did not get along well. The AOL managers came from a relatively free-wheeling environment. Time Warner's people were used to a more traditional and bureaucratic environment.

The most visible acknowledgement of the cultural difficulties within the firm was the pressured resignation of Robert Pittman in July 2002. Pittman was seen as a good liaison between the firms. He had worked for Time Warner before moving to AOL. Pittman was placed in charge of integrating the two firms, and later he was moved to the chief operating officer post of the combined company. The two stories that emerged when Pittman left were: (1) he had done a poor job of delivering synergies and earnings that were expected; (2) he was simply a scapegoat and the company was too troubled to be able to deliver on any of its earnings targets.

Ultimately, the dramatic decline in AOL's value gave former Time Warner employees the justification to take full control of the upper management of the combined firm. As AOL began to be investigated for its accounting practices, a former Time Warner executive was even put in charge of the AOL unit.

SEC Investigations into AOL Accounting Practices

In 2002, fraudulent accounting began to emerge in several large firms. In the wake of the collapse of firms such as WorldCom and Enron, investors began to become more vigilant about accounting practices. As the SEC commenced an investigation into AOL's accounting, it was revealed that AOL had improperly accounted for $49 million of revenues, some of which involved dealings with WorldCom. Although this total was relatively small, investors were wary that more improprieties would be discovered. Skepticism continued after AOL Time Warner's CEO and CFO waited until the SEC-imposed deadline to personally guarantee the firm's financial statements.

Potentially even worse for AOL, a *Washington Post* article detailed numerous incidents of question-able accounting decisions. The article alleged that certain executives of AOL had bent accounting rules to keep the stock price of AOL up during the year between the announcement of the merger with Time Warner and the time the firms actually combined. The anecdotes included stories of advertisements being run repeatedly right before the end of the fiscal quarter to allow booking as revenue, questionable barter deals with Internet firms that were booked improperly, and other bending of the rules. This article was another reason the SEC began its investigation of the firm.

QUESTIONS

C20.3.1 Was the AOL/Time Warner merger beneficial to AOL and/or Time Warner shareholders?

C20.3.2 In the summer of 2002, there was discussion that AOL Time Warner should essentially reverse the merger and spin off, sell, or otherwise remove the AOL unit. Do you agree of disagree with this idea?

References

Agrawal, Anup, and Charles R. Knoeber, "Firm Performance and Mechanisms to Control Agency Problems Between Managers and Shareholders," *Journal of Financial and Quantitative Analysis* 31, September 1990, pp. 377–397.

Agrawal, Anup, Jeffrey F. Jaffe, and Jonathan M. Karpoff, "Management Turnover and Governance Changes Following the Revelation of Fraud," *Journal of Law and Economics* 42, April 1999, pp. 309–342.

Alchian, A. A., "Property Rights, Specialization and the Firm," Chapter 1 in *Corporate Enterprise in a New Environment*, J. Fred Weston and Michael E. Cranfield (eds.), New York: KCG Production, Inc., 1982, pp. 11–36.

———, and S. Woodward, "The Firm Is Dead: Long Live the Firm: A Review of Oliver E. Williamson's *The Economic Institutions of Capitalism,*" *Journal of Economic Literature* 20, March 1988, pp. 65–79.

Amihud, Yakov, B. Lev, and N. G. Travlos, "Corporate Control and the Choice of Investment Financing," *Journal of Finance* 45, June 1990, pp. 603–616.

"AOL's Merger Accounting Could Lead to Problems, Too," *Wall Street Journal,* August 2, 2002, p. C1.

"AOL Time Warner: Down But Not Out," JP Morgan, analyst report, July 10, 2002.

"AOL Time Warner: TW's Results Dwarfed by AOL'S Ills," First Albany analyst report, August 5, 2002.

Bagnani, Elizabeth Strock, Nikolaos T. Milonas, Anthony Saunders, and Nickolaos G. Travlos, "Managers, Owners, and the Pricing of Risky Debt: An Empirical Analysis," *Journal of Finance* 40, June 1994, pp. 453–477.

Barclay, Michael J., and C. G. Holderness, "Negotiated Block Trades and Corporate Control," *Journal of Finance* 46, July 1991, pp. 861–878.

Becht, Marco, Patrick Bolton, and Alisa Röell, "Corporate Governance and Control," NBER working paper 9371, December 2002.

Becker, Gary S., "What the Scandals Reveal: A Strong Economy," *BusinessWeek,* December 30, 2002, p. 30.

Berle A. A., Jr., and G. C. Means, *The Modern Corporation and Private Property,* New York: Macmillan, 1932.

Borokhovich, Kenneth A., Robert Parino, and Teresa Trapani, "Outside Directors and CEO Selection," *Journal of Financial and Quantitative Analysis* 31, September 1996, pp. 337–355.

Borstadt, Lisa F., and T. J. Zwirlein, "The Efficient Monitoring of Proxy Contests: An Empirical Analysis of Post-Contest Control Changes and Firm Performance," *Financial Management* 21, Autumn 1992, pp. 22–34.

Bradley, Michael, Anand Desai, and E. Han Kim, "The Rationale Behind Interfirm Tender Offers: Information of Synergy," *Journal of Financial Economics* 11, April 1983, pp. 183–206.

Bristow, Duke K. "Time Series and Cross Sectional Properties of Management Ownership and Valuation," manuscript, May 16, 1998.

Bruner, Robert F., "An Analysis of Value Destruction and Recovery in the Alliance and Proposed Merger of Volvo and Renault," *Journal of Financial Economics* 31, 1999, pp. 125–166.

Byrne, John, "The Best and Worst Boards," *BusinessWeek*, November 25, 1996, pp. 82–106.

Campbell, C. J., S. L. Gillan, and C. M. Niden, "Current Perspectives on Shareholder Proposals: Lessons from the 1997 Proxy Season," *Financial Management* 28, Spring 1999, pp. 89–98.

Carleton, Willard T., James M. Nelson, and Michael S. Weisbach, "The Influence of Institutions on Corporate Governance Though Private Negotiations: Evidence from TIAA-CREF," *Journal of Finance* 53, August 1998, pp. 1335–1362.

Chew, Donald H., ed., *Studies in International Corporate Finance and Governance Systems,* New York: Oxford University Press, 1997.

Cho, Myeong-Hyeon, "Ownership Structure, Investment, and the Corporate Value: An Empirical Analysis," *Journal of Financial Economics* 47, 1998, pp. 103–121.

Copeland, Thomas E., and J. Fred Weston, *Financial Theory and Corporate Policy,* Reading, MA: Addison-Wesley Publishing Company, 1988.

Core, J. E., R. W. Holthausen, and D. F. Larcker, "Corporate Governance, Chief Executive Officer Compensation, and Firm Performance," *Journal of Financial Economics* 51, 1999, pp. 371–406.

Cornell, Bradford, and Alan Shapiro, "Corporate Stakeholders and Corporate Finance," *Financial Management* 16, Spring 1987, pp. 5–14.

Coughlan, A. T., and R. M. Schmidt, "Executive Compensation, Managerial Turnover, and Firm Performance: An Empirical Investigation," *Journal of Accounting and Economics* 7, 1985, pp. 43–66.

DeAngelo, Harry, and Linda DeAngelo, "Proxy Contests and the Governance of Publicly Held Corporation," *Journal of Financial Economics* 25, 1989, pp. 29–60.

Demsetz, H., and K. Lehn, "The Structure of Corporate Ownership," *Journal of Political Economy* 93, 1985, pp. 1155–1177.

Denis, David J., and Diane K. Denis, "Performance Changes Following Top Management Dismissals," *Journal of Finance* 50, September 1995, pp. 1029–1057.

Dodd, Peter, and Jerold B. Warner, "On Corporate Governance: A Study of Proxy Contests," *Journal of Financial Economics* 11, 1983, pp. 401–438.

The Economist, "A Survey of Corporate Governance," January 29, 1994, special supplement, pp. 1–18.

Fama, E. F., "Agency Problems and the Theory of the Firm," *Journal of Political Economy* 88, 1980, pp. 288–307.

———, and Michael C. Jensen, "Separation of Ownership and Control," *The Journal of Law and Economics* 26, June 1983a, pp. 301–325.

———, and "Agency Problems and Residual Claims," The Journal of Law and Economics 26, 1983b, pp. 327–349.

"For WorldCom, Acquisitions Were Behind Its Rise and Fall," *New York Times*, August 8, 2002, p. 1.

Franks, J., and C. Mayer, "Bank Control, Takeovers and Corporate Governance in Germany," *Journal of Banking & Finance* 22, 1998, pp. 1985–1403.

——, "Ownership and Control of German Corporations," *The Review of Financial Studies* 14, 2001, pp. 943–977.

Gillan, Stuart, and Laura T. Starks, "Corporate Governance Proposals and Shareholder Activism: The Role of Institutional Investors," *Journal of Financial Economics* 57, August 2000, pp. 275–305.

Gorton, Gary, and Frank A. Schmid, "Universal Banking and the Performance of German Firms," *Journal of Financial Economics* 58, January 2000, pp. 29–80.

Haubrich, Joseph G., "Risk Aversion, Performance Pay, and the Principal-Agent Problem," *Journal of Political Economy* 102, April 1994, pp. 258–276.

Holderness, C. G., and D. P. Sheehan, "The Role of Majority Shareholders in Publicly Held Corporations: An Exploratory Analysis," *Journal of Financial Economics* 20, 1988, pp. 317–346.

Holderness, Clifford G., Randall S. Kroszner, and Dennis P. Sheehan, "Were the Good Old Days that Good? Changes in Managerial Stock Ownership Since the Great Depression," *Journal of Finance* 54, April 1999, pp. 435–469.

Ikenberry, David, and Josef Lakonishok, "Corporate Governance Though the Proxy Contest: Evidence and Implications," *Journal of Business* 66, July 1993, pp. 405–435.

"In Shift, AOL Time Warner to De-Emphasize 'Convergence,'" *Wall Street Journal*, May 13, 2002, pp. B1, B6.

Jensen, Michael C., "Agency Costs of Free Cash Flow, Corporate Finance and Takeovers," *American Economic Review,* Papers and Proceedings 76, May 1986, pp. 323–329.

Jensen, Michael C., and Jerold B. Warner, eds., "Symposium on the Distribution of Power Among Corporate Managers, Shareholders, and Directors," *Journal of Financial Economics* 20, January/March 1988.

Jensen, Michael C., and Kevin J Murphy, "Performance Pay and Top-Management Incentives," *Journal of Political Economy* 98, April 1990, pp. 225–264.

Jensen, Michael C., and Richard S. Ruback, eds., Symposium on the Structure and Governance of Enterprise, *Journal of Financial Economic* 27, Part I, September 1990: Part II, October 1990.

Jensen, Michael C., and W. H. Meckling, "Theory of the Firm: Managerial Behavior, Agency Costs and Ownership Structure," *Journal of Financial Economics* 3, 1976, pp. 305–360.

John, Kose, and Lemma W. Senbet, "Corporate Governance and Board Effectiveness," *Journal of Banking & Finance* 22, 1998, pp. 371–403.

Jordan, Jerry L., "Not As Easy As It Looks: Regulating Effective Corporate Governance," *Economic Commentary Federal Reserve of Cleveland*, January 1, 2003.

Kaplan, Steven N., "Top Executive Rewards and Firm Performance: A Comparison of Japan and the United States," *Journal of Political Economy* 102, June 1994, pp. 510–546.

Klein, Alec, "Creative Transactions Earned Team Rewards," *Washington Post,* July 19, 2002, p. A1.

Klein, Alec, "Unconventional Transactions Boosted Sales," *Washington Post*, July 18, 2002, p. A1.

La Porta, Rafael, Florencio Lopez-de-Silanes, and Andrei Shleifer, "Corporate Ownership Around the World," *Journal of Finance* 54, April 1999, pp. 471–517.

Logue, Dennis E., and James K. Seward, "Anatomy of a Governance Transformation: The Case of Daimler-Benz," *Journal of Law & Contemporary Problems* 87, Summer 1999, pp. 87–111.

Malatesta, Paul, and John McConnell (eds.), Special Issue on International Corporate Governance, *Journal of Financial and Quantitative Analysis* 38, March 2003.

McConnell, John J., and Henri Servaes, "Additional Evidence on Equity Ownership and Corporate Value," *Journal of Financial Economics* 27, 1990, pp. 595–612.

Millstein, Ira M., and Paul W. MacAvoy, "The Active Board of Directors and Performance of the Large Publicly Traded Corporation," *Columbia Law Review* 985, June 1998, pp. 1283–1321.

Mitchell, Mark L., and J. Harold Mulherin, "The Impact of Industry Shocks on Takeover and Restructuring Activity," *Journal of Financial Economic* 41, 1996, pp. 193–229.

Monks, Robert A. G., and Nell Minow, *Corporate Governance*, Cambridge, MA: Blackwell Publishers, 1995.

Morck, R., A. Shleifer, and R. W. Vishny, "Alternative Mechanism for Corporate Control," *American Economic Review* 79, 1989, pp. 842–852.

——, "Management Ownership and Market Valuation: An Empirical Analysis," *Journal of Financial Economics* 20, 1988, pp. 293–315.

Mulford, Charles W., and Eugene E. Comiskey, *The Financial Numbers Game: Detecting Creative Accounting Practices,* New York: John Wiley & Sons, 2002.

Mulherin, J. H., and A. B. Poulsen, "Proxy Contests and Corporate Change: Implications for Shareholders Wealth," *Journal of Financial Economics* 47, 1998, pp. 279–313.

Pound, John, "Proxy Contests and the Efficiency of Shareholder Oversight," *Journal of Financial Economics* 20, 1988. pp. 237–265.

Rappaport, Alfred, *Creating Shareholder Value*, New York: The Free Press, 1986.

Rosenstein, Stuart, and J. G. Wyatt, "Outside Directors, Board Independence, and Shareholders Wealth," *Journal of Financial Economics* 26, 1990, pp. 175–191.

Safieddine, Assem, and Sheridan Titman, "Leverage and Corporate Performance: Evidence from Unsuccessful Takeovers,"*Journal of Finance* 54, April 1999, pp. 547–580.

Schilit, Howard, *Financial Shenanigans*, 2nd ed., New York: McGraw-Hill, 2002.

Schwert, G. William, "Markup Pricing in Mergers and Acquisitions," *Journal of Financial Economics* 41, 1996, pp. 153–192.

Scism, Leslie, "Labor Unions Increasingly Initiate Proxy Proposals," *Wall Street Journal*, March 1, 1994, pp. C1, C16.

Seward, James K., and James P. Walsh, "The Governance and Control of Voluntary Corporate Spin-Offs," *Strategic Management Journal* 17, 1996, pp. 25–39.

Shleifer, Andrei, and Robert W. Vishny, "A Survey of Corporate Governance," *Journal of Finance* 35, June 1997, pp. 737–783.

Slovin, Myron B., and Marie E. Sushka, "Ownership Concentration, Corporate Control Activity, and Firm Value: Evidence from the Death of Inside Blockholders, *Journal of Finance* 48, September 1993, pp. 1293–1391.

Sridharan, Uma V., and M. R. Reinganum, "Determinants of the Choice of the Hostile Takeover Mechanism: An Empirical Analysis of Tender Offers and Proxy Contests," *Financial Management* 24, Spring 1995, pp. 57–67.

Strickland, Deon, Kenneth W. Wiles, and Marc Zenner, "A Requiem for the USA — Is Small Shareholder Monitoring Effective?" *Journal of Financial Economics* 40, February 1996, pp. 319–338.

Stulz, R. M., "Managerial Control of Voting Rights: Financing Policies and the Market for Corporate Control," *Journal of Financial Economics* 20, 1988, pp. 25–54.

Wahal, Sunil, "Pension Fund Activism and Firm Performance," *Journal of Financial and Quantitative Analysis* 31, March 1996, pp. 1–23.

Warner, J. B., R. L. Watts, and K. H. Wruck, "Stock Prices and Top Management Changes," *Journal of Financial Economics* 20, 1988, pp. 461–492.

Weinberg, Neil, "Asleep at the Switch," *Forbes*, July 22, 2002, pp. 38–39.

Weisbach, M., "Outside Directors and CEO Turnover," *Journal of Financial Economics* 20, 1988, pp. 431–461.

Williamson, Oliver E., "Strategy Research: Governance and Competence Perspectives," *Strategic Management Journal* 20, 1999, pp. 1087–1108.

"WorldCom," Hilliard Lyons, analyst report, July 2, 2002.

"WorldCom Restatement a Major Problem for Sector," Morgan Stanley, analyst report, June 26, 2002.

"WorldCom's Sorry Legacy," *BusinessWeek*, July 8, 2002, pp. 38–41.

CHAPTER 21
MERGER ARBITRAGE

The mention of merger arbitrage often conjures up images of Ivan Boesky, famed arbitrageur, or Gordon Gekko in the box-office hit *Wall Street*. However, Ivan Boesky went to federal prison for buying takeover targets in advance of merger announcements. Gordon Gekko was a corporate raider who attempted to buy entire companies based on illegal inside information. In contrast to purchasing takeover targets prior to the merger announcement or engaging in insider information, merger arbitrage is the purchase of a target's stock after the merger announcement.

After the announcement of a merger, the target's stock price typically trades at a small discount, often 1% to 2%, relative to the consideration offered by the acquirer. This discount reflects the time value of money because the deal usually takes a few months to complete, and it reflects the possibility that the merger might fail, in which case the target stock often plummets. In evaluating the discount, commonly referred to on Wall Street as the deal spread, the arbitrageur will translate the spread into an annualized rate of return, estimate the probability of deal failure, and then decide whether or not the spread compensates for the time value of money and for the possibility of deal termination. If the spread is sufficiently large, the arbitrageur will purchase shares in the target firm.

On the opposite side of the trade are investors, who typically have received a substantial windfall, usually ranging from 20% to 30%, due to the large appreciation of the value in the target stock at the merger announcement. These investors face the choice of selling the target stock and realizing the large windfall or holding onto the stock in order to obtain the remaining premium that is the result of the target trading at a small discount relative to the consideration offered. The cost of holding onto the target stock until merger consummation is that if the deal breaks, albeit with a low degree of probability, the investor will lose the previous gain on the target stock due to the large appreciation at merger announcement and might lose considerably more, as well. Many investors choose to insure against this downside by locking in the gains and avoiding the potential for deal failure. Arbitrageurs step in and buy the target shares from the investors, thereby in effect selling insurance against deal failure to those investors. Merger arbitrageurs are compensated for bearing this transaction risk.

Several distinct characteristics of mergers are important for understanding merger arbitrage.

- Aggregate merger activity tends to be procyclical with respect to the stock market.
- Times-series clustering of merger activity can occur with heavy concentrations in certain sectors at each point in time.
- Merger agreements sometimes fall apart and, therefore, fail.

- Merger failure is typically idiosyncratic but is occasionally due to aggregate market conditions.
- There are many forms of payment to the target shareholders, which determines the trades required to capture the merger arbitrage spread.

Many notable financial experts have excelled at merger arbitrage at some point during their career, including Warren Buffett, chairman of Berkshire Hathaway (invested in merger arbitrage during the 1970s and 1980s), Ace Greenberg, former chairman of Bear Stearns (spent 54 years at Bear Stearns and continues to sit on the arbitrage trading desk), and Robert Rubin, vice chairman of Citigroup and former U.S. Treasury Secretary (famed Goldman Sachs merger arbitrageur during the 1970s and 1980s). Today, numerous types of financial institutions engage in merger arbitrage, including proprietary trading desks of Wall Street investment houses, hedge funds, and even some corporate pension funds and endowment funds. Indeed, on a much smaller scale, individual investors often invest in target firms after mergers are announced and hold until deal consummation or failure.

This chapter will describe the investment practice of merger arbitrage and will discuss the risk and return to this investment strategy. The chapter is organized into the following sections: (1) merger arbitrage scenarios, (2) empirical research of merger arbitrage, and (3) merger arbitrage in action.

MERGER ARBITRAGE SCENARIOS

Arbitrage is the zero-investment purchase of a security financed by the sale of an identical security at a higher price. Because arbitrage has a zero probability of a loss on the investment and a positive probability of a profit, it is risk free. Merger arbitrage, however, is risky due to the occasional deal failure, and is thus often referred to as risk arbitrage. Merger arbitrageurs specialize in bearing deal-failure risk and typically attempt to avoid overall market risk as much as possible. As we will see, insulating just the deal-failure risk sometimes involves fairly complicated trading strategies and cannot be done completely. Failing to fully appreciate the risks of merger arbitrage has proven to be costly for many investors. This section describes the mechanics of various types of merger arbitrage.

CASH DEALS

The most straightforward merger arbitrage trade involves cash mergers or cash tender offers. An example will illustrate the arbitrage trade. At 7:29 A.M. on May 13, 2002, Sears, Roebuck and Company announced a definitive agreement for Sears to acquire Lands' End, Inc. (LE), the successful catalog apparel retailer, in a cash tender offer for $62 per LE share, or roughly $1.9 billion. The merger announcement followed months of extensive discussions regarding the strategic merits of the merger and how to structure the actual transaction. Management of the merging parties believed that the merger would be helpful in addressing key strategic issues that each party faced. Sears had recently done an excellent job at cutting costs, but it had fared poorly at enhancing revenue growth, especially in the apparel offerings. The addition of LE clothes to all 870 Sears department stores would increase the annual sales at Sears greatly. For LE, the merger brought huge growth opportunity because it would allow exposure to a large group of consumers who do not buy clothing through catalogs or the Internet.

The stock price of LE increased substantially in response to the definitive merger agreement, closing at $61.73 on the announcement date, up from $51.02 at the close of the prior trading day, an increase of 21%. A merger arbitrageur would calculate the expected return to an investment of purchasing LE stock and holding it until merger completion or termination. See Table 21.1 for the calculation. Assuming that the arbitrageur could purchase the stock at the closing price of $61.73 and would pay commission costs of 2 cents per share, the net dollar return would be 25 cents ($62.00–$61.73–$0.02), representing a 0.405% return ($0.25/$61.75). Note that arbitrageurs also would account for any dividends to be received during the period that they hold the target stock. In the case of LE, management did not plan to pay any dividends prior to merger closing. The commission cost of 2 cents per share was simply an estimate of what the arbitrageur would pay. It could range from less than 1 cent per share for an arbitrageur who employs an electronic trading system to 5 cents per share at a full-service investment house, which provides research guidance to the arbitrageur regarding the merger.

In order to determine whether or not to invest in LE, a comparison should be made to the opportunity cost of capital. In order to make this comparison, the arbitrageur must assess the risk of the transaction. Because Sears and LE signed a definitive agreement, management of both firms had full intentions of consummating the merger. Moreover, Gary Comer, founder and chairman of LE, and certain other shareholders had agreed to tender their shares, representing roughly 55% of the total shares outstanding. The tender offer was conditional on obtaining at least 67% of the shares, and thus with the 55% already in favor, probability was low that target shareholders would block the merger. Both companies were in good financial shape and thus little problem was anticipated in financing the cash tender offer. Indeed, Sears had in excess of $1 billion in cash at the time of the merger announcement, more than half of the total cost of the acquisition. In addition, LE had more than $100 million in excess cash, and hence the actual purchase price was $1.8 billion rather than the stated $1.9 billion. Sears knew it would be able to finance the rest of the acquisition easily with its near-term cash flow from operations.

TABLE 21.1	Expected Payoff in Lands' End Incorporated–Sears, Roebuck and Company Merger
Expected Payoff	
Tender Offer	$62
Current Price	$61.73
Gross Spread	$0.27
Commission Costs	$0.02
Cost of Purchase	$61.75
Net Spread	$0.25
Promised Return	0.405%
Price if Deal Breaks	$51.02
Net Sale Price	$51
Probability of Deal Failure	0.01
Expected Return	0.227%
Time to Completion	40 days
Expected Annualized Return	2.09%
Annualized Risk-free Rate	1.70%

An unlikely deal blocker was the failure to obtain government approval. Arbitrageurs often spend considerable resources and time attempting to predict the government's reaction to a deal. In light of the low market share and minor overlapping operations held by the merging parties, and given the competitive marketplace in which they were operating, arbitrageurs assigned a small probability to the FTC or the Department of Justice blocking the merger on antitrust grounds. In addition to assessing the strategic benefits of the merger, evaluating the financial positions of the merging parties, forecasting antitrust action, and so on, arbitrageurs also attempt to account for any other potential factor that could derail the deal.

Once arbitrageurs have evaluated the likelihood of a merger being completed, they assign a probability to deal completion versus termination and make the appropriate adjustment to the expected return. For purposes of illustration, assume that arbitrageurs assigned a probability of 99% of Sears acquiring LE at the stated terms. Thus, arbitrageurs believed there was little probability of any factor derailing the merger. To complete the calculation of the expected return, they needed to forecast the price of LE stock in case of merger failure. This forecast is difficult to make with a high degree of certainty, because it is hard to forecast the reason for merger failure. If the merger failed due to LE receiving a higher bid from another acquirer, then its price would go up. However, if the merger failed due to accounting fraud issues at LE, the price would plummet likely well below where it was trading prior to the merger announcement. In the LE example, assume that its price would drop to the premerger announcement price of $51.02 in the event of deal failure. Accounting for the probability of deal failure, the expected return can be calculated as 0.227% [99% × ($62/$61.75 − 1) + 1% × ($51.02/$61.75 − 1)], considerably less than the 0.405% promised return.

Once the arbitrageur has calculated the expected return, the next step is to compare to the opportunity cost of capital. Merger arbitrageurs typically assume that the investment is market neutral and hence has no beta risk (this will be discussed in greater detail later in the chapter). Many arbitrageurs use the 3-month Treasury bill return as the comparable benchmark. At the time of the LE merger, the annualized 3-month Treasury bill return was about 1.70%. In order to annualize the expected return to the arbitrage investment in LE, the expected time to completion must be forecasted. During the conference call on May 13, 2002, when the deal was announced, management indicated that the deal would be expected to close in mid to late June. Given this guidance by management, coupled with the low likelihood of a second request from the FTC and the fact that it was a cash tender offer without substantial outside financing, arbitrageurs forecasted the deal would take about 40 days to complete. Consequently, the expected annualized return was $[(1.00227)^{365/40} − 1]$, or 2.09%. In that the expected return exceeded the benchmark return, the merger arbitrageur would invest in LE.

Alternatively, merger arbitrageurs could calculate the market's expectation of deal failure and then compare this estimate to their own estimate of deal failure likelihood. To the extent that arbitrageurs' estimates of deal failure are less than the market's estimate of deal failure, they would choose to invest in the deal. To compute the market's expectation of deal failure, arbitrageurs would use the following equation:

$$\frac{[(1 - p) \times \text{Offer Price} + p \times \text{Failure Price}]}{[1 + \text{Treasury Bill Rate}]^T} = \text{Current Price}$$

where p is the probability that the merger fails. If we use the same inputs (Offer Price = $62.00, Failure Price = $51.02, Annualized Treasury Bill Rate = 1.70%, Time to Completion as proxied by T = 40 days, and Current Price = $61.73) as before, the implied probability failure is equal to

1.40%. To the extent that the merger arbitrageurs believe that the probability of deal failure is less than 1.40%, they will invest in the deal.

Sears completed the merger with LE on the evening of June 17, which was 1 week ahead of the completion date as forecasted by the merger arbitrage community. When Sears announced the acquisition on May 13, management revealed that it would commence the formal tender offer shortly, which it did on May 17. On May 28, the FTC notified Sears and LE that it granted early termination of the waiting period under HSR. Figure 21.1 displays the daily gross spread on LE from May 13 through June 18, calculated as the tender offer price of $62 minus the closing price on each day during the window. As the deal progressed to completion, the spread tightened. By June 17, the spread was 1 cent, as the LE stock price closed at $61.99. The gross spread of 1 cent would have yielded an annualized return of nearly 6% assuming arbitrageurs had have received their tender offer payment on the next day, but any adjustment for commission would have eliminated the risk-free profit opportunity.

STOCK MERGERS

In a stock merger, the arbitrageur does not merely buy the target stock after the merger announcement and hold it until deal consummation or failure. Rather, in a stock merger, the arbitrageur also will short the stock of the acquiring firm in order to eliminate any overall stock

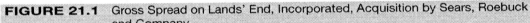

FIGURE 21.1 Gross Spread on Lands' End, Incorporated, Acquisition by Sears, Roebuck and Company

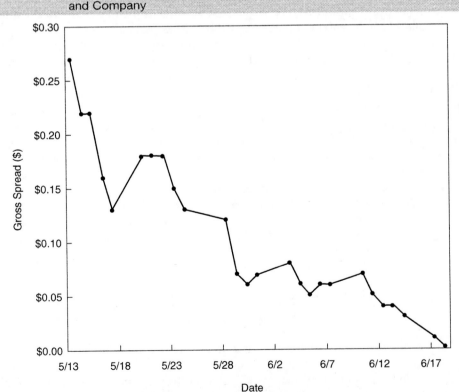

market risk associated with the trade because the merger arbitrageur specializes in deal failure risk. A recent high-profile example of a stock merger that received enormous attention from the merger arbitrage community in addition to an extraordinary amount of discussion by the corporate governance community was the merger of Compaq Computer Corporation ("Compaq") and Hewlett-Packard Company ("HP") that was announced in September 2001 and completed in May 2002. In this chapter, we will describe the merger from the perspective of the merger arbitrageur rather than from the corporate finance and governance view.

HP and Compaq announced the $25 billion merger at 10:31 P.M. on Labor Day, September 3, 2001. Under the terms of the agreement, unanimously approved by both boards of directors, Compaq stockholders received 0.6325 shares of a newly issued share of HP for each share of Compaq. Management predicted that the merger would be substantially accretive to HP's earnings in the first full year of combined operations. Cost synergies of $2 billion and $2.5 billion were forecasted for 2003 and 2004, respectively. Based on HP's closing price of $23.21 on August 31, the Friday before the announcement, the 0.6325 stock-exchange offer represented a premium of 18.9% [(0.6325 × $23.21)/$12.35 − 1] over Compaq's closing price of $12.35. As displayed in Table 21.2, the offer consideration was simply the exchange ratio of 0.6325 times HP's share price of $23.21, yielding an offer price of $14.68.

Despite the synergies proclaimed by management, the stock market did not respond positively to the merger announcement. By the close of trading on September 4, HP's stock price had dropped to $18.87, a decline of 18.7% ($18.87/$23.21 − 1). As a result of HP's large stock price decline and the newly established link between the two stocks, Compaq stock dropped as well, down to $11.08 from the prior close of $12.35, representing a 10.3% ($11.08/$12.35 − 1) decline. Academicians, journalists, and Wall Street analysts criticized the merger decision, claiming that it would not generate the synergies suggested, but rather would destroy the value of the two firms, especially HP. For example, David Yoffie, a professor at Harvard Business School, in his strong criticism of the merger contended that "no large-scale, high-tech merger has ever worked—ever" (*Wall Street Journal*, December 17, 2001, p. A18).

To the merger arbitrage community, the issue was not so much whether the merger would result in increased profit margins in the long term, but rather whether the merger would be completed, whether the terms would change even if completed, and if completed, the actual timing of completion. Merger arbitrageurs were mindful of HP's recent failed attempt to acquire the consulting unit of Price Waterhouse for $17 billion, a failure that was attributed to

TABLE 21.2 Announcement-Period Stock Price Information for Compaq Computer and Hewlett-Packard Merger

Announcement Period Price Information		
	Compaq Computer	*Hewlett-Packard*
Premerger Price	$12.35	$23.21
Merger Exchange Ratio		0.6325
Offer Price	$14.68	
Premium	18.87%	
Announcement-day Closing Price	$11.08	$18.87
Announcement-day Return	−10.28%	−18.70%

the sharp negative price reaction of HP stock to the acquisition announcement. Arbitrageurs also were mindful of the EU's rejection of the General Electric and Honeywell merger only 3 months prior. Given the large size of the Compaq merger, it was possible that antitrust authorities would label the merger as anticompetitive due to the potential for the new HP to bundle its personal computer/server/printer products to the detriment of the consumer.

Based on HP's closing stock price of $18.87 on September 4, 2001, the offer price was $11.94 ($18.87 × 0.6325), yielding a gross spread of 86 cents (7.8% relative to Compaq's closing price of $11.08. This 7.8% spread is large relative to the 0.4% (27 cents) gross spread in the Lands' End merger.

In the LE cash tender offer, the arbitrageur locked in the gross spread of 27 cents by purchasing stock in LE and waiting until tender offer completion to collect the payment. It is more difficult to lock in the 86 cent gross spread in the Compaq merger. For example, suppose the arbitrageur simply purchases Compaq shares at a price of $11.08. The merger closes on schedule several months later, and by that time, HP stock has dropped from $18.87 to $12.87. Because the stock-swap ratio is 0.6325, the arbitrageur receives $8.14 in HP stock (0.6325 × $12.87). Thus, arbitrageurs would lose 27% ($8.14/$11.08 − 1) on their investment, and yet the merger was completed successfully at the agreed-upon terms. Had HP stock increased subsequent to the arbitrageurs' purchase of Compaq stock, they would have made more than the 86 cent spread. For example, if HP's price were $24.87 at the close of the merger, arbitrageurs would have made $4.65 on their investment (0.6325 × $24.87 − $11.08). Only if HP's stock price at the merger close equaled $18.87 would the arbitrageur receive the gross spread of 86 cents. Because arbitrageurs seek to neutralize market risk and focus on deal failure risk, the arbitrageur will short HP stock contemporaneous with the purchase of Compaq. Specifically, the arbitrageur will short 0.6325 shares of HP for every share purchased in Compaq. Table 21.3 illustrates the payoff from the hedged investment versus that of the unhedged investment. For the hedged investment, whereby the arbitrageur shorts 0.6325 shares of HP for every share purchased in Compaq, the net profit is 86 cents, irrespective of HP's price when the merger closes. For example, when HP's price at merger close is $12.87, the arbitrageur loses $2.94 on the Compaq long position (0.6325 × $12.87 − $11.08) but makes $3.80 on the HP short position [0.6325($18.87 − $12.87)], yielding the net profit of 86 cents. By hedging in the exact proportion as the merger exchange ratio, the arbitrageur will neutralize the market risk associated with movements in HP's stock price.

Before making the hedged investment in Compaq, the arbitrageur will assess the probability of deal failure, the expected time to completion, and so forth. As mentioned earlier, arbitrageurs would be concerned about HP's large price decline upon the announcement of the merger, and also would have concerns about antitrust issues. In addition, the Compaq merger would be expected to take considerably longer than the Lands' End merger. Due to the complexities in due diligence involved with integrating the two firms and the antitrust issues, arbitrageurs forecasted that the merger would take 7 months to complete and predicted a merger closing date of March 31, 2002. During the merger conference call on the announcement date, management indicated that they expected the merger to close in the first half of 2002 but were not more specific. In light of the lengthy period prior to merger completion, the arbitrageur would need to forecast the expected dividend payments by Compaq and HP. Both companies would be paying dividends with record dates in September, December, and March. Compaq pays a quarterly dividend of 3 cents, and HP pays a quarterly dividend of 8 cents. Thus, assuming the merger closes on schedule, arbitrageurs will receive 9 cents in dividends for each Compaq share held and will have to pay out 15 cents in dividends (3 × $0.08 × 0.6325) on their

TABLE 21.3   Payoff of Unhedged Versus Hedged Investment in Compaq–Hewlett-Packard Merger

Unhedged Investment

Unhedged Investment	Purchase (number of shares)	Price
Compaq	1	$11.08
HP	0	

Outcome	Value of HP Stock Received	Compaq Profit/Loss
HP Price = $12.87	$ 8.14	−$2.94
HP Price = $18.87	11.94	0.86
HP Price = $24.87	15.73	4.65

Hedged Investment

Hedged Investment	Purchase (number of shares)	Price	Short Sale (number of shares)	Price
Compaq	1	$11.08		
HP			0.6325	$18.87

Outcome	Value of HP Stock Received	Compaq Profit/Loss	HP Profit/Loss	Net Profit/Loss
HP Price = $12.87	$ 8.14	−$2.94	$3.80	$0.86
HP Price = $18.87	11.94	0.86	0.00	0.86
HP Price = $24.87	15.73	4.65	−3.80	0.86

0.6325 short position in HP. Another financial consideration in the hedged investment is the expected short-interest rebate on the short position in HP stock. Professional investors typically receive short-interest proceeds at a rate slightly less than the federal funds rate. At the time of the merger announcement, the federal funds rate was 3.5%. Assuming arbitrageurs would receive 80% of this rate, they would expect to receive roughly 19 cents ($18.87 × 0.6325 × 0.035 × 0.80 × 7/12) in short-interest proceeds. Finally, there is the matter of actual transactions costs in setting up the trade. The arbitrageur often will pay a higher rate on setting up a stock-swap trade than on setting up the simple long-only trade. The higher rate is due to the added complexities in simultaneously buying Compaq stock and short selling HP stock. Rather than attempt to place the trades directly, the arbitrageur often will have a merger arbitrage trading desk at a major investment house set up the trade. A large investment house typically will have substantial trading volume in both stocks, thereby making it easier to put on the hedged position. A typical rate on such a trade is 5 cents per share. Thus, in the case of the Compaq merger, the commission costs would be 8.2 cents, consisting of the 5 cents on the long position and 3.2 cents (0.6325 × $0.05) on the short position. If the merger closes successfully, the long position simply crosses with the short position and no further commission costs are incurred. However, if the merger fails, the arbitrageur will incur added transactions costs associated with liquidating the position.

Table 21.4 displays the various inputs to convert the gross spread of 86 cents to a net spread of $0.91. Based on the net spread of $0.91, the return to the arbitrageur if the deal is completed is 8.25% ($0.91/$11.03). Note that the $11.03 is the net investment cost and is equal to the offer

TABLE 21.4	Deal Spread on Compaq-Hewlett Packard Merger
Deal Spread	
Gross spread	$0.86
Compaq dividends	$0.09
HP dividends	−$0.15
Short interest proceeds	$0.19
Commission costs	−$0.08
Net spread	$0.91

price of $11.94 minus the net spread. Assuming the deal closes on schedule as of the end of March, the annualized return would be 14.6% ($1.0825^{12/7} - 1$). This spread is large relative to the 2.1% annualized spread associated with the Lands' End merger, highlighting the perceived greater likelihood of failure. If arbitrageurs believe that the spread is sufficiently large enough to offset the likelihood of deal failure, then they will put on the position. Otherwise, they will delay an investment until there is either an increase in the spread or a decrease in their estimate of deal failure, holding all other factors constant.

Figure 21.2 displays the gross dollar spread for the Compaq-HP merger. On the far left side of the chart, the spread is 86 cents as described previously. A relatively sharp increase in the spread occurs on September 17 from 97 cents to $1.38, the first day of trading subsequent to the tragic events of September 11, 2001. By November 5, the gross spread had gapped out to $1.69 on

FIGURE 21.2 Gross Spread on Compaq-Hewlett Packard Merger

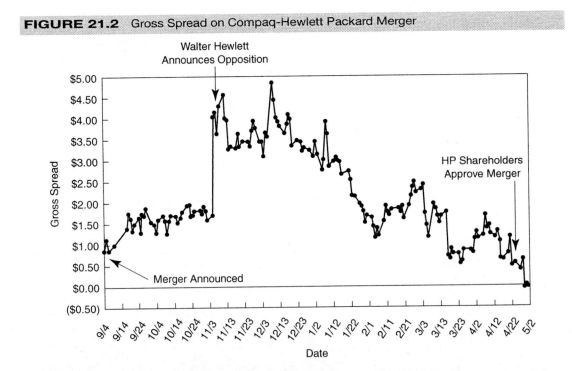

fears that the merger would be canceled or the exchange ratio reduced as a consequence of deteriorating performance numbers at Compaq. Assuming the forecasted closing date of March 31, 2002, the gross annualized return would be 53.8% if the merger was completed on schedule:

Prices on 11/5/01   Compaq $8.99

                                 HP $16.89

Gross spread = $16.89 × 0.6325 − $8.99 = $1.69

Gross return = $1.69/$8.99 = 18.8%

Number of days from 11/5/01 to 3/31/02 = 146 days

Gross annualized return = $(1 + 0.188)^{(365/146)} - 1 = 53.8\%$

In a surprising development, Walter Hewlett, son of the HP cofounder William Hewlett, publicly announced on the afternoon of November 6 that he and the rest of the Hewlett family members, along with a foundation in the family's name, would vote against the merger. The Hewlett family held a 5% stake in HP and thus accounted for 10% of the votes necessary to block the merger (HP is incorporated in Delaware which mandates 50% approval for shareholder voting). Arbitrageurs were stunned by the announcement because Walter Hewlett was not merely a member of the cofounder's family but was also a board member of HP and had earlier voted in favor of the merger at the board meeting. Upon the release of this announcement, the spread more than doubled to greater than $4. The news also caught HP management by surprise as they were given only a half-hour warning by Mr. Hewlett before the news was made public. Soon after, the Packard family, with a stake of 10% indicated its intention to vote against the merger. Several large institutional investors indicated their intention to vote against the merger, as well.

Due to the large increase in the spread, many arbitrageurs reduced their position in Compaq in order to prevent further losses. Several arbitrageurs went so far as completely exit their investment in Compaq, and a few even chose to speculate against the deal by shorting Compaq and buying HP. Eventually, management prevailed, winning slightly more than 50% of the shareholder vote in a proxy election that was bitter until the end, climaxed by a vote recount demanded by Walter Hewlett. Once it finally became official that the merger would be completed, the spread closed to zero in early May 2002. The merger was formally consummated after the close of trading on May 3, 2002.

COMPLEX MERGER TRANSACTIONS

Cash mergers (Lands' End) and fixed-exchange ratio stock mergers (Compaq Computer) are straightforward merger arbitrage investments and account for more than half of all mergers. However, several different types of complex merger transactions are more difficult to hedge. Examples include transactions in which some of the payment to the target shareholders include securities such as debentures and preferred stock, transactions in which investors have a choice in the form of payment received (often a choice of either cash or stock), and stock transactions in which the exchange ratio is not known at the initial merger announcement date.

Without going into detail of explaining the hedging strategies for these complex transactions, we will describe briefly why they are more difficult to hedge from the viewpoint of the merger arbitrageur. Considerable market risk arises in a merger in which the form of payment is a security, such as preferred stock or debentures, that is not publicly traded, yet it is difficult to hedge the risk therein. One could hedge out a basket of publicly traded preferred stocks or debentures; however, there is considerable pricing risk in these hedges, especially considering that spreads on arbitrage deals are often only 1 or 2%, thereby leaving little room for error.

In many mergers, the form of payment is a combination of cash and stock. In some of these cases, the acquirer offers a fixed-dollar amount of cash per share and a fixed exchange ratio. These mergers are relatively straightforward because they simply offer a cash component and a stock component, and the arbitrageur will hedge out the stock component in the same manner as in the Compaq merger. However, in some cash/stock combination mergers, the acquirer allows the target shareholders to elect to receive either cash or acquirer stock as payment. A recent example was the merger of RGS Energy and Energy East Corporation. Under the terms of the merger agreement, shareholders of RGS Energy could elect to receive either $39.50 in cash or 1.7626 shares in Energy East stock, subject to proration so that 55% of the RGS shares would be exchanged for cash and 45% would be exchanged for Energy East stock. Shareholders had to elect their preference within 3 days after the merger had closed. On June 28, 2002, the last day of trading in RGS stock, RGS closed at $39.20 and Energy East closed at $22.60. As of this date, electing stock would yield the higher value of $39.83 ($22.60 × 1.7626) versus cash of $39.50. However, 3 days later, at the time of the election deadline, Energy East stock had dropped to $22.07, thereby yielding a decreased value of $38.90 to the stock electors. Thus, an investor who chose to elect at the close of trading on the election deadline date would prefer cash, all else being equal. From the arbitrageur's viewpoint, the problem is not knowing how other investors plan to elect. That is, arbitrageurs who elect cash because it generates the highest value might find out a few days subsequent that they have received stock in addition to cash due to the fact that nearly all of the investors elected cash. Consequently, the arbitrageurs would have an unhedged position in the acquirer stock and would thus bear considerable risk if the acquirer stock dropped during the period in which the investors made the election and learned of the outcome of the election. As a result, it is important for arbitrageurs to be able to forecast accurately how other investors will choose to elect, a difficult task because most investors do not pre-announce their election decision. As described, arbitrageurs do not always know the optimal hedge ratio near the end of the merger; however, in these election mergers, this is a problem throughout the life of the merger period.

Whereas the exchange ratio was fixed as of the merger announcement date in the Compaq and HP merger, in many stock mergers the exchange ratio is not known as of the merger announcement date but is instead dependent on the acquirer's stock price near the close of the merger. An example is the 2001 merger of American General and AIG International. According to the merger agreement, the exchange ratio would be determined based on the 10-day average price of AIG's daily high and low share prices ending 3 days prior to the closing of the merger. If AIG's average price during this 10-day period was less than $76.20, the exchange ratio was to be fixed at 0.6037. If AIG's average price during this period was greater than $84.22, the exchange ratio was fixed at 0.5462. If AIG's average price was between $76.20 and $84.22, the shareholders of American General were to receive a fractional amount of AIG shares equal to $46 per share of AIG. The payoff to the American General shareholder is displayed in Figure 21.3, and this payoff is referred to as a collar. There are numerous varieties of these collar transactions, many of them more complicated than the American General merger. To the arbitrageur, these mergers are relatively more difficult to hedge because the merger-closing price of the acquirer is not known at the time that the deal is announced. However, the payoff to the target shareholder can be modeled as a portfolio of options on the acquirer's stock price. As with the straightforward, fixed-exchange ratio merger, the goal is to isolate market risk as proxied by changes in the stock price of the acquiring firm. With the fixed-exchange ratio merger, the arbitrageur simply sets the hedge ratio as equivalent to the stock-swap exchange ratio. To obtain market neutrality in the collar deals, many arbitrageurs employ

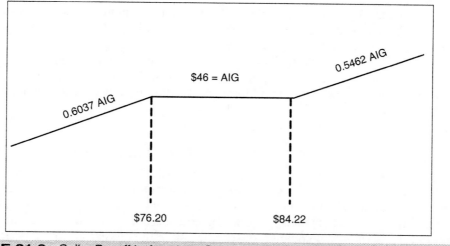

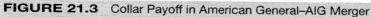

FIGURE 21.3 Collar Payoff in American General–AIG Merger

option-pricing models to determine the optimal hedge ratio for these mergers and then continually adjust the hedge as the acquirer price changes during the course of the merger.

EMPIRICAL RESEARCH ON MERGER ARBITRAGE

Until recently, merger arbitrage has received little attention in academic literature. However, recent work has focused on many aspects of merger arbitrage, ranging from investment management issues such as the risk and return of merger arbitrage, to corporate finance/market microstructure issues, such as the impact of arbitrage short selling on stock prices of acquiring firms around merger announcements. This section describes the recent literature.

RISK AND RETURN TO MERGER ARBITRAGE

Many merger arbitrageurs view their occupation as one of selling insurance. When a merger is announced, the target shareholder can hold on the shares to receive the higher payoff assuming the deal goes through. However, the target shareholder then bears the risk of deal failure, which can cause the stock price to drop considerably, often well below what it was trading at prior to the merger announcement. Consider, for example, an investor who purchased stock in Lands' End at $29.91 on September 17, 2001. Upon the May 13, 2002, announcement of Sears' plan to acquire LE for $62 in a cash tender offer, the stock price of LE immediately increased to $61.73. As of that date, investors would have realized a 106% return ($61.73/$29.91 − 1) on their investment in LE during a period in which the overall stock market was virtually flat. Many investors would choose to recognize their profits rather than to wait for the deal to be completed. If the deal is completed, their incremental return is less than half a percent. Moreover, they face the possibility of substantial downside risk in case the deal fails, say due to the exposure of accounting fraud at LE. In such a case, the stock potentially could be delisted, as was the recent case of Enron following its failed acquisition by Dynegy. To the extent that these target shareholders demand liquidity to avoid the blow-up risk, merger arbitrageurs step in to provide such liquidity. Indeed, it is the occasional deal failure that allows the arbitrageur to collect the insurance premium via the deal spread. Absent deal failure, the spread would not bear a risk premium and thus would only reflect the time value of money.

The merger arbitrageur diversifies across several deals so as to reduce the risk of the portfolio. When a merger fails, the reason for failure often is unrelated to the other deals in the merger arbitrageur's portfolio. In addition, deal failure usually is uncorrelated with the overall stock market and is thus viewed as a market-neutral investment. The risk/return to merger arbitrage can be considered in the context of the CAPM:

$$R_{MA,t} - R_{F,t} = \alpha_{MA} + \beta_{MA}(R_{MKT,t} - R_{F,t})$$

where $R_{MA,t}$ is the return at time t to the merger arbitrage portfolio, $R_{F,t}$ is the return at time t to the risk-free rate, α_{MA} is the excess return to the merger arbitrage portfolio, β_{MA} is the measure of systematic risk of the merger arbitrage portfolio, and $R_{MKT,t}$ is the overall stock market return at time t. To the extent that merger arbitrage is market neutral, the beta should be equal to zero. That is, there should be no systematic risk in the merger arbitrage portfolio if the deal failure risk is unrelated to the overall stock market. Assuming market efficiency and that the CAPM is the correct asset pricing model by which to examine the risk and return to merger arbitrage, the alpha term also should be equal to zero.

What is the risk and return to arbitrageurs who purchase target stocks after takeover announcements? Several recent studies have reported large returns to merger arbitrage, inconsistent with the efficient market hypothesis. For example, Dukes, Frohlich, and Ma (1992) reported annualized returns of 220% for a sample of 761 cash tender offers during the period 1971 to 1985. Jindra and Walkling (1999) reported annualized excess returns of 102% for a sample of 361 cash tender offers during the period 1971 to 1995. Karolyi and Shannon (1999) focused on Canadian targets of 37 cash and stock mergers and reported an annualized return of 26%, which is more than twice the return on the overall Canadian stock market during the corresponding period. Geczy, Musto, and Reed (2002) documented annualized excess returns of 65% for a sample of 227 stock mergers during the period 1998 to 1999. Geczy, Musto, and Reed noted that even after accounting for various short-selling constraints with respect to shorting the acquirer, the excess return still exceeded 30% on an annualized basis.

The aforementioned studies largely relied on the CAPM or a similar asset-pricing model to calculate the returns to merger arbitrage. For the most part, these studies reported a beta near zero in support of the view that merger arbitrage is a market-neutral investment. In addition, the large excess returns to merger arbitrage as documented by these studies suggest that the stock market is not efficient at pricing merger targets. Using a large sample of 1,901 cash and stock mergers over the period 1981 to 1996, Baker and Savasoglu (2002) searched for the source of the perceived market inefficiencies in merger arbitrage. Similar to the other studies, Baker and Savasoglu also documented large annualized excess returns, roughly 10%, though not nearly as large as that of the other studies. Baker and Savasoglu suggested that the positive excess returns reflect limited arbitrage (capital is limited in erasing arbitrage opportunities; see Shleifer and Vishny [1997]). In their model, merger arbitrageurs are risk averse and must be compensated for bearing idiosyncratic risk. They performed a cross-sectional analysis of the returns to merger arbitrage and showed that returns are higher when deal failure is more likely, and returns are higher when targets are larger. Thus, arbitrageurs are relatively averse to holding deals that have a substantial probability of failure, and they are averse to holding large positions in deals. In addition, Baker and Savasoglu found that returns are higher when the supply of merger arbitrage capital is low.

Mitchell and Pulvino (2001) constructed a sample of 4,750 cash and stock mergers that occurred during the period 1963 through 1998. They created a portfolio series that mimics the returns from a hypothetical merger arbitrage manager. The hypothetical manager is seeded with $1 million in cash at the beginning of 1963. Similar to active merger arbitrageurs, the hypothetical manager incurs transactions costs, including direct transactions costs such as brokerage commissions and indirect transactions costs such as price impact. In addition, the maximum weight in a deal cannot exceed 10% of the overall portfolio as of the time that the investment is made in the deal. Mitchell and Pulvino attempted to account for the various transactions costs and practical constraints that an active merger arbitrageur is subject to, and then imposed these costs and constraints on the hypothetical manager. However, unlike active merger arbitrageurs, Mitchell and Pulvino's hypothetical merger arbitrageur did not discriminate between deals that the arbitrageur believed would succeed versus fail. Rather, this arbitrageur can be thought of as a monkey that will invest in every target when it is first publicly revealed. Accounting for the various transactions costs and real-world constraints, the hypothetical merger arbitrageur generated an excess return of roughly 4% per annum.

By using a much larger sample of mergers and a considerably longer time series, in conjunction with accounting for transactions costs and practical constraints, the excess return documented by Mitchell and Pulvino was much smaller than that of the other studies; however, it was still economically and statistically significant. Thus, where is the risk in merger arbitrage, often referred to as risk arbitrage? Mitchell and Pulvino argued that the excess returns to merger arbitrageurs simply reflect compensation for bearing extraordinary risk. Although most of the other merger arbitrage studies controlled for risk such as market risk, they all assumed that a linear asset pricing model such as CAPM was appropriate to analyze merger arbitrage investments.

In contrast, Mitchell and Pulvino accounted for market risk in a nonlinear way. The intuition is that in flat and appreciating markets, a merger arbitrage portfolio generates positive returns that are largely uncorrelated with the overall market (see Figure 21.4 for an illustration).

Deals occasionally fail in these environments, but failure is typically unique to the specific deal and not systematic. However, in depreciating markets, for example when the overall monthly stock market return is −5% or worse, they conjectured that deals are more likely to either fail outright, be revised to the detriment of the target shareholders, or take longer to complete (note that in Figure 21.4, the slope of the relation between the excess return to merger arbitrage and the excess return to the overall stock market is much steeper during stock market downturns). For example, as discussed by Mitchell and Netter (1989), takeover targets suffered enormous losses around the crash of October 1987. During the late 1980s, most mergers were financed with cash, often with borrowed funds, and in the aftermath of the crash, many acquirers either terminated their bids or revised the offers downward. Merger arbitrageurs were hard hit as a result, and many exited the business. An example was Comdisco, a computer-leasing firm that invested excess cash of $130 million along with borrowed funds of $70 million in merger arbitrage. Comdisco ended up losing nearly $100 million on the total invested capital of $200 million, a loss in excess of 75% of its own capital. Every merger arbitrage firm was hit hard during the crash of 1987 as virtually every single takeover target dropped considerably in value during the crash period. Moreover, most of the arbitrage funds were levered, as in the case of Comdisco, and thus accentuated the losses to the funds' equity capital.

More recently, merger arbitrageurs realized large losses in September 2001 as a result of the stock market downturn due to the tragic events of September 11. Many deals were delayed, and some were outright canceled. For example, on September 21, 2001, Felcor Lodging terminated

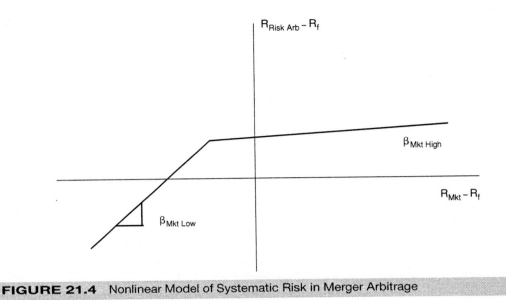

FIGURE 21.4 Nonlinear Model of Systematic Risk in Merger Arbitrage

Source: Mitchell, Mark, and Todd Pulvino, *Journal of Finance,* December 2001, p. 2139.

its agreement to acquire Meristar Hospitality. The merger agreement contained a walk-away provision at $18.40 per share of Felcor whereby either party could terminate the agreement without penalty. Felcor's stock price closed at $19.95 on September 10, 2001, but it traded as low as $11.95 on September 21, due to concerns that the travel industry would be hard hit by the events of September 11. Due to Felcor's stock price trading so far below the walk-away price, both parties agreed to mutually terminate the merger. On September 10, Felcor stock closed at $19.95 and Meristar closed at $20.16. The terms of the deal called for a stock swap of 0.784 plus $4.60 in cash. Thus, the value of the offer was $20.24 on September 10 (0.784 × $19.95 + $4.60), yielding a gross spread of just 8 cents ($20.24 − $20.16). Just 11 days later, when the deal was terminated on September 21, Felcor closed at $12.70 and Meristar closed at $8.65, resulting in a gross spread that had increased from 8 cents to $5.91 (0.784 × $12.70 + $4.60 − $8.65), thereby causing huge losses to any arbitrageur who was betting on the deal being completed.

Consistent with the anecdotal evidence of October 1987 and September 2001, Mitchell and Pulvino documented that merger arbitrage does indeed offer a nonlinear payoff. In flat and appreciating market months, merger arbitrage yields a positive return with zero beta, but in negative market months, merger arbitrage suffers large losses and has a beta of roughly 0.50. Thus, merger arbitrage generates positive returns in most environments, but in infrequent cases, it generates large negative returns. Consequently, Mitchell and Pulvino argued that the 4% annualized excess return reflects a risk premium to merger arbitrageurs for providing liquidity to other investors, especially during periods of severe market stress.

DO MERGER ARBITRAGEURS ACCURATELY FORECAST MERGER SUCCESS?

Merger arbitrageurs attempt to uncover information regarding the probability of deal completion and to forecast the stock prices of the merging parties in the occasion of deal failure. In assessing the probability of deal completion, they consider issues such as the form of payment, method of financing, intent of the acquirer, intent of the target, underlying economic conditions, historical and forecasted performance of the merging parties, and antitrust considerations. Merger arbitrageurs also purchase advice from Wall Street equity research analysts who cover the merging parties and from law firms and economics consulting firms that have expertise in antitrust matters. Are arbitrageurs able to use their proprietary databases, trading systems, and information-gathering processes and networks to generate excess profits versus that of the hypothetical merger arbitrageur who invests in all deals? Specifically, do arbitrageurs know in advance which mergers will succeed versus those that will fail? As indicated previously, many arbitrageurs view their occupation as one of selling insurance. The evidence amassed by Mitchell and Pulvino is consistent with this notion. However, many arbitrageurs claim they are able to beat the market and avoid investing in deals that fail. Some of these arbitrageurs will even trade in and out of the same deal numerous times as their probability of deal failure differs from that of the market as proxied by the deal spread.

Research by Brown and Raymond (1986) and Samuelson and Rosenthal (1986) provided evidence that the deal spread, calculated as the difference between the offer price and the post-merger announcement price of the target, distinguishes between those mergers that succeed versus those that fail. That is, for those deals that eventually fail, the spreads are much larger prior to failure than for those deals that are completed. A recent study by Jindra and Walkling (2001) examined the deal spread for a sample of 362 cash tender offers during 1981 through 1995. They found that the deal spread is positively related to the length of time that it takes to complete the tender offer and negatively related to the magnitude of price revision. Thus, for tender offers that are expected to take a relatively long time to complete, the spread is larger than for tender offers that are expected to be completed in a short period. For deals with tight spreads or even negative spreads (a negative spread is the case of the target stock trading higher than the proposed tender offer price), it is more likely that the acquirer will increase the offer compared with deals that have wide spreads.

The empirical evidence from these papers provides support for the notion of an efficient merger arbitrage market, namely that the market is able to distinguish the winners from the losers, as well as to distinguish along the dimensions of length of time to deal completion and the likelihood of deal terms revision. Consistent with this evidence, Figure 21.5 (adapted from Figure 1 of Mitchell and Pulvino, 2001) indicates that for a large sample of mergers and a long-time series, the market is able to distinguish mergers that succeed from mergers that fail. Specifically, spreads are much wider for mergers that eventually fail versus those mergers that succeed. Of added interest is the fact that although the market is able to *ex ante* select between the winners and the losers, the failure itself is a major surprise to the stock market, as demonstrated by the near doubling of the spread when failure occurs. In all likelihood, professional arbitrageurs are also unlikely to have forecasted deal failure accurately; otherwise, the spread would have begun to widen well in advance of the deal failure date as a result of arbitrageurs reducing their positions in the deal. Just as arbitrageurs generally keep deal spreads fairly tight for secure deals, any threat of a deal failure will send arbitrageurs rushing to unload their deal positions by selling their target shares and buying to cover the acquirer shares. To the extent that many arbitrageurs exit the deal, the spread will widen immediately and often by a large amount.

To directly assess the ability of active merger arbitrageurs to outperform the market, Mitchell and Pulvino examined the merger arbitrage return series published by Hedge Fund Research, a consulting firm that tracks the hedge fund industry. The active merger arbitrage series is an index of several merger arbitrage funds since 1990. Mitchell and Pulvino found that the payoff profile of the active merger arbitrageurs is similar to that of the hypothetical manager

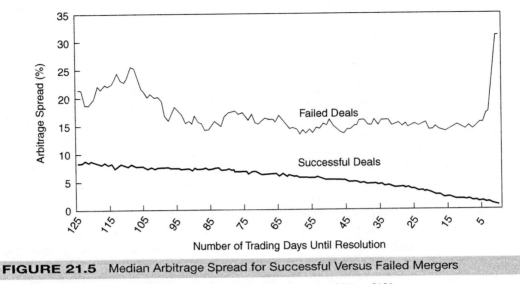

FIGURE 21.5 Median Arbitrage Spread for Successful Versus Failed Mergers

Source: Mitchell, Mark, and Todd Pulvino, *Journal of Finance,* December 2001, p. 2139.

who does not pick deals but rather invests in every merger target. The excess returns are similar, and the nonlinear relation of large betas in down markets and near-zero betas in flat and appreciating markets is also the case for the active arbitrageurs.

Overall, the empirical evidence suggests that the market is able to distinguish quickly between deals that will fail versus deals that will succeed. However, even though the arbitrage community can assess on average the likelihood of failure, the active arbitrageurs do not appear to be able to avoid all the failed deals, as evidenced by the fact that their payoff profile is similar to the index approach to merger arbitrage.

PRICE PRESSURE AROUND MERGERS

As described earlier, when HP announced the acquisition of Compaq on September 4, 2001, its stock price dropped from $23.21 to $18.87. Numerous commentators ranging from academicians to journalists blasted the merger, saying it would destroy value rather then create synergies. As support for their arguments, they pointed to the immediate negative response that the stock market gave to the merger announcement. These commentators argued that the stock market response to the merger reflected a negative NPV merger from the point of view of the acquiring-firm shareholders. However, as this book has discussed earlier, a negative stock-price reaction does not necessarily reflect the market's dissatisfaction with the merger, but rather some merger announcements signal low growth opportunities for the acquirer on a stand-alone basis, and thus the merger was a necessary adjustment to the changing environment. Indeed, according to this line of reasoning, the merger may well generate positive NPV, yet the merger announcement generates a negative stock-price reaction due to the revelation of the diminishing stand-alone prospects of the acquirer. An alternative explanation, and one that is given frequently in the case of stock mergers, is that the negative price reaction reflects a signal that the acquirer's stock was previously overvalued. A fourth explanation, and one that is often suggested by merger arbitrageurs, is that their selling pressure on acquirer stocks due to hedging the deal spread is the reason for the price decline. When mergers are announced, merger arbitrageurs act quickly and begin to make large investments in the target stock on the announcement date. Thus, if the merger involves a stock swap, the arbitrageurs will simultaneously short sell the acquirer's stock. To the extent that they short a relatively large amount of the acquirer's stock, arguably these arbitrageurs exert downward price pressure on the acquirer's stock price. This does not mean that arbitrageurs accounted for the entire price decline in the case of the Compaq merger, but rather that arbitrage short selling could potentially account for some of the price decline.

Recent research by Mitchell, Pulvino, and Stafford (2003) examined a sample of 2,130 mergers announced during the period 1994 to 2000 to assess the importance of price pressure around various merger event dates attributable to arbitrageurs. Consistent with merger arbitrage activity, they noted that the level of short interest increases substantially around fixed-exchange ratio stock mergers on the order of about 40% but does not increase around cash mergers. This evidence is also consistent with an information explanation of the negative price reaction to stock mergers whereby fundamental investors short stock acquirers and buy cash acquirers. However, Mitchell, Pulvino and Stafford (2003) also documented that when the stock merger closes, the short interest drops back to its forecasted level, consistent with the activity of merger arbitrageurs who are taking the deal off, and inconsistent with fundamental short sellers who would not necessarily pick the merger closing date as the period during which to take off the short position in the acquirer. These authors construct measures of price pressure caused by merger arbitrage short selling on merger announcement days, and provide evidence that such price pressure accounts for nearly half of the stock price decline associated with fixed-exchange ratio stock mergers on announcement days.

FLOATING-EXCHANGE RATIO MERGERS

Most stock mergers are of the Compaq and HP variety where the exchange ratio is fixed as of the announcement date. However, in a subset of stock mergers, the exchange ratio is not known until nearly the date of the merger completion. Recall that we briefly discussed collar stock mergers earlier. Another subset is a floating-exchange ratio merger, which specifies the value of the acquirer's stock to be exchanged for each target share rather than the number of shares. The number of acquirer shares that will be exchanged for each target share is determined later by dividing the offer value by the acquirer's stock price measured during a prespecified pricing period, usually just before the merger closing. It is during this pricing period that merger arbitrageurs short sell the acquirer's stock. An example is detailed next.

In 1998, First Union agreed to purchase Money Store for $34 in First Union stock for each share of Money Store. The merger agreement specified that the number of shares of First Union that ultimately would be exchanged would be determined by dividing $34 by the average closing price of First Union stock over the 5 trading days prior to the merger closing date. To capture the arbitrage spread, an arbitrageur would buy Money Store stock immediately after the merger announcement. However, unlike a fixed-exchange ratio offer, the arbitrageur would not immediately short sell the stock of First Union, the acquiring company. The reason is that by doing so, the arbitrageur would bear significant market risk. Recall that in the Compaq and HP example, as long as merger arbitrageurs shorted 0.6325 HP shares for each share long of Compaq on September 4, 2001, the date of the merger announcement, they would lock in the gross spread of 86 cents, irrespective of what happened to the price of HP over the ensuing months, assuming the merger was completed. In the case of the Money Store merger, the stock price of Money Store closed at $31.75, and the stock price of First Union closed at $52 on

March 4, 1998, the announcement date of the merger. Because the agreement called for share-holders of Money Store to receive $34 in First Union stock, the deal spread based on March 4 closing prices was $2.25, or 7.1%. Based on First Union's closing price of $52 on the merger announcement day, the pro forma exchange ratio was 0.6538 ($34/$52). Assuming that 0.6538 was the actual exchange ratio used in the merger, the arbitrageur who shorts 6,538 shares of First Union for every 10,000 shares purchased in Money Store would realize a profit of $2.25 per share.

However, as indicated previously, the merger agreement stated that the number of First Union shares that would be exchanged would be determined by dividing $34 by the average closing price of First Union stock over the 5 trading days prior to the merger closing date. The merger formally closed on June 30, 1998, prior to the market open. First Union set the exchange ratio at 0.5851, equal to $34 divided by $58.1125, where the latter is the average closing price of First Union during June 23 to 29, 1998, the 5 trading days preceding the merger close. Reconsider the arbitrageurs who shorted 0.6538 shares of First Union for each share purchased in Money Store on March 4. Based on First Union's closing price of $58.0625 on June 29, the value of the arbitrageurs' long position in Money Store would be worth $33.97 ($58.0625 × 0.5851), yielding a per-share profit on the long position of $2.22 ($33.97–$31.75). However, because the arbitrageurs were short 0.6538 shares of First Union for every share held in Money Store, they would have lost $3.96 on their short position (0.6538 × ($58.0625 – $52)), yielding a net loss per share of $1.74. The problem was that the arbitrageurs had shorted too many shares of First Union, and because its stock price increased subsequent to the merger announcement date, the loss on the short position exceeded the profit realized on the long side of the trade. Note also that because the arbitrageurs had shorted 0.6538 shares but actually received only 0.5851 shares, they would have a net short position in First Union after the merger had closed and thus must buy to cover the additional shares short in order to completely close out the trade.

Because the exchange ratio is not determined until the pricing period, the arbitrageur will purchase the stock of Money Store at merger announcement but will wait until the pricing period before shorting the stock of First Union. In order to minimize pricing risk, the merger arbitrageur would short sell First Union near the close of each of the 5 trading days of the pricing period. In the simple case where First Union's share price remained constant at $58.1125 during the pricing period, the arbitrageur who had purchased 10,000 shares of Money Store at merger announcement would short sell 1,170 (10,000 × 0.5851 / 5) shares of First Union on each of the pricing period days to hedge the position. Note that substantial price changes during the pricing period can result in large changes in the number of shares to short each day. For example, in the case of a rapidly declining acquirer price during the pricing period, the arbitrageur would increase the number of shares sold short each day.

Thus, from the arbitrageur's perspective, floating-exchange ratio mergers are similar to cash mergers before the pricing period begins and similar to fixed-exchange ratio mergers after the pricing period ends. In The Money Store merger just discussed, the pricing period ended the day before the merger closed. Often, however, the target trades for a couple of days after the pricing period ends, in which case the exchange ratio is fixed. In the case of Money Store, the fixed-exchange ratio would have been 0.5851 had trading continued in Money Store during the post-pricing period.

Mitchell, Pulvino, and Stafford (2003) argued that price pressure effects on the acquirer's stock are expected to be greatest during the pricing period when arbitrageurs are shorting the acquirer's stock. The pricing period does not begin until after the merging parties have met the milestones necessary to complete the merger and generally precedes the closing of the merger by only a day or so. Consistent with their arguments, Mitchell, Pulvino, and Stafford (2003) found that during the pricing period (10 days on average), acquirers' stock prices declined 3.2% in floating-ratio stock mergers. On the announcement date of these mergers, when it is fully known that stock will be used as currency for the merger, the acquirer's stock price increases, 0.6% on average, in comparison with a 2.7% decline on the announcement date for fixed-exchange ratio mergers. Indeed, they found that the announcement period stock price reaction for the floating-ratio stock mergers is similar to the 1.0% positive price reaction associated with the cash mergers in their sample. Consistent with the short interest patterns around fixed-exchange ratio mergers, this evidence suggests that a large part of the negative price reaction to fixed-exchange ratio mergers might be due to price pressure caused by merger arbitrageurs rather than solely due to fundamental sellers for information reasons.

MERGER ARBITRAGE IN ACTION

Merger arbitrageurs are active throughout the takeover process from the date of the merger announcement until the merger formally closes or terminates. These arbitrageurs are employed at various institutions, primarily at proprietary trading desks of Wall Street investment houses, merger arbitrage boutiques, and multistrategy hedge funds. To a lesser extent, some large endowments and pension funds manage merger arbitrage strategies in house, and even some nonfinancial corporations invest excess cash in merger arbitrage (note, however, that the latter can yield sharp losses to the firm's excess capital at the very time when such capital is needed). This section describes some of the typical portfolio management activities that the merger arbitrageur undertakes.

Most mergers are announced during the morning prior to the opening of the stock market. On a highly active day during periods of market expansion, 10 mergers could be announced during the 2-hour period preceding the market open. During recessionary periods, a few days could pass without the occurrence of an investable target. When a merger is announced, the arbitrageur will act quickly. The first step is to record all of the terms associated with the transactions and then cross-check these terms with various sources. The arbitrageur will first learn of the merger from one of several potential sources, including news sources such as Bloomberg, CNBC, Dow Jones News Service, Reuters, and *Wall Street Journal*; merger arbitrage research desks of brokerage firms where the arbitrageur sends trade orders; and merger arbitrage consulting firms.

After reading the various press releases and news accounts of the merger, the arbitrageur will listen to the merger conference call held for investors by the merging parties. This call usually takes place on the day of the merger announcement, and in most cases during the morning. During the call, management will review the terms of the merger, discuss expected revenue synergies and cost savings, forecast the expected closing date, and so forth. Following the presentation by management, a question-and-answer session occurs in which investors are able to raise questions about the merger. Both fundamental investors and merger arbitrageurs will address concerns during this session. The questions by the arbitrageurs generally focus on making sure of the exact deal terms, on understanding the perceived risks that could stop the merger such as antitrust complications, and on the expected time to completion.

Many arbitrageurs will begin to build their position in the target firm as soon as possible following the merger announcement. Some arbitrageurs will wait until all terms have been verified either via the merger conference call or via discussions with management at the target or acquirer firm. Other arbitrageurs might wait until they have spent considerable time scrutinizing the deal, including building financial spreadsheets to determine their own valuation of the target, talking with outside legal counsel to better understand the antitrust issues surrounding the merger, and reading research reports by Wall Street analysts about the merger.

THE MECHANICS OF TRADING

The actual mechanics of trading vary considerably across merger arbitrageurs. In some cases, a distinction is evident between the analyst and the trader. In other cases, the analyst also acts as the trader. Generally, the larger the merger arbitrage firm is, the more likely it is that a dedicated trader will be used. To the extent that the investment philosophy is to trade numerous times throughout the course of a deal, it is also more likely that the firm will employ a dedicated trader. For example, many merger arbitrageurs will trade a particular deal multiple times during a given day. One approach would be to increase the position size as the deal spread gaps out on an intraday basis, and then reduce the position size as the deal spread subsequently tightens. This approach can cause huge losses to the portfolio if the deal spread continues to gap out and the merger eventually fails. At the opposite end of the spectrum is the arbitrageur who builds a position, sometimes building the entire position in the deal soon after the announcement, and other times, increasing the position as the deal hits various milestones but not cutting back on the position to take profits until there is resolution of either deal completion or failure.

Trading venues also need to be considered. Historically, the standard approach was to conduct trading through a brokerage firm. Many brokerage firms have merger arbitrage desks that specifically cater to merger arbitrageurs. These desks provide research and trading support. The research support ranges from answering questions about a specific merger regarding deal terms, closing dates, antitrust issues, and so on, to providing lengthy research reports on the current M&A landscape. With respect to trading support, the broker will handle all types of trades on behalf of the arbitrageur.

In the case of a straightforward cash merger, arbitrageurs typically will use a limit order specifying the highest price they are willing to pay for the target firm. Consider the recent acquisition of Garan by Berkshire Hathaway in a cash merger of $60, which was completed in early September 2002. Two weeks prior to the close of the merger, Garan was trading at around $59.88 with a bid price of $59.87 and an ask price of $59.89. Because the merger was near completion, there was little liquidity in Garan's stock. A market order to buy 10,000 shares of Garan would not simply be executed at the ask price of $59.89 but could go much higher before other sellers would step in. Consequently, if the average price per share paid turned out to be $59.95, the return to the arbitrageur would be extremely low, even on an annualized basis, especially if the broker charged a high commission for the trade. For instance, commission costs range from 1 cent to 5 cents per share. At a commission cost of 5 cents per share the arbitrageur would expect to receive a zero rate of return on the deal if the average price per share on a market order turned out to be $59.95. Thus, arbitrageurs would place limit orders to ensure that they do not end up paying an especially high price via market orders. A downside to the limit order approach is that it might take considerable time to ever build a position in the target, specifically relatively small targets of $500 million or less in equity value. However, by going through a major brokerage house, there are often occasions for which some of the broker's major customers are looking to sell large blocks of the target stock and thus the broker can facilitate the large trade, thereby allowing arbitrageurs to fill their positions more rapidly before all the available shares are in the hands of other arbitrageurs. Indeed, it is this benefit of obtaining trade flow that allows some brokerage houses to charge higher commissions.

THE CHALLENGE OF STOCK MERGERS

Stock mergers are much more difficult to set up. As discussed, the arbitrageur must short the stock in the acquiring firm in addition to buying the stock in the target firm. Consider the merger of Conoco and Phillips Petroleum, which was announced in November 2001 and was completed in September 2002. The terms of the merger agreement called for Conoco shareholders to receive 0.4677 shares of stock in Phillips Petroleum for each share held in Conoco. Appendix A displays a Trading Summary Recommendation and Risk Capital Analysis for the Conoco merger prepared by DealAnalytics.com. DealAnalytics is a Web-based company that provides research and analytical support to merger arbitrageurs. DealAnalytics continuously updates the Trading Summary Recommendation for mergers involving publicly traded U.S. targets with equity values in excess of $100 million. The snapshot of the Trading Strategy Recommendation for Conono was taken on midday August 22, 2002, roughly 6 weeks prior to the expected merger close. Terms of the merger are listed at the top of the Trading Strategy Recommendation. The pricing period information on the right of the table pertains to collar deals and floating-ratio deals. Because the Conoco merger is a fixed-exchange ratio deal, the pricing period entries are blank. The Sample Trading Strategy in the second frame details the arbitrage potential profits from putting the deal on. Based on the stock price of $52.74 for Phillips Petroleum and the stock price of $24.54, the gross spread per share is calculated as 12.6 cents (52.74 × 0.4677 – 24.54). Both companies paid a dividend on September 3, 2002, with an ex-dividend date prior to August 22, 2002. Because the merger was expected to close at the end of September, DealAnalytics.com was not forecasting any dividends on either the long or the short side of the position. The brokerage commission of 7.3 cents is for the long and the short trade, reflecting a 5-cent commission per share traded (7.3 cents = 5 cents + 5 cents × 0.4677). The short rebate of 4.2 cents refers to the interest rate that the merger arbitrageur would expect to receive from shorting 0.4677 share of Phillips Petroleum. Typically, institutional investors receive a rate that is slightly below the federal funds rate (the federal funds rate is the interest rate at which a depository institution lends immediately available funds balances at the Federal Reserve to another depository institution overnight). On August 22, 2002, the federal funds rate was 1.73%. For stocks such as Phillips Petroleum that are easily shortable, the short rebate rate is equal to the 1.73% less a haircut of 0.25%. Accounting for the time to completion, this yields the 4.2 cents short rebate from shorting the 0.4677 share of Phillips Petroleum. Finally, note that DealAnalytics.com does not make an adjustment for price impact. Specifically, their calculation of the net spread of 9.4 cents assumes that the arbitrageur can buy and sell at the latest traded price. However, if one assumes instead that the purchase takes place at the ask price and that the short sale takes place at the bid price, then the net spread would be lower. The annualized net spread as calculated is 3.42%, roughly twice that of the current 3-month Treasury bill rate.

As alluded to in the previous discussion, it is more difficult to build a position in a stock merger than in a cash deal. In the example of Conoco, the arbitrageur will short 4,677 shares of Phillips Petroleum for every 10,000 shares purchased in Conoco. The objective is to lock in the gross spread of 12.6 cents on the trade. However, in order to do so, first there must be shares in Phillips Petroleum available to short. Arbitrageurs will first check with their prime broker (prime brokers provide clearing, custody, settlement, financing, stock lending, and other services to hedge funds) to determine whether the shares in Phillips are available for shorting and what short interest rebate the prime broker will pay with respect to the short. Note that the short interest rebate is not always simply a straight haircut of 0.25% off the prevailing federal funds rate, as it also depends on the demand for shorting. The greater the demand is for shorting, the higher the price will be namely the lower the short rebate that the arbitrageur will receive from the broker. In certain cases, the rebate will be negative; that is, the arbitrageur will pay the prime broker for the right to short shares in a particular company. There are instances in which the gross spread on a stock merger yields a sufficiently high annualized return to invest in, yet an inability to receive full rebate will render the trade unprofitable.

Once arbitrageurs are ready to begin trading, they must decide on the actual mechanics as to putting on the position. In order to short the acquirer stock, the arbitrageur must wait on an uptick (an uptick is when the trade takes place at a price higher than the previous trade, or if the trade takes place at a price equal to the previous trade, then the previous trade took place at a price higher than its previous trade, and so forth). In the event of the acquirer declining in price when the arbitrageur is attempting to put the deal on, it will be more difficult to lock in the deal spread. This is especially true on the merger announcement day when price pressure from the arbitrageur results in substantial downward pressure on the price of the acquirer.

In light of the potential difficulty in setting up the short side of the trade, many arbitrageurs will set up the short side in the acquirer before purchasing any shares in the target. They might either put the entire short position on first and then put on the long position, or instead they might build the position in increments; for example, in the Conoco merger, they would short 46.77 shares of Phillips Petroleum and then buy 100 shares of Conoco, repeat the sequence of trades, and so forth. The latter method of incrementally building the position is more likely to be used if the arbitrageur is using a proprietary, in-house electronic trading system. It should be noted that with the first approach, arbitrageurs face substantial stock market risk because they might have built a substantial short position before purchasing the target. Some arbitrageurs decide which side of the trade to put on first based on what they think will happen to the stock market that day. For example, if arbitrageurs believe that the market will be strong throughout the day, they might put on the long position first, and then hedge it out at the end of the day. In doing so, they are taking on considerable market risk.

Given the complexities in building a position in a stock deal, especially in a deal with a relatively tight spread where the margin for error is slight, many arbitrageurs will have a broker execute a paired transaction. Arbitrageurs often will send the entire trade for the day on a deal they wish to put on or add to and will specify either a gross spread or a spread net of commission costs to the broker. The broker is then responsible for setting up the trade, and if the broker only manages to set up one side, the arbitrageur is not liable for the trade. In return for accepting the risk, the broker generally will charge a fairly high commission for these types of orders, often up to 5 cents per share.

THE MONITORING PROCESS

Once merger arbitrageurs have invested in a deal, they will monitor it constantly and often will either increase or decrease the weight on the deal based on their assessment of the deal completing on time. This monitoring process can be time consuming and involves not only reading press releases and analysts' reports about the progression of the merger, it also involves conversations with the involved parties, expert consultants, and so on. Brokerage firms with merger arbitrage desks often will provide periodic reports of ongoing deals. As mentioned previously, DealAnalytics.com is an example of a company that provides analysis and commentary about ongoing deals. Appendix B provides selected commentary from DealAnalytics.com regarding the attempted merger of HotJobs.com, Limited, and TMP Worldwide, Incorporated, in 2001. We provide a brief discussion of this commentary below.

On July 2, 2001, the date of the Hotjobs.com and TMP Worldwide merger announcement, DealAnalytics.com described the transaction, forecasted a closing date of October 15, indicated there should be minimal antitrust risk, and noted that HotJobs.com had poor financial performance and thus the downside risk would likely be severe should the deal break. DealAnalytics.com regarded the gross spread of 41 cents (13.9% annualized) as a bit high, given HotJobs's poor operating performance. On August 14, DealAnalytics.com questioned the HSR second request issued by the FTC, noting that the FTC staff has some difficulty with basic market concepts. However, DealAnalytics.com still believed that the merger would close on schedule. By October, the spread had more than doubled due to antitrust concerns, and DealAnalytics.com moved the closing date to mid-January. Concerns about the merger continued in November, and DealAnalytics.com at that time assigned only a 60% likelihood of FTC approval. Both merging parties were starting to become extremely frustrated with the entire process. By December, DealAnalytics.com noted that the FTC was preparing to block the merger on the grounds that it would greatly reduce competition in the recruitment industry. Arbitrageurs were rapidly unwinding their positions, and the gross had increased to $3.43—more than $3 higher than the initial spread. Soon after, and just before the FTC was to block the merger, Yahoo! entered the picture with a bid of $10.50. On December 13, 2001, the date of the Yahoo! offer, the stock price of HotJobs.com increased from $6.47 to $10.30, an increase of 59%. On December 28, DealAnalytics.com announced that HotJobs.com was terminating the merger with TMP Worldwide.

In most cases, arbitrageurs have the same opinion of a deal. This is especially true for safe deals with tight spreads. However, arbitrageurs can differ widely in their assessment of a deal such as HotJobs.com. A few invested in the deal at the initial merger announcement in July and held until HotJobs.com was acquired successfully by Yahoo!, but many arbitrageurs exited the deal when the spread widened in November and December and then reinvested when Yahoo! made its bid. Other arbitrageurs traded in and out of the deal numerous times, often speculating against the deal going forward by reversing the natural trade (these arbitrageurs bought TMP Worldwide and shorted HotJobs.com).

In addition to paying considerable attention to each deal, the arbitrageur devotes substantial effort to managing the overall portfolio. Merger arbitrageurs do not invest all of their available funds in a single deal, but rather invest across a number of deals in order to diversify the largely idiosyncratic deal-failure risk. Consequently, they set maximum weights on the amount invested in any one deal. These maximum weights range from as low as 2% to as high as 20%. In addition, they will limit their exposure to a particular type of deal based on characteristics such as form of payment, friendliness of merging parties, deal spread, downside risk, and industry clustering. To further increase the level of diversification, many merger arbitrageurs will allocate a small part of the portfolio to similar trading strategies such as negative stub-investments associated with parent/subsidiary stocks (See Mitchell, Pulvino, and Stafford, 2002). Appendix C displays Portfolio Recommendations from DealAnalytics.com for 52 live mergers as of August 13, 2002. The methodology for these recommendations is provided in Appendix D.

Summary

An important role in the merger process is played by merger arbitrageurs. These arbitrageurs begin their investment in a target firm after a merger is announced, and generally continue to own the target stock up until the date that it is delisted. Many investors seek to exit their investment in a company after it has agreed to a takeover. Merger arbitrageurs provide these investors with the liquidity to exit without a price impact. In so doing, arbitrageurs facilitate the merger occurring as planned. During the course of the merger, arbitrageurs are not only active investors, but also actively provide information about how the deal is proceeding. In some cases, they will even provide information to the merging parties regarding how to better structure the deal to avoid deal termination.

The potential for blow-up risk is considerable. Mergers sometimes fail to be completed, and when they do, the target stock typically plummets. In some cases, the losses are compounded if the acquirer stock increases, assuming it is a stock merger and the arbitrageur has shorted the acquirer. To some extent, the arbitrageur can mitigate the blow-up risk by pooling across a large number of mergers, similar to the sale of insurance. However, although merger arbitrage typically is viewed as a market-neutral investment strategy, deal stocks often are hit hard during severe market downturns. As compensation for bearing this risk, arbitrageurs receive a risk premium.

For a long time, researchers have viewed the negative stock market response to stock acquirers as signaling either a negative NPV investment or overvalued stock. However, recent evidence suggests that a portion of the negative stock price reaction to stock acquirers might reflect shorting by merger arbitrageurs. This evidence has implications for interpretations of stock price reactions around stock mergers.

Questions

21.1 What is the difference between a merger arbitrageur and a textbook "perfect capital market" arbitrageur?

21.2 On August 23, 2002, McAfee.com Corporation agreed to a takeover offer by Network Associates to acquire each outstanding share of McAfee.com's stock in exchange for $8.00 in cash plus 0.675 of a share of Network Associates. At the close of trading on the merger agreement date, McAfee.com's stock was $17.72 and Network Associates's stock price was $14.56. The merger was expected to be completed by September 14, 2002. At the time, the 3-month Treasury bill rate was 1.75%. Arbitrageurs were receiving short interest rebates of 1.50% and were paying commission costs of 3 cents per share. What is the arbitrage investment? Should the merger arbitrageur undertake this investment?

21.3 Evaluate the stock-picking ability of a merger arbitrageur who is able to identify takeover targets and purchase their stocks during the month immediately prior to the merger announcement.

21.4 Why are acquirers more likely to terminate mergers during stock market downturns? How does this impact merger arbitrageurs?

21.5 What is the price pressure explanation of negative stock price reactions to acquiring firms at stock merger announcements?

Case 21.1 CHEAP TICKETS, INCORPORATED–CENDANT CORPORATION

On August 13, 2001, Cendant Corporation and Cheap Tickets, Incorporated, announced a definitive agreement for Cendant to acquire all of the outstanding common shares of Cheap Tickets at a share price of $16.50. With 25.76 million shares outstanding, the total buyout would be about $425 million. In addition, Cheap Tickets had about $145 million in excess cash, and thus the net purchase price would be about $280 million. To execute the transaction, Cendant planned to begin a cash tender offer within 10 days for any and all shares of Cheap Tickets. Subject to meeting customary closing conditions, including HSR approval, Cendant expected to complete the merger in the fall of 2001.

Cheap Tickets was a leading seller of discount leisure travel products, with the majority of sales coming from airline tickets. The company was founded in 1986 as a traditional travel agency, and since launching its Web site in 1997, roughly 40% of its bookings had come from the Internet. Cendant is a diversified global provider of business and consumer services primarily within the real estate and travel sectors. Cendant's travel operations consist of hotel management car rentals; and computer reservation services to airlines, hotels, car rental agencies, and other travel suppliers. The acquisition would permit Cendant to continue the rapid expansion of its global business in the leisure travel marketplace.

On the day of the merger announcement, the stock price of Cheap Tickets rose from $11.85 to $16.33. Trading volume on that date was extremely high at roughly 6 million shares, more than three times the highest trading volume day to date in 2001. In light of the 38% increase in the stock price of Cheap Tickets, many investors chose to sell their positions rather than hold out for the remaining 1%. Merger arbitrageurs responded by providing liquidity to these selling shareholders. Arbitrageurs forecasted that the merger would close at the end of September

or early October. They expected that the merger would easily pass FTC muster as Cheap Tickets competed with numerous online travel brokers such as Priceline.com, Expedia.com, and Travelocity.com, and with traditional travel agents.

Cendant began the tender offer on August 23, 10 days after the announcement date, as planned. In addition, Cendant already had filed HSR on August 16, and the 15-day waiting period was scheduled to expire on August 31. Given that the deal was proceeding on a relatively fast track, many arbitrageurs were now forecasting the merger to close on September 21, which was 1 day after the 20-day tender offer was expected to expire.

By Monday, September 10, 2001, the stock price of Cheap Tickets had climbed to $16.44 with a gross spread of only 6 cents ($16.50 – $16.44). However, following the tragic events of the morning of Tuesday, September 11, the stock market was closed for the rest of the week. On Monday, September 17, 2001, the first day of trading in a week, the stock price of Cheap Tickets was hard hit, declining to $12.55. Arbitrageurs feared that Cendant would terminate the merger due to the impact of September 11 on the travel industry. For example, during the week following September 11, online air travel bookings were down 50%.

In light of the high level of deal-failure risk, arbitrageurs began to focus on termination clauses in the merger agreement. The agreement provided for Company Material Adverse Changes (MACs) that would allow Cendant or Cheap Tickets to terminate the merger. For example, if either company were found to have committed fraud and such fraud would have a material impact on the viability of the merger, the harmed party could terminate the merger.

However, these MACs excluded any change in the market price of Cheap Ticket's stock or negative conditions (including changes in economic, financial market, regulatory, or political conditions) affecting generally the travel industry in which Cheap Tickets operated. Thus, the merger agreement appeared to be secure, barring any extraordinary events. Of special interest to the arbitrage community was that the MAC included a commencement of a war, armed hostilities, or other international or national calamity directly or indirectly involving the United States. Thus, although a general economic condition would not impair the merger going forward, a war arguably could allow either party to terminate the merger agreement.

On September 24, Cendant chose to extend the tender offer for an additional 10 days. Upon the release of this information, the stock market responded quickly, sending Cheap Ticket's stock price up from $14.85 to $16.24. Despite the events of September 11, the merger was completed successfully on October 5 at the agreed-upon terms. ▓

QUESTIONS

C21.1.1 What is the expected arbitrage return to purchasing Cheap Tickets at the closing price on the day of the merger announcement? Should a merger arbitrageur buy the stock? Note that at the time of the merger announcement, the 3-month U.S. Treasury bill rate was roughly 3.5%. Assume commission costs of 2 cents per share.

C21.1.2 In light of the huge downward pressure in Cheap Tickets's stock price on September 17, what should the merger arbitrageur do?

References

Baker, Malcolm, and Serkan Savasoglu. "Limited Arbitrage in Mergers and Acquisitions," *Journal of Financial Economics* 64, April 2002, pp. 91–115.

Brown, Keith, and Michael Raymond, "Risk Arbitrage and the Prediction of Successful Corporate Takeovers," *Financial Management* 15, Autumn 1986, pp. 54–63.

Dukes, William, Cheryl Frohlich, and Christopher Ma, "Risk Arbitrage in Tender Offers: Handsome Rewards—And Not for Insiders Only," *Journal of Portfolio Management* 18, 1992, pp. 47–55.

Geczy, Christopher, David Musto, and Adam Reed, "Stocks Are Special Too: An Analysis of the Equity Lending Market, *Journal of Financial Economics* 66, November 2002.

Jindra, Jan, and Ralph Walkling, "Arbitrage Spreads and the Market Pricing of Proposed Acquisitions," working paper, Ohio State University, 1999.

Jindra, Jan, and Ralph Walkling, "Speculation Spreads, Arbitrage Profits, and Market Pricing of Proposed Acquisitions," working paper, Ohio State University, 2001.

Karolyi, G. Andrew, and John Shannon, "Where's the Risk in Risk Arbitrage?" *Canadian Investment Review* 12, Spring 1999, pp. 11–18.

Mitchell, Mark, and Jeffry Netter, "Triggering the 1987 Stock Market Crash: Antitakeover Provisions in the House Ways and Means Tax Bill?" *Journal of Financial Economics* 24, September 1989, pp. 37–68.

Mitchell, Mark, and Todd Pulvino, "Characteristics of Risk and Return in Risk Arbitrage," *Journal of Finance* 56, December 2001, pp. 2135–2175.

Mitchell, Mark, Todd Pulvino, and Erik Stafford, "Limited Arbitrage in Equity Markets," *Journal of Finance* 57, April 2002, pp. 551–584.

Mitchell, Mark, Todd Pulvino, and Erik Stafford, "Price Pressure Around Mergers," forthcoming in *Journal of Finance*, 2003.

Samuelson, William, and Leonard Rosenthal, "Price Movements as Indicators of Tender Offer Success," *Journal of Finance* 41, June 1986, pp. 481–499.

Shleifer, Andrei, and Robert Vishny, "The Limits of Arbitrage," *Journal of Finance* 52, March 1997, pp. 35–55.

APPENDIX A

—————— ✒/✒/✒ ——————

CONOCO INCORPORATED–
PHILLIPS PETROLEUM

CONOCO INCORPORATED–PHILLIPS PETROLEUM

Trading Strategy Recommendation and Risk Capital Analysis
Last Trading Strategy Update 08/15/02

Deal Summary
Target Ticker COC/Acquirer Ticker P

Date Announced	11/18/01	Pricing Period Begins	N/A
Estimated Closing	09/30/02	Pricing Period Ends	N/A
Trading Days Remaining	27	Trading Days Remaining	N/A
Calendar Days Remaining	39	Current Average Price	N/A
		Current Stock Ratio	0.4677

	Terms	*Amount*	*Value per Share*
Stock Ratio	0.4677	100%	$24.6660
Cash per Share	$0.0000	0%	0
Other	$0.0000	0%	0
Current Parity Value			$24.6660

Minimum Ratio 0.0000/Maximum Ratio 0.0000

SAMPLE TRADING STRATEGY

Target Ticker COC/Acquirer Ticker P

Target Positions

	Ticker	Type	Month	Strike	Contracts	# of Shares	Price			
Stock	COC	—	—	—	—	10,000	$24.5400			

Gross Spread per Share	$0.1260
Long Dividends	$0
Short Dividends	$0
Options Adjustment[a]	$0
Pre-Carry Spread	$0.1260
Cost of Carry	$0

Acquirer Positions

	Ticker	Type	Month	Strike	Contracts	# of Shares	Price
Stock	P	—	—	—	—	–4,677	$52.7400

Brokerage Commissions	–$0.0730
Short Rebate	$0.0420
Net Spread[a]	$0.0940
Net Annual Return	3.42%
Adj. Net Spread[a]	$0.0940
Adj. Net Annual Return	3.42%

[a]Options Adjustment equals the cost of any respective options strategy reflected as an addition to or subtraction from the Gross Spread per Share. The Pre-Carry Spread reflects the adjusted spread per share, including the premium from or cost of any short or long options contracts. The Net Spread compares the Net Spread and Net Return versus an options-based Adjusted Net Spread and Net Return.

RISK/RETURN SUMMARY

	Amount	% of Total Capital	% of Total P&L
Total Capital Invested[a]	$245,400	100.0%	19,476.2%
Total P&L at Parity	1,260	0.5	100.0
Maximum Loss[b]	260,342	106.1	20,662.1
Risk Capital[c]	42,371	17.3	3,362.8

[a]Total Capital Invested equals the absolute sum of all long and short positions aggregated.
[b]Maximum Loss equals total loss if deal terminates and position prices exceed historic averages by more than two standard deviations.
[c]Risk Capital equals estimated loss if deal terminates.

RISK/RETURN MATRIX

Acquirer Price	Implied Parity	Positions		Deal Close-Results	
		Target P&L	Acquirer P&L	Total P&L	Annualized Net Return
$36.740	$17.183	−$73,570	$74,832	$1,262	3.42%
38.740	18.119	−64,210	65,478	1,268	3.45
40.740	19.054	−54,860	56,124	1,264	3.43
42.740	19.989	−45,510	46,770	1,260	3.42
44.740	20.925	−36,150	37,416	1,266	3.44
46.740	21.860	−26,800	28,062	1,262	3.42
48.740	22.796	−17,440	18,708	1,268	3.45
50.740	23.731	−8,090	9,354	1,264	3.43
52.740	24.666	1,260	0	1,260	3.42
54.740	25.602	10,620	−9,354	1,266	3.44
56.740	26.537	19,970	−18,708	1,262	3.42
58.740	27.473	29,330	−28,062	1,268	3.45
60.740	28.408	38,680	−37,416	1,264	3.43
62.740	29.343	48,030	−46,770	1,260	3.42
64.740	30.279	57,390	−56,124	1,266	3.44
66.740	31.214	66,740	−65,478	1,262	3.42
68.740	32.150	76,100	−74,832	1,268	3.45

Source: DealAnalytics.com.

APPENDIX B

PROPOSED HOTJOBS.COM, LTD. AND TMP WORLDWIDE, INC. MERGER SELECTED COMMENTARY BY *DEALANALYTICS.COM*

07/02/01, 08:26 A.M.

TRANSACTION SUMMARY

The new definitive agreement was announced late Friday, June 29, 2001:

- Terms: fixed ratio providing 0.2195 TMPW per share of HOTJ
- Accounting: pooling-of-interests (not a condition to the merger)
- Projected closing date: October 15, 2001
- Competing entities: HotJobs.com and Monster.com (owned by TMPW)

From the press release:

- TMP Worldwide Inc. (NASDAQ: TMPW), the world's leading supplier of human capital solutions, including the pre-eminent Internet career portal Monster.com(R), announced today that it has entered into an agreement to acquire HotJobs.com, Ltd. (NASDAQ: HOTJ). Under the terms of the acquisition, each share of HotJobs common stock outstanding will be exchanged for 0.2195 shares of TMP common stock. TMP intends to maintain HotJobs.com as a stand-alone site and brand. Monster and HotJobs will be a formidable combination in the online recruitment industry, with a total of more than 14 million resumes and more than 650,000 jobs.
- As a result, TMP anticipates issuing a total of approximately 8.3 million shares of its common stock, with a value of approximately $460 million, based on the 10-day average TMP closing stock price, representing a 20.9% premium to HotJobs' June 28, 2001, closing price.
- The Board of Directors of both companies have approved the transaction, which is expected to be tax free to the shareholders of both companies. The merger is subject to the approval of

HotJobs' shareholders, regulatory approval, and other customary closing conditions, and is expected to close in the fourth quarter of 2001. The transaction is being accounted for as a pooling of interests under U.S. generally accepted accounting principles.

BUSINESS SUMMARY

A brief summary of the companies follows from their press release:

- HotJobs.com is a leading Internet recruiting solutions company that develops and provides companies with innovative recruiting solutions and services. HotJobs.com (www.hotjobs.com), the company's popular consumer job board, provides a direct exchange of information between opportunity seekers and employers, and includes features such as HOTBLOCK, which enables job seekers to block specific companies from searching their resumes. In addition, HotJobs also offers an Agency Desktop, which provides a direct, business-to-business exchange between corporate hiring managers and staffing agencies. Over 10,600 companies subscribe to HotJobs' online employment exchanges. HotJobs also provides employers with progressive recruiting solutions such as its Resumix® and Softshoe® hiring management software, Career Expos, its HotReach affiliate program, and Diversity Marketing Solutions.
- Founded in 1967, TMP Worldwide Inc., with more than 9,500 employees in 32 countries, is the online recruitment leader, the world's largest Recruitment Advertising agency network, and one of the world's largest Executive Search and Executive Selection agencies. TMP Worldwide, headquartered in New York, is also the world's largest Yellow Pages advertising agency and a provider of direct marketing services. The

company's clients include more than 90 of the Fortune 100 and more than 480 of the Fortune 500 companies. In June 2001, TMP Worldwide was added to the S&P 500 Index.

- Monster.com, headquartered in Maynard, Mass., is the leading global careers Web site, recording over 26.9 million unique visits during the month of May 2001 according to independent research conducted by I/PRO. Monster.com connects the most progressive companies with the most qualified career-minded individuals, offering innovative technology and superior services that give them more control over the recruiting process. The Monster.com global network consists of local content and language sites in the United States, United Kingdom, Australia, Canada, the Netherlands, Belgium, New Zealand, Singapore, Hong Kong, France, Germany, Ireland, Spain, Luxembourg, India, and Italy.

We will post our initial Pending Transaction analysis shortly, but we foresee no antitrust with this transaction despite the obvious overlap. We are using an initial October 15, 2001, projected closing date.

07/02/01, 09:33 A.M.

ANTITRUST COMMENTARY

HOTJ and Monster.com are the two leading Internet-based job placement services. On the conference call this morning, management cited (i) low barriers to entry and (ii) "thousands of competitors" as the primary reasons for the lack of antitrust concern. We tend to agree, particularly with the second point, noting that competitors include:

- Online services—both general and industry-specific
- Traditional headhunting services
- Company Web sites—many companies offer their own "Job Opportunities" sections on their Web sites

Despite the "60% market share" created by combining the top two Internet companies, we cannot see how the FTC will have any problems with the merger. We suppose a second request is a possibility, but we view this deal as having minimal, if any, antitrust risk.

The transaction will be subject to only the expiration of the HSR waiting period.

We will post our Financial Analysis summary shortly.

07/02/01, 10:25 A.M.

FINANCIAL ANALYSIS SUMMARY

HOTJ is bleeding cash. On an operating basis, since 1998 the company has lost $60.6 million on total cumulative revenue of $120.6 million. Its most recent results have shown some signs of improvement and are as follow (for the period ending March 31, 2001):

- LTM revenue = $116.3 million (up 20.5% versus fiscal 2000 and up 464% versus 1999)
- LTM EBIT = −$34.7 million (versus −$41.3 million in fiscal 2000 and −$17.1 million in 1999)
- LTM EBITDA = −$13.3 million (versus −$25.7 million in fiscal 2000 and −$16.3 million in 1999)

Between December 31, 2000 and March 31, 2001, HOTJ's cash balance declined from $99.1 million to $82.7 million. Net of cash, the TMPW acquisition values HOTJ at $2.9 \times$ LTM revenue, which equates to the following premiums paid:

- 90-days Average Prior to Announcement ($5.89) = 115.4%; 90-days High Prior to Announcement ($10.10) = 25.8%; 90-days Low Prior to Announcement ($3.09) = 311.3%

TRADING RECOMMENDATION

We are maintaining our October 15, 2001, projected closing date and our "3" Portfolio Rating (Monitoring Key Issues).

At $0.41 gross, the arbitrage spread yields a 13.9% net annualized return to our projected closing date, a level which we view as somewhat rich given HOTJ's operating performance. If the deal terminates for any reason, we view the downside in HOTJ as quite substantial. Note that HOTJ was trading below $4.00 per share as recently as April 2001.

08/07/01, 4:40 P.M.

COMMENTARY

Despite recent complaints to the FTC from one of the company's competitors, FreeJob.com, regarding the "monopolistic" threat of a merged HOTJ/TMPW, we view the antitrust associated with this merger as nil. The relevant market is not defined simply by on-line job search engines. It includes printed media, company Web sites, other portals (such as Bloomberg), and a variety of other job-hunting resources. We see absolutely no risk associated with the efforts of New York-based FreeJob.

In today's *WSJ*, for example, FreeJob is quoted as having sent a letter to the FTC warning of Monster. com's "monopolistic practices." The company has also filed a lawsuit against Monster.com.

08/14/01, 09:03 A.M.

ANTITRUST COMMENTARY

Once again demonstrating that the staff of the FTC has difficulty with basic market concepts, the FTC yesterday issued an HSR second request, as disclosed this morning by the companies:

TMP Worldwide Inc. (Nasdaq: TMPW) and HotJobs.com, Ltd. (Nasdaq: HOTJ) announced today that they each received a request for additional information from the Federal Trade Commission ('FTC') in connection with TMP's pending acquisition of HotJobs. TMP and HotJobs will comply with the request for additional information promptly. The merger is subject to the expiration of the Hart-Scott-Rodino waiting period, the approval of HotJobs' shareholders, and other customary closing conditions, and is expected to close in the fourth quarter of 2001. TMP and HotJobs remain committed to working cooperatively with the FTC as it conducts its review of the merger.

We expected the HSR waiting period to expire yesterday, and we find the FTC's action disturbingly inappropriate. True, the FTC may simply be on a fishing expedition to learn more about the online job-recruiting market, but its issuance of an HSR second request is irrational (unless the companies' filings were somehow deficient, in which case we would have believed a re-filing was warranted). We cannot imagine any scenario that would entail remedial action.

The FTC's response would be analogous to issuing a second request for the merger of two Internet-based research services while ignoring the mountains of research provided by sell-side competitors through hard-copy, email, and fax.

In any event, we believe the HSR second request should be resolved within the timeframe provided by our mid-October projected closing date.

TRADING RECOMMENDATION

We are maintaining our "3" Portfolio Rating (Monitoring Key Issues).

10/03/01, 10:00 A.M.

COMMENTARY

Observations based upon a follow-up conversation with HOTJ's CFO this morning:

1. Delayed timing: The companies have realized that the FTC's inquiry will simply take longer than they had hoped. The FTC remains in the discovery phase of its investigation. HOTJ and TMPW believe a year-end closing remains possible, but the companies are trying to be realistic and anticipate that a two-month post-compliance period will be likely in order to obtain approval.
2. Second request compliance: Both HOTJ and TMPW still expect to fully comply with the HSR second request prior to October month-end.
3. Remedial action: HOTJ's CFO does not believe any remedial action should be mandated; however, he acknowledges that the process is moving slowly and speculation is premature.
4. Market definition: The companies have not received enough specific inquiry from the FTC to determine the staff's position on market definition. The staff's questions have been broad and general so far, although the companies expect focused inquiries once full compliance is certified.
5. Full compliance: The companies are committed to working together with the FTC to resolve the second request expeditiously. They will not seek to force the FTC's hand by adhering to a specific deadline once compliance is certified.
6. HeadHunter.net: Neither TMPW (during the conference call this morning) nor HOTJ had any meaningful comments regarding the HHNT/CareerBuilder deal.

We continue to believe that the FTC should approve the transaction without remedial action. We are extending our forecasted closing date to January 15.

10/10/01, 10:28 A.M.

COMMENTARY

Excerpt from the FTC Watch "In Brief" column (dated today, October 10):

[T]he FTC's Northwest Regional Office in Seattle, assisted by investigators in Washington,

D.C., is considered likely to recommend injunctive action to block the proposed merger of Monster.com and HotJobs, two of the Internet's largest personnel recruiters.

We would find this action, if taken, to be nearly inconceivable.

10/10/01, 4:06 P.M.

COMMENTARY

We spoke at length with HOTJ's CFO this afternoon:

- Nature of FTC Watch article. He characterized the article as "ridiculous," noting that the companies have not even fully complied with the HSR second request.
- Second request. The companies continue to furnish information to the FTC (both Washington and Seattle), and the inquiries from the FTC have evolved into a "second round of responses" that are more focused in nature.
- Timing. He reiterated that the companies remain firmly committed to closing the merger by year-end (despite TMPW's acknowledgement that the closing could slip into early 2002).

We are maintaining our January 15, 2002, projected closing date.

TRADING RECOMMENDATION

We are maintaining our "3" Portfolio Rating (Monitoring Key Issues). The spread widened to as much as $1.50 gross this morning before trading throughout the afternoon at $1.00 gross and closing at $0.86 gross.

10/16/01, 07:30 A.M.

ANTITRUST COMMENTARY

To continue our antitrust review, posted Friday, October 15, we estimate that the entire "job recruitment" market will equal $8.5 billion in total revenue, with $2.0 billion derived from companies in the online sector, for the current year. These figures supply the denominator for the following analysis.

Our analysis follows.

INDUSTRY OVERVIEW

As a starting point, we excerpt a description of the entire market from TMPW's most recent 10-K:

1. Interactive: The Internet is an increasingly significant global medium for communications, content, and commerce. The increasing functionality, accessibility and overall usage of the Internet and online service have made them an attractive commercial medium. Thousands of companies have created corporate Web sites that feature information about their product offerings and advertise employment opportunities. Online recruiting is also proving to be attractive to employers and recruiters because online job advertisements can be accessed by job seekers anywhere in the world at anytime and more cost-effective than print media. Forrester Research estimates that online spending by employers for recruitment will grow from $1.2 billion in 2000 to $7.1 billion in 2005.

2. The Recruitment Advertising Market: Recruitment advertising traditionally consists of creating and placing recruitment advertisements in the classified advertising sections of newspapers. While the recruitment advertising market has historically been cyclical, during the period of 1995 through 2000, the U.S. market grew at a compound annual rate of approximately 12% according to the Newspaper Association of America. For the year ended December 31, 2000, global spending (billings) in the recruitment classified advertisement section of newspapers was approximately $8.7 billion according to the Newspaper Association of America. Agencies which place recruitment classified advertising are paid commission rates historically ranging from approximately 10% in Australia to 15% in the U.S. and the United Kingdom of recruitment advertising placed in newspapers and earn fees for providing additional recruitment services. Based on experience with our clients, we believe that only 20% to 30% of open job positions are placed using traditional print media.

3. Executive Search: The market for executive search firms is generally separated into two broad categories: retained executive search firms and contingency executive search firms. Retained search firms are generally engaged on an exclusive basis and paid a contractually agreed-to fee. Contingency executive search firms typically do not focus on the senior executives and are generally paid a percentage of the hired candidate's salary only when a candidate is successfully placed.

4. The Yellow Page Advertising Market: Currently, approximately 6,000 yellow page directories are published annually by 200 publishers and, in the U.S., many cities with populations in excess of 80,000 are served by multiple directories. The percentage of adults who use the yellow pages has remained relatively constant over the last ten years at over 56%, and such readers consult the yellow pages approximately two times weekly. Accordingly, yellow page directories continue to be a highly effective advertising medium. According to the Yellow Page Publishers Association, for the year ended December 31, 2000, total spending on yellow page advertisements in the U.S. was $12.0 billion. Of this amount, approximately $10.0 billion was spent by local accounts and approximately $2.0 billion was spent by national accounts.

5. Selection and Temporary Contracting: The mid-market selection finds for our clients those professional candidates who typically earn between $50,000 and $150,000. Temporary contracting supplements our management selection and permanent placement services and allows our clients to quickly respond to staffing needs that are a result of growth or changing business conditions. According to the Staffing Industry Report, the United States temporary staffing market grew from approximately $62 billion in revenue in 1998 to approximately $86 billion in revenue in 2000, and the U.S. total staffing industry is at more than $140.0 billion.

FINANCIAL SUMMARY

TMPW operates five segments:

- Interactive (including Monster.com and Monstermoving.com)
- Advertising
- eResourcing
- Executive Search
- Directional Marketing

Within each segment, commissions and fees are earned from the following activities: (a) job postings placed on its career Web site, Monster.com, (b) resume and other database access, (c) executive placement services, (d) moving related advertisements on its website, Monstermoving.com, (e) mid-level employee selection and temporary contracting services, (f) selling and placing recruitment advertising and related services, (g) resume screening services, and (h) selling and placing yellow page advertising and related services.

TMPW earns fees through the following activities:

1. Interactive: For the placement of job postings on the Internet primarily its careers Web site, Monster.com. In addition, it earns fees for resume and other database access. The company also derives commissions and fees for job advertisements placed in newspapers and other media, plus associated fees for related services. Commissions and fees are generally recognized upon placement date for newspapers and other media.

2. Permanent placement: For permanent placement services provided, a fee equal to between 20% and 30% of a candidate's first year estimated annual cash compensation is billed in equal installments over 3 consecutive months (the average length of time needed to successfully complete an assignment). For eResourcing's temporary contracting business, commission and fees are recorded when the contracted services are performed.

3. Executive Search: Services and these are recognized as clients are billed. Billings begin with the client's acceptance of a contract. A retainer equal to 33 1/3% of a candidate's first year estimated annual cash compensation is billed in equal installments over 3 consecutive months.

4. Advertising: Quarterly commissions and fees for the Advertising and Communications Division are typically highest in the second quarter and lowest in the fourth quarter; however, the timing of yellow page directory closings is currently concentrated in the third quarter.

For fiscal 2000, Monster.com's gross billings and commissions and fees were $364.0 million and $362.0 million, respectively, and the company's total Interactive gross billings and commissions and fees were $485.9 million and $435.2 million, respectively, including Monster.com, MonsterMoving.com and related advertising revenue.

TMPW Fiscal 2000 Gross Billings:

- Interactive = $485.9 million
- Advertising = $877.8 million
- EResourcing = $391.7 million
- Executive Search = $178.3 million

- Directional Marketing = $545.8 million
- Total Gross Billings = $2.48 billion

TMPW Fiscal 2000 Total Net Revenue (commissions and fees):

- Monster.com/Interactive = $372.9 million, including $10.9 million from Monstermoving.com
- Advertising = $225.7 million
- EResourcing (temporary employment) = $408.4 million
- Executive Search = $178.4 million
- Other = $106.3 million
- Total gross revenue = $1.29 billion

For 2001, we estimate the following for TMPW:

- TMPW total commission revenue = $1.5 billion (18% of total $8.5 billion)
- TMPW total Monster.com Interactive online segment revenue = $462 million (23% of total $2.0 billion)

For 2001, we estimate the following for HOTJ:

- HOTJ total revenue = $125 million (1.4% of total $8.5 billion)
- HOTJ online segment revenue = $125 million (6.2% of total $2.0 billion)

Pro forma combined HOTJ/TMPW:

- Total revenue = $1.525 billion = 18% of total industry
- Online revenue = $587 million = 30% of online segment

By comparison, the #2-ranked HHNT/Career-Builders estimated 2001 pro forma is as follows:

- HHNT ($67 million) + CareerBuilders ($47 million) = $114 million = 6% of online segment.

MARKET SHARE CONCLUSIONS

The FTC seeks to prevent business practices that restrain competition. The agency's analysis consists of many components, including:

- Market definition
- Pricing power
- Barriers to entry

Market Definition

Most FTC investigations are led by its Bureau of Competition. In this case, the Bureau of Competition is being assisted by lawyers in the FTC's Seattle branch who are familiar with e-commerce. This issue in this case is not how many competitors have significant market shares because of one simple fact, the merger of HOTJ and TMPW will further consolidate TMPW's already sizable lead in the online/interactive segment of the job recruiting industry.

We believe that the market should be defined more broadly than the online/interactive segment. However, to assume the FTC's role, we will proceed under the assumption that the merger will create an entity with 30% to 33% of the online/interactive market.

Pricing Power

The issue then becomes clear. Assuming the segment is defined narrowly, can the merger entity restrain competition? To reach a conclusion, one needs to examine the competitive landscape within the online/interactive segment. As we posted on October 12, the top five firms, ranked by "eyeball" share (time spent on site) are as follow:

1. Monster.com = 58.2%
2. Headhunter.net = 13.5%
3. HotJobs = 12.7%
4. JobsOnLine.com = 4.6%
5. CareerBuilder = 4.4%

Pro forma for the two pending mergers:

1. HOTJ/TMPW = 70.9%
2. HHNT/CareerBuilders = 17.9%
3. JobsOnLine.com = 4.6%

This appears overwhelming; however, shopping does not equal buying. Thus, we are led to ask who are the customers and how do TMPW and HOTJ derive revenue? The companies customers consist of three categories: (1) job seekers, (2) companies seeking help, and (3) advertisers.

The ability of Monster.com and HotJobs to "restrain competition" depends on the elasticity of demand for their services. If the companies raise prices for posting resumes, job searches, and executive recruiting, then what happens? Job seekers will use the newspaper classified ads, as will companies seeking help. Or they will use traditional headhunting firms who use phones and fax machines. Or the weaker players will gain market share by discounting. Or well capitalized firms will move into the online/interactive space because . . . there are no barriers to entry.

Barriers to Entry

We will make this comment brief. The only barrier to entry is capital. In fiscal 2000, TMPW, HOTJ, and HHNT spent the following on marketing, related salaries, and promotion:

- TMPW spent $161.4 million (up 112% versus $75.8 million in 1999), or 12% of net revenue, excluding salaries. Total salary expense equaled $667.4 million. Combined, these expenses equaled $828.8 million, or 64% of net revenue.
- HOTJ spent $82.5 million (up 236% versus $24.5 million in 1999), or 85% of net revenue.
- HHNT spent $50.9 million (up 500% versus $9.9 million in 1999), or 103% of net revenue.

Interestingly, compare net revenue growth rates since 1999:

- TMPW (Monster.com only) = 181% (19% for LTM)
- HOTJ = 368% (30% for LTM)
- HHNT = 442% (33% for LTM)

This trend leads to two conclusions: (1) The online/interactive sector is well penetrated and thus sustained revenue growth will be achieved by buying market share and lowering prices, and (2) access to capital is essential to fund growth.

As HHNT summarizes in its most recent 10-K:

We compete against other online recruiting services, such as Monster.com, HotJobs, and CareerBuilder, as well as:

ONLINE
- corporate Internet sites,
- not-for-profit Web sites operated by individuals,
- educational institutions, and
- government job sites.

OTHER
- classified print advertising,
- radio, and
- television.

Many of our current and potential competitors, including those mentioned above, have significantly greater financial, technical and marketing resources, longer operating histories, better name recognition, and more experience than we do. Many of our competitors also have established relationships with job posters.

Note two points raised in the final paragraph: (1) "current and potential competitors," and (2) "marketing resources."

Our conclusions remain that:

- HOTJ/TMPW should be approved by the FTC.
- HHNT/CareerBuilders will be approved by the FTC.

In the final analysis, the HHNT/CareerBuilders merger is pro-competitive under any scenario. Although we find that the HOTJ/TMPW merger is not pro-competitive, we fail to see how the merger will, in the FTC's own words, "restrain competition."

11/06/01, 09:42 A.M.

COMMENTARY

We have three additional observations regarding the conference call:

1. The HOTJ acquisition was barely mentioned during the call. In fact, TMPW management failed to discuss the merger in any detail until asked specifically about the transaction during Q&A. We found that surprising.
2. TMPW's new president, Jim Treacy, seemed to imply that TMPW is frustrated with the FTC and that the company may be less willing to continue to cooperate than previously assumed. although he stated that the company "intends to work" with the FTC, the inference we took away from his remark was that TMPW may become less committed to the acquisition if the FTC fails to approve the merger shortly after TMPW certifies compliance with the pending second request. This worries us.
3. Timing. TMPW will complete its document dump "within the next few weeks" (late November). TMPW then intends to certify compliance, which gives the FTC an additional 30 days to review the submitted material (late December). Assuming, for the moment, that TMPW works with the FTC without adhering to the 30-day deadline, closing could occur in early January.

TRADING RECOMMENDATION

We are maintaining our "3" Portfolio Rating (Monitoring Key Issues), which we will review after speaking with TMPW management.

The current $0.95 gross arbitrage spread yields a 67.5% net annualized return to our January 15, 2002, projected closing date. This date is probably the earliest possible closing date and could easily extend deeper into the first quarter—assuming the companies continue to work toward completing negotiations with the FTC and closing the merger.

11/06/01, 10:11 A.M.

COMMENTARY

We spoke with a contact in TMPW management after the conference call:

- Questions we asked:

  Q. Is TMPW committed to closing the acquisition?

  A. "Yes, fully."

  Q. Will TMPW continue to work with the FTC staff?

  A. "We don't work with the FTC, we comply. If someone at the FTC has a position against the merger, we'll aggressively pursue our position."

  Q. Will TMPW certify compliance and then adhere to the 30-day deadline?

  A. "Absolutely not. When they ask for an extension, you give it to them. We'll be happy to give them additional time, but we won't give them forever."

  Q. Why was HOTJ not emphasized on the call?

  A. "We were happy to answer any question regarding them on the call . . . We believe our shareholders know as much as we know."

  Q. What is management's attitude regarding the FTC?

  A. "The FTC has its own pace without regard to our business or shareholders or market conditions. We want this done, and we want HotJobs to be part of the family. Willing or not, we have to comply with the FTC, and we'll supply them with tons and tons, truckloads, of paperwork. They've asked for 5 years of material, but this is not the time to lose sight of our commitment."

  Q. What other steps are being undertaken by TMPW?

  A. "We've supplied the FTC with several white papers, position papers, that we didn't go into on the call."

- Our conclusions:

  1. TMPW wants to close the acquisition but seems very frustrated by the second request and the depth of the FTC's investigation.
  2. TMPW will not allow this process to continue indefinitely.
  3. We are maintaining our 60% probability of FTC approval.

12/04/01, 10:25 A.M.

TRADING COMMENTARY

We are growing somewhat more disillusioned with the situation, but not for reasons espoused by Robert Doyle in yesterday's Bloomberg report[1]. The definitive proxy statement has not been filed despite the objective of having the HOTJ shareholder meeting in December, which is now impossible. HOTJ needs TMPW a great deal more than TMPW needs HOTJ, and we fail to sense a burning commitment from TMPW's management.

We have no new checks regarding the status of the FTC's legal staff's views on the merger. We believe, though, that Monster.com remains viewed by regulators as an overzealous competitor. Our doubts remain, however, whether the FTC would be able to win an injunction against the merger-assuming TMPW persists. The termination drop-dead date is not until March 31, 2002.

As we have discussed previously, we do not believe HOTJ's share price downside is substantial when compared with the HHNT transaction multiples (see our posting dated October 18 in the Pending Transaction file). Despite poor liquidity and a large overhang, we believe HOTJ should not trade significantly below $5.00 per share in the event of a deal termination, subject to the market remaining relatively stable.

The arbitrage spread is now at its widest level since announcement (June 29):

- Current gross spread = $2.64
- Average Since Announcement = $0.61
- Previous Wide Spread Since Announcement = $2.01
- Tightest Spread Since Announcement = $0.14

---

[1] Robert Doyle, a former FTC staff lawyer, is in the Washington, DC, office of Powell, Goldstein (202-624-7231).

12/06/01, 3:33 P.M.

COMMENTARY

To summarize our views:

1. FTC staff recommendation: We have little doubt at this point that the legal staff is preparing to recommend seeking to block the merger. Its actions are consistent with preparing to litigate and, frankly, Jim Treacy's comments and tone at the CS First Boston conference convince us that TMPW is well aware of the position of the FTC staff. Plans to meet with the Commissioners are not made lightly and certainly not unless a last resort effort is in the works.
2. TMPW's commitment: TMPW's motivation is one aspect of this transaction that has always troubled us. In our opinion, TMPW has never really cared about acquiring HOTJ; instead, we believe HOTJ needs TMPW much more than TMPW needs HOTJ. We tend to think that TMPW's original objective remains to eat the competition.
3. Probabilities: We continue to view the FTC's position as weak (despite the undoubted presence of damning internal documents contained in the companies' data dump), and we believe that the Commission has only a 40% chance of prevailing in winning an injunction. However, we now view the likelihood of a Commission vote to block as 60% based upon deepening evidence of the legal staff's conviction. Much will depend on TMPW's true commitment to closing the acquisition in determining whether the company will call the FTC's bluff or simply walk away from trying to acquire HOTJ.
4. Market definition: We still believe the relevant market includes newspapers, trade journals, geo-specific Web sites, company-specific Web sites and many other sources of job-seeking and job-posting. Recently, the *New York Times* and *Boston Globe* announced plans to consolidate their job-listing Web sites. Furthermore, Dow Jones and the *WSJ* operate a joint venture with Korn-Ferry, a major international recruiting firm, called FutureStep.com. However, the FTC legal staff seems hell-bent on forging ahead with a new market definition.

If the FTC choose this path, then we firmly believe that its decision will look as ridiculous 3 years from now as its decision on Office Depot/Staples looks today.

In terms of technicals, we believe that many arbitrage accounts have unwound most or all of their positions, which, along with Jim Treacy's remarks, accounts for the continuing lack of trading support for HOTJ.

12/12/01, 12:43 P.M.

COMMENTARY

We interviewed Stephen Axinn at length earlier today. Mr. Axinn is acting as lead counsel on behalf of TMPW in connection with the company's negotiations with the FTC. Mr. Axinn seemed clearly interested in promoting TMPW's views, as well as clarifying certain recent published reports in the media.

A review of topics discussed follows:

GENERAL OBSERVATIONS

1. TMPW is "hopeful" that the FTC will approve the transaction.
2. TMPW believes "at the moment" that no remedy is required.
3. TMPW argues that the barriers to entry should exclude promotional and advertising expenses.
4. TMPW believes strongly that the broad market definition is relevant and, even in a narrow definition, that the barriers to entry are sufficiently low enough to invite serious competition in the near future as major media players devote more resources to the online segment.

Discussion of Issues

APPROVAL

- Mr. Axinn stated that he is hopeful that the FTC will "come around" to the company's views regarding market definition and barriers to entry. He added that his optimism is based generally upon "the government's reaction to the information we've provided." He would comment specifically beyond this remark other than to say his view is predicated on "compelling facts and precedents," including the FTC's recent approval of the RAL/Nestle transaction, which initially encountered "the same knee-jerk reactions" by the FTC's staff.

ISSUES

- Barriers to entry. TMPW's view is that few, if any, credible barriers to entry exist. "A well defined concept for antitrust analysis is that a barrier to entry is an obstacle faced by a new entrant that was not faced by the incumbent." Mr. Axinn's position is that advertising and promotion expenses are ongoing operating expenses, not a prerequisite to entering the market segment. He added that "branding is not a barrier, whether it's renting a blimp to fly over the Super Bowl, or anything else." His view is that "patents, copyrights, and expertise," are barriers, not simply raising and spending capital. Mr. Axinn pointed out the new site Gator.com, which directs Web-surfers from a sought site to an advertisement pop-up for a competing site. Services like Gator.com illustrate competitive advertising alternatives geared directly at users of specific types of searches (such as job-hunting). He concluded, "There are no barriers to entry in this business."

- **New entrants.** The job recruiting market has experienced "extraordinarily dynamic level" of change over the past few years. Monster.com continues to view itself as a "new entrant" into a market dominated by deep-pocketed media companies (e.g., Knight-Ridder, Dow Jones, the New York Times). Furthermore, any major Web-based company possesses the ability to enter the segment, including Yahoo!, AOL, and Microsoft. Mr. Axinn stated: "Can TMP dictate to them? We're still a small company compared to some" of the major media players, several of which are making strides in switching from printed classified ads to Internet-based content.

- **Market segment.** The "ultimate" issue to resolve is whether HOTJ "can be replaced" (i.e., whether TMPW's acquisition of HOTJ will result in a less competitive market)—not whether Monster.com can be replaced. TMPW's position is that only 3%–4% of all job placements result from Internet based recruiting, with the vast majority continuing to result from classified ads and word-of-mouth. In antitrust analysis the acquisition of a competitor must be considered within the context of the competitive realities of the marketplace. Mr. Axinn stated that "any of [the major media players] can decide to plant their flags" at any time. In fact, any search engine, such as Google.com or Alta Vista.com, will find multiple job postings from a variety of sources on an objective, non-discrimi-

natory basis, which may or may not include "Monster.com, HotJobs, or Headhunter."

STATUS OF FTC NEGOTIATIONS

- **TMPW's attitude.** The company realizes that Jim Treacy's recent remarks were inappropriate and only "reflected a level of frustration" based upon the FTC staff's level of demands (additional documentation, studies, depositions, etc.). According to Mr. Axinn, Jim Treacy "saw the KRI [Headhunter] deal go through and felt like the FTC was singling out Monster.com." About Mr. Treacy's public frustration, Mr. Axinn said that "We're not denying that it happened, but that's history. He never intended to be insulting." Mr. Axinn confirmed that senior executives have met with Joe Simons (Director of the Bureau of Competition) recently and that the FTC and the company is "communicating" more effectively, with both sides "listening to each other . . . Diplomacy is an art."

- **Negotiations.** Mr. Axinn would not discuss the level of "conversations" with the FTC staff or the FTC's more senior officials, stating that he would not comment "on any solution or whether any solution is necessary." He added: "Our opinion at the moment is that no solution will be necessary."

We pressed Mr. Axinn about whether TMPW would consider behavioral remedies as a compromise solution. We discussed the specific remedies suggested in our previous commentaries (of which he was aware), but Mr. Axinn would not comment on their viability. Throughout the interview, it struck us that TMPW is willing to agree to certain behavioral modifications. Mr. Axinn repeated the phrase "at the moment" more than once when discussing his view that no remedies would be required. He presented a compelling argument which, as a litigator, is to be expected, but our view is that some progress has been made recently with the FTC.

TRADING RECOMMENDATION

We are maintaining our "3" Portfolio Rating (Monitoring Key Issues). The arbitrage spread is currently $3.43 gross, which is approximately $0.60 tighter than the recent widest level.

12/28/01, 4:14 P.M.

COMMENTARY

We have confirmed with HOTJ's CFO that the breakup fee has been wired to TMPW.

For the record, as filed on Form 8-K with the SEC this afternoon:

- On December 27, 2001, HotJobs.com, Ltd. ("HotJobs") announced that it had terminated the agreement and plan of merger by and among TMP Worldwide Inc., TMP Tower Corp. and HotJobs (the "TMP Merger Agreement"), dated as of June 29, 2001, and that it had entered into an agreement and plan of merger (the "Yahoo! Merger Agreement") by and among Yahoo! Inc., ("Yahoo!"), HJ Acquisition Corp., a wholly owned subsidiary of Yahoo!, and HotJobs.

We will move the Pending Transaction file to the Archive shortly.

Source: DealAnalytics.com, August 18, 2002.

APPENDIX C

ILLUSTRATIVE PORTFOLIO RECOMMENDATIONS

ILLUSTRATIVE PORTFOLIO RECOMMENDATIONS: AUGUST 13, 2002

Target/Acquirer	Ticker/ Ticker	Industry	Portfolio Rating	Parity Value	Gross Spread	Net Spread	Date Announced	Estimated Closing	Annual Net Return	Latest Update
American Water Works/RWE A.G.	AWK/ N/A	IND	3	$46.000	$2.530	$2.970	9/14/01	1/31/03	13.10%	8/7/02
AT&T Canada/AT&T Corp.	ATTC/ T	TEL	3	33.340	1.820	1.770	3/4/99	10/8/02	36.83	8/12/02
AT&T Corp./Comcast Corp.	T/ CMCSA	TEL	3	10.464	0.064	0.076	7/8/01	11/30/02	4.73	8/12/02
Bancorp Connecticut/Banknorth Group	BKCT/ BKNG	BAN	1	28.000	0.040	−0.010	4/11/02	8/30/02	−0.59	7/23/02
Centennial Bancorp/Umpqua Holdings	CEBC/ UMPQ	BAN	2	9.058	0.458	0.452	7/23/02	11/29/02	17.13	7/24/02
Chase Industries/Olin Corp.	CSI/ OLN	IND	3	11.885	0.335	0.287	5/8/02	9/30/02	5.08	8/6/02
ChemFirst Inc./DuPont	CEM/ DD	IND	2	29.200	0.270	0.420	7/23/02	12/15/02	4.30	7/29/02
Conoco, Inc./Phillips Petroleum	COC/P	IND	2	23.769	0.009	0.003	11/18/01	9/30/02	−0.26	8/9/02
Datum/Symmetricom, Inc.	DATM/ SYMM	TEC	4	9.111	1.221	1.074	5/23/02	10/31/02	54.75	8/13/02
Dave & Buster's/Investcorp	DAB/ N/A	OTH	3	13.500	0.490	0.440	5/30/02	9/30/02	22.74	8/2/02
DeWolfe Companies/NRT Corp. (Cendant)	DWL/ NRT	OTH	2	19.000	0.140	0.090	8/12/02	9/20/02	4.05	8/12/02
Donnelly Corp./Magna International	DON/ MGA	IND	3	26.406	0.906	0.933	6/25/02	9/30/02	32.73	8/13/02
Dreyer's Grand Ice Cream/ Nestle SA	DRYR/ N/A	OTH	2	83.000	16.070	16.860	6/17/02	1/1/06	7.49	8/7/02
Echo Bay/TVX Gold/Kinross Gold	ECO/ KGC	OTH	4	0.946	0.036	−0.036	6/10/02	10/31/02	−22.09	8/13/02
EEX Corp./Newfield Exploration	EEX/ NFX	IND	2	1.866	0.026	−0.022	5/29/02	9/27/02	−3.85	8/9/02
EXCO Resources/Management LBO	EXCO/ N/A	IND	4	17.000	1.040	0.990	8/7/02	12/31/02	19.13	8/9/02
Expedia Inc./USA Networks	EXPE/ USAI	INT	3	59.305	8.365	8.180	7/16/01	12/31/02	43.71	8/9/02

FEI Corp./Veeco Instruments	FEIC/ VECO	TEC	2	18.658	0.269	0.236	7/12/02	10/31/02	5.09	8/13/02
Garan Inc./Berkshire Hathaway	GAN/ BRK/A	IND	1	60.000	0.120	0.070	7/02/02	9/4/02	2.49	8/5/02
Golden State Bancorp/Citigroup	GSB/C	BAN	2	34.724	0.554	0.530	5/21/02	9/30/02	11.51	8/9/02
Hispanic Broadcasting/Univision Communications	HSP/ UVN	MED	4	18.827	0.627	0.744	6/12/02	2/28/03	4.70	8/8/02
Hollywood Casino/Peran National Gaming	HWD/ PENN	OTH	3	12.750	0.730	0.680	8/7/02	5/31/03	7.55	8/11/02
Hughes Electronics/EchoStar Communications	GMH/ DISH	TEL	3	11.556	1.626	1.631	8/5/01	12/31/02	42.59	8/13/02
International Speciality Products/ Management LBO	ISP/ N/A	IND	3	10.000	0.050	0	7/8/02	12/31/02	.00	7/25/02
McAfee.com Inc./Network Associates	MCAF/ NET	TEC	2	15.108	0.158	0.087	3/18/02	9/12/02	6.29	8/13/02
MCI Group/WorldCom, Inc.	MCWE/ WCOE	TEL	3	0.190	0.010	–0.103	5/22/02	12/31/03	–40.81	8/12/02
Medford Bancorp/Citizens Financial	MDBK/ N/A	BAN	1	35.000	0.150	0.250	6/13/02	10/15/02	3.85	8/7/02
Mississippi Valley Bancshares/ Marshall & Ilsley	MVBI/ MI	BAN	2	52.158	0.458	0.506	6/17/02	10/31/02	5.21	7/24/02
NCS HealthCare/Genesis Health Ventures	NCSS/ GHVI	HEA	3	1.590	–0.830	–0.885	7/29/02	10/31/02	–159.83	8/9/02
Nortek, Inc./Keiso & Co.	NTK/ N/A	IND	3	46.000	1.700	1.650	4/8/02	10/31/02	18.53	8/9/02
Oplink Communications/Avanex Corp.	OPLK/ AVNX	TEC	4	0.928	0.018	–0.052	3/19/02	8/19/02	–319.89	8/5/02
P&O Princess Cruises/Carnival Corp.	POC/ CCL	OTH	4	30.352	6.532	6.661	12/16/01	12/31/02	64.16	7/31/02
PanAmSat/EchoStar Communications	SPOT/ DISH	TEL	3	22.470	0.070	0.020	8/5/01	12/31/02	.22	7/12/02
Paradigm Geophysical/Fox Paine & Co.	PGEO/ N/A	IND	3	5.150	0.029	–0.021	5/22/02	8/13/02	–37.42	8/13/02
PayPal Inc./eBay Inc.	PYPL/ EBAY	INT	3	23.014	2.354	2.466	7/8/02	12/31/02	31.48	8/12/02
Penn Virginia/BP Capital	PVA/ N/A	IND	3	40.000	6.150	6.550	6/25/02	11/25/02	68.34	8/09/02
Pennzoil-Quaker State/Royal Dutch Shell	PZL/ RD	IND	2	22.000	0.300	0.275	3/25/02	9/30/02	9.05	8/1/02
Petroleum Geo-Services/Veritas DGC	PGO/ VTS	IND	3	0	–0.500	–0.550	11/27/01	12/31/02	–268.03	8/13/02
Pharmacia Corp./Pfizer Inc.	PHA/ PFE	HEA	3	45.402	–0.168	–0.091	7/15/02	2/15/03	–0.26	8/13/02
Prime Group Realty/American Realty Investors	PGE/ ARL	OTH	3	10.500	5.270	5.220	8/24/01	12/31/02	270.96	8/13/02
Rainbow Media/Cablevision Systems	RMG/ CVC	MED	2	6.419	0.019	–0.087	8/5/02	8/20/02	–26.25	8/8/02
Royal Caribbean/P&O Princess Cruises	RCL/ POC	OTH	3	20.637	3.097	3.219	11/20/01	12/31/02	45.02	7/31/02
SkillSoft Corp./SmartForce plc	SKIL/ SMTF	TEC	4	7.765	0.015	–0.141	6/10/02	9/6/02	–49.60	8/6/02
Spectrain Corp./REMEC Inc.	SPCT/ REMC	TEC	4	7.900	1.500	1.350	5/20/02	9/30/02	192.75	8/12/02
SpeedFam-IPEC/Novellus Systems	SFAM/ NVLS	BAN	3	4.892	0.092	0.063	8/12/02	11/29/02	3.33	8/13/02
Syncor International/Cardinal Health	SCOR/ CAH	HEA	2	32.302	0.222	0.225	6/14/02	9/30/02	5.74	8/08/02
Three Rivers Bancorp/Sky Financial	TRBC/ SKYF	BAN	1	16.958	–0.192	–0.231	5/8/02	9/30/02	–9.24	7/29/02
TRW Inc./Northrop Grumman	TRW/ NOC	IND	2	59.998	5.248	5.171	2/22/02	10/31/02	37.45	8/8/02
Unilab Corp./Quest Diagnostics	ULAB/ DGX	HEA	3	21.256	3.466	3.443	4/2/02	9/30/02	120.09	8/13/02
VIB Corp./Rabobank Group	VIBC/ N/A	BAN	1	15.100	0.160	0.110	7/31/02	12/31/02	1.68	8/2/02
Warren Bancorp/Banknorth Group	WRNB/ BKNG	BAN	1	15.750	0.170	0.225	8/8/02	12/31/02	3.88	8/9/02
Wink Communications/Liberty Media	WINK/ L	MED	3	3.000	0.020	–0.030	6/24/02	8/19/02	–44.39	8/1/02

Source: DealAnalytics.com.

APPENDIX D

ILLUSTRATIVE PORTFOLIO RECOMMENDATIONS SUMMARY

PORTFOLIO RECOMMENDATIONS SUMMARY

Portfolio Recommendations provides specific rankings of recommended investment positions from DealAnalytics Transaction Database. Each Portfolio Recommendation is weighted by its overall merits and risks, and each is reviewed on a daily basis. A key to the rankings is set forth:

Portfolio Recommendations Ratings Key[a]:

	Maximum Allocation[a]:		Summary of Current Recommendations:	
	Assets	Risk Capital	Total	Average Return
1 = Core Portfolio Holding	7.5%	3.5%	6	0.3%
2 = Developing Trading Position	4.0	1.5	14	5.9
3 = Monitoring Key Issues	2.5	0.5	25	5.8
4 = Sell Position/No Position	0.0	0.0	8	−7.0
5 = Short/Reverse	2.5	0.5	0	0

[a]Maximum Allocation of Assets represents the maximum percentage of an unleveraged portfolio's total assets or a leveraged portfolio's net assets. Maximum Allocation of Risk Capital represents the maximum "equity risk capital" expressed as a percentage of an unleveraged portfolio's total equity value or a leveraged portfolio's net equity value.

PORTFOLIO RECOMMENDATIONS METHODOLOGY

Investment Strategy

I.   Announced deals (mergers, acquisitions, and restructurings)
II. Hedged approached to portfolio management (utilizing options when appropriate)
III. Short-term trading strategies (60 days average)
IV. Minimize risk of loss, market correlation, and volatility

Research Process

I.   General Philosophy: To eliminate uncertainty in two areas—deal risk and market volatility.
II. Two distinct disciplines:

Fundamental Research—three objectives:
  • Determine whether transaction makes strategic business sense (financial analysis)
  • Research regulatory challenges to the deal (legal analysis)
  • Estimate timing and project what can delay closing (trading analysis)

Quantitative Research—two objectives:
  • Quantify maximum loss and "risk capital" (hedging analysis)
  • Quantify effect of potential market volatility (P&L analysis)

Portfolio Diversification

I.   General Philosophy: To diversify based upon risk of loss rather than capital allocation.
II. Combine Fundamental Research with Quantitative Research

III. Create trading strategies designed to:
- Minimize "risk capital" and market correlation
- Maximize short-term IRR
- Hedge maximum loss

IV. Diversify portfolio investments with:
- No more than 3.5% "risk capital" in any one position
- No more than 7.5% maximum asset allocation in any one position
- Increased risk capital percentage as deal-closing nears
- Actively traded and rebalanced hedges

Source: DealAnalytics.com, August 13, 2002.

CHAPTER 22

IMPLEMENTATION AND MANAGEMENT GUIDES FOR M&As

—————◆◇◆—————

World business faces new uncertainties since the economic downturn began in early 2000, aggravated by the September 11, 2001, terrorist attacks, the decline in stock markets, and increased geopolitical tensions. The economic, financial, political, cultural, and international environments have become increasingly turbulent. Communications, transportation, computer, and Internet developments have increased globalization and changed the way business is conducted. Interactions with competitors, suppliers, customers, complementary firms, and other stakeholders continue to be adjusted. In these adjustment processes, M&As (broadly defined) continue to perform increasingly important roles.

M&A activities have important economic and business functions in enabling firms to adjust to changing environments and to enhance long term enterprise values. But combining organizations can pose considerable challenges causing M&A failures. A widely held view is that about 67% of acquisitions do not earn the buyers' cost of capital. Mergers fail for a variety of reasons as listed in Table 22.1. The purpose of this concluding chapter is to help management avoid the mistakes listed in Table 22.1.

While merger failures occur, the overall performance record of mergers is encouraging. Chapter 8 summarized the evidence. A comprehensive study of combined returns in a large sample of 3,688 mergers from 1973–1998 found that the combined return in excess of market required returns to targets and bidders was a positive 2% (Andrade, Mitchell, and Stafford, 2001). A paper by Moeller, Schlingemann, and Stulz (2003) looks at the absolute dollar amounts of losses to acquiring firms from 1980 to 2001. They report that small firms gained $8 billion while large firms lost $226 billion. Their figure 1, p. 28 shows that dollar returns to acquiring firms was a breakeven activity from 1980 to 1999. Most of the dollar losses occurred in 2000–2001, a difficult economic environment during which the market value of domestic corporations declined from $17.1 trillion to $13.3 trillion, a loss of $3.8 trillion. They found "no evidence that acquirers have poor long-term performance" (p. 21). Since the Moeller et al. (2003) data were limited to acquiring firms, no evidence is provided on combined returns for merger activities during the 1980–1999 period. In this chapter our emphasis is on guidelines that will assist firms in achieving value increasing M&A programs.

TABLE 22.1 Why Mergers Fail

1. Pay too much
2. Overoptimistic expected synergies
3. No business-economic logic to the deal
4. Businesses unrelated—bad fit
5. Did not understand what they bought—Internet, high tech
6. Unduly hyped by investment bankers, consulting firms, and/or lawyers
7. Underestimated regulatory delays or prohibitions
8. Hubris of top executives—ambition to run a bigger firm and increase salary
9. Top executives want to cash out stock options
10. Culture clashes
11. Ineffective integration—poorly planned, poorly executed, too slow, too fast
12. Suppression of effective business systems of target firms, destroying the basis of their prior success
13. Too much debt—future interest payments a burden
14. Too much short term debt—repayment before synergies are realized
15. Power struggles or incompatibility in new boardroom
16. Mergers of equals delay requisite decisions
17. Target resistance—white knights, scorched earth, antitrust
18. Multiple bidders cause overpayment
19. Hostile takeovers prevent obtaining sufficient information, fail to uncover basic incompatibilities or create resentment and persistent ill will
20. Basic industry problems such as overcapacity (autos, steel, telecoms)

M&As IN A STRATEGIC, LONG-RANGE PLANNING FRAMEWORK

Sometimes M&A activities can help a firm improve its capabilities and performance, but sometimes M&A activities would represent a diversion from the fundamental adjustments that must be made. M&A planning must fit into the framework of the firm's overall strategic planning processes (Chung and Weston, 1982; Weston, 1970).

GOALS AND OBJECTIVES

General goals can be formulated with respect to size, growth, stability, flexibility, and technological breadth. Size objectives are established in order to use effectively the fixed factors the firm owns or buys. Size objectives also have been expressed in terms of critical mass. Critical mass refers to the size a firm must achieve in order to attain cost levels that will enable it to operate profitably at market prices.

Growth objectives can be expressed in terms of sales, total assets, earnings per share, or the market price of the firm's stock. These are related to two valuation objectives. One is to attain a favorable price/earnings multiple for the firm's shares. A second is to increase the ratio of the market value of the firm's common stock to its book value.

Three major forms of instability can be distinguished. The first is exemplified by the defense market, which is subject to large, erratic fluctuations in its total size and abrupt shifts in individual programs. Another form of instability is the cyclical instability that characterizes producers of industrial and consumer durable goods. Other instabilities are major discontinuities of the type that have taken place in the computer and media industries.

The goal of flexibility refers to the firm's ability to adjust to a wide variety of changes. Such flexibility can require a breadth of research, manufacturing, or marketing capabilities. Of increased interest in recent years is technological breadth. With the faster pace of technological change in the U.S. economy, a firm may consider it important to possess capabilities in the rapidly advancing technologies.

Goals may be stated in general or specific terms, but both are subject to quantification. For example, growth objectives can be expressed in relationship to the growth of the economy or the firm's industry. Specific objectives may be expressed in terms of percentage of sales in specified types of markets. The quantification of goals facilitates comparisons of goals with forecasts of the prospects for the firm. If it is necessary for the firm to alter its product-market mix or range of capabilities to reduce or close the planning gap, a diversification strategy may be formulated.

Efforts to achieve multiple goals suggest a broader range of variables in the decision processes of the firm. Decisions involve trade-offs and judgments of the nature of future environments; the policies of other firms with respect to the dimensions described; and new missions, technologies, and capabilities. In short, to the requirements of operating efficiency and optimal output adjustments has been added the increased importance of the planning processes (Weston, 1972; Weston and Copeland, 1992).

THE ROLE OF STRATEGY

The literature views long-range planning and strategic planning as essentially synonymous (Steiner, 1979). The emphasis of strategic planning is on areas related to the firm's environments and constituencies, not just operating decisions (Summer, 1980). In our view, the modern literature on long-range planning indicates that long-range strategic planning involves at least the following elements:

1. Environmental reassessment for new technologies, new industries, and new forms of competitors.
2. A consideration of capabilities, missions, and environmental interactions from the standpoint of the firm and its divisions.
3. An emphasis on process rather than particular goals or objectives.
4. An emphasis on iteration and on an iterative feedback process as a methodology for dealing with ill-structured problems.
5. Recognition of the need for coordination and consistency in the resulting long-range planning processes with respect to individual divisions, product-market activities, and optimization from the standpoint of the firms as a whole.
6. Recognition of the need to relate effectively to the firm's changing environment and constituencies.
7. Integration of the planning process into a reward and penalty (incentive) system, taking a long-range perspective.

Earlier, the emphasis of long-range strategic planning was on doing something about the so-called gap. When it is necessary to take action to close a prospective gap between the firm's objectives and its potential based on its present capabilities, difficult choices must be made. For example, should the firm attempt to change its environment or capabilities? What would be the costs of such changes? What are the risks and unknowns? What are the rewards of success? What are the penalties of failure? Because the stakes are large, the iterative process is employed. A tentative decision is made. The process is repeated, perhaps from a different management function orientation, and at some point the total enterprise point of view is brought to bear on the problem. At some point, decisions are made and must involve entrepreneurial judgments.

Alternatively, the emphasis may be on broader orientations to the effective alignment of the firm with its environments and constituencies. Different approaches may be emphasized. One approach seeks to choose products related to the needs or missions of the customer that will provide large markets. A second approach focuses on technological bottlenecks or barriers, the solution of which may create new markets. A third strategy chooses to be at the frontiers of technological capabilities on the theory that attractive product fallout will result from such competence. A fourth approach emphasizes economic criteria including attractive growth prospects and manageable instability.

Other things being equal, a preferred strategy is to move into a diversification program from the base of existing capabilities or organizational strengths. Guidance may be obtained by answering the following questions: Is there strength in the general management functions? Can the company provide staff expertise in the new areas? Does the firm's financial planning and control effectiveness have a broad carryover? Are there specific capabilities such as research, marketing, and manufacturing that the firm is seeking to spread over a wider area?

The firm should be clear on its strengths, its limitations, and the changing environments in which it operates. To remedy weaknesses, the firm should clearly define the specific new capabilities it is seeking to obtain. If the firm does not possess sufficient breadth of capability to use as a basis for moving into other areas, an alternative strategy may be employed—one that would establish a beachhead of capabilities in one or more selected areas. The firm is then in a position to develop concentrically from each of these nuclei.

Changing product requirements and changing market opportunities require new technologies and new combinations of technologies. To illustrate, the aircraft industry moved through stages in which the critical competence shifted from structures; to engine and other propulsion methods; to guidance; and finally to the interaction of structures, propulsion, and guidance as reflected in the concept of aerospace systems. Similarly, in office equipment, products have moved from manual operation to electromechanical, to electric, to electronic, and to the interactions of specialized units in systems. Electronics technology has moved from electron tubes to semiconductors to integrated circuitry, involving a fusion with chemistry and metallurgy. Competitive factors caused Intel to drop its production of memory chips and focus its resources on microprocessors. Telecommunications is shifting from hard wire to microwave, fiber optics, broadband, and so on. Internet systems have created many new types of businesses and have impacted many "Old Economy" businesses.

In the consumer nondurable goods industries (such as food, cleaning products, and paper goods), product changes have characteristically been labeled product differentiation, with the unfavorable connotation that fundamental characteristics of products have not been altered. Yet even in these industries, fluctuations in consumer income patterns and tastes have created needs and opportunities for basic changes. For example, the need to understand the nature of the impact of foods on people has increased the requirements for competence in the chemical and biological sciences in the food industry.

THE ROLE OF PLANNING

A number of misconceptions are held with respect to the significance of planning in the firm. The misconceptions range between two extremes. One view holds that we have always planned—that planning is nothing new—as the practice antedates biblical times. This view misses the real significance of modern planning, however. Certainly business firms have been planning for decades, with accounting and financial budgeting activities representing one kind of planning. However, the important developments that set the new managerial technology of planning apart from its predecessor activities are (1) coordinating research, sales, production, marketing, facilities, personnel, and financial plans, making them consistent with one another and resolving them into comprehensive planning for the enterprise as a whole; (2) a feedback system; and (3) integration with reward and penalty (incentive) systems. Some U.S. firms developed and practiced such integrated and coordinated planning by the 1920s, but the broad extension of the practice did not occur until after World War II, with substantial gaps still persisting in the understanding and implementation of effective planning among a large number of firms.

The other erroneous view about business planning holds that the heavy investments of capital by large corporations have led them to devise methods for controlling demand and that planning has replaced the market mechanism. Such a view led one author to sweeping generalizations, unsupported by systematic evidence, such as the following: "It is a feature of all planning that, unlike the market, it incorporates within itself no mechanism by which demand is accommodated to supply and the reverse" (Galbraith, 1967, p. 35). This statement represents a basic misconception. Those with experience with purposive organization planning processes recognize that the development of integrated planning is an effort to adapt more responsively to increasingly dynamic environments. Planning and management controls do not remove the uncertainty of market influences; rather, they seek to help the firm adjust more sensitively to change, to new threats, and to opportunities.

MANAGERIAL CAPABILITIES PERSPECTIVE

The capabilities concept encompasses important management technologies including planning, information sciences, computerization of information flows, Internet technologies, formal decision models, problem-solving methodologies, and behavioral sciences. Thus, managerial capabilities include competence in the general management functions of planning, organizing, directing, and controlling, as well as in the specific management functions of research, production, personnel, marketing, and finance. In addition, they include a range of technological capabilities. Another important dimension is coordinating and achieving an effective organization system, aided by real-time information systems.

The development of such a range of capabilities requires substantial investments in the training and experience of people. This includes investments required to hold organizations together during periods of depressed sales. Market demand and supply forces place a high value on executive talent and staff expertise. Their importance in the competitive performance of firms leads to new forms of fixed investment in managerial organizations. The effective utilization of augmented fixed factors leads to firms of larger size and increased diversification. Fixed factors include investments in plant and equipment or the development and holding of a group of scientists, engineers, and other highly trained and experienced executives. The pharmaceutical and Internet industries are clear examples.

The theory of the firm set forth by Coase (1937) predicted these developments. In explaining the role of firms in relation to markets, Coase identified two functions as determinants of the scope and size of firms. One was the relative efficiency of making transactions within the firm compared to conducting transactions in the external marketplace. The other was the effectiveness with which the elements of the firm were coordinated or managed. Coase described possible developments that would affect the size of firms compared to the relative scope of market transactions. Coase's model predicted that the broadening of capabilities encompassed by a firm and developments in managerial technology would result in an increase in the absolute size of business firms and in the degree of their diversification with respect to capabilities, missions, and markets.

Potential competition has thus been enlarged. Industry boundaries defined by products or production methods become less meaningful than those defined by the ability to perform the critical functions for meeting customers' needs or missions. The case of entry into industries can be affected because the critical factor for success in changing environments may be a range of technologies, experience developed in international markets, or even more general organizational performance capabilities.

Because of the critical role of managerial capabilities, some firms have emphasized hiring key executives rather than buying companies. This policy might have some validity on theoretical grounds, but it also can stir up ill will in the companies that have been raided. Companies that have succeeded in hiring new top executives with recognized capabilities have experienced an immediate increase in the market value of their common stock.

THE FOUNDATION FOR SOUND M&A DECISIONS

Sound M&A planning must take into account the many factors involved in M&A activities. Of central importance is the understanding that M&As should fit into the broad framework of the firm's overall strategic planning processes. The basic elements of strategic planning include an assessment of the firm's environment and an analysis of the firm's resources and capabilities as they relate to the environment. Goals are formulated, and adjustments, which may include mergers and acquisitions, are made to move the firm closer to these goals. The process is never complete but rather is performed iteratively as the firm's capabilities and environments change over time.

Increasingly, firms are defined less in terms of products and markets and more by their range of capabilities. This creates opportunities and increasing competitive threats in a dynamic economy. M&As provide a means of preserving the organization capital of those firms that have been less able to adapt to change. They allow more successful firms to acquire needed capabilities faster and with less risk than developing them internally. Even pure conglomerate M&As that start with transferability of only generic management capabilities provide an avenue for the eventual development of increased skills in specific management functions such as production and marketing.

M&A decisions involve the use of principles from finance, business economics, and strategy in a dynamic framework. They recognize multiple dimensions of successful business operations. Operating activities must be efficient, but efficient operations must be a part of sound planning processes. The firm must continuously adjust to its changing economic, financial, political, and social environments. It must adjust to, and be proactive toward, potential competitors, suppliers, customers, and complementary firms. A successful firm must be a part of processes that involve many change forces, such as changes in technology, changes in production processes, changes in product quality, new products, and changes in the organization of industry. It is within this broad framework that M&A decisions are made and contribute to increases in the value of organizations.

STRATEGIC PLANNING FRAMEWORK

The aforementioned concepts are summarized in Figure 22.1, which illustrates the iterative "going around the loop" concept in the strategic planning process. The overview of relationships presented demonstrates that strategic planning is a continuous process. It begins with strategic planning to achieve competitive advantages, which produce superior growth in economic profits and returns to shareholders. Strategic planning guides the firm's choice of a product-market scope and its resource requirements. The economic nature of the industry or industries in which the firm operates determines the patterns of its financial statements reflected in traditional financial ratio analysis. Based on a business economic analysis of the industry and the firm's competitive position, projections of financial relationships provide a basis for valuation estimates. Because these are subject to error and change, further analysis based on identification of the key drivers of value are made. This facilitates study of the impact of operating performance on the value driver levels and the resulting valuations. Intrinsic value estimates are related to alternative performance measurements. Compensation systems should be linked to performance metrics. Periodic reviews lead to strategy revisions, as well as to changes in policies and operations. Repeated iterations of the process shown in Figure 22.1 are made.

FIGURE 22.1 Strategic Planning Loop

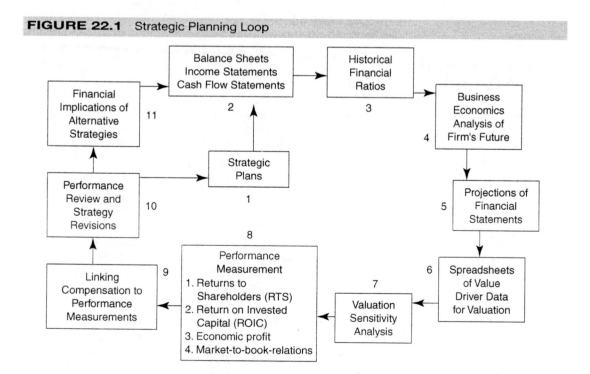

REAL OPTIONS FRAMEWORK

The performance measurements in block 8 in Figure 22.1 provide a basis for reassessments of the firm's strategies and product market areas. For example, Dell Computer, to continue its high rate of revenues growth, announced in 2001 that it would enter the printer market, competing against Hewlett-Packard. In 2002, Dell announced that it would enter the handheld personal digital assistant (PDA) market. These are examples of the types of performance reviews and strategy revisions covered in block 10 of Figure 22.1. The financial results of alternative strategy revisions are initiated in the next step depicted in block 11.

The performance review and analysis depicted in block 10 involve assessments of a wide range of alternatives. These are illustrated in Figure 22.2, which depicts a real options framework. A real options analysis (RO) places a value on the benefits of decision flexibility. A firm might acquire real options through intellectual property rights (patents, licenses, leases), ownership of natural resources (real estate, oil field), technological know-how, reputation/brand name, strategic alliances/market position, and organizational capabilities/infrastructure and employees.

A real options analysis has a potential for important benefits. RO helps systematize the analytical process and structures decisions to uncover the important dimensions and to provide deeper insights. A common language for communication among different functions (R&D, finance, strategy, marketing) is provided. RO achieves a better interface among strategic planning, capital budgeting, incentives, and control systems. RO provides intuition and insights that might challenge conventional thinking. For example, accepting negative NPV projects or delaying positive NPV projects might increase value.

Figure 22.2 illustrates the wide range of strategic options under continuous review by the firm. Existing activities of the firm can be augmented for value enhancement. The framework presented in Figure 22.2 depicts five major decision areas for developing new growth opportunities: internal changes, financial restructuring, external opportunities, alternative contracting relationships, and restructuring operations. The roles of M&As (in a broad sense) also are depicted in relation to other alternatives. This illustrates one of the key ideas in real options analysis of reassessment of alternative forms of growth opportunities.

Each of the important decision areas in Figure 22.2 can be analyzed in a more detailed framework. Table 22.2 depicts multiple strategies for growth. The relative contributions and limitations of six major alternatives are depicted. The criteria in the first column reflect the important potential benefits of each alternative growth strategy. Compared with internal growth, mergers have the advantage of speed in adding capabilities, product, and markets. Joint ventures reduce antitrust problems, investment requirements, and risk. Alliances provide opportunities for gaining knowledge about new areas but the relationships have greater ambiguity. Licensing quickly adds revenues but might create competitors. Investments in other companies might provide new knowledge and high returns, and lead to joint ventures and mergers.

Table 22.3 illustrates alternative approaches to asset restructuring. The strength of divestitures is in raising funds and enabling the parent to focus on its core business. Equity carve-outs raise funds as an initial step toward a spin-off. Spin-offs may facilitate performance measurements and strengthen incentives. Tracking stocks achieve similar results but give the parent continuing control over the operations.

In Table 22.4, financial engineering and changes in financial structure are evaluated by a different set of criteria. ESOPs provide tax benefits and help owners maintain control. A leveraged recap maintains control by a capital infusion to pay a large dividend to existing shareholders;

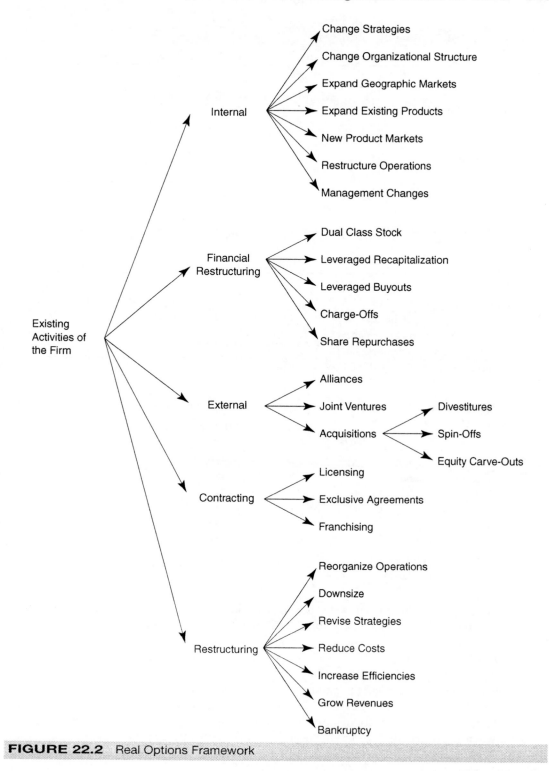

FIGURE 22.2   Real Options Framework

TABLE 22.2 Multiple Strategies for Growth[a]

	Internal	*Merger*	*JV*	*Alliance*	*Licensing*	*Investment*
Speed	L	H	M	M	H	M
Cost known	L	M	H	M	L	H
Add capabilities	L	H	H	M	L	H
Add products	L	H	M	L	L	L
Add markets	L	H	M	M	H	L
Avoid antitrust	H	L	H	H	H	M
Clarity	H	M	M	L	H	M

[a]Strength of benefit: *High, Medium, Low.*

TABLE 22.3 Asset Restructuring[a]

	Divestiture	*Equity Carve-Out*	*Spin-Off*	*Tracking Stock*
Raise funds	H	H	L	L
Improve efficiency by focus	M	M	H	H
Measure performance better	L	H	H	H
Tie compensation to performance	L	H	H	H
Parent focus on core business	H	H	H	M

[a]Strength of benefit: *High, Medium, Low.*

TABLE 22.4 Changes in Ownership Structure (Financial Engineering)[a]

	ESOP	*Leveraged Recap*	*LBO or MBO*	*Dual-Class Recap*	*Share Repurchase*	*Proxy Contest*
Infusion of new capital	M	H	H	M	L	L
Achieve a turnaround	L	M	H	M	L	M
Tax benefits	H	H	H	L	L	L
Takeover defense	H	H	H	H	M	H
Leverage is increased	H	H	H	L	H	L
Maintain control	H	H	H	H	M	L
Management incentives	L	M	H	L	L	M

[a]Strength of benefit: *High, Medium, Low.*

management is compensated by additional shares of stock, which increase their ownership percentage. Dual-class recapitalizations enable management, often a founding group, to trade higher income to other shareholders in return for a class of stock with higher voting power. Share repurchases provide flexibility in returning cash to shareholders in a tax-advantaged form and also offset dilution from the exercise of stock options. A proxy contest represents an effort to change the management control group in a company.

Tables 22.2, 22.3, and 22.4 provide a form of summary of the role of M&As in broad terms. Sixteen alternative forms of ownership structure, asset restructuring, and forms of relationships between firms are analyzed with respect to different potential benefits and limitations. The analysis is aimed at providing perspectives on a wide range of options for improving firm performance.

THE ACQUISITION PROCESS

Within the framework of strategy as process and the relationships between structure and strategy, this section outlines practical aspects of formulating and implementing M&A programs. It is a review of the central topics. These materials are developed more fully in the preceding chapters. Many books and articles have been written on the M&A subject. Each appears to recommend a particular approach. Our view is that different approaches are likely to be required by different circumstances.

One logical basis for organizing the acquisition process is to divide it into four categories: strategy, screening, acquisition/execution, and integration. Other groupings might add accounting and tax issues, due diligence, and human resources considerations. Our emphasis is on a set of dynamic, interrelated processes with consideration of the firm's characteristics and needs or goals. We organize the acquisition process into 14 interacting activities:

1. Strategic processes for growth in value
2. The economics of the industry
3. The firm's organization system
4. Multiple strategies for value growth
5. Search processes
6. Economic basis—synergy potentials
7. Restructuring potentials
8. Due diligence—legal and business
9. Cultural factors
10. Valuation
11. Negotiation
12. Deal structuring
13. Implementation and integration
14. Reviews and renewal processes

Our emphasis is on the dynamic, interrelated activities. Feasible strategies are related to the quality of the firm's capabilities and resources. Cisco Systems, Incorporated successfully implemented an expanding strategy because of the high quality of its management and execution, including a financial information and control system that provides real-time feedback. We discuss each item of the preceding list in sequence.

STRATEGY FORMULATION

The firm must formulate the strategies that define its character and scope. From this analysis, the firm can articulate its goals. It can then assess its strengths and weaknesses in relationship to its goals. We emphasized in Chapter 5 that we begin with a powerful strategic vision.

Strategy deals with problems that cannot be put in neat mathematical equations with solutions readily obtained by the computer. The complex, ill-structured, dynamic environmental changes in competitive thrusts are the challenges that strategy seeks to meet. The central methodological procedure is a rapid review process to identify weaknesses to be eliminated and resources and capabilities to be added to enforce strengths.

THE ECONOMICS OF THE INDUSTRY

The firm is defined by the business economic characteristics of its industry. Industries are classified in different ways for different purposes. From an economic standpoint, some useful distinctions are consumer versus producer products, durable versus non durable, products versus services versus information, stage in life cycle, tangible versus intangible, and the pace of technological and other changes.

All business activities in recent years have been greatly influenced by the increased dynamism of their economic, political, and cultural environments. Rapid change defines the environment of most business activities. Industries have characteristics that influence responses to change. Change is reflected in economic activity measured by rates of growth in gross domestic product (GDP). Some industries are affected more than others. For example, a 5% change in the rate of growth of GDP will be magnified in the growth or decline in durable goods industries but have a smaller impact on nondurable goods industries. The strong upward thrust of growth in high-tech industries may dominate cyclical changes in business activity.

The nature of the industry may influence the relative advantages of large and smaller firms. Industry characteristics will influence opportunities for industry roll ups or the need for consolidation to reduce industry excess capacity. This discussion suggests the many dimensions of industry characteristics; it is not meant to be exhaustive.

An example of an industry assessment is our summary outline of the characteristics of the pharmaceutical industry.

1. Research-intensive—R&D about 11% to 13% of sales.
2. Small investment in plant and equipment; major investment in research Ph.D. staffs; patent protection, but only 11 years after FDA approval.
3. Scale advantages—it costs about $300 million to bring a new drug to FDA approval, which takes 7 to 11 years; then "me-too" drugs surround them.
4. Many dry holes; even if drugs are approved by the FDA, most are not blockbusters; only about 10% earn their cost of capital.
5. Risk of liability suits—can ruin an otherwise good company.
6. Number of new chemical entities (NCEs) per time period—key to market share and profitability.
7. A leader in a therapeutic product class does not hold its position beyond 3 to 5 years; needs continual stream of NCEs to succeed.
8. Generally price-skimming policy; start with high prices and then reduce them as they get "me too'd" and better NCEs take their market share.
9. Needs backup of strong marketing and sales effort; key role of detail salespeople.
10. Needs to be worldwide to spread fixed costs; approximately 50% of sales in foreign countries by majors.
11. Purchase decision made by doctor, not by patient; doctor not sensitive to costs; doctor wants it (drug) to be effective and safe; continue with what works.
12. For many decades, drug prices increased at a rate less than CPI; in past decade, the reverse occurred. Also, if drugs prevent surgery, long hospital stay, and death, they are cheap and relatively effective.
13. Accounting profits have been higher than the average for all manufacturing industries; does not take into account value of capitalized marketing and R&D outlays.
14. Increasingly vulnerable to political pressure. This is aggravated by the demographics—higher-percentage of individuals over 65, many of whom spend their income on drugs to keep alive and much of their time on voting to protect their interests. Paradox: Successful drugs extend the life expectancy of people who criticize the drug companies because the aged spend so much on drugs to stay alive longer.

15. Data on the drug industry have "survivor" biases; companies that survive were successful; the companies that failed are not in the data. If data on unsuccessful are included, the picture is different.
16. Exotic new areas like biotechnology.
17. No company strong across full 64 therapeutic product classes (TPCs).
18. Subject to considerable political surveillance and pressure.
19. New research efforts and areas require large investment and outlays. Pressures for larger size. Cause of major mergers.

Because of demographic and political factors, the pressure to keep prices down is strong. Yet the costs of developing new chemical entities continues to rise. Investments required for newer types of research methods such as gene description are large. Individual companies run into periods when research efforts result in "dry holes" and product pipelines begin to empty. As a result alliances and mergers among pharmaceutical companies have taken place to attain larger size to afford the larger investments for new forms of research. Mergers to reduce costs and to balance product lines also are stimulated. These are some of the factors behind the major drug combinations: Glaxo Wellcome with SmithKline Beecham, Ciba Geigy and Sandoz into Novartis, and Pfizer with Warner-Lambert and then Pharmacia.

THE ORGANIZATION SYSTEM

The firm must have an organizational structure consistent with its strategies and operations. It must have resources and capabilities consistent with its product-market activities. It must have an effective information flow system related to meaningful performance measurement. Compensation systems must be based on contributions to value creation.

We have described how the unitary form (U-form) of organization based on functions such as production, marketing, or geographic areas must change as the scope of a firm's activities expands. The multidivisional form (M-form) provides a more flexible framework for expanding products and widening geographic areas of operations. We also noted that in the Internet age, firms are developing virtual organizations. Through Internet processes, suppliers, for example, become virtual segments of end firm activity. Early examples are Dell and the new arrangements Ford and GM have made with their suppliers.

Thus, a clearly articulated strategic vision and strong organizational framework are required to embrace expanded and new activities. In addition, operational efficiency must be achieved. The firm must have a solid basis for adding capabilities and resources to align more effectively to changes and opportunities through acquisitions. However, if the firm is underperforming, it is more likely to be a target for a takeover.

MULTIPLE STRATEGIES FOR VALUE GROWTH

The firm has a wide variety of strategies for growth. Potentials for internal growth through product expansion and new product programs deserve full consideration. Alliances and joint ventures extend possibilities with smaller investment requirements. Licensing *from* other firms provides knowledge, and licensing *to* other firms provides revenues with small incremental direct costs. Firms may use divestitures to harvest successes or to correct mistakes. Spin-offs can be a source of funds, as well as increased corporate focus. Financial policies such as the use of debt and share repurchases also can enhance value.

SEARCH PROCESSES

In a firm that is seeking to grow by acquisitions, how are prospective candidates selected? Our recommendation is that this must be an ongoing activity of the firm. Organizationally, the firm should have a dedicated business development group. It is essential to have a core group that builds up experience and expertise in the acquisition process. Much basic information about the universe of candidate firms can be obtained from Web sites on the Internet. The business development group should train all employees to regard themselves as a source of research information on potential acquisition candidates.

In the ordinary course of business, the firm has customers, suppliers, and competitors. Customers can provide information on product and marketing effectiveness in relation to competitors. Continued surveillance of competitors provides information on whether the firm is in the forefront of best practices. Interactions with suppliers can be a source of information on potential product improvements and may uncover opportunities for vertical integration of operations. Trade shows and technical forums provide information. Financial analysts and market analysts develop considerable knowledge about the best practices and superior performance.

ECONOMIC BASIS—SYNERGY POTENTIALS

A wide range of valid economic reasons for mergers may be considered. The explosive growth in the Internet sector has been driven by new technologies, new information systems, and new distribution systems. Internet companies such as Yahoo! and Amazon.com have formulated a concept and expanded it rapidly by acquisitions. The high-technology area has stimulated acquisition programs based on a critical set of technological capabilities expanded and improved by acquisitions, as illustrated by Cisco Systems.

Deregulation also has stimulated acquisition programs. Deregulation usually reflects new technologies and intensified competition, which puts pressure on incumbent firms. AT&T has had to adjust to new technologies, new forms of competition, and changed opportunities by acquisitions to reinvent itself. Excess capacity in the automobile industry and intense product competition have stimulated alliances, joint ventures, and mergers such as the Daimler-Chrysler transaction.

Globalization has created strong pressures for cross-border mergers. Economic reversals in developing countries have resulted in "invasions of the bargain snatchers." Industry roll ups represent the consolidation of a highly fragmented industry through aggressive programs of acquiring similar businesses. Industry characteristics favorable for a roll up include initial fragmentation, substantial industry annual revenues, companies with robust cash flows, and economies of scale.

Thus, a wide range of valid economic reasons exist for acquisitions, alliances, and joint ventures. Others can be formulated in terms of management strategies. A classic example is Beatrice Foods. Baker (1992) described how Beatrice engaged in a dairy industry geographic roll up under its president, Clinton Haskell. His successor, William Karnes, expanded the roll-up efforts. However, Federal Trade Commission intervention against horizontal acquisitions led to diversifying acquisitions. Instead of integrating the more weakly related activities, Karnes moved to a decentralized organizational structure, avoiding intervention in the management of the new divisions. Karnes extended the logic of the earlier acquisition program. Small firms were acquired to avoid competitive bidders. Many were privately held, family run firms with relatively informal management procedures. Beatrice provided professional management expertise in functional areas and developed a program of management education for the company managers. This program produced increased efficiency, profitability, and growth for which Beatrice provided the requisite financing. Beatrice also used the knowledge and opinions of managers of previously acquired companies as well as their contacts with other companies to expand horizontally within the new diversified areas. The Beatrice example illustrates how management and organization policies can reinforce the economic basis for making synergistic acquisitions.

RESTRUCTURING POTENTIALS

A strong economic rationale for an acquisition can be reinforced by restructuring gains. The collection period for receivables can be moved closer to contractual terms of credit. Inventory costs can be reduced by utilization of Internet arrangements. Investments in fixed assets can be controlled by improved models of production management and material flows. Firms also have demonstrated savings in the management of financing forms and sources. The increased use of share repurchases illustrates innovations in dividend policy. In general, leveraging best practices between the buying and selling firms can contribute to achieving the kinds of efficiency increases described. Products can be improved, new products can be developed, and more effective utilization of investments can be achieved through incorporating the knowledge and best practices of the combined firms.

DUE DILIGENCE

Due diligence may begin with legal aspects but must be extended to business and management considerations. It involves all of the following. An examination of all aspects of prospective partners should be performed. Firms should be sure there are no legal problems, such as pension funding, environmental problems, or product liabilities. Inspection should determine important factors like the relevance of accounting records, the maintenance and quality of equipment, and the possibility of maintaining cost controls. It also should be determined whether the firm has potentials for product improvement or superiority.

Broader business aspects also need to be taken into account. In particular, management relationships must be analyzed. A business combination should fill gaps in managerial capabilities and also extend capabilities. The firm's resources should be extended in multiple dimensions. Consideration must be given to how the two management systems will fit together and whether managers will have to be hired or fired. Firms should be aware of new developments that will benefit the firm or require adjustments. Ultimately, the acquired unit should be worth more as a part of the acquiring firm than alone or with any other firm.

EXPANDING DUE DILIGENCE

It is important to identify in an Operations and Integration planning checklist the key decision areas.[1] This provides an overview of the tasks to be accomplished in each of the four typical phases of the M&A process: strategy, screening, acquisition execution, and integration. In performing due diligence, representatives from all important areas of activities, as well as outside expert consultants, should work together to think through what is required for successful operations and integration performance. By considering the total process at the due diligence stage, the critical requirements for success can be identified. Then, in addition to the legal aspects, the

---

[1]Thanks to Richard S. Parenteau, managing partner of Quick-Cycle Consulting, for these insights.

operating and integration relationships between the combining companies can be evaluated to determine whether the hoped-for synergies can be achieved. This orientation can change all of the planning and execution activities involved. It represents a focused approach that is more informative and efficient.

CULTURAL FACTORS

Corporate culture is defined by an organization's values, traditions, norms, beliefs, and behavior patterns. Corporate culture may be articulated in formal statements of organization values and aspirations. Corporate culture also is expressed in informal relationships and networks. Corporate cultures may be reflected in a company's operating style, including formal and informal influences. More concretely, corporate culture may be conveyed by the kinds of behavior that are rewarded in an organization.

Differences in organization cultures may be illustrated by the following examples:

- Strong top leadership versus team approach.
- Management by formal paperwork versus management by wandering around.
- Individual decision versus group consensus decisions.
- Rapid evaluation based on performance versus long-term relationship based on loyalty.
- Rapid feedback for change versus formal bureaucratic rules and procedures.
- Narrow career paths versus movement through many areas.
- Risk taking encouraged versus "one mistake and you're out."
- Big-stakes (bet-your-company) decisions versus low-risk activities.
- Learn from the customer versus "we know what is best for the customer."
- Narrow responsibility assignments versus "everyone in this company is a source of new or improved product ideas or sources of sales effort or sources of cost efficiencies, and so on."

We argue that a firm must manage its own corporate culture effectively before engaging in merger activity. If its organizational culture house is not in order, combining companies and their cultures will aggravate problems. The firm must be consistent in its formal statements of values and the kinds of actions that are rewarded. The firm must already have a program of proactive employee training and communications systems that convey the importance of the value of individual development and recognition of contributions to organizational effectiveness.

The foregoing emphasizes that in planning for external growth through mergers, alliances, and other relationships, the firm must recognize cultural factors in addition to products, plant and equipment, and financial factors. The firm must be sensitized to recognizing the requirement for pulling together all the systems, informal processes, and cultures required for organizational effectiveness. Due diligence must include coverage of cultural factors in all their dimensions. A wise acquirer puts culture on the table at the earliest planning sessions.

Cultural differences have caused mergers to fail or prevented them from achieving their potentials. Cultural differences are almost certain to be involved when companies are combined. Cultural differences are increasingly important in the rising number of cross-border transactions.

Pitfalls begin with simply ignoring the problem. Another is to promise equal treatment and respect but impose culture from one firm onto another. Problems inherent in inconsistent cultures can escalate to conflict.

Information on how the acquiring firm has handled cultural factors in the past or how the firm has handled organizational change can be developed. Formal tools are available for assessing cultural problems and potentials. Potential partners might be asked to complete a questionnaire describing the cultural dimensions of the prospective merger partners. Focus groups might be employed to conduct sessions with senior officers and directors of the combining firms.

End solutions can take various forms. One is to recognize cultural differences and to respect them. This might occur in firms with vertical relationships in which required management styles may vary at different levels of activity such as research, production, marketing, and finance. Another practice is to exchange executives across the organizations that have been brought together.

Ultimately, the cultures might move toward similarity, or differences might even be valued as sources of increased efficiency. Diversity of patterns may be the result in different types of industrial activities or between firms with different histories. A general recommendation is to involve the human resources managers in the process so that modern concepts and tools can be used.

VALUATION

The purpose of a careful valuation analysis is to provide a disciplined procedure for arriving at a price. If the buyer offers too little, the target may resist and, because it is in play, seek to interest other bidders. If the price is too high, the premium might never be recovered from post-merger synergies. These general principles are illustrated by the following simple model.

The Model

Mergers increase value when the value of the combined firm is greater than the sum of the pre-merger values of the independent entities.

$$NVI = V_{BT} - (V_B + V_T)$$

where

NVI = Net value increase
V_B = Value of bidder alone
V_T = Value of target alone
V_{BT} = Value of firms combined

A simple example will illustrate. Company B (the bidder) has a current market value of $40 (it is understood that all the numbers are in millions). Company T (the target) has a current market value of $40. The sum of the values as independent firms is, therefore, $80. Assume that as a Combined Company (CC), synergies will increase the value to $100. The amount of value created is $20.

How will the increase in value be divided? Targets always (usually) receive a premium. What about the bidders? If the bidder pays a premium of less than $20, it will share in the value increase. If B pays a premium larger than $20, the value of the bidder will decline. If the bidder pays $50 for the target, a premium of 25% has been paid to T. The value increases are shared equally.

If B pays $60 for T, all gains go to the target. B achieves no value increase. If B pays $70 for T, the value of B will decline to $30.

The Use of Stock in Acquisitions

A high percentage of the large transactions between 1992 and 2000 were stock-for-stock transactions. Some hold the view that this does not represent real money, but that view is not valid.

Suppose B exchanges 1.25 of its shares for 1 share of T. Because B is valued at $40, T will receive 1.25 × $40, which equals $50. The premium paid is 25%. Based on their previous $40 values, B and T each owned 50% of the premerger combined values. Postmerger, the percentages of ownership will remain 50–50.

If B exchanges 1.5 of its own shares per share of T, this is equivalent to paying $60 in value for the target. T shareholders will own 60% of the combined company. None of the synergy gains will be received by the bidder shareholders. Also note that the target shareholders will have 1.5 shares in the new company for every 1.0 share held by the bidder shareholders.

The situation is even worse if B pays more than $60 for the target. Assume B pays $70 for the target. Because the combined company has a value of $100, the value of the bidder shares must decline to $30. The consequences are terrible. The shares of the bidder will decline in value by $10, or 25%. Furthermore, the B shareholders will own only 30% of the combined company; for every 1.0 share that they own, the target shareholders will own 2.3 shares.

NEGOTIATION

We believe that the area of M&As (mergers and acquisitions, alliances, and joint ventures) offers attractive opportunities for principled negotiation. By this we mean using standards of fairness in seeking to meet the interests of both parties. Because firms are being combined, it is important to produce agreements that build good future relationships.

With that foundation in principle, the literature offers guides for negotiation strategy and techniques. A basic requirement is to start with good preparation. Recall the previous topics in this summary statement on the M&A (defined broadly as stated previously) process. We need a strategic vision. The firm needs to assess its strengths and weaknesses. The firm identifies the resources and capabilities required and what it brings to the deal.

A key factor in M&As is realistic identification of gains, synergies, and their sources, whether in revenue enhancement and/or cost reductions and/or possibilities for new and strengthened strategies. This is the basis for developing a solid quantification of the firm's best alternative to a negotiated agreement (BATNA). In merger valuation, quantification of BATNA is facilitated. Value relationships can be analyzed with references to comparable companies and comparable transactions. Other more formal methods of valuation, as described in Chapters 9 and 10, can be used. The active markets for buying and selling business entities and segments provide quantitative information. In addition, all the parties can benefit. For the buyer, it is imperative that the premium paid have a sound foundation in estimates of synergy and savings.

DEAL STRUCTURING

Deal structuring begins with understanding the tax consequences of combining firms. A second important area is to understand whether the accounting treatment employed has any true economic consequences. A third issue is the method of payment: cash, stock, debt, or a combination thereof. A fourth variable is whether an explicit contingency payout should be used and how the standard for the bonus or penalty should be formulated. The use of cash reduces uncertainty for the seller but has tax consequences. The use of stock makes the actual return to the seller dependent upon the future success of the combination.

IMPLEMENTATION

A key challenge in doing M&As is implementation. Some discussions propose that implementation and integration start when the merger agreement has been signed. Our view is that implementation starts as a condition for thinking about M&As. The firm must have implemented all aspects of effective operations before it can combine organizations effectively. This means that the firm must have a shareholder value orientation. It must have strategies and organizational structures compatible with its multiple business units.

Companies should pursue only mergers that further their corporate strategy: strengthening weaknesses, filling gaps, developing new growth opportunities, and extending capabilities. Integration leadership is required. The demands of regular business operations and integration are too much for one person to handle. The integration leader should have management experience, experience with external constituencies, and credibility with the various integration participants.

REVIEWS AND RENEWAL PROCESS

Strong change forces in the environments in which a firm operates and the continued impacts of competitors represent continued challenges. No plan or set of policies can remain in force without change for long. The firm must adjust continuously to new opportunities and challenges.

It is to be hoped that the firm has a broad strategy that guides success in its business markets. For example, Dell Computer began with the central strategy of selling directly to customers. However, Dell has continuously integrated new concepts into its operations. The initial vision of Cisco Systems was to provide business customers with network routers. From this base, Cisco moved to become a provider of complete data networking solutions. When the new technologies for long-distance telephone communications gave cost advantages to the use of microwave and fiber-optic systems, AT&T had to reinvent itself.

In more mature industries such as food and automobiles, similar continuing challenges had to be managed. Food sales are tied to population growth, which in the United States is only 1% to 2% per annum. Growth rates that low would not make it possible for firms to compete for executives seeking promotions and stock options. Nor do low-growth firms receive respect or support from the financial markets. Food companies over a period of years were able to achieve earnings growth at two-digit levels by introducing new products and promoting strong brands and by expanding abroad in faster growing markets. In recent years, this has been increasingly difficult to accomplish. Similarly, the automobile industry has persistently faced a world production capacity of some 80 million units per year, but with quantity demanded at around 60 million units per year. Strong continuing competitive pressures have resulted. Automobile companies have sought to develop innovative new products, such as sport utility vehicles (SUVs). They also have engaged in a wide range of M&A and restructuring activities. The cross-border Daimler-Chrysler merger in 1998 is a notable example. Many consolidating automobile mergers and alliances have taken place in Europe. General Motors has made investments in a number of manufacturers in Asian countries, including mainland China.

So the adjustment processes for firms are a continuous activity. Learn from the past, manage well in the present, and plan imaginatively for the future! These are the precepts that make M&A and restructuring continuing activities. The fundamental characteristics of strategic planning processes are illustrated: assessment of needs; evaluation of alternative strategies; selection of strategies and plans; fast feedback on results; reassessment of strategies, plans, policies, and decisions; modifications and adjustments; and continued repetitions of the process. Alliances, joint ventures, mergers, restructuring, and financial engineering all perform significant roles in these dynamic processes. That is why our subject is highly important for the well-being of firms, as well as economies.

Summary

The case studies and systematic empirical studies suggest the following guidelines for successful merger and acquisition activity.

1. The M&A program must be part of long-range strategic planning.

2. Recognize that in seeking new areas with higher growth potentials and improved opportunities for value enhancement, internal investments and restructuring can be used in conjunction with external investments and M&A activity.

3. Know the industry and its competitive environment as a basis for making projections for the future.

4. Be sure there is an element of relatedness, but don't be too restrictive in defining the scope of potential relatedness.

5. Combine firms that have relatively unique relationships that other firms cannot match, thus avoiding multiple bids that drive up the price of the target to excessively high levels. The acquired unit should be worth more as part of the acquiring firm than alone or with some other firm.

6. There is a time to buy. There is a time to sell. Sometimes a firm may seek to augment its position in an industry by acquiring related firms. If the prices received by sellers reflect overoptimistic expectations, it might make sense to reverse the strategy and become a seller rather than a buyer.

7. Top executives must be involved in M&A activity as well as other major investment programs.

8. Combining two companies is an activity that involves substantial trauma and readjustment. Therefore, a strong emphasis on maintaining and enhancing managerial rewards and incentives is required in the postmerger period. The managements of all the companies combined in a merger must receive incentives to stay and to make contributions to the combined company.

9. Communicate as soon as possible when major investment and restructuring decisions are made.

10. Postmerger coordination must be another top management responsibility. This does not happen automatically. Top executives must be involved, as well as all members of the organization.

11. For future promotions, distinctions based on employment in different segments of the company should disappear. If employees have to be separated, it should be done in as enlightened a way as possible including assistance with insurance coverages and placement activities. This is ethically sound behavior and has an important impact on the future morale and culture of the firm.

12. Managing the integration of cultures and coordinating all the systems and informal processes of the combining firms are absolute musts. Cultural integration usually works best when the combining firms have similar cultures. When cultures are greatly different, each should be respected for its values. Initially, each component company may be encouraged to operate within its own culture. As each component learns to appreciate the strengths and weaknesses of cultural differences, a blended culture may develop over time.

13. The risk of mistakes stemming from wishful thinking is especially great in mergers. The planning might be sound from the standpoint of business of financial complementarities or relatedness, but if the acquiring firm pays too much, the result will be a negative net present value investment.

14. The restructuring and renewal requirements for an organization represent a continuing challenge to be addressed in the firm's strategic planning processes.

Questions

22.1 What are the basic principles to keep in mind in mergers and acquisitions planning?

22.2 In evaluating an individual merger or takeover, why is it useful to start with an analysis of the business economics of the industry?

22.3 Why is industry important in influencing the pace of M&A activity?

22.4 According to Coase, what are the determinants of the scope and size of firms?

22.5 What is the value of a real options framework for making decisions with regard to mergers and acquisitions as we have defined them covering a wide range of strategies as depicted in Figure 22.2?

References

Andrade, Gregor, Mark Mitchell, and Erik Stafford, "New Evidence and Perspectives on Mergers," *Journal of Economic Perspectives* 15, Spring 2001, pp. 103–120.

Baker, George P., "Beatrice: A Study in the Creation and Destruction of Value," *Journal of Finance* 47, 1992, pp. 1081–1120.

Chung, Kwang S., and J. Fred Weston, "Diversification and Mergers in a Strategic Long-Range-Planning Framework," Chapter 13 in *Mergers and Acquisitions*, M. Keenan and L. J. White (eds.), Lexington, MA: D. C. Heath & Co., 1982, pp. 315–347.

Coase, Ronald H., "The Nature of the Firm," *Economica* 4, November 1937, pp. 386–405.

Galbraith, John K., *The New Industrial State*, Boston: Houghton Mifflin, 1967.

Moeller, Sara B., Frederik P. Schlingemann, and Rene M. Stulz, "Do Shareholders of Acquiring Firms Gain From Acquisitions? National Bureau of Economic Research Working Paper 9523, February 2003.

Steiner, George A., *Strategic Planning*, New York: Free Press, 1979.

Summer, Charles E., *Strategic Behavior in Business and Government*, Boston: Little, Brown and Company, 1980.

Weston, J. Fred, "Mergers and Acquisitions in Business Planning," *Rivista Internazionale di Scienze Economiche e Commerciali* 17, April 1970, pp. 309–320.

——, "ROI Planning and Control," *Business Horizons* 15, August 1972, pp. 35–42.

——, "The Rules for Successful Mergers," *Midland Corporate Finance Journal* 1, Winter 1983, pp. 47–50.

——, and Thomas E. Copeland, *Managerial Finance*, 9th ed., Fort Worth, TX: The Dryden Press, 1992.

GLOSSARY[1]

Abnormal return In event studies, the part of the return that is not predicted; the change in value caused by the event. Also excess return, benchmark adjusted.

Acquisition The purchase of a controlling interest in a firm, generally via a tender offer for the target shares.

Acquisition MLP Also called start-up master limited partnership; the assets of an existing entity are transferred to an MLP, and the business is henceforth conducted as an MLP. The Boston Celtics's conversion into an MLP is an example.

Adjusted present value (APV) A method of valuation in which operating free cash flows are discounted at the cost of equity and tax shields are discounted at the cost of debt.

Adverse selection Without a basis for buyers to identify good products, bad products will always be offered at the same price as good products; said to be a characteristic of the used-car market in which buyers have to consider the probability that they are being offered a lemon.

Agency problem The conflict of interest between principal (e.g., shareholders) and agent (e.g., managers) in which agents have an incentive to act in their own self-interest because they bear less than the total costs of their actions.

Anergy Negative synergy, instead of a "2 + 2 = 5" effect, anergy implies "2 + 2 = 3." Business units actively interfere with each other and may have more value if separated.

Announcement data In event studies, typically, the day information becomes public.

Antigreenmail amendment Corporate charter amendment that prohibits targeted share repurchases at a premium from an unwanted acquirer without the approval of nonparticipating shareholders.

Antitakeover amendment A corporate charter amendment that is intended to make it more difficult for an unwanted acquirer to take over the firm.

Any-or-all offer A tender offer that does not specify a maximum number of shares to be purchased, but none will be purchased if the conditions of the offer are not met.

Appraisal right The right of minority shareholders to obtain an independent valuation of their shares to determine the appropriate back-end value in a two-tier tender offer.

Arbitrage The purchase of an asset for near-term resale at a higher price. In the context of M&As, risk arbitrage refers to investing in the stock of takeover targets for short-term resale to capture a portion of the gains that typically accrue to target shareholders.

Arbitrage pricing theory A general approach to asset pricing that allows for the possibility that multiple factors may be used to explain asset returns, as opposed to the capital asset pricing model. (See *Capital asset pricing model.*)

Atomistic competition Numerous small sellers and buyers, none of which have the power to influence market prices or output.

Atomistic shareholders Each shareholder has only a small amount of stock. Small shareholders have less incentive to monitor management than large block shareholders.

Auction Two or more bidders competing for a single target. An auction increases the price target shareholders receive.

Back-end value The amount paid to remaining shareholders in the second stage of a two-tier or partial tender offer.

Bear hug A takeover strategy in which the acquirer, without previous warning, mails the directors of the target a letter announcing the acquisition proposal and demanding a quick decision.

Benchmark A company, group of companies, or portfolio used as a standard of performance.

Beta In the capital asset pricing model, the systematic risk of the asset; the variability of the asset's return in relation to the return on the market.

Bidder The acquiring firm in a tender offer.

---

[1]Technical terms used in explanations are defined in their alphabetical position.

Blended price The weighted average price in a two-tier tender offer. The front-end price is weighted by the percent of shares purchased in the first step of the transaction, and the lower, back-end price is weighted by the percent of shares purchased to complete the transaction.

Blockholder The holder of a significant percentage of the ownership shares.

Board-out clause A provision in most super-majority antitakeover amendments that gives the board of directors the power to decide when and if the supermajority provision will be in effect.

Bootstrap transaction A highly leveraged transaction (HLT).

Bottom-up An approach to firm strategy formulation based on the aggregation of segment forecasts.

Bounded rationality Refers to the limited capacity of the human mind to deal with complexity.

Brand-name capital Firm reputation; the result of nonsalvageable investment, which provides customers with an implicit guarantee of product quality for which they are willing to pay a premium.

Breach of trust Unilaterally changing the terms of a contract.

Business judgment rule A legal doctrine that holds that the board of directors is acting in the best interests of shareholders unless it can be proven by a preponderance of the evidence that the board is acting in its own interest or is in breach of its fiduciary duty.

Bust-up takeover An acquisition followed by the divestiture of some or all of the operating units of the acquired firm, which can be sold at prices greater than their current value.

Buyback See *Share repurchase.*

Calls Options to buy an asset at a specified price for a specified period of time.

Capital asset pricing model Calculates the required return on an asset as a function of the risk-free rate plus the market risk premium times the asset's beta.

Capital budgeting The process of planning expenditures whose returns extend over a period of time.

Capital cash flow valuation A method of valuation in which capital cash flows are discounted at the expected or required return on assets.

Capital cash flows (CCF) Operating free cash flows (FCF) plus tax shields.

Capital intensity In economics, the ratio of investment required per dollar of sales. In finance, the sales-to-investment ratio. The steel industry and manufacturing generally are more capital intensive than the wholesale or retail industries.

Cash cows A Boston Consulting Group term for business segments that have a high market share in low-growth product markets and thus throw off more cash flow than needed for reinvestment.

Chinese wall The imaginary barrier separating investment banking and other activities within a financial intermediary.

Classified board Also called a staggered board. An antitakeover measure that divides a firm's board of directors into several classes, only one of which is up for election in any given year, thus delaying effective transfer of control to a new owner in a takeover.

Clayton Act Federal antitrust law originally passed in 1914 and strengthened in 1950 by the Celler-Kefauver amendment. Section 7 gives the Federal Trade Commission (FTC) power to prohibit the acquisition of one company by another if adverse effects on competition would result, or if the FTC perceives a trend that ultimately might lead to decreased competition.

Clean-up merger Also called a take-out merger. The consolidation of the acquired firm into the acquiring firm after the acquirer has obtained control.

Clientele effect A dividend theory that states that high–tax bracket shareholders will prefer to hold stock in firms with low dividend payout rates and low–tax bracket shareholders will prefer the stock of firms with high payouts.

Coercive tender offer Any tender offer that puts pressure on target shareholders to tender by offering a higher price to those who tender early.

Coinsurance effect The combination of two firms with cash flows that are not perfectly correlated will result in cash flow of less variability for the merged firm, thus decreasing the risk to lenders to the firm and thereby increasing its debt capacity.

Collar The range of the exchange ratios in an acquisition in which the equity of the buyer is a part of the payment to the target. The range is specified in terms of the relative market values during the period before final approval of the transaction.

Collateral restraints Agreements between the parties to a joint venture to limit competition between themselves in certain areas.

Collusion Illegal coordination or cooperation among competitors with respect to price or output.

Complementarity The strengths of one firm offset the weaknesses of another firm with which it combines. For example, one firm that is strong in marketing combines with one that is strong in research.

Concentration Measures of the percentage of total industry sales accounted for by a specified number of firms, such as 4, 8, or 20.

Concentric merger A merger in which there is carry-over in *specific* management functions (e.g., marketing) or complementarity in relative strengths among *specific* management functions rather than carryover complementarities in only generic management functions (e.g., planning).

Conglomerate A combination of unrelated firms; any combination that is not vertical or horizontal.

Conjectural variation The reaction of rival firms as one firm, Firm A, restricts output or raises prices. Ranges from −1 to +1; a negative conjectural variation indicates competitive behavior (i.e., Firm A's action is offset by the reactions of competing rival firms).

Contingent voting rights Rights to vote in corporate elections that become exercisable upon the occurrence of a particular event. Examples: Preferred stockholders might win the right to vote if preferred dividends are missed; convertible debt might be viewed as having voting rights contingent upon conversion.

Convergence of interests hypothesis Predicts a positive relationship between the proportion of management stock ownership and the market's valuation of the firm's assets.

Cost leadership A business strategy based on achieving lower costs than rivals.

Covenant See *Indenture.*

Crown jewels The most valuable segments of a company; the parts most wanted by an acquirer.

Cumulative abnormal return (CAR) In event studies, the sum of daily abnormal returns over a period relative to the event.

Cumulative voting Instead of one vote per candidate selected, shareholders can vote (the number of shares they hold times the number of directors to be elected) for one candidate or divide the total votes among a desired number of candidates. Example: A shareholder has 100 shares; six directors are to be elected. With cumulative votings the shareholder has 600 votes to distribute among six candidates however he or she chooses.

De novo entry Entry into an industry by forming a new company as opposed to combining with an existing firm in the industry.

Decision control Fundamental ownership rights of shareholders to select management, to monitor management, and to determine reward/incentive arrangements.

Decision management Decision functions related to day-to-day operations that may be delegated to managers. Includes initiation and implementation of policies and procedures.

Defensive diversification Entering new product markets to offset the limitations of the firm's existing product-market areas.

Defined benefit plan A pension plan that specifies in advance the amount beneficiaries will receive based on compensation, years of service, and so on.

Defined contribution plan A pension plan in which the annual contribution are specified in advance. Benefits upon retirement depend on the performance of the assets in which the contributions are invested.

Delphi technique An information gathering technique in which questionnaires are sent to informed individuals. The responses are summarized into a feedback report and used to generate subsequent questionnaires to probe more deeply into the issue under study.

Differential managerial efficiency hypothesis A theory that hypothesizes that more efficient managements take over firms with less efficient managements and achieve gains by improving the efficiency of the target.

Discounted cash flow valuation (DCF) The application of an appropriate cost of capital to a future stream of cash flows.

Discriminatory poison pill Antitakeover plans that penalize acquirers who exceed a given shareholding percentage (the kick-in or trigger point).

Dissident A shareholder or group of shareholders who disagrees with incumbent management and seeks to make changes via a proxy contest to gain representation on the board of directors.

Diversification The holding of assets whose returns are not perfectly correlated.

Divestiture Sale of a segment of a company (assets, a product line, a subsidiary) to a third party for cash and/or securities.

Dividend growth valuation model The application of an appropriate discount factor to a future stream of dividends.

Dividend method dual-class recapitalization Most widely used method of converting to dual-class stock ownership. A stock split or dividend is used to distribute new, inferior voting stock. The previously existing common stock is redesignated as superior-vote class B stock.

Dogs A Boston Consulting Group term for business segments characterized by low market shares in product markets with low growth rates.

Dual class recapitalization Corporate restructuring used to create two classes of common stock with the superior-vote stock concentrated in the hands of management.

Dual-class stock Two (or more) classes of common stock with equal rights to cash flows but with unequal voting rights.

DuPont system A financial planning and control system that focuses on return on investment by relating asset turnover (effective asset management) to profit margin on sales (effective cost control).

Dutch auction repurchases (DARs) Shareholders are permitted to put their shares to the company within a range of prices; at a price at which the company's target level of shares is reached, all shares offered receive that price.

Dynamic competition theory A model of industrial organization theory that extends the traditional models of price and output decisions of firms in a static environment to decisions on product quality, innovation, promotion, marketing, and so on in changing environments.

Dynamic oligopoly Although an industry might be dominated by a few large firms (oligopoly), recognized interdependence does not occur because decisions must be made on so many factors that actions and reactions of rivals cannot be predicted or coordinated.

Earnings before interest and taxes (EBIT) Net operating income (NOI) plus net nonoperating income.

Earnings before interest, taxes, and depreciation and amortization (EBITDA) Earnings before interest and taxes (EBIT) plus depreciation and amortization.

Earnout Part of the payment to a target based on some measures of future performance.

Economic profit Return on invested capital (ROIC) less the weighted average cost of capital (WACC) multiplied by invested capital.

Empirical test Systematic examination of data to check the consistency of evidence with alternative theories.

Employee Retirement Income Security Act (ERISA) Federal legislation enacted in 1974 to regulate pension plans including some ESOPs. Sets vesting requirements, fiduciary standards, and minimum funding standards. Established the Pension Benefit Guarantee Corporation (PBGC) to guarantee pensions.

Employee stock ownership plan (ESOP) Defined contribution pension plan (stock bonus and/or money purchase) designed to invest primarily in the stock of the employer firm.

End of regulation A theory hypothesizing that takeovers occur following deregulation of an industry as a result of increased competition, which exposes management inefficiency that might have been masked by regulation.

Entrenchment See *Managerial entrenchment hypothesis.*

Equity carve-out A transaction in which a parent firm offers some of a subsidiary's common stock to the general public to bring in a cash infusion to the parent without loss of control.

ERISA-type ESOP Employee stock ownership plans other than tax credits ESOPs (i.e., includes leveraged, leveragable, and nonleveraged ESOPs recognized under ERISA rather than under the Tax Reduction Act of 1975).

Event returns A measure of the stock price reaction to the announcement of significant new information such as a takeover or some type of restructuring.

Event study An empirical test of the effect of an event (e.g., a merger, divestiture) on stock returns. The event is the reference date from which analysis of returns is made regardless of the calendar timing of the occurrences in the sample of firms.

Excess return See *Abnormal return.*

Exchange method dual-class recapitalization Means of converting to a dual-class stock corporate structure. High-vote stock is issued to insiders in exchange for their currently outstanding (low-vote) stock. The remaining low-vote stock, in the hands of outside share-holders, generally receives a higher dividend.

Exchange offer A transaction that provides one class (or more) of securities with the right or option to exchange part or all of their holdings for a different class of the firm's securities (e.g., an exchange of debt for common stock). Enables a change in capital structure with no change in investment.

Exit-type firm In Jensen's free cash flow hypothesis, a firm with positive free cash flows. The theory predicts that for such a firm, stock prices will increase with unexpected increases in payout.

Extra merger premium hypothesis The possibility that a higher price will be paid for superior vote shares if a dual-class stock firm becomes a takeover target and causes the price of superior vote stock to be higher even in the absence of a takeover bid.

Failing firm defense A defense against a merger challenge alleging that in the absence of the merger, the firm(s) would fail. The 1982 Merger Guidelines spell out the conditions under which this defense will be acceptable.

Fair-price amendment An antitakeover charter amendment that waives the supermajority approval requirement for a change of control if a fair price is paid for all purchased shares. Defends against two-tier offers that do not have board approval.

Fallen angel A bond issued at investment grade whose rating is subsequently dropped to below investment grade, below BBB.

Financial conglomerates Conglomerate firms in which corporate management provides a flow of funds to operating segments, exercises control and strategic planning functions, and is the ultimate financial risk taker but does not participate in operating decisions.

Financial Institutions Reform, Recovery, and Enforcement Act (FIRREA) A 1989 law changing the regulatory rules for savings and loan companies as well as other financial institutions.

Financial synergy A theory that suggests a financial motive for mergers, especially between firms with high internal cash flows (but poor investment opportunities) and firms with low internal cash flows (and high investment opportunities which, absent merger, would require costly external financing). Also includes increased debt capacity or coinsurance effect and economies of scale in flotation and transactions costs of securities.

Fixed-price tender offers (FPTs) A method of share repurchase in which a put price is specified for a specified number of company shares.

Flip-in poison pill plan Shareholders of the target firm are issued rights to acquire stock in the target at a substantial discount when a bidder has reached a designated percentage ownership trigger point.

Flip-over poison pill plan Shareholders of the target firm are issued rights to purchase the common stock of the surviving company at a substantial discount when a bidder has reached a designated percentage ownership trigger point.

Formula approach A discounted cash flow valuation in which key variables or value drivers are used to calculate the net present value of a project or firm.

Four-firm concentration ratio The sum of the shares of sales, value added, assets, or employees held by the largest four firms in an industry. A measure of competitiveness according to the structural theory.

Free cash flow Cash flows in excess of positive net present value investment opportunities available.

Free cash flow hypothesis Jensen's theory of how the payout of free cash flows helps resolve the agency problem between managers and shareholders. Holds that bonding payout of current (and future) free cash flows reduces the power of management as well as subjecting it more frequently to capital market scrutiny.

Free-rider problem Atomistic shareholder reasons that its decision has no impact on the outcome of the tender offer and refrains from tendering to free ride on the value increase resulting from the merger, thus causing the bid to fall.

Front-end loading A tender offer in which the offer price is greater than the value of any unpurchased shares. Resolves the free-rider problems by providing an incentive to tender early.

Full ex post setting up A manager's compensation is adjusted frequently over the course of his or her career to fully reflect his or her performance, thus eliminating an incentive to shirk.

Gambler's ruin An adverse string of losses that could lead to bankruptcy, although the long-run cash flows could be positive.

Game theory An analysis' of the behavior (actions and reactions) of participants under specified rules, information, and strategies.

General Utilities doctrine An IRS rule that allowed firms to not recognize gains on the distribution of appreciated property in redemption of its shares (e.g., in a "legal" liquidation). Repealed by the Tax Reform Act of 1980.

Generic management functions Those functions that are not industry specific and are thus transferable even in conglomerate mergers. Include planning, organizing, directing, and controlling.

Going-concern value The value of the firm as a whole over and above the sum of the values of each of its parts; the value of organization learning and reputation.

Going private The transformation of a public corporation into a privately held firm (often via a leveraged buyout or a management buyout).

Golden parachute Provision in the employment contracts of top managers providing for compensation for loss of jobs following a change of control.

Goodwill The excess of the purchase price paid for a firm over the book value received. Recorded on the acquirer's balance sheet, to be amortized over not more than 40 years (amortization not tax deductible).

Greenmail The premium over the current market price of stock paid to buy back the holdings accumulated by an unwanted acquirer to avoid a takeover.

Gross cash flows Net operating profit after taxes (NOPAT) plus depreciation.

Gross present value An appropriately discounted stream of future cash flows before the deduction of investment costs.

Growth-share matrix A guide to strategy formulation that emphasizes attainment of high market share in industries with favorable growth rates.

Harassment hypothesis Ellert's theory that Federal Trade Commission antitrust complaints are brought against firms with abnormally good stock price performance at the instigation of the firms competitors who are threatened by their superior performance.

Hart-Scott-Rodino Antitrust Improvements Act of 1976 (HSR) Expands power of Department of Justice in antitrust investigations; provides for waiting period (15 days for tender offers, 30 days for mergers) following submission of information to Department of Justice and Federal Trade Commission before transaction can be completed; expands power of state attorneys general to institute triple-damage antitrust lawsuits on behalf of their citizens.

Herfindahl-Hirschman Index (HHI) The measure of concentration under the 1982 Merger Guidelines, defined as the sum of the squares of the market shares of all the firms in the industry.

Hidden equity Undervalued assets whose market value exceeds their depreciated book value but is not reflected in stock price.

High-yield bond See *Junk bond*.

Highly leveraged transaction (HLT) Use of debt in relation to equity in excess of average industry ratios.

Holding company An organization whose primary function is to hold the stock of other corporations but that has no operating units of its own. Similar to the multidivisional organization, which has profit centers and a single central headquarters; however, the segments owned by the holding company are separate legal entities that in practice are controlled by the holding company.

Holdup Whenever a resource is dependent on (specialized to) the rest of the firm, there may be a temptation for others to try to expropriate the quasi-rent of the dependent resource by withholding their complementary resources; this is holdup. However, each resource in the team (firm) may be dependent on all the others, and thus all are vulnerable to expropriation.

Horizontal merger A combination of firms operating in the same business activity.

Hostile takeover A tender offer that proceeds even after it has been opposed by the management of the target.

Hubris hypothesis (Winner's curse) Roll's theory that acquiring firm managers commit errors of overoptimism in evaluating merger opportunities (due to excessive pride, animal spirits) and end up paying too high a price for acquisitions.

Implicit claim A tacit rather than contractual promise of continuing service and delivery of expected quality to customers and job security to employees.

Incentive stock option (ISO) An executive compensation plan to align the interests of managers with stockholders. Executives are issued options whose exercise price is equal to or greater than the stock price at the time of issue and thus have value only if the stock price rises, giving managers incentives to take actions to maximize stock price.

Increased debt capacity hypothesis A theory that postmerger financial leverage increases are the result of increased debt capacity (as opposed to the firms involved having been underleveraged before the merger) due to reduced expected bankruptcy costs.

Indenture The contract between a firm and its bondholders that sets out the terms and conditions of the borrowing and the rights and obligations of each party (covenants).

Industry life cycle A conceptual model of the different stages of an industry's development. (1) Development stage—new product, high investment needs, losses. (2) Growth stage—consumer acceptance, expanding sales, high profitability, case of entry. (3) Maturity stage—sales growth slows, excess capacity, prices and profits decline—key period for merger strategy. (4) Decline stage—substitute products emerge, sales growth declines, pressure for mergers to survive.

Inferior-vote stock In dual-class stock firms, the class of common stock that has less voting power (e.g., may be able to elect only a minority on the board of directors; may be compensated with higher dividends).

Information asymmetry A game or decisions in which one party has more information than other players.

In play Because of a bid or rumours of a bid, the financial community regards the company as receptive or vulnerable to takeover bids.

Initial public offering (IPO) The first offering to the public of common stock (e.g., of a former privately held firm) or a portion of the common stock of a hitherto wholly owned subsidiary.

Insider trading Some parties take action based on information not available to outside investors.

Internal rate of return (IRR) A capital budgeting method that finds the discount rate (the IRR) that equates the present value of cash inflows and investment outlays. The IRR must equal or exceed the relevant risk-adjusted cost of capital for the project to be acceptable.

Investment Advisers Act of 1940 (IAA) Federal securities legislation providing for registration and regulation of investment advisers.

Investment Company Act of 1940 (ICA) Federal securities legislation regulating publicly owned companies in the business of investing and trading in securities; subjects them to SEC rules. Amended in 1970 to place more controls on management compensation and sales charges.

Investment requirements Include capital expenditures and additions to working capital. Can be expressed as a percentage of revenues or as a percentage of changes in revenues.

Investment requirements ratio A firm's investment expenditures (or opportunities) in relation to after-tax cash flows.

Joint production Production using complementary inputs in which the output cannot be unambiguously attributed to any single input and in which the output is greater than the sum of the inputs (i.e., synergy). Problems in assigning returns may arise if the inputs are not owned by the same entity.

Joint venture A combination of subsets of assets contributed by two (or more) business entities for a specific business purpose and a limited duration. Each of the venture partners continues to exist as a separate firm, and the joint venture represents a new business enterprise.

Junk bond High-yield bonds that are below investment grade when issued, that is, rated below BBB (Standard & Poor's) or below Baa3 (Moody's).

Kick-in or trigger point The level of share ownership by an acquiring firm that activates a poison pill antitakeover defense plan.

Kick-in-the-pants hypothesis Attributes the increase in a takeover target's stock price to the impetus given by the bid to target management to implement a higher-valued strategy.

Latent debt capacity hypothesis A theory that postmerger increases in financial leverage are due to underleverage in the premerger period.

Learning-by-doing A means of transferring knowledge that is complex or embedded in a complex set of technological and/or organizational circumstances and thus difficult or impossible to transfer in a classroom setting. May motivate knowledge acquisition joint ventures.

Learning curve An approach to strategy formulation that hypothesizes that costs decline with cumulative volume experience, resulting in competitive advantage for the first entrants into an industry.

Leveraged buyout (LBO) The purchase of a company by a small group of investors, financed largely by debt. Usually entails going private.

Leveraged cash-out (LCO) See Leveraged recapitalization.

Leveraged ESOP An employee stock ownership plan recognized under ERISA in which the ESOP borrows funds to purchase employer securities. The employer then makes tax-deductible contributions to the ESOP sufficient to cover both principal repayment and interest on the loan.

Leveraged recapitalization A defensive reorganization of the firm's capital structure in which outside shareholders receive a large, one-time cash dividend and inside shareholders receive new shares of stock instead. The cash dividend is largely financed with newly borrowed funds, leaving the firm highly leveraged and with a greater proportional ownership share in the hands of management. Also called leveraged cash-out.

Life cycle model of firm ownership A theory that suggests that firms will attract different shareholder clienteles (high- or low-tax bracket investors) over different periods of firm development depending on changing investment needs and profitability.

Line and staff An organizational form characterized by the separation of support activities (staff) from operations (line).

Liquidation Divestiture of all the assets of a firm so that the firm ceases to exist.

Liquidation MLP The complete liquidation of a corporation into a master limited partnership.

Lock-in amendment A corporate charter amendment that makes it more difficult to void previously passed (antitakeover) amendments (e.g., by requiring supermajority approval for a change).

Lock-up option An option to buy a large block of newly issued shares that target management may grant to a favored bidder, thus virtually guaranteeing that the favored bidder will succeed. Target management's ability to grant a lock-up option induces bidders to negotiate.

Logical incrementalism A process of effecting major changes in strategy via a series of relatively small (incremental) changes.

Macroconcentration An overall measure of the share of sales or value added by a specified number of firms; their share is the aggregate concentration ratio (ACR).

Management buyout (MBO) A going-private transaction led by the incumbent managers of the formerly public firm.

Managerial conglomerates Conglomerate firms that provide managerial expertise, counsel, and interaction on decisions pertaining to operating units. Based on the transferability of generic management skills even across nonrelated businesses.

Managerial entrenchment hypothesis A theory that antitakeover efforts are motivated by managers' self-interests in keeping their jobs rather than in the best interests of shareholders.

Managerialism A theory that managers pursue mergers and acquisitions to increase the size of the organizations they control and thus increase their compensation.

Marginal cost of capital (MCC) The relevant discount factor for a current decision.

Mark-to-market accounting At statement dates, assets and liabilities are restated to measures of their current market values.

Market-adjusted return The return for a firm for a period is its actual return less the return on the market index for that period.

Market extension merger A combination of firms whose operations had previously been conducted in nonoverlapping geographic areas.

Market model In event studies, the most widely used method of calculating the return predicted if no event took place. In this method, a clean period (with no events) is chosen, and a regression is run of firm returns against the market index return over the clean period. The regression coefficient and intercept are then used with the market index return for the day of interest in the event period to predict what the return for the firm would have been on that day had no event taken place.

Market value rule The principle that all decisions of a corporation should be judged solely by their contribution to the market value of the firm's stock.

Markup return The event return measured from the announcement date to various designated dates thereafter.

Master limited partnership (MLP) An organizational form in which limited partnership interests are publicly traded (like shares of corporate stock) while retaining the tax attributes of a partnership.

Matrix organization Company that has functional departments assigned to subunits organized around products or geography. Employees report to a functional manager as well as a product manager.

Maximum limit offer A stock repurchase tender offer in which all tendered shares will be purchased if the offer is undersubscribed, but if the offer is oversubscribed, shares may be purchased only on a pro rata basis.

Mean adjusted return The actual return for a period less the average (mean) return calculated for a time segment before, after, or both in relation to the event.

Merger Any transaction that forms one economic unit from two or more previous units.

Mezzanine financing Subordinated debt issued in connection with leveraged buyouts. Sometimes carries payment-in-kind (PIK) provisions, in which debt holders receive more of the same kind of debt securities in lieu of cash payments under specified conditions.

Microconcentration A measure of the market share of individual firms or groups such as the four-firm concentration ratio or a measure of inequality of market shares such as the HHI.

Minority squeeze-out The elimination by controlling shareholders of noncontrolling (minority) shareholders.

Misappropriation doctrine A rationale for insider trading prosecution of outsiders who trade on the basis of information that they have "misappropriated" (e.g., stolen from their employers or obtained by fraud).

Money purchase plan A defined contribution pension plan in which the firm contributes a specified annual amount of cash as opposed to stock bonus plans in which the firm contributes stock, and profit-sharing plans in which the amount of the annual cash contribution depends on profitability.

Monopoly A single seller.

Moral hazard One party (principal) relies on the behavior of another agent), and it is costly to observe information or action. Opportunistic behavior in which success benefits one party and failure injures another (e.g., high leverage benefits equity holders under success and injures creditors under failure).

Muddling through An approach to strategy formulation in which policy makers focus only on those alternatives that differ incrementally (i.e., only a little) from existing policies rather than considering a wider range of alternatives.

Multidivisional corporation (M-form) An organizational form to achieve greater efficiency via profit centers to reduce the need for information flow across divisions and to guide resource allocation to the highest-valued uses. Benefits from large fixed investment in general management expertise (especially strategic planning, monitoring, and control) spread over a number of individual decentralized operations (at which level decision making on specific management functions takes place).

Multinational enterprise (MNE) A business organization with operations in more than one country, beyond import-export operations.

NASDAQ Stock quotation system of the National Association of Securities Dealers for stocks that trade over the counter as opposed to being traded on an organized exchange.

National Association of Attorneys General (NAAG) An organization of state attorneys general.

Negotiated share repurchase Refers to buying back the stock of a large blockholder (an unwanted acquirer) at a premium over market price (greenmail).

Net operating income (NOI) Revenues minus all operating costs including depreciation.

Net operating loss carryover Tax provision allowing firms to use net operating losses to offset taxable income over a period of years before and after the loss. Available to firms that acquire a loss firm only under strictly specified conditions.

Net operating profit after taxes (NOPAT) Net operating income (NOI) multiplied by one minus the actual cash tax rate applicable to a line of business.

Net present value (NPV) Capital budgeting criteria that compares the present value of cash inflows of a project discounted at the risk-adjusted cost of capital to the present value of investment outlays (discounted at the risk-adjusted cost of capital).

Niche opportunities A business strategy that aims at meeting the needs or interests of specific consumer groups.

No-shop agreement The target agrees not to consider other offers while negotiating with a particular bidder.

Nolo contendere A legal plea in which a defendant, without admitting guilt, declines to contest allegations of wrongdoing.

Nondiscriminatory poison pill Antitakeover defense plans that do not penalize acquirers exceeding a given shareholding limit. Include flip-over plans, preferred stock plans, and ownership flip-in plans that permit cash offers for all shares.

Nonleveraged ESOP An employee stock ownership plan recognized under ERISA that does not provide for borrowing by the ESOP. Essentially the same as a stock bonus plan.

Normal return In event studies, the predicted return if no event took place, the reference point for the calculation of abnormal, or excess, return attributable to the event.

Oligopoly A small number (few) of sellers.

Omnibus Budget Reconciliation Act of 1993 (OBRA) A tax law that included the conditions under which the excess purchase price over the accounting value of a target could be amortized as a taxdeductible expense.

Open corporations Fama and Jensen's term for large corporations whose residual claims (common stock) are least restricted. They identify the following characteristics: (1) They have property rights in net cash flows for an indefinite horizon; (2) stockholders are not required to hold any other role in the organization; (3) common stock is alienable (transferable, salable) without restriction.

Open-market share repurchase Refers to a corporation buying its own shares on the open market at the going price just as any other investor might buy the corporation's shares, as opposed to a tender offer for share repurchase or a negotiated repurchase.

Operating free cash flows (FCF) Gross cash flows minus investment requirements.

Operating synergy Combining two or more entities results in gains in revenues or cost reductions because of complementarities or economies of scale or scope.

Opportunism Self-interest seeking with guile, including shirking, cheating.

Organization capital Firm-specific informational assets that accumulate over time to enhance productivity. Includes information used in assigning employees to appropriate tasks and forming teams of employees, and the information each employee acquires about other employees and the organization. Alternatively, defined by Cornell and Shapiro as the current market value of all future implicit claims the firm expects to sell.

Organization culture An organization's "style" or approach to problem solving, relations with employees, customers, and other stakeholders.

Organization learning The improvement in skills and abilities of individuals or groups (teams) of employees through learning by experience within the firm. Includes managerial learning (generic as well as industry specific) and non-managerial labor learning.

Original plan poison pill Also called preferred stock plan. An early poison pill antitakeover defense in which the firm issues a dividend of convertible preferred stock to its common stockholders. If an acquiring firm passes a trigger point of share ownership, preferred stockholders (other than the large blockholder) can put the preferred stock to the target firm (force the firm to redeem it) at the highest price paid by the acquiring firm for the target's common or preferred stock during the past year. If the acquirer merges with the target, the preferred can be converted into acquirer voting stock with a market value no less than the redemption value at the trigger point.

Ownership flip-in plan A poison pill antitakeover defense often included as part of flip-over plan. Target stockholders are issued rights to purchase target shares at a discount if an acquirer passes a specified level of share ownership. The acquirer's rights are void, and his or her ownership interest becomes diluted.

Pac Man defense The target makes a counterbid for the acquirer.

Parking A securities law violation in which traders attempt to hide the extent of their share ownership (to avoid the 5% trigger requiring disclosure of takeover intentions and keep down the price of target stock) by depositing, or parking, shares with an accomplice broker until a later date (e.g., when the takeover attempt is out in the open).

Partial tender offer A tender offer for less than all target shares: specifies a maximum number of shares to be accepted but does not announce bidder's plans with respect to the remaining shares.

Payment-in-kind (PIK) provision A clause that provides for issuance of more of the same type of securities to bondholders in lieu of cash interest payments.

Payroll-based ESOP (PAYSOP) A type of employee stock ownership plan in which employers could take a tax credit of 0.5% of ESOP covered payroll. Repealed by the Tax Reform Act of 1986.

Pension plan A fund established by an organization to provide for benefits to plan participants (e.g., employees) after their retirement.

Perfect competition Set of assumptions for an idealized economic model: (1) Large numbers of buyers and sellers so none can influence market prices or output; (2) economies of scale exhausted at relatively small size, and cost efficiencies are the same for all companies; (3) no significant barriers to entry; (4) constant innovation, new product development; (5) complete knowledge of all aspects of input/output markets is costlessly available.

Plasticity (Alchian and Woodward) Resources are considered plastic when a wide range of discretionary uses can be employed by the user. If monitoring costs are high, moral hazard problems are likely to develop.

Poison pill Any antitakeover defense that creates securities that provide their holders with special rights (e.g., to buy target or acquiring firm shares) exercisable only after a triggering event (e.g., a tender offer for or the accumulation of a specified percentage of target shares). Exercise of the rights would make it more difficult and/or costly for an acquirer to take over the target against the will of its board of directors.

Poison put A provision in some new bond issues designed to protect bondholders against takeover-related credit deterioration of the issuer. Following a triggering event, bondholders may put their bonds to the corporation at an exercise price of 100% to 101% of the bond's face amount.

Pooling of interests accounting Assets and liabilities of each firm are combined based solely on their previous accounting values.

Portfolio balance strategy A balance in business segments based on market growth–market share criteria. Combine high growth–high market share (stars), low growth–high market share (cash cows), and low growth–low market share (dogs) segments to achieve favorable overall growth, profitability, and sufficient internal cash flows to finance positive NPV investment opportunities.

Potential competition Firms not in an industry at the present time but that could enter.

Predatory behavior A theory that holds that a dominant firm may price below cost or build excess capacity to inflict economic harm on existing firms and to deter potential entrants.

Premium buyback Refers to repurchasing the stock of a large blockholder (an unwanted acquirer) at a premium over market price (greenmail).

Price-cost margin (PCM) Defined as (Price minus Marginal Cost) divided by Price; that is, operating profit as a percentage of price. A zero PCM reflects perfect competition (i.e., Price = Marginal Cost).

Price pressure A theory that the demand curve for the securities of an individual company is downward sloping and that this causes negative stock price effects resulting from large supply increases such as large block offerings.

Price trader Outside investors who trade in response to price changes in securities regardless of whether or not they understand the cause of the price change.

Product breadth Carryover of organizational capabilities to new products.

Product differentiation The development of a variety of product configurations to appeal to a variety of consumer tastes.

Product-extension merger A type of conglomerate merger; a combination between firms in related business activities that broadens the product lines of the firms; also called concentric mergers.

Product life cycle A conceptual model of the stages through which products or lines of business pass. Includes development, growth, maturity, and decline. Each stage presents its own threats and opportunities.

Production knowledge A form of organization learning; entrepreneurial or managerial ability to organize and maintain complex production processes economically.

Profit-sharing plan A defined contribution pension plan in which the firm's annual contributions to the plan are based on the firm's profitability.

Proxy contest An attempt by a dissident group of shareholders to gain representation on a firm's board of directors.

Public Utilities Holding Company Act of 1935 Federal securities legislation to correct abuses in financing and operation of gas and electric utility holding company systems.

Purchase accounting The total assets of the combined firm reflect the purchase price of the target.

Pure conglomerate merger A combination of firms in nonrelated business activities that is neither a product-extension nor a geographic-extension merger.

Puts An option to sell an asset at a specified price for a designated period of time.

q-ratio (Tobin's q-ratio) The ratio of the market value of a firm's securities to the replacement costs of its physical assets.

Quasi-rent The excess return to an asset above the return necessary to maintain its current service flow.

Racketeer Influenced and Corrupt Organizations Act of 1970 (RICO) Federal legislation that provides for seizure of assets upon accusation and triple damages upon conviction for companies that conspire to defraud consumers, investors, and so on.

Real options The use of an analytical framework that calculates the value of flexibility.

Recap See *Leveraged recapitalization.*

Recapture of depreciation The amount of prior depreciation that becomes taxable as ordinary income when an asset is sold for more than its tax basis.

Redistribution hypothesis A theory that value increases in mergers represent wealth shifts among stakeholders (e.g., a wealth transfer from bondholders to shareholders) rather than real increases in value.

Residual analysis The examination of asset returns to determine if a particular event has caused the return to deviate from a normal or predicted return that would have resulted if the event had not taken place. The difference between the actual return and the predicted return is the residual.

Residual claims The right of owners of an organization to cash flows not otherwise committed.

Restricted vote stock In dual-class stock firms, the stock with inferior voting rights.

Restructuring Significant changes in the strategies and policies relating to asset composition and liability and equity patterns as well as operations.

Retention ratio The percentage of free cash flows retained in the firm.

Return on invested capital (ROIC) The percentage of net operating profit after taxes (NOPAT) to total operating assets.

Returns to scale As scale of operations becomes larger, marginal and average costs decline.

Reverse LBOs Firms, or divisions of firms, that go public again after having been taken private in a leveraged buyout transaction.

Reverse mergers The uncombining of firms via spin-offs, divestitures, and so on.

Risk-free rate The return on an asset with no risk of default. In theory, the return on short-term government securities.

Risk premium The differential of the required return on an asset in excess of the risk-free rate.

Roll-out MLP Also called spin-off MLP. A corporation transfers some of its assets to an MLP to avoid double taxation; for example, MLP units are initially distributed to corporate shareholders, and corporate management serves as the general partner.

Roll-up MLP The combination of several ordinary limited partnerships into a master limited partnership.

Royalty trust An organizational form used by firms that would otherwise be taxed heavily (due to declining depreciation and increasing pretax cash flows) to transfer ownership to investors in low tax brackets.

Runup return The event return measured for some period ending with the announcement date.

Sample selection bias Criteria for sample may exclude some relevant categories. Examples: Completed spin-offs will not include spin-offs announced but not completed. Measures of industry profitability will not include firms that have failed. Studies of leveraged buyouts that have a subsequent public offering will represent the most successful and exclude the failures or less successful.

Saturday night special A hostile tender offer with a short time for response.

Scale economies The reduction in per-unit costs achievable by spreading fixed costs over a higher level of production.

Schedule 13D A form that must be filed with the SEC within 10 days of acquiring 5% or more of a firm's stock; discloses the acquirer's identity and business intentions toward the target. Applies to all large stock acquisitions.

Schedule 14D A form that must be filed with the SEC by any group or individual making solicitations or recommendations that would result in its owning more than 5% of the target's stock. Applies to public tender offers only.

Scorched earth defenses Actions taken to make the target less attractive to the acquiring firm and that also might leave the target in weakened condition. Examples are sale of best segments (crown jewels) and incurring high levels of debt to pay a large dividend or to engage in substantial share repurchase.

Second-step transaction Typically the merger of an acquired firm into the acquirer after control has been obtained.

Secondary initial public offering (SIPO) The reoffering to the public of common stock in a company that initially was public but then was taken private (e.g., in an LBO).

Securities Act of 1933 (SA) First of the federal securities laws of the 1930s. Provides for federal regulation of the sale of securities to the public and registration of public offerings of securities.

Securities Exchange Act of 1934 (SEA) Federal legislation that established the Securities and Exchange Commission (SEC) to administer securities laws and to regulate practices in the purchase and sale of securities.

Securities Investor Protection Act of 1970 (SIPA) Federal legislation that established the Securities Investor Protection Corporation empowered to supervise the liquidation of bankrupt securities firms and to arrange for payments to their customers.

Securities parking An arrangement in which a second party holds ownership of assets to avoid identification of the actual owner in order to avoid rules and regulations related to securities trading.

Sell-off General term for divestiture of part or all of a firm by any one of a number of means—sale, liquidation, spin-off, and so on.

Shareholder interest hypothesis The theory that shareholder benefits of antitakeover defenses outweigh management entrenchment motives and effects.

Share repurchase A public corporation buys its own shares, by tender offer, on the open market or in a negotiated buyback from a large blockholder.

Shark repellent Any of a number of takeover defenses designed to make a firm less attractive and less vulnerable to unwanted acquirers.

Shark watcher A firm (usually a proxy solicitation firm) that monitors trading activity in its clients' stock to detect early accumulations by an unwanted acquirer before the 5% disclosure threshold.

Shelf registration The federal securities law provision in Rule 415 that allows firms to register at one time the total amount of debt or equity they plan to sell over a 2 year period. Securities can then be sold with no further delays whenever market conditions are most favorable.

Sherman Act of 1890 Early antitrust legislation. Section 1 prohibits contracts, combinations, and conspiracies in restraint of trade. Section 2 is directed against actual or attempted monopolization.

Short-swing trading rule Federal regulation under Section 16 of the Securities Exchange Act that prohibits designated corporate insiders from retaining the profits on any purchase and sale of their own firm's securities within a 6 month period.

Signaling An action that conveys information to other players; for example, seasoned new equity issues signal that the stock is overvalued.

Silver parachutes Reduced golden parachute provisions that extend to a wider range of managers.

Sitting-on-a-gold mine hypothesis Attributes the increase in a takeover target's stock price to information disclosed during the takeover process that the target's assets are undervalued by the market.

Small numbers problem When the number of bidders is large, rivalry among bidders renders opportunistic behavior ineffectual. When the number of bidders is small, each party seeks terms most favorable to it through opportunistic representations and haggling.

Specialized asset An asset whose use is complementary to other assets. For example, a pipeline from oil-producing fields to a cluster of refineries near large consumption markets.

Specificity The degree to which an asset or resource is specialized to and thus dependent on the rest of the firm or organization.

Spin-off A transaction in which a company distributes on a pro rata basis all of the shares it owns in a subsidiary to its own shareholders. Creates a new public company with (initially) the same proportional equity ownership as the parent company.

Split-off A transaction in which some, but not all, parent company shareholders receive shares in a subsidiary in return for relinquishing their parent company shares.

Split-up A transaction in which a company spins off all of its subsidiaries to its shareholders and ceases to exist.

Spreadsheet approach Analysis of data over a number of past and projected time periods.

Squeeze-out The elimination of minority shareholders by a controlling shareholder.

Staggered board Also called a classified board. An antitakeover measure that divides a firm's board of directors into several classes, only one of which is up for election in any given year, thus delaying effective transfer of control to a new owner in a takeover.

Stake-out investment Preliminary investment for a foothold in anticipation of the future possibility of a larger investment.

Stakeholder Any individual or group who has an interest in a firm; in addition to shareholders and bondholders, includes labor, consumers, suppliers, the local community, and so on.

Standard Industrial Classification (SIC) The Census Bureau's system of categorizing industry groups, mainly product or process oriented.

Standstill agreement A voluntary contract by a large block shareholder (or former large blockholder bought out in a negotiated repurchase) not to make further investments in the target company for a specified period of time.

Start-up MLP Also called acquisition MLP. The assets of an existing entity are transferred to a master limited partnership, and the business is henceforth conducted as an MLP. The Boston Celtics's conversion into an MLP is an example.

Stepped-up asset basis The provision allowing asset purchasers to use the price paid for an asset as the starting point for future depreciation rather than the asset's depreciated book value in the hands of the seller.

Stock appreciation right (SAR) Part of an executive compensation program to align managers' interests with those of shareholders. SARs are issued to managers, giving them the right to purchase stock on favorable terms; the exercise price can be as low as 50% of the stock price at issuance; maximum life is 10 years.

Stock bonus plan A defined contribution pension plan in which the firm contributes a specified number of shares to the plan annually. The benefits to plan beneficiaries depend on the stock performance.

Stock lockup An option to buy some fraction of the target stock at the first bidder's initial offer when a rival bidder wins.

Strategy The long-range planning process for an organization. A succession of plans (with provisions for implementation) for the future of a firm.

Strip financing A type of financing, often used in leveraged buyouts, in which all claimants hold approximately the same proportion of each security (except for management incentive shares and the most senior bank debt).

Structural theory An approach to industrial organization that argues that higher concentration in an industry causes less competition due to tacit coordination or over collusion among the largest companies.

Stub New shares issued in exchange for old shares in a leveraged recapitalization.

Subchapter S corporation A form of business organization that provides the limited liability feature of the corporate form while allowing business income to be taxed at the personal tax rates of the business owners.

Superior-vote stock In dual-class stock firms, the class of stock that has more power to elect directors; usually concentrated in the hands of management.

Supermajority A requirement in many antitakeover charter amendments that a change of control (for example) must be approved by more than a simple majority of shareholders; at least 67% to 90% approval may be required.

Supernormal growth Growth due to a profitability rate above the cost of capital.

Swaps Exchanges of one class of securities for another.

SWOT Acronym for Strengths, Weaknesses, Opportunities, and Threats; an approach to formulating firm strategy via assessments of firm capabilities in relation to the environment.

Synergy The "2 + 2 = 5" effect. The condition of the output of a combination of two entities being greater than the sum of their individual outputs.

Take-out merger The second-step transaction that merges the acquired firm into the acquirer and thus "takes out" the remaining target shares that were not purchased in the initial (partial) tender offer.

Takeover A general term that includes mergers and tender offers (acquisitions).

Takeover defenses Methods employed by targets to prevent the success of bidders' efforts.

Target The object of takeover efforts.

Targeted share repurchase Refers to repurchasing the stock of a large blockholder (an unwanted acquirer) at a premium over market price (greenmail).

Tax credit ESOP (TRASOP, PAYSOP) An employee stock ownership plan that allowed employers to take a credit against their tax liability for contributions up to a specified amount, based on qualified investment in plant and equipment (TRASOP) and/or covered payroll (PAYSOP). Repealed by the Economic Recovery Tax Act of 1981 and the Tax Reform Act of 1986.

Tax-free reorganization A takeover transaction in which the primary consideration paid to obtain the voting stock or assets of the target must be the voting stock of the acquiring firm. (In fact, tax is deferred only until target shareholders sell the stock received.)

Team effects A form of organization capital; information that helps assign employees for an efficient match of capabilities to tasks and that helps match managers and other employees to form efficient teams.

Team production Alchian and Demsetz's distinguishing characteristic of a firm. Team output is greater than the sum of the outputs of individual team members working independently (synergy). Increased output cannot be unambiguously attributed to any individual team member.

Tender offer A method of effecting a takeover via a public offer to target firm shareholders to buy their shares.

Termination fee The payment or consolation prize to unsuccessful bidders.

Third market Trading conducted off the organized securities exchanges by institutional investors.

Tin parachutes Payments to a wide range of the target's employees for terminations resulting from a takeover.

Tobin's q The ratio of the current market value of the firm's securities to the current replacement costs of its assets; used as a measure of management performance.

Toehold The initial fraction of a target firm's shares acquired by a bidder.

Top-down planning An approach to overall firm strategy based on companywide forecasts from top management versus aggregation of segment forecasts.

Total capital requirements A firm's financing requirements. Two alternative measures: (1) Change in operating working capital plus capital expenditures plus change in net other assets; (2) Change in sum of Interest-Bearing Debt plus Shareholders' Equity.

Total capitalization The sum of total debt, preferred stock, and equity.

Tracking stock The parent corporation issues a separate class of common stock whose value is based on the cash flows of a specific division.

Transaction cost The cost of transferring a good or service across economic units or agents.

Transferable put rights (TPRs) A share repurchase plan in which puts for a limited time period issued to current shareholders can be resold to others.

Trigger point The level of share ownership by a bidder at which provisions of a poison pill antitakeover defense plan are activated.

Trust Indenture Act of 1939 (TIA) Federal securities regulation of public issues of debt securities of $5 million or more. Specifies requirements to be included in the indenture (the agreement between the borrower and lenders) and sets out the responsibilities of the indenture trustee.

Two-tier tender offer Tender offers in which the bidder offers a superior first-tier price (e.g., higher or all cash) for a specified maximum number of shares it will accept and simultaneously announces its intentions to acquire remaining shares at a second-tier price (lower and/or securities rather than cash).

Type A, B, C reorganization Forms of tax-free reorganizations. Type A: Statutory mergers (target merged into acquirer) and consolidations (new entity created). Type B: Stock for stock transaction in which target is liquidated into the acquirer or maintained as a separate operating entity. Type C: Stock-for-asset transaction in which at least 80% of fair market value of target's property is acquired; target then dissolves.

Undervaluation A firm's securities are selling for less than their intrinsic, or potential, or long-run value for one or more reasons.

Underwritten offerings Public securities issues that are sold by a firm to an investment banker at a negotiated price; the investment banker then bears the risk of price fluctuations before the securities are sold to the general public.

Unitary company (U-form) An organization form that is highly centralized under the president. Departments are organized by functions such as research, manufacturing, and marketing. It facilitates rapid decision making. Difficulties arise with multiple products.

Value additivity principle (VAP) A quality of the NPV method of capital budgeting that enables managers to consider each project independently. The sum of project NPVs represents the value added to the corporation by taking them on.

Value-Based Management (VBM) Relating the firm's strategies and operating decisions to measures of economic value created.

Value chain An approach to strategy that analyzes the steps or chain of activities in the firm to find opportunities for reducing cost outlays while adding product characteristics valued by customers.

Value drivers Operating measures that have a major influence on the value of a firm.

Vertical merger A combination of firms that operate in different levels or stages of the same industry (e.g., a toy manufacturer merges with a chain of toy stores—forward integration; an auto manufacturer merges with a tire company—backward integration).

Virtual organization The links of the value chain are brought together by contracts the company makes with its suppliers and customers. This is a form of virtual integration facilitated by a networked computer system or through the Internet.

Voting plan A poison pill antitakeover defense plan that issues voting preferred stock to target firm shareholders. At a trigger point, preferred stockholders (other than the bidder for the target) become entitled to supervoting privileges, making it difficult for the bidder to obtain voting control.

Voting trust A device by means of which shareholders retain cash flow rights to their shares while giving the right to vote those shares to another entity.

Wealth transfer The gain of one type of stakeholder in relation to the associated losses of other stakeholders.

Weighted-average marginal cost of capital (WACC) The relevant discount rate or investment hurdle rate based on targeted capital structure proportions.

White knight A more acceptable merger partner sought out by the target of a hostile bidder.

White squire A third party friendly to management who helps a company avoid an unwanted takeover without taking over the company on its own.

Williams Act of 1968 Federal legislation designed to protect target shareholders from swift and secret takeovers in three ways: (1) Generating more information during the takeover process; (2) requiring minimum period for tender offer to remain open; (3) authorizing targets to sue bidders.

Winner's curse The tendency that in a bidding contest or in some types of auctions, the winner is the bidder with the highest (overly optimistic) estimate of value. This explains the high frequency of negative returns to acquiring firms in takeovers with multiple bidders.

WOTS UP Acronym for Weaknesses, Opportunities, Threats, and Strengths; a technique to identify these key elements as part of the alternative process used to develop strategy.

AUTHOR INDEX

SUBJECT INDEX